Italy

a photo essay

1 Andagna, Liguria

2

3

2 Capri, Campania
3 Menaggio, Lombardy

4 The Marches

5 An isolated chapel, Piemonte

6 Olive trees, Puglia
7 Italian grapes, ingredients of some of the world's best wines
8 *Cantuccini* and Vin Santo

9 Norcineria, selling pork and cheese, Umbria
10 Local women, the Dolomites, Venetia

11 Delicatessen window display

FOTOCOPIE
ELIOGRAFIA
NEL PALAZZO
BAR
TRATTORIA
E. D'ANDREA
DISCHI
DI IMPORTAZIONE

13

12 A bustling street, Naples, Campania
13 Designer fashion, Milan, Lombardy
14 A Chianti wine cellar, Tuscany

14

15 Piazza del Popolo, Todi, Umbria
16 Santa Croce, Florence, Tuscany

16

17

17 Backwater canal, Venice, Venetia
18 Peppers, a staple of the healthy Mediterranean diet
19 Passata Festival, Lazio

20 Byzantine mosaics, Ravenna, Emilia-Romagna
21 Poplar avenue, Emilia-Romagna

22 Monster Park, Bomarzo, Lazio

23

24

23 Santa Maria Maggiore, Pianella, Abruzzo
24 Colonnade on the Duomo, Ferrara, Emilia-Romagna
25 Paestum, Campania

26 The Due Torri, Bologna, Emilia-Romagna

27 Rooftop view of the Duomo, Siena

28 Campidoglio, Rome, Lazio

Dana Facaros and
Michael Pauls

ITALY

"You must write all the beautiful things of Italy,' said the Venetian on the train, but the man from Bologna vehemently shook his finger. 'No, no,' he insisted. 'You must write the truth!'

CADOGANguides

Contents

Introducing

The Guide

Reference

Maps

About the authors

Dana Facaros and Michael Pauls lived in Italy for three years before moving to France, but get back as often as they can. For this edition they revisited and updated Piemonte and Valle d'Aosta, and Liguria.

About the updaters

Leonie Loudon updated Travel, Practical A–Z, Venetia (excluding Venice), Emilia-Romagna, and Puglia, **Gabriella Giganti** Lombardy and the Lakes, Campania (excluding Naples and Bay of Naples), and Calabria and the Basilicata, **Georgina Palffy** The Marches, and Umbria, **Mary-Ann Gallagher** Abruzzo and Molise, and Lazio (excluding Rome), and **Nicky Swallow** Tuscany.

Cadogan Guides, Highlands House,
165 The Broadway, London SW19 1NE
info@cadoganguides.co.uk
www.cadoganguides.com

The Globe Pequot Press
246 Goose Lane, PO Box 480, Guilford,
Connecticut 06437–0480

Book design by Andrew Barker
Cover photographs by John Ferro Sims
Maps © Cadogan Guides,
drawn by Map Creation Ltd
Managing Editor: Antonia Cunningham
Editor: Rhonda Carrier
Layout: Sarah Rianhard-Gardner
Proofreading: Daphne Trotter
Indexing: Isobel McLean
Production: Navigator Guides

Printed in Italy by Legoprint
A catalogue record for this book is available from
the British Library
ISBN 1–86011–113–0

Extract from Petrarch and corresponding English translation on p.53 from *Some Love Songs of Petrarch*, translated and annotated with a biographical introduction by William Dudley Foulke LL.D. (OUP CAT 1920, OUP 1915), included by permission of Oxford University Press.

Please help us to keep this guide up to date. We have done our best to ensure that the information in this guide is correct at the time of going to press, but places and facilities are constantly changing, and standards and prices in hotels and restaurants fluctuate. We would be delighted to receive any comments concerning existing entries or omissions. Authors of the best letters will receive a copy of the Cadogan Guide of their choice.

Introduction

01

Italy dangles from the centre of western Europe like a Christmas stocking, stuffed to the brim with marvels, some as soaring and grand as a Verdi opera or Brunelleschi's dome over Florence cathedral, some as weird and unexpected as the pagan tombs buried underneath St Peter's in Rome, or Galileo's erect middle finger, carefully, significantly preserved in a reliquary in Florence's science museum. Even first-time visitors, with eyes and brains spinning, soon become uneasily aware that for every over-familiar image, every Mount Vesuvius, St Mark's Basilica and Leonardo's *Last Supper*, Italy has 100 other natural wonders and artistic showpieces that any other nation would die for. Someone once tried to count up all the works of art, and concluded that there was at least one per inhabitant.

This national heritage is echoed by even the most ephemeral arts, whether they are cranked out by the fashion and design workshops or simmered in the kitchen: for every Italian dish or wine you've been craving to try on its home turf, expect myriad other delights that you've never heard of before. Even the common, everyday Italy that coexists next to the overflow of museums, art cities, ruins and rivieras is an extravagant, daunting place to digest, and as the headlines over the past few years confirm (the Mafia trials, the *tangentopoli* bribery scandals), this is a country that operates on rules entirely unlike those in force back home, full of contradictions and paradoxes, depths and shallows.

As an Umbrian friend told us, you cry twice in Italy: when you first arrive and when you have to leave. In the meantime, make sure to pack your intellect, gird your senses and watch out – not only for pickpockets but for a country that might just pick your heart.

A Little Geography

This is not a complex subject: there are tall mountains, and there are not-so-tall mountains. From the Alps down through the Apennines, the Italians are often at a loss to find enough level ground on which to plant a football field. In all Italy, you'll find only three substantial flatlands: the broad valley of the Po, separating the Alps and the Apennines, offering forgettable scenery but Italy's richest farmlands and a score of her most interesting cities; the coastal plain that includes the Maremma of southern Tuscany and northern Lazio; and the thoroughly flat *Tavoliere* stretching across Puglia. Most of the really impressive mountains are in the Alps (Mont Blanc, the Matterhorn and the fantastical Dolomites), but the tallest within Italy is the Gran Sasso d'Italia (the 'Big Rock of Italy'), the centre of a mighty patch of snow-clad peaks in the Abruzzo.

Not counting the islands, there are approximately 260,000 square kilometres of Italy – this is roughly the size of the island of Britain (Americans can think of it as a Colorado). Even with some 55 million Italians, busily tending the world's fifth or sixth most opulent economy, the country rarely seems too crowded. Large patches of urban sprawl do exist – in the Po valley, for example, or around the Bay of Naples – but the Italian people enjoy one another's company, and generally live in tightly packed cities, hill towns and villages, with plenty of good green countryside in between. It is about 1,000 kilometres as the crow flies (1,400 kilometres if you're driving) from Mont Blanc to the furthest corner of Puglia, which constitutes the 'heel' of the Italian boot, and the long peninsula is in most places approximately 150–250 kilometres across.

There are very few easy routes over the Apennines between the Adriatic and the Tyrrhenian; now as in ancient times the main highways parallel the coast or converge on Rome from all points. The long coastline is unevenly blessed; at one extreme there's the delicious Amalfi coast, the Riviera, the Gargano in Puglia and a few isolated lovely expanses (Calabria's Tyrrhenian coast, Monte Cónero near Ancona, around Terracina and Gaeta in Lazio, the cliffs by Trieste), while most of the rest is surprisingly dull – much of Tuscany and Lazio, and the greater part of the Adriatic and Ionian coasts.

Some Features of the Landscape

North: the beautiful, jagged Dolomites, made of coral of aeons past; the 'seven seas', a string of lagoons from Venice to Ravenna along the Adriatic; the caves and underground streams of the karst topography around Trieste and the Friuli; the Italian Lakes, formed by alpine rivers that can't reach the sea, large enough to form Mediterranean micro-climates on the edge of the Alps; the Ligurian Alps, blocking off the Italian Riviera from the rest of the continent and giving it the mildest winter weather north of Calabria.

Centre: the Apennines flanked by rolling hills in Tuscany, Umbria and the Marches; in Umbria and Lazio, a string of lakes, mostly of volcanic origin, of which the largest is Lake Trasimeno; the Gran Sasso and Monte Terminillo, the tallest of the Apennines.

South: the volcanic playground of coastal Campania, which is rammed with extinct volcanoes, dangerous volcanoes, baby volcanoes and bubbling pits; the exotic Gargano peninsula in Puglia, which geologically has nothing to do with the rest of Italy; and the rough, mountainous toe of Calabria, enclosing a green alpine plateau known as the Sila. Southern Italy is hot and dry, and wanton deforestation in the late 19th century has turned many of its mountain regions into barren wastelands. It is a bit wetter on the coastal plains – enough for most of them to have been malarial wastelands until the Allied occupation forces bathed them in DDT at the end of the Second World War.

As for **trees**, some very striking ones decorate the landscape, including the beautiful parasol pine, tall erect Lombardy poplars and cypresses, all of which make Italy Italy. Old forests have large numbers of oaks, beeches and evergreens, and palms can be seen around the deep south and in Liguria. Koala bears would thrive in Calabria if anyone wanted to introduce them – a century ago the government planted millions of eucalyptus trees to dry out the wet ground where the malaria mosquitoes lived. However, Italian hunters blast anything that moves, so wildlife is kept to a minimum. Even in country districts it's rare to hear many birds singing. Up in the mountains there are still plenty of boar, the famous Abruzzo bears still hang on in the Abruzzo National Park, and in the Alps mountain chamois and wolves are still occasionally seen. If you're out in the woods, especially in late spring and summer, watch out for vipers. The late spring is also the best time for wildflowers, of course; they are at their best in the Alps and the mountainous regions in the south.

FRANCE
GERMANY
SLOVAAKIA
AUSTRIA
HUNGARY
SWITZERLAND
TRENTINO-ALTO ADIGE
Dolomites
FRIULI-VENEZIA GIULIA
SLOVENIA
A l p s
Lake Como
11
LOMBARDY & THE LAKES
Trento
12
VENETIA
Trieste
Aosta
VALLE D'AOSTA
Lake Maggiore
CROATIA
VENETO
Milan
Turin
9
PIEMONTE & VALLE D'AOSTA
Lake Garda
Venice
Po
PIEMONTE
13
EMILIA-ROMAGNA
Bologna
Genoa
Savona
10
LIGURIA: THE ITALIAN RIVIERA
BOSNIA-HERZEGOVINA
FRANCE
SAN MARINO
A p e n n i n e s
Arno
Florence
Ancona
Ligurian Sea
Livorno
16
TUSCANY
14
THE MARCHES
Adriatic Sea
Capraia
Piombino
Lake Trasimeno
Perugia
17
UMBRIA
Elba
Gran Sasso d'Italia
15
ABRUZZO & MOLISE
CORSICA
Giglio
Lake Bolsena
Tiber
L'Aquila
Tremiti Islands
Civitavecchia
18
LAZIO
ABRUZZO
Gargano Peninsula
ROME
MOLISE
Campobasso
Anzio
Bari
21
PUGLIA
Olbia
Naples
19
CAMPANIA
Brindisi
Porto Torres
Pontine Islands
Ischia
Potenza
Matera
Salerno
Capri
BASILICATA
Otra
SARDINIA
Tyrrhenian Sea
Gulf of Taranto
Arbatax
20
CALABRIA & THE BASILICATA
La Sila
Cagliari
CALABRIA
Aeolian Islands
Catanzaro
Mediterranean Sea
Egadi Islands
Messina
Reggio di Calabria
Trapani
Palermo
Nebrodi
Straits of Messina
SICILY
Catania
Ionian Sea
Agrigento
Sicilian Channel
Syracuse
Pantelleria
Malta Channel
TUNISIA
Linosa
MALTA
Lampedusa
200
100 miles

A Guide to the Guide: Italian Regions, Italian Art

To the geographical features mentioned above, add a preposterous amount of history, tradition and language, and you have the political map of Italy, which only acquired its present divisions in the 1960s. There are now 21 amazingly diverse regions with various degrees of political autonomy, two of which are Sicily and Sardinia; the rest are described in this book from north to south according to regional boundaries, except where from a visitor's viewpoint it made more sense to combine parts of one region with another. This is a brief guide to the Guide, introducing the regions in the order they are presented in this book.

Northern Italy

This is the wealthiest third of the republic, the most industrial, expensive and dramatically scenic, the land of Alps and lakes. Beginning in the northwestern corner, you have **Piemonte** (Piedmont), the birthplace of modern Italy. At the 'mountains' feet', as the name implies, green Piemonte encompasses both excellent ski slopes in its western alpine arc and table-flat rice paddies to the east. Car-manufacturing Turin is the region's capital, a rather unexpected and quirky Baroque city that some love and others hate. Southern Piemonte, around Asti and Alba, produces Barolo, Asti Spumante and other vinous delights. The proximity of France scents the Piemontese kitchen; white truffles are the speciality in autumn.

The northwest's most spectacular scenery, however, is contained in the small, autonomous, bilingual (French and Italian) region of the **Valle d'Aosta**. The Aosta valleys are one of Italy's great holiday playgrounds, with Courmayeur, Breuil-Cervinia and other stunning resorts on the south slopes of Mont Blanc (Monte Bianco) and the Matterhorn (Cervino), near legendary passes such as the Great St Bernard, and in lovely Gran Paradiso National Park. Aosta, the handsome capital, is nicknamed the 'Rome of the Alps' for its extensive ruins.

Over the lush Maritime Alps lies Italy's smallest region, **Liguria**, a rugged rainbow of a coast better known as the Italian Riviera. In the centre lies Genoa, Italy's greatest seaport, while on either side shimmer famous resorts such as San Remo, Alassio, Rapallo, Portofino, Portovenere and the magnificent Cinque Terre. The climate is especially mild: palms, olives, flowers and vines grow in profusion. The seafood and the dishes with *pesto* are reason enough to linger.

To the east of Piemonte lies the large and dynamic region of **Lombardy**. First in its chapter is Milan, the adopted city of Leonardo da Vinci, a feverish centre of fashion and finance, the home of one of Europe's greatest cathedrals and opera houses, and a vision of the new Italy. This is followed by the three jewels of Lombardy's Po plain: medieval, scholarly Pavia, curlicue violin-making Cremona, and Renaissance Mantua, product of the exquisite Gonzaga dukes.

Northern Lombardy, and a piece of eastern Piemonte and western Veneto, form the **Italian Lakes**, that fabled district beloved of poets since Roman times. From west to east you'll find charming little Lake Orta; Lake Maggiore with the Borromean Islands and the world-famous resort of Stresa; zigzagging Lake Lugano, which Italy shares with Switzerland; and romantic Lake Como, forked in the middle, with villas at Bellagio, Cernobbio, Tremezzo and Menaggio. To the north of Como extends the great alpine valley, the Valtellina, which is splendid but scarcely known outside Italy. To the south of the Valtellina are some more lakes – sweet Iseo and tiny Idro – and two fascinating art cities: Bergamo and Brescia. Westernmost is dramatic Lake Garda, the 'Riviera of the Dolomites', its shores dotted with lovely villages: Sirmione, Gardone, Limone and more, and Italy's biggest theme park, Gardaland.

The next three regions to the east, which were for centuries either influenced or governed by the Most Serene Republic, are collectively known as Venetia. The main attraction of the **Veneto** is of course Venice itself, which becomes only more remarkable the more you learn about it, but there are a number of other lovely cities that shouldn't be overlooked by visitors – St Anthony's (and Giotto's) Padua; Palladio's Vicenza; and lovely Verona, of rose-coloured marble, the Scaligeri, Valpolicella and – as if we could forget – Romeo and Juliet. Magnificent white villas dot the lush landscapes of the Euganean Hills and foothills of the Dolomites; to the south lie the haunting flatlands of the Po Delta.

Rising up in northern Venetia, the strange and fabulous peaks of the Dolomites are the most beautiful mountains in the world. The eastern half, which is still part of the Veneto, includes Cortina d'Ampezzo, which hosted the 1956 Winter Olympics, while the western mountains are in the confines of the large autonomous region of **Trentino-Alto Adige**. Trento, the capital of Trentino, is a fine old town that was associated with the 16th-century Counter-Reformation council; nearby are the rugged Brenta Dolomites, valleys of apple orchards, castles and vineyards. Bilingual Alto Adige, on the Austrian border, prefers to be known as Süd Tirol – it's an intriguing mix of strudel and pasta, fairy-tale castles and resorts, vineyards and spas. Bolzano is its capital, Merano its most celebrated watering hole. Much of the western portion of Alto Adige is occupied by Stelvio National Park, Italy's largest, where glaciers permit year-round skiing.

East lies the third region of Venetia, **Friuli-Venezia Giulia**, a rich ethnic mix wedged in the corner between Austria and Slovenia, with the neoclassical seaport of Trieste as its capital, a city now regaining some of its lustre with the opening of eastern Europe. The region has popular resorts on the coast, such as Grado and Lignano, intriguing towns such as Ùdine and Cividale, Alps in the north, and more wine than you can shake a stick at in between.

Between north and central Italy, **Emilia-Romagna** nearly crosses the entire peninsula, occupying the Po plain and the northern Apennines. The home of Italy's finest cuisine, it also has some delicious cities: the arty medieval university town of Bologna; elegant Parma, a city of cheese and ham; Modena, of Ferrari, Lambrusco and balsamic vinegar fame; Busseto, the home of Verdi; Ferrara, fief of the great Renaissance patrons, the Este; Faenza, city of faïence ware; and Ravenna, with its unique and utterly luminous mosaics from the Dark Ages. Here, too, the string of Adriatic resorts begins, with Rimini, the biggest and brashest of all, with a Renaissance pearl in its heart. Just a short ride from Rimini, up in the mountains, is San Marino, the world's smallest and oldest republic.

Central Italy

Here, for many, lies the archetypal Italy: those rolling hills, faded ochre farmhouses and villas, cypresses, olive groves, hill towns, and the pines of Rome. This was the birthplace of two momentous chapters in western history – the Roman Empire and the Renaissance.

The first chapter begins where Emilia-Romagna left off, in the **Marches** (Le Marche), one of the lesser-known corners of central Italy, although its landscapes resemble those of Tuscany. Here are two exceptional cities: Urbino, which was built around Duke Federico's perfect Renaissance palace; and lovely, medieval Ascoli Piceno. In between them are a score of pleasant, seldom-visited hill towns, a major pilgrimage target – Loreto – and a string of modest resorts, on either side of the salty old port city of Ancona.

South of the Marches are two even less familiar regions, **Abruzzo and Molise**. The first, containing the loftiest peaks in the Apennines, is Rome's winter and summer mountain playground; Abruzzo National Park is the home of the Abruzzo bear and other fauna. The coast is fairly nondescript, lined with family resorts; inland there's a fascinating collection of unspoiled medieval villages and churches. With the highest villages in the Apennines, Molise is a small rather poor region south of Abruzzo, utterly obscure, quiet and artlessly unprepared for mass tourism.

Back on the western or Tyrrhenian coast, **Tuscany** probably needs no introduction. There's more to it, however, than the charmed trio of art cities, Florence, Siena and Pisa. Lucca, Pistoia, Prato and Arezzo have also accumulated more than their share of notable art and architecture, and the rolling, civilized landscape has beautiful hill towns in every direction: San Gimignano, with its medieval 'skyscrapers', brooding Etruscan Volterra, Cortona, Montepulciano and dozens more.

Landlocked, vaguely otherworldly Umbria is in many ways a more rustic version of Tuscany, spangled with historic hill towns such as Perugia, the capital and cultural centre; Orvieto with its famous cathedral; Spoleto, synonymous with Italy's most important arts festival; medieval Gubbio; Assisi, city of St Francis; and a dozen others, set in lovely green valleys and hills.

Lazio, ancient *Latium*, includes Rome and a good deal more; despite being right at the centre of things, its attractions are not well known. Northern Lazio was the homeland of the Etruscans and has fascinating archaeological sites such as those at Tarquinia and Cerveteri. There's plenty to see in Viterbo and Anagni, two places that contributed much to the history of the Popes in the Middle Ages, some extraordinary Renaissance villas and gardens (as at Caprarola, Tivoli and Bomarzo), major Roman ruins at Ostia Antica and Tivoli (not to mention in Rome itself), and a pretty stretch of coast between Cape Circeo and Formia.

Southern Italy

The four regions of Italy's **Mezzogiorno** often seem an entirely different country from the green and tidy north. Not many visitors ever make it further south than **Campania**, where Naples and its famous bay make up the south's prime attraction – including *Pompeii*, Vesuvius, Capri, Sorrento, the infernal volcanic Phlegraean Fields, dozens of Roman ruins and much more. The wonderful Amalfi Drive between Sorrento and Salerno covers the most spectacular bit of coastline in Italy, passing the truly unique towns of Positano, Amalfi and Ravello. Naples itself, famous for pizza and animated *italianità*, is the best antidote to the decaffeinated control-freak Europe being forged in Brussels, as well as the south's great art capital. The rest of Campania has venerable and interesting towns such as Salerno, Caserta, Capua and Benevento; well-preserved Greek temples at Paestum; and the unspoiled Cilento coast.

Lovers of fine Italian art and cuisine will not find them in **Calabria and the Basilicata**, once the most backward corners of the nation, now struggling gamely to catch up. The west coast from Maratea to Reggio di Calabria, the 'Calabrian Riviera', offers some clean beaches and beautiful scenery (especially around Maratea and Cape Vaticano), and the heavily forested mountain plateau west of Cosenza, the Sila, attracts hikers and nature-lovers. Of the once-mighty Greek cities of the Ionian Coast, there's little left but the great museum at Reggio and scanty ruins at Metaponto. The bare, eroded hills of the inland Basilicata are not particularly inviting, unless you want to see the famous *sassi* (cave dwellers' quarters) of Matera.

Puglia (Apulia) will for many be the real find in the south. The flat cornfields of the *Tavoliere* cover most of the region, but the rocky limestone Gargano Peninsula offers scenery unique in Italy, along with expanding but enjoyable resorts such as Vieste. Puglia did quite well in the Middle Ages, as is seen in its fine Romanesque cathedrals, including that of Bari, the south's prosperous second city and the burial place of Santa Claus. The *Tavoliere* also grows robust wines; on it Emperor Frederick II built his mysterious Castel del Monte. Tàranto, founded by the ancient Greeks, has a museum full of Greek vases, great seafood and a wonderful maritime atmosphere. You won't see anything in Italy like the *trulli*, the whitewashed houses with conical stone roofs that turn the areas around Alberobello into a fairy-tale landscape; further south on Italy's 'heel', on the Salentine Peninsula, Baroque Lecce is the south's most beautiful city.

History

02

The First Italians

Some 50,000 years ago, when the Alps were covered by an ice cap and the low level of the Mediterranean made Italy a much wider peninsula than it is now, Neanderthal man graced the Ligurian Riviera with his low-browed presence. Even that, however, is not the beginning of the story. Relatively recently, scientists have become excited about the discovery of a new type, *Homo Aeserniensis*, the first known inhabitant of Europe, who lived in caves around Isernia in Molise a million years ago.

Italy makes a convenient bridge from Africa to Europe, and it seems that there was a constant stream of traffic throughout prehistory. Nevertheless, none of the earliest inhabitants of Italy left much in terms of art or culture, and the peninsula remained a backwater until about the 8th century BC. At that time, most of the population were lumped together as **Italics**, a number of powerful, distinct tribes with related languages. Among them were the Samnites, who dominated much of Campania and the south, the dolmen-building Messapii in Puglia, the Piceni and Umbrii along the northern Adriatic coast, and a boiling kettle of contentious peoples in the centre: Sabines, Aequi, Volscii and Latins. The mighty 'Cyclopean walls' of their cities can still be seen today around southern Lazio.

Two of Italy's most culturally sophisticated peoples lived on the islands: the Siculi of Sicily and the castle-building, bronze-working Sards of the Nuraghe culture. Both kept to themselves and interfered little with affairs on the mainland. Much of the north, the classical Cisalpine Gaul, was the stomping ground of Celtic Ligurians; at the time this area north of the Po was not really thought of as part of Italy.

750–509 BC: Greeks and Etruscans

The most interesting nations of the time, however, were two relative newcomers who contributed much towards bringing Italy out of its primitive state, the **Etruscans** and the **Greeks**. With their shadowy past and as yet undeciphered language, the Etruscans are one of the puzzles of ancient history. According to their own traditions, they arrived from somewhere in western Anatolia about 900 BC – Etruscan inscriptions have been found on the Greek island of Lemnos – probably as a sort of warrior aristocracy that imposed itself on the existing populations of Tuscany and Lazio. By the 8th century BC they were the strongest people in Italy, grouped in a loose confederation of 12 city states called the *Dodecapolis*. At the same time the Greeks – whose trading routes had long covered Italy's southern coasts – began to look upon that 'underdeveloped' country as a New World for exploration and colonization. Cumae, on the Campanian coast, became the first Greek foundation in 750 BC, a convenient base for trading with the Etruscans and their newly discovered iron mines. A score of others soon followed, in Sicily and along the Ionian Sea, and soon they were rivalling the cities of Greece itself in wealth and culture. A third new factor in the Italian equation also appeared at this time, without much fanfare: the year 753 BC, according to the legends, saw the foundation of **Rome**.

Italy was ripe for civilization. In the centuries that followed, the Etruscans spread their rule and their culture over most of the north while the Italic tribes learned from Etruscans and Greeks alike. Some of them, especially the Latins and the Samnites, developed into urbanized, cultured nations in their own right. For the Greek cities, it was a golden age, as Taras (Táranto), Metapontum, Sybaris, Croton, and especially the Sicilian cities such as Syracuse and Akragas grew into marble metropolises that dominated central Mediterranean trade and turned much of inland Italy into tribute-paying allies. In the 6th century BC, the Greeks had more wealth than was probably good for them; stories are told of the merchants of Sybaris sending across the Mediterranean, offering fortunes for a cook who could produce the perfect sauce for seafood, and of the sentries of Akragas' army going on strike for softer pillows. From the first, also, these cities dissipated their energies by engaging in constant wars with each other. Some, like Sybaris, were completely destroyed, and by *c.* 400 BC the failure of the rest to work together sent them into a slow but irreversible economic decline.

The Etruscan story is much the same. By about 600 BC the 12 cities and their allies ruled almost all northern Italy (excluding Cisalpine Gaul), and wealth from their Tuscan mines made them a political force on a Mediterranean scale. Their decline was to be as rapid as that of Magna Graecia. Repeated defeats at the hands of the wild Gauls weakened their confederation, but the economic decline that led to Etruria's virtual evaporation in the 4th century BC is harder to account for. Rome, a border city between the Etruscans and Latins, threw out its Etruscan king and established a **Republic** in 509 BC (*see* Rome's history, p.778). Somehow, probably by the absorption of conquered populations, this relatively new city grew to include perhaps 100,000 people, ranking it with Taras and Capua, an Etruscan colony in the growing region of Campania, as the largest on the peninsula. With an economy insufficient to support so many Romans, the city could only live by a career of permanent conquest.

509–268 BC: The Rise of Rome

After the expulsion of the Etruscans, Rome spent 100 years at war with the various cities of Etruria, while gradually subjugating the rest of the Latins and neighbouring tribes. It was successful on all fronts, and a sacking by marauding Gauls in 390 BC proved only a brief interruption in its march to conquest. Southern Etruria and Latium were swallowed up by 358 BC, and Rome next turned its attention to the only power in Italy capable of competing with it on an equal basis: the Samnites.

These rugged highlanders of the southern Apennines, with their capital at Benevento, had begun to seize parts of coastal Campania. The Romans drove them out in 343–1 BC, but in the **Second Samnite War** the Samnites dealt them a severe defeat (Battle of Caudine Forks, 321 BC). In the third war, feeling themselves surrounded by Roman allies, the Samnites formed an alliance with the Northern Etruscans and Celts, leading to a general Italian commotion in which the Romans beat everybody, annexing almost all of Italy by 283 BC.

A strange interlude, delaying Rome's complete domination of Italy, came with the arrival of **Pyrrhus of Epirus**, a Greek adventurer with a large army who was invited in by the cities of Magna Graecia as a protector. From him we get the term 'Pyrrhic victories', for he outmatched the Romans in one battle after another but was never able to follow up his advantage. After finally losing at Benevento in 275 BC, he quit and returned to Epirus, while the Romans took the deserted Greek cities one by one.

Now the conquest was complete. All along, the Romans had been diabolically clever in managing their new demesne, maintaining most of the tribes and cities as nominally independent states, while planting Latin colonies everywhere (re-founded cities such as Paestum, Ascoli Piceno and Benevento were such colonies, together with new ones in the north such as Florence). The great network of roads centred on Rome was extended with great speed, and a united Italy seemed close to becoming a reality.

268–91 BC: Empire Abroad, Disarray at Home

After all this, Rome deserved at least a shot at the Mediterranean heavyweight title. The current champ, the powerful merchant thalassocracy of Carthage, was alarmed enough at the successes of its precocious neighbour, and proved happy to oblige. Rome won the first bout, beating Carthage and her ally Syracuse in the **First Punic War** (264–41 BC), and gained Sicily, Sardinia and Corsica. For the rematch, the **Second Punic War** (219–02 BC), Carthage sent **Hannibal** and his elephants from Spain into Italy over the Alps to bring the war into the Romans' backyard. Undeterred by the brilliant African general's victory at Cannae in 216 BC, where four legions were destroyed, the Romans hung on even when Hannibal appeared at the gates of Rome. In Hannibal's absence, they took Spain and much of Africa, and after Scipio Africanus' victory at Zama in 202 BC, Carthage surrendered. The **Third Punic War** was a sorry affair: Rome only waited long enough for Carthage to miss a step in its treaty obligations before razing the city to the ground. The west conquered, Rome looked east. Already by 200 BC it had been interfering in Greek affairs. The disunited Greeks and successor states of Alexander's empire proved easy targets, and by 64 BC the legions were camped on the Cataracts of the Nile, in Jerusalem and over Asia Minor.

Nothing corrupts a state like easy conquests, and all this time things in Italy were going wrong. Taxation ceased for Roman citizens, as booty provided the state with all the revenues it needed, and tens of thousands of slaves were imported. Italy became a parasite nation. Vast amounts of cheap grain from Africa and Egypt ruined Italian farmers, who had the choice of selling their freehold and becoming a sharecropper, joining the army, or moving to Rome as part of the burgeoning lumpen proletariat. The men who profited most from the wars bought up tremendous amounts of land, turning Italy into a country of huge estates (latifundia), and becoming an aristocracy powerful enough to stifle any attempts at reform. Only Rome, of course, and a few other cities prospered. In this period many of the Greek and Etruscan towns withered. Many country districts became abandoned, and rural Italy knew constant famine and plagues, while in Rome the new rich were learning the delights of orgies, gladiatorial combats, and being carried around by slaves.

Not that degeneracy and social disintegration had proceeded far enough for Italy to fail to resist. Rome, and indeed all Italy, divided into extremist factions: the reactionary 'Senatorial Party' and the radical 'Popular Party'. (The Senate and the senatorial class were not yet a nobility per se. A hefty fortune was all that was needed for entry. Their populist opponents included not only the poor, but most of the businessmen, and the hard-pressed middle class.) In 133 BC a remarkable reformer named **Tiberius Gracchus** was elected Tribune, but his plans for land reforms earned him assassination the following year. His brother, **Gaius Gracchus**, went even further when he gained the Tribunate in 123 BC, attempting to expand citizenship to most Italians; but he, too, was murdered after the Senate declared martial law that same year. By this time Rome's constitution was reduced to a travesty, and both sides realized that the only real power lay with the legions. The populists staked their hopes on **Gaius Marius**, an illiterate but good-hearted general who saved Italy from the last surprise Celtic raid in 113 BC. Marius' ascent to power proved a disappointment, and a whole new generation of populist statesmen was assassinated one by one.

91–31 BC: Sixty Years of Civil War

Italy had had enough; the year 91 BC saw a coordinated revolt among the southern peoples called the **Social Wars**, defeated by the campaigns of Marius and Sulla and by an offer to extend Roman citizenship to all Italians. A military coup by **Sulla** followed, with the backing of the Senate; it was the first time armed Roman soldiers ever actually entered Rome, a religious and constitutional taboo. However, when Sulla's army left for conquest and booty on the Black Sea, a populist countermovement took power and ruled Rome for the next three years. Sulla's triumphal return threw them out, and the haughty general unleashed a bloody reign of terror unlike anything Italy had ever seen. An effective dictatorship was created, and all opponents murdered or exiled (a redoubtable populist general named Quintus Sertorius still held Spain, and defeated five separate legions sent against him). Italy spiralled into anarchy, with many rural districts reverting to bandit-ridden wastelands, a setting for the remarkable revolt in 73 BC of **Spartacus**, an escaped gladiator who led a motley army of dispossessed farmers and runaway slaves – some 70,000 of them – back and forth across the south until the legions finally defeated him in 71 BC.

All this had exhausted both sides, and finally discredited senatorial rule. After Sulla's death, no one minded when the consulship and real power passed to **Pompey**, another successful general but one who cared little for politics. Like Sulla before him, Pompey soon set out for the east, where the most glory and booty were to be gained, and his departure left the stage in Rome open to 33-year-old **Julius Caesar**, a tremendously clever soldier–politician, but a good man anyhow. With his two great talents, one for rhetoric and the other for attracting money, he took up the popular cause in better style than anyone before. A taint of connection to the **Catiline conspiracy** of 68 BC, a revolt of adventurers, disaffected nobles and other loose ends, proved a temporary setback, just as it advanced the fortunes of **Marcus Tullius Cicero**, the great orator, writer and statesman who dreamed of founding a real republic with a real constitution, opposing both extreme parties and pinning his hopes on the still-surviving Italian middle class. Few people in Rome cared for such principles, however, and after Pompey returned from bashing the Pontic Kingdom and the Cilician pirates, he, Caesar, and a wealthy building contractor named Licinius Crassus sliced up the republic between them, forming the **First Triumvirate** in 59 BC.

What Caesar really wanted, of course, was a military command. Following the accepted practice, he managed to buy himself one in the north, and undertook the conquest of most of Gaul, with well-known results. When Pompey grew jealous and turned against him, Caesar led his army back into Italy, defying the Senate by 'crossing the Rubicon', the river boundary between Italy and Gaul that Roman armies were not allowed to cross without senatorial authorization. Resistance collapsed before him, and he became the unchallenged master of Rome while not even holding public office. Pompey and most of the Senate fled to Greece, where Caesar caught up with them three years later. In his four years as ruler of Rome, Caesar surprised everyone, even his enemies; everything received a good dose of reform, even the calendar, and a beginning was made towards sorting out the economic mess and getting Italy back on its feet. Caesar's assassination by a clique of republican bitter-enders in 44 BC plunged Italy into civil war again, and left historians to ponder the grand question of whether he had really intended to make himself a king and finally put the now senile republic to sleep. A **Second Triumvirate** was formed, of Caesar's adopted son Octavian, a senatorial figurehead named Lepidus, and Caesar's old friend and right-hand man, a talented, dissipated fellow named **Marcus Antonius** (Mark Anthony), who according to one historian spent the equivalent of $3 billion (of other people's money) in his brief lifetime. While he dallied in the east with Cleopatra, Octavian was consolidating his power in Italy. The inevitable battle came in 31 BC, at Actium in Greece, and was a complete victory for **Octavian**.

31 BC–AD 251: The Empire

With unchallenged authority through all the Roman lands, Octavian – soon to rename himself **Augustus** – was free to complete the reforms initiated by Caesar. He maintained the forms of the republic while accumulating enough titles and offices for himself to have constitutional justification for his absolute rule. The title he chose for public use was 'first citizen', while behind the scenes the machinery was being perfected for the deification of the Caesars (a practical policy in the eastern half of the empire, where such things were common practice), and for a stable monarchy after his death. It all worked brilliantly: peace was restored, an effective administration created, and Italy was able to recover from its time of troubles with the help of Augustus' huge programmes of public works.

To find out about his career, and those of his successors, read the gossipy, shocking and wonderfully unreliable *Lives of the Caesars* of Suetonius. All Rome tittered at the scandals of the later **Julian emperors**, but reality was usually much more prosaic. **Tiberius** (AD 14–37) may have been a monster to his girlfriends and boyfriends, but he proved an intelligent and just ruler; his criminally insane successor **Caligula**, or 'Bootkin', lasted only four years (37–41) while the bureaucracy kept things going. **Claudius** (41–54) governed well and conquered southern Britain, while his stepson **Nero** (54–68) generally made a nuisance of himself in Rome but otherwise did little to disturb the system. Nevertheless, a commander in Spain called **Galba** declared him unfit to be emperor and marched on Rome; Nero managed to commit suicide just before they caught him. The genie was out of the bottle again, as the soldiers once more realized that the real power lay with them. Another general, **Otto**, commander of the emperor's Praetorian Guard, toppled Galba, and soon lost out in turn to **Vitellius**, commander on the Rhine.

The fourth emperor of the fateful years AD 68–9 was **Vespasian**, leader of the eastern armies. He had the strongest legions and so got to keep the job; his reign (69–79) and those of his sons **Titus** (79–81) and **Domitian** (81–96), the three **Flavian emperors**, were remembered as a period of prosperity. Vespasian began the Colosseum; whether intentionally or not, this incomparable new charnel house made a perfect symbol for the renewed decadence and militarization of the state.

For the moment, however, things looked rosy. After the assassination of **Domitian**, another bad boy but not an especially calamitous ruler, Rome had the good fortune to be ruled by a series of high-minded and intelligent military men, who carefully chose their successors in advance to avoid civil war. The so-called **Antonine emperors** presided over the greatest age of prosperity the Mediterranean world ever knew; in Italy they ran a surprisingly modern state (though one still based on slave labour) that would seem familiar to us today, with public libraries, water boards to maintain the aqueducts, rent control, agricultural price supports, low-cost loans for starting new businesses and many other such innovations. The first of the Antonines was **Nerva** (96–8), followed by **Trajan** (98–117) and **Hadrian** (117–38); they were both great soldiers and builders on a monumental scale, especially in Rome. After them came **Antoninus Pius** (138–61), little known only because his reign was so peaceful, and **Marcus Aurelius** (161–80), soldier, statesman and Stoic philosopher. His successor was his useless son **Commodus** (180–93) – whose cowardice was immortalized in the Hollywood blockbuster *Gladiator* – and the string of good emperors was broken.

The 2nd-century prosperity was not without its darker side. The arts were in serious decline, as if the imagination of the Graeco-Roman Mediterranean was somehow failing. Education was in poor shape, and every sort of fatuous mysticism imported from the east permeated the minds of the people. Economically, this period saw the emergence of the well-known north–south split in Italy. The rural south, impoverished by the Roman Republic, now sank deeper into decline, while even the commerce of wealthy Campania began to fail, ruined by foreign competition. In the north, especially Cisalpine Gaul, a sounder, more stable economy led to the growth of new centres, Milan, Padua, Verona and Ravenna the most prominent, beginning the economic divide that continues even today. In the balance, though, Italy was becoming an ever less significant part of the empire, both politically and economically. Of the 2nd-century emperors, fewer came from Italy than from Spain, Illyria or Africa.

251–475: Decline and Fall

For all it cost to maintain them, the legions were no longer the formidable military machine of Augustus' day. They were bureaucratic and a little tired, and their tactics and equipment were also falling behind those of the Persians and even some of the more clever German barbarians. The **Goths** were the first to demonstrate this, in 251, when they overran the Balkans, Greece and Asia Minor. Five years later **Franks** and **Alemanni** invaded Gaul, and in 268 much of the east detached itself from the empire under the leadership of Odenathus of Palmyra. Somehow the empire recovered and prevailed, under dour soldier–emperors such as **Aurelian** (270–75), who built Rome's walls, and **Diocletian** (284–305) who completely revamped the structure of the state and economy. His fiscal reforms, such as the fixing of prices and a decree that every son had to follow the trade of his father, ossified the economy and made the creeping decline of Italy and all western Europe harder to arrest. A gigantic bureaucracy was created, taxes reached new heights as people's ability to pay them declined, and society became increasingly militarized in every respect. The biggest change was the division of the empire into halves, each ruled by a co-emperor equally called 'Augustus'; Diocletian, significantly, chose the wealthier east for himself. The new western emperors usually kept their court at army headquarters in Mediolanum (Milan), and later at impregnable **Ravenna** on the Adriatic, and Rome itself became a marble-veneered backwater.

More than ever, the empire had become an outright military dictatorship, in a society whose waning energies were entirely devoted to supporting a bloated, all-devouring army and bureaucracy. Medieval feudalism actually had its origins in this period, as the remaining freehold farmers sold their lands and liberty to the local gentry – for protection's sake, but also to get off the tax rolls. In cities, the high taxes and uncertain times ruined business and trade; throughout Italy and the west, towns both large and small began their fatal declines. Diocletian reduced Italy to the status of a mere province, and the peninsula had little to do with imperial events thereafter. The confused politics of the 4th century are dominated by **Constantine** (306–37), who ruled both halves of the empire, defeated various other contenders (Battle of the Milvian Bridge, outside Rome, in 312), and founded the eastern capital of Constantinople. He adroitly moved to increase his and the empire's political support by favouring **Christianity**. Though still a small minority in most of the empire, the Christians' strong organization and determination made them a good bet for the future. The religious revolution that followed was unexpected and remarkable. Diocletian had been the most ferocious of Christianity's persecutors; by 400, it was the turn of the pagans and Jews to be persecuted. In the next decades, as the empire's cities became Christianized, the **Church** itself became the most powerful and coherent instrument of the Roman élite.

The military disasters began in 406, with Visigoths, Franks, Vandals, Alans and Suevi overrunning Gaul and Spain. Italy's turn came in 408, when the western emperor **Honorius**, ruling from the new capital of Ravenna, had his brilliant general Stilicho (who happened to be a Vandal) murdered. A Visigothic invasion followed, leading to **Alaric's sack of Rome** in 410. St Augustine, probably echoing the thoughts of most Romans, wrote that the end of the world must be near. Rome should have been so lucky; judgment was postponed long enough for **Attila the Hun** to pass through Italy in 451. Then **Gaiseric the Vandal**, who had set up a pirate kingdom in Africa, raided Italy and sacked Rome again in 455. So completely had things changed, it was scarcely possible to tell the Romans from the barbarians. By the 470s, the real ruler in Italy was a Gothic general named **Odoacer**, who led a half-Romanized Germanic army and probably thought of himself as the genuine heir of the Caesars. In 476 he decided to dispense with the lingering charade of the Western Empire. The last emperor, young, silly Romulus Augustulus, was packed off to premature retirement in Naples, and Odoacer was crowned King of Italy at Pavia.

475–1000: The Dark Ages

At the beginning, the new Gothic–Latin state showed some promise. Certainly the average man was no worse off than he had been under the last emperors; trade and cities even revived a bit. In 493, Odoacer was replaced (and murdered) by a rival Ostrogoth, **Theodoric**, nominally working on behalf of the eastern emperor at Byzantium. Theodoric proved a strong and able, though somewhat paranoid ruler; his court at Ravenna witnessed a minor rebirth of Latin letters with Cassiodorus, Symmachus and the great Christian philosopher Boethius. Nevertheless, stability was compromised by religious quarrels between the Arian Christian Goths and the orthodox Catholic populations in the cities.

A disaster as serious as those of the 5th century began in 536, with the invasion of Italy by the Eastern Empire, as part of the relentlessly expansionist policy of **Justinian**. The historical irony was profound; in the ancient homeland of the Roman Empire, Roman troops now came not as liberators but as foreign, largely Greek-speaking conquerors. His brilliant generals, **Belisarius** and **Narses**, ultimately prevailed over the Goths in a series of terrible wars that lasted until 563, but the damage to an already stricken society and economy was incalculable.

Italy's complete exhaustion was exposed only five years later, when the **Lombards**, a Germanic tribe that worked very hard to earn the title of barbarian, overran northern Italy and some parts of the south, establishing a kingdom at Pavia and separate duchies in Benevento and Spoleto. A new pattern of power appeared, with semi-independent Byzantine dukes defending many coastal areas, the **Byzantine Exarchs of Ravenna** controlling considerable territory on the Adriatic and in Calabria, and Lombard chiefs ruling the majority of the interior. The popes in Rome, who occasionally allied with the Lombards against Byzantium, became a force during this period, especially following the papacy of the clever, determined **Gregory the Great** (590–604). Scion of the richest family in Italy, Gregory took political control in Rome during desperate times, and laid the foundations for the papacy's claims to temporal power.

With trade and culture at their lowest ever ebb, the 7th century marks the rock bottom of Italian history. The 8th showed some improvement; while most of the peninsula lay in feudal darkness, **Venice** was beginning its remarkable career as a trading city, and independent **Amalfi** and **Naples** emulated its success on the Tyrrhenian coast. The popes, along with other bishops who had taken advantage of the confused times to become temporal powers, intrigued everywhere in order to increase their influence; they finally cashed in with a Frankish alliance in the 750s. At the time the Lombard kings were doing well, finally conquering Ravenna (751) and considerable territories formerly under the dominion of the popes, who invited in **Charlemagne** to protect them. He eliminated the last Lombard king, Desiderius (his father-in-law, incidentally), and tucked all Italy as far south as Rome (with the exception of Venice) into his short-lived patchwork empire, sanctified by a papal coronation as the heir of the Roman Empire. A Lombard Duchy of Benevento survived for centuries up in the mountains, and the Byzantines kept a tenuous hold on the heel and toe; the Greek villages and relics of troglodyte Greek monasticism in

Calabria and Puglia date from this period. Arabs from Tunisia were beginning a gradual conquest of Sicily, and their raiders menaced all the peninsula's coasts; they sacked Rome itself in 746.

When Charlemagne's empire disintegrated following his death in 814, Italy reverted to a finely balanced anarchy. Altogether the 9th century was a bad time, with Italy caught between the Arab raiders and the endless wars of petty nobles and battling bishops in the north. The 10th century proved somewhat better – perhaps much better than the scanty chronicles of the time attest. Even in the worst times, Italy's cities never entirely disappeared. Sailing and trading overseas always lead to better technologies, new ideas and economic growth, and Italy's maritime cities had become the most advanced in Europe; even inland cities such as Florence and Milan were developing a new economic importance and self-consciousness. Cities do not grow by magic in such unpromising times; even though few had attained complete freedom of action, it is clear that even in the 900s many were looking to their own resources, defending their interests against the Church and nobles alike.

A big break for the cities, and for Italy, came in 961 with the invasion of the German **Otto the Great**, heir to the imperial pretensions of the Carolingians. He deposed the last feeble King of Italy, Berengar II of Ivrea, and was crowned Holy Roman Emperor in Rome the next year. Not that any of the Italians were happy to see him, but the strong government of Otto and his successors beat down the great nobles and allowed the growing cities to expand their power and influence. A new pattern was established; Germanic Emperors would meddle in Italian affairs for centuries, not powerful enough to establish total control but usually able to keep out important rivals.

1000–1154: The Rise of the *Comuni*

On the eve of the new millennium, the majority of Christians were convinced that the turn of the calendar would bring with it the end of the world. If there had been economists and social scientists around, however, they would have had ample evidence to reassure everyone that things were looking up. Especially in the towns, business was very good, and the political prospects even brighter. The first mention of a truly independent *comune* (plural: *comuni*; a term used throughout this book, meaning a free city state; the best translation might be 'commonwealth') was in Milan, where in 1024 a popular assembly is recorded, deciding which side the city would take in the Imperial Wars.

Throughout this period the papacy had declined greatly in power and prestige, and was a political football kicked between the emperors and the piratical Roman nobles. Beginning in the 1050s, a remarkable Tuscan monk named Hildebrand controlled papal policy, working behind the scenes to reassert the influence of the Church. When he became pope himself, in 1073, **Gregory VII** immediately set himself in conflict with the emperors over the issue of investiture – whether the Church or secular powers could name Church officials. The various Italian (and European) powers took sides on the issue, and 50 years of intermittent war followed, including the famous penance in the snow of Emperor Henry IV at Canossa in 1077 (*see* p.480). The result was a big revival for the papacy, but more importantly the cities of Lombardy and the rest of the north used the opportunity to increase their influence, and in some cases achieve outright independence, defeating the local barons in war, razing their castles and forcing them to move inside the towns.

Southern Italy knew a different fate. The first **Normans** arrived about 1020, on pilgrimages to Monte Sant'Angelo in the Gargano. They liked the opportunities they saw for conquest, and soon the younger sons of Norman feudal families were moving into the south, first as mercenaries but gradually gaining large tracts of land for themselves in exchange for their services. Usually allied to the popes, they soon controlled most of Puglia and Calabria. One of their greatest chiefs, **Roger de Hauteville**, began the conquest of Sicily from the Arabs in 1060, six years before William the Conqueror sailed for England. Roger eventually united all the south into the 'Kingdom of Sicily', and by the 1140s, under **Roger II**, this strange Norman–Arab–Italian state with its glittering, half-oriental capital of Palermo had become the cultural centre of the Mediterranean, as well as one of the strongest, best-organized states in Europe.

1154–1300: Guelphs and Ghibellines

While all this was happening, the **First Crusade** (1097–1130) occupied the headlines. It was, in part, a result of the new militancy of the papacy begun by Gregory VII. For Italy, especially Pisa and Venice, the two states with plenty of boats to help ship Crusaders, the affair meant nothing but pure profit. Trade was booming everywhere, and the accumulation of money helped the Italians create modern Europe's first banking system. It also financed the continued independence of the *comuni*, which flourished everywhere, with a big enough surplus for building projects such as Pisa's cathedral complex, perhaps the biggest undertaking since the time of Trajan and Hadrian. Culture and science were flourishing, too, with a big boost from contact with the Byzantines and the Muslims of Spain and Africa. By the 12th century, far in advance of most of Europe, Italy had attained a prosperity unknown since Roman times. The classical past had never been forgotten – witness the attempt of Arnold of Brescia (1154) to recreate the Roman Republic. Similarly, free *comuni* in the north called their elected leaders 'consuls', and artists and architects turned ancient Roman styles into the Romanesque. Even Italian names were changing, an interesting sign of the beginnings of national consciousness; quite suddenly the public records (such as they were) show a marked shift from Germanic to classical and Biblical surnames, with fewer Ugos, Othos and Astolfos and more Giuseppes, Giovannis and Giulios.

Emperors and popes were still embroiled in the north. **Frederick I, Barbarossa** of the Hohenstaufen – or Swabian – dynasty, was strong enough in Germany, and he made it the cornerstone of his policy to reassert imperial power in Italy. Beginning in 1154, he crossed the Alps five times, molesting free cities that asked nothing more than the right to fight one another continually. He spread terror, utterly destroying Milan in 1161, but a united front of cities called the **Lombard League** defeated him in 1176. Frederick's greatest triumph in Italy came by arranging a marriage with the Normans, leaving his grandson **Frederick II** not only Holy Roman Emperor but also King of Sicily, giving him a strong power base in Italy itself.

The second Frederick's career dominated Italian politics for 30 years (1220–50). With his brilliant court, in which Italian was used for the first time (alongside Arabic and Latin), his half-Muslim army, his incredible processions of dancing girls, eunuchs and elephants, he provided Europe with a spectacle the like of which it had never seen. Frederick founded universities (as at Naples), gave Sicily a written constitution (perhaps the world's first), and built geometrically arcane castles and towers all over the south. The popes excommunicated him at least twice; the battle of pope and emperor had become serious. All Italy divided into factions: the **Guelphs**, under the leadership of the popes, supported religious orthodoxy, the liberty of the *comuni* and the interests of their emerging merchant class. The **Ghibellines** stood for the emperor, statist economic control, the interests of rural nobles, and religious and intellectual tolerance. Frederick's campaigns and diplomacy in the north met with very limited success, and his death in 1250 left the outcome very much in doubt.

His son **Manfred**, not emperor but merely King of Sicily, took up the battle with better luck; Siena's defeat of Florence in 1260 gained that city and most of Tuscany for the Ghibellines. The next year, however, **Pope Urban IV** began an ultimately disastrous precedent by inviting in **Charles of Anjou**, a powerful, ambitious leader and brother of the King of France. As protector of the Guelphs, Charles defeated Manfred (1266) and murdered the last of the Hohenstaufens, **Conradin** (1268). He held unchallenged sway over Italy until 1282, when the famous revolt of the **Sicilian Vespers** started the party wars up again. By now, however, the terms Guelph and Ghibelline had ceased to have much meaning; men and cities changed sides as they found expedient, and the old parties began to seem like the black and white squares on a chessboard. If your neighbour and enemy were Guelph, you became for the moment Ghibelline, and if he changed so would you. (Strangely enough, black and white were respectively the Ghibelline and Guelph colours. They also had distinctive styles of architecture. When you see a castle in Italy with simple rectangular crenellations along the walls, you know that Guelphs built it; ornate 'swallow-tail' crenellations are Ghibelline.)

Some real changes did occur out of all this sound and fury. In 1204 Venice hit its all-time biggest jackpot when it diverted the **Fourth Crusade** to the **sack of Constantinople**, winning for itself a small empire of islands in the Adriatic and Levant. Genoa emerged as its greatest rival in 1284, when its fleet put an end to Pisa's prominence at the Battle of Meloria. And elsewhere around the peninsula, some cities were falling under the rule of military *signori* whose descendants would be styling themselves counts and dukes – the **Visconti** of Milan, the **Della Scala** of Verona, the **Malatesta** of Rimini. Everywhere the freedom of the *comuni* was in jeopardy; after so much useless strife the temptation to submit to a strong leader often proved overwhelming. During Charles of Anjou's reign the popes extracted the price for their invitation. The **Papal State**, including much of central Italy, was established in 1278. But most importantly, the Italian economy never seemed to mind the trouble. Trade and money flowed as never before; cities built new cathedrals and acquired incredible skyscraper skylines with the tall tower-fortresses of the now urbanized nobles. And it was, in spite of everything, a great age for culture – the era of Guelphs and Ghibellines was also the time of Dante (*b.* 1265) and Giotto (*b.* 1266).

1300–1494: Renaissance Italy

This paradoxical Italy continued into the 14th century, with a golden age of culture and an opulent economy side by side with almost continuous war and turmoil. With no serious threats from the emperors or any other foreign power, the myriad Italian states were able to menace each other without outside interference. One of the secrets to this state of affairs was that war had become a sort of game, conducted on behalf of cities by bands of paid mercenaries led by a *condottiere*, who were never allowed to enter the cities. The arrangement suited everyone. The soldiers had lovely horses and armour, and no real desire to do each other serious harm. The cities were usually free from grand ambitions; everyone was making too much money to want to wreck the system. Without heavy artillery, walled towns and castles were nearly impossible to take, making the incentives to try hard even less. Best of all, the worst schemers and troublemakers on the Italian stage were fortuitously removed from the scene. Shortly after the election of the French **Pope Clement V** in 1305, the papacy moved to **Avignon**, becoming a puppet of the French king that temporarily had little influence in Italian affairs.

By far the biggest event of the 14th century was the **Black Death** of 1347–8, in which it is estimated that Italy lost a third of its population. The shock brought a rude halt to what had been 400 years of almost continuous growth and prosperity, though its effects did not prove a permanent setback for the economy. In fact, the plague's grim joke was that it actually made life better for most of the Italians who survived; working people in the cities, no longer overcrowded, found their rents lower and their labour worth more, while in the country farmers were able to increase their profits by tilling only the best land.

It is impossible to speak of 'Italian history' in this period, with the peninsula split up into long-established, cohesive states pursuing different ends and warring against one another. Italian statesmen understood the idea of a balance of power long before political theorists invented the term and, despite all the clatter and noise, most probably believed Italy was enjoying the best of all possible worlds. Four major states, each a European power in its own right, dominated the region's politics: first **Venice**, the oldest and most glorious, with its oligarchic but singularly effective constitution, and its exotic career of trade with the east. The Venetians waged a series of wars against arch-rival Genoa, finally exhausting her after the War of Chioggia in 1379. After that, they felt strong enough to make a major change in policy. Once serenely aloof from Italian politics, Venice now carved out a small land empire for itself, by 1428 including Verona, Padua, Vicenza, Brescia and Bergamo.

Florence, the richest city–state thanks to its banking and wool trade, also enjoyed good fortune, extending its control over most of Tuscany, and gaining a seaport with its conquest of now-decadent Pisa in 1406. In 1434, **Cosimo de' Medici**, head of the largest banking house, succeeded in establishing a de facto dictatorship. Even though the forms of the old republic were maintained, Florence was well on its way to becoming a signorial state like its greatest rival, **Milan**. Under the Visconti, Milan had become rich and powerful, basing its success on the manufactures of the city (arms and textiles) and the bountiful, progressively managed agriculture of southern

Lombardy. Its greatest glory came during the reign of **Gian Galeazzo Visconti** (1385–1402), who bought himself a ducal title from the emperor and nearly conquered all north Italy, before his untimely death caused his plans to unravel.

In the south, the huge **Kingdom of Naples** suffered from the heritage of the Normans, who had made it the only part of Italy where north European style feudalism had ever taken root. When times changed, the backward rural barons who dominated the south held back its commerce and its culture. Despite promising periods such as the reign of the King of Aragon, **Alfonso the Magnanimous** (1442–58), a Renaissance prince and patron of the arts who seized Naples and added it to his domains, the south was falling far behind the rest of Italy. The other Italian states included Genoa, a nasty little oligarchy that made money but contributed nothing to the cultural life of the times; the Duchy of Savoy-Piedmont, a quiet backwater more closely tied to France than Italy; the tiny, stalwart republics of Lucca and Siena; refined independent courts in Ferrara, Mantua, Modena and Rimini, surviving the rough seas of Italian politics; and finally the Papal States, anarchic while the popes were in France (until 1378), and woefully misgoverned when they came back.

And what of the Renaissance? No word has ever caused more mischief for the understanding of history and culture – it suggests that Italy had been Sleeping Beauty, waiting for some Prince Charming of classical culture to come and awaken it from a 1,000-year nap. Nothing could be further from the truth – Italy even in the 1200s was richer, more technologically advanced, and far more artistically creative than it had ever been in the days of the Caesars. The new art and scholarship that began in Florence in the 1400s and spread across the nation grew from a solid foundation of medieval accomplishment. The gilded, opulent Italy of the 15th century felt complacently secure in its long-established cultural and economic pre-eminence. A long spell of freedom from outside interference lulled the nation into believing that its political disunity could continue safely forever; except perhaps for the sanguinely realistic Florentine Niccolò Machiavelli, no one realized that Italy in fact was a plum waiting to be picked.

1494–1529: The Wars of Italy

The Italians brought the trouble down on themselves, when Duke Lodovico Sforza of Milan invited the French king Charles VIII to cross the Alps and assert his claim to the throne of Milan's enemy, Naples. Charles did just that, and the failure of the combined Italian states to stop him (at the inconclusive Battle of Fornovo, 1494) showed how helpless Italy was at the hands of emerging monarchies such as **France** or **Spain**. When the Spaniards saw how easy it was, they, too, marched in, and restored Naples to its Spanish king the following year (an Aragonese dynasty, cousins to Ferdinand and Isabella, had ruled Naples since 1442). Before long the German emperor and even the Swiss entered this new market for Italian real estate. The popes did as much as anyone to keep the pot boiling. Alexander VI and his son **Cesare Borgia** carried the war across central Italy in an attempt to found a new state for the Borgia family, and **Julius II**'s madcap policy led him to egg on the Swiss, French and Spaniards in turn, before finally crying 'Out with the barbarians!' when it was already too late.

By 1516, with the French ruling Milan and the Spanish in control of the south, it seemed as if a settlement would be possible. The worst luck for Italy, however, came with the accession of the insatiable megalomaniac **Charles V** to the throne of Spain that year; in 1519 he bought himself the crown of the Holy Roman Empire, making him the most powerful ruler in Europe since Charlemagne. Charles felt he needed Milan as a base for communications between his Spanish, German and Flemish possessions, and as soon as he had emptied Spain's treasury, driven her to revolt, and plunged Germany into civil war, he turned his attentions to Italy. The wars began anew, and were bloodier than anything Italy had seen for centuries, climaxing with the defeat of the French at Pavia in 1525, and the sack of Rome by an out-of-control imperial army in 1527. The French invaded once more, in 1529, and were defeated this time at Naples by the treachery of their Genoese allies. All Italy, save Venice, was now at the mercy of Charles and the Spaniards.

1529–1600: Italy in Chains

The final treaties left **Spanish viceroys** in Milan and Naples, and pliant dukes and counts toeing the Spanish line almost everywhere else. Besides Venice and the very careful Republic of Lucca, the last bastions of Italian liberty were **Siena** and **Florence**, where the Medici had been thrown out and the republic re-established. Charles' army besieged and took the city in 1530, giving it back to the Medici, who gained the title of Grand Dukes of Tuscany. They collaborated with Spain in extinguishing Siena's independence, despite a desperate resistance of seven years (1552–59), and the new Medici state assumed roughly the borders of Tuscany today.

The broader context of these events, of course, was the bitter struggles of the Reformation and **Counter-Reformation**. In Italy, the new religious angle made the Spaniards and the popes natural allies. One had the difficult job of breaking the spirit of a nation that, though conquered, was still wealthy, culturally sophisticated and ready to resist; the other saw an opportunity to recapture by force the hearts and minds it had lost long before. With the majority of the peninsula still nominally controlled by local rulers, and an economy that continued to be sound, both the Spanish and the popes realized that the only real threat would come not from men, but from ideas. Under the banner of combating Protestantism, they commenced a reign of terror across Italy. In the 1550s, the revived **Inquisition** began its manhunt for freethinkers of every variety; the Index of Prohibited Books followed in 1559 (some works of Dante included), accompanied by public book-burnings in Rome and elsewhere. A long line of Italian intellectuals trudged to the stake, while many more buried their convictions or left for exile in Germany or England. The job of re-educating Italy was put in the hands of the new Jesuit order; their schools and propaganda campaigns bore the popes' message deeply into the Italian mind, while their sumptuous new churches and dramatic sermons helped redefine Catholicism.

Despite the oppression, the average Italian at first had little to complain about. Spanish domination brought peace and order to a country that had long been a madhouse of conflicting ambitions. Renaissance artists attained a virtuosity never seen before, just in time to embellish the scores of new churches, palaces and villas of the mid 16th-century building boom. The combined Christian forces had turned back the Turkish threat at Malta (1566) and Lepanto (1571), and some Italians were benefiting to a great extent from Spanish imperialism in the **New World** – especially the Genoese, who rented ships, floated loans and even snatched up a surprising amount of the gold and silver arriving from America.

1600–1796: The Age of Baroque

However, the first signs of decay were already apparent. Palladio's country villas for the Venetian magnates, and Michelozzo's outside Florence, are architectural landmarks but also one of the earliest symptoms. In both cities, the old mercantile economies were failing, and the wealthy began to invest their money unproductively in land instead of risking it in business or finance. **Venice**, between its wars with the Turks and its loss of the spice trade when the Portuguese discovered the route to the Indies, suffered the most. By 1650 it no longer had an important role to play in European affairs, though the Venetians kept their heads and made their inevitable descent into decadence a serene and enjoyable one.

The troubles were not limited to these two cities. After 1600 nearly everything started to go wrong for the Italians. The textiles and banking industries of the north, which had long been the engines of the economy, both withered in the face of foreign competition, and the old port towns (with the exceptions of Genoa and the new city of Livorno) began to look half empty as the English and Dutch muscled them out of the declining Mediterranean trade. Worst off of all was the south, under direct Spanish or papal rule. Combining incompetence and brutality with outrageously high taxes (the Spaniards' to finance foreign wars, the popes' to build up Rome), they rapidly turned the already-poor south into a nightmare of **anarchic depravity**, haunted by legions of bandits and beggars, and controlled more tightly than ever by its violent feudal barons. To everyone's surprise, the south rose up and staged an epic rebellion. Beginning in Naples (**Masaniello's Revolt**, 1647), the disturbances soon spread all over the south and Sicily. For more than a year peasant militias ruled some areas, and makeshift revolutionary councils defended the cities. When the Spanish finally defeated them, however, they massacred some 18,000 people, and tightened the screws more than ever.

Bullied, humiliated and increasingly impoverished, 17th-century Italy at least tried hard to keep up its ancient prominence in the arts and sciences. Galileo Galilei looked through telescopes, Monteverdi wrote the first operas, and hundreds of talented though uninspired artists cranked out pretty pictures to meet the continuing high demand. Bernini and Borromini turned Rome into the capital of Baroque – the florid, expensive coloratura style that serves as a perfect symbol for the age itself, an age of political repression and thought control where art became a political tool. Baroque's heavenly grandeur and symmetry helped impress everyone with the majesty of Church and State. At the same time, Baroque scholars wrote books that went on for hundreds of pages without saying anything but avoided offending the government and the Inquisition. Baroque impresarios managed the wonderful pageantry of Church holidays, state occasions and carnivals that kept the ragged crowds amused.

Manners and clothing became decorously berserk, and a race for easily bought noble titles occurred that would have made a medieval Italian laugh out loud. Italy was being rocked to sleep in a Baroque cradle.

By the 18th century there were very few painters, or scholars, or scientists. There were no more heroic revolts either. Italy in this period hardly has any history at all; with Spain's increasing decadence, the great powers decided the futures of Italy's major states, and used the minor ones as a kind of overflow tank to hold surplus princes and those dispossessed by wars elsewhere (Napoleon on Elba was the last and most famous of these). In 1713, after the War of the Spanish Succession, the Habsburgs of **Austria** came into control of Milan and Lombardy, Mantua and the Kingdom of Naples. The **House of Lorraine**, related to the Austrians, won Tuscany upon the extinction of the Medici in 1737.

These new rulers improved conditions somewhat. Especially during the reigns of the **Empress Maria Theresa** (1740–80) and her son Joseph II (1780–92), two of the most likeable Enlightenment despots, Lombardy and the other Austrian possessions underwent intelligent economic reforms – giving them the headstart over the rest of Italy that helped Milan to its industrial prominence today. Naples' hard luck carried on when the Austrians transferred it to a branch of the **House of Bourbon** (1731); under them the southern kingdom was independent, but just as poorly governed as before. A new player in Italian affairs, and from the start an important one, was **Piedmont**, which during the War of the Austrian Succession shook loose from the tutelage of France and joined the winning side, earning a royal title in 1720 for **Vittorio Amedeo II**. The infant kingdom, with its brand-new capital of Turin, was poor and a bit backward in many ways, but as the only strong and free state in Italy it would be able to play the leading role in the events of the next century, and in Italian unification.

1796–1830: Napoleon, Restoration and Reaction

Napoleon, that greatest of Italian generals, arrived in Italy in 1796 on behalf of the French revolutionary Directorate, sweeping away the Piedmontese and Austrians and setting up republics in Lombardy (the 'Cisalpine Republic'), Liguria, and Naples (the 'Parthenopean Republic'). Italy woke with a start from its Baroque slumbers, and local patriots gaily joined the French cause. In 1799, however, while Napoleon was off in Egypt, the advance through Italy by an Austro-Russian army, aided by Nelson's fleet, restored the status quo. This was often accompanied by bloody reprisals, as peasant mobs led by clerics. such as the 'Army of the Holy Faith', marched across the south massacring liberals and French sympathizers.

In 1800 Napoleon returned in a campaign that saw the great victory at **Marengo**, giving him the opportunity once more to reorganize Italian affairs. He crowned himself King of Italy; Joseph Bonaparte and later Joachim Murat ruled at Naples. Elisa Bonaparte and her husband got Tuscany. Rome was annexed to France, and the Pope was carted off to Fontainebleau. Napoleonic rule lasted only until 1814, but in that time important public works were begun and laws, education and everything else reformed after the French model; immense Church properties were expropriated, and medieval relics everywhere put to rest – including the Venetian Republic, which

Napoleon for some reason took a special delight in liquidating. The French, however, soon wore out their welcome. Besides hauling much of Italy's artistic heritage off to the Louvre, implementing high war taxes and conscription (some 25,000 Italians died in the invasion of Russia), and brutally repressing a number of local revolts, they systematically exploited Italy for the benefit of the Napoleonic élite and the crowds of speculators who came flocking over the Alps. When the Austrians and English came to chase all the little Napoleons out, no one was sad to see them go.

The experience, though, had given Italians a taste of the opportunities offered by the modern world, as well as a sense of **national feeling** that had been suppressed for centuries. The 1815 Congress of Vienna put the clock back to 1796; indeed the Habsburgs and Bourbons seemed to think they could pretend the Napoleonic upheavals never happened, and the political reaction in their territories was fierce. The only major change from the *ancien régime* was that Venice and its inland empire now belonged to Austria. (Two name changes help to confuse students of this period; Piedmont is often referred to as the 'Kingdom of Sardinia', and Naples acquired the name 'Kingdom of the Two Sicilies'.)

Almost immediately, revolutionary agitators and secret societies such as the famous Carbonari emerged that would keep Italy convulsed in plots and intrigues. A large-scale revolt in Naples forced the reactionary **King Ferdinand** to grant a constitution (1821), but when Austrian troops came down to crush the rebels he revoked it. The French July Revolution of 1830 also spread to Italy, encouraged by the liberal **King Carlo Alberto** in Piedmont–Savoy, but once more the hated Austrians intervened.

1848–1915: The Risorgimento and United Italy

Conspirators of every colour and shape, including the legendary **Giuseppe Mazzini**, had to wait another 18 years for their next chance. Mazzini, a sincere patriot and democrat, agitated frenetically all through the years 1830–70, beginning by founding the Young Italy movement. Generally followed by a small cloud of cops and spies, he started parties, issued manifestos, plotted dozens of doomed revolts, defined great theories and strategies, checked in and out of exile, and chaired meetings of eternal committees, all with little practical effect. In retrospect, his career as a revolutionary can bear a slight comparison with Marx's – though less Karl than Groucho. It was typical of the times, and the disarray and futility among republicans, radicals and those who simply wanted a united Italy set the stage for the stumbling, divisive process of the Risorgimento.

The big change came in the revolutionary year of **1848**, when risings in Palermo and Naples (in January) anticipated even those in Paris itself. Soon all Italy was in the streets. Piedmont and Tuscany won constitutions from their rulers, and the people of Milan chased out the Austrians after a month of extremely bloody fighting; at the same time the Venetian Republic was restored. Carlo Alberto, the hope of most Italians for a war of liberation, marched against the Austrians, but his two badly bungled campaigns allowed the enemy to re-establish control over the peninsula. By June 1849, only Venice, under Austrian blockade, and the recently declared Roman Republic were left. Rome, led by Mazzini, and with a small army under **Giuseppe**

Garibaldi, a former sailor who had fought in the wars of independence in Latin America, beat off several attacks from foreign troops invited in by the Pope. The republic finally succumbed to a large force sent by, of all people, the republic of President Louis Napoleon (soon to declare himself Napoleon III) in France. Garibaldi's dramatic escape to safety in San Marino (he was trying to reach Venice, itself soon to surrender) gave the Risorgimento one of its great heroic myths.

Despite failure on a grand scale, at least the Italians knew they would get another chance. Unification was inevitable, but there were two irreconcilable contenders for the honour of accomplishing it. On one side, the democrats and radicals dreamed of a truly reborn, revolutionary Italy, and looked to the popular hero Garibaldi to deliver it; on the other, moderates wanted the Piedmontese to do the job, ensuring a stable future by making **Vittorio Emanuele II** king of Italy. His minister, the polished, clever **Count Camillo Cavour**, spent the 1850s getting Piedmont in shape for the struggle, building its economy and army, participating in the Crimean War to earn diplomatic support, and plotting with the French for an alliance against Austria.

War came in 1859, and French armies did most of the work in conquering Lombardy. Tuscany and Emilia revolted, and Piedmont was able to annexe all three. In May 1860, Garibaldi and his red-shirted '**Thousand**' sailed from Genoa (Cavour almost stopped them at the last minute), landed in Sicily, and electrified Europe by repeatedly beating the Bourbon forces in a quick march across the island. The Thousand had become 20,000, and when they crossed the straits bound for Naples it was clear that the affair was reaching its climax. On 7 September Garibaldi entered Naples, and though he proclaimed himself temporary dictator on behalf of Vittorio Emanuele, the Piedmontese were alarmed enough to occupy Umbria and the Marches. The King met Garibaldi on 27 October, near Teano, and after finding out what little regard the Piedmontese had for him, the greatest and least self-interested leader modern Italy has known went off to retirement on the island of Caprara.

Just as the French made all this possible, some more unexpected help from outside allowed the new Italy to add two missing pieces and complete its unification. When the Prussians defeated Austria in the war of 1866, Italy was able to seize the Veneto. Only Rome was left, defended by a French garrison, and when the Prussians beat France at Sedan in 1870, the Italian army marched into Rome without opposition.

The first decades of the **Italian Kingdom** were just as unimpressive as its wars of independence. A liberal constitutional monarchy was established, but the parliament almost immediately decomposed into cliques and political cartels representing various interests. Finances started in disorder and stayed that way, and corruption became widespread. Peasant revolts occurred in the south, as people felt cheated by inaction after the promises of the Risorgimento, and organized brigandage became a problem, partially instigated by the Vatican as part of an all-out attempt to discredit the new regime. The outlines of foreign policy often seemed to change monthly, though like the other European powers Italy felt it necessary to snatch up some colonies. The attempt revealed the new state's limited capabilities, with highly embarrassing military disasters at the hands of the Ethiopians at Dogali in 1887, and again at Adowa in 1896.

After 1900, with the rise of a strong socialist movement, strikes, riots and police repression often occupied centre stage in Italian politics. Even so, important signs of progress, such as the big new industries in Turin and Milan, showed that at least the northern half of Italy was becoming a fully integral part of the European economy. The 15 years before the war, prosperous and contented ones for many, came to be known by the slightly derogatory term *Italietta*, the 'little Italy' of modest bourgeois happiness, an age of sweet Puccini operas, the first motorcars, blooming 'Liberty'-style architecture, and Sunday afternoons at the beach.

1915–45: War, Fascism and War

Italy could have stayed out of the First World War, but let the chance to do so go by for the usual reasons – a hope of gaining some new territory, especially Trieste. Also, a certain segment of the intelligentsia found the *Italietta* boring and disgraceful: Irredentists of all stripes, some of the artistic Futurists, and the perverse, idolized poet **Gabriele D'Annunzio**. The groups helped Italy leap blindly into the conflict in 1915, with a big promise of boundary adjustments dangled by the beleaguered Allies. Italian armies fought with their accustomed flair, masterminding an utter catastrophe at Caporetto (October 1917) that any other nation but Austria would have parleyed into a total victory. No thanks to their incompetent generals, the poorly armed and equipped Italians somehow held firm for another year, until the total exhaustion of Austria allowed them to prevail (at the battle of Vittorio Veneto that you see so many streets named after), capturing some 600,000 prisoners in November 1918.

In return for 650,000 dead, 1 million casualties, severe privation on the home front, and a war debt higher than anyone could count, Italy received Trieste, Gorizia, the South Tyrol, and scraps. Italians felt cheated, and nationalist sentiment increased, especially when D'Annunzio led a band of freebooters to seize the half-Italian city of Fiume in September 1919, after the peace conferences had promised it to Yugoslavia. The Italian economy was in shambles and, at least in the north, revolution was in the air; workers in Turin raised the Red Flag over the Fiat plants and organized themselves into soviets. The troubles had encouraged extremists of both right and left, and many Italians became convinced that the liberal state was finished.

Enter **Benito Mussolini**, a professional intriguer in the Mazzini tradition with bad manners and no fixed principles. Before the war he had found his real talent as editor of the Socialist Party paper *Avanti* – the best it ever had, in fact, tripling the circulation in a year. When he decided that what Italy really needed was war, he left to found a new paper, and contributed mightily to the jingoist agitation of 1915. In the post-war confusion, he found his opportunity. A little bit at a time, he developed the idea of **Fascism**, at first less a philosophy than an astute use of mass propaganda and a sense for design. (*Fascis*, from which the name comes, were bundles of rods carried before ancient Roman officials, a symbol of authority. *Fascii* also referred to organized bands of rebellious peasants in 19th-century Sicily.) With a little discreet money supplied by frightened industrialists, Mussolini had no trouble recruiting for his black-shirted gangs, who found their first success beating up Slavs in Trieste and working as a sort of private police for landowners in stoutly socialist Emilia-Romagna.

The basic principle, combining left- and right-wing extremism into something the ruling classes could live with, proved attractive to many, and a series of weak governments stood by while the Fascist *squadre* cast their shadow over more and more of Italy. Mussolini's accession to power came on an improbable gamble. In the particularly anarchic month of October 1922, he announced that his followers would march on Rome. King Vittorio Emanuele III refused to sign a decree of martial law to disperse them, and there was nothing to do but offer Mussolini the post of prime minister. At first, he governed Italy with undeniable competence. Order was restored, and the economy and foreign policy were handled intelligently by non-Fascist professionals. In the 1924 elections, despite the flagrant rigging and intimidation, the Fascists only won a slight majority. One politician who was not intimidated was **Giacomo Matteotti**, and when some of Mussolini's close associates murdered him, a major scandal erupted. Mussolini survived it, and in 1925 and 1926 the Fascists used parliamentary methods to convert Italy into a permanent Fascist dictatorship.

Compared to the governments that preceded him, Mussolini looked quite impressive. Industry advanced, great public works were undertaken, with special care for the backward south, and the Mafia took some heavy blows at the hands of a determined Sicilian prefect named Mori. The most lasting achievement was the **Concordat** of 1929 with the Pope, founding the Vatican State and ending the Church's isolation from Italian affairs. The regime evolved a new economic philosophy, the 'corporate state', where labour and capital were supposed to live in harmony under syndicalist government control. But the longer Fascism lasted, the more unreal it seemed to be, a patchwork government of Mussolini and his ageing cronies, magnified and rendered heroic by cinematic technique – stirring rhetoric before oceanic crowds, colourful pageantry, magnificent, larger-than-life post offices and railway stations of travertine and marble, dashing aviators and parades of winsome gymnasts from the Fascist youth groups. In a way it was the Baroque all over again, and Italians tried not to think about the consequences. As one of Mussolini's favourite slogans, painted on walls all over Italy, summed it up: 'Whoever stops is lost.'

Mussolini couldn't stop, and the only possibility for new diversions lay with the chance of conquest and empire. His invasion of Ethiopia and his meddling in the Spanish Civil War, both in 1936, compromised Italy into a close alliance with Nazi Germany. Mussolini's confidence and rhetoric never faltered as he led an unprepared nation into the biggest ever war. Once more, Italian ineptitude at warfare produced embarrassing defeats on all fronts, and only German intervention in Greece and North Africa saved Italy from being knocked out of the war as early as 1941. The Allies invaded Sicily in July 1943, and the Italians began to look for a clever way out. They seized Mussolini during a meeting of the Grand Council, packed him into an ambulance and sent him off first to Ponza, then to a little ski hotel up in the Apennines (*see* p.576). The new government under Marshal Badoglio didn't know what to do, and confusion reigned supreme.

While British and American forces slogged northwards with the help of the free French, Brazilians, Costa Ricans, Poles, Czechs, New Zealanders and Norwegians, the Germans poured in divisions to defend the peninsula. They rescued Mussolini, and set him up in a puppet state called the Italian Social Republic in the north. In September 1943, the Badoglio government signed an armistice with the Allies, but it was too late to keep the war from dragging on another year and a half, as the Germans made good use of Italy's difficult terrain to slow the Allied advance. Meanwhile Italy finally gave itself something to be proud of – a determined, resourceful Resistance that established free zones in many areas, and harassed the Germans with sabotage and strikes. The *partigiani* caught Mussolini in April 1945, while he was trying to escape to Switzerland; after shooting him and his mistress, they hung him by his feet from the roof of a petrol station in Milan.

1945–the Present

Post-war Italian *cinema verità* – Rossellini's *Rome, Open City*, and De Sica's *Bicycle Thieves* – captures the atmosphere better than words ever could. In a period of serious hardships that older Italians still remember, the nation slowly picked itself up and returned to normal. A referendum in June 1946 made Italy a **republic**, but only by a narrow margin. The first governments fell to the new Christian Democrat party (DC) under Alcide de Gasperi, which ran the show for decades with a preposterous band of smaller parties. The main opposition was provided by the Communists (PCI), surely one of the most remarkable parties of modern European history. With the heritage of the only important socialist philosopher since Marx, Antonio Gramsci, and democratic, broadminded leader Enrico Berlinguer, Italian communism is unique, with its stronghold and showcase in the well-run, prosperous cities of Emilia-Romagna.

The 1950s, when Italian style and Italian cinema caught the imagination of the world, was Rome's decade. Gradually, a little economic miracle was happening; *Signor Rossi*, the average Italian, started buzzing around in his first classic Fiat *cinquecento*, northern industries boomed, and life cruised slowly back to normal. The south still lagged behind, despite the efforts of the government and its special planning fund, the Cassa per il Mezzogiorno. Though the extreme poverty and despair of the post-war years gradually disappeared, the region has still not caught up with the rest of Italy. Nationally, the *Democristiani*-controlled government soon evolved a **Byzantine style of politics** that only an Italian could understand. Through the constantly collapsing and reforming cabinets, nothing changed; all deals were made in the backrooms and everyone, from the Pope to the Communists, had a share in the decision making. One wouldn't call it democracy with a straight face, but for four decades it worked well enough to keep Italy on its wheels.

The dark side of the arrangement was the all-pervasive **corruption** that the system fostered. It is fascinating to read the work of journalists only a decade ago and see how almost without exception they politely sidestepped the facts; Italy was run by an unprincipled political machine, whose members raked in as much for themselves as they could grab, and everyone knew it, but it couldn't be said openly, for lack of proof. Even more sinister was the extent to which the machine would go to keep on top. The 1970s, Italy's 'years of lead', witnessed the worst of the political sleaze, along with a grim reign of extreme left- and right-wing terrorism, culminating in the kidnap and murder in 1978 of honourable DC prime minister Aldo Moro, who had attempted to forge a *compromesso storico* between mainstream left and right to balance power. The attacks were attributed to 'leftist groups', though even at the time many suspected that some of the highest circles in the government and army were manipulating them, with the possible collusion of the CIA. They were indeed; only relatively recently has some of the truth of Moro's 'sacrifice' begun to seep out. On another front, Italians woke up one morning in 1992 to find that the government had magically vacuumed seven per cent of the money out of all their savings accounts, an 'emergency measure' to meet the nation's colossal budget deficit, which was caused largely by the thievery of the political class and its allies in organized crime.

Italians are a patient lot, but the lid was about to blow. It all started in the judiciary, the one independent and relatively uncorrupt part of the government. In the early 1990s, heroic prosecutors Giovanni Falcone and Paolo Borsellino went after the Sicilian Mafia with some success, and were spectacularly assassinated for it, causing national outrage. Meanwhile, in Milan, a small group of prosecutors found a minor political kickback scandal that led them, through years of painstaking work, to the golden string that unravelled the whole rotten tangle of Italian political depravity – what Italians called *tangentopoli*, or 'bribe city'. For a year, the televised hearings of Judge Antonio di Pietro and his Operation Mani Pulite ('clean hands') team from Milan were the nation's favourite and most fascinating serial.

All the kingpins fell, notably Socialist leader Bettino Craxi. Others, especially former prime minister Giulio Andreotti, lost their parliamentary immunity. Andreotti was put on trial on two counts – association with the Mafia, and ordering the assassination of a journalist who had come perilously close to uncovering sinister facts surrounding Moro's murder. The trials continue to this day, and the impossibility of upholding the convictions of Andreotti and others in the appeals courts has been a factor in Italians' dwindling faith in their country's ability to make a clean sweep of its past.

If all the big fish escaped jail, it was definitely the end for the two criminal ruling parties, the DC and the Socialists. The 1993 municipal elections, held at the height of the *tangentopoli* hearings, saw a major political realignment: a big victory for the new PDS, the former Communists, as well as advances by the neo-fascist MSI (now reborn and santized as the 'National Alliance') and the Lega, a coalition of northern separatist parties led by the bumptious and eccentric Umberto Bossi.

Many of the same old faces, unsurprisingly, could still be seen thronging the corridors of power, but a power vacuum had been created, and to fill it in rushed the unlikely figure of Silvio Berlusconi, the former lounge singer and Craxi protégé whose political connections allowed him to assemble an unprecedented empire in television and publishing, and to become Italy's richest man in the process. Berlusconi thinks big: his empire was threatened by a possible PDS government, and the only way out was to buy the government for himself. He used his big bankroll and media control (he owns half of Italy's TV audience, a third of its magazine readership, books, newspapers and AC Milan) to create a new, totally synthetic party, Forza Italia, and to sell it to Italians the same way as soap and sex; prospective candidates were selected through auditions. Meanwhile, Berlusconi managed an improbable three-way alliance with the neo-fascists and Bossi's Lega. It all worked brilliantly: in the 1994 parliamentary elections, the first of what many Italians called their 'Second Republic', his rightist alliance won an impressive victory, and 'Mr TV' himself became prime minister. It soon became apparent that government under Berlusconi only meant business as usual. The media mogul's refusal to distance himself from his empire while in office, and his heavy-handed attempt to cripple the *Mani Pulite* probes, made many Italians feel the egg on their faces – they had struggled so hard to topple a malodorous old order, only to vote it back into office at the first chance.

It wasn't long before Judge Di Pietro resigned from the *Mani Pulite* investigations under a cloud of phony political allegations. His departure was followed by that of Berlusconi himself, who – surrounded by his own fog of allegations of scandal and bribery – was forced out of office in early 1995 when Bossi withdrew his support. The political mess that remained was such that President Scalfaro called in a political outsider to straighten out the country and institute reforms. This was a banker, Lamberto Dini, whose lack of a political past and steady head were virtues enough to keep him in office while the politicians got their house in order.

Dini, the finance man, started reforms, but it was Romano Prodi and his left-centre 'Olive Tree' coalition who brought in the necessary political will. Prodi, one of the country's biggest Europhiles, rallied the republic to swallow a difficult financial pill: stringent economic measures that allowed Italy to squeak into the first round of the Euro in 1999. Prodi had little time to bask in the glory: the same strict measures led to the Communists withdrawing their support of his government in late 1998, giving it to a new prime minister, left-wing darling Massimo D'Alema of the DS, who formed Italy's 60th government since the war. D'Alema didn't last long either, and was replaced by yet another coalition of the left, headed by former Craxian minister Giuseppe Amato.

The left's disarray and poor economic performance made it possible for Berlusconi and his piquant allies to come roaring back in the 2001 elections. Since then, the man who calls himself 'the world's greatest politician' has seldom been out of the headlines. Mostly, he's been busy keeping himself and his henchmen out of courtrooms; laws have been passed granting him immunity against all charges, while another innovative bill threatens judges with jail terms for giving 'incorrect sentences'. Berlusconi's rough vulgarity in publicly insulting Germans, Muslims and others, coming in a year when Italy held the EU presidency, has proved a major embarrassment, while his strong support of the American adventure in Iraq, in the face of massive public opposition, has started to chip away at his popularity.

Now fully in control of nearly all of Italian television and much of the press, Berlusconi has been able to avert any serious national discussion of all this. He may not be another Mussolini – to start with, he's 67 years old – but the idea of this Italian model of political power through media dominance spreading to other countries is beginning to cause increasing alarm across Europe.

Art and Architecture

03

You'd have to spend your holiday in a baggage compartment to miss Italy's vast piles of architecture and art. The Italians estimate there is at least one work of art per capita in their country, which is more than anyone could see in a lifetime – especially when so much of it is locked away in museums that are undergoing semi-permanent 'restoration'. Although you may occasionally chafe at not being able to see certain frescoes, or at finding a famous palace wrapped in the ubiquitous green netting of the restorers, the Italians on the whole bear very well the burden of keeping their awesome patrimony dusted off and open for visitors. Some Italians find living with the stuff all around them insupportable; the Futurists, for instance, were worried St Mark's might be blown up by foreign enemies in the First World War – but only as they wanted to do it themselves, which they deemed their right as Italian citizens.

Pre-Etruscan

To give a chronological account of the first Italian artists is an uncomfortable task. The peninsula's mountainous terrain saw many isolated ancient cultures even during the days of the sophisticated Etruscans and Romans. Most ancient of all, however, is the Palaeolithic troglodyte culture on the Riviera, credited with creating some of the first artworks in Europe – chubby images of fertility goddesses. These and other curious trappings may be seen in the Ligurian museums at **Balzi Rossi**, **Pegli** and **Finalborgo**. The most remarkable works from the Neolithic period until the Iron Age are the thousands of graffiti rock incisions in several isolated alpine valleys north of Lake Iseo, especially in the **Val Camonica** national park. After 1000 BC, Italic peoples all over the peninsula were making geometrically painted pots, weapons, tools and bronze statuettes. The most impressive culture, however, was the tower-building, bronze-working Nuraghe civilization on **Sardinia**, of which echoes are seen on the mainland. Among the most intriguing and beautiful artefacts to have survived are those of the Villanova culture in **Bologna**; the statues and inscriptions of the little-known Middle Adriatic culture at **Chieti** in Abruzzo, and the steles of an unknown people at **Pontrémoli**, north of Viareggio; others, of the Luini culture, are in **La Spezia**. Dolmens and strange little temples survive in many corners of central and southern **Puglia**. If you wish to see what was going on across the Mediterranean at the same time, there's also one of the best Egyptian museums in the world in **Turin**.

Etruscan and Greek (8th–2nd centuries BC)

With the refined, art-loving Etruscans we begin to have architecture as well as art. Not much has survived, thanks to their habit of building in wood and decorating with terracotta, but we do have plenty of distinctive rock-cut tombs, the best of which are at **Cerveteri** and **Tarquinia**; many of them contain exceptional frescoes that reflect Aegean Greek styles. The best of their lovely sculptures, jewellery, vases and much more are in **Rome** (where there's also a temple façade), **Chiusi**, **Volterra** and **Tarquinia**. There are also fine Etruscan holdings in **Perugia**, **Florence** and **Bologna**.

The Etruscans imported and copied many of their vases from their ancient Greek contemporaries, from Greece proper and the colonies of Magna Graecia in southern Italy. The Doric temple at **Paestum** is the best Greek structure on the peninsula (there are many more in Sicily); **Cumae**, west of Naples, and **Metapontum**, near Táranto, also merit a visit; of the many excavated Greek cities, usually only foundations remain. **Reggio di Calabria, Táranto, Naples, Bari** and the **Vatican** are the homes of the most impressive collections of ancient Greek vases, statues and other types of art.

Roman (3rd century BC–5th century AD)

Italian art during the Roman hegemony is mostly derivative of Etruscan and Greek, bearing witness to a talent for mosaics, wall paintings, glasswork and portraiture; architecturally, the Romans were brilliant engineers, the inventors of concrete and grand exponents of the arch. Even today their aqueducts, amphitheatres, bridges, baths – and the Pantheon – are impressive.

Of course, **Rome** itself has no end of ancient monuments; also nearby is **Ostia Antica**, Rome's ancient port, and the great **Villa Adriana**. Rome also has the stellar museums of Roman antiquities: the Museo Nazionale Romano, the Vatican Museums, the Capitoline Museums and the Museum of Roman Civilization at EUR. **Naples** is the other main destination for Roman art, with the ruins of ancient **Pompeii** and **Herculaneum,** and a spectacular museum of Pompeiian artefacts and of statues from Rome dug up by Renaissance collectors such as the Farnese.

Other impressive Roman monuments may be seen in **Benevento** (the best triumphal arch and some unusual Roman–Egyptian art); **Capua** (a huge amphitheatre and Mithraeum); **Verona** (the arena, gates and theatre complex); **Aosta** (a theatre and gates); the excavations of **Aquileia** in Friuli and **Sepino** in Molise; the temples in **Brescia** and **Assisi**; 'the villa of Catullus' in **Sirmione** on Lake Garda; villas, tunnels, canals, markets and other surprises in **Pozzuoli**, **Baia**, and the western Bay of Naples, and odds and ends in **Fiesole**, **Bologna**, **Trieste**, **Perugia**, **Cori** (in Lazio), **Spoleto**, **Rimini**, **Ancona**, **Susa**, **Lecce** and **Alba Fucens** in Abruzzo.

Early Middle Ages (5th–10th centuries)

After the fall of the Roman Empire, civilization's lamp flickered brightly in **Ravenna**, where Byzantine mosaicists adorned the glittering churches of the Eastern Exarchate. Theirs was to be the prominent pictorial and architectural style until the 13th century.

There are fine mosaics and paintings in **Rome** too, in the churches of San Clemente and Santa Prassede. In Rome, Italy's preference for basilican churches and octagonal baptistries began in Constantine's day; the growth of Christian art and architecture through the Dark Ages can best be traced there. The catacombs of Rome and **Naples** are packed with paintings. Ravenna-style mosaics may also be seen in the cathedrals of **Aquileia** and Torcello in **Venice**, where the fashion lingered until St Mark's. In the vicinity of **Táranto** there are the remains of Greek monasteries and cave paintings, and early-Christian churches at **Nocera** in Campania, and in Benevento. In **Albenga**, on the Riviera, and **Novara**, you'll find unusual 5th-century baptistries with artworks.

'Lombard' art, really the work of natives under Lombard rule, revealed new talent in the 7th–9th centuries, seen in the churches of **Cividale del Friuli**, works in the cathedral of **Monza**, in and around **Spoleto**, and in the abbey of San Salvatore in **Brescia**. A new style, presaging the Romanesque, may be seen in Sant'Ambrogio in **Milan**.

Romanesque (11th–12th centuries)

At this point an expansive society made new advances in art possible. North and south went separate ways, each contributing distinctive sculptural and architectural styles. We begin to learn the identities of the makers: the great Lombard cathedrals, masterworks of brick art, adorned with blind arcading, reliefs and lofty campaniles, are best exemplified at **Modena** (by master builder–sculptor Wiligelmo), San Michele in **Pavia, Cremona** cathedral, and Santo Stefano in **Bologna**. In **Verona** the cathedral and San Zeno were embellished by Guglielmo's talented student Nicolò; in **Parma** Antelami's baptistry is a milestone in the synthesis of sculpture and architecture.

Pisa's wealth permitted the largest building programme in Italy in 1,000 years – its cathedral. The exotic style owed something to the Muslim world, but the inspiration was completely original – in part a conscious attempt to recapture the grandeur of the ancient world. **Florence** developed its own black and white style, exemplified in buildings such as the baptistry and San Miniato. Variations appeared in the other Tuscan cities, each showing some Pisan stripes or Florentine rectangles.

In the south, Byzantine and Muslim influences created a different tendency. **Amalfi** and **Caserta** built a Saracenic cathedral and cloister, Amalfi's adorned with incised bronze doors from Constantinople in a style that was copied all over the south, notably at **Trani** and **Monte Sant'Angelo** in Puglia. The Byzantine painting and mosaics tradition continued, mostly in Sicily, though there is a fine example at Sant'Angelo in Formis near **Capua**. From Muslim geometrical patterns, southern artists acquired a taste for intricate designs using enamel or marble chips in church furnishings and architectural trim – as seen in pulpits and candlesticks in the churches of **Salerno** and **Ravello**. The outstanding advance of this period is the Pugliese Romanesque, as shown in cathedrals in almost every Puglian city (**Troia**, **Sipontum**, **Monte Sant'Angelo**, **Ruvo di Puglia**, **Trani**, **Altamura** and **Bari**), a style closely related to contemporary Norman and Pisan work – it's difficult to say who should get the credit for being first. Another impressive southern Romanesque cathedral is that of **Anagni** in Lazio; in the same region are the two unusual church façades in **Tuscània**. The Norman influence also appears in churches such as the Abbazia della Trinità in **Venosa** (Basilicata) and in the wonderful mosaic pavement of **Ótranto** cathedral.

This period also saw the erection of urban skyscrapers by the nobility – family fortress–towers built when the *comuni* forced barons into the towns. Larger cities had hundreds of them, before the townspeople demolished them. **San Gimignano** and **Ascoli Piceno** have the most surviving examples. In many cases tall towers were built simply for decoration and prestige. **Bologna**'s Due Torri, along with **Pisa**'s Campanile, are the best examples of medieval Italy's occasional disdain for the horizontal.

Late Medieval–Early Renaissance (13th–14th centuries)

In many ways this was the most exciting and vigorous phase in Italian art history, an age of discovery when the artist was like a magician. Great imaginative leaps occurred in architecture, painting and sculpture, especially in Tuscany. From Milan to Assisi, a group of masons and sculptors known as the Campionese Masters built magnificent brick cathedrals and basilicas. Some of their buildings reflect the Gothic style of the north (most spectacularly **Milan**), while in **Como** cathedral you can see the transition from Gothic to Renaissance. In **Venice** an ornate, half-oriental style called Venetian–Gothic still sets the city's palaces and public buildings apart, and influenced **Padua**'s exotic Basilica di Sant'Antonio.

This was also an era of transition in sculpture, from stiff Romanesque stylization to the more realistic, classically inspired works of the great Nicola Pisano, his son Giovanni (in the churches of **Pisa, Pistoia** and **Siena**), and his pupil Arnolfo di Cambio (**Florence**). Other outstanding works of the 14th century are Lorenzo Maitani's cathedral in **Orvieto** and the Scaligeri tombs of **Verona** by the Campionese Masters.

Painters in Rome and Siena learned from the new spatial sculpture. Most celebrated of the masters of the dawning Renaissance is, of course, the solemn Giotto, whose greatest works are the fresco cycles in **Padua** and **Assisi**. In St Francis' town you can also see excellent works by Giotto's merrier contemporaries from **Siena**. That city's artists, Duccio di Buoninsegna, Simone Martini and Pietro and Ambrogio Lorenzetti, gave Italy brilliant exponents of International Gothic, who were also precursors of the Renaissance. Their brightly coloured scenes, embellished with a thousand details, made Siena into a medieval dream city; the style carried on into the quattrocento with the courtly frescoes of the northerner Pisanello. In **Florence**, works by Orcagna, Gentile da Fabriano and Lorenzo Monaco laid a unique foundation for the Renaissance. Cathedral and public buildings in the north, especially at **Siena** and **Pistoia**, show a sophisticated understanding of urban design and an original treatment of established forms. Northern European Gothic never made much headway, though French Cistercians did build fine abbey churches such as those at **San Galgano** in Tuscany, **Fossanova** in Lazio, and Sant'Andrea in **Vercelli**. The south had little to contribute during this period, but **Naples** developed its own neo-Gothic architecture, and unique geometrically patterned church façades appear at **L'Aquila** and **Brindisi**.

Rome, for once, achieved artistic prominence with home-grown talent. The city's architecture from this period (as seen in the campanile of Santa Maria in Cosmedin) has largely been lost under Baroque remodellings, but the paintings and mosaics created by Pietro Cavallini and his school, and the intricate, inlaid stone pavements and architectural trim of the Cosmati and their followers, derived from the Amalfi Coast style, can be seen all over the city; both had an influence that extended far beyond Rome itself.

The Renaissance (15th–16th centuries)

The origins of this high noon of art are very much the accomplishment of quattrocento **Florence**, where sculpture and painting embarked on a totally new way of educating the eye. The idea of a supposed 'rediscovery of antiquity' has confused the understanding of the time. In general, artists broke new ground when they expanded from the traditions of medieval art; when they sought merely to copy the forms of ancient Greece and Rome, the imagination often faltered. Florentine art soon became recognized as the standard of the age, and examples can be seen everywhere in Tuscany. By 1450 Florentine artists were spreading the new style to the north, especially **Milan**, where Leonardo da Vinci and Bramante spent several years;

the collections in the Brera and other galleries, the *Last Supper*, and the nearby **Certosa di Pavia** are essential works of the Renaissance. There are other good museum collections in **Rome, Parma, Turin** and **Bergamo**; the core of Bergamo is a Renaissance masterpiece. **Mantua** has important works by Alberti and Mantegna, and nearby lies the 'ideal' Renaissance town: **Sabbioneta**. Michelangelo and Bramante, among others, carried the Renaissance to **Rome**, where it thrived under the patronage of enlightened popes. Other Renaissance diversions can be seen in **Rimini**: its remarkable Malatesta Temple; and **Urbino**: the lovely palace and art collection of the archetypal Renaissance prince, Duke Federico da Montefeltro.

The most significant art in the north came out of **Venice**, which had its own distinct school led by Mantegna and Giovanni Bellini; one of the best painters of the school, the fastidious Carlo Crivelli, did much of his work in the Marches (**Ascoli Piceno** and **Ancona**). Under the patronage of the Este family, Renaissance **Ferrara** produced its own school of quattrocento painters (Cosmè Tura, Ercole Roberti). In **Perugia**, Perugino was laying the foundations of the Umbrian school, in which Raphael and Pinturicchio earned their stripes. In **Orvieto** cathedral, the Tuscan painter Signorelli left a Last Judgment that inspired Michelangelo. Piero della Francesca was the most important non-Florentine painter before Raphael; his revolutionary works are at **Urbino, Sansepolcro** and **Arezzo**. Southern Italy, trapped in a decline that was even more artistic than economic, hardly participated at all, though examples of the northerners' art can be seen in **Naples** (the triumphal arch in the Castel Nuovo).

Despite the brilliant triumphs in painting and sculpture, the story of Renaissance architecture is partially one of confusion and retreat. **Florence**, with Brunelleschi, Alberti and Michelozzo, achieved its own special mode of expression – a dignified austerity that proved difficult to transplant elsewhere. In most of Italy the rediscovery of the works of Vitruvius, representing the authority of antiquity, killed off Italians' appreciation of their own architectural heritage; with surprising speed, the dazzling imaginative freedom of medieval architecture was lost forever. Some fine work still appeared, however, notably Codussi's palaces and churches in **Venice**.

High Renaissance and Mannerism (16th century)

At the beginning of the cinquecento, Michelangelo, Raphael and Leonardo held court at the summit of European art. But as Italy was losing her self-confidence, and soon her liberty, artistic currents tended toward the dark and subversive. Michelangelo, more than anyone, tipped the balance from the cool, classical Renaissance into turgid, emotionally fraught **Mannerism**. Among the few painters left in exhausted Florence, he had the brilliant Jacopo Pontormo and Rosso Fiorentino to help. Other painters lumped in with the Mannerists, such as Giulio Romano in Mantua and Il Sodoma around Siena, broke new ground while maintaining the discipline and intellectual rigour of the early Renaissance. Elsewhere, and especially among fashionable Florentine painters and sculptors, art was decaying into mere interior decoration.

For **Venice** it was a golden age, with Titian, Veronese, Tintoretto, Sansovino and Palladio, whose works may be seen throughout Venetia. Another art centre of the epoch, **Parma**, is embellished with the Mannerist brushes of Correggio and Parmigianino.

In **Cremona**, Milan, and other lucky galleries, you can see works by Arcimboldo, the cinquecento surrealist. In architecture, attempts to recreate ancient styles and the classical orders won the day. In **Milan,** and later in **Rome**, Bramante was one of the few architects able to do anything interesting with it, while Michelangelo's great dome of St Peter's put a cap on the accomplishments of the Renaissance. Other talented architects found most of their patronage in Rome, which after the 1520s became Italy's centre of artistic activity; Ligorio, Peruzzi, Vignola and the Sangallo family were among them.

Baroque (17th–18th centuries)

Rome continued its artistic dominance to become the Baroque capital, where the socially irresponsible genius of artists such as Bernini and Borromini was approved by the Jesuits and indulged by the tainted ducats of the popes. As an art designed to induce temporal obedience and psychical oblivion, its effects are difficult to describe, but the three great churches along Corso Vittorio Emanuele, Bernini's Piazza Navona fountains and St Peter's colonnades, are fine examples. More honest cities such as Florence and Venice chose to sit out the Baroque, though **Florence** at first approved the works of 16th-century proto-Baroque sculptors such as Ammannati, Giambologna and Cellini. Not all artists fit the Baroque mould; genius could survive even in a dangerous, picaresque age, most notably in the person of Michelangelo (works in **Milan** and **Rome**), not to mention other painters such as Mattia Preti, with works in Naples and **Taverna**, in his native Calabria.

The south of Italy, with its long tradition of religious emotionalism, found the Baroque entirely to its tastes, though few towns could afford to build much. **Naples** could, and the monastery of San Martino by Cosimo Fanzago marks the apotheosis of Neapolitan Baroque. Painting and sculpture even flourished while they were dying in northern Renaissance towns; southern art's eccentricity climaxed in the Sansevero chapel. A very different sort of Baroque appeared in the deep south, where the studied excess seemed to strike a deep chord in the popular psyche. Much of it is in Sicily, though the Spanish-looking city of **Lecce** developed a Baroque style that lasted from the 16th to the late 18th century, consistent and beautiful enough to make as impressive an architectural ensemble as any medieval or Renaissance city in the north. **Turin**'s town plan, churches, palaces and royal hunting lodges, designed by the priest Guarini and the early 18th-century Sicilian Juvarra, are the most elegant representations of the Baroque spirit in northern Italy. This was a great age of palaces and ornate Italian gardens, most famously in **Tivoli**, Isola Bella in **Lake Maggiore**, Villa Borghese and innumerable other locations in and around **Rome**, as well as around **Padua** and **Vicenza**.

Neoclassicism and Romanticism (late 18th–19th centuries)

Baroque was a hard act to follow, and at this time Italian art and architecture almost cease to exist. Two centuries of stifling oppression had taken their toll on the national imagination, and for the first time Italy not only ceased to be a leader in art, but failed even to make significant contributions. The one bright spot was **Venice**, where Giambattista Tiepolo and son adorned the churches and palaces of the last days of the Serenissima; their works can be seen in many places in the Veneto, and in **Ùdine** in Friuli. Other Venetians, such as Canaletto and Guardi, painted their famous canal scenes for Grand Tourists. In the 19th century the Macchiaioli, the Italian Impressionist movement that was led by Giovanni Fattori, was centred in **Florence**. In sculpture the neoclassical master Canova stands almost alone, a favourite in the days of Napoleon. His best works may be seen in the Villa Carlotta, on **Lake Como**, in **Rome**'s Villa Borghese and at **Possagno**. In architecture it was the age of grand opera houses, many of which were designed by the Bibiena family of Bologna. The Gallerie in **Milan** and **Naples** (late 19th century) and the extravagances of the Piemontese Alessandro Antonelli (**Turin** and **Novara**) are among the most impressive public buildings, and the neoclassical royal palaces at **Caserta** and **Stra** near Venice the grandest private addresses.

20th Century

The turn-of-the-19th-century Italian Art Nouveau – known as Liberty Style – failed to spread as widely as its counterparts in France and central Europe. There are a few good examples in **Milan**, but the best are linked with the burgeoning tourist industry: the construction of grand hotels, casinos and villas, especially in **Venice**, the **Lakes**, the **Riviera, Pésaro, Viareggio** and the great spas at **Merano, Montecatini** and **San Pellegrino**. Two art movements attracted international attention: Futurism, a response to Cubism, concerned with relevancy to the present, a movement led by Boccioni, Severini and Balla (best seen in the National Gallery of Modern Art, **Rome**, and in **Milan**); and the mysterious, metaphysical world of De Chirico; while Modigliani, Morandi and Carrà were masters of silences. Their works, among others, are displayed in the museums of **Rome, Venice** and **Milan**. Architecture in this century reached its (admittedly low) summit in the Fascist period (the **EUR** suburb in Rome, and public buildings everywhere in the south). Mussolinian architecture often makes us smile, but as the only Italian school in the last 200 years to have achieved a consistent sense of design, it presents a challenge to all modern Italian architects – one they have so far been unable to meet.

In **Turin** and **Milan** you can see the works of the most acclaimed Italian architect of this century, Pier Luigi Nervi; good post-war buildings are very difficult to find, and the other arts have never yet risen above the level of dreary, saleable postmodernism. Much of the Italians' artistic urge has been sublimated into the shibboleth of Italian design – clothes, sports cars, suitcases, kitchen utensils and the like. At present, though business is good, Italy is generating little excitement in these fields. Europe expects more from its most artistically talented nation; after the bad centuries of shame and slumber, a free and prosperous Italy may well find its own voice and its own style to help interpret the events of the day. If Italy ever does begin to speak with a single voice, whatever it has to say will be worth hearing.

Topics

04

Bella Figura

The longer you stay in Italy, the more inscrutable it becomes. Nothing is ever quite as it seems here, and part of the reason for this is the obsession with making a good impression – *'fare una bella figura'* – a singular Italian trait. You notice it almost immediately: not only are many Italians immaculate fashion victims (they are by far the biggest consumers of their own fashion industry), but they always seem to be modelling their spiffy threads – posing, gesturing, playing to an audience when they have one, which is nearly always because they rarely move about except in small herds. Their cities are their stage, the piazzas and streets like movie sets, with lights suspended over the middle. Longtime observers have even noted that each city's women dress in colours that complement the local brick or stone.

The Italians' natural grace and elegance may be partly instinctive; even back in the 14th century, visitors noted their charming manners and taste for exquisite clothes. Many a painting of the Madonna served not only for piety's sake, but also to advertise Milanese silks or Venetian brocades. In the Renaissance, appearance supplanted reality in a thousand ways, especially artificial perspective, which made artistic representations much cleverer than the real thing. Fake, painted marble supplanted real marble, even if it cost more; Palladio built marble palaces out of stucco; *trompe l'œil* frescoes embellished a hundred churches; glorious façades on cathedrals and palaces disguise the fact that the rest is unfinished brick. Even castles were built to impress rather than to keep out the enemy, in a day when battles had become brilliant bloodless games, and gorgeous Italian armour deflected few blows.

Castiglione's *The Courtier* advises that it is no use doing a brave and noble deed unless someone is watching; honour, like almost every other virtue, is something bestowed from without. After the French and Spanish burst the Italians' bubble of superiority in the 16th century, Italy's history becomes a saga of trying to do everything to keep up appearances, of nobles mending their socks in the half-light to save up for hiring a servant when visitors were expected.

Bella figura pleases the eye but irritates just about everything else. Fashionable conformity spreads from clothing to opinions, especially in the provinces; Italians remain the masters of empty flattery, and will say anything to please: 'Yes, straight ahead!' they'll often reply when you need directions, hoping it will make you happy even if they've never heard of your destination. Nor does fashion slavery show any sign of abating; now that more Italians have more money than ever before, they are using it for rarely necessary fur coats, and for designer clothes for the whole family. Even little children go to bed with visions of fashion dancing in their heads; Italy is the last stand of Barbie and Ken dolls, where each little girl owns at least a dozen.

Brick Italy, Marble Italy

'Italy', begins the 1948 Constitution, 'is a Republic based on labour' – an unusual turn of phrase, but one entirely in keeping with a time when a thoroughly humbled Italy was beginning to get back on its feet after the war. The sorrows of the common man occupied the plots of post-war *cinema verità*, and artists and writers began to celebrate themes of Faith, Bread and Work as if they were in the employ of the Church's *Famiglia Cristiana* magazine. To outsiders it seemed Italy was undergoing a serious change, but careful observers noted only another oscillation in the grandest, oldest dichotomy in Italian history. Brick Italy was once more in the driver's seat.

Brick Italy is a nation of hard work, humility and piety that knows it must be diligent and clever to wrest a comfortable living from the thin soil of this resource-poor, rocky peninsula. Marble Italy knows its citizens have always done just that, and celebrates by turning their diligence and cleverness into opulence, excess and foreign conquest. The two have been contending for Italy's soul ever since Roman quarrymen discovered Carrara marble. Brick Italy's capital was once brilliant, republican Siena; right now it is hard-working socialist Bologna. Its triumphs came with the age of the *Comuni*, with the modest genius of the Early Renaissance, and with the hard-won successes of the last 40 years. Marble Italy reached its height in the days of Imperial Rome; its capital is Rome, always and forever.

After the medieval interlude, marble made its great comeback with the High Renaissance and Michelangelo, the high priest of marble. The age of Baroque belonged to it, as did the brief era of Mussolini. Confirmed marble cities are Naples, Genoa, Turin, Pisa, Parma, Trieste, Perugia and Verona. Brick partisans include Pavia, Livorno, Lucca, Arezzo, Cremona and Mantua. Florence and Venice, the two medieval city-republics that became important states on their own, are the two cities that successfully straddle the fence. Look carefully at their old churches and palaces – you will often find marble veneer outside and solid brick underneath.

Keep all this in mind when you ponder the infinite subtleties of Italian history. It isn't always a perfect fit; medieval Guelphs and Ghibellines each had a little brick and a little marble in them, and the contemporary papacy changes from one to the other with every shift of the wind. Mussolini would have paved Italy over in marble if he had been able – but look at the monuments he could afford, and you'll see travertine and brick more than anything else. For a while in the 1980s, with Italy's economic boom and the glitz of Milanese design, it looked as if Marble Italy was about to make another comeback. But today, with Italy in the midst of its long and tortuous revolution, the situation is unclear. If and when a new regime emerges, will its monument to itself be a beautiful symbol of republican aspirations, such as Siena's brick Palazzo Pubblico, or a florid marble pile such as Rome's Altar of the Nation, the monument to Italian unification (and one of the biggest lumps of kitsch on this planet)?

Commedia dell'Arte

The first recorded mention of Arlecchino, or Harlequin, came in 1601 – the year that saw the debut of *Hamlet* – when the part was played by Tristano Martinelli. Theatre was blooming all over Europe, with Shakespeare and Marlowe in England, Calderón and Lope de Vega in Spain, and the predecessors of Molière in France. All had learned their craft from late Renaissance Italy, where the *commedia dell'arte* had created a fashion that spread across the continent. The great companies – the Gelosi, the Confidenti and the Accesi – toured the capitals, while others shared the provinces. Groups of 10 or 12 actors, run as co-operatives, they could do comedies, tragedies or pastorals to their own texts, and provide music, dance and juggling between acts.

The audiences liked the comedies best, with their set of masked stock characters, playing off scenes between the *magnifici* (great lords) and the *zanni* (servants), who provide the slapstick, half-improvised comic relief. These represented every corner of Italy: Arlecchino is a Bergamese; Balanzone,, the wise doctor who 'cures with Latin', from Bologna; Pulcinello, white-clad and warbling, a true Neapolitan; Meneghino, the piratical warrior, Milanese; the drunkard Rugantino, a Roman; and the nervous rich merchant Pantalone, a Venetian. To spring the plot there would be lovers (*innamorati*) – unmasked to remind us that love is life.

Arte doesn't mean art, but a guild; these companies were made up of professional players. The term was invented by Goldoni (*Arlecchino, servitore di due padroni*) in 1745; in the 1500s the companies were often known as the *commedia mercenaria* – they would hit town, set up a stage and start their show within the hour. Cultured Italians deplored the way the 'mercenary' shows were driving out serious drama, written by scholarly amateurs in the princely courts. In the repressive climate, caught between the Inquisition and the Spanish, a culture of ideas survived only in free Venice. Theatre retreated into humorous popular entertainment, but even then the Italians found a way to say what was on their minds. A new stock character appeared, the menacing but slow-witted *Capitano*, who always spoke with a Spanish accent; and the Italians learned from the French, using Arlecchino to satirize the hated Charles V – playing on the pronunciation of the names *harlequin* and *Charles Quint*.

Arlecchino may come from Oneta, a village north of Bergamo, but he carries a proud lineage that goes back to the ancient Greeks and Romans. From his character and appearance, theatre historians trace him back to the antique *planipedes*, comic mimes with shaven heads (everyone knew Arlecchino wore his nightcap to cover his baldness). He's been linked to German and Scandinavian mythological tricksters too, and it's been claimed that his patched costume is that of a Sufi dervish. No doubt he had a brilliant career all through the Middle Ages, but it was only in the 1500s that he took the form of the Arlecchino we know. At that time, young rustics from the valleys of Bergamo would go to Venice, Milan and other cities to get work as porters (*facchini*). They all seemed to be named Johnny – *Zanni* in dialect, which became the common term for any of the clownish roles in the plays; hence our word 'zany'.

The name of Arlecchino was a French contribution: at the court of Henri III, an Italian actor who played the role became a protégé of a Monsieur de Harlay, and people started calling him Harlequin. He became a stock role, the most beloved of the *commedia dell'arte* clown masks: simple-minded and easily frightened, an incorrigible prankster, a fellow as unstable as his motley dress. His foil was usually another servant, the Neapolitan Pulcinella/Punchinello – Punch – more serious and sometimes boastful, but still just as much of a buffoon. Try to imagine them together on stage, and you'll get something rather like Laurel and Hardy. No doubt they have always gone through the world together, and we can hope they always will.

That Etruscan Smile

Everything about the Etruscans is mysterious, and that's the way they liked it: their everyday lives were wrapped in magic and superstition, and we know only superficial details of their religion in the *Fanum Voltumnae* or sacred wood, around Viterbo, where no outsider was allowed. No one is sure of their origins, though they seem to have come from western Anatolia; their sudden decline and eventual complete disappearance after the 4th century BC was just as shadowy and unaccountable.

What the Etruscans did leave behind are portraits of themselves, and these are some of the most remarkable achievements of ancient art. They weren't the most original of artists, but every style that came from Greece was given an Etruscan twist. Even more than the Greeks, they had a talent for capturing expression and character on every level, from the astute, gentlemanly *Orator* in the Florence museum, to the happy, worldly couples lounging on their stone sarcophagi, the terracotta heads of children in the Villa Giulia and the grinning, rosy-cheeked grotesques that peer out from all Etruscan decoration. Usually they are smiling, a faraway mysterious smile.

Battered by dour Romans on one side and crazed Celts on the other, the Etruscans faded away – unless they went right into the ground, like the lost people that became the Irish fairies. But their presence is still felt in central Italy, especially in its art: the Romans and the other Italic nations learned much about art from the Greeks, but when you look at their painting – at Pompeii, in Naples, or in Nero's Golden House – it is clear that something essential, something in the soul, was their heritage from Etruria.

The thread of it has never been lost in all the centuries since. When you get to know Etruscan art, you'll see subtle reflections of it in everything that came after, from Botticelli's paintings to Mussolini's post offices. From the grotesques, revived by Raphael and now gazing out at us from the cornices of old buildings everywhere, one gets the feeling that somehow those mysterious Etruscans are still with us.

Fungus Fever

If you've brought the children, ignore their scoffing. That's not spaghetti with dirt on your plate, but *spaghetti al tartufo*, with truffles, the most prized gourmet delicacy in Italy – earthy, aromatic and aphrodisiac. It's true they're not much to look at, these subterranean lumpy *funghi*, these bulbous tubers that consent to sprout only in certain corners of France and Italy with the proper calcareous soils, oak trees and exposure. Per ounce they are the most expensive comestibles in the world; luckily, a little goes a long way.

Two types of truffles are considered outstanding – the black, found in southwest France and the Apennines; and the white, found in the Alba and Asti area of Piemonte. The white is the more prized, being rarer. It's a creamy colour, smooth and irregularly shaped, and can vary in size from that of a walnut to something more like a football. Truffles actually have very little intrinsic taste – it's their power to impart flavour to other foods that makes them so valued. They are usually eaten raw, sliced very finely over meat, fish or pasta, or added to stuffing for meat, poultry or game.

Truffles are so expensive because they are so hard to track down. An aura of mystery hangs over their origins; according to legend they are spawned by lightning bolts zapping through oak groves. Prices have led to experiments in cultivation, but most truffles are still brought to market by truffle hunters with keen-nosed truffle hounds; unlike the French, who use pigs, the Italians swear by dogs, suckled on teats rubbed with truffle juice.

The truffle season is short, lasting from October until the snows fall around Christmas. During this time daily auctions take place in Asti and Alba in the wee hours of the morning, when the secretive truffle-hunters arrive to sell the night's harvest (do truffles smell strongest at night, or is it that the best ones are always on someone else's property?).

If you're offered *tartufo* ice cream, by the way, don't despair for the sanity of the Italian kitchen – it's made of cream and chocolate, and like French chocolate *truffes* just looks like its namesake.

Leaning Towers

It isn't always a subject the Italians like to discuss. They'll be happy to sell you as many plastic souvenirs as you like of the most celebrated of the species, in Pisa, but a mention of the dozens of other listing landmarks scattered around Italy makes them uneasy. Italians, of course, think of themselves as the most skilled engineers on this planet. They built the Roman roads and aqueducts, the Pantheon and the dome of St Peter's, the biggest in the world. They invented concrete. Their endless *autostrade* zoom through long tunnels and skim over deep valleys on stilts, remarkable *tours de force* of engineering. They have built more railway tunnels, perhaps, than the rest of Europe put together. So why can't they keep their towers from drooping?

The answer may well be that they built them that way. For centuries there has been a dark undercurrent of thought that claims Pisa's tower was meant to lean. Goethe thought so, and architects who carefully measured the foundation stones came to the same conclusion. More than 100 years ago a Professor Goodyear exposed the whole business as 'symmetrophobia' – not fear of the symmetrical, but disdain for it. Italy's medieval master builders, not yet squeezed into the Renaissance straitjacket of monumental symmetry, could still be playful – witness the *parfait* stripes on so many cathedrals, or the floral print that covers Florence's Duomo.

The Italians of today do not like this explanation any better; they brusquely reject any suggestion that their ancestors were tempted away from the perpendicular on a whim. You can judge for yourself at Pisa – the campanile of which would not look right without the tilt – or at the Garisenda and Asinelli towers of Bologna, a pair of elephantine monstrosities that seem ready to topple at any minute. None of Venice's, except for the new St Mark's, are close to being straight; Ravenna has two that are even more precarious, and other examples can be seen at Rovigo and Rome. In Naples they have tilting domes – nothing intentional, but perhaps Providence's reminder that nothing around the Bay of Naples is allowed to stand forever.

Non-Leaning Towers

In most of Italy, when there are no billboards and power lines to block the view, you will see landscapes that have not changed since 1500. Long ago, Italian farmers began the job of making the country into one great formal garden, planting olives and vines in neat rows, and creating avenues of Lombardy poplars or parasol pines. Medieval designers added cities, towns and castles in constantly changing styles, each one complementary to those that came before. The basic feature in many parts of the rugged peninsula is the hill town, orderly and compact, its buildings draped carefully on a peak as if arranged there by a sculptor. By 1500, after 500 years of prosperity, the builders' work was done, and the Italian garden was perfect, cohesive and complete.

Visitors from over the Alps were impressed by the richness and size of Italian towns, and especially by their monumental urge to the vertical. By 1150 Italians were building towers on a scale unmatched until the American cities of the 1900s. Indeed, larger Italian cities had a Manhattanish aspect, with hundreds of tall, square defence towers creating incredible skylines – as with skyscrapers, it soon became a matter of prestige among baronial families to have the tallest; many reached over 200ft. In those rough times the towers weren't just for show; city officials had to take constant complaints from neighbours about siege engines parked on the street, stray showers of boiling oil, and noisy, pitched battles keeping the children up at night. The *comuni* managed to get most of these towers pulled down by about 1350. The great bell-towers of the cathedrals and city halls survive, and they are usually still the tallest buildings in the city. To give some idea of how ambitiously Italy could build, here are the 10 tallest structures completed before the year 1500:

1. **Cremona**, campanile, 370ft
2. **Florence**, cathedral, 364ft
3. **Milan**, cathedral, 351ft
4. **Siena**, Palazzo Pubblico, 338ft
5. **Venice**, campanile, 332ft
6. **Bologna**, Torre Asinelli, 318ft
7. **Florence**, Palazzo Vecchio, 308ft
8. **Modena**, Ghirlandina, 276ft
9. **Verona**, Torre dei Lamberti, 275ft
10. **Florence**, Giotto's campanile, 280ft

Pasta

Croton and Sybaris, other Greek cities, introduced the Italians to their future hearts' delight. *Makaria*, a small, cylindrical form of pasta – perhaps the original *maccheroni* – was eaten at funeral banquets; by 600 BC the Sybarites had invented the rolling pin and were making the equivalent of tagliatelle and maybe even lasagne. In a nation that has trouble baking a decent loaf of bread this delicious and practical new staple found a warm welcome nearly everywhere.

Pasta's triumphal march northwards finally slowed to a halt in the rice paddies and treacherous polenta morasses of Lombardy; everywhere else it remains in firm control of the country's menus. Pasta does have its cultural ramifications. The artists of the Futurist movement declared war on spaghetti, and many of today's Italian *nouveaux riches* wouldn't be caught dead ordering pasta in a restaurant (while their counterparts in northern Europe and America wax ever more enthusiastic about it).

Do you think that pasta is all the same? Well, so do millions of Italians, though an equal number revel in the incredible variety of pasta forms and fashions; during your travels you'll find the same mixture of flour and water turned into broad *pappardelle* and narrow *linguini* ('tiny tongues'), stuffed delights such as ravioli and tortellini, and regional specialities such as Puglian *orecchiette* ('little ears'). Other inviting forms, among the 400 or so known shapes, include vermicelli ('little worms'), *lumacconi* ('slugs'), *bavette* ('dribbles'), and *strozzapreti* ('priest-chokers'). But even these fail to satisfy the nation's culinary whims, and every so often one of the big pasta companies commissions a big-name fashion designer to come up with a new form.

The Pinocchio Complex

The Italians, much as they adore their *bambini*, have produced but one classic of children's literature, the story of a wooden puppet who must pass through trials and tribulations before he can become a real boy and a blessing to his father in his old age.

Since the Risorgimento, the Italian government has been a bit of a Pinocchio to the country that painfully carved it out of wood, admittedly half-petrified and half-rotten from the start. Each ring of the thick trunk told a dire tale of defeat and tyranny, corruption, papal misgovernment, foreign rule and betrayal. From this piece of flotsam the Italians created a new creature, a national state that sits in the class of real governments like an exasperating puppet, the bad boy of the EU, with more violations of its trade rules than any other nation. Every day its parliament is in session, its nose grows a little bit longer. With its creaky bureaucracy, unpredictable and not blessed with the soundest of judgments, it is constantly led astray – by the Mafia, power-hungry cabals of 'freemasons', Mussolinis, southern landowners, popes, Jesuits and whale-sized special interests that threaten to gobble it down whole. The parties that make up its *commedia dell'arte* coalitions, like flimsy wooden limbs and joints, are liable to trip up or fly off at any moment, making the poor thing collapse (something that since 1946 has occurred on average once every 11 months).

Just as Pinocchio is somehow able to walk without strings, so Italy functions with remarkable smoothness, and even prospers. As Europe grows ever closer together, having a wooden-headed political system becomes rather embarrassing, however. Constitutional reform, with the 1993 referendum that changed the electoral system, may prove the biggest threat to this puppet's career. And, with the revelations of the last few years, Italians are beginning to interest themselves in the all-important question of who, all this time, has been pulling the strings.

Italian Culture

05

Cinema

After the Second World War, when Italy was at its lowest ebb, when it was financially and culturally bankrupt, and when its traditional creativity in painting, architecture and music seemed to have dried up, along came a handful of Italian directors who invented a whole new language of cinema. Neorealism was a response to the fictions propagated by years of Fascism; it was also a response to the lack of movie-making equipment after the Romans, their eyes suddenly opened after a decade of deception and mindless 'White Telephone' comedies, pillaged and sacked Cinecittà in 1943. Stark, unsentimental, often shot in bleak locations and featuring non-professional actors, the genre took shape with directors such as Roberto Rossellini (*Rome, Open City*, 1945), Vittorio de Sica (*Bicycle Thieves*, 1948) and Luchino Visconti (*The Earth Trembles*, 1948).

Although neorealism continued to influence Italian cinema (Rossellini's films with Ingrid Bergman, such as *Europa 51* and *Stromboli*, Fellini's classic *La Strada* with Giulietta Masina and Anthony Quinn, Antonioni's *The Scream*), Italian directors began to go off in their own directions. The post-war period was the golden age of Italian cinema, when Cinecittà, Italy's Hollywood, produced scores of films every year. Like the artists of the age of Mannerism, a new generation of individualistic (or egoistic) directors created works that needed no signature, from Sergio Leone's ultra-popular kitsch Westerns to the often jarring films of the Marxist poet Pasolini (*Accattone, The Decameron*). This was the period of Visconti's *The Damned*, Antonioni's *Blow Up*, Lina Wertmüller's *Seven Beauties*, De Sica's *Neapolitan Gold*, Bertolucci's *The Conformist*, and the classics of the *maestro* Federico Fellini – *I Vitelloni, La Dolce Vita, Juliet of the Spirits, The Clowns, Satyricon*.

In the 1970s the cost of making films soared and the industry went into recession. Increasingly, directors went abroad or sought out actors with international appeal to help finance their films (Bertolucci's *Last Tango in Paris* with Marlon Brando and *1900* with Donald Sutherland; the overripe Franco Zeffirelli's *Taming of the Shrew* with Taylor and Burton; Visconti's *Death in Venice*). Fellini was one of the few who managed to stay home (*Roma, Amarcord*, and later *Casanova* – admittedly with Donald Sutherland in the lead role – *City of Women, The Ship Sails On, Orchestra Rehearsal* and *Intervista*, a film about Cinecittà itself).

Although funds for films became even scarcer in the 1980s, new directors appeared and recharged Italian cinema, often with a fresh lyrical realism and sensitivity. Bright stars of the decade included Ermanno Olmi (the singularly beautiful *Tree of the Wooden Clogs* and *Cammina, Cammina*), Giuseppe Tornatore's sentimental and nostalgic *Cinema Paradiso* (1988), Paolo and Vittorio Taviani (*Padre Padrone, Night of the Shooting Stars, Kaos* and *Good Morning, Babilonia*), Francesco Rosi (*Christ Stopped at Eboli, Three Brothers, Carmen* and *Cronaca di una Morte Annunciata*), and Nanni Moretti (*La Messa è Finita*), unfortunately rarely seen outside of festivals and film clubs, while Zeffirelli (*La Traviata*) and Bertolucci (*1900, The Last Emperor*) continued to represent Italy in the world's cinemas. Comedy found new life in Mario Monicelli's hilarious *Speriamo che sia Femmina* and in Bruno Bozzetto, whose animation features (especially *Allegro non Troppo*, a satire of Disney's *Fantasia*) are a scream.

The 1990s served up some fairly thin gruel, in a recession of inspiration that went with that of the economy. Worthy exceptions were *Il Ladro di Bambini* (1992) by Gianni Amelio, *Mediterraneo* (1991) by Gabriele Salvatores, about Italian soldiers marooned on a Greek island, Nanni Moretti's travelogue to the Ionian islands, *Caro Diario* (1994), Franco Zeffirelli's *Hamlet* (1990), with a surprise casting of Mel Gibson in the leading role, and *Il Postino* (1995), directed by Michael Radford – a very Italian story about the relationship of a local postman with the poet Pablo Neruda, exiled on an Italian island.

This was also the decade that Fellini spun his final reel. Though critics both at home and abroad sometimes complained he repeated himself in his last films, his loyal fans eagerly awaited each new instalment of his personal fantasy, his alternative hyper-Italy that exists on the other side of the looking glass. He was the last director regularly to use Cinecittà ('Cinecittà is not my home; I just live there,' he famously said), and his demise may well bring about the end of Rome's pretensions as Hollywood on the Mediterranean.

In the past few years, Bernardo Bertolucci has returned to the scene with *Stealing Beauty* (1996), a lush Tuscan coming of age drama, and *Besieged* (1998), the story of the romance between an Italian composer and an African political refugee, filmed in Rome (although his latest work, *The Dreamers*, returns to the Paris of *Last Tango*). But all in all the most acclaimed recent Italian film has been Roberto Benigni's unlikely comedy on the Holocaust, the Oscar-winning *La Vita è Bella* (1999),

Italian films are windows on the nation's soul, but if you don't understand Italian you may want to see them at home, where you have the advantage of subtitles. English-language films in Italy rarely receive the same courtesy, however – Italians like their movies dubbed. Check current events listings for films labelled *versione originale* – you'll find a few in Rome , Milan and Bologna, and often in other big cities. There are also Italy's film festivals (where films tend to be subtitled); the most important one is in Venice (last week of August to first week of September); Florence hosts a documentary festival in December.

Literature

Few countries have as grand a literary tradition – even Shakespeare made extensive use of Italian stories for his plots. Besides the great Latin authors and poets of ancient Rome, the peninsula has produced a small shelf of world classics in Italian; read a few before you come, or bring them along for train trips. (All the books mentioned below are available in English translation and may be found in the English sections of Italian bookshops.) Once you've visited some of the settings of Dante's *Divine Comedy*, and come to know at least historically some of the inhabitants of the *Inferno*, *Purgatorio* and *Paradiso*, the old classic becomes even more fascinating.

Dante (1265–1321) was one of the first poets in Europe to write in the vernacular, and in doing so he incorporated a good deal of topographical material from his 13th-century world. His literary successor, Petrarch (1304–74), has been called by many 'the first modern man'; in his poetry the first buds of humanism were born, deeply thought and felt, complex, subtle and fascinating today as ever (his *Canzoniere* is widely available in English).

The third literary deity in Italy's late medieval/early Renaissance trinity is Boccaccio (1313–75), whose imagination, humour and realism is most apparent in his 'Human Comedy', the *Decameron* – 100 stories 'told' by a group of young aristocrats who fled into the countryside from Florence to escape the plague of 1348. Boccaccio's detached point of view had the effect of disenchanting Dante's ordered medieval cosmos, clearing the way for the renaissance of the secular novel.

Dante, Petrarch and Boccaccio exerted a tremendous influence over literary Europe, and in the 15th and 16th centuries a new crop of writers continued in the vanguard – Machiavelli in political thought (*The Prince*), though he also wrote two of the finest plays of the Renaissance (*Mandragola* and *Clizia*); Ariosto in the genre of knightly romance (*Orlando Furioso*, the antecedent of Spenser's *Faerie Queene*, among others); Cellini in autobiography; Vasari in art criticism and history (*The Lives of the Artists*); Castiglione in etiquette, gentlemanly arts and behaviour (*The Courtier*); Alberti in architecture and art theory (*Della Pintura*); and Leonardo da Vinci in a hundred different subjects (the *Notebook* and so on). Even Michelangelo had time to write a book of sonnets, now translated into English. Other works include the writings and intriguing play (*The Candlemaker*) of the great philosopher and heretic Giordano Bruno (perhaps the only person excommunicated from three different churches); the risqué, scathing writings of Aretino, the 'Scourge of Princes'; the poetry and songs of Lorenzo de' Medici; and the *Commentaries* by Pope Pius II (Enea Silvio), which provides a rare view into the life, opinions and times of one of the most accomplished Renaissance men, and is the only autobiography ever written by a pope.

Baroque Italy was a quieter place, dampened by the censorship of the Inquisition. The Venetians kept the flame alight with Casanova's picaresque *Life*, the tales of Carlo Gozzi, and the plays of Goldoni. Modern Italian literature has an official birthdate – 1827, with the publication of Alessandro Manzoni's *I Promessi Sposi* ('The Betrothed'), which not only spoke with sweeping humanity to the concerns of pre-Risorgimento Italy, but spoke in its language – an everyday Italian that nearly everyone understood, no matter what their regional dialect; the novel went on to become a symbol of the aspiration of national unity.

The next writer with the power to capture the turbulent emotions of his time was Gabriele D'Annunzio, whose life of daredevil patriotism and superman cult contrast with the lyricism of his poetry and some of his novels, which are still widely read in Italy. Meanwhile, and much more influentially, Pirandello, the philosophical Sicilian playwright and novelist who was obsessed with absurdity, changed the international vocabulary of drama before the Second World War.

The post-war era saw the appearance of neorealism in fiction as well as in cinema, and the classics, though available in English, are among the easiest books to read in Italian – Cesare Pavese's *La Luna e i Falò* ('The Moon and the Bonfires'), Carlo Levi's tragic *Cristo Si è Fermato a Eboli* ('Christ Stopped at Eboli)', and Vittorini's *Conversazione in Sicilia*. Other acclaimed works of the post-war period include

Non è questo 'l terren, ch' i' toccai pria?
Non è questo il mio nido,
Ove nudrito fui sí dolcemente?
Non è questa la patria in ch' io mi fido,
Madre benigna e pia,
Che copre l'un e l'altro mio parente?
Per Dio, questo la mente
Talor vi mova; e con pietà guardate
Le lagrime del popol doloroso,
Che sol da voi riposo,
Dopo Dio, spera: e, pur che voi mostriate
Segno, alcun di pietate,
Vertú contra furore
Prenderà l'arme; e fia 'l combatter corto;
Ché l'antiquo valore
Ne l' italici cor non è ancor morto.

Petrarch (1304–74)

Is not this precious earth my native land?
And is not this the nest
From which my tender wings were taught to fly?
And is not this soil upon whose breast,
Loving and soft, faithful and true and fond,
My father and my gentle mother lie?
'For love of God,' I cry,
Some time take thought of your humanity
And spare your people all their tears and grief!
From you they seek relief
Next after God. If in your eyes they see
Some marks of sympathy,
Against this mad disgrace
They will arise, the combat will be short
For the stern valour of our ancient race
Is not yet dead in the Italian heart.

trans. William Dudley Foulke LLD (1915)

The Garden of the Finzi-Contini (about a Jewish family in Fascist Italy) by Giorgio Bassani and, also set during the Fascist era, *That Awful Mess on Via Merulana* by Carlo Emilio Gadda. Then there's the Sicilian classic that became famous around the world, as well as being made into a classic film – *The Leopard* by Giuseppe di Lampedusa.

The late Italo Calvino, perhaps more than any other Italian writer in the past two decades, enjoyed a large international following – his *If on a Winter's Night a Traveller, Italian Folktales, Marcovaldo* and *The Baron in the Trees* were all immediately translated into English; perhaps the best of them is *Invisible Cities*, an imaginary dialogue between Marco Polo and Kublai Khan. Much maligned, Sicily continued to produce some of Italy's best literature, from the pens of Leonardo Sciascia and Gesualdo Bufalino. The current celebrity of Italian literature is Umberto Eco, professor of semiotics at Bologna university, whose *The Name of the Rose* kept readers all over the world at the edge of their seats over the murders of a handful of 14th-century monks in a remote Italian monastery, while magically evoking, better than many historians, the political and ecclesiastical turmoil of the period.

Italy has inspired countless of her visitors, appearing as a setting in more novels, poems and plays than tongue can tell. There is also a long list of non-fiction classics, some of which make fascinating reading and are readily available in most bookshops: Goethe's *Italian Journey*, Ruskin's *The Stones of Venice*, D.H. Lawrence's *Etruscan Places* and *Twilight in Italy*, Hilaire Belloc's *The Path to Rome*, Norman Douglas' *Old Calabria*, James/Jan Morris' *Venice*, Mary McCarthy's *The Stones of Florence* and *Venice Observed*, and many others, including the famously over-the-top travellers' accounts of Edward Hutton and the ever-entertaining H.V. Morton.

For a rare Italian point of view from the outside looking in, read *The Italians* by the late Luigi Barzini, one-time correspondent for the *Corriere della Sera* in London.

Music and Opera

Italy has contributed as much to western music as any country – perhaps a little more, in fact. It was an Italian monk, Guido d'Arezzo, who devised the musical scale; it was a Venetian printer, Ottaviano Petrucci, who invented a method of printing music with movable type in 1501 – an industry that Italian printers monopolized for years (which is why we play *allegro* and not *schnell*). Italy also gave us the piano, originally the pianoforte because, unlike the harpsichord, it could be played both soft and loud, the accordion, invented in the Marches, and the violins of the Guarneri and Stradivarius of Cremona, which set a standard for the instrument that has never been equalled. But Italy is most famous as the mother of opera, in many ways the most Italian of arts.

Italian composers came into their own in the 14th century, led by the blind Florentine Landini, whose *Ecco la Primavera* is one of the first Italian compositions to have come down to us. Although they were following international trends that had been introduced by musicians from France and the Low Countries, the earliest Italian works bear witness to a special love of melody, as well as a preference for vocal music.

Landini was followed by the age of the *frottolas* (secular verses accompanied by lutes), which were especially prominent in the court of Mantua. The *frottolas* were forerunners of the *madrigal*, the greatest Italian musical invention of the Renaissance. The text of the madrigals, though they were sung in three or six parts, was given serious consideration and was sung to be understood; at the same time church music had become so polyphonically rich and sumptuous (most notoriously at St Mark's in Venice) that it drowned out the words of the Mass. Many melodies used were from secular and often bawdy songs, and the bishops at the Council of Trent (1545–63) seriously considered banning music from the liturgy. The day was saved by the Roman composers, led by Palestrina, whose solemn, simple but beautiful melodies set a standard for all subsequent composers.

Two contrasting strains near the end of the 16th century led to the birth of opera: the Baroque love of spectacle and the urge to make everything, at least on the surface, more beautiful, more elaborate, more showy. Musically, there were the lavish Florentine *intermedii*, performed on special occasions between the acts of plays; the *intermedii* used elaborate sets and costumes, songs, choruses and dances to set a mythological scene. At the same time, in Florence, a group of humanist intellectuals who called themselves the Camerata came to the conclusion from their classical studies that ancient Greek drama was not spoken, but sung, and took it upon themselves to try to recreate this pure and classical form. One of their chief theorists was Galileo's father Vincenzo, who studied Greek, Turkish and Moorish music and advocated the clear enunciation of the words, as opposed to the Venetian tendency to merge words and music as a single rich unit of sound.

One of the first results of the Camerata's debates was court musician Jacopo Peri's *L'Euridice*, performed in Florence in 1600. Peri used a kind of singing speech (recitative) to tell the story, interspersed with a few melodic songs. No one, it seems, asked for an encore; opera had to wait a few years until the Duchess of Mantua asked her court composer, Claudio Monteverdi (1567–1643), to compose something similar to what she had heard in Florence. Monteverdi went far beyond Peri, bringing in a large orchestra, designing elegant sets, adding dances and many more melodic songs, or arias. His classic *L'Orfeo* (1607), still heard today, and *L'Arianna* (unfortunately lost but for fragments) were the first operatic 'hits'. He moved on to bigger audiences in Venice, which soon had 11 opera houses. After he died, Naples took over top opera honours, gaining special renown for its clear-toned *castrati*.

Other advances were developing in the more pious atmosphere of Rome, where Corelli was busily perfecting the concerto form and composing his famous *Christmas Concerto*. In Venice, Vivaldi expanded the genre by composing some 400 concerti for whatever instruments happened to be played in the orchestra of orphaned girls where he was concertmaster.

The 18th century saw the sonata form perfected by harpsichord master Domenico Scarlatti. Opera was rid of some of its Baroque excesses and a division was set between serious works and the comic *opera buffa*; Pergolesi (1710–36; his *Il Flaminio* was the basis for Stravinsky's *Pulcinella*) and Cimarosa (1749–1801) were the most sought-after composers, while the now infamous Salieri, antagonist of Mozart, charmed the court of Vienna. Italian composers held sway throughout Europe; with others, such as Sammartini, who helped develop the modern symphony, they contributed more than is generally acknowledged today towards the founding of modern music.

Italy was less innovative in the 19th century, when most of its musical energies were devoted to opera, the reviving nation's clearest and most widely appreciated medium of self-expression. All of the most popular Italian operas were written in the 19th and early 20th century, most of them by the 'Big Five' – Bellini, Donizetti, Rossini, Verdi and

Puccini. For Italians, Verdi (1813–1901) is supreme, the national idol even in his lifetime, with rousing operas that were practically the battle hymns of the Risorgimento. Verdi, more than anyone else, re-established Italy on the musical map; his works provided Italy's melodic answer to the ponderous turbulence of Richard Wagner.

After Verdi, Puccini held the operatic stage, though not entirely singlehandedly; the later 19th century gave us a number of composers who are best remembered for only one opera: Leoncavallo with *Pagliacci*, Mascagni with *Cavalleria Rusticana*, Cilea with *Adriana Lecouvreur*, and many others, down to obscure composers such Giordano, whose *Fedora*, famous for being the only opera with bicycles on stage, is revived frequently in his home town of Fóggia.

Of more recent Italian and Italian-American composers, there's Ottorino Respighi (whose works were among the few 20th-century productions that the great Toscanini deigned to direct) and Gian Carlo Menotti, surely the best loved – not only for his operas but for founding the Spoleto Festival. Later there were the innovative post-war composers Luigi Nono and Luciano Berio, two highly respected names in contemporary academic music.

Next to all of this big-league culture, however, there survive remnants of Italy's traditional music – the pungent tunes of Italian bagpipes (*zampogne*), the ancient instrument of the Apennine shepherds, which is often heard in big cities (especially in the south) at Christmas time; the lively *tarantella* of Puglia; country accordion music, the fare of many a rural *festa*; and the great song tradition of the country's music capital, Naples, the cradle of everyone's favourite cornball classics but also of many haunting, passionate melodies of tragedy and romance rarely heard abroad – or, to be honest, in Italy itself these days. Naples now prides itself on being the capital of Mediterranean rock 'n' roll – a spurious claim, and not too impressive even if it were true. Listen for yourself; on the *bancarelle* in the street markets of Naples you'll have ample opportunity to audition a wide range of locally produced cassettes and see if anything catches your fancy. Italian pop climbs to the top of its modest plateau every February at the San Remo song festival, the national run-off for the Eurovision Song Contest and just as hilariously tacky; the likes of *Volare* are nowhere to be heard.

The opera season in Italy runs roughly from November to May. Be sure not to limit your explorations to the prestigious La Scala in Milan. The San Carlo in Naples is equally old and impressive, and La Fenice in Venice, finally restored, is impressive once more – both are in cities with a longer and richer operatic tradition. The Teatro dell'Opera in Rome and the Teatro Comunale in Florence can both put on excellent, innovative productions too. On the next rung down (in size and finances, though not necessarily in quality) are the houses in Parma, Trieste, Genoa, Bergamo, Turin, Modena, Bari and Fóggia. Summer festivals are also an excellent place to hear music.

Food and Drink

06

In Rome people spend most of their time having lunch. And they do it very well – Rome is unquestionably the lunch capital of the world.

Fran Lebowitz, *Metropolitan Life*, 1978

There are those who eat to live and those who live to eat, and then there are the Italians, for whom food has an almost religious significance, unfathomably linked with love, *la mamma,* and tradition. In this singular country, where millions of otherwise sane people spend many of their waking hours worrying about their digestion, standards both at home and in the restaurants are understandably high. Few Italians are gluttons, but all are experts on what is what in the kitchen; to serve a meal that is not properly prepared and more than a little complex is tantamount to an insult.

For the visitor, this national culinary obsession comes as an extra bonus to the senses, along with Italy's remarkable sights, its music, and the feel of the warm sun on your back. Here you can enjoy some of the best tastes and smells the world can offer, prepared daily in Italy's kitchens and fermented in its countless wine cellars. Eating *all'italiana* is not only delicious and wholesome, but now undeniably trendy. Foreigners flock here to learn the secrets of Italian cuisine and the even more elusive secret of how the Italians can live surrounded by such delights and still fit into their sleek Armani trousers.

Restaurant Generalities

Breakfast (*colazione*) in Italy is no lingering affair, but an early-morning wake-up shot to the brain: a *cappuccino* (*espresso* with hot foamy milk, often sprinkled with chocolate – first thing in the morning is the only time of day any self-respecting Italian will touch the stuff), a *caffè latte* (white coffee) or a *caffè lungo* (a generous portion of *espresso*), accompanied by a croissant-type roll, called a *cornetto* or *brioche*, or a fancy pastry. This repast can be consumed in any bar and repeated during the morning as often as is felt necessary. Breakfast in most Italian hotels seldom represents great value.

Lunch (*pranzo*), generally served around 1pm, is the most important meal of the day for the Italians, with a minimum of a first course (*primo piatto* – any kind of pasta dish, broth or soup, or rice dish or pizza), a second course (*secondo piatto* – a meat dish, accompanied by a *contorno* or side dish – usually a vegetable, salad or potatoes), followed by fruit or dessert and coffee. You can begin with a platter of *antipasti* – the appetizers Italians do so brilliantly, ranging from warm seafood delicacies to raw ham (*prosciutto crudo*), salami in 100 varieties, lovely vegetables, savoury toasts, olives, pâté and much much more. There are restaurants that specialize in *antipasti*, and they usually don't take it amiss if you decide to forget the pasta and meat and just nibble on these scrumptious hors d'œuvres (though in the end this may well cost more than a full meal). Most Italians accompany their meal with wine and mineral water – *acqua minerale*, with or without bubbles (*con* or *senza gas*), which supposedly aids digestion – and conclude it with a *digestivo* liqueur.

Cena, the **evening meal,** is usually eaten around 8pm – earlier in the north and later in the south. This is much the same as *pranzo* but lighter, without the pasta; a pizza and beer, eggs or a fish dish. In restaurants, they offer all the courses, so if you have only a sandwich for lunch you can have a full meal in the evening.

In Italy the various terms for types of **restaurants** – *ristorante*, *trattoria* and *osteria* – have been confused. A *trattoria* or *osteria* can be just as elaborate as a restaurant, though rarely is a *ristorante* as informal as a traditional *trattoria*. Unfortunately, the old habit of posting menus and prices in the windows has fallen from fashion, so it's often difficult to judge variety or prices. Invariably, the least expensive eating place is the *vino e cucina*, a simple establishment serving simple cuisine for simple everyday prices. It is essential to remember that the fancier the fittings, the fancier the **bill** will be, though neither of these points has anything at all to do with the quality of the food. If you're uncertain, do as you would at home – look for lots of locals.

People who haven't visited Italy for years and have fond memories of eating full meals for under a pound will be amazed at how much **prices** have risen, though in some respects eating out in Italy is still a bargain, especially when you figure out how much all that wine would have cost you at home. In many places you'll find restaurants offering a *menu turistico* – set meals of usually meagre inspiration for a reasonable set price. More imaginative chefs often offer a *menu degustazione* – a set-price gourmet meal that allows you to taste their daily specialities and seasonal dishes. Both of these are cheaper than if you had ordered the same food *à la carte*.

As the pace of modern urban life militates against traditional lengthy, home-cooked repasts with the family, followed by a siesta, alternatives to sit-down meals have mushroomed. Many office workers now behave much as their counterparts elsewhere in Europe and consume a rapid snack at lunchtime, returning home after a busy day to throw together some pasta and salad in the evenings.

The Italian fast-food alternative, a buffet known as the 'hot table' (*tavola calda*), is becoming harder to find among the international and made-in-Italy fast-food franchises; bars often double as *paninotecas* (which make sandwiches to order, or serve *tramezzini* – little sandwiches on square white bread); outlets selling pizza by the slice (*al taglio*) are common in city centres. You can get material for outdoor or hotel-room picnics at a grocer's (*alimentari*) or market (*mercato*); some will make sandwiches for you.

Regional Specialities

What comes as a surprise to many visitors is the tremendous regional diversity at the table; often next to nothing on the menu looks familiar, once dishes are disguised by their local or dialect name. Expect further mystification – many Italian chefs have wholeheartedly embraced the concept of nouvelle cuisine, or rather *nuova cucina*, and are constantly inventing dishes with even more names.

In **northern Italy**, look for heavier dishes prepared with butter and cream. *Pasta all'uovo* and risotto are favourite first courses, while game dishes, liver, *bollito misto* (mixed boiled meats), *fritto misto* (mixed fried meats), sausages and seafood appear as main courses. **Piemonte** is a gourmet region that's particularly renowned for its white truffles and cheeses. It also boasts the unique *bagna cauda,* a rich hot dip that's made with butter, olive oil, garlic, anchovies and cream and eaten with winter salad, *cardi* (a raw artichoke-like thistle), or roasted meats. **Liguria**'s cuisine, on the other hand, matches the criteria of the perfect Mediterranean diet – this is the *cucina povera* of olive oil, lots of vegetables, a little cheese and wine, and seafood. Liguria also gave the world *pesto,* the tangy, rich, addictive sauce of basil, pine nuts, garlic, olive oil and cheese, usually served with local *trenette* pasta.

The **Lombards** like their food substantial too: *antipasti* include meats (raw *carpaccio,* or *bresaola* – dried salt beef served with lemon, oil and rocket); popular *primi* are saffron-tinted *risotto alla milanese* and pasta stuffed with pumpkin and cheese; meat courses include classics such as *ossobuco alla milanese* (veal knuckle braised with white wine and tomatoes) and the hearty regional pork and cabbage stew, *cazzoela* or *cassuoela* (two of 25 different spellings). If you're really hungry, plump for brick-heavy polenta, a cake of yellow maize flour, served with various sauces – a Lombard classic is *polenta e osei* (topped with roast birds); another, more rare, is *stu'a'd'asnin cünt la pulenta* (stewed donkey with polenta).

In the **Veneto**, a typical seashore meal might include oysters from Chioggia or *sarde in saor* (marinated sardines) followed by the classic *risi e bisi* (rice and peas, cooked with Parma ham and Parmesan) or Venice's favourite pasta, *bigoli in salsa* (thick spaghetti, served with a piquant onion, butter and anchovy sauce). *Secondi* range from *fegato alla veneziana* (liver and onions) to *seppie alla veneziana* (cuttlefish in its own ink). In Vicenza try *baccalà alla vicentina* – salt cod cooked with onions, cheese and anchovies. Inland, the rivers yield ingredients for the famous *brodetto di pesce* (fish soup), and *anguilla* or *bisato in umido* (eel stew). The province is also renowned for its *radicchio,* red chicory, and for its white asparagus in springtime. The further north or east you go, the more ethnic the cuisine. Towards the **Trentino-Adige**, the cooking displays hearty Austrian influences: try goulash and smoked meats with rye bread, and the ubiquitous *speck,* a chewy, dry smoked ham. Desserts in **Friuli** are an epiphany: don't miss poppyseed strudel, Hungarian-style *rigojanci* (whipped cream and chocolate) or Slovenian-style *gibanica* (ricotta, honey, poppyseeds and pine nuts).

Emilia-Romagna ranks as Italy's gourmet region *par excellence* – this is the land of delicious *tortellini* and lasagne, Parmesan cheese, Parma ham, balsamic vinegar and a hundred other delicacies. *A panzu pina u s'ragiona mej* – 'You think best with a full belly', they say in the region. A typical *antipasto* would be a selection of *salumi* (cured pork) cuts that might include *mortadella* or *culatello* – tenderest pig's bottom. Pasta is the classic *primo*: *tortelli* (or *anolini*, in Parma, or *cappelletti*) filled with pork, ham, *mortadella* and Parmesan; or *tortellini d'erbetta* filled with herbs and ricotta, served with melted butter and freshly grated Parmesan. Alternatively, there's tagliatelle with *ragù* (or *alla bolognese*), a smooth sauce of finely minced pork and veal, *prosciutto,* onions, carrots, celery, butter and tomato (the lofty original of the humble British 'spag bol'), or the third great Bolognese pasta dish, lasagne. Meat dishes can be heavy: *stracotto*, topside of beef, cooked for hours in wine with herbs and vegetables until it becomes incredibly tender, is one.

Central Italy is the land of beans and chick peas, game, tripe, salt cod (*baccalà*), *porchetta* (whole roast pork cooked with rosemary), Florentine steaks, *saltimbocca alla romana* (veal scallops with ham and sage), and freshwater fish in interesting guises. Pasta, which seems to come in more intriguing shapes than elsewhere, might be served with rabbit or stewed boar. **Tuscan and Umbrian** cooking uses fresh, simple, high-quality ingredients flavoured with herbs and olive oil, and the local *porcini* mushrooms or truffles. Seafood is more prominent in the **Marches**, along with a fancier version of lasagne called *vincisgrassi*, and stuffed fried olives.

Modern **Romans** are as adventurous at the table as their classical ancestors; their capital is an excellent place in which to delve into any style of regional cooking, with dozens of restaurants from all over Italy. Lots of cooks in Roman restaurants come from the central Apennines, so you can easily get a taste of the **Abruzzo** – a region known for its game dishes, sheeps' cheese, saffron, and the quality of its pasta. The **Molise** is much the same, but the Molisani are especially fond of hot red peppers.

The further south you go, the spicier things get, and the richer the puddings and cakes. **Southern Italy** is the land of home-made pasta, wonderful vegetables and superb seafood, frequently fried or laced with olive oil. Southern specialities are often seasoned with capers, anchovies, lemon juice, oregano, olives and fennel. **Campania**'s favourites are simple: *pasta e fagioli* (pasta and beans) and *spaghetti alle vongole* (with baby clams); its seafood is exceptional – mussels (*zuppa di cozze*, in a hot pepper sauce) appear frequently, along with oily fish such as mackerel and sardines. Aubergines and zucchini crop up in many local dishes, especially *melanzane parmigiana* (aubergine baked with tomato and mozzarella) and *misto di frittura* (deep-fried potato, aubergine and zucchini flowers). Naples invented both **pizza** and spaghetti; a genuine Neapolitan pizza cooked in a wood-fired brick oven is the classic local eating experience. *Calzoni*, half-moon envelopes of pizza dough, often filled with ham and cheese, and *mozzarella in carrozza*, a fried cheese sandwich, are excellent street snacks.

Calabria and Basilicata boast the best swordfish anywhere, caught fresh from the straits of Messina. In more prosperous **Puglia** you'll taste varieties of shellfish seen nowhere else: *fasulare*, small and roundish with tan-coloured shells, and *piedi di porco*, small rugged black shells; you'll even encounter *vongole imperiali*, giants among the clams. A favourite pasta dish is *orecchiette* ('little ears'), often served with greens on top. The local olive oil is dark and strong, similar to that of Greece. Also look out for the strongly flavoured *ricotta forte*.

Wine and Spirits

Italy is a country where everyday wine is cheaper than Coca-Cola or milk, and where nearly every family owns some vineyards or has some relatives who supply most of their daily needs. Yet though they live in one of the world's largest wine-growing countries, Italians imbibe relatively little – when they do drink, it's usually only at meals. That said, if Italy has an infinite variety of regional dishes, there is an equally bewildering array of regional wines, many of which are rarely exported because they

Italian Menu Vocabulary

Antipasti (Starters)

These treats can include almost anything; among the most common are:

antipasto misto mixed antipasto
bruschetta garlic toast (with olive oil and sometimes tomatoes)
carciofi (sott'olio) artichokes (in oil)
frutti di mare seafood
funghi (trifolati) mushrooms (with anchovies, garlic and lemon)
gamberi ai fagioli prawns (shrimps) with white beans
mozzarella *(in carrozza)* soft cow/buffalo cheese (fried with bread in batter)
prosciutto (con melone) cured ham (with melon)
salsicce sausages

Minestre (Soups) and Pasta

agnolotti ravioli stuffed with meat
cappelletti small ravioli, often in broth
crespelle crêpes
frittata omelette
orecchiette ear-shaped pasta
panzerotti ravioli with mozzarella, anchovies and egg
pasta e fagioli soup with beans, bacon and tomatoes
pastina in brodo tiny pasta in broth
polenta cake or pudding of corn semolina
ravioli flat, stuffed pasta parcels
spaghetti all'amatriciana with spicy bacon, tomato, onion and chilli sauce
spaghetti alle vongole with clam sauce
stracciatella broth with eggs and cheese
tortellini crescent-shaped pasta parcels

Carne (Meat)

agnello lamb
anatra duck
arrosto misto mixed roast meats
bollito misto mixed boiled meats, or stew
braciola chop
brasato di manzo braised beef with vegetables
bresaola dried raw meat
carpaccio thinly sliced raw beef
cassuoela pork stew with cabbage
cervello brains
cervo venison
coniglio rabbit
costoletta/cotoletta chop
lumache snails
manzo beef
osso buco braised veal knuckle
pancetta bacon
piccione pigeon
pizzaiola beef in tomato and oregano sauce
pollo chicken
polpette meatballs
rognoni kidneys
saltimbocca veal, prosciutto and sage, in wine
scaloppine thin slices of veal sautéed in butter
stufato beef and vegetables braised in wine
tacchino turkey
vitello veal

Pesce (Fish)

acciughe or ***alici*** anchovies
anguilla eel
aragosta lobster
baccalà dried salt cod
bonito small tuna
calamari squid
cappesante scallops
cozze mussels
fritto misto mixed fried fish
gamberetti shrimps
gamberi prawns
granchio crab
insalata di mare seafood salad
merluzzo cod
ostriche oysters
pesce spada swordfish
polipi/polpi octopus
sarde sardines
sogliola sole
squadro monkfish
stoccafisso wind-dried cod
tonno tuna
vongole small clams
zuppa di pesce fish in sauce or stew

Contorni (Side Dishes, Vegetables)

aglio garlic
asparagi asparagus
carciofi artichokes
cavolo cabbage
ceci chick peas
cetriolo cucumber
cipolla onion
fagiolini French (green) beans
fave broad beans

funghi (porcini) mushrooms (boletus)
insalata (mista/verde) salad (mixed/green)
lenticchie lentils
melanzane aubergines
patate (fritte) potatoes (fried)
peperoncini hot chilli peppers
peperoni sweet peppers
peperonata stewed peppers
piselli (al prosciutto) peas (with ham)
pomodoro(i) tomato(es)
porri leeks
rucola rocket
verdure greens
zucca pumpkin
zucchini courgettes

Formaggio (Cheese)

bel paese soft white cow's cheese
cacio/caciocavallo pale yellow, sharp cheese
caprino goat's cheese
parmigiano Parmesan
pecorino sharp sheep's cheese
provolone sharp, tangy cheese; *dolce* is less strong
stracchino soft white cheese

Frutta (Fruit, Nuts)

albicocche apricots
ananas pineapple
arance oranges
banane bananas
ciliegie cherries
cocomero watermelon
fragole strawberries
frutta di stagione fruit in season
lamponi raspberries
limone lemon
macedonia di frutta fruit salad
mandorle almonds
mele apples
more blackberries
nocciole hazelnuts
noci walnuts
pesca peach
pesca noce nectarine
pompelmo grapefruit
prugna/susina prune/plum
uva grapes

Dolci (Desserts)

amaretti macaroons
crostata fruit flan
gelato (produzione propria) ice cream (home-made)
granita flavoured ice, usually lemon or coffee
panettone cake with candied fruit and raisins
semifreddo refrigerated cake
spumone a soft ice cream
torta cake, tart
zabaglione eggs and Marsala wine, served hot
zuppa inglese trifle

Bevande (Beverages)

acqua minerale mineral water
con/senza gas sparkling/natural
aranciata orange soda
birra (alla spina) beer (draught)
latte (intero/scremato) milk (whole/skimmed)
succo di frutta fruit juice
vino (rosso, bianco, rosato) wine (red, white, rosé)

Cooking Terms (Miscellaneous)

aceto (balsamico) vinegar (balsamic)
affumicato smoked
bicchiere glass
burro butter
conto bill
coltello knife
cucchiaio spoon
forchetta fork
forno oven
fritto fried
ghiaccio ice
griglia grill
in bianco without tomato
marmellata jam
menta mint
miele honey
olio oil
pane (tostato) bread (toasted)
panini sandwiches (in a roll)
panna cream
pepe pepper
ripieno stuffed
rosmarino rosemary
sale salt
salvia sage
tavola table
tovagliolo napkin
tramezzini sandwiches (in sliced bread)
uovo egg
zucchero sugar

are best drunk young. Even wines that are well-known and often-derided clichés abroad, such as Chianti and Lambrusco, can be wonderful new experiences when tasted on their home turf. Unless you're dining at a restaurant with an exceptional cellar, do as the Italians do and order the local wine (*vino locale* or *vino della casa*). You won't often regret it.

Most Italian wines are named after the grape and the district they come from. If the label says DOC (*Denominazione di Origine Controllata*), it means the wine comes from a specially defined area and was produced according to a certain traditional method. DOCG (*Denominazione di Origine Controllata e Garantita*) is allegedly a more rigorous classification, indicating that the wines not only conform to DOC standards but are tested by government-appointed inspectors. At present, few wines have been granted this status, but the number should increase steadily. *Classico* means that a wine comes from the oldest part of the zone of production, though is not necessarily better than a *non-Classico*. *Riserva, superiore* or *speciale* denotes a wine that has been aged longer and is more alcoholic; *recioto* is a wine made from the outer clusters of grapes, with a higher sugar and therefore alcohol content.

Other Italian wine terms are *spumante* (sparkling), *frizzante* (pétillant), *amabile* (semi-sweet), *abboccato* (medium dry), *passito* (strong sweet wine made from raisins). *Rosso* is red, *bianco* white; between the two extremes lie *rubiato* (ruby) and *rosato, chiaretto* or *cerasuolo* (rosé). *Secco* is dry, *dolce* sweet, *liquoroso* fortified and sweet. *Vendemmia* means vintage, a *cantina* is a cellar, and an *enoteca* is a wine shop or museum where you can taste and buy wines.

The regions of Piemonte, Tuscany and Veneto produce Italy's most prestigious red wines, while Friuli-Venezia Giulia and Trentino-Alto Adige are the greatest regions for white wines. King of the Tuscans is the mighty Brunello di Montalcino (DOCG), an expensive blockbuster. Pinot Grigio and the unusual Tocai make some of the best whites. But almost every other corner of Italy has its vinous virtues, be it the Lambrusco of Emilia-Romagna, the Orvieto of Umbria, the Taurasi of Campania or the Frascati of Lazio. The well-known Valpolicella, Bardolino and Soave are produced on the shores of Lake Garda. Even in the south, with much of its stronger, rougher wine shipped north for blending, you will find some wonderful varieties, such as the Sicilian Corvo (red and white).

Italy turns its grape harvest to other uses too, producing Sicilian Marsala, a famous fortified wine fermented in wooden casks, ranging from very dry to flavoured and sweet, and *vin santo* ('sacred wine'), a sweet Tuscan speciality that is often served with almond biscuits. Vermouth, originating from Turin, is made of wine flavoured with alpine herbs and spices. Italians are fond of post-prandial brandies (to aid digestion) – Stock or Vecchia Romagna appear on the best-known Italian brandy bottles. *Grappa* is a rough, schnapps-like spirit drunk in black coffee after a meal (*caffè corretto*). Other drinks that you'll see in Italian bars include Campari, a red bitter that's drunk on its own or in cocktails; *Fernet Branca, Cynar* and *Averno* (popular aperitif/digestifs); and a host of liqueurs such as *Strega*, the witch potion from Benevento, almond-flavoured *Amaretto*, cherry *Maraschino*, aniseed *Sambuca* and herby *Millefiori*.

Travel

07

Getting There

By Air from the UK and Ireland

There are currently direct flights to more than 20 Italian destinations from more than half a dozen British airports. Rome, Milan, Pisa and Venice have the greatest choice of year-round services, and there are plenty of regular flights to the business cities of Genoa and Bologna too. Flights to coastal or island resort destinations may be much more seasonal. Florence and Turin have more limited air links with Britain, but are well connected by rail to Pisa, Milan and Rome.

It's much cheaper flying to Italy from the UK now that competition from **no-frills carriers** has forced the traditional airlines to lower their prices. Travelling midweek is normally cheaper with the budget airlines, but it's worth shopping around for weekend flights – often flights offered by the 'low-cost' airlines are more expensive than established scheduled flights.

Scheduled return fares vary greatly, depending on the season in which you travel. The best-value deals are usually **APEX** fares, which have to be booked 7–14 days ahead, and must include a Saturday night in Italy – no alterations or refunds are possible without penalties. Return scheduled fares range from around £130 off-season to midsummer fares of well over £350. Full fares on the major carriers, especially to some of the less popular destinations such as Turin, can be as high as £500. Cheaper fares often have restrictions and may involve flying via another European destination.

There are many inexpensive **charter flights** to popular Italian destinations in summer, although you are unlikely to find the same sort of rock-bottom bargains as you can, say,

Major Carriers

From the UK and Ireland

Alitalia, London, **t** 0870 544 8259, Dublin, **t** (01) 677 5171, *www.alitalia.co.uk*

British Airways, **t** 0870 850 9850, *www.britishairways.com*

KLM Direct, **t** 0870 243 0541, *www.klm.com*

Meridiana, **t** (020) 7839 2222, *www.meridiana.it*

SN Brussels, **t** 0870 735 2345, *www.flysn.be*

Lufthansa, **t** 08457 737 747, *www.lufthansa.com*

Aer Lingus, Dublin, **t** 0818 365 000; or Belfast, 045 084 4444, *www.aerlingus.com*

From the USA and Canada

Alitalia, (USA) **t** 800 223 5730, *www.alitaliausa.com*

British Airways, **t** 800 AIRWAYS, *www.britishairways.com*

Continental, **t** 800 231 0856; 800 361 8071 (hearing impaired), Canada 800 521 0280, *www.continental.com*

Delta, **t** 800 241 4141, *www.delta.com*

Air Canada, **t** 1 888 247 2262, *www.aircanada.com*

Northwest Airlines, **t** 800 447 4747, *www.nwa.com*

United Airlines, **t** 800 433 7300, *www.ual.com*

Low-cost Carriers (UK)

easyJet, **t** 0870 600 0000, *www.easyjet.com*. Daily flights between London Stansted and Bologna, Venice, Rome, Milan and Naples.

Ryanair, **t** 0871 246 000, *www.ryanair.com*. Flights from Stansted to Rome, Milan, Turin, Bologna, Pisa, Treviso, Ancona, Brescia, Genoa, Rimini, Alghero, Palermo, Pescara and Trieste.

Other no-frills airlines flying to Italy at the time of writing are **Air Scotland** (**t** (0141) 848 4990, *www.airscotland.com*), **BmiBaby** (**t** 0870 264 2229, *www.bmibaby.com*), **Duo** (**t** 0871 700 0700, *www.duo.com*), **Fly Globespan** (**t** 08705 561 522, *www.flyglobespan.com*), **Flybe** (**t** 0870 567 6676, *www.flybe.com*), **Jet 2** (**t** 0870 737 8282, *www.jet2.com*), **Now** (**t** 0845 458 9737, *www.now-airlines.com*), and **Volare** (**t** 0800 032 0992, *www.volareweb.com*).

Charters, Discounts, Youth Fares and Special Deals

From the UK and Ireland

Italy Sky Shuttle, 227 Shepherd's Bush Rd, London W6 7AS, **t** (020) 8748 1333, *www.travelshop.com*

to Spain. You may find cheaper fares by combing the small ads in the travel pages, or from a specialist agent (a reputable ABTA-registered one), which offer good student and youth rates.

The main problems with cheaper flights are inconvenient schedules, and restrictions – especially on changing travel times. Make sure that you take out good travel insurance, however cheap your ticket.

By Air from the USA and Canada

The main Italian air gateways for direct flights from **North America** are Rome and Milan, but if you're doing a grand tour, fares to other European destinations (Paris or Amsterdam, for example) may be cheaper. Most US airlines have partnered up with a main European provider, which cuts costs and saves checking in twice. It may be worth catching a cheap flight to London (New York–London fares are always competitive) then flying on from there using one of the British low-cost carriers (*see* box).

Prices are higher from **Canada**, so you may be better off flying via the United States.

By Air from Mainland Europe

Air travel between Italy and other parts of Europe can be expensive, especially when it comes to short hops. Some airlines (for example **Alitalia, Qantas** and **Air France**) offer excellent rates on the European stages of intercontinental flights, and Italy is a touch-down for many long-haul services to the Middle or Far East and some parts of Africa. Amsterdam, Paris and Athens are good centres to find cheap flights.

Italflights, 125 High Holborn, London WC1V 6QA, **t** (020) 7405 6771.

Trailfinders, 225 Kensington High St, London W8, **t** (020) 7937 1234, *www.trailfinders.co.uk*

Budget Travel, 134 Lower Baggot St, Dublin 2, **t** (01) 661 1866.

United Travel, 2 Old Dublin Rd, Stillorgan, County Dublin, **t** (01) 283 2555.

Besides saving 25% on regular flights, people under the age of 26 can fly on special discount charters.

STA, 6 Wright's Lane, London W8 6TA, **t** 0870 1600 599, *www.statravel.co.uk*, and branches.

USIT Now, 19–21 Aston Quay, Dublin 2, **t** (01) 602 1600, and other branches in Ireland, *www.usitnow.ie*

From the USA and Canada

For discounted flights, hunt through the small ads in the newspaper travel pages (*New York Times, Chicago Tribune, Toronto Globe & Mail* and so on).

There are are number of travel clubs and agencies that specialize in discounted fares, but these may well charge an annual membership fee.

Airhitch, 2790 Broadway, Suite 100, New York, NY 10025, **t** (212) 247 4482, **t** 1-877-AIRHITCH, *www.airhitch.org*

Now Voyager, 74 Varick St, Suite 307, New York, NY 10013, **t** (212) 431 1616, *www.nowvoyagertravel.com*. Courier flights.

STA, **t** 800 329 9537, *www.statravel.com*, with branches at most universities and also at 315 West 49th St, Plaza Arcade, New York, NY 10019, **t** (212) 459 1616, and ASUC Building, 2nd Floor, University of California, Berkeley, CA 94720, **t** (510) 642 3000.

TFI, 34 West 32nd St, New York, NY 10001, **t** (212) 736 1140, **t** 800 745 8000.

Travel Cuts, 187 College St, Toronto, Ontario M5T 1P7, **t** (416) 979 2406, *www.travelcuts.com*. Canada's largest student travel specialists; with branches in most provinces.

You could also try comparing the prices offered on some of the US cheap flight websites, which include:

www.priceline.com (bid for tickets)
www.bestfares.com
www.travelocity.com
www.eurovacations.com
www.cheaptrips.com
www.courier.org (courier flights)
www.ricksteves.com
www.xfares.com (carry-on luggage only)
www.smarterliving.com

By Rail

With Eurostar from London, the journey to Rome takes 15½hrs (12hrs 40mins to Milan). Services run daily in summer and return fares range from £187 to £250. Travelling by train and ferry takes about 24hrs but you can stop off as often as you like. There are also Motorail links from Denderleeuw in Belgium to Milan, Rimini, Rome, Bologna and Venice (frequently in winter: contact **RailChoice**, *see* box).

Fares, Passes and Discounts

In the age of low-cost airlines, rail travel is not much of an economy unless you can get student, youth, family, young children and senior citizen discounts. Interail (UK) or Eurail (USA/Canada) **passes** offer a bewilderingly large variety of opportunities for discounts—for groups, families, under 26's, for varying lengths of time, and for travel within combinations of Italy and France or other countries, not to mention complete holiday packages (contact **Rail Europe**, *see* box)

Various rail passes are also available directly from the Italian railroads; one, the Trenitalia Pass, can be organized before leaving home at **Rail Choice** (*see* box). The Trenitalia pass allows 4–10 days' unlimited travel within a 2-month period (small supplements are charged on Eurostars). Rail Choice have further discounts for students and under-26s using Eurostar. Other passes are available only from stations within Italy (*see* Getting Around, p.72, for details).

CIT offices, which act as agents for Italian State Railways, also offer various deals. In Italy, a good bet for discounted train tickets and flights is **CTS**, the Italian student agency.

Rail Agencies

Rail Europe (Eurostar tickets and Inter-Rail passes), (UK) 179 Piccadilly, London W1V OBA, **t** 08705 848 848, *www.raileurope.co.uk*; (USA) 1-877 257 2887, *www.raileurope.com*

RailChoice (rail passes in Italy and Motorail), (UK) 15 Coleman House, Empire Square, High St, Penge, London SE20 7EX, **t** 0870 165 7300, *www.railchoice.co.uk*; (USA) 1-800 361 RAIL, *www.railchoice.com*

CIT (agents for Italian state railways), (UK) Marco Polo House, 3–5 Lansdowne Rd, Croydon, Surrey, **t** (020) 8686 0677, *www.citalia.co.uk*; (USA) 875 3rd Ave, mezz. level, New York, NY 10022, **t** 1-800 CIT-TOUR, *www.cittours.com*; (Canada) 80 Tiverton Court, Suite 401, Markham, Toronto L3R O94, **t** 800 387 0711; Montreal, **t** 800 361 7299, *www.cittours-canada.com*

CTS (flights, rail tickets) Corso P. Ticinese 83, Milan, **t** (02) 837 2674, *www.cts.it.*

Italian Railways (tickets and timetables) *www.trenitalia.com.*

Italwings (travel & accommodation), (UK) 162–6 Regent St, London W1R 5TB, **t** (020) 7287 2117.

Venice-Simplon Orient Express (UK) Sea Containers House, 20 Upper Ground, London SE1 9PF, **t** (020) 7805 5060; (US) (212) 302 5055; *www.orient-express.com*

Timetables

A pocket-sized **timetable** detailing the main and secondary Italian railway lines is available in the UK for £9 (plus 50p postage; contact **Italian Railways** or **Italwings**). In Italy you can pick up an annual Italian timetable (about €4) at any station.

Venice-Simplon Orient Express

The Orient Express whirls passengers from London through Paris, Zurich, Innsbruck and Verona to Venice in a cocoon of 1920s and '30s glamour in beautifully restored Pullman/wagon-lits. Prices (including meals) are about £1,200 pp one-way; Venice–London one-way tickets include a free flight out. Several operators offer packages including smart Venice hotels and return flights home (contact **Venice-Simplon Orient Express**, *see* box).

By Road

By Bus and Coach

Eurolines, 52 Grosvenor Gardens, London SW1Q OAU, **t** 01705 808 080, *www.nationalexpress.com*, are booked in the UK through National Express (return ticket London–Rome £120; single £88; under-26s and senior citizens return £109 or single £88).

Within Italy itself, you can get information on long-distance bus services from any CIT office (*see* above).

By Car

Italy is the best part of 24hrs' driving time from the UK, even if you stick to fast toll roads. Calais–Florence via Nancy, Lucerne and Lugano is about 1,042km.

The most scenic and hassle-free route is via the Alps, but if you go through Switzerland expect to pay for the privilege (around £15.50 for motorway use). In winter the passes may be closed and you will have to use expensive tunnels. Current motorway tunnel tolls are:

Mont Blanc, *www.tunnelmb.com*, from Haute Savoie (France) to Aosta, €25.60–€31.90.

Fréjus Tunnel, *www.tunneldufrejus.com*, from Modane (France) to Bardonècchia, €25.60–€31.90.

Gran San Bernardo, *www.grandsaintbernard.ch*, from Bourg St Pierre (Switzerland) to Aosta, €18.20–€25.60.

You can avoid some of the driving by putting your car on the train (*see* p.68, By Rail). The **Italian Auto Club** (ACI), **t** 800 313 535, offers reasonably priced breakdown assistance.

To bring a GB-registered car into Italy, you need a **vehicle registration document, full driving licence**, and **insurance papers** (these must be carried at all times when driving). If your driving licence is the old-fashioned sort without a photo you are strongly recommended to apply for an international driving permit (available from the AA or RAC). Non-EU citizens should preferably have an **international driving licence,** which has an Italian translation incorporated. Your vehicle should display a nationality plate indicating its country of registration. Before travelling, check everything is in perfect order. **Red hazard triangles** and **headlight converters** are obligatory; also recommended are a spare set of bulbs, a first-aid kit and a fire extinguisher. Spare parts for non-Italian cars can be difficult to find. Before crossing the border, fill your car up; *benzina* is very expensive in Italy.

For more information on driving in Italy, contact the **AA**, **t** 0870 500 600 or 0800 444 500 (5-star breakdown cover), or **RAC**, **t** 0800 550 550 in the UK, and **AAA**, **t** (407) 444 4000, in the USA.

Entry Formalities

Passports and Visas

EU nationals with a valid passport can enter and stay in Italy as long as they like. Citizens of the USA, Canada, Australia and New Zealand need only a valid passport to stay up to 90 days in Italy.

If you mean to stay longer than 90 days, you have to get a *permesso di soggiorno*. For this you will need to state your reason for staying and be able to prove a source of income and medical insurance. After a couple of exasperating days at a Questura (police station) filling out forms, you should walk out with your permit.

UK, 38 Eaton Place, London SW1X 8AN, **t** (020) 7838 6991/6961; 32 Melville St, Edinburgh EH3 7HW, **t** (0131) 226 3631 (also deals with Northern Ireland); 2111 Piccadilly, Manchester (also deals with Wales), **t** (0161) 236 9024, *www.embitaly.org.uk*

Ireland, 63–5 Northumberland Rd, Dublin, **t** (01) 660 1744; *www.italcult.ie*, *www.italianembassy.ie*

USA, 101 Boylston St, Suite 900, Boston, MA 02166, **t** (617) 542 0483, *www.italyemb.org/consulati*. There are Italian consulates in Chicago, Detroit, Houston, LA, Miami, New York, Newark, Philadelphia and San Francisco.

Canada, 275 Slater St, 21st fl., Ottawa (ON), K1P 5H9, **t** (613) 232 2401, *www.italyincanada.com*, *www.italconsulate.org*. There are Italian consulates in Montreal, Vancouver, Edmonton and Toronto.

Australia, 61 Macquarie St, Sydney 2000 NSW, **t** (02) 9392 7900, *www.ambitalia.org.au*.

New Zealand, 34 Grant Rd, PO Box 463, Thorndon, Wellington, **t** (04) 4735 339, **t** (04) 4727 255, *www.italy-embassy.org.nz*. There are consulate agencies in Auckland, Christchurch, Dunedin and Wellington.

By law you should register with the police within 8 days of arrival in Italy. In practice this is done automatically for most visitors when they check in at their first hotel.

Customs

EU nationals over the age of 17 can import an unlimited amount of goods for personal use. Non-EU nationals have to pass through

Italian customs. which are usually benign. They'll let you be if you don't look suspicious and haven't brought along more than 200 cigarettes or 100 cigars, or not more than a litre of hard drink or three bottles of wine, a couple of cameras, a movie camera, 10 rolls of film for each, a tape recorder, a radio, a hi-fi, one canoe measuring less than 5.5m in length, sports equipment for personal use, and one television set.

You can take the same items that are listed above home with you without hassle. Citizens of the US may return with up to $400 worth of merchandise – make sure that you keep your receipts.

Pets travelling with you must always be accompanied by a current bilingual Certificate of Health that's been provided by your local Veterinary Inspector.

Getting Around

Italy has an excellent network of airports, railways, highways and byways, and you'll find getting around fairly easy – until one union or another takes it into its head to go on strike, that is (to be fair they rarely do it during the high holiday season). There's plenty of talk about passing a law to regulate strikes, but it won't happen soon, if ever. Learn to recognize the word in Italian: *sciopero* (SHO-pe-ro), and do as the Romans do – quiver with resignation. There's always a day or two's notice, and strikes usually last only one day – just long enough to throw a spanner in the works if you have to catch a plane. Keep your ears open – ask bartenders and hotel receptionists, and watch for notices in the stations.

Courses for Foreigners and Special-interest Holidays

The Italian Institute, 39 Belgrave Square, London SW1X 8NX, **t** (020) 7235 1461, and 686 Park Avenue, New York, NY 10021, **t** (212) 879 4242, is the chief source of information on courses for foreigners in Italy. Graduate students should also contact their nearest Italian consulate to find out about scholarships – many go unused each year because no one knows about them.

A selection of specialist companies are listed below. Not all are necessarily ABTA-bonded; check before booking.

In the UK

Abercrombie & Kent, St George's House, Ambrose St, Cheltenham, Glos GLO 3LG, **t** 0845 0700 610, *www.abercrombiekent.co.uk*. City breaks in all the major cities, country retreats and island-hopping cruises, plus a range of walking holidays in Tuscany, the Italian Lakes and Umbria and combi-holidays (Rome, Venice, Florence, and Sicily–Amalfi).

ACE Study Tours, Babraham, Cambridge CB2 4AP, **t** (01223) 835 055, *www.study-tours.org*. Cultural and garden tours all over Italy (Piero della Francesca, Vasari, the Visconti and the Sforza, popes and princes, etc).

Alternative Travel, 69–71 Banbury Rd, Oxford OX2 6PJ, **t** (01865) 315 678, *www.atg-oxford.co.uk*. Walking, wild flower-spotting, garden and cycling tours; Piero della Francesca, the Palio in Siena, Renaissance Tuscany, Venice, Sardinia and Sicily art routes; truffle hunts and painting courses.

American Express Europe, branches across UK, **t** 0870 600 1060, *www.americanexpress.co.uk*. City breaks and fly-drive holidays.

Arblaster & Clarke Wine Tours, Farnham Rd, West Liss, Petersfield, Hants GU33 6JQ, **t** (01730) 893 344, *www.winetours.co.uk*. Wine tours, truffle hunts and gourmet cooking tours in Rome, southern Italy, Tuscany, Verona, the Veneto and northern and central Italy, plus cruises.

British Museum Traveller, 46 Bloomsbury St, London WC1B 3QQ, **t** (020) 7436 7575, *www.britishmuseumtraveller.co.uk*. Tours with guest lecturers, looking at art and architecture in Tuscany and Umbria (especially Florence).

Brompton Travel, Brompton House, 64 Richmond Rd, Kingston-upon-Thames, Surrey KT2 5EH, **t** (020) 8549 3334, *www.BromptonTravel.co.uk*. Tailor-made and opera tours in Verona, Naples, Venice, Milan, Turin and Genoa.

Citalia, Marco Polo House, 3–5 Lansdowne Rd, Croydon CR9 1LL, **t** (020) 8686 5533, *www.citalia.co.uk*. Resorts, self-catering holidays and honeymoons throughout Italy, including Florence, Rome, Venice, Puglia,

By Air

Air traffic within Italy is intense, with up to 10 flights a day on popular routes. Domestic flights are handled by Alitalia, ATI (its internal arm) or Avianova.

Air travel makes most sense when you're hopping between the north and the south. Shorter journeys are often just as quick (and usually much less expensive) if you go by train or even bus, if you take travelling to the airport and check-in times into account.

Mainland cities with airports include Ancona, Bari, Bergamo, Bologna, Brindisi, Florence, Genoa, Lamezia Terme (near Catanzaro), Milan, Naples, Parma, Pisa, Reggio di Calabria, Turin, Trieste, Venice and Verona, all of which have direct flights to and from Rome.

Domestic flight prices are comparable to those in other European countries, and a complex system of discounts is available. Each airport has a bus terminal in the city; ask about schedules when you purchase your ticket to avoid hefty taxi fares. Baggage allowances vary between airlines. Tickets can be bought at CIT and other travel agencies, and at the airport (note that online bookings can often only be made with credit cards registered in Italy).

There are several domestic airlines, including various new ones:

Air Dolomiti (Verona-based; *www.airdolomiti.it*)

Air Emilia (Reggio-Emilia based; *www.airemilia.it*)

Air One (serving the Sicilian islands in summer; *www.air-one.it*)

Campania (Maori, Paestum and Positano), the Lakes, Umbria and Venice (the Carnival).

Cox & Kings, Gordon House, 10 Greencoat Place, London SW1P 1PH, **t** (020) 7873 5000, *www.coxandkings.co.uk*. Short breaks, gastronomic and escorted cultural tours with guest lecturers in Rome and the Lakes, plus cruises.

Fine Art Travel, 15 Savile Row, London W1S 3PG, **t** (020) 7437 8553, *www.bellinitravel.com*. Cultural, art and historical tours in Umbria, Venice and Naples.

Gordon Overland, 76 Croft Road, Carlisle, Cumbria CA3 9AG, **t** (01228) 26796. Annual month-long language and painting holidays in Tuscany and the Veneto, plus garden and villa tours in northern Italy.

Inscape Fine Art Tours, Austins Farm, High St, Stonesfield, Witney, Oxfordshire OX8 8PU, **t** (01993) 891 726, *www.inscapetours.co.uk*. Escorted art tours with guest lecturers in Venice, the Veneto, Sicily, Umbria and Tuscany.

Italiatour, 9 Whyteleafe Business Village, Whyteleafe, Surrey CR3 0AT, **t** (01883) 621 900, *www.italiatour.co.uk*. Resort holidays and city breaks all over Italy, plus vegetarian cookery courses in Umbria, horse-riding in Umbria, football tickets, opera in Rome, Venice and Verona, and *agriturismo*.

JMB, Suite 4, High Tree House, 4 Cromwell Rd, Powick, Worcester WR2 4QJ, **t** (01905) 830 099, *www.jmb-travel.co.uk*. Opera holidays in Florence, Palermo, Milan, Turin, Torre del Lago, Rome and Venice.

Kirker, 3 New Concordia Wharf, Mill St, London SE1 2BB, **t** (020) 7231 3333, *www.kirkerholidays.com*. City breaks, tailor-made tours throughout Italy, and trips to the Verona Opera.

Magic of Italy, 227 Shepherd's Bush Rd, London W6 7AS, **t** 0870 888 0228, *www.magictravelgroup.co.uk*. City breaks and villa holidays throughout Italy.

Martin Randall Travel, Voysey House, 45F Barley Mow Passage, Chiswick, London W4 4GF, **t** (020) 8742 3355, *www.martinrandall.com*. Imaginatively put-together cultural tours with guest lecturers: architecture and painting, history, Florence, Venice, Verona at Christmas, wines, Venice music festival, gardens and villas.

Page & Moy, 135-40 London Rd, Leicester LE2 1EN, **t** 08700 106 212, *www.page-moy.co.uk*. City breaks, gastronomy and cultural tours: Sicily, northern Italy, gardens of the Italian Lakes, plus river cruises and air and coach tours throughout the country.

Ramblers, Box 43, Welwyn Garden City, Hertfordshire AL8 6PQ, **t** (01707) 331 133, *www.ramblersholidays.co.uk*. Walking holidays in Abruzzo, Umbria, Tuscany, Sicily, Sorrento, Urbino, Assisi, the Lake Garda region, Florence, Venice, Siena and Liguria.

Alitalia (*www.alitalia.it*)
Alpieagles (*www.alpieagles.com*)
Meridiana (especially Sardinia; *www.meridiana.it*)
Minerva (Trieste-based; *www.minerva-airlines.it*)
Volare (*www.volare-group.it*)

By Rail

Trenitalia information from anywhere in Italy: ***t*** *892 021*; *www.trenitalia.com*.

Italy's national railway, now repackaged as Trenitalia (including the old FS, Ferrovie dello Stato and the Italian Eurostar lines), is well run, inexpensive (despite recent price rises) and often a pleasure to ride. There are also several private rail lines that may not accept Interail or Eurail passes. Some of the trains are sleek and high-tech, but much of the rolling stock hasn't been changed for fifty years. Possible unpleasantnesses you may encounter, besides a strike, are delays, crowding (especially at weekends and in the summer), and crime on overnight trains, where someone rifles your bags while you sleep. The crowding, at least, becomes less of a problem if you reserve a seat in advance (*fare una prenotazione*); the fee is small and can save you hours standing in some train corridor. On the more expensive trains, reservations are mandatory. Do check that the date on your ticket is correct; tickets are only valid the day they're purchased unless you specify otherwise. Sleepers and couchettes on overnight trains must also be reserved in advance. At sleepy rural train stations the

Simply Tuscany & Umbria, Kings Place, Wood Street, Kingston-upon-Thames, Surrey KT1 1SG, **t** (020) 8541 2222,*www.simply-travel.com*. Tailor-made itineraries, plus art, architecture and vegetarian cookery courses, balloon flights, spa resorts and painting holidays.
Swan Hellenic, Richmond House, Terminus Terrace, Southampton SO14 3PN, **t** 0845 355 5111, *www.swanhellenic.com*. Cruises.
Tasting Places, Unit 108, Buspace Studios, Conlan St, London W10 5AP, **t** (020) 7460 0077, *www.tastingplaces.com*. Cookery courses in Umbria, Sicily, the Veneto, Tuscany and Piedmont.
The Travel Club of Upminster, Station Rd, Upminster, Essex RM14 2TT, **t** (01708) 225 000, *www.travelclub. org.uk*. Painting holidays, garden tours, art and gastronomy in Piemonte and the Italian Lakes.
Travelsphere, Compass House, Rockingham Rd, Market Harborough, Leics LE16 7QD, **t** (01858) 410 818, *www.travelsphere.co.uk*. Themed air and coach cultural tours: art, gardens, food, wine, walking and singles holidays.
Voyages Jules Verne, 21 Dorset Square, London NW1 6QG, **t** (020) 7616 1000, *www.vjv.co.uk*. Swish resorts all over Italy, especially Venice, Venice Lido, Ravello, Sorrento, Taormina and Capri.
Wallace Arnold, Gelderd Road, Leeds LS12 6DH and travel shops across UK, **t** (0113) 2310 739, *www.wallacearnold.com*. Coach holidays all over Italy, including Tuscany and Venice.

In the USA/Canada

Abercrombie & Kent, Suite 212, 1520 Kensington Rd, Oak Brook, IL 60523 2141, **t** 800 323 7308, *www.abercrombiekent.com*. City breaks, walking holidays, country retreats and island-hopping cruises.
Archaeological Tours Inc, Suite 904, 271 Madison Avenue, New York, NY 10016, **t** (866) 740 5130, *www.museumstuff.com*. Expertly led archaeological tours for small groups.
Bike Riders' Tours, PO Box 130254, Boston, MA 02113, **t** 800 473 7040, *www.bikeriderstours.com*. Cycling tours in Umbria, Tuscany, the Veneto, Emilia-Romagna and Sicily.
CIT Tours (USA) 875 3rd Ave, New York, NY 10022, **t** 1-800 CIT-TOUR, *www.cittours.com*; (Canada) 80 Tiverton Court, Suite 401, Markham, Toronto L3R O94, **t** 800 387 0711; Montreal **t** 800 361 7299, *www.cittours-canada.com* General and skiing holidays.
Dailey-Thorp Travel, PO Box 670, Big Horn, Wyoming,**t** (307) 673 1555, *www.daileythorp.com*. Luxury escorted tours to Milan opera.
Europe Train Tours, **t** (877) 257 2887, 800 361-RAIL (Canada). Escorted tours by train and car.
Italiatour, 666 5th Avenue, New York, NY 10103, **t** (800) 845 3365 (US) and (888) 515 5245 (Canada), *www.italiatourusa.com*. Fly-drive holidays and sightseeing tours by Alitalia.
Travel Concepts, 191 Worcester Rd, Princeton, MA 01541, **t** (978) 464 0411. Wine and food.

Riding the Rails

The FS may have its strikes and delays, its petty crime and its bureaucratic inconveniences, but when you catch it on its better side it will treat you to a dose of the real Italy before you even reach your destination. If you have a choice, aim for one of the older cars, which are depressingly grey on the outside but fitted with comfortably upholstered seats, Art Deco lamps and old pictures of the towns and villages of the country. The washrooms are invariably clean and pleasant (they're one of the only places in Italy to provide toilet paper!). Best of all, the FS is relatively reliable, and even if there has been some delay you'll have an amenable station full of clocks – albeit all telling different times – to wait in. Some of the station bars have astonishingly good food (some don't), but at any you can expect a well-brewed cappuccino. All this said, try to avoid travelling on Friday evenings, when the major lines out of the big cities are packed (or at least book a seat).

imminent presence of a train is signalled by a platform bell.

Tickets may be purchased not only in the stations, but at many travel agents in the city centres. Fares are strictly determined by the kilometres travelled. The system is computerized and runs smoothly, at least until you try to get a reimbursement for an unused ticket (usually not worth the trouble). Be sure you ask which platform (*binario*) your train arrives at; the big permanent boards in the stations are not always correct. Always remember to stamp your ticket (*convalidare*) in the not-very obvious yellow machines at the head of the platform before boarding the train. Failure to do so could result in a fine. If you get on a train without a ticket you can buy one from the conductor, with an added 20% penalty. You can also pay a conductor to move up to first class or get a couchette, if there are places available.

There is a fairly straightforward hierarchy of trains. At the bottom of the pyramid is the humble *Regionale* which often stops even where there's no station in sight; it can be excruciatingly slow. When you're checking the schedules, beware of what may look like the first train to your destination – if it's a *Regionale*, it will be the last to arrive. A *Diretto* or *Interregionale* stops far less. *Intercity* trains whoosh between the big cities and rarely deign to stop. *Eurocity* trains link Italian cities with major European centres. Both of these services require a supplement – some 30% more than a regular fare. Some of the latter two services run the ETR 500 'Pendolino' similar to the French TGV, which can travel at up to 186mph. Reservations are free, but must be made at least five hours before the trip, and on some trains there are only first-class coaches. Sitting on the pinnacle are the true Kings of the Rails, the super-swish and super-fast *Eurostars*. These make very few stops, have both first- and second-class carriages, and carry a supplement which includes an obligatory seat reservation.These are much more expensive than *Intercity* trains, which are almos as fast; travelling by 1st-class *Intercity* is nicer than going by 2nd-class *Eurostar*.

The FS offers a range of discount cards. For non-Italians, there are Trenitalia Passes, which can be purchased abroad at approved agents outside Italy or at big-city rail stations within Italy. They come in versions for individuals, under-26s and groups of up to five, and are good for all trains on 4-10 travel days; with a lot of fringe benefits for ferries, hotels, etc., these can be a very good deal.

If you're going to be spending some time in Italy, check out the other discount cards on offer, available at most stations; though mostly good for one year, they can still offer a bargain if you mean to ride a lot of trains. There's a Carta Verde for under-26s, a Carta Argento for over 60's, an Intercity card and a Club Eurostar card for frequent riders on those lines: The Carta Amicotreno costs [euro] 50 for a year, and offers discounts of 10-50% on certain trains

Besides trains and bars, Italy's stations offer other **facilities** (although most *depositi*, where you can leave your bags for hours or days for a small fee, are closed these days because of fears of terrorism). Larger stations have porters (but be aware that thieves often masquerade as porters – ask one of the guards to point you out a bona fide one), and some have luggage trolleys. Major stations have showers, information offices, currency exchanges open at weekends (not at the most advantageous rates, though), hotel-finding and reservation services, kiosks selling foreign newspapers, restaurants, etc. You can also have a rental car waiting at your destination – Avis, Hertz and Maggiore are the firms most widespread in Italy (*see* box, opposite).

By Coach and Bus

Inter-city coach travel is sometimes quicker than train travel, but it's also a bit more expensive; you will find regular coach connections between big towns only where there is no train to offer competition. For smaller towns and villages, the system is top-class; you'll be able to reach more destinations conveniently by public transport in Italy than almost anywhere in western Europe.

City buses are the traveller's friend. Most cities (at least those in the north) label routes well; all charge flat fees for rides within the city limits and immediate suburbs (€0.77–€1). Bus tickets must be purchased before you get on board, at either a tobacconist, a newspaper kiosk or a bar, or from ticket machines near the main stops.

Once you get on, you have to 'obliterate' your ticket in the machines at the front or back of the bus; controllers stage random checks to make sure you've punched your ticket. Fines for cheaters are about €50, and the odds are about 12 to 1 against a check, so many passengers take a chance. If you're good-hearted, however, you'll buy a ticket and help some overburdened municipal transit line meet its annual deficit.

By Car

The advantages of driving in Italy generally outweigh the disadvantages, but before you bring your own car or hire one, consider the kind of holiday you're planning. For a tour of Italy's great art cities, you'd be better off not driving at all: parking is impossible, traffic is impossible, and deciphering one-way streets, signals and signs is impossible. (You'll find the only good times to get in and out of any town is at night, or during the afternoon lunch break.) In Naples, don't even think about it. If you're touring the countryside, however, a car gives you immeasurable freedom.

Third-party **insurance** is a minimum requirement in Italy (and you should be a lot more than minimally insured, as many of the locals have none whatsoever!). Obtain a Green Card from your insurer, which gives proof that you are fully covered. Also get hold of a **European Accident Statement** form, which may simplify things if you are unlucky enough to have an accident. Always insist on a full translation of any statement you are asked to sign. Break-down assistance insurance is obviously a sensible investment: **Europ Assistance**, Sussex House, Perrymount Road, Haywards Heath, West Sussex RH16 1DN, **t** (01444) 442 211, can arrange both this and general insurance for trips abroad.

Petrol (*benzina*: unleaded is *benzina senza piombo*, and diesel *gasolio*) is still expensive in Italy (around €1 per litre). Many petrol stations close for lunch in the afternoon, and only a few stay open late at night, though you may find a 'self-service' where you feed a machine nice, smooth €5 notes. Services can be hard to find in remote areas, where they are generally closed all afternoon.

Motorway (*autostrada*) **tolls** are quite high (the journey from Milan to Rome on the A1 will cost you around €30). Rest stops and petrol stations along the motorways stay open 24hrs but are notorious spots for getting robbed: don't leave conspicuous valuables in the car.

Italians are famously anarchic behind a wheel, and the only way to cope with being on the road here is by developing an assertive and constantly alert driving style. Bear in mind the maxim that he/she who hesitates is lost (especially at traffic lights, where the danger is less great of crashing into someone at the front than of being rammed from behind). All drivers tempt providence by overtaking at the most dangerous bends, and no matter how fast you're driving along the *autostrada*, plenty whizz past at supersonic rates.

North Americans used to leisurely speeds and gentler road manners may find the Italian interpretation of the highway code especially stressful. **Speed limits** (which are generally ignored) are officially 130km/hr on motorways, 110km/hr on main highways, 90km/hr on secondary roads, and 50km/hr in built-up areas. Speeding fines may be as much as €32, those for dangerous driving €1,000.

All this said, new legislation that came into force in summer 2003 – based on a severe points system – seems to be having an effect (and not before time – this is a country that sees 40 deaths and hundreds of injuries on an average weekend). Take extra care in mist, fog and heavy rain.

And you may actually enjoy driving in Italy, at least away from the congested tourist centres. Signposting is generally good, and the roads are well maintained (some are feats of engineering that the Romans themselves would have admired: bravura projects suspended on cliffs, crossing valleys on vast stilts and winding up hairpins).

Make sure you invest in a good road map (the Italian Touring Club series is excellent). The **Automobile Club of Italy** (ACI; *www.aci.it*) is a good friend to the foreign motorist: besides offering bushels of useful information and tips, they can be reached from anywhere by dialling **t** 116 (you can also use this number to find the nearest service station). If you need major repairs, the ACI will make sure that the prices you are charged concord with their guidelines.

Hiring a Car

Hiring a car in Italy (*autonoleggio*) is a simple process but not particularly cheap. You need to remember to take into account that some hire companies will require a deposit amounting to the estimated cost of the hire. The minimum age limit is usually 25 (sometimes 23) and the driver must have held their licence for more than a year.

Car Hire

In the UK

Avis, t 08700 100 287, *www.avis.co.uk*
Budget, t (0541) 565 656.
Europcar, t (0870) 607 5000, *www.europcar.co.uk* (Italy **t** 02 70 299 700).
Hertz, t 08708 448 844, *www.hertz.co.uk*
Thrifty, t (01494) 751 600, *www.thrifty.co.uk*

In the USA

Auto Europe, 888 223 5555, *www.autoeurope.com*
Avis Rent a Car, t 1-99 100 133, *www.avis.com*
Europcar, t 877 940 6900, *www.europcar.com*
Europe by Car, t 800 223 1516, *www.europebycar.com*
Hertz, t 800 654 3001, *www.hertz.com*

Most major rental companies have offices in airports or main stations, though it may be worthwhile checking out the prices offered by local firms. If you need a car for longer than three weeks, leasing may be a more economic alternative. The National Tourist Office has a list of firms in Italy that let caravans (trailers) or camper vans. Non-residents are not allowed to buy cars in Italy.

It is probably easiest to arrange your car hire with a domestic firm before you depart (*see* box) and, in particular, to find out about fly-drive discounts.

Be forewarned that car hire firms in Italy are rarely able to provide baby/child seats (no one uses them here), so it is wise to check in advance (and to book one if they're available), or to bring your own.

Hitchhiking

It is illegal to hitch on the *autostrade*, though you can pick up a lift near one of the toll booths or service areas. Don't hitch from the city centres; head for suburban exit routes instead.

For the best chances of getting a lift, travel light, look respectable and take your shades off. Hold a sign indicating your destination if you can. Risks for women are lower in north Italy than in the more macho south, but don't hitch alone. Two or more men may encounter some reluctance.

On major roads out of town, the scantily clad women that you may see standing or sitting on stools on the edges of cornfields are not hitchhikers.

By Motorcycle or Bicycle

Mopeds, vespas and scooters are the vehicles of choice for a great many Italians, and you'll see them everywhere. In the traffic-congested towns, this is a ubiquity born of necessity; when driving space is limited, two wheels are always better than four.

Despite the obvious dangers, there are clear benefits to moped-riding in Italy. For one thing it is cheaper than hiring a car and can prove an excellent way of covering a town's sites in a limited space of time. Furthermore, because Italy is such a scooter-friendly place, car drivers are more conditioned to their presence and so are less likely to hurtle into them when taking corners.

Nonetheless, you should only really consider hiring a moped here if you have ridden one before (Italy's hills and alarming traffic are definitely no place to learn) and, despite what you may see the locals doing, you should always wear a helmet. Also, you should be aware that some travel insurance policies exclude claims resulting from scooter or motorbike accidents.

You can hire a bicycle in most Italian towns. Alternatively, if you decide to bring along your own bike, make sure that you check in advance the airline's policy on transporting them. Bikes can be transported by train in Italy, either at the same time as you or within a couple of days: you'll need to apply at the baggage office (*ufficio bagagli*).

Practical A-Z

08

Children

Children are the royalty of Italy, pampered, often obscenely spoiled, fashionably dressed and never allowed to get dirty. Most also somehow manage to be well-mannered little charmers, with the exception of teenagers en masse – school trips to museums in Mar and Apr may spoil your enjoyment.

If you're bringing your own *bambini*, they'll receive a warm welcome everywhere. Many hotels offer advantageous rates for kids and most larger cities have permanent **luna parks**, or funfairs. Rome's, in EUR, is huge and charmingly old-fashioned (it makes a great trade-off for a day in the Vatican Museums).

Apart from the endless quantities of pizza, spaghetti and ice cream, children love the **Bomarzo Monster Park** in northern Lazio (a collection of huge, weird 16th-century follies); the Disneyesque amusement parks of **Edenlandia** near Naples and **Gardaland** on Lake Garda; **Minitalia** between Bergamo and Milan (a relief model of Italy studded with replica monuments); **Pinocchio Park** in Collodi, near Pisa; the fairy-tale playground of **Città della Domenica** in Perugia; and the whole city of **Venice**.

If a **circus** visits town, you're in for a treat: it will be a sparkling showcase of daredevil skill or a poignant, family-run version of Fellini's *La Strada*. Try to catch one or two of Italy's more vivacious **festivals** or **carnivals** – the most famous ones are in Venice and Viareggio.

Climate and When to Go

Just as everywhere else, global warming has had a serious effect on Italy's weather. **Summer** temperatures and humidity levels are now well nigh tropical – in summer 2003, 48°C (110°F) was recorded in Sardinia and the average temperature was around 36°C (99°F). Especially high humidity levels are found in the centre (Tuscany/Umbria) and towards the north (Veneto, Emilia-Romagna, Lombardy): if you suffer from the heat, make sure your room has air-conditioning (that works!) – most hotels from the moderate price range upwards do. Drink plenty of **water**, and try not to drink too much wine at lunchtime: it is all too easy to get sunstroke. Wear a hat if you're walking in the sun, and remember that it's usually hottest at 3–4pm, when the ground, buildings and air have heated to boiling point.

Average Temperatures in °C (°F)

	January	April	July	October
Bari	8.8 (48)	13.5 (56)	21.9 (71)	17.8 (64)
Florence	6.5 (44)	13.3 (56)	21.7 (71)	16.2 (61)
Genoa	8.9 (48)	13.9 (57)	21.1 (70)	17.5 (64)
Milan	5.0 (41)	12.5 (55)	20.9 (70)	14.0 (57)
Cortina	-2.3 (28)	5.0 (41)	15.0 (60)	7.0 (45)
Naples	9.1 (48)	13.7 (57)	21.8 (71)	18.0 (64)
Rome	7.3 (45)	12.9 (55)	21.2 (70)	17.0 (63)
Venice	3.3 (38)	12.3 (54)	20.6 (69)	14.2 (58)
Lake Garda	3.3 (38)	13.5 (56)	23.3 (74)	13.4 (56)

Average Monthly Rainfall in Millimetres (inches)

	January	April	July	October
Bari	55.1 (2)	30.8 (1)	23.1 (1)	56.8 (2)
Florence	51.1 (2)	80.1 (3)	109 (4)	120 (5)
Genoa	47.0 (2)	102 (4)	26.0 (1)	158 (6)
Milan	45.5 (2)	111.5 (4)	51.9 (2)	103 (4)
Cortina	28.0 (1)	46.0 (2)	109 (4)	56.0 (2)
Naples	78.0 (3)	81.8 (3)	23.7 (1)	112 (4)
Rome	53.8 (2)	67.9 (3)	16.6 (1)	121 (5)
Venice	33.0 (1)	58.9 (2)	68.4 (3)	93.5 (4)
Lake Garda	43.0 (2)	55.0 (2)	79.0 (3)	77.5 (3)

In summer, **mosquitoes** are a big problem, especially in the Veneto (all those canals). Bring lots of repellent (industrial strength) and an ammonia stick to relieve the pain and itch – it's the only thing that seems to work.

For average touring, **August** is probably the worst month: public transport is jammed to capacity, prices are at their highest, and Rome, Milan, Florence, Venice and the other large cities are abandoned to hordes of tourists while the locals take to the beach. In Milan, especially, so many restaurants close down that you could starve, and the few staff left behind to man the galleys are sullen captives.

Spring and **autumn** are perhaps the best times to go; spring for the wildflowers in the countryside, autumn for the colour of the trees in the hills and vineyards. The weather is mild, places aren't crowded, and you won't need an umbrella too much, at least until Nov.

Winter can be very cold and damp – make sure that you get a hotel with central heating. Even in the south, temperatures can fall to below freezing.

Crime

There is a lot of petty crime here (if little violent crime), and unless you are extremely vigilant it can ruin your holiday. Particular hotspots are **train stations**, inside and out – be especially wary on *Eurostar* platforms, and never let anyone distract you or make you put your bags down – the person may have an accomplice who steals your bags or frisks your pockets while you're trying to be helpful. Often, station 'porters' will put your bags on their trolley and run off into the night (ask a guard on the platform to point out the real McCoy). In **trains** themselves, don't leave possessions unattended when you go to the toilet or bar.

Cities with particularly bad crime are more often than those in the **south**, where there is the highest unemployment and greatest poverty. In Naples, Bari, Taranto and Palermo, holidaymakers stick out like a sore thumb and may find themselves unwelcome centres of attention. Avoid wearing expensive jewellery or watches, and strap cameras across your body; avoid looking at maps in the street; and carry the bare minimum of cash and credit cards – leave the rest in the hotel safe. Keep loose change and small notes in your pocket – the last thing you want to do is get your wallet/purse out in public.

Men should keep wallets in their breast pocket or front trouser pocket with their hand on it (don't let anyone make you take your hands out of your pockets). If your bag doesn't have a long strap, carry it on your shoulder and wear a jacket/cardigan over the strap. Keep valuables in rustly plastic bags so you will hear anyone trying to steal them. In crowded places, especially buses and metros, wear your rucksack in front of you. Scooter-borne purse-snatchers can be foiled if you stay on the inside of the pavement and keep a firm hold on your property (sling your bag strap across your body, not dangling from one shoulder).

Tourists in Rome and other art cities, such as Florence, are particularly targeted by petty criminals. The gypsies in Rome are especially ingenious and usually work in groups – many now dress like anyone else (gone are the headscarves and long skirts). Beware of groups of scruffy-looking women or children begging – the classic trick is for one child to thrust a placard at you while other children rifle your pockets. If you're targeted, the best technique is to grab hold of your possessions and pockets and shout furiously – the fuss usually puts them off, and passers-by or plain-clothes police may come to your assistance.

Always park your **car** in garages, guarded car parks or on well-lit streets, with temptation well out of sight.

Purchasing a small quantities of soft **drugs** for personal consumption is technically legal, but anyone found carrying more than 1 'dose' is considered a dealer.

Political terrorism, once the scourge of Italy, has declined greatly, mainly thanks to the quasi-military squads of black-uniformed national police, the *Carabinieri*. Local matters are usually in the hands of the *Polizia Urbana*; the nattily dressed *Vigili Urbani* direct traffic and hand out parking fines. If you need to summon any of them, dial **t** 113.

Disabled Travellers

Italy has been slow off the mark in provision for disabled visitors. Cobblestones, uneven or nonexistent pavements, appalling traffic conditions, crowded public transport and endless flights of steps in many public places are all inconveniences. Progress is being made, however, and a national support organization in your own country may have details on facilities in Italy, or will at least be able to provide general advice.

The Italian tourist office, or CIT (travel agency), can also advise on hotels, museums with ramps, and so on. If you book rail travel through CIT, you can request assistance. Once you're in Italy, call the Coin Sociale, **t** 800 271 027 (freephone) for advice on accommodation and travel, or see *www.italiapertutti.it/english* or *www.accessibleeurope.com*.

Every May Modena hosts the International Festival of Different Abilities; for details see *www.tour-web.com*.

Specialist Organizations

In the UK

See also *www.canbedone.co.uk*.

RADAR (Royal Association for Disability & Rehabilitation), 12 City Forum, 250 City Rd, London ECIV 8AF, **t** (020) 7250 3222, *www.radar.org.uk*. Information and books about travelling abroad.

Holiday Care Service, 7th floor, Sunley House, 4 Bedford Park, Croydon, CR0 2AP, **t** 0845 124 9971, *www.holidaycare.org.uk*. A charity that disseminates access and disability information to holiday-makers.

In the USA and Canada

See also *www.disabilitytravel.com*.

Alternative Leisure Co., 165 Middlesex Turnpike, Suite 206, Bedford, MA 01730, **t** (781) 275 0023, *www.alctrips.com*. A company organizing vacations abroad for disabled people.

Mobility International USA, PO Box 10767, Eugene, OR 97440, **t**/TTY (541) 343 1284, *www.miusa.org*. An organization providing information about international educational exchange programmes and volunteer services overseas for the disabled.

SATH (Society for Accessible Travel and Hospitality), 347 5th Ave, Suite 610, New York, NY 10016, **t** (212) 447 7284, *www.sath.org*. An association providing travel and access information; it also has details of other access resources on the web.

Internet Sites

Access Tourism, *www.accesstourism.com*. A pan-European website with information on hotels, travel agencies and specialist tour operators aware of access issues affecting disabled travellers.

The Able Informer, *www.sasquatch.com/ableinfo*. An online magazine with travel tips for disabled people going abroad.

Emerging Horizons, *www.emerginghorizons.com*. An online travel newsletter for people with disabilities.

Dress Codes

It's not that the Italians are very formal; they just like to dress up and adorn their cities as much as those old Renaissance churches and palaces. The few places with dress codes are the major churches and basilicas (no shorts, sleeveless shirts or strappy sundresses – women should carry a light scarf to throw over their shoulders), casinos, and some posh restaurants.

Embassies and Consulates

Bari, (UK) Via Dalmazia 127, **t** 080 554 3668.

Florence, (UK) Lungarno Corsini 2, **t** 055 284 133; (USA) Lungarno Vespucci 38, **t** 055 266 951.

Milan, (Australia) Via Borgagna 2, **t** 02 7770 1330; (Canada) Via Vittorio Pisani 19, **t** 02 67581; (UK) Via San Paolo 7, **t** 02 723 001; (USA) Via Principe 2/10, **t** 02 290 351.

Naples, (UK) Via dei Mille 40, **t** 081 423 8911; (USA) Piazza Repubblica 2, **t** 081 583 8111.

Rome, (Australia) Via Alessandria 215, **t** 06 852 721; (Canada) Via Zara 30, **t** 06 445 981; (Ireland) Piazza di Campitelli 3, **t** 06 697 9121; (New Zealand) Via Zara 28, **t** 06 441 7171; (UK) Via XX Settembre 80/a, **t** 06 4220 0001; (USA) Via Vittorio Veneto 121, **t** 06 46741.

Festivals

There are thousands of festivals answering to every description in Italy. Every *comune* has at least 1 or 2 honouring patron saints, at which the presiding Madonna is paraded through the streets decked in fairy lights and gaudy flowers. Shrovetide and Holy Week are great focuses of activity.

Calendar of Events and Festivals

Jan–July Opera and ballet season at La Scala, **Milan**.

Jan 5–6 Child-oriented Epiphany celebrations throughout Italy, honouring the good stocking-filling witch La Befana, who brings lumps of coal and sweets.
Three Kings Procession, **Milan**.

Late Jan Festival of Italian Popular Song, **San Remo** – the Italian Eurovision, a must in any kitsch-lover's diary, at least on TV.

30–31 Jan Sant'Orso craft fair, **Aosta**.

Feb–Mar Shrovetide Carnivals all over Italy, especially in **Venice** – boat procession; **Viareggio**, Sa Sartiglia – medieval tournament and masquerade.

Mar Fashion collections shown, **Milan**.
Sant'Ambrogio carnival, **Milan**.

Mar–Apr Holy Week and Easter celebrations: processions in **Táranto Bari**, and **Brìndisi**; Scoppio del Carro ('Explosion of the Cart'), **Florence**; Good Friday procession from St Peter's to the Colosseum, led by the Pope, **Rome**; concerts at San Maurizio church in Monastero Maggiore, **Milan**.

Apr Ortafiori flower festival, **Orta San Giulio**.

May Feast of San Nicola, **Bari**.
Festival of Snakes, **Cocullo** (Abruzzo).
Palio del Carroccio, **Legnano** (Milan) – celebrates the defeat of Barbarossa by the Lombard League in 1176 (medieval parade and horse race).
Feast of San Gennaro, the first of 2 such occasions when the faithful assemble in **Naples** cathedral to await the miraculous liquefaction of a phial of their patron saint's blood. Corsa dei Ceri ('Race of the Candles'), **Gubbio** (Umbria) – huge wooden shrines are raced up the town's steep hill to the basilica. Palio della Balestra ('Crossbow Palio'), **Gubbio** – medieval contest with antique weapons. **Vogalonga, Venice** – the 'long row' from San Marco to Burano.

May–June Maggio Musicale Fiorentino, **Florence**.

June Historical Regatta of the Four Ancient Maritime republics (boat race between the rival ports and former rulers of the sea, **Pisa, Venice, Amalfi** and **Genoa** – each takes it in turn to host the regatta).
Gioco del Ponte ('Game of the Bridge'), **Pisa** – mock battle.

June 21 Infiorata, **Genzano** (Rome) and **Spello** (Umbria) – Corpus Domini celebrations with flower decorations.
Feast of St Antonio, **Padua**.
Gioco del Calcio, **Florence** – football in medieval costume.
Festa dei Gigli, **Nola** (Naples) – 'lily' procession; the lilies here are actually large wooden towers.

Mid-June–July Festival of Two Worlds, **Spoleto** (Umbria) – the biggest arts festival in the country.

July Joust of the Bear, **Pistoia**.
Feast of the Redeemer (Il Redentore), **Venice** – fireworks display and gondola procession.
Umbria Jazz Festival, **Perugia**.
Archery contest, **Fivizzano** (Massa).

July and Aug Palio, **Siena** – bareback horse race (held twice).
Summer Operetta Festival, **Trieste**.
Outdoor opera season, **Verona**.

Aug Joust of the Quintana, **Ascoli Piceno** (the Marches).
Bravo delle Botti, **Montepulciano** – a barrel race taking place around the hill town's streets.
International Film Festival, **Venice**.
Regatta, **Ventimiglia**.
Wheat Festival, **Foglianise** (Benevento) – decorated tractors.

Aug–Sept Settimane Musicali ('Musical Weeks'), **Stresa** – concerts galore.

Sept Joust of the Saracen, **Arezzo** – knights in armour.
Historic Regatta, **Venice** – antics in boats.
Living chess game, **Maròstica** (Veneto) (even years).
Feast of San Gennaro, **Naples**.
Luminaria di Santa Croce, **Lucca** – torchlit procession.
Italian Grand Prix, **Monza**.
Neapolitan song contest, **Piedigrotta**.

Oct Truffle fair, **Alba**.
Feast of St Francis, **Assisi**.

Nov Festa della Salute, **Venice**.

Dec Start of Opera Lirica season throughout Italy. Advent and Christmas celebrations.
Christmas Fair of the *presepi*, **Naples**.
Sausage and polenta festival, **Benevento**.

Carnival, after being suppressed and ignored for decades, has been revived in many places, displaying the gorgeous music and pageantry of the *Commedia dell'Arte* with Harlequin and his motley crew. In Venice, the handmade carnival masks now constitute a new art form and make popular souvenirs.

Holy Week celebrations take on a dirgelike Spanish flavour in the south, where robed and hooded penitents haul melodramatic floats through the streets. In Rome the Supreme Pontiff himself officiates at the Easter ceremonies. Other festivals are more earthily pagan, celebrating the land and the harvest with giant phallic towers. Some are purely secular affairs sponsored by political parties (especially the Communists and Socialists), where everyone goes to hang out.

There are great costume pageants dating back to the Middle Ages or Renaissance, such as the Sienese *Palio* (a bareback horse race), an endless round of carnivals, music festivals, opera seasons and antique fairs. Relaxed village *festas* can even more enjoyable than the national crowd-pullers. Outsiders are nearly always welcome.

Whatever the occasion, eating is a primary pastime at all Italian jamborees, and all kinds of regional specialities are prepared.

Check at the local tourist office for precise dates, which alter from year to year, and often slide into the nearest weekend. See also *www.italiantourism.com* for updates of events all over the country.

Food and Drink

When you eat out, you need to mentally add to the bill (*conto*) the bread and cover charge (*pane e coperto*, between €1.20 and €4). A **service charge** is often included in the bill (*servizio compreso*); if not, it will say *servizio non compreso*, and you'll have to do your own arithmetic (15% is standard, but no Italian would leave this much). Additional **tipping** is at your own discretion, but never do it in family-run places (you may offend).

We have divided restaurants into **price categories** (*see* box). Prices have risen considerably in recent years, and these days it is well nigh impossible to get a 3-course meal, including wine, water and coperto, for less than €20. However, few people go for 3 courses except on special occasions, and certainly not twice a day.

Restaurant Price Categories

very expensive over €45
expensive €30–45
moderate €20–30
cheap up to €20

A typical meal in a *cheap–moderate* restaurant breaks down as follows:

coperto €2
water €3
wine (*quartino*) €3–5
starter €4–7
main course €8–12
dessert €3–5
coffee €1–2

Your final bill will obviously depend on how many courses you have, whether you have water and coffee, and, most importantly, the type of **wine** you choose. Some places offer house wine by the litre (for one person you have a *quartino*, or 1/4), which is usually very cheap; others, at the upper end, only offer wine by the bottle, so prices are much higher.

Water is generally not expensive apart from in Venice, Capri and the like, where they charge extortionate prices for small bottles (€5; they don't seem able to procure large bottles!). The best places to buy water are *salumerie* (delis), where you can also get sandwiches made up for a couple of euros.

To identify good restaurants in Italy, look out for the Gamberi Rossi (the equivalent of the AA) and the **Slow Food** symbol – a snail. 'The International Movement for the Defence of the Right to Pleasure', Slow Food is very popular in France and Italy and many excellent restaurants adhere to its ideology – that of meticulously prepared food and leisurely eating (the antithesis of fast food). For more information about the movements, the guidebooks it publishes and related events, see *www.slowfood.com*.

When you leave a restaurant you'll be given a receipt (*scontrino* or *ricevuto fiscale*), which according to law you must take with you out of the door and carry for at least 60 metres. If you aren't given one, it means the restaurant is probably fudging on its taxes and pocketing the extra. There is a slim chance that the tax police (*Guardia di Finanza*) may have their eye on you and the restaurant, and if you can't produce your receipt they could slap you with a heavy fine.

For further information about eating in Italy, including regional specialities, wines and a menu decoder, *see* the **Food and Drink** chapter on p.57.

Health and Emergencies

You can insure yourself against almost any possible mishap before you leave – cancelled flights, stolen or lost baggage, and health. Check any current insurance policies you hold to see if they cover you while abroad, and if so under what circumstances, and judge whether you need a special **traveller's insurance** policy for the journey. Travel agencies, as well as insurance companies and banks, sell special travel packages; it's worth shopping around, but do read the small print.

EU citizens are entitled to **reciprocal health care** in Italy's national health service and a 90% discount on prescriptions (bring **form E111** with you, which you can obtain in the UK from any main post office). The E111 should cover you for emergencies, but does not cover all medical expenses (repatriation costs, for example, and private treatment); it is still advisable to take out travel insurance.

Citizens of non-EU countries should check carefully that they have adequate insurance for any medical expenses, and the cost of returning home. Australia has a reciprocal health care scheme with Italy, but New Zealand, Canada and the USA do not. If you already have health insurance, a student card, or a credit card, any of these may entitle you to some medical cover abroad.

In an **emergency**, dial **t 115** for fire and **t 113** for an ambulance (*ambulanza*) or to find the nearest hospital (*ospedale*). Less serious problems can be treated at a *pronto soccorso* (casualty/first aid department) at any hospital clinic (*ambulatorio*), or at a local health unit (Unità Sanitaria Locale – USL). Airports and main railway stations also have **first-aid posts**. If you have to pay for any health treatment, make sure you get a receipt so you can claim for reimbursement later.

Dispensing **chemists** (*farmacie*) are generally open 8.30–1 and 4–8. Pharmacists are trained to give advice for minor ills. Any large town will have a *farmacia* that opens 24hrs; others take turns to stay open (the rota is generally posted in windows).

No specific **vaccinations** are required or advised for citizens of most countries before visiting Italy; the main health risks are the usual travellers' woes of upset stomachs or the effects of too much sun. Take a supply of **medicaments** with you (insect repellent, anti-diarrhoeal medicine, sun lotion and antiseptic cream), and any drugs you need regularly.

Most Italian doctors speak basic English; if you can't find one, contact your embassy or consulate. Standards of health care are generally higher in the north than the deep south.

Living and Working in Italy

Registration and Residency

If you are planning to stay in Italy long-term without working, you should register with the police within 8 days of arrival and apply for a *permesso di soggiorno* from the local **Questura** (police station). Get there early in the morning as most state offices close in the afternoon, though you'll probably still have to wait. EU citizens are given priority. However frustrating the process of obtaining documentation, try to appear calm and remain polite, or things will only get worse.

You need a *permesso* in order to open a bank account in Italy, or to buy a car. They vary in duration. If you can prove you have enough money to live on and a reason to be here (a job offer, a study place or the like), a renewal is usually granted, though non-whites may have a harder time. Make sure to take your passport, photographs, as much ID as you can muster and plenty of photocopies of any supporting documentation.

If you wish to be registered as a resident you should apply to the local **Ufficio Anagrafe** (registry office). If you're here for work, your employer should help you with the red tape, though many small businesses prefer to employ unregistered foreigners (so they don't have to declare them and pay tax).

Students attending courses at Italian universities must obtain a declaration from the Italian consulate in their home countries before departure, certifying their 'acceptability' for further study, and that they have adequate health insurance. A surprising number of scholarships are offered to foreign students (especially post-graduates) by the Italian Ministry of Foreign Affairs; many go unclaimed. The Italian cultural institutes attached to consulates and embassies have details.

Maps

The maps in this guide are for orientation only; for exploring it is worth investing in a good, up-to-date regional map before you arrive. The following sources are recommended:

Stanford's, (UK) 12–14 Long Acre, London WC2 9LP, **t** (020) 7836 1321.

The Travel Bookshop, (UK) 13 Blenheim Crescent, London W11 2EE, **t** (020) 7229 5260.

The Complete Traveler, (USA) 199 Madison Ave, New York, NY 10016, **t** (212) 685 9007.

Excellent maps are produced by the **Touring Club Italiano, Michelin** and the **Istituto Geografico de Agostini**. They are available at major bookshops in Italy, and sometimes on news-stands. Italian tourist offices are helpful and can often supply good area maps and town plans.

Money

It's a good idea to order a wad of euros from your home bank to have on hand when you arrive in the land of strikes, unforeseen delays and quirky banking hours. Take great care how you carry it, however, and don't keep it all in one place. Most hotels now have safe boxes.

Obtaining money is often a frustrating business involving a great deal of queueing and form-filling. Major banks and exchange bureaux licensed by the Bank of Italy give the best exchange rates for currency or traveller's cheques. Hotels, private exchanges in resorts and FS-run exchanges at railway stations usually have less advantageous rates, but are open outside normal banking hours. Thomas Cook, which joined forces with Travelex in 2001, is widespread and charges no commission.

Weekend Exchange Offices

Milan: Banca Ponti, Piazza del Duomo 19; Banca delle Comunicazioni, Stazione Centrale; American Express, Via Larga 4.

Florence: Thomas Cook, Lungarno Acciaiuoli 6r and American Express, Via Dante Alighieri 22r.

Rome: Banca Nazionale delle Comunicazioni, Stazione Termini; Thomas Cook, Piazza Barberini 21, and Largo Caduti di El Alamein 9.

Naples: Thomas Cook, airport branch; and Dusila Travel (AmEx agent), Via Santa Lucia 145.

Venice: American Express, San Marco 1471; CIT, Piazza San Marco; Thomas Cook, Piazza San Marco 142.

In addition there are exchange offices at most airports. Remember that Italians indicate decimals with commas and thousands with full points.

Most British banks have an arrangement with their Italian counterparts whereby you can (for a significant commission) use your bank card to withdraw money from Italian ATMs (*Bancomats*), but check with your bank first. Bancomats also take credit cards (if know your PIN number), and banks will advance you cash on a credit card.

Visa, American Express and Diners are more widely accepted than MasterCard. Large hotels, resort area restaurants, shops and car hire firms all accept plastic; smaller places may not.

National Holidays

Most museums, as well as banks and shops, close on the following national holidays:

1 Jan (New Year's Day)
6 Jan (Epiphany)
Easter Monday
25 Apr (Liberation Day)
1 May (Labour Day)
15 Aug (Assumption, which is also known as *Ferragosto*, the official climax of the Italian holiday season)
1 Nov (All Saints' Day)
8 Dec (Immaculate Conception)
25 Dec (Christmas Day)
26 Dec (*Santo Stefano*, St Stephen's Day)

In addition to these general holidays, many towns also take their patron saint's day off.

Opening Hours and Museums

Though it varies from region to region, with the north bearing more resemblance to the rest of Europe than the Mediterranean south, most of Italy closes down at 1pm until 3–5pm to eat and digest the main meal of the day. Afternoon hours are from 4–7, often 5–8 in summer. Bars are often the only places open in the early afternoon.

Some cities (notably Milan) close down during **August**, when locals flee to the hills, lakes or coast. Emila-Romagna closes down at weekends in July and Aug.

Don't be surprised if you find anywhere in Italy unexpectedly closed (or open), whatever its official stated hours.

Offices

Banks: open Mon–Fri 8.30–1 and 3–4, closed weekends and local and national holidays (*see* p.84).

Shops: food shops open Mon–Sat 8–1 and 3.30–7.30; clothes shops and department stoes often don't open until 10). Some supermarkets and department stores stay open all day; hours vary according to season and are shorter in smaller centres.

Government-run dispensers of red tape (such as **visa departments**) often stay open for limited periods, usually during the mornings (*Mon–Fri*). It pays to get there as soon as they open (or before) to spare your nerves in an interminable queue. Take something to read.

Museums and Galleries

Italy has a difficult time financing the preservation of its national heritage; enquire at the nearest tourist office to find out what is open and what is 'temporarily' closed (which can sometimes mean 10 years!) before setting off on a wild-goose chase.

Opening hours change frequently.

Churches

Italy's churches have always been a prime target for art thieves and are usually kept locked up when there isn't a sacristan or a caretaker to keep an eye on things. If a church you'd like to visit is closed, ask at the nearest tourist office if they can arrange access.

All churches, except the really important cathedrals and basilicas, close in the afternoon at the same hours as shops; little ones tend to stay closed. Always have a pocketful of coins for the light machines, or the works of art will remain in ecclesiastical gloom.

Don't do your visiting during services, and don't come to see paintings and statues the week before Easter – you'll probably find them covered with mourning shrouds.

In general, Sun afternoons and Mon are dead periods for the sightseer, so you may want to make them your travelling days. Places without specified opening hours can usually be visited on request, but it is best to go before 1pm.

We have listed the hours of important sights and museums, and specified which charge admission. Entrance charges vary widely; major sights can be fairly steep (€6–8), but others may be free; the Vatican continues a long papal tradition with its high admission charges. EU citizens under 18 and over 65 get free entry to state museums, at least in theory (you'll need to show ID).

Post Offices

Usually open Mon–Sat 8–1; large cities 8–6/7.

Dealing with *la posta italiana* is frustrating and time consuming; even buying the right stamps requires research and patience (you have to check your envelope size and weight before posting). Stamps (*francobolli*) are sold in post offices and at tobacconists (*tabacchi*, identified by blue signs with a white T). Letters sent *Posta Prioritaria* (€0.65) are supposed to take a day to arrive (within Italy).

This is also one of Europe's most expensive and slowest postal services. The Vatican City's special postal service knocks spots off the rest of the country for speed and efficiency, so if you're anywhere in Rome, post your mail in the Holy See (using Vatican stamps).

To receive your mail *poste restante*, have it addressed to the central post office (*Fermo Posta*) of the town or city in question and expect it to take 3–4 weeks to arrive. Make sure that your surname is clearly written in block capitals. In order to pick up your mail you have to present your passport and pay a nominal charge.

You can have money telegraphed to you via the post office; if all goes well, this can happen in a mere 3 days, but expect a fair proportion of it to go into commission.

Shopping

'Made in Italy' has long been a byword for style and quality, not just in fashion and leather but also in home design, ceramics, pots and pans, jewellery, lace and linens, glass and crystal, chocolates, hats, art books, handmade stationery, gold and silver, bicycles, sports cars, woodwork, liqueurs, aperitifs, coffee machines, gastronomic specialities, antiques and more.

You'll find the greatest variety of goods in Milan, Rome, Florence and Venice – the cities where the money is. Design-conscious Milan is Italy's major shopping centre and a cynosure of innovative style and fashion throughout the world.

If you're buying antiques, be sure to get a certificate of authenticity – reproductions can be very good. To get antique or modern art purchases home, you have to apply to the Export Department of the Italian Ministry of Education and pay an export tax; your seller should know the details. Non-EU citizens should save all receipts for Customs.

Italians don't much like department stores, but there are a few chains – the classiest is the oldest, Rinascente. COIN stores often have good buys in the latest fashions (or almost).

Sports and Activities

Cycling

About 75% of Italy is hilly or mountainous, so a cycling holiday is no soft option. It's best to bring your own bike (preferably a mountain bike) and spare parts; cycling is growing fast, but is nowhere near as fanatically practised in Italy as, say, in France or Denmark. Facilities for hiring or repairing bikes are less widespread, but you can buy a good bike for €150.

Good **biking regions** include Tuscany and Umbria, Veneto, Puglia and the alpine areas, where there are fine trails. Emilia-Romagna is a cyclist's paradise. Most airlines and rail companies transport bikes quite cheaply.

Fishing

You don't need a permit for sea-fishing (without an aqualung), but Italy's polluted, over-exploited coastal waters may disappoint. Many freshwater lakes and streams are stocked, and if you're more interested in fresh fish than the sport of it, there are innumerable trout farms where you can practically pick the fish out of the water with your hands. To fish in freshwater you need to purchase a year's membership card from the **Federazione Italiana della Pesca Sportiva** (*www.fipsas.it*), which has an office in every province; they can tell you about local conditions and restrictions. Bait and equipment are readily available.

Football

Soccer (*il calcio*) is a national obsession. For many Italians its importance far outweighs tedious issues such as the state of the nation, the government of the day, or any momentous international event – not least because of the chance (slim) of winning the Lotteria Sportiva.

All major cities, and most minor ones, have at least one team. Rivalry is intense, and scandals, usually involving bribery and cheating, are rife, but crowd violence is rare, except during 'derbies' between the likes of Lazio and Roma, Juventus and Torino, and Internazionale and AC Milan.

Big-league matches are played on Sun afternoons (*Sept–May*). For info, contact the Federazione Italiana Giuoco Calcio, Via Gregorio Allegri 14, 00198 Rome, **t** 06 84911, *www.figc.it*. To see the results of all the Italian league matches, log on to *www.livescore.com*.

Golf

The north is a good place to practise, particularly around Lake Como. Contact the Federazione Italiana Golf, Via Tiziano 74, 00196 Rome, **t** 06 323 1825, *www.federgolf.it*, for more information.

Hiking and Mountaineering

These sports are becoming steadily more popular among Italians every year. Walking in the Alps is generally practicable between May and Oct, though most chairlifts close from early or mid Sept. Tuscany and the Apennines (Abruzzo National Park) offer less strenuous but equally enjoyable walking country.

Strategically placed **alpine refuges** (*rifugi alpini*) open from the end of June to the end of Sept (so if you come in early June or Oct you need to carry camping gear). In July and Aug it's wise to book a bed in advance. Many are owned by the Italian Alpine Club; others are privately owned, usually by ski resorts. Some are along trails, others are reached via cable car. All offer bed and board; nearly all now require that you bring a sleeping sheet, or buy one on site. The higher up they are and more difficult the access, the more expensive they are.

There are also custodian-less *baite* (wooden huts), *casere* (stone huts) and *bivouacs* (with beds but no food) along some of the higher trails. For information, contact the **Italian Alpine Club**, **t** 02 2614 1378, *www.cai.it* (*www.turismo.fvg.it* for Friuli). Regional websites are also very helpful: see *www.infodolomiti.it* (Veneto), *www.trentino.to* (Trentino) and *www.altoadige.com* and *www.suedtirol.info* (Alto Adige).

Non-Italian sources of information include *www.alpine-club-org.uk*, *www.borntowalk.com* and *www.american-alpineclub.org*.

Some alpine resorts offer Settimane Verdi ('Green Weeks') – good-value accommodation and activity packages for summer visitors, similar to skiers' White Weeks.

Motor and Motorbike Racing

The homeland of Ferrari, Maserati and Alfa Romeo, as well as Ducati, Aprilia and Valentino Rossi, naturally fosters a keen interest in motor sports (the proof of which can be witnessed along any Italian road, which many Italians regard as practice tracks).

Monza, near Milan, hosts the Italian Grand Prix every September. The Formula Uno track, built in 1922, is 15km from town.

Riding Holidays

Riding holidays are available in many parts of Italy, particularly in areas where *agriturismo* (*see* p.91) is popular, such as Tuscany, Umbria and Lazio; in these areas tours based at country estates are offered. There also are riding stables in most cities and resorts.

For more information, contact local Agriturist offices, or the Associazione Nazionale per il Turismo Equestre, Piazza Mancini, 00196 Rome, **t** 06 3265 0230.

Rome's International Riding Show in the Villa Borghese draws a big crowd each May. Horse racing is staged in many large cities, but easily the most exciting race is Siena's bareback Palio (*see* p.504 and p.674).

Rowing and Canoeing

Good rowing spots are the Arno and Lombardy's lakes. Mountain rivers provide exciting white-water sport; kayak races take place in the Dolomites. For information contact the Federazione Italiana Canoa e Kayak, Viale Tiziano 70, 00196 Rome, **t** 06 368 58454, *www.federcanoa.it*.

Spectator-wise, the annual regatta between the four Ancient Maritime republics of Venice, Amalfi, Genoa and Pisa (held in turn at each city, *see* p.81) is splendidly colourful. Lake Piediluco in Umbria hosts an international rowing championship.

Skiing and Winter Sports

Italy still lacks the cachet of neighbouring Switzerland or Austria among the skiing fraternity but has caught up significantly, and now has a better reputation for safety and efficiency (though erratic snow cover is always a problem). The 2006 Winter Olympics in Turin will give winter sports in Italy a boost. Useful websites are *www.goski.com* and *www.fisi.org*.

The main resorts are in the Alps, particularly the scenic Dolomites. As well as downhill and cross-country (*sci di fondo*) skiing, there are exotic variants (for experts only) such as helicopter skiing. Equipment hire is generally not too expensive, but lift passes and hotels can push up the cost of a winter holiday.

Some of the most fashionable (and expensive) resorts are **Cortina** and **Courmayeur**. The Sella Ronda links several resorts in an exhilarating day's circuit. The Marmolada glacier in Trentino-Adige and Cervinia at the foot of the Matterhorn are year-round sources of snowy runs. Lombardy's most famous ski resort is **Bormio**, at the entrance to Italy's largest national park.

Prices are highest during the Christmas and New Year holidays, in Feb and at Easter. Most resorts offer Settimane Bianche ('White Weeks') – off-season packages at economical rates. Other winter sports such as ice-skating and bobsleighing are available at resorts.

Tennis

Every *comune* has public courts for hourly hire, especially resorts. Private clubs may offer temporary membership to visitors, and hotel courts can often be used by non-residents for a reasonable fee. Contact local tourist offices for information.

Italy's big tennis event is the Grand Prix tournament at Rome's Villa Borghese in May.

Water Sports

Despite Italy's coastal pollution, water sports are immensely popular, especially sailing and windsurfing. The best areas for sailing include the Ligurian Riviera and the Tuscan and Lazio coasts. Lakes Como and Garda also have good sailing and windsurfing schools. Water-skiing is possible on all the major lakes, as well as at many coastal resorts.

There are a few good areas for diving, notably Alassio (Liguria) and Capri. Boat and equipment hire is often quite expensive.

Mainland Italy is not remarkable for its **beaches**. Much of the coast is disappointingly flat and dull and many resorts are plagued by the concessionaire, who parks lines of sunbeds and brollies along the best stretches of beach and charges all comers handsomely for the privilege of spending time at the seaside.

Beaches in the south (Calabria, Basilicata and Puglia) are generally cleaner and less developed than those further north; those around the Bay of Naples, Rome's Lido di Ostia and the Venetian Lido are best avoided by swimmers; head for the islands for cleaner water and prettier scenery.

In Lombardy, the smaller, less crowded lakes such as Viverone, Varese and Mergozzo are preferable to the larger lakes for swimming.

No one bats an eye at topless bathing, especially in Rimini, although you see it less often in the south.

For further information on water sports, contact the following organizations:

Federazione Italiana Vela (Italian Sailing Federation), Via Brigata Bisagno 2/17, Genoa, **t** 010 565 723, *www.federvela.it*.

Federazione Italiana Motonautica (Italian Motorboat Federation), *www.fimconi.it*; and **Federazione Italiana Sci Nautico** (Italian Waterskiing Federation), Via Piranesi 44b, Milan, **t** 02 761 050, *www.coni.it*

Telephones

You can find public phones for international calls in the offices of **Telecom Italia**, Italy's telephone company. These are the only places where you can make **reverse-charge calls** (*a erre*, collect calls), but be prepared for a wait, as calls go through the operator in Rome. Rates for long-distance calls are among the highest in Europe. Calls within Italy are cheapest after 10pm; international calls after 11pm. Italy's streets are dotted with these orange phones.

Phone booths rarely take coins; phonecards (*schede telefoniche*), available in €2.50 and €5, are sold at tobacconists and news-stands – you have to snap off the small perforated corner to use them. In smaller villages you can usually find *telefoni a scatti*, with meters on, in at least one bar (a small commission is generally charged). Try to avoid telephoning from hotels, which often add 25% to the bill.

Direct calls can be made by dialling the **international prefix** (for the UK 0044, Ireland 00353, USA and Canada 001, Australia 0061, New Zealand 0064). If you're calling Italy from abroad, dial +39 first. Many places have public fax machines, but the speed of transmission may make costs very high.

Time

Italy is on Central European Time, 1hr ahead of Greenwich Mean Time and 6hrs ahead of Eastern Standard Time. From the last weekend of Mar to the end of Sept, Italian Summer Time (daylight saving time) is in effect – clocks go back 1hr in Mar.

Toilets

You will only find public conveniences in places such as train and bus stations and bars; ask for the *bagno, toilette* or *gabinetto*, and don't confuse Italian plurals; *signori* (gents) and *signore* (ladies)! In stations and smarter bars and cafés there are attendants who expect €0.20–0.50 for keeping the place decent.

Carry tissues and wipes with you, as finding paper (*carta*), soap *and* running water in one place is extremely rare. In the Veneto, 'Turkish loos' (holes in the ground) are very common.

Tourist Offices

Tourist information offices are generally open 8.30/9–12.30/1 and 3–7, possibly longer during the summer. Few open Sat afternoon or Sun.

Known as EPT, APT or IAT, **information booths** provide hotel lists, town plans and terse information on local sights and transport. Queues can be maddeningly long. If you're stuck, you may get more sense out of a friendly travel agency than an official tourist office. If there's no official tourist office, there's often a **Pro Loco**, an association whereby local people give tourist advice.

Nearly every city and province now has a **web page**, and you can often book your hotel direct through the Internet.

UK, Italian State Tourist Board, 1 Princes St, London W1B 8AY, **t** (020) 7408 1254, *www.enit.it/www.italiantourism.com*; Italian Embassy, 14 Three Kings Yard, Davies St, London W1Y 2EH, **t** (020) 7312 2200, *www.embitaly.org.uk*.

USA, 630 Fifth Ave, Suite 1565, New York, NY 10111, **t** (212) 245 5618/4822; 12400 Wilshire Blvd, Suite 550, Los Angeles, CA 90025, **t** (310) 820 1898/9807; 500 N. Michigan Ave, Suite 2240, Chicago 1 IL 60611, **t** (312) 644 0996, *www.italiantourism.com*.

Australia, Level 26–44 Market Street, Sydney, NSW 2000, **t** (02) 92 621 666.

Canada, 175 Bloor St East, Suite 907, South Tower, M4W 3R8 Toronto (ON), **t** (416) 925 4882/925 3870, *www.italiantourism.com*.

New Zealand, c/o Italian Embassy, 34 Grant Rd, Thorndon, Wellington, **t** (04) 947 178.

Tourist and travel information may also be available from **Alitalia** (Italy's national airline) or **CIT** (Italy's state-run travel agency) offices in some countries.

Where to Stay

All accommodation in Italy is classified by the Provincial Tourist boards. Price control, however, has been deregulated since 1992, at which point hotels began to set their own tariffs. Prices rocketed in some places, but after a period of rapid and erratic fluctuation, are settling down to more predictable levels under the influence of market forces.

Good-value, interesting accommodation in cities can be very difficult to find. Milan has the most expensive and heavily booked hotels in Italy; check the calendar of events with the tourist office – a major trade fair or conference could put your travel plans in jeopardy.

The quality of furnishings and facilities has generally improved in all categories in recent years. At the top end of the market are some exceptionally sybaritic hotels, furnished and decorated with real panache. But you can still find plenty of older-style hotels and *pensioni* with eccentricities of character and architecture (in some cases undeniably charming) that may be at odds with modern standards of comfort or even safety.

Hotels and Guesthouses

Italian *alberghi* are rated from 1 to 5 stars, depending on what facilities they offer (not their character, style or charm), such as lift, car park and air-conditioning. The **star ratings** are some indication of price levels, but for tax reasons not all hotels advertise themselves at the rating to which they are entitled, so you may find a modestly rated hotel just as comfortable (or more so) than a more highly rated one. Conversely, you may find a hotel offers few stars in hopes of attracting budget-conscious travellers but charges just as much as a higher-rated neighbour.

Pensioni are generally more modest, though the distinction between these and ordinary hotels is becoming rather blurred. *Locande* are traditionally an even more basic form of hostelry, but these days the term may denote somewhere fairly chic. Other inexpensive accommodation is sometimes known as *alloggi* or *affittacamere*. There are usually plenty of cheap dives around railway stations; for somewhere more salubrious, head for the historic quarters. Whatever the shortcomings of the décor, furnishings and fittings, you can usually rely at least on having clean sheets.

Price lists, by law, must be posted on the back of the door of every room, along with meal prices and any extra charges (such as air-con or cable TV). Many hotels display 2 or 3 rates, depending on the season. **Low-season** rates may be about a third lower than peak-season tariffs. Some resort hotels close down for several months a year. During **high season** you should always book ahead to be sure of a room (an email may be easier than post or telephone, and you'll have the advantage of written confirmation to print out and take along with you). Major city business hotels may offer significant **discounts** at weekends.

Tourist offices publish annual regional lists of hotels and *pensioni* with current rates, but don't generally make reservations for visitors, although they can check availability. Main train stations have **accommodation booking desks**, which charge fees.

Chain hotels or motels are generally the easiest hotels to book, though not always the most interesting to stay in. Top of the list is CIGA (*Compagnia Grandi Alberghi*), with some of the most luxurious establishments in Italy, many grand, turn-of-the-century places that have been wonderfully restored (Venice's legendary Cipriani is one of its flagships). The French *Relais & Châteaux* consortium specializes in tastefully indulgent hotels, often in historic buildings. At a more affordable level, one of the biggest chains in Italy is the reliable Jolly Hotels; these can be found near the centre of larger towns. Many motels are operated by the ACI (Italian Automobile Club) or by AGIP (the oil company) and are usually located along major exit routes.

If you arrive without a reservation, begin looking or phoning round early in the day. If possible, inspect the room (and bathroom) before you book , and check the tariff carefully. Italian hoteliers can legally alter their rates twice a year, so printed tariffs or tourist-board lists (and prices quoted in this book!) may be out of date. Hoteliers who wilfully overcharge should be reported to the local tourist office. When you check in, you will be asked for your passport to register.

Prices listed in this guide (*see* below) are for **double rooms in high season, with en suite bath where available**; expect to pay about half to two-thirds the rate for single occupancy – though in high season you may be charged the full rate in some popular beach resorts. Extra beds are usually charged at about a third more of the room rate. Rooms without en suite bathrooms are generally 20–30% less, and most hotels offer discounts for children sharing parent's rooms, or children's meals. A single room (*camera singola*) may cost anything from about €35; double rooms (*camera doppia*) go from about €60 to €250 or more. If you want a double bed, you need to request a *camera matrimoniale*.

If you've paid a **deposit**, your booking is valid under Italian law, but don't expect it to be refunded if you have to cancel.

Breakfast is often 'included' by hotels (especially in high season; you may be charged €11 or more on top of the room rate), and obligatory in *pensioni*. You can get better value by eating breakfast in a bar or café. In high season you may be expected to take half board in resorts if the hotel has a restaurant, and one-night stays may be refused.

Hotel Price Categories

Category	Double with bath/shower
luxury	over €230
very expensive	€150–230
expensive	€100–150
moderate	€60–100
cheap	up to €60

Hostels and Budget Accommodation

There aren't many youth hostels (*alberghi* or *ostelli per la gioventù*) in Italy, but they are generally pleasant and sometimes located in historic buildings. The **Associazione Italiana Alberghi per la Gioventù** (Italian Youth Hostel Association, or AIG) is affiliated to the International Youth Hostel Federation. For a list of hostels, contact AIG at Via Cavour 44, 00184 Roma (**t** 06 487 1152). An international membership card enables you to stay in any of them. You can purchase them on the spot in many hostels, or get one in advance from:

UK, Youth Hostels Assocation of England and Wales, **t** (01629) 592 600, *www.yha.org.uk*.

USA, Hostelling International, **t** (301) 495 1240, *www.hiayh.org*.

Canada, Hostelling International, *www.hihostels.ca*.

Australia, Australian Youth Hostel Association, **t** (02) 926 1111, *www.yha.com.au*.

Discounts are available for senior citizens, and some family rooms are available. You generally have to check in after 5pm, and pay for your room before 9am. Most hostels close for the best part of the daytime, and many operate a curfew. In spring, noisy school parties cram hostels for field trips. Book ahead during the summer.

Religious institutions also run hostels; some are single sex, others accept Catholics only. Rates are usually somewhere between €10–20, including breakfast.

Villas, Flats and Chalets

If you're travelling in a group or with a family, self-catering can be the ideal way to experience Italy. The Italian State Tourist Office has lists of agencies in the UK and USA that rent places on a weekly or fortnightly basis. The small ads in the weekend papers are crammed with suggestions, especially for Tuscany.

If you have set your heart on a region, write to its tourist office for a list of agencies and owners, who will send brochures or particulars of their accommodation. Maid service is included in the more glamorous villas; ask whether bed linen and towels are provided. The agencies in the box below are all reliable.

Rural Self-catering

For a breath of rural seclusion, the gregarious Italians head for a spell on a **working farm**, in accommodation (usually self-catering) that often approximates to the French *gîte*. Often, however, the real pull of such places is cooking by the hosts and the chance to sample home-grown produce. Outdoor activities offered by such places may include riding and fishing.

This branch of the Italian tourist industry is run by **Agriturist**. It has burgeoned in recent years, and every region now has several offices. Prices of farmhouse accommodation, compared with those of over-hyped Tuscan villas, are still reasonable. To make the most of your rural hosts, it's as well to have a little Italian under your belt.

Local tourist offices have information on this type of accommodation in their area; full listings are compiled by the national organization **Agriturist**, *www.agiturist.it*, and **Turismo Verde**, *www.cia.it*.

Alpine Refuges

See p.87.

Camping

Life under canvas is not the fanatical craze here that it is in France, nor is it necessarily any great bargain, but there are more than 2,000 sites in Italy, and they are particularly popular with holiday-making families in Aug, when you can expect to find many sites at bursting point.

You can obtain a list of local sites from any regional tourist office. Charges are generally about €8 per adult; tents and vehicles carry an additional cost of about €6 each. Small extra charges may also be levied for hot showers and electricity.

Accommodation and Self-catering

www.venere.com is a useful hotel/B&B booking service with lots of feedback from previous guests.

In the UK and Ireland

Abercrombie & Kent, Sloane Square House, Holbein Place, London SW1W 8NS, **t** 0845 0700 618, *www.abercrombiekent.co.uk*.

Accommodation Line, 46 Maddox St, London W1R 9PB, **t** (020) 7499 4433.

Citalia, *see* p.70.

Individual Travellers Co, Manor Courtyard, Bignor, Pulborough, West Sussex RH20 1QD, **t** (01798) 869 461/08700 780 193, *www.indiv-travellers.com*.

Inghams, 10–18 Putney Hill, London SW15 6AX, **t** (020) 8780 4400, *www.inghams.co.uk*.

Interhome, 383 Richmond Rd, Twickenham, Middx TW1 2EF, **t** (020) 8891 1294, *www.interhome.co.uk*

Magic of Italy, *see* p.71.

Topflight, 3rd floor, Jervis House, Jervis St, Dublin 1, Ireland, **t** (01) 2401 700, *www.topflight.ie*.

In the USA

CIT Tours, *see* p.72.

Hideaways International, 767 Islington St, Portsmouth, NH 03801, **t** (603) 430 4433, (800) 843 4433, *www.hideaways.com*.

RentVillas.com, 700 E Main St, Ventura, CA 93001, **t** 800 726 6702, *www.rentvillas.com*.

RAVE (Rent-a-Vacation-Everywhere), Market Place Mall, Rochester, NY 14607, **t** (716) 427 0259.

To obtain a camping carnet and to book ahead, write to:

Centro Internazionale Prenotazioni Campeggio, Casella Postale 23, 50041 Calenzano, Firenze, **t** 055 882 381 (ask for their list of campsites with the booking form).

Touring Club Italiano (TCI), Corso Italia 10, 20122 Milano, **t** 02 85261/02 852 6245, *www.touringclub.it*. This publishes a comprehensive annual guide to campsites throughout Italy, available on the website for €20.

Unofficial camping is generally frowned on. Camper vans (and facilities for them) are increasingly popular.

Women Travellers

The old horror stories of gangs following the innocent tourist maiden and pinching her bottom are way behind the times. These days Italian men are often supremely polite and flirt on a much more sophisticated level, especially in the more 'Europeanized' north: Milan or Venice are easier cities for women than Rome or Naples.

Still, women travelling alone may receive hisses, wolf-whistles and unsolicited comments, and 'assistance' from local swains – usually of the balding, middle-age-crisis variety. The best policy is usually a confident, indifferent poise; failing that, a polite 'I am waiting for my *marito*' followed by a firm '*No!*' or '*Vai via!*' (Scram!) will generally solve the problem.

Any risks can be greatly reduced if you use common sense and avoid lonely streets or parks and train stations after dark, as you would anywhere. Choose hotels and restaurants within easy and safe walking distance of public transport. Although travelling with a companion of either sex will buffer you considerably from such nuisances, two women travelling together may still find they attract unwanted advances, particularly in the south. Avoid hitchhiking alone.

Piemonte and Valle d'Aosta

9

Piemonte (Piedmont), 'the foot of the mountains', is not only the birthplace of the modern Italian state, the source of its greatest river, the cradle of its industry, and the originator of such indispensable Italian staples as vermouth, Fiats and breadsticks, but also a beautiful region full of surprises. To the north and west tower some of the tallest Alps, soon to host the 2006 Winter Olympics, while the autonomous region of Valle d'Aosta just north is home to such world-class heavyweights as Mont Blanc, the Matterhorn and Monte Rosa. Southern Piemonte is walled off from Liguria by the lush green Maritime Alps, which, like most of the rest of Piemonte, are practically untouched by mass tourism. Wedged between the Maritime Alps and the Po, Le Langhe and Monferrato are home to miles of rolling hills clad in the noble pinstripes of Italy's most prestigious vineyards and the Slow Food movement.

To the north of the Po the scene changes again, into a flat plain that's crisscrossed by a complicated web of small canals that water Europe's most important rice fields. And in the centre of the hills, plains and mountains lies the regional capital of Turin, not an industrial by-product of Flat as one might suppose, but a Baroque, regal and often strange city.

If the Italy you seek includes sensational alpine scenery and emerald valleys, and all the skiing and hiking possibilities they offer; if it includes un-hyped medieval hill towns and castles standing like islands above rolling seas of vines; if it includes fantastic wines and regional cuisine; or if you have a special interest in white truffles, caves, Saint Bernards, trout fishing, Egyptology, Romanesque or Baroque architecture, Gothic frescoes, rare flowers, wildlife or kayaking, you will love Piemonte and Aosta. On the other hand, if your Italy consists of Renaissance art, lemon groves and endless sunshine, you'd better do as Hannibal did and just pass right on through.

Food and Wine in Piemonte

Grissini (breadsticks), invented in Turin, so charmed Napoleon that he introduced them to France. *Tartufi bianchi* (white truffles) from Alba are a local obsession, often served grated in a *fonduta*, with melted fontina cheese from Aosta – just one of a score of great regional cheeses; Piemonte is the one region of Italy where restaurants regularly do a cheese course.

The winter speciality, *bagna cauda*, a rich hot dip made with butter, olive oil, garlic, anchovies and cream, is often served with *cardi*, a raw artichoke-like thistle, or with roasted meats. The classic first course is *agnolotti* – pasta squares similar to ravioli, stuffed with meat or cheese. The pastries and desserts are superb: the Bocca di Leone is a sinfully rich calorific heavyweight, *torta di nocciole* a divine hazelnut cake.

The hills of Piemonte yield superb wines – Barbaresco, Barolo, Dolcetto, Nebbiolo and Barbera. To promote them there are 10 regional wine shops (*enoteche regionali*) in historic castles and buildings along the wine roads. Note that all close for lunch (although some also have fine restaurants) and in January; some charge for tasting. **Grinzane Cavour**, **Barbaresco**, **Barolo**, **Mango, Canelli** and **Canale d'Alba** are all near Alba (*see* p133). Others are at **Vignale Monferrato** (*see* p.132), **Acqui Terme** (*see* p.138) and **Róppolo**, by Lake Viverone (*see* p.130) and **Grattinara** (*see* p.130).

Piemonte and Valle d'Aosta

Highlights

1 Turin's Baroque geometry, museums and ring of royal pleasure palaces
2 Aosta, the 'Rome of the Alps'
3 The heartstopping Mont Blanc funiculars
4 The incredible Sacra di San Michele
5 White truffles and famous wines in the pretty hill villages of Le Langhe

Piemonte

By Italian standards, Piemonte is a relatively recent creation. Even the name only dates back as far as the 13th century, and only gradually did 'Piemonte' spread to encompass a patchwork of feudal lands collected by the counts and dukes of Savoy, who first got a foothold in Italy by marriage in the 11th century. Right from the beginning, they kept a tight reign on their border realm. Juices flowing elsewhere – the rise of independent *comuni* and the medieval Italian republics and the Renaissance – failed to penetrate their fastness. For centuries the population didn't even consider itself Italian, and instead spoke Provençal (or Occitan), which still survives in most of the alpine valleys.

Yet, as stodgily uninspired as Piemonte remained throughout Italy's Golden Age, it was the first region to re-surface after the cruel Spanish–French wars that were fought in Italy in the 16th century, Piemonte's French occupation, begun in 1539, ended 20 years later, when Duke Emanuele Filiberto won back his lands in the battle of Saint-Quentin. From that point on, the Dukes linked their destiny with Italy, moving their capital to Turin and treading the troubled political waters of the day with an astute (and occasionally unscrupulous) choice of alliances and diplomatic manoeuvring that earned them the title of King of Sardinia in 1713, and then, in the Risorgimento, the crown of Italy herself. For all that, Turin lacked the historical credentials to remain the seat of power (besides being too close to France for comfort). Turin rioted, but the first king of Italy, Vittorio Emanuele II, moved his capital to Florence, en route to Rome.

Rather than collect dust, the Piemontese began Italy's industrial revolution, building the first wool mills in the torrent-sliced valleys of Biella, the first cars in Turin, the first typewriters in Ivrea, and creating a felt-hat empire in Alessandria. Piemonte's economy has always been one of the strongest in Italy, with tourism playing only an insignificant supporting role.

Turin

Detroit without the degradation; the absolutist capital of the Savoys; a stately, masculine Baroque city of avenues, porticos and squares; the home of the famous shroud, of Juventus, the Red Brigades, breadsticks and vermouth; and the reputed centre of black magic in the Mediterranean – Turin (Torino, population 900,000) makes a rather unexpected 'Gateway to Italy'. It stands on the Po, so close to its alpine sources that this longest of Italy's rivers is almost clean. Its cuisine is influenced by that of France; its winters are colder than those of Copenhagen; its most renowned museum is Egyptian.

In 1563, a time when King Philip II of Spain held the rest of Italy by the bootstrap, feisty 'iron-headed' Emanuele Filiberto of Savoy, descendant of Europe's most ancient ruling house, drove the French and Spanish troops from his territory and moved his capital from Chambéry to Turin, previously little more than a fortified Roman outpost

(*Augusta Taurinorum*) and medieval university town. It was a move symbolizing the dynasty's new identity with the Italian portion of Savoy, or Piemonte – a move that was to have the greatest impact on the future. No one at the time suspected that the absolutionist duchy in this hitherto neglected corner of the peninsula would one day unite the land, and that Turin would be the first capital of the Kingdom of Italy.

In 1899, the first Giovanni Agnelli founded Turin's new dynasty, Fiat (Fabbrica Italiana Automobili Torino). His employees became Italy's first and most organized proletariat: during the First World War, Antonio Gramsci, the great philosopher of the Italian Communist Party, led the workers' councils in occupying the Fiat works in what he hoped would become an Italian Petrograd. The failure taught him that Italians required a different solution, and made him rightly fear that extremism would be the end result; he was arrested in 1926 and died in a Fascist prison in 1937.

The post-war years were equally troubled, as thousands of southerners came up to work in the factories. Paradoxically, although Turin took credit for Italy's unification, it also suffered the consequences of that union most acutely in the bigotry against the newcomers. Nor had conditions for workers improved much; in the early 1970s, when the Red Brigades, 'the armed instrument of class struggle', were born on the factory floors of Milan and Turin, they had plenty of support.

Despite the agitation, these were also the years when Giovanni Agnelli's grandson, the flamboyant Gianni, turned Fiat into a huge conglomerate (with help from the government in Rome) and made Italy into a world economic power. Automobiles are now only a small part of their interests, which is just as well – agreements with Japan on restricting car imports have expired, and Fiat's former 60 per cent market share in Italy has been cut in half. Since the death of Gianni Agnelli in January 2003, there has been speculation on what GM (Fiat Auto's part owner) will do next. But the decades of crisis have helped to make Turin stronger, and in the 1990s it has emerged as a dynamic, multicultural city of hi-tech service industries, arts and culture, food and tourism, ready to show off to the world in the 2006 Winter Olympics

Turin's Centre: along Via Roma

Central Turin is laid out in a stately rhythm of porticoed streets and squares. Few stations in Italy will deposit you in a piazza as elegant as Porta Nuova's **Piazza Carlo Felice**. Fashionable **Via Roma**, lined with designer shops, leads from here into the heart of the city, passing through an impressive gateway formed by the churches of **Santa Cristina** (1639) and **San Carlo** (begun in 1619), dedicated to St Charles Borromeo, whose nearly twin façades overlook Turin's finest square, **Piazza San Carlo**, a 17th-century set piece with a flamboyant bronze **equestrian statue of Duke Emanuele Filiberto**, 'the Iron Head', sheathing his sword after defeating the French at the battle of Saint-Quentin. This is a city of elegant cafés, and in Piazza San Carlo you can sip your cappuccino in the most celebrated all, the 19th-century **Caffè Torino**, a veritable palace of java with chandeliers and frescoed ceilings. Just west, the **Museo della Marionetta** at Via Santa Teresa 5 (***t** 011 530 238; open daily by appointment; adm*) has a collection of Italian puppets from the 19th century. Nearby, the glass-roofed **Galleria San Federico** has a great Art Deco cinema.

Turin
S. Maria Ausiliatrice
Porta Palazzo
to Stazione Dora
Piazza della Repubblica
Porta Palatina
Piazza C. Augusto
Museo delle Antichità
Teatro Romano
Duomo
Palazzo Reale
Giardino Reale
Biblioteca / Armeria Reale
Piazzetta Reale
S. Lorenzo
Piazza Castello
Galleria Subalpina
Teatro Regio
Università
Palazzo Carignano
Piazza Carignano
Piazza Carlo Alberto
Accademia Albertina
Mole Antonelliana/ Museo Nazionale del Cinema
SS. Annunziata
Museo di Arte Decorative
Piazza Vittorio Veneto
Ponte Vittorio Emanuele I
to Villa della Regina
Piazza Gran Madre di Dio
Gran Madre di Dio
Parco Michelotti
Fiume Po
Fiume Dora
Museo Nazionale della Montagna Duca degli Abruzzi
SS. Sudario/ Museo della Sindone
S. Consolata
Piazza Em. Filiberto
Piazza D. Consolata
S. Domenico
Largo IV Marzo
Pza S. Giovanni
Piazza Savoia
Church of the Carminer
Palazzo di Città
SS. Martiri
Piazza Statuto
Pza Arbarello
S. Maria di Piazza
Giardino Cittadella
Museo Egizio e Gall. Sabauda
S. Filippo Neri
Piazza Carlo Emanuele II
Stazione Porta Susa
Piazza XVIII Dicembre
Museo Civico Pietro Micca
Museo Storico dell' Ariglieria
Mastro della Cittadella
Galleria S. Federico
Piazza S. Carlo
Piazza Solferino
S. Carlo
Sta Cristina
Fondazione Palazzo
Museo Regionale di Scienze Naturali
Piazza Cavour
Pza Bodoni
Pza Paleocapa
Piazza Carlo Felice
Pza Lagrange
Fondazione Italiana per la Fotografia
Largo Vittorio Emanuele
Galleria Civica d'Arte Moderna e Contemporanea
Stazione Porta Nuova
Air Terminal
To Lingotto
Parco del Valentino
Orto Botanico
Ponte Umberto I
Piazza Crimea
Largo Montebello
Pza Santa Giulia
Corso Regina Margherita
Corso Principe Oddone
Corso Inghilterra
Corso S. Martino
Corso Valdocco
Corso Palestro
Corso Pr. Eugenio
Corso 11 Febbraio
Corso San Maurizio
Corso Casale
Corso G. Matteotti
Corso Vittorio Emanuele II
Corso Re Umberto I
Corso G. Ferraris
Corso Vinzaglio
Corso Bolzano
Corso Cairoli
Corso Moncalieri
Corso Giovanni Lanza
Corso M. D'Azeglio
Lungo Dora Firenze
Lungo Po Machiavelli
Lungo Po Cadorna
Murazzi del Po
Via Cottolengo
Via Sta Chiara
Via S. Domenico
Via del Carmine
Via C. Giulio
Via della Consolata
Via Bligny
Via Corte d'Appello
Via Milano
Via XX Settembre
Via V. D. Basilica
Via Giuseppe Garibaldi
Via Barbaroux
Via Juvarra
Via Sta Maria
Via Monte di Pietà
Via P. Micca
Via Bertola
Via Cernaia
Via Sta Teresa
Via Alfieri
Via D. Arcivescovado
Via Gramsci
Via S. Quintino
Via Magenta
Via V. Vela
Via Allioni
Via Passalacqua
Via Manzoni
Via Botero
Via S. Francesco d'Assisi
Via Roma
Via Acc. Scienze
Via Lagrange
Via Carlo Alberto
Via San Francesco da Paola
Via Accademia Albertina
Via Principe Amedeo
Via Maria Vittoria
Via Giovanni Giolitti
Via Camillo Cavour
Via Giuseppe Mazzini
Via Giuseppe Verdi
Via Po
Via G. Rossini
Via Montebello
Via C. Balbo
Via Santa Giulia
Via degli Artisti
Via Giulia di Barolo
Via Napione
Via Plana
Via Giardino
Via Guicciardini
Via Avogadro
Via Sacchi
Via Nizza
Via Goito
Via Madama Cristina
250 metres
250 yards
N

Getting There

By Air

Turin's Caselle **airport**, **t** 011 567 6361, is 15km north of the city. Every 30mins an airport bus, **t** 011 300 0611, stops at the air terminal, at Corso Vittorio Emanuele II by Porta Nuova Station; tickets can be bought from a kiosk in the arrivals hall, at bars near the bus stops, or on board. The journey time is about 40mins. GTT trains, with a station right by the airport (reached by a covered walkway), run every 30mins to Turin's Dora station (20mins).

By Rail

Turin's **Porta Nuova** station, **t** 892021, near the centre, has connections to France and Genoa (2hrs), Milan (1½hrs), Aosta (2½hrs) and Venice (5hrs).

Porta Susa station, on the west side of town, can be a convenient getting-off point; a 3rd station, **Dora** (Via Giachino 10), serves the local line to the airport, Ciriè, Lanzo and Ceres.

By Bus

The SADEM **bus** terminal, **t** 011 300 0611, is on Corso Inghilterra, at the west end of Corso Vittorio Emanuele II; many buses also stop by Porta Susa station. Buses serve Aosta's ski resorts as far as Chamonix, towns in the province, Milan Malpensa airport (3 times daily).

Getting Around

Most of Turin's sites are within **walking** distance of each other in the historic centre, where cars have been banned. Otherwise, its regular grid of streets is served by old-fashioned **trams** and **buses** (a new automatic metro, linking Collegno to Porta Nuova and Porta Nuova to Lingotto, is scheduled to open in late 2005).

The city transport office at Porta Nuova station provides a good free bus map (also available from tourist offices). The TurismoBus (day pass available on board) stops at 14 points of interest (10am–7pm weekends; daily during hols and July to mid-Sept).

Parking is very restricted in the old city centre. There are **taxi ranks** in many of the main piazzas, or call **t** 011 5730 or **t** 011 3399).

Tourist Information

Piazza Castello 161, **t** 011 535 181/011 535 901 (*open Mon–Sat 9.30–7, Sun 9.30–3*); Porta Nuova station, **t** 011 531 327; and Caselle airport; *www.turismotorino.org*.

The tourist board's Torino Card (48/72hrs) includes travel on city buses and boats and the TurismoBus, admission to 120 museums and sites, and half-price concert and theatre tickets and tours.

Shopping

Turin's big-name designer shops are in **Via Roma** and in the majestic shopping arcades off it – **Galleria San Federico** and **Galleria Subalpina** – while arty boutiques and food shops fill the pedestrian-only Quadrilatero Romano north of Via Garibaldi. A good buy in Turin is fine chocolates or **gianduiotti**, named after comic figure Gianduia; one of the best places to get them is **Giordano** at Piazza Carlo Felice 69.

Turin has Europe's largest covered market (Mon–Fri until 1.30, Sat until 6.30), at **Porta Palazzo** in Piazza della Repubblica, with nearly 700 stands. The Sat morning **'Balôn' flea market** takes place in the streets behind Porta Palazzo; there's a much bigger **'Gran Balôn'** the second Sun of the month.

The Egyptian Museum and Galleria Sabauda

These treasure troves are just off Piazza San Carlo, sharing the big brick **Palazzo dell'Accademia delle Scienze** (1679, by Guarino Guarini), a former Jesuit college. The **Museo Egizio** (***t*** *011 561 7776; open Tues–Sun 8.30–7.30; adm exp*) is rated (except by the directors of the Louvre) as the second most important Egyptian collection in the world, after Cairo's. It was begun as a cabinet of curios in 1628 by Carlo Emanuele I, but later Savoys took their pharaohs and mummies more seriously, especially Carlo

Sports and Activities

The **Stadio delle Alpi**, Strada Altessano 131, on the northern outskirts of town (tram no.9b), is home to **Torino**, in the Italian 2nd division, and **Juventus**, often at the top of the 1st division. It's generally acknowledged that the Italian league produces the highest standard of football in the world and that no one (except emergent Roma and Lazio, or perhaps AC Milan in a good year) plays it better than Juventus.

The season is May–Sept and tickets can be bought at tobacconists, or on **t** 011 65631/*www.juventus.it*. Steer clear of any match involving Juventus and Fiorentina (Florence), referred to in the Italian media as the 'derby of poison'.

For information on the 2006 **Winter Olympics**, contact Torino 2006, **t** 011 631 0511, *www.torino2006.org*.

Where to Stay

Turin ✉ 10100

Turin's hotels tend to be expensive, modern and business oriented, or cheap and a bit seedy. Most are within walking distance of Porta Nuova station. The tourist office runs a free hotel and B&B finding service (contact them 48hrs in advance, **t** 011 440 7032).

Luxury

****Turin Palace**, Via Sacchi 8, **t** 011 562 5511, *www.thi.it*. A traditional grand hotel across from Porta Nuova station, Turin's top hotel since 1872. The public rooms are sumptuous, the restaurant elegant, and the soundproofed bedrooms luxurious.

****Villa Sassi**, Via Traforo di Pino 47, **t** 011 898 0556, *www.villasassi.com*. The city's most evocative hotel, in a lovely park in the hills east of the Po. Converted from a 17th-century patrician villa, it has many original features – marble floors, Baroque fireplaces and portraits. You'll need a car to get here, and there's a minimum 3-night stay. *Closed Aug.*

****Grand Hotel Sitea**, Via Carlo Alberto 35, **t** 011 517 0171, *www.thi.it*. A hotel in a quiet street near the centre, with plush bedrooms (half-price at weekends). The restaurant, **Carignano** (*expensive*), serves local fare.

Very Expensive

***Victoria**, Via Nino Costa 4, **t** 011 561 1909, *www.hotelvictoria-torino.com*. A delightful, quirkily furnished hotel. Staff are friendly and helpful, and there's a bright and airy breakfast room overlooking the garden.

Expensive

***Roma & Rocca Cavour**, Piazza Carlo Felice 60, **t** 011 561 2772. A somewhat impersonal option. Some of the rooms are lovely, with old-fashioned furnishings; others are merely adequate but may be available at reduced rates for tourists. Rates drop out of season.

Moderate

Sila, Piazza Carlo Felice 80, **t** 011 544 086. A slightly gloomy hotel with a great location and views, near the airport bus stop and good for a last-night stopover.

Cheap

Mobledor, Via Acc. Albertina 1, **t** 011 888445, *www.paginegialle.it/mobledor*. Comfortable rooms decorated with murals, with shower and TV, by Porta Nuova.

Ostello Torino, Via Alby 1, **t** 011 660 2939. The town's youth hostel, near Piazza Crimea (bus no.52 from the station), with decent cheap rooms, and bed and breakfast. *Reception open 7–10 and 3.30–11.30. Closed mid-Dec–Feb.*

Felice, who acquired the collection of Piemonte native Bernardo Drovetti (the French consul general of Egypt and a confidant of Mehmet Ali) and in 1824 founded the world's first Egyptian museum. Two 20th-century Italian expeditions added to the collections, and the museum played a major role in the Aswan Dam rescue digs. It was rewarded with one of the Aswan temples: the 15th-century-BC rock-cut **temple of Ellessya**, complete with a relief of Thothmes III, now reconstructed on the ground floor – it's best viewed in the early evening, when the half-light allows the reliefs to stand out properly.

Eating Out

Very Expensive

Del Cambio, Piazza Carignano 2, **t** 011 546 690. A place for a trip back to the old royal capital of the Savoys, opened in 1757. The décor and waiters' uniforms have been preserved, as has Prime Minister Cavour's favourite corner. The recipes have been lightened to appeal to modern tastes. Try Cavour's favourite dish, *finanziera* – veal, sweetbreads, cockscombs and *porcini* cooked in butter and wine. *Closed Sun, Aug and 1st wk Jan.*

Vintage 1997, Piazza Solferino 16, **t** 011 535 948. A refined restaurant in a historic house, popular with local VIPs for its delicate fusion of Mediterranean and Piemontese cuisine. *Closed Sat lunch, Sun and Aug.*

Expensive

Al Garamond, Via Pomba 14, **t** 011 812 2781. An atmospheric gourmet haven in the centre, serving the likes of seafood and broccoletti *lasagnette. Closed Sun, Sat lunch and Aug.*

Savoia, Via Corte d'Appello 13, **t** 011 436 2288. Inventive dishes featuring some surprising ingredients, including duck breast with fava beans and cumin. *Closed Sat lunch and Sun.*

Moderate

Sotto La Mole, Via Montebello 9, **t** 011 521 2810. A charming restaurant serving Piemontese classics and creative dishes such as chestnut gnocchi. *Closed lunch, Weds eve and few wks Jan and June.*

L'Agrifoglio, Via Accademia Albertina 38/d, **t** 011 837 064. A delightful family-run place serving mountain dishes with a French touch. *Closed lunch, Sun, Mon and part of Aug.*

Il Gatto e la volpe, Via Fontanesi 33, **t** 011 812 6882. Well-prepared seafood. *Closed lunch and Mon.*

Cheap

Arcadia, Galleria Subalpina 16, **t** 011 561 3898. A popular lunchtime spot for *antipasti*, pasta and country-style meat dishes. *Closed Sun.*

Cafés

Turin's grand cafés aren't cheap, but their famous hot chocolate, cakes, sandwiches and ice cream are usually superb. **Baratti & Milano** in Piazza Castello is largely unchanged since 1873; **Caffè Torino**, Piazza San Carlo 204, is famed for its cocktails; **Al Bicerin**, Piazza della Consolata, opened in 1763 and still serves *bicerin*, a mix of coffee, chocolate and cream that was Cavour's favourite drink; and the early 1900s **Mulassano**, Piazza Castello 15, was the birthplace of the *tramezzini*.

Entertainment and Nightlife

For information on concerts, film times and so on, check the listings in *La Stampa*, or visit the Vetrina per Torino booth at Piazza San Carlo 159, freephone **t** 800 015 475.

The **Teatro Regio** in Piazza Castello stages ballet, concerts and opera year round, **t** 011 881 5241/2, or freephone **t** 800 807 064.

Summer sees a **jazz festival**, and in July the **ForinoExtra** festival draws big-name musicians from around the world. **Settembre Musica** features mostly classical concerts in theatres and churches.

The **Torino Film Festival**, held in Nov, is a hugely popular showcase for both new and up-and-coming directors of independent art-house films.

Nightowls haunt the **clubs** in the old boat sheds in the Murazzi (the defensive walls along the Po) and in the Quadrilatero Romano.

The same floor houses an excellent collection of monumental public sculpture, notably the 13th-century BC black granite Ramses II, the 15th-century BC Thothmes III, and the sarcophagus of Ghemenef-Har-Bak, a vizier of the 26th Dynasty. Upstairs there is an immense papyrus library; after cracking the Rosetta Stone, Champollion came here to complete his study of hieroglyphics. Elsewhere, you can spend hours just wandering amid the essentials and the trivialities of ancient Egypt; there's a reconstruction of the 14th-century BC **tomb of the architect Khaiè and his wife Meriè** that managed to escape the grave robbers – even the bread and beans for their afterlife remain intact. Other rooms contain some mummies in various stages of deshabille, wooden models of boats and funerary processions, paintings, statuettes, jewellery, clothing and textiles.

The basement holds finds from the Gebelein, Assiut and Qau el Kebir sites, which were excavated by representatives of the museum between 1905 and 1920. There are more reconstructed tombs, painted sarcophagi and dozens of beautifully preserved wooden models recovered from tombs: boats with crews and oars, kitchens and granaries, servants performing everyday tasks, as well as scale models of the dead.

On the top two floors, the **Galleria Sabauda** (*t 011 547 440; open Weds, Thurs, Sat and Sun 8.30–7.30, Tues and Fri 8.30–2; adm*) has one of Italy's top hordes of paintings, collected by the House of Savoy. It starts with some choice Florentine works by the likes of Beato Angelico and Antonio and Piero del Pollaiuolo, which are followed by other Italian schools (Giovanni Bellini, Mantegna, Taddeo Gaddi, Il Sodoma, Tintoretto, Titian, Veronese, Bergognone and Piemontese masters Jacques Iverny (a 15th-century triptych) and Gaudenzio Ferrari (*Crucifixion*). The Savoys were equally fond of Flemish and Dutch art: look out for Jan Van Eyck's exquisite *St Francis*, Memling's drama-filled *Scenes from the Passion*, Van Dyck's beautiful *Children of Charles I of England*, and his *Equestrian Portrait of Prince Tommaso di Savoia Carignano* (1634), popular scenes by Jan Brueghel, *Deinira tempted by the Fury* by Rubens, *Portrait of a Doctor* by Jacobs Dirk, and Rembrandt's *Old Man Sleeping*. The French have a room to themselves, with works by Poussin, Claude and Clouet.

Cater-corner from here, the Baroque **Palazzo Carignano** has a bold undulating brick façade billowing like a wave across Piazza Carignano. Begun in 1679 for the Savoia-Carignano branch of the ducal family, this is one of the finest secular buildings of the age in northern Italy, a key work by Guarino Guarini, the Theatine priest and mathematician who moonlighted as an architect and came to work for Carlo Emanuele II in 1668. The interior is full of historical fossils: the reconstructed bedroom in Oporto where Carlo Alberto died; Cavour's study; and the chamber of the Piemontese Parliament preserved as it was during its final session in 1860, all chandeliers, gilt and plush. Here its successor, the first Italian Parliament, proclaimed Vittorio Emanuele II King of Italy on 14 March 1861. Rooms on the *piano nobile* contain the **Museo Nazionale del Risorgimento** (*t 011 562 1147; open Tues–Sun 9–7; adm*), covering the Siege of Turin in 1706 up to the Second World War.

Just north of the Palazzo Carignano, the **Galleria Subalpina** was inspired by Milan's Galleria Vittorio Emanuele. Nietzsche was living in a room nearby when he collapsed here in 1889, consumed by syphilis; he would live another 11 years, but in the silence of a sanitorium.

Piazza Castello: the Royal Command Centre

The Galleria Subalpina leads to the elegant **Caffè Baratti & Milano** and the huge expanse of Turin's main **Piazza Castello**, with the **Palazzo Madama** in the middle. This has a long history; it started as the Roman gate, the fortified Porta Decumana, and was converted into a medieval castle and inherited by the Savoys in 1418. When Emanuele Filiberto I moved here, he restored the castle as a showplace for his court.

In the 17th century, two 'Madame' regents chose to live here, and gave it its name. In 1718, Juvarra was given the task of doing up the old place, but only the beautiful, articulated façade inspired by Versailles and the magnificent palace-width **staircase** were ever built. Visitors can now walk up the stairs again after a meticulous 13-year restoration (*t 011 442 9912, open Tues–Sun 10–8, Sat 10am–11pm*). Restoration of the rest is due to be finished in 2005, when the **Museo Civico di Arte Antica** may return, with its stunning *Heures de Milan* illustrated by Jan Van Eyck, the superb *Portrait of an Unknown Man* (1476) by Antonello da Messina, and much more.

The west end of Piazza Castello is closed by the **Teatro Regio**, which was built in 1738, although only the façade survived a fire in 1936; the innards are from the 1970s. Under the portico on the north side of Piazza Castello, the **Armeria Reale** (*t 011 543 889; open Tues–Sun 8.30–7.30; adm*) contains one of Europe's top collections of weaponry and armour; the adjacent **Biblioteca Reale** contains works by Leonardo da Vinci, including a self-portrait in red ink that looks for all the world like that of a magician grown weary of his own magic (*written permission needed for viewing from library director*).

The Palazzo Reale, the Duomo and the Shroud of Turin

The **Palazzo Reale** (*t 011 436 1455; guided tours Tues–Sun 9–7.30; adm*) lies just off Piazza Castello, behind a gate framed by equestrian statues of the Dioscuri; according to those in the know, Turin lies in the centre of two great triangles of black and white magic, and this is where they intersect. The palace, begun by Emanuele Filiberto I, was the main residence of the Savoys until 1865, and they lavished a considerable amount of their subjects' taxes on heavy chandeliers and fluffy frescoes, although there are some brilliant touches by Juvarra – the 'scissors' stair and laquered 'Chinese cabinet'.

The **Giardini Reali,** behind the palace, is central Turin's only real park; here the Mole Antonelliana rises over the trees like the headquarters of Ming the Merciless. The royal chapel of **San Lorenzo** (1668–80) stands on the corner, a bland 19th-century civic façade hiding Guarini's dynamic, pulsating Baroque fantasia, with a concave-convex octagonal drum culminating in a dome that, supported on pendentives pierced by large Palladian windows, floats in streams of light and geometry.

Around the corner, just off Via XX Settembre, Turin's cathedral, the **Duomo di San Giovanni**, was built by three dry 15th-century Tuscan architects and houses a fine polyptych of SS. Crispin and Crispinian by Defendente Ferrari. What it lacks in presence it compensates for with one of the most provocative and arguably the most precious relic in Christendom: the **shroud of Turin**, brought from the old Savoy capital of Chambéry in 1587 by Emanuele Filiberto. To house it, Guarini built the striking black marble **Cappella della Sacra Sindone** (1694) weaving a diaphanous cone of restless dissonate patterns zigzagging ever upwards, suggesting infinity, reaching its climax in a dome that looks forward to some of the wilder moments of Art Deco. In 1997, when it went up in flames (arson is suspected) a heroic fireman broke through the bulletproof glass to rescue the shroud. After its narrow escape, the relic (the next public display is slated for 2025) lies in a side chapel to the left of the cathedral's high altar, laid out flat under protective glass, beneath a simple altar.

Although theories of its history abound, the shroud was only first recorded in 1356 in Lirey, France, when it belonged to a knight whose descendants sold it to the Savoys in 1453; in 1983, the former King Umberto II willed it to the Pope, on condition it stayed in Turin. Forensic scientists believe it would have been impossible to forge the unique front and back impressions of a crucified man with a wound in his side and bruises from a crown of thorns, but a carbon-dating test in 1989 declared the shroud a medieval forgery. However, now that test has been called into dispute by recent studies of pollen in the threads that seem to place it in the right place at the right time. A secret restoration in summer 2002 has many sindonologists or 'shroudies' fearing that any further scientific investigation may have been compromised.

The Duomo stands on the east end of the Roman core of Augusta Taurinorum, now a pedestrian area of trendy restaurants and bars known as the **Quadrilatero Romano**. Near the campanile are bits of a Roman theatre, while across the piazza stands the impressive Roman **Porta Palatina**, with a pair of 16-sided towers. More of the ancient city can be found at Via XX Settembre 88 in the **Museo delle Antichità** (***t*** *011 521 1106; open Tues–Sun 8.30–7.30; adm*), located in the former royal greenhouse. Nearby, on Via Consolata, the **Santuario della Consolata** is another Baroque one-off, consisting of two churches, a hexagon and an oval, knitted together by Guarini.

The shroud is the subject of the **Museo della Sindone**, southwest at Via San Domenico 28 (***t*** *011 436 5832; open daily 9–12 and 3–7, adm*), in the crypt of the chapel of the **SS. Sudario** (1735), the base of a confraternity dedicated to the relic. There are displays on its history and scientific studies, and the beautiful 16th-century reliquary used until 1998 to house the shroud, when it was rolled up on a cylinder.

The Mole Antonelliana and down Via Po

East of Piazza Castello, Turin's idiocyncratic landmark, the **Mole Antonelliana** ('Antonelli's massive bulk'), was begun as a synagogue in 1863 but left unfinished a decade later, when funds ran low. Distraught, its architect Alessandro Antonelli asked the city to take on the project and re-dedicate it to Vittorio Emanuele II, in whose glory it should be allowed to grow like Topsy, an extra 400 ft or so. Turin, weened on the Baroque extravaganzas of Guarini and Juvarra, gave him the thumbs up. Standing 549ft, the Mole is an engineering and aesthetic feat, bizarre and harmonious at the same time – a vaguely Classical temple façade topped by a colonnade and windows, a majestic sloping glass pyramid, then a double-decker Greek temple, and a pinnacle crowned with a star lit up at night. If Turin is a city of magic, the Mole is its cosmic transmitter. A new glass-walled **lift** offers a unique view over Turin and the Alps (on a clear day); inside, the fun new **Museo Nazionale del Cinema** (***t*** *011 812 5658; open Tues–Sun 9–8, Sat 9am–11pm; adm*) focuses on the history of moving images, from magic lanterns to the present day, with explanations in English.

Lively, arcaded **Via Po**, two blocks away, was laid out in 1673 and serves as the main funnel to the river from Piazza Castello and the main artery for students attending the university of Turin, founded in 1404. Its seat since 1720, the **Palazzo Università** is at Via Po 17; the courtyard has a plaque to Erasmus, the most renowned of its alumni. In the 1820s, Carlo Alberto moved the royal art school, the **Accademia Albertina** (***t*** *011 817*

7862; open Tues–Sun 9–1 and 3–7, adm), to just off Via Po at Via Accademia Albertina 8; its has works by Filippo Lippi, Defendente Ferrari, plenty of *caravaggeschi*, a beautiful Flemish tapestry, and cartoons by Gaudenzio Ferrari.

Via Po flows into long Piazza Vittorio Veneto, the centre of a lively night scene along the **Murazzi**, the walled banks of the Po. On the far bank the landmark is an imitation Pantheon of a church, the **Gran Madre di Dio** (1831); behind it on the hillside is the **Villa della Regina** (*currently being restored, along with the gardens with their fountains, pavilions and 'theatre of waters'*), built by the son of Carlo Emanuele in the early 1600s in the style of a Roman villa and later the favourite residence of Anne d'Orléans, wife of Vittorio Amedeo II. It has an original vineyard that is being replanted (*guided tours sometimes available Aug–Nov, call* ***t*** *800 829 829*).

South of the Gran Madre di Dio at Via Giardino 39, the **Museo Nazionale della Montagna Duca degli Abruzzi** (***t*** *011 660 4104; open daily 9–7; adm*), founded in 1874 by the Club Alpino Italiano, is dedicated to Italy's mountains, climbing and folk traditions.

South along the Po

Back along the Po's west bank stretches Turin's largest park, the **Parco del Valentino**, named after a French château, the Castello del Valentino, rebuilt in 1660 by Madama Reale Cristina, sister of the king of France. Uniquely, its splendid interior stuccoes and paintings are intact, but as it now serves as the university's school of architecture, visiting possibilities are limited (*open Sat 9–12 by appointment only,* ***t*** *011 564 6216*). Its 16th-century **Orto Botanico** has fine old trees, native fruit trees, a small lake and more (***t*** *011 661 244; open for tours in Italian Apr–Sept Sat, Sun and hols 9–1 and 3–7; adm*).

This isn't the only castle on the block; Turin built another one, along with a mock medieval hamlet, the **Borgo e Rocca Medioevale** (***t*** *011 443 1707; open daily 9–7; guided tours of castle Tues–Sun 9–7; adm*), as part of the Italian Exhibition of 1884. The houses are modelled on traditional Piemonte styles, while the castle has baronial fittings. There's a place near the castle loaning out bicycles, another hiring out rowing boats for a duck's-eye view of Turin; alternatively, can take a Po river cruise on the *Valentino* (***t*** *011 744 892*), moored at the Borgo Mediovale.

More Museums

Further south, at Via Nizza 230, just in from the Po, Fiat's **Lingotto** plant was one of the most avant-garde factories in the world when it was built in 1916. It closed in 1983, and the cars have been replaced by a shopping mall, a heliport, an exhibition centre (host to the Auto Salon in even-numbered years), cinemas, a hotel, a suspended glass bubble for meetings and the **Pinacoteca Giovanni e Marella Agnelli** (***t*** *011 006 2713; open Tues–Sun 9–7; adm*). The late Gianni Agnelli collected art even more diligently than he did starlets (Rita Hayworth and Anita Eckberg were among his conquests), and he commissioned Renzo Piano to build what the architect nicknamed the *Scrigno* ('coffer') projecting over the roof, to house his choice works by Balla, Matisse, Renoir, Canaletto, Picasso, Modigliani, Canova and others. Trams, buses no.1, 18, 34 and 35 or a lift can take you there; if you arrive by taxi you can ask to be taken up to the entrance of the Pinacoteca by way of the famous south ramp and rooftop test track.

Further south at Corso Unità d'Italia 40, the **Museo Nazionale dell'Automobile Carlo Biscaretti di Ruffia** (*buses no.45 or 45/ from Corso Marconi by Porta Nuova station;* ***t*** *011 677 666; open Tues–Sat 10–6.30, Thurs 10–10, Sun 10–8.30; adm*), is housed in a 1960s exhibition hall; highlights include the classics of Italian car design – Lancias, Maseratis, Alfa Romeos, Italas and Fiats – as well as oddities such as the asymmetrical 1948 Tarf 1. Further along Corso Unità d'Italia are other exhibition halls, built for the 1961 centenary of the Risorgimento: the **Palazzo del Lavoro** by Pier Luigi Nervi and the hexagonal roofed **Palazzo a Vela** by Annibale and Giorgio Rigotti.

One of Italy's best collections of modern art, the **Galleria Civica d'Arte Moderna e Contemporanea** (***t*** *011 562 9911; open Tues–Sun 9–7; adm*) is west of Porta Nuova station, off Corso Vittorio Emanuele II at Via Magenta 31; it has works by Klee, Chagall, Modigliani, Picasso and others, contemporary installations, photos and more.

Basilica di Superga

Bus no.61 from Via Po or Porta Nuova station, or tram no.15 from Piazza Castello, takes you northeast along the Po to the **Funiculare Sassi-Superga** *(open Mon, Weds, Thurs and Fri 8–12 and 2–8, Tues 7pm–12, Sat, Sun and hols 9–8)*, which climbs slowly up through the greenwood to the Baroque **Basilica di Superga** *(**t** 011 898 0083; open Mon–Fri 9.30–12 and 3–6, Sat and Sun 1–7)*, Filippo Juvarra's masterpiece, enjoying what Le Corbusier called 'the world's most charming setting' on a 2,205ft hill, to fulfil a vow made by Vittorio Amedeo II in 1706 during the French siege of Turin. Two towers flank a magnificent drum dome set above a deep neoclassical porch; the crypt (*adm*) contains the tombs of Vittorio Amedeo II and later kings of Sardinia. The views from the dome *(adm)* stretch to the Alps. The cloister houses the **Museo di Grande Toro,** dedicated to Turin's 'other' football club, Torino.

Around Turin: a Garland of Pleasure Domes

The Savoys, never ones to stint on themselves, built a ring of magnificent residences around Turin; in 1997 UNESCO declared the lot of them a World Heritage Site. **Rivoli**, west of Turin (*take bus no.36 from Piazza Statuto; at the last stop in Rivoli, shuttle bus no.36 continues to the castle; at weekends a bus runs direct to the art museum from Piazza Castello at the corner of Via Po*), preserves their imposing **Castello di Rivoli**, an 11th-century fort Baroqued into a palace. The family sold it to the town council in 1883; since 1984 the frescoed figures in its huge rooms have been bemused by an embalmed horse and other works of the **Museo dell'Arte Contemporanea** (***t*** *011 956 5220; open Tues–Fri 10–5, Sat and Sun 10–7, also 1st and 3rd Sat of month 10–10; adm exp*).

On the southwest edge of Turin, **Stupinigi** is the site of Vittorio Amedeo II's hunting lodge, a star-shaped rococo palace designed by Juvarra in 1730 and known modestly as the **Palazzina di Caccia** (*bus no. 63 from centre to Piazza Caio Mario, then bus no.41;* ***t*** *011 358 1220; open Tues–Sun 10–5; adm*). The statue of a stag on the top, frescoes of hunting scenes by Carle Van Loo, and *trompe-l'œil* scenes of hanging game make sure that no one forgets what the palace was for, although the superb oval salon in the centre was lovely enough to host royal wedding receptions. A few rooms have charming non-hunting frescoes of birds and Chinese legends.

In the southern suburbs of Turin, the **Castello di Moncalieri** (*bus no.36 from Porta Nuova;* ***t*** *011 640 2883; open Thurs, Sat and Sun 8.30–6.30; adm*) with its four sturdy towers, dates back to *c.* 1200 and is now occupied by a battalion of *carabineri*; three richly furnished royal apartments are open for visits.

Northwest of Turin is the vast complex of the **Venaria Reale** (*bus no.72 from Via Bertola near Via Roma,* ***t*** *011 459 3675; open Tues, Thurs, Sat and Sun 9–11.30 and 2.30–5.30; adm*), begun in 1660 as Carlo Emanuele II's answer to Versailles. Long a barracks, it's now the biggest restoration project in Europe; you can currently visit the stables, chapel of St Hubert and Galleria di Diana,a 272ft hall of windows by Juvarra, covered with Baroque stuccoes. Bus no.72 also goes to the **Castello de la Mándria** (***t*** *011 499 3322; open by appointment; adm*) with its toy palace of a hunting lodge where Vittorio Emmanuele II dallied with his mistress, the Bella Rosina, and where earlier Savoys raised prize thoroughbreds in a beautiful 16,230-acre walled park; you can hire a bike to explore.

West of Turin: the Olympic Mountains

Some of the most spectacular scenery in Piemonte lies just west of Turin in the Valle di Susa, where mountain resorts, especially Sestiere, are preparing to host the alpine events in the 2006 Winter Olympics. Turn the clock back 1,000 years and you'd see pilgrims trundling to Rome – a history recalled by several fascinating churches.

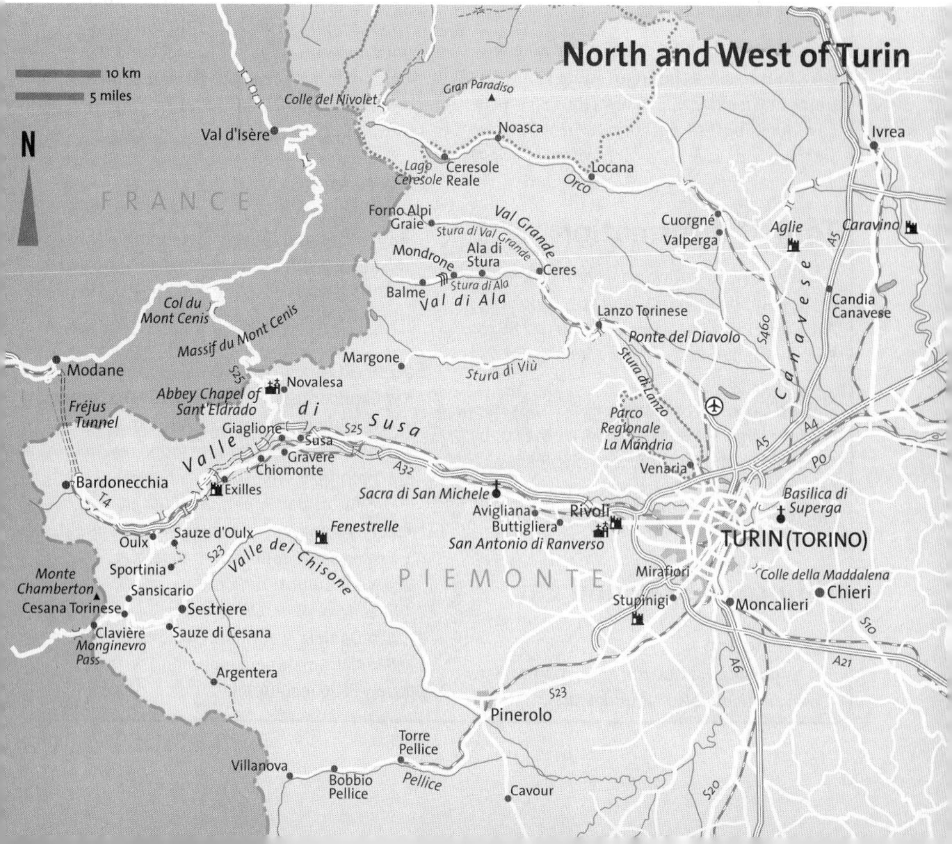

Turin to Susa

From Rivoli, it's five kilometres west to **Buttigliera Alta** and the monastery of **Sant' Antonio di Ranverso**, founded in 1188 by Count Umberto III (***t*** *011 936 7450; open Tues–Sun Mar–Oct 9–12 and 2.30–6, Nov–Apr until 5; adm*). The church has a striking 15th-century Gothic façade with three high-pitched gables, and inside there are some beautiful frescoes representing the best surviving work by the early 15th-century International Gothic master Giacomo Jaquerio, which were only discovered in 1912, long after the abbey had closed: the turmoil-filled *Ascent to Calvary* in the sacristy is his masterpiece. A polyptych (1531) by another Piemontese painter, Defendente Ferrari, adorns the altar.

The next town, **Avigliana**, sprawls around a handsome car-free medieval core on a hill, with two fine churches and a 12th-century Savoy castle in Piazza di Conde Rosso. From here it's 14 kilometres to Piemonte's most extraordinary church, the **Sacra di San Michele** (***t*** *011 939 130; open Tues–Sun mid-Mar–mid-Oct 9.30–12.30 and 3–6, Sun and hols 9.30–12 and 2.40–6; closes at 5 rest of year; adm*), founded in the 900s on a 2,018ft rock, piled on 90ft of substructures and visible all across the Dora Riparia valley. Located along the Via Francigena, the French pilgrimage route to Rome, the Sacra is an uncanny place, built like a seal over a dragon's lair, similar to other mountain shrines dedicated to God's generalissimo (*see* p.938, Monte Sant'Angelo). A kilometre

Getting There

Trains from Turin go through the Valle di Susa to France via the Fréjus Tunnel (only local trains make more than a few stops en route).

Frequent **buses** from Turin to Susa, Pinerolo, Sestriere and Claviere, call at most valley villages.

Tourist Information

Contact the following via *www.montagnedoc.it*; they also do online ski and hotel bookings.

Avigliana: Piazza del Popolo 2, **t** 011 932 8650,
Susa: Porta d'Italia, Fraz. San Giuliano, **t** 0122 623 886.
Sauze d'Oulx: Piazza Assietta 18, **t** 0122 858 009.
Bardonecchia: Via della Vittoria 4, **t** 0122 99032.
Claviere: Via Nazionale 30, **t** 0122 878 856.
Sestriere: Via Louset 14, **t** 0122 755 444.
Pinerolo: Viale Giolitti 7/9, **t** 0121 795 589.

Where to Stay and Eat

Susa ✉ 10059

*****Napoleon**, Via Mazzini 44, **t** 0122 622 855, *www.hotelnapoleon.it* (*moderate*). The top place to stay in the town, although you shouldn't expect unbridled luxury – it's unpretentious but friendly, and the bedrooms have the bare 3-star essentials. The restaurant (*cheap*) is uninspiring. *Restaurant closed Jan.*

Oulx ✉ 10056

Al Vecchio Mulino, Fraz. Beaulard, **t** 0122 851 669 (*moderate*) A lovely restaurant in the meadows, with dishes such as duck stuffed with chestnuts, sausage and honey. *Closed Mon and Tues lunch, half Oct and May.*

Sauze d'Oulx ✉ 10050

******Capricorno**, in Le Clotes, **t** 0122 850 273, *www.chaletilcapricorno.it* (*very expenisve*). An intimate, quiet, 8-room lodge reached by chairlift. Reserve well in advance. *Closed May–mid-June and mid-Sept–Nov.*

****Stella Alpina**, Via Miramonti, **t** 0122 858 731, *www.mysauzedoulx.com* (*moderate*). A decent English-run option. *Closed May–June, Oct and Nov.*

****Villa Daniela**, Via Monfol 9, **t** 0122 850 196 (*cheap*). A small, personal choice with a lovely little restaurant.

up from the car park, the steep, covered **Scalone dei Morti**, the 154-step 'Staircase of the Dead' hewn out of the rock (it's well-named, as the climb seems designed to test your mortality) leads up to the 11th-century **Porta dello Zodiaco**, carved with mermaids, mermen and other mysterious creatures. The ceiling of the mostly 12th-century church is supported by a massive stone pillar; early dukes and princes of the House of Savoy–Carignano are buried here.

Susa

The old town of Susa (Roman *Segusio*) may sound Persian but was actually the seat of Gaulish chieftain Cottius, the kind of fraternizing Gaul whom Asterix and Obelix would have liked to slap with a menhir, one who so admired the Romans that he erected the **Arco di Augusto**, carved with reliefs of a triumphant procession. Augustus returned the compliment by making Cottius a prefect, and naming the local Cottian Alps after him. Other remains of Segusio lie above the Arco di Augusto: there's part of a 3rd-century aqueduct and the Roman castle, and a rock where druids are said to have sacrficed victims and told the future by the direction in which the blood flowed.

In the adjacent *centro storico* are the **Castello della Contessa Adelaide** (who gave her hand to Otho of Savoy in 1045), and the **Duomo di San Giusto** (1020) in the shadow of its own massive tower, containing a sculpted quattrocento choir, a prized

Sestriere ✉ 10058

★★★★**Grand Hotel Sestriere**, Via Assietta 1, **t** 0122 76476 (*moderate–luxury*). The most luxurious and elegant place to stay on the slopes, with an indoor swimming pool, spacious rooms and a fairly good restaurant. *Closed May–Nov.*

★★**Duchi d'Aosta** and ★**La Torre**, **t** 0122 799 800, *www.clubmed.com* (*expensive–luxury*). The Club Méditerranée's hotels in the twin towers that dominate Sestriere. Full board is compulsory. *Closed May–mid-Dec.*

La Baita, Via Louset 4/a, **t** 0122 77496 (*moderate*). A restaurant famous for its polenta, served with hare or boar, but also offering tamer dishes. *Closed Tues and May.*

La Tana della Volpe, Monte Banchetta Sestiere, **t** 0335 362 054 (*cheap*). A restaurant in the mountains above town, offering delicious meals, after which guests ski back to town bearing flaming torches. Book in advance. *Closed May–Nov.*

Bardonecchia ✉ 10052

★★★★**Des Geneys-Splendid**, Viale Einaudi 21, **t** 0122 99001, *www.hoteldesgeneys.com* (*expensive–very expensive*). A characterful option among the resort hotels, with a tranquil setting in the trees. *Closed mid-Sept–mid-Dec and mid-Apr–June.*

★★**Bucaneve**, Viale della Vecchia 2, **t** 0122 999 332,*www.hotelbucanevebardonecchia.it* (*moderate*). A warm, traditionally decorated wooden chalet within walking distance of the lifts, with ample rooms. Half board only. *Closed mid-Sept–Nov.*

★★**La Quiete**, Viale San Francesco 26, **t** 0122 999 859 (*cheap*). A quiet, warm, cosy hotel in the style of a log cabin, with good-sized rooms, some with balcony. Full board is required in season.

Tabor, Via della Stazione 6, **t** 0122 999 857 (*cheap*). A simple option, one of very few that does more than slap out plates of mediocre pasta for the crowds. *Closed Apr–June, Oct and Nov.*

Pinerolo ✉ 10064

Taverna degli Acaja, Corso Torino 106, **t** 0121 794 727 (*expensive*). A picturesque restaurant in the centre, serving up tasty mountain cuisine, followed by one of the finest cheese boards this side of the Alps. *Closed Sun, Mon lunch and last 2wks Aug,*

Flemish brass, the *Triptych of Rocciamelone* (1358), a polyptych by Bergognone, and a 10th-century baptismal font made of serpentine. The **Museo Diocesano**, in the refectory of the Madonna del Ponte at Via Mazzini 1 (***t*** *0122 622640; open July–Sept Tues–Sun 9.30–12 and 3.30–7; Oct–June Sat and Sun 2.30–6; or by appointment*) has fine art from churches across the valley, including works going back to the Lombards.

North of Susa, **Novalesa** is synonymous with its **Abbazia di Novalesa**, founded in 725 and patronized by Charlemagne. Rebuilt after destruction by the Saracens in 906, it was repopulated in the 1970s by Benedictines specializing in the restoration of antique books. It has four chapels, one of which, **Sant'Eldrado**, has good 11th-century frescoes (***t*** *0122 653210; open Mon–Sat 9–12 and 3.30–6.30; Sun 9–12*). In the heart of the village, there's another diocesan **museum** (*open by appointment,* ***t*** *0122 622640*) in the 16th-century church of Santo Stefano.

The road to the **Mont Cenis Pass** begins north of Susa; it has always been a favoured route into Italy, especially by conquerors; Napoleon began the carriage road in 1808.

The Upper Valley

From Susa the road ascends steeply past the venerable villages of **Gravere** and **Chiomonte. Exilles**, further on, lies under a tremendous **fort** (***t*** *0122 58270; open Tues–Sat 10–7; Nov–Apr until 2; adm*) that has controlled the valley since the 10th century. Rebuilt in the 1800s, it spills over its hill like molten gold when lit at night.

The last town before France, **Bardonecchia**, grew up during the digging of the Fréjus Tunnel, absorbing an older village of stone houses or *grangie*. Now a major resort, it has summer skiing on the Sommeiller glaciers (9,843ft), and four separate ski areas with their own lifts. The **Museo Civico** on Via Des Geneys 6 (***t*** *0122 999 350; open Mon–Sat 5.30–7.30; Sun and hols 10–12.30 and 5.30–7.30*) houses local artefacts, old costumes and tools. For the best views in the neighbourhood, take the chairlift up Monte Colomion (6,645ft).

The **Fréjus Tunnel**, at 12.8 kilometres the second-longest road tunnel in Europe, opened in 1980, though the rail tunnel was finished in 1871, cutting the 10-hour coach journey over the Moncenisio pass to a mere 30 minutes. Now even this isn't fast enough: a new tunnel exclusively for high-speed trains was begun in 2001.

A Milky Way of Ski Resorts

Sauze d'Oulx, the 'Balcony of the Alps', and its plateau, Sportinia, are the first of a string of winter resorts extending to Montgenèvre in France, called the Via Lattea or 'Milky Way', with a total of 140 ski runs. They are also adored, in summer, by hikers and motorcyclists, some of whom attempt to scale Mont Chaberton, the highest point in Europe accessible by bike. The Milky Way sweeps around the upper Susa valley to **Cesana** and its ultra-modern satellite Sansicario, lying at the junction of the road to Oulx. Just to the west, **Claviere** lies just below the **Col di Monginevro** (the Roman *Mons Janus*), favoured pass of the Roman emperors. The Roman god Janus had two faces, and his mountain does, too – Italian Claviere and French Montgenèvre – which share lifts and ski passes. If you continue down the road into France, there are wonderfully vertiginous views over the mountaintop forts of Briançon.

Sestriere (6,676 ft), Piemonte's trendiest playground, was planned as a resort by Senator Giovanni Agnelli in the 1930s and will host Olympic downhill events in 2006. It has exceptional slopes , cross-country trails, ice tracks, a skating rink and Europe's highest 18-hole golf course. Above it are the old villages of **Sauze di Cesana** and **Grangesises**, with traditional alpine houses, and the tiny village and wooded valley of **Argentera**, popular with cross-country skiers and hikers.

The Valle del Chisone and Val Péllice

Pinerolo, 38 kilometres southwest of Turin, was the capital of the princes of Acaja, predecessors of the Savoys. Set at the junction of the Valle del Chisone and Val Pellice, it preserves several memories of its glory days, including the 14th-century **Palazzo dei Principi d'Acaja**, the **Duomo di San Donato** (1044, but unkindly restored in the 1800s) containing the princes' tombs, and the Baroque **Palazzo Vittone**. In the 17th century the citadel of Pinerolo (or Pignerol) was rebuilt by Sebastien Vauban for France, and deemed strong and remote enough to serve as the prison of the Man in the Iron Mask from 1668 to 1678. A decade later the French destroyed the fort and retreated over the Alps. Today Pinerolo's biggest attraction is Europe's largest collection of parrots (along with other birds, animals and reptiles) at the **Parco Ornitologico Martinat** (***t*** *0121 303199; open daily 10–6, or sunset in winter; adm exp*).

Between Pinerolo and Sestriere, the **Forte di Fenestrelle** (***t*** *0121 83600; open daily July and Aug 10–12 and 2.30–6, closed Tues and Weds rest of year; adm)*, Piemonte's 'Great Wall of China' (1728–1850), was built by the Savoys to make sure the French stayed away. It consists of three mountain forts linked by an extraordinary two-kilometre subterranean stair; to see it all (or most of it), book ahead for one of three guided tours (in Italian) of varying lengths, wear sturdy shoes and bring a torch.

Pinerolo and the Waldenses

The Valle del Chisone and the Val Péllice, south of Pinerolo, are commonly known as the **Valli Valdesi**, or Waldensean valleys. The Waldenses were followers of Peter Waldo of Lyon. Like St Francis of Assisi, Waldo was the son of a wealthy merchant who renounced all his possessions to preach the gospel; unlike Francis, he criticized the corruption of the Church and was branded a heretic instead of a saint.

Condemned by a Lateran Council in 1184, his followers, many from the south of France, took refuge in Piemonte's secluded valleys. The Waldenses joined up with Protestantism during the Swiss Reformation but were frequently persecuted, especially under Carlo Emanuele and Louis XIV of France. They briefly took refuge in Switzerland, but returned in 1698 to reconquer their mountain valleys. Vittorio Amedeo of Savoy agreed to tolerate them as his subjects, though they had to wait until 1848 to gain complete freedom of religion.

Today, nearly every town in northern Italy has a small community of Waldenses – Torre Péllice is their centre, with a Waldensean college and museum. It is also a base for scenic excursions up the valley to Bobbio Péllice and Villanova, which still has a flood embankment built with money sent by the Waldenses' supporter Oliver Cromwell.

Getting There

Trains on a regional rail line head north from Dora station in Turin into the Valli di Lanzo, as far as Ceres, and to Cuorgné.

For the valleys further north, trains run from Turin to Aosta about once every 2hrs, stopping at Ivrea.

Any destinations not on the rail line can easily be reached by SADEM **buses**.

North of Turin: the Valli di Lanzo and the Canavese

The Valli di Lanzo

The valleys north of Turin are much less visited than the Valle di Susa, and pride themselves on their authenticity. In pretty **Lanzo Torinese**, a base for excursions into branching valleys, is the soaring Gothic **Ponte del Diavolo** (1378); as with many startling medieval bridges, the architect is said to have been none other than the devil himself.

The railway line from Turin peters out at **Ceres**, a summer resort at the fork of two valleys. Buses from Ceres continue up the **Val Grande** to **Forno Alpi Graie**, a base for walks; another bus winds up the **Valle d'Ala** to the small ski resort of **Balme**, passing by way of **Ala di Stura**, which has a chairlift, and **Mondrone** with its lovely waterfall.

Turin to the Valle d'Aosta

The **Canavese**, a glacier-carved amphitheatre, stretches north of Turin along the Dora Báltea river. **Ivrea**, which is the big news here, reached its peak of influence in the year 1002, when its Marquis Arduin was crowned king of Italy; not long afterwards, Ivrea built its **cathedral**, which is hidden by a big neoclassical façade; the interior resembles an ancient Roman basilica all in pseudo-marble, while below is an authentically ancient crypt with Roman columns; in the sacristy, look for Defendente Ferrari's *Adorazione del Bambino*. Behind the cathedral, the four-towered brick **castle** was built in 1358, when the town passed to the Savoys. Famous for its historic carnival featuring battles with oranges, Ivrea used to be synonymous with Olivetti and its office machines, founded in 1908 but now only a memory after Telecom Italia gobbled up the firm. Ivrea is busily finding new uses for its array of empty office buildings; the Olivetti plant by the river encompasses the church of **San Bernardino**, with good 15th-century frescoes by Martino Spanzotti.

Ivrea is surrounded by lakes: one of the prettiest is **Candia** to the south, guarded by a 14th-century castle. For something totally different, head 20 kilometres southwest of Ivrea,to **Baldissero Canevese**, where the nation of **Damanhur** (with a population of 800-plus) was founded in 1977 as a 'centre of spiritual research'. Their masterpiece is the astonishing Temple of Humankind dug by hand into a mountain; you can only visit if you pre-book a day of 'spiritual preparation' (see *www.damanhur.org*).

Further west, **Cuorgné** has a cluster of fine medieval buildings on Via Arduino, where King Arduin once lived. **Valperga**, just south, has an attractive castle and 15th-century church. From Cuorgné the N460 follows the Orco river along the southern edge of the Gran Paradiso National Park, becoming increasingly beautiful as it nears the waterfalls by Noasca; further west, the snowy giants tumble over the meadows and deep blue lake of **Ceresole Reale**.

Valle d'Aosta

At **Pont-St-Martin**, the road from Turin enters the Valle d'Aosta. Rimmed by the highest mountains in Europe – **Mont Blanc** (15,780ft), the **Matterhorn** (or Cervino, 14,690ft), **Monte Rosa** (15,200ft) and **Gran Paradiso** (13,402ft), the Aosta valleys are one of Europe's most popular summer and winter playgrounds, dotted with lakes and serenaded by rushing streams. Sparkling green meadows lie beneath great swathes of woodlands; hills and gorges are defended by fairy-tale castles.

Amedeo IV of Savoy conquered Occitan-speaking Aosta in 1242, but into the 18th century these valleys maintained their own assembly, council and body of law, the *Coutumier*. Union with Italy aggravated linguistic differences,and Mussolini rubbed in the salt with his Italian-only cultural policy. The Valdaostans played a leading role in the Resistance, and in 1945 the region was granted its current semi-autonomy.

The Aosta valleys have been compared to a leaf, traversed by a main vein (the Dora Báltea valley) with a dozen smaller valleys branching off. Each has its own character, and many still speak French or Provençal; most towns are officially bilingual.

The Eastern Valleys

Pont-St-Martin and the Val du Gressoney

A remarkable Roman bridge from the 1st century BC lies just within the region, in the handsome old wine of town of **Pont-St-Martin**. According to legend, the devil made a pact with the village – the bridge in exchange for the first soul to wander across – only to be cheated by St Martin, who sent a dog over at dawn.

Pont-St-Martin stands at the entrance of the **Val di Gressoney** (or Val de Lys), which meanders up to the crystal glaciers of Monte Rosa. In the 12th century, the Walser (Swiss Germans from the Valais) settled here and in the nearby Valsesia (*see* p.130), where they continued to speak medieval German into the early 1900s – now linguists

Skiing

The major resorts are **Courmayeur, Breuil-Cervinia, St-Vincent, Brusson, Pila** and **Cogne**, but there are many smaller, quieter and less expensive bases; write to the tourist board for the region's ski handbook with maps of slopes, lifts and facilities.

Prices on the sunny side of the Alps are, like the weather, milder than in France or Switzerland, but can be very high by Italian standards. In high season at the resorts (*Christmas–first week Jan, second week Feb–mid-March, Easter holidays and July–Aug*) prices go up by about 15 per cent. If you come during peak periods, reserve at least three months in advance. Buying a week's package (*settimana bianca*), including hotel and ski pass, from a travel agent is the easiest and least expensive way to go, but families and groups of more than two can save money by writing in advance to the Aosta tourist office for its list of privately owned self-catering flats in the region (*elenco di appartamenti da affittare*).

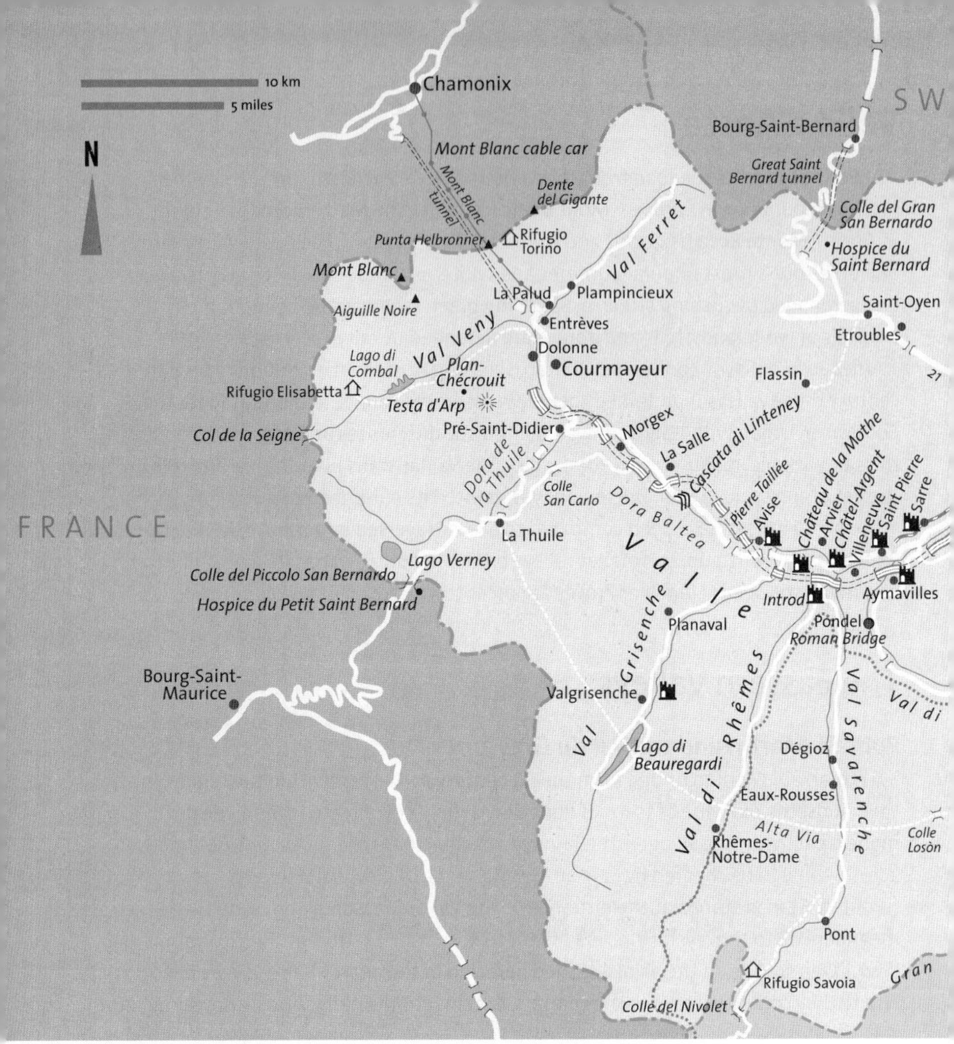

come to study the last 1,500 elderly speakers. Their valley is as wholesome as Heidi, dotted with traditional chalets. Even the church facades promote goodness: at **Issime**, 15 kilometres from Pont-St-Martin, **San Giacomo Maggiore** has a fresco of sinners taking their licks in the *Last Judgement* (1698) as a warning to passers-by.

Stone houses predominate at **Gaby**, an island of Provençal four kilometres away. Further up, **Gressoney-St-Jean,** under the Lys glacier, is the site of the neo-medieval **Castel Savoia** (*t 0125 355 396; open for guided tours of 20 people at a time, daily 10–12 and 1.30–5.30; adm*), built by Queen Margherita, widow of Umberto I. The interior is mostly Art Nouveau; in summer the visit includes an alpine rock garden. Further up, **Gressoney-la-Trinité** has lifts up Monte Rosa, Europe's second highest peak, with the continent's highest shelter, the Rifugio Regina Margherita (14,957ft) and Monterosa, Aosta's largest ski resort, with lifts that make it possible to ski down into the neighbouring valleys, to Champoluc (*see* p. 117) or Alagna (*see* p.131).

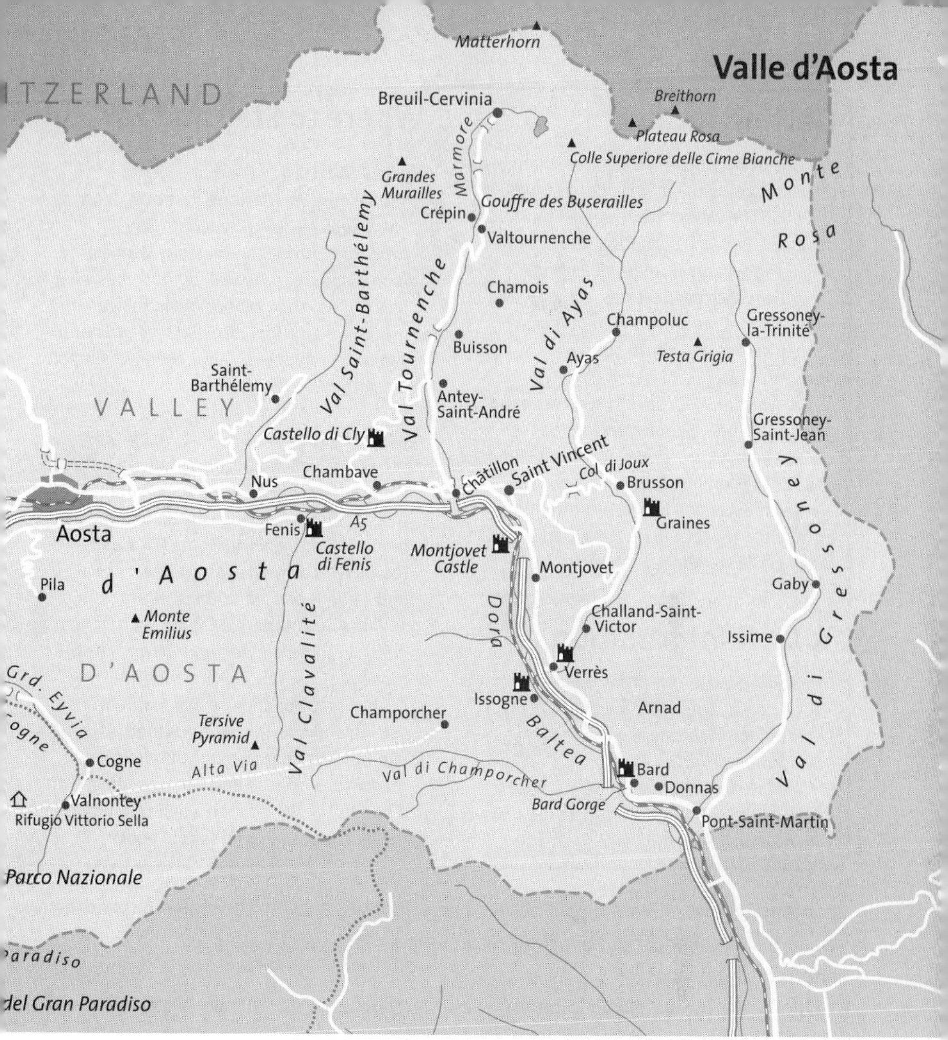

Pont-St-Martin to Issogne

From Pont-St-Martin the main valley road continues past **Donnaz**, where there are the remains of a Roman road hewn 200 yards into the living rock, parallel to the modern road, and then through the narrow **Gorge de Bard**, where the gloomy **fortress of Bard** looms up on its promontory; in 1800 Napoleon slipped his cannons past in the night, spreading the road with sacking and straw to muffle their wheels. Picturesque **Arnad**, the next village, has medieval houses and a church from *c.* 1000, with 15th-century frescoes.

Another old town, **Verrès**, lies at the junction of the Val d'Ayas, a crossroads defended by the massive late Gothic cube of the **Castello di Verrès**, 'one of the mightiest manors ever built by a vassal in a sovereign state' (***t*** *0125 929 067; open Mar–June and Sept daily 9–5; July and Aug daily 9–7.30; Oct–Feb Mon–Weds and Fri–Sun 10–12 and 1.30–4.30; adm*). Built in the 14th century by Ybelt de Challant,

Getting Around

Trains from Turin or Milan (5hrs, changing at Chivasso) go up the main valley as far as Pré-St-Didier. The valleys are all served by SAVDA **buses, t** 0165 262 027, though services to smaller valleys are infrequent.

Regular **coach** connections include: Turin/Milan–Courmayeur/Chamonix; Turin–Chamonix–Geneva (2 a day); Aosta–Val d'Isère–Col Iseran (1 a day); Aosta–Martigny (2 a day). In summer extra services include: Genoa–Alessandria–Courmayeur; Courmayeur–San Remo–Rimini; and Aosta–Florence–Rome.

Regular **excursion buses** in summer run from Aosta to Mont Blanc, Lake Geneva and the two Savoys/Annecy.

Tourist Information

Gressoney-St-Jean: Villa Margherita, **t** 0125 355 185, *www.aiatmonterosawalser.it*
Champoluc: Via Varasc 16, **t** 0125 307 113, *www.monterosa.it*
St Vincent: Via Roma 48, **t** 0166 512 239.
Breuil-Cervinia: Via J.A. Carrel 29, **t** 0166 949 136, *www.montecervino.it*

Where to Stay and Eat

Verrès ✉ 11029

*****Da Pierre**, Via Martorey 73, **t** 0125 929 376, *www.dapierre.com* (*moderate–very expensive*). An elegant hostelry with comfy rooms and fine seasonal food, served by the blazing hearth in winter, and in the garden in summer. Try *agnolotti alla savoiarda* and venison in blueberry sauce, then warm apple pie with cream. *Closed Tues.*

Ayas ✉ 11020

*****Castor**, Via Ramey 2, **t** 0125 307 117 *www.hotelcastor.it* (*cheap–moderate*). A beautifully sited, English-run hotel with breathtaking views of Monte Rosa, panelled rooms with all mod cons, plenty of space and a good restaurant (*moderate*).

*****Villa Anna Maria**, Via Croues 5, **t** 0125 307 128, *www.hotelvillaannamaria.com* (*cheap–moderate*). A lovely old chalet brimful of simple, rustic bonhomie, in a magnificent setting and offering delicious food.

Le Goil, Loc. Barmasc, **t** 0125 306 370 (*cheap*). An *agriturismo* in an enchanting setting, with a handful of simple rooms and traditional meals at weekends; be sure to book.

Captain General of Piemonte, it has delicate windows relieving the stone mass of the walls; inside the most noteworthy features are a monumental staircase and some enormous fireplaces.

Yblet's nearby **Castello di Issogne** (*t 0125 929 373; open Mar–June and Sept daily 9–5; July and Aug daily 9–7.30; Oct–Feb Mon, Tues and Thurs–Sun 10–12 and 1.30–4.30; guided tours on the half-hour; adm*) may look plain from the outside, but his less austere heirs called in some early Renaissance decorators to liven things up. The garden courtyard, with its lunettes frescoed with scenes of daily life *c.* 1500 (the apothecary's, the butcher's, and a grocer's with the oldest known portrayal of fontina cheese) lacks only knights and ladies fair dallying around the beautiful iron pomegranate fountain. The bedroom of the king of France is ornate with fleurs de lys; the baronial hall has frescoes of landscapes, hunting scenes and a Judgement of Paris distantly inspired by Botticelli.

Val d'Ayas

Thickly forested with pines and chestnut groves, the **Val d'Ayas** winds northwards, with Monte Rosa on the right and Cervinia (aka the Matterhorn) on the left. It's a walker's paradise and a good place to find traditional alpine architecture. Just up from Verrès, **Challand-St-Victor** was the cradle of the medieval Viscounts of Aosta,

St Vincent ✉ **11027**

★★★★**Grand Hotel Billia**, Viale Piemonte 72, **t** 0166 5231, *www.grandhotelbillia.com* (*luxury*). A grand turn-of-the-19th-century hotel built to take advantage of St Vincent's curative mineral springs, though it's also a magnet for those who come to get soaked at its roulette tables. Amenities include a sauna, an outdoor swimming pool, tennis courts and a lovely park.

★★★**Elena**, Via Biavaz, **t** 0166 512 140 (*moderate*). A hotel offering large pleasant rooms with balconies and good views of the surrounding countryside. Its only drawback is its proximity to the parish church, with its busy bells.

★★★**Haiti**, Via E. Chanoux 15/17, **t** 0166 512 114, (*cheap–moderate*). A modest place with modern rooms (some with en suite baths) with lots of space.

Il Viale, Viale Piemonte 7, **t** 0166 512569 (*very expensive*). The place to come to celebrate a lucky streak at the roulette tables, intimate and elegant. It specializes in home-made pasta (including potato tagliatelle) and seafood selected in Turin by the chef, and offers a range of fabulous desserts. *Closed lunch and Thurs.*

La Rosa Bianca, Via Chanoux 38, **t** 0166 512 691 (*moderate*). A small, friendly diner in the centre of town – the place to come if your luck hasn't held out at the roulette tables. *Closed Weds.*

Breuil-Cervinia ✉ **11021**

★★★★**Hermitage**, Strada del Cristallo, **t** 0166 948 998, *www.hotelhermitage.com* (*luxury; discounts in summer*). A member of the prestigious Relais & Châteaux group, located just outside the village (there's a shuttle bus). It's a veritable mountain oasis, offering every creature comfort, including a beauty farm and an elegant restaurant (*very expensive*) serving wonderful seasonal dishes. *Closed May, June and Sept–Nov.*

★★**Les Neiges d'Antan**, Perrères, 4km from town, **t** 0166 948 775, *www.lesneigesdantan.it* (*very expensive*). A pretty alpine chalet located in tranquil surroundings, with the resort's skyscrapers hidden from view. The restaurant (*expensive*) is the best in the area, so even if you don't stay at the hotel you can drop by for a traditional meal of salt beef, polenta, cheeses, Valdostana wines and home-made desserts. *Closed June and mid-Sept–Dec.*

the Challants; their derelict but impressive Castello de Graines with its ruined Romanesque chapel is just up at **Brusson**, a low-key summer resort. A scenic road rises from here through the pine forests of the **Col di Joux** down to St Vincent, or you can walk up to the miniature mountain lakes under **Punta Valfredda**.

The most important resort in the Val d'Ayas, **Champoluc**, shares the large Monterosa ski complex with Gressoney-la-Trinité, plus a cable car and chairlift to the slopes just below **Testa Grigia** (10,875ft), one of the grandest belvederes of the western Alps, offering a breathtaking panorama of Mont Blanc, the Matterhorn, Gran Paradiso and Monte Rosa, towering over a sea of peaks.

Saint Vincent and Châtillon

The main valley widens at **Saint Vincent**, dubbed the 'Riviera of the Alps', which was a spa for the rich and dissipated from the 18th century and is now home to Europe's largest casino, the **Casinò de la Vallée** (***t*** *0166 5221, open daily 3pm–3am; adm exp, half-price weekdays; hotel guests usually get in free; bring your passport*).

Besides playing blackjack, you can make a trip through the chestnut groves to **St Germain castle** in Montjovet, take the funicular up to the spa of the **Fons Salutis** to imbibe the famous water (which is said to be a tonic for most anything that ails you), or make a culture call at Saint Vincent's frescoed Romanesque church, which was built over the baths of a Roman villa (*closed 12–2*). The main road continues to the Valle d'Aosta's second city, industrial **Châtillon**, where travellers leave the train to catch a bus up the Valtournenche.

Under the Matterhorn: the Valtournenche and Breuil-Cervinia

The **Valtournenche** is Italy's picture window on the majestic, rakish pyramid of the Matterhorn. The first small resort, **Antey-St-André**, has a healthy, mild climate that first attracted inhabitants in the Bronze Age. Cable cars from nearby **Buisson** ascend to the lovely old hamlet of **Chamois** (you can't get there by car); from here a chairlift continues up to the green banks of the Lago di Lod.

Valtournenche, the flowery valley capital, is a popular resort built on several levels. Most of the Matterhorn guides call it home – memorial plaques posted around the church are a grim reminder of the dangers they face. From Valtournenche you can get a cable car up the **Cime Bianche**, or take a dramatic walk along the specially constructed galleries through the **Gouffre des Busserailles**, a narrow gorge carved out by the Marmore river above Crépin.

The valley road ends at the resort of **Breuil-Cervinia**, in a truly grand setting with the Matterhorn to the north, the sweep of the **Grandes Murailles** to the west, and the **Furggen massif** to the east. The resort dates from the construction of the road in the late 1930s and has all the charms of a frontier boom town, but the mountains are everything here – there are more than 200 kilometres of ski runs, and summer skiing on the glacier at **Plateau Rosa** (11,482ft). A cable car and lift from here take you to the top of **Piccolo Cervino** ('the little Matterhorn'; 12,739ft), from where fantastic ski trails continue down to Zermatt in Switzerland, or along the valley to Valtournenche; the descents are so lengthy that the KL time trials for the world speed record are held here. Other winter sports include ice-skating, bobsledding and hockey. In summer, Breuil-Cervinia is the base for ascents of the **Matterhorn**, a feat first achieved from this side in 1867; the route's most precipitous passages are now fitted out with ropes. Other far less demanding excursions include the easy hike from Plateau Rosa over the Colle Superiore delle Cime Bianche, either to Lago Goillet and its view over the Val d'Ayas, or to the summit of the **Breithorn** (13,684ft).

Up the Main Valley: Chambave and Nus

West of Châtillon, **Chambave** lies under a crag draped with the ruins of the **Castello di Cly**; the vineyards that skirt the environs produce a rare and prized golden dessert wine, Passito di Chambave. More wine and a modest amount of tourism are the industries of **Nus**, the next town, where the Challants built their mid 14th-century **Castello di Fénis** (***t** 0165 764 263; open for guided tours Mar–June and Sept daily 9–6.30; July and Aug daily 9–7.30; Oct–Feb Mon and Weds–Sun 10–11.30 and 2–4.30; adm*), a genuine fairy-tale castle where the kitchen has a chimney big enough to smoke an ox and the hall of judgement and courtyard have lovely courtly frescoes from *c.* 1425 by an artist inspired by Giacomo Jaquerio. From Nus you can visit the remote **Val Clavalité**, under the striking Punta Tersiva, and **Val Saint-Barthélemy**, with its scattered hamlets in the trees, or continue 13 kilometres to Aosta.

Aosta: the 'Rome of the Alps'

Aosta, regional capital, easygoing resort and everyday workplace, has an enchanting setting ringed by mountains holding the sky on their shoulders; on clear mornings they wrap the city in a shimmering blueness, while their bright snows merge with the clouds to form a magic circle high above.

Aosta's street plan has changed little since 23 BC, when the Romans founded it after conquering the diehard Salassian Gauls, the last Celtic nation to hold out against their legions. *Augusta Praetoria* they called it; the name had contracted into Aosta by the Middle Ages, when the town was ruled by the Challants. Not only are many of its monuments from the period, but every 31 January the city holds the oldest continuous markets in Europe, the **Sant'Orso Fair**, dating back to 1000; here, Aosta's woodworkers sell everything from ladders to fine sculpture. In July the town hosts a series of organ concerts, and in October you can see the finals of a peculiar Valdostana sport, the **Bataille des Reines**, in which battling heifers butt heads.

Place Emile Chanoux

Aosta's Roman streets branch out from central Place Emile Chanoux, home of the neoclassical town hall (1839), tourist office and regional handicrafts association. From here, Via Porta Praetoria leads to the square tower of the Signori di Quart and the double arches of the **Porta Praetoria**, the Roman gate, its strength a compliment to the ferocity of the Salassians. To the left, a tall section of the façade (*currently under scaffolding*) and some seats remain of the **Roman theatre** (*open daily 9–6.30*); in a section of the Roman walls nearby, the stout **Tour Fromage** (Cheesemakers' Tower) houses a contemporary art gallery. Aosta's main street, **Via Sant'Anselmo,** awash with stuffed Saint Bernards and garish alpine elixirs, begins through the Porta Praetoria. The city's most famous son, St Anselm, an archbishop of Canterbury, the founder of scholasticism and a doctor of the Church, was born at No.66 in 1033.

Turn left on Via Sant'Orso to reach the Romanesque–Gothic **Collegiata di Sant'Orso** (***t*** *349 804 1239, open daily Apr–Sept 9–7, Oct–Mar 10–5*), founded in the late 10th century over the tomb of Aosta's patron, a 6th-century Irishman named Urso who came here preaching against Arian heretics. The church has rare Ottonian frescoes dating from its foundation, and a delightful little cloister (1133) of short columns and marble capitals sculpted with Biblical and mythological scenes. Across the lane are the ruins of the **Basilica di San Lorenzo**, built in the 6th century and destroyed in the 9th (*open daily Mar–June and Sept 9–7, July and Aug 10–8, Oct–Feb 10–5*). Via Sant'Anselmo ends at the **Arco di Augusto**, erected by the Romans to celebrate their final victory over the Salassians; the roof was added in 1716. On the other side of the arch, a single-span Roman bridge is still used by Aostans to pass over the river bed.

The Cathedral and Forum

From Place Emile Chanoux, Via Xavier de Maistre leads, on the right, to the scanty remains of the **Roman amphitheatre** and the 12th-century **Torre dei Balivi.** To the left, off Via Monseigneur de Sales, the **cathedral of the Assunta** has a neoclassical façade

Tourist Information

Aosta: Place Chanoux 8, **t** 0165 236 627, *www.regione.vda.it*
Rome: Via Sistina 9, **t** 06 474 4104.

Both offices have information on skiing and hiking trails in the Aosta valleys.

Where to Stay and Eat

Aosta ✉ 11100

Aosta is the central transport hub for the region and is more likely than most resorts to have rooms if you haven't booked in advance.

★★★★**Europe**, Via Ribitel 8, **t** 0165 236 363, *www.valdhotel.com* (*very expensive–luxury*). An excellent, friendly hotel in the centre, with all mod cons and a restaurant.

★★★**Rayon de Soleil**, Viale Gran San Bernardo, Saraillon, above town, **t** 0165 262 247, *www.rayondesoleil.it* (*moderate*). A pleasant, medium-sized hotel convenient if you're driving, with fine views, a garden and an indoor swimming pool.

★★★**Bus**, Via Malherbes 18, **t** 0165 4364 (*moderate*). An option in a quiet street off Via Aubert, with comfortable, tasteful rooms and a good restaurant (*cheap*).

★**Monte Emilius**, Via G. Carrel 11, **t** 0165 261 270 (*cheap*). A little gem by the station, with some large, high-ceilinged Art Deco style rooms with balconies (some have lovely views of the mountains, others terrible views of the railway tracks). There's a good restaurant.

Vecchio Ristoro, Via Tourneuve 4, **t** 0165 33238 (*very expensive*). A restaurant located in an old windmill, with excellent hot *antipasti*, smoked trout and salmon, and a fabulous selection of local cheeses. *Closed Sun, and Mon lunch.*

Pretoria, Via A. Anselmo 9, **t** 0165 44356 (*moderate*). A wonderful, extremely popular family-run trattoria serving simple but faultless dishes such as *pasta e fagioli*, suckling pig and apple pie. *Closed Thurs.*

Taberna ad Forum, Piazza della Cattedrale, **t** 0165 400111 (*cheap*). An atmospheric wine shop built into the Roman forum, offering light lunches, afternoon teas and fresh pasta, steaks and cheeses at night. *Closed Mon.*

La Cave, Via Challand 34, **t** 0165 44164 (*cheap*). A popular place just off Via Aubert, where you can nibble the evening away on cheese, salads, smoked salmon and other treats, to accompany wines by the glass. *Closed Sun.*

Papa Marcel's, Via Croix de Ville (*cheap*). The only place in town with any real character, with graffiti over the walls and hundreds of bottles containing weird liquids on the shelves. Just off the main drag, it's good for an informal bite or a nightcap.

hiding a Gothic cross-vaulted interior. The 23 stained-glass windows are 15th- and 16th-century Swiss workmanship, while the choir contains finely inlaid 15th-century stalls and two excellent mosaics, one a 12th-century Labours of the Months, the other a 14th-century scene featuring 'ferocious beasts' from Mesopotamia. The suspended wooden crucifix with a life-size Jesus dates from the late 14th century. Next to the choir is the well-arranged **Museo del Tesoro** (***t*** *0165 40413; ring bell for custodian; adm*), containing some lovely old things: an ivory diptych of the Emperor Honorius from 406 AD; the 13th-century effigy of Tommaso II of Savoy, visible in the choir; and some medieval reliquaries and statues.

Opposite, in Piazza Giovanni XXIII, are the remains of the **Roman forum** and a huge 302ft by 285ft **Cryptoportico**, or underground gallery. No one knows what it was for – it may have been a storeroom for wheat, or a place for the great and the good to perambulate on hot days – but the temperature here is always several degrees cooler than outside. You can also make out the foundations of a Roman temple under the **Casa Arcidianale**. Via San Bernard de Monthon leads into Piazza Roncas, which is the site of the handsome **Palazzo Roncas** (1606) and the **Museo Archeologico Regionale** (***t***

0165 275902; open daily 9–7), where you can see some Neolithic steles, a silver bust of Jupiter, a beautiful ceremonial breastplate for a horse (3rd century AD) and more items from recent digs.

Beyond the forum stands a nearly intact portion of the Roman wall, with the 11th-century cylindrical **Tour Neuve**, built by the Challants. Other sections of the walls have survived in the south, close to the train station, along with three towers: the Roman **Torre Pailleron**, set in a garden by the station; the large round 13th-century **Torre di Bramafam**, which was built by the Challants; and the **Torre del Lebbroso** (*open for temporary exhibitions Tues–Sun 9.30–12.30 and 2.30–6.30*), which earned its sad name from a family of lepers who were incarcerated here from 1733 until the last survivor died in 1803.

Around Aosta

Pila, 20 kilometres south of Aosta, is the city's winter and summer resort, located up the **Col di Chamolé** (7,546ft). Trails up the slopes of **Monte Emilius** (11,677ft), by way of Chamolé, offer stupendous views over the ranges to the north.

Castles bristle over the valley to the west of Aosta, beginning with the 13th-century **Castello Reale di Sarre**, which was rebuilt in the 18th century. After the Risorgimento, the Savoy kings of Italy, who spent 99.5 per cent of their time hunting, used it as a lodge, and filled it with trophies bagged in the surroundings (***t** 0165 257539; open Mar–June and Sept daily 9–6.30; July and Aug daily 9–7.30; Oct–Feb Tues–Sat 10–12 and 1.30–4.30, Sun 10–12 and 1.30-5.30; adm*).

Two other medieval castles guard the pretty village of **Saint-Pierre**: one is home to the **Museo Regionale di Scienze Naturali**, dedicated to Aosta's flora, fauna and minerals (***t** 0165 903485; open daily Apr–Oct 9–7; adm*); the other, the 14th-century **Sarriod de la Tour**, is used for art exhibitions.

The Western Valleys

Aosta to the Great St Bernard Pass

From Aosta, at least two buses a day make the 34-kilometre trip to the Great St Bernard Pass (Colle del Gran San Bernardo; *closed Oct–May*), the importance of which is now diminished by a tunnel. Before St Bernard, the pass was known as Mont Jovis, after a temple of *Jupiter Poeninus*; Celts, Romans and Holy Roman Emperors marched to and fro on a regular basis, and in 1800 Napoleon moved 40,000 troops through to defeat the Austrians at Marengo. The road up is uncommonly pretty, with some splendid vistas down the valleys and back towards Aosta itself. **Etroubles** is the main resort; **Saint Oyen**, in the midst of vivid green meadows, is a quieter holiday centre, with skiing at Flassin.

The legendary 11th-century **Hospice de St Bernard** (***t** 0041 277 871 236*) lies just over the Swiss border (bring your passport). St Bernard, the archdeacon of Aosta, founded the monastery at the exposed summit of the pass (8,100ft), and the canons from **Martigny** who ran it made it their business to minister to weary travellers, many of them pilgrims or churchmen on the road to Rome. To help find people lost in the heavy snows, the canons developed their famous hardy breed of dog. Magnificent specimens abound near the hospice, and when not engaged in saving the lives of intrepid skiers they happily mug for the cameras of the intrepid tourist.

Val di Cogne and the Parco Nazionale del Gran Paradiso

From Aosta and St Pierre, the Val di Cogne stretches south towards the blunt peak of the **Gran Paradiso massif** (13,323ft). The mouth of the valley is defended by the picturesque **Castello di Aymavilles** (*closed indefinitely*), which was built by the Challants, though its four round towers date from the 18th century. Further up, at **Pondel**, signs point the way down, down, down to the torrent of the stunning **Grand Eyvia** gorge spanned by a steep Roman bridge.

A breathtaking drive through forested ravines and lush valleys leads to **Cogne**, a pleasant, busy town built beside a huge meadow, its old livelihood as a mining town commemorated with a cast-iron fountain of 1819. Cogne is now best known as the main gateway to the **Parco Nazionale del Gran Paradiso**. Set aside as a Savoy hunting reserve in the 19th century, the park was donated to the state by Vittorio Emanuele III in 1919 and played a leading role in preserving the ibex (*stambecco*), a pretty creature with long, ridged horns, so hunted that by 1945 only 420 remained, all in the confines of Gran Paradiso. Since then their numbers have ballooned, allowing them to be reintroduced across the Alps. They share their paradise with the shorter-horned chamois, who are more easily spotted – if not here, then on local menus. The flowers are spectacular from late June to mid July – more than 1,000 species from the region and other mountains grow in the **Giardino Alpino Paradisia** in nearby **Valnontey** (***t** 0165 74147; open 15 June–15 Sept daily 9.30–12.30 and 2.30–6.30; adm*).

Cogne tourist office can provide maps and advice on paths through the park. One easy walk starts in Valnontey and continues up a gorgeous riverside trail towards the glaciers. Cogne has eight alpine refuges – the best one to aim for (by foot or horse) is the **Rifugio Vittorio Sella** (8,478ft), a lovely walk through the vast meadow of Sant'Orso up into the deep, flower-spangled vale of **Losòn**, a favourite rendezvous of ibex and chamois now that the refuge is no longer a hunting lodge. You can return to Cogne through Valnontey.

The western reaches of the park – the lush, unspoiled **Val Savarenche** and the **Val di Rhêmes** – can be reached from Villeneuve on the Courmayeur road. In the Val Savarenche, the ideal base is **Eaux-Rousses**; from here you can take the Alta Via path east to the Rifugio Vittorio Sella or west to **Lake Djovan** for the **Entrelor pass** and the prettily situated old village of **Rhêmes-Notre-Dame** in the Val di Rhêmes. The Valsavarenche bus terminus, at **Pont**, is the base for ascents of **Gran Paradiso** and the **Nivolè Pass** (8,569ft), site of yet another royal hunting lodge, the **Rifugio Savoia**.

Up the Main Valley again: Villeneuve to Pré-St-Didier

Every medieval Tom, Dick and Harry seems to have built a castle in these parts. **Villeneuve** sprawls under the massive, ruined, 12th-century **Châtel-Argent**, while the next town to it, **Arvier**, sits under the slightly later **Château de la Mothe** and makes a helluva wine, called *Vin de l'Enfer*. Here there's a road that forks for the wild and rocky **Val Grisenche**; its two main villages, **Planaval** and **Valgrisenche,** have the shimmering **Rutor Glacier** for a backdrop, while just beyond towers the massive Beauregard dam (1957) and its lake.

Back in the main valley, **Avise** is a charming village with two medieval castles at the foot of a romantic gorge, where the **Pierre Taillée** has remains of the Roman road cut into the rock. Just past Avise you'll catch your first memorable glimpse of Mont Blanc. Above the road to the left, **Derby** has a fine collection of fortified medieval houses, a little Gothic church, and a waterfall, the **Cascata di Linteney**. To the right of the road the landmark is the 13th-century **Châtelard tower** in La Salle.

The medieval winemaking town of **Morgex** was the administrative seat of the Savoys; its church of Santa Maria Assunta has preserved a Gothic portal and frescoes dating back to 1492. **Pré-St-Didier**, which lies just beyond it, is situated at the confluence of the Dora de la Thuile and Dora Baltea. Its warm springs are used for a variety of skin complaints; its station is the last rail link in the Valle d'Aosta. From here you can pick up buses to La Thuile or Courmayeur.

Little St Bernard Valley

At Pré-St-Didier begins the road up the **Little St Bernard Valley**, threading through forests and dizzily skirting the ravine of the Dora de la Thuile. The valley's only town, **La Thuile**, is a busy resort with excellent skiing on the slopes of Chaz Dura. In summer you can drive up to the **Colle San Carlo** and the **Testa d'Arpy**, which has an azure lake and a remarkable view of Mont Blanc.

Above La Thuile, Mont Blanc also forms a stunning backdrop to pretty **Lac Verney**, which sits like a mirror in a setting of lovely meadows. A little beyond it, the **Little St Bernard Pass** (Colle del Piccolo San Bernardo, 7,178ft; *open June–Oct*) was the main link between France and Aosta before the Mont Blanc tunnel opened. The pass is marked by a statue of St Bernard on a column, as well as a cromlech (a Neolithic stone burial circle), with the ruins of two structures to the side.

Just over the French frontier, the ancient **Hospice du Petit St Bernard** was founded *c.* 1000, even before St Bernard, with the same purpose of sheltering destitute travellers. Bombed during the Second World War, it was ceded to France, and then abandoned until 1993, when reconstruction began; it now contains a **museum on the history of the pass** *(open daily July and Aug 9.30–12.30 and 2–6)*. In 1897, the abbot Pierre Chanous planted an **alpine botanical garden** here, which, after years of neglect, reopened in 1967 with some 1,600 plants.

Courmayeur and Mont Blanc

In more ways than one, the Valle d'Aosta reaches its climax in **Courmayeur**, one of the most stunning, best-equipped and most congenial resorts in the Alps. Lying at the foot of the 'Roof of Europe', 15,771ft Mont Blanc, it is one of Italy's most fashionable winter and summer resorts, rivalling Chamonix in chic but warmer both in climate and atmosphere. The skiing is matchless, the scenery mythic in its grandeur, and the accommodation and facilities among the best in the Alps.

Getting Around

The 11.6km Mont Blanc tunnel connecting Courmayeur and Chamonix (France) reopened in 2002 with some new safety features and escape routes.

Tourist Information

Cogne: Place Chanoux 36, **t** 0165 74040, *www.cogne.org*

Courmayeur: Piazzale Monte Bianco 13, **t** 0165 842 060, *www.courmayeur.net*

Where to Stay and Eat

Cogne ✉ 11012

******Bellevue**, Rue Grand Paradis 22, **t** 0165 74825, *www.hotelbellevue.it* (*expensive, luxury in season*). The best-located hotel in Cogne, if not all Aosta, with majestic views from its excellent restaurant of a glacial valley carpeted with meadow flowers in summer and covered with cross-country skiers in winter . It's family-run, with very friendly staff in traditional costume. There's a limousine service, and a pool and Jacuzzi in the basement. *Closed Nov–Christmas hols.*

*****Sant'Orso**, Via Bourgeois 2, **t** 0165 74821, *www.cognevacanze.com* (*cheap–moderate*). A hotel offering splendid views at more affordable prices, and boasting an excellent restaurant (*moderate*).

Lou Ressignon, Via Mines de Cogne 22, **t** 0165 74034 (*moderate*). A restaurant set in an attractive chalet, serving good, honest Valdostan specialities such as chamois (*camoscio*), rounded off by good home-made desserts. *Closed Mon eve and Tues out of high season.*

Brasserie du Bon Pec, Rue Bourgeois 72, **t** 0165 749 288 (*moderate*). An excellent, cosy little diner where big meaty grills and fondues are served by waiters in Cogne traditional dress. The wine list is extensive and expensive. It's very popular, so book ahead. *Closed Mon Nov–mid-Dec.*

Courmayeur ✉ 11013

******Palace Bron**, Plan Gorret, just over 1km above town, **t** 0165 846 742, *www.palacebron.it* (*expensive-luxury*). A luxurious white chalet among pine forests, with beautiful views over Mont Blanc from nearly every room. It's convenient for the slopes, but far enough away to enjoy a rarefied tranquillity. The restaurant and piano bar are elegant. Next door to the hotel there's lake-like pool. *Closed Mar–June, Oct and Nov.*

******Royal e Golf**, Via Roma 87, **t** 0165 831 611, *www.ventaglio.com* (*expensive–luxury*).

Besides the 100 kilometres of downhill ski runs at **Chécrouit-Val Veny**, which is served by nine cable cars, seven chairlifts, 13 ski lifts, and helicopters for jet-set thrills, Courmayeur offers some magnificent cross-country skiing, ice skating and an indoor pool: in summer there is skiing on the glacier of **Colle del Gigante**, a rock-climbing school, golf, tennis, riding, hang-gliding, fishing and spectacular walks. There are some 20 alpine refuges in the area.

La Palud, just to the north of Courmayeur, near the medieval fortress-village of **Entrèves**, is the base for one of the world's most thrilling journeys: the ride on the **Funivie Mont Blanc**, which whisks you up and over the glaciers of Mont Blanc to Chamonix, France – it's a truly unforgettable trip, especially if you're lucky enough to catch the big mountain without its veil of mist (***t*** *0165 89925; packages return by bus through Mont Blanc tunnel*). It's possible to ascend to the first three stations all year round: to the **Pavillion du Mont Frety** (6,988ft), home to a restaurant and the **Giardino Alpino Saussurea**, the highest botanical garden in Europe (*open daily July–Sept 9.30–6; adm*); to the **Rifugio Torino** (11,073ft); and to **Punta Helbronner** (11,358ft), which offers a magnificent panoramic view over the Alps, and has a

The top choice, with excellent facilities and service. The views, especially those from the excellent restaurant, are fantastic, and the bedrooms are beautifully furnished. There is an indoor pool and a piano bar. *Closed Oct, Nov, and Mar–end-June.*

*****Bouton d'Or**, SS26 No.10, **t** 0165 846 729, *www.hotelboutondor.com* (*expensive*). A friendly, central option with small but comfortably furnished rooms, some with balconies with views of Mont Blanc.

*****Croux**, Via Circonvallazione 94, **t** 0165 846 735, *www.hotelcroux.it* (*expensive*). A hotel in the centre of town, with outstanding views. Bedrooms are modern and well-equipped. *Closed mid-May–late June and Sept–Nov.*

*****Del Viale**, Viale Monte Bianco, **t** 0165 846 712,*www.hoteldeviale.com* (*expensive*). An old-fashioned alpine chalet with pleasant views. The cosy, folksy lobby and restaurant have stripped wooden floors and an open fire, and most bedrooms have a balcony or sun terrace.

***Venezia**, Via Delle Villette 2, **t** 0165 842 461 (*cheap*). A good budget option offering a range of good-sized rooms boasting fantastic views.

Le Vieux Pommier, Piazzale Monte Bianco 25, **t** 0165 842 281 (*expensive*). A tourist favourite, with a rustic interior and solid Valdostana cuisine. *Closed Mon.*

Frebouzie, Loc. Val Ferret, **t** 335 563 3291 (*moderate*). A fairy-tale setting for tasty alpine dishes. *Closed mid-Sept–May.*

La Palud/Entrèves ✉ 11013

Accommodation here is generally more reasonably priced.

*****La Brenva**, Strada La Palud 12, **t** 0165 869 780, *www.labrenva.com* (*moderate*). A simple royal hunting lodge that has been a hotel since 1897. The décor has changed little since then, though the amenities are up-to-date.

*****Astoria**, Strada La Palud 23, **t** 0165 869 740, *www.hotelastoria-courmayeur.com* (*moderate*). An excellent choice with big, modern rooms in a cosy old style.

****Funivia**, Via San Bernardo, **t** 0165 89924, *www.hotelfunivia.com* (*cheap-moderate*). Big rooms, modern bathrooms, old wooden furniture and priceless views. *Closed May, Oct and Nov.*

Maison de Filippo, **t** 0165 869 797, *www.lamaison.com* (*expensive*). A jovial temple of alpine cuisine; some customers don't mind paying the tunnel fares just to feast here. The décor is charming – rustic but unfussy – and in summer you can dine in the garden. The food is delicious, from *antipasti* of salami and ham, ravioli stuffed with *porcini*, fondue, trout and game, to the wonderful desserts. *Closed Tues, June and Nov.*

display of crystals and minerals that were found on Mont Blanc. From here there's a *telecabina* (*June–Oct*) that continues high over Mont Blanc's glaciers to the **Aiguille du Midi** (12,604ft). At whatever time of year you go, make sure to douse yourself in sunscreen and to wrap up warm – even in summer the temperatures on Mont Blanc are near freezing.

Another summer excursion is to take the **Funivia Courmayeur** west of town to the **Plan Chécrouit** (which has a pool) and walk from there up to **Mont Chétif**, the peak just before Mont Blanc, offering views into the mighty abyss of the **Aiguille Noire**. Or take another cable car from the Plan Chécrouit to **Testa d'Arpy** (9,039ft), with more fantastic views and a ski run descending all the way to Dolonne by Courmayeur.

Two gorgeous valleys run in opposite directions from Entrèves. The **Val Veny** can be ascended by bus as far as the **Lago di Combal**, the base for a fairly easy hike to the **Rifugio Elisabetta** and, from there, a three-hour walk up to the **Col de la Seigne** on the French border, with fabulous views in either direction. **The Val Ferret** is enchanting and serene, filled with meadows and trout streams; there is accommodation in **Plampincieux**, a quiet resort in the pines.

East of Turin: Vercelli, Novara and Rice, Rice, Rice

East of Turin and north of the Po is a landscape that encompasses the gamut of scenery from flood plain to alpine splendour. This includes **Vercelli** and **Novara**, two cities close enough to Lombardy to join in Italy's medieval and Renaissance cultural boom. They had the money: rice was introduced here by the Arabs, and grew like kudzu: today several million plates of risotto are born each year in this patchwork of fields, divided by canals, dating back to the 15th century. In summer, when they're newly flooded, they reflect the clouds and sunset in an irregular checkerboard of mirrors. It's a landscape bordering on the abstract: desolate, melancholy and beautiful.

Vercelli

Vercelli was not only stirring in the Renaissance; in the 16th century it produced an excellent school of painters, though the most brilliant one, Il Sodoma (*b.* 1477), soon escaped to more promising territory in Tuscany. Even so, as a minor 'city of art', Vercelli is an atmospheric old place. If you have only an hour between trains, make sure to take in its chief marvel, the **Basilica di Sant'Andrea** (*open daily 7–11.30 and 3–6)* opposite the station. It was begun in 1219 by Cardinal Guala Bicchieri, papal legate and 'saviour' of England's Henry III. To thank him for his aid in obtaining the throne, Henry gave the cardinal the revenues of the Abbey of St Andrew in Chesterton, near Cambridge, and he used the money to finance another St Andrew's in Vercelli. Completed only nine years later – a lightning clip in those days – the basilica, though basically Romanesque, is famous as one of the first in Italy to display signs of the new Gothic style from the Île de France; it whispers in its twin bell towers, its flying buttresses, the vaulting in the nave and in the plan of the church and cloister.

Money, however, ran out halfway up the cladding of the façade, giving Sant' Andrea the air of a 1960s woody station wagon. The three Romanesque portals have fine sculpted lunettes; in the majestic interior, note the choir, decorated with intarsia still lifes and city views (1513) and the Gothic tomb of the abbot Tommaso Gallo (*d.* 1246). The lovely cloister, with its cluster columns and sculptural details, offers the best view of the unusual tower. The massive campanile was added in 1407.

Vercelli's grand 16th-century **cathedral** is nearby (take Corso De Gasperi to Piazza Sant'Eusebio), next to a Romanesque campanile. The one saintly member of the House of Savoy, the Blessed Amedeo IX, who died in Vercelli in 1472, is buried in a splendid octagonal chapel on the right side of the church. The altar has a precious silver crucifix from the year 1000, made by Lombard goldsmiths, and the library has a famous collection of *codices*, including 11th-century Anglo-Saxon poems that were perhaps brought to Vercelli by Cardinal Bicchieri.

From the cathedral, Via Duomo leads past the **Castello d'Amedeo** (left, behind Santa Maria Maggiore) to Via Gioberti and Via Borgogna, site of the neoclassical *palazzo* housing the **Pinacoteca Borgogna** (***t*** *0161 252 776; open Tues–Fri 3–5.30, Sat and Sun 10–12.30; adm*), the second most important collection in Piemonte after the Sabauda in Turin, featuring paintings by Vercelli natives (Il Sodoma, Gaudenzio and Defendente Ferrari), plus works by Titian, Palma il Vecchio and Luini and more.

Via Borgogna gives onto old Vercelli's main street, Corso Libertà; if the door's open at No.204, be sure to look in at the lovely courtyard of the 15th-century **Palazzo Centori**. The Corso continues to Vercelli's main Piazza Cavour, where markets are held under the **Palazzo Municipio**. Down Via Lucca, **San Cristoforo** has some excellent frescoes (1529–33) by Gaudenzio Ferrari, including his lovely *Madonna of the Oranges*.

In Via Verdi, off Piazza Cavour, there is a good archaeological and historical collection in the **Museo Leone** (*t 0161 253 204; open Tues, Thurs and Sat 3–5.30, Sun 10–12 and 3–6; adm*), spread between a 15th-century house with charming frescoes and a Baroque palace. From Piazza Cavour, Corso Libertà continues into the newer part of town; in Piazza Zumaglini, rice prices are decided in the Rice Exchange, or **Borsa Risi**; here, too, is the national rice board's headquarters.

Novara

Novara became a *municipium* under Julius Caesar, and the street plan of its *centro storico* still reflects its Roman origins. The cobbled Corso Cavour and Corso Italia, which are lined with tearooms and fashionable shops, are pleasant places for a stroll, perhaps after you've digested Novara's unmissable landmark: the 396ft dome of **San Gaudenzio**. The church was designed in the 16th century by Pellegrino Tibaldi, a rather eccentric campanile was added in 1786 by Benedetto Alfieri. The dome is a 19th-century addition by Italy's most phallically minded architect, Antonelli, the author of Turin's Mole; its spire is topped by the shining figure of Jesus, poking into the sky. Inside, St Gaudenzio's relics lie in a raised crypt; among the paintings look for a polyptych by Gaudenzio Ferrari and Tanzio da Varallo's nightmarish *Battle of Sennacherib* (1627).

Central Piazza della Repubblica boasts Novara's **Broletto** (old city hall), which was contained in four buildings on a central courtyard, built and rebuilt between the 12th and 18th centuries; it now houses the **Museo Novarese** (*t 0321 623 021; open Tues–Sun 9–12 and 3–6; adm*), which has exhibits on the province's art, history and archaeology. The Broletto shares the piazza with the **Duomo**, rebuilt in the 1860s by the inimitable Antonelli, who gave it one of the largest doorways in Europe (38ft by 19ft). He saved parts of the earlier Romanesque cathedral, including the campanile, the 12th-century frescoed chapel of **San Siro** (*open by request*), the red-brick cloister, and a mosaic in the chancel showing Adam, Eve and the Serpent and four rivers flowing from Paradise. In the main body are some frescoes and paintings by Gaudenzio Ferrari and others of the Vercelli school, and some 16th-century Flemish tapestries on the Life of King Solomon. The **baptistry** dates back to the 5th century, and contains unusual frescoes of the apocalypse, added 500 years later and considered among the most important paintings of that period in Italy.

Biella, the Santuario d'Oropa, and Around

Biella was Italy's little Manchester, and to this day its mills supply the big design houses in Milan and Florence with their wool, especially cashmere. More than 50 factory outlets make it a popular destination for shoppers: the very keen can follow the Strada della Lana ('Wool Road') from Biella to Valle Mosso and Borgosesia.

Getting Around

This area is especially well served by rail, with frequent **trains** travelling to Vercelli and Novara from Turin and Milan; both cities are also linked with Biella (1hr), which is the base of a network of **buses** into the alpine valleys.

The main rail and **road** approach to the Valsesia is from Novara (if you're coming from Turin, you have to change trains at Romagnano) and goes as far as Varallo (1½hrs from Novara), where you can catch a bus up to Alagna. Rail links from Vercelli continue south to Casale Monferrato, Asti and Alessandria, while Novara has trains to lakes Orta and Maggiore and beyond.

Tourist Information

Vercelli: Viale Garibaldi 90, **t** 0161 58002, *www.turismovalsesiavercelli.it*
Novara: Baluardo Quintino Sella 40, **t** 0321 394 059, *www.turismonovara.it*
Biella: Piazza V. Veneto 3, **t** 015 351 128, *www.atl.biella.it*
Varallo: Corso Roma 38, **t** 0163 51280.

Where to Stay and Eat

Vercelli ✉ 13100

★★**Il Giardinetto**, Via L. Sereno 3, **t** 0161 257 230, (*moderate*). A reasonable, central option for a stopover, with 8 modern rooms and an attractive restaurant rated by many the best in town (*expensive*). *Restaurant closed Mon. Hotel and restaurant closed Aug.*

Il Paiolo, Via Garibaldi 72, **t** 0161 250 577 (*expensive*). An elegant place serving Piemontese classics and regional wines. *Closed Thurs.*

Novara ✉ 28100

★★★★**Italia**, Via Solaroli 8/10, **t** 0321 399 316, *www.panciolihotels.it* (*expensive*). An elegant, comfortable and modern hotel in the centre of town, containing one of the best restaurants in Novara. The food includes good rice dishes and surprises such as chicken curry.

★★★**Parmigiano**, Via dei Cattaneo 4/6, **t** 0321 623 231 (*moderate–expensive*). A sparkling modern interior behind an old façade. The bedrooms are simple, and there's an excellent restaurant (*cheap*) where you can try various local specialities. *Restaurant closed Sun.*

Trattoria Tri Scalin, Via Sottile 23, off Via Paganini, **t** 0321 623 247 (*moderate*). A shrine to Novarese cuisine, with excellent food, including local *salame della duja, risotto al Barolo* and *pasta e fagioli*, accompanied by a good list of Piemontese wines. *Closed Sat lunch, Sun and Aug.*

Caffè Groppi, Via Mameli 20, Trecate, 9km east of Novara, **t** 0321 71154 (*very expensive*). One of the most exciting and talked about new fusion restaurants in northern Italy, in what looks like an old-fashioned café near the train station. It's small, so book in advance. *Closed Sun eve, Mon and Aug.*

Biella ✉ 13900

★★★★**Astoria**, Viale Roma 9, **t** 015 402 750, *www.astoriabiella.com* (*moderate*). Biella's grandest hotel, specializing in what it terms 'sober elegance' – which seems to mean lots of comfort but little style. There's a bar but no restaurant.

★★★★**Augustus**, Via Italia 54, **t** 015 27554, *www.augustus.it* (*moderate*). A no-nonsense business hotel with comfortable rooms. *Closed Christmas and Aug.*

Ca' Verna, Via Avogadro 10, Biella Piazzo, near the funicular, **t** 015 22724 (*moderate*). A restaurant serving superb veal and pizza dishes. It's popular with the locals, and the general air of bonhomie is shared by the helpful staff. *Closed Thurs.*

Il Baracca, Via Sant'Eusebio 12, on the road to Oropa, **t** 015 21941 (*moderate*). The oldest and best place to eat in the area, offering a range of Piemontese treats such as *bagna cauda, salame della duja*, rice dishes and mixed roast or boiled meats. *Closed Sat and Sun.*

Varallo ✉ 13019

★**Monte Rosa**, Via Regaldi 4, **t** 0163 51100, *www.albergomonterosa.com* (*cheap*). A wonderful little family-run hotel with a red façade, offering a number of large, old-fashioned, beautifully furnished rooms, with balconies and lovely views.

There are two Biellas – Biella Piano and the upper Biella Piazzo. **Biella Piano**'s social focus is **Via Italia**, a pretty cobbled street where the great and the good promenade in the sun, its monuments clustered in Piazza Duomo. These include the lovely little **baptistry** (*ask in the cathedral to visit*) from the late 10th century, constructed from Roman bits, the mighty Romanesque **campanile** from the same period, and the Gothic **Cattedrale di Santo Stefano**, over-prettified in the 19th century but preserving 14th-century frescoes and fine choir stalls decorated with fruit trees and labourers. Left of the altar, by the old entrance, is a 'Sunday Christ' (*c.* 1470), a once-popular if surreal depiction of Jesus under attack by hoes, hammers, rakes, scissors and other tools – a reminder of what it was forbidden to take up on the Sabbath.

Nearby, in Via G. Ferrero, the elegant Renaissance basilica of **San Sebastiano** (1504) hides behind a 19th-century façade. It houses works by the Vercelli school, notably Bernardino Lanino's *Assumption* (1543) and choir stalls embedded with 12th-century enamels from Limoges. In 2001 the cloister reopened as home to the **Museo del Territorio** *(**t** 015 252 9345; open Thurs and Sat 10–12 and 3–7, Fri and Sun 3– 7)*, containing everything from a mummy to artworks by Joan Miró.

Upper **Biella Piazzo,** linked to Bella Piano by a jaunty little **funicular** (*open daily 7am–midnight, Fri and Sat till 2am*), enjoys fine views over the city and mountains. It was founded in 1160 by the Bishop of Vercelli; to encourage other swells to move in with him, he granted Piazzo the right to administer justice, hold a weekly market, and slaughter animals. In the Renaissance, wealthy textile merchants added their showy mansions; the grandest residence, the 17th-century **Palazzo Lamarmora**, has lavish 17th- and 18th-century frescoes (*open by appointment*, ***t*** *015 352 533*).

On the map the environs of Biella look like spaghetti, all squiggly valley roads between the mountains, and finding the right one on the ground can be a challenge. A short drive south of town is the stately 16th-century castle at **Gagliànico**, and north-west at **Pollone** (follow the Oropo signs) is the lovely **Parco Burcina Felice Piacenza**, where rhododendrons and azaleas burst into a dazzling blast of colour in May.

North of here, the road winds up to the oldest, most venerated shrine in Piemonte, the **Santuario d'Oropa**, set in a mountain hollow. Legend has it that this was founded by St Eusebius, Bishop of Vercelli, when he took refuge here from Roman persecutions in the 4th century, leaving behind a black Madonna and Child carved by St Luke that he brought from Jerusalem (art historians say it's really 12th century). This now holds pride of place in the Basilica Antica. The sanctuary also includes a huge new basilica, a Sacro Monte with 19 chapels, inspired by the original in Varallo (*see* p.130), three vast quadrangles, plus restaurants, cafés and pleasant suites and rooms to lodge hundreds of pilgrims (*for information call* ***t*** *015 245 5927*). It also houses the **Museo dei Tesori**, displaying historical items, ornate copes and crowns, and jewels donated by the Savoys, and a **botanical garden** (*open May–Sept daily 10.30–6; adm*), which is near the base of the funivia that ascends **Monte Mucrone** (7,661ft), with its lake, hiking and mountain-biking in summer and skiing in winter.

To the north, the **Oasi Zegna**, a beautiful natural reserve, is crossed by the **Strada Panoramica Zegna** (SS232), which winds from Rosazza across to Trivero. The Oasi has spectacular views of Monte Rosa; entomologists know it as the home of a rare golden beetle (*Caravus olympiae Sella*). West of Biella, little roads twist up to another shrine, the Baroque **Santuario di Graglia**, with four Sacro Monte chapels – it was a bit of a comedown for the founder, who planned to build 100.

To the southwest, at **Donato**, begins a district of morainic ridges called **La Serra**, where oaks, chestnuts, birches and vines grow in arcadian harmony with quiet villages. At the end of the ridge lies the clear, spring-fed **Lago di Viverone**, an unglamorous but soothing place to camp, swim or mess about on a boat. The medieval **Castello di Róppolo** in a lovely setting over the lake houses the regional **Enoteca della Serra** (***t** 0161 98501; open Weds–Sun*), which has a fine restaurant.

The Valsesia, Varallo and Sacro Monte

North of the Oasi Zegna, the **Valsesia** claims to be the greenest valley in Italy. More textile mills dot the lower river, as well as vines producing Piemonte's prized Nebbiolo wine; taste it at the **Enoteca Regionale** at Corso Valesesia 112, **Grattinara** (***t** 0163 834 070; open Tues–Sun*). The scenery turns dramatic as you approach **Varallo**, a friendly town embraced by wooded slopes; here the Sesia froths and tumbles, offering exciting white-water rafting. Varallo's good **Pinacoteca**, with works by the Vercelli school, shares space with the natural history museum in the **palace of museums** (***t** 0163 51424; open June–Sept Tues–Sun 10–12.30 and 2–6; Oct–May by request; adm*). The church of **San Gaudenzio**, picturesquely piled up on top of a stair, has a polyptych by Gaudenzio Ferrari, but best of all is the convent church of **Santa Maria delle Grazie**, with an entire wall of his work, the striking *21 Scenes from the Life of Christ* (1513); the slight 3D effects of the Roman armour are a preview of Varallo's five-star attraction, the **Sacro Monte**, easily reached by the nearby funicular (or winding road).

There are dozens of other Sacro Montes in northern Italy, most, like this one, in beautiful settings. But this is the original, begun in 1491 by the Blessed Bernardo Caimi. A visit to the Holy Land gave him the idea of recreating an ideal city or New Jerusalem housing displays of Christianity's holiest scenes for the people back home. The idea caught the fancy of St Charles Borromeo, Archbishop of Milan and a leading figure of the Counter-Reformation, who saw it as a means to give an emotional immediacy to the faith. The result is a sincere if slightly nutty extravaganza, a Disneyland of piety: Sacro Monte's 50 chapels, in fact, contain the world's first 3D dioramas – Biblical scenes featuring 800 life-sized statues, many with real hair (some by Gaudenzio Ferrari), with 4,000 painted figures in the backgrounds. The chapels featuring the Passion are clustered, city-like, in **Piazza del Tempio**. At the end of the line is the **Basilica**, a mass of exploding Baroque; its choir features 145 sculpted figures and 500 frescoed children in heaven's vortex; the crypt, its walls covered in heart-rending tributes to dead children, provides the final flourish of fervour.

North of Varallo extends the **Val Mastallone**, a valley of deep ravines and alpine scenery, settled in the 12th century, like much of the Valsesia, by the Walser (German-speakers from the Swiss Valais). **Rimella** has lovely traditonal wood and stone houses in the hamlet of Gottardo. In the main **Val Grande**, **Riva Valdobbia** enjoys great views of Monte Rosa and has a parish church with exterior frescoes of the Last Judgement and a giant St Christopher (1597). A number of walks begin here, including the hike over the **Colle Valdobbia** to the Val Gressoney in the Valle d'Aosta. **Alagna**, the last town in the valley, is a popular summer and winter resort under **Monte Rosa**. In the hamlet of **Pedemonte**, three kilometres from Alagna, the Walser have converted one of their handsome 17th-century houses into a **Walser museum** (***t*** *0163 922 935; open July daily 2–6; Aug daily 10–12 and 2–6; Sept–June Sat and Sun 2–6; adm*).

Southeast Piemonte: Monferrato and Le Langhe

When the Turinese or Milanese come here at weekends, their thoughts, even more than normal for Italians, are focused on lunch and dinner. Here, some of Italy's most prestigious wines are born in a civilized landscape of ridges receding as far as the eye can see, while southeast Piemonte's other speciality, *tartufi bianchi* (white truffles), are harvested in autumn and a barrage of ecstatic festivals are devoted to gluttony.

This rich area was a much-disputed prize from the early Middle Ages; nearly every hill has its fort. Monferrato managed to remain an independent marquessate until 1707, while the sweet hills of Le Langhe around Alba are equally dotted with feudal castles, many once owned by the great families of Turin.

Coming from Turin: Martini, Chieri and the Abbazia di Vezzolano

Turin takes the credit for more than 300 innovations, including Italian vermouth, which was invented in 1786 when Benedetto Carpano combined wine with alpine herbs. The Carpano firm still bottles his bittersweet Punt e Mes; the competition, Martini & Rossi and Cinzano, are known for their classic dry *bianco* and red elixir of many an Italian happy hour. In Pessione, 24 kilometres southeast of Turin, the **Museo Martini di Storia dell'Enologia** at Martini headquarters (***t*** *011 94191; open Tues–Fri 2–5, Sat and Sun 9–12 and 2–5; closed hols*) tells the story of wine and aperitifs. Five kilometres north, **Chieri** has one of Piemonte's finest Gothic churches, dating from 1436 and boasting a lofty gable.

The main sight in these parts, however, is to the northeast: the **Abbazia di Santa Maria di Vezzolano**, the finest Romanesque building in Piemonte (***t*** *011 992 0607; open Tues–Sun Apr–Sept 9–1 and 2–6, Oct–Mar 9–1 and 2–5*). Set in the countryside near the hill town of **Albugnano**, the abbey was founded – so they say – in 773 by Charlemagne, who had a vision while hunting. It has a handsome façade dating from the early 12th century, adorned with blind arcades and sculpture, and an even more remarkable French-style *jubé* in stone, dividing the nave in two and decorated in the 13th century with wonderful painted high reliefs, depicting the Four Evangelists and the Deposition, Assumption and Coronation of the Virgin, while below a highly animated band of 35 patriarchs, the ancestors of Mary, sit in a row, with their names draped over their chests like beauty contestants. On the high altar, 15th-century terracotta figures of the Virgin and Child are worshipped by St Augustine and Charlemagne, while the apse contains beautiful reliefs of the Annunciation from *c.* 1180. Part of the cloister is even older than the church, while the newer section has 13th-century frescoes, including some of Charlemagne.

Casale Monferrato and Around

Casale Monferrato has the unglamourous claim to fame of being Italy's biggest producer of cement. Once, however, this little city on the Po held the snazzier title of capital of the marquessate of Monferrato, ruled by the Paleologi, cousins to the Byzantine emperors; it subsequently passed in 1536 to the Gonzaga, and in 1707 to the Savoys, when its citadel became a barracks. Its Romanesque cathedral, **Sant'Evasio** (1107), was redone in the 1800s but has a remarkable narthex that is worthy of the Hagia Sophia itself – as is the 11th-century gilded crucifix suspended over the altar, brought from Constantinople. Under the Gonzaga humanists, Monferrato was an important safe haven for Jews; Casale's **synagogue** at Vicolo S. Olper 44 (***t*** *0142 71807; open Sun 10–12 and 3–5, or by appointment*) was built in 1595, then lavishly Baroqued; it now doubles as a **Jewish museum**.

South of Casale, in the pretty hills off the Moncalvo road, a venerable Madonna is the focus of the **Sacro Monte di Crea**, which was founded in 1589; its 23 chapels culminate in Paradiso, which has an explosion of earnest Counter-Reformation putti and saints. Moncalvo, the gastronomic capital of Monferrato, holds wine and truffle festivals in October. It also has a good Gothic church, San Francesco; a pretty Gothic house in Via Testafochi; and a spectacular view of the countryside from Piazza Carlo Alberto. To the southeast of it, a sea of vine-clad hills surrounds **Vignale Monferrato**, which is host to a major dance festival in summer and to Monferrato's **enoteca** in the 18th-century Palazzo Callori (***t*** *0142 933 243; open Mon and Weds–Sat 9–1 and 1.30–4.30, Sun 10–1 and 2–7*).

Asti and its Palio

One time rival of Milan, **Asti** is a noble old city that gave Italy one of its great poets, Vittorio Alfieri (1749–1803), who was also famous for running off with the young wife of the not-so-bonny Prince Charlie. Corso Alfieri is the main street; at its east end, at No.2, stands the 15th-century church of **San Pietro in Consavia**, with an intriguing octagonal baptistry, the **rotonda** (12th century), supported by eight thick columns with cubic capitals. There's a **museo archeologico** in the cloister, with Neolithic to Roman finds and a small Egyptian collection (***t*** *0141 353 072; all open Tues–Sun Apr–Sept 10–1 and 4–7; Oct–Mar 10–1 and 3–6; adm*).

Heading west, the Corso passes by large **Piazza Alfieri,** where Asti's bareback horse race, or Palio, takes place on the third Sunday of September, coinciding with Douja d'Or wine fair. This tradition of neighbourhood rivalry dates back to 1275, and as in Siena, it combines medieval pageantry and daredevil riding with much feasting and celebration afterwards. A week before the Palio, Asti holds the Festival delle Sagre, when people from surrounding villages parade in traditional 19th-century costumes and recreate cooking and working practices from that era.

Just west of Piazza Alfieri and south of the Corso, the attractive Romanesque–Gothic **Collegiata di San Secondo** houses the relics of Asti's patron saint; the *Palio Astigiano* (the banner awarded at the horse race – whoever comes in last gets anchovy and lettuce); a model of the medieval *carroccio* (ox-drawn cart) the Astigiani once led into battle; and a polyptych by Asti's greatest Renaissance artist, Gandolfino d'Asti.

Medieval towers loom over the rooftops – the tall, elegant **Torre Troyana** across the Corso; the **Torre Comentina** further down, with the swallowtail merlins of the Ghibellines; and then the octagonal **Torre dei De Regibus**.

Vittorio Alfieri was born in **Palazzo Alfieri** at Corso Alfieri 357, which now contains a small museum in his honour *(**t** 0141 538 284; currently closed for restoration)*. In the neighbouring Liceo at No. 365/A, you can visit the 8th-century **crypt of Sant'Anastasio**, with it carved capitals and other old stone bits in the **Museo Lapidario** (*__t__ 0141 399 460; open Apr–Sept Tues–Sun 10–1 and 4–7; Oct–Mar Tues, Fri and Sun 10–1 and 3–6; adm*). Two streets back, Asti's great Gothic **cathedral** (1309–54, with a porch from 1470) is covered with Baroque frescoes and contains good paintings by Gandolfino d'Asti and some painted terracotta statues of the Pietà, dating from 1502. The Corso ends by another medieval tower, the **Torre Rossa**, an unusual cylinder built on a Roman foundation, with a checkerboard crown.

On a hill four kilometres northeast of Asti, the Romanesque–Gothic **Chiesetta di Viatosto** has quattrocento frescoes and enchanting views over the countryside.

Alba and Le Langhe

South of Asti lie the pale, steep hills of **Le Langhe** ('ridges'), swathed with the vines that produce Italy's finest red wines – Barolo, Barbera, Barbaresco, Dolcetto and Nebbiolo. **Alba**, the capital of Le Langhe, of wine, white truffles and the Ferrero chocolate company, has an austere medieval centre of narrow winding alleys and brick towers. At the beginning of the 16th century it produced its greatest painter, Macrino, whose *Vergine Incoronata* (1501) hangs in the council chamber of the **Palazzo Comunale**, along with the *Piccolo Concerto* by Mattia Preti. The 14th-century **Duomo** has a much redone interior but beautiful choir stalls, inlaid with town views and still lifes created in 1500 by Bernardino Fossato da Codogno. Traditionally a bitter enemy of Asti, Alba is now content to send up its old rival in a donkey Palio complete with clown jockeys the first Sunday in October. But it can be serious when needs be: its resistance fighters were the bravest in Italy and defended the 'Free Republic of Alba' from the Germans for 23 days in 1944.

The lovely rolling country around Alba is scattered with hilltop villages, castles and *enoteche* waiting to introduce you to the nectar from their vineyards. **Montegrosso**, between Asti and Alba, is the main producer of Barbera wine; the regional **enoteca**, west in **Canale d'Alba**, at Via Roma 57 (*__t__ 0173 978 228; open Mon, Tues and Thurs–Sat*), also has a superb restaurant (*see* p.137). **Costigliole d'Asti** and **Canelli**, to the east, are the centre of Barbera and Moscato production; Canelli has an **enoteca** at Corso Libertà 65A (*__t__ 0141 832182; open Tues–Sun*); and Costigliole's castle is now the home of the **Italian Culinary Institute for Foreigners** (*www.icif.com*). There's another regional **enoteca** west of Alba at **Mango** in the Baroque **Castello dei Marchesi di Busca** *(**t** 0141 89291; open Weds–Sun 10–12.30 and 3.30–7)*.

There are more, south of Alba: the enoteca at **Grinzane Cavour** is in the striking medieval castle Count Cavour called home when he served as village mayor; now the seat of the Premio Grinzane Cavour, one of Italy's most prestigious literary prizes, it

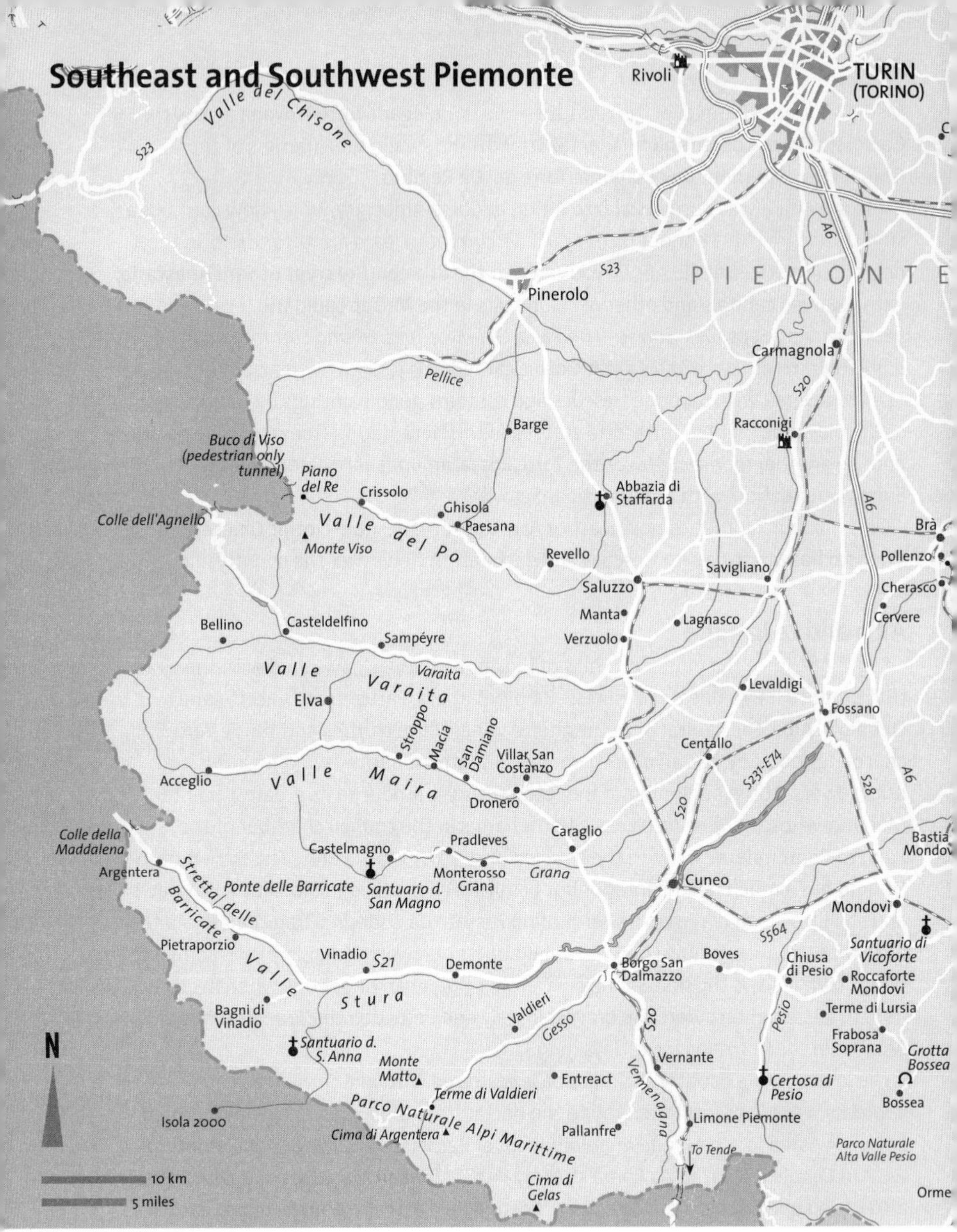

also has a fine restaurant and a museum dedicated to wine, folklore and Cavour himself (***t*** *0173 262 159; open for guided tours Mon and Weds–Sun 9.30–12.30 and 2.30–6.30; adm*). Charming **Barolo**, further south, has a well-stocked **enoteca** in the 16th-century **Castello Falletti**, where the eponymous wine was born (***t*** *0173 56277; open for guided tours of upper rooms Mon–Weds and Fri–Sun 10–12.30 and 3–6.30; adm; tastings Sat and Sun only*). **Barbaresco**, east of Alba, has an **enoteca** in the former church of San Donato at Via Torino 8/a (***t*** *0173 635 251; closed Weds and 1st wk July*).

The village of **La Morra**, the belvedere of Le Langhe, makes a good base for walks through the vineyards, and for visiting the former Abbazia dell'Annunziata, now the **Ratti wine museum** (***t*** *0173 50185; open Mon–Fri 8.30–12 and 2.30–5, but call ahead; closed Jan and Aug*). Nearby **Verduno** is dominated by a 17th-century castle in Juvarra's elegant Baroque style, used as a summer residence by King Carlo Alberto. Another castle, the handsome 12th-century **Castello Falletti di Barolo**, guards the concentric wine village of **Serralunga d'Alba** to the east.

Getting Around

Alessandria, Casale Monferrato, Acqui Terme, Asti and Alba are all connected by **rail**, and Alessandria and Asti also have good links to Turin, Genoa and Milan.

Tourist Information

Asti: Piazza Alfieri 29 , **t** 0141 530 357, *www.atasti.it*

Casale Monferrato: Piazza Castello, **t** 0142 444 330, *www.comune.casale-monferrato.al.it*

Alba: Piazza Medford 3, Alba, **t** 0173 35833, *www.langheroero.it*

Alessandria: Piazza Santa Maria di Castello 14, **t** 0131 251 021, *www.alexala.it*

Novi Ligure: Viale dei Campionissimi, **t** 0143 72585

Acqui Terme:Via Maggironi Ferraris 5, **t** 0144 322 142.

Each summer the provinces of Alessandria, Asti and Cuneo sponsor the 'Open Castles' season, with visits and cultural activities; pick up the annual brochure at any tourist office.

Where to Stay and Eat

Casale Monferrato ✉ 15033

La Torre, Via Garoglio 3, **t** 0142 70295 (*very expensive*). A restaurant that the Turinese and Milanese drive out of their way for, with dishes based on fresh ingredients from the immediate environs, including risotto with crayfish, spinach-filled *tortelli*, and breast of duck. *Closed Christmas and Aug.*

Asti ✉ 14100

******Reale**, Piazza Alfieri 6, **t** 0141 530 240, *www.hotel-reale.com* (*expensive*). Large, sumptuous, modern rooms with the best position in town, with balconies looking out on to the square. Reserve ahead for the Palio.

******Aleramo**, Via E. Filiberto 13, **t** 0141 595 661, *www.hotel.aleramo.it* (*expensive*). An excellent hotel with superb views over the town's rooftops from its top two floors.

******Hasta**, Valle Benedetta 25, just outside town, **t** 0141 213 312 (*moderate–expensive*). A tranquil, cosy option convenient for those with cars, boasting tennis courts, a garden and a good restaurant (*expensive*).

****Cavour**, Piazza Marconi 18, **t** 0141 530 222, (*cheap*). Clean, modern hotel just off the Campo del Palio.

Gener Neuv, Lungo Tanaro 4, **t** 0141 557 270, (*very expensive*). An elegant gourmet haven on the river, with a superb *menu degustazione* based on Piemontese traditions. The light desserts are beautiful to behold; the list of Piemontese wines is matchless. Reserve ahead. *Closed Sun, Mon and Aug.*

Tacabanda,Via Al Teatro Alfieri 5, **t** 0141 530999 (*moderate*). A pleasant cellar *osteria* with a limited menu of very tasty dishes. *Closed Weds and Aug.*

Alba ✉ 12051

*****Locanda del Pilone**, Fraz. Madonna di Como 34, **t** 0173 366616, *www.locandadelpilone.com* (*very expensive*). Romantic rooms and a superb elegant restaurant in the vaulted cellars, offering home-made bread, delicious mountain-inspired cuisine and a giant cheese cart. *Closed Mon, Weds and Thurs lunch, and most of Jan and Aug.*

*****Savona**, Via Roma 1, **t** 0173 440 440, *www.hotelsavona.com* (*moderate*). Very stylish, comfortable and modern rooms, plus a restaurant and bar.

Osteria dell'Arco, Piazza Savona 5, **t** 0173 363 974 (*moderate*). A restaurant situated in a historic building in the very centre of town, with a small but excellent-value menu including tarragon risotto and stuffed guinea fowl, and a good selection of wine. *Closed Sun and Mon.*

West of Alba, **Brà** is the HQ of the Slow Food Movement (*see* p.82), dedicated to the preservation of gastronomic traditions in the face of global standardization. Each September, in odd-numbered years, the town hosts the world's most prestigious cheese fair, featuring 'art cheeses' you can nibble while sipping wines from Le Langhe. The tall curvaceous church of **Santa Chiara** (1742), designed by Bernardo Vittone, has a

Barolo ✉ 12060

★★**Del Buon Padre**, Via delle Viole 30, Vergne, **t** 0173 56192 (*moderate*). A number of peaceful rooms and a restaurant serving good, solid Piemontese cuisine, accompanied by some divine wines. *Closed Weds, Jan and last 2wks July.*

Locanda nel Borgo Antico, Piazza Municipio 2, **t** 0173 56355 (*very expensive*). Well-prepared, traditional Le Langhe dishes served in a romantic setting. *Closed Weds, Thurs July and Christmas.*

Canale d'Alba ✉ 12043

Enoteca del Roera, Via Roma 57, **t** 0173 95857 (*very expensive*). An elegant, intimate restaurant above a wine shop, presided over by one of Piemonte's best young chefs and offering a 6-course *menu degustazione*. *Closed Weds, and Thurs lunch.*

La Morra/Verduno ✉ 12064

Belvedere, Piazza Castello 5, **t** 0173 50190 (*expensive*). Great *agnolotti* and *finanziera*, plus good mushroom and truffle dishes in autumn. *Closed Sun eve and Mon.*

Real Castello, Via Umberto I 9, **t** 0172 470 125 (*expensive*). King Carlo Alberto's castle in Verduno, where you can royally feast on the favourite local pasta, *tajarin* (tiny tagliatelle), roast guinea fowl and hazelnut torte. *Closed Dec–mid-Apr.*

Cervere (9km south of Brà) ✉ 12040

Antica Corona Reale, Via Fossano 13, **t** 0172 47132 (*expensive*). One of Piemonte's finest restaurants, founded in 1835 and serving culinary masterpieces made from the finest foie gras, white truffles, Cherasco snails and so on. *Closed Tues eve, Weds and Aug.*

Alessandria ✉ 15100

★★★★**Alli Due Buoi Rossi**, Via Cavour 32, **t** 0131 234598 (*very expensive*). The comfiest hotel in town, with a fine restaurant (*expensive*) serving the full range of local specialities. *Closed Sun.*

★★★★**Domus**, Via T. Castellani 12, **t** 0131 43305, (*expensive*). A central option with small, modern rooms.

★★**Rex**, Via S. Francesco d'Assisi 48, **t** 0131 252 297 (*cheap*). A bright and modern choice if you're on a budget.

Il Grappolo, Via Casale 28, **t** 0131 253 217 (*expensive*). A smart, modern restaurant situated in a 19th-century *palazzo*, offering a particularly fine selection of local wines. *Closed Mon eve and Tues.*

Acqui Terme ✉ 15011

★★★**Grand Hotel Nuove Terme**, Piazza Italia 1, **t** 0144 322 106, *www.grandhotelnuoveterme.it* (*moderate*). A pampered environment where you can indulge in a water or mud cure.

★★**San Marco**, Via Ghione 5, **t** 0144 322 456 (*cheap*). A family-run place offering the best deal in town, including optional full board. *Closed last 2wks July and Christmas.*

Cappello, Strada Visone 62, **t** 0144 356340, (*expensive*). A restaurant situated outside town but worth the trip for its delightful, imaginative dishes and *menu degustazione*. Reserve in advance.

La Schiavia, Vicolo della Schiavia, **t** 0144 55939 (*expensive*). A refined watering-hole situated on the first floor of a 15th-century *palazzo*; try the *stoccafisso* (stock fish). *Closed Sun and 3wks Aug.*

La Curia, Via alla Bollente 72, **t** 0144 356 049 (*expensive*). A lively enoteca with the best cellar in town and dishes to match. There's a good set lunch menu. *Closed Mon.*

Da Bigät, Via Mazzini 30, **t** 0144 324 283 (*cheap*). A restaurant famous for its hearty Ligurian *farinata*, made from chick peas, and its local specialities, including Roccaverano cheese. No credit cards. *Closed Weds, Sun eve, 2wks July and 2wks Feb.*

delightful rococo interior, while the handsome Gothic **Palazzo Traversa** on Via Parpera has odds and ends from Brà's predecessor, nearby **Pollenzo** (Roman *Pollentia*), where archaeologists have excavated the forum, theatre and 17,000-seat amphitheatre. Pollenzo also has a neo-Gothic Savoy castle, restored to become the Slow Food Movement's Università del Gusto, the world's first 'university of taste'.

South of Brà, atmospheric **Cherasco**, the 'Italian capital of snails', has a **Torre Civica** with a clock showing the phases of the moon. Its castle is a comfortable residence built by the Visconti in the 14th century.

Piemonte's Southeast Corner: Hats and Hot Water

East of Asti, **Alessandria**, city of Borsalino hats, was founded in the 12th century by disgruntled nobles from Monferrato who opposed Emperor Frederick Barbarossa and named their new town after his arch-enemy, Pope Alexander III. When the Savoys picked it up in the early 1700s, they built the vast **Cittadella** on the left bank of the Tanaro, destroying an entire village in the process. The cathedral has the second tallest **campanile** in Italy after Cremona's. But the best things here are a bit smaller: a remarkable cycle of 15 frescoes from the 1390s, discovered in 1971 in a medieval tower, with themes inspired by the Arthurian legends; they're now displayed in the **Stanze di Artù**, a former convent at Via Cavour 39 (***t** 0131 234 794; open Fri–Sun 3–7*). There's also a **museo etnografico** in Piazza del Gambarina (***t** 0131 40030, open Mon, Tues and Thurs Sat 9–12 and 4–7, Sun 4–7, adm*), dedicated to life in the 18th and 19th centuries. Or you can take in a collection of keys, wrought iron, weapons, fossils, Mongolian art and Robespierre's guillotine in the **Museo Francesco Janniello** at Via S. Ubaldo 1 (***t** 0131 226368; open Mon, Tues and Thurs–Sat 9–12 and 3–6.30, Sun 9–12*).

Eight kilometres south of Alessandria, Napoleon defeated the Austrians on 14 June 1800 in what he considered the greatest battle of his career, **Marengo**. The battlefield is marked by a column; in the village of Marengo are monuments to Napoleon and General Desaix, who perished on the field. The **museum of the battle of Marengo,** with weapons, helmets, plans and more, is in nearby **Spinetta Marengo** (***t** 0131 216 344; open Weds–Sat 10–12 and 2–6, Sun 10–12 and 3–7; adm*).

Six kilometres south, **Bosco Marengo** was the birthplace of Pius V (1504–72), whose papacy saw the great victory over the Turks at Lepanto. Pius built the church of **Santa Croce** in the village to serve as his tomb, a masterpiece of green marble and porphyry, but the Romans buried him in Santa Maria Maggiore.

Tortona, Novi Ligure and Aquae Terme

East of Alessandria, **Tortona** has been a transport hub since it was Roman *Derthona*, and still has a sprinkling of Roman remains, including the **Necropoli Monumentale** north of town at Fitteria, and part of the city walls, discovered in 1999.

Achey Romans soaked in the hot sulphuric waters of *Acquae Statiellae*, now the attractive spa town of **Aquae Terme**; four arches of a Roman aqueduct stand near the Antiche Terme hotel, and the **Museo Civico Archeologico** (***t** 0144 575 55, open Weds–Sat 9.30 –12.30 and 3.30–6.30, Sun 3.30–6.30; adm*) in the half-ruined **Castello dei Paleologi** has mosaics and remains from the ancient baths. Next door is the fine Romanesque **cathedral** (1067) with a good campanile, spectacular apses, and a marble doorway from 1481. There's an **enoteca** in the ancient cellars of the **Palazzo Robellini** at Piazza Levi 7 (***t** 0144 770 273*), but the most memorable sight in Acqui is the **Bollente**, a hot sulphuric spring that bubbles up at 75°C beneath an octagonal neoclassical pavilion, leaving the earth in cloud of steam that fills the square on cold winter days.

Southwest Piemonte: Cuneo and the Maritime Alps

Although it's just up from the Riviera, the lofty Maritime Alps have made this corner of Piemonte something of a well-kept secret. The French influence is strong, and the difficulty of access has also meant that folk traditions and festivals have lingered longer than they have almost anywhere else on the peninsula.

South from Turin to Saluzzo

Carmagnola, 27 kilometres south of Turin, was for four centuries a fortified outpost of the Marquis of Saluzzo. Students of French history will recognize the name as the origin of the hit song of the Revolution, the *Carmagnole,* a tune originally sung about an early 15th-century *condottiere* nicknamed Il Carmagnola; how it made Danton's hit parade, with very different lyrics, is anyone's guess. Silk-making **Racconigi**, further south, has the Savoys' **Castello Reale**, begun in 1676 and finished in 1842, with a Chinese apartment and rooms dedicated to various mythological deities (***t*** *0172 84005; open Tues–Sun 8.30–7.30; adm*); behind the castle extends a lovely **park** designed by French landscape architect André Le Notre, with ancient trees and a lake (*open Apr–Oct, Sun and hols 10–1hr before sunset; adm*).

Mellow old **Saluzzo**, the 'little Siena of the Alps' was the capital of a courtly Occitan-speaking marquissate, founded in 1142. It knew its golden age in the 15th century and lost independence in the wars between Emperor Charles V and France, becoming part of Savoy in 1601. In the steep lanes below the brick **Castiglia** (the castle of the marquis, rebuilt in the 19th century to serve as a prison), it retains much of its character. In the Middle Ages, the Salita Castello was the centre of town; here you visit the **Torre Civica** (1462), with pretty views over the medieval roofs into the Alps (*open Thurs–Sun Apr–Sept 10–1 and 2–6, Oct–Mar till 5; Tues and Weds by request; adm*). Nearby, in Via San Giovanni, the Dominican church of **San Giovanni** (1280) has a Romanesque–Gothic campanile, good quattrocento frescoes, and the Gothic tomb of Saluzzo's greatest marquis, Ludovico II (*d.* 1503). On the same street, the charming 15th-century Casa Cavassa, restored in the 1880s, houses the **Museo Civico** (***t*** *0175 41455; same hrs as Torre Civica*), which contains, amongst other things, a splendid carved altarpiece of the Madonna della Misericordia (1499) by Hans Clemer.

The marquises had a favourite residence at the hilltop **Castello di Manta**, four kilometres south of Saluzzo (***t*** *0175 87822, open Tues–Sun 10–1 and 2–6, Oct–Dec until 5; adm*). Here, more than anywhere, you can get a feel for the polished court of Saluzzo, in the **Sala Baronale**, which is decorated with exquisite, refined frescoes (1420s) of nine sumptuously dressed heroes and nine heroines – believed to be the marquises and their wives. The opposite wall has a very seductive Fountain of Youth.

Saluzzo's Alpine Valleys: the Po, Varaita and Maira

The apple-growing **Valle del Po**, now a natural park, was an important route to France for Saluzzo, and **Revello** was fortified early on by the marquises. Their palace is now incorporated in the Municipio, including their frescoed chapel, the **Cappella Marchionale** (1519), with portraits of the marquises and a Leonardoesque Last Supper

Getting Around

Cuneo's airport, 20km north at Levaldigi, has daily connections to Rome and Strasbourg, and summer flights to Olbia, Split, Ibiza, Gerona and Bastia.

Cuneo is linked by **rail** with Turin via Saluzzo, and with Genoa via Ceva and Mondovì. It is also linked by **one of Italy's most spectacular railways** to southwest Piemonte's main mountain resort, Limone Piemonte, then via French territory to Ventimiglia (*c*. 3hrs).

Buses also run from Cuneo to all the towns in the province and to Turin and Genoa.

Tourist Information

Saluzzo: Via Griselda 8, **t** 0175 240 352, *www.terredelmarchesato.it*.

Cuneo: Via Vittorio Amedeo II 13, **t** 0171 690 217, *www.cuneoholiday.com*.

Parco Naturale Alpi Marittime: Corso DL Bianco 5, 12010 Valdieri, **t** 0171 97397, *www.parcoalpimarittime.it*

Limone Piemonte: Via Roma 30, **t** 0171 929 515, *www.limonepiemonte.it*.

Mondovì: Corso Statuo, **t** 0174 47428

Where to Stay and Eat

Saluzzo ✉ 12037

★★**Persico**, Vicolo Mercati, **t** 0175 41213 (*cheap*). A nice bohemian hotel (with resident artist) in the centre, with comfy if oddly furnished rooms. The good restaurant serves a tasty wild boar stew. *Closed Fri.*

La Gargotta del Pellico, Piazzetta dei Mondagli 5, **t** 0175 46833 (*expensive*). An exceptional restaurant in the birthplace of Saluzzo's republican patriot, Silvio Pellico. Try quail in pastry, or the *raviolini* with marjoram and mushroom butter, followed by superb pear mousse and exquisite Piemontese cheese. *Closed Tues, and Weds lunch.*

Sampeyre ✉ 12020

★★★**Monte Nebin**, Via Cavour 26, **t** 0175 977 112, (*cheap*). A large modern base for trips into the mountains, with a good restaurant serving Italian classics. *Restaurant closed Weds.*

Cuneo ✉ 12100

★★★★**Lovera Palace**, Via Savigliano 12, **t** 0171 690 420, *www.loverapalace.com* (*expensive*). An elegant central hotel that once hosted

(*to visit call ahead,* **t** *0340 534 6767*). Revello has another fine church, the 15th-century **Collegiata dell'Assunta**, with an elegant marble portal by Matteo Sanmicheli (1534) and three 16th-century polyptychs by Hans Clemer and Pascale Oddone.

According to tradition, when Charlemagne exiled the last Lombard king of Italy, Desiderius, in 774, the latter took refuge in **Ghisola**, a tiny, ancient hamlet situated up the Po valley near **Paesana**. Further up, the little resort of **Crissolo** lies under the great pyramid of **Monviso** (the 'Stone King'; 12,600ft), the highest peak in the Maritime Alps; from Crissolo, it's a short walk from the **Grotta del Rio Martino**, with its stunning 140ft waterfall.

Above Crissolo, the lovely **Pian del Re** (9,455ft) is the source of Italy's longest river (652 kilometres); if you've ever wanted to drink a glass of Po, this is the place. Above Pian del Re, you can walk through the very first alpine tunnel, the 246ft **Buco di Viso**, which was dug in 1480 by the Marquis of Saluzzo Ludovico II, in a remarkable feat of engineering that facilitated the passage of mule caravans between Saluzzo and France (*best done July–Sept; bring a torch*). The Col de la Traversette, above Pian del Re, may have been used by even bigger freight – Hannibal's elephants.

At **Verzuolo** (south of Manta) you can take a lovely detour into the luxuriant **Valle Varaita**, an Occitan-speaking valley that has retained many of its traditions. Aim for **Sampeyre**, where the church of SS. Pietro e Paolo has a number of good 15th-century frescoes by the Biazaci brothers. During Carnival, Sampeyre celebrates the *Baio*, a

King François I of France. It has a fitness centre and offers tours and cooking lessons with the chefs of its excellent restaurant, the **Antica Contrade** (*very expensive*). *Closed Thurs.*

****Principe**, Piazza Duccio Galimberti 5, **t** 0171 693 355, *www.hotel-principe.it* (*expensive*). One of the town's best hotels, right in the centre with 42 modern rooms.

Ligure, Via Savigliano 11, **t** 0171 681942, *www.ligurehotel.it* (*cheap*). A slightly worn option in the oldest quarter, brightened by old-fashioned courtesy and offering tasty meals of home-made pasta and roast meat or trout. *Restaurant closed Sun eve. Hotel closed Jan.*

Rododendro, Frazione San Giacomo, Boves, 9km from town, **t** 0171 380 372 (*very expensive*). The wood-surrounded atelier of Mary Barale, one of Italy's top woman chefs, whose leek soup, truffles with eggs, and tender *Chateaubriand* have put this place on Italy's gourmet map. There's an extensive wine list of French and Italian bottles. *Closed Sun eve, Mon and part of June.*

Osteria della Chiocciola, Via Fossano 1, **t** 0171 66277 (*moderate*). Traditional Piemontese fare, including mouthwatering *agnolotti del plin* (stuffed with meat and vegetables), duck, and rabbit with olives. *Closed Sun and 2–3wks Jan.*

Pradleves (Valle Grana) ✉ 12100

Tre Verghe d'Oro, **t** 0171 986 116 (*cheap*). An old-fashioned mountain inn with a restaurant (*moderate*) serving *gnocchi al Castelmagno* and other mountain specialities. *Restaurant closed Tues. Hotel closed Jan.*

Limone Piemonte ✉ 12015

***Le Ginestre**, Via Nizza 68, **t** 0171 927 596, *www.albergosiesta-e-leginestre.com* (*moderate*). A cosy little option convenient for the slopes.

Lu Taz, Loc. San Maurizio, 1km from town, **t** 0171 929061 (*expensive*). An attractive stone house in the woods, with traditional Piemontese dishes prepared with flair. *Closed Tues, 2wks June and 2wks Nov.*

La Crubarsela, Via Comm. Beltrandi 7, **t** 0171 92391 (*cheap*). An excellent, homely, family-run eatery just down from the tourist office, serving fine local dishes and boasting an unusually good wine selection. *Closed Mon, May and 2wks Nov.*

1000-year-old pageant featuring historical characters and dramas in Napoleonic-era costumes and brightly ribboned hats. Another village, **Casteldelfino**, recalls in its name the 14th century, when it was the capital of the Dauphin's Cisalpine lands; in good weather you can continue along the road to France, over the **Colle dell'Agnello**. The other road west of Casteldelfino leads to **Bellino**, famous for its 32 sundials.

The **Valle Maira**, the next valley south, is known for its lush orchards. It begins at **Dronero**, which has an attractive 15th-century bridge – yet another one built by Old Nick. Nearby, **Villar San Costanzo** has a beautiful crypt of 1091, a survivor of a Benedictine abbey, now under the **parish church**; one chapel has frescoes on the Golden Legend by Pietro di Saluzzo. Another church, **San Costanzo al Monte**, marks the martydom of St Costanzo under Diocletian; a few 8th century sculptures have survived from the original Lombard building, and there are some good capitals from the 12th century. Villar San Costanzo is also the base for visiting the **Ciciu** ('Puppets') – weird standing rocks wearing large stone caps, left behind by glaciers; they are up to 26ft in height, and are a haunting sight in winter or at night.

Further up the valley, above **Stroppo**, the beautiful, isolated 12th-century church of **San Peyre** has remarkable frescoes. In **Elva**, a *comune* dispersed in a gorge-lined valley, people were once famous for their specialized trade: travelling around Italy and buying women's tresses, which they wove into skeins to sell to wigmakers in France and England. Elva's church of **Santa Maria Assunta,** built in the 1400s, has a triumphal arch in the choir, sculpted with figures straight out of the Middle Ages, and an important fresco cycle, culminating in a majestic Crucifixion (*pick up keys at La Fernisolo, in front of church*) by Hans Clemer.

The upper Valle Maira, around **Acceglio**, is completely unspoiled; there are lovely hikes, especially to the **Cascate Stroppia**, a long waterfall ground into the rock, and the Lago dei Novi Colori ('nine colours').

Cuneo: Piemonte's Cheesy Wedge

A pleasant leafy provincial capital, **Cuneo** stands at the confluence of the rivers Gesso and Stura, which here form a wedge, or *cuneo* that forced railway engineers in the early 1930s to build the city's landmark, the **Viadotto Soleri**, to carry the tracks. On the main Nice–Turin road, Cuneo was often besieged by France, and was largely rebuilt in the 1800s. The Turin-style, vast, porticoed **Piazza Galimberti** marks the centre and hosts an enormous market every Tuesday. **San Francesco** (1227), a church with a good Gothic portal dating from 1481, now houses the **Museo Civico**, which contains a small gathering of Piemontese paintings from the 18th and 19th centuries and a number of prehistoric, Roman and medieval artefacts, and folk items, including dolls in local costumes (***t** 071 634 175; open Tues–Sat 8.30–1 and 2.30–5, Sun 10–12.30 and 2.30–6; adm*).

Buses from Cuneo will take you up the surrounding valleys, which are famous for their small, locally made cheeses. The closest valley, the chestnut-forested little **Valle Grana**, contains the tiny village of **Monterosso Grana**, spread under its ruined watchtower, with a 15th-century frescoed chapel. There's a small **ethnographic museum** in Santo Lucio di Coumboscuro (***t** 0171 98707; open daily 8–12 and 2–6*), as well as a school aimed at reviving the old crafts of furniture-making and weaving.

Pradleves is a small resort, while **Castelmagno**, further up, is synonymous with the much loved 'king of cheeses'. A serpentine road twists to the **Santuario di San Magno**, built over a temple of Mars and dedicated to a Roman legionary martyred on this lonely site; its oldest section dates back to the 1400s and has frescoes by Pietro di Saluzzo (*open daily June–Sept 9–6*).

Into the Parco Naturale delle Alpi Marittime

South of Cuneo, **Borgo San Dalmazzo** is named after another martyr, Dalmatius, but is more famous these days for its snails, the main attraction of the Fiera Fredda ('Cold Fair'), an early-December market founded by Emanuele Filiberto.

A trio of valleys convene at Borgo San Dalmazzo. The longest, the **Valle Stura**, once a major route of salt merchants and armies, is a botanical paradise with rare flowers. Its chief town is medieval **Demonte**; on the mountain of Podio stand the ruins of the once-mighty **Fortezza di Consolata**, which was destroyed by the French in 1796.

Further up the valley, **Bagni di Vinadio** is a small, hot sulphur spring-spa (*open summer only*); at **Pietraporzio** begins the **Stretta delle Barricate**, a narrow ravine closed in by sheer walls. **Argentera**, the last and highest *comune*, is a cool summer resort; above Argentera, the **Colle della Maddalena**, the pass into France, is open from May to mid-October, lined with pastures brimful of flowers.

The **Valle Gesso** leads into the heart of the Maritime Alps, where three peaks over 10,000 ft – Argentera, Gelas and Matto – are part of the **Parco Naturale delle Alpi Marittime**. These lofty altitudes so close to the sea bring plenty of rain, and the park is exceptionally rich in flora and fauna; even wolves have recently returned, without even being formally invited. In the middle of the park, the old spa of the Savoy dukes and kings, **Terme di Valdieri**, was rebuilt in the 1950s and is famed for its hot sulphur springs; waters flow down steps covered with a unique algae called *muffa* (*Ulva labyrinthiformis*), famed for its healing properties.

East of Borgo San Dalmazzo, the steep, wooded **Valle Vermenagna** is the route of the Cuneo–Ventimiglia railway and the SS20. From **Vernante** (proud to be 'the only village in Italy where the houses are covered with Pinocchio frescoes'), there's an eight-kilometre side road up to **Palanfre**, on the fringe of an enchanting ancient beech forest, in a lush microclimate supporting more than 650 trees and flowers.

Back in Valle Vermenagna, near the French border, **Limone Piemonte** is a popular winter sports centre, with skiing until Easter. Its citrusy name derives from *leimon*, Greek for meadow, one of the town's most charming features. Amidst all the new development stands the Gothic **San Pietro in Vincoli**, housing a hodgepodge of frescoes, carvings and plaques.

The next valley east, the **Valle del Pesio**, rises to the **Parco Naturale Alta Valle Pesio**, with karstic formations and pine forests under Mt Marguareis. In May and June you can make an hour-and-a-half walk up to the **Pis del Pesio**, a spectacular 100ft jet of subterranean water shooting into a void, which resembles just what it sounds like. The **Certosa di Pesio**, founded by St Bruno himself in 1173 and dominated by an oversize cloister, was abandoned after Napoleon but is now inhabited by brothers of the Istituto Missioni Consolate (***t*** *0101 738123; open daily 9–12 and 2.30-6*).

In the bosquey little valley just to the east, the trendy spa of **Terme di Lurisia** was visited by a certain Marie Curie in 1918 – not to soak but to study its radioactive waters.

Mondovì and the Monregalese

Founded rather late by Italian standards, in 1198, by three villages united against the nasty bishop of Asti, **Mondovì** was originally known as Monregalese, a name that survives for its environs. The first buildings went up in the lofty *centro storico* of **Piazza**, in attractive, asymmetrical **Piazza Maggiore**; here the city's best church, the **Chiesa della Missione** (1675–1733) adds an elegant Baroque touch; inside *trompe-l'œil* figures by Andrea Pozzo float in the vault. Mondovì native Francesco Gallo (1672–1750) was one of the busiest architects of his day in Piemonte, and left his home town its **cathedral** with a chapel dedicated to Universal Suffrage – a notion introduced in Italy by five-time prime minister Giovanni Giolitti, also from Mondovì. Don't miss the views from the belvedere next door. Down in **Breo**, the commmercial centre, the city's symbol, the 'Moor', sounds the hours from the top of the church of **SS. Pietro e Paolo** (1489).

In the mountainous, unspoiled Monregalese is **Bastia Mondovì**, where the interior of the 11th–15th-century **San Fiorenzo** is covered with 51 late Gothic Provençal-style frescoes. Just east of Mondovì, the huge sanctuary in **Vicoforte,** founded in 1596, has an enormous elliptical dome by Francesco Gallo and a suitably impressive interior (*open daily 7–12 and 2.30–7*). To the south, **Frabosa Soprana** is a popular winter and summer resort. Buses from Mondovì to Frabosa continue south to the spectacular **Grotta di Bossea** (***t*** *0174 349 240, guided tours daily July and Aug 10–12 and 2–6, rest of year at 10, 11.30, 2.30, 4 and 5.30; adm; dress warmly*) with its beautiful stalactite formations, underground river, lakes and waterfall.

From the rail junction at Ceva, you can take a train south along the Tanaro river as far as Ormea, by way of **Garessio**, a picturesque collection of four hamlets, where you can ski, take a spa cure at **San Bernardo**, source of 'the lightest water in the world', or visit yet another palatial hunting lodge of the Savoys, the **Castello di Casotto**, built in 1800 over an 11th-century Carthusian monastery, parts of which have recently been excavated (***t*** *0174 351 131 ; open 9–12 and 2–6; adm*). Pretty **Ormea** with its narrow lanes is a woodsy summer resort, its ruined **castle** a nest of Saracen corsairs in the 10th and 11th centuries, when they controlled the coast.

Liguria
The Italian Riviera

10

Highlights

1. Genoa's renovated *centro storico* and aquarium
2. Liberty-style San Remo, a grand 1890s resort
3. Albenga's Romanesque cathedral
4. Exquisite Portofino and its promontory
5. The Cinque Terre and their vines

In Liguria the shore ('riviera') is *the* Riviera, a rainbow of coast endowed with a rare Italian commodity – beautiful, refined beaches, in magical settings beneath steep cliffs and hanging gardens, backed by old fishing towns squeezed between the rock, or palm-fringed resorts that fit like an old pair of shoes. You'd have to continue all the way down to the Bay of Naples to find a shore as good. And if you're approaching from the French Riviera, the Italian version seems genteelly laid back – no one cares if your socks don't match, or you've brought the kids, and the splendid grand hotels are outnumbered by unpretentious old-school *pensioni*.

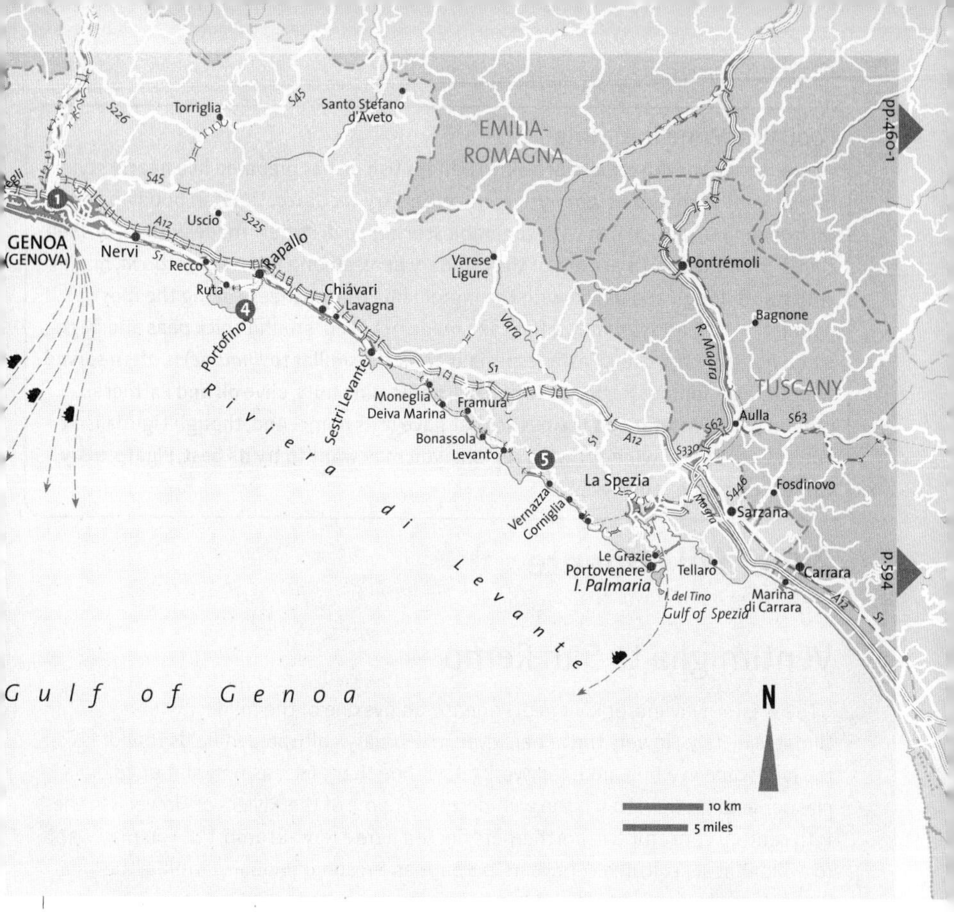

Although August is peak season these days, people first came to this fabled shore for its mild winter climate. Sheltered by the Maritime Alps and Apennines from the fogs and chills of the north, Liguria has sensuous yields of lemons, oranges and flowers – one of the region's principal exports – while the oil from its ancient olive groves is legendary. Bathed in a luminous, warm light, the Riveria dazzles with its reds, blues, yellows, yet just a few dozen hairpin turns up into the hinterland you're in another world altogether, lush and cool and green; Liguria is the most forested region of Italy.

The delights of sun and sea are only part of what the region has to offer. Long isolated from the rest of Italy by difficult mountains, Liguria has a distinct identity. Poor in resources but full of intrepid, tenacious seamen and merchants, it has looked to the sea for its survival since the early Middle Ages. After the Crusades, the Republic of Genoa grew to become a seapower and east–west wheeler-dealer rivalled only by Venice, and in the 17th century it did so well financing Spain's treasure fleet that it became the wealthiest corner of Europe. All these experiences formed the Ligurian character – tough, feisty, shrewd, adventurous, independent and stubborn. Columbus, of course, came from Liguria, as did the great admiral Andrea Doria, and the Risorgimento heroes Garibaldi and Mazzini.

Food and Wine in Liguria

Liguria's wonderful regional cuisine includes fish dishes prepared in a hearty style reminiscent of that of neighbouring Provence – try *cacciucco*, Ligurian bouillabaisse; *cappon magro*, pickled fish with vegetables; or *zuppa di datteri*, made with razor shell clams. Even the snacks are out of the ordinary here; among them are *focaccia*, made with a soft dough and baked with the ingredients (runny cheese being the most popular) inside; and *farinata*, a flat cake made of baked, ground chick peas and best eaten hot from the oven. Pasta (especially *trenette*, similar to *linguine*) is often served with Genoa's famous *pesto* sauce of basil, garlic, pine nuts, olive oil and Parmesan, ground with a mortar and the pestle that gave it its name. And, though Liguria isn't one of Italy's great wine-growing regions, you may want to try its best, Pigato, a dry white, or Rossese, a dry red.

Riviera di Ponente

Ventimiglia to San Remo

The western Riviera, or Riviera di Ponente, enjoys one of the mildest winter climates in Italy. Flowers thrive here even in February, cultivated in fields that dress the landscape in a brilliant patchwork (albeit one that's increasingly shrouded in plastic), lending this stretch the well-deserved name of the 'Riviera of Flowers'. In the 19th century, consumptive northerners flocked here every autumn, but you may want to avoid that season; in recent years, perhaps as a result of global warming, the area has been hit by tempestuous rains and floods.

Ventimiglia

Ventimiglia is a bit like the elephant and blind men, and your impression of it may well depend on where you touch down: its medieval core is a typical Ligurian hillside town, overlooking the swan-filled Roja river; some of the modern town is dull and boring but other parts by the sea are charming and flower filled. Roses and carnations are the main crops, and in July the town stages the 'Battle of the Flowers'.

Ventimiglia is also a garden of history, with the most ancient roots in Liguria. Between 100,000 and 200,000 BC, members of Europe's first sophisticated culture – the Neanderthal – lived in the **Balzi Rossi** caves (***t** 0184 381 113; open Tues–Sun 9–7; adm; closed during strong winds or heavy rain*) on the beach at Grimaldi near the French frontier. At their entrance, the **Museo Preistorico** (*same hours*) displays what was found there – seashell finery, tools, weapons and lumpy 'Venuses', the first ever sculptures. The caves hold traces of elaborate burials, and the Grotto del Caviglione has an etching of a horse, of a breed now common only on the Russian steppes.

A bus from Ventimiglia serves Mortola Inferiore and the **Hanbury Gardens** (***t** 0184 229 507; open Mon, Tues, Thurs–Sun Apr–Sept 9–6, Oct–Mar 10–4; adm*), one of Italy's most important botanical paradises. They were founded in 1867 by Londoner Sir

Thomas Hanbury, who acclimatized some 5,000 rare plants from Africa and Asia to co-exist with native flora. Nearby, a section of the ancient Via Aurelia has a plaque listing VIPs who have passed this way, from St Catherine of Siena to Napoleon. The main road, passing underneath the gardens, leads to the former customs post at Ponte San Ludovico, with its **castle** where Serge Voronoff performed his experiments, seeking the Fountain of Youth in monkey glands.

Ventimiglia's Roman incarnation, **Albintimilium**, a kilometre east of the modern town, was an important stop on the Via Aurelia; best-preserved among its ruins is the small 2nd-century AD **theatre** (*open Weds and Fri 3–7, Thurs and Sat 9–1*). The finds are on view in the **Museo Archeologico** at nearby Via Verdi 41 (***t*** *0184 351 181; open Tues–Sat 9.30–12.30 and 3–5, Sun 10–12.30; adm*).

Ventimiglia itself is divided into old and new by the Roja. The modern town is centred around the huge Friday market and lined with seaside promenades; the old town, with its twisting medieval lanes, has the attractive 11th–12th-century **cathedral** and **baptistry** as a focal point. Another Romanesque church, **San Michele**, was built from Roman columns and milestones. Guarding the coast to the west of town, the ruined 12th-century **Castel d'Appio** was the HQ of the piratical Counts of Ventimiglia.

Dolceacqua

Among the valleys cutting inland from Ventimiglia, the Val Nervia is perhaps the most appealing (buses run there hourly from Ventimiglia). Aim for Dolceacqua, a picturesque village linked by the single arch of a medieval bridge and crowned by the 16th-century **Castello di Doria**, reputedly haunted by villains who took full advantage of their *droit du seigneur* with the local brides. On St Sebastian's Day (20 January), the village holds a unique religious procession led by the 'tree man', who bears a huge tree branch hung with large, coloured communion hosts in a curious mixture of Christianity and ancient fertility rites.

The hills around Dolceacqua are terraced with vineyards producing Rossese, a good red wine available in local cafés. Further up, **Pigna**, the 'pine cone', looks like one with its concentric walls, which shelter two fine churches containing paintings by Giovanni Canevesio. Some three kilometres away, **Castelvittorio** has changed little since the 13th century, when its thick walls kept out arch-enemy Pigna, with whom it conducted non-stop war in the Middle Ages.

Bordighera

Once a favourite winter retreat of chilblained Britons (who sometimes outnumbered locals), Bordighera is now one of the most jovial resorts on the Riviera, blessed with a good beach, regal promenades and a September festival of humour. As at Ventimiglia, the environs contain fields of cultivated flowers, but here the speciality is palms; ever since Sant'Ampelio supposedly brought the first date palm seeds from Egypt in 411, the town has had a monopoly in supplying the Vatican with fronds during Easter week. Monet painted here in 1884, captivated by 'this brilliance, this magical light'. In the summer the tourist office runs free tours that point out the Giardino Moreno, Valle di Sasso and other places that caught his eye.

PIEMONTE
LIGURIA
FRANCE
Cuneo
Grana
S20
S231-E74
S28
A6
Bastia Mondovì
Bormida di Millesimo
Mondovì
Ceva
Santuario di Vicoforte
S564
Borgo San Dalmazzo
Gesso
Pesio
Frabosa Soprana
Grotta di Bossea
Bossea
Vernante
Vermenagna
Certosa di Pesio
Limone Piemonte
Pallanfre
Tanaro
Garessio
Ormea
Grotte del Toirano
Castelvecchio di Rocca Barbena
Balestrino
Toirano
Gorges de Saorge
Triora
Argentina
VIA AURELIA
Alassio
Laigueglia
Andora
Capo Mele
Marina di Andora
Pigna
Castel Vittorio
Baiardo
Nervia
Monte Bignone
Pontedassio
A10
Cervo
Bartolomeo al Mare
Diano Marina
Dolcedo
Oneglia
Imperia
Porto Maurizio
Taggia
Dolceacqua
Arma di Taggia
Bussana Vecchia
Grimaldi
S1
SAN REMO
Colidrodi
Ospedaletti
Bordighera
Ventimiglia
Mortola Inferiore
Villa Hanbury
Balzi Rossi
Ponte San Ludovico

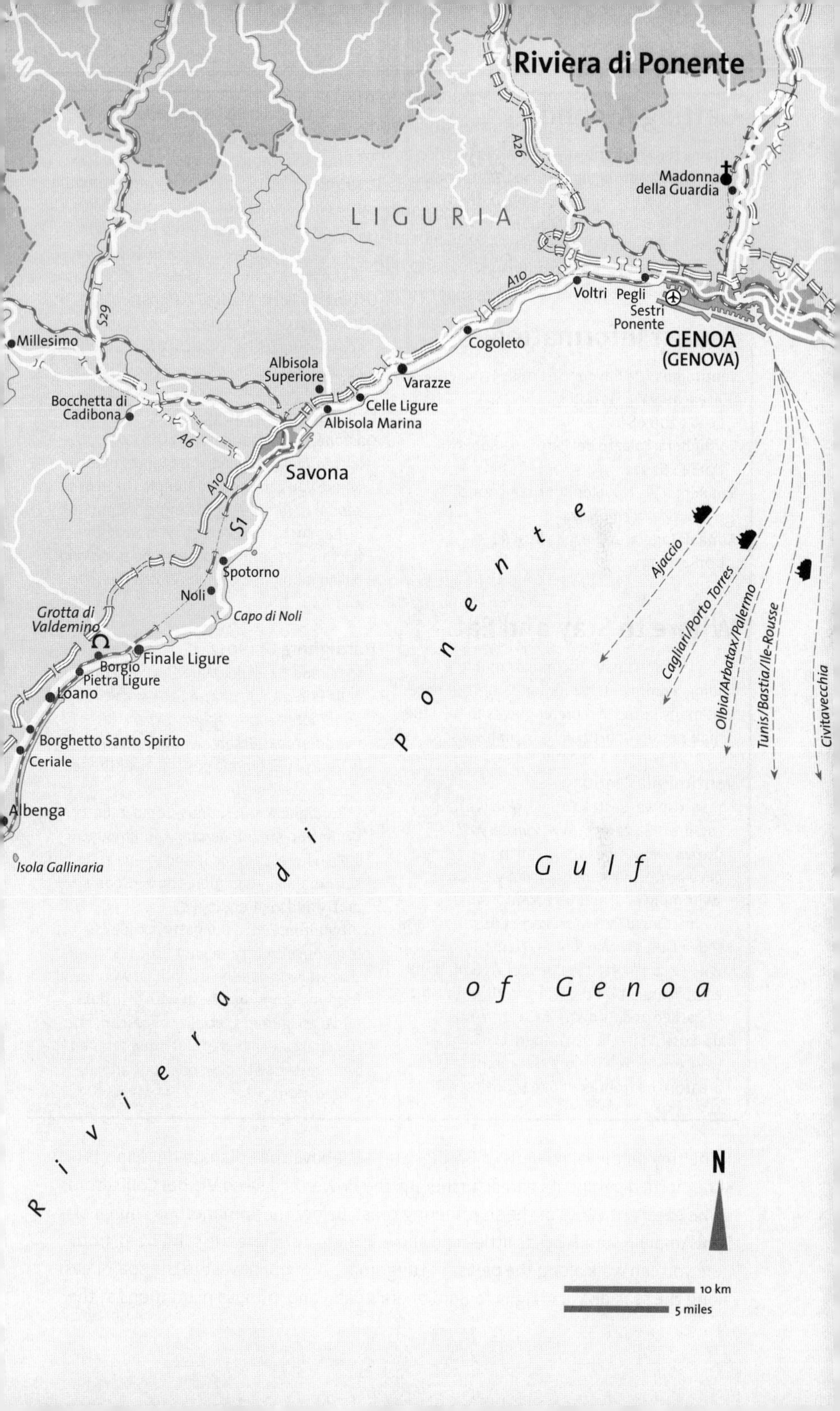
Riviera di Ponente
LIGURIA
A26
Madonna della Guardia
A10
Voltri
Pegli
Sestri Ponente
GENOA (GENOVA)
Cogoleto
Varazze
Celle Ligure
Albisola Superiore
Albisola Marina
Savona
S29
Millesimo
Bocchetta di Cadibona
A6
S1
Spotorno
Noli
Capo di Noli
Grotta di Valdemino
Borgio
Finale Ligure
Pietra Ligure
Loano
Borghetto Santo Spirito
Ceriale
Albenga
Isola Gallinaria
Ajaccio
Cagliari/Porto Torres
Olbia/Arbatax/Palermo
Tunis/Bastia/Ile-Rousse
Civitavecchia
Riviera di Ponente
Gulf of Genoa
N
10 km
5 miles

Getting Around

Trains run frequently up and down the coast; from Ventimiglia the line that branches off for Cuneo, in Piemonte, is one of the country's most scenic rail routes.

Inland, the hill towns are easily reached by **bus** from their nearest coastal towns.

Tourist Information

Ventimiglia: Via Cavour 61, **t** 0184 351 183.
Dolceacqua: Via Patrioti Martiri 58, **t** 0184 206 681.
Bordighera: Palazzo del Parco, Via Roberto 1, **t** 0184 262 322.
San Remo: Via Nuvoloni 1, **t** 0184 59090, *www.rivieradeifiori.org*
Arma di Taggia: in the Villa Boselli, **t** 0184 43 733.

Where to Stay and Eat

You shouldn't have too much trouble finding a room outside July and Aug, but note that many hotels still prefer guests to take full or half pension, particularly in high season.

Ventimiglia ✉ 18039

*****La Riserva**, Castel d'Appio, 5km west of town, **t** 0184 229 533, *www.lariserva.it* (*expensive*). A fine family-run inn up in the olive groves, with magnificent views, a swimming pool and very comfortable rooms. *Closed Oct–Mar except Christmas hols.*

*****Sea Gull**, Via Marconi 24, **t** 0184 351 726, *www.seagullhotel.it* (*moderate*). A comfortable establishment on the waterfront, with a bit of garden and its own beach.

Balzi Rossi, Piazzale De Gasperi, **t** 0184 38132 (*very expensive*). The top restaurant in the area, on the frontier at San Lodovico, with a flower-filled dining room overlooking the Med. The cuisine, which blends the best of France and Liguria, includes a legendary *terrina di coniglio*, pasta with fresh tomatoes and basil, scallops of sea bass and divine desserts. Book ahead. *Closed Mon, Tues lunch, Sun lunch in July and Aug, 2wks Mar and 2wks Nov.*

Usteria d'a Porta Marina, Via Trossarelli 22, **t** 0184 351 650 (*moderate*). A restaurant specializing in fish, particularly sea bass in Rossese wine. *Closed Tues eve and Weds.*

Dolceacqua ✉ 18035

Gastone, Piazza Garibaldi 2, **t** 0184 206 577 (*expensive*). A relaxed and friendly place where you can come to sample the likes of *capron magro*, alongside more imaginative dishes such as *gnocchetti* with zucchini flowers and shrimp, followed by traditional baked rabbit in casserole. *Closed Mon eve and Tues.*

Bordighera ✉ 18012

******Grand Hotel del Mare**, Via Portico della Punta 34, **t** 0184 262 201, *www.grandhoteldelmare.it* (*very expensive*). A modern, extremely elegant hotel in a beautiful panoramic position over the sea. *Closed Nov–Christmas.*

*****Bordighera & Terminus**, Corso Italia 21, **t** 0184 260 561 (*moderate*). A luminous, stylish hotel situated in the town centre but surrounded by a garden. The bedrooms are pretty and well-equipped.

Le Chaudron, Piazza Bengasi 2, **t** 0184 263 592 (*expensive*). A very elegant little restaurant that will win your heart with its wonderful food, including spaghetti with artichokes, and the Ligurian speciality of *pesce al sale* (fish baked in a bed of salt, then skinned and dressed with olive oil). Book ahead. *Closed Mon.*

The tiny medieval nucleus of Bordighera, set above the Spianata del Capo, is shoe-horned behind its gates; further up, the flower-bedecked **Via dei Colli** affords some excellent views of the shimmering coast. Below, the Romanesque church of **Sant'Ampelio** stands on its little cape above the grotto where the saint lived; from here you can walk along the pleasant Lungomare Argentina west to the spa, or east along the seaside Via Arziglia to Bordighera's palm and mimosa plantations at the

La Reserve Tastevin, Via Aurelia 20, Capo Sant'Ampelio, **t** 0184 261 322 (*expensive*). The most spectacular place to eat in town, in a restaurant set in the cliffs themselves, with fantastic views and delightful dishes combining ingredients from the sea and the Valle Argentina.

Ristorante dei Marinai, Via Marinai 2, **t** 0184 261 511 (*moderate*). A restaurant specializing in all things marine, with a menu that is based on the day's catch. The *stoccafisso mantecato alla Liguria* is particularly good. *Closed Weds.*

San Remo ✉ 18038

There's a hotel-finding service in the station, **t** 0184 80172 (*closed Sun*).

★★★★★**Royal**, Corso Imperatrice 80, **t** 0184 5391, *www.royalhotelsanremo.com* (*luxury*). A turn-of-the-19th-century *grande dame* surrounded by lush gardens with palms. Accommodation varies from imperial suites to modest doubles. There's a hotel orchestra to serenade guests in the afternoon and get them dancing in the evening.

★★★★**Astoria West End**, Corso Matuzia 8, **t** 0184 65541, *www.astoriasanremo.it* (*expensive*). One of the region's oldest hotels, with chandeliers, elaborate stucco ceilings and carved lifts. Situated opposite the sea, it has luxuriant gardens with a pool and a pretty outdoor terrace.

★★★**Paradiso**, Via Roccasterone 12, **t** 0184 571 211, www.*paradisohotel.it* (*moderate–expensive*). The perfect place if you seek peace and quiet, set just back from the seafront, above most of the hurly-burly, with a terrace and balconies enveloped with flowers. There's a distinguished, glass-enclosed restaurant and a lovely sunny breakfast room. *Closed Nov and early Dec.*

★★★**Eletto**, Corso Matteotti 44, **t** 0184 531 548 (*moderate*). A very pretty 19th-century hotel situated in the town centre, furnished with antiques and blessed with a welcoming little garden.

★★★**Lolli Palace**, Corso dell'Imperatrice 70, **t** 0184 531 496, *www.lollihotel.it* (*moderate*). A lovely little seafront hotel with a decent restaurant. The sea-facing rooms are large, bright and airy with great big bay windows and cute little balconies; they're all tastefully decorated in white and wood.

★★**Sole Mare**, Via Carli 23, **t** 0184 577 105, *www.solemarehotel.com* (*cheap*). A comfortable option with 8 rooms, popular with Italians.

Da Giannino, Corso Trento e Trieste 23, **t** 0184 504 014 (*very expensive*). Wonderful dishes based on fresh, natural ingredients, including the local speciality of *tagliolini al sugo di triglia* (wholewheat pasta with red mullet sauce), polenta with cheese and vegetable sauce, and pigeon with ginger. The wine list is excellent. *Closed Sun.*

Paolo e Barbara, Via Roma 47, **t** 0184 531 653 (*very expensive*). A very highly acclaimed restaurant serving inventive dishes based on Riviera traditions, including famous *gamberoni San Remo* flambéed in whisky. Book ahead. *Closed Weds and Fri.*

Bagatto, Via Matteotti 145, **t** 0184 531 925 (*expensive*). One of the brightest, most relaxed restaurants in San Remo, offering tempting *antipasti, risotti* and other dishes with sun-ripened vegetables, plus delicious seafood and lamb. *Closed Sun and July.*

Arma di Taggia ✉ 18011

La Conchiglia, Via Lungomare 33, **t** 0184 43169 (*expensive*). One of the most highly regarded restaurants on the Riviera, serving Ligurian delights based on seafood, local cheese and delicate olive oil – the prawn and white bean salad is superb. There's a very good set lunch. Reserve in advance. *Closed Weds except July and Aug, 2wks Jan and wks July.*

winter garden and the **Giardino Madonna della Ruota**, a 45-minute walk. On Via Bicknell, the **Museo Bicknell** (*t 0184 263 601; open Mon–Fri 9.30–1 and 1.30–4.45; closed first 2wks Aug*) contains some plaster casts of the curious Neolithic rock-engravings from the Valle delle Meraviglie (part of France since the Second World War), discovered by the Reverend Clarence Bicknell. This whole neighbourhood is packed with British hotels and villas.

San Remo

San Remo is the opulent queen of the Italian Riviera, her grand hotels and villas as beautiful and slightly out of date as antimacassars on an armchair. Yet even if the old girl isn't young, she's a corker with a Mae West twinkle in her eye. Other resorts may have more glamour, but few have more character.

Set on a huge, sheltered bay, San Remo was long a watering hole for a variety of drifting aristocrats, most famously Empress Maria Alexandrovna, the wife of Czar Alexander II. She played the Pied Piper to a sizeable Russian colony, including Tchaikovsky, who composed *Eugene Onegin* and his Fourth Symphony during his stay here in 1878. The duke of nonsense, Edward Lear, ended his lifelong travels in the Mediterranean here in 1888, as did the father of dynamite and famous prizes, Alfred Nobel, who died in 1896 in the **Villa Nobel**, on the eastern edge of town by the Parco Ormond (***t** 0183 704 304; guided tours 3 and 4 Sun Mar–June, Sept, Oct and Dec, Weds May, June and Sept; 8pm and 10pm Weds and Sun July and Aug; adm*).

Modern San Remo consists of three distinct parts: the shopping quarter, the dusty old town and the smart west end, where the grand hotels are situated. To get the full flavour make the *passeggiata* down the lovely, palm-lined **Corso dell'Imperatrice**; here, springing out of semi-tropical foliage, are the incongruous onion domes of a **Russian Orthodox church** (*open summer Tues, Thurs and Sat 9.30–12.30 and 4–7; winter 3–6.30*), a dainty jewel box built in the 1920s by the exiled nobility and containing the tombs of deposed members of the Royal House of Montenegro. This part of town reaches its zenith at the white, brightly lit, Liberty-style **casino**, still the lively heart of San Remo's social life, with its gaming rooms, roof-garden cabaret and celebrated restaurant with live orchestra (*open 10am–3am; roulette wheels in operation from 2pm; over-18s only; dress code for some rooms but jackets can be loaned; adm*).

West on Corso Matteotti lies the lively, commercial heart of San Remo. In February, the Corso's **Teatro Ariston** hosts the biggest event in Italian pop, the unabashedly tacky Festival della Canzone, a five-day lip-synch ritual of glitter and hype during which this once gloriously musical nation parades its current talents with all the confidence of the emperor in his new clothes. All year long, early risers can take in the intoxicating colour and scent of the **flower market** on Corso Garibaldi, just off Piazza Colombo – it's a working, wholesale market, but a fascinating one nonetheless.

The old town, **La Pigna**, is San Remo's 'casbah' – a tangled mesh of steep lanes and stairs weaving under archways and narrow tunnels, fortified around the year 1000 as a refuge against the Saracens. Get there via Piazza San Siro, site of the 12th-century but much-altered **Duomo di San Siro**, with an unusual black crucifix by an unknown sculptor and the Baroque **Oratorio dell'Immacolata Concezione**. The large covered food market (*open Tues–Sat 8.30–1*) is nearby on Piazza Eroi Sanremesi. From here you can wend your way up through the casbah to the **Giardini Regina Elena**, which is rather dull as a garden but has fantastic views of the town and harbour.

Standing majestic at the top of La Pigna is the 17th-century **Santuario Madonna della Costa** (*open daily Apr–Sept 9–12 and 3–6.30, Oct–Mar 9–12 and 3–5.30; regular buses from San Remo*). The madonna inside saved a local sailor from shipwreck, and he subsequently donated a gold coin to establish the shrine. On Ferragosto, 15 August, this event is celebrated with fireworks and a feast, in one of the Riviera's most appealing traditional festivals.

The panoramic **Corso degli Inglesi** begins at the casino and passes the old funicular that goes up to **Monte Bignone** (4,281ft), the highest peak in the amphitheatre of hills around San Remo. You can drive or take a bus part way to the top, past the **Ulivi Golf Club** (***t*** *0184 557 093*), for great views of the Riviera.

Around San Remo

San Remo has some interesting neighbours, all of them easily reached by buses from the train station. Just to the west, the quiet seaside resort of **Ospedaletti** is shaded by luxuriant pines, palms and eucalyptus; Katherine Mansfield lived here in the early 1900s. Its name comes from the Knights Hospitallers of Rhodes, who ran a pilgrims' hospice here in 1300. They also bestowed their name on the nearby hill town of **Coldirodi**, known for its **Rambaldi art gallery** (*open Thurs 10–12 but call ahead;* ***t*** *0184 531 942*), with a collection of great forgeries – of Veronese, Reni and Rembrandt – along with some originals.

On 23 February 1887 an earthquake turned **Bussana Vecchia** into a picturesque ruin and killed thousands; the survivors built a Bussana Nuova two kilometres closer to the sea. Though Bussana Vecchia no longer officially exists, it now has some arty inhabitants who have restored the interiors of the ruins and hooked them up with water, lights and phones. The quake knocked in the roof of the Baroque church (which was packed at the time for the Ash Wednesday service), but nearly all the parishioners escaped death by taking shelter in the side chapels; one survivor, Giovanni Torre detto Merlo, went on to invent the ice-cream cone in 1902. The church remains open to the sky; its stucco decorations sprout weeds, trees grow in the nave and apse, and cherubs smile down like broken dolls on a shelf.

Further inland, **Bajardo**, which is spread out over a conical hill against a backdrop of mountains and forests, was also devastated by the earthquake but was rebuilt on the same site. Don't miss the ruined church, with its 13th-century capitals carved roughly in the shape of Mongols' heads, some of whom are believed to have accompanied the Saracens to Liguria. Bajardo celebrates the Festival della Barca on Pentecost Sunday, when a large tree trunk topped by a smaller pine tree is erected in the middle of the piazza, around which the people slowly dance and sing a tale of tragic love from the year 1200, when the Count beheaded his daughter rather than let her marry against his will.

To the east, **Arma di Taggia** has one of the finest sandy beaches in the area, lying at the mouth of the Valle Argentina; inland, picturesque, medieval **Taggia** is the site of an antiques fair on the fourth Saturday and Sunday of every month. The **Convento di San Domenico** (*open Mon–Sat 9–12 and 3–5, summer until 6; donation requested*) contains fine paintings by members of the 15th-century Ligurian school; the monks introduced the olive trees that have made Taggia's fortune. Within its walls, noble palaces with coats of arms line the streets, and a remarkable, dog-leg 16-arched **medieval bridge** crosses the Argentina. Come on the third Sunday of July for the ancient Festival of Mary Magdalen – the latter once paid Taggia a call (or so they claim) and is remembered by members of her red-capped confraternity with an eerie Dance of Death performed by two men, one playing the role of 'the man' and the other the role of Mary, who dies and is brought back to life with a sprig of lavender.

There are a number of attractive hill villages above the Valle Argentina, the most intriguing of which is **Triora**, the Riviera's very own Salem, a fortified 15th-century village where, in 1588, during a famine, 13 women and girls were denounced as witches before the Inquisition; five died before their accusers themselves were excommunicated. The **Museo Etnografico e della Stregoneria** (***t*** *0184 94477; open Mon–Sat 2.30–6, Sun 10.30–12 and 2.30–6; adm*) tells the story. The **Collegiata** has a lovely Baptism of Jesus (1397) by Taddeo di Bartolo, and in summer you also can bungee jump here.

Imperia to Savona

Imperia divides the 'Riviera of Flowers' from the rockier, silvery 'Riviera of Olives'. Connoisseurs of olive oil rate Liguria's the best in Italy, although of course there are plenty of other regions ready to dispute this most slippery of crowns.

Imperia

In 1923 two towns, Porto Maurizio and Oneglia, were married by Mussolini to form a slightly schizophrenic provincial capital, Imperia. The bustling oil port (olive oil, that is) of Oneglia was the birthplace of the great Genoese Admiral Andrea Doria, while the old quarter of Porto Maurizio has most of Imperia's charm, with steep lanes and steps and a palatial hill, the Paraxio, though even here Imperia lacks the typical Riviera resort ambience.

The Porto Maurizio side of town has a **naval museum** at Piazza Duomo 11 (***t*** *0183 651 541; open summer Weds–Sat 9pm–11; winter Weds and Sat 3–7.30*), with ships' models and nautical instruments. Behind the train station in Oneglia, at Via Garessio 13, is the **Museo dell'Olivo** (***t*** *0183 295 762; open Weds–Mon 9–12 and 3–6*), dedicated to the history and practice of olive-growing. Imperia is also the base for exploring old villages in the hinterland, including **Dolcedo**, home to the most renowned olive groves in Liguria, with numerous *frantoii* (presses) that sell the local oil, as well as medieval bridges, one built by the Knights of St John in 1292. In another valley, further east, the main SS28 leads to pretty **Pontedassio**.

To the east of Imperia lie a string of popular resorts: **Diano Marina**, with its long beach and palms and the small **Museo Civico** (***t*** *0183 496 112; currently closed for restoration*), which contains items from a 1st-century BC Roman shipwreck; modern **San Bartolomeo al Mare**; and pretty **Cervo**, a curl of white, cream and pale yellow houses sweeping up from the sea, with a delightful, sunny, Moorish atmosphere. At the top of the curl stands the cream-pastry Baroque **Chiesa dei Corallini** ('coral fishers'), with its concave façade emblazoned with a stag, or *cervo* in Italian. Although it hosts a chamber music festival in July and August, Cervo has only three small hotels near its shingle beach.

Andora, next along the coast, consists of a marine quarter with a beach and, up in the Merula valley, a fortified hamlet, Castello Andora, reached by way of a medieval bridge, with a picturesque ruined castle, a tower-gate and the lovely 13th-century Romanesque-Gothic church of **SS. Giacomo e Filippo**. On the other side of Capo Mele ('Cape Apples') lies the attractive old fishing town of **Laigueglia**, which has a majestic Baroque church dating from 1754.

Alàssio and Albenga

The coastal road, the Via Aurelia, bucks inland to skirt above Alàssio, a long-standing resort with a fine beach. Old *palazzi* on its main street, pretty **Sant'Ambrogio** (1597) with its Romanesque campanile, and a defence tower recall the town before such things as holidays. Visiting celebrities, beginning with Hemingway, have left their autographs in ceramic plaques on the 'Muretto' ('little wall'), Alàssio's Hollywood Boulevard; in August there's even a 'Miss Muretto' beauty contest.

Between 15 June and 15 September you can take a boat to tiny **Isola Gallinara**, a kilometre and a half off the coast. Named after the wild hens that used to populate it, the island sheltered St Martin when he fled Arian persecution in the 4th century. For more than 1,000 years it was home to a powerful abbey, now in ruins; today it is a nature reserve, popular with skin-divers. Another pleasant outing from Alàssio is up to the 13th-century Benedictine church of **Santa Croce**, with one of the best views in the area. From here you can walk the Roman road down to Albenga.

East of Alàssio, **Albenga**, the Roman port of *Album Ingaunum*, remained prosperous through the Middle Ages, until its harbour shifted away with the course of the Cento river; nowadays the town stands a kilometre from the sea and grows asparagus in the old river bed. Its impressive collection of 13th-century towers, built during its days as a *comune*, stand like bridesmaids around the elegant campanile (1391) of the Romanesque **cathedral**. One (*c.* 1300) belongs to the Palazzo Vecchio del Comune and now houses the **Museo Civico Ingauno** (***t*** *0182 51215; open Tues–Sun summer 9.30–12.30 and 3.30–7.30, winter 10–12.30 and 2.30–6; adm*), which contains finds from Roman to medieval times, plus frescoes by Giovanni Canevasio. Admission includes Albenga's 5th-century **baptistry**. Early Christians were fond of difficult geometrical forms, and this is a minor *tour de force*, fitting a 10-sided exterior around an octagonal interior. The blue and white mosaics prefigure the mosaics of Ravenna; they depict 12 doves, symbols of the Apostles, circling the monogram of Christ.

North of the cathedral, on Via Episcopio, the bishop's palace with its exterior frescoes houses the **Museo Diocesano** (***t*** *0182 50288, open Tues–Sun 10–12 and 3–6; adm*), with 17th-century Flemish tapestries, paintings, reliquaries and illuminated manuscripts. The 13th-century **Loggia dei Quattro Canti**, nearby, marks the Roman town centre. On Piazza San Michele, the 14th-century **Palazzo Peloso Cepolla** ('Hairy Onion Palace') contains the **Museo Navale Romana** (***t*** *0182 51215; open Tues–Sun summer 9.30–12.30 and 3.30–7.30, winter 10–12.30 and 2.30–6; adm*), featuring amphorae and other items salvaged from a 1st-century BC Roman shipwreck discovered near the Isola Gallinara, plus blue and white 16th–18th-century pharmacy jars from Albisola.

Tourist Information

Imperia: Viale G. Matteotti 54/a, **t** 0183 660 140, *www.rivieradeifiori.it*
Cervo: Piazza Santa Caterina 2, **t** 0183 408 197.
Alassio: Piazza della Libertà 5, **t** 0182 647 027, *www.italianriviera.it*
Albenga: Viale Martiri della Libertà 1, **t** 0182 558 444.
Finale Ligure: Finalmarina, **t** 019 681 019.
Savona: Corso Italia 157r, **t** 019 840 2321.

Where to Stay and Eat

Imperia ✉ 18100

There are any number of indistinguishable 1- and 2-star establishments around Viale Matteotti in the port of Oneglia.

★★★★**Hotel Miramare**, Viale Matteotti 24, **t** 0183 667 120, *www.rrhotels.it* (*expensive*). A 19th-century villa with a garden, pool and private beach. The dining area has great views of the Duomo and the sea below.

★★★**Croce di Malta**, Via Scarincio 148, Porto Maurizio, **t** 0183 667 020, *www.hotelcrocedimalta.com* (*moderate*). A good comfortable, seaside hotel with a pretty breakfast terrace.

Lanterna Blù, Via Scarincio 32, Borgo Marina, Porto Maurizio, **t** 0183 63859 (*very expensive*). An excellent restaurant offering fine dishes using ingredients from two local farms; try the hot seafood *antipasti*. *Closed Weds.*

Ristorante Beppa, Calata Cuneo 24, Oneglia, **t** 0183 294 286 (*moderate*). Good fresh fish in a no-frills, no-fuss atmosphere opposite the fishing boats.

Alassio ✉ 17021

This is the biggest resort in the area.

★★★★**Grand Hotel Diana**, Via Garibaldi 110, **t** 0182 642 701 (*very expensive*). A fine hotel boasting its own beach, beach bar and beach restaurant, plus a heated indoor swimming pool and bike loan. The seafront rooms are large and have balconies (those without a sea view are much cheaper) and there's a small restaurant.

★★★**Beau Sejour**, Via Garibaldi 102, **t** 0182 640 303 (*expensive*). A hotel directly on the beach, with well-furnished rooms, a terrace and a garden. A good option for a longer stay. *Closed Oct–Mar.*

★★★**Milano**, Piazza Airaldi e Durante 11, **t** 0182 640 597 (*moderate*). An excellent hotel right on the beach. Bedrooms are well equipped, with balconies and fine sea views, and there's a very good restaurant serving Ligurian specialities.

★★**Bel Air**, Via Roma 40, **t** 0182 642 578 (*cheap*). A wonderful-value hotel with modern rooms and its own beach.

Monti e Mare, Via F. Giancardi 47, 2km from town, **t** 0182 643 036, *www.mmapartments.it* (*cheap*). Pretty, fully equipped flats sleeping up to 6 in a tranquil lush setting overlooking the sea, with friendly owners.

To the west and along the Cento, you can stroll through the scattered remains of Album Ingaunum – the old Roman road and tombs on the hill, the amphitheatre below, and the foundations of the city on the river banks. A short walk from here, along Viale Pontelungo, will take you to part of the ancient Via Aurelia and the impressive 13th-century, 495ft-long **Ponte Lungo**; apparently this only spanned the Cento for a few years before the river changed its course. Along the road, note the ruins of the 4th-century basilica of **San Vittore**, one of the oldest in Liguria.

The Paleolithic Grottoes of Toirano

Heading east from Albenga, **Ceriale** is a small seaside resort with a long beach lined with palms. **Borghetto Santo Spirito**, the next coastal town, is the junction (and bus pick-up point) for **Toirano**, a medieval village that seems spanking new next to the relics of its Middle Palaeolithic inhabitants (80,000 BC), who were discovered in the limestone cliffs just up the valley. These Cro-Magnons, like modern Italians, had

La Palma, Via Cavour 5, **t** 0182 640 314 (*very expensive*). A gourmet palace with 2 *menu degustazione*, one highlighting basil, totem herb of Liguria, and the other Provençal–Ligurian specialities, with an emphasis on seafood. Book ahead. *Closed Weds.*

La Cave, Passeggiata Italia 7, **t** 0182 640 693 (*expensive*). An atmospheric old restaurant in the heart of the old town, serving typical Ligurian dishes such as *troffie al pesto* and fish soups. *Closed Weds lunch.*

Garlenda ✉ 17033

★★★★**La Meridiana**, Via ai Castelli 11, **t** 0182 580 271 (*expensive–luxury*). A golfer's paradise next to the course, amid pretty olive groves, ancient oaks and vineyards. A member of the Relais et Châteaux group, it is in a contemporary building constructed with traditional stone walls and wooden ceilings, and furnished simply but attractively. The restaurant serves gourmet Franco-Italian dishes, including delicious breast of duck with caramelized pears.

Finale Ligure ✉ 17024

Hotels here cater mainly to families. If you arrive without a booking try the room-finding service, **t** 019 694 252 (*open June–Sept*).

★★★**Park Hotel Castello**, Via Caviglia 26, Finalmarina, **t** 019 691 320 (*moderate*). A hotel near the top of the town, with more personality than most and a pretty garden. It's one of the few that remain open all year.

★★★**Conte**, Via Genova 16, Finalmarina, **t** 019 680 234 (*moderate*). A characterful old establishment with a secluded garden in a lovely setting, old prints on the walls and period furniture in reception.

Torchi, Via dell'Annunziata, Finaleborgo, **t** 019 690 531 (*expensive*). A restaurant offering warm *antipasti*, herb-filled ravioli and a couple of meat dishes, as well as good fish dishes. *Closed Tues except Aug.*

Entertainment and Nightlife

In summer this is one of the liveliest areas on the Italian coast. Events include the **Musica nei Castelli di Liguria** classical music festival, held in castles of the region throughout the season. Details are available from local tourist offices.

Ceriale, just east of Albenga, has the only **aquapark** in the region, at Le Caravelle, Via Sant'Eugenio, **t** 0182 931 755 (*open June–Sept daily 10–7; July and Aug Weds and Thurs until 10pm; adm exp*).

Finale is a hotspot for nightowls, with plenty of **bars** lining the seafront, including Clipper, with an old-style atmosphere. Of the **nightclubs**, Caligola on Via Colombo plays mainly dance, and El Patio on Lungomare Italia provides less frantic music for a slightly older crowd; the **outdoor clubs**, Covo and Covo Nord Est, are the trendiest of all.

excellent taste, and chose as their abode the **Grotte di Toirano** (***t** 0182 98062; open daily Jan–Nov 9.30–12.30 and 2–5, until 5.30 in summer; adm*), three of the loveliest caves in the region, tarted up by Mother Nature with draperies of pastel-coloured stalactites. They seem to have had company: the largest cave, the Grotta della Bàsura ('witch's cave'), has a 'Bear Cemetery' full of bones accumulated over the course of thousands of years; a 'Corridor of Imprints', where human hand, foot and knee prints mingle with the imprints of bear claws, as if left over from a prehistoric boogie-woogie; and a 'Room of Mystery', where the inhabitants threw clay balls at the walls, perhaps just to see if they'd stick. The tour includes the Grotte di Santa Lucia, with a miraculous eye-curing spring.

Another medieval village nearby, **Balestrino**, is still defended by a picturesque Del Carretto **castle**; the same clan of lordlings built the castle up at **Castelvecchio di Rocca Barbena**, high on a crag, dating from the 11th century (but altered since) and encircled by the walled village, with magnificent views down the valley.

Loano to Noli

Loano is an attractive, palm-shaded town and resort, long a fief of the Doria; in their 16th-century **Palazzo Doria** (now the Municipio), you can see a rare 3rd-century AD mosaic pavement, and there are fine views from the Carmelite convent (1608). Another old seaside town and modern beach resort, **Pietra Ligure**, boasts the ruins of a Genoese fortress.

Finale Ligure is the big news here, a lively resort spread between Finale Marina and the medieval village of Finalborgo, two kilometres inland. Finale is pocked with caves filled with debris left by palaeolithic man and woman, most famously the **Grotta delle Arene Candide**. Although none are open to visitors, there are pottery, tools, tombs, Venuses and another huge bear skeleton on display in the **Museo Civico del Finale**, which is housed in the 14th-century cloister of Santa Caterina (***t** 0196 90020; open Tues–Sun summer 10–12 and 4–7, winter 9–12 and 2.30–7; adm*).

Finalborgo itself is spread under an impressive if derelict Del Carretto **castle** and the splendid 13th-century octagonal campanile of the **Basilica di San Biagio**. One of the prettiest excursions from Finalborgo is to make your way along the **Roman Via Julia Augusta**, which weaves through the Valle di Ponci to the northeast of Finale Pia, traversing five Roman bridges dating back to 124 AD; one, the **Ponte delle Fate**, is in perfect condition.

Although it never made the big time like Pisa or Genoa, **Noli** thrived as a small maritime republic from 1192 to 1796 – a fact that is celebrated every September in a regatta between its four neighbourhoods. Lying between Capo Noli and Monte Ursino, the town still has eight of its original 72 medieval towers. Its most important monument, however, is the 11th-century church of **San Paragorio**; the treasures contained here include a 13th-century bishop's throne and a 12th-century crucifix called a *Volto Santo* because its picture is said to be a true portrayal of Christ (it's similar to the more famous one in Lucca). There's a good beach here, and an even better one nearby at **Spotorno**.

Savona

The provincial capital, Savona is a working city rather than a resort, as well as one of Italy's busiest ports; if you have small children to amuse, hang around the docks and watch the aerial cable cars unload coal for the ironworks at San Giuseppe di Cairo. The harbour tower, the **Torre di Leon Pancaldo**, dates from the 13th century but was renamed to honour Magellan's unlucky pilot, born nearby. Other natives include the Della Rovere family, which gave the world two popes: Sixtus IV, who built the Sistine Chapel, and his nephew, Julius II, who hired Michelangelo to paint it. The two also left their mark on Savona. Giuliano da Sangallo designed the **Della Rovere palace** (now the law courts) for Julius; in the next street back the **cathedral** has a 6th-century Byzantine font, a sculpted choir and, in its cloister, Savona's own **Sistine Chapel** (*often locked*), built by Sixtus and redone *à la* rococo to house the marble tomb of his parents.

The best art here is tucked away in the **Museo del Tesoro** (***t** 019 825960; open Weds 4–5.30, Thurs 9.30–11.30, Sat 4–5*), including a fine Adoration of the Magi by the Hoogstraeten master, some 14th-century English alabaster statues, and items donated by the popes. There's more fine art nearby in the **Pinacoteca Civica** in Piazza Chabrol (*t 019 811 520; open Mon, Weds and Fri 8.30–1, Tues and Thurs 2–7, Sat 8.30–1 and 3.30-6.30, Sun 3.30–6.30, Sat and Sun also 8pm–11 in summer; adm*), containing Renaissance paintings by Donato de' Bardi and Giovanni Mazzone, Baroque works, and a modern collection donated by Savonese writer Milena Milani, which includes works by Picasso, De Chirico, Miró and Magritte.

The cathedral's medieval predecessor was demolished by the Genoese in 1528 to make way for the huge **Fortezza Priamàr**, built not to protect Savona but to put a damper on its ambition. It houses two museums – the **Museo Sandro Pertini** (*t 019 811 520; open Mon–Sat 8.30–1; adm*) of modern paintings donated by the former president (one of Italy's most revered for his probity); and the **Museo Archeologico** with Bronze Age to medieval finds (*t 019 822 708; open June–Sept Tues–Sat 10–12.30 and 4–6, Sun 4–6; Oct–May Tues–Sat 10–12.30 and 3–5, Sun 3–5; adm*).

From Savona, rail lines branch off for Turin and Milan. The first route passes the traditional boundary between the Alps and the Apennines at **Bocchetta di Cadibona** and **Millesimo** (to which there's a bus from Savona), a charming, fortified hill town where even the bridge, the **Gaietta**, has a watch tower. Now a popular excursion destination, it has a clutch of artisans' workshops and pastry shops selling delicious rum chocolates called *millesimini*.

Savona to Genoa

Although the bathing quality declines the closer you get to the big city, there are some tempting stopovers: **Albisola**, Liguria's ceramics centre, with plenty of shops and art along the shore, and the resorts of **Celle Ligure** and **Varazze**, the latter still partly surrounded by walls that incorporate the façade of the 10th-century church of **Sant'Ambrogio**. The rebuilt Sant'Ambrogio (1535), which has a lovely medieval campanile, contains some fine Renaissance and Baroque art. Further east, **Cogoleto**, according to one tradition, was the birthplace of Columbus; at least everyone in the village thinks so, and they've erected a statue to him in the piazza.

Pegli, which was a long-time weekend retreat of the Genoese, has been sucked into the metropolis. Green spaces here are provided by the parks of two grand villas. One of them belonged to the frescoed 16th-century **Villa Centurione Doria**, which now houses the **Museo di Storia Navale** (*t 010 696 9885; open Tues–Thurs 9–1, Fri and Sat 9–7, 1st and 3rd Sun of month 9–12.30; adm*), the future of which is currently in question since the opening of the Padiglione del Mare e della Navigazione (*see* p.173); it may or may not still have its famous portrait of Columbus and view of Genoa in 1481. The **Villa Durazzo-Pallavicini** (*entrance next to the train station; t 010 698 2776; open Tues–Sun Apr–Sept 9–6, Oct–Mar; adm*), in spite of the *autostrada* below, retains its romantic 19th-century garden with statuary, rotundas, temples and a pond. The villa itself now contains the **Museo Archeologico** (*t 010 698 1048; open Tues–Thurs 9–7, Fri and Sat 9–1, 2nd and 4th Sun of month 9–12.30*), containing prehistoric and Roman finds; the star exhibit is the unique palaeolithic burial of the 'Young Prince', discovered in the Grotta delle Arene Candide, with a seashell headdress and a dagger in his hand.

Genoa

There's always a tingling air of danger, excitement, unexpected fortune or sudden disaster in real port cities. The streets are enlivened by sailors, travellers and vagrants of all nationalities, and there's always the volatility of the sea itself, ready to make or break a fortune. Of the country's four ancient maritime republics (Venice, Amalfi and Pisa are the others), only Genoa (Genova) has retained its salty tang. It is Italy's largest port, and any possible scenographic effect it could have, enhanced by its beautiful location of steep hills piling into the sea, has been snuffed out by the more important affairs of the port. An elevated highway, huge docks, warehouses, stacks of containers and unloading facilites hog the shoreline, so that from many points you can't even see the sea. And behind the docks wind dishevelled alleys where you can still find a few piquant portside establishments that cater to men of indeterminate nationality, old pirates and tattooed ladies of the old school.

Counterbalancing this fragrant zone of stevedores is the Genoa that Petrarch called *La Superba* – the Superb City (or 'Proud City', as in one of the Seven Deadly Sins) of palaces, gardens and art; the city whose merchant fleet once reigned supreme from Spain as far as the southern Russian ports on the Black Sea; the city that gave the Spaniards Columbus but that in return cunningly controlled the contents of Spain's American silver fleets, becoming the New York City of the 16th century, flowing with money, capitalist before capitalism was invented, ruled by factions of bankers and oligarchs, populated by rugged individualists and entrepreneurs, and leaving a mark in the fashion industry with its sturdy blue cotton trousers the French called de Gênes.

Genoa is a neon-flashing, kinetic antidote to the Riviera's resortarama. Even its impossible topography is exciting: squeezed between mountains and sea, the city stretches out for a total of 30 kilometres – there are people here who commute to work by lift or by funicular, tunnels that bore under green parks in the very centre of the city, and apartment houses that hang over the hills so that the penthouse is at street level.

The old quarter, which is said to be the largest historic district in Europe, is a warren of alleys, or *caruggi* – miniature canyons under eight-storey palaces and tenements, streaming with banners of laundry. There are streets full of Renaissance palaces and Art Nouveau mansions, lots of art (although the Genoese produced relatively few painters or sculptors of note, they amassed fine collections), and one of the most amazing cemeteries on earth. And since the Columbus fair in 1992, Genoa has a new razzmatazz, concentrated in the redevelopment of the Porto Antico; today the city is looking especially well scrubbed and pretty, ready to assume its role as European Cultural Capital in 2004.

History

Genoa's destiny was shaped by its position, as not only the northernmost port on the Tyrrhenian Sea but one that is protected and isolated by a crescent of mountains. It was already a trading post in the 6th century BC, when the Phoenicians and Greeks came to barter with the Ligurians. Later the city was a stalwart outpost of the Roman Empire, and as such suffered the wrath of Hannibal's brother Mago; rebuilt after his sacking, it remained relatively happy and whole until the Lombards took it in 641, initiating a dark, troubled period. While the merchants of Amalfi, Pisa and Venice were creating their maritime republics in the 10th and 11th centuries, Genoa was still an agricultural backwater, far from the main highways of the Middle Ages, its traffic dominated by Pisa, its coasts prey to Saracen corsairs.

Adversity helped to form the Genoese character. Once it rallied to defeat the Saracens in the 12th century, the city began a dizzy rise to prominence, capturing Sardinia and Corsica, and joining the Normans to conquer Antioch, where Genoa established its first of many trading colonies in the Middle East. In 1155 the walls had to be enlarged as the city expanded and competition with Pisa grew into a battle of blows as well as of trade. The turning point for their duel for supremacy in the western Mediterranean came in 1284, when Genoa soundly pummelled Pisa into naval obscurity at the Battle of Meloria – a victory that Genoa followed up by defeating a more troublesome rival, Venice, at the Curzonali Islands in 1298.

By this time Genoa had merchant colonies stretching from the coast of North Africa to Syria, along the Black Sea and in Spain, where Genoese captains were the first to sail to the Canary Islands and the Azores. Genoa itself was the most densely populated city in Europe, as its patricians constructed their towering houses that seemed so 'superb' to visitors; its fame was so widespread that it served as a setting for a tale in the *Arabian Nights*, the only western city to be so honoured.

Genoa's first golden age was marred, however, as all subsequent ones would be, by civic strife and turmoil that were disgraceful even by Italian standards. The individualistic, stubborn Genoese refused to accept communal unity; nearly every enterprise was privately funded, down to the city's military expeditions. Genoa itself was divided into factions – nobles against one another, nobles against the mercantile classes, merchants against artisans – while the ruling families each dominated their own quarter, forming *alberghi*, or brotherhoods, of their partisans, and running their own prisons and armies.

In 1339 the popular classes, envying the superior government of Venice, won a victory by electing Genoa's first doge, Simone Boccanegra, the hero of Verdi's opera. Boccanegra raised taxes to support his habits: the nobles responded by inviting in the Visconti of Milan; Boccanegra was exiled to Pisa; the Visconti were thrown out; Boccanegra returned as Doge – Genoese civic history is an ignoble chronicle of one faction momentarily gaining the upper hand, and all the others doing everything to undermine it, even inviting in a foreign lord.

The Banco di San Giorgio

The real power in Genoa turned out to be a bank. When the city sank deep into debt during its prolonged war with Venice for the eastern Mediterranean (which ended in Genoa's traumatic defeat at Chioggia in 1380), its creditors – Genoa's oligarchs – formed a syndicate, the Banco di San Giorgio, to guarantee their increasingly precarious loans. This the bank did by gradually assuming control of

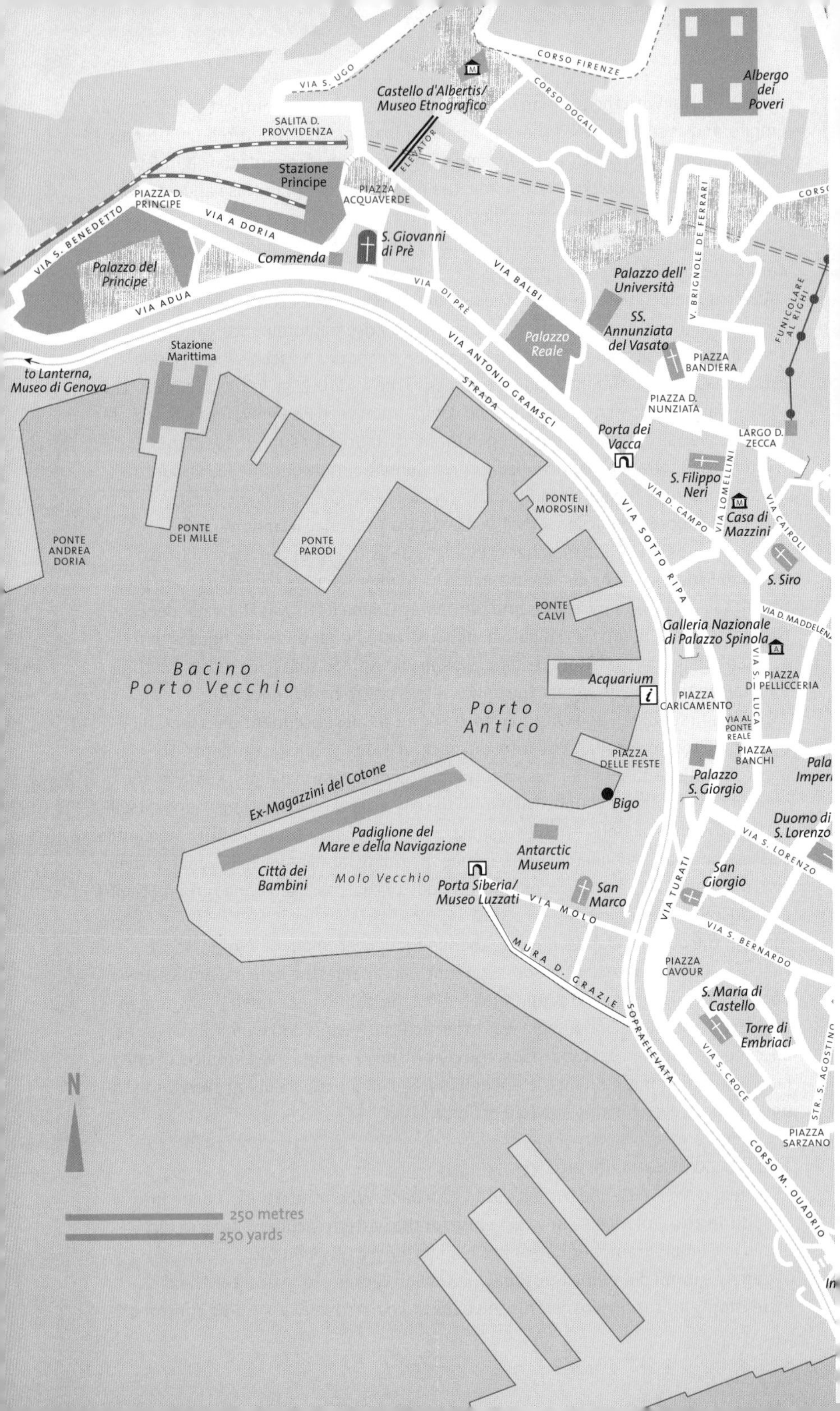

Castello d'Albertis/ Museo Etnografico
Albergo dei Poveri
CORSO FIRENZE
VIA S. UGO
CORSO DOGALI
SALITA D. PROVVIDENZA
ELEVATOR
Stazione Principe
PIAZZA ACQUAVERDE
PIAZZA D. PRINCIPE
VIA A DORIA
VIA S. BENEDETTO
S. Giovanni di Prè
Commenda
Palazzo del Principe
VIA ADUA
VIA DI PRÈ
VIA BALBI
V. BRIGNOLE DE FERRARI
FUNICOLARE AL RIGHI
Palazzo dell' Università
SS. Annunziata del Vasato
Palazzo Reale
PIAZZA BANDIERA
VIA ANTONIO GRAMSCI
STRADA
Stazione Marittima
to Lanterna, Museo di Genova
PIAZZA D. NUNZIATA
Porta dei Vacca
LARGO D. ZECCA
S. Filippo Neri
VIA D. CAMPO
VIA LOMELLINI
Casa di Mazzini
VIA CAIROLI
PONTE MOROSINI
PONTE DEI MILLE
PONTE ANDREA DORIA
PONTE PARODI
VIA SOTTO RIPA
S. Siro
PONTE CALVI
VIA D. MADDELENA
Galleria Nazionale di Palazzo Spinola
VIA S. LUCA
PIAZZA DI PELLICCERIA
Bacino Porto Vecchio
Acquarium
PIAZZA CARICAMENTO
Porto Antico
VIA AL PONTE REALE
PIAZZA BANCHI
PIAZZA DELLE FESTE
Palazzo S. Giorgio
Ex-Magazzini del Cotone
Bigo
Duomo di S. Lorenzo
VIA S. LORENZO
Padiglione del Mare e della Navigazione
Antarctic Museum
Città dei Bambini
Molo Vecchio
Porta Siberia/ Museo Luzzati
San Marco
VIA MOLO
San Giorgio
VIA TURATI
VIA S. BERNARDO
MURA D. GRAZIE
PIAZZA CAVOUR
S. Maria di Castello
Torre di Embriaci
SOPRAELEVATA
VIA S. CROCE
STR. S. AGOSTINO
PIAZZA SARZANO
CORSO M. QUADRIO
N
250 metres
250 yards

Genoa
to Santuario della Madonnetta
S. Bartol Degli A
To Casella
Strada delle Mura
Salita di San Rocchino
Via C. Cabella
Carbonara
Corso Firenze
Corso Paganini
Corso Magenta
Via Caffaro
Funicolare di S. Anna
Castelletto
Elevator
Villa Grüber
Corso Solferino
Piazza Manin
Corso Armellini
To Cimitero Staglieno
Via A. Bertani
Via G. Mameli
Via Palestro
S. Bartolomeo Degli Armeni
Galleria Garibaldi
Palazzo Bianco
Palazzo Tursi
Piazza D. Portello
Villa di Negro/ Museo d'Arte Orientale
Via Assarotti
Via Garibaldi
Palazzo Rosso
Palazzo Podestà
Palazzo Parodi-Lercari
Piazza Fontane Marose
Galleria N. Bixio
Palazzo Doria-Spinola
Piazza Corvetto
Via Peschiera
Salita Santa Caterina
Piazza Soziglia
Via Luccoli
Palazzo Spinola dei Marmi
Via Serra
Via Orefici
Campetto
Vico Casana
Case dei Doria
V. XXV Aprile
Via Roma
Galleria Mazzini
S. Marta
Piazza San Matteo
S. Matteo
Teatro Carlo Felice
Via XXII Ottobre
Viale IV Novembre
Via E. De Amicis
Via Galata
Palazzo Ducale
Accademia Ligustica di Belle Arti
Piazza Matteotti
Piazza De Ferrari
Via S Vincenzo
Via P. Soprana
Gesù
Via XX Settembre
S. Stefano
Stazione Brignole
Piazza D. Erbe
V. Dante
N.S. della Consolazione
Piazza Colombo
Piazza Verdi
S. D. Prione
S. Donato
Columbus House & cloister of Sant'Andrea
Ponte Monumentale
Mercato Orientale
Via Fiume
Vico del Fico
Porta Soprana
Piazza Dante
Via XX Settembre
V. Ravecca
Museo di S. Agostino
Corso Podestà
Via Frugoni
Via Cesarea
Via Cadorna
Galleria C. Colombo
Via Ravasco
Via Fieschi
Via Brigata Liguria
Via Ipp. D'Aste
Arco dei Caduti
Viale Brigata Bisagno
Piazza Carignano
Via Alessi
Via Corsica
Via Ruffini
Museo di Storia Naturale
To Fiera Internationale
Santa Maria Assunta Carignano
Via N. Bixio
To Museo d'Arte Contemporanea Villa Croce
Via A. Diaz

The Famous Insult to the Genoese

In 1316 occurred an event that became the subject of one of the most beloved anecdotes of Genoese history: a Genoese merchant, Megollo Lercari, the guest of the Eastern Emperor at Trebizond, disagreed with one of the emperor's pages, who slapped him across the face. The Emperor refused to let the Genoese strike back, though he apologized for the youth's behaviour. It was not enough. Seething, Megollo returned to Genoa, got up a private fleet, sailed back to Trebizond, and demanded the page. When the Emperor refused, the Genoese besieged the city, capturing whoever they could and chopping off their ears or noses. Finally his subjects' despair made the Emperor give in and he handed over the youth, and watched, first in trepidation and then in amazement, as Megollo made the page stoop over, then gave him a smart kick in the seat of the pants. Honour thus regained, the merchant returned the youth, lifted the siege and sailed back to Genoa.

the city's overseas territories, castles and towns, and even its treasury. Genoa from then on, for all practical purposes, was run as a business proposition – once, in 1421, when the bank was short of cash, it sold Livorno to Florence for a tidy sum. The Genoese never had any reason to identify with their government but, as Machiavelli noted, they were very loyal to their bank. Under its bankers, Genoa recovered from the defeat at Chioggia by transforming its economy from the mercantile to the financial sphere. The cinquecento found the city Europe's leading economic power, a position Genoa maintained thanks to the foresight of Andrea Doria (1468–1560), the 'Saviour of Genoa' and the greatest admiral of his day.

During the Wars of Italy between Charles V of Spain and Francis I of France, Doria drove Genoa's traditional French allies from the city and welcomed Spanish protection. He then wrote a new Republican constitution for the strife-torn city, institutionalizing the shared rule of the 28 *alberghi*. Charles V rewarded Doria with the title of Prince of Melfi, and he and other Genoese were given prominent posts throughout the Empire. Meanwhile the Banco di San Giorgio became fat and sleek financing the wars in the Low Countries for Charles V and Philip II, processing Spain's silver and taking over the international money market from Besançon and Antwerp: millions of *scudi* passed through Genoa every year. Doria was also Genoa's first great patron of the arts, introducing the Renaissance to the city that had formerly managed without it.

Nevertheless, after the crusty old admiral Genoa began to decline, Spain's bankruptcies came too frequently; Atlantic commerce overtook the old Mediterranean trade; and the Ottoman Empire gobbled up Genoa's last colonies in the east. The French besieged (1668), and the Austrians took briefly (1746), the city itself; Corsica, Genoa's last colony, revolted in 1768, and the Banco di San Giorgio could do nothing but sell it to France. By the 1815 Treaty of Vienna, Genoa and Liguria joined Piemonte, and at once the city became a hotbed of Italian unification sentiment, led by the conspiring philosopher of the Risorgimento, Giuseppe Mazzini, and such patriot luminaries as Nino Bixio, Goffredo Mameli, the Ruffini brothers and, of course, Garibaldi himself.

Getting There

By Air

Genoa's international **airport**, Cristoforo Colombo (**t** 010 601 5410), is 6km from the city in Sestri Ponente. It has direct flights to the UK and many European destinations, as well as to Italian cities. **AMT** shuttle buses to the airport depart every 30mins from Stazione Brignole, Stazione Principe and Piazza De Ferrari.

By Rail

Genoa has two main stations: **Principe**, in Piazza Acquaverde, just west of the centre, and **Brignole**, northeast. Principe generally handles trains from the north and France; Brignole takes trains from the south (though most long-distance trains call at both). City bus no.37 links the stations. For train info, call **t** 147 888 088.

By Coach

Intercity buses to the rest of the province and the Riviera, **t** 010 599 7414, depart from Piazza della Vittoria south of Stazione Brignole, or from Piazza Acquaverde in front of Stazione Principe.

By Sea

There are ferries to Rome (Civitavecchia), Sardinia, Sicily. Corsica and Tunisia from the **Stazione Marittima**, just south of the Stazione Principe; see *www.fun.informare.it*

Getting Around

Most of Genoa's points of interest are located within walking distance of one another in the centre, between the train stations, though public transport (by bus, train, metro, lift and *funivia*) is relatively cheap. **Tickets** must be purchased before embarking, either from tobacconists or the transport authority (AMT; **t** 010 558 2414) offices and information kiosks around town. Note that you can also use main line trains for getting around (to Nervi, for example); the AMT and FS sell convenient joint tickets.

Funiculars run from Piazza del Portello and Largo della Zecca to the city's upper residential quarters; the one served by the latter, **Righi**, has splendid views over the city and harbour. There's also a **lift** from Piazza Portello to the belvedere at Castelletto. **Taxis** are plentiful; for a radio taxi, call **t** 010 5966.

Genoa has an unnecessarily complicated street-numbering system: any commercial establishment has a red number, any residence a black or blue numberplate.

Tourist Information

Porto Antico: Palazzina Santa Maria B5, **t** 010 253 0671, *www. apt.genova.it*. There are branch offices at Stazione Principe, **t** 010 246 2633, at the airport, **t** 010 601 5247, at the Stazione Marittima). **t** 010 246 3686 (it opens to meet arriving ferries in summer).

Genoa's main cultural event is its annual **boat show**, held around the Fiera di Genova in early October. For a closer look at the sea itself, **tours of Genoa's port** are run by Cooperativa Battellieri, **t** 010 265 712, and Alimar, **t** 010 256 775; both depart from the aquarium.

Where to Stay

Genoa ✉ 16100

Very Expensive–Luxury

****__Bristol Palace__, Via XX Settembre 35, **t** 010 592 541, *www.hotelbristolpalace.com*.

Stazione Principe to Via Garibaldi

Both of Genoa's two main stations are lovely – the Stazione Principe could serve as the setting for a fancy-dress ball. In Piazza Acquaverde, travellers are greeted by a **statue of Columbus**, a view of the port, and the stately and now spruced-up Via Balbi. If you're catching a ferry, take Via Andrea Doria down to the Stazione Marittima, passing the **Palazzo del Principe Doria Pamphili** (*t 010 255 509; open Sat 3–6, Sun 10–3; adm exp; call for details of guided tours outside opening hours*) on the way, the only

An elegant choice near Brignole station and the Teatro Carlo Felice, with sumptuous antique furnishings, beautiful rooms and a pleasant English bar.

****Britannia, Via Balbi 38, t 010 26991, *www.britannia.it*. A smart and slick hotel, perhaps the best upper-range hotel near Principe station (although the black and red colour scheme is a little garish). The top-floor rooms have fantastic views.

Expensive

****Astor, Viale delle Palme 16, Nervi 16167, t 010 329 011, *www.astorhotel.it*. An elegant, fashionable hotel in an enchanting garden near the sea, far from the hurly-burly of the city centre.

Moderate

***Agnello d'Oro, Via Monachette 6, t 010 246 2084, *www.hotelagnellodoro.it*. A hotel in a 17th-century property of the Doria family, close to Via Balbi. Most of the old-fashioned charm is concentrated in the lobby, but bedrooms are very comfortable.

***La Capannina, Via T. Speri 7, t 010 317 131. An option out in the eastern residential zone, by the fishing port of Boccadasse, with a lovely breakfast terrace and simple, tranquil rooms (plus some much cheaper rooms in the *dipendenza*). In summer, the hotel's boat goes out on diving expeditions.

***Vittoria & Orlandini, Via Balbi 33, t 010 261 923, *www.vittoriaorlandini.com*. A charming, slightly eccentric hotel with an inner garden, comfortable bedrooms and a pretty breakfast room with views over the centre.

**Cairoli, Via Cairoli 14/4, t 010 246 1454, *www.hotelcairoligenova.com*. A very centrally located choice that seems more like a 3-star, with sparkling, modern bedrooms and a relaxed, friendly and personal atmosphere.

**Villa Bonera, Via Sarfatti 8, Nervi, t 010 372 6164. A very attractive hotel with 26 charming rooms in a 17th-century villa surrounded by an attractive garden.

Cheap

*Major, Vico Spada 4, t 010 247 4174. A hotel in a great location just inside the *centro storico*, close by Piazza de Ferrari and Via Garibaldi. The clean, modern rooms are a real bargain.

*Argentina, Via Gropallo 4/4, t 010 839 3722. One of a number of small hotels close to Brignole station, clean and friendly. If it's fully booked try *Carola, t 010 839 1340, in the same building.

Eating Out

Besides serving up various forms of pasta with *pesto*, the Genoese are fond of putting basil in dishes: *pansotti* are little ravioli filled with spinach and served in a walnut sauce; *torta pasqualina* is vegetables and hard-boiled eggs rolled in a pastry; *cima alla Genovese* is breast of veal filled with similar ingredients.

Very Expensive

Gran Gotto, Viale Brigata Bisagno (near Piazza della Vittoria), **t** 010 564 344. One of Genoa's classic eateries, first opened in 1939 and seemingly getting better all the time. You can feast on imaginative, delicately prepared seafood, such as turbot in radicchio sauce, warm seafood *antipasti*, famous *rognone* (kidney) dishes and delectable desserts. *Closed Sat lunch and Sun.*

'royal' palace built during the secular history of the Genoese Republic. The royal in this instance was Andrea Doria, whose decision in 1528 to commission Raphael's pupil, Perin del Vaga, to decorate the interior marked the beginining of Genoa's Renaissance.

Genoa's landmark lighthouse, the 384ft **Lanterna** (1543), is a 10-minute walk west around the port. Originally open fires on top welcomed home the city's fleet, who now rely on a beam of yellow light extending 33 kilometres. Climb the 375 stairs for spectacular views of the city and coast (*guided tours by appointment; **t** 010 246 5346*). The area around the Lanterna is currently being redeveloped, and the fortifications around the lighthouse are to house the new **Museo di Genova** from 2004. Back near

Expensive

Toe Drue, Via Corsi 441, **t** 010 650 0100. One of Genoa's most famous restaurants, situated in the working-class district of Sestri Ponente to the west of the city centre. 'Toe Drue' means 'hard table', and this is a fashionable restaurant that has kept the furnishings of the rustic inn that used to occupy the site. Many of the delightful and unusual Ligurian specialities on offer feature seafood. Book in advance. *Closed Sun and Sat lunch.*

Rina, Mura delle Grazie 3/r, **t** 010 246 6475. A restaurant that's been run by the same family since 1946 and was a favourite of one-time president Sandro Pertini. It's still popular with politicians and film stars, thanks to its simple, good food and unpretentious surroundings. Try the *branzino in salsa di asparagi* – to die for. Book ahead. *Closed Mon and Aug.*

Moderate

Archivolto Mongiardino, Archivolto Mongiardino 2, **t** 010 247 7610. A place in the maze of streets in the southern old city, offering a range of excellent seafood dishes. *Closed lunch, Sun and Mon.*

Ostaja Do Castello, Salita Santa Margherita del Castello, **t** 010 246 8980. A restaurant serving some of the best food in town, including good Genoese specialities. *Closed Tues.*

Trattoria Da Vittorio, Via Sottoripa 59, **t** 010 247 2927. A restaurant with an enticing display of fish and shellfish, where you can get half a lobster with *linguine*, wine and coffee for less than €20. You need to book a table in advance, or be prepared to wait. No credit cards.

Cheap

Da Maria, Vico Testadora 14/r, **t** 010 581 080. A wonderfully authentic trattoria just off Via XXV Aprile, near Piazza de Ferrari, serving up filling meals for next to nothing. *Closed Sat.*

Fulvio, Piazza delle Erbe, **t** 010 251 3886. A place serving excellent seafood, including grilled fish, kebabs and a locally famous *zuppa di pesce*, at outside tables in Genoa's medieval marketplace. Reserve a table in advance. *Closed Sun and Mon.*

La Santa, Vico Indoratori 1, **t** 010 247 2613. The ultimate bargain spot for seafood in the *centro storico*, including swordfish, *spaghetti alle vongole*, and a great risotto. *Closed Mon.*

Entertainment and Nightlife

For information about special events and what's on in general , have a look at the city's daily paper, *Il Secolo XIX*.

There's plenty of music Paganini's home town: the **Genoa Opera** in Teatro Carlo Felice in Piazza de Ferrari presents its main season from Jan to June; in summer it sponsors the prestigious **ballet festival** in the park in Nervi. For schedules and ticket information see *www.carlofelice.it* or call **t** 010 570 1650 (Tues–Fri 2–5).

Every 4 years, Genoa hosts the **regatta of the Ancient Maritime republics,** when it competes with Venice, Pisa and Amalfi

The main centre of **café and bar** life is around Via XX Settembre and in the medieval city, around Piazza delle Erbe. The **Britannia Pub** on Vico della Casana just off Piazza De Ferrari is very popular with both foreigners and Italians.

the Stazione Principe, **La Commenda** is Genoa's oldest hotel, where pilgrims lodged while awaiting ships to the Holy Land. In 1180 the Knights of St John built the next-door two-storey church, **San Giovanni di Pré**, with its spire-clustered campanile.

Via Balbi is lined with late-Renaissance palaces, including the yellow and red **Palazzo Reale** (***t** 010 271 0236; open Mon and Tues 8.15–1.45, Weds–Sun 8.15–7.15; adm exp*), with its lavish 18th-century ballroom and Hall of Mirrors, and paintings by Veronese and Guercino, plus a Crucifixion by Van Dyck, who spent several years in Genoa. Via Balbi gives on to Piazza della Nunziata, site of **SS. Annunziata del Vastato**, a church with a neoclassical façade of 1867 hiding a voluptuous Baroque interior.

From the next square, **Largo della Zecca**, you have several options: browsing through the district's antiques shops; a thrilling funicular ride to Righi, where you can dine at the top of the town; walking through the tunnel to Piazza Portello and taking the lift up to the Castelletto belvedere; or continuing round on Via Cairoli to Genoa's most famous street, **Via Garibaldi**. This, the former *Strada Nuova* laid out in 1558, was for centuries Genoa's 'Millionaires' Row', with lines of 16th- and 17th-century *palazzi*. Many have since been converted into banks and offices, but the street's unique and elegant character has been carefully maintained.

Two of the palaces hold important art collections: the **Palazzo Bianco** (***t** 010 557 3499; open Tues–Fri 9–7, Sat and Sun 10–7; adm*), at No.11, former residence of the Grimaldi, is no longer very white but has the most noteworthy collection in the city, with a good assortment of Italian paintings, including Filippino Lippi's *Madonna with Saints*, Pontormo's *Florentine Gentleman*, Veronese's *Crucifixion*, and an even more impressive collection of Flemish art. Among the latter are Gerhard David's sweetly domestic *Madonna della Pappa*, paintings by Cranach, Van der Goes, Van Dyck and Rubens (who worked for a while in Genoa); there is also a fine San Bonaventura by Zurbarán. The portrait of Andrea Doria by Jan Matsys is remarkable for its hands.

Across the street at No.18, the **Palazzo Rosso** (***t** 010 247 6351, same hrs as Palazzo Bianco*), retains some of its palatial fittings, as well as a picture gallery with a good collection of portraits by Van Dyck, Pisanello and Dürer, and works by Caravaggio and his follower Mattia Preti, Veronese and Guercino.

Opposite the Palazzo Rosso, the **Palazzo Tursi-Doria**, now Genoa's Municipio, will in 2004 form part of a Strada Nuova indoor–outdoor museum (***t** 010 557 2223*) that will make the city's most beautiful courtyard and treasures such as native son Paganini's violin and three letters from Columbus more accessible. You can enter the courtyard of No.7, the **Palazzo Podestà**, which has an elaborate fountain in the shape of a grotto. The façade of No.3, the 16th-century **Palazzo Parodi-Lercari**, was built by the descendants of Megollo Lercari, who recalled his 'Insult to the Genoese' at Trebizond (*see* p.166) with earless and noseless caryatids.

The Villa di Negro

Via Garibaldi ends at Piazza Marose, where you can see more palaces, including the 15th-century **Palazzo Spinola dei Marmi**, embellished with black and white bands and statues of the Spinola family. From here, Salita Santa Caterina leads into circular **Piazza Corvetto**, a major junction of city bus lines and the entrance to the **Villa di Negro**, an urban oasis that takes full advantage of Genoa's crazy topography, with streams, cascades, grottoes and walkways, culminating at the top in the **Museo di Arte Orientale** (***t** 010 542 285; open Tues–Fri 9–7, Sat and Sun 10–7; adm*), Italy's finest museum of Oriental art, with a lovely collection of statues, paintings and theatre masks, and an extraordinary set of Samurai helmets and armour, all well displayed in a sun-filled modern building.

At the corner of Piazza Corvetto and Via Roma, you can stop off for a historical coffee break at the early 19th-century **Caffè Mangini**. Via Roma continues down to tumultuous **Piazza de Ferrari**, which on one side is marked by the neoclassical **Teatro**

Carlo Felice, built in 1829, bombed in 1944, and then left until 1992, when it was restored for the Columbus year. Across the piazza is the giant, black and white mass of the 16th-century **Palazzo Ducale** (*see* p.172).

The Old City

From Piazza de Ferrari you can walk down into Old Genoa; the most picturesque route is down Via Dante to Piazza Dante and through the tall twin-towered **Porta Soprana**, which was built in 1155 as part of the Barbarossa walls designed to repel the Frederick of that name. Columbus' father was gatekeeper here; the explorer's 'boyhood home' is nearby, as are the ruins of the 12th-century cloister of **Sant'Andrea**, out on the lawn.

Within the Porta Soprana are the tall houses of medieval Genoa, sliced up by corridor-like *caruggi*; some of these are so narrow that they live in perpetual shade. Partly bombed in the Second World War and now mostly restored, leaning ever so gently towards the harbour below, many of the houses have white marble and black slate portals, which were permitted only to those families who performed a deed of benefit to the city; corners and wall niches are decorated with hundreds of shrines called *madonnette* ('little Madonnas').

The old town is for exploring. To see the highlights of the quarter, take Via Ravecca down from Porta Soprana to the 13th-century Gothic church of Sant'Agostino, its ruined cloisters converted into the well-designed **Museo di Sant'Agostino** (***t*** *010 251 1263; open Tues–Fri 9–7, Sat and Sun 10–7; adm*), which contains art and architectural fragments that were salvaged from demolished churches. One of the finest works is the fragment of the tomb of Margherita of Brabant, wife of Emperor Henry VII, sculpted in 1312 by Giovanni Pisano. Margherita died suddenly in Genoa while accompanying her husband to Rome for his coronation, and Henry, whom Dante and many others had hoped would be able to end the feud between Italy's Guelphs and Ghibellines, died in Siena two years later, many believe of sorrow; his last request was that his heart be taken to Genoa to be interred with his wife. There are also some Roman works, Romanesque sculpture, frescoes and the 14th-century wooden *Christ of the Caravana*.

From Sant'Agostino, the Stradone di Sant'Agostino leads to another good church, the 12th-century Romanesque **San Donato**, which boasts an exceptionally lovely octagonal campanile, portal and interior, combining a mix of ancient and medieval columns. Nearby Via San Bernardo, which is one of the few straight streets in the old city, was laid out by the Romans.

Their castle up the hill (take the Salita della Torre degli Embriaci to get there) provided the foundations for Genoa's most venerable church, the evocative **Santa Maria di Castello**, which incorporates some Roman columns and stones in its Romanesque structure. The crusaders used Santa Maria's complex as a hostel. The fairest of its art is the 15th-century fresco of the Annunciation in the cloister, while the strangest is the *Crocifisso Miracoloso*, kept in a chapel near the high altar – it is miraculous in that the Christ's beard is said to grow whenever Genoa is threatened with calamity.

Around Piazza Matteotti

An alternative entrance into the historic centre from Piazza de Ferrari is by way of the huge monumental stair once used for the Republic's most theatrical processions to Piazza Matteotti, dominated by the main façade of the grandiose **Palazzo Ducale**. Built in the 16th century, this was greatly altered in the following century to serve as the law courts. It stood neglected for years, but like the Carlo Felice theatre was restored for 1992; you can now walk through its attractive courtyards, sample its restaurants, bars and shops, and visit its exhibitions (*call **t** 010 557 4004 for times of guided tours of monumental rooms, tower, chapel and prison*). Sharing the square is the Baroque church of the **Gesù**, designed in the 1600s by Jesuit Giuseppe Valeriani. The interior is all lavish stuccoes, frescoes and *trompe l'œil* stage effects that highlight its frothy treasures: a Circumcision and St Ignatius Exorcising the Devil by Rubens, and an Assumption by 'il Divino' Guido Reni.

Just off the square is Genoa's jaunty black-and-white-striped **Duomo di San Lorenzo**, begun in the 12th century and modified several times; the façade was last restored in 1934. Odds and ends from the ages embellish the exterior: two kindly 19th-century lions by the steps, and a carving of St Lawrence toasting on his grill above the central of three French Gothic portals. On the north side is a pretty 12th-century **portal of San Giovanni**; on the south are Hellenistic sarcophagi, another Romanesque portal and a 15th-century tomb. The rather morose interior also wears jailbird stripes. The first chapel on the right contains a good marble Crucifixion of 1443, and a British shell fired from the sea 500 years later that hit the chapel but miraculously failed to explode. On the left, note the sumptuous Renaissance **Cappella di San Giovanni Battista**, with fine sculptures and marble decorations, and a 13th-century sarcophagus that once held the Baptist's relics.

The well-arranged **Museo del Tesoro** (***t** 010 247 1831; guided tours Mon and Sat 9–12 and 3–5.30; adm*) in the vaults to the left of the nave contains a number of genuine treasures acquired during the heyday of Genoa's mercantile empire: a crystal plate said to have been part of the dinner service of the Last Supper, the blue chalcedony dish on which John the Baptist's head was supposedly served to Salome, an 11th-century arm reliquary of St Anne, the golden, jewel-studded Byzantine Zaccaria Cross, and the elaborate 15th-century silver reliquary of John the Baptist. In 2001, after a long restoration, the mid 12th-century cloister of the Cannons of San Lorenzo in Via Tommaso Reggio 20 opened as the **Museo Diocesano** (***t** 010 254 1250; open Mon–Fri 9–12, Sat and Sun 9–12 and 3–6; adm*), with an important collection of sacred Genoese art, including two altarpieces by Gregorio de Ferrari.

The Salita del Fonaco follows the back of the Palazzo Ducale, then veers off to the right to reach **Piazza San Matteo**, a beautiful little square that's completely clothed in the black and white bands of illustrious civic benefactors – it's no wonder, for this was the public foyer of the Doria family, encompassed by their *palazzi* and their 12th-century church of **San Matteo**, inscribed with their great deeds and adorned with a charming early 14th-century cloister. Andrea Doria's palace was No.17 on the square, while No.14, belonging to Branca Doria, has a portal guarded by Genoa's patron St George.

Between Via San Lorenzo and Via Garibaldi, and the Porto Antico

This northern section of the historic centre, which was built mostly during the Renaissance, has survived somewhat better than the district around Porta Soprana, and has, amidst its monuments, a number of shops, bars, restaurants and cafés. From Piazza San Matteo it's a short walk to the **Campetto**, a lovely square adorned with the ornate 16th-century **Palazzo Imperiale**, now **Museo Fabrorum della Filigrana** (***t*** *010 247 3536; open Tues–Sat 9–6; free*) dedicated to gold, silver and filigree work. In nearby Piazza Soziglia you can take a break at the oldest coffeehouses in Genoa, **Kainguti**, at No.98/r, or **Romanegro**, at No.74/r, both founded in the early 1800s.

From Piazza Soziglia and the Campetto, pretty Via degli Orefici meanders down to the most important intersection of old Genoa, **Piazza Banchi**, with its Renaissance Loggia dei Mercanti. From here Via Ponte Reale descends to the portside **Piazza Caricamento**, which is lined with the medieval arcades and shops of Via Sottoripa and dominated by the gaudily decorated **Palazzo San Giorgio**. This was originally built in 1260 for the Capitani del Popolo but was taken over in 1408 by the Banco di San Giorgio in order that the shrewd bankers could scrutinize all the comings and goings. It's now occupied by the Harbour Board, but you can ask the guard to show you the rooms that have been refurbished in the 13th-century style.

Seawards, on the other side of the *Sopraelevata* highway from Piazza Caricamento, the whole of the old quay or **Porto Antico** was the showcase for the 1992 celebrations; it is home to the **Museo Nazionale dell'Antartide** (***t*** *010 254 3690; open Tues–Sat 9.45–6.15, Sun 10–7 or June–Sept 2–10; adm*), dedicated to the Antarctic; to Italy's largest cinema complex; to the **Citta dei Bambini** (***t*** *010 247 572; open daily June–3rd wk Sept 11.30–6.15; 2nd wk Oct–May 10–4.45; adm*), the *ne plus ultra* of playgrounds, full of climbing frames and giant plastic insects, as well as a building site where kids can dress up in hard hats and overalls and push around plastic wheelbarrows full of sand; and to Europe's largest **aquarium** (***t*** *010 234 5678; open Mon–Weds 9.30–6, Thurs 9.30–8.30, Sat and Sun 9.30–7; July and Aug 9am–9.30pm; adm exp*), housed in a converted ship and home to seals, dolphins, sharks, penguins and reconstructed coral reefs (it's Italy's third most popular 'museum' in terms of visitor numbers).

This is also where you'll find the **Gran Bigo**, or 'Great Crane', designed by Renzo Piano and towering over the port; a panoramic, revolving lift goes to the top, from which there are superb views (*adm*). Finally, the **Padiglione del Mare e della Navigazione** (***t*** *010 24 3678; open Mon–Fri 10.30–5.30, Sat and Sun 10.30–6; longer hrs in summer; adm exp*) displays artefacts from 16th- and 17th-century ships, and contains a reconstruction of a medieval shipyard.

Returning to the old city, **Via San Luca**, the main street passing through Piazza Banchi, used to be the principal thoroughfare of medieval Genoa and, in its day, was the home turf of another prominent Genoese family, the Spinola. The latter donated one of their palaces, located just off Via San Luca in little Piazza di Pellicceria and boasting 16th–18th-century décor and paintings, to provide a home for the **Galleria Nazionale di Palazzo Spinola** (***t*** *010 270 5300; open Tues–Sat 8.30–7.30, Sun 1–8; adm*). The paintings, which are still arranged as they would be in a private residence, include Antonello da Messina's sad and beautiful *Ecce Homo*, Joos Van Cleve's magnificent *Adoration of the Magi*, works by Van Dyck (*Portrait of a Child* and the *Four Evangelists*), and a statue of Justice, another fragment of Giovanni Pisano's tomb of Margherita di Brabante.

A little further to the north, back towards Largo Zecca, stands one of the chief shrines of 19th-century Italian history, the **Casa Mazzini**, at Via Lomellini 11, where the romantic prophet of Italian unification, Giuseppe Mazzini, was born in 1805. It now houses Genoa's **Museo del Risorgimento** (*t 010 246 5843; open Tues–Fri 9–1, Sat 10–7; adm*), with a collection centred on relics of Mazzini himself.

East Genoa

East of the Piazza de Ferrari runs arcaded **Via XX Settembre**, the main thoroughfare of 19th-century Genoa, adorned here and there with Liberty-style touches. This is still the city's main shopping street, and it and the area around Stazione Brignole make up a lively neighbourhood, aglow with neon. Via XX Settembre is traversed by the Ponte Monumentale, which carries the Corso A. Podesta overhead. Next to the bridge is a lane leading up to another of Genoa's striped medieval churches, **Santo Stefano**, which contains a Martyrdom of St Stephen by a less flamboyant than usual Giulio Romano. Beyond the bridge, the avenue continues to the large Piazza della Vittoria, a Fascist-era square presided over by a war memorial arch of 1931.

The Hills and Staglieno Cemetery

Some of the loveliest bits of Genoa are to be found up in the surrounding hills. The **Circonvallazione a Monte** is a scenic route that skirts the slopes, followed by city bus no.33 from Stazione Brignole or Piazza Manin. Not far from Piazza Manin, the church of **San Bartolomeo degli Armeni** in Corso Armellini houses Genoa's holiest relic, the *Santo Volto*, said to be the oldest true portrait of Jesus, painted on a piece of linen recently dated by scientists to Roman imperial times. The hill route continues east, passing the pretty English gardens of the **Villa Grüber**, then the imposing medieval **Castello d'Albertis**, rebuilt in the 19th century and home to the **Museo Etnografico** (*due to reopen in 2004*) with items from the Americas, Oceania, New Guinea and southeast Asia; it can also be reached by lift from Piazza Acquaverde.

Just over the mountains, along the Torrente Bisagno, lies the remarkable **Cimitero di Staglieno** (*open daily 8–5; bus no.34 from Piazza Acquaverde or Piazza Corvetto*). Founded in 1844, the cemetery covers 160 hectares, and even has its own internal bus system. The Genoese have a reputation for being tight-fisted, but when it comes to post-mortem extravagance they have few peers: Staglieno is a veritable Babylon of the dead, with miniature cathedrals, Romanesque chapels, Egyptian temples and Art Nouveau palaces and statuary, creating a fantastic, often surreal ensemble. In the centre of the hills, Genoa's revolutionary idealist of the Risorgimento, Giuseppe Mazzini, is buried in a simple tomb behind two massive Doric columns, surrounded by laudatory inscriptions by Tolstoy, Lloyd George, D'Annunzio and others. After a life of plots and exile, Mazzini died in semi-exile in Pisa, hiding under the assumed name of American abolitionist John Brown. Mrs Oscar Wilde is buried in the Protestant section.

Around Genoa

Just to the east of Genoa, **Nervi**, one of the oldest resorts on the Riviera, has been incorporated into the metropolis (it's linked by bus no.17 from Piazza de Ferrari). Two of the town's oldest Genoese villas have been converted to museums: the **Galleria d'Arte Moderna** in the Villa Serra Gropallo at Via Capolungo 3 has a large collection of 19th- and 20th-century Italian art (***t** 010 557 4739; call for opening hours*) and a pretty English park. The other, the **Museo Giannettino Luxoro** (***t** 010 322 673; open Tues–Fri 9–1, Sat 10–1; adm*), is further east in one of the Riviera's loveliest parks, at Viale Mafalda di Savoia 3. It, too, has a modern art collection, but it's most noteworthy for its decorative arts: clocks (some of the first luminous timepieces), furniture, fabrics and lace, and paintings by Alessandro Magnasco. Nervi also has a beautiful coastal walk, the **Passeggiata Anita Garibaldi**, named after Garibaldi's heroic wife, which takes in enticing views of Monte Portofino.

There are also two popular excursions into the hinterland from Genoa: to **Casella**, a small mountain resort reached in an hour by a train pulled by a 1924 electric locomotive (***t** 010 837321; every 2hrs from Piazza Manin*) and **Torriglia** (reached by bus, or by car on the SS45 towards Piacenza), a small resort offering skiing in winter and pretty walks in summer, with an impressive if derelict medieval castle.

Riviera di Levante

Recco to Sestri Levante

East of Genoa, the coast, fairly tame up to this point, becomes a creature of high drama and romance. The beaches aren't as prominent, nor the climate quite as mild, but from the Monte di Portofino to the once nearly inaccessible villages of the Cinque Terre, the mountains and sea tussle and tumble in a voluptuous chaos of azure, turquoise and piney green. Against these deep-coloured coves, cliffs and inlets rise the villages of weathered pastels and ochres and villas under the palms, gazing out over bobbing fleets of fishing craft, sailing boats and sleek white yachts.

Recco and Camogli

Of all the nubs and notches in the Italian coast, one of the best loved comes into view as you leave Nervi: the squarish promontory of Monte di Portofino and Golfo Paradiso. **Recco**,the first town, was bombed to bits during the war, but has come back to life as a gourmet mecca, thanks to its legendary cheese *focaccia* and fine restaurants. In the green hills above Recco, the main village, **Uscio**, manufactures campanile clocks and has a great climate, and one of Italy's oldest health farms to go with it.

The bombers spared picturesque **Camogli**, tucked under the promontory on its piney slope. This is a serious nautical town; its renowned republican fleet fought with Napoleon, and its fishing and merchant vessels were prominent along the Riviera in the 1800s; it still has a school training Italy's merchant marines. Its name derives from *Casa Mogli* ('home of wives') – the menfolk were almost always at sea. The port, piled high with tall, faded houses, hosts the famous Sagra del Pesce, with spectacular fireworks on the second Saturday in May, followed on Sunday by a fish fry in Italy's largest pan (13ft across), during which thousands of sardines are distributed free to all comers – a display of generosity and abundance that carries with it the hope that the sea will provide the same in the coming year.

A small promontory separates Camogli's little pebble beach from its fishing port. Near here, the **Castello della Dragonara**, built against the Saracens, is undergoing restoration to become a multimedia centre. Camogli recalls its proud history in its **maritime museum** at Via Gio Bono Ferrari 41 (***t** 0185 729 049; open Mon, Thurs and Fri 9–12, Weds, Sat and Sun 9–11.45*), which has an array of ship's models, more than 100 'ships' portraits', nautical instruments, and diaries recalling the town's thrilling days as a rough-and-tumble sea power. The archaeological section contains artefacts from, and a reconstruction of, an Iron Age settlement discovered nearby

The Parco Naturale di Portofino and San Fruttuoso

After Camogli, the road winds up inland to Ruta, where you can can continue by car to the church of **San Rocco** or to **Portfino Vetta**, an hour's walk from the summit of Monte di Portofino (2,001ft), which has views as far as Elba. But to take in the best of this enchanting corner of the Gulf of Paradise, the **Parco Naturale di Portofino**, you have to go by sea (*see* p.180) or by foot. From San Rocco it's a very strenuous but gorgeous three-hour hike to the isolated fishing village of **San Fruttuoso**. A branch of the path descends to **Punta Chiappa**, a rocky toe in the sea, famous for the changing colours of the water.

San Fruttuoso, surrounded by a lush growth of palms and olives, is named after its **abbey**, founded in 711 by the Bishop of Tarragona, who fled the Moors in Spain, with the relics of St Fruttuosus in his grip. The abbey came under the protection of the Doria, and in the 16th century Andrea Doria built the powerful **Torre dei Doria** to defend it from the Turkish corsairs, employed by the King of France. In 1981 the Dorias donated the abbey and surrounding land to the FAI, the Italian National Trust, and now you can stroll through the abbey, and the pretty white 11th-century church with its Byzantine cupola and tiny cloister (***t** 0185 772 703; open Mar and Apr Tues–Sun 10–4; May Tues–Sun 10–6; June–Sept daily 10–6; Oct Tues 10–4; Dec–Feb Sun and hols 10–4, adm*). Another sight, at least for skin-divers or trippers in glass-bottomed boats, is the bronze **Cristo degli Abissi** eight fathoms under the sea, a memorial set up in 1954 to those lost at sea and protector of all who work underwater. The sea here, among the most pristine in Italy, is part of a 'whale sanctuary' that extends along the coasts of Tuscany, Corsica and Sardinia; this is the one corner of the Mediterranean where you have a good chance of spotting one of the giants.

Santa Margherita Ligure

Santa Margherita, with its beautiful harbour, beaches and mild climate, was a fashionable 19th-century winter hideaway among the British; now 'Santa' becomes more fashionable by the year in summer among Italians. Near the **Basilica di Santa**

Margherita, a rococo extravaganza with Italian and Flemish art that gave the town its name, you can wander through the luxuriant **Parco di Villa Durazzo,** complete with allegorical statues, and visit the big square villa itself, built just after 1560 and decorated with architectural frescoes and stuccoes, Murano chandeliers, and tapestries (***t** 0185 293135; villa open Tues–Sun summer 9.30–6.30, until 4.30 in winter, adm; park open daily summer 9–7, until 5 in winter*).

Just outside the town, towards Portofino, the 14th-century **Abbazia della Cervara** and its Italian gardens, a private residence in the 1930s, has recently undergone a long and loving restoration (***t** 800 652 110; open for guided tours 1st and 3rd Sun of month 10, 11 and 12*). Over the centuries it hosted many passing celebrities, including King François I of France, imprisoned here in 1525 after the Battle of Pavia.

Portofino

At the end of the Second World War, a Nazi officer was ordered to blow Portofino and all its munitions to bits, but an elderly German noblewoman talked him into disobeying. She deserves a statue. One of Italy's most romantic nooks, Portofino has the stunning looks and seclusion that have long made it a favourite hideaway among the yachting set and paparazzi-shy celebrities. This exclusiveness still exists to a certain extent – although Portofino was linked to the rest of the Riviera by the construction of a narrow cliffside road, no new development was allowed to ensue.

Yet though there are only a handful of hotels, Portofino's seclusion vanishes every weekend and every day in summertime, when thousands of trippers pour into people-watch in the portside bars of the *piazzetta* or to take a stroll up into in the cyprus-lined hills. In the evening, however, the yachties and residents descend once again and reclaim Portofino as their own.

Portofino's name is derived from the Roman *Portus Delphini*, which had a *mithraeum* (dedicated to the Persian god Mithras, a favourite of Roman soldiers) on its isthmus. This is now the site of the church of **San Giorgio**, which was rebuilt after war damage in 1950 but still housing the relics of the now de-sainted George; as often as not there's a cat snoozing under the altar. Further up, **Castello di San Giorgio**, which was built in the 1500s as a defence against the Turks, affords enchanting views of the little port (*open Weds–Mon 10–6 , until 5 in winter; adm*); from here you can continue to the Punta del Capo and the **Faro**, the old lighthouse, taking in magnificent views of the gulf of Tigullio.

The other thing to do while you're in Portofino is to find a table at one of the two drinking holes that have long competed for the biggest celebrities: **La Gritta American Bar** and **Scafandro American Bar** – both are elegant, glamorous, studiously laid-back and *very* expensive.

Rapallo and Inland

Tucked in the innermost corner of the gulf of Tigullio, Rapallo is the best-known resort on the Riviera di Levante after Portofino, counting among its blessings certain things that Portofino lacks: affordable hotels, a good beach, an 18-hole golf course, and indoor pool and a riding stables. This was the longtime home of Max Beerbohm,

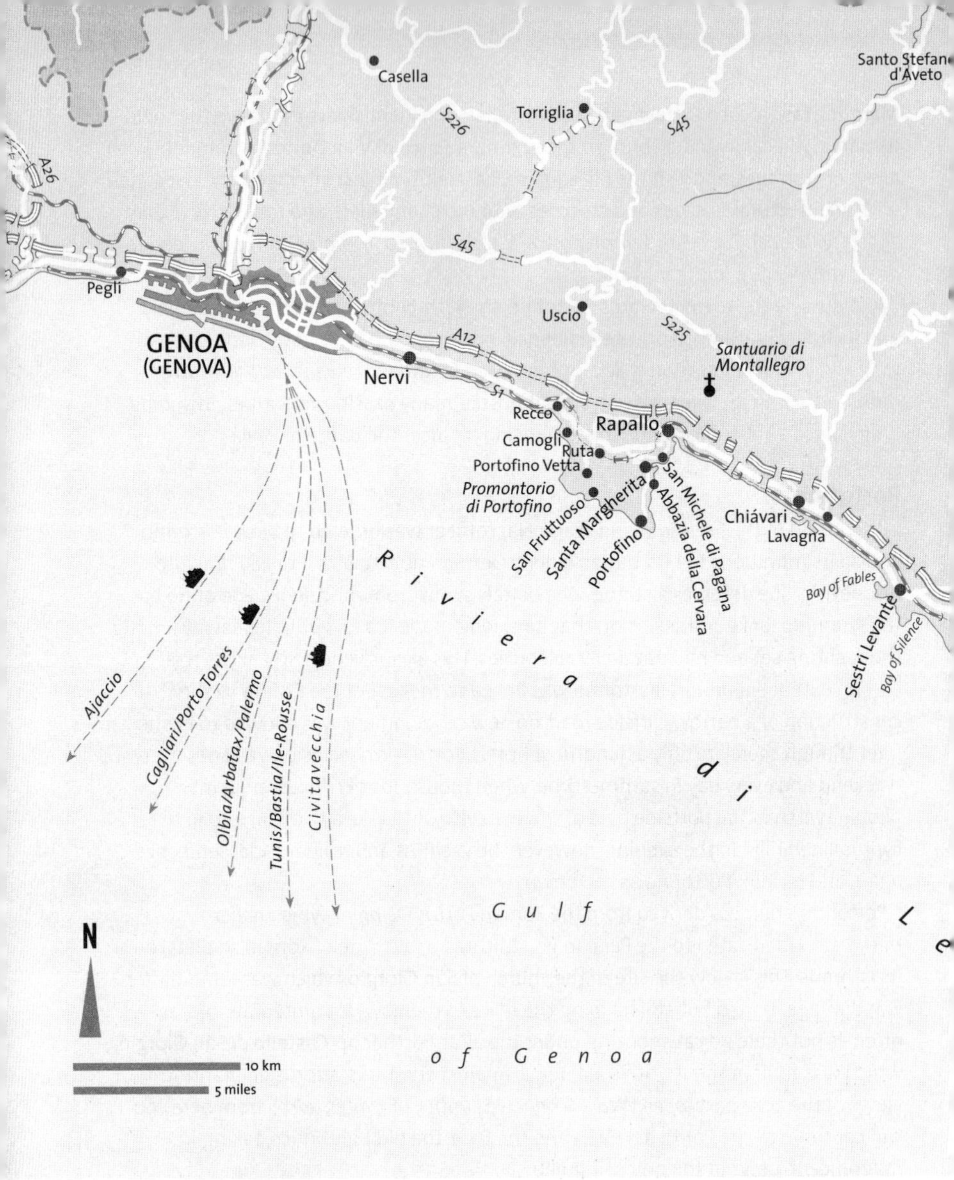

who lived in the Villino Chiaro and attracted a literary circle; it is also a venue for conferences – at the **Villa Spinola**, Italy and Yugoslavia signed the Treaty of Rapallo in 1920. The latter is on the Santa Margherita road, not far from **San Michele di Pagana**, a seaside hamlet with firework festivals in July and September, and a parish church containing an excellent Crucifixion by Van Dyck and a Nativity by Luca Giordano.

In Rapallo itself, the **Castello del Mare**, which literally soaks its feet in the port, hosts changing exhibitions. Further along the shore, eight rooms in the Villa Tigullio by the Parco Casale have been arranged as the **Museo del Merletto** (***t*** *0185 63305; open Tues, Weds and Fri 3–6.45, Thurs 9.30–12.30 but call ahead to check; adm*), dedicated to the

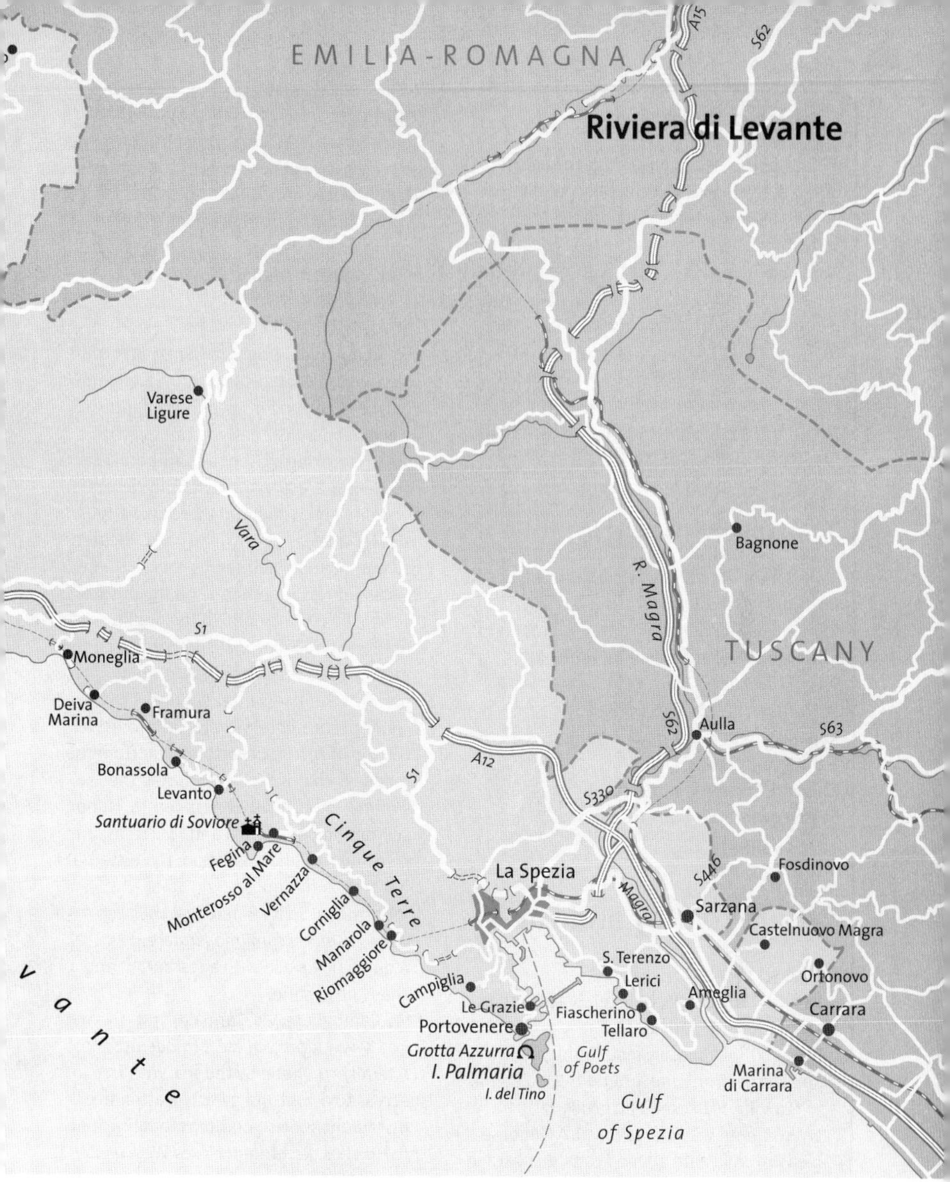

town's old craft of bobbin lace, with pieces going back to the 16th century. Rapallo's **funivia** (***t*** *0185 273444; daily Mar–Oct 8–12.30 and 2–sunset, Nov–Feb 8.30–12.30 and 2–5*) takes in spectacular views of the coast as it climbs 7,707ft to the 16th-century **Santuario di Montallegro**, built where the Virgin appeared to a farmer, leaving behind a Byzantine icon miraculously flown in from Dalmatia. Behind its neo-Gothic façade, look for the pala of the Pietà by Luca Cambiaso and hundreds of ex-votos.

From Montallegro, it's about an hour's drive up a winding road to **Santo Stefano d'Aveto**, up in the Ligurian Apennines under the 13th-century **Castello Malaspina**; in winter locals head up here for a taste of snow and skiing at 3,300ft.

Getting Around

The Genoa–Pisa **railway** hugs the coastline, but in many places you can only get glimpses of the scenery between the tunnels.

The most scenic road is the old coastal Via Aurelia (SS1), which is also the route used by most of the **buses**.

Camogli, San Fruttuoso, Portofino, Santa Margherita and Rapallo are linked by **boat** services run by the Battellieri del Golfo Paradiso, Via Scalo 2, **t** 0185 772 091; in summer they do jaunts as far as Portovenere, for lovely sea views of the Cinque Terre.

Tourist Information

All the tourist offices below share a website, *www.apttigullio.liguria.it*

Camogli: Via XX Settembre 33, **t** 0185 771 066.

S. Margherita Ligure: Via XXV Aprile 2/b, **t** 0185 287 485.

Portofino: Via Roma 35, **t** 0185 269 024.

Rapallo: Lungomare Vittorio Veneto, **t** 0185 230 346.

Chiávari: Corso Assarotti 1, **t** 0185 325 198.

Sestri Levante: Piazza S. Antonio 10, **t** 0185 457 011.

Where to Stay and Eat

Recco ✉ 16036

Besides *focaccia*, Recco is celebrated for its *trofie* with *pesto* and *pansotti*.

For good, inexpensive restaurants, look along the seafront and around the Via Roma.

****La Villa**, Via Roma 274, **t** 0185 720 779, www.*manuelina.it* (*expensive*). A Genoese pleasure villa with all mod cons, in a garden with a pool. Its older restaurant, the celebrated **Manuelina**, is a good place to try wonderful *trofie* with *pesto*, and seafood in a variety of styles for *secondo*. *Closed Weds.*

***Da-ö Vittorió**, Via Roma 160, **t** 0185 74029, *www.daovittorio.it* (*expensive*). A renowned restaurant dating back more than a century, with 20 recently added and comfortable bedrooms. The specialities of the kitchen include an utterly superb *minestrone di verdura alla Genovese* and *trofie al pesto*. *Restaurant closed Thurs.*

Vitturin, Via dei Giustiniani 50, **t** 0185 720 225 (*moderate*). A restaurant that's been owned by successive generations of the same family since 1860. Nibble on cheese *focaccia* while choosing from the market-based menu, which features good lamb and fish, and prawns in cognac. *Closed Mon.*

Camogli ✉ 16032

****Cenobio dei Dogi**, Via Cuneo 34, **t** 0185 7241, *www.cenobio.it* (*luxury*). A former ducal palace at the water's edge, with fantastic views – on a clear day you can see the steady winking of Genoa's Lanterna. The bedrooms are airy and tastefully decorated in white and wood, and there are various sun terraces, a flower-filled park, a heated swimming pool and tennis courts. The two excellent **restaurants**, one on the private pebble beach, are open to the public.

****Portofino Kulm**, Viale Bernardo Gaggini 23, Portofino Vetta. **t** 0185 7361, *www. portofinokulm.it* (*very expensive*). A sumptuous hotel situated in a forest at the top of Monte di Portofino, far from the madness that is Portofino during the summer months. Its fitness centre, indoor swimming pool, sauna and Jacuzzi assure plentiful rest and relaxation. The restaurant is run by Zefferino.

***Casmona**, Salita Pineto 13, **t** 0185 770 015, *www.casmona.com* (*moderate–expensive*). A quiet, tidy place with a restaurant and a shady little patio.

La Camogliese, Via Garibaldi 55, **t** 0185 771 402, *www.lacamogliese.it* (*moderate*). A family-run hotel by the sea, with free access to a pool and gym. The attractive restaurant serves good, reasonably priced fish dishes. *Restaurant closed Weds. Hotel closed Nov and half of Dec.*

Nonna Nina, Loc. S Rocco, Via Molfino 126, **t** 0195 773 835 (*expensive*). A restaurant set in a pretty garden, offering fragrant Ligurian classics, including an exceptional *pansotti* in walnut sauce. *Closed lunchtimes except Sat and hols.*

San Fruttuoso ✉ 16030

*Da Giovanni**, **t** 0185 770 047 (*expensive*). A charming little hotel with its own seafood restaurant.

Santa Margherita Ligure ✉ 16038

★★★★★**Imperiale Palace**, Via Pagana 19, **t** 0185 288 991, *www.hotelimperiale.com* (*luxury*). A former private villa on the outskirts of town, converted into a hotel at the turn of the 19th century; in 1922, in one of the marble- and gilt-encrusted public rooms, the Weimar Republic signed an agreement with Russia to reopen diplomatic relations. Antiques furnish the public rooms and more expensive bedrooms, and there are concerts in the music room some afternoons. There's also a heated outdoor pool, a lush tropical garden and a seafront terrace. The refined restaurant leads on to a wonderful breakfast room overlooking the garden. *Closed Nov–Feb.*

★★★★**Grand Hotel Miramare**, Via Milite Ignoto 30, **t** 0185 287 013, *www.grandhotelmiramare.it* (*very expensive–luxury*). A palatial place built as a posh winter hotel in the early 1900s. Surrounded by a lovely garden, it has a heated salt-water pool (and a pebbly beach across the road) and lovely bedrooms with balconies, many with views of the gulf.

★★★**La Vela**, Via N. Cuneo 21, **t** 0185 284 771, *www.lavela.it* (*moderate–expensive*). A former villa just above town, with a friendly, intimate atmosphere and 16 rooms with good sea views. *Closed Nov–Christmas.*

★★**Fasce**, Via L. Bozzo 3, **t** 0185 286 435, *www.hotelfasce.it* (*moderate*). A very friendly and welcoming option, good for families. The rooms are modern and immaculate, and there's a laundry service, bike loan, parking facilities, a sun roof and a small garden. There's also an excellent, good-value restaurant where you can enjoy Ligurian specialities. *Restaurant open high season only. Hotel closed Nov–Christmas.*

★★**Europa**, Via Trento 5, **t** 0185 287 187, *www.hoteleuropa-sml.it* (*cheap–moderate*). A recently refurbished family-run hotel close to the Villa Durazzo.

Cesarina, Via Mameli 2/c, **t** 0185 286 059 (*very expensive*). The finest restaurant in town, located under an arcade in the old part of town. The fresh and modern décor goes well with food, which includes *zuppa di datteri* (razor clam soup) and spaghetti with red mullet (*triglie*) sauce. Book in advance. *Closed Tues and Jan.*

Il Faro, Via Maragliano, **t** 0185 286 867 (*moderate*). A delightful family-run place offering excellent *trenette* with *pesto*, and meat and seafood specialities. *Closed Tues and 2wks Nov.*

Portofino ✉ 16034

★★★★**Nazionale**, Via Roma 8, **t** 0185 269 575, *www.nazionaleportofino.com* (*luxury*). A hotel on the port, with a faded charm, furnished with antiques or reproductions. The best rooms have Venetian furniture and overlook the harbour. It has no parking, which can be a headache in Portofino.

★★★★**Splendido**, Viale Baratta 16, **t** 0185 267 801, *www.orient-expresshotels.com* (*luxury*). One of the best hotels in Liguria, if not Italy. The views alone, of olive- and-cypress-clad hills framing the town, its tiny harbour and the sea beyond, are worth the astronomical fees. Bedrooms are sumptuous, the restaurant refined and the breakfast terrace, beneath a huge sub-tropical canopy, simply delightful. Swim in the heated outdoor pool, or hire the hotel's speedboat for a day. The wall of fame includes the likes of Groucho Marx, Liz Taylor, Madonna and Bill Gates, attracted by the secluded hillside location. *Closed Feb.*

★★★★**Splendido Mare**, Via Roma 2, **t** 0185 267 802, *www.orient-expresshotels.com* (*luxury*). The Splendido's smaller younger sibling on the piazza by the harbour, less grand and slightly cheaper, with a delightful alfresco restaurant, the Chuflay Bar. *Closed Feb.*

★★★**Eden**, Vico Dritto 18, **t** 0185 269 091, *www.italyhotels.it* (*very expensive*). The least expensive option in town, in the centre with 12 charming rooms, a fine garden and a good Ligurian restaurant.

Most restaurants are clustered around Portofino's little piazza and port.

Il Pitosforo, Molo Umberto I 9, **t** 0185 269 020 (*very expensive*). A restaurant serving some of the finest Ligurian cuisine available anywhere, including bouillabaisse, spaghetti with prawns and mushrooms, red mullet and sea bream with olives. A tree grows in the middle of the dining room, and one wall is lined with a collection of spirits from around the world. At 10pm the lights are switched off to highlight the magical view of the port. *Closed Tues.*

Da Puny, Piazza Martiri dell'Olivetta 5, **t** 0185 269 037 (*expensive*). A good restaurant with delicious pasta and seafood starters and well-prepared main fish dishes, such as sea bass baked in salt. Bookings essential; no credit cards. *Closed Thurs, and mid-Dec–mid-Feb.*

Taverna del Marinaio, Piazza Martiri dell' Olivetta 36, **t** 0185 269 103 (*moderate*). As reasonably priced a place as you'll find here. The fish and pasta are excellent. *Closed Tues.*

Rapallo ✉ 16035

★★★**Riviera**, Piazza IV Novembre 2, **t** 0185 50248, *www.hotelriviera.biz* (*expensive*). A converted villa near the sea in the centre, with a popular terrace at the front and a garden at the rear.

★**Bandoni**, Via Marsala 24/3, **t** 0185 50423, *www.bandoni.supereva.it* (*cheap*). A simple, comfortable hotel close to the seafront in the middle of town.

U Giancu, S. Massimino 78, a few km from town, **t** 0185 261 212 (*moderate*). A delightful family restaurant among the olives, with every cranny filled with cartoon characters, a small playground, and good, traditional food. Book ahead. *Open lunchtimes and Weds.*

Chiávari ✉ 16043

Lord Nelson Pub, Corso Valparaiso 27, **t** 0185 302 595 (*very expensive*). A misleadingly named place with 5 suites with sea views and Jacuzzis, a bar modelled on HMS *Victory*, and the most elegant restaurant in town, with delicate seafood dishes such as ravioli with smoked ricotta and shrimp. Save room for the great desserts. *Closed Weds.*

★★**Zia Piera**, Via Marina Giulia 25, **t** 0185 307 686, *www.angelfire.com/ok/ziapiera* (*cheap*). A modern hotel on the beach, refurbished to 3-star standard.

Ca' Peo, Strada Panoramica, Leivi, 6km from town, **t** 0185 319 696 (*very expensive*). One of the best restaurants on the Riviera, elegant and charming, with imaginative food featuring ingredients such as radicchio from Treviso and truffles from Alba, followed by excellent desserts. Reservations are a must. *Closed Mon, Tues lunch and Nov.*

Felice, Via L. Risso 71, **t** 0185 308 016 (*moderate*). A popular little place serving a delicious *zimino* (fish soup) and other Ligurian dishes. Book ahead. *Closed Mon.*

Sestri Levante ✉ 16039

★★★★★**Grand Hotel dei Castelli**, Via Penisola 26, **t** 0185 487 220, *www.rainbownet.it/htl.castelli* (*very expensive*). A hotel built in the 1920s at the tip of the Isola peninsula on the site of a Genoese castle, and constructed from the castle's stone. The views of both bays and the sea crashing against the cliffs around the park are magnificent, especially from the dining terrace. There's also a sea pool cut into the rock for safe swims. *Closed Nov–Apr.*

★★★★**Villa Balbi**, Viale Rimembranza 1, **t** 0185 42941, *www.villabalbi.it* (*very expensive*). A supremely stately pink palace on the seafront, built at the beginning of the 17th century for the Brignole family and full of unexpected treasures, including a preserved library and a room decorated entirely with paintings of fish, as well as oak-beamed bedrooms and antique-laden public rooms. Much of the original garden remains, including a large camphor tree growing in the middle (and through the roof) of the restaurant. *Closed Nov–Mar.*

★★★**Helvetia**, Via Cappuccini 43, **t** 0185 41175, *www.hotelhelvetia.it* (*expensive*). A welcoming little hotel set in the prettiest part of town, right on the Bay of Silence, with a large terraced garden.

★★★**Mira**, Via Rimembranza 15, **t** 0185 41576, *www.sestrilevante.hotels.com/ph/mire.htm* (*moderate*). A family-run hotel with rooms with a view, plus a restaurant where you can feast on excellent fish specialities, including *riso marinara* and *nasello alla mira*, on a covered terrace by the sea. *Closed Mon.*

Fiammenghilla Fieschi, Via Pestella 6, **t** 0185 481 041 (*very expensive*). A great place for seafood and traditional Ligurian cuisine, especially marinated swordfish, lobster, *focaccia* and *pansotti*. There's also a very good Ligurian wine list. *Closed lunchtimes and Mon.*

Angiolina, Piazza Matteotti 51, **t** 0185 41198 (*expensive*). An excellent seaside dining room, serving up a wonderful *zuppa di pesce*. *Closed Tues.*

Polpo Mario, Via XXV Aprile 163, **t** 0185 480 203 (*moderate*). A cosy family restaurant a few streets back from the Bay of Silence, very popular with locals, with generous portions.

Chiávari and Lavagna

To the east of Rapallo, **Zoagli**, with its striking setting under the cliffs, was bombed in the Second World War because of its rail viaduct, leaving a castle folly from the 1920s as its landmark. The village has produced silks, patterned velvets and damasks ever since they were all the rage during the Middle Ages, although nowadays people prefer it for dressing their furniture instead of themselves; the tourist office can arrange visits of a velvet mill. A seaside path cut into the rock offers lovely views over the gulf. Just off the Via Aurelia towards Chiávari, the late 15th-century **Santuario della Madonna delle Grazie** has some fine frescoes, especially a Last Judgement by Luca Cambiaso.

The coast flattens out for the last time at **Chiávari**, which was founded as a colony of Genoa in 1178, and is laid out in a nice tidy grid of porticoed lanes. Although tourism is now the big earner here, traditional crafts have yet to die out completely, in particular fine wooden chairs and macramé – an art that was brought back by the town's sailors from the Middle East, and is used to create intricate fringes and tassels for towels and tablecloths. Central **Piazza Mazzini** has a lively morning market, a tower, stern palaces and a monument dedicated to Liguria's favourite revolutionary. A few streets away at Via Costaguta 4, the **Palazzo Rocca**, which was designed by Bartolomeo Bianco in 1629, houses the up-to-date **Museo Archeologico** (***t*** *0185 320 829; open Tues–Sat and 2nd and 4th Sun of month 9–1.30*), containing finds from the nearby 8th–7th-century BC necropolis that demonstrate ancient trade links with the Phoenicians, Greeks and Egyptians. Afterwards, treat yourself to an ice cream at **Caffè Defilla**, on Via Garibaldi 4, founded in 1883.

Just to the east, over the bridge, there's a big beach and lots of new building at **Lavagna**, the town of slate (it gave its name to 'blackboard' in Italian). The Fieschi family who ruled it produced a pope, Innocent IV, who reigned from 1243 to 1254. In 1230, the marriage of Innocent's older brother, Opizzo, to Bianca dei Bianchi, was celebrated with a cake so large each of his subjects got a slice; the anniversary (14 August) is re-enacted in costumes each year, climaxing with the eating of the 1,500kg Torta dei Fieschi. Innocent IV is himself more soberly remembered in the beautiful early Gothic church he built, the **Basilica di San Salvatore dei Fieschi**, a few kilometres inland (*signposted*).

Sestri Levante

The coastal train tracks delve inland at delightful Sestri Levante, built on a curving peninsula that divides the **Bay of Silence** from what Hans Christian Andersen himself named the **Bay of Fables** in 1833. The private garden on the peninsula belongs to a hotel, but you can take a path to the old Genoese tower where Marconi performed his experiments with ultra short radio waves and navigation, in 1934. The peninsula also has the fine Romanesque church of **San Nicolò**. By the Bay of Silence, the **Galleria Rizzi** at Via Cappuccini 8 (***t*** *0185 41300; open Apr–Oct Sun 10.30–1, May–Sept also Weds 4–7, July and Aug also Fri and Sat 9pm–11; adm*), has works by the Florentine, Emilian and Ligurian schools, including two 15th-century female wooden busts from Tuscany and pieces by Denis Calvaert and Sebastiano Ricci.

From Sestri there's a bus that heads up the tortuous SS523 to **Varese Ligure**, the chief town of the Val di Vara. Its core, the perfectly circular Borgo Rotundo, was laid out in the late 1400s by the Fieschi, who offered land to any merchant who would build a house in a ring around the market. The Fieschi also owned the 15th-century **castle** with it lovely slate roof. North of Varese, the scenery is lush, dotted with tiny slate-roofed hamlets.

The Cinque Terre and La Spezia

Before sliding down to the comparatively flat coast of Tuscany, the Riviera bows out with a flourish around the rugged, almost inaccessible cliffs of the Cinque Terre, the rocky peninsula of Portovenere, and La Spezia's lovely 'Gulf of Poets'.

Sestri Levante to the Cinque Terre

After Sestri Levante, the Apennines crowd the coast, admitting here and there little glens and sandy strands. A coastal tunnel makes it easy to reach **Moneglia** (from the Latin *monellia*, or jewel), with its quiet stretch of beach framed by two medieval castles, Monleone and Villafranca. It also provides access to the busy resort, numerous campsites and kilometre-long beach of **Deiva Marina**, situated close to the pretty village of Framura. The road then delves inland to redescend at **Bonassola** and **Lèvanto**, which has a good sandy beach, gardens, and some monuments dating from its 13th-century heyday as a free *comune* – the **Loggia** in Piazza del Popolo, the striped church of **Sant'Andrea** with its ornate rose window and parts of its walls, the castle, and the **Torre dell'Orologio** (1265).

To the southeast of Lèvanto rises the startlingly vertical coast of the **Cinque Terre**, as these five remarkable villages have been known since the Middle Ages. They represent the concentrated essence of Liguria at its most tenacious. Fishing was a traditional livelihood here, and, amazingly, wine-making – more than 7,000 kilometres of dry stone terraces corrugate their precipitous slopes, the labour of generations of men and women, forming one of Europe's most stunning artificial landscapes.

Once accessible only by sea or by cliff-skirting footpaths, the five villages have maintained much of their charm, though nowadays they are far from being undiscovered. Declared a UNESCO World Heritage site in 1997, the Cinque Terre and their surroundings were designated a National Park and a Marine Protected Area two years later, which should spare them from the worst ravages of development made possible by construction of the new road; sustainable, eco-friendly tourism is the new key phrase.

Westernmost **Monterosso al Mare** is the only one of the villages with beaches (free and 'organized'), and has the biggest choice of accommodation. Much of this is in the new half of town, Fegina, which is separated from the old part by a hill crowned with the **Convento dei Cappuccini** (1622) and a medieval tower. The parish church, striped **San Giovanni**, has a lovely sculpted marble rose window – the Cinque Terre's status symbol.

A path (and a road) leads high up to the 18th-century **Santuario di Soviore**, which was built over an older church. From Monterosso it's a momentary train ride, a nerve-wracking drive, or an hour-and-a-half's walk to the next *terre*, pretty **Vernazza**, which was founded by the Romans on a rocky spit. Its curious split-level church, Santa Margherita of Antioch, was built in 1318.

It's another 90-minute walk from Vernazza to **Corniglia,** the Cinque Terre wine centre; this one of the most strenuous sections to do on foot, for Corniglia, unlike the other towns, is high up on the cliffs, 365 steps up from the sea and the train station, though it does have the longest (pebbly) beach.

From Corniglia, it's an hour's walk through splendid scenery to picture-postcard **Manarola**, piled on a great black rock. This is linked in 20 minutes or so to Riomaggiore by the most popular section of the footpath, the 'Via dell'Amore' ('Lovers' Lane'), which is carved into the cliff face over the sea. **Riomaggiore**, one of the prettiest of the Cinque Terre towns, also sees plenty of visitors, who crowd its lively cafés and rocky beaches.

La Spezia

The provincial capital and a major naval base, La Spezia was bombed heavily during the Second World War and presents a modern but cheerful face to the world, standing as it does at the head of one of Italy's prettiest gulfs. Often overlooked by visitors, it has its fair share of attractions, including some often peculiar Liberty-style touches in its architecture, a promenade of swaying palms, lush public gardens, and a trio of fine museums.

Leave a couple of hours to fully appreciate the superb horde of art that's on display in the **Museo Amedeo Lia**, housed in a 17th-century convent on pedestrian-only Via Prione (***t** 0187 731 100; open Tues–Sun 10–6; adm exp*). The collection includes paintings by Gentile Bellini, Pontormo, Sebastiano del Piombo and Titian, plus a number of Renaissance bronzetti, medieval ivories, illuminated antiphonals and much much more. To the north of it, on Via XXVII Marzo, the medieval Castello San Giorgio is now home to the **Museo del Castello** (***t** 0187 751 142; open Weds–Sun summer 9.30–12.30 and 5–8, winter 9.30–12.30 and 2–5; adm*), which houses an excellent archaeological collection that includes prehistoric and Roman finds, as well as 19 Ligurian statue stelae dating from the Copper and Iron ages (4th–3rd millenia BC) – figures that look uncannily like prehistoric spacemen (others are in Pontrémoli; *see* p.652).

Next to the Arsenale, off Piazza Chiodo, is the **Museo Tecnico Navale** (***t** 0187 770 750; open Mon–Sat 8.30–6, Sun 10.15–3.45; adm*) with its old-fashioned maritime collection begun in 1560 by Emanuele Filiberto and including relics of the Battle of Lepanto, figureheads, models, and a section on the *maiali*, or 'pigs' – Italy's secret weapon during the Second World War

Portovenere

To the south of La Spezia is a winding road that passes by way of the pretty cove of **Le Grazie** before ending at delightful **Portovenere**, the long promontory of which is draped with a castle and colourful houses on the seafront. The town was named for

Getting Around

The easiest way to reach the Cinque Terre is by **train** from Lèvanto or from La Spezia. Each of the five towns has a station, which are only a few minutes apart and are separated by long tunnels.

The Cinque Terre National Park runs **electric buses** to the sanctuaries and to a variety of other lofty places; the **Carta Cinque Terre** (which is available at train stations) gives unlimited train travel between Lèvanto and La Spezia and bus travel in the park for periods of 1, 3 or 7 days.

There are several **boat** lines that connect La Spezia, Lerici, Portovenere and the villages of the Cinque Terre, including **NGP**, **t** 0187 732 987, which goes as far as Genoa's aquarium and Viareggio in Tuscany; and **Fratelli Rossignoli**, **t** 0187 817 456, which sails between Monterosso al Mare and Viareggio during the summer.

There are **buses** that run from La Spezia to Portovenere (every 15mins), Lérici, Sarzana and the remainder of the province, operated by the ATC, **t** 800 322 322 (freephone within Italy); the departure points vary, so you'll need to ask

Avoid driving in the Cinque Terre if you possibly can. The tunnels to the east of Sestri Levante were built for steam trains and are only one lane wide. An often narrow **road** connects the villages of the Cinque Terre, but once you arrive, you'll find parking in the tiny villages difficult at the best of times (although some of them have expensive car parks a long walk up the hill).

Tourist Information

Lèvanto: Piazza Cavour, **t** 0187 808 125.
Monterosso al Mare: Via Fegina 40, **t** 0187 817 059,
Vernazza: Via Roma 51, **t** 0187 812533
Riomaggiore: Piazza Rio Finale 26, **t** 0187 920633.
La Spezia: Viale Mazzini 45, **t** 0187 770 900, *www.aptcinqueterre.sp.it*
Portovenere: Piazza Bastreri 7, **t** 0187 790 691, *www.portovenere.it*
Lerici: Via Biaggini 6, **t** 0187 967 346.
Sarzana: Piazza S. Giorgio, **t** 0187 620 419.

Where to Stay and Eat

Moneglia ✉ 16030

***__Villa Edera__**, Via Venino 12, **t** 0185 49291, *www.villaedera.com* (*moderate*). A quiet, pleasant, bright-pink, family-run hotel in the hills, 150m from the beach, with a swimming pool and lovely **restaurant** where you can sample various regional specialities. The same family offer B&B (*expensive*) in the neighbouring early 19th-century **Castello di Monleone** with its lovely garden and many original fittings (*minimum 3-night stay*).

Il Frantoio,Via Torrente S. Lorenzo 150, **t** 0185 401 105 (*expensive*). A restaurant that's situated, as the name suggests, in the cellar of an old olive mill, serving up a wide selection of seafood dishes. Be sure to try the home-made basil liqueur as a *digestivo Closed Tues.*

Monterosso al Mare ✉ 19016

****__Porto Roca__**, Via Corone 1, **t** 0187 817 502, *www.portoroca.it* (*very expensive*). The top choice in town, set on the headland with lovely views of the sea from all rooms. *Closed mid-Oct–Feb.*

***__Degli Amici__**, Via Burranco 36, **t** 0187 817 544, *www.hotelamici.it* (*expensive*). An option in the old part of town, 150m from the beach. Rooms are light and airy; some have a balcony. There's a lemon garden to sit in and an excellent restaurant.

La Cambusa, Via Roma 6, **t** 0187 817 546 (*cheap*). A restaurant in a 13th-century building in the heart of the village, offering tasty seafood, from ravioli to swordfish grilled with sundried tomatoes, with an emphasis on the local anchovies. *Closed Mon, mid-Jan–mid-Feb and Nov.*

Vernazza ✉ 19018

*__Sorriso__, Via Gavino 4, **t** 0187 812 224 (*moderate*). An honest little inn with several annexes on the same street.

Gambero Rosso, Piazza Marconi 7, **t** 0187 812 265 (*moderate*). A well-known restaurant partly carved out of the rock; try tasty *tegame di acciughe*, made with Cinque Terre anchovies. There are also some rooms (*cheap*) with lovely views. *Closed Mon and late Nov–Mar.*

Manarola ✉ 19010

***Marina Piccola, **t** 0187 920 103, *www.hotelmarinapiccola.com* (*moderate*). A good place to get away from it all, with simple rooms and a pleasant restaurant.

Aristide, Via Roma, **t** 0187 920 000 (*moderate*). A choice trattoria by the train tracks, serving delicious *minestra* and fish, plus rabbit, game and other meat in season, accompanied by the owner's wine. No credit cards. *Closed Mon.*

La Spezia ✉ 19100

****Jolly, Via XX Settembre 2, **t** 0187 739 555, *www.jollyhotels.it* (*moderate–very expensive*). A modern, stylish member of the Italian chain.

*Flavia, Vicolo dello Stagno 7, off Via del Prione, **t** 0187 736 060 (*cheap*). One of the best bargain options in town, not far from the station.

Il Sogno di Angelo, Via del Popolo 39, **t** 0187 514 041 (*very expensive*). *The* place for a big night out in La Spezia, with a classy ambience and classy, imaginative food, including good desserts. *Closed Sun.*

Osteria All'Inferno, Via Lorenzo Costa 3, **t** 0187 29458 (*moderate*). An inconspicuous place that is housed in an old coal cellar and has been run by the same family since 1905. Try the *mesciüa* (cannellini bean, chick pea and cereal soup) and *porcetta al forno*. *Closed Sun and Aug.*

Da Dino, Via de Passano 17, **t** 0187 736 157 (*cheap*). A charming, unpretentious place with an excellent-value fixed-price menu. *Closed Sun eve and Mon.*

Portovenere ✉ 19025

****Grand Hotel Portovenere, Via Garibaldi 5, **t** 0187 792 610, *www.village.it/ghp* (*expensive–luxury*). A hotel in a 17th-century Franciscan convent by the sea, with views across the gulf and Palmaria. The cells have been converted into stylish rooms, and the restaurant has a terrace.

***Paradiso, Via Garibaldi 34, **t** 0187 790 612, *www.hotelportovenere.it* (*expensive*). A little family-run hotel boasting lovely views from its seaside terrace and cosy, well-equipped rooms.

Genio, Piazza Bastreri 8, **t 0187 790 611 (*moderate*). A pleasant inexpensive choice with a little garden.

Da Iseo, **Calata Doria 9**, **t** 0187 790 686 (*expensive*). Portovenere's best-known restaurant, with a lovely setting and faithful renditions of the classics, including delicious spaghetti with seafood. *Closed Weds and Christmas hols.*

Lerici ✉ 19032

***Byron, Via Biaggini 19, **t** 0187 967 104, *www.byronhotel.com* (*moderate–expensive*). A good choice on the left as you approach the town, with smallish rooms that are compensated for by views across the bay and some huge balconies.

***Shelley & Delle Palme, Lungomare Biaggini 5, **t** 0187 968 204, *www.hotelshelley.it* (*moderate–expensive*). One of the largest and most comfortable hotels on the 'Gulf of Poets', with fine views.

Del Golfo, Via Gerini 37, **t 0187 967 400, *www.hoteldelgolfo.com* (*cheap–moderate*). The only inexpensive hotel in Lerici, situated just up from the tourist office. Some of the bedrooms have balconies.

Due Corone, Via G Mazzini, **t** 0187 967 417 (*very expensive*). An award-winning restaurant with superb seafood; don't miss the *cocktail di antipasti mare* and the *grigliata mista*. *Closed Tues.*

Ameglia ✉ 19031

***Locanda delle Tamerici, Via Litoranea 106, Fiumaretta, **t** 0187 64262 (*expensive*). An wonderful option situated down by the sea, with a number of cosy, tranquil rooms and a romantic flower-filled garden. Its restaurant (*very expensive*) offers very tasty seafood and vegetable dishes. *Restaurant closed Tues.*

***Paracucchi Locanda dell'Angelo, Ca' di Scabello, Viale V Aprile 60, **t** 0187 64391/2, *www.paracucchilocanda.it* (*expensive*). A modern slick hotel just a couple of minutes away from a pool and the sea. Its top-notch restaurant (*very expensive*) was founded by one of Italy's most famous chefs, Angelo Paracucchi, and is now run by son Marco. The menu changes often, but you can count on each dish being superb – and often amazingly simple. Among the great desserts is a wonderful fruit flambée. *Closed Sun eve and Mon out of season.*

the goddess of love, who was also a protectress of fisherfolk; she had her temple at the tip of the promontory, until she was upstaged by Christianity's top fisherman. His strange little church with its black and white stripes, **San Pietro**, dates from 1277; below it are a few remains of its 6th-century predecessor. It enjoys splendid views of Palmaria and the Cinque Terre coast; the lovely bay below once held the Grotta Arpaia, where Byron wrote *The Corsair*, and from where he swam across the gulf to visit Shelley. It collapsed in the 1930s.

Portovenere is Italy's champion kitty city, and the best thing here to do is join the cats as they wander through its narrow lanes, past the tall houses with their decorated doorways built by the Genoese, who fortified the town in the early 12th century to counter their Pisan rivals, who had fortified Lerici across the gulf. Don't miss the lovely church of **San Lorenzo**, built in 1130 and featuring a bas-relief of St Lawrence being toasted on his gridiron over the door; inside is Portovenere's most precious relic, the *Madonna Bianca*, which is said to have floated to the town encased in a cedar log in the 13th century. A steep walk will take you up to the 16th-century Genoese **Castello Doria** with its marvellous views (*open Apr–Oct daily 10–12 and 2–6; Nov–Mar Sat and Sun 10–1 and 2–5*).

Boats cross the half-kilometre channel to **Isola Palmaria**, mostly carrying visitors over to its sea cave, the Grotta Azzurra. Little **Isola del Tino** has a lighthouse and the remains of the 8th-century **monastery of San Venerio**, which used to be home to a dragon-whacking hermit, while the even tinier **Tinetto** has the ruins of a 5th-century oratory – they're part of a military zone, and visits are only possible on 13 September, the feast of St Venerio.

Lerici and the Gulf of Poets

At La Spezia the gulf may seem all business, but head east towards the marbly Apuan Alps and it becomes the lovely 'Golfo dei Poeti', where the likes of Dante, Petrarch, George Sand, and Gabriele D'Annunzio loitered. Shelley, his wife Mary and her stepsister lived in the Casa Magni, now in the centre of charming **San Terenzo**; it was from here that he sailed, in 1822, to meet Leigh Hunt at Livorno, only to shipwreck and drown by Viareggio. The multimedia **Museo P.B. Shelley** *(open Tues–Sun 10.30–12.30 and 3–5.30; adm)*, dedicated to the couple, has recently been opened in San Terenzo's 11th-century castle, which, appropriately enough, has some of the Gothic atmosphere of Mary Shelley's *Frankenstein*.

Just to the south, **Lérici** is a colourful medieval port with a long beach, although yachts have long-since replaced the galleys. Tit for Portovenere's tat, the Pisans built Lérici's landmark castle in 1242; inside you can visit their chapel of Sant'Anastasia and the new state-of-the-art, interactive **Museo Geopaleontologico** (***t*** *0187 969 042; open Sept–June Tues–Fri 10.30–12.30, Sat and Sun 10.30–12.30 and 2.30–5.30; July and Aug Tues–Sun 10.30–12.30 and 6.30–midnight; adm*), which is dedicated to the dinosaurs who once stomped here.

To the south is the enchanting cove and beach of **Fiascherino**, where D.H. Lawrence and his Frieda lived in a flat pink fisherman's house on the Mediterranean in 1913 and 1914, with a garden with orange and lemon trees; beyond it you'll find the unspoiled

Heaven and Hell: the Shelleys in the Casa Magni

Mary Shelley had already written her masterpiece, *Frankenstein* (published in 1817), by the time she and her poet husband took up summer residence at the isolated Casa Magni in 1822. But the atmosphere Mary found at the beach house was something straight out of the pages of a Gothic novel, and the landscape oppressed her. Indeed, early on during their stay, she suffered a near-fatal miscarriage there – Shelley saved her by making her sit on ice to halt the bleeding.

Shelley himself loved the place and enjoyed a productive spell there, but his happiness was marred by nightmares of strangling Mary, of meeting his own double (who asked him, 'How long do you mean to be content?'), and of the sea overwhelming the house. One night, the couple's friend Jane Williams saw Shelley walk past the window twice, but when she looked onto the terrace he was gone. Meanwhile, Mary was woken by Shelley rushing into her room after dreaming that Jane and another friend, Edward Trelawney, had come to him as he lay in bed, their bodies lacerated.

The terrible visions soon came to seem prophetic, when on 8 July the 30-year-old Shelley met his end in the gulf of Spezia while sailing home from a trip to Livorno. His decomposed body, half eaten by fishes, was washed up on the shore and cremated right there on the beach, after the heart had been removed and given to Mary, who was eventually buried with it.

Despite or perhaps because of her terrible ordeals in Italy (she also lost two children there), Mary later returned to the country and in 1844 her *Rambles in Germany and Italy* was published.

medieval hamlet of **Tellaro**, where Lawrence attended a peasant wedding. Another scenic road from Lérici continues up around the promontory towards **Montemarcello**, which boasts beautiful views from its botanical garden, then descends towards the Magra river, where **Bocca di Magra** is a popular beach resort and pretty hilltop **Ameglia** has a 10th-century castle, some slate portals along its narrow *caruggi*, and a couple of hotels containing excellent restaurants (*see* p.187).

Sarzana and Ancient Luni

Across the Magra river, **Sarzana**, the main town in these parts, was fought over by Pisa and Florence before Genoa won the prize: from those days it retains a Medici citadel in the centre and the **Fortezza di Sarzanello** a mile to the east (***t*** *0187 622 262; open Tues–Sat 4.30–7.30, Sun 9.30 –12.30 and 4.30–7.30, Aug also Fri and Sat 9pm–midnight; adm*), which from one angle resembles a great stone steam iron. Sarzana's **cathedral**, begun just after 1204, contains one of the first signed and dated works of Italian art, a Crucifixion of 1138 by Master Guglielmo. Other churches of note here include **Sant'Andrea** and **San Francesco**, which contain some good sculptures.

To the north in **Fosdinovo** is the Malaspina castle that hosted Dante in 1306; he also visited the ruined 13th-century castle in **Castelnuovo Magra**. Castelnuovo's lavish church of Santa Maria Maddalena contains a superb, moody Crucifixion by Brueghel the Younger.

Ortonovo lies near the site of the ancient Roman marble-shipping city of **Luni**, (***t*** *0187 66811; open Tues–Sun 9–7; adm*) – the 'Port of the Moon' – which was founded in 177 BC as a bulwark against the fierce Ligurians. Lombards, Normans and floods had done it in by 1204, when its bishopric was moved to Sarzana. Excavations have revealed the remains of a sizeable amphitheatre, a forum, houses with mosaics and frescoes, the old cathedral and so on. The site contains the **Museo Nazionale di Luni** (*same hrs*), where you can see marble statuary, coins, jewellery, portraits, and more.

If you're continuing down the coast from here, *see* 'The Tuscan Coast', p.652.

Lombardy and the Lakes

11

Highlights

1 Milan's cathedral, Galleria and museums
2 The Gonzaga frescoes in Mantua
3 The resort villages and Borromean Islands of Lake Maggiore
4 The refined art city of Bergamo
5 Lake Garda: palms, lemon groves and castles at the foot of the Alps

Of all the barbarians who took part in the desecration of the corpse of the Roman Empire, none were more barbaric than the Lombards (otherwise known as the Longobards), a tall Germanic tribe who bled much of the peninsula dry before going on to settle down in the region that still bears their name. Even today, the inhabitants of Milan are taller than the average Italian person, although whether this is because of their Lombard blood or due to prosperity is up for discussion. Since the Middle Ages, Lombardy has assumed the role of economic powerhouse of the country. The complaint that Milan makes money while Rome wastes it is almost as old as the city itself.

Frenetic Milan, the pounding, racing economic heart of modern Italy, is the centre of gravity for the north. It always has been, for its geography has meant that the destinies of entire empires and kingdoms have been decided here, not to mention religions – Christianity was made the religion of the Roman Empire in Milan.

Lombardy has its gentle side as well. This was the homeland of epic Virgil and lyric Catullus, of composers Donizetti and Monteverdi, of violin masters Amati, Guarneri and Stradivarius. And since the 18th century, poets, composers and weary aristocrats have come for the peace and beauty of the Italian Lakes – which, although partially in Piemonte, Switzerland and the Veneto, have been included here for convenience.

Milan

Most tourists don't come to Italy looking for slick and feverishly busy Milan, and most of those who find themselves here take in only the obligatory sights – Leonardo's *Last Supper*, La Scala, the Duomo, and the Brera art gallery – before rushing off to shop. And most Italians (apart from the 4 million Milanese, that is) have little good to say about their second city: all the Milanese do is work, all they care about is money, they are just as corrupt as everyone else, and they defiantly refuse to indulge even in the myth of *la dolce vita*.

Yet the Italians who deride Milan are mostly envious, and the tourists who whip through it in a day are mostly ignorant of what this great city has to offer. Milan is certainly atypical, devoid of the usual Italian daydreams and living-museum mustiness. Like Naples, it lives for the present, and as one of Europe's major financial centres and a capital of fashion, Milan dresses in a well-tailored, cosmopolitan three-piece suit. The skills of its workers, above all in the luxury clothing trades, have been known for centuries – as evoked in the English word 'millinery'.

And yet, as the Milanese are the first to admit, Milan has made its way in the world not so much by native talent as through the ability to attract and make use of those from other places, from St Ambrose and Leonardo da Vinci to its most celebrated designer of the moment. It has produced no great music of its own, but La Scala opera house is one of the world's most prestigious places to sing; it has produced very few artists but has amassed enough treasures to fill four superb galleries. Milan is the Italian melting pot, Italy's picture window on the modern world, where the young and ambitious gravitate to see their talents rewarded. Here history seems to weigh less; here willowy Japanese models slink down the pavement with natty young gents whose parents immigrated from Calabria. Roiling, moiling, toiling, constantly evolving, Milan is *sui generis*; in Milanese dialect they have said simply, long before Gertrude Stein's 'a rose is a rose', *Milan l'e Milan*, Milan is Milan.

History

Milan was born cosmopolitan. Although far from any sea or river, in the midst of the fertile but vulnerable Lombard plain, it occupies the natural junction of trade routes through the alpine passes, from the Tyrrhenian and Adriatic ports and from

St Ambrose (Sant'Ambrogio)

No sooner had Christianity received the imperial stamp of approval than it split into two hostile camps: the orthodox, early-Catholic traditionalists and the followers of the Egyptian bishop Arius. Arians denied that Christ was of the same substance as God; the sect was widespread among the peoples on the fringes of the Roman Empire. An early bishop of Milan was an Arian and persecutor of the orthodox, and a schism seemed inevitable when he died. When the young consular governor Ambrose spoke to calm the crowd during the election of the new bishop, a child's voice piped up: 'Ambrose Bishop!' The cry was taken up, and Ambrose, who hadn't even been baptized, suddenly found himself thrust into a new job.

According to legend, when Ambrose was an infant in Rome, bees had flown into his mouth, attracted by the honey of his tongue. Ambrose's eloquence as bishop (374–97) is given much of the credit for preserving the unity of the Church; when the widow of Emperor Valentine desired to raise her son as an Arian, demanding a Milanese basilica for Arian worship, Ambrose and his supporters held the church through a nine-day siege, converting the empress's soldiers in the process. His most famous convert was St Augustine, and he also set what was to become the standard in relations between Church and Empire when he refused to allow Emperor Theodosius to enter church until he had done penance for ordering a civilian massacre in Thessalonika.

Ambrose left such an imprint on Milan that to this day genuine Milanese are called *Ambrosiani*. Their church, which was practically independent from Rome until the 11th century, still celebrates Mass according to the Ambrosian rite and holds its own carnival of Sant'Ambrogio in March.

the Po river. This commercially strategic position has also put Milan square in the path of every conqueror tramping through Italy.

Mediolanum, as it was called for its first millennium and a half, first came to prominence in the twilight of Rome when, as the headquarters of the Mobile Army and the seat of the court and government of the west, it became the de facto capital of the empire; Diocletian preferred it to Rome, and his successors spent much of their time here. The official Christianization of the empire began here in 313, when Constantine the Great established religious toleration with his **edict of Milan**.

The Rise of the *Comune*

During the barbarian invasions of the following few centuries, Mediolanum was shortened to *Mailand*, the prized Land of May – for so it seemed to the frostbitten Goths and Lombards who came to take it for their own. In the early 11th century, Milan evolved into one of Italy's first *comuni* under the leadership of another great bishop, **Heribert**, who organized a *parlamento* of citizens and a citizen militia. The new *comune*, Guelph in defiance of imperial pretensions, at once began subjugating the surrounding country and especially its Ghibelline rivals Pavia, Lodi and Como. To inspire the militia, Heribert also invented that unique Italian war totem, the *carroccio* – a huge ox-drawn cart that bore the city's banner, altar and bells into battle.

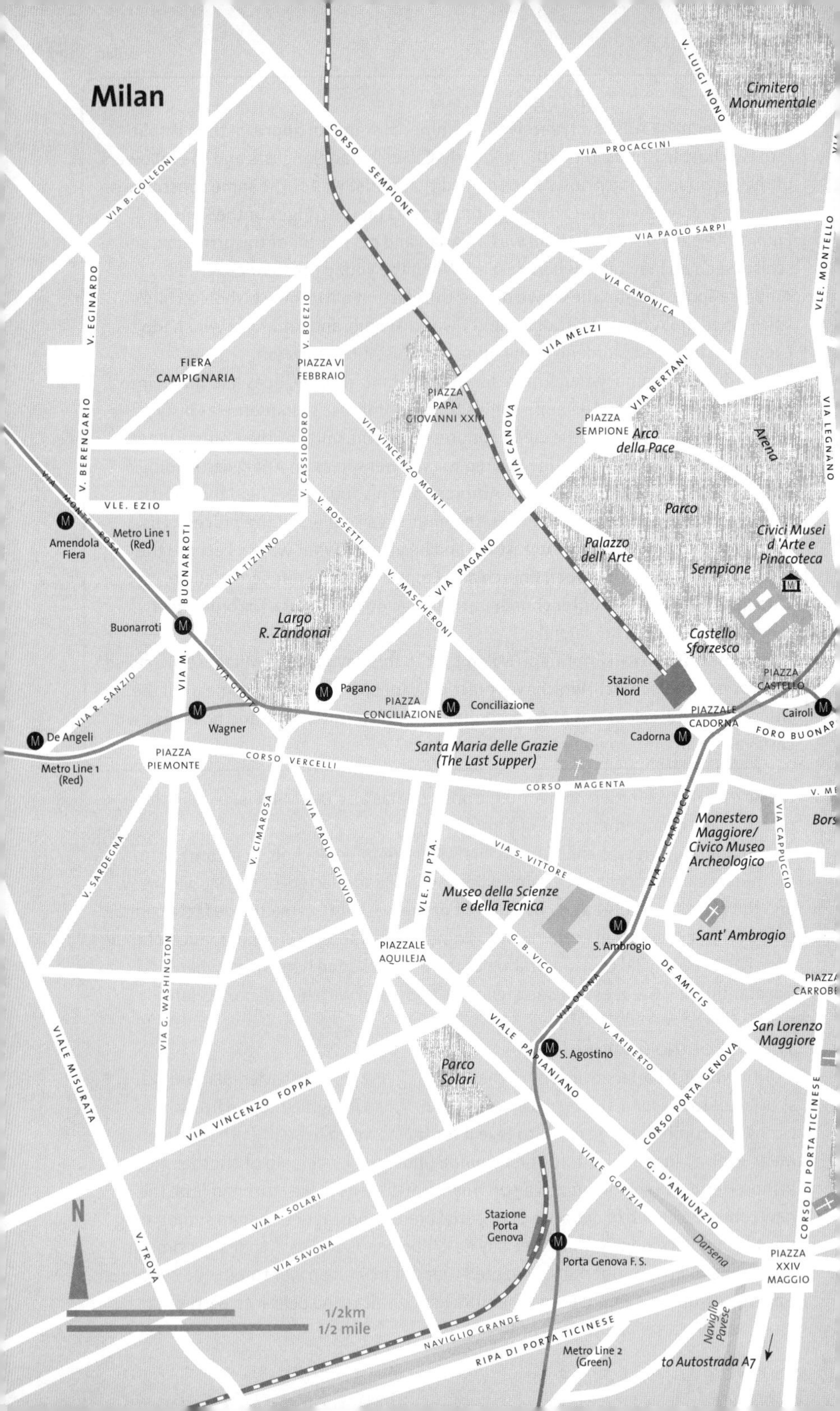

Milan
Cimitero Monumentale
V. LUIGI NONO
VIA PROCACCINI
CORSO SEMPIONE
VIA B. COLLEONI
VIA PAOLO SARPI
VLE. MONTELLO
VIA CANONICA
V. EGINARDO
V. BOEZIO
VIA MELZI
FIERA CAMPIGNARIA
PIAZZA VI FEBBRAIO
PIAZZA PAPA GIOVANNI XXIII
VIA BERTANI
PIAZZA SEMPIONE
Arco della Pace
Arena
VIA LEGNANO
VIA CANOVA
V. BERENGARIO
V. CASSIODORO
VIA VINCENZO MONTI
Parco
VLE. EZIO
V. ROSSETTI
VIA MONTE ROSA
Amendola Fiera
Metro Line 1 (Red)
V. BUONARROTI
VIA TIZIANO
VIA PAGANO
Palazzo dell' Arte
Civici Musei d'Arte e Pinacoteca
Sempione
V. MASCHERONI
Largo R. Zandonai
Buonarroti
Castello Sforzesco
VIA R. SANZIO
VIA M.
VIA GIOTTO
Pagano
PIAZZA CONCILIAZIONE
Conciliazione
Stazione Nord
PIAZZA CASTELLO
Cairoli
Wagner
PIAZZALE CADORNA
De Angeli
Cadorna
FORO BUONAP
PIAZZA PIEMONTE
CORSO VERCELLI
Santa Maria delle Grazie (The Last Supper)
Metro Line 1 (Red)
CORSO MAGENTA
V. ME
V. CIMAROSA
VIA PAOLO GIOVIO
VIA G. CARDUCCI
Monestero Maggiore/ Civico Museo Archeologico
VIA CAPPUCCIO
Bors
V. SARDEGNA
VIA S. VITTORE
VLE. DI PTA.
Museo della Scienze e della Tecnica
Sant' Ambrogio
S. Ambrogio
PIAZZALE AQUILEJA
G. B. VICO
DE AMICIS
PIAZZA CARROB
VIA G. WASHINGTON
VIA OLONA
San Lorenzo Maggiore
VIALE PAPINIANO
V. ARIBERTO
S. Agostino
VIALE MISURATA
Parco Solari
CORSO PORTA GENOVA
CORSO DI PORTA TICINESE
VIA VINCENZO FOPPA
VIALE GORIZIA
G. D'ANNUNZIO
N
VIA A. SOLARI
Stazione Porta Genova
Darsena
V. TROYA
VIA SAVONA
Porta Genova F. S.
PIAZZA XXIV MAGGIO
1/2km
1/2 mile
NAVIGLIO GRANDE
RIPA DI PORTA TICINESE
Naviglio Pavese
Metro Line 2 (Green)
to Autostrada A7

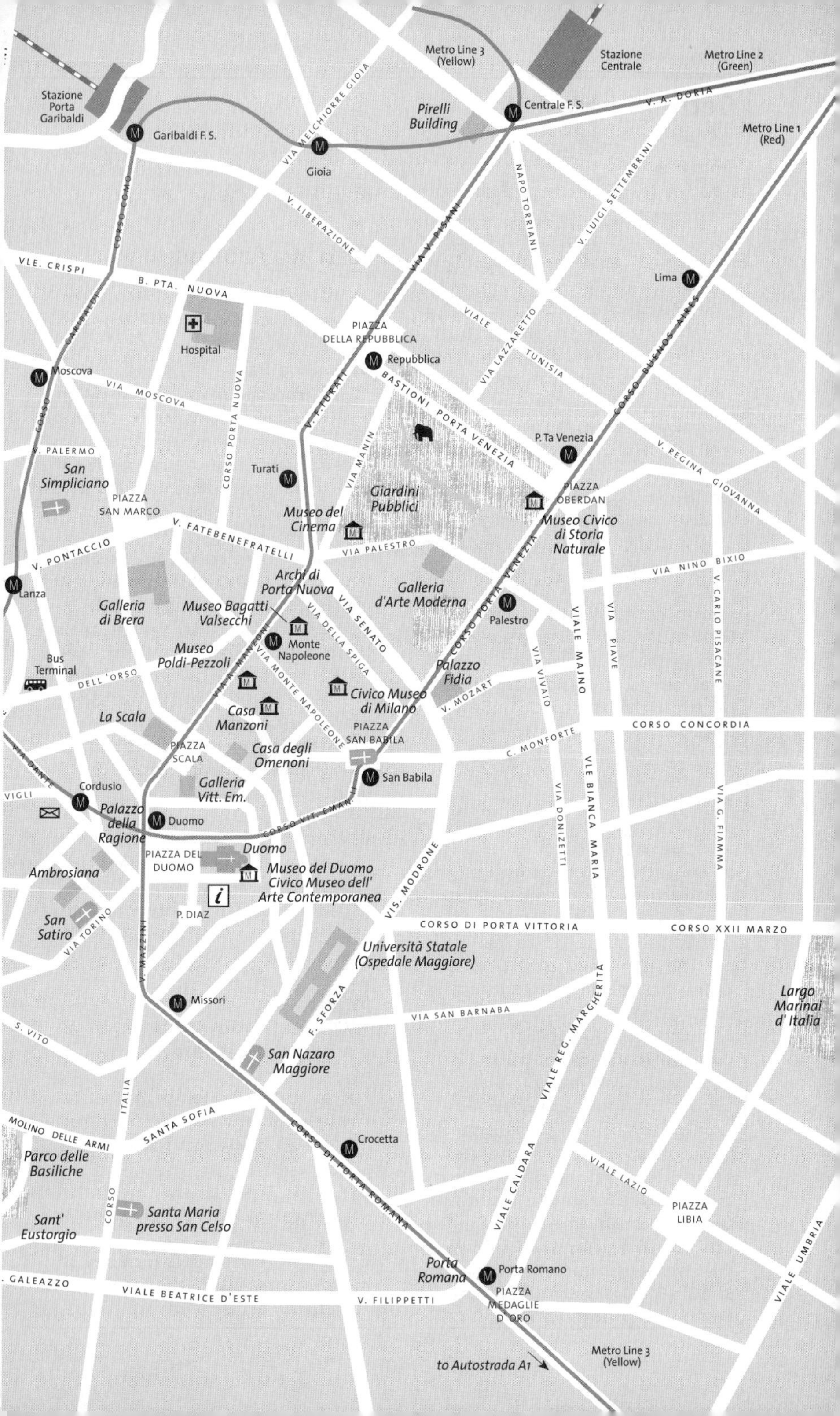

Stazione Porta Garibaldi
Garibaldi F. S.
Metro Line 3 (Yellow)
Stazione Centrale
Metro Line 2 (Green)
Centrale F. S.
V. A. Doria
Pirelli Building
Via Melchiorre Gioia
Gioia
Metro Line 1 (Red)
Corso Como
V. Liberazione
Napo Torriani
V. Luigi Settembrini
Via V. Pisani
Vle. Crispi
B. Pta. Nuova
Lima
Viale Tunisia
Via Lazzaretto
Corso Buenos Aires
Hospital
Piazza della Repubblica
Repubblica
Garibaldi
Moscova
Via Moscova
Corso Porta Nuova
V. F. Turati
Bastioni Porta Venezia
Corso
V. Palermo
P. Ta Venezia
V. Regina Giovanna
San Simpliciano
Turati
Via Manin
Giardini Pubblici
Piazza Oberdan
Piazza San Marco
Museo del Cinema
Museo Civico di Storia Naturale
V. Fatebenefratelli
V. Pontaccio
Via Palestro
Via Nino Bixio
Lanza
Archi di Porta Nuova
Galleria d'Arte Moderna
Galleria di Brera
Museo Bagatti Valsecchi
Via Senato
Palestro
Corso Porta Venezia
Viale Majno
Via Piave
V. Carlo Pisacane
Via della Spiga
Monte Napoleone
Museo Poldi-Pezzoli
Bus Terminal
Via A. Manzoni
Via Monte Napoleone
Palazzo Fidia
Via Vivaio
Dell' Orso
Civico Museo di Milano
V. Mozart
Casa Manzoni
La Scala
Piazza San Babila
Corso Concordia
Piazza Scala
Casa degli Omenoni
C. Monforte
Via Dante
Galleria Vitt. Em.
San Babila
Vle Bianca Maria
Cordusio
Vigli
Palazzo della Ragione
Duomo
Corso Vit. Eman. II
Via Donizetti
Via G. Fiamma
Piazza del Duomo
Duomo
Ambrosiana
Museo del Duomo
Civico Museo dell' Arte Contemporanea
V.S. Modrone
P. Diaz
San Satiro
Via Torino
Corso di Porta Vittoria
Corso XXII Marzo
Università Statale (Ospedale Maggiore)
V. Mazzini
Missori
Viale Reg. Margherita
Largo Marinai d' Italia
Via San Barnaba
S. Vito
F. Sforza
San Nazaro Maggiore
Italia
Molino delle Armi
Santa Sofia
Crocetta
Corso di Porta Romana
Parco delle Basiliche
Viale Caldara
Viale Lazio
Piazza Libia
Corso
Santa Maria presso San Celso
Sant' Eustorgio
Viale Umbria
Porta Romana
Porta Romano
Galeazzo
Viale Beatrice d'Este
V. Filippetti
Piazza Medaglie d'Oro
Metro Line 3 (Yellow)
to Autostrada A1

Getting There

From the Airport

Milan has two main airports, **Linate** (8km from the centre) and **Malpensa** (50km west); as a rule, Linate handles most European and domestic traffic and intercontinental flights use Malpensa. For flight info call **t** 02 7485 2200.

The quickest way to the centre from Malpensa is by **Malpensa Express** rail shuttle, **t** 02 27763, to Cadorna North railway station, running every 30mins 5am–11pm, taking 40mins. STAM buses, **t** 035 318 472, run between Linate and Stazione Centrale every 30mins 5.40am–9pm, taking about 20mins. **City bus 73** also runs between Linate and Piazza San Babila every 10mins from 5.30am–2am.

Air Pullman bus shuttles, **t** 02 5858 3185, link Malpensa to Stazione Centrale every 20mins from 4.15am–midnight, taking 1hr. An hourly service stops at the Fiera di Trade Fair on request. There is a direct Air Pullman link between Linate and Malpensa, leaving hourly 6am–8pm and taking about 75mins. Taxis from Malpensa to Milan cost a fortune.

Charter flights often use **Orio al Serio** near Bergamo, **t** 035 326 323. STAM buses, **t** 035 318 472, link it to Milan's Stazione Centrale.

By Train

Milan's main **Stazione Centrale** (connected to metro lines nos.2 and 3) on Piazza Duca d'Aosta northeast of the centre handles nearly all international trains and most of domestic routes, **t** 147 888 088. Useful **trams** and **buses** from Centrale include tram no.1 to Piazza Scala and Nord Station, tram no.33 to Stazione Garibaldi and the Cimitero Monumentale, bus no.60 to Piazza del Duomo, and bus no.65 down Corso Buenos Aires, Corso Venezia and through the centre to Corso Italia.

Stazione Garibaldi (metro no.2) is the terminus for car-train services, plus trains for Pavia, Monza, Varese, Como and Bergamo. Stazione Lambrate (metro no.2), on the east side of the city, has links to Genoa, Bergamo and towards the Simplon Pass. Stazione Cadorna (**metro Cadorna**) is the main station of Lombardy's regional Milan Nord railway, **t** 02 20222, with connections to Como, Varese, Saronno, Erba and Laveno (Lake Maggiore).

By Coach

Inter-city coaches arrive in Piazza Castello (metro Cairoli), where several bus companies have offices. Contact the tourist office for info on destinations, schedules and prices.

Getting Around

Most of Milan's sights are in the walkable innermost ring, the Cerchia dei Navigli.

By Bus and Tram

Buses, trams and trolleys run by the **Milan transport authority** (ATM), freephone **t** 800 016 857, are convenient, with well-marked routes. The ATM publishes a useful **map** showing all bus routes and metro stops, the *Guida Rete dei trasporti pubblici*, available at the tourist office and Stazione Centrale.

Tickets and carnets can be purchased at tobacconists, newsstands, metro stations and machines at main stops. Stamp them in machines on board; a ticket is valid for 75 mins' travel regardless of how many transfers you make, but can't be used twice on the metro. One- and 2-day passes valid for buses, trams and the metro are available.

Most bus routes run from about 6am to midnight, after which **night bus** routes operate with reasonable frequency.

By Metro

The Metropolitana Milanese is sleek and well run, with three lines, **Red** (no.1), **Green** (no.2) and **Yellow** (no.3). It's open daily 6am–midnight; tickets are the same as those for buses and trams.

By Taxi

Milanese taxis are white; their drivers are generally honest and reliable (if averse to coins). You can't flag cabs; you must call (**t** 02 8383, **t** 02 6767 or **t** 02 5251) or go to a stand or rank (i.e. Stazione Centrale, Piazza del Duomo and in several other central piazzas).

By Car

Bringing a vehicle into the centre 8am–8pm is not only foolhardy, but illegal unless you have a foreign number plate. There are ATM **car parks** on the outskirts and large car parks at the termini of the metro lines.

Tourist Information

Piazza del Duomo, Via Marconi 1, **t** 02 7252 4301/2/3 (*open Mon–Fri 8.30–7, Sat 9–1 and 2–6, Sun 9–1 and 2–5*).

Stazione Centrale (*open Mon–Sat 8–7, Sun 9–12.30 and 1.30–6*).

Galleria Vittorio Emanuele II, Piazza della Scala, **t** 02869 0734 (*open Mon–Sat 8–7, Sun 9–12.30 and 1.30–6*).

Shopping

Milan is Italy's best shopping city hands down, especially for clothes and anything capable of being 'designed'. The big **sales** begin the 2nd week of Jan and around 10 July.

Most shops close all day Sun, Mon mornings (except over Christmas), and in Aug. Food stores tend to close on Mon afternoons.

The Quadrilatero d'Oro

Many of the big names in fashion have their boutique 'headquarters' in what is known as the Quadrilatero d'Oro, defined by Via Monte Napoleone, Via della Spiga, Via Sant'Andrea and Via Borgospesso (metro Monte Napoleone). Nearly all the shops here have branches elsewhere in Milan and in other cities.

The jewellers arrived first, in the 1930s; since then an address on Via Monte Napoleone has meant status and quality. **Buccellati** (No.4), considered by many the best jewellery designer in Italy, has delicate gold work and jewels, each piece individually crafted. Other classics on Monte Napoleone are **Faraone** (No.7a), **Martignetti** (No.10), **Cartier** (corner Via del Gesù), **Damiani** (No.16), **Cusi** (No.21a) and **Calderoni**, the city's oldest (No.23). For **Bulgari** head for Via della Spiga (No.6); for antique jewellery try **Romani Adami**, Via Bagutta 3.

As for clothing and accessories: **Missoni**'s ravishing knits are at Via Sant'Andrea, corner of Via Bagutta; **Valentino** is at Via Santo Spirito 3; and **Armani** is at Via Durini 23–5. **Armani's Megastore**, Via Manzoni 31, has 3 floors dedicated to the home collection and Emporio lines, plus a sushi bar and a Mediterranean café and restaurant (*see* p.202).

Via della Spiga is chock-a-block with top designers: **Byblos, Krizia, Luciano Soprani** and **Dolce e Gabbana** are all here. Via Monte Napoleone also has its share: **Alberta Ferretti, Roccobarocco, Prada, Ungaro** and **Versace**. On Via S. Andrea are **Chanel, Prada** (again, and Via della Spiga as well), **Helmut Lang, Fendi, Ferré, Trussardi** and **Moschino**, also at Via Durini 14.

Italian leather is known in most parts of the world through the name **Gucci**, Monte Napoleone 5, but also have a look at **Bottega Veneta**, Via della Spiga 5; **Nazareno Gabrielli**, Monte Napoleone 23; **Ferragamo**, Via Monte Napoleone 3, on corner of Via Borgospesso; **Fendi**, Via Sant'Andrea 16; and **Fratelli Rossetti**, Via Monte Napoleone. **Pollini**, Corso Vittorio Emanuele II 30, has designer shoes.

City Centre

Besides the great **Galleria Vittorio Emanuele II**, several minor galleries branch off Corso Vittorio Emanuele II, each an arcade lined with good-quality and reasonably priced shops. In Piazza del Duomo is Milan's biggest and oldest department store, **La Rinascente**, with especially good clothing and kitchen gear. The top-floor café has great views over the cathedral.

Near the Duomo, Via Spadari is a food lover's heaven; at No. 9, is **Peck**, home of Milanese gastronomy. Peck has extended the original **Casa del Formaggio** on nearby Via Speronari (selling the best cheeses since 1894), and **Bottega del Maiale** (cheese and pork shops) to include delicacies (from escargots to exotic fruits), a wine cellar, and an exclusive restaurant (*see* p.202). **Peck Rosticceria**, with a *tavola calda* where you can have lunch, is in nearby Via Cantù, and there is a **Peck Bottega del Vino**, a wine bar, in Via Victor Hugo.

Rizzoli, Galleria Vittorio Emanuele 79, one of the city's best-stocked bookshops (with many English titles), is owned by the family that founded the *Corriere della Sera*.

Cutting-edge designer homewares stores and showrooms near the centre include **Artemide**, Corso Monforte 19; **Flos**, Corso Monforte 7; **Fontana Arte**, Via Santa Margherita 4; **De Padova**, Corso Venezia 14; **Dilmos**, Piazza San Marco 1; **Cassini**, Via Durini 18; and **Alias**, Via V. Monti 2.

Elsewhere in Milan

Brera has some of Milan's most original shops and boutiques, as well as old standbys such as **Surplus**, Corso Garibaldi 7, with its marvellous array of secondhand clothes, and the **COIN** department store, Piazza 5 Giornate 1/a, a good bet for reasonably priced fashions.

Via Paolo Sarpi (metro Moscova), formerly the city's Chinatown, has excellent wares at reasonable prices. Further south, Corso di Porta Ticinese and Corsa Porta Romana have several quirkier, smaller designer shops; try **Dibiemme Fashion,** Corso di Porta Romana 121, a label gold mine.

Outside the centre are several outlets offering designer labels at up to 70% off: **Dolce & Gabbana Industria**, Via Rossini 70 in Legnano (metro Palestro), is worth the trek; **Il Salvagente**, Via Fratelli Bronzetti 26 (tram no.27), stocks surplus exclusive labels.

Markets

The tourist office publishes a complete list. Most markets open mornings 9–1; nearly all close in Aug.

The **Mercato del Sabato** clothes market on Viale Papiniano (metro Sant'Agostino; Tues and Sat mornings) sometimes has cast-offs from fashion shows.

Antiques markets include the **Mercatone dell'Antiquariato**, along the Naviglio Grande (metro Porta Genova; last Sun of month except July), and the **Mercato Antiquariato di Brera**, Via Fiori Chiari (metro Lanza, 3rd Sat of month).

The **Mercato della Darsena** along the banks of the Darsena (metro Porta Genova) is an excellent daily food market, as is the lovely old covered **Mercato di Piazza Wagner** (metro Wagner).

Sports and Activities

Milan's 1st-division **football** clubs, **AC Milan** (*www.acmilan.com*) and **Inter** (*www.inter.it*), play on alternate Suns Sept–May at San Siro stadium, Via Piccolomini 5 (metro Lotto). **Tickets** for matches are available at the stadium, or from Milan Point, Via P. Verri 8, **t** 02 780398. For Inter matches, you can also buy tickets at branches of Banca Popolare di Milano; for AC games you can get tickets from branches of the Banca Cariplo.

San Siro Stadium also has a **football museum** that offers guided stadium tours, **t** 02 404 2432 (*open daily 10–6, except match days; adm exp*).

Where to Stay

Basically, Milan has smart hotels for expense accounters and seedy dives for new arrivals from the provinces. The pleasure traveller has the choice of paying a lot for an up-to-date modern room with little atmosphere, or less for a place where they may not feel very comfortable (or, worse, safe).

Reserve in advance, because exceptions to the rule are snapped up fast. During the trade fairs (especially the big fashion shows in Mar and autumn, and the April Fair) you may find no room at the inn, whereas in Aug much of Milan closes down and it can be surprisingly easy to find a hotel.

Milan Hoteliers Association: Corso Buenos Aires 77, **t** 02 674 8031, *www.traveleurope.it*.

Milano Hotels Central Booking: **t** 02 805 4242, *www.hotelbooking.com*.

Luxury

*******Excelsior Gallia**, Piazza Duca d'Aosta 9, 20124 (metro Centrale), **t** 02 67851, *www.excelsiorgallia.it*. A hotel that opened in 1932 and has been stayed in by Toscanini and Gorbachev, with spacious, elegant, air-conditioned rooms with satellite TV, plus a health centre offering Turkish baths and beauty treatments.

*******Four Seasons**, Via Gesù 8, 20121 (metro Montenapoleone), **t** 02 77088, *www.fourseasons.com*. A beautiful hotel in a 15th-century monastery – the church is the lobby and most of the spacious rooms overlook the cloister. There are enormous bathrooms, plush sofas around a blazing fire in the winter, and a private garage.

*******Grand Hotel et de Milan**, Via Manzoni 29, 20121 (metro Montenapoleone), **t** 02 723 141, *www.grandhoteletdemilan.it*. Open since 1863 and a favourite with Verdi, Hemingway and Nureyev, now fashion HQ. Rooms are furnished with antiques; the atmosphere is grand and gracious.

*******Principe di Savoia**, Piazza della Repubblica 17, 20124 (metro Repubblica), **t** 02 6230 5555. An elegant and prestigious hotel built in 1927 and patronized by the Duke of Windsor, Aristotle Onassis and Maria Callas. The presidential suite is considered by *Architectural Digest* one of the world's most beautiful retreats.

Very Expensive

****Cavour, Via Fatebenefratelli 21, 20121 (metro Montenapoleone), **t** 02 657 2051, *www.hotelcavour.it*. An elegantly furnished hotel with a display of drawings of costumes at La Scala by Gio Ponti.

****De La Ville, Via Hoepli 6, 20121 (metro Duomo), **t** 02 867 651. A modern place with antique furnishings, courteous staff, comfy lounges, a bar and an excellent restaurant.

****Manin, Via Manin 7, 20121 (metro Turati), **t** 02 659 6511. A hotel facing the Giardini Pubblici, with a friendly welcome, quiet, modern, comfy rooms and a garden.

****Sheraton Diana Majestic, Viale Piave 42, 20129 (metro Porta Venezia), **t** 02 20581. A fashionable Liberty-style hotel with charming rooms, views over a garden and a lovely breakfast buffet.

****Hotel Spadari, Via Spadari 11, 20123 (metro Duomo), **t** 02 7200 2371, *www.spadarihotel.com*. A swanky designer hotel.

***Antica Locanda dei Mercanti, Via San Tomaso 6, 20121 (metro Duomo), **t** 02 805 4080, *www.locanda.it*. A charming, discreet but very central inn. Top-floor rooms have canopy beds and roof terraces.

***Ariosto, Via Ariosto 22, 20145 (metro Conciliazione), **t** 02 481 7844, *www.brerahotels.com*. A characterful early 20th-century mansion with a lovely courtyard.

***Ariston, Largo Carrobbio 2, 20123 (south end of Via Torino; tram no.2, 5 or 14), **t** 02 7200 0556, *www.brerahotels.com*. An eco-lover's paradise with 100% cotton futons, hydro-massage water-saving showers and ion-emitting machines in every room.

***Gala, Viale Zara 89, 20159 (metro Zara), **t** 02 6680 0891. A fine mid-sized hotel with wrought-iron beds, set in a quiet garden.

***Manzoni, Via Santo Spirito 20, 20121 (metro Montenapoleone), **t** 02 7600 5700. A pleasant hotel near the centre, with a garage and soundproofed rooms. Book ahead.

Expensive

****Hotel Regency, Via Giovanni Arimondi 12, 20155 (tram no.12), **t** 02 3921 6021. An Art Nouveau style hotel.

****Pierre Milano, Via de Amicis 32 (tram no.2), 20123, **t** 02 7200 0581. A friendly hotel with well-designed rooms and all the amenities.

Antica Locanda Solferino, Via Castelfidardo 2, 20121 (metro Moscova), **t 02 657 0129. An atmospheric 19th-century inn. Book ahead.

Moderate

****Hotel Regina, Via Cesare Correnti 13, 20123 (metro Sant'Ambrogio), **t** 02 5810 6913, *www.hotelregina.it*. A stylish but keenly priced option.

***Hotel Promessi Sposi, Piazza Oberdan, 20129 (metro Porta Venezia), **t** 02 2951 3661. A romantic hotel with all the amenities.

***Hotel Vittoria, Via Pietro Calvi 32, 20129, (tram no.27, bus 60), **t** 02 545 6520. A small, friendly hotel with comfortable rooms.

Cheap

Albergo Commercio, Via Mercato 1, entrance on Via Erbe, 20121 (metro Lanza), **t** 02 8646 3880. A clean, good-value hotel. Book ahead.

La Cordata (Casa Scout), Via Burigozzo 11, 20122 (metro Missori), **t** 02 5831 4675. A private hostel with kitchen facilities.

Ostello Piero Rotta, Via Salmoiraghi 2, near San Siro stadium, 20148 (metro QT 8), **t** 02 3926 7095. A modern youth hostel, with a maximum 3-night stay. *Closed 22 Dec–13 Jan; open 7–9.30am and 3.30–midnight.*

Hotel Ullrich, Corso Italia 6, 20124 (metro Missori), **t** 02 8645 9156. A pleasant *pensione* on the 6th floor of a *palazzo*.

Eating Out

Moneyed Milan has some of Italy's finest restaurants and the widest range of global cuisine, but an average meal costs considerably more here than almost anywhere else in Italy. The best places to find cheaper restaurants are the Brera, Ticinese and Navigli districts.

Unless otherwise stated, restaurants close in Aug; so few remain open that their names are printed in the paper.

Saffron, the city's fetish spice, appears in most dishes *alla milanese*.

Very Expensive

Aimo e Nadia, Via Montecuccoli 6 (metro Bande Nere), **t** 02 416 886. High-quality and highly popular Lombard and national cuisine. Book ahead. *Closed Sat eve and Sun. Book ahead.*

Antica Osteria del Ponte, on Naviglio Grande, Cassinetta di Lugagnano (20km from Milan), **t** 02 981 8663. A temple of Italian traditional cuisine. *Closed Sun and Mon.*

Don Lisander, Via Manzoni 12 (metro Duomo), **t** 02 7602 0130. A creative global menu, served in a garden in summer. *Closed Sun.*

La Galleria, Piazza della Repubblica 17 (metro Repubblica), **t** 02 6230 2026. Excellent Paduan food in the luxurious Hotel Principe di Savoia.

Nino Arnaldo, Via Carlo Poerio 3 (metro Porta Venezia), **t** 02 7600 5981. The elegant base of one of the city's most creative chefs, whose repertoire includes wonderful desserts such as cinnamon ice cream and *zabaione*. *Closed Sat lunch and Sun.*

Nobu, Armani flagship store, Via Manzoni 31 (metro Montenapoleone), **t** 02 7231 8645. Sushi downstairs and a chic New York-style restaurant upstairs. *Closed eves except Mon.*

Peck, Via Victor Hugo 4 (metro Duomo), **t** 02 876 774. A deli (*see* p.199) with a modern restaurant offering a hard-to-beat *risotto alla milanese*. *Closed Sun, hols and 3wks July.*

Ran, Via Bordoni 8 (metro Gioia), **t** 02 669 6997. An elegant sushi bar. *Closed Sun.*

Savini, Galleria Vittorio Emanuele II, **t** 02 7200 3433 (metro Duomo). A bastion of Milanese tradition since 1867, with faultless Lombard classics. *Closed Sat lunch and Sun.*

La Scaletta, Piazzale Stazione Porta Genova 3 (metro Porta Genova), **t** 02 5810 0290. The culinary workshop of Italy's *nuova cucina* sorceress, Pina Bellini, who does stunning things to pasta and risotto, fish and rabbit. Book ahead. *Closed Sun, and Mon lunch.*

Expensive

Antica Trattoria della Pesa, Viale Pasubio 10, close to Porta Comasina (metro Garibaldi), **t** 02 655 5741. A traditional trattoria dating back to 1880, which has fed generations of Milanese publishers and journalists, plus Maria Callas and Visconti. *Closed Sun.*

Aurora, Via Savona 23, in the Navigli (metro Porta Genova), **t** 02 8940 4978. Lovely *belle époque* dining rooms in which to enjoy lovely Piemonte cuisine, with an emphasis on mushrooms and truffles. Save room for the bewildering array of cheeses and superb *tarte tatin*. *Closed Mon.*

Bice, Via Borgospesso 12 (metro Montenapoleone), **t** 02 7600 2572. Sophisticated, traditional cuisine and impeccable service. *Closed Mon.*

Centro Ittico, Via Aporti 35 (metro Loreto), **t** 02 614 3774. Fish direct from the market counter. *Closed Sun and Mon.*

Hong Kong, Via Schiaparelli 5 (metro Centrale), **t** 02 670 1992. A secluded place combining Chinese *haute cuisine* with refined décor. *Closed Mon.*

Piccolo Sogno, Via Stoppani 5 (metro Porta Venezia), **t** 02 2024 1210. Faultless traditional and regional cuisine. *Closed Sat lunch and Sun.*

Al Porto, Piazzale Generale Cantore, **t** 02 832 1481 (metro Porta Genova). A fish restaurant in a 19th-century toll house with a beautiful winter garden. *Closed Sun and Mon lunch.*

Quattrocento, Via Campazzino 14 (tram no.79), **t** 02 895 1777. A 15th-century monastery transformed into a stylish and popular minimalist shrine with delicious nouveau cuisine. Booking essential. *Closed Mon.*

La Terrazza, Via Ozanam 1 (metro Lima), **t** 02 204 8433. Alfresco traditional dining on the top floor of the Hotel Galles Milano, with a view over the Duomo.

13 Giugno, Via Carlo Goldoni 44 (metro Porta Venezia), **t** 02 719 654. Sicilian seafood dishes in a 1930s ambience. *Closed Sun.*

Al Vecchio Porco, Via Messina 8 (tram no.12 or 14), **t** 02 313 862. A trendy pizzeria serving such delights as *pizza del Porco*, with sausage, gorgonzola and egg. *Closed lunch and Sun.*

Vini e Cucina, Via P. Castaldi 38 (metro Repubblica), **t** 02 2951 9840. An acclaimed New York-style fish restaurant. *Closed Mon eve.*

La Volpe e l'Uva, Via Senato 45 (metro Montenapoleone), **t** 02 7602 2167. Imaginative cooking in intimate surroundings. *Closed Sun, Mon, and Weds and Sat eves.*

Moderate

Armani Caffè, Via Croce Rossa 2 (metro Montenapoleone), **t** 02 7231 8680. Mediterranean dishes in non-smoking designer surroundings. *Closed eves.*

La Compagnia dei Naviganti e Viaggiatori, Naviganti e Sognatori, Via Cuccagna 4 (metro Porta Romana), **t** 02 551 6154. A Japanese place run by Italians and Brazilians in an old country house. *Closed lunch, Sun and Mon.*

Endo, Via Fabio Filzi 8 (metro Loreto), **t** 02 6698 6688. Milan's oldest Japanese restaurant, with a good-value lunch menu and takeaway. *Closed Mon.*

La Felicità, Via Rovello 3 (metro Cairoli), **t** 02 865 235. A romantic central Chinese. *Closed Mon eve.*

Geppo, Viale Brianza 30 (metro Loreto), **t** 02 284 6548. A big name in Milan pizza lore, with 50 varieties. *Closed Sun.*

Innocenti Evasioni, Via Bindellina, San Siro (tram no.14), **t** 02 3300 1882. An escape from the city, with country-style rooms overlooking a garden and an eclectic, ever-changing menu. *Closed lunch, Sun and Mon.*

Jucker Zupperia, Via Pasquale Sottocorno 50 (tram no.9, 20 or 23), **t** 02 700 9813. Soups made from natural ingredients, to take away or enjoy at the diner bar. *Closed Mon eve.*

Kota Radja, Piazzale Baracca 6 (metro Conciliazione), **t** 02 468 850. Excellent Chinese cuisine in an elegant setting. *Closed Mon.*

Latteria San Marco, Via San Marco 24 (metro Moscova), **t** 02 659 7653. A busy family-run inn favoured by media types, with excellent puddings. No bookings or credit cards. *Closed Sat and Sun.*

Officina 12, Alzaia Naviglio Grande 12 (metro Porta Genova), **t** 02 8942 2261. A huge hi-tech loft meets traditional pizzeria. *Closed Mon.*

Osteria delle Vigne, Ripa di Porta Ticinese 61 (metro Porta Genova), **t** 02 857 5617. A relaxed, good-value, friendly restaurant in a buzzy district, serving delicious food. *Closed Sat–Mon and lunchtimes.*

Al Pont de Ferr, Via Ripa Ticinese 55 (metro Porta Genova), **t** 02 8940 6277. Fine dishes such as pigeon with mushrooms and polenta, and superb wines. Arrive early to avoid the queues. *Closed lunch and Sun.*

Ponte Rosso, Via Ripa di Porta Ticinese 23 (metro Porta Genova), **t** 02 837 3132. A romantic old-world bistro combing traditional Trieste dishes with Lombard specialities. *Closed Sun and Weds eve.*

Sadler Wine & Food, Via Montebianco 2/a (metro Lotto), **t** 02 481 4677. Elaborate, creative traditional dishes to accompany more than 350 wines. *Closed Sun.*

Tipica Osteria Pugliese, Via Tadino 5 (metro Lima), **t** 02 2952 2574. A place where you can eat cheaply by filling your dish of *antipasti* from a selection of 40 specialities from Puglia. *Closed Sun.*

Trattoria all'Antica, Via Montevideo 4, Ticinese area (metro Sant'Agostino), **t** 02 5810 4360. Abundant, simply prepared Lombard fare. *Closed Sat lunch and Sun.*

Trattoria Milanese, Via Santa Maria 11 (*metro Duomo*), **t** 02 864 51991. A homely, family-run trattoria with genuine local fare. *Closed Tues.*

Trattoria Toscana, Corso Porta Ticinese 58 (tram 3, 20), **t** 02 8940 6292. A jolly, late-opening place offering the likes of gnocchi filled with ricotta, and swordfish with thyme. *Closed lunchtimes, and Sun.*

Cheap

Milan has many US and Italian fast-food outlets. Self-service chains Brek and Pastarito are recommended for their pasta dishes, which are so large that a portion often feeds 2.

Da Rino Vecchia Napoli, Via Chavez 4, between Stazione Centrale and Parco Lambro (metro Pasteur), **t** 02 261 9056. A vast selection of prize-winning pizzas, plus good *antipasti*, gnocchi and fish. Booking advisable. *Closed Sun lunch and Mon.*

Govinda, Via Valpetrosa 3/5 (metro Duomo), **t** 02 862 417. Very good vegetarian and macrobiotic food, with takeaway. *Closed Sun, and Mon lunch.*

Joya, Via P. Castaldi 18 (metro Porta Venezia), **t** 02 2952 2124. One of the best vegetarian restaurants in Italy (*expensive–moderate in the evening*). *Closed Sat lunch and Sun.*

Il Naviglio, Via Casale 5 (metro Porta Genova), **t** 02 8940 0768. Very good vegetarian food. *Closed Mon, and Tues eve.*

Osteria del Treno, Via S. Gregorio 46 (metro Porta Venezia), **t** 02 669 1706. An atmospheric ex railworkers' club with excellent, good-value self-service lunches, and very good (*moderate*) sit-down dinners. *Closed Sat.*

Osteria Tagiura, Via Tagiura 5, San Siro (bus no.50, 90 or 91), **t** 02 4895 0613. A friendly, family-run *osteria* where you can have a good full meal or just a piece of cake or dish of salami. No credit cards. *Open daily for lunch, and Thurs and Fri eves.*

Ristorante San Tomaso, Via San Tomaso 5 (metro Cairoli), **t** 02 874 510. A popular lunch choice with working Milanese for its self-service buffet. *Closed Sat lunch and Sun.*

Cakes, Brunches and *Panini*

Acerba 2, Via Orti 4 (metro Porta Romana). Daily brunch in an old carriage garage, and an excellent choice of cakes. *Closed Mon.*

Art & Soul Café, Smeraldo theatre, Piazza XXIV Aprile 10 (metro Garibaldi). New Age veggie brunches. *Closed Sun eve.*

Bar Quadronno, Via Quadronno 34 (metro Crocetta). Milan's oldest sandwich-maker, with a loyal clientele. *Closed Mon and eves.*

Berlin Café, Via G. Mora 7 (metro Porta Genova). Sunday brunches in a historical bar.

Le Biciclette, Via Torti (tram no.2 or 14). A trendy café in an old bike shed, with good Sunday brunches. *Closed Sun eve.*

Caffè Cova, Via Monte Napoleone 8 (metro Montenapoleone). A Milanese institution famous for its pastries since 1837. *Closed Sun.*

Caffè Sant'Ambroeus, Corso Matteotti 7 (metro Montenapoleone). A 1936 bar with wonderful period décor. *Closed Mon.*

10 Corso Como Caffè, Corso Como 10 (metro Garibaldi). Mediterranean sushi, truffle omelettes and other minimal brunches, plus late-night cocktails. *Closed Mon lunch.*

Al Panino, Viale Crispi 5 (metro Garibaldi). Eighty types of sandwich plus warm *focaccia*, cold dishes and fries. *Closed Mon.*

Panino del Conte, Via Broletto (metro Duomo). Excellent sandwiches, including the famous *Piadina del Conte*. *Closed Sun.*

Panino Giusto, Piazza Beccaria 4 (metro Duomo), Piazzale XXIV Maggio (metro Porta Genova) and elsewhere. A good sandwich chain.

Gelaterie

Antica Gelateria del Corso, Galleria del Corso 4 (metro Duomo). Three floors of delicious ice creams, sandwiches, pastries, weekend brunches, salads and cocktails.

Cremeria Buonarroti, Via Buonarroti 9 (metro Buonarroti). The crème de la crème, with goodies such as strawberries bathed in Gianduja chocolate. *Closed Mon.*

Ecologica, Corso di Porta Ticinese 40 (tram no.3 or 20). Natural ice-cream treats. *Closed Weds.*

Rossi, Viale Romagna 23 (metro Piola). A tiny place serving some of the best ice cream in Milan, plus exquisite chocolates and *tiramisù*. *Closed Tues.*

Viel, Foro Buonaparte 71 (metro Cairoli). Ice creams in surprising flavours. *Closed Weds.*

Entertainment and Nightlife

Check listings in the daily *Corriere della Sera* and *La Repubblica*'s Weds *Tutto Milano* magazine. Other sources include the free *Milano Mese* and *Hello Milan*, from the main tourist office.

Tickets are sold at **Virgin Megastore**, Piazza Duomo 8; **Ricordi**, Galleria Vittorio Emanuele II; **La Biglietteria**, Via Molino delle Armi 3; **Box Ticket**, Largo Cairoli; and at Stazione Cadorna.

Cinema

Anteo on Corso Via Milazzo 9 (metro Moscova), **t** 02 659 7732, regularly shows films in English – make sure it says *versione originale*.

Opera and Classical Music

For many people, **La Scala** (metro Duomo), is the reason for visiting Milan (*see* p.210). Tickets can be booked on **t** 02 860 775 from about 2mths in advance of the show, or at *www.teatroallascala.org*. Finding a good seat at a moment's notice is all but impossible; you could try through your hotel's concierge, or show up at the box office an hour or so before the performance starts to see what's available; chances are it'll be a vertiginous gallery seat, or squeezed in under the ceiling. The CIT office in Galleria Vittorio Emanuele II, **t** 02 863 701, has a number of tickets to sell to foreign tourists who book hotels through them.

The **Auditorium di Milano**, Corso San Gottardo, Navigli district (tram no.3 or 15), **t** 02 8942 2090, *www.auditoriumdimilano.org*, hosts concerts by the Symphonic Conservatory Giuseppe Verdi, plus jazz, choral and chamber music. The **Giuseppe Verdi Conservatorio**, Via del Conservatorio 12 (metro San Babila), **t** 02 762 1101 or **t** 02 7600 1854, is another classical venue (mid-Sept–June).

The city sponsors a series of (sometimes free) Renaissance and Baroque music concerts in the lovely church of **San Maurizio** on Corso Magenta and in **San Marco**, Piazza San Marco.

Theatre

Italy's best theatre company, the **Piccolo Teatro**, Via Rovello 2, near Via Dante (metro Cordusio), **t** 7233 3222, *www.piccoloteatro.org*, has a repertory ranging from *commedia dell'arte* to the avant garde. Tickets are cheap, but book ahead. Performances are held in the historical venue in Via Rovello, at **Teatro Giorgio Strehler**, Largo Greppi, at **Teatro Studio**, Via Rivoli 6, and occasionally at the much bigger **Teatro Lirico**, near the Duomo at Via Larga 14, **t** 02 809 665.

The **Teatro Nazionale**, Piazza Piemonte 12 (metro Wagner), **t** 02 4800 7700, *www.teatronazionale.com*, hosts plays and musicals.

Jazz

Blues Canal, Via Casale 7, Navigli (metro Porta Genova). Top live jazz in the evenings (spot Louis Armstrong's trumpet hanging on the wall) and American/Irish Sunday brunches.

Blues House, Via S. Uguzzone 26, off Viale Monza, Sesto San Giovanni, northeast of city, **t** 02 2700 3621. Live blues. *Closed Mon.*

Gimmies, Via Cellini 2 (metro San Babila), **t** 02 5518 8069. An exclusive piano bar favoured by Italian celebs and theatre types.

Grilloparlante, Alzaia Naviglio Grande 36 (metro Porta Genova), **t** 02 8940 9321. An old Navigli house with jazz and blues by amateurs and professionals.

Martinique Café, Via P. da Cannobio 37 (metro Missori). A jazz and soul bar serving sushi at happy hour. *Closed Mon.*

Scimmie, Via Ascanio Sforza 49 (metro Porta Genova), **t** 02 8940 2874. High-quality jazz, on a barge in summer. *Closed Tues.*

Tangram, Via Pezzotti 52 (metro Famagosta), **t** 02 8950 1007. Jazz, funk, rhythm and blues. *Closed Sun.*

Bars

Atiemme, Bastioni di Porta Volta 15 (metro Moscova), **t** 02 655 2365. A trendy former train station with good cocktails. *Closed Sun.*

Atomic Bar, Via F. Casati 24 (metro Repubblica). An avant-garde dance bar. *Closed Tues.*

Bar Basso, Via Plinio 39, Città Studi (metro Lima). More than 500 cocktails and home-made ice creams in a venue with a 19th-century *salotto*. *Closed Tues.*

La Bodeguita del Medio, Via Col di Lana (tram no.9 or 15), **t** 02 8940 0560. A popular cigar bar with Cuban music, food and atmosphere.

Casablanca, Corso Como 14 (metro Garibaldi), **t** 02 626 0186. A trendy cocktail bar/restaurant with dancing in the garden in summer. *Closed Mon.*

Diana Garden, Viale Piave 42 (metro Porta Venezia), **t** 02 20581. A fashionable *aperitivo* spot in the 'tropical' garden of the Diana hotel.

Light, Via Maroncelli 8 (metro Garibaldi), **t** 02 6269 0631. The definitive late lounge.

Magenta, Via Carducci 13 (tram no.19 or 24), **t** 02 805 3808. A historical Art Nouveau bar and beer house. *Closed Mon.*

Moscatelli, Corso Garibaldi 93 (metro Moscova), **t** 02 655 4602. Milan's oldest wine bar.

Matricola Pub, Viale Romagna 43 (tram no.23). A Guinness-owned place, with full pub lunches and 'English' breakfasts. *Closed Sun.*

Speakeasy, Via Castelfidardo 7 (metro Moscova). A 1930s US-style bar in front of Ponte delle Gabelle, with Sunday brunch, happy hours and a vast choice of US dailies. *Closed Mon.*

Le Trottoir, Corso Garibaldi 1, Brera (metro Garibaldi). An artists' bar with live music and a good restaurant. In summer people often play chess on the pavement.

Xe Mauri, Via Confalonieri 28 (metro Garibaldi), **t** 02 3360 8697. A laguna bar ideal for early evening drinks. *Closed Mon.*

Zythum, Via Rutilia 16 (metro Porta Romana), **t** 02 569 1616. A brewery/fusion restaurant with a sushi corner and live music and events.

Clubs and Discos

Clubs generally open daily until 3am (often later at weekends), and the pricey admission entitles you to a free drink.

Nuova Idea, Via De Castilla 30 (metro Garibaldi). Milan's foremost gay club. *Closed Mon–Weds.*

Plastic, Viale Umbria 120 (metro Porta Romana). A chic place with an eclectic clientele, drag-queen shows and fussy doormen; Thurs is gay night. *Closed Mon–Weds.*

Shocking, Via Bastioni di Porta Nuova 12 (metro Repubblica). A popular club among models, designers and fashion victims: *Closed Sun and Mon.*

Propaganda, Via Castelbarco 11 (metro Porta Genova). Dance nights and live concerts. *Closed Thurs.*

Sottomarino Giallo, Via Donatello 2 (metro Loreto). A gay hotspot with dance music; most nights are for women only. *Closed Thurs.*

Tropicana Club Latino, Viale Bligny 52 (metro Porta Romana). Latin American dancing. *Closed Sun, Mon and Weds.*

It was Lodi's complaint about Milan's bullying to the Holy Roman Emperor **Frederick Barbarossa** that first brought old Red Beard to Italy in 1154. It was to prove a momentous battle of wills and arms between the emperor and Milan. Barbarossa sacked Milan in 1158; the *Ambrosiani* promised to behave but attacked his German garrison as soon as the emperor was back safely over the Alps. Undaunted, Barbarossa returned again and for two years laid waste to the countryside around Milan, then grimly besieged the defiant city. When it surrendered, he was merciless, demanding the surrender of the *carroccio*, forcing the citizens to kiss his feet with ropes around their necks, and inviting Milan's bitterest enemies, Lodi and Como, to raze the city to the ground, sparing only the churches of Sant'Ambrogio and San Lorenzo.

But this total humiliation of Milan, meant as an imperial lesson to Italy's other *comuni*, had the opposite effect; it galvanized them to form the **Lombard League** against the foreign oppressor (only Pavia hated Milan too much to join). Barbarossa, on his next trip over the Alps, found the *comuni* united against him, and in 1176 he was soundly defeated by the Lombard League at Legnano. Now the tables had turned and the empire itself was in danger of total revolt. To preserve it, Barbarossa had to do a little foot-kissing himself in Venice – the privileged toe in this case belonging to Pope Alexander III, whom Barbarossa had exiled from Rome in order to set up another pope more malleable to his schemes. To placate the Lombard *comuni*, the **Treaty of Constance** was signed after a six-year truce in 1183, in which the signatories of the Lombard League received all that they desired: their municipal autonomy and the privilege of making war – on each other. The more magnanimous idea of a united Italy was still centuries away.

The Age of the Big Bosses

If Milan invented government by *comune*, it was also one of the first cities to give it up. Unlike their counterparts in Florence, Milan's manufacturers were varied in their trades; they limited themselves to small workshops, and failed to form the companies of merchants and trade associations that were the power base of a medieval Italian republic. The first to fill the vacuum at the top were the Torriani (della Torre), feudal lords who became the city's *signori* in 1247, losing their position to the Visconti in 1277.

The Visconti, created dukes in 1395, made Milan the strongest state in Italy, and marriages with French and English royalty brought the family into European affairs. Most ambitious of all the Visconti was Gian Galeazzo (1351–1402), married first to the daughter of the king of France, then to the daughter of his powerful and malevolent uncle Bernabò, whom Gian Galeazzo sent to prison before conquering northern Italy, the Veneto, Romagna and Umbria. His army was ready to march on Florence when he died of the plague. In his ruthlessness and his dependence on astrology, his love of art and letters (he founded the Certosa of Pavia, began the Duomo, held a lavish court and supported the university of Pavia), Gian Galeazzo was one of the first 'archetypal' Renaissance princes. The Florentines and Venetians took advantage of his demise to carry off pieces of his empire; while his sons, the obscene Giovanni Maria (who fed his enemies to the dogs) and the gruesome, paranoid Filippo Maria, tried to regain their father's conquests, Milan's influence was reduced to Lombardy.

Filippo Maria left no male heirs but betrothed his wise and lovely daughter, Bianca, to his best *condottiere*, Francesco Sforza (1401–66). After Filippo's death the Golden Ambrosian Republic was declared by the Milanese, but it crumbled after three years, when Francesco Sforza returned peacefully to accept the dukedom. One of Milan's best rulers, he continued the scientific development of Lombard agriculture, navigable canals and hydraulic schemes, and kept the peace through an alliance with the Medici. His son, Galeazzo Maria, was assassinated, but not before fathering Caterina Sforza, the great Renaissance virago, and a son, Gian Galeazzo II.

Lodovico il Moro

It was, however, Francesco Sforza's second son, **Lodovico il Moro** (1451–1508), who took power and became Milan's most cultivated ruler, helped by his wife, the delightful **Beatrice d'Este**, who ran one of Italy's most sparkling courts until her early death in childbirth. Lodovico was a great patron of the arts, commissioning from Leonardo the *Last Supper*, engineering schemes and magnificent theatrical pageants. But Lodovico also bears the blame for one of the greatest political blunders in Italian history, when his quarrel with Naples grew so touchy that he invited Charles VIII of France to come and claim the Kingdom of Naples for himself. Charles took him up on it and marched unhindered down Italy. Lodovico soon realized his mistake, and joined the last-minute league of Italian states that united to trap and destroy the French at Fornovo. They succeeded, partially, but the damage was done: the French invasion had shown the Italian states, beautiful, rich, in full flower of the Renaissance, to be disunited and vulnerable. Charles VIII's son, **Louis XII**, took advantage of a claim on Milan through a Visconti grandmother and captured the city, and Lodovico with it. The Duke of Milan died a prisoner in a Loire château, an unhappy Prospero covering the walls of his dungeon with bizarre graffiti that perplexes visitors to this day. After more fights between French and Spanish, Milan ended up a strategic province of Charles V's empire, ruled by a Spanish viceroy.

In 1712 the city came under the **Habsburgs** of Austria, and along with the rest of Lombardy it profited from the enlightened reforms of **Maria Theresa**, who did much to improve agriculture, rationalize taxes and increase education; her rule saw the creation of La Scala, the Brera Academy and the majority of central neoclassical Milan. After centuries of hibernation the Ambrosiani were stirring again, and when Napoleon arrived the city welcomed him fervently. With a huge festival, Milan became the capital of Napoleon's 'Cisalpine Republic', linked to Paris via the new Simplon Highway.

The Powerhouse of United Italy

After Napoleon's defeat in 1814 the Austrians returned, but Milan was an important centre of Italian nationalist sentiment during the Risorgimento and rebelled against the repressive Habsburg regime in 1848. The city's greatest contribution during this period, however, was the novelist **Manzoni**, whose masterpiece *I Promessi Sposi* caused a nationwide sensation and sense of unity in a peninsula that had been politically divided since the fall of Rome (*see* p.211 and p.271).

After joining the new **kingdom of Italy**, Milan rapidly took its place as the country's economic and industrial dynamo, attracting thousands of workers from the poorer sections of Italy. Many joined the new Italian Socialist Party, which was strongest in the regions of Lombardy and Emilia-Romagna. In Milan, too, **Mussolini** founded the Fascist Party and launched its first campaign in 1919. The city was bombed during the **Second World War**. In May 1945 Milan's well-organized partisan forces liberated it from the Germans before the Allies arrived, and when Mussolini's corpse was hung on a meat hook in the Piazzale Loreto the Milanese turned out to make sure the duke of delusion was truly dead before beginning to rebuild their battered city.

Milan was, again, the centre of Italy's postwar miracle when it began to take off in the late 1950s, drawing in still more thousands of migrants from the south. Despite ups and downs and a few hiccups, the city's wealth has continued to grow ever since. In the early 1990s, however, the whole structure came crashing down, for it was here that the first allegations of the large-scale taking of *tangenti* (bribes) came to light, initially involving the Socialists and their ineffable boss, Bettino Craxi, though the mud spread to all established parties. Craxi and his cronies have disappeared from the political map, and power in Milan is held by a right-wing government, after being disputed between a left/green alliance and Umberto Bossi's Lega Nord, though Italian PM Silvio Berlusconi, who calls Milan home, also has a strong political influence.

Piazza del Duomo

Duomo

Open Tues–Sun 9.45–5.45; adm free except for baptistry (tickets at bookshop, closed 1–3), treasury and crypt. Roof open daily Nov–Feb 9–4.45, Mar–Oct 9–5.45; adm. Metro Duomo. Façade covered for restoration work until late 2004.

In the exact centre of Milan towers its famous **Duomo**, a monument of such imposing proportions (the third largest in the world after St Peter's and Seville) that on clear days it is as visible from the distant Alps as the Alps are visible from its dome. Bristling with 135 spires, defended by 2,244 marble saints and one cheeky sinner (Napoleon, who crowned himself King of Italy here in 1805), guarded by 95 leering gargoyles, energized by sunlight pouring through the largest stained-glass windows in Christendom, Milan cathedral is a remarkable bulwark of the faith. And yet for all its monstrous size, for all the hubbub of its busy piazza, traversed daily by tens of thousands of Milanese and tourists, the Duomo is utterly ethereal, a rose-white vision of pinnacles and tracery woven by angels. In Vittorio de Sica's *Miracle in Milan* (1950) it serves its natural role as a stairway (or launching pad) to heaven for the broomstick-riding heroes. Gian Galeazzo Visconti began the Duomo in 1386 as a votive offering to the Mother of God, hoping she would favour him with an heir. His prayers were answered in the form of Giovanni Maria, a loathsome degenerate who was assassinated soon after he attained power; as the Ambrosiani have wryly noted, the Mother of God got the better of the deal.

The Cathedral Interior

The remarkable dimensions of the interior challenge the eye to take in what seems like infinity captured under a canopy. Its tremendous volume is defined into five aisles by 52 pillars of titanic dimensions, unusually crowned by rings of niches and statues, and is dazzlingly lit by acres of stained glass, embellished with flamboyant Gothic tracery; the oldest windows, from the 15th century, are along the naves at the crossing. All other decorations seem rather small (the better to emphasize the vast size), but you may want to seek out in the right transept Leone Leoni's fine Mannerist tomb of the Marquess di Marignano, Gian Giacomo de' Medici, Il Medeghino, the pirate of Lake Como – erected by his brother Pope Pius IV. Fine bronze statues of Peace and Military Virtue sit on either side of a statue of the hero, portrayed with sword on hand, ready to go to war again. A relief of the Adoration of the Magi on top is the only nod towards religion, and its placement covers up part of the window. His sarcophagus was originally here as well, until his nephew, St Charles Borromeo, removed it in accordance with the edict from the Council of Trent that 'receptacles and vain trophies' be removed from church interiors and buried under the floor.

In the same transept you'll find one of the most peculiar of the cathedral's thousands of statues: that of San Bartolomeo holding his own skin, with an inscription assuring us that it was made by Marco Agrate and not by Praxiteles, just in case we couldn't tell the difference. Other treasures include the beautiful walnut choir stalls, which were carved between 1572 and 1620, and the 12th-century bronze Trivulzio Candelabrum by Nicola da Verdun, as well as medieval ivory, gold and silverwork in the Treasury, located below the main altar by the crypt, where the mastermind of the Counter-Reformation, St Charles Borromeo (1538–84), lies in state. The latter was lucky that he didn't die in the cathedral as well – when he returned to Milan as the resident archbishop at the end of the Council of Trent, he infuriated many members of Milan's then cosy clergy by making them toe the line of the new reforms in order to set a good example to other bishops. One dissident of many shot him during mass, but he was saved by the heavy brocade of his vestments. Throughout the Duomo you can see the alchemical symbol adopted as the Visconti crest, now the symbol of Milan: a twisting serpent in the act of swallowing a man. The story goes that in 1100, in the Second Crusade, the battling bishop Ottone Visconti (the founder of the family fortunes) fought a giant Saracen, and when he slew him he took the device from his shield.

Near the cathedral entrance you'll find a door that leads down to the 4th-century remains of the baptistry of San Giovanni delle Fonti, which was excavated in the 1960s and contains the octagonal baptismal font where St Ambrose baptized St Augustine, as well as remains of the Roman road and other churches that were demolished to make way for the Duomo.

For a splendid view of Milan, take a walk through the enchanted forest of spires and statues on the **cathedral roof**. The 15th-century dome by Amadeo of Pavia, topped by the main spire with the gilt statue of La Madonnina (who at 12ft really isn't as diminutive as she seems 354ft from the ground), offers the best view of all – on a clear morning, you can see all the way to the Matterhorn.

Museo del Duomo and Palazzo Reale

*Piazza del Duomo 12 and 14, **t** 02 7202 2656; open daily 9.30–12.30 and 3–6; adm.*

On the south side of the cathedral, the Palazzo Reale was for centuries the HQ of Milan's rulers, from the Visconti down to the Austrian governors, who had the place redone in their favourite neoclassical style. In one wing, the **Museo del Duomo** contains art and artefacts made for the cathedral over six centuries, including original stained glass and fine 14th-century French and German statues, gargoyles, tapestries and a Tintoretto. Other rooms document the cathedral's construction, including a magnificent 16th-century wooden model and castings from the bronze doors.

The main core of the Palazzo Reale used to accommodate the Civico Museo dell'Arte Contemporanea (CIMAC); though there are tentative plans to see the Palazzo Reale host all the city's contemporary art in the future, the museum is now closed for major restructuring, its collections divided between the Civica Galleria d'Arte Moderna and the Esposizione Permanente delle Belle Arti (for both, *see* p.213). Behind the palace, on Via Palazzo Reale, note the beautiful 14th-century apse and octagonal campanile of the royal palace's church of **San Gottardo** (***t** 02 8646 4500; open daily 8–12 and 2–5.45*), which also contains the reconstructed funerary monument of Azzone Visconti by Giovanni di Balduccio, and part of a fresco of the Crucifixion by the school of Giotto. The porticoes around Piazza del Duomo house some of the city's oldest bars; in its centre Vittorio Emanuele II on his horse looks ready to charge into action.

North of the Duomo

Piazza della Scala and Around

The Piazza della Scala is the address of one of the world's great opera houses, the neoclassical **La Scala** (*see* p.204); its name was derived from the church of Santa Maria alla Scala that stood on the site. Inaugurated in 1778 with Salieri's *Europa Riconosciuta*, it saw the premières of most 19th-century classics of Italian opera; when bombs smashed it in 1943, it was rebuilt as it was in just three years, reopening under the baton of its great conductor Arturo Toscanini. A current €49million refurbishment of the stage, dressing rooms and storage areas is scheduled to be complete by late 2004.

Nearby is the **Galleria Vittorio Emanuele II**, an elegant glass-roofed arcade linking Piazza Duomo and Piazza della Scala. It was designed by Giuseppe Mengoni, who slipped and fell from the roof the day before its inauguration in 1878. Here are more elegant bars and some of the city's finest shops. In the centre, under a marvellous 157ft glass dome, is a mosaic figure of Taurus; the Milanese believe it's good luck to step on the bull's testicles. It has seen a number of historical events, including a parade of elephants on their way to play the part in a production of *Aida* at La Scala.

Next to La Scala, **San Giuseppe** (***t** 02 805 2320; open Mon–Sat 9.30–12.30 and 3.30–6, Sun 9–1*) was a great architectural landmark in its day; if it looks like hundreds of other churches in Italy, it proves the old adage that imitation is the sincerest form of flattery. Begun in 1607, it was the first independent project of Milan's most innovative

Baroque architect Francesco Maria Ricchino, before his patron Cardinal Federico Borromeo sent him to Rome to finish his training. When he returned, this was the result: a church designed on the basis of two simple Greek crosses with abbreviated arms. The dome rises over the congregation on arches, but here Ricchino added a high arch between the congregation and sanctuary to fuse the two spaces in a new and exciting way that would be endlessly repeated by later Baroque architects, who loved its rich possibilities for scenographic effects.

The façade, designed at the same time as the church but not added until 1630, was another innovation. Previous Italian façades had been merely decorative, hardly related to the structure of the church itself. Here Ricchino strove for integration: the façade, designed as a pair of aedicules (compositions of a pediment over paired columns), one set inside the other, reflects the proportions and decorative style of the interior, and draws the eye to the other visible parts of the exterior rather than just the immediate 'show front'. The impression of unity is so immediate that Ricchino's aedicule façade became the favourite in the Baroque style – it was so common, in fact, that most people walk past this once cutting-edge church without a second glance. Originally a convent was attached to it, but it was demolished to allow La Scala to build a deeper stage.

An unloved 19th-century statue of Leonardo stands in the middle of Piazza della Scala, while opposite the theatre the imposing **Palazzo Marino** (*courtyard only open to the public*) is a fine 16th-century building hiding behind a 19th-century façade; now the Palazzo Municipale, it contains one of the city's loveliest courtyards. A few steps away, on Via Catena, the unusual 1565 **Casa degli Omenoni** (*closed to the public*) was built by sculptor Leone Leoni for his retirement. He made his house into a tribute to his hero, the philosopher emperor Marcus Aurelius; the six large and rather uncomfortable-looking *telamones* he sculpted for the façade probably represent members of the barbarian tribes subdued by the emperor.

Around the corner of cobblestoned Piazza Belgioioso, at Via Morone 1 (*metro Montenapoleone*), the handsome old home of Alessandro Manzoni (1785–1873) is now a shrine, the **Museo Manzoniano** (***t** 02 8646 0403; open Tues–Fri 9–12 and 2–4*), filled with items relating to the Milanese novelist's life and work, including some illustrations from *I Promessi Sposi* and an autographed portrait of his friend Goethe. For more on the man, *see* p.271.

Museo Poldi-Pezzoli

In front of La Scala runs one of Milan's busiest and most fashionable boulevards, **Via Manzoni**. Verdi lived for years and died in a room in the Grand Hotel (No.29); at No.10 is the lovely 17th-century palace of Gian Giacomo Poldi-Pezzoli, who rearranged his home to fit his fabulous art collection, then willed it to the public in 1879. Repaired after bomb damage during the war, the **Museo Poldi-Pezzoli** at No.10 (*metro Montenapoleone;* ***t** 02 796 334; open Tues–Sun 10–6; adm*) houses a lovely collection of 15th- to 18th-century paintings, including one of Italy's best-known portraits, the 15th-century *Portrait of a Young Woman* by Antonio Pollaiuolo, depicting an ideal Renaissance beauty.

She shares the most elegant room of the palace, the **Salone Dorato**, with the other jewels of the museum: Mantegna's Byzantinish *Madonna*, Giovanni Bellini's *Pietà*, Piero della Francesca's *San Nicolò* and, from a few centuries later, Francesco Guardi's *Grey Lagoon* (*c.* 1790), a beautiful, dreamlike visionary work. Other outstanding paintings include Vitale da Bologna's *Madonna*, a polyptych by Cristoforo Moretti and works by Botticelli, Luini, Foppa, Turà, Tiepolo, Crivelli, Lotto, Cranach (including portraits of Luther and wife) and a crucifix by Raphael. The collection is also rich in decorative arts, including Islamic metalwork and rugs – note the magnificent Persian carpet (1532) depicting a hunting scene in the Salone Dorato – medieval and Renaissance armour, Renaissance bronzes, Flemish tapestries, and Murano glass.

Quadrilatero d'Oro

Just up Via Manzoni is the entrance to Milan's high-fashion vortex, the **Quadrilatero d'Oro**, concentrated in the palace-lined Via Monte Napoleone and elegant Via della Spiga. Even if you're not in the market for astronomically priced clothes by Italy's top designers, these exclusive lanes make for good window-shopping and perhaps even better people-watching. It's hard to remember that until the 1970s, Florence was the centre of the Italian garment industry. When Milan took over this status – it has the airports Florence lacks – it added the essential ingredients of business savvy and packaging to the Italians' innate sense of style to create a high-fashion empire.

The sumptuous 18th-century Palazzo Morando Bolognini at Via S. Andrea 6, between 'Montenapo' and Via della Spiga, contains the **Civico Museo di Milano** (*call* ***t*** *02 783 797 for opening hours*), with paintings of old Milan, the **Civico Museo di Storia Contemporanea** (*call* ***t*** *02 8846 5933 for opening hours*), devoted to Italian history between 1914 and 1945, and the **Civico Museo Marinaro Ugo Mursia** (*call* ***t*** *02 7600 4143 for opening hours*), a collection of nautical models, English figureheads, scrimshaw and mementoes founded by a Milanese scholar obsessed with Joseph Conrad. At Via Santo Spirito 10, the **Museo Bagatti Valsecchi** (*metro Montenapoleone;* ***t*** *02 7600 6132; open Tues–Sun 1–5.45; adm*) was the life's work of brothers Fausto and Giuseppe Bagatti Valsecchi, who built a neo-Renaissance palace to integrate the period fireplaces, ceilings and friezes they'd collected, carefully disguising 19th-century conveniences such as the bathtub. Some of the city's top designers have made unique creations inspired by the museum's displays, sold in the shop in the lobby.

Near the intersection of Via della Spiga and Via Manzoni, the **Archi di Porta Nuova**, the huge stone arches of a gate, are a rare survival of the city walls of 1171. If you look around the inside of the arches, you can see some of the old Roman tombstones used to build the wall; a Gothic tabernacle has statues of the saints. The moat around the walls was enlarged into a canal to bring in marble for building the cathedral; it was covered in the 1880s when its stench outweighed any economic benefit.

The Giardini Pubblici

From Piazza Cavour, Via Palestro curves between the two sections of Milan's public gardens, the romantic **Giardini di Villa Reale** (*metro Palestro*) laid out in 1790 for the Belgioioso family by Leopoldo Pollak, who later built the Villa Reale, Napoleon's residence while he was in the Cisalpine Republic. The neoclassical villa is now the **Civica Galleria d'Arte Moderna** (*t 02 7600 2819; open Tues–Sun 9.30–5.30*), which includes the **Vismara collection** of paintings by Picasso, Matisse, Modigliani, De Pisis, Tosi, Morandi and Renoir) and the Marino Marini sculpture collection. Marini (*d.* 1980), generally held to be the top Italian sculptor of the 20th century, spent most of his career in Milan. The first floor hosts a collection of 17th-century Italian art, which includes the famous *Fourth State* by Pelizza da Volpedo, fine paintings by the self-consciously romantic *Scapigliati* (Wild-Haired Ones) of Milan, and work by **Italian Impressionists**. The second floor hosts the **Grassi collection** by French painters Gauguin, Bonnard, Manet and Toulouse-Lautrec and work by **Italian Futurists** Balla and Boccioni, including the latter's *Spiral Construction* of 1913.

The **Giardini Pubblici** proper, a shady arcadia between Via Palestro and the Corso Venezia, was laid out in 1782; artificial rocks compensate for Milan's flat terrain. A good place to take children, with its zoo, swans, pedal cars and playgrounds, it is also the site of Italy's premier **natural history museum** (*t 02 8846 3280; open Tues–Fri 9–6, Sat and Sun 9.30–6.30*), near the Corso Venezia. Look out for the Madagascar aye-aye and the 40-kilo topaz. The gardens also contain the **Museo del Cinema** (*t 02 655 4977; open Fri–Sun 3–6; adm*), located in the late 17th-century Palazzo Dugnani, with a small collection on early animation techniques, posters, cameras and so on.

Close to the Giardini Pubblici in a classy 1800s palace at Via Turati 34, the **Esposizione Permanente delle Belle Arti** (Fine Arts Society and Permanent Exhibition; *metro Turati; t 02 659 9803; open Tues–Fri 10–1 and 2.30–6.30, Thurs until 10pm; Sat, Sun and hols 10–6.30; adm*) has 100 20th-century sculptures and paintings from the Civico Museo dell'Arte Contemporanea, as well as 40 contemporary works of the **Jucker collection**, with paintings by Picasso, Klee, Kandinsky, Boccioni and Modigliani.

Corso Venezia itself is lined with neoclassical and Liberty-style palaces – most remarkably, the 1903 **Palazzo Castiglione** at No.47 and the neoclassical **Palazzo Serbelloni**, Milan's press club, on the corner of Via Senato. The district just to the west of the Corso Venezia was the city's most fashionable during the 1920s, and there are a smattering of rewarding buildings here: the **Casa Galimberti** with its colourful ceramic façade at Via Malpighi 3, off Piazza Oberdan; the good Art Deco foyer at Via Cappuccini 8; the eccentric houses on Via Mozart (especially No.11); and the romantic 1920s **Palazzo Fidia** at Via Melegari 2.

To the northwest of the Giardini Pubblici, the Piazza della Repubblica has many of the city's hotels; the Mesopotamian-scale **Stazione Centrale** (1931), blocking the end of Via Vittor Pisani, is the largest train station in Italy. Designed in 1906, it was built between 1925 and 1931. The five metal roofs extending over the tracks are an impressive 236ft across and 118ft high. The nearby skyscraper, the **Pirelli building**, known as *Pirellone* (big Pirelli), is one that the Milanese are especially proud of, built in 1959 by Gio Ponti (Pier Luigi Nervi designed the concrete structure). It's now the seat of Lombardy's regional government, and you can see most of the city from its terrace (*call ahead to visit, t 02 67651*). In early 2002, a small, private plane flew into the top of the Pirelli building; subsequent investigation interpreted the incident as an act of suicide.

Lo Stile Liberty

'Liberty style' is the name given in Italy to Art Nouveau, the short-lived artistic and architectural movement that flourished in many European countries around the turn of the 19th century. It refers, curiously, to Liberty's, the London department store; its William Morris-influenced flower-patterned fabrics and ceramics were some of the first articles in the style imported into Italy, and became hugely popular (the style is also, less commonly, known as the *stile floreale*).

The ethos behind the movement was an avoidance of architectural precedents, an embracing of 'naturalistic' ornament and flowing lines, and a desire to 'integrate' all the arts – hence the importance given not just to painting and fine art, but to architecture and interior design. Decoration, an integral part of every design, was key.

Liberty style was never as important in Italy as were its equivalents in France, Austria or Catalunya, nor was it usually as extravagant as they often were, but it did for a time become the vogue among the newly wealthy middle classes of Italy's industrializing north. As the prosperity of this class grew in the 1900s, so did the demand for Liberty buildings and products – seen most notably in the hotels and villas around the lakes and along the Riviera. Perhaps the most important figure working in the style in Italy was Giuseppe Sommaruga (1867–1917), whose achievements include the Palazzo Castiglione, a pair of villas at Sárnico on Lake Iseo, and the Hotel Tre Colli near Varese, characterized by their ornamental lines and uninhibited use of space. Similar but more refined is the architecture of Raimondo D'Aronco (1857–1932), who worked mainly on public buildings, particularly for exhibitions, and whose most famous work is the Palazzo Comunale in Udine.

Further to the northwest, at Via Petteri 56, the Palazzo Martinitt houses the **Museo del Giocattolo e del Bambino** (*metro Lambrate;* ***t*** *02 2641 1585; open Tues–Sun 9.30–12.30 and 3–6; adm*) with a beautiful display of toys dating back to 1700.

Brera and its National Gallery

Another street alongside La Scala, Via Giuseppe Verdi, leads into the **Brera**, which has been compared to Montmartre or Portobello Road. It's hip and arty, yet fails to quite measure up, however – partly because Italians never let their hair down enough to be truly bohemian. Yet in this city that was heavily bombed in the Second World War, the district's cobbled and narrow streets were left relatively unscathed, so that it retains an appealing old-world artiness that the Milanese have cashed in on. This is best seen in atmospheric **Via Fiori Chiari** ('Street of Light-coloured Flowers'), which offers a very Milanese impression of *la dolce vita*, with its chic boutiques, small art galleries, and trendy bars and restaurants. The quarter's banner street, **Via Brera**, once poor and arty, is now lined with achingly exclusive bars and shops, though once a month, for those who would like a taste of what life used to be like here, it hosts a more down-to-earth, though still pricey, antiques market (*see* p.200).

At the corner of Via Brera and Via Fiori Oscuri ('Street of the Dark Flowers') is the elegant courtyard of the **Galleria Nazionale di Brera** (*metro Lanza or Montenapoleone,* ***t*** *02 722 631; open Tues–Sun 8.30–7.15, may close at 6 in winter; adm*), one of the world's finest hoards of art, especially 14th–18th century northern Italian painting. The collection was compiled by Napoleon, whose bronze statue, draped in a toga, greets visitors; a believer in centralized art as well as centralized government, he had north Italy's churches and monasteries stripped of their treasures to form a Louvre-like collection for Milan, the capital of his Cisalpine Republic. The museum opened in 1809; after Waterloo, Milan had become used to its role as the capital of northern Italy and the paintings stayed put. A private collection, the **Donazione Jesi**, was added, and there are plans to expand into the 18th-century Palazzo Citterio at Via Brera 12–14. Ongoing improvements and restoration work since 1988 may mean that certain sections are closed at any given time.

Perhaps the best known of the Brera's scores of masterpieces is Raphael's *Marriage of the Virgin*, a Renaissance landmark because of its evocation of an ideal, rarefied world, where even the disappointed suitor snapping his rod on his knee performs the bitter ritual in a graceful dance step, all acted out before a perfect but eerily vacant temple in the background. In the same room hangs Piero della Francesca's last painting, the *Pala di Urbino*, featuring among its holy personages Federico da Montefeltro, Duke of Urbino, with his famous nose. The Venetian masters are well represented – Carpaccio, Veronese, Titian, Tintoretto, Jacopo Bellini and the Vivarini, and especially Giovanni Bellini, with several of his loveliest Madonnas and the great *Pietà*, as well as a joint effort with his brother Gentile of St Mark Preaching in Alexandria. *The Flagellation* by Luca Signorelli of Cortona is his first documented work (it's signed *Opus luce cortonensis* on the building in the background).

There are also some luminous works by Carlo Crivelli (the golden, gorgeously dressed *Madonna della Candeletta*, framed in an arch of Crivelli's trademark fruit and cucumbers) and by Cima da Conegliano, plus several paintings by Mantegna, including his remarkable study in foreshortening, the *Cristo Morto;* Mantegna's subdued colouring was an inspiration for Bramante. Other famous works include *Christ at the Column* by Bramante (transferred to canvas); Caravaggio's striking *Supper at Emmaus*; the *Pala Sforzesca* by a 15th-century Lombard artist, depicting Lodovico il Moro and his family; a polyptych by Gentile da Fabriano; and fine works by the Ferrarese masters Da Cossa and Ercole de' Roberti.

Outstanding among the works on display by non-Italians are Rembrandt's *Portrait of his Sister*, El Greco's *St Francis* and Van Dyck's *Portrait of the Princess of Orange*. When the Great Masters become indigestible, you can take a breather in the new 20th-century wing of the gallery, which is populated mainly by Futurists such as Severini, Balla and Boccioni, who believed that to achieve speed was to achieve success, and by the Metaphysical followers of De Chirico, who seem to believe just the opposite.

Brera's other principal monument is **San Simpliciano** just off Corso Garibaldi (*metro Lanza;* ***t*** *02 862 274; open daily 7–12 and 3–7*). Possibly founded by St Ambrose, this retains its essential palaeo-Christian form in a 12th-century wrapping, with an octagonal drum. The apse has a beautiful fresco of the *Coronation of the Virgin* (1515) by Bergognone, and the larger of the two cloisters, from the mid-16th century, is especially charming with its twin columns.

Castello Sforzesco

Marking the western limits of the Brera, the **Castello Sforzesco** (*metro Cairoli*) is one of Milan's best-known landmarks. It was originally a fortress; the Visconti made it their base, but it was razed to the ground by the Ambrosian Republic in 1447. It was rebuilt three years later under Francesco Sforza, and again after air raids in the Second World War; this time, water cisterns were disguised in its stout towers.

Today the castle houses the city's excellent collections, the **Civici Musei d'Arte e Pinacoteca del Castello** (*open Tues–Sun 9–5.30*). The entrance, by way of a tower rebuilt on a design by Filarete (1452) and the huge Piazza d'Armi, is through the lovely Renaissance Corte Ducale and the principal residence of the Sforza. There are intriguing fragments of Milanese history – the equestrian tomb of Bernabò Visconti and a beautiful 14th-century monument of the Rusca family; reliefs of Milan's triumph over Barbarossa, and the city's gonfalon. Leonardo designed the ilex decorations of the **Sala delle Asse**; the next room, the **Sala dei Ducali**, contains a superb relief by Duccio from Rimini's Tempio Malatestiano. The **Sala degli Scarlioni** contains the two finest sculptures in the museum, the *Effigy of Gaston de Foix* (1525) by Bambaia and Michelangelo's unfinished *Rondanini Pietà*, a haunting work that the aged sculptor worked at off and on during his last nine years, repudiating all of his early ideals of physical beauty in favour of blunt, expressionistic figures.

Upstairs, among the fine collection of Renaissance furnishings and decorative arts, are the 15th-century Castello Roccabianca frescoes illustrating the popular medieval tale of Patient Griselda. The **Pinacoteca** has a tender Madonna with Child by Giovanni Bellini, his brother-in-law Mantegna's more austere, classical Madonna in the Pala Trivulzio, and the lovely *Madonna dell'Umiltà* by Filippo Lippi. Lombards, unsurprisingly, predominate: Foppa, Solario, Magnasco (who spent most of his life in Milan), Bergognone (especially the serene *Virgin with SS. Sebastian and Gerolamo*) and Bramantino, with his eerie *Noli me tangere*. There's a room of Leonardo's followers, then the *Primavera*, by Milanese Giuseppe Arcimboldo (1527–1593), who was no one's follower and the first surrealist – the *Primavera* is a woman's face made of flowers. From 18th-century Venice, Francesco Guardi's *Storm* looks ahead to Impressionism.

The third court, the beautiful **Cortile della Rocchetta**, was designed by Florentines Bramante and Filarete, both of whom worked for several years for Francesco Sforza. The courtyard basement has a large collection of Egyptian funerary artefacts and prehistoric items found in Lombardy's Iron Age settlements, notably the 6th-century BC bronzes from the tomb of the warrior of Sesto Calende. The first floor has a **museum of musical instruments**, with a beautiful collection of 641 string and wind instruments and a spinet played by Mozart. The **Sala della Balla**, where the Sforza family played ball, now contains the *Tapestries of the Months* designed by Bramantino.

The **Museo Teatrale alla Scala**, at nearby Palazzo Busca at Corso Magenta 71 (*metro Cadorna;* ***t*** *02 805 3418; open Tues–Sun 9–6; adm*), was moved here to a larger abode in front of *The Last Supper*. It has an excellent collection of opera memorabilia (especially on Verdi), including scores, letters, portraits and photos of legendary stars, and set designs; there's even an archaeological section related to ancient Greek and Roman drama, and a great collection of costumes on the top floor.

Parco Sempione and Cimitero Monumentale

Behind the Castello stretches the Parco Sempione, Milan's largest park, where you can find De Chirico's **Metaphysical Fountain**; the 1930s **Palazzo dell'Arte**, used for exhibitions, especially the **Milan Triennial** of modern architecture and design; the **Arena**, designed in 1806 after Roman models, where 19th-century dilettantes staged mock naval battles; and an imposing triumphal arch, the **Arco della Pace**, marking the terminus of Napoleon's highway (Corso Sempione) to the Simplon Pass. At Corso Sempione 36, the **Casa Rustici** (1931), designed by Giuseppe Terragni of Como on the proportions of the Golden Rule, is considered by many Milan's finest modern building. Also in the park is the panoramic steel **Fernet Branca tower** (*open Weds, Thurs, Sat and Sun 11–6; adm*). Reminiscent of the Eiffel Tower, it was designed by Gio Ponti and erected in 1933 in just two and a half months, in time for the Triennale. The views from the top are lovely.

Further out, the **Cimitero Monumentale** (*tram no.14; open Tues–Sun 8.30–5*) is the last rendezvous of Milan's well-to-do burghers. Their lavish monuments – Liberty-style temples and pseudo-ancient columns and obelisks – are just slightly less flamboyant than those of the Genoese, the Italian champions for post-mortem splendour. The cemetery keeper has guides to the tombs – Manzoni, Toscanini and Albert Einstein's father are among the best-known names. New acquisitions include Italian novelists Eugenio Montale and Elio Vittorini, and opera diva Maria Callas. The memorial to the 800 Milanese who perished in German concentration camps is very moving.

West of the Duomo

Santa Maria delle Grazie and the *Last Supper*

Metro Cadorna, then Via Boccaccio and left on Via Caradosso; open Tues–Sun 8.15–6.45 in summer; adm exp. Booking compulsory on **t** *02 8942 1146 at an extra charge; only 15 visitors admitted at a time.*

Milan's greatest painting, Leonardo da Vinci's *Last Supper*, or the *Cenacolo* (*see* box p.218), is displayed in the refectory of the convent of **Santa Maria delle Grazie**. Before entering, get yourself into the proper Renaissance mood by going for a walk around the 15th-century church and cloister. Built by Guiniforte Solari, with later revisions by Bramante under Lodovico il Moro, it is perhaps the most beautiful Renaissance church in Lombardy. Its exterior is articulated with fine brickwork and terracotta that respects the local delight in a bit of fancy stuff – Bramante would never do anything as lavish again. His greatest contribution, however, is the majestic tribune, added in 1492 – it was inspired by Brunelleschi in Florence but with an eye towards the imposing style of the ancient Romans, which in the next decade Bramante would take back to Rome itself. Nearly every element in the tribune is based on the circle, from the decorative motifs to the play of geometric forms to the great cupola that crowns it all. Bramante also designed the choir, the sacristy and the elegant little cloister, all simple, geometric and pure.

The *Last Supper*

Leonardo painted three of his masterpieces in Milan: the two versions of the enigmatic *Virgin of the Rocks*, and the *Last Supper*. The former are in London and the Louvre; the latter would have been in Paris too, had the French figured out how to remove the wall.

Since the 14th century, it had been the fashion in Italy to paint a *Cenacolo* or scene of the Last Supper on the walls of monastic refectories, and as the Dominicans at Santa Maria were favourites of Lodovico il Moro, he sent them his favourite artist. When Leonardo unveiled his Last Supper (1494–98), it was acclaimed as the greatest work of the greatest living artist, a masterful psychological study. Vasari wrote in his *Lives of the Artists:* 'In all the faces one can read the fearful question: who will betray the Lord? And each expresses in his own way not only his love for Jesus, but also fear, anger and indeed sorrow, because they cannot understand his words.'

According to Vasari, Leonardo left the portrait of Christ purposely unfinished, believing himself unworthy to paint divinity; Judas, the isolated traitor, also posed a problem, but the artist eventually nailed down the expression of a man caught guiltily unawares but still nefariously determined and unrepentant.

Unfortunately for posterity, damp was a problem even as Leonardo worked on the fresco, and the ever-experimental genius was not content to use established fresco technique (where paint is applied quickly to wet plaster) but painted with tempera on glue and plaster as if on wood, enabling him to achieve the subtlety of tone and depth he desired. He knew that it wouldn't last, but the fact only stimulated his mind, fascinated with the unfinished and the transitory. Almost immediately the moisture in the walls began its deadly work of flaking off particles of paint.

Though it was considered a 'lost work' by the 17th century, various restorers tried their hand. In the Second World War the refectory was massively damaged by a bomb, and the *Last Supper* was only saved thanks to piles of mattresses and other measures. In 1953, master restorer Mauro Pellicioli covered what remained of the work with a protective shield of glue; by then, only an estimated 20 per cent of what was visible was by Leonardo's hand.

In 1977, the Ministry of Arts let communications company Olivetti pay €3.5 million to make the *Last Supper* a showcase restoration project. The protective coating was chipped off and the work cleansed of its previous restorations and repaintings, the wall was stablized to prevent further damage, and finally the gaps were painted. The project leader, Pinin Brambilla (who was quoted as saying she communed daily with Leonardo's ghost while working on the project), notoriously even went where the living Leonardo feared to tread and put some finishing touches on Christ's face.

In 1999, when the last scaffolding was taken down (the restoration took more than five times as long as it took Leonardo to paint it), the work was displayed to howls of fury from art critics around the world. One of the harshest detractors, James Beck of Columbia University, said: 'What you have is a modern repainting of a work that was poorly conserved. It doesn't even have an echo of the past. At least the older over-paintings were guided by Leonardo's work.' Italians, for the most part, have tried to hold their chins up.

Monastero Maggiore and the Archaeology Museum

From Santa Maria delle Grazie, the Corso Magenta leads back towards the centre. At the corner of Via Luini stands the Monastero Maggiore, with its pretty 16th-century church of **San Maurizio** (*metro Cadorna; open Sept–June daily 4–6*) containing some exceptional frescoes by Bernardino Luini, one of Leonardo's most accomplished followers. The former Benedictine convent houses the city's Etruscan, Greek and Roman collections in the **Civico Museo Archeologico** (*entrance at Corso Magenta 15; open Tues–Sun 9–5.30*). As important as Milan was in the late Roman Empire, relatively little has survived the razings and rebuildings: the 3rd-century tower in the garden, Roman altars, sarcophagi, stelae, glass, ceramics, bronzes and mosaics. Other sections are Greek, Etruscan, Indian, Goth and Lombard. Opposite the church, Francesco Maria Ricchini's **Palazzo Litta** (1648) has a rococo façade by Bartolomeo Bolli, added 100 years later, and a lovely courtyard with twinned columns.

Sant'Ambrogio

Just off San Vittore and Via Carducci (*metro Sant'Ambrogio*), the stern 12th-century gate, the **Pusterla di Sant'Ambrogio**, bristles with the armour, antique weapons and torture instruments of the **Museo della Criminologia e Armi Antiche** (*open daily 10–7; adm*). The Pusterla guards the last resting place of Milan's patron saint and the city's holy of holies, the beautiful church of **Sant'Ambrogio**. Founded by Ambrose in 379, this was enlarged and rebuilt several times; its current appearance dates from the 1080s.

The church (*open daily 9–12 and 2–8*) is entered through a porticoed atrium, which in 1140 replaced the Carolingian paved court or *parvis*. It sets off the simple, triangular façade with its rounded arches and towers; the right one, the Monks' Campanile, was built in the 9th century; the more artistic Canons' Campanile on the left was finished in 1144. The bronze doors, in their decorated portals, are 10th century. In its day the finely proportioned if shadowy interior was revolutionary for its rib vaulting; rows of arches divide the aisles, supporting the women's gallery. On the left is a 10th-century bronze serpent and richly sculpted pulpit, a masterpiece carved in 1080, set on a huge late Roman sarcophagus. The apse is adorned with 10th–11th-century mosaics of the Redeemer and saints, and the sanctuary has two ancient treasures: the 9th-century ciborium on columns, and a magnificent gold, silver, enamel and gem-studded altarpiece (835), both signed '*Wolvinus magister phaber*'. In the crypt moulder the bones of saints Ambrose, Gervasio and Protasio. At the end of the south aisle the 4th-century *Sacello di San Vittore in Ciel d'Oro* ('in the sky of gold') contains brilliant 5th-century mosaics in its cupola and a presumed authentic portrait of St Ambrose.

After working on Santa Maria delle Grazie, Bramante spent two years on Sant' Ambrogio, contributing the unusual Portico della Canonica and the two cloisters, now part of the Università Cattolica; these display his new interest in the ancient orders of architecture, an interest he developed when he moved to Rome. In the upper section of the Portico is the **Museo della Basilica di Sant'Ambrogio** (*open Mon and Weds–Fri 10–12 and 3–5, Sat and Sun 3–5; adm*), housing illuminated manuscripts, the saint's bed, Romanesque capitals, ancient fabrics and 4th-century vestments called the *Dalmatiche di Sant'Ambrogio*, tapestries, and frescoes by Luini and Bergognone.

Museum of Science and Technology

From Sant'Ambrogio, Via San Vittore leads to the Olivetan convent of San Vittore, home to the **Leonardo da Vinci Museo Nazionale della Scienza e Tecnica** (*t 02 4855 5330; open Tues–Sun 9.30–5, Sat and Sun until 6.30; adm*). Most of this vast and diverse collection is mysterious for the uninitiated; if you're not fascinated by smelting and the evolution of batteries, head straight for the Leonardo da Vinci Gallery, lined with pretty wooden models and explanations of his machines and inventions.

In 1481 Leonardo applied to Lodovico il Moro for a job. He had been recommended to the duke as musician and player of the lyre (he played a beautiful lyre he had made himself, of silver, in the shape of a horse's head); in his letter of introduction he boasts of his talents as a military engineer, designer of war machines and fortifications, canal builder, arranger and festival decorator, sculptor and caster of bronzes. Only at the end does he mention that he can paint too, if required. In Milan he filled notebook after notebook (many are on display in the Ambrosiana) with studies of nature, weather and anatomy and ideas for inventions in the applied sciences. His most practical work in the canal-building city, however, was in hydraulic engineering. He painted occasionally; besides the *Virgin of the Rocks* and the *Last Supper*, he did a range of portraits, including one of Sforza's mistress, Cecilia Gallerani, *Lady with an Ermine* (in Cracow).

Other rooms include musical instruments and displays on optics, radios, computers, clocks and astronomy; downstairs you can push buttons and make waterwheels turn. Other buildings are devoted to trains, and to ships and naval history.

Milan's Financial District

For centuries, the area between Sant'Ambrogio and the Duomo has been the HQ of Milan's merchant guilds, bankers and financiers, concentrated in bank-filled **Piazza Cordusio**, Via degli Affari and Via Mercanti, just off Piazza del Duomo (*metro Cordusio or Duomo*). Milan's imposing **Borsa** in Piazza Affari was founded by Napoleon's viceroy Eugène de Beauharnais and is now the most important stock exchange in Italy. The current imposing Palazzo della Borsa dates from 1931 and sits smack on the ruins of Mediolanum's ancient theatre; bits remain in the cellars and in the lower parts of the buildings along Via Vittore al Teatro. On Via Mercanti, the **Palazzo della Ragione** (1233), the old hall of justice, was given an extra floor with oval windows by Maria Theresa.

On the side facing Piazza Mercanti, look for a beautiful early 13th-century equestrian relief. Facing Via Mercanti don't miss the bas-relief of a sow partly clad in wool – according to legend, a tribe of Gauls under their chief Belloveso defeated the local Etruscans in the 6th century BC and wanted to settle in the area. An oracle told them to found their town on the spot where they found a sow half-covered in wool, and to name it after her. When the Romans conquered the Gauls, they translated the Celtic name of the town into the Latin Mediolanum, 'half-woolly'.

The Ambrosiana

In Piazza Pio XI (off Via Spadari and Via Cantù), this is Milan's most enduring legacy of its leading family, the Borromei. Cardinal Federico Borromeo (cousin of Charles) founded one of Italy's greatest libraries here in 1609, housing 30,000 rare manuscripts, including ancient Middle Eastern texts collected to further the cardinal's efforts to produce a translation of the Bible; a 5th-century illustrated *Iliad*; Leonardo da Vinci's famous *Codex Atlanticus*, early editions of *The Divine Comedy*; and much, much more (*open for study or special exhibits; call* **t** *02 8645 1436*).

The Cardinal's art collection or **Pinacoteca** (*open Tues–Sun 10–5.30; adm exp*) in the same building is essentially a monument to one man's taste – which showed a marked preference for the Dutch and the peculiar, and ranges from the truly sublime to some of the funniest paintings ever to grace a gallery. Here are Botticelli's lovely *Tondo*, and his *Madonna del Baldacchino* nonchalantly watering lilies with her milk; a respectable Madonna by Pinturicchio; paintings by Bergognone (including the altar from Pavia's San Pietro in Ciel d'Oro), and a lovely portable altar by Geertgen tot Sint Jans. A small room, illuminated by a pre-Raphaelitish stained-glass window of Dante by Giuseppe Bertini (1865), contains the glove Napoleon wore at Waterloo, a 17th-century bronze of Diana the Huntress so ornate that even the stag wears earrings, and entertaining paintings by the Cardinal's friend Jan Brueghel the Younger.

These are followed by more masterpieces: a Page, perhaps by Giorgione, Luini's *Holy Family with St Anne* (from a cartoon by Leonardo), Leonardo's *Portrait of a Musician*, a portrait of Beatrice d'Este attributed to Leonardo's follower Ambrogio da Predis, and Bramantino's *Madonna in Trono fra Santi*, a scene balanced by a dead man on the left and an enormous dead frog on the right. Challenging this for absurdity is the nearby *Female Allegory* by 17th-century Giovanni Serodine, in which the lady, apparently disgruntled with her lute, astrolabe and books, is squirting herself in the nose.

The magnificent cartoon for Raphael's *School of Athens* in the Vatican is as interesting as the fresco itself; here too is a copy of Leonardo's *Last Supper*, painted by order of the Cardinal, who sought to preserve what he considered a lost work. The 16th-century *Washing of Feet* from Ferrara has one apostle blithely clipping his toenails. Another room has pages of drawings from Leonardo's *Codex Atlanticus*. The first Italian still life, Caravaggio's *Fruit Basket*, is also the most dramatic; it shares the space with more fond items such as Alessandro Magnasco's *The Crow's Singing Lesson*. Further on is Titian's *Adoration of the Magi*, painted for Henri II of France and in its original frame.

San Satiro

Via Torino (metro Duomo), **t** *02 7202 1804. Open Mon–Sat 8.30–11.30 and 3.30–5.30, Sun 9.30–10.30 and 4.30–5.30.*

A bland 19th-century façade conceals one of the most remarkable Renaissance churches in Italy, officially named Santa Maria presso San Satiro. It was rebuilt by Bramante in 1476, his first project in Milan. Faced with a lack of space in the T-shaped interior, he created a perfect illusion of a deep choir extending back by three bays under a coffered vault, in a space only a few feet long. He also designed the beautiful octagonal baptistry off the right aisle, with terracottas by Agosto de Fondutis; to the left, San Satiro's 9th-century Cappella della Pietà is one of the finest examples of Carolingian architecture in north Italy, though it was touched up in the Renaissance, with decorations and a Pietà by De Fondutis.

South of the Duomo: Porta Romana

Trams no.4 and 24 take you to **San Nazaro Maggiore** on Corso Porta Romana, a church dedicated in the 4th century and last restored in the Romanesque style. Its most original feature is the hexagonal *Cappella Trivulzio* by Bramantino (1512–47), built to contain the tomb of the *condottiere* Giangiacomo Trivulzio, a native Milanese who disliked Lodovico Sforza so much he led Louis XII's attack on Milan in 1499.

Just behind San Nazaro, in Via Festa del Perdono, the **Ospedale Maggiore**, or **Ca' Grande**, was commissioned in 1456 by Francesco Sforza, who asked Filarete to design one building to incorporate all the little hospitals across Milan. The result, now the centrepiece of the Università degli Studi, is a beautiful early Renaissance work with ornate brickwork and terracotta and the first cross-shaped wards. North, at Via Bellini 2, is **Santa Maria della Passione** (*metro San Babila;* ***t*** *02 7602 1370; open daily 7–12 and 3–6.15*), which was begun as a Greek cross in 1482, with a fine octagonal dome added in 1530. The Laternesi monks who worshipped here converted it into a Latin cross and in 1729 gave it its Baroque façade. In the fine Renaissance interior are important works by Baroque painter Daniele Crespi, including *St Charles Borromeo at Supper* (1628), a Deposition by Luini in the right transept, and a Redeemer and the Apostles by Bergognone, who also painted the pretty frescoes in the 15th-century sacristy.

On Corso Italia, **Santa Maria presso San Celso** (1490–1563) offers a fine example of the Lombard love of ornament, with its handsome, lively façade by Alessi. The interior has an exceptional marble floor and High Renaissance paintings by Paris Bordone, Bergognone and Moretto; local brides and grooms traditionally pray in the chapel of the Madonna on the way to their weddings. The adjacent 10th-century church of **San Celso** has a charming interior restored in the 19th century and a good original portal.

South Milan: The Ticinese and Navigli Districts

Southwest of the centre, Via Torino leads into the artsy quarter named for the Ticino river, traversed by Corso di Porta Ticinese (*tram no.3 from Via Torino*). In the Ticinese are pieces of Roman Mediolanum, which had its forum in modern **Piazza Carrobbio**: there's a bit of the Roman circus on Via Circo, off Via Lanzone, and the **Colonne di San Lorenzo** on the Corso – 16 Corinthian columns, originally part of a temple or bath, transported here in the 4th century to construct a portico in front of the **Basilica di San Lorenzo Maggiore** (***t*** *02 8940 4129; open daily 7.30–6.30*), the oldest surviving church in Milan. This acquired its octagonal form, encircled by an ambulatory and crowned with a dome, in the 4th century, predating the church it resembles most, San Vitale in Ravenna. Carefully spared by Barbarossa in the sack of Milan in 1164, it has suffered severe fires, and in the 16th century when it was near total collapse it was rebuilt, conserving as much of the old structure as possible. Luckily, the beautiful **Cappella di Sant'Aquilino** (*adm*) has come down intact, with 4th- or 5th-century mosaics of Christ and his disciples and an early Christian sarcophagus. Below are blocks from a Roman building from the 2nd century.

A green walkway, the Parco delle Basiliche, links San Lorenzo to the **Basilica di Sant'Eustorgio** (*tram no.3, 15 or 20;* **t** *02 5810 1583*), one of the most important medieval churches in Milan. This was rebuilt in 1278 along the lines of Sant'Ambrogio, with a lofty campanile (1309). The first chapel on the right has a tryptych by Bergognone, while the transept has a chapel dedicated to the Magi, where a Roman sarcophagus held the relics of the Three Kings until Frederick Barbarossa hauled them off to Cologne. But the highlight is the pure Tuscan Renaissance **Cappella Portinari** (1468) built for Pigello Portinari, an agent of the Medici bank in Milan (*open Tues–Sun 9.30–12 and 3.30–6; adm*). Attributed to Michelozzo and often compared with Brunelleschi's Pazzi Chapel in Florence in its elegant cubic simplicity and proportions, it is crowned by a lovely dome, adorned with stucco reliefs of angels. This jewel is dedicated to the Inquisitor St Peter Martyr (axed in the head on the shores of Lake Como in 1252), whose life of intolerance was superbly frescoed on the walls by Vincente Foppa. Foppa's remains are buried in the magnificent marble Arca di San Pietro Martire (1339) by the Pisan Giovanni di Balduccio. Balduccio also added the relief of saints on the nearby 14th-century **Porta Ticinese** built in the Spanish walls.

The **Navigli** district (*metro Porta Genova, tram no.2 or 14*) is named for its medieval navigable canals, the Naviglio Grande and Naviglio Pavese that meet to form the docks, or Darsena, near Porta Ticinese. Until the 1950s, Milan, through these canals, handled more tonnage than seaports such Brindisi, and the Navigli was a working-class district of warehouses, workshops, sailors' bars and public housing blocks. It's now a relaxed, bohemian zone, with artists' studios, jazz clubs and cheap restaurants.

Short Excursions from Milan

Monza

Only 15 minutes by train from Milan's Garibaldi station, Monza is unfairly slighted by most visitors to Lombardy, except in early September, when it hosts the Italian Grand Prix. Back in the late 6th century, it was the darling of Queen Theodolinda, who founded its first cathedral after her conversion from Arianism by Pope Gregory the Great. Rebuilt in the 13th century, the **Duomo** on Via Napoleone (*open Tues–Sat 9–11.30 and 3–5.30, Sun and hols 10.30–12 and 3–5.30*) has a green and white striped marble façade by the great Matteo da Campione (1396). The huge campanile dates from 1606, when the interior was given its Baroque facelift. To the left of the presbytery, **Theodolinda's chapel** has charming 1444 frescoes by the Zavattari brothers, depicting the life of the queen who left Monza its most famous relic, preserved in the high altar: the gem-encrusted **iron crown of Italy** (*open Tues–Sat 9–11.30 and 3–5.30, Sun and hols 10.30–12 and 3–5.30; adm*). The story goes that when his mother Helena unearthed the True Cross in Jerusalem, Emperor Constantine had one of its iron nails embedded in his crown. It became a tradition in the Middle Ages for every newly elected emperor to stop in Monza or Pavia to be crowned King of Italy before heading to Rome to receive the Crown of Empire from the pope. The Duomo's **museum** (*same hours; combined adm*) contains Theodolinda's treasures.

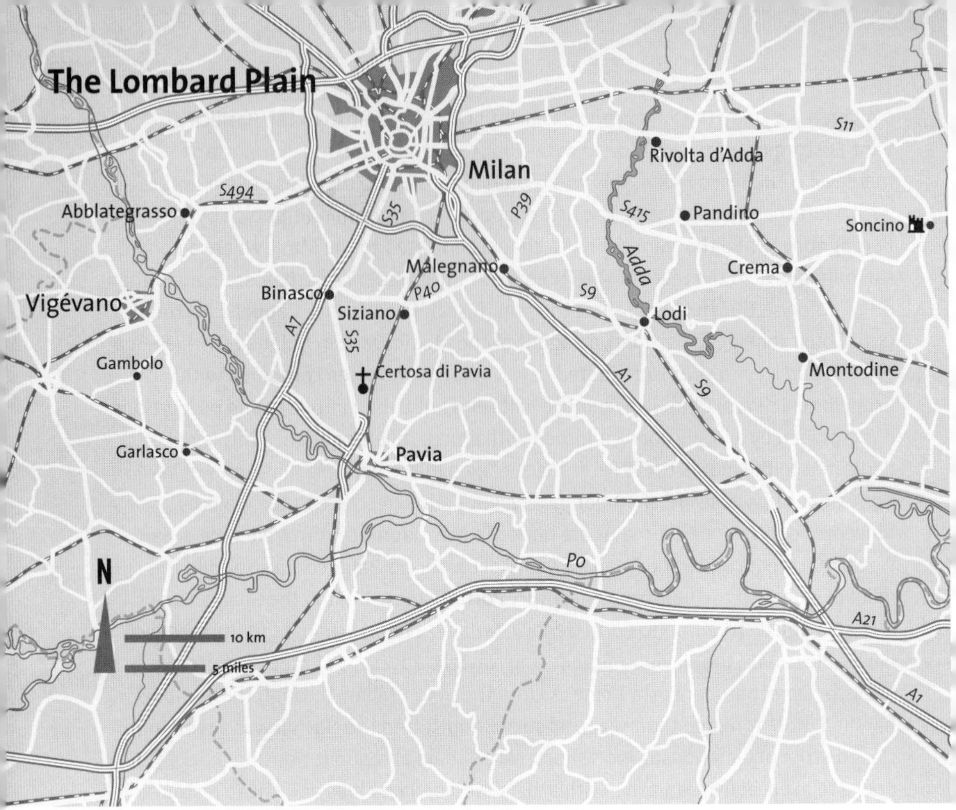

Just north of the Duomo, the 13th-century Palazzo Comunale or **Arengario** is the city's finest secular building. From here, Via C. Alberto leads north to the beautiful 800-hectare **Parco di Monza** (*open 7.30–6.30, until 7.30 in summer*), home to a horse-racing course and site of the Italian Grand Prix. Until 1806 the park was the grounds of the neoclassical **Villa Reale** (*open to groups of 20 or more by appointment; book 10 days ahead on* ***t*** *02 323 222; adm*), built by Archduke Ferdinand of Austria and the favourite residence of Napoleon's viceroy Eugène de Beauharnais. Behind the 18th-century residence an expiatory chapel built by Vittorio Emanuele III marks the spot where his father Umberto was assassinated by an anarchist in 1900.

Alfa Romeos and Saronno

Northwest of Milan, **Arese** has been the home town of Lombardy's car industry, the *Associazione Lombarda Fabbrica Automobilistiche*, since 1910 and you can visit the six-floor 'family album', the **Museo Storico dell'Alfa Romeo** (***t*** *02 9392 8111; open Mon–Fri 9–12.30 and 2–4.30, closed Aug and Christmas hols; book at least 10 days in advance*).

Further towards Varese, **Saronno** is synonymous with *amaretto*, either in the liqueur glass or in the biscuits. Its **Santuario della Madonna dei Miracoli** (***t*** *02 960 3027; open daily 7–12 and 3–7*) was built by Giovanni Antonio Amadeo in 1498. The façade with its trumpeting angels was added in the next century by Pellegrini. Inside, don't miss the dome's startling, innovative fresco, the *Concert of Angels* by Gaudenzio Ferrari (1534) and Bernadino Luini's beautiful frescoes in the chapel of the Madonna (1531).

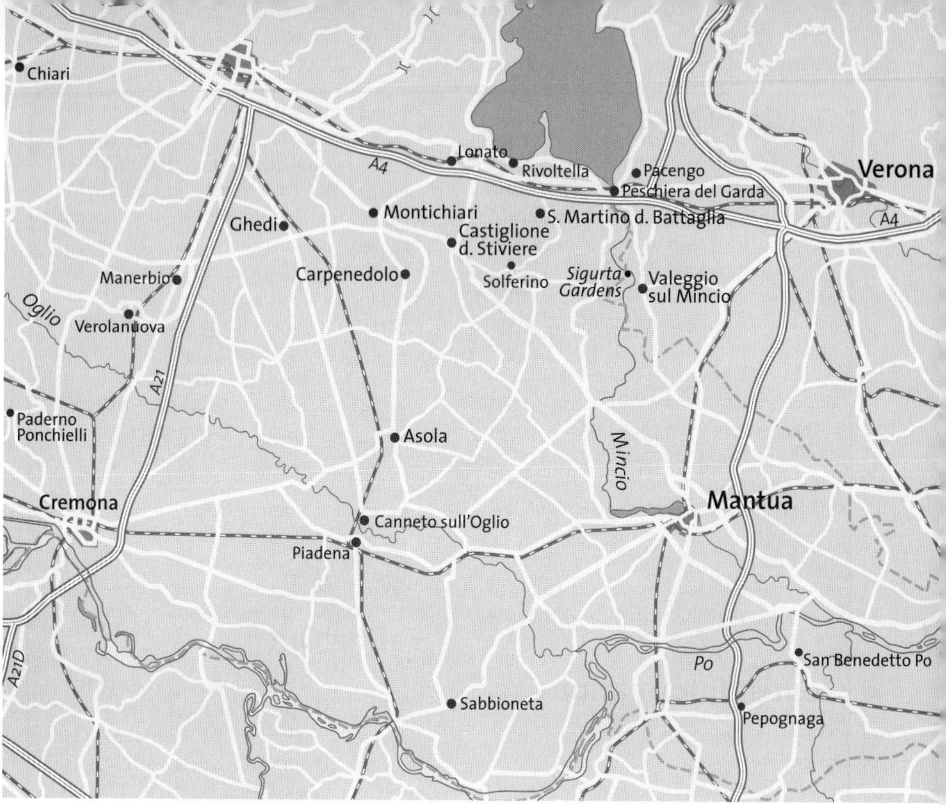

The Lombard Plain

The three provincial capitals of the Lombard plain are among Italy's most rewarding art cities: **Pavia**, capital of the ancient Lombards and the region's oldest centre of learning, with Romanesque churches and its famous Renaissance Certosa; **Cremona**, the graceful city where the medieval fiddle was reincarnated as the lyrical violin; and **Mantua**, the dream shadow capital of the wealthy Gonzaga dukes and Isabella d'Este.

Pavia

Pavia is a distinctly serious, no-monkey-business place. It is one of those rare cities that had its golden age in the three-digit years before the millennium, that misty half-legendary time that historians have shrugged off as the Dark Ages. But these were bright days for Pavia, when it served as capital of the Goths and saw Odoacer proclaimed King of Italy after defeating Romulus Augustulus, the last Roman emperor in the west. In the 6th century, the heretical Lombards led by King Alboin captured it from the Goths and formed a state the equal of Byzantine Ravenna and Rome, making Pavia the capital of their *Regnum Italicum* – a position the city maintained into the 11th century. Charlemagne came here to be crowned (774), as did the first King of Italy, Berenguer (888), and Emperor Frederick Barbarossa (1155).

Getting There

Pavia is quite close to Milan's **airports** (Linate 58km, Malpensa 85km). SGEA's direct **coach** service , **t** 0382 375 405/513 506, runs about every 2hrs from both to the Certosa di Pavia.

Frequent **trains** link Pavia to Milan (30mins) and Genoa (1½hrs), and there are less frequent services to Cremona and Mantua, Alessandria and Vercelli, and Piacenza. The train station is a 10-min walk from the centre at the end of Corso Cavour and Viale Vittorio Emanuele II.

There are **buses, t** 02 8954 6132, between Milan and Pavia roughly every 30mins; this is also the best way to travel if you want to stop off and visit the Certosa 8km north of Pavia. The station is on Via Trieste.

By **car**, Pavia can be quickly reached from Milan by the A7 *autostrada*, or in a more leisurely fashion by the SS35, via the Certosa.

Tourist Information

APT Pavia: Via Filzi 2, **t** 0382 22156, *www.apt.pavia.it*.

Where to Stay

Pavia ✉ 27100

The countryside around Pavia has many *agriturismi*; ask at the tourist office for a list.

Very Expensive–Expensive

★★★★**Castello di San Gaudenzio**, Via Mulino 1, San Gaudenzio, Cervesina, 30min drive from Pavia, **t** 0383 3331, *www.castellosangaudenzio.com*. A 14th-century castle in a century-old park with statues. Most accommodation is in an adjacent modern builiding.

★★★★**Moderno**, Viale Vittorio Emanuele II 41, near railway station, **t** 0382 303 401, *www.hotelmoderno.it*. The comfiest hotel in town.

Moderate

★★★**Ariston**, Via A. Scopoli 10/d, **t** 0382 34334/5, A central, slightly old-fashioned place.

★★★**De La Ville**, Via al Ticino 44, Bereguardo, 8km from centre, **t** 0382 928 100, *www.hotel-delaville.com*. A good choice for families and countryside lovers, with mountain-bike hire, tennis courts,and a playground.

★★**Aurora**, Via Vittorio Emanuele II 25, **t** 0382 23664. A convenient hotel for the station.

Azienda Agrituristica Torrazzetta, Torrazzetta, Borgo Priolo, 25km from town, **t** 0383 871 041, *www.torrazzetta.it*. Modern service and country hospitality in the Oltrepò wine-producing area. The restaurant (*cheap*) uses organic local produce.

Castello di Stefanago, La Boatta, near Borgo Priolo, **t** 0383 875 227/413. An *agriturismo* in a hilltop castle with suites, plus rooms (*cheap*) in the nearby Cascina La Boatta. There are riding facilities and a good restaurant.

Cheap

Locanda della Stazione (ring bell), Viale Vittorio Emanuele II 14, **t** 0382 29231. A good budget option in a private house.

Eating Out

Specialities include frogs, Varzi salami and *zuppa pavese* (raw egg on toast in hot broth); good local wines are from the Oltrepò Pavese region, one of Lombardy's best. Cortese is a dry white, Bonarda a dry red, Pinot a fruity white.

Very Expensive

Al Cassinino, Via Cassinino 1, Giovi highway, **t** 0382 422 097. Pavia's temple of fine cuisine, sitting on the Naviglio and offering market-inspired dishes such as pheasant breast with apples and *risotto alla Certosino*. Booking required. *Closed Weds and Christmas.*

Expensive

Antica Osteria del Previ, Via Milazzo 65, **t** 0382 26203. An old-fashioned place on the banks of the Ticino, serving home-made salami, risotto with frog or radicchio and speck, and river fish and snails. *Closed Sun.*

Moderate–Cheap

Osteria del Naviglio, Via Alzaia 39b, **t** 0382 460 392. The former rest point for sailors of the Naviglio, now a gourmet wine bar and restaurant. Delicacies include *pappardelle* with duck. There's a *menu degustazione* and excellent desserts. *Closed Mon.*

Osteria della Madonna del Peo, Via Cardano 63, **t** 0382 302 833. A homely central inn serving typical Lombard dishes. *Closed Sun.*

At the turn of the millennium, the precursor of Pavia's modern university, the *Studio*, was founded. Among its first students of law was the first Norman archbishop of Canterbury, Lanfranc, born here in 1005. Pavia was a Ghibelline *comune* and a rival of Milan, to whom it lost its independence in 1359. It was favoured by the Visconti, especially Gian Galeazzo, who built the castle housing his art collection and founded the Certosa di Pavia, which, with other churches, bears the mark of Pavia's great, half-demented sculptor–architect of the High Renaissance, Giovanni Antonio Amadeo.

The Duomo and San Michele

Pavia's core retains its street plan from the days when it was Roman *Ticinum*; the *cardus* (Corso Cavour) and *decumanus* (Corso Strada Nuova) intersect by the town hall or **Broletto**, begun in the 12th century. The adjacent **Duomo** (*under restoration; front entrance may be hard to access*), one of the ugliest churches in Italy, was begun in 1488 and owes its imposing design to Amadeo, Leonardo da Vinci, Bramante and a dozen others. Its appearance, like corrugated cardboard (its façade was to be covered by polychrome marble), led to a lack of interest in finishing it. The vast cupola was added in the 1880s; the last two apses in the transept were added in 1930. Next to the Duomo is the rubble of the unattractive 12th-century **Torre Civica**, the 1989 collapse of which prompted serious attention to be paid to its famous Pisan relation.

The Strada Nuova continues south down to the river and the pretty **covered bridge**, which replaced the Renaissance model damaged in the last war. On the opposite shore lies **Borgo Ticino**, the borough of the *bursan*, who are of Sabaudian origin and claim to be the true people of Pavia. From Strada Nuova, Via Maffi leads to the small brick 12th-century **San Teodoro**, notable for its early 16th-century fresco of Pavia when it still had 100 towers and the original covered bridge. East of the Strada, Via Capsoni leads in a couple of blocks to Pavia's most important church, the Romanesque **Basilica di San Michele Maggiore**, founded in 661 but rebuilt in the 12th century after destruction by lightning. Unlike other churches in Pavia, San Michele is made of sand-stone, mellowed into a fine golden hue, though the weather has been less kind to the intricate friezes across its front, depicting an 'apocalyptic vision' with its medieval bestiary, monsters and human figures involved in the fight between Good and Evil.

The solemn interior, where Frederick Barbarossa received the Iron Crown of Italy, contains more fine carvings on the capitals of the columns; the fourth on the left portrays the 'Death of the Righteous'. Along the top runs a Byzantine-style women's gallery, and in the chapel to the right of the main altar is a 7th-century silver crucifix.

The University and Castello Visconteo

The great yellow neoclassical quadrangles of the **university of Pavia**, famous for law and medicine, occupy much of the northeast quadrant of the ancient street plan. The ancient *Studio* was officially made a university in 1361. St Charles Borromeo, a former student, founded a college here in 1561 for talented but poor young men, and Pope Pius V founded another, the Collegio Ghislieri, in 1569. In the 18th century Maria Theresa brought the university back to life after scholarship had hit the skids, financing the construction of the main buildings. The university's history is traced in the **Museo per la Storia Dell'Università** at Corso Strada Nuova 65 (*t 0382 23724; open Mon 3.30–5, Fri 9.30–12*). Three of Pavia's medieval skyscrapers or **Torri** survive in the middle of the university, in Piazza Leonardo da Vinci; the roof in the piazza shelters what is believed to be the crypt of the demolished 12th-century **Sant'Eusebio** church.

At the top of Strada Nuova looms the mighty **Castello Visconteo**, built in 1360–5 by the Campionese masters for Gian Galeazzo II but partly destroyed in the Battle of Pavia in 1525, when Emperor Charles V captured Francis I of France. Three sides of the castle and its beautifully arcaded courtyard with terracotta decorations survived and house the **Musei Civici** (*t 0382 33853; open Mar–June and Sept–Nov Tues–Fri 9–1.30, Sat and Sun 10–7; Dec, Jan, July and Aug Tues–Sat 9–1.30, Sun 9–1; adm*). The archaeological and medieval sections contain finds from Roman and Gaulish Pavia, as well as robust Lombard and medieval carvings salvaged from now-vanished churches, and colourful 12th-century mosaics. The picture gallery on the first floor contains works by Giovanni Bellini, Correggio, Foppa, Van der Goes and others.

San Pietro in Ciel d'Oro

Behind the castle, Via Griziotti leads to Pavia's second great Romanesque temple, **San Pietro in Ciel d'Oro** ('St Peter in the Golden Sky'), built in 1132 and named for its once-glorious gilded ceiling, mentioned by Dante in Canto X of the *Paradiso*. The main altar is one of the greatest works of the Campionese masters – the **Arca di Sant' Agostino**, a 14th-century monument built to shelter the bones of St Augustine which, according to legend, were retrieved in the 8th century from Carthage by the Lombard king Luitprand, staunch ally of Pope Gregory II, against the iconoclasts of Byzantium. Luitprand is buried in a humble tomb to the right; in the crypt lies another Dark Age celebrity, the philosopher Boethius, slain by Emperor Theodoric of Ravenna in 524.

In the centre of town (towards Piazza Petrarca), **Santa Maria del Carmine** (1390s) is an excellent example of Lombard Gothic, with a fine façade and, inside, a beautifully sculptured lavabo by Amadeo. A 15-minute walk west (Corso Cavour to Corso Manzoni and Via della Riviera) is the rather plain, vertical, 13th-century **San Lanfranco**, notable for its memorial, the Arca di San Lanfranco, sculpted by Amadeo in 1498 and his last work.

The Certosa di Pavia

Off SS35 road from Milan–Pavia, along Naviglio Pavese; open Nov–Feb Tues–Sun 9–11.30 and 2.30–4.30; Mar, Apr and Oct until 5; May–Sept until 6; adm.

According to Jacob Burckhardt 'the greatest decorative masterpiece in all of Italy', the charterhouse was built over 200 years. Gian Galeazzo Visconti laid the cornerstone in 1396, with visions of the crown of Italy and the desire to build a pantheon for his hoped-for royal self and his heirs. Many architects and artists worked on it, but it bears the greatest imprint of Giovanni Antonio Amadeo, who with his successor Bergognone worked on its sculptural programme for 30 years and designed the lavish façade. Napoleon disbanded the monastery, but in 1968 a small group of Cistercians reoccupied it, living the same contemplative life as the old Carthusians, maintaining vows of silence (although a couple are released to take visitors around).

Through the main gate and **vestibule** adorned with frescoes by Luini, a large grassy court opens up, lined with buildings that served as lodgings for visitors and stores for the monks. At the far side the façade of the **church** is a marvel of polychromatic marbles, medallions, bas-reliefs, statues, and windows covered with marble embroidery from the chisel of Amadeo, who died before the upper, less elaborate level was begun.

The interior plan is Gothic but the decoration is Renaissance, with Baroque additions. Works of art include Bergognone's five statues of saints in the chapel of Sant'Ambrogio; the tombs of Lodovico il Moro and his young bride by Cristoforo Solari; the inlaid choir stalls, with the main altar in marble and lapis lazuli; and the tomb of Gian Galeazzo Visconti. All date from the 1490s and are surrounded by fine frescoes. The old sacristy has an early cinquecento ivory altarpiece by the Florentine Baldassarre degli Embriachi.

The tour continues into the **little cloister**, with delicate terracotta decorations and a dream-like view of the church and its cupola. A lovely doorway by Amadeo leads back into the church. The **great cloister** with its long arcades is surrounded by the 24 monks' 'cells', each with a chapel, study/dining room, a bedroom and a walled garden.

Around Pavia: Lomello and Vigévano

To the west of Pavia and the Certosa lies the little-known Lomellina, a major rice-growing and frog-farming district irrigated by canals dug by the Visconti in the 14th century. The feudal seat, **Lomello**, has some fine early medieval buildings, notably a lovely little 5th-century polygonal baptistry near the main church, the 11th-century Basilica di Santa Maria.

Also in the Lomellina is the old silk town of **Vigévano** (better known these days for its high-fashion shoes), the site of another vast castle of the Visconti and Sforza clans; it was the birthplace of Lodovico il Moro, and has been undergoing a lengthy restoration. Below it lies the majestic Piazza Ducale, designed in 1492 by Bramante (with help from Leonardo) as Lombardy's answer to Venice's Piazza San Marco. Originally a grand stairway connected the piazza to one of the castle towers; now the three sides are adorned with slender arcades, while on the fourth stands the magnificent concave Baroque façade of the cathedral, designed by a Spanish bishop, Juan Caramuel de Lobkowitz. Inside there's a 15th-century Lombard polyptych on St Thomas of Canterbury, and a rich treasury (*open Sun and hols 3–6, or by request*), containing illuminated codices, Flemish tapestries and golden reliquaries.

Tourist Information

Ufficio Turismo Vigévano, **t** 0381 299 269 (*open Mon–Thurs 8.30–1 and 3–5.30, Fri 8.30–1.30*).

Eating Out

I Castagni, Via Ottobiano 8/20, Vigévano, 2km south of centre, **t** 0381 42860 (*very expensive*). An old Lombard farmhouse with a young chef specializing in creative takes on traditional dishes, including pigeon in summer truffle sauce, spinach with roasted nuts, and foie gras with smoked duck breast in a ginger and onion jam. *Closed Sun eve, Mon, Jan and Aug.*

Trattoria Guallina, Via Molino Farenza 19, Guallina, near Mortara, **t** 0384 91962 (*expensive*). The place to come for excellently cooked local goose, served as an *antipasto*, in home-made ravioli, roasted, and as foie gras. *Closed Thurs.*

Station
VIA BERGAMO
PIAZZA STAZIONE
Bus Station
PIAZZA RISORGIMENTO
VIA F. GHINAGLIA
VIA DANTE
VIALE TRE
CORSO GARIBALDI
San Luca
PIAZZA FIUME
VIA BERTESI
VIA PALESTRO
VIA G. FAERNO
Palazzo Raimondi
Palazzo Stanga Trecco
VIA GRADO
PIAZZA XXIV MAGGIO
Museo Stradivariano
Sant' Agata
VIA DEI MILLE
Palazzo Cittanova
VIA MASSAROTTI
VIA STEFANO LEONIDA BISSOLATI
Palazzo Trecchi
CORSO GARIBALDI
VIA VILLA GLORI
VIA RUGGIERO MONNA
VIA MILAZZO
Sant' Agostino
VIA PLASIO
PIAZZA S. LUCIA
VIA TREBBIA
PIAZZA LUIGI CADORNA
Teatro Ponchielli
San Pietro al Po
PIAZZA SAN PIETRO
VIA DEL GIORDANO
VIALE PO
N
300 metres
250 yards

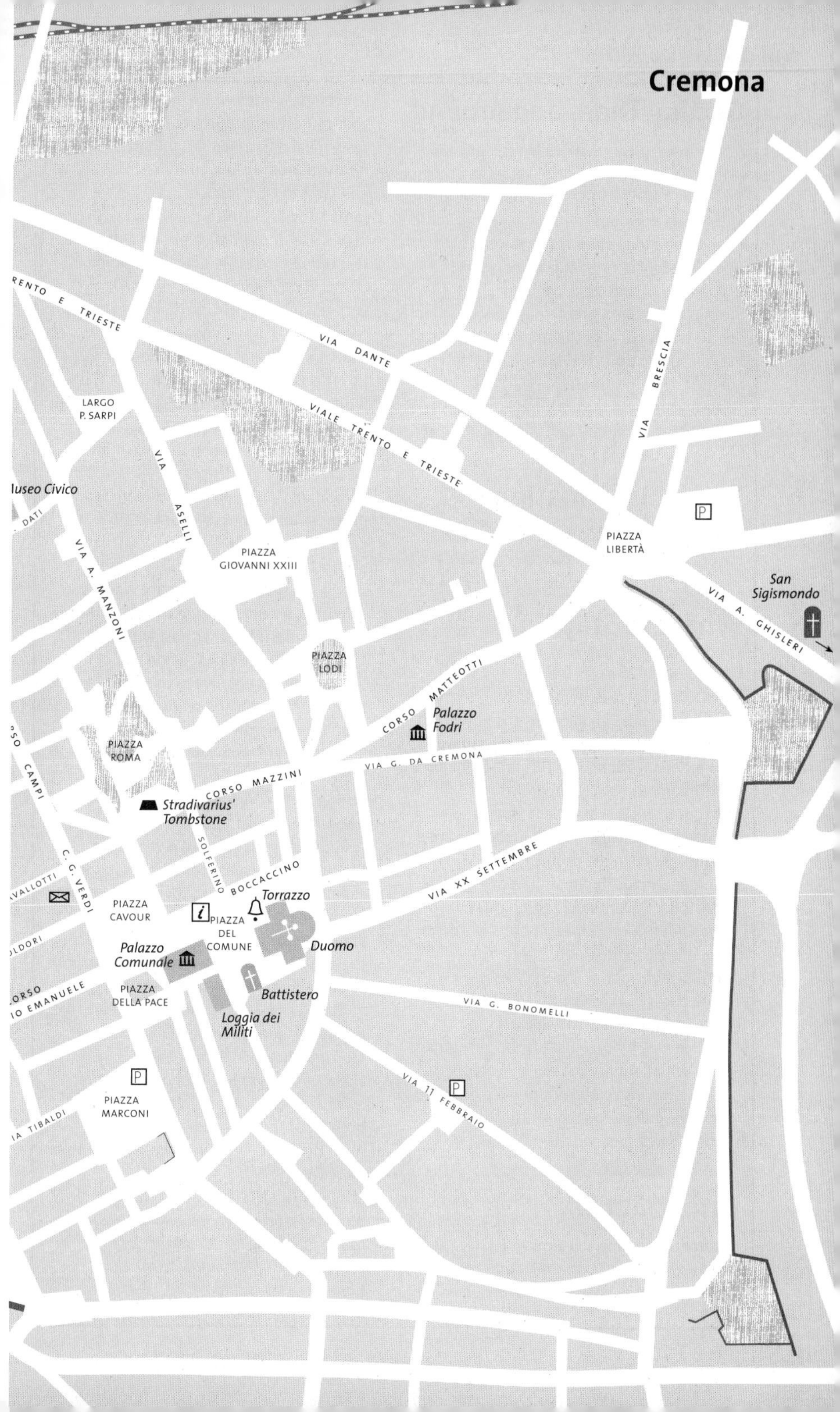

Cremona
VIA DANTE
VIALE TRENTO E TRIESTE
RENTO E TRIESTE
VIA BRESCIA
LARGO P. SARPI
VIA ASELLI
Museo Civico
DATI
VIA A. MANZONI
PIAZZA GIOVANNI XXIII
PIAZZA LIBERTÀ
VIA A. GHISLERI
San Sigismondo
PIAZZA LODI
CORSO MATTEOTTI
Palazzo Fodri
PIAZZA ROMA
CAMPI
VIA G. DA CREMONA
CORSO MAZZINI
Stradivarius' Tombstone
SOLFERINO
C. G. VERDI
VALLOTTI
BOCCACCINO
Torrazzo
VIA XX SETTEMBRE
PIAZZA CAVOUR
PIAZZA DEL COMUNE
Duomo
Palazzo Comunale
PIAZZA DELLA PACE
Battistero
Loggia dei Militi
VIA G. BONOMELLI
ORSO
IO EMANUELE
OLDORI
PIAZZA MARCONI
VIA TIBALDI
VIA 11 FEBBRAIO

Getting There and Around

The closest **airports** are Milan's Linate and Malpensa, and Bergamo's Orio al Serio. Gruppo Quattrini, **t** 02 670 6487, offers **bus** services for individuals or groups from Linate (*1hr 30mins*).

Cremona's **train** station, **t** 0372 407 911, has frequent services from Milan (*1hr 15mins; regional trains may be slower*), Pavia, Mantua, Brescia and Piacenza, and 3 a day from Bergamo. The station is north of the centre, at the end of Via Palestro. The **bus station** is in Via Dante, next to the train station.

Leave your **car** in the Via Villa Gloria car park, **t** 0372 28243, where you get free use of a **bike**.

Tourist Information

Cremona: Piazza del Comune 5, **t** 0372 23233, *www.aptcremona.it (open daily 9–12.30, 3–6).*

Where to Stay

Cremona ✉ 26100

★★★×**Delle Arti**, Via Bonomelli 8, **t** 0372 23131, (*very expensive*). An idiosyncratic hotel with ultra-modern designer décor, a video wall for art installations, helpful staff, fabulous bathrooms and excellent breakfasts.

★★★★**Continental**, Piazza della Libertà 26, **t** 0372 434 141 (*expensive*). A modern, comfy, friendly hotel in the centre, with a display of Cremona-made fiddles and its own garage.

★★★**Astoria**, Via Bordigallo 19, **t** 0372 461 616 (*moderate*). A very pleasant hotel in a quiet street close to the Duomo, with tidy, comfortable rooms. The cheapest have en suite baths but communal showers.

★★★**La Locanda**, Via Pallavicino 4, **t** 0372 457 834 (*cheap*). A hotel just off the pedestrian area, with a simple but stylish restaurant (*expensive–moderate*) offering regional fare – try the guinea fowl cooked in Marsala wine. *Closed Tues.*

Eating Out

Ristorante Il Violino, Via Sicardo 3, **t** 0372 461 010 (*expensive*). A classy restaurant located just behind the baptistry and renowned for its regional dishes, which include melt-in-your-mouth *antipasti*, *tortelli di zucca* and zesty meat or seafood *secondi*. Advance reservations are required. *Closed Mon eve and Tues.*

Osteria La Sosta, Via Sicardo 9, **t** 0372 456 656 (*expensive–moderate*). A good-value restaurant offering a range of traditional dishes. Try the *gnocchi vecchi*, based on a 500-year-old recipe. *Closed Sun eve and Mon, carnival and Aug.*

Porta Mosa, Via Santa Maria in Betlem 11, **t** 0372 411 803 (*expensive–moderate*). A tiny family-run place where you can choose from a selection of delicious traditional dishes such as *tortelli* stuffed with squash, and locally caught sturgeon steamed with herbs and capers. Make sure to save room for the mean *tiramisù*. Booking is advisable. *Closed Sun and Aug.*

Trattoria La Prima, Via Cavitelli 8, **t** 0372 411 383 (*moderate*). A restaurant where you can count on experiencing truly local dishes and attitude: the owner, host and chef selects his clientele by keeping half of the tables reserved even when they aren't. If you pass muster, the service is very hospitable and the cooking excellent. Specialities are the home-made *primi*. *Closed Mon and Sun eve.*

Trattoria Mellini, Via Bissolati 105, **t** 0372 30535 (*moderate*). An older, rather more traditional restaurant at the western end of town, featuring hard-core meat dishes such as casseroled donkey and baby horse, and raw baby horse with truffle. For those who can't stomach such things, there is other hearty regional fare, including a kind of risotto with salami and savoy cabbage, and fresh pasta with sausage. Advance booking is advisable, especially in the evenings. *Closed Sun eve, Mon and Aug.*

Hai Xia, Corso Garibaldi 85, **t** 0372 39153 (*cheap*). A restaurant where you can get both pizza and Thai and Chinese food. All of them are delicious, especially the Thai. *Closed Mon.*

Lanfranchi, Via Solferino 30. A historic *pasticceria* offering a range of traditional cakes, including *Pan Cremona*, a soft confection that's made with almonds, honey and chocolate.

Cremona

Cremona has been the capital of the violin industry since 1566, when Andrea Amati invented the modern violin from the old medieval fiddle. It soon became fashionable, and demand across Europe initiated a golden age of fiddle-making, when Andrea's son Nicolò Amati, and his pupils Stradivarius and Giuseppe Guarneri, made the best violins ever. Walking around, you can easily pick out in the elegant curves and scrolls on the brick and terracotta palaces that inspired the instrument's Baroque form, while the sweetness of the violin's tone seems to have something of the city's culinary specialities in it – not only nougat but *mostarda di Cremona* (candied cherries, apricots and melons in a sweet or piquant mustard sauce, served with boiled meats). Today some 50 *liutai* (violin-makers) keep up the tradition, using similar methods and woods (poplar, spruce, pear, willow and maple); a school and research institute are devoted to the craft, and every third October the city hosts a festival of stringed instruments.

Milan captured the once feisty *comune* in 1344 and in 1441 gave the city to Bianca Maria Visconti when she married Francesco Sforza, marking the change of the great Milanese dynasties. The city enjoyed a fruitful Renaissance as the apple of Bianca's eye, producing Claudio Monteverdi, the father of opera, the prolific Campi family of painters, and Sofonisba Anguissola, the Renaissance portrait painter admired by Michelangelo, Van Dyck and Philip II for her ability to depict a sitter's soul.

Via Palestro to the Piazza del Comune

Cremona can be easily explored on foot, starting from the station and Via Palestro. Here, behind a remodelled Baroque façade at No.36, the **Palazzo Stanga Trecco's** 15th-century courtyard is an excellent introduction to the Cremonese fondness for elaborate terracotta ornament. The nearby **Museo Civico 'Ala Ponzone'** at Via Ugolani Dati 4 (***t** 0372 407 770; open Tues–Sat 9–6, Sun and hols 10–6; adm*) includes the **art gallery**, **archeological museum** and **Museo Stradivariano**; the last provides a good introduction to the cream of Cremona's best-known industry, featuring casts, models, items from the master's workshop and drawings explaining how Stradivarius did it. Around the corner, the **Palazzo Affaitati** (begun in 1561) houses a theatrical staircase that was added in 1769 and the **Museo Civico**, with sections devoted to amazingly dreary paintings by the Cremonese school (Boccaccino and the Campi family) and Caravaggio's *Francesco in Meditation*. The archaeology museum includes a fine labyrinth mosaic with Theseus and the Minotaur in the centre (*c.* 2nd century AD) from the Roman *colonia* at Cremona; another section houses the cathedral treasury, with some fine illuminated codices and corals. The palace opposite, at Via U. Dati 7, has a pretty frescoed courtyard.

Via Palestro becomes Corso Campi, and at an angle runs into the boxy, Mussolini-era Galleria Venticinque Aprile, leading to **Piazza Roma**, a nice little park; along Corso Mazzini is Stradivarius' red marble tombstone, transferred from a demolished church. Corso Mazzini forks after a block; near the split, at Corso Matteotti 17, is the city's prettiest palace, the 1499 **Palazzo Fodri** (owned by the Banca Cariplo; ask the guard to open the gate), with a courtyard adorned with frescoed battle scenes and terracottas.

Piazza del Comune: The Torrazzo and Duomo

Cremona's medieval Piazza del Comune could compete in any urban beauty contest. The 370ft **Torrazzo** (*under restoration; call tourist office for opening times*) with its curious pointed crown is the tallest bell tower in Italy. Only slightly shorter than Milan cathedral, it was built in the 1260s, has battlements as well as bells, and even tells the time, thanks to a fine astronomical clock added in 1583 by Giovanni Battista Divizioli (*visits by appointment with tourist office*). The stout-hearted can climb 487 steps for an eye-popping view; otherwise buy a famous Cremona TTT postcard (Torrazzo, *torrone* and tits). The lower level houses a reproduction of a violin=maker's shop of Stradivarius' time (*visits by appointment with tourist office; adm exp*).

Linked to the Torrazzo in 1525 by a double loggia, the **Portico della Bertazzola**, the **Duomo** (***t** 0372 27386; open Mon–Sat 7.30–12 and 3.30–7, Sun and hols 7.30–1 and 3.30–7*) is the highest and one of the most exuberant expressions of Lombard Romanesque, with a trademark Cremonese flourish in the graceful scrolls on the marble front. Built by the Comacini masters after a quake destroyed its predecessor in 1117, the main door or **Porta Regia** remains as it was originally, flanked by two nearly toothless lion *telamones* and four flat prophets, and crowned by a small portico, the Rostrum, where 13th- and 14th-century statues of the Virgin and two saints silently but eloquently hold forth above a frieze of the months by the school of Antelami.

The cathedral was begun as a basilica, but as Gothic came into fashion the arms of a Latin cross were added; the new transepts are almost as splendid from the outside as the main façade. The restored interior reveals primitive frescoes under the opulent 16th-century works by Romanino, Boccaccino and Pordenone (who painted the Crucifixion under the rose window); the right transept has some sweet and simple paintings on the ceiling and Flemish tapestries. The twin pulpits have nervous, delicate reliefs by Amadeo or Pietro da Rho. The choir has lovely stalls inlaid in 1490 by G.M. Platina, with nearly all secular scenes, views of Cremona and still lifes. Also of interest is the 15th-century *Grande Croce* or 'Great Cross', created by the 'Fabbrica del Duomo' craftsmen. A true masterpiece, the gold cross, which furnished the main altar, is now in a glass display case nearby. In the crypt with the tomb of Omobono Tucenghi (*d.* 1197), patron saint of tailors and the first layman to be canonized (in 1199), are the remains of medieval mosaics, plus a painting of Jesus, the Virgin Mary and Joseph, with old Cremona and its Manhattan skyline of towers in the background.

Completing the sacred ensemble in Piazza del Comune is the octagonal **Battistero di San Giovanni** of 1167 (***t** 0372 27386; visits by prior appointment; ask at Duomo's sacristy*), with another pair of lions supporting the portico and two sides of marble facing to match the cathedral. Across from the Duomo, the **Loggia dei Militi** (1292) was used as a rendezvous by the captains of the *comune*'s citizens' militia; the outdoor pulpit between two of the arches is a relic of charismatic, itinerant preachers such as San Bernadino of Siena, whose sermons were so popular they had to be held outside.

Behind it, the **Palazzo del Comune** (***t** 0372 22138, open Tues–Sat 9–6, Sun and hols 10–6*) was begun in 1206 as the lavish seat of the Ghibelline party and is now the town hall. On show are paintings salvaged from churches, a superb marble fireplace of 1502 by Giovan Gaspare Pedone in the Sala della Giunta, Baroque furniture and the **Saletta dei Violini** (*adm; buy tickets in advance at bookshop across courtyard*), once the chapel of the palace, now with a collection of eight violins (not all always on display). The star is Stradivarius' golden 'Cremonese 1715', retaining its original varnish, which is almost as mysterious as the embalming fluids of ancient Egypt. Another of the master's secrets was in the woods he used – like Michelangelo seeking the right piece of marble in the Carrara mountains, Stradivarius would visit the forests of the Dolomites looking for perfect trees. Other violins include 'Charles IX of France' by Andrea Amati (1566), one of 24 violins commissioned in the 1560s by the French sovereign. Free listening sessions are held in the Saletta (***t*** *0372 22138; book ahead*).

Take time to visit the Sala della Consulta and Sala della Giunta (if there's not a plenary session) for their original décor, as well as the Salone dei Decurioni, housing a splendid luxury coach, the 18th-century Corrozza Crotti, as well as a cycle of restored paintings on the life and miracles of Saint Omobono by Partolomeo Bersani.

Back Towards the Station

Behind the Palazzo del Comune are Piazza Cavour and Corso Vittorio Emanuele, leading to the Po. En route it passes one of Italy's earliest and best-known small-town theatres, the **Teatro Ponchielli**, built in 1734 and rebuilt after a fire in 1808, named for Amilcare Ponchielli who premièred several of his operas on its little stage. A street to the right of it leads back to Piazza San Pietro and **San Pietro al Po**, with its 16th-century stuccoes and frescoes by Antonio Campi.

Cremona has several lofty churches with interiors strikingly similar to ancient Roman basilicas, including the 14th-century **Sant'Agostino** north of the Corso Vittorio Emanuele on Via Plasio (***t*** *0372 22545*). Its striking red-brick façade has fine terracotta decorations, and the centre nave is lined with statues of the virtues. There are good Renaissance frescoes in the right aisle by Bonifacio Bembo and a lovely pala of the Madonna with Saints (1494) by Perugino (*currently undergoing restoration*). For something different, seek out the sinuous terracottas on the Liberty-style building nearby at Via Milazzo 16.

Further up, Via Plasio joins Corso Garibaldi, site of the 11th-century church of **Sant' Agata** (***t*** *0372 22951; open daily 7.30–12 and 4–7.30*) hiding behind a neoclassical façade; the interior, a perfect Roman basilica, has excellent frescoes by Giulio Campi of the unpleasant Martyrdom of St Agata in the choir, a painting in the left aisle of the holy family by Lucia Anguissola, sister of the famous Sofonisba, and a medieval masterpiece, the 13th-century wooden panel painted with the life of St Agatha.

Opposite, the restored Gothic **Palazzo Cittanova** of 1256 was the HQ of the Guelph party: adjacent, note the flamboyant, phoney façade of the **Palazzo Trecchi**. Further along, the pink and white **Palazzo Raimondi** (1496) houses the Scuola Internazionale di Liuteria, where students learn to make violins (*selected visits by appointment,* ***t*** *0372 38689*); its **Museo Organologico-Didattico** (***t*** *0372 38689; open Sept–July Mon and Fri 9–12*) is worth a look if you're interested in fiddle-making. Across the street is the city's most peculiar palace, crowned with strange iron dragons. Near the station, **San Luca** (***t*** *0372 20262; open 6.45–11.45 and 3.30–7*) has a beautiful terracotta façade and a detached octagonal temple of 1503, a votive offering for the end of a plague.

San Sigismondo, east of Piazzale Libertà at Via A. Giuseppina (**t** *0372 431 919; open daily 8.30–12 and 3–6 except during Mass*), was built in 1463 by Bianca Maria Visconti to commemorate her marriage to Francesco Sforza. Inside are rich pastel frescoes and *trompe l'œil* décors by Giulio, Antonio and Bernardino Campi, Camillo Boccaccino and Bernardino and Gervasio Gatti. The choir stalls are by Domenico and Gabriele Capra (1590); in the cloister is a fresco of the Last Supper by Tommaso Aleni (1508).

Around Cremona

Soncino and Paderno Ponchielli

The strategic agricultural province of Cremona is well fortified with castles and towers recalling the glorious days when the Italian *comuni* had nothing better to do than beat each other up. The most imposing, the **Rocca Sforzesca** (*open Apr–Oct Tues–Fri 10–12, Sat, Sun and hols 3–7; Nov–May Tues–Fri 10–12, Sat, Sun and hols 10–12.30 and 2.30–5.30; adm*) rears up over **Soncino**, a walled town north of Cremona. Built in the 12th century, it was enlarged in 1473 by Galeazzo Maria Sforza as an advance base against the Venetians, holed up in the Brescian town of Orzinuovi across the river. The moat and sinister towers are intact, as is the dungeon, which in 1259 hosted the most hated man in Italy: Emperor Frederick II's henchman, Ezzelino da Romano. Ezzelino's own army and Ghibelline allies turned on him as he crossed the Oglio on his way to surprise Milan; aged 65, he kept his reputation as a tough *hombre*, refusing to speak or receive medical treatment, ripping the bandages from his wounds until he died in agony. Details of other castles are available from the tourist office in Soncino.

Delicious painted terracottas and frescoes (*c.* 1500) by Giulio Campi and others cover the interior of **Santa Maria delle Grazie** (**t** *0374 86883; open Sun summer 10–12 and 4–7; winter 10–12 and 3–6; by request during week*). In the late 15th century the Sforzas invited a community of Jewish refugees to settle in Soncino, one of whom, Israel Nathan, founded a press and printed his first ornate book in Hebrew in 1483. The site is now a little **Museo della Stampa** (*open same hours as the castle*).

Between Cremona is **Paderno Ponchielli**, where 'the Italian Tchaikovsky', Amilcare Ponchielli (1834–86), teacher of Puccini and Mascagni, was born. His humble birthplace is the **Museo Ponchiellano**, with old scores and memorabilia (**t** *0374 367 200*).

Crema

In 1159, during Frederick Barbarossa's third war with Milan, the emperor, realizing he lacked enough troops to besiege the big city, turned his German army on Milan's little ally. Four hundred Milanese came to Crema's defence; Frederick hung hostages from Crema and Milan outside the gates, and when that didn't bring about surrender strapped their infants to moving siege towers, so the Cremaschi could not repulse the towers without harming their own children. The parents asked their fellow citizens to kill them, while shouting to their children to be brave and give up their lives for their country. Crema held out for six months, but at last, starving and exhausted, surrendered on condition the citizens could withdraw to Milan as their town was razed.

Three hundred years later, in 1449, Francesco Sforza offered the most loyal town of Crema to Venice when the Serenissima offered to support his dukedom. It proved a more pleasant occupation, lasting three centuries and endowing Crema with a tidy elegance rare in the Lombard plain. To this day it bears a white Istrian marble lion of St Mark on its gates and town hall, the latter by the pink-brick **Duomo**, a delightful Romanesque Gothic work built after Barbarossa sent the original up in flames.

The incomplete but utterly romantic Baroque **Palazzo Terni de' Gregori** (or Bondenti) at Via Dante Alighieri 49 houses the library and **Museo Civico** (*t 0373 257 161; open Mon 2.30–6.30, Tues–Fri 9–12 and 2.30–6.30, Sat, Sun and hols 10–12 and 4–7*), with everything from medieval Lombard armour, Risorgimento mementoes, scores by local composers, and two dramatic paintings of the Miracles of Christ by Alessandro Magnasco, with backgrounds by Clemente Spera, an expert on painting theatrical landscapes of ruins. Ask the curators to unlock the refectory to see the restored frescoes of the Last Supper and **Crucifixion** (1498) by Giovan Pietro da Cemmo.

Just to the north of the walls, at the end of a long tree-lined avenue, an apparition of the Virgin is marked by the basilica of **Santa Maria della Croce** (*t 0373 259 597; open daily 7–12 and 2.3–7, summer until 8.30*), a lovely Renaissance 1490–1500 drum church that was inspired by Bramante. Encircled by three orders of loggias and four polygonal chapels with spherical cupolas, the interior is octagonal and contains a fine Assumption by Diana.

West of Crema towards Milan, **Pandino** has a large 14th-century Visconti hunting lodge-cum-castle, one of the best preserved of the area. The fortress now hosts the *Comune* offices, but its court, loggia, frescoes and two restored halls can be visited (*call* **t** *0373 973 313 for times and details of guided tours*). **Rivolta d'Adda**, another eight kilometres on, has the 11th-century church of San Sigismondo, dwarfed by its battlemented campanile and containing some good carvings. Rivolta also offers Jurassic-era fun in its **Parco della Preistoria** (**t** *0363 78184 or* **t** *0363 370 250; open daily Feb–Nov 9–dusk; adm*), where a zoo train chugs past 23 life-size reproductions of dinosaurs, prowling the wooded banks of the Adda.

Tourist Information

Crema: Via dei Racchetti 8, **t** 0373 81020 (*open Tues–Fri 8.30–12.30 and 3–6, Sun 10–12), www.crema.net/proloco.*

Soncino: **t** 0374 86883.

Where to Stay and Eat

Crema ✉ 26013

******Park Hotel Residence**, Via IV Novembre 51, **t** 0373 86353 (*expensive*). An upmarket hotel with a good restaurant, the **Openhouse**, with a Sicilian chef who does great fish.

******Ponte di Rialto**, Via Cadorna 7, **t** 0373 82342 (*moderate*). A small, pleasant choice.

The local speciality, *tortelli cremaschi*, is pasta filled with amaretti, raisins, lemon, peppermint, nutmeg and cheese, served in melted butter, sage and cheese.

In late Nov–Dec, many places offer moderately priced set menus as part of the **Rassegna Eno-Gastronomica** wine and food fair.

Mario, Via Stazione 118, **t** 0373 204 708 (*moderate*). Good local dishes. *Closed Tues eve and Weds.*

Trattoria Gobbato, Via Podgora 2, **t** 0373 80891 (*cheap*). A little place that's fed workers local specialities for decades; try the local salami and hare with polenta. *Closed Mon.*

Pasticceria Dossena, Via Mazzini 56 (*cheap*). A good place to get *Spongarda Dolce*, a typical local cake.

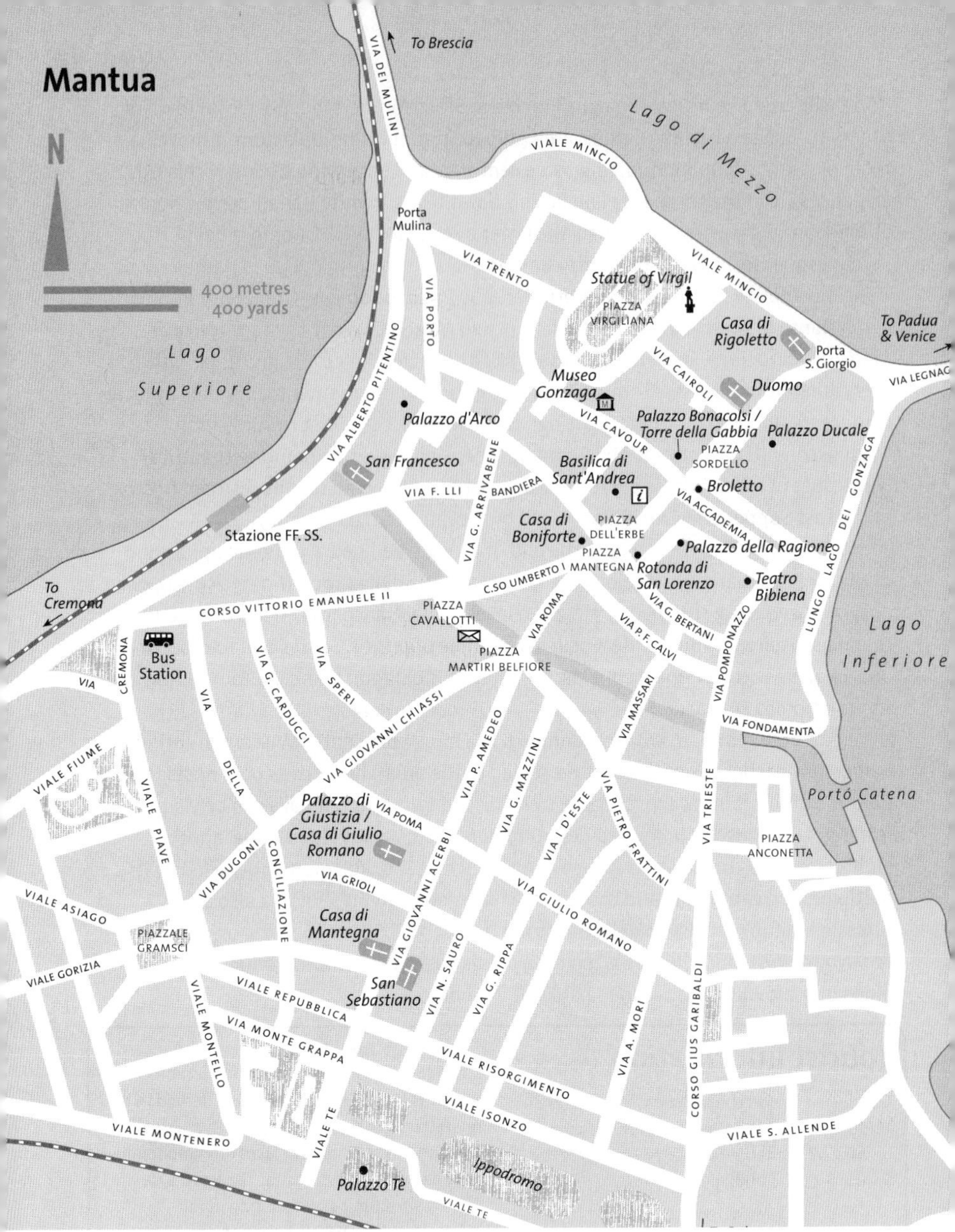

Mantua (Mantova)

Mantua sits in the midst of a flat plain, on a wide thumb of land protruding into three swampy, swollen lakes formed by the Mincio river. Its climate is moody: soggy with heat and humidity in summer, frosty under blankets of fog in winter. The local dialect is harsh, and the Mantuans, when they feel chipper, dine on braised donkey with macaroni. Verdi made it the sombre setting of *Rigoletto*. Yet this former capital of the art-loving, fast-living Gonzaga dukes is one of the most atmospheric old cities in the country – 'a city in the form of a palace' as Castiglione called it. Masculine, dark and handsome, with few of Cremona's sweet architectural arpeggios it is poker-faced, but holds a royal flush of dazzling Renaissance art.

History

Mantua gained its fame in Roman times, as the beloved home town of Virgil, who recounts the legend of its founding by Theban soothsayer Manto, daughter of Tiresias, and her son, the hero Ocnus. Virgil was born around 70 BC, and not much else was heard from Mantua until the 11th century, when the city formed part of the vast domains of Countess Matilda of Canossa. Matilda was a great champion of the pope against the emperor; her advisor Anselmo, Bishop of Lucca, became Mantua's patron saint. Even so, Mantua soon allied itself with the opposition, beginning an unusually important and lengthy career as an independent Ghibelline *comune*, dominated first by the Bonacolsi family, then the Gonzaga.

Naturally defended on three sides by the Mincio, enriched by river tolls and enjoying the protection and favour of the emperor, Mantua became a prominent neutral buffer state between the expansionist powers of Milan and Venice. The three centuries of Gonzaga rule, beginning in 1328, brought unusual peace and stability, and the refined tastes of the marquesses brought out artists of the highest calibre: Pisanello, Alberti and especially Andrea Mantegna, court painter from 1460 until his death in 1506.

Gianfrancesco I Gonzaga invited the great Renaissance teacher Vittorino da Feltre to open a school in the city in 1423, where his sons and courtiers, with the children of Mantua's poorer families, were taught according to Vittorino's educational theories, which gave equal emphasis to the intellectual, the physical and the moral. His star pupil was Ludovico (1412–78), one of the most just princes of his day, who did much to create Mantua according to Florentine humanist principles. Ludovico's grandson, Gianfrancesco II, was a military commander who led the Italians against the French at Fornovo but is perhaps best known as the husband of the brilliant and cultivated Isabella d'Este, the foremost culture vulture of her day and an astute diplomat, handling most of Mantua's affairs of state for her not very clever husband.

The family fortunes reached their apogee under Isabella's two sons. The elder, Federico II (1500–40), the godson of Cesare Borgia, married Margherita Palaeologo, the heiress of Monferrato, acquiring that duchy for the family as well as a ducal title for the Gonzaga. He hired Raphael's assistant, the Mannerist Giulio Romano ('that rare Italian master', Shakespeare called him in *The Winter's Tale*), to design and adorn his pleasure dome, the Palazzo Tè. When he died his brother, Cardinal Ercole, served as regent for his son Guglielmo, and both of these men, too, proved to be busy builders and civic improvers.

The last great Gonzaga, Vincenzo I, was a patron of Rubens, Fetti and Monteverdi, who composed the first modern opera, *L'Orfeo*, for the Mantuan court in 1607. But times got hard, and in 1628 Vincenzo II sold off many of the Gonzaga's treasures to Charles I of England, including Mantegna's *Triumphs of Caesar*. It's just as well that he did; two years later Mantua suffered a near mortal blow when the Gonzaga's claims

Getting There and Around

Mantua is 20km from Verona airport and has direct **train** links Verona, Vicenza, Florence, Rome, Milan, Modena and Cremona, and indirect links with Brescia (change at Piadena). The train station, **t** 0376 321 667 or freephone **t** 1 678 88088, is at Piazza Don Leoni.

There are **buses**, **t** 0376 327 237, to Lake Garda and towns in the province. The bus station is at Via Mutilati e Caduti del Lavoro 4, a 10min walk from the centre near Piazza Porta Pradella.

You can rent **bicycles** at the station; ask at the ticket office. For **taxis**, call **t** 0376 368 866.

Tourist Information

APT Mantua: corner of Piazza delle Erbe and Piazza Mantegna 6, **t** 0376 328 253, *www.aptmantova.it*.

Where to Stay

Mantua ✉ 46100

Mantua's few hotels tend to fill up fast.

Very Expensive

*****__Villa dei Tigli__, Via Cantarana 20, Rodigo, 15km from town, **t** 0376 650 691, *www.hotelvilladeitigli.it*. A patrician villa in its own park, with all modern facilities, including a pool and a beauty/fitness centre.

Expensive

****__Rechigi__, Via Calvi 30, **t** 0376 320 781, *www.rechigi.com*. A hotel in the historic centre, with permanent and temporary exhibitions of contemporary art. The comfortable air-conditioned rooms have satellite TV and there's parking (extra charge) and bikes for hire.

****__San Lorenzo__, Piazza Concordia 14, **t** 0376 220 500, *www.hotelsanlorenzo.it*. A restored late Renaissance building in the central pedestrian zone, with views over Piazza delle Erbe. Rooms have most of the comforts.

Moderate

***__Bianchi Stazione__, Piazza Don Leoni 24, **t** 0376 326 465. An option near the station, with soberly furnished rooms and good bathrooms. Most rooms open on a quiet inner courtyard, and from the top floor you can see the water lilies of Lago Superiore.

***__Broletto__, Via Accademia 1, **t** 0376 326 784. A cosy, family-run hotel in the city centre. Rooms are a bit small but have all modern amenities, including satellite TV and air-con.

__ABC Superior__, Piazza Don Leoni 25, **t 0376 323 347. A hotel by the station, with air-conditioned rooms, most opening on to an inner courtyard. Some rooms are *cheap*. There's free bike loan.

Cheap

*__Maragò__, Virgiliana, just outside centre , **t** 0376 370 313. Thirteen simple rooms, some with bath, and private parking.

Corte Bersaglio, Via L. Guerra 15, Migliaretto, just outside town, **t** 0376 320 345. An *agriturismo* with a riding stable.

Corte Feniletto, Via Francesca Est 86, Rodgio, 13km from town, **t** 0376 650 262. A farm offering accommodation in the midst of the regional park of the Mincio. *Open Apr–Oct.*

Corte Prada Alta, Strada San Girolamo 9, on cycle route to Peschiera on Lake Garda, **t** 0376 391 144. An *agriturismo* with bike hire. *Closed Tues and last 2wks Jan.*

Corte Schiarino-Lena, Porto Mantovano, Via Martorelli 45, **t** 0376 398 238. An *agriturismo* on the other side of Lago Superiore, with a 16th-century courtyard. *Open May–Nov.*

to Monferrato came into conflict with those of the Habsburgs, who were never ones for legal niceties and sent imperial troops to capture and sack the town. The duchy, under a cadet branch of the family, limped along until the Austrians snatched Mantua in 1707, eventually making it the southwest corner of their Quadrilateral. Until they became part of the Italian nation in 1866, the towns and the surrounding area remained part of the Austro-Hungarian Empire (except during Napoleonic rule between 1797 and 1814).

Eating Out

Mantua ✉ 46100

Stracotto di asino (donkey stew) heads the list of local dishes; Mantuans also like to add Lambrusco to broth and soup. Classic *primi* include *agnoli* stuffed with bacon, salami, chicken livers and cheese cooked in broth, *risotto alla pilota* (with onion, butter and local grana cheese), *risotto con salamelle* (with fresh salami) and *tortelli di zucca* (little pasta caps stuffed with pumpkin, mustard and cheese, served with melted butter). The local lake and river fish – catfish, eel, crayfish, pike (the delicious *luccio in salsa* is prepared with peppers and capers) and bass – and deep-fried frogs' legs are traditional second courses.

Mantua is also a good place to taste true, natural **Lambrusco**, which must be drunk young (a year or so old) to be perfectly lively and sparkling; the test is to see if the foam vanishes when it's poured. There are three main kinds: the grand Lambrusco di Sorbana, the mighty Lambrusco di Santa Croce and the amiable Lambrusco di Castelvetro.

From May to Sept, there are **wine tastings** in Mantua's main squares, **t** 0376 204 244. A local food and wine route map is available at *www.mantovastradaviniesapori.it*.

Very Expensive

Aquila Nigra, Vicolo Bonacolsi 4, **t** 0376 327 180. A lovely place with marble and traces of frescoes, serving wonderful dishes, both regional and from further afield. The pasta courses (ravioli filled with truffled duck, for instance) are superb. *Closed Mon, Jan and Aug.*

Trattoria dei Martini, Piazza C. d'Arco 1, **t** 0376 327 101. A restaurant overlooking an inner garden, with a seasonal menu based on local cuisine – try the tagliatelle with duck. *Closed Mon, Tues and 1st half Jan.*

Expensive

Ai Garibaldini, Via S. Longino 7, **t** 0376 328 263. A restaurant in a fine old house with a shady garden in the historic centre, with Mantuan dishes, including especially good risotto and *tortelli di zucca. Closed Weds and Jan.*

San Gervasio, Vicolo San Gervasio 13, **t** 0376 323 873. A restaurant in a superbly renovated 14th-century palace, with an excellent *menu mantovano. Closed Weds and Aug.*

Moderate

Antica Osteria Fragoletta, Piazza Arche 5, **t** 0376 323 300. A trendy restaurant with good food appreciated by the local clientele. Booking advised. *Closed Mon.*

Due Cavallini, Via Salnitro 5, near Lago Inferiore, off Corso Garibaldi, **t** 0376 322 084. Donkey dishes and other, less ethnic fare. *Closed Tues and late July–late Aug.*

L'Ochina Bianca, Via Finzi 2, **t** 0376 323 700. An ever-changing menu that might include smoked beef dressed with olive oil, and deep-fried zucchini flowers. The owners were founders of the 'Slow Food' association (*see* p.82). *Closed Mon, and Tues lunch.*

Il Portichetto, Via Portichetto 14, **t** 0376 360 747. A menu revolving around local river fish and vegetarian dishes. *Closed Mon.*

Ristorante Pavesi dal 1918, Piazza delle Erbe 13, **t** 0376 323 627. Particularly good local cuisine. *Closed Thurs and mid-Dec to Feb.*

Trattoria Quattrotette, Vicolo Nazione 4, **t** 0376 329 478. A small restaurant away from the obvious tourist areas, attracting hordes of locals who relish the vegetable dishes and salads (*melanzana grillata, carciofi alla giudia* and *peperonata*), the steaming bowls of pasta, and the *pasticceria*. In autumn make sure you try the crepes with pumpkins, and the *sugolo*, a special vine sorbet. *Closed Sun.*

Piazza Mantegna

From the station, Corso Vittorio Emanuele and Corso Umberto I lead straight into the Renaissance heart of Mantua, where the narrow cobbled streets are lined with inviting porticoes providing shelter from the sun or rain. Rising above the rest of the city in Piazza Mantegna is the great basilica of **Sant'Andrea** (*open daily 7.30–12 and 3–7*), designed by the great Florentine humanist Leon Battista Alberti in 1472 to house the Gonzaga's most precious holy relic: two ampoules of Christ's blood, said to have been given to St Andrew by St Longinus, the Roman centurion who pierced Christ's side with his lance. The finding of the relic is celebrated on 12 March, and the ampoules are exhibited during the Good Friday ceremonies. Ludovico Gonzaga had asked Alberti to create a truly monumental edifice to house the relic and form a fitting centrepiece for the city, and Alberti complied. In Florence Alberti had found himself constrained as an architect by his patrons' tastes, but in Mantua he was able to experiment and play with the ancient forms he loved. Sant'Andrea is based on Vitruvius' idea of an Etruscan temple, with a single barrel-vaulted nave supported by side chapels, fronted with a unique façade combining a triumphal arch and a temple. The lofty dome, designed by Juvarra, was completed in 1782. The interior is as imposing as the outside. Andrea Mantegna (*d.* 1506) is buried in the first chapel on the left, with a stern self-portrait in bronze. The other chapels have fine altarpieces as well, especially the second one on the left, by Lorenzo Costa.

On the east side, the unfinished flank of the basilica is lined with the porticoes and market stalls of delightful **Piazza delle Erbe**. Sunk below the level of the modern pavement, the **Rotonda di San Lorenzo** (*open daily mid-Mar–mid-Nov 10–12 and 3–7; mid-Nov–mid-Mar 11–12*), modelled on the Church of the Holy Sepulchre in Jerusalem, was built by the Countess Matilda in 1082; an ambulatory supports a matroneum for the ladies and there are damaged Romanesque frescoes by the altar.

Opposite the tourist office, the **Casa di Boniforte da Concorezzo** has elegant stucco decoration that has remained almost unchanged since it was built in 1455, while the 13th-century Palazzo della Ragione has a stout clock tower topped by an odd little temple and astronomical clock, added during Ludovico's restoration of the palace in 1475. The piazza is closed by the **Broletto**, built in 1227, facing Piazza del Broletto; note the niche holding a 13th-century statue of Virgil seated near the door.

In Piazza Broletto another local hero, a racing driver this time, is remembered in the **Museo Tazio Nuvolari** (*open Apr and Oct Tues, Weds and Fri–Sun 10–1 and 3.30–6.30; Mar, Nov and Dec, Sat and Sun 10–1 and 3.30–6.30; in Jan and Feb by appointment on* ***t*** *0376 325 691 or* ***t*** *0376 220 892; adm*). In the third weekend of September an **antique car race** is held there.

An archway leads into grand cobbled **Piazza Sordello**, traditional seat of Mantua's bosses. On one side rise the sombre palaces of the Bonacolsi, the Gonzaga's predecessors, with their **Torre della Gabbia**, named for the iron torture cage they kept to suspend prisoners over the city (though the Mantuans claim it was only used once). At the head of the piazza stands the **Duomo** (*open daily 7–12 and 3–7*), with a silly 1756 façade topped by wedding-cake figures that hides a lovely interior with five naves designed by Giulio Romano in 1545. Renaissance tapestries hang in the choir, and the enormous Trinity in the apse is by Domenico Fetti, another Roman painter who worked in Mantua in the early 17th century. The 15th-century house at No.23 has become the '**Casa di Rigoletto**' to satisfy the longings of Verdi buffs.

The new **Museo Archeologico Nazionale** in Piazza Castello (***t*** *0376 329 223; open Tues–Fri 8.30–1.30, Sat 8.30–6.30, Sun and hols 9.30–2.30*) contains a permanent exhibition on the archaeology of the Mantuan territory, as well as a number of prehistoric findings.

The Palazzo Ducale

Open Tues–Sun 8.45–7.15 (reduced tour after 6pm; ticket office closes at 6.30), June–Sept also Sat 9am–11pm; to see Camera degli Sposi, groups must book on **t** *0376 382 150; adm.*

Opposite the Bonacolsi palaces stands that of the Gonzaga, its unimpressive façade hiding one of Italy's most remarkable Renaissance abodes, both in sheer size and in the magnificence of its art. The insatiable Gonzaga kept adding until they had some 500 rooms in three main structures – the original **Corte Vecchia**, first built by the Bonacolsi in 1290, the 14th-century **Castello**, with its large towers overlooking the lake, and the **Corte Nuova**, designed by Giulio Romano. Throw in the Gonzaga's **Basilica di Santa Barbara** and you have a complex that occupies the entire northeast corner of Mantua (more than 34,000 square metres). It was the focal point of Mantuan life and politics and represented Gonzaga's taste and love for the arts; the most important artists of the time were invited to court and asked to adorn the rooms. If you go in winter, dress warmly – it's as cold as a dead duke.

Though stripped of its furnishings and most of its moveable art, the Palazzo Ducale remains imposing and seemingly endless. One of the first rooms on the tour, the former **chapel**, has a dramatic, half-ruined 14th-century fresco of the Crucifixion, attributed by some to Tommaso da Modena, while another contains a painting of a battle between the Gonzaga and the Bonacolsi in Piazza Sordello, in which the former crushed their rivals once and for all in 1328 – although the artist, Domenico Monore, painted the piazza as it appeared in 1494. Even more fascinating than this real battle is the vivid **fresco of Arthurian knights** by Pisanello, Italy's International Gothic master. Recorded as damaged in the 1480s, the fresco was believed lost until 1969, when layers of plaster were stripped away to reveal a remarkable work commissioned by Gianfrancesco Gonzaga in 1442 to commemorate his receiving from Henry VI the concession to use the heraldic SS collar of the House of Lancaster – an insignia that forms the border of Pisanello's mural, mingled with marigolds, a Gonzaga emblem.

Beyond this are the remodelled **neoclassical rooms**, holding a set of Flemish tapestries from Raphael's *Acts of the Apostles* cartoons (now in the Victoria and Albert Museum in London). Woven in the early 1500s, these copies of the Vatican originals are in a much better state of preservation. Beyond, the **Sala dello Zodiaco** has vivacious 1580 frescoes by Lorenzo Costa; the **Sala del Fiume** is named for its fine views over the river; and the **Galleria degli Specchi** has mirrors and mythological frescoes and, by the door, a note from Monteverdi on the musical evenings he directed there in the 1600s.

The Gonzaga were mad about horses and dogs and had one room, the **Salone degli Arcieri**, painted with *trompe l'œil* frescoes of their favourite steeds standing on upper ledges; the family used to play a kind of guessing game with them, when curtains would be drawn over the figures. Sharing the room are works by Tintoretto and a family portrait by Rubens, court painter under Vincenzo I, a picture so large that Napoleon's troops had to cut it up to carry it off. The duke's apartments hold a fine collection of classical statuary: busts of the emperors, a Hellenistic torso of Aphrodite, and the 'Apollo of Mantova', inherited from Sabbioneta after Vespasiano's death. The

Sala di Troia has vivid 1536 frescoes by Giulio Romano and pupil Rinaldo Mantovano; another ducal chamber has a beautiful 17th-century labyrinth painted on the ceiling, each path inscribed in gold with 'Maybe Yes, Maybe No'. From some rooms you can look out over the grassy Cortile della Cavallerizza, with rustic façades by Giulio Romano.

The oldest part of the palace complex, the 14th-century **Castello San Giorgio**, is reached by a low spiral ramp, built for the horses the Gonzaga could never bear to be without. Here, in the famous **Camera degli Sposi**, are the remarkable frescoes painted by Mantegna in 1474. Restored to their brilliant original colours, they depict the life of Ludovico Gonzaga, with his wife Barbara of Brandenburg, his children, dwarves, servants, dogs and horses, and important events. The portraits are those of real people and not for public display, almost like a family photo album. And there is a lingering sorcery here, for these frescoes are the fruit of Mantegna's fascination with the science of perspective. The beautiful backgrounds of imaginary cities and ruins reflect Mantegna's other love, classical architecture, but add an element of unreality in their realistic vividness, as do his *trompe l'œil* ceiling frescoes.

From here the tour continues to the **Casetta dei Nani**, tiny rooms with low ceilings and shallow stairs where the dwarves lived. The last stop is the **suite of Isabella d'Este**, designed by her as a retreat after her husband's death. In these rooms she held court as the Renaissance's most imperious patron, practically commanding Leonardo and Titian to paint her portrait; at one point she commissioned an allegorical canvas from Perugino so exacting that she sketched what she wanted and set spies to make sure the painter followed orders. Given an excellent classical education in her native Ferrara, she surrounded herself with humanists, astrologers, poets and scholars. Her fabulous art collection has long gone to the Louvre, but the emblems and symbols she devised with her astrologers remain like faint ghosts from a lost world on the ceiling.

Around Town

Within walking distance of the Palazzo Ducale at Via Accademia 47 east of the Broletto is the **Teatro Accademico Bibiena** (***t*** *0376 327 653; open Tues–Sun 9.30–12.30 and 3–6; adm*), a gem built by Antonio Galli Bibiena, of the famous Bolognese family of theatre builders. Mozart performed at the inaugural concert in 1770 aged 13; his father Leopold said it was the most beautiful theatre he had ever seen.

West of Piazza Sordello, Via Cairoli leads to the city's main park, **Piazza Virgiliana**, with a marble statue of Virgil from 1927 (in time for the poet's 2,000th birthday) and the **Museo Gonzaga** (***t*** *0376 320 602; open mid-Mar–June, Sept and Oct Tues–Sun 9.30–12 and 2.30–5; July and Aug Thurs, Sat and Sun 9.30–12 and 2.30–5; Nov–mid-Mar Sun 9.30–12 and 2.30–5; adm*), containing artefacts and treasures that belonged to the family. Further west, in Piazza d'Arco, the **Palazzo d'Arco** (***t*** *0376 322 242; open Mar–Oct Tues–Sun and hols 10–12.30 and 2.30–5.30; Nov–Feb Sat, Sun and hols 10–12.30 and 2–5; adm*) was rebuilt in 1784 over a 15th-century palace for the arty counts from Garda's north shore and has been left more or less as it was, with furnishings, paintings, instruments, a superb kitchen and, in a room preserved from the original palace, fascinating frescoes of the zodiac attributed to Giovanni Maria Falconetto of Verona and painted *c.* 1515 in the period between Mantegna's death and Giulio Romano's arrival. The nearby 1304 **church of San Francesco** (*open daily 7–12 and 3–9*) was rediscovered in 1944, when a bomb hit the arsenal that had disguised it for a century and a half. Now restored, it contains frescoes by Tommaso da Modena.

South of the medieval nucleus, just off main Via Principe Amedeo at Via Poma 18, the **Casa di Giulio Romano** was designed by the artist in 1544 while working on the Palazzo Tè. He also gets credit for the quaint palace decorated with monsters nearby. Mantegna designed his dream house, the **Casa del Mantegna** at Via Acerbi 47, in the same neighbourhood (***t** 0376 360 506; open Mon–Fri 10–12.30, Tues–Sun 10–12.30 and 3–6 for exhibitions*). As a cube built round a circular courtyard, he intended it partially as his personal museum and embellished it with classical 'Mantegnesque' decorations.

A Renaissance Pleasure Dome: the Palazzo Tè

*Viale Tè, **t** 0376 323 266; open Mon 1–6, Tues–Sun 9–6; adm.*

Giulio Romano's masterpiece got its name from *tejeto*, a local term for drainage canal. Work began on a former swamp in 1527, when Federico II had Giulio Romano expand the stables to create a little palace for his mistress, Isabella Boschetti, of whom his mother, Isabella d'Este, disapproved. The project expanded over the decades to become a guesthouse suitable for the Emperor Charles V, who visited twice.

Giulio Romano had moved from Rome to Mantua in 1524 to escape prison for designing pornographic prints. In his Palazzo Tè, one of the very first great Mannerist buildings – which took 10 years to complete – he had the same desire to shock and and to upset the cool classicism exemplified in Mantua by Alberti, and along the way he created one of the great Renaissance syntheses of architecture and art, combining *trompe l'œil* with a bold play between the structure of the room and the frescoes. Most of the art still has classical themes: the **Sala della Metamorfosi** is inspired by Ovid and Roman frescoes, which Giulio discovered with his master Raphael in Nero's Golden House in Rome. Gonzaga emblems fill the **Sala delle Imprese**: putti holding a cup, a belt, a bird catching fish, a muzzle, Mount Olympus and the salamander (a symbol of Federico's love, which is consumed, but doesn't burn); the chariot of the sun on the ceiling is a first hint of Giulio's love of wacky perspectives. The next room has more life-size Gonzaga horses on ledges, and in the next, the **Sala di Psiche**, are intensely coloured, exuberant scenes from The Golden Ass of Apuleius. The **Camera dei Venti** was Federico's private study, designed with the most precious materials and with a complex iconographic programme based on ancient astrological texts.

The **Loggia di Davide**, which was quickly thrown up for Charles V's second visit in 1532, is decorated with scenes dear to Federico's heart – he identified himself with the king, and Isabella with Bathsheba, both of whom were relieved of their husbands in suspicious circumstances. The next room has incredible antiquated stuccoes by Francesco Primaticcio, who later went on to Fontainebleau to work for François I. The climax, however, is the famous **Sala dei Giganti**, Giulio's most startling work, frescoed from floor to ceiling. Above, Zeus and company rain lightning, thunder, boulders and earthquakes down on the uppity Titans, creating so powerful an illusion of chaos that it seems as if the very room is about to cave in around the spectator.

Around Mantua

Mantua's western lake, **Lago Superiore**, is noted for its delicate lotus blossoms, planted in the 1930s as an experiment, which turn the lake violet and pink in July and August around the city's park, the **Valletta Belfiore**. Another park, the **Bosco della Fontana** (*open Mon, Weds, Thurs, Sat and Sun Mar–Oct 9–7; Nov–Feb 9–5; adm Sun and hols*) lies five kilometres to the north off the road to Brescia. Once a Gonzaga hunting reserve, with a moated little castle built as a hunting lodge in 1595 (*visits by request*), the Bosco has ancient, broad-leafed trees that are a last relic of the ancient forest that covered the Po plain.

San Benedetto Po

Some 22 kilometres southeast of Mantua, San Benedetto Po grew up around the Benedictine abbey of **Polirone** (*open daily 8–12 and 2.30–7*), the 'Monte Cassino of the North', established in 1007 by the Canossa counts of Tuscany. It was especially favoured by the last of their line, feisty Countess Matilda (*d.* 1115), whose alabaster sarcophagus survives in the richly appointed Basilica di San Benedetto, rebuilt in the 1540s by Giulio Romano and linked to the 12th-century church of **Santa Maria**, which has a fine 1151 mosaic. The three cloisters and refectory with frescoes by Correggio are now part of the **Musei Civici Polironiani** (***t*** *0376 623 036; open Mar–mid-Nov Mon 9–12.30, Tues–Fri 9–12.30 and 2.30–6.30, Sat and Sun 9–12.30 and 3–7; mid-Nov–Feb Tues–Fri by appointment; adm*), which includes the **Museo dell'Abbazia** and **Museo della Cultura Popolare Padana**, devoted to the traditions and culture of the surrounding countryside.

Sabbioneta

Midway between Mantua, Cremona and Parma, this was a rural village backwater until 1556, when its new prince, Vespasiano Gonzaga Colonna, decided to rebuild it from scratch as the capital of his little Ruritania. His Sabbioneta would be a rational expression of humanistic ideals, with a content and a military, civic and cultural function. He gets credit as the first to consider urban planning as an act of government, but unfortunately for Sabbioneta, humanism was out of fashion even before it was built. When its creator died without an heir his principality reverted to Mantua and became a backwater once more, a little museum city of unfulfilled expectations with the haunting, empty air of a De Chirico painting. In the last 15 years, however, interest has been rekindled, and much has been restored; antique shops and restaurants have begun to fill some of the houses. The interiors of the principal monuments, however, can only be seen by guided tour (*Tues–Sat 10–1 and 2–5, Sun and hols 10–1 and 2.30–6.30; ring Ufficio del Turismo del Comune to book 1½hr tour in English; adm*).

Along one side of **Piazza Castello**, where Vespasiano constructed his castle (demolished in the 18th century) and erected a column topped with a statue of Sabbioneta's patroness, the goddess of wisdom, Athena, runs a long brick atrium to Vespasiano's pleasure palace, a mini-version of the Palazzo Tè in Mantua called the **Palazzo e Giardino**. Its rich frescoes and stuccoes by the school of Giulio Romano and Bernardino Campi remain fairly intact. The Palazzo was linked to the castle by the

Galleria degli Antichi, a long frescoed corridor, the height of architectural fashion in Renaissance France and Italy. The next stop on the tour, the **Teatro all'Antica** (1588), was designed by Vicenzo Scamozzi, Palladio's greatest pupil. Restored remnants includes *trompe l'œil* boxes of chatting spectators and musicians.

Sabbioneta's second piazza contains the **Palazzo Ducale**, the first building erected by Vespasiano, which has kept its stately façade. A number of frescoed rooms with intricately carved Venetian ceilings have survived. It shares the square with the pink and white marble church of the **Assumption**, begun in 1578, its interior given a lovely rococo treatment in the 18th century. Continue to the octagonal church of the **Incoronata** (1586) with its impressive *trompe l'œil* dome from 1769 and Vespasiano's tomb in rare and antique marbles, with a bronze statue of the prince in Roman garb by Michelangelo's student Leone Leoni (1588). Near here, the **synagogue** (***t*** *0375 52039; open Tues–Sat 9.30–12 and 2.30–5, Sun and hols 9.30–12.30 and 2.30–6.30; adm*) rebuilt in the 1820s and still consecrated, has displays on the history of Judaism in the region.

In the countryside of Casalmaggiore on the way to Cremona, the imposing **Santuario della Madonna della Fontana** was built around a miraculous spring in medieval times. The painter Parmigianino is buried there.

Tourist Information

Curatone: Pro Loco, **t** 0376 369 122; Ufficio Cultura del Comune di Curtatone, **t** 0376 358 128.

Sabbioneta: Pro Loco, Via Gonzaga 27, **t** 0375 52039; Ufficio del Turismo del Comune, Piazza d'Armi 1, **t** 0375 221044, *www.unh.net/sabbioneta/index.html*.

Where to Stay and Eat

Sabbioneta ✉ 46018

★★**Al Duca**, Via della Stamperia 18, **t** 0375 52474 (*cheap*). A central hotel with comfortable enough rooms with en suite baths and TVs.

★**Giulia Gonzaga**, Via V. Gonzaga 65, **t** 0375 528 169 (*cheap*). A slightly simpler option.

Dal Pescatore, Loc. Runate 13, Canneto sull'Oglio, 20km north of town, **t** 0376 723 001 (*very expensive*). One of Lombardy's finest, most tranquil restaurants,. set in an elegant country villa and presided over by Italy's most talented female chef. The light cuisine uses the best and freshest produce, much of it picked that morning at the family farm. Book well in advance. *Closed Mon, Tues, Weds lunch, Aug and 2wks Jan.*

Il Capriccio, Via Solazzi 51 (Mantua–Parma road), **t** 0375 52722 (*moderate*). Delicious creative cuisine based on Mantuan tradition, including prawn risotto with truffles. *Closed Mon eve and Tues.*

Parco Cappuccini, Via Santuario 30, **t** 0375 52005 (*moderate*). An elegant restaurant in an 18th-century villa with a veranda on the park, offering classic Mantuan cuisine such as *risotto alla mantovana. Closed Mon and Wed eves, and 24 Dec–mid-Jan.*

Casalmaggiore ✉ 26041

Hotels here may be more comfortable than at Sabbioneta 3km away.

★★★**Bifi**, **t** 0375 200 938, *www.bifihotel.it* (*expensive*). A modern hotel with all amenities.

★★★**Il Leone**, Piazza Quattro Martiri 2, Pomponesco, 15km from town, **t** 0375 86077, (*moderate*). A good-value choice in a little Renaissance piazza close to the banks of the Po, with frescoed walls and wooden ceilings. A flower-filled patio leads to the 8 sunny rooms, and there's a swimming pool and an excellent restaurant serving specialities of the low Mantuan region.

Country Club Corte Lavadera, Cogozzo di Viadana, Via Pangona 6, **t** 0375 790 260, (*cheap*). A farmhouse complete with a swimming pool, tennis courts, a sauna, hydromassage facilities and a fully equipped horse-riding centre.

The Italian Lakes

The Lakes evoke a dreamy image of gentlemen and gentle ladies strolling through gardens, sketching landscapes, and indulging in a round of whist on the villa verandah in the evening. The backgrounds to their fond pleasures are snow-capped peaks tumbling into ribbons of blue, trimmed with the silver tinsel of olives and the daggers of dark cypress; mellowed villas gracing vine-clad hillsides and gold-flecked citrus groves; and lakes drunken with colour as azaleas, rhododendrons and camellias spill over the banks. For though the Swiss border is just around the corner, the Lakes cover enough area to create their own climatic oases of Mediterranean floras.

Lake holidays faded from fashion in the post-war era, when a suntan became a symbol of leisure, not manual labour, and a mass trek to the seashore became a summer ritual. But these lakes are too lovely to stay out of fashion for long, and today a new generation is rediscovering what their grandparents took for granted. For better or worse, the Italians have ringed the lakes with finely engineered roads, making them perhaps too accessible, although all still have their leisurely steamers.

Between July and September rest and relaxation may seem a Victorian relic, unless you book into one of the grander villa hotels. Quiet havens, however, still exist on the smaller, less developed lakes of Iseo and Orta, the east shores of Maggiore and Como. Lake resorts are generally open from April to October. The best times to visit are spring and autumn –not only to avoid the crowds, but because the lakes are less subject to winter mists and summer haze. In the restaurants, look for lake fish, served fresh or sun-dried. The finest wines from the lakes district come from the Franciacorta near Iseo, Bardolino on Lake Garda, the Valtellina, and La Brianza near Lake Como.

The lakes are described geographically from west to east, from Piemonte's Lake Orta and the valleys around Domodossola, through Lombardy's lakes and the Valtellina, Bergamo and Brescia, and then to Lake Garda on the border of the Veneto.

Lake Orta

The calm green waters of Orta hold a magical isle, illuminated on summer nights like a golden fairy-tale castle. Just 13 kilometres long, this is a lake 'made to the measurements of man'. Nietzsche, who never fell in love, did so on its soft green shores. He didn't get the girl, but the world got *Thus Spake Zarathustra*.

Orta San Giulio, its Island and its Sacro Monte

Set on its own garden peninsula, the lake's 'capital', Orta San Giulio, is a fetching little town. Narrow lanes lead into handsome lakeside **Piazza Motta**, nicknamed the *salotto* or drawing room, with the bijou 1582 **Palazzotto** decorated with faded frescoes. A lovely 40- to 60-minute walk (Movero/Lungolago) from the bottom of Via Motta follows the shoreline around the promontory and allows a glimpse at the patrician villas through their gardens. It ends at Via Panoramica, close to the tourist office.

Isola di San Giulio was inhabited by serpents and monsters until AD 390, when Julius (Giulio), a Christian preacher from Aegina, showed up. Local fishermen, fearing he would anger the dragons, refused to row him across, so Julius spread his cloak on the waters and surfed across. He sent the dragons packing, then built the precursor to the island's basilica by yoking a team of wolves to his ox cart – a feat good enough to make him the patron of builders, who gather here on his feast day, 31 January.

Around 1,000, the **Basilica** (***t*** *0322 90324; open Mon 11–12.15 and 2–6.45, Tues–Fri 9.30–12.15 and 2–6.45, until 5.45 in winter*) was rebuilt for the first time. The chief relic of this rebuilding, the startling black marble **pulpit**, shows Giulio in high relief, wearily leaning on the hilt of his sword after chasing the dragons, along with symbols of the Evangelists. There are some good 15th-century frescoes by Gaudenzio Ferrari and his

Getting There and Around

The main lake resorts, Orta San Giulio, Pettenasco and Omegna, are easily reached from Turin or Milan, by **car** via the A26, and on **trains** heading north to Domodossola and the Simplon Pass. Orta is also easy to reach from Lake Maggiore: **buses** run from Stresa to Orta, from Arona to Borgomanero with connections to Orta, and from Verbania to Omegna.

Navigazione Lago d'Orta, **t** 0322 844 862, provides a **boat service** at least twice a day between Oria, Omegna, Punta di Crabbia, Pettenasco, L'Approdo, Orta, Isola San Giulio, Pella, San Filiberto and Lagna. There's also a boat service to Isola San Giulio from Orta, leaving Piazza Motta every 15–20mins, **t** 333 605 0288, or there are **taxi-boats** for 10 people.

Tourist Information

Orta San Giulio: Via Panoramica, **t** 0322 905 614, and Via Bossi 47, **t** 0322 911 937.

Where to Stay and Eat

Orta San Giulio ✉ 28016

★★★★**Villa Crespi**, Via G. Fava 8/10, **t** 0322 911 902, *www.lagodortahotels.com* (*luxury*). Lake Orta's most luxurious hotel, in a restored Moorish folly in a garden at the top of town. Rooms each have romantic canopied beds, marble baths and Jacuzzis. In the elegant dining room (*very expensive*) you can enjoy sophisticated dishes combining Mediterranean and alpine flavours, such as macaroni with lobster ragout, cherry tomatoes and light pesto sauce. The wine list is vast. *Closed Tues in winter, Jan and Feb.*

★★★★**San Rocco**, Via Gippini 11, **t** 0322 911 977, *www.hotelsanrocco.it* (*very expensive*). A 17th-century monastery in Orta's historic centre, with modern rooms, a pretty garden and a heated outdoor pool. In Aug it hosts a series of jazz and classical music concerts.

★★★**La Bussola**, Via Panoramica 24, **t** 0322 911 913, *www.orta.net/bussola* (*very expensive–expensive*). A hotel on a quiet hill, with 16 rooms and panoramic views over the lake. There's a pretty garden with a pool, and a good restaurant. *Closed Nov.*

★★★**Orta**, Piazza Motta, **t** 0322 90253, *www.orta.net/hotelorta* (*very expensive–expensive*). A hotel brimming over with old-fashioned Italian character, run by the same family for more than a century, with big rooms and bathrooms and a charming dining terrace on the lake.

★★★**La Contrada dei Monti**, Via Contrada dei Monti 10, **t** 0322 905 114, *www.orta.net/lacontradadeimonti* (*expensive–moderate*). A charming hotel in Orta's centre, with individually furnished rooms and bathrooms overlooking quiet inner courtyards or the enchanting sidestreets .

★★★**Leon d'Oro**, Piazza Motta, **t** 0322 911 991, *www.orta.net/leondoro* (*expensive–moderate*). The place where, in 1882, Nietzsche and Lou Salomé spent their love-troubled week; the lake terrace and bar remain just as amenable to such breaks from philosophy. The bedrooms are small but immaculately furnished, and there is an à la carte restaurant.

★★★**Santa Caterina**, Via Marconi 10, **t** 0322 915 865, *www.orta.net/s.caterina* (*moderate*). A peaceful hotel set on the hills overlooking the town, near Sacro Monte. The owner also has several apartments to let on a weekly basis (with reduced rates for 2 weeks, higher rate for 2–3-night stays).

★★**Olina**, Via Olina 40, **t** 0322 905 656, *www.orta.net/olina* (*moderate*). Very pleasant rooms, some with whirlpool shower, and an elegant restaurant offering specialities such as home-made pasta, lake fish and meat cooked in an earthenware pot. *Closed Weds.*

Venus, Piazza Motta, **t** 0322 90256 (*moderate*). A restaurant that's always packed for lunch because of its location, though standards have dropped and prices risen of late.

Omegna ✉ 28026

★★**Vittoria**, Via Zanoia 37, **t** 0323 62237, *www.albergo-vittoria.it* (*moderate*). A family-run hotel with 10 tidy rooms, all with bath and TV, and a reasonably priced restaurant.

Ponte Bria, Via Ponte, Bria, near Cireggio di Omegna a few km from town , **t** 0323 863 732 (*moderate*). A restaurant in the woods, offering home-made *crespelle*, ravioli and gnocchi, and grilled trout directly from its lake. *Closed Mon out of season, and Nov–Feb.*

school (note the *Story of San Giulio* in the left aisle) and a marble sarcophagus belonging to the Lombard duke Meinulphus, who had betrayed the island to the Franks and was beheaded by King Agilulf; his decapitated skeleton was found inside in 1697. You can see what's left of Giulio in a glass casket, as well as some fragments of his 4th-century church.

Orta is framed by sacred places; a road winds up the promontory behind town to its holy acropolis or **Sacro Monte** (*t 0322 911 960; park always open; chapels open daily 9–5.30 in summer, until 4.30 in winter*), begun in 1591 and dedicated to Italy's patron St Francis. Twenty-one numbered slate-roofed chapels in a wooded grove spiral to the top of the hill; in each, life-sized statues in 17th-century garb enact an important event in Francis' life. What sets Orta's Sacro Monte apart from the others is its delicious setting, with its distracting views over Isola San Giulio. While you're here, spare a thought for poor, shy, awkward Nietzsche who, beguiled by the nightingales of Sacro Monte, fell head over heels for Lou Salomé, his Russian poet travelling companion. He advanced; she, surprised, retreated. He never tried love again.

Lake Orta to Domodossola

The Valle Anzasca

North of Lake Orta, the road passes into the shadow of the mighty granite dome of Mount Orfano, which locals are slowly whittling away to make flowerpots. Orfano guards an orphan lake, the small but deep **Lago Mergozzo**, one of the cleanest lakes in Europe – motorboats are banned. Between the mountain and lake, the hamlet of **Montorfano** has a striking Romanesque church in the shape of a Latin cross, with a 5th-century baptismal font. The lake's attractive main town, also called **Mergozzo**, has been a quiet place ever since it lost its role as a transit centre with the construction of the Simplon road and tunnel. It has a 12th-century church of Orfano granite, **San Giovanni** (*ring **t** 0323 80347 or **t** 0323 80593 for key*).

The first valley splitting off to the west, the enchanting **Valle Anzasca**, leads straight towards the tremendous east face of Monte Rosa. Among the woods and vineyards is **Cimamulera**, where one of the oldest horse chestnut trees in Italy grows next to the church (the old mule path from here to Piedimulera is especially lovely). The slate roofs of tiny **Colombetti** huddle under a cliff; **Bannio-Anzino**, 'capital' of the valley, has a 1st-century BC Gallo-Roman necropolis and a parish church with a 6ft, 16th-century bronze Christ from Flanders. At **Ceppo Morelli** the vertiginous bridge over the Anza traditionally divides the valley's Latin population from the Walser – German-speaking Swiss settlers from the Valais who came to these valleys in the 13th century. Beyond Ceppo the road plunges through a gorge to the old Walser mining town of **Pestarena**.

The hamlets that comprise **Macugnaga**, the Valle's popular mountain resort, seem tiny under the tremendous 'cathedral of stone and ice', **Monte Rosa** (15,305ft). Macugnaga's Walser culture and traditions are recalled in the **Museo Casa Walser** in the hamlet of Borca (*open Sat and Sun June and 1st week of Sept 3.30–5.30; daily July,*

*Aug and Christmas period 3–5.30; to visits at other times call **t** 0324 65056; adm*). At Fornarelli, the **Museo della Miniera Aurifera** (***t*** *0324 65656; open June–Sept daily 9–12 and 2–5.30; Oct–May Tues–Sun 1.30–5; Christmas daily 9–12; other periods by request; adm*) is dedicated to gold-mining; there's also a guided visit of part of the 18th-century mine (dress warmly). Macugnaga has some 40 kilometres of ski runs and two cross-country tracks; a dozen ski lifts; a chairlift to the magnificent **Belvedere** with views over the Macugnaga glacier, and a *funivia* to the **Passo Monte Moro** (9,410ft), used by skiers in winter and spring. From Macugnaga walkers can make a three-day trek over the mountains to Gressoney-St-Jean in the Valle d'Aosta (trail map essential).

To the north, the pretty, wooded **Val d'Antrona** is famed for its trout fishing and old-fashioned ways: the older women wear traditional costumes and make Venetian lace.

Domodossola

The capital of the Valle d'Ossola, Domodossola was a Roman settlemnent. After his victory at Marengo, Napoleon, to make French meddling in Italy easier, built the first transalpine highway from Geneva to Domodossola through the Simplon Pass (Passo del Sempione), a major engineering feat completed in 1805. Exactly 100 years later, the even more remarkable Simplon rail tunnel was completed – at the time it was the longest in the world, at 19.8 kilometres.

In the heart of Domodossola's compact historic centre, the **Motta**, is pretty **Piazza Mercato**, lined with 15th-century porticoes. A few steps away, the old church of **SS. Gervasio e Protasio** was rebuilt in the 18th century but conserves a Baroque porch and a curious Romanesque architrave carved with the *Dream of Constantine*, informing the emperor that he would conquer under the sign of the cross. Opposite SS. Gervasio e Protasio, the town's finest Renaissance building, the Palazzo Silva contains the **Museo Civico**, with Etruscan and Roman finds from the 3rd century AD necropolis in the Val Cannobina, Egyptian mummy bits and costumes (***t*** *0324 249001; open by appointment only, some guided visits in summer; adm*). At the other end of Piazza Mercato, the Palazzo San Francesco contains the **Museo G.G. Galletti**, part of the Museo Civico (*visits upon request, as above*). This incorporates a medieval church and holds something for every taste, from paintings to natural history exhibits to displays on the construction of the Simplon tunnel and the flight of Peruvian Jorge Chavez, the first man to fly over the Alps (in 1910), only to die in a crash near Domodossola (he also has a monument in Piazza Liberazione). In 1944 the adjacent **Palazzo di Città** was the seat of the Repubblica Partigiana dell'Ossola for 40 days in one of the most significant acts of the Italian resistance.

From the centre, Via Mattarella leads up to the site of a ruined castle, where two Capuchin friars founded a **Sacro Monte** (***t*** *0324 241 376; open daily till dusk*) in 1656, with 15 Baroque chapels dedicated to the Via Crucis. Unfortunately the first and best one exploded in 1830, when it was used to store powder – this shouldn't happen again, now the Sacro Monte is part of a special reserve. Domodossola has its own ski station 10 kilometres away, **Domobianca**, or, if pounds of polenta are weighing you down, relax at the hot mineral springs at **Bognanco** just up the next valley to the west (***t*** *0324 234 127; open May–Oct*).

Lake Maggiore

Have you not read in books how men when they see even divine visions are terrified? So as I looked at Lake Major in its halo I also was afraid ...

Hilaire Belloc, *The Path to Rome*

Italy's second-largest lake, Maggiore winds majestically between Piemonte and Lombardy, its north corner lost in the Swiss Alps. In Roman times it was *Lacus Verbanus*, for the verbena that still grows on its shores. What really sets the lake apart, though, are the Borromean Isles and their gardens, property of the Borromeo family of Milan, who have owned the lake's fishing rights since the 1500s. Otherwise, the western shore, especially the resorts of Stresa, Baveno and Verbania, are the most scenic.

Arona

Approaching Maggiore from the south, **Arona** is a sprawling market town with the 15th-century **Casa del Podestà** with its portico of pointed arches in cobbled Piazza del Popolo, and, in the old upper part, **Santa Maria** with a Borromeo family chapel with a 1511 polyptych by Gaudenzio Ferrari, and **SS. Martiri** with a painting by Bergognone. A medieval fief of the Visconti, the town passed to the Borromei in 1439. A few walls remain of their **castle** up on top of the town; it was the birthplace of Charles Borromeo (1538–84), an event commemorated with a church, three chapels of an unfinished Sacro Monte and **San Carlone**, a 115ft copper and bronze jug-eared colossus blessing the lake (*open daily Mar–Sept 9.30–6, Oct and Nov 9.30–5; adm*).

The World's Biggest Saint

Charles Borromeo was the most influential churchman of his day, appointed 'Cardinal Nephew and Archbishop of Milan' at the age of 22 by his maternal uncle, Pope Pius IV. In Rome he was a powerful voice calling for disciplinary reform within the Church, and he instigated the Council of Trent, the decade-long Counter-Reformation strategy session. There was one legendary point in Trent when the cardinals wanted to ban all church music, which by the 16th century had degenerated to the point of singing lewd love ballads to accompany the *Te Deum*. Charles and his committee decided to let the musicians have one more chance, and asked Palestrina to compose three Masses that reflected the dignity of the words of the service. Palestrina succeeded, and sacred music was saved.

After his uncle's death, Charles went to live in his diocese of Milan, the first archbishop to do so in 80 years. Following the codex of the Council of Trent to the letter, he began reforming the once-cosy clergy to set the example for other bishops. The Milanese weren't exactly thrilled: Charles escaped an assassination attempt in the cathedral, when the bullet bounced off his brocade vestments. He was a bitter enemy of original thought; if New York has a Statue of Liberty, Arona has a Statue of Tyranny.

For a weird sensation walk up the steps through his hollow viscera (no access for children under eight due to its steep steps): his head can hold six people, who can peer out of his eyes, each a foot and a half wide.

Getting There and Around

Trains from Milan's Stazione Centrale to Domodossola stop at Arona and Stresa; others from Milan's Porta Garibaldi station go to Luino. The regional railway from Milano-Nord passes by way of Varese to Laveno. Trains from Turin and Novara go to Arona and Stresa; Stresa is also linked by train to Orta 4 times a day.

From Lake Orta, **buses** run from Omegna to Verbania every 20mins. Buses connecting the two lakes also run from Stresa and Arona stations; others serve all the villages along the west shore.

Navigazione Lago Maggiore, **t** 0322 233 200, runs **steamers** to all corners of the lake, with the most frequent services in the central area between Stresa, Baveno, Verbania, Pallanza, Laveno and the islands; **hydrofoils** buzz between the main Italian ports and Locarno (Switzerland). There are frequent services by steamer or hydrofoil from Stresa, Baveno, Pallanza and Laveno to the Borromean Isles – a ticket for the furthest, Isola Madre, lets you visit all. **Car ferries** run between Intra and Laveno.

Tourist Information

A good source of information on the region is *www.lagomaggiore.it*.

Arona: Piazzale Duca d'Aosta, **t** 0322 243 601.

Stresa: Via Canonica 3, **t** 0323 30150, and Piazza Marconi 16, **t** 0323 31308.

Baveno, Piazza Dante Alighieri 14, **t** 0323 924 632, *www.comune.baveno.vb.it*.

Where to Stay and Eat

Arona ✉ 28041

Taverna del Pittore, Piazza del Popolo 39, **t** 0322 243 366 (*very expensive*). One of Lake Maggiore's finest restaurants, with lovely views from its terrace and dishes such as seafood *lasagnette* with saffron. *Closed Mon and end of Dec–Jan.*

Vecchia Arona, Lungolago Marconi 17, **t** 0322 242 469 (*expensive*). Delicious dishes based on the market and the day's catch. *Closed Fri, and 2wks June and Nov.*

Stresa ✉ 28838

*****Des Iles Borromées**, Corso Umberto I 67, **t** 0323 938 938, *www.stresa.net/hotel/borromees* (*luxury*). A stylish hotel mixing *belle époque* furnishings with all the mod cons. Overlooking the islands and a palm-shaded garden, it has a pool, beach, tennis courts, gym, 'wellbeing centre' and heli-pad.

****Regina Palace**, Corso Umberto I 29, **t** 0323 936 936, *www.stresa.net/hotel/regina* (*luxury*). A lovely Liberty-style palace in its own large park, with original décor in the halls, stylish bedrooms, a pool, tennis courts, a sauna, a Turkish bath, a gym, a beach and splendid views. *Closed Nov–mid-Mar.*

****Milan au Lac**, Piazza Marconi 9, **t** 0323 31190, *www.milansperanza.it* (*luxury–very expensive*). A lake-front hotel with good-sized rooms, many with balconies. There are also tennis courts, a swimming pool and a garage. *Closed Nov–Feb.*

Stresa, the 'Pearl of Verbano'

Beautifully positioned on the lake overlooking the Borromean Islands, under the majestic peak of Mottarone, this is Maggiore's most beautiful town, bursting with flowers and sprinkled with fine old villas. A holiday resort since the last century, famous for its lush gardens and its mild climate, it soared in popularity after the construction of the Simplon tunnel; Hemingway used its **Grand Hôtel des Iles Borromées** as Frederick Henry's refuge from war in *A Farewell to Arms*.

Little triangular **Piazza Cadorna** in the centre, shaded by age-old plane trees, is the social centre, its number of habitués swollen by participants in international congresses and music lovers attending the **Settimane Musicali di Stresa** in August and September. Two of Stresa's lakeside villas are open to the public: **Villa Pallavicino** (1850) and its colourful gardens, where saucy parrots rule the roost, along with a few other animals (***t*** *0323 31533; open daily Mar–Oct 9–6; adm*), and **Villa Ducale** (1771),

***Du Parc, Via Gignous 1, t 0323 30335, (*expensive*). A charming family-run hotel in a period private villa in its own grounds not far from the lakeside. *Open Mar–Oct.*

***Italie & Suisse, Piazza Marconi, t 0323 30540, *www.italiesuisse.com* (*expensive–moderate*). A good choice by the steamer landing.

***Primavera, Via Cavour 39, t 0323 31286 (*expensive–moderate*). A friendly, stylish hotel with pretty balconies.

*Elena, Piazza Cadorna 15, t 0323 31043, *www.hotelelena.com* (*expensive–moderate*). A good option with a garage and big modern rooms, most with balconies, and satellite TV.

*Fiorentino, Via Anna Maria Bolongaro 9, t 0323 30254 (*moderate*). A simple, central, family-run place with a good restaurant serving local and international cuisine.

*La Locanda, Via Leopardi 19, near Mottarone cable car, t 0323 31176 (*moderate*). A quiet family-run hotel with 14 comfy en suite rooms, most with balcony (but no lake view).

Piemontese, Via Mazzini 25, t 0323 30235 (*very expensive*). A restaurant with tables in a garden and dishes such as divine spaghetti with melted onions, basil and pecorino, and excellent fish. *Closed Mon, Jan and half Feb.*

Red Baron Pub, Via Roma 63. A lively English-run place serving great sandwiches, imaginative salads and draught beer.

Borromean Islands ✉ 28838

***Verbano, Isola dei Pescatori, t 0323 30408, *www.hotelverbano.it* (*very expensive*). A lovely, quiet, well-decorated hotel with a restaurant with romantic views (if brusque service and average food). *Closed Jan and Feb.*

Ristorante Belvedere, Isola dei Pescatori, t 0323 32292 (*cheap*). A busy place, popular with tourists. *Open mid-Mar–Nov.*

Delfino, Isola Bella, t 0323 30473 (*moderate*). A restaurant where you should expect more of the views than the food.

La Piratera, Isola Madre, t 0323 31171 (*moderate*). A similar option to the Delfino.

Baveno ✉ 28831

****Grand Hotel Dino, Via Garibaldi 20, t 0323 922 201, *www.grandhoteldino.com* (*luxury*). The lake's biggest hotel, right on the water, with 360 modern rooms and a beach.

***Hotel Beau Rivage, Viale della Vittoria 36, t 0323 924 534 (*expensive*). A family-run place on the lakefront road in the centre, with a pleasant back garden and old-style furniture and atmosphere on the ground floor.

***Carillon, Via Nazionale del Sempione 2, Feriolo, t 0323 28115, *www.hotelcarillon.it* (*expensive–moderate*). A hotel on the beach on the northern edge of town, with private mooring and parking. *Closed Nov–Mar.*

**Elvezia, Via Monte Grappa 15, t 0323 924 106, *www.elveziahotel.com* (*moderate–inexpensive*). A charming, bright hotel up by the church, with a little garden and parking. Wine tastings are offered. *Closed Nov–Mar.*

**Serenella, Via 42 Martiri 5, Feriolo, t 0323 28112 (*moderate*). Delicious home-made pasta and risotto and good lake fish, served in a garden in summer. *Closed Weds, Jan and Feb.*

once the property of Catholic philosopher Antonio Rosmini (*d.* 1855); besides the gardens, there's a small museum on Rosmini's life and works (*t 0323 30091; open daily 9–12 and 3–6; donation requested*).

From Stresa you can ascend **Monte Mottarone** (4,920ft) via the cable car from Piazzale Lido in Carciano di Stresa (*t 0323 30295; open daily 9.20–12 and 1.40–5.30*). On a clear day the famous views take in not only all seven major Italian lakes, but also glacier-crested peaks from Monviso to the far west and Monte Rosa over to the eastern ranges of Ortles and Adamello, as well as much of the Lombard plain. If you drive, walk or take the bus from Stresa, you can also visit the alpine rock gardens of the **Giardino Alpinia** (*t 0323 31308; open Tues–Sat Apr–15 Oct 9.30–6*), with more than 500 species of plants and flowers; or visit **Gignese**, with its **Museo dell'Ombrello** (*t 0323 208 064; open Tues–Sun Apr–Sep, 10–12 and 3–6; adm*), recalling the history and making of umbrellas and parasols, a traditional industry in the Colle Vergante.

The Borromean Islands

Lake Maggiore became a private fief of the Borromei in the 1470s, and they still own some of the finest bits, including the sumptuous gardens and villas of the Borromean Islands. The closest island to Stresa, **Isola Bella**, was a scattering of barren rocks until the 17th century, when Count Carlo III Borromeo made it a garden in the form of a ship for his wife Isabella (hence the name). Architect Angelo Crivelli arranged it in 10 terraces to form a pyramid-shaped 'poop deck', to create the kind of architectural perspectives beloved by Baroque theatre. The project was continued by Vitaliano VI Borromeo, who added the palace and grottoes but left it unfinished at his death in 1670.

The Borromei completed the **palace** according to the original plans in 1948–59 and left it a fine collection of art, with works by Annibale Carracci, Luca Giordano, Pannini, Giambattista Tiepolo and a certain Pietro Mulier, or 'Il Tempesta' (*d.* 1701), a longtime guest of the family. The room in which Napoleon slept in 1797 is done up in the Directory style in his honour, while the music room, with its antique instruments, hosted the 1935 Stresa Conference, where Italy, Britain and France tried to decide what to do in the face of Hitler's rearmament and ended up doing nothing. A stair leads down to six artificial grottoes on the lake, covered with shells and pebbles, while the Tapestry Gallery has six 16th-century Flemish tapestries with the favourite Borromeo family emblem, the unicorn, who also holds pride of place in the gardens. Stendhal wrote that the panorama from the top is 'equal to the Bay of Naples [...] It seems to me that these islands waken the emotions even more than St Peter's...'

The Borromei opened the delightful, larger **Isola Madre** to the public in 1978. Here they planted a luxuriant botanical garden dominated by Europe's largest Kashmir cypress; its camellias begin to bloom in January. On its best days, few places are more conducive to a state of perfect languor, at least until one of the isle's bold pheasants, peacocks or parrots tries to stare you out. The 16th-century villa has a collection of 18th- and 19th-century puppet theatres, marionettes, portraits and furnishings.

The **Isola dei Pescatori** is home to an almost too quaint fishing village. A private islet just off the shore at Pallanza, **San Giovanni**, has a villa once owned by Toscanini.

Beyond Stresa

Baveno is Stresa's quieter sister, connected by a beautiful, villa-lined road. Known for its quarries (source of the pink stone in Milan's Galleria Vittorio Emanuele and the Basilica of St Paul's in Rome), it made the society pages in 1879, when Queen Victoria spent a summer at the Villa Clara, now Castello Branca; Wagner also spent a holiday here, and Umberto Giordano composed his opera *Fedora* in his Villa Fedora. In the centre, the 11th-century church of **Santi Gervasio e Protasio** has retained its original plain square façade, though the interior was redone in the 18th century; the charming little octagonal baptistry adjacent dates from the 5th century.

The main shore road carries on to **Pallanza**, with its famously mild winter climate and Renaissance **Madonna di Campagna** on the edge of town, up Viale Azari. Inspired by Bramante, the church has a curious gazebo-like arcaded drum and a Romanesque campanile, inherited from its predecessor; the lavish interior has good 15th-century frescoes by Gerolamo Lanino (*St Bernardo*). In the centre of Pallanza, the 16th-century

Palazzo Dugnani houses the **Museo del Paesaggio** (*open Tues–Sun Apr–Oct 10–12 and 3–6; adm*) with a collection of 19th- and 20th-century landscapes of Lake Maggiore and the vicinity, plus plaster casts and sculptures by Giulio Branca of Cannobio, Paolo Troubetzkoy, born in Intra of noble Russian parents (*d.* 1938), and Arturo Martini (*d.* 1947). In **Palazzo Biumi Innocenti** on Salita Biumi there's a section dedicated to religious artefacts, with more than 5,000 *ex-votos*.

Pallanza united with Suna and Intra in 1939 to form **Verbania** (from the old Roman name of the lake), now the capital of a province. The glory of greater Verbania is the **Villa Taranto** (***t*** *0323 31533; open daily Mar–Oct 8–6; adm exp*), built on the Castagnola promontory between Pallanza and Intra by a certain Count Orsetti in 1875. In 1931 the derelict villa was purchased by a Scots captain, Neil McEacharn, who imported some 20,000 varieties of plants from the tropics, including giant Amazonian water lilies and copper-coloured Japanese maples. He left his masterpiece to the state; the villa is occasionally used by the Italian prime minister for special conferences. Intra is the departure point for a ferryboat across to Laveno, and buses up to the mountain resort of **Premeno**.

The Eastern Shore and Santa Caterina del Sasso

Interest on the Lombard shore is focused around the deserted Carmelite convent of **Santa Caterina del Sasso** (*open Apr–Oct daily 8.30–12 and 2.30–6; Nov–Feb Sat, Sun and hols 9–12 and 2–5; Christmas hols and Mar daily 9–12 and 2–5*). Visible only from the lake, it is visited by boats between April and September; if you're driving, follow the signs from the shore road and walk down from the car park. According to legend, in the 12th century wealthy merchant and usurer Alberto Besozzi was sailing on the lake when his boat sank. He prayed to St Catherine of Alexandria, who cast him upon this rock-bound shore. Impressed, Alberto repented of his usury and lived as a hermit in a cave. When his prayers brought an end to a local plague, he asked that as an *ex voto* the people construct a church to St Catherine. Over the centuries, a convent was added next to the cave of 'Beato Alberto', and it became a popular pilgrimage destination, especially after a huge boulder fell on the roof only to be miraculously wedged just above the altar, directly over the head of the priest saying Mass. Inside are medieval fresco fragments; don't miss the 16th-century *Danse Macabre*, high up in the loggia of the Gothic convent.

Laveno-Mombello, the ferry terminus from Intra, was known until recently for its ceramics, which are recalled in the **Museo Internazionale Design Ceramico** at Via Lungolago Perabo 5 in Cerro (***t*** *0332 666 530; open Sept–June Tues–Thurs 2.30–5.30, Fri–Sun 10–12 and 2.30–5.30; July and Aug Tues–Thurs 3.30–6.30, Fri–Sun 10–12 and 3.30–6.30; adm*). The best thing to do here is take the cable car up to the **Sasso del Ferro** (3,483ft), from where you can walk up for a marvellous view over the lake. Or come at Christmas, when Laveno has Italy's only underwater *presepio* (crib), floodlit and visible from *terra firma*. On the northern reaches of the lake on the eastern side, **Luino**, a pleasant town with plane trees along the lake, is the presumed birthplace of Leonardo da Vinci's chief follower Bernadino Luini, who left a fresco up at the cemetery church, the **Oratorio di Santi Pietro e Paolo**.

Lake Varese and Castiglione Olona

Between Lake Maggiore and Milan is quiet **Lago di Varese**, eight and a half kilometres long and the big sleepyhead of the 'minor lakes'. There's a Renaissance vision of it just outside the centre of Varese in the **Castello di Masnago** (*t 0332 220 256; open Tues–Sun 10.30–12.30 and 2.30–6.30; adm*), where in 1938 two sets of 15th-century secular frescoes were discovered under the whitewash: a courtly scene by the lake and, upstairs, female vices and virtues, including Vanity, preening her elaborate muffin of hair. The museum also contains a *pinacoteca* with modern and contemporary art.

Lake Varese's main settlement, **Gavirate**, is famous for its hand-carved pipes, and has a collection from around the world in its **Museo della Pipa** (*t 0332 743 334; open by appointment*). For carvings of a different nature go to Voltorre just south of Gavirate, where the 11th-century Cluniac monastery of **San Michele** (now a cultural centre) has a cloister (*t 0332 743 914; open Tues–Sun 10–12.30 and 2.30–6.30*), with beautifully sculpted capitals, attributed to Comacino master Lanfranco. It also hosts temporary exhibitions. The campanile has one of the oldest bells in Italy, and sounds like it too.

Catch the boat from **Biandronno** on the west shore for **Isolino Virginia**, a wooded islet inhabited three millennia ago by people who built their homes on pile dwellings just offshore. Its **Museo Preistorico di Villa Ponti** (*t 0332 281 590; open Sat and Sun Apr–Oct 2–6, or by appointment*) chronicles the settlement, which lasted into Roman times.

The little Renaissance nugget of **Castiglione Olona**, eight kilometres from Varese, is wrapped in suburban sprawl; you need locate the ghastly new church and take the winding road down to the bottom of the valley to find the **Borgo**, which owes its quattrocento Tuscan charm to Cardinal Branda Castiglioni (1350–1443), who was so enchanted by the blossoming Renaissance in Florence he brought Masolino da Panicale, Lorenzo di Pietro (Il Vecchietta) and other artists to do up Castiglione. The Borgo, the Cardinal's 'ideal citadel', is essentially unchanged since the 15th century. In tiny central Piazza Garibaldi, the **Chiesa di Villa** was inspired by Brunelleschi, a cube surmounted by an octagonal drum, its exterior decoration limited to framing bands of grey and two giant statues either side of the door, of St Christopher and St Anthony Abbot. Inside, nearly all the art dates from the 1400s: the Annunciation, the tomb of Guido Castiglioni by the school of Amadeo, and the terracotta *Doctors of the Church*.

Opposite, the cardinal's **Palazzo Branda Castiglioni** is a museum (*t 0331 858 301; open Apr–Sept Tues–Sat 9–12 and 3–6; Sun and hols 10.30–12.30 and 3–6; Oct–Mar Tues–Sat 9–12 and 3–6; hols 10.30–12.30, Sun 3–6; adm*). The cardinal's bedroom has charming frescoes of children playing under fruit trees by an unknown Lombard painter.

Ancient plane trees line the steep Via Cardinale Branda that leads up to the Gothic **Collegiata** (*open Tues–Sun Apr–Sept 9.30–12 and 3–6.30; Oct–Mar 10–12 and 2.30–5.30; adm*), built in 1421 over the Castiglioni castle (the gate survives). The brick church contains beautiful frescoes, especially Masolino's Life of the Virgin in the vault, while Il Vecchietta painted the Life of St Stephen and Paolo Schiavo frescoed the Life of St Lawrence; the Crucifixion in the apse is attributed to another Tuscan master, Neri di Bicci. In 1435 Masolino frescoed the entire **baptistry** (once the castle tower), a work commonly considered the culmination of his evocatively lyrical and refined style.

The **Monastero di Torba,** in the woods just off the road in **Gornate Olona** (*t 0331 820 301; open daily Feb–Sept 10–1 and 2–6; Oct–mid-Dec 10–1 and 2–5; adm*) was founded in the 5th century as a Lombard defence tower. Acquired by the Fondo per l'Ambiente Italiano (Italian National Trust), it has restored 8th-century frescoes in the tower, along with the original crypt and tombs. The tower defended **Castelséprio** to the south, a Lombard *castrum* on the Roman model; ruins of the walls, churches and castle moulder under the trees a short way from the centre, though the main reason to stop is **Santa Maria Foris Portas**: its unique 8th-century frescoes in an Eastern Hellenistic style were found during World War II by a partisan hiding here (*t 0331 820 438; open Nov–Feb Tues–Sat 9–6; Sun and hols 9.30–6.30; Mar–Oct Tues–Sat 9–7.30*).

Varese

Varese, a city of gardens and shoes, and increasingly a bedroom suburb of Milan, spills over a plateau between Lake Maggiore and the Olona river. Founded by the Celts, it has avoided history for most of its career. Maria Theresa gave it briefly to the Duke of Modena, Francesco III d'Este (1765–80), whose main contribution was to build himself the vast **Palazzo Estense**, now the Municipio; its gaudiest room, the Salone Estense, can only be visited by written request, or with a guide. The duke's park, modelled on Vienna's Schönbrunn, and the adjacent English garden of the eclectic **Villa Mirabello** are now a city park; the villa houses the **Musei Civici** (*t 0332 281 590; open Tues–Sun 9.30–12.30 and 2–5, Sat and Sun until 5.30; adm*), with a hodgepodge of paintings, local archaeology and the butterfly collection of the great tenor Tamagno.

Central Piazza Monte Grappa received a stern Mussolini facelift and is stylish but not exactly cosy. Just beyond it, Varese's landmark, the garlic-domed 17th-century **Campanile del Bernascone**, rings the chimes for the **Basilica di San Vittore** (*t 0332 236 019*), an ancient foundation rebuilt by Pellegrino Tibaldi with a neoclassical façade pasted on; inside the most important paintings are by Il Morazzone.

Varese's **Sacro Monte** (*t 0332 223 223*) has 14 chapels filled with frescoes and stuccoes on the Mystery of the Rosary; you can get there on the renovated funicular from Stazione Vallone (*Mon–Fri 9–6, Sat–Sun 9–8.20*). The seventh chapel (*The Flagellation*) was frescoed by Il Morazzone. The devotional tour climaxes at **Santuario di Santa Maria del Monte**, founded in the 5th century by St Ambrose. Rebuilt in 1473 and later lavishly Baroqued, it has an ornate marble altar, a revered 14th-century 'Black Virgin' attributed to St Luke, and trecento frescoes in the crypt. The Sacro Monte sculptures are so expressive that experts think Lombard mountain theatre originated from the sacred monument, the static chapels representing an *in itinere* meditation on Christ's death, just as in a religious festival, and the statues representing the actors, who seem to move as soon as you turn your head.

The nearby **Museo Baroffio Dall'Aglio**, or Museo del Santuario (*t 0331 777 472; open Thurs, Sat and Sun Apr–Sept 9.30–12.30 and 3–6.30; ring for winter hours; booking advised; adm*) houses works of art donated to the sanctuary, and the **Museo Pogliaghi** (*closed for restoration*) has Egyptian, Greek and Roman antiquities, and works by the villa's former owner Ludovico Pogliaghi, including a full-size plaster cast of his Milan cathedral door.

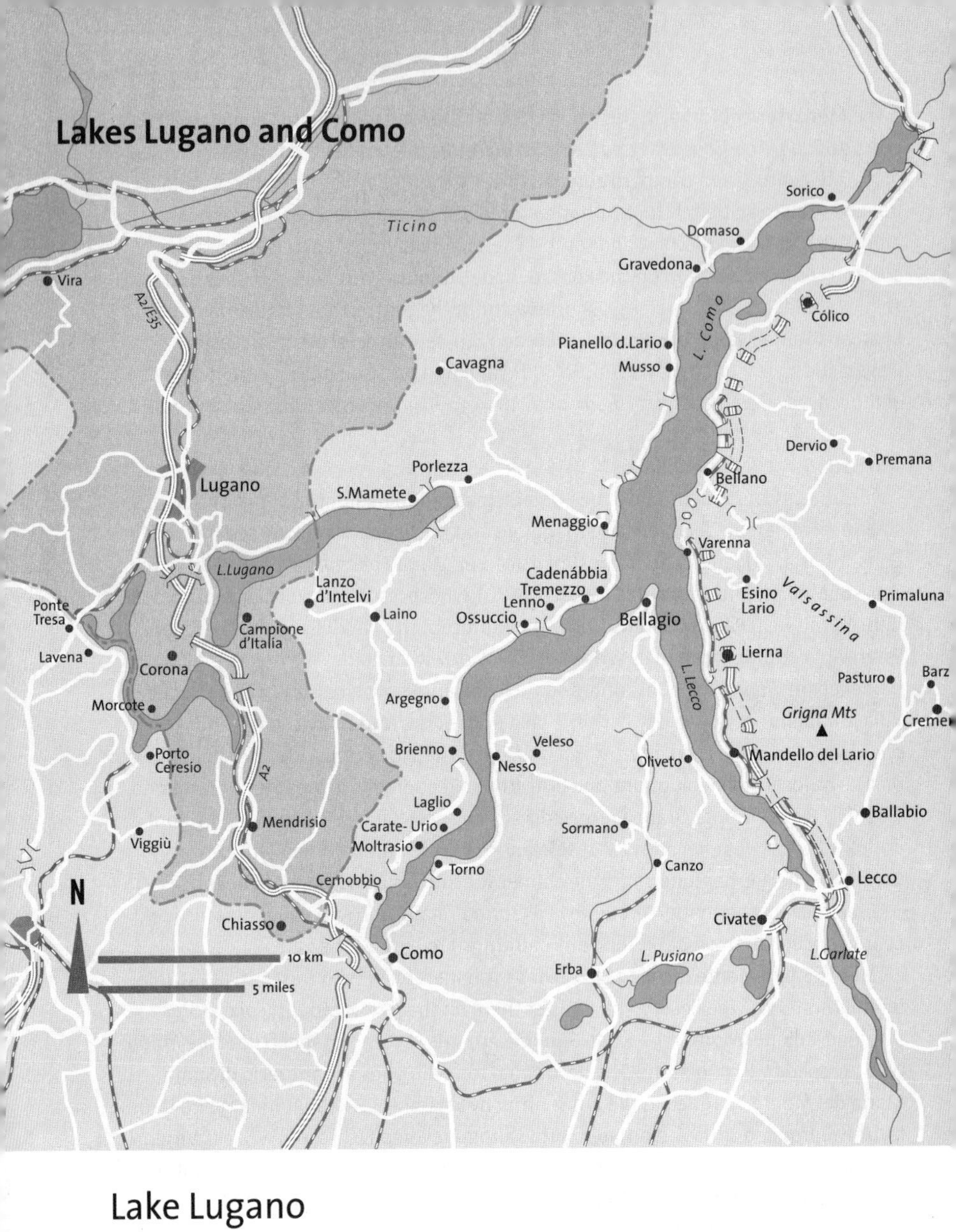

Lake Lugano

With its steep, fjorded shores, Lugano is a striking sight, especially in the centre, where its curious shape and narrow span closed in by mountains give it a rare intimacy and benign climate. In a few places, especially around the city of Lugano, the lake has become a victim of its own attractiveness; other shores, too steep for building, still darken the waters with emerald-green and white reflections of the wooded cliffs. Lugano's extremities are Italian, but its heart has been part of the Canton Ticino ever since the Swiss snatched the province from French-occupied Milan back in 1512. Two centuries later, when Ticino had a chance to return to Italy, it refused: as part of its

Getting There and Around

Lugano's **airport** in Agno, **t** 04191 610 1111, has links with Swiss flights from London, Paris, Nice, Rome, Florence and Venice as well as the major Swiss airports. A shuttle service, **t** 079 221 4243 (ring in advance), connects it with the city centre. Lugano is also easily reached from Milano's Malpensa on a shuttlebus service via Chiasso, **t** 091 807 8520.

From Varese, **trains** go as far as Porto Ceresio at the west end of Lugano; from Milan trains to Como continue to Lugano by way of Chiasso, while Lugano itself is linked by a local train line (FLP) to points west as far as Ponte Tresa.

Porlezza, on the east end of the lake, is linked by **bus** to Como or Menaggio; buses from Lugano or Como go direct to Campione d'Italia.

All lakeside towns are served by **steamers**, **t** 091 971 5223, on the Società Navigazione Lago di Lugano line. They also organize tours.

Tourist Information

Caslano: Ente Turistico del Malcantone, Piazza Lago, **t** 606 2986, *www.malcantone.ch*

Campione d'Italia: Via Volta 3, **t** 649 5051 (*open Mon–Fri 10–12 and 3–5*); *www.campioneitalia.com*

Lugano: Riva Albertolli 5, **t** 913 3232 (*open Apr–Oct Mon–Fri 9–6.30, Sat 9–11.30 and 1.30–5, Sun 10–4; Nov–Mar Mon–Fri 9–12.30 and 1.30–5.30*), *www.lugano-tourism.ch;* and at airport, **t** 04191 605 1226 (*open Mon–Sun 8–8*).

Where to Stay and Eat

Lugano ✉ CH6900, t (004191–)

There's a **hotel reservation service** at the train station, **t** 091 923 5120.

*******Villa Principe Leopoldo**, Via Montalbano 5, **t** 985 8855, *www.leopoldohotel.com* (*luxury*). A 19th-century Relais & Châteaux hotel in a beautiful hillside park overlooking the city, with a health centre and restaurant with gourmet international cuisine.

*****International au Lac**, Via Nassa 68, **t** 922 7541, *www.hotel-international.ch* (*very expensive*). A very comfortable option near in the city centre, with a pool, garden terrace and parking. *Closed end Oct–1st wk Apr.*

****Fischer's Seehotel**, Sentiero di Gandria 10, **t** 971 5571 (*moderate–expensive*). A simple and pleasant choice smack on the lake, far from traffic. The kitchen closes at 8.30pm. *Closed Nov–Feb.*

***Montarina**, Via Montarina 1, **t** 966 7272, *www.montarina.ch* (*moderate*). A hotel and hostel in a 19th-century villa in a palm garden near the station, welcoming families and backpackers. It has pretty lake views, a pool and a chicken farm. *Closed Nov–Feb.*

Parco Saroli, Via Stefano Franscini 6, **t** 923 5314 (*expensive*). A fashionable place with excellent, unusual home-made pasta, seafood, superb breads, cheeses and desserts, and an award-winning wine list. *Closed Sat and Sun.*

Antica Osteria Gerso, Piazzetta Solaro 24, Massagno, **t** 966 1915 (*moderate*). An utterly simple restaurant with a discriminating menu: try onion soup with tangy pecorino cheese or *tortelli di zucca alle mandorle*. Book a day or two ahead. *Closed Sun.*

Campione d'Italia ✉ CH22060, t (004191–)

The only hotels here at present are some rather Swissified places just before the entry arch to Campione.

******Lago di Lugano**, in Bissone, **t** 649 8591, *www.hotellagodilugano.ch* (*expensive*). Mini-apartments with terraces, adults' and kids' pools, a playground, a kids' club, *boules*, bikes to rent, windsurfing, canoeing, pedalos and a fitness centre. *Closed Jan and Feb.*

****La Palma**, Piazza Borromini, Bissone, **t** 649 8406 (*moderate–inexpensive*). A family-run hotel with a restaurant serving pizza (also to take away).

Da Candida, Via Marco 4, **t** 41 91 649 7541 (*expensive*). A charming, romantic restaurant offering an unparalleled mix of French and Italian cuisine, including house pâté de foie gras, bread and pasta, and oysters direct from Brittany. Book in advance for dinner. *Closed Sun, Mon lunch, Mar and July.*

La Taverna, Piazzale Roma 2, **t** 649 4797 (*expensive*). Delicious truffle and mushroom dishes. *Closed Weds.*

Tavola di Totone, Casino, **t** 41 91 640 1111 (*expensive*). The Casino's top-floor restaurant, offering a set-price menu (including drinks) and shows on Sat eves.

punishment, the Italians insist on calling the lake by its Latin name, Ceresio. Another punishment is to have a border rimmed with petrol stations. And a crumb of Italian territory, **Campione d'Italia**, survives in the middle of the lake, just big enough to support a casino that more than welcomes Swiss wallets. If you can't beat 'em, soak 'em.

Lugano

Warm, palmy Lugano is an arty resort city piled between Monte Brè and Monte San Salvatore – a lovely setting that has been compared to that of Rio de Janeiro. To go with its sumptuous lake views, it has a Renaissance gem in waterfront Piazza Luini: plain **Santa Maria degli Angioli**, built in 1510 by the Franciscans and frescoed in 1529 with a nearly life-size Crucifixion by Bernardino Luini: his masterpiece, full of colour and detail. Ruskin, who wrote that Luini was 'ten times greater than Leonardo', saw it and gushed, 'Every thought he conceives is beauty and purity...'

Art from the late Gothic period and 19th and 20th centuries, including works by Renoir, Degas and Klee, is in the **Museo Cantonale d'Arte**, in three 15th-century *palazzi* (*entry at Via Canova 10;* ***t*** *091 910 4780; open Tues 2–5, Weds–Sun 10–5; adm*). On the other side of town at Via Pietro Cappelli, the **Villa Favorita** (***t*** *091 972 1741*) has Baron Heinrich von Thyssen-Bornemisza's collection of European and American modern art, with a special emphasis on the Luminists and Hudson River School.

Further along the lake, along Via Cortivo (bus no.1 or 11 from Piazza Manzoni to San Domenico, then a five-minute walk), the neoclassical Villa Heleneum is the **Museo delle Culture Extraeuropee** (***t*** *091 911 5380; open Weds–Sun 10–5; adm*), containing a fascinating collection of wooden figures and cult objects from Oceania, Africa and Asia donated by Surrealist artists Serge and Graziella Brignoni.

Every 30 minutes until almost midnight, a funicular (***t*** *091 971 3171*) runs up 3,150ft **Monte Brè**, 'Switzerland's sunniest mountain', at the top of which is a restaurant and the little village of Brè. Another funicular (***t*** *091 985 2828; open Mar–end Oct*) leaves Lugano's suburb of Paradiso every 30 minutes until 11pm for **Monte San Salvatore** (3,000ft), with more fine views over the lake and Alps, a restaurant and nature trails. Alternatively, catch the steamer down the south arm of the lake to Capolago and take the rack railway (40 minutes) up 5,623ft **Monte Generoso** (***t*** *04191 648 1105*), where you can go mountain biking, paragliding, climbing, birdwatching and potholing. Lastly, boats from Lugano call at Gandria for visits to the **Museo Doganale Svizzero** (***t*** *091 923 9843; open daily 1.30–5.30*), where you can learn about all the cracks and crevices Swiss Customs have found in cars, false passports, counterfeit goods: children like the night-vision tunnel and the 'catch-the-smuggler' computer games.

Lake Como

Sapphire Lake Como has been Italy's most romantic lake since the earliest days of the Roman Empire, when the Plinys wrote of the luxuriant beauty surrounding their villas on its shores. It was just the sort of beauty that enraptured the children of the Romantic era, inspiring operas from Verdi, Rossini and Bellini, as well as enough good

Getting There and Around

There are frequent FS **trains** from Milan's Porta Garibaldi, Centrale and Cadorna stations to Como's main San Giovanni station, **t** 147 888 088 (40mins). Slow trains run on the regional Milano-Nord line to the lakeside station of Como-Lago. From Como, trains to Lugano and Lecco depart from San Giovanni. **Buses** from Como run to nearly every lakeside town.

A **steamer** (July–Aug), motorboats and hydrofoils are operated by Navigazione Lago di Como, Via per Cernobbio 18, **t** 031 573 211. The most frequent connections are between Como, Tremezzo, Menaggio, Bellagio, Varenna and Cólico, with additional services in the central lake, and at least 1 boat a day to Lecco. **Car ferries** run between Bellagio, Menaggio, Varenna and Cadenábbia; some just in summer.

Tourist Information

Via Cavour 17, **t** 031 269 712, *www.lakecomo.com*, *www.lagodicomo.com*

Where to Stay

Como ✉ 22100

★★★★**Albergo Terminus**, Lungo Lario Trieste 14, **t** 031 329 111 (*very expensive*). An elegant 1902 hotel in the heart of town, with its original Liberty-style halls, reading room and bar, and a panoramic terrace on the lake. Rooms are stylish with all modern comforts.

★★★★**Villa Flori**, Via Cernobbio 12, just outside town on west shore, **t** 031 33820, *www.hotelvillaflori.com* (*very expensive*). A classy, romantic 19th-century hotel, with stylish rooms with terraces overlooking the lake. It also has the finest restaurant in town,the **Ristorante Raimondi**, **t** 031 338 233 (*expensive*), where wonderful renditions of classic Lombard and other cuisine are served on the lakeside terrace or in the luminous dining room. *Closed Mon.*

★★★★**Le Due Corti**, Piazza Vittoria 12/13, **t** 031 328 111, (*very expensive–expensive*). A former monastery and post house with atmospheric rooms arranged around the former cloister. Concessions to modernity include satellite TV, air conditioning, mini bars, Jacuzzis in some bathrooms, and a small outdoor pool. There's an adjoining Art Deco bar, a wine bar under the Roman bricked vaults of the basement and a good restaurant.

★★★**Marco's**, Via Coloniola 43, **t** 031 303 628, (*expensive*). Eleven small rooms with TV, phone and balcony near the lake front, the city centre and the cable car to Brunate.

★★**Posta**, Via Garibaldi 2, **t** 031 266 012, *www.hotelposta.net* (*moderate*). A hotel designed by Terragni in 1930, minus the original décor.

Ostello dell'Olmo, Via Bellinzona 6, Villa Olmo Park, **t** 031 573 800 (*cheap*). A decent youth hostel. *Closed Dec–Feb.*

Eating Out

Sant'Anna, Via Filippo Turati 1/3, **t** 031 505 266 (*very expensive*). Seasonal menus of *nouvelle cuisine*. You need a car to get here. *Closed Sun, Sat lunch and late July–late Aug.*

Terrazzo Perlasca, Piazza De Gasperi 8, **t** 031 300 263 (*very expensive*). A restaurant run by four brothers, with a daily-changing menu featuring the likes of pasta with local mushrooms, and wonderful views over the lake. *Closed Mon and 2wks Aug.*

Locanda dell'Oca Bianca, Via Canturina 251, Trecallo (a 5min drive on the road to Cantù), **t** 031 525 605 (*expensive*). Startlingly good Italian and French food, including foie gras, served on a terrace in summer. *Open for lunch by reservation only. Closed Mon.*

Osteria Angolo del Silenzio, Via Lecco 25, **t** 031 337 2157 (*expensive*). A place just outside the walls, with home-made pasta, fish and meat, local game and mushrooms in season, and an inner court for outdoor dining. A *cheap* one-course lunch menu is available weekdays. *Closed Mon, Tues lunch, 2wks Jan and Aug,*

Le Sette Porte, Via A. Diaz 52A, **t** 031 267 939, (*expensive*). Two stylish vaulted rooms inside the walls where you can feast on Italian delicacies imaginatively mixed with unusual ingredients, such as ravioli with carrots and yoghurt. *Closed Sun.*

Villa Olmo Parco, Via Cantoni 1, **t** 031 572 321 (*moderate*). Well-prepared food and fine wines near the beach. *Closed Tues.*

Ristorante Teatro Sociale, Via Maestri Comacini 8, **t** 031 264 042 (*cheap*). A traditional inn for post-theatre refuelling. *Closed Tues.*

and bad English verse to fill an anthology. And it is still there, the Lake Como of the Shelleys and Wordsworths, the villas and lush gardens, the mountains and wooded promontories. The English still haunt their traditional English shore, but most of the visitors to Como these days are Italian, and there are times when the lake seems schizophrenic, its mellowed dignity battered by modern expectations of a Milanese Riviera. Even so, Como is large and varied enough to offer retreats where, to paraphrase Longfellow's ode to the lake, no sound of Vespa or high heel breaks the silence of the summer day.

The third largest of the lakes, measuring 50 kilometres in length but just four and a half kilometres at its widest point, Como (or Lario) is one of the deepest lakes in Europe, plunging down 1,345ft near Argegno. It forks in the middle like a pair of legs; the east branch is known as the **Lago di Lecco** for its biggest town, while the prettiest region is the centre, where Como appears to be three separate lakes, and where towns such as Tremezzo and Bellagio have been English enclaves for 200 years. One legacy of the English are the seven golf courses in the province, while the waters around Domaso are excellent for windsurfing. The further you go from the city of Como, the cleaner the lake.

The City of Como

Magnificently located at the southern tip of the lake's left leg, Como is a lively little city that has long had a bent for science, silk and architecture. In AD 23 it was the birthplace of Pliny the Elder, the compiler of antiquity's greatest work of hearsay, the *Natural History*, and later it produced his nephew and heir Pliny the Younger, whose letters are one of our main sources for information on the cultured Roman life of the period. From *c.* 1050 to 1335, when Como enjoyed a period as an independent *comune*, it produced a school of master builders, known generally as the Maestri Comacini, rivals to Lugano's Maestri Campionesi.

Como's historic centre, its street plan almost unchanged since Roman times, opens up to the lake at **Piazza Cavour**, with its cafés, hotels, steamer landing and pretty views. Two landmarks in the public gardens just to the west offer an introduction to Como's more recent scientists and architects. The first, the circular **Tempio Voltiano** (***t*** *031 574 705; open Tues–Sun Apr–Sept 10–12 and 3–6; Oct–Mar 10–12 and 2–4; adm*), was built in 1927 to house the manuscripts, instruments and inventions of Como's electrifying native son, self-taught physicist Alessandro Volta (1745–1827), who lent his name to volts in 100 languages.

A bit further on, the striking **Monumento ai Caduti** – a memorial to the fallen of the First World War – was designed by the young Futurist architect Antonio Sant'Elia of Como (1888–1916), who himself died in action on the Front; his plans and drawings in particular have established him as one of the most important visionary planners of the 20th century. The monument was actually built by Giuseppe Terragni (1904–43), a native of Como province and the most inspired Italian architect to work during the Fascist period. His buildings are spread throughout Como (the 1927 Hotel Metropole Suisse in Piazza Cavour is one) and the tourist office offers a special Terragni town plan. One ends up wishing that he, like Sant'Elia, had lived a little longer.

The Historic Centre

From Piazza Cavour, Via Plinio leads back to Como's elegant salon, Piazza Duomo. Unusually, the chief monuments here are all joined: the **Torre del Comune** to the charming white, grey and red marble striped town hall or **Broletto** (both built in 1215), one of the rare Romanesque (not Gothic) symbols of civic might in the north; and this in turn to the magnificent **Duomo** (1396), the most harmonious example of transitional architecture in Italy, although Gothic dominates in the façade and lovely rose window and pinnacles. The majority of the sculpture and reliefs are by the Rodari family (late 15th–early 16th century), who also sculpted the lateral doors. The two statues flanking the central door, under delicate stone canopies, are of famous pagans Pliny the Elder (on the left) and Pliny the Younger – though the latter did write a letter to Trajan on the subject of Christians, praising their hard work and suggesting they be left in peace, the fact is that Renaissance humanists regarded all noble figures of antiquity as honorary saints, especially if they were home-town boys.

Inside, the three Gothic aisles combine happily with a Renaissance choir and transept, crowned by a dome that was designed by the great late Baroque master Filippo Juvarra in 1744. Nine 16th-century tapestries hang along the nave, lending the place an air of palatial elegance; a pair of Romanesque lions near the entrance are survivors from the cathedral's 11th-century predecessor. But most of the art dates from the Renaissance: in the right aisle are six reliefs with scenes from the Passion by Tommaso Rodari, and fine canvases by two of Leonardo's followers, Gaudenzio Ferrari (*Flight into Egypt*) and Luini (*Adoration of the Magi*); the latter's famous *Madonna with Child and Four Saints* adorns the high altar. The left aisle has more by the same trio: Rodari's *Deposition* on the fourth altar, Ferrari's *Marriage of the Virgin* and Luini's *Nativity*, as well as a 13th-century sarcophagus.

For a contrast, take a walk behind the Duomo and across the train tracks to Piazza del Popolo, where Giuseppe Terragni's ex-Casa del Fascio, now the **Palazzo Terragni,** stands out in all its functional, luminous beauty. Built in 1931 but completely unlike the typically ponderous travertine buildings that were constructed under Mussolini, the Palazzo is 50 years ahead of its time – practically transparent, it's an essay in light and harmony, the masterpiece of the only coherent architectural style that Italy produced in the 20th century. Its present occupants, the Guardia di Finanza, will let you in to visit the ground floor.

From the cathedral, main Via Vittorio Emanuele leads to Como's old cathedral, **San Fedele**, which was first built in 914. It has a unique pentagonal apse and a doorway carved with chubby archaic figures and a griffon; the interior is lavishly decorated with 18th-century frescoes and stuccoes. Further up, in Piazza Medaglie d'Oro Comasche, the **Museo Civico**, **Museo Archeologico** and **Museo Storico** (***t*** *031 271 343; open Tues–Sat 9.30–12.30 and 2–5, Sun 10–1; adm*) constitute the city's attic of artefacts, dating from the Neolithic era until the Second World War, with some interesting Roman finds and frescoes along the way.

From Piazza Medaglie d'Oro Comasche, continue down Via Giovio to reach the **Porta Vittoria**, a striking skyscraper of a gate from 1192, its immaculate tiers of arches rising to a height of 72ft.

Near here, Como's small **Pinacoteca** at Via Diaz 84 (*closed for restoration, call* ***t*** *031 269 869*) has carved capitals and wonderful medieval paintings from the old monastery of Santa Margherita del Broletto. A short walk from the Porta Vittoria, at the beginning of Via della Regina (the road built by Lombard queen Theodolinda around Lake Como), is Como's Romanesque gem **Sant'Abbondio**, consecrated by Pope Urban II in 1095. The twin campaniles are believed to be of Norman inspiration; the interior, with its lofty vaults and forest of columns forming five aisles, offers a kind of preview of coming great events in Italian architecture. Its unadorned majesty is relieved by the rich bands of reliefs around the windows of the nave and apse, imitating the intricate patterns of damasks from the Near East.

If you've brought your walking shoes or car, continue three kilometres south to the **Castello Baradello**, built by Emperor Barbarossa in 1158. In 1277 it became the military headquarters of the Archbishop of Milan, Ottone Visconti, exiled by Milan's arrogant Guelph boss Napo della Torre. Napo marched out to capture the archbishop, but so carelessly disdained his opponent that he was captured instead, spending his last 19 months suspended in a metal cage from its 112ft tower; you can enjoy the view that tormented him (***t*** *031 592 805; open Thurs, Sat and Sun 10–5, other days by appointment*).

There's a funicular every 15–30 minutes up to **Brunate**, a mountain village with views across the lake and Alps as far as Monte Rosa (***t*** *031 303 608; adm*). Industrious **Cantù**, a hop away on the Lecco train or SPT bus, provides Milan's handmade lace and some of its furniture. Its landmark is the tall, minaret-like Romanesque campanile of its church, but the main point of interest, the 10th-century **Basilica di San Vincenzo** and **Battistero di San Giovanni**, lies a kilometre east of the station in neighbouring Galliano (*open daily 9–11.30 and 3–5; call* ***t*** *031 714 126 before setting out*). Isolated in the pines, the basilica has a remarkable fresco cycle painted just after the first millennium; the baptistry with its little cupola is one of the oldest in Lombardy.

Around Lake Como

The steamer is the ideal way to travel around the lake, allowing you to drink in the scenery. The first steamer landing, **Cernobbio**, is an old resort, the 1816–17 retreat of Queen Caroline of England, who held wild parties in what is now the fabulous Grand Hotel Villa d'Este. Across the lake, at **Torno**, the 16th-century **Villa Pliniana** so charmed Shelley he tried to buy it; its name is derived from its intermittent spring, described in a letter of Pliny the Younger. The area has been fertile soil for operas; Rossini wrote *Tancredi* in the Villa Pliniana, and Bellini composed *Norma* in other villas nearby.

Back on the west shore, **Argegno** has views of mountains to the north and access to the west into the pretty Val d'Intelvi, which ascends to Lake Lugano. North is the pretty islet of **Comacina**, sprinkled with ruined ancient churches, the entrance to the lush mid-lake area of **Tremezzina**, where calling Como the 'mirror of Venus' hardly seems extravagant. **Lenno**, the southernmost village, was the site of Pliny the Younger's villa 'Comedia'; in a letter he describes fishing from his bedroom window. It was in this idyllic spot, in front of a posh villa in nearby Mezzegra, that Mussolini and his mistress Claretta Petacci were executed by partisans. They'd been captured on the north shore, attempting to flee in a German truck.

Tourist Information

Cernobbio: Via Regina 33b, **t** 031 510 198 (*open May–Oct*).

Tremezzo: Via Regina 3, **t** 0344 40493 (*open May–Oct*).

Bellagio : Piazza Mazzini, **t** 031 950 204, *www.bellagiolakecomo.com (open Apr–Oct 9–12 and 3–6; Nov–Mar Mon and Weds–Sat 9–12 and 3–6)*.

Menaggio: Piazza Garibaldi, **t** 0344 32924, *www.menaggio.com*.

Varenna:Via Venini 6, **t** 0341 830 367, *www.varenna.net* (*open Tues–Sat 10–12.30 and 3–5, Sun 10–12.30*).

Lecco: Via Nazario Sauro 6, **t** 0341 362 360, *www.aptlecco.com*.

Where to Stay and Eat

Cernobbio ✉ 22012

*******Grand Hotel Villa d'Este**, Via Regina 40, **t** 031 3481, *www.villadeste.it* (*luxury*). A glittering showcase built in 1557 by Pelligrini for Cardinal Tolomeo Gallio, who became one of the most powerful men in the Vatican. Bedrooms are furnished with antiques or fine reproductions, public rooms are regal, and the restaurant is superb (jacket and tie required in the evening; there's a more informal grill). There are glorious gardens, a floating swimming pool, a golf course, squash and tennis courts, sailing facilities, a Turkish bath, a spa, a nightclub and more. *Closed mid-Nov–Feb.*

*****Asnigo**, Via Noseda 2, Piazza S. Stefano, **t** 031 510 062 (*very expensive–expensive*). A good hotel with a lovely terrace overlooking Cernobbio and Como, pretty rooms, friendly service and a good restaurant. *Closed Mon.*

***La Vignetta**, Via Monte Grappa 32, **t** 031 334 7055 (*moderate*). An excellent-value, clean and cosy choice with a good restaurant (*cheap–moderate*). Some rooms have shared bathrooms. *Restaurant closed Tues.*

****Terzo Crotto**, Via Volta 1, **t** 031 512 304 (*cheap*). A hotel in peaceful grounds, with 9 rooms, all with bath, and an excellent family-run restaurant. No credit cards. *Closed Mon.*

Trattoria Gatto Nero, Via Monte Santo 69, Rovenna, a 5min drive from centre, **t** 031 512 042 (*expensive*). A characterful rustic place with lake views and delicious food. Booking advised. *Closed Mon and Tues lunch.*

Giardino, Via Regina 73, **t** 031 511 154 (*cheap–moderate*). A popular restaurant and pizzeria with an inner court for outside dining, and some standard rooms (*moderate*). *Closed Weds.*

Ossuccio ✉ 22018

Locanda dell'Isola Comacina, private boat from Cala Comacina and Ossuccio **t** 0344 55083 (*expensive*). A 50-year-old restaurant where you will be regaled with a set meal of *antipasti* followed by grilled trout, fried chicken, wine and dessert, and a rendition of poetry while you sip your flambéed coffee, *caffè all'uso delle canaglie in armi. Closed Tues except summer, and Nov–Feb.*

Tremezzo ✉ 22019

*******Grand Hotel Tremezzo**, Via Regina 8, **t** 0344 42491, *www.grandhoteltremezzo.com* (*luxury*). The comforts and charm of a large 19th-century hotel combined with modern facilities, including a sports centre, a sauna and a helipad. *Grand Hotel* starring Greta Garbo was shot here, *A Month by the Lake* by John Irving had the hotel as a background. and George Lucas 'secretly' stayed here while filming an episode of the *Star Wars* saga nearby. A monumental staircase at the back leads out into the park with its modern art sculptures and breathtaking views of Bellagio, Varenna, Lecco and the Grignean mountains. The lakeside restaurant offers a five-course menu. *Closed mid-Nov–Feb.*

*****Villa Marie**, Via Regina 30, **t** 0344 40427, *www.hotelvillamarie.com*, (*moderate*). An intimate Victorian-style hotel overlooking the lake and a shady garden, with pleasant rooms and an outside pool. *Closed Nov–Mar.*

****Azalea**, main lakeside road, **t** 0344 40424 (*cheap*). Decent rooms with all comforts, en suite baths and bags of family atmosphere.

Cadenábbia ✉ 22011

The following hotels may host package tours in the high season:

*****Bellevue**, **t** 0344 40418 (*moderate*). A large, charmingly old-fashioned place on the lake, with sun terraces, a garden and a pool. *Closed mid-Oct–mid-Mar.*

★★★**Britannia Excelsior**, **t** 0344 40413, (*moderate*). A cosy old hotel in the piazza, overlooking the lake. Many rooms have balconies. *Closed Nov–Mar.*

Bellagio ✉ 22021

★★★★★**Grand Hotel Villa Serbelloni**, Via Roma 1, **t** 031 950 216, *www.villaserbelloni.it* (*luxury*). A magnificent, ornate hotel in a garden at the tip of the headland, with palatial frescoed public rooms. There's a heated pool and private beach, tennis courts, a gym, a spa, boating and water-skiing, and a hotel orchestra. You can also swim in the lake and bask on an anchored raft. *Closed Nov–Mar.*

★★★**Firenze**, Piazza Mazzini 42, **t** 031 950 342 (*expensive*). A 19th-century villa next to the harbour, with stylish rooms and a coffee bar with live music once a week. The terraces and many of the rooms have lake views, and there's a restaurant under an arbour by the lake. *Closed Nov–Mar.*

★★★**Hotel Du Lac**, Piazza Mazzini 30–32, **t** 031 950 320 (*expensive*). A genial, family-run hotel in a 16th-century building near the centre, with fine views from the rooftop terrace and a traditional restaurant. Some rooms have wonderful lake views. There is also a sports club with swimming pool, tennis courts, football and Turkish baths. *Closed Nov–late-Mar.*

★★★**Excelsior Splendide**, Lungo Lago Manzoni, **t** 031 950 225 (*expensive–moderate*). A lakefront hotel with faded Liberty-style charm, big old rooms (most with a view), a pool and a garden. *Closed Nov–mid-Mar.*

★★**La Pergola**, Piazza del Porto, Pescallo, a 10min walk from town, **t** 031 950 263 (*moderate*). A charming little olde-worlde place in a tiny fishing harbour, with stylish rooms with all comforts, and a waterside restaurant (*cheap–moderate*) with a nice pergola above the lake. *Closed Tues out of season.*

★★**Silvio**, Via Carcano 12, Loppia, road to Como, **t** 031 950 322, *www.bellagiosilvio.com* (*moderate*). Good-value, comfortable rooms with lake or garden views, friendly service, peaceful surroundings and excellent home cooking, including home-made pasta. The fresh fish is caught daily by the father and son; try the fish ravioli and the *tiramisù*, approved by Pavarotti and Robert de Niro.

La Genzianella, San Primo forest, **t** 031 964 734 (*cheap*). A hotel and restaurant serving local mountain dishes such as polenta *uncia* (or *oncia*) and game. *Closed Weds Sept–June.*

Barchetta, Salita Mella 13, **t** 031 951 389, (*expensive*). The best place to eat in Bellagio, on a terrace overlooking the deep narrow streets. Feast on creatively revisited Lombard cuisine, including foie gras, pasta dishes and lake delicacies. The wine list is outstanding. Booking advised for evenings. *Closed Tues, and lunchtimes in winter*

Bilacus, Salita Serbelloni 30–32, **t** 031 95080 (*moderate*). One of the nicest places to dine in central Bellagio, with a romantic terrace and excellent *spaghetti alle vongole*, saffrony mushroom risotto, and simple grilled fish. *Closed winter.*

Mella, Piazza San Giovanni 7, **t** 031 950 205 (*moderate*). The place to go for a feast of fish, a pleasant half-hour walk through the Villa Melzi. Try mixed fish *antipasto*, mixed grilled fish and a bottle of lemony Soave. *Closed Tues and winter.*

Chalet Gabriele, Piano Rancio hamlet, **t** 031 963 624 (*cheap*). A place up in the green mountains behind Bellagio, offering typical local cheese *tocc*, polenta and a variety of fondues. *Closed Tues.*

Pasticceria Bar Sport, Piazza della Chiesa (*cheap*). An ice-cream shop and *pasticceria* where you can get *mataloc*, a typical Bellagio cake with raisins.

Rifugio Capanna Martina, Alpe dei Picetti, above Lezzeno, 15km from Bellagio, **t** 031 964 695 (*cheap*). Mountain food and a beautiful lake view from the garden terrace. *Closed weekdays in winter.*

Menaggio ✉ 22017

★★★★**Grand Hotel Victoria**, Lungolago Castelli 7, **t** 0344 32003, *www.palacehotel.it* (*very expensive*). An 1806 hotel by the lake, with original décor alongside modern creature comforts such as designer bathrooms, TVs, minibars, and a swimming pool in the garden.

★★★★**Grand Hotel Menaggio**, Via IV Novembre 69, **t** 0344 30640, *www.grandhotelmenaggio.com* (*very expensive–expensive*). A hotel in its own grounds on the lake, with fully equipped rooms, most with stunning views, and a heated pool. *Closed Nov–Feb.*

*****Bellavista**, Via IV Novembre 21, **t** 0344 32136 (*expensive–moderate*). A central option right on the lake, with pleasant rooms. *Closed Nov–Feb.*

****Corona**, Largo Cavour 3, **t** 0344 32006 (*cheap*). A hotel near the centre, with lake views.

Ostello La Primula, Via IV Novembre 86, **t** 0344 32356, *www.menaggiohostel.com* (*cheap*). A very fine youth hostel, with a restaurant serving some of the best cheap meals in the area. *Closed Nov–Feb.*

Vecchia Menaggio, Via al Lago 13, **t** 0344 32082 (*moderate*). A friendly, low-key restaurant with great pizzas and pasta, plus several rooms (*cheap*) to stay in, four with en suite baths. *Closed Tues and Nov–mid-Dec.*

Varenna ✉ 22050

******Hotel du Lac**, **t** 0341 830 238 (*very expensive*). A hotel on the lakeside in the quiet medieval part of the centre, with fully equipped, well-decorated rooms and suites with marvellous views. There's also a lovely terrace, a pergola, mooring and a good restaurant at lake level (*expensive*).

*****Albergo Milano**, Via XX Settembre 29, **t** 0341 830 298 (*expensive*). A beautifully located place in the village, offering 8 rooms with balconies and wonderful views. *Closed Dec–Feb.*

*****Villa Cipressi**, Via IV Novembre 18, **t** 0341 830 113 (*expensive*). A hotel with a gorgeous garden and lake terraces, if somewhat disappointing rooms in comparison.

****Olivedo**, Piazza Martiri 4, near steamer terminal, **t** 0341 830 115, *www.olivedo.it* (*cheap–moderate*). A cosy hotel with atmospheric old furnishings and décor. All bedrooms face the lake; some have shared baths. The food, served on a terrace if the weather's good, is excellent.

Vecchia Varenna, Via Scoscesa 10, **t** 0341 830 793 (*expensive*). Splendid views matched by dishes prepared with the finest ingredients from France and Italy: the lake fish is wonderful. *Closed Mon and Jan.*

Lecco ✉ 22053

******Il Griso**, Via Provinciale 51, Malgrate, 1km from town, **t** 0341 202 040 (*expensive*). A moderate-sized, elegant hotel with fine views of the lake from its wide terrace, plus a sauna, gym and billiards room. The food and beautiful views compensate for the faded 1970s décor. There's a swimming pool in the garden, and one of the region's best restaurants, with *menu degustazione*. Reservations are essential.

*****Don Abbondio**, Piazza Era 10, Pescarenico, **t** 0341 366 315 (*moderate*). Simple rooms with small bathrooms in a charming little fishing village, with views over the Adda river and the fishing boats. Some rooms have private terraces.

*****Moderno**, Piazza Diaz 5, **t** 0341 286 519 (*moderate*). Adequate rooms with all mod cons. There are no breakfasts.

***Marchett**, Via per Erna 11, up the funicular at the Piani d'Erna, **t** 0341 505 019 (*cheap*). Simple rooms with views, plus a good restaurant with a set menu.

Al Porticciolo, Via Valsecchi 5, **t** 0341 498 103, (*very expensive*). Lecco's best restaurant, offering seafood dishes where the natural flavours are allowed to come through. You pick your fish from the tanks. *Closed Mon, Tues, early Jan and Aug.*

Nicolin, Via Ponchielli 54, Maggianico Sud, behind Pescarenico, **t** 0341 422 122 (*very expensive*). A gourmet restaurant with surprises such as home-made foie gras with a marmalade of figs and *pan brioche*, and rice with watercress and *ragù* of frogs. There's a good choice of cakes, an excellent wine list, and cheaper working lunch menus. *Closed Tues and Aug.*

Trattoria Vecchia Pescarenico, Via Pescatori 8, Pescarenico, **t** 0341 368 330 (*moderate*). A restaurant in a fishing village, offering dishes with lake fish. *Closed Mon.*

Taverna ai Poggi, Via ai Poggi 14, road to Pian d'Erni funivia, **t** 0341 497 126 (*cheap–moderate*). Regional specialities such as local salami, *brigioli* with Valsassina cheese, and lake fish, plus good sandwiches and soup. You can sit outside in summer. A *menu lavoro* (working lunch) is available. *Closed Mon.*

Viganò Brianza ✉ 22048

Pierino Penati, Via XXIV Maggio 36, **t** 039 956 020 (*very expensive*). Delcious regional specialities, including innovative dishes such as *gnocchetti* in saffron-scented prawn bisque. *Closed Sun eve, Mon, Jan and Aug.*

Beautiful villas are chock-a-block along the shore at **Tremezzo**, including the early 18th-century **Villa La Quiete** at Bolvedro, with its stone balustrades, and, from the same period, the celebrated **Villa Carlotta** (*open daily Apr–Sept 9–6; Mar and Oct 9–11.30 and 2–4.30; adm exp*), at the north end of Tremezzo. Originally built in 1747, it took its name from Princess Carlotta of the Netherlands, who received it as a wedding gift from her mother in the 1850s, but most of what you see was the work of the counts Sommariva, who laid out the magnificent gardens and park. The neoclassical interior is filled with cool, virtuoso neoclassical statuary.

Bella Bella Bellagio

Enjoying one of the most beautiful sites in Italy, spilling over the promontory in the centre of Lake Como, Bellagio (from the Latin *bi-lacus*, 'between the lakes') is as charming as its setting, with steep, stepped lanes of handsome old houses, ornate balconies spilling over with flowers and an endlessly fascinating waterfront. Its first mention in history is in relation to Pliny the Younger's Villa Tragedia, which most scholars place in the spectacular grounds of the **Villa Serbelloni**, now the Study and Conference Centre of the Rockefeller Foundation. The park and gardens (English, Italian and Mediterranean), commissioned by Count Alessandro Serbelloni at the beginning of the 19th century, are worth a visit (*daily guided tours Apr–Oct Tues–Sun 11 and 4; tickets available from Promo Bellagio tourist office up to 10mins beforehand; in season morning tour is often booked up by groups*) for their beauty and views. Also open for visits is the neoclassical **Villa Melzi** (*open late Mar–Oct 9–6.30; adm*), built in 1808 for one of Napoleon's henchmen, the Duke of Lodi, Francesco Melzi d'Eril. It has a rare Montezuma pine, a lily pond and a little Moorish temple where in 1837 Liszt composed his sonata dedicated to Dante and Beatrice.

The last really stylish address for villas and hotels on the west shore, **Menaggio** was a favourite of Venice's Cardinal Roncalli (later Pope John XXIII) and Churchill, who came here to sketch. Wedged on a promontory under the mountains, picturesque **Varenna**, the ferry port for Bellagio, Cadenábbia and Menaggio, makes a fine base for visiting the lake but it is worth exploring in its own right. It proudest lakeside villas are now used as congress centres; the oldest, **Villa Monastero**, was built on the site of a 13th-century convent; the garden (***t** 0341 830 129; open May–Oct 10–12.30 and 2.30–6; adm*), with statues and bas-reliefs, is famed for its citrus trees. Nearby **Villa Cipressi** built 1400–1800, also has a fine garden (***t** 0361 830 113; open daily spring 9–6, summer 9–7*) under its towering cypresses. The **Museo Ornitologico** (*currently closed; call Pro Loco Varenna for info*) houses 700 bird species that frequent Como's shores.

Higher up, the partially ruined **Castello di Vezio** (***t** 0341 814 011; call for open hours adm*), founded in the 7th century by Lombard queen Theodolinda, has a fantastic view over the Bellagio headland. Recently restored, it frequently hosts exhibitions. South of Varenna, the scenic path to the cemetery continues up (15 minutes) to the headspring of Lake Como's most curious natural wonder, the **Fiumelatte** ('river of milk'), Italy's shortest river, lasting only 820ft before blasting down in creamy foam into the lake. Not even Leonardo da Vinci could discover its source, or find out why it abruptly begins to flow in the last days of March and abruptly ceases at the end of October.

South again, **Bellano** lies at the bottom of the steep gorge or **Orrido** of the Pioverna torrent, where steps and gangways thread through the rocky chasm, offering views of the thundering water just below (*open daily spring 10–12 and 2.30–5, summer 9–12 and 2.30–7; adm*). It has a fine Lombard church, **Santi Nazzaro e Celso** (*open most days for religious services*), built by the Campionese and Intelvi masters in 1348.

Up the coast, **Musso** is gathered under the **Sasso di Musso**, the almost inaccessible rocky abutment dominating the Via Regina. Its castle was the stronghold of Lake Como's notorious pirate Gian Giacomo de' Medici (Il Medeghino), who made it the base for a fleet of armed ships that terrorized the lake for a decade, until Duke Francesco II, with help from the Swiss, dislodged him and demolished his citadel. The site of the castle, by the little church of Sant'Eufemia, was made into an eclectic Giardino di Merlo in the 1850s; you can imagine it while you get lost in its labyrinth of paths.

To the north, **Dongo**, **Gravedona** and **Sorico** formed the independent republic of the Tre Pievi or Three Parishes, a hotbed of Paternene (or Cathar) heresy, and scores of their citizens were sent to the stake by Peter of Verona for doubting, among other things, that the pope was Christ's representative on earth. Gravedona remains the most important town. By its parish church of **San Vicenzo** (with a 5th-century crypt), the tall 12th-century grey and white striped **Santa Maria del Tiglio** was founded as a detached baptistry, and rebuilt reusing palaeo-Christian carvings; the solemn interior has damaged frescoes and a stark 13th-century crucifix over the altar.

Lecco and its Lake

South of Varenna, the shores close in around the **Lago di Lecco**, a brooding fjord where mountains plunge down into the water, entwined in rushing streams and waterfalls and carved with shadowy abysses – landscapes that so enchanted Leonardo da Vinci when he visited Lecco to plan Milan's water schemes that he used them as backgrounds in his *Virgin of the Rocks* and *The Virgin and St Anne*. Lecco was the birthplace of Alessandro Manzoni (1785–1873) and the setting of his novel, *I Promessi Sposi* ('The Betrothed'), the 19th-century Italian classic. Literary pilgrims flock to the museum in his boyhood home, the **Villa Manzoni** at Via Guanella 7 (*from Piazza Manzoni, walk up Viale Dante; open Tues–Sun 9.30–2; adm*). Also to see are the 14th-century fortified bridge over the Adda, built by the Visconti, which survives minus its towers, and Lecco's **basilica**, with 14th-century Giottesque frescoes.

La Brianza

South of the mountainous Triangolo Lariano, this is a gentle region of little lakes that span the legs of Lake Como like blue footprints. Its villages spun the silk that was woven into cloth in Como and Lecco, and Milanese nobles erected summer villas on their shores in the 18th and 19th centuries. Today La Brianza, close to the big-name designers in Milan, is the most important furniture-making region in Italy.

The lake just south of Lecco, the **Lago di Garlate**, was also closely associated with the silk industry. In 1950 the Abegg silk mill, on the SS30 in the town of Garlate, was converted into the **Museo Civico della Seta**, or Silk Museum (*open Sun 10–12 and 2–6 or by request, **t** 0341 701 139; adm*).

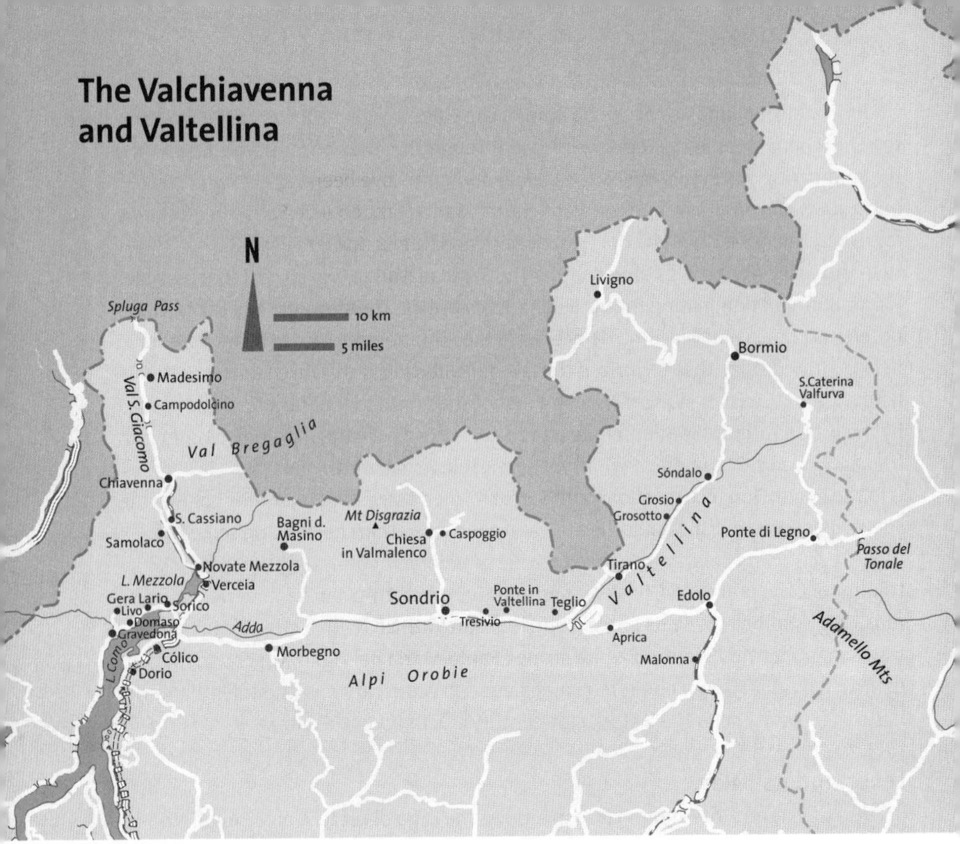

Beyond Como: the Valli del Sondrio

North and east of Lake Como lies mountainous Sondrio, sandwiched between the Orobie Alps and Switzerland. Its glacier-fed rivers flow into Como and the Med, through the Danube to the Black Sea, and through the Rhine into the North Sea. Only four roads link the two main valleys, the **Valchiavenna** and the **Valtellina**, with the rest of Italy. The province is among the least-exploited alpine regions, offering plenty of opportunities to see more of the mountains and fewer of your fellow creatures.

When the Spanish Habsburgs took Milan, the Valtellina, with its many Protestants, joined the Swiss Confederation. It was of prime importance to the Spaniards in the Counter-Reformation, assuring the route between Milan, Austria and the Netherlands. In 1620 the Spanish in Milan instigated the 'Holy Butchery' of 400 Protestants by their Catholic neighbours. The valley rejoined Italy only in the Napoleonic partition of 1797.

The Valchiavenna

The Valchiavenna stretches from Novate Mezzola north of Lake Como to the Spluga and Maloja passes, threading through the Lepontine and Rhaetic Alps. Many towns here started as stations along the Roman road and prospered thanks to the thick veins of potstone in the mountains – turned on a lathe and carved into cooking pots (*laveggi*), or sculpted into decorations, especially on windows and portals.

Chiavenna, the valley metropolis, is a pleasant town along the Mera river. Its natural rock cellars, the ***crotti***, maintain a year-round temperature of 4–8°C and have long been used for ripening local cheeses and hams; some have been converted into restaurants and wine cellars. Chiavenna's most important church, **San Lorenzo** (*open summer Tues–Sun 3–6, Sat also 10–12; winter Tues–Sat 2–4, Sat also 10–12, Sun 2–5; adm*), was begun in the 11th century and contains a 12th-century golden gem-studded 'Pax' cover for the Gospels. In the Romanesque baptistry (*open Mar–May Sat and Sun 9–12 and 2–5; June–Sept Tues–Sun 9–12 and 2–5*), the octagonal font (1156) is carved from a single chunk of potstone.

Above the 15th-century Palazzo Baliani you can walk up to the **Parco Botanico Archeologico Paradiso** (*open summer Tues–Sun 10–12 and 2–6; winter Tues–Sat 2–5, Sun 10–12 and 2–5; adm*), an ancient potstone quarry where workers once cut out stones and pots for architectural details. It has a natural history section, the **Torione** (*open summer Tues, Thurs, Sat and Sun 2.30–5.30*), and the **Mulino di Bottonera** (windmill), now a museum of industrial archaeology (*open 30 Mar–8 June Sat–Sun and hols 2.30–5.30; 15 June–15 Sept Tues–Sun 3–6, Sat also 10–12; 21 Sept–3 Nov, Sat, Sun and hols 2.30–5.30*). Further up, the **Parco Marmitte dei Giganti**, the 'Giants' Kettles', is named for its remarkable round glacial potholes, Europe's finest collection (*call **t** 0343 33795 for guided tours*).

East of Chiavenna on the St Moritz road in the Val Bregaglia, a magnificent waterfall (frozen in winter), the **Cascate dell'Acqua Fraggia**, is just above **Borgonuovo**; 2,000 steps lead up past *crotti* to the ancient hamlet of Savogno at the top of the waterfall. In 1618 a landslide off Monte Conto buried **Piuro**, next to Borgonuovo; you can visit the excavations of this humble 17th-century Pompeii, once an important potstone quarrying town; finds are displayed in the church of **Sant'Abbondio** in Borgonuovo (***t*** *0343 33795; open end Mar–end Oct Sat and Sun 3–5; adm*). Before it was buried, Piuro had fine mansions such as the 16th-century **Palazzo Vertemate Franchi** in nearby **Prosto di Piuro** (*open for guided tours June–Sept Tues–Fri 10, 11, 2, 3 and 4; Sat, Sun and hols 10, 11, 3, 4 and 5; adm*), with beautiful carved ceilings and lush mythological frescoes by the Campi brothers of Cremona.

North of Chiavenna, the **Valle San Giacomo** becomes increasingly rugged and steep, with dramatic landslides, glaciers and waterfalls. The village of **Campodolcino**, with its Roman bridge and a church with florid rococo altars, shares the 45km 'Skirama' ski slopes with **Madesimo**, watched over by a 44ft gilt statue of the **Madonna d'Europa**. Madesimo is a high-rise, high-altitude international summer and winter resort before the 6,948ft **Splügen Pass** (*generally closed Dec–Apr*).

The Valtellina

East of Cólico and Lake Como the traffic-swollen SS38 enters the Valtellina, giving a false first impression: the rest of the great valley of the Adda, where villages and vineyards hang precariously on the faces of the mountains, is as unadulterated and fresh as any, a great alpine playground a couple of hours from smoggy Milan. In 1989, the Orobie Alps south of the Adda were set aside as the **Parco Regionale delle Orobie Valtellinesi** (***t*** *0342 211 236*), to protect, among other things, the local wood grouse.

Getting There and Around

At Cólico the **railway** from Milan and Lecco forks, one line heading north to Chiavenna. **Buses** from there link up to Madesimo and other valley towns.

Tourist Information

Chiavenna: Via Vittoria Emanuele II 2, **t** 0343 36384, *www.valchiavenna.com*
Morbegno: Piazza Bossi, **t** 0342 610 015, *www.panvaltellina.com*
Sondrio: Via Trieste, **t** 0342 512 500, *www.valtellinaonline.com*
Bormio: Via Roma 131, **t** 0342 903 300.
Valli Orobiche Consortium: *www.vallidelbitto.it*

Where to Stay and Eat

Local specialities include *violino*, a special ham of *pecora*; goat, marinated in brine with aromatic herbs and dried in the open air; brown *bisciola* cakes with nuts, figs, raisins and honey, and *torta di fioretto* with anis seeds.

Chiavenna ✉ 23022

Passerini, Via Dolzino 128, **t** 0343 36166 (*expensive*). A family-run restaurant in the 17th-century Palazzo Salis, with a good-value lunch menu. Don't miss ravioli with sea bass or spaghetti with scampi and chilli. Booking advised. *Closed Mon, 2wks Jan and all July.*

Al Cenacolo, Via Pedretti 16, **t** 0343 32123 (*moderate*). A stylish mix of regional dishes and innovative cuisine based on local seasonal ingredients, cooked on a traditional potstone. In summer you can eat on a small balcony overlooking the river. Booking advised. *Closed Tues eve, Weds and June.*

La Lanterna Verde, Villa di Chiavenna, 10km west of town, **t** 0343 38588 (*very expensive*). The best place to taste regional cuisine elevated to a gourmet level, known for its trout and meat dishes, and its beautifully served desserts. The huge wine list comprises a good selection of half-bottles. Booking advised. *Closed Weds, Thurs lunch, last 2wks Nov, and 10 days end of June.*

Morbegno ✉ 23017

***Margna**, Via Margna 36, **t** 0342 610 377, (*moderate*). A modernized 1886 hotel with a roof-terrace solarium. The stylish restaurant offers the likes of crêpes filled with *bitto* cheese, and venison cutlets in juniper. Ask about the special wine and food weekends.

Sondrio ✉ 23100

****Della Posta**, Piazza Garibaldi 19, **t** 0342 510 404, *www.hotelposta.so.it* (*expensive–moderate*). A grand old family-run hotel in the former stage post, with big rooms with lots of charm, a cosy reading room, an American bar and an excellent restaurant, **Sozzani**. Garibaldi is one of several illustrious guests to have slept here.

****Vittoria**, Via Bernina 1, **t** 0342 533 888 (*moderate*). A hotel with lots of comforts, including no-smoking rooms and a courtesy laptop computer for Internet access from the privacy of your room.

***Campelli**, Via Moia 6, Albosaggia, 5km south of town, **t** 0342 510 662 (*cheap–moderate*). A pretty family-run hotel with a restaurant offering light, modern versions of the Valtellina's rich delights, plus excellent wines. There's a pleasant park in the back, a solarium, a health farm and a disco. *Closed Sun and most of Aug.*

Torre della Sassella, Loc. Sassella 17, a few km outside town, **t** 0342 218 500 (*expensive*). Four elegant yet rustic dining rooms on different levels of a 16th-century tower on a hill, where you can enjoy fine cured fish,

To enter the lower valley from Cólico is to enter the territory of the Cèch, a people whose origin is as mysterious as their name. One interpretation is that Cèch comes from *ciechi* (blind) as the locals were the last to convert to Christianity. Located just above and north of the Adda, the nine old vine-wrapped villages of the **Costiera dei Cèch** are veritable suntraps and make for pretty, not too demanding walks; there's also an 18th-century wine press and museum, the **Museum del Vino** and **Torchio di** risotto and meats, and excellent wines. The menu combines traditional dishes with more unusual fare, such as *tagliata* of ostrich meat. Booking advised. *Closed Weds.*

Cima 11, Via Pelosi 3, **t** 0342 515 040 (*cheap*). A traditional inn near Piazza Campello, with long tables and benches where diners feast on hearty old-style Valtellina cooking. *Closed Sun, hols and Aug.*

Eden, Via Nazario Sauro 40, **t** 0342 214 038 (*cheap*). Excellent-value national cuisine. *Closed eves, Sun and 2nd and 3rd wk Aug.*

Amici Vecchie Cantine, Via Parravicini 6, **t** 0342 512 590 (*cheap*). A wine bar serving excellent locally cured meats, cheeses and vegetables in oil. *Closed Sun.*

Chiesa in Valmalenco ✉ 23023

★★★★**Tremoggia**, Via Bernina 4, **t** 0342 451 106 (*expensive*). A welcoming hotel with sauna, gym and hydromassage pool. The restaurant serves good, cheesy *sciatt* and beef marinated in juniper. *Closed Weds and Nov.*

★★★**Chalet Rezia**, Via Marconi 27, **t** 0342 451 271, *www.hotelrezia.it* (*cheap–moderate*). A nice if slightly run-down little place with a covered swimming pool.

La Volta, Via Milano 48, **t** 0342 454 051 (*expensive*). Local cuisine creatively revisited. Booking advised. *Closed Wed exc summer and Christmas, 10 days May and 3wks Oct.*

Il Vassallo, Vassalini hamlet, **t** 0342 451 200 (*expensive*). An old stone chalet with both traditional and original recipes, including excellent home-made gnocchi. *Closed Mon.*

Ponte in Valtellina ✉ 23026

Cerere, Via Guicciardi 7, **t** 0342 482 294 (*moderate–expensive*). One of the region's best restaurants, occupying a 17th-century palace. The classic Valtellina cuisine includes *sciatt* and *pizzoccheri*; the wine list features the valley's finest. *Closed Weds, Jan and July.*

Grosio ✉ 23022

★★★**Sassella**, Via Roma 2, **t** 0342 847 272, (*moderate*). A fine old hotel with big rooms with private bath. The restaurant serves refined local specialities such as *bresaola condita* (with olive oil, lemon and herbs) and an unparalleled *sciatt. Closed Mon in winter.*

Bormio ✉ 23032

★★★★**Baita dei Pini**, Via Don Peccedi 15, **t** 0342 904 346, *www.baitadeipini.com* (*very expensive*). A central choice with very good rooms and a fitness centre. *Closed Dec–Apr and 15 June–Sept.*

★★★★**Palace**, Via Milano 54, **t** 0342 903 131 (*very expensive*). An upmarket modern option with tennis courts, a swimming pool and very comfortable rooms. *Closed May.*

★★★★**Rezia**, Via Milano 9, **t** 0342 904 721 (*very expensive*). One of the town's cosiest hotels, furnished with local handcrafted furniture. The very good restaurant (*moderate*) serves solid Valtellina home cooking. *Closed Mon.*

★★★**Hotel Chateaux les Bains**, Valdidentro, just outside town on way to Stelvio, **t** 0342 910 1331 (*moderate–expensive*). A renovated turn-of-the-19th-century hotel at the Bagni Vecchi thermal waters and Roman caves, with access to the thermal facilities.

★★**Everest**, Via S. Barbara 11, **t** 0342 901 291 (*cheap*). A hotel with flowery balconies, a little back garden and private bathrooms. *Closed Oct and Nov.*

Al Filo, Via Dante 6, **t** 0342 904 771 (*moderate–expensive*). A stylish old *taulà* (hayloft) offering Valtellinese cuisine. *Closed Tues, Weds lunch, May, June, Oct and Nov.*

Kuerc, Piazza Cavour 7, **t** 0342 904 738 (*moderate*). Good local dishes in an attractive setting. *Closed Tues and 25 Sept–25 Oct.*

La Rasiga, Via Marconi 5, **t** 0342 901 541 (*cheap–moderate*). A restaurant in an old sawmill across the river. *Closed Mon.*

Cerido (*open Thurs and Sun 3–5 or call **t** 0342 611 342*). In the Cèchs' pleasant main town, **Morbegno** just over the river, the **Museo Civico** in the Palazzo Gualteroni (***t** 0342 612 451; open Tues, Thurs, Sat and Sun 2.30–5.30*) is strong on natural history. From here buses make excursions towards the south into two scenic valleys, the **Valli del Bitto** (named for the local cheese) and **Valle di Albareto e Valgerola**, both of which have iron ore deposits that made them a prize for the Venetians for two centuries; the

Pescegallo ski resort sits up on top. There's also the rural **Val Tartano**, a 'lost paradise', dotted with alpine cottages, woods and pastures, its declining population farming as their ancestors did. Many hamlets even today are accessible only by foot or mule.

A third valley running to the north, the wild granite **Val Másino**, is the beginning of the magnificent 'Sentiero Roma', the six-day path to the Valchiavenna laid out in the 1920s. It begins at the little 15th-century spa **Bagni di Masino** at 3,845ft (***t** 0342 641 010; open May–Sept*), although other paths from Bagni can be walked in a single day, especially up to the meadows and torrents of the Piano Porcellizzo.

The provincial capital **Sondrio** (from the Lombard *sonder*, changed into the Latin *sundrium*, the land Lombard lords gave to their peasants) is a mostly modern town, built on either side of the flood-prone Torrente Mallero that devastated the city in 1987. Many of its surviving old mansions have been put to new uses: the 18th-century Palazzo Sassi De' Lavizzari houses the new **Museo Valtellinese di Storia e Arte** (***t** 0342 566 269; open Tues–Sat summer 10–12 and 3–6; winter 9–12 and 3–5*) with statues, gold work and frescoes salvaged from churches, and an exceptional collection of rococo drawings, etchings and oils by the 18th-century Ligari family. At the time of writing, the **Collezione Fulvio Grazioli**, one of Italy's most important collections of rocks and minerals, nearly all from the Valmalenco (*see* below), was in Palazzo Martinengo in Via Dante (***t** 0342 526 280; open Tues–Thurs 5–6, Fri and Sat 10–12 and 5–6*).

No valley in all the Alps comes close to matching the 260 minerals found in the lovely **Val Malenco**, with its chestnut forests and glacier lakes, including commercially mined serpentine (green marble) and potstone. **Chiesa in Valmalenco** and **Caspoggio** are the main towns and ski resorts in the valley; the former has a small **Museo Storico Etnografico e Naturalistico della Valmalenco** in the former church of SS. Giacomo e Filippo (*open July–Aug Weds–Mon 5–7; Sept Sat 5–7; Feb–Mar Sat 4.30–6.30; Christmas and Easter daily 4.30–6.30; groups by request, call **t** 0342 451 150; adm*), containing stone objects found in the valley from Roman times to the present.

The Upper Valtellina

East of Sondrio the SS38 rises relentlessly. If you're not in a hurry take the scenic 'Castel road' through the vineyards north of the highway, beginning at Tresivio and the melancholy ruins of Grumello castle, then continuing to the old patrician town of **Ponte in Valtellina**, mostly visited for its church of **San Maurizio** (***t** 0362 482 158*), with an unusual bronze *cimborio* or lantern (1578), and frescoes by Luini. In 1746, Ponte was the birthplace of astronomer Giuseppe Piazzi, discoverer of the first asteroid.

Further east, charming **Teglio** gave its name to the entire valley (from Tellina Vallis). Its Renaissance **Palazzo Besta** is the finest in the region (***t** 0342 781 218; open Tues–Sat May–Sept 9–12 and 2–5; Oct–Apr 8–2; also open 1st, 3rd and 5th Sun of month, 2nd and 4th Mon and hols, 8–2; closed 1 May, Christmas and 1 Jan; adm*). Built in 1539, it has an arcaded courtyard with fine *chiaroscuro* frescoes from the *Aeneid* and *Orlando Furioso*; inside, the Sala della Creazione has a world map dated 1549. Downstairs, the **Antiquarium Tellinum** (*same ticket*) houses the Stele di Caven, known as the Mother Goddess, an exceptional example of the prehistoric rock incisions common in these parts, which the locals once believed were made by the claws of witches.

Among the old lanes in the centre, look for 11th-century **San Pietro**, with geometric decorations, a fine campanile and a Byzantine-style fresco of Christ Pantocrator in the apse; the **Oratorio dei Bianchi**, its exterior frescoed with a ruined 15th-century *danse macabre*; and the **Ca' del Boia** with blackened arcades, once the home of a particularly adept executioner. These days Teglio takes special pride in its wines and *pizzoccheri*, narcotic grey noodles with butter and vegetables.

East of Teglio, the SS39 runs east to **Aprica** (3,897ft), a winter and summer resort convenient for visiting the protected areas of Pian di Gembro, San Antonio valleys, and the park of the Orobie Valtellinesi. At **Corteno Golgi** you can hire a horse (***t** 0342 746 208*) to explore the remote **Val Brandet** and **Val Camovecchio**, part of a little-known park of firs, rhododendrons, tiny lakes, wooden bridges and old stone huts.

The vines begin to give way to lush apple orchards as you approach **Tirano**, a historic crossroads: mule trains from Venice and Brescia would pass up the Valle Camonica and at Tirano turn west to trade in the Valtellina or continue north into Switzerland and Germany. Today the town is the terminus of the FS trains from Milan, as well as the narrow-gauge **Trenino rosso del Bernina** (***t** 0342 701 353*), which plunges and twists through 70 kilometres of dramatic gorges to St Moritz; in July and August open cars make it even easier to drink in the stupendous scenery.

Tirano's most famous building, the **Santuario della Madonna di Tirano** a kilometre outside the centre, marks the spot where the Virgin made a appearance in 1504. It became the focal point of Catholicism during the Counter-Reformation, and was exuberantly Baroqued, painted and stuccoed and given an impressive wood-inlaid organ to keep the faithful dazzled when the Valtellina was quickly sliding away into the Protestant camp. In the 18th-century Casa del Penitenziere in Piazza Basilica, the **Museo Etnografico Tiranese** (*open June–Sept Tues–Sun 10–12 and 3.30–6.30; Oct–May Sat 10–12 and 3–6*) documents rural activity and traditional furnishings, tools and objects, some dating back to the Bronze Age.

Bormio and Stelvio National Park

Bormio, splendidly situated in a mountain basin 4,019ft up, is both a year-round sports destination and picturesque old town of narrow medieval lanes and frescoed palaces, recalling the days of prosperity when Venice's Swiss trade passed through. It's also the western gateway to the **Parco Nazionale dello Stelvio** (***t** 0342 911 654*), Italy's largest national park, which was founded in 1935 around the grand alpine massif of Ortles-Cevedale and is linked to Switzerland's Engadine National Park. A tenth of Stelvio is permanently covered with 100 glaciers, including one of Europe's largest, the *Ghiacciaio dei Forni*. The peaks offer many exciting climbs, especially **Grand Zebrù** (12,631ft), **Ortles** (12,811ft) and **Cevedale** (12,395ft). The park embraces Europe's second-highest pass, the **Passo dello Stelvio** (9,048ft), where you can ski all summer and continue into the South Tyrol between the months of June and October. Building the road here was such an engineering feat that its mastermind has a small museum in the pass, the **Museo Carlo Donegani** (***t** 0342 903 030 or **t** 0342 904 534; open June–Oct Mon and Sat 9–12 and 1.30–5, Tues–Fri 9–1 and 1.30–5, Sun 9–11.30 and 1.30–5*).

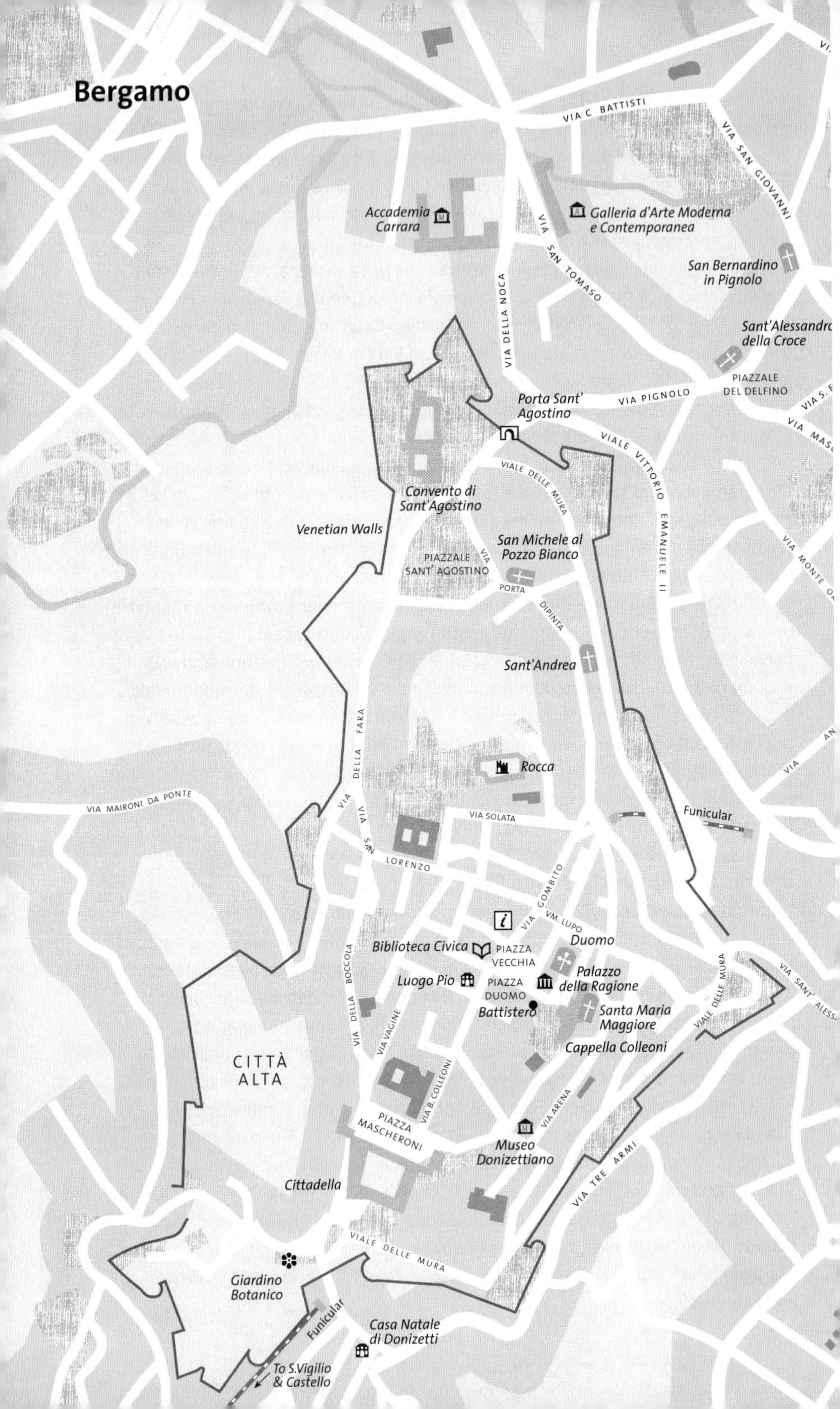
Bergamo
VIA C BATTISTI
VIA SAN GIOVANNI
Accademia Carrara
Galleria d'Arte Moderna e Contemporanea
VIA SAN TOMASO
VIA DELLA NOCA
San Bernardino in Pignolo
Sant'Alessandro della Croce
PIAZZALE DEL DELFINO
Porta Sant' Agostino
VIA PIGNOLO
VIALE VITTORIO EMANUELE II
VIALE DELLE MURA
Convento di Sant'Agostino
Venetian Walls
San Michele al Pozzo Bianco
PIAZZALE SANT' AGOSTINO
PORTA DIPINTA
Sant'Andrea
VIA MONTE
VIA DELLA FARA
Rocca
VIA MAIRONI DA PONTE
VIA SOLATA
Funicular
VIA SAN LORENZO
VIA GOMBITO
VM. LUPO
Duomo
Biblioteca Civica
PIAZZA VECCHIA
Luogo Pio
PIAZZA DUOMO
Palazzo della Ragione
Battistero
Santa Maria Maggiore
Cappella Colleoni
VIA DELLA BOCCOLA
VIA VAGINE
VIALE DELLE MURA
VIA SANT' ALESS
CITTÀ ALTA
VIA B. COLLEONI
PIAZZA MASCHERONI
VIA ARENA
Museo Donizettiano
Cittadella
VIA TRE ARMI
VIALE DELLE MURA
Giardino Botanico
Funicular
Casa Natale di Donizetti
To S.Vigilio & Castello

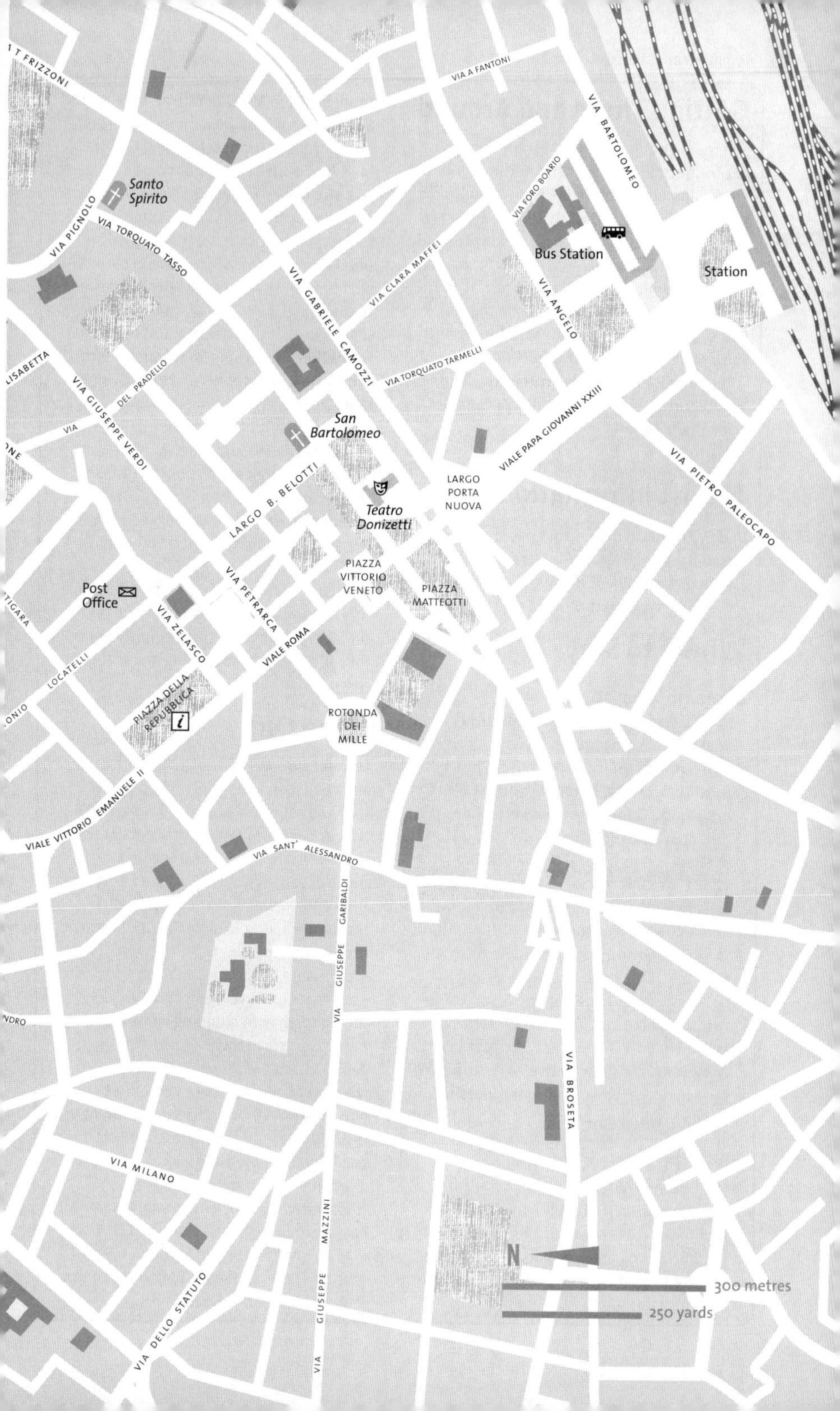

Santo Spirito
San Bartolomeo
Teatro Donizetti
Bus Station
Station
Post Office
LARGO PORTA NUOVA
PIAZZA VITTORIO VENETO
PIAZZA MATTEOTTI
ROTONDA DEI MILLE
PIAZZA DELLA REPUBBLICA
LARGO B. BELOTTI
VIA A FANTONI
VIA BARTOLOMEO
VIA FORO BOARIO
VIA ANGELO
VIA CLARA MAFFEI
VIA GABRIELE CAMOZZI
VIA TORQUATO TARMELLI
VIALE PAPA GIOVANNI XXIII
VIA PIETRO PALEOCAPO
VIA PIGNOLO
VIA TORQUATO TASSO
VIA GIUSEPPE VERDI
VIA DEL PRADELLO
VIA PETRARCA
VIA ZELASCO
VIALE ROMA
VIALE VITTORIO EMANUELE II
VIA SANT' ALESSANDRO
VIA GIUSEPPE GARIBALDI
VIA BROSETA
VIA MILANO
VIA DELLO STATUTO
VIA GIUSEPPE MAZZINI
LOCATELLI
N
300 metres
250 yards

Getting There and Around

Bergamo's **airport**, Orio al Serio, **t** 035 326 111, has connections to Rome and Ancona.

Bergamo is a 1hr **train** ride from Milan, and also has frequent links with Brescia, and a few trains a day to Cremona and Lecco, **t** 1478 88088.

There are regular **bus** services, **t** 035 289 011, to Milan, Como, Lake Garda (via Brescia), the Bergamasque valleys and Boario in the Val Camonica. The train and bus stations are at the end of Viale Papa Giovanni XXIII.

Bergamo is hell for those with **cars**. There's supervised parking in Piazza del Mercato del Fieno in the Città Alta.

Tourist Information

Viale Vittorio Emanuele 20, **t** 035 210204.
Città Alta, Vicolo dell'Aquila Nera 2, **t** 035 242 226, *www.apt.bergamo.it*

Where to Stay

Bergamo ✉ 24100

********Excelsior San Marco****, Piazzale della Repubblica 6, **t** 035 366 111, *www.hotelsanmarco.it* (*very expensive*). The city's most comfortable hotel, with an excellent restaurant, **Colonna** (*expensive*) and a roof terrace with a 360° view.

******Best Western Hotel Cappello d'Oro**, Viale Giovanni XXIII 12, **t** 035 232 503 (*very expensive*). Well-equipped modern rooms and a very good restaurant.

******San Lorenzo**, Piazza L. Mascheroni 9/A, **t** 035 237 383 (*expensive*). A convenient option for drivers, in Bergamo Alta outside the pedestrian area, with all comforts.

*****San Vigilio**, Via S. Vigilio 15, **t** 035 253 179, *www.sanvigilio.it* (*expensive*). A hotel first built by a local bank for its employees' holidays, with just 7 rooms – 5 with splendid views – and an olde-worlde atmosphere. It's reached by the S. Vigilio cable car.

*****Il Gourmet**, Via San Vigilio 1, **t** 035 437 3004 (*moderate*). A family-run place at the foot of the cable car, with a terrace for outdoor dining and free parking for guests. The gourmet cuisine includes Iranian caviar and fresh foie gras. *Closed Tues.*

****Agnello d'Oro**, Via Gombito 22, **t** 035 249 883, *www.agnellodoro.it* (*moderate*). The most atmospheric hotel in the Città Alta, built in 1600, with modern rooms with bath. The excellent restaurant (*moderate–expensive*) offers regional dishes. *Closed Mon, and Sun eve.*

****Sole**, Via B. Colleoni 1, **t** 035 218 238 (*moderate*). A homely option with baths in all rooms and a restaurant specializing in traditional cuisine. *Closed Thurs Nov–Feb.*

La Peta, Via Peta 3, Costa Serina, about 15km from city, **t** 0345 97955 (*moderate*). A 15th-century inn, with rooms and local cuisine.

****San Giorgio**, Via S. Giorgio 10, **t** 035 212 043, (*cheap*). Quiet rooms near the station, with private baths, TVs and other comforts.

***Caironi**, Via Torretta 6, a 20min walk from station or bus nos.5, 7 or 8, **t** 035 243 083 (*cheap*). A friendly family-run locanda in Bergamo Bassa, with shared bathrooms. *Closed Mon and Aug.*

Agriturismo Ardizzone, Via Ripago, Nese hamlet, Alzano Lombardo, 6km from city, **t** 035 510 060 (*cheap*). A 15th-century country house in the hills, offering horseriding and archery.

Eating Out

Look for *casoncelli* (ravioli filled with tangy sausagemeat in a sauce of melted butter, bacon and sage) and *polenta taragna* (with butter and cheese). Bergamo is a major fish market so many places have seafood.

Baretto di San Vigilio, Via Castello 1, **t** 035 253 191 (*very expensive*). A stylish, secluded restaurant specializing in fish. It's best to reserve. *Closed Mon.*

La Colombina, Via Borgo Canale 12, **t** 035 261 402 (*very expensive*). A pretty Liberty-style dining room with stunning views and the best *casoncelli* in town. *Closed Mon, Tues, 2wks Jan and 2wks June.*

Taverna del Colleoni, Piazza Vecchia 7, **t** 035 232 596 (*expensive*). A celebrated restaurant in a historic palace, with faultless classical Italian cuisine. *Closed Mon and 2wks Aug.*

Da Ornella, Via Gombito 15, **t** 035 232 736 (*moderate*). Good *polenta taragna*, served in cast-iron bowls. *Closed Thurs, and Fri lunch.*

San Vigilio, Via San Vigilio 34, **t** 035 253 188 (*cheap*). Pizzas and more, plus views of the Paduan plain. *Closed Wed.*

Bergamo

At the end of *A Midsummer's Night Dream*, Bottom and his pals dance a bergamask to celebrate the happy ending. Bergamo itself has the same stomping spirit as its peasant dance, mixing a rugged edge with refinement: it has given the world not only a dance but the maestro of *bel canto*, Gaetano Donizetti, the Renaissance painter of beautiful women, Palma il Vecchio, and the great portrait master, Gian Battista Moroni.

Piled on a promontory on the edge of the Alps, the city was founded by mountain Celts, who named it 'Bergheim' or hill town. To this day the Bergamasques speak a dialect that puzzles even their fellow Lombards; their language, courage and upfront character set them apart. Though old Bergamo owes many of its grace notes to the rule of Venice (1428–1797), it was by no means a one-way traffic of culture: Bergamo contributed not only artists but the Serenissima's most brilliant and honourable *condottiere*, Bartolomeo Colleoni (1400–75). The city prospered to the extent that in the 16th century another Bergamo, Bergamo Bassa, grew up on the plain below.

Bergamo Bassa

The heart of Bergamo's pleasant Città Bassa was laid out in the 1920s by Marcello Piacentini; it's wide and stately, lined with trees and always full of cars. Viale Giovanni XXIII goes up from the station to elongated **Piazza Matteotti**, where the pedestrian *Sentierone* ('Big Path') is flanked by cafés, the 18th-century **Teatro Donizetti**, and **San Bartolomeo**, housing a 1516 altarpiece of the Madonna by Venetian Lorenzo Lotto.

The oldest part of Bergamo Bassa, a few blocks east, is **Via Pignolo**, lined with 16th-century *palazzi* built for local cloth merchants, and their three churches, each with paintings by Lotto: Renaissance **Santo Spirito** on Via Torquato Tasso, part of a monastery rebuilt in the 16th century to a design by Pietro Isabello, with paintings by Bergamo native Previtali and Bergognone (*open Sept–June Mon–Sat 7–11.30 and 4–6.30, Sun and hols 8–12 and 4–7; July and Aug Mon–Sat 7–11 and 5–6.30, Sun and hols 8.30–12 and 5–9*); **San Bernardino in Pignolo** on Via San Giovanni, with a superb Pala of the Madonna and Saints (1521) by Lotto; and, near Piazzetta del Delfino, **Sant'Alessandro della Croce** (St Alexander is the city's patron saint), with a Trinity by Lotto and excellent works by Costa and Previtali, all a preview to the Accademia Carrara.

The Accademia Carrara

*Piazza dell'Accademia 82/A, **t** 035 399 643; open Tues–Sun Oct–Mar 9.30–1 and 2–5.45; Apr–Sept 9.30–1 and 2.30–6.45; guided visits by appointment; adm.*

This is one of the top provincial art museums in Italy, founded in 1796 by Count Giacomo Carrara and housed in this neoclassical palace since 1810. It has exquisite portraits – Botticelli's haughty *Giuliano de' Medici*, Pisanello's refined *Lionello d'Este*, Gentile Bellini's *Portrait of a Man*, Lotto's *Portrait of Lucina Brembati*, and a strange painting of uncertain origin, believed to be of Cesare Borgia. Other portraits (especially the *Young Girl*, one of the most beautiful portraits of a child) are by Bergamo's Gion Battista Moroni (1520–78), the master to whom Titian sent the *Rectors of Venice* with the advice that only Moroni could 'make them natural'. There are beautiful Madonnas by the Venetians, three superlative ones by Giovanni Bellini, others by Mantegna, Fra Angelico, Landi and Crivelli. The anti-plague St Sebastian is portrayed by three contemporaries from remarkably different aspects – naked and pierced with arrows before a silent city by Giovanni Bellini; well dressed and rather sweetly contemplating an arrow, by Raphael; and sitting at a table in a fur-trimmed coat, by Dürer. Other works are by Cariani, Fra Galgario, Palma il Vecchio and Previtali (all from Bergamo), Bergognone, the Venetians Carpaccio, Vivarini, Titian, Veronese, Tintoretto, Tiepolo and Guardi; also Cosmè Tura, Foppa, Luini, Savoldo, Moretto, Clouet, Van Dyck and Bruegel.

Opposite, at Via San Tommaso 53, the **Galleria d'Arte Moderna e Contemporanea** (*__t__ 035 399 527; open Tues–Sun 10–9, Thurs until 10; hours may vary*) hosts temporary exhibitions of mostly 20th-century art. Follow Via della Noca up to Piazzale Sant' Agostino, where the 16th-century **Porta Sant'Agostino**, bearing the Lion of St Mark, is the main gate to the Città Alta. From just inside the gate, the Viale delle Mura circles the top of the mighty **Venetian walls**, built 1561–88; the impressive underground passage in one of the ramparts, the **Cannoniera di San Michele**, has recently been restored (*call __t__ 035 251 233 for weekday guided tours June–Sept; adm*).

The Città Alta: Piazza Vecchia

Its domes and towers rising boldly on the hill against a background of mountains, the Città Alta is one of the most arresting urban views in Italy. The **funicular** was built in 1887 to rise to its heart, a short walk from beautiful **Piazza Vecchia**. Architects as diverse as Frank Lloyd Wright and Le Corbusier heaped praise on this square, encased in magnificent medieval and Renaissance buildings overlooking a dignified fountain with marble lions donated by the Contarini of Venice in 1780. At the lower end, the **Biblioteca Civica** (*__t__ 035 399 430; open Mon, Tues, Thurs and Fri 8.30–6.30, Weds and Sat 8.30–12.30; closed Sat July and Aug, week of Ferragosto and hols*) was begun in 1604 to a design by Palladio's student Vincenzo Scamozzi, modelled after Sansovino's famous library in Venice; it holds Donizetti's autograph score of *Lucia di Lammermoor*. Next is the 12th-century **Torre Civica** (*call __t__ 035 224 700 for open hours; adm*), with a 15th-century clock and curfew bell that still vainly orders Bergamasques to bed at 10pm.

The 12th-century **Palazzo della Ragione** has a relief of the Lion of St Mark, added in 1800 to commemorate Bergamo's golden days under Venice. In the 15th century, the ground-floor walls of the Palazzo were removed to allow glimpses of a second square, **Piazza Duomo**, and the jewel box **Colleoni Chapel** (*__t__ 035 210 061; open Apr–Oct daily 9–12.30 and 2–6.30; Nov–Mar Tues–Sun 9–12.30 and 2–4.30*), designed for the old *condottiere* by Giovanni Antonio Amadeo in 1476, moonlighting while working on the Certosa at Pavia. The chapel is even more ornate and out of temper with the times than the Certosa, a crazy quilt of medieval motifs and flourishes that spits in the face of Renaissance proportion and serenity. Amadeo also sculpted the double-decker tomb inside for Colleoni and his wife. Another wall has the calmer tomb of Colleoni's young daughter Medea, brought here in the 19th century from another church. The fine paintings under the dome were done by G.B. Tiepolo in 1733, and on the altar is a Holy Family by Goethe's companion in Rome, Swiss painter Angelica Kauffmann.

Flanking the chapel are two works by Giovanni, a master from Campione: the octagonal **baptistry** of 1340 (*open by appointment, **t** 035 210 223*) in white and red marble from Verona, and the colourful porch (1353) of the **Basilica of Santa Maria Maggiore** (***t** 035 223 327; open Apr–Oct daily 9–12.30 and 2.30–6; Nov–Mar Mon–Sat 9–12.30 and 2.30–5, Sun and hols 9–1 and 3–6*). Its palatial late 16th-century interior has sumptuous 16th-century tapestries on the walls: nine are scenes from the Life of the Virgin by Alessandro Allori, others are more secular. Here also is Donizetti's tomb, and a florid confessional by Fantoni. The best art is up in the chancel and choir, where Lorenzo Lotto designed 33 Old Testament scenes, beautifully executed in intarsia in 1552 by Capodiferro ('Ironhead') di Lovere. Only the four along the chancel rail are generally visible, and then only on Sunday or by arrangement with the sacristan; at other times their unfathomable locked wooden covers are food for thought.

Piazza Vecchia is also the address of the 6th-century **Duomo** (*open 7.30–11.45 and 3–6.30*), designed by Florentine humanist Filarete in 1459, remodelled by Carlo Fontana 200 years later and given a pseudo-but-pleasing late Baroque façade in 1886.

Around the Città Alta

The Visconti, who ruled Bergamo until 1428, built the 14th-century **Rocca** at the highest point in the Città Alta; the *torrione* (fortified tower) has been restored (***t** 035 224 700; open Sat, Sun and hols May–15 Sept 10–8; 16 Sept–Oct 10–6; Nov–Feb 10.30–12.30 and 2–4; Mar–Apr 10.30–12.30 and 2–6*). Below, Via Porta Dipinta curves around to the Porta Sant'Agostino, passing neoclassical **Sant'Andrea**, housing a superb altarpiece of the Madonna and saints by Moretto, and Romanesque **San Michele al Pozzo Bianco** (***t** 035 247 651; open daily 8–6; no visits during Mass*), rebuilt in the 1400s, its solemn interior illuminated with frescoes from the 1200s and 1500s and frescoes by Lotto.

Bartolomeo Colleoni lived at Via B. Colleoni 9/11, where he founded the **Luogo Pio** religious charity; among the frescoes is a portrait of the *condottiere* (*call **t** 035 217 185 to visit*). Via Colleoni continues to the west end of the Città Alta, closed off by the 14th-century **Cittadella**, former residence of the Venetian captains, now the **Museo di Scienze Naturali E. Caffi** (***t** 035 399 422; open Apr–Oct Tues–Fri 9–12.30 and 2.30–6, Sat–Sun 9–7; 25 Oct–Mar Tues–Sun 9–12.30 and 2.30–5.30; open most hols*) with stuffed animals and birds, and the **Museo Civico Archeologico** (***t** 035 242 839; open Apr–Sept Tues–Fri 9–12.30 and 2.30–6, Sat 9–midnight, Sun 9–7; Oct–Mar Tues–Sun 9–12.30 and 2.30–6*). The **Giardino Botanico** nearby, at the top of the Scaletta Colle Aperto (*open Apr–Aug 9–12.30 and 2–6, Sat, Sun and hols 9–7; Sept 9–12.30 and 2–6; Oct 9–12 and 2–5*), has more than 600 species of mostly medicinal plants.

Near the Cittadella, a funicular rises to **San Vigilio**, where the **Castello** (***t** 035 236 284; open daily Apr–Sept 9–8; Mar–Oct 10–6; Nov–Feb 10–4*), has superb views over the Parco dei Colli, dotted with old farmhouses and villas. Near the lower funicular station on Via Borgo Canale is the **Casa Natale di Donizetti** (*open Sat and Sun 11–6.30, or call **t** 035 399 208 1wk in advance*), where the composer was born. From the Cittadella, medieval Via Arena leads around to the back of the cathedral, passing the **Museo Donizettiano** (***t** 035 399 269; open Apr–Sept Tues–Sun 10–1 and 2.30–5; Oct–Mar Tues–Fri 10–1, Sat, Sun and hols 10–1 and 2.30–5*).

Around Bergamo

The year after Bartolomeo Colleoni was appointed Captain General of Venice, he purchased the ruined **Castello di Malpaga** in Cavernago, eight kilometres southeast of Bergamo (*t 030 840 003; open Feb–Nov Sun 3–6.30, or by booking for groups*), which he had restored for his old age. His heirs added frescoes by Romanino (or someone similar) commemorating a visit by Christian I of Denmark in 1474, portraying Colleoni hosting the splendid banquets, jousts, hunts and pageants of Renaissance hospitality.

At **Trescore Balneario**, 14 kilometres east of Bergamo, the chapel of the **Villa Suardi** (*call t 035 944 777 Weds–Sat 9–12.30 to arrange a visit*) has a charming fresco cycle by Lorenzo Lotto, painted in 1524 during his 15-year stint in Bergamo. The subject is the apocryphal story of St Barbara, patroness of artillerymen, architects and gravediggers, whose pagan father locked her in a tower and had her martyred for being a Christian, though he paid for his wickedness by being struck down by a bolt of lightning.

Southwest of Bergamo, **Caravaggio** was the birthplace of Michelangelo Merisi da Caravaggio, who left not a smear of oil paint behind, at the **Santuario della Madonna del Fonte** (*t 0363 3571; open summer Mon–Sat 6.30–12 and 2–7, Sun 6.30am–7pm; winter Mon–Sat 6.30–12 and 2–5, Sun 6.30–6*), designed in a cool Renaissance style by Pellegrino Tibaldi (1575) on the site of a 1432 apparition of the Virgin.

In **Capriate San Gervasio**, the **Parco Minitalia Fantasy World** (*open Mar daily 9.30–6; Apr–July daily 9.30–7.30; Aug daily 9.30am–11pm; Sept daily 9.30–6; Oct Sat and Sun 9.30–6; Nov–Feb Sat and Sun 9.30–5; adm*) cuts Italy down to size – 1,310ft from tip to toe, with mountains, seas, cities and monuments all in their proper place. Due east of Bergamo, **Sotto il Monte** was the birthplace of the beloved Pope John XXIII, and is an increasingly popular pilgrimage destination; there's a **Museo Papa Giovanni** (*open Tues–Sun 8.30–11.30 and 2.30–6.30; until 5.30 in winter*) filled with memorabilia.

The Bergamasque Valleys

North of Bergamo the two Bergamasque valleys plunge into the stony heart of the Orobie Alps, the mighty wall of mountains isolating the Valtellina further north. The Val Brembana was the main route for Venetian caravans transporting minerals from the Valtellina; the eastern Valle Seriana is Bergamo's favourite summer retreat.

The Val Brembana

In **Almenno San Bartolomeo**, just off the main road, the tiny, late 11th-century church of **San Tomè** (*open May–Sept Sat, Sun and hols 2–6; Oct–Apr Sun and hols 2–4; or call t 035 549 3337*) is a jewel of Lombard Romanesque built by the Comaschi masters. Composed of three stacked cylinders, it contains sturdy pillars and arches circled by a matriorum, and lovely capitals. **Zogno**, further up the valley, has the **Museo della Valle Brembana** (*t 0345 91673; open Tues–Sun 9–12 and 2–5; adm*) on the valley's history. Next up the valley, **San Pellegrino Terme** (*t 0345 22455; open May–Nov*) is synonymous with delicious mineral water and still has some claim as Lombardy's most fashionable spa, especially recommended for recuperating heart-attack patients.

According to legend, the humorously frescoed 15th-century **Casa dell'Arlecchino** (*call **t** 0345 43555 to book a visit*) at Oneta hamlet in **San Giovanni Bianco** was the birthplace of Harlequin (*see* p.44) – the role was supposedly invented by a *commedia dell'arte* actor named Ganassa who lived there, though more likely it is a reminder of the many men and women who, like Harlequin, chose to forsake their poor hills to become servants in Venice or Bergamo. There are any number of lovely, forgotten hamlets like Oneta in these mountains; many of them lie in a mini-region called the Val Taleggio, on the other side of the spectacular gorge of the **Torrente Enna**.

The next town north, medieval **Cornello dei Tasso**, is down to 30 inhabitants but preserves its appearance as a relay station on the merchants' road, with an arcaded lane to protect mule caravans. In the 13th century, much of the business of expediting merchandise here was in the hands of the Tasso family, one branch of which went on to run the post between Venice and Rome; another organized the first European postal service for emperors Maximilian I and Charles V in the 1500s. A third branch of the family in Sorrento produced the Renaissance poet Torquato Tasso; Cornello preserves the ruins of the Tasso ancestral home.

Beyond **Piazza Brembana** the road branches out into several mountain valleys. The most developed resort is **Foppolo**; besides winter sports it offers an easy ascent up the **Corno Stella** , with marvellous views north and east. **Carona** is a good base for summer excursions into the mountains and alpine lakes. East of Piazza Brembana, a lovely road rises to **Roncobello**; from here you can drive as far as the Baite di Mezzeno, the base for a bracing three-hour walk up to the **Laghi Gemelli**.

The Valle Seriana

Bergamo's eastern valley, industrial in its lower half and ruggedly alpine in the north, is known for the whirling Baroque wood sculptures and carvings by the Fantoni and Caniana families. One of their finest works, a fabulous pulpit covered with reliefs and soaring cherubs, is in the **Basilica di San Martino** in **Alzano Lombardo** (***t** 035 516 579; open Sun and hols 3–6, or by advance booking; guided visits 3.30; adm*).

In the Middle Ages, **Gandino** was the chief producer of a heavy, inexpensive cloth of wool and goat hair called bergamot, and the picturesque centre of town has changed little since. The 17th-century **Basilica di Santa Maria Assunta**, with its garlic-domed campanile, has confessionals and other works by the Fantoni and Caniana. The basilica museum (***t** 035 745 425; open by appointment only*) has relics of the textile industry.

Clusone is the capital of the Valle Seriana and its prettiest town. In Piazza dell'Orologio, the 11th-century **Palazzo Comunale** has a beautiful 16th-century astronomical clock, the **Orologio Planetario Fanzago** (*ring tourist office for opening hours; guided tours Thurs July–Sept*). Near it, the **Oratorio dei Disciplini** is adorned with an eerie 1485 fresco of the Danse Macabre and the Triumph of Death. There are more frescoes inside from the same period, and a Deposition by the Fantoni.

Further up, **Castione della Presolana** is the biggest resort in the Valle Seriana, surrounded by striking dolomitic mountain scenery. One of the biggest attractions is the lovely **Passo della Presolana** (3,691ft) near sheer dolomite walls and Monte Pora, a ski resort, with tremendous views over Lake Iseo.

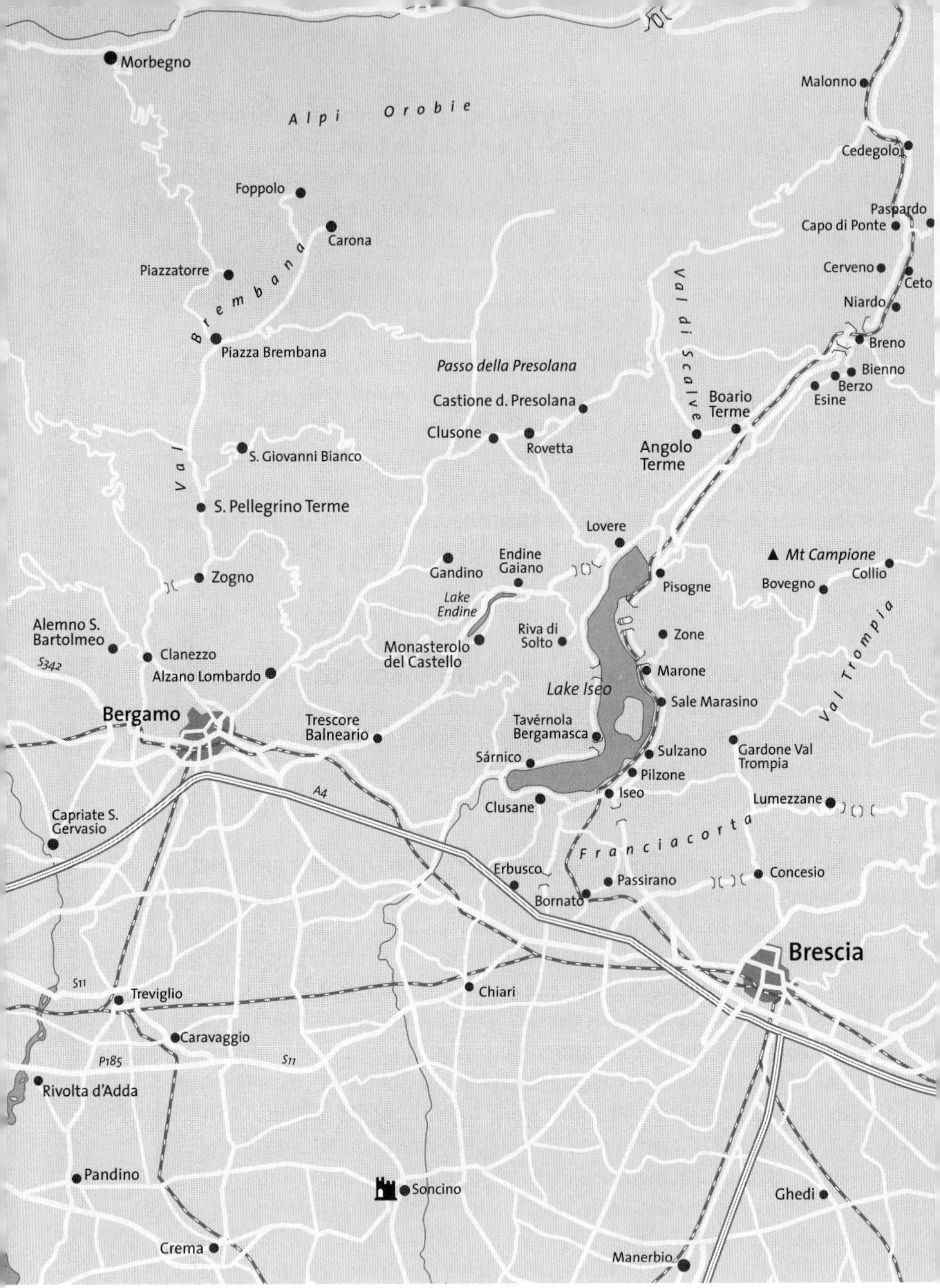

Lake Iseo, Franciacorta and the Valle Camonica

Lake Iseo (known as *Lacus Sebinus* in Roman times) is only the fifth in size but one of the first in charm, being well endowed with what it takes to get under your skin; even back in the 1750s it was the preferred resort of the Italophile Lady Montagu,

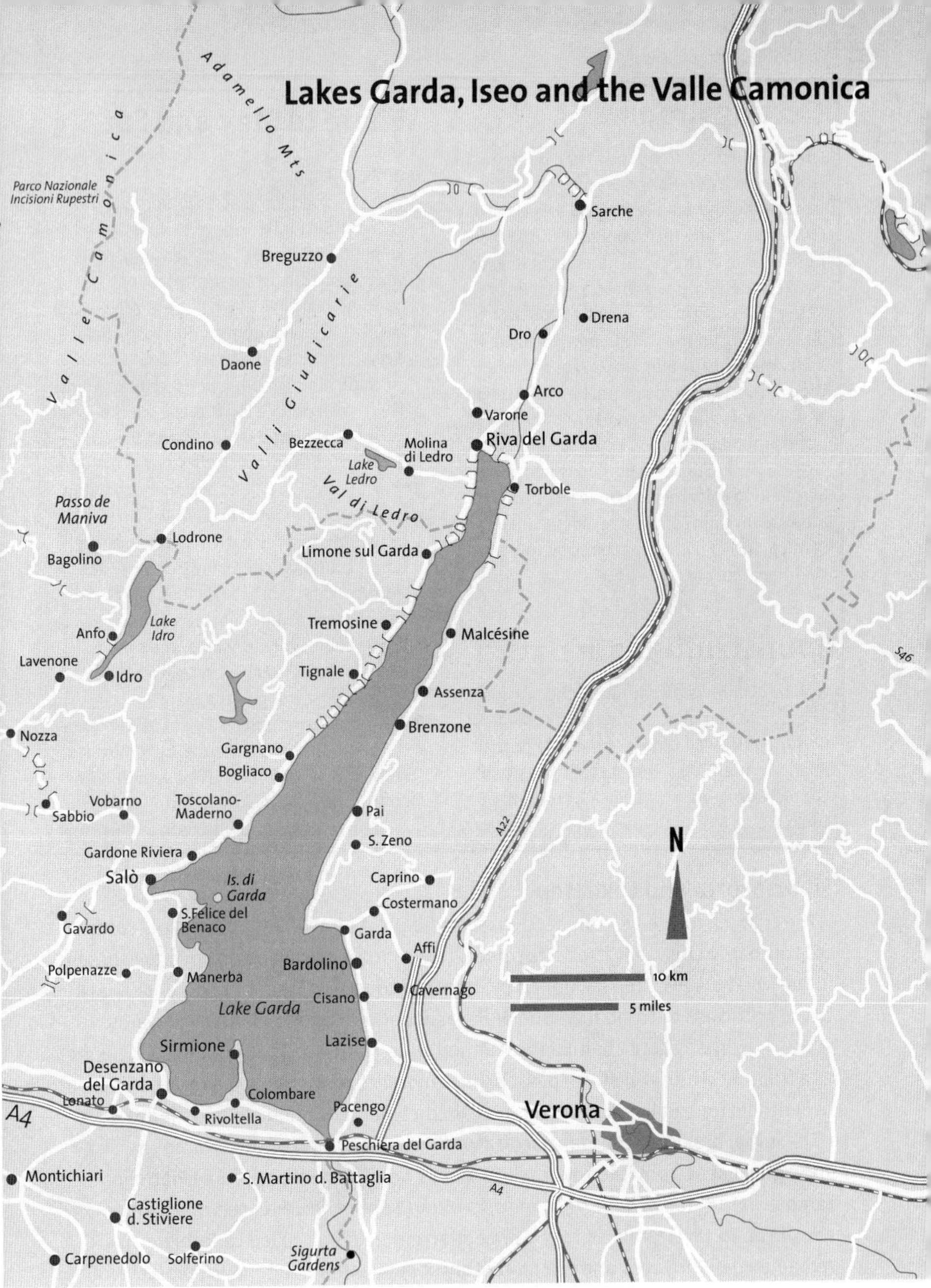

who turned her aristocratic nose up at the English that 'herd together' by the larger lakes. The southeastern shore of the lake borders on the lovely wine-growing region of Franciacorta; its main source, the river Oglio, runs through the lovely Valle Camonica, which provides the rocky palette for some of the world's most intriguing prehistoric art.

Getting Around

Buses run quite frequently from Bergamo to lake towns Tavèrnola and Lovere. Iseo town has frequent buses from Brescia, and a local **railway**, FNME, runs along the east shore of Lake Iseo from Brescia or the FS rail junction at Rovato, between Bergamo and Brescia. From Pisogne at the lake's north end, several FNME trains a day continue up the Valle Camonica to Edolo.

Steamers run by Bergamo's Navigazione Lago d'Iseo, **t** 035 971 483, sail between Lovere and Sárnico, calling at 15 ports and Monte Isola. Timetables are posted by the quays.

On summer Suns and hols, FS **trains** from Bergamo to Palazzolo sul Oglio link up to the little **steam train** Ferrovia del Basso Sebino to Sárnico, with direct connections on to the lake steamers; call **t** 035 910 900.

Tourist Information

www.bresciaholiday.com covers the province.
Iseo: Lungolago Marconi 2, **t** 030 980 209.
Clusane: OTC, Via Punta 14, **t** 030 982 9142.
Boario Terme: Piazza Einaudi 2, **t** 0364 531 609.
Capo di Ponte, Via S. Briscioli 42, **t** 0364 42080.
Edolo: Piazza Martiri della Libertà 2, **t** 0364 71065.

Where to Stay and Eat

Iseo ✉ 25049

★★★★**I Due Roccoli**, Via Silvio Bonomelli, Fraz. Invino di Sotto, 4km above town in the hills (direction Polaveno), **t** 030 982 2977, *www.idueroccoli.com* (*expensive*). Part of an old hunting lodge in its own large gardens, with lovely suites and rooms with garden or lake views. There's a sun terrace, a pool and an intimate dining room (*open to non-residents Thurs–Mon*) with a log fire; the superb food (much of it from the hotel farm), includes *antipasto* of salad and truffles. *Closed Oct–Mar.*

★★★★**Iseolago**, Via Colombera 2B, **t** 030 98891, *www.iseolagohotel.it* (*expensive*). An ideal retreat for families, with a a fitness centre, tennis courts, a pool, a playground, beach volleyball and football facilities, a pizzeria, a restaurant, a supermarket and an *enoteca*. Sports courses are available, and canoes, pedalos and bikes are available for hire. It's close to the cycling paths of the Franciacorta area and the natural reserve of Le Torbiere.

★★★**Ambra**, Via Porto G. Rosa 2, **t** 030 980 130, *www.ambrahotel.3000.it* (*moderate*). A hotel on the lake near the town centre, with modern rooms, most with bath and balcony.

Franciacorta and Lake Iseo

The triangle formed by Lake Iseo, Brescia and the A4 is a sweet and mellow corner of old Lombardy. Originally the *corte franca*, 'free court', it was wild and poverty-stricken in the Middle Ages, then reclaimed by monastic courts. The lack of taxes endeared it to the patricians of Lombardy, who built castles and villas and planted vineyards, producing an excellent champagne-method wine, Franciacorta Spumante DOC, as well as a fragrant white wine from pinot bianco and/or chardonnay, and a ruby herbaceous red with an unusually mixed pedigree: cabernet, barbera, nebbiolo and merlot.

The initial project in the Franciacorta was the reclamation of the swamps in **Provaglio** just in from Iseo town, when monks from Cluny founded **San Pietro in Lamosa** in 1083 (*open daily 9–12 and 2.30–6 but book in advance weekdays in low season;* ***t*** *030 383 477*). Part of their project, an emerald bog called **Le Torbiere**, has remained defiantly wet, and after a century of peat extraction is now a protected area; in late spring it becomes an aquatic garden of pink and white water lilies navigable by hired rowing boat.

Cluny also founded the abbey of San Nicola at **Rodengo Saiano** (***t*** *030 610 182; open daily 9–12 and 3–6; guided visits Sat 3–6 and Sun, hols 4–6; donations welcome*), with three cloisters now occupied by Olivetan monks; there are frescoes by Romanino and Moretto in the church, and a **Museo del Ferro** (*same hours*) dedicated to iron.

***Albergo Rosa, Via Roma 47, t 030 980 053 (*cheap*). A neat family-run hotel.

**Milano, Lungolago Marconi 4, t 030 980 449 (*cheap*). Small old-fashioned rooms, many with lake views, and a small restaurant and bar.

Il Volto, Via Mirolte 33, **t** 030 981 462 (*expensive–very expensive*). An old-fashioned inn with Italian and French cuisine, including lake fish (excellent with *tagliolini*) and tasty land dishes such as roast pigeon in mustard cream sauce. It's best to reserve. *Closed Weds and Thurs lunch, end Jan and 2wks July.*

Osteria del Vicolo, Via Pieve 4/a, **t** 030 982 1616 (*cheap*). A restaurant run by a local doctor and his wife, offering local cuisine. *Closed Tues.*

Monte Isola ✉ 25050

**Bellavista, t 030 988 6106 (*cheap*). Small, simple but comfy rooms with outstanding views, and a nice little restaurant.

**Canogola, t 030 982 5310 (*cheap*). A quiet, romantic hotel with 7 rooms in the trees by the lake, all with bath. *Closed Nov–Feb.*

Boario Terme ✉ 25041

****Rizzi, Via Carducci 11/Corso Italia 12, t 0364 531 617 (*moderate*). The most comfy rooms in town, some with soundproofing and air-conditioning. There's also a garden, an outside veranda and a very pleasant restaurant. *Closed Nov–Mar.*

***Brescia, Via Zanardelli 6, t 0364 531 409 (*moderate*). A slightly old-fashioned option with fully equipped rooms, a very stylish dining room, and a pub/disco downstairs.

***Armonia, Via Manifattura 11, t 0364 531 816 (*cheap*). Simple rooms with TV and bath, and a restaurant serving perhaps the most generous lunches and dinners in all Italy.

***Diana, Via Manifattura 10, t 0364 531 403 (*cheap*). A stylish modern hotel with good-sized rooms with all mod cons, large bathrooms and wonderful mountain views. There's also a garden and a candle-lit restaurant. *Closed Nov–Mar.*

**Ariston, Piazzale Einaudi 9, station forecourt, t 0364 531 532 (*cheap*). Small, clean rooms with modern fittings and old-fashioned hospitality. *Closed Nov–Mar.*

Capo di Ponte ✉ 25044

**Cumili, Viale della Stazione 1, t 0364 42034, *www.italiaabc.it* (*cheap*). Small, simple rooms with baths, plus a restaurant. Full board is compulsory.

Bornato is surrounded by 18th-century villas, including **Villa Rossa** with its lovely garden, stair and belvedere. **Villa Lana da Terzo** in **Colombaro** has the country's oldest cedar of Lebanon in its garden. **Erbusco** has the fine 17th-century Villa Lechi and a 13th-century church of Santa Maria, and an excellent Franciacorta vineyard that welcomes visitors, **Longhi-De Carli** (*t 030 776 8280*). Ask the Iseo tourist office for information on Franciacorta's Via dei Vini, a guided tour of the local vineyards.

Iseo is the lake's endearing, low-key and fetching 'capital', where flowers spill out of every window and the narrow alleys have kept their medieval names; its 11th-century **Pieve di Sant'Andrea** has an air of benign neglect. **Clusane**, west of Iseo, is crowned by an abandoned Castello di Carmagnola – it briefly belonged to the Venetian captain – and has a fleet of white-, blue- and pink- rimmed boats called *naêcc* that spend the day bagging the ingredients of *tinca al forno* (baked lake tench with polenta), an old recipe served in 20 restaurants, seating 4,000 – in a village with a population of 1,500.

The west shore of Iseo is the quieter one,. The road from Bergamo meets the lake at **Sárnico**, a pleasant town with a sprinkling of Liberty-style villas. The rugged scenery around **Riva di Solto** further north is best seen from the little lake steamers; the view of its coves, rugged rocks, ravines and formidable Adamello mountains in the distance is said to have caught the fancy of Leonardo, who used it as the background for the *Mona Lisa*: the black marble columns of St Mark's in Venice were quarried here.

From Endine Gaiano north of Riva di Solto the main road rejoins Lake Iseo at **Lovere**, the largest town of the west shore, with a medieval core dating from its days as a Venetian textile centre. In 1630 it shifted from cloth to steel, and to this day it mixes grit with art. There are 16th-century frescoes in the restored Baroque interior of **Santa Maria in Valvendra** (***t*** *035 983 567; open mid-Apr–Oct Mon–Sat 10–12 and 4–6, Sun 4–6; Nov–mid-Apr daily 4–6*), a Martyrdom of St George by Palma il Giovane on the altar of **San Giorgio**, a church partly built into a medieval tower; and fine paintings in the **Galleria dell'Accademia Tadini** in a neoclassical palace on Via Nazionale (*open late Apr–Oct Mon–Sat 3–6, Sun 10–12 and 3–6; adm*), including works by Tiepolo, Lorenzo Veneziano, Strozzi, Parmigianino and Bordone, and a lovely Madonna by Jacopo Bellini.

From Lovere, the road circles the north of the lake to reach the sprawling village of **Pisogne**, with the 15th-century church of **Santa Maria della Neve** (*open Tues–Sun 9.30–11.30 and 3–6; if closed, ask for key at Bar Romanino next door*), covered in 1532–43 with frescoes of the Passion, and Prophets and Sibyls by Romanino. South, beyond the tunnels, **Marone** overlooks the cute private Isolina di Loreto and is at the crossroads of the little **Val Valeriana**, an ancient road, now a walking path (you can get a map at Iseo's bookshop) through uncanny scenery: debris that was deposited by glaciers on the dolomitic rock aeons ago has been eroded into spiky 'earth pyramids', many balancing boulders on top like something out of *Road Runner*. There's a famous view of the pyramids – locally known as 'the fairies' – at **Cislano**.

Back on the lake, olive groves surround **Sale Marasino**, a pretty little resort built around a 16th-century town; **Sulzano**, just south, is the main port for the Arcadian, car-less (but well motorbiked) island of **Monte Isola**, the largest lake island in Europe at 45 kilometres in width. Once a hunting reserve of the local nobles and Visconti, it is now home to some 200 souls in its genteelly decaying hamlets.

Valle Camonica

From Pisogne, the road and railway continue northeast of Lake Iseo into the fertile Valle Camonica. Its name is derived from a Rhaetian tribe, the Camuni, whose ancestors used its smooth, glacier-seared Permian sandstone as tablets to engrave enigmatic solar discs and labyrinths, mysterious figures and geometric designs, animals, weapons and people. The oldest have been dated to the 9th millennium BC, and the last date from 16 BC, the year the Romans conquered the valley. Though one can only hazard guesses at the significance the etchings had for their makers, their magic must have been extraordinary: some 180,000 examples have been discovered so far. Some are beautiful, some ungainly and peculiar, some utterly mystifying; a few fuel crackpot theories. UNESCO has shortlisted them as part of the artistic patrimony of humanity.

Boario Terme, 12 kilometres north of Pisogne, has medicinal springs protected by a pretty Liberty-style cupola, set in a lavish garden at Terme di Boario (***t*** *0364 5391*). The first inhabitants, however, were into rocks: in the **Parco delle Luine** (***t*** *0348 737 4467; open Tues–Sun 9–12 and 1–5, until 6 in summer*), a kilometre and a half up from the spa, they scratched the oldest incisions yet discovered in the Valle Camonica (8000 BC) and others from the Bronze Age. Sadly, the rock has weathered here more than at other sites and the graffiti can be hard to decipher. A favourite excursion from Boario is up the Val di Scalve to a smaller spa, **Angolo Terme** (**t** *0364 54244*), near pretty little sapphire **Lago Moro**, then into the wild and narrow **Dezzo Ravine**.

Heading up the Valle Camonica, there's a brief but scenic detour east into the Vallata della Grigna, to see churches with some surprisingly good art: **Santa Maria Assunta** at **Ésine** (*open 9–5, summer until 6; ask priest for key,* **t** *0364 360 522*) is a national monument, with its trecento campanile and charming frescoes by the valley's Giovan Pietro Da Cemmo (1493), who also contributed to the 15th-century **Santa Maria Annunziata** in **Bienno** (*ring tourist office; open Mon–Fri 9–4.30, Sat and Sun until 6*).

Below Bienno, **Breno**, the Valle's modern capital, has an imposing 14th-century castle with a spooky dungeon (**t** *347 769 0133; open daily 2pm–2am mid-June–mid-Sept*) and the **Museo Civico Camuno** (*temporarily closed; call* **t** *0364 220 421*) with an ethnographic collection and paintings from the valley. **Sant'Antonio** (*open Mon pm, Tues and Sat; ask at nearby foodstore,* **t** *0364 22412*) has excellent frescoes (1535) by Romanino.

Four kilometres south of Breno, guarded by a stout medieval tower, **Cividate Camuno Archeologico** was the Romans' administrative centre in the valley; its small **Museo** (**t** *0364 344 301; open Tues–Sun 8.30–2*) has mosaics, tombstones and other finds.

Capo di Ponte and its National Park

In the centre of the Valle Camonica, near Capo di Ponte, are the most extensive and best-preserved prehistoric engravings: the tourist office (**t** *0364 42080*) has maps. The most notable and accessible are in the **Parco Nazionale delle Incisioni Rupestri Preistoriche** (**t** *0364 422 140; open Tues–Sun 8.30–4.30, until 7.30 in summer; adm*), where the enormous **Naquane rock** attracted artists from the Neolithic to Etruscan periods. More than 1,000 figures are etched into the rock: labyrinths, dogs, hunters and deer; enigmatic processions, armed warriors and horsemen; priests, a funeral; looms, carts, huts, even an Iron Age smithy. Certain symbols are repeated so often as to suggest a code: 'blades', slashes and four-petalled, dotted 'Camuna roses'.

Capo di Ponte's **Centro Studi Preistorici** has a small museum (**t** *0364 42091; open Mon–Fri 9–4*), with plans of Camuni sites among other explanatory items; just up beyond a car park, two great lumps of sandstone, the **Massi di Cemmo**, formed part of a much longer megalithic alignment, covered with engravings of deer, oxen, other animals and human figures from the 3rd millennium BC. A bit further up, **Archeodromo** (**t** *0364 42148; open daily Sept–June 8.30–12.30 and 1.30–5.30, July and Aug 1.30–6; adm*), the 'Centre of Experimental Archaeology', has a reconstruction of an Iron Age Camuni village; above is a path to the lovely 11th-century Romanesque **San Siro** (*open Mon and Fri 9–12 and 2.30–4.30, Sat 9–12; also Sun 9–12 in summer; key at Capo di Ponte Pro Loco*). Across the Oglio, the equally beautiful Cluniac church of **San Salvatore** (*open 9–11 and 3–5; ring keeper on* **t** *0364 42389, or call Capo di Ponte Pro Loco*) was built in the late 11th century in the Burgundian style; its monastic grounds are protected by walls.

A few kilometres south, another great concentration of engravings was found in 1975 in what is now the **Riserva Regionale Incisioni Rupestri Ceto-Cimbergo-Paspardo** (**t** *0364 433 465, open daily 9–12 and 2–5, until 6 in summer; adm*). The main entrance is in tiny **Nadro**, where from the small museum a path leads up to Foppe di Nadro, dotted with rocks etched from Neolithic to Etruscan times: scenes of solar worship, five-pointed stars, weapons, a village, footprints and what looks like a god by praying figures. The reserve also encompasses the rocks of Campanine, just under the ruined castle and village of **Cimbergo**, where Iron Age graffiti mingle with a Latin dedication to Jove and early Christian symbols, and Iron Age etchings in three sites in **Paspardo**.

Down on the main Valle Camonica road, below Ceto, is the crossroads for **Cerveno**, up in the hills to the west, where the Sacro Monte-style chapels of the **Santuario della Via Crucis-San Martino** (*t 0364 434 014; open daily Oct–May 8–12 and 2.30–5; June–Sept until 6*) have 198 life-size figures from the 18th century acting out the Passion of Christ.

Further up the Valle, the mountain scenery becomes grander as the Adamello Dolomites (11,733ft) loom to the right. Beautiful excursions into the range are possible from **Cedegolo**, into the lovely **Val di Saviore** with its mountain lakes. Further north, from **Malonno**, there's a scenic road through the chestnut woods of the **Valle Malga**, with more pretty lakes and easy ascents.

Surrounded by majestic mountains, **Edolo**, where the railway ends, is a busy market town at the crossroads of the Valle Camonica and the Valtellina (*see* p.273) and the Passo di Tonale. To the west are the ski stations of the **Valle di Corteno** and to the north that of **Ponte di Legno**, the most developed. From there a daring stretch of road engineering rises north through Stelvio National Park to Bormio (*see* p.277); the main road continues to the **Passo del Tonale**, with more skiing. From the Passo di Tonale the road goes east into Trentino's lovely Val di Sole.

Brescia

Lombardy's second city, Brescia is a busy and prosperous place with some of the best-preserved Roman and Lombard relics in northern Italy. This is no one's favourite town, though – perhaps it's the vaguely sinister aura of having been Italy's chief arms manufacturer for the last 400 years, or perhaps it's because local Fascists punched out the heart of the old city and replace it with a piazza frosty and heavy as an iceberg.

History

Brescia was founded by the Gauls – the name *Brixia* came from the Celtic *brik* (hill). A willing ally of Rome from early on, it achieved the favoured status of a *Colonia Civica Augusta* in 26 BC, when it was embellished with splendid monuments. By the 8th century, Brescia had recovered enough from the barbarian invasions to become the seat of a Lombard duchy under King Desiderius, whose daughter Ermengarda was wed by Charlemagne – the condition imposed by the Italians before they crowned him emperor. He later repudiated her, and she returned to Brescia to die in the abbey of San Salvatore. When Brescia joined the Lombard League against Frederick Barbarossa, its opposition had a voice: that of a Benedictine monk, Arnold of Brescia, who studied under Peter Abelard in Paris and went to Rome, preaching eloquently against the tyranny of the emperor and the materialism of the Church. In 1155, Barbarossa, with Adrian IV, arrested the troublesome monk and handed him over to the pope, who burned Arnold alive at the stake in front of Castel Sant'Angelo.

Getting There and Around

Brescia is easily reached from 3 **airports**: Verona's Catullo, Bergamo's Orio al Serio and Montichiari's Gabriele D'Annunzio, halfway between Brescia and Lake Garda.

Brescia is on the main Milan–Venice **rail** line, (55mins from Milan, 1hr from Verona), and has links to Desenzano del Garda, the main Lake Garda station. There are also frequent services to Bergamo (1hr), Lecco (2hrs), Cremona (just over 1hr), and Parma via Piadena (2hrs). For FS rail info, call **t** 892921. The local FNME line, **t** 02 20222, winds north along Lake Iseo's east shore and up the Valle Camonica to Edolo (2½hrs).

The extensive **bus** network has frequent links to the towns of lakes Garda and Iseo, and less frequent services to Idro. There are also buses to Turin and Milan, Padua and the Euganean Hills, Marostica, Bassano del Grappa and Belluno; Trento via Riva and the resorts of Pinzolo and Madonna di Campiglio in Trentino, as well as to all points within the province.

The rail station and SIA bus station serving the Brescia province, **t** 030 377 4237, are next to each other just south of the centre on Viale Stazione. Just around the corner, at Via Solferino 6, is the station where buses serving all other destinations, including Garda and Cremona, depart, **t** 030 34915.

Bus C connects the stations to the city centre, or it's a 10min walk up the Corso Martiri della Libertà.

Tourist Information

Regional Tourist Office: Piazza della Loggia 6, Monte di Pietà Nuova, Brescia, **t** 030 297 8988. *Open Apr–Sept Mon–Sat 9.30–6.30; Oct–Mar Mon–Fri 9.30–12.30 and 2.30–5, Sat 9.30–12.30.*

APT Brescia: Corso Zanardelli 34, **t** 030 43418 or **t** 030 45052, *www.bresciaholiday.com*.

Where to Stay

Brescia caters mainly to business clients, and its best hotels are comfortable if uninspiring.

*****__Vittoria__, Via X Giornate 20, **t** 030 280 061, *www.hotelvittoria.com* (*very expensive*). A rather soulless, Fascist-era building with large, sumptuous rooms, palatial bathrooms and marble and chandeliers throughout.

****__Ambasciatori__, Via Crocifissa di Rosa 92, **t** 030 399 114, *www.ambasciatori.net* (*moderate–expensive*). A modern, welcoming, family-run option just outside the centre, with a garage and air-conditioned rooms.

***__Master__, Via L. Apollonio 72, **t** 030 399 037, *www.hotelmaster.net* (*moderate–expensive*). A central, family-run choice with parking, a pleeant gazebo in the garden, a restaurant (*cheap*) and simple, spacious rooms.

***__Antica Villa__, Via San Rocchino 90, **t** 030 303 186 (*cheap–moderate*). A hospitable place in a secluded 18th-century villa at the

Brescia itself was too tempting to be left in peace. Firmly in the Guelph camp, for the freedom of cities against imperial pretensions, it held tight when Frederick II besieged it for 68 days, then suffered under his lieutenant, Ezzelino da Romano, in 1258; in 1421, when the detested Visconti horned in, the weary Brescians asked Venice to adopt them. Venice brought peace and prosperity, and also initiated an artistic flowering. The Brescian Vincenzo Foppa (1485–1566) was a key figure in the Lombard Renaissance, while Alessandro Bonvincino (who was better known as 'the little Moor' or *Moretto*; 1498–1554), an ardent student of Titian, contributed the first Italian full-length portrait and taught Giovanni Battista Moroni of Bergamo. His contemporary Giovanni Girolamo Savoldo, a Brescian who later worked in Venice, was neglected in his lifetime but is now recognized for his lyricism, especially in his use of light. Recently, Giacomo Antonio Ceruti (1698–1767) has been the centre of interest for his realist, un-romanticized genre paintings of Brescia's humble, demented and down-and-out – a unique subject for the time. His nickname was *Il Pitocchetto* ('the little skinflint').

foot of the Ronchi hills, with soundproofed and air-conditioned rooms and a car park.

★★★**Astron**, Via Togni 14, **t** 030 48220 (*cheap–moderate*). Clean, simple rooms overlooking the station.

★★**Trento**, Piazzale Cesare Battisti 31, **t** 030 380 768 (*cheap–moderate*). Rooms with all mod cons within walking distance of the centre, plus a good-value restaurant.

Eating Out

Kid, stews, *risotti*, skewered meats and polenta have favoured here since the Renaissance. A typical dish is *casonséi* – huge ravioli filled with eggs, hard cheese or ricotta, spinach or meat, served with sage and melted butter.

Castello Malvezzi, Via Colle San Giuseppe 1, **t** 030 200 4224 (*very expensive*). A lovely medieval place just north of the centre, with delicious French and Italian food. *Closed Mon, Tues, 2wks Jan and 2wks Aug.*

I Templari, Via Matteotti 19, **t** 030 375 2234 (*very expensive*). Seafood with a Tuscan touch. *Closed Sat lunch, Sun and Aug.*

La Sosta, Via San Martino della Battaglia 20, **t** 030 295 603 (*very expensive*). An elegant 17th-century stable with first-class fish and Italian classics. *Closed Mon, Sun eve, and Aug.*

L'Artigliere, Via Forcella 6, Gussago, 5km west of town, **t** 030 277 0373 (*expensive*). Gourmet local cuisine in an old country *osteria*.

Vasco da Gama, Via dei Musei 42, **t** 030 375 4039 (*expensive*). Dishes such as octopus with zucchini and cream, and Andalucían soup with crayfish tails.

Locanda dei Guasconi, Via Beccaria 11/G, **t** 030 377 1605 (*moderate–expensive*). A trendy setting for traditional dishes and more unusual fare. Book for dinner. *Closed Mon.*

Duomo Vecchio, Via Trieste 3, **t** 030 40088 (*moderate*). Excellent southern Italian dishes. *Closed Sun.*

Al Granaio, Piazzale Arnaldo, **t** 030 375 9345 (*moderate*). A popular late-opening meeting place specializing in meat. *Closed Mon.*

La Vineria, Via X Giornate 4, **t** 030 280 477 (*moderate*). Excellent cured meats and salami, herby risotto, *casoncelli* and home-made tarts. *Closed Tues and Aug.*

Bersagliera, Corso Magenta 38, **t** 030 375 0569 (*cheap*). A good, popular pizzeria. *Closed Mon.*

Due Stelle, Via San Faustino 48, **t** 030 42370 (*cheap*). One of Brescia's oldest *osterie*, with an inner courtyard for summer dining. Local tripe, *casoncelli* and old peasant dishes are revisited, including chicken and bread dumplings in broth. *Closed Mon, and Tues and Weds lunch.*

Osteria Al Bianchi, Via Gasparo da Salo' 32, **t** 030 292 320 (*cheap*). A noisy, typical *osteria* with hearty local fare. *Closed Tues eve, and Weds.*

Osteria dell'Elfo, Piazza Vescovato 1/B, **t** 030 377 4858. A popular late-opening place for an *aperitivo* and snack. *Closed Mon.*

The Central Squares

The closed, Venetian-style **Piazza della Loggia** was named for the **Palazzo della Loggia**, Brescia's town hall, a neo-Roman confection begun in 1492 and designed in part by Venice's top architects, Sansovino and Palladio; its public areas can be visited during office hours. Opposite, the **Torre dell'Orologio** (*under restoration*) is a copy of the clock tower in St Mark's Square, complete with two bell-ringing figures on top. The other chief buildings on the square are the old and new municipal pawn shops, **Monte di Pietà Vecchia** (1489) and **Monte di Pietà Nuova** (1590s); the Roman inscriptions embedded in the façade of the former constitute Italy's very first lapidary collection.

Behind the clock tower rises the third-highest dome in Italy, that of the **Duomo**, built in 1602 by Gianbattista Lantana (*open Mon–Sat 7.30–12 and 4–7*). The adjacent **Duomo Vecchio** or La Rotonda (*open Apr–Oct Tues–Sun 9–12 and 3–7*), a singular old cathedral built in the 11th century over the ruins of the Basilica of San Filastrio and ancient Roman baths, is the only one in Italy in the shape of a top hat. Its altarpiece, an Assumption by Moretto, is one his greatest works.

Roman and Lombard Brixia

The ancient *Decumanus Maximus*, now **Via dei Musei**, leads to the heart of Roman Brixia. Its forum, now narrow **Piazza del Foro**, lies under the mighty columns of the **Capitolium temple**, erected by the Emperor Vespasian in AD 73 and preserved by a medieval mud-slide. In 1955, a Republican-era Capitoline temple was found beneath Vespasian's, with unusual mosaics of natural stone. The temple is divided into three *cellae* containing the lapidarium, tablets, altars and architectural fragments. Next to the temple is the unexcavated *cavea* of the **Roman theatre**, while down Via Carlo Cattaneo, in Piazza Labus, are the columns and lintels of the third building of the forum: the **Curia**, or senate, imprinted like a fossil in a house wall.

From Piazza del Foro, Via dei Musei continues to the **Monastero San Salvatore-Santa Giulia**, founded in the 700s by the wife of Lombard king Desiderius and now the **Museo della Città** (*call **t** 030 277 7833 for open hours*). At the entrance are the remains of a large Roman *domus*, with original mosaics and frescoes. The museum documents Brescian history from the prehistoric period to the Venetian age, with more than 11,000 finds. The heart of the complex, the 8th-century **Basilica of San Salvatore**, was modelled on the 6th-century churches of Ravenna. In the nave, the capitals are either ancient Roman or made of stucco, an art at which Lombards excelled.

The **Civico Museo Romano** (*closed for refurbishment; call **t** 030 46031*) has a large collection of Roman remains, including six gilded bronze busts of emperors found in the temple. Contents of the other sections of the museum include the 8th-century golden Lombard Cross of Desiderius, with 212 gems and cameos, and a 4th-century ivory coffer, the *Lipsanoteca*, adorned with beautiful bas-reliefs of scriptural scenes.

The Cydnean Hill

Poet Catullus, who considered Brixia the mother of his native Verona, was the first to mention the hill that rises behind the Via dei Musei. Named after Ligurian king Cidno, legendary founder of Brixia, the site has been inhabited since the Bronze Age and was the core of Gaulish and early Roman Brixia – on Via Piamarta are the ruins of the city's last surviving **Roman gate**. Up on top is the **Castello** with its round 14th-century Mirabella tower on a Roman foundation. Built in 1443, in the brief reign of the Visconti, it houses the **Museo Civico delle Armi Antiche Luigi Marzoli** (*open Tues–Sun June–Sept 10–5; Oct–May 9.30–1 and 2.30–5; adm*), with a special collection of 15th–18th-century firearms. The Venetian granary houses the **Museo del Risorgimento** (*same hours*) with paintings, uniforms, decrees and weapons.

The Pinacoteca and Around

The **Pinacoteca Civica Tosio-Martinengo** (***t** 030 377 4999; open June–Sept Tues–Sun 10–5; Oct–May 9.30–1 and 2.30–5; adm*), which is housed in a 16th-century patrician palace on Piazza Moretto, showcases Brescia's talent, including works by Foppa, Savoldo, Moretto, Romanino, Moroni and Ceruti; there's also a lovely Adoration of the Magi by Lorenzo Lotto, a portrait of Henri III by Clouet and two early works by Raphael. The Pinacoteca also houses paintings to be exhibited in the Galleria d'Arte Moderna e Contemporanea.

South on Via Crispi, there's more art in little 16th-century **Santa Angela Merici**, by Tintoretto and Francesco Bassano (*open Mon–Sat 7.30–9.30, Sun 3–5.30*), and at Via Monti 9, in the Istituto Paolo VI's **Museo Arte e Spiritualità** (*open Sat and Sun 4–7, other days by appointment; call* **t** *030 375 3002*), devoted to contemporary religious art. **Sant'Alessandro** on Via Moretto (*open Mon–Sun 6.30–11*) has a pretty Annunciation by Jacopo Bellini; further north, in elegant, porticoed Corso Zanardelli, the **Teatro Grande** (**t** *030 297 9311*) is one of the most lavish theatres in Lombardy.

West Side Churches

Just west of Via S. Faustino are the unusual **San Faustino e Giovita** (*open Mon–Weds, Fri and Sat 7.30–11 and 3–7, Thurs 7.30–10, Sun 7.30–12 and 3.30–7*), a cylindrical, steep-roofed drum of a 12th-century church, and, on Contrada Carmine, the 15th-century **Santa Maria del Carmine** (*closed at the time of writing, call* **t** *030 40807*), crowned with a set of Mongol-like brick pinnacles; it contains frescoes by Foppa, among his finest work, and a 15th-century terracotta Deposition by Mazzoni. Just off Corso G. Mameli, Renaissance **San Giovanni Evangelista** (*open daily 7–11 and 4–6.30*) has good works by Moretto, Romanino and Bolognese painter Francia. Via della Pace heads south to the 1265 **San Francesco** (*open daily 7–11.30 and 3–5; cloister open Mon–Sat 8–12 and 2.30–6.30*) with its cloister in red Verona marble and frescoes, and nearby **Santa Maria dei Miracoli** (*open daily 6–8, 10–12 and 3–6*) with a 15th-century Lombard Renaissance marble façade. Further south, on Corso Matteotti, the 18th-century **Santi Nazzaro e Celso** (*open during Mass, Sat 6pm and Sun 9, 10, 11 and 6; or call* **t** *030 375 4387*) houses the Averoldi polyptych (1522), considered the masterpiece of Titian's youth.

Around Brescia

North of Brescia, the **Val Trompia** is named for an ancient Ligurian tribe, the Triumplini. The lower valley is known for its guns: the handguns produced in **Gardone Val Trompia** since the 1500s were so valuable the town enjoyed the protection of Venice. North of here are the popular resorts of **Bovegno** and **Collio**. Beyond Collio a road goes up to the scenic **Passo del Maniva** (5,453ft) and over to the Passo di Croce Dóminii.

In the next valley east, the Val Sabbia, the Chiese forms a fjord in the mountains, **Lake Idro**. A scattered collection of hamlets form **Idro**, at the south tip of the lake; one, Castel Antinco, has the ruins of a 1st-century BC village. **Anfo**, on the west bank, has a 15th-century castle built by the Venetians, where Garibaldi briefly had his HQ in 1866.

Lake Garda

The Italian lakes culminate in Garda, the largest and most dramatic, its 'Madonna blue' waters, as Churchill described them, lapping the feet of the Dolomites. Its shores recall two of Italy's greatest poets of pure passion: ancient, lovelorn Catullus, and that 20th-century Italian fire hazard, Gabriele D'Annunzio. Venice's 'little sea', Garda has a genuine Mediterranean climate – open to the south and blocked off from the cold winds of the north by the Dolomites, its great volume make it a giant solar battery,

Lake Garda
Arco
Varone
Riva del Garda
Bezzecca
Condino
Molina di Ledro
Lake Ledro
Valli Giudicarie
Val di Ledro
Torbole
Passo de Maniva
Lodrone
Bagolino
Limone sul Garda
Lake Idro
Tremosine
Malcésine
Anfo
Campione
Tignale
Idro
Lavenone
Assenza
Brenzone
Gargnano
Lake Garda
Bogliaco
Sabbio
Vobarno
Toscolano-Maderno
Pai
A22
Gardone Riviera
S. Zeno
Salò
Torri del Benaco
Caprino
Is. di Garda
Gavardo
S.Felice del Benaco
Costermano
Garda
Affi
Polpenazze
Manerba
Bardolino
Cavernago
Moniga
Cisano
Padenghe
Lazise
Sirmione
Desenzano del Garda
Lonato
Colombare
A4
Rivoltella
Pacengo
Peschiera del Garda
S. Martino d. Battaglia
N
Castiglione d. Stiviere
5 km
2.5 miles
Solferino
Carpenedolo
Sigurta Gardens
Valeggio sul Mincio

Getting Around

There are 2 **railway** stations, freephone **t** 848 888 088, at the southern end of Lake Garda, at Desenzano and Peschiera, both landings for the lake's **hydrofoils** (*aliscafi*) and **steamers**.

Buses from Brescia, Trento and Verona go to their respective shores; Desenzano, gateway to Lake Garda, is served by buses from Brescia, Verona and Mantua. Frequent buses connect Sirmione to Desenzano and Peschiera. Other local bus lines run along the road around the lake shores, *La Gardesana*, Occidentale (SS45) on the west and Orientale (SS249) on the east.

Boat services are run by Navigazione sul Lago di Garda, Piazza Matteotti 2, Desenzano, freephone **t** 800 55180, where you can pick up a timetable. There are 2 **car ferries**, from Maderno to Torri, and Limone to Malcésine; between Desenzano and Riva there are several hydrofoils a day, calling at various ports (2hrs full trip), and more frequent steamers (4½hrs). Services are much reduced Nov–Mar.

Tourist Information

www.rivadelgarda.com has a hotel search and list of local websites. Other good sites are *www.gardalake.it*, *www.hotels promotion.com*, *www.gardainforma.com*, *www.lagodigarda.it* and *www.bresciaholiday.com*.

Desenzano del Garda: Via del Porto Vecchio 34, **t** 030 914 1510, *www.desenzano.net*

Sirmione: Viale Marconi 2, **t** 030 916 114, *www.sirmione.net*

Salò: Lungolago Zanardelli 39, **t** 0365 21423.

Gardone Riviera: Corso Repubblica 35, **t** 0365 20347.

Gargnano: Piazza Feltrinelli 2, **t** 0365 71222, *www.prolocogargnano.it* (*open Mon 9–12 and 3.30–6.30, Weds–Sat 9–12*).

Limone sul Garda: Via Comboni 15, **t** 0365 954 070; there is also a seasonal tourist office at Piazzale A. De Gasperi, **t** 0365 954 265.

Where to Stay and Eat

In high season many hotels require you to send a deposit or have your credit card debited to confirm the reservation.

Desenzano del Garda ✉ 25015

★★★★**Piccola Vela**, Via T. dal Molin 36, **t** 030 991 4666, *www.gardalake.it/piccolovela* (*expensive*). A hotel a short walk from the town pier, with an olive grove, pool, lake views. and flats suitable for families.

★★★**Tripoli**, Piazza Matteotti 18, **t** 030 914 1305, *www.hotel-tripoli.it* (*moderate–expensive*). A small, well-equipped lakefront hotel.

★★★**Hotel Piroscafo**, Via Porto Vecchio 11, **t** 030 914 1128, *www.hotelpiroscafo.it* (*moderate*). A family-run hotel in the centre of town. Rooms are simple, but have air-con; some have balconies overlooking the old quay.

★★★**Mayer e Splendid**, Via U. Papa 10, **t** 030 914 2253, *www.hotelmayersplendid.it* (*cheap*). A good bargain by the quay, with some en suite rooms and parking. *Closed Dec–Feb.*

Cavallino, Via Gherla 30, **t** 030 912 0217 (*very expensive*). Imaginative seasonal fare based on lake fish, duck, pigeon and offal. Booking advised. *Closed Mon and Tues lunch.*

Bagatta alla Lepre, Via Bagatta 33, **t** 030 914 2313 (*very expensive*). Creative Mediterranean cuisine. *Closed Weds lunch and 3wks Jan.*

Caffè Italia, Piazza Malvezzi 19, **t** 030 914 1243 (*expensive*). A wine bar and restaurant with a good choice of hot and cold dishes, ideal for breakfast, brunch and late-night snacks. *Closed Mon, Jan and Feb.*

Trattoria Bicocca, Vic. Molini 6, **t** 030 914 3658 (*moderate*). A picturesque trattoria offering a wide variety of lake fish with fresh herbs. *Closed Thurs, 1wk at Christmas.*

Sirmione ✉ 25019

★★★★★**Villa Cortine**, Via C.V. Catullo, **t** 030 990 5890, *www.hotelvillacortine.com* (*luxury*). A romantic, tranquil neoclassical villa in a

heating the surrounding hills in winter and keeping deadly frosts and clammy mists at bay. For Goethe and generations of chilblained travellers from Middle Europe, its olives, vines, citrus groves and palm trees have long signalled the beginning of their dream Italy. No tourist office could concoct a more scintillating oasis to stimulate what Icelanders call 'a longing for figs', that urge to go south.

century-old garden occupying almost a third of the peninsula, with fountains running to the water's edge, a private beach and dock, a pool and a tennis court. Half board is compulsory in high season. *Closed Jan and Feb.*

*****__Grand Hotel Terme__, Viale Marconi 7, **t** 030 916 261, *www.terme disirmione.com* (*expensive–luxury*). A top hotel with a private beach, a pool, a gym and a lovely lakeside restaurant. *Closed Jan and Feb.*

***__Catullo__, Piazza Flaminia 7, **t** 030 990 5811, *www.hotelcatullo.sirmione.de* (*expensive*). Good-sized rooms in the old town, with beautiful views. *Closed early-Nov–end Mar.*

***__Corte Regina__, Via Antiche Mura 11, **t** 030 916 147 (*moderate*). A central option with all modern amenities and family rooms.

__Grifone__, Via Bocchio 4, **t 030 916 014 (*cheap*). A well-located budget choice overlooking the Rocca Scaligera. *Closed Nov–Feb.*

La Rucola, Via Strentelle 7, **t** 030 916 326 (*very expensive*). An intimate place near the Scaliger castle, with seasonal gourmet fish and meat specialities in which aromatic herbs and fruit flavours are combined with traditional Mediterranean cuisine. Reserve in advance. *Closed Thurs, Fri lunch and Jan.*

Vecchia Lugana, Piazzale Vecchia Lugana 1, **t** 030 919 012 (*very expensive*). One of Garda's finest restaurants, near the base of the peninsula, with a wonderful menu based on lake fish. *Closed Mon eve, Tues, Jan and Feb.*

Osteria al Torcol, Via San Salvatore 30, **t** 030 990 4605 (*moderate*). A late-opening place for cold or hot snacks or meals and great wines and oils to taste. *Closed Weds and lunchtimes.*

Al Progresso, Via Vittorio Emanuele 16, **t** 030 916 108 (*cheap–moderate*). A central choice with a family atmosphere and homely dishes. *Closed Thurs, Dec and Jan.*

Salò ✉ 25087

****__Laurin__, Viale Landi 9, **t** 0365 22022, *www.laurinsalo.com* (*expensive–luxury*). A lovely Liberty-style villa with period décor in the public rooms. The charming grounds include a swimming pool and beach access. The stylish gourmet restaurant has frescoes and Art Nouveau windows. *Closed Dec–Feb.*

****__Duomo__, Lungolago Zanardelli 63, **t** 0365 21026, *www.hotelduomosalo.it* (*expensive–very expensive*). Large modern rooms (those situated on the first floor lead out to a huge geranium-laden balcony overlooking the lake), a fine restaurant, a sauna, a solarium and a fitness hall.

***__Vigna__, Lungolago Zanardelli 62, **t** 0365 520 144, *www.hotelvigna.it* (*moderate–expensive*). Comfortable modern rooms, with scene-stealing views.

Il Bagnolo, Bagnolo di Serniga, in hills between Salò and Gardone di Riviera, **t** 0365 20290, *www.gardalake.it/ilbagnolo* (*moderate*). An 18th-century *cascina* and newer farmhouse convenient for trekking, with a restaurant using milk and meat produced in house, and local wine, oil and cheeses. *Closed weekday Nov–Mar. Restaurant closed Tues.*

__Lepanto__, Lungolago Zanardelli 67, **t 0365 20428 (*cheap*). Eight rooms overlooking the lake, plus a restaurant (*moderate*) with a garden terrace. Booking advised. *Restaurant closed Thurs. Hotel closed Feb.*

Il Melograno, Via del Panorama 5, Campoverde, south of town, **t** 0365 520 421 (*expensive*). A hidden jewel specializing in home-made foie gras dishes – try *scaloppa* filled with foie gras – as well as risottos and lake fish soups. *Closed Mon eve, Tues and Nov.*

Osteria dell'Orologio, Via Butturini 26, **t** 0365 290 158 (*moderate*). A beautifully restored old inn offering dishes such as polenta and gorgonzola, lake fish and skewered wild birds. Book ahead and be prepared to wait to be served. *Closed Weds.*

Cantina Santa Giustina, Salita S. Giustina 8, **t** 0365 520 320 (*cheap*). Cold snacks of cheeses and local *affettati*, salted *coregone* and grilled vegetables, and an excellent selection of local wines. *Closed Mon and lunchtimes.*

Perhaps it's because Lake Garda seems more 'Italian' that it has traditionally been less stuffy and status-conscious than its sister lakes. It attracts more families (thanks to Gardaland), partygoers (at Desenzano), beach bums (the water's very clean) and older package tourists (especially Germans and Austrians). Sailors and windsurfers come to test their mettle on the winds, first mentioned by Virgil: the *sover* that blows

Gardone Riviera ✉ 25083

★★★**Villa Fiordaliso**, Corso Zanardelli 132, **t** 0365 20158, *www.villafiordaliso.it* (*very expensive–luxury*). A Liberty-style palace in luxuriant gardens on the lake, with 7 fine rooms plus the suite in which Mussolini and his mistress spent their last few weeks. There's a private beach and pier, and the best restaurant in Gardone, with classic Lombard dishes. *Hotel closed Dec–Jan. Restaurant mid-Nov–mid-Feb.*

★★★★**Grand Hotel**, Corso Zanardelli 84, **t** 0365 20261, *www.grangardone.it* (*expensive–luxury*). One of the largest resort hotels in Europe when built in 1881 and still a landmark, with countless chandeliers glittering as brightly as when Churchill stayed here in the 1940s. Almost all the palatial rooms look on to the lake; guests can luxuriate on the garden terraces or swim in the heated outdoor pool or off the private beach. *Closed Nov–Feb.*

★★★**Bellevue**, Corso Zanardelli 81, **t** 0365 20235, *www.hotelbellevuegardone.com* (*moderate*). A hotel on the main road overlooking the lake, with a garden sheltering it from the traffic and a pool. The modernized rooms have private bathrooms. *Closed Nov–Mar.*

★★★**Monte Baldo**, Via Zanardelli 110, **t** 0365 20951, *www.hotelmontebaldo.it* (*cheap–moderate*). A lakeside hotel with a stylish modern interior, a garden, a pool, and a terrace for breakfast, meals, snacks and drinks. The slightly more expensive annexe has atmospheric rooms with lake views. Half or full-board are compulsory at Easter and mid-July–mid-Sept. *Open Mar–Oct.*

Ristorante Casinò, Corso Zanardelli 42, **t** 0365 20387 (*expensive*). A restaurant with old-style atmosphere and service, offering lake and sea fish and meat dishes right on the lake. *Closed Mon, Jan and Feb.*

Locanda Agli Angeli, Piazza Garibaldi 2, Gardone Sopra, **t** 0365 20832 (*moderate*). A very good family-run place where you can eat the likes of home-smoked *magatello di manzo* (beef) with local capers. Booking advised. There are also 9 comfy rooms (*moderate*), some with air-con. *Restaurant closed Mon. Locanda closed 16 Nov–Feb except Christmas and New Year.*

Gargnano ✉ 25084

★★★**Baia d'Oro**, Via Gamberera 13, Villa, just outside town, **t** 0365 71171, *www.hotelbaiadoro.it* (*expensive*). A small but charming old place on the lake front, with a private beach and picturesque terrace. *Closed Nov–mid-Mar.*

★★★**Du Lac**, Via Colletta 21, Villa, **t** 0365 71107, *www.hotel-dulac.it* (*moderate*). A salmon-tinted charmer on the water. All rooms have baths and satellite TV and are furnished with antiques. *Open Mar–Jan.*

La Tortuga, Via XXIV Maggio 5, **t** 0365 71251 (*very expensive*). A celebrated gourmet restaurant with just 7 tables near the port, specializing in delicate dishes based on lake fish and seasonal ingredients. Book ahead. *Closed Mon eve, Tues in winter, and mid Jan–Feb.*

Lo Scoglio, Via Barbacane 3, Bogliaco di Gargnano, **t** 0365 71030 (*moderate*). A highly recommended restaurant offering all kinds of lake fish, home-made pasta and cakes. *Closed Fri, Jan and Feb.*

Osteria del Restauro, main square, **t** 0365 72643 (*cheap*). Good hot and cold dishes at a place overlooking the small harbour. *Closed Weds.*

Limone ✉ 25010

★★★★**Le Palme**, Via Porto 36, **t** 0365 954 681, *www.sunhotels.it* (*moderate–expensive*). A pretty Venetian villa in the historic centre, preserving much of its original charm alongside modern amenities. It has a good fish restaurant. *Closed Nov–Feb.*

★★★**Hotel Coste**, Via Tamas 11, 10mins from centre, **t** 0365 954 042, *www.hotelcoste.com* (*moderate*). A hotel in an olive grove, with a pool, *boules* area and playground. There's a minimum 3-night stay. *Closed Dec–Mar.*

★★★**La Limonaia**, Via Sopino Alto 3, **t** 0365 954 221, *www.chincherini.com*

from the north from midnight and through the morning, and the *ora* that puffs from the south in the afternoon and evening. White caps and storms are not uncommon, but the breezes are delightfully cool in summer. Though services drop to a minimum, winter is a good time to visit, when the jagged peaks shimmer with snow and you can better take in the voluptuous charms that brought visitors here in the first place.

(*cheap–moderate*). A superbly sited hotel above the centre, with adult and children's pools and a playground. *Closed Nov–Feb.*

****Mercedes**, Via Nanzello 12, **t** 0365 954 073, *www.mercedeshotel.com* (*cheap*). A lovely little hotel in a prime location, with great views and friendly owners. *Closed Nov–Feb.*

Tovo, Via Tamas, **t** 0365 954 064 (*moderate*). A pretty restaurant high above Limone and the Gardesana road, with a terrace overlooking the lake, serving great pizzas and local dishes.

Riva del Garda ✉ 38066

Ask the tourist office for a list of cheap rooms to rent in private houses.

******Hotel du Lac et du Parc**, Viale Rovereto 44, **t** 0464 551 500, *www.hoteldulac-riva.it* (*very expensive–luxury*). A modernized, spacious, tranquil hotel in a large lakeside garden – German intellectuals from Nietzsche to Günter Grass have flocked here to chill out. Facilities include indoor and outdoor pools, a beach, a sailing school, a gym, a sauna and tennis courts. *Closed Nov–Mar.*

******Grand Hotel Liberty**, Viale Carducci 3/5, **t** 0464 551 144, *www.grandhotelliberty.it* (*very expensive*). A Liberty-style villa in its own grounds, with a pool and whirlpool baths.

******Grand Hotel Riva**, Piazza Garibaldi 10, **t** 0464 521 800, *www.gardaresort.it* (*expensive*). A turn-of-the-19th-century hotel with a majestic position on the main square, with 87 modern rooms looking out over the lake. The rooftop restaurant combines fine food with incomparable views. *Closed Nov–Feb.*

******Sole**, Piazza III Novembre 35, **t** 0464 552 686, *www.hotelsole.net* (*expensive*). A hotel right on the port in Riva's main square, with a lovely terrace. All rooms have baths. Some of the interior character has been lost, but it's an atmospheric building from outside.

*****Centrale**, Piazza III Novembre 27, **t** 0464 552 344 (*moderate*). Fully equipped and spacious rooms and bathrooms right beside the harbour.

*****Portici**, Piazza III Novembre 19, **t** 0464 555 400 (*moderate*). A pleasant refurbished option offering modern rooms, all of them complete with en suite bathrooms. *Closed Dec–Mar.*

***Restel de Fer**, Via Restel de Fer 10, **t** 0464 553 481, *www.restel-de-fer.de* (*moderate*). An atmospheric hotel built in 1400, with just 5 rooms and a good restaurant. In summer you can dine in the former cloister.

***Villa Moretti**, Via Mazzano 7, Varone, 3km from town, **t** 0464 521 127, *www.rivadelgarda.com/villamoretti* (*cheap*). A family-run hotel offering peace and quiet in a panoramic spot, plus a garden and pool.

Ostello Benacus, Piazza Cavour 10, **t** 0464 554 911, *www.ostelloriva.com* (*cheap*). Riva's youth hostel. Cheap meals are available, and you can also get packed lunches made up for you. *Closed Nov–Feb.*

Villa Negri ai Germandri, Via Bastione 31/35, **t** 0464 555 061 (*very expensive*). The historic villa of architect Maroni (of D'Annunzio's Vittoriale), just below the castle overlooking the lake and town centre (there's a shuttle service in golf carts from Riva's car park). It's an exclusive place, with silver cutlery and silk tablecloths, napkins and wall covers, and two circular terraces perched over the lake. There's a 9-dish daily 'itinerary' of creatively revisited local cuisine. At the back, the less formal, cheaper terrace bistro has an outdoor grill; Mozart evenings are held Fri nights in summer. The cellar is a former First World War shelter excavated in the rocks, with more than 1800 labels. *Closed Tues, Nov and lunchtimes. Open eves only.*

Al Volt, Via Fiume 73, **t** 0464 552 570 (*very expensive*). A restaurant located in a 17th-century palace, where you can feast on specialities such as onion soup, *salmerino* (stream fish), and pork fillet with a gorgonzola sauce. There's a 5-course *menu degustazione* that changes twice a week. *Closed mid-Feb–mid-Mar.*

The South Shore: Desenzano and Solferino

Lively and colourful, **Desenzano del Garda**, on a wide gulf dotted with beaches, is Garda's largest town. Life centres around its portside cafés; the lakefront **High Speed monument** celebrates an air speed record set here in 1934 by Francesco Agello. On the other end of the technological scale, Desenzano's Bronze Age inhabitants lived in pile dwellings, recently discovered in peat bogs southwest of town and yielding the contents of the **Museo Archeologico Rambotti** in the cloister of Santa Maria de Senioribus at Via Anelli 7 (***t** 030 314 4529; open Tues, Fri, Sat, Sun and hols 3–7*).

Desenzano was on the Bergamo–Verona Via Gallica, and towards the end of the empire, the rich and powerful retreated from the anarchy to their country estates – the origins of feudalism. One of the most important was Desenzano's **Villa Romana** at Via Crocifisso 22 (***t** 030 914 3547; open Mar–mid-Oct Tues–Fri 8.30–7.30, Sat and Sun 9–5.30; mid-Oct–Feb Tues–Fri 8.30–4.30, Sat and Sun 9–4.30; park closes 5; adm*). Begun in the 1st century BC, it was fitted in the 4th century with heated baths, a *triclinium* (dining hall) with three apses, and the most extensive mosaic floors in northern Italy.

Desenzano is also a base for visiting the low, war-scarred hills to the south, where, on 24 June 1859, the Italians and their French allies pounded the Austrian occupier twice, when King Vittorio Emanuele II and his Sardinian army crushed the Austrian right wing at **San Martino della Battaglia**, while Napoleon III defeated Emperor Franz Joseph at **Solferino**, 11 kilometres southwest. The first (*Via Ossario; **t** 030 331 0370; open daily; adm*) commemorates the victory in a monumental complex. In an **ossuary** in a 13th-century chapel are the bones of 2,619 dead from both sides, while, at the highest point of the hill, the round 213ft **Torre Monumentale** has rooms with frescoes and statues on the events and heroes of the Risorgimento. Behind it is a **museum** containing photos, weapons, letters and other mementoes from the campaign.

Solferino saw the single bloodiest battle of the war; the **Cappella Ossuaria** (*open daily; adm*) has the remains of 7,000 mostly French and Austrian troops. The **museum** (*open daily; adm*) traces the history of Italy from 1796 to 1870, and contains weapons, arms and documents from the battle: there's other memorabilia in Solferino's mighty tower, the **Spia d'Italia** '(Italy's Spy'), built in 1022 by the Scaligers of Verona and restored in the 17th century. Nearby is a simple **Memorial to the Red Cross**, erected in 1959 to commemorate the centenary of the battle and Henry Dunant's founding of what was first known as the Committee to Aid the Wounded in War. You can learn more about it in the **Museo della Croce Rossa** in **Castiglione delle Stiviere** (***t** 0376 638 505; open Tues–Sun Apr–Oct 9–12 and 3–7; Nov–Mar 9–12 and 2–5; donation required*).

Sirmione

Few towns enjoy the dramatic position of Sirmione, strung out along the narrow peninsula that pierces Lake Garda's broad bottom like a pin. Lake views and palms, cypresses and parasol pines keep it medieval core from feeling claustrophic, even in summer, but for fewer day-trippers and more of the atmosphere that inspired Catullus, Dante, Goethe, Byron, and later Pound and Joyce, come before June or after September.

Large car parks signal the entrance into the historic centre; only residents and hotel guests can drive over the bridge of the fairy-tale castle, the **Rocca Scaligera** (*open Tues–Sun Nov–Mar 8.30–4.30, Apr–Oct 9–7; adm*), built by Mastino I della Scala, *signore* of Verona in the 13th century, and surrounded by a moat with mallards and swans. There's not much to see inside, but the views from its battlements and lofty tower are lovely. A second set of battlements protect 15th-century **Santa Maria Maggiore**, overlooking a slender beach.

Between bouts with his fickle mistress, 'Lesbia', lyric poet Catullus cooled his heels at the family villa at Sirmione, though chances are the opulent late 1st-century BC **Grotte di Catullo** at the tip of the promontory wasn't it. Still, the superb site (***t** 030 916 157; open Tues–Sun 1 Mar–14 Oct 8.30–7; 15 Oct–28 Feb 9–4.30; adm*), set among ancient olives and rosemary hedges, is romantic with a capital R. There's a small **museum** with bits from the ruins and prehistoric and medieval remains found around Lake Garda.

Near the Grotte, on the peninsula's highest point, the Romanesque **San Pietro in Mavino** was built of scavenged Roman bricks; inside are frescoes from the 13th–16th centuries by the school of Verona. Also nearby is the thermal **Stabilimento Termale Catullo** (***t** 800 802 125; open Apr Mon–Sat 7–12; May–Oct daily 7–12 and 4–6.30; Nov Mon–Sat 7–12*), where a pipe brings up steaming sulphuric water from the bottom of the lake, just the thing for respiratory ailments.

Peschiera del Garda, Gardaland and the Sigurtà Gardens

East of Sirmione, **Peschiera** has been fortified since Roman times, though the imposing walls you see today are 16th-century Venetian, reinforced by the Austrians when the town was one of the corners of the empire's 'Quadrilateral'. Today it's best known as the site of **Gardaland**, Italy's largest and most popular theme park (*on SS149 between Peschiera and Lazise, **t** 045 644 9777; open late Mar–mid-June, last 3wks Sept and 1st weekend Nov daily 9.30–6; mid-June–early Sept daily 9am–midnight; Oct Sat and Sun 9.30–6; adm*). Recent additions include the Flying Island, an orbiting space station that offers a wonderful panorama of the lake and surroundings.

The region south of Peschiera is known for its dry white wine, Bianco di Custoza, and for the pretty gardens and groves that line the Mincio river. The Anglo-Italian **Sigurtà Gardens** (***t** 045 637 1033; open daily Mar–Nov 9–7; adm*), eight kilometres from Peschiera, are considered one of the world's five most beautiful gardens and were the 40-year project of Dr Count Carlo Sigurtà, 'Italy's Capability Brown'; there are 13 parking areas on the seven-kilometre route so you can get out and walk as much as you like.

Up the West Shore to Gardone Riviera

The west or Lombard shore of Garda is its most prestigious, with the oldest villas and grandest hotels. Six kilometres north of Desenzano, **Padenghe** marks the start of an olive- and wine-growing and white-truffle-finding corner of gentle hills called the Valtenesi. The old Valtenesi villages, especially **Moniga**, preserve tracts of their walls going back to the 10th century. The Valtenesi's fortress, the **Rocca di Manerba**, sits high on a headland; beneath it the shore, with Mediterranean flora and beaches, is a natural park. The Rocca looks out over the **Isola di Garda**, the lake's largest island. Its ruined monastery, visited by St Francis, provided the foundations for a neo-Venetian–Gothic-style palace, owned by the Borghese and tantalizingly off limits.

Salò (Roman *Salodium*), traditionally Garda's 'capital', seat of the Venetian magistrates, enjoys a privileged location on a deep bay with a grand promenade. It was rebuilt with Liberty-style flourish after an earthquake in 1901; among the fine older buildings that survived is a late Gothic **cathedral** with a Renaissance portal of 1509 stuck in its unfinished façade.

The **Museo del Nastro Azzuro** at Via Fantoni 49 (***t*** *0365 20804; open Easter–Sept Tues–Sat 5–7, Sun and hols 10–12.30 and 5–8; adm*) is dedicated to 'blue-ribboned' Italian military figures from 1797 to 1945: there's a collection of uniforms, weapons and portraits, and a room on the Fascist period and the puppet 'Republic of Salò' of 1943–5, Il Duce's dismal last stand formed after the Nazis 'rescued' him from an Abruzzo ski lodge (*see* p.576).

North of Salò, sumptuous old villas, gardens and hotels line the lovely promenade at **Gardone Riviera**, which became the lake's most fashionable resort in 1880, when a scientist noted the almost uncanny consistency of its climate. The **Giardino Botanico Hruska** (***t*** *0336 410 877; open daily Mar–Oct 9–6.30; adm*) profits from this mildness, with 8,000 exotic blooms and plants growing between imported tufa cliffs.

D'Annunzio's Folly

t *0365 296 511; guided tours daily Apr–Sept 8.30–8, Oct–Mar 9–5; D'Annunzio house (the Prioria) open Tues–Sun Apr–Sept 9.30–7, Oct–Mar 9–1 and 2–5; Museo della Guerra open Thurs–Tues Apr–Sept 3.30–7, Oct–Mar 9–1 and 2–5; adm exp but cheaper tickets for museum and grounds only (Vittoriale).*

In an incomparable setting above the botanical garden, the Liberty-style villa designed for a German family by Giancarlo Maroni was presented to writer Gabriele D'Annunzio (1863–1938) by Mussolini in 1925, ostensibly as a reward for his patriotism and heroism in the First World War, but really as a sop to keep the volatile poet out of politics. D'Annunzio dubbed his new home Il Vittoriale degli Italiani after Italy's victory over Austria in 1918; with Maroni's help he recreated it in his own image, leaving posterity a mix of eccentric beauty and self-aggrandizing kitsch. The villa is a pack rat's paradise, its every nook and cranny filled with quirky junk, more or less all left as it was in 1938 when a brain haemorrhage put an abrupt end to the poet's hoarding. Your eyes will need time to adjust to the gloom: D'Annunzio hated daylight and had the windows painted over, preferring low-watt electric lamps.

Past the entrance gate, note the double arch, a copy of the bridge pier on the Piave, where the Italians held the line against the Central Powers in 1917–18. Near the courtyard are two of D'Annunzio's favourite fast cars – one is the 1913 Fiat he drove in triumph to Fiume. The tour begins with the 'cool reception' room for guests he disliked, including Mussolini. The ornate organs in the music room and library were played by his young American wife, who gave up a promising musical career to play for his ears. In his spare bedroom, adorned with leopardskins, is a coffin he liked to lie in to think cosmic thoughts. He designed the entrance to his study low so visitors had to bow as they entered; here he kept a bust of Duse, covered to prevent her memory from distracting his genius.

In the **museum**, in the Art Deco Casa Schifamondo ('escape the world') D'Annunzio built but never moved into, you can ponder his death bed and death mask, casts of Michelangelo's sculptures, paintings and biographical memorabilia. In the adjacent auditorium is the biplane he used to fly over Vienna to drop propaganda leaflets in the war. The recently opened **private garden** occupies an 18th-century lemon terrace,

More Italian than Any Other Italian

Born Gaetano Rapagnetta into a modest family in the Abruzzo, the self-styled angel Gabriel of the Annunciation went on to become the greatest Italian poet of his generation, a leading figure in the fin-de-siècle Decadent school who managed to have nearly all of his works placed on the pope's Index but who scoffed at the idea that the pen is mightier than the sword. A right-wing nationalist, he clamoured for Italy to enter the First World War, and when it was over he was so furious that Fiume (Rijeka), a town promised as a prize to Italy, was to be ceded by the Allies to Yugoslavia that he invaded Fiume with a band of volunteers. In Italy he was proclaimed a hero, stirring up a diplomatic furore before being forced to withdraw.

Luigi Barzini has described D'Annunzio as 'perhaps more Italian than any other Italian' for his love of gesture and spectacle – what can you say about a man who boasted he had once dined on roast baby? Yet for Italians of his generation, whatever their politics, he exerted a powerful influence in thought and fashion; he seemed a breath of fresh air, a new kind of 'superman' – hard, passionate yet capable of writing intoxicating verse, the spiritual father of the technology-infatuated Futurists, ready to destroy the old bourgeois *Italia vile* of museum curators and parish priests and create in its stead a great modern power, the 'New Italy'.

He lived a life of total exhibitionism, living extravagantly, decadently and beyond his means, at every moment incarnating the role of the trend-setting, aristocratic aesthete, with his borzois and his melodramatic affairs with 'the Divine' actress Eleanora Duse and innumerable other loves (usually duchesses). He thought the New Italians should all be as flamboyant and clever, and disdained the corporate state of the Fascists. For Mussolini, the still-popular old nationalist was a loose cannon and an embarrassment, and he decided to pension him off into gilded retirement on Lake Garda, correctly calculating that the villa would appeal to his delusions of grandeur.

where a magnolia grove contains D'Annunzio's war memorial, with a throne and stone benches for nationalist legionary ceremonies, which must have been a hoot. The open-air theatre, designed by Maroni after the ancient Greek theatre in Taormina, has a magnificent view from the top seats, stretching from Monte Baldo to Sirmione; in July and August it hosts D'Annunzio's plays. The **mausoleum**, the poet's last ego trip, is a perverse wedding cake in glaring white travertine; within three concentric stone circles, the sarcophagi of the Fiume legionnaires pay court to the plain tomb of D'A himself, raised up on columns like a pagan sun-king.

Toscolano-Maderno and Gargnano

The *comune* of Toscolano-Maderno has one of the finest beaches on Lake Garda and the car ferry to Torri. Toscolano traces its origins to the Etruscans, while Maderno was the site of *Benacum*, the main Roman town on the lake. In the 12th century, many of its Roman bits were incorporated into the elegant **Sant'Andrea**, a Romanesque beauty benignly restored in the 16th century by St Charles Borromeo; inside, the capitals, some with their original paint, are sculpted with fighting animals. The 18th-century parish church has a Sant'Ercolano by Paolo Veronese and a Martyrdom of St Andrew by Palma il Giovane. Toscolano was the chief manufacturer of nails for Venice's galleys and had a famous printing press in the 15th century; the Cartiera di Toscolano paper mill remains Garda's largest industry. The cool, green **Valle delle Cartiere** – the valley of the paper mills – is a favourite excursion.

To the north, **Gargnano**, the last town before the towering cliffs, has hosted the Centomiglia regatta since 1950. The Franciscans were among the first to live here, in the 13th century; their church has been Baroqued inside and the cloister's capitals have carvings of lemons and oranges – a reminder of the tradition that the Franciscans were the first to cultivate citrus fruits in Europe.

After the Borghese ranch on Isola di Garda, the largest villa on the lake, just south of Gargnano in Bogliaco, is the 18th-century **Villa Bettoni** (*ask at villa for opening hours*), used as a set in a dozen films. In another villa, built for publisher Feltrinelli (whose chain of bookstores is a blessing for English-speaking travellers in Italy), the university of Milan runs summer courses for foreign students; a second **Villa Feltrinelli**, designed by Milanese architect Belgioioso in 1854, was Mussolini's home during the Republic of Salò. D.H. Lawrence stayed in Gargnano in 1912–13 and wrote *Twilight in Italy* here.

Limone sul Garda

North of Gargnano the lake narrows, the cliffs plunge sheer into the water, and the Gardesana road pierces tunnel after tunnel. In the morning, when the wind's up, windsurfers flit across the waves; on weekends their cars are parked all along the road around **Campione**, a tiny hamlet huddled under the cliffs. For tremendous views, take one of several turnings inland that wind precipitously up to the cliffs: to peaceful **Tignale**, with its church on the edge of a spectacular viewpoint, and **Tremósine**, on a 1,000ft precipice looking across the lake to mighty Monte Baldo.

The inland route from Tremósine rejoins the lake and the Gardesana shore road at **Limone sul Garda**, a popular resort with a tiny port and a long beach. Its name comes from the Latin *limen* (border), although by happy coincidence it was one of the main citrus-producing towns on Lake Garda, and to this day its lemon terraces with their white square pillars are a striking feature.

Riva del Garda

North of Limone the charming town of Riva sits snug beneath an amphitheatre formed by Monte Brione. A commercial port for the bishops of Trento from 1027, it was much fought over through the centuries, ruled at various times by Verona, Milan and Venice before being handed back to the bishop-princes in 1521. In 1703, in the War of the Spanish Succession, French general Vendôme sacked it and the surroundings, leaving only a ghost of the former town to be inherited by Napoleon in 1796.

With its long beaches and summer breezes, it revived as a resort under Austrian rule (1813–1918); Stendhal, Thomas Mann, D.H. Lawrence and Kafka were among habitués. The lakefront was defended by the grey bulk of the 12th-century castle, the **Rocca**, surrounded by a swan-filled moat, now home to the **Museo Civico** (***t** 0464 573 869; open Apr–Aug Tues–Sat 9.30–12.30 and 3.30–6.30, Sun until 5.30; Sept–Mar Tues–Sat*

9.30–12.30 and 2–5, Sun until 5.30; adm) with finds from the Bronze Age settlement at Lake Ledro, six statue-stelae with human features from the 4th–3rd millennia BC, items from Roman Riva, and paintings, detached frescoes and sculpture from the surrounds.

Three kilometres north, a 287ft waterfall, the **Cascata del Varone** (*open Mar and Oct daily 10–12.30 and 2–5; Apr and Sept daily 9–6; May–Aug daily 9–7; Nov–Feb Sun and hols 10–12.30 and 2–5; adm*), crashes down a tight grotto-like gorge by the village of Varone; walkways allow you to get close to the thundering water.

From the west side of Riva, the exciting Ponale road rises five kilometres to **Lake Ledro**, noted both for its scenery and the remains of a Bronze Age settlement of pile dwellings (*c.* 2000 BC), discovered in 1929. One has been reconstructed near the ancient piles around **Molina di Ledro**, where the **Museo delle Palafitte** (***t** 0464 508 182; open Tues–Sun 16 June–10 Sept 10–1 and 2–6, 11 Sept–15 June 9–1 and 2–5; adm*) houses pottery, axes, daggers and amber jewellery recovered from the site; the visit includes the new prehistoric botanical garden, dedicated to plants cultivated by northern Italian farmers in the Bronze Age.

One of the most dramatic sights on Garda, just behind Riva in a natural balcony of hills overlooking the lake, is the **Castello di Arco** (***t** 0464 510 156; open daily Apr–Sept 10–7, Oct–Mar 10–4; adm*), on a jagged crag crowned with ancient sharp cypresses. Built to defend the Valle di Sarca, the main funnel of northern armies into Italy, it was controlled from the 12th century by the cultured Counts of Arco, who tugged their forelocks at various stages to Verona, Milan and Trento. The path up (20 minutes) is lovely, if tiring on a hot day, and, despite the damage wrought by Vendôme's troops, there are a few frescoes left, including one of a courtly game of chess.

Arco itself, once heavily fortified and moated, became, like Riva, an Austro-Hungarian resort in the 1800s, prized for its climate. In the centre the Palladian-inspired **Collegiata dell'Assunta** (1613) was another Madruzzo project, this time by Trentino architect Giovanni Maria Filippi, who became court architect of Emperor Rudolph II in Prague. There's a pretty public garden full of Mediterranean plants, near the equally pretty 19th-century **Casino**. On the edge of town, the park laid out at the end of the 19th century by Habsburg archduke Albert is an **arboretum** (*open daily 9–4, summer until 7*).

The East Shore: Riva to Peschiera

Garda's east shore belongs to the province of Verona. The silvery groves gracing the hills gave it its name, the Riviera degli Olivi, but its outstanding feature is **Monte Baldo**, a ridge of limestone stretching 35 kilometres from Lake Garda to the Adige valley. Cresting at 6,989ft, Baldo is anything but bald: it supports an astonishing variety of flora, from Mediterranean palms to Arctic tundra; some 20 flowers discovered here bear its name and it is home to the Best Corna Piana botanical park. The southern third of the Riviera degli Olivi is the land of one of Italy's finest reds – Bardolino.

Torbole

Back on Garda's northeast shore, Monte Baldo looms over **Torbole** and the mouth of the Sarca, the most important river feeding the lake. An old fishing village and a pleasant resort, Torbole is famous in the annals of naval history: in 1438, during a war

Getting There and Around

APT **buses** run up the east coast from Verona and Peschiera as far as Riva, **t** 045 805 7911. A bus service around the lake is provided by SIA, **t** 030 377 4237. There's a year-round **car ferry** from Torri del Benaco to Maderno.

Tourist Information

Useful websites include *www.torbole.com*, *www.malcesine.com*, *www.torridelbenaco.com* and *www.bardolino.net*.

Malcésine: Via Capitanato 6/8, **t** 045 740 0044.
Torri del Benaco: Viale F.lli. Lavanda, **t** 045 722 5120.
Garda: Via Don Gnocchi 23, **t** 045 627 0384, *www.aptgardaveneto.com*
Bardolino: Piazzale Aldo Moro, **t** 045 721 0078, *www.info-bardolino.it*

Where to Stay and Eat

Hotels on the east shore tend to be cheaper than on the west shore.

Malcésine ✉ 37018

****Park Hotel Querceto**, Campiano, **t** 045 740 0344, *www.parkhotelquerceto.com* (*expensive–very expensive*). A romantic place south of the centre, with lovely views, a pool, a garden, and one of the best restaurants in the area. *Closed Nov–Mar.*

***Vega**, Viale Roma 10, **t** 045 657 0355, *www.malcesine.com/vega* (*expensive*). An inviting lakefront hotel in the centre, with big, modern rooms with satellite TV and air-con, and a private beach. There's a minimum 3-day stay; half board is obligatory.

****Val di Sogno**, Val di Sogno, **t** 045 740 0108, *www.hotelvaldisogno.com* (*moderate–very expensive*). A hotel in its own grounds on the shore; with a pool, a sauna, a gym, tennis courts, a lakeside restaurant, and rooms with balconies. There's a minimum 3-day stay, and half board is obligatory in high season.

***International Sailing Centre**, Via Molini 3, Campagnola 3, **t** 045 740 0055 (*moderate*). Rooms in low houses in a lakefront garden north of the centre. It has a beach, sailing and windsurf schools, a sauna and a pool. Half board only; minimum 3-day stay. *Closed Nov–Feb.*

***Malcésine**, Piazza Pallone, **t** 045 740 0173, *www.chincherini.com* (*cheap–moderate*). A beautifully sited hotel on the lake in the centre, with a garden with a swimming terrace. Half board only.

Erika, Via Campogrande 8, **t** 045 740 0451, *www.malcesine.com/erika* (*cheap–moderate*). Family-run, cosy hospitality behind the centre, with parking.

San Marco, Via Capitanato, **t**045 740 0115, *www.malcesine.com/sanmarco* (*cheap–moderate*). A central option where Goethe slept in 1786, with simple rooms with baths.

with the Visconti, the Venetians had to get supplies to Brescia past the southern reaches of Lake Garda, controlled by Milan. A Greek sailor suggested they sail a fleet of provision-packed warships up the Adige to its furthest navigable point, then transport them over Monte Baldo on to Lake Garda. Anyone who's seen Herzog's film *Fitzcarraldo* will appreciate the difficulties involved, and the amazing fact that, with the aid of 2,000 oxen, the 26 ships were launched at Torbole only 15 days after leaving the Adige. After all that trouble, the supplies never reached Brescia, but the same trick, perhaps even suggested by the same Greek, enabled Mohammed II to bring the Ottoman fleet into the upper harbour of Constantinople the following year and capture the city.

Malcésine and Monte Baldo

South of Torbole, the forbidding cliffs of Monte di Nago hang perilously over the lake before Malcésine, the loveliest town on the east shore. The Veronese lords protected this coast and, in the 13th century, over the old Lombard castle, built their magnificent **Rocca Scaligera** (*t 045 940 0044; open daily Apr–Oct 9.30–7, Nov–Mar 11–5; adm*) on a

Restaurant food here is generally dreadful and touristy.

Trattoria Vecchia Malcesine, Via Pisort 6, **t** 045 740 0469 (*very expensive*). A romantic escape from the hurly burly, with high-quality fare such as *canederli di speck* (ham-flecked dumplings) with Monteveronese cheese. Lake recipes include poached pike with caper sauce. Booking advised. *Closed lunch, Weds and Feb.*

Trattoria la Pace, Via Casella 1, **t** 045 740 0057 (*moderate*). A popular seafood place by the Porto Vecchio, with lakeside tables.

Torri del Benaco ✉ 37010

***Gardesana**, Piazza Calderini 20, **t** 045 722 5411, *www.hotel-gardesana.com* (*moderate–expensive*). A comfortable hotel in a 1442 building on the old harbour, with splendid views of the lake and castle. Vivien Leigh, Maria Callas and André Gide all stayed here. In fine weather meals are served on the harbour patio. The restaurant, deemed by many the best on the Veronese shore, serves lake specialities with a creative touch. Try lake sardine marinated in cider, trout *carpaccio* or pike with polenta. There's a minimum 3-night stay. *Restaurant closed lunchtimes, and Tues out of season. Hotel and restaurant closed end Nov–end Feb..*

***Al Caval**, Via Gardesana 186, **t** 045 722 5666, *www.alcaval.com* (*cheap–moderate*). A plain hotel in a park near the lake, with a very good restaurant (*expensive*) with vegetarian and *degustazione* menus. *Restaurant closed lunch Tues–Fri; Sat and Sun eve. All closed Jan–Mar.*

Garda ✉ 37016

****Locanda San Vigilio**, Punta San Vigilio, **t** 045 725 6688, *www.locanda-sanvigilio.it* (*very expensive–luxury*). A little inn by a private harbour, with 7 romantic rooms, a beach and an old tavern. *Closed Dec–Feb.*

****Hotel Regina Adelaide**, Via Francesco D'Assisi 23, **t** 045 725 5977, *www.regina-adelaide.it* (*moderate–very expensive*). A central option with a health centre.

***Flora**, Via Giorgione 22 and 27, **t** 045 725 5348, *www.hotelflora.net* (*moderate–very expensive*). A slick, modern hotel above town in its own grounds, with spacious rooms, tennis courts, mini-golf and two pools. *Closed Nov–Easter.*

***Continental**, Via Giorgione 14, **t** 045 725 5100, *www.hotelcontinental.vr.it* (*moderate*). A reasonable hotel in its own grounds, with a swimming pool. *Closed Nov–Easter.*

*Ancora**, Via Manzoni 7, **t** 045 725 5202, *www.chincherini.com* (*moderate*). A good-value lakefront option in the centre, with clean, comfy rooms. *Closed end Oct–end Mar.*

Stafolet, Via Poiano 12, **t** 045 725 5427 (*very expensive*). *Tagliolini* with truffles, grilled meat and fish, and pizza. *Closed Tues, and Jan.*

Al Ponte Sel, Via Monte Baldo 71, **t** 045 725 5419 (*cheap*). Good, stout local cooking, plus 4 rooms with en suite bathrooms.

sheer rock over the water; inside are natural history exhibits, prehistoric rock etchings and a room on Goethe, accused of spying while sketching the castle. Note also the 16th-century **Palazzo dei Capitani del Lago** in Malcésine's medieval web of streets.

Every half-hour a pair of cable cars run vertiginously up **Monte Baldo** (***t*** *045 740 0206; daily from 4pm; adm*); their rotating cabins enable you to further enjoy the ravishing views, and the ski slopes at the top are very popular with the Veronese. Malcésine also has pretty walks through the olives, and the shore has lovely places to swim and sunbathe, especially around the cove called the Val di Sogno.

Torri del Benaco and Garda

Further south, past a steep, sparsely populated stretch of shore, are two pretty towns, one on either side of Punta di San Vigilio, that played minor roles in the 10th century. The first, laid-back **Torri del Benaco**, owes its name to a rugged old tower in the centre that served as the HQ of Berengario, first king of Italy, in his 905 campaign against the Magyars. Later, it was defended by another **Scaliger castle** (1383), now a museum (***t** 045 629 6111; open daily Jan–May and Oct 9.30–12.30 and 2.30–6, June–Sept 9.30–1 and 4.30–7.30; adm*) with displays on olive oil, citrus fruits, fishing, and rock engravings found in the area from *c.* 2000 BC, similar to those in the Valle Camonica. The church of **Santa Trinità** has good 14th-century Giottesque frescoes.

One of the many lovely walks in the region is up to the old village of **Albisano**, with its beautiful views, then on to Crer and Brancolino, where the largest of Torri's prehistoric etchings can be seen, especially near Crer's church. The first recorded pleasure tourist in Torri was the great Medicean poet Poliziano in the 15th century; more recent fans have included André Gide and Stephen Spender. Laurence Olivier preferred enchanting **Punta di San Vigilio** with its Sirens' rocks, occupied by the lovely **Villa Guarienti** (*not open to the public*) designed by the great Venetian Renaissance architect Sammicheli, the old church of San Vigilio, and a 16th-century tavern, now an inn (*see* p.309). The Mermaid bay, a private beach accessible via a park shaded with olive trees, has playgrounds and two refreshment bars.

On the other side of a green soufflé of a headland, the Rocca del Garda, lies **Garda** itself, a fine old town with Renaissance *palazzi* and villas. It gave the lake its modern name, from the Lombard *Warthe*, 'the watch'. After Charlemagne defeated the Lombards, Garda became a county, and in its long-gone castle wicked Count Berenguer secretly held Queen Adelaide of Italy prisoner in 960, after he had murdered her husband Lotario and she had refused to marry his son. After a year she was discovered by a monk, who spent another year plotting her escape. She then received the protection of Otto I of Germany, who defeated Berenguer, married the widowed queen, and became Holy Roman Emperor.

Bardolino

To the south, Bardolino is synonymous with its lively red wine with a bitter cherry fragrance that goes well with fishy *antipasti*; learn all about it at the Cantine Zeni's **Museo del Vino** at Via Costabella 9 (***t** 045 721 0022; open Mar–Oct daily 9–1 and 2–6*), or by following the wine route through the soft rolling hills, dotted with 19th-century villas. There are two important churches in Bardolino itself: the 8th-century **San Zeno** and the 12th-century **San Severo**, which has frescoes and a landmark campanile. **Cisano**, to the south of Bardolino, has a museum dedicated to the Riviera degli Olivi's other cash crop, the **Museo dell'Olio d'Oliva** at Via Peschiera 54 (***t** 045 622 9047; open Mar–Oct Mon–Sat 9–12.30 and 3–7, Sun 9–12.30; Jan–Feb Mon, Tues and Thurs–Sat 9–12.30 and 2.30–6*).

The next town, **Lazise**, was the main Venetian port; near the harbour is an ensemble of Venetian buildings, as well as another castle, built in the 9th century by the Magyars and taken over and rebuilt by the Scaligers. Just inland, at Bussolengo, the **Parco Natura Viva** (***t** 045 717 0052; open Mar–May and Oct daily 9–5; June, July and Sept daily 9–6; Aug daily 9–7; Feb Suns and hols 9–5*) is a private foundation devoted to the protection of endangered species; it's divided into a zoo (*open daily 9–6*), complete with a tropical aviary and dinosaur models, and a drive-through safari park (*open Mar–Nov Mon, Tues and Thurs–Sun 9–4; Jan Sat or Sun 9–6*) with a host of animals from the African savannah. Near here you'll also find Gardaland (*see* p.303).

Venetia

12

Highlights

1 A ride down the Grand Canal in Venice
2 Padua: Giotto's Cappella degli Scrovegni
3 Vicenza's Palladian villas and theatre
4 The High Trails of the Dolomites
5 The Mitteleuropean ambience of Trieste

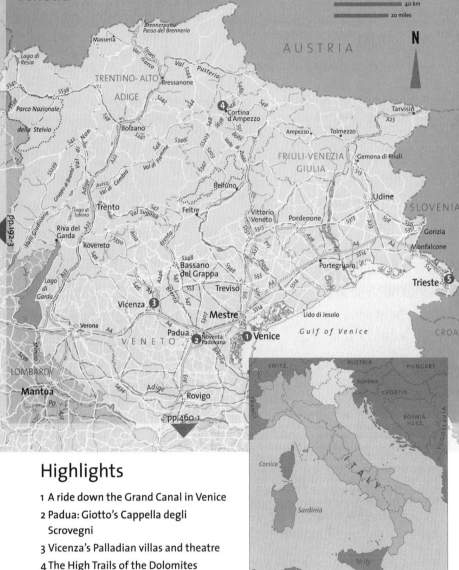

Venetia (the Tre Venezie in Italian) encompasses three regions: the Veneto, the autonomous region of Trentino-Alto Adige (including a good part of the Dolomites), and Friuli-Venezia Giulia, stretching east to Slovenia. As the local economic powerhouse for more than 1,000 years, Venice's influences are strong everywhere; in wealth Venetia rivals Lombardy, and in culture it rivals Tuscany: Venice, Verona, Vicenza, Treviso, Padua, Trento and Ùdine are major art cities. Lagoons and sandy

beaches line the coast, while the Dolomites are dotted with fairy-tale castles and vineyards, as well as resorts equipped for every summer and winter sport. In between are lush landscapes littered with thousands of villas built in the 16th–18th centuries, including 18 by Palladio, master of the genre. Friuli, a top wine region, has a variety of other attractions, especially its Roman–medieval capital Aquileia, the most important archaeological site in northern Italy, and the fascinating Lombard town of Cividale.

Because Venetia has so much to offer, especially for families (the seashore, Lake Garda and its theme parks, and the mountains), avoid coming in August if you can, when the crowds and prices can be overwhelming. At any time of year you can get along without a car, although they do come in handy for visiting villas or castles. Venice is the obvious place to start, and has frequent links to Padua and Treviso; Verona, with quick connections to Lake Garda, is another good base, although Palladiophiles will want to stay in Vicenza. The Dolomites are served by an excellent bus system; Trento, Bolzano and Cortina are important hubs and have beautiful routes to explore in all directions. Ùdine makes a good base for Friuli-Venezia Giulia, with connections to Aquileia, Trieste and the coast.

Venice

Venice seduces, Venice irritates, but Venice rarely disappoints. On the surface she is little changed from the days when Goethe called her the 'market-place of the Morning and the Evening lands', when her amphibious citizens dazzled the world with their wealth and pageantry, their fleet, their half-Oriental doges, their crafty merchant princes, their luminous art, their silken debauchery and their decline and fall into a seemingly endless carnival. One can imagine Julius Caesar bewildered by today's Rome, or Romeo and Juliet missing their rendezvous in the hubbub of modern Verona, but Marco Polo could take a familiar gondola up the familiar Grand Canal to his house in the Rialto, astonished more by the motorboats than anything else. Credit for this unique preservation goes to the Lagoon, the amniotic fluid of Venice's birth, her impenetrable 'walls' and the formaldehyde that has pickled her more thoroughly than many far more venerable cities on the mainland.

For 1,000 years Venice called herself the Most Serene Republic (*La Serenissima*), and at one point she ruled 'a quarter and a half' of the Roman Empire. The descent to an Italian provincial capital was steep and bittersweet; and sensitive souls find gallons of melancholy or, like Thomas Mann, even death, brewed into the city's canals. In winter, when the streets are silent and evocative, you have to kick the ghosts out of the way to pass down the narrower alleys. But most people show up in summer and, like their ancestors, have a jolly good time. For Venice is an experienced old siren. Global organizations pump in funds to keep her petticoats out of the water and smooth her wrinkles. Notices posted throughout the city acknowledge that she 'belongs to everybody', while with a wink she slides a hand deep into your pocket. Venice has always lived for gold, and you can bet she wants yours. You might as well give it to her, in return for the most enchanting, dream-like favours any city can grant.

Venice

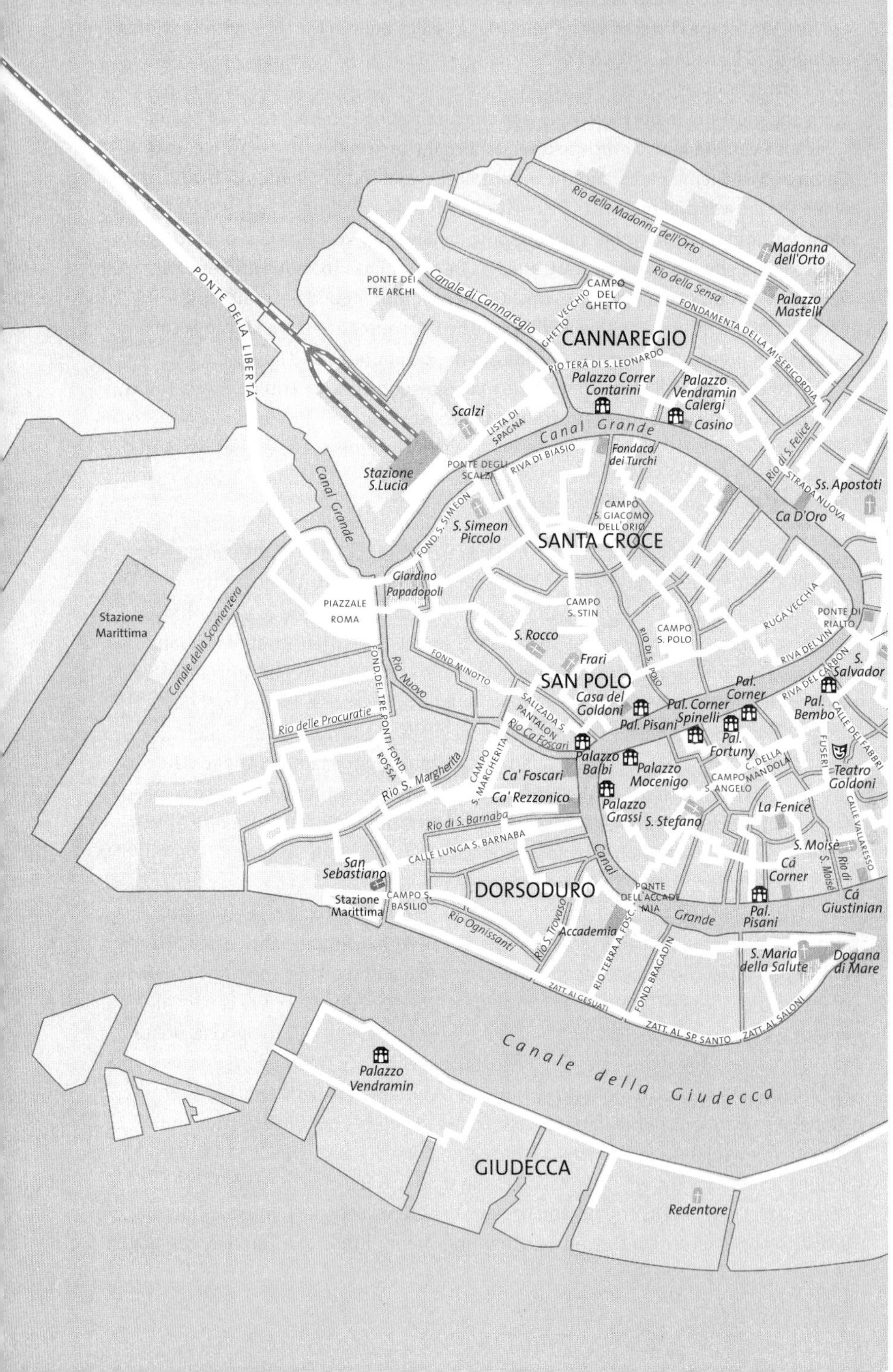

PONTE DELLA LIBERTÀ
PONTE DEI TRE ARCHI
Canale di Cannaregio
Rio della Madonna dell'Orto
Madonna dell'Orto
Rio della Sensa
Palazzo Mastelli
CAMPO DEL GHETTO
GHETTO VECCHIO
FONDAMENTA DELLA MISERICORDIA
CANNAREGIO
RIO TERÀ DI S. LEONARDO
Palazzo Correr Contarini
Palazzo Vendramin Calergi
Casino
Scalzi
LISTA DI SPAGNA
Canal Grande
Stazione S.Lucia
PONTE DEGLI SCALZI
RIVA DI BIASIO
Fondaco dei Turchi
Rio di S. Felice
STRADA NUOVA
Ss. Apostoti
Ca D'Oro
FOND. S. SIMEON
S. Simeon Piccolo
CAMPO S. GIACOMO DELL'ORIO
SANTA CROCE
Giardino Papadopoli
PIAZZALE ROMA
Stazione Marittima
Canale della Scomenzera
CAMPO S. STIN
RUGA VECCHIA
PONTE DI RIALTO
S. Rocco
CAMPO S. POLO
RIO DI S. POLO
RIVA DEL VIN
Frari
FOND. MINOTTO
Rio Nuovo
FOND. DEL TRE PONTI
SAN POLO
RIVA DEL CARBON
S. Salvador
Casa del Goldoni
Pal. Corner
Pal. Corner Spinelli
Pal. Bembo
CALLE DEI FABBRI
SALIZADA S. PANTALON
Rio Ca Foscari
Pal. Pisani
Rio delle Procuratie
FOND. ROSSA
Pal. Fortuny
FUSERI
Palazzo Balbi
Palazzo Mocenigo
C. DELLA MANDOLA
Teatro Goldoni
CAMPO S. MARGHERITA
Rio S. Margherita
Ca' Foscari
CAMPO S. ANGELO
Ca' Rezzonico
Palazzo Grassi
S. Stefano
La Fenice
CALLE VALLARESSO
Rio di S. Barnaba
CALLE LUNGA S. BARNABA
S. Moisè
Rio di S. Moisè
San Sebastiano
Cá Corner
Stazione Marittima
CAMPO S. BASILIO
DORSODURO
PONTE DELL'ACCADEMIA
Cá Giustinian
Rio Ognissanti
Rio S. Trovaso
Accademia
RIO TERRA A. FOSC.
Grande
Pal. Pisani
FOND. BRAGADIN
S. Maria della Salute
Dogana di Mare
ZATT. AI GESUATI
ZATT. AL SP. SANTO
ZATT. AL SALONI
Canale della Giudecca
Palazzo Vendramin
GIUDECCA
Redentore

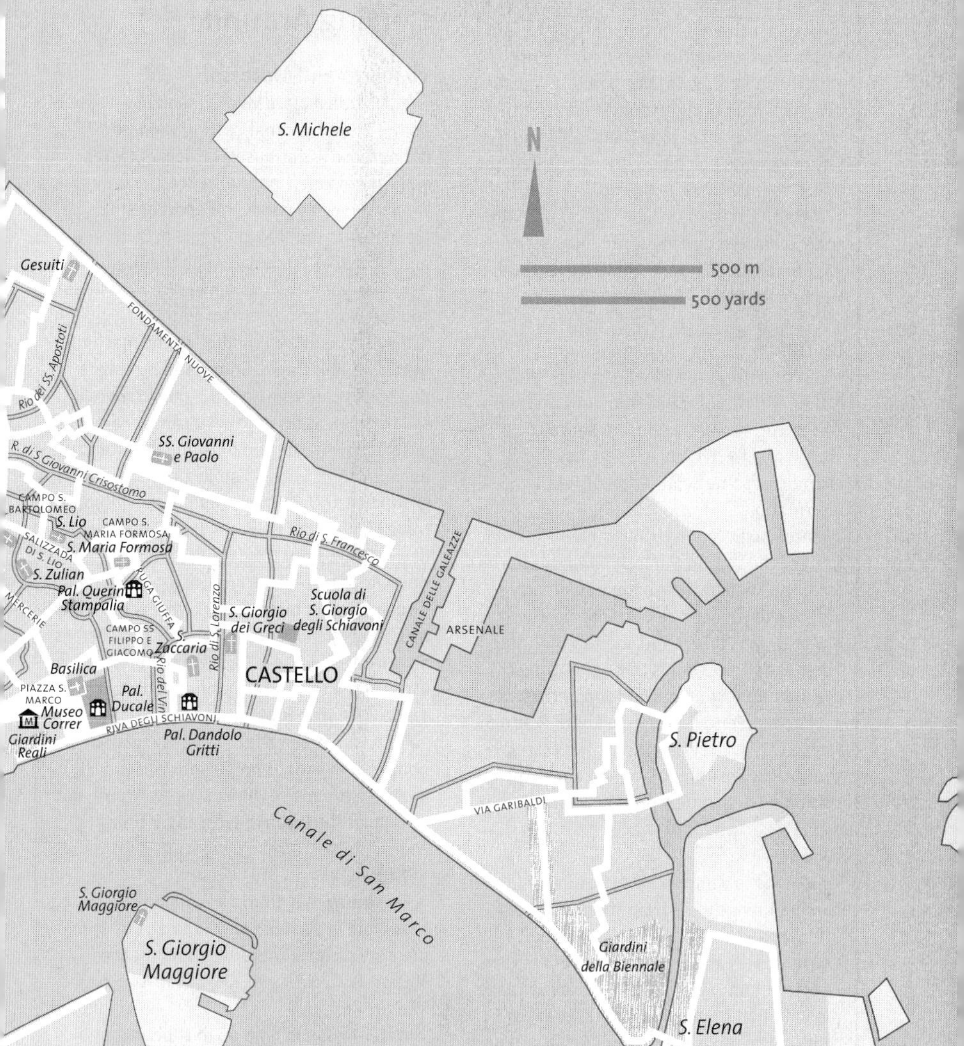

S. Michele
N
500 m
500 yards
Gesuiti
FONDAMENTA NUOVE
Rio dei SS. Apostoli
SS. Giovanni e Paolo
R. di S Giovanni Crisostomo
CAMPO S. BARTOLOMEO
S. Lio
CAMPO S. MARIA FORMOSA
S. Maria Formosa
SALIZZADA DI S. LIO
S. Zulian
Rio di S. Francesco
Pal. Querini Stampalia
RUGA GIUFFA
MERCERIE
Rio di S. Lorenzo
S. Giorgio dei Greci
Scuola di S. Giorgio degli Schiavoni
CANALE DELLE GALEAZZE
ARSENALE
CAMPO SS FILIPPO E GIACOMO
S. Zaccaria
Rio del Vin
Basilica
CASTELLO
PIAZZA S. MARCO
Pal. Ducale
Museo Correr
RIVA DEGLI SCHIAVONI
Pal. Dandolo Gritti
Giardini Reali
S. Pietro
VIA GARIBALDI
Canale di San Marco
S. Giorgio Maggiore
S. Giorgio Maggiore
Giardini della Biennale
S. Elena
S. Elena

Getting There

By Air

Marco Polo Airport, **t** 041 260 9260, 13km north of the city, has regular connections with other Italian and European cities, and New York (via Milan). It is linked with Venice by water-taxi (**t** 041 966 870 or **t** 041 523 5775), the most expensive option; or *motoscafi* to San Marco (Zecca) roughly every hour, connecting with most flights from Mar to Oct; boats (**t** 041 541 5084) run hourly 4.50am–midnight, taking 1hr 10mins to San Marco. There is also an ATVO bus to Piazzale Roma and, cheapest of all, the twice-hourly ACTV city bus no.5.

Some charter and budget flights go to Treviso, 30km away. If a transfer is not included with your ticket, catch bus no.6 into Treviso, which has frequent trains and buses to Venice.

By Train

Venice's Stazione Santa Lucia (the Ferrovia) is the terminus of trains from Italy and the rest of Europe. All trains from Santa Lucia stop in Mestre, where you may have to change for some destinations. For rail information call **t** 1478 88088.

Water-taxis, *vaporetti* and gondolas wait in front of the station. Venice's infamous **porters** (distinguished by their badges) will carry your luggage to your choice of transport and, if you pay their fare, take it and you to your hotel. There are porter stands throughout the city at the main tourist points and *vaporetto* stops; Accademia, Ferrovia, Piazzale Roma, Rialto, San Marco, etc, or call **t** 041 522 4891 or **t** 041 520 5308. Rates are unregulated except at the station, so negotiate a price in advance.

By Car

All roads to Venice end at the municipal parking towers in Piazzale Roma, **t** 041 523 7763, or their cheaper annexe, Tronchetto, **t** 041 520 7555, the largest car park in Europe. The Italian Auto Club also has three car parks (open to non-members): Fusina, **t** 041 547 0160, at the mouth of the Brenta Canal south of Marghera (summer only; *vaporetto* no.16 to Venice); San Giuliano, in Mestre near the causeway (bus service to Venice), and Punta Sabbioni, **t** 041 530 1096, between the Lido and Jesolo (ferry no.17 from Tronchetto).

By Sea

Adriatica (Zattere 1412, **t** 041 520 4322 or **t** 041 522 8018) sails every 10 days June–Sept to Split (15hrs) and Dubrovnik (24hrs). There are also daily car-ferries between Venice, Corfu and Patras, Greece (2 days), and Alexandria (3½ days).

Getting Around

Vaporetti and *Motoscafi*

Public transport in Venice means by water, on the grunting, canal-cutting ***vaporetti*** (all-purpose water-buses) or sleeker, faster ACTV ***motoscafi*** (**t** 041 528 7886). The only canals served by public transport are the Grand Canal, Rio Nuovo, Canale di Cannaregio and Rio dell'Arsenale; between them, you have to rely on your feet, though Venice is so small you can walk across it in an hour.

Tickets should be validated in the machines at the landing stages. Some landing stages don't sell tickets, so stock up (most *tabacchi* sell them in blocks of 10). You can buy a single ticket on board, but you must tell the attendant as soon as you get on. Family tickets and group tickets are a bit cheaper. If you intend travelling by boat at least 3 times in a given day, get a **24-hour tourist pass**, valid for unlimited travel on all lines, or a **3-day pass**.

Lines of most interest to visitors are listed on pp.334–5; most run until midnight. There is also an all-night line. Precise schedules are listed in the tourist office's free fortnightly guide, *Un Ospite di Venezia*.

From San Marco, a number of **excursion boats** run to various points in the Lagoon; they are more expensive than public transport, but may be useful if you're pressed for time.

Water-taxis

These are really tourist excursion boats – they work in a similar way to taxis, but their fares are de luxe. There are stands at the station, Piazzale Roma, Rialto, San Marco, Lido and the airport.

Water-taxis can hold up to 15 people, and fares are set for destinations beyond the historic centre, or you can pay by the hour. There are surcharges for baggage, holiday or nocturnal service (after 10pm), and for using a radio taxi (**t** 041 522 2303 or **t** 041 723 112).

Gondolas

Once used by all and sundry, gondolas now operate frankly for tourists (and weddings). Be sure to agree with the gondolier on where you want to go and how long you expect it to take before setting out.

Gondolas retired from the tourist trade are used for **gondola *traghetti*** services across the Grand Canal at various points between its three bridges – your only chance to enjoy an economical, if brief, gondola ride. *Traghetto* crossings are signposted in the streets nearby. For appearance's sake you have to stand up.

Hiring a Boat

Perhaps the best way to spend a day in Venice is by bringing or hiring your own motor boat (chauffeured or self-drive):

Cooperativa San Marco, San Marco 4267, **t** 041 523 5775.

Veneziana Motoscafi, San Marco 4179, **t** 041 716 000.

Serenissima Motoscafi, Castello 4545, **t** 041 522 4281.

Tourist Information

Palazzina dei Santi, Giardini Reali (by Piazza San Marco), **t** 041 522 5150, *www.turismovenezia.it*

There are branches at Palazzetto Selva, by the San Marco *vaporetto* stop, at the train station and at the bus station in Piazzale Roma; all offer accommodation booking services. There are also offices on the Rotonda Marghera, at Marco Polo airport, and on the Lido at Gran Viale 6.

Many churches belong to **Chorus** (**t** 041 275 0462), which sells a collective entry ticket, available from the churches, VELA ticket offices, and the Venice Pavilion tourist office. All Chorus churches have the same opening times (*Mon–Sat 10–5 and Sun 1–5*).

Shopping

Venice has long been one of Italy's best shopping cities, whether you're looking for tacky bric-a-brac (walk down the Lista di Spagna or Riva degli Schiavoni, or through the Rialto) or hand-crafted Venetian design.

Shops generally open Mon–Sat 8–1 or 9–1 and 4–7.30, but many tourist shops have longer hours. Many shops (except grocers) are closed Mon am; markets and grocers tend to close Weds pm. Many shops don't have a name, so some of those listed are just addresses.

Art and Antiques

In the Dorsoduro, **Antichità**, Calle Toletta, has antique glass beads, jewellery, lace, children's clothes, and other bits and pieces, while the shop at **Dorsoduro 2609**, Fondamenta del Soccorso, has curiosities ranging from Baroque clocks to bills printed by the 1848 revolutionary government. **Madera**, Campo San Barnaba, sells contemporary *objets* handmade using traditional methods.

In San Marco, you'll find **Bastianello Arte**, Campo San Bartolomeo, specializing in western and oriental antiques, Art Nouveau items and jewellery, and in San Polo, **Sabbie e Nebbie**, Calle dei Nomboli, has Japanese ceramics, ethnic papers and Italian ceramics.

Books

Try Calle Larga XXII Marzo in San Marco, where the **Libreria Cassini** has old prints and rare editions, and **Sangiorgio** sells books in English, many about Venice, and hefty art tomes. At Calle dei Fabbri, **Libreria Goldoni** is Venice's largest general bookstore. **Sansovino**, Bacino Orseolo (just outside the Procuratie Vecchie), has art and coffeetable books, and lots of postcards.

In Castello, **Filippi**, Calle del Paradiso, specializes in Italian books on Venice, including facsimiles of books from the days when it was one of Europe's chief printing centres. **The Museum Shop**, Fondamenta Venier dei Leoni, Dorsoduro, **t** 041 240 5410, sells art and photography books, children's books in English, gifts and postcards. More art and architecture books can be found at **Punto Libri**, Salizzada di San Pantalon, Santa Croce.

Fashion

Most of the big-name designer boutiques (Gucci, Prada, Versace, Louis Vuitton, Armani) are clustered around the outskirts of Piazza San Marco, along streets such as Mercerie, Frezzeria, Calle dei Fabbri, Calle Larga XXII Marzo and Salizzada San Moisè. Venetians buy their clothes at the **COIN** department store, Fontego Salizzada San Giovanni Grisostomo, Cannaregio, while tourists buy their 'Vuitton' and 'Prada' bags from the street-sellers paving the way to Piazza San Marco along Calle Larga XXII Marzo. Their first offer will be about three times what you should end up paying.

Trois, Campo San Maurizio, San Marco, is a Venetian institution selling Fortuny fabrics made to traditional specifications on the Giudecca. At Calle Larga XXII Marzo 2403 and Merceria San Zulian, both in San Marco, **Venetia Studium** has pleated silk Fortuny scarves, Fortuny lamps, pochettes and more.

For fabulous handmade shoes, from the elegant to the eccentric, go to **Rolando Segalin**, Calle dei Fuseri, San Marco. The greatest name in Venetian leather is **Vogini**, Calle Larga XXII Marzo 1300, San Marco, with articles by local designer Roberta di Camerino.

Food and Drink

For Venice's tastiest, most exotic pastas – *al cacao* (chocolate), *al limone* (lemon), beetroot, garlic, mushroom and more – make tracks for **Pastificio Artigiano**, Strada Nuova, Cannaregio. **Il Pastaio**, in the Rialto Markets at Calle del Varoteri, has pasta in a score of colours and shapes, including tagliatelle made with cuttlefish ink or curry. In the Dorsoduro, **Pantagruelica**, Campo San Barnaba (also in the Giudecca at Fondamenta Sant' Eufemia) stocks cheeses, hams and salamis, pastas, rice, preserves, wines, bread, oils and vinegars, all carefully sourced and much of it organic.

Sacchi, Rio Terrà San Leonardo, Cannaregio, is possibly the best fruit and veg shop in the city, with a spectacular display. Alternatively, seek out the last floating greengrocer's in Venice, by the Ponte dei Pugni near Campo San Barnabà in the Dorsoduro. If you need a supermarket, **Punto**, Rio Terrà Canal, Dorsoduro, is one of the few in the *centro storico*.

Glass and Ceramics

CAM, Piazzale Colonna 1/b, has one of the largest selections of glassware on Murano, and exceptionally friendly, unpushy staff. Also on Murano are **Carlo Moretti**, Fondamenta Manin 3, stocking contemporary glassware, and **Domus Vetri d'Arte**, Fondamenta Vetrai 82, with tasteful work by top Italian designers.

In San Marco, **Pauly**, Calle Larga San Marco, has classic blown glassware, while **San Vio**, 669, Campo San Vio, Dorsoduro 669, offers striking modern designs.

Jewellery

Jewellers are concentrated in Piazza San Marco and on the Ponte Rialto. **Missiaglia**, near Quadri in Piazza San Marco, has some of the most elegant work by Venetian gold and silversmiths, as well as necklaces and the like. **Nardi**, next to Florian, is one of Venice's luxury establishment jewellers, celebrated for its series of 'Othellos', elaborate jewelled pieces of carved ebony, each unique. Grace Kelly and Liz Taylor both shopped here.

Still in San Marco, **Codognato**, Calle dell' Ascensione, one of the oldest jewellers in Venice, has rare pieces by Tiffany and Cartier, plus Art Deco baubles. **Perle e Dintorni**, Calle della Mandola and Calle della Bissa (and also Campo Santi Apostoli, Cannaregio), has glass beads you can buy or have transformed into necklaces and bracelets in a couple of hours.

Lace

This is hard to avoid on Burano, though any bargains you might find are unlikely to be either hand-made or Buranese. In San Marco, try **La Fenice Atelier**, Campo Sant'Angelo, **t** 041 523 9578, which has bed linens, towels and nightwear in superb silks, satins and cotton lawn, decorated with lace and embroidery. **Jesurum** in Piazza San Marco stocks a vast quantity of lace (tablecloths, lingerie, and so on) in a former 12th-century church. In the Dorsoduro, **Annelie**, Calle Lunga San Barnabà, **t** 041 520 3277, has gorgeously worked items, new and antique.

Markets

The **Rialto Markets**, Venice's major markets, sell everything under the sun on the bridge and in all the streets to the north. There is a morning fish market (*Tues–Sat*) and a fruit and veg market (*Mon–Sat*) in the **Peschiera, Fabbriche Vecchie** and **Fabbriche Nuove**. At **Rio Terrà San Leonardo** you can get clothes, fish and other food daily.

There's a periodic flea market in **Campo San Maurizio**, in the heart of Venice's main antiques area.

Masks and Costumes

Some of the best masks in town (camels, sphinxes, moonfaces and more) are sold at **Mondonovo**, Rio Terrà Canal, Dorsoduro. In the Castello, **Papier-mâché**, Calle Lunga Santa Maria Formosa, has lovely paintwork and masks decorated in the style of Kandinsky, and in San Polo, **Tragicomica**, Calle dei Nomboli, has an extraordinary variety of wonderfully shaped masks and costumes.

Paper and Stationery

For exquisite hand-made paper and other gifts, visit **Legatoria Piazzesi**, Campiello Feltrina, **which bills itself as the** 'oldest paper shop in Italy'. Also in San Marco is **Alberto Valese-Ebrû**, Campo Santo Stefano, selling Persian and Italian paper, as well as silk ties and masks. **Paolo Olbi**, Calle della Mandola (near Campo Sant'Angelo), has wonderful hand-made paper, notebooks and photo albums, some leather-bound.

In the Dorsoduro are **Carta da Casetti**, tucked away in a tiny piazzetta between the Salute and the Guggenheim and selling original paper designs, and **Il Pavone**, Fondamenta Venier dei Leoni, offering paper products covered in unusual designs made on the premises, bound books and other gifts.

Wood

Livio de Marchi, Salizzada San Samuele, San Marco, is world renowned for its everyday objects sculpted in natural wood – benches in the form of giant paintbrushes, desks made from piles of oversized wooden books and so on. In San Polo, **Franco Furlanetto**, Calle dei Nomboli, and **La Scialuppa**, Calle Seconda dei Saoneri, sell gondola oars and oar-locks .

Where to Stay

All classes of hotel here cost around a third more than on the mainland, even without the often outrageous breakfast charge. Booking is near-essential Apr–Oct and for Carnival. Many hotels close in winter; many that don't offer hefty discounts. The tourist offices at the station and Piazzale Roma have a free room-finding service. The office in Piazza San Marco has a list of agencies letting self-catering flats.

Luxury

*******Cipriani**, Giudecca 10, Fondamenta San Giovanni, **t** 041 520 7744, *www.orientexpresshotels.com*. One of Italy's most luxurious hotels, in a lush garden at one end of the Giudecca that's so quiet you could forget Venice exists, though it's only a few minutes away by the hotel's 24hr private launch. An Olympic-size pool, sauna, jacuzzis in each room, tennis courts and a superb restaurant are just some of its facilities.

*******Danieli**, Castello 4196, Riva degli Schiavoni, **t** 041 522 6480, *www.luxurycollection.com*. The largest, best-known and most gloriously located hotel in Venice, overlooking the Lagoon and rubbing shoulders with the Palazzo Ducale. Set in a Gothic *palazzo*, it has been a hotel since 1822; Dickens, Proust, George Sand and Wagner stayed here. Nearly every room has a story to tell, in a beautiful setting of silken walls, Gothic staircases, gilt mirrors and oriental rugs. The new wing is comfortable but lacks the charm.

*******Gritti Palace**, San Marco 2467, Campo Santa Maria del Giglio, **t** 041 794 611, *www.starwood.com/grittipalace*. The 15th-century Grand Canal palace of glutton and womanizer Doge Andrea Gritti, now an elegant retreat. All rooms are furnished with Venetian antiques; for a real splurge do as Somerset Maugham did and stay in the Ducal Suite. The delightful restaurant, **Club del Doge**, has a terrace overlooking the canal.

******Des Bains**, Lido, Lungomare Marconi 17, **t** 041 526 5921, *www.sheraton.com*. A grand old luxury hotel in a large park designed for dalliance. Thomas Mann stayed here, and had Aschenbach sigh his life away on the private beach. It has a saltwater pool, tennis courts, a motorboat service and a breezy veranda dining room. *Closed Dec–mid-Mar.*

******Londra Palace**, Castello 4171, Riva degli Schiavoni, **t** 041 520 0533, *www.hotelondra.it*. Two former palaces with elegant interiors and canal views from more than half the rooms; Tchaikovsky wrote his *Fourth Symphony* in room 108. There is also an excellent restaurant, **Les Deux Lions**.

*****San Moisè**, San Marco 2058, Piscina San Moisè, **t** 041 520 3755, *www.sanmoise.it*. A quiet hotel with a clean look and a tub in most bathrooms. Book early for canal views.

Very Expensive

******Accademia**, Dorsoduro 1058, Fondamenta Bollani, **t** 041 521 0188. A 17th-century villa with a garden just off the Grand Canal and 26 rooms furnished with antiques. Book well in advance.

******American**, Dorsoduro 628, Fondamenta Bragadin, **t** 041 520 4733, *www.hotelamerican.com*. An elegant, traditional hotel overlooking the lovely San Vio canal (the best rooms are 201 and 202, with windows on two sides). There's a pretty first-floor breakfast terrace.

******Locanda Cipriani**, Torcello, Piazza Santa Fosca, **t** 041 730 150, *www.locandacipriani.com*. A famous yellow-painted, green-shuttered country house hotel in the most rural spot in Venice. Some of the 6 rooms have views over the garden; in one Hemingway wrote *Across the River and Into the Trees*. The restaurant is excellent (*see* p.321). *Closed Jan.*

******Locanda del Ghetto**, Cannaregio 2892, Campo del Ghetto Nuovo, **t** 041 275 9292, *www.veneziahotels.com*. A delightful hotel with a pretty canalside breakfast room and 9 stylish bedrooms, 2 with terraces overlooking the *campo*.

******Pausania**, Dorsoduro 2824, San Barnaba, **t** 041 522 2083. A traditional hotel in an old *palazzo* in a quiet corner of the Dorsoduro. The courtyard has an old well and a stone staircase leading to some of the rooms.

Expensive

******Do Pozzi**,San Marco 2373, Via XXII Marzo, **t** 041 520 7855, *www.hoteldopozzi.it*. A hotel with 29 rooms on a charming square where tables are set out for breakfast or a drink.

*****San Fantin**, San Marco 1930A, Campiello Fenice, **t** 041 523 1 401. A spotless hotel in a quiet little *campo* around the corner from La Fenice, dated in a rather refreshing way.

****Antica Locanda Montin**, Dorsoduro 1147, Fondamenta di Borgo, **t** 041 522 7151. An old-fashioned hostelry with 10 characterful rooms and an infamous arty restaurant.

Ca' del Dose, Castello 3801, Calle del Dose, **t** 041 520 9887, *www.cadeldose.com*. One of the new generation of good-value *affitta camere* or small B&Bs, located just off the Campo Bandiera e Moro. The 6 comfortable, stylish rooms have dark parquet floors and elegant fabrics.

Moderate

*****Hotel Iris**, San Polo 2910A, Calle del Cristo, **t** 041 522 2882. Clean, pleasant rooms, one with a pretty ceiling fresco. *Closed Jan*.

****Silva**, Castello 4423, Fondamenta del Remedio, **t** 041 522 7643. A basic, quiet option on one of Venice's most photographed little canals, between San Zaccaria *vaporetto* stop and Santa Maria Formosa (it's a bit hard to find).

Inexpensive

****Casa Boccassini**, Cannaregio 5295, Calle del Fumo, **t** 041 522 9892. Clean rooms In a quiet neighbourhood, plus a delightful garden.

****Doni**, Castello 4656, Calle del Vin, **t** 041 522 4267. A basic but clean family-run hotel. The three best rooms (with wooden floors and pretty canal views) share a bathroom.

Hostels and Campsites

The tourist office has a list of hostels. Contact **Assocamping**, **t** 041 968 071, *www.cavallino.net*, for a list of Venice campsites.

*****Fusina**, Via Moranzini 79, **t** 041 547 0055, *www.camping-fusina.com*. A site with 1,000-plus places, 20mins from Venice (*vaporetto* no.16 from San Zaccaria runs every hour until 11pm in summer). It has a restaurant and pizzeria, a bar, and Internet access. There are also small self-catering bungalows.

*****Serenissima**, Via Padana 334, Oriago, Mira, **t** 041 920 286, *www.camping serenissima.com*. Three hundred camping places and 60 bungalows just off the Brenta Canal; bus no.53 connects with Venice every half-hour. *Open Apr–Oct*.

Foresteria Valdese, Castello 5170, Palazzo Cavagnis, **t** 041 528 6797, *www.diaconiavaldese.org/venezia*. An old *palazzo* converted into a dormitory/*pensione* by the Waldensians.

Istituto Canossiano, Giudecca 428, Fondamenta del Ponte Piccolo, **t** 041 522 2157. A women's hostel run by nuns, with a 10.30pm curfew.

Ostello di Venezia, Giudecca 86, Fondamenta delle Zitelle, **t** 041 523 8211. One of the best located youth hostels in Italy, on the Giudecca Canal with views of San Marco. Phone bookings are not taken; for a place in July or Aug, write well in advance. At other times, either chance it or book in person any day after 6pm (doors open for queueing at midday). Curfew is 11.30pm.

Eating Out

The Venetians are traditionally the worst cooks in Italy, and the city has the highest percentage of dud restaurants per capita, though prices tend to be about 15% higher. Even moderate ones can give you a nasty surprise with excessive service and cover charges, while the cheap ones, serving up 500 tourist menus a day, are mere providers of sustenance to keep you on your feet.

Very Expensive

Antico Martini, San Marco 1983, Campo San Fantin, **t** 041 522 4121. An 18th-century Turkish coffeehouse turned elegant Venetian classic known for its seafood, *pennette al pomodoro*, and superb wine list. The intimate piano bar-restaurant is open until 2am. *Closed Tues, and Weds lunch.*

Cipriani, Giudecca 10, **t** 041 240 8507. Romance and atmosphere aplenty, especially in summer when tables are laid on a magical terrace and a piano tinkles in the background. The wide variety of dishes, local and otherwise, are well prepared and presented. Try fillet of John Dory in a potato crust with asparagus, or duck breast with polenta soufflé. Booking is advised. No children under 8 are allowed in for dinner. For a less wallet-busting (but less romantic) experience, lunch at the Cip's club. *Closed Nov–Mar.*

La Corte Sconta, Castello 3886, Calle del Pestrin, **t** 041 522 7024. An off-the-beaten-track trattoria with a reputation for its molluscs and crustaceans. Be sure to order the house wine. Booking essential. *Closed Sun, Mon and mid-July–mid-Aug.*

Danieli Terrace, Danieli Hotel, Castello 4196, Riva degli Schiavoni, **t** 041 522 6480. The Danieli hotel's rooftop restaurant, renowned for its classic cuisine (try *spaghetti alla Danieli*, prepared at your table) and faultless service.

Da Fiore, San Polo 2202A, Calle del Scaleter, **t** 041 721 308. A place were food is taken very seriously indeed, with none of the pretentious frills of many other Venetian eateries. Start with *misto crudo* (marinated raw fish) or scallops *gratinati* with thyme, then try the classic *bigoli in salsa* (hand-made spaghetti with mashed anchovies and onions), penne with scallops and broccoli, or squid-ink risotto. Main courses include *involtini* of sole wrapped round radicchio. *Closed Sun and Mon, early Jan and Aug.*

Harry's Bar, San Marco 1323, Calle Vallaresso, **t** 041 528 5777. A favourite of Hemingway and other luminaries, and as much a Venetian institution as the Doge's Palace. Avoid the restaurant upstairs and sample a sandwich or the famous cocktails (a Bellini, a Tiziano or a Tiepolo) at a table downstairs near the bar.

Harry's Dolci, Giudecca 773, Fondamenta San Biagio, **t** 041 522 4844. A restaurant decked out like a trattoria, with tiled walls and wooden tables, affording stunning views across the canal. The food is similar to that at Harry's Bar, though considerably cheaper. *Closed Mon, Tues and Nov–Mar.*

Hostaria da Franz, Castello 754, Fondamenta San Giuseppe, **t** 041 522 0861. An intimate dining room with an enchanting canalside terrace. Traditional fish dishes given a creative twist include giant prawns marinated in citrus fruits. Eels are a speciality. Booking is advised. *Closed Jan.*

Da Ignazio, San Polo 2749, Calle dei Saoneri, **t** 041 523 4852. A cosy, traditional trattoria that's been serving classic Venetian fish dishes for more than 50 years, as well as such oddities as *moeche* (small, soft-shelled crabs eaten whole), *castraure* (spring artichokes) and *sparesee* (wild asparagus). There is a pretty courtyard. Booking advised. *Closed Sat and 3wks July–Aug.*

Locanda Cipriani, Torcello, Piazza Santa Fosca 29, **t** 041 730 150. An idyllic place to eat (as Hemingway and Chaplin discovered) off sleepy Torcello's main square. Rustic and cosy, it has a lovely vine-covered terrace. The food is a bit of an afterthought. There are 6 elegant bedrooms (*see* p.320). *Closed Tues.*

Da Remigio, Castello 3416, Ponte dei Greci, **t** 041 523 0089. A neighbourhood seafood favourite. *Closed Mon eve and Tues.*

Il Sole Sulla Vecia Cavana, Cannaregio 4624, Rio Terrà SS Apostoli, **t** 041 528 7106. An elegant restaurant with both traditional and innovative dishes, including seafood salad with 'pearls' of melon and cucumber, and *margherite* (ravioli) stuffed with sea bass. *Closed Mon, and 2 wks Jan and Aug.*

Expensive

Al'Aciugheta, Castello 4357, Campo SS. Filippo e Giacomo, **t** 041 522 4292. One of the best restaurants and bars near Piazza San Marco, with a good atmosphere. Avoid the touristy pizzeria at the front, and go early to the back room for great *cicheti* and excellent wines.

Le Bistrot de Venise, San Marco 4685, Calle dei Fabbri, **t** 041 523 6651. A cosy place offering historical local dishes with unusual herbs and spices, such as pumpkin and cheese gnocchi with cinnamon, sturgeon with prunes, grapes and balsamic vinegar, and Turkish spiced rice pudding. Poetry readings, live music and other cultural events are held.

L'Incontro, Dorsoduro 3062, Rio Terrà Canal, **t** 041 522 2404. A Sardinian restaurant serving only meat and vegetable dishes (no fish): gnocchi with tomato and *pecorino*, ravioli flavoured with saffron, and roast suckling pig. *Closed Mon, and Tues lunch.*

Alla Nuova Speranza, Castello 145, Campo Ruga, **t** 041 528 5225. A friendly trattoria packed with local workmen at lunchtime, serving fat *capparossoli* (clams) sautéed in garlic and wine or tossed into spaghetti, plus other seafood. The tourist menu is good value. Book for dinner (or the cook will go home early). No credit cards.

Al Mascaron, Castello 5225, Calle Lunga Santa Maria Formosa, **t** 041 522 5995. A favourite Venetian *osteria*, noisy and unpretentious. Wine is served out of huge containers in the front, and Venetian specialities are served at marble-topped tables. Try liver and sardines served *in saor* – with pine nuts, raisins and marinated onions. *Closed Sun and Jan.*

Osteria San Marco, San Marco 1610, Frezzeria, **t** 041 528 5242. A stylish *osteria/enoteca* with white walls, exposed bricks and interesting food, including gnocchi with crab and rosemary, guinea fowl with balsamic vinegar, and fillet steak cooked with coffee (an ancient recipe). It's open all day for a snack and a glass of wine. *Closed Sun and Jan.*

Ribò, Santa Croce 158, Fondamenta Minotto, **t** 041 524 2486. A small restaurant with an elegant modern look and food to match. Try carpaccio of octopus with shallot vinegar, risotto with scampi and asparagus, and tempura of scallops. There's a delightful garden. *Closed Mon.*

Vecio Fritolin, Santa Croce 2262, Calle della Regina, **t** 041 522 2881. A calm, civilized restaurant offering the day's catch cooked without fuss: you might get baby shrimp on a bed of sautéed artichoke hearts, or steamed fillet of turbot with asparagus in a buttery vinaigrette. *Closed Sun eve and Mon.*

Vini da Gigio, Cannaregio 3628A, Fondamenta San Felice, **t** 041 528 5140. A small restaurant with canal views, always crowded with local foodies. The traditional food includes raw, marinated fish, sautéed scallops, and lagoon duck (*masorini*) . The superb wine list has some 600 labels from both Italy and beyond. Booking is essential. *Closed Mon, 3wks Jan–Feb and 3wks July–Aug.*

Moderate

Anice Stellato, Cannaregio 3272, Fondamenta della Sensa, **t** 041 720 744. A new-generation, family-run *bacaro*/trattoria near remote Sant'Alvise church, offering traditional dishes with a creative twist – spaghetti with sardines and balsamic vinegar, tagliatelle with scampi and zucchini, and *dorade* flavoured with curry. Booking advised. *Closed Mon and 3wks Aug–Sept.*

Bancogiro: Osteria da Andrea, San Polo 122, Campo Giacometto, **t** 041 523 2061. A modern *osteria* overlooking the Grand Canal. The bar has excellent wines and snacks, the upstairs restaurant creative dishes such as fish salad with apple and mandarin, and roast tuna with pine nuts. Booking is essential. *Closed Sun eve and Mon.*

Gam-Gam, Cannaregio 1122, Sottoportico di Ghetto Vecchio, **t** 041 715 284. A modern kosher bar and restaurant by the entrance to the ghetto, with tables on the canal. There's an excellent choice of *antipasti* (houmous, baba ganoush and the like), fish, meat and vegetable couscous, *shawarma*, *latkes*, the odd Italian dish, and vegetarian options. No credit cards. *Closed Sat.*

Osteria ai Assassini, San Marco 3695, Rio Terrà dei Assassini, **t** 041 528 7986. A popular *osteria* on a quiet street north of La Fenice, serving fish on Thursdays and Fridays, meat the rest of the week, plus a range of *cicheti*. The ambience is rustic (low ceilings, wood panelling and brickwork) and lively. *Closed Sat lunch and Sun.*

Mistra, Giudecca 212A, **t** 041 522 0743.
A first-floor trattoria located among the boatyards, with watery views. Specialities are fish and dishes from Liguria (expect lots of pesto). Booking is advised. *Closed Mon eve, Tues and Jan.*

Al Pantalon, Dorsoduro 3958, Calle del Scaleter, **t** 041 710 849. A popular rustic *osteria* near the Frari, serving *cicheti* at a front counter and full meals at tables in an adjoining room. *Closed Sun.*

Ai 4 Feri, Dorsoduro 2754, Calle Lunga San Barnabà, **t** 041 520 6978. A traditional *osteria* run along traditional lines, with excellent *cicheti* and full meals at honest prices: pumpkin soup, spaghetti with artichokes and shrimps, simple grilled fish, *seppie* with polenta, and fresh tuna *in saor*, a speciality. No credit cards. *Closed Sun.*

Alla Vedova, Cannaregio 3912, Ramo Ca' d'Oro, **t** 041 528 5324. One of the oldest, best-known *bacari* in Venice, where locals crowd round the bar to eat excellent *cicheti* (including wonderful spicy *polpette* or meatballs) and hungrier punters sit at wooden tables in the adjoining room to enjoy tagliatelle with duck, *fritto misto*, *fegato alla veneziana* and vegetarian options. Booking is essential. *Closed Sun lunch, Thurs, Fri and Aug.*

Cheap

Il Réfolo, Santa Croce 1459, Campo San Giacomo dell'Orio, **t** 041 524 0016.
An excellent pizzeria run by the same team behind the legendary Da Fiore (*see* p.321). *Closed Tues and Dec and Jan.*

Rosticceria San Bartolomeo, San Marco 5424, Calle della Bissa, **t** 041 522 3569. A no-frills trattoria with an even cheaper snack bar downstairs (eat in or take away).

Da Toni, Dorsoduro 1642, Fondamenta San Basegio, **t** 041 528 6899. A simple local trattoria offering the likes of scallops with parsley, garlicky sea snails, and excellent grilled monkfish. No credit cards.
Closed Mon and 3wks Aug.

Vino Vino, San Marco 2007A, Calle del Caffettier, **t** 041 523 7027. A pleasant little wine bar near La Fenice, offering some 350 vintages from all over Italy and further afield. Enjoy snacks at the bar or reasonably priced meals in the adjoining room.

Bacari

The *bacaro* is Venice's answer to a tapas bar, though many also serve full meals, often at long tables in a back room. They come in all shapes and sizes, from gloomy holes in the wall with standing room only to slick, trendy establishments. They all offer wines by the glass (*un ombra*) and *cicheti* – tasty little snacks, usually arranged on the counter. You either spear them with a toothpick off the main serving dish, or ask for a selection to be put on a plate, pointing at whatever takes your fancy. Prices are not usually displayed on each item, and the bill can quickly mount up.

Venice is full of *bacari*, usually hidden down narrow alleys. Most are open all day (some have a couple of hours' siesta mid-afternoon) but close at around 8pm; some newer ones stay open late. They rarely accept credit cards.

Algiubagiò, Cannaregio 5039, Fondamenta Nuove, **t** 041 523 6084. A good place for a drink, snack or light meal, right by the *vaporetto* stop for the islands, with a large terrace and friendly staff. *Closed Jan.*

Al Bacareto, San Marco 3447, Calle delle Botteghe, **t** 041 528 9336. A traditional *bacaro* with great *cicheti*, plus heartier dishes. Booking advised. *Closed Sat eve, Sun and Aug.*

Al Bottegon, Dorsoduro 992, Fondamenta Nani, **t** 041 523 0034. An old-fashioned wine shop serving snacks. *Closed Sun pm.*

Da Codroma, Dorsoduro 2540, Fondamenta Briati, **t** 041 524 6789. A smoky, laid-back venue with live jazz and blues on Tues. At lunch the long communal tables are packed with students. *Closed Sun and 3wks Aug.*

Ai Do Mori, San Polo 429, Calle dei Do Mori, **t** 041 522 5401. A historic '*locale*' in a long, rather gloomy, wood-panelled room, with standing room only. *Closed Sun and 3wks Aug.*

Alla Patatina, San Polo 2741A, Ponte San Polo, **t** 041 523 7238. A lively place famous for its chips. *Closed Sat eve, Sun and 2wks Aug.*

Al Volto, San Marco 4081, Calle Cavalli, **t** 041 522 8945. A cosy *bacaro* near Campo San Luca, with both snacks and daily-changing dishes such as *bigoli in salsa* or *calimari in umido*. *Closed Sun.*

Enoteca Due Colonne, Cannaregio 1814C, Rio Terrà del Cristo, **t** 041 524 0453. A fun, noisy bar full of Venetians, serving *cicheti*, panini and a wide variety of drinks. *Closed Sat.*

Cafés and Bars

Between 5pm and dinner Venetians indulge in a beer and *tramezzini* (finger sandwiches).

Il Caffè, Dorsoduro 2963, Campo Santa Margherita, **t** 041 528 7998. A lively local hang-out offering cocktails, coffee, pastries and snacks. *Closed Sun.*

Caffè Costarica, Cannaregio 1337, Rio Terrà San Leonardo. Venice's strongest *espressos*, plus great iced coffee (*frappé*). *Closed Sun.*

Caffè Florian, San Marco 56/59, Piazza San Marco, **t** 041 520 5641. The place every Venetian learns to favour over Quadri (*see* below), with a charming, cosy 18th-century décor. Sitting on the outside terrace when there is live music carries an extra charge.

Gran Caffè Lavena, San Marco 133, Piazza San Marco, **t** 041 522 4070. Excellent coffee in a beautiful 1750 setting, less touristy (and less pricey) than Florian or Quadri.

Gran Caffè Quadri, San Marco 120, Piazza San Marco. **t** 041 522 2105. A historic coffeehouse that fell from grace during the Second World War. There's a gorgeous restaurant and a terrace hosting live music (extra charge).

Marchini, San Marco 676, Calle Spadaria, **t** 041 522 9109. Chocolates, cakes and pastries; try the prize-winning *Torta del Doge*. *Closed Sun.*

Nico, Dorsoduro 922, Fondamenta Zattere ai Gesuati, **t** 041 522 5293. A must on anyone's ice-cream tour, with long late-night queues.

Paolin, San Marco 2962, Campo Santo Stefano, **t** 041 522 5576. The best *gelateria* in the city, with a divine pistachio.

Rizzardini, San Polo 1415, Campiello dei Meloni, **t** 041 522 3835. An old-fashioned pastry shop and *caffè* with traditional cakes and biscuits. *Closed Tues and Aug.*

Rosa Salva, Castello 6779, Campo SS Giovanni e Paolo, **t** 041 522 7949; San Marco 4589, Campo San Luca, **t** 041 522 5385. One of the city's best cake shops, with outside tables.

Entertainment and Nightlife

For a city made for revelry and romance, life after dark here is strangely moribund. Locals take an evening stroll to their nearest *campo* for an *aperitivo*, then head home. The hot-blooded may go on to bars and discos in Mestre, Marghera or the Lido. If you want to become even poorer, go to the **Casinò di Venezia**, Cannaregio 2040, Ca' Vendramin-Calergi, **t** 041 529 7111 (*open daily 3pm–2.30am; dress smartly*). A moonlit gondola ride is a comparative bargain.

That said, Venice has a packed calendar of special events. For up-to-date listings of exhibitions, shows, films and concerts, consult the fortnightly English magazine *Un Ospite di Venezia*, free at tourist offices and hotels, or local dailies *Il Gazzettino* and *Nuova Venezia.*

VELA, part of the ACTV transport company, is a ticket office not only for bus/boat tickets but for some concerts, operas, dance events and the Biennale. All are available from main *vaporetto* stops (Accademia, Ferrovia, Rialto, Tronchetto, Vallaresso, San Zaccaria, Lido) and VELA agencies (Calle dei Fuseri, **t** 041 241 8029, *open 7.30–7*, and Piazzale Roma, **t** 041 272 2249; *open 8.30–6.30*).

Festivals

The **Biennale** (*odd-numbered years; June–Sept*) is the world's most famous contemporary art show, with 40 or so countries exhibiting in permanent pavilions in the Giardini Pubblici. The other great cultural junket is the **Film Festival** (*late Aug/early Sept*), in the Palazzo del Cinema and the Astra Cinema on the Lido. You may get into a film if you arrive really early.

Venice's **Carnival** (*10 days before Shrove Tues*), first held in 1094, was revived in 1979 after decades of dormancy. It attracts huge crowds, but faces an uphill battle against the Italian love of *bella figura* – getting dressed up, wandering down to San Marco and taking one another's picture is as much as most revellers get up to. Concerts and shows take place, with city and corporate sponsorship, but there's little spontaneity or serious carousing.

In 1988 Venice revived another crowd-pleaser, **La Sensa** (*first Sun after Ascension Day*), in which the Doge married the sea. The mayor now plays the groom, in a replica of the state barge or *Bucintoro*. It's corny and pretentious, but the gondoliers racing in the **Vogalonga** ('long row') is worth watching.

The most spectacular festival is **Il Redentore** (*third Sun in July*), with its bridge of boats (*see* p.356). The best part is the previous Saturday night, when Venetians row out for a picnic on the water, and to watch fabulous fireworks over the Lagoon. For landlubbers the prime viewing and picnic spots are towards the eastern ends of the Giudecca or the Zattere.

The **Regata Storica** (*first Sun in Sept*) is a splendid pageant of historic vessels with crews in Renaissance costumes, and races by gondoliers and others down the Grand Canal.

Another bridge of boats is built on 21 Nov, across the Grand Canal to the Salute, for the feast of **Santa Maria della Salute**, which commemorates the end of a plague in 1631. It's the only opportunity to see Longhena's basilica as it was when it was built, doors thrown open on to the Grand Canal.

Opera, Classical Music and Theatre

The famous **La Fenice** opera house, **t** 041 786 511 (*see* p.347), finally reopened in Dec 2003 with an inaugural performance by the theatre orchestra and chorus. At the time of writing, opera was slated to recommence in autumn 2004, beginning with *La Traviata*.

The **Palazzo delle Prigioni**, Riva degli Schiavoni, **t** 041 984 252, an ex-prison next to the Palazzo Ducale, hosts Venetian Baroque and classical concerts (*Jan–May and summer*). Regular church concerts are held in **I Frari**, San Polo, Campo dei Frari, **t** 041 522 2637, *see* p.350 (*9pm Fri May–July, Sept and Oct*); and in **La Pietà**, Castello, Riva degli Schiavoni, **t** 041 523 1096, *see* p.351. Prices at the latter are usually high, but the acoustics are well-nigh perfect.

The beautiful state-run **Teatro Goldoni**, San Marco 4650B, Calle del Teatro, **t** 041 240 2011, puts on classic Italian dramas (Goldoni, Pirandello and so on), with big-name directors and actors appearing regularly. Occasional concerts also take place here.

Pubs, Clubs and Other Nightspots

The few late-night bars and music venues can be fun, or posey and dull; what you find is pretty much pot luck.

Bacaro Jazz, San Marco 5546, Salizzada del Fóndaco dei Tedeschi, **t** 041 528 5249. A lively bar with occasional live jazz and blues. *Closed Weds.*

Caffè Blu, Dorsoduro 3778, Salizzada San Pantalon, **t** 041 710 227. A crowded bar with live music (blues, Latin, jazz) on Fri (*Oct–Apr*). *Open Sun.*

Casanova Disco, Cannaregio 158A, Lista di Spagna, **t** 041 275 0199. A large nightclub with pop, rock, chart and house nights.

Al Delfino, Lido, Lungomare Marconi 96, **t** 041 526 8309. An 'American bar' with music, snacks and billiards.

The Fiddler's Elbow, Cannaregio 3847, Campiello Testori, **t** 041 523 9930. An Irish pub behind Palazzo Fontana.

Iguana, Cannaregio 2515, Fondamenta della Misericordia, **t** 041 713 561. A Latin club with great cocktails (*happy hour 7–9*), spicy food, dancing and live acts on Tues. *Closed Sun and Mon.*

Margaret Duchamp, Dorsoduro 3019, Campo Santa Margherita, **t** 041 528 6255. A designer 'disco bar' frequented by trendy Venetians and foreigners. *Closed Tues in winter.*

L'Olandese Volante, Castello 5658, Campo San Lio, **t** 041 528 9349. One of Venice's answers to a pub, open late and serving snacks. *Closed Sun.*

Paradiso Perduto, Cannaregio 2540, Fondamenta della Misericordia, **t** 041 720 581. The city's best-known and most popular late-night bar/restaurant, with a relaxed, bohemian atmosphere; live concerts (jazz and roots), parties and exhibitions. *Closed Weds and 2wks Aug.*

Piccolo Mondo, Dorsoduro 1056, Calle Contarini-Corfù, **t** 041 520 0371. One of the few real clubs in Venice, tiny and a little sleazy. *Closed Mon.*

Sound Code, Mestre, Via delle Industrie 32, **t** 041 531 3890. The best disco in the area. *Open Fri and Sat.*

T.A.G. Club, Mestre, Via Giustizia 19, **t** 041 921 970. An excellent little club with live blues, jazz and rock. *Closed Sun–Tues.*

Teranga, Mestre, Via della Crusca 34, **t** 041 531 7787. A popular, lively club playing mainly African sounds, with regular live music. Membership required. *Open Fri and Sat.*

Al Vapore, Marghera, Via Fratelli Bandiera 8, **t** 041 930 796. A small venue near Mestre station, with excellent live jazz and blues concerts by known and lesser-known names. *Closed Mon.*

Vitae, San Marco 4118, Calle Sant'Antonio, **t** 041 520 5205. A small, smoky venue with designer décor, loud, laid-back music and good cocktails. *Closed Sun.*

History

Venice has always been so improbable that one can easily believe the legend that the original inhabitants sprang up from the dew and mists on the mud banks of the Lagoon. Historians who don't believe in fairies say Venice was born of adversity: the islands and treacherous shallows of the Lagoon provided citizens of the Veneto with a refuge from **Attila the Hun** and the Arian heresies sweeping the mainland. According to Venetians' own legends, the city was founded at noon on 25 March 413, when the refugees laid the first stone on the Rialto. Twelve Lagoon townships grew up between modern Chioggia and Grado; in 523 Theodoric the Great's secretary Cassiadorus wrote that they were 'scattered like sea-birds' nests over the face of the waters'.

In 697 the 12 townships united to elect their first duke, or Doge. Fishing, trading – in slaves, among other things – and their unique knowledge of the Lagoon brought Venetians their first prosperity, but their key position between the Byzantine empire and the 'barbarian' kings on the mainland also made them a bone of contention. In 810 the Franks, who had defeated the Lombards in the name of the Pope and claimed dominion over the whole of northern Italy, turned their attention to the last holdout, Venice. Doge Obelario de' Antenori, engaged in a bitter feud with other Venetian factions, even invited Charlemagne's son Pepin to send his army into the city.

The quarrelling Venetians, until then undecided whether to support Rome or Constantinople, united at the approach of Pepin's fleet, deposed the Doge, declared for Byzantium, and entrenched themselves on the Rialto. The shallows and queer humours of the Lagoon confounded Pepin, and after a gruelling six-month siege he threw in the towel. A subsequent treaty between the Franks and the Eastern Emperor Nicephorus (814) recognized Venice as a subject of **Byzantium**, with important trading concessions. As Byzantine authority over the city was never more than words, it in effect marked the birth of an independent republic.

The Venetians lacked only a dynamic spiritual protector; their frumpy St Theodore with his crocodile was simply too low in the celestial hierarchy to fulfil the destiny they had in mind. In 829 Venetian merchants, supposedly on secret orders from the Doge, carried off one of the Republic's greatest coups when they purloined the body of St Mark from Alexandria, smuggling him past Egyptian customs by claiming that the saint was pickled pork. To acquire an Evangelist for themselves was, in itself, a demonstration of the Venetians' new ambition.

Marriage to the Sea

As east–west trade expanded, the Venetians designed their domestic and external policies to accommodate it. At home they required peace and stability, and by the beginning of the 11th century had squelched all notions of a hereditary dogeship by exiling the most hyperactive families. Raids by Dalmatian pirates spurred them to fight and win their first major war in 997, under **Doge Pietro Orseolo**. The Venetians celebrated the event with a splendidly arrogant ritual every Ascension Day, the Sensa or 'Marriage of the Sea', in which the Doge sailed out to the Lido in his sumptuous barge, the *Bucintoro*, and cast a diamond ring into the sea, proclaiming 'We wed thee, O sea, in sign of our true and perpetual dominion'.

When to Go

In no other city will you be so aware of the light; on a clear, fine day no place could be more limpid and clear, no water as crystal-bright as the Lagoon. The rosy dawn igniting the domes of St Mark's, the splash of an oar fading in the cool mist of a canal, the pearly twilit union of water and sky are among the city's oldest clichés.

If you seek solitude and romance, go in January. Pack a warm coat, waterproof shoes and an umbrella, and expect frequent fogs and mists. It may even snow – in 1987 you could ski-jump down the Rialto bridge. But there are also plenty of radiant diamond days, brilliant, sunny and chill; any time after October you take your chances.

As spring approaches there's Carnival, a game and beautiful but bland attempt to revive a piece of old Venice; Lent is fairly quiet, though Venetians are building up for their first major invasion of sightseers at Easter. By April the tourism industry is cranked up to full capacity; the gondolas are de-mothballed and the café tables have blossomed in the Piazza. In June even Italians are considering a trip to the beach.

In July and August elbow-room is at a premium. Peripheral campsites are packed, queues at the tourist office room-finding service are ever longer, and the police are kept busy reminding the hordes there's no picnicking in Piazza San Marco. The heat can be sweltering, the ancient city gasping under a flood of cameras, sunglasses and rucksacks. Scores head off to the Lido for relief; a sudden thunderstorm over the Lagoon livens things up, as do the many festivals, especially the Redentore and its fireworks in July. In autumn the city starts to unwind, the rains begin, and you can watch them pack up the parasols and cabanas on the Lido with a wistful sigh.

As far as hotels are concerned, high season is from Carnival to mid-November, with prices coming down a bit in midsummer.

Venice, because of her location and fleet, supplied a great deal of the transport for the first three Crusades, and in return she received her first important trading concessions in the Middle East. Her arch-rival Genoa became increasingly envious, and in 1171 convinced the Byzantine Emperor to all but wipe out the Venetian merchants in Constantinople. Rashly, the Doge Vitale Michiel II set off in person in order to launch a revenge attack upon the Empire. He failed utterly, and on his return was killed by an angry mob. The Venetians learned from their mistakes: the Great Council, the Maggior Consiglio, was created to check the power of the Doge and thus avert future calamities.

Vengeance stayed on the backburner until the next Doge, the spry and crafty Enrico Dandolo, was contracted to provide transport for the Fourth Crusade. When the Crusaders turned up without their fare, Dandolo offered to forgo it in return for certain services: first, to reduce Venice's rebellious satellites in Dalmatia, and then, in 1204, to sail to Constantinople instead of Egypt. Aged 90 and almost blind, Dandolo personally led the attack; Christendom was scandalized, but Venice had gained, not only a glittering hoard of loot, but three-eighths of Constantinople and 'a quarter and a half' of the Roman Empire – enough islands and ports to control the trade routes in the Adriatic, Aegean, Asia Minor and the Black Sea.

To ensure their dominance at home, in 1297 the merchant élite limited membership in the *Maggior Consiglio* to themselves and their heirs (an event known as the **Serrata**, or Lock-out), their names inscribed in the famous **Golden Book**. The Doges were reduced to honorary chairmen of the board, bound up by an increasingly complex web of laws and customs to curb any possible ambitions; for the patricians, fear of revolution from above was as powerful as fear of revolt from below.

A Rocky 14th Century

First the people (1300) and then the snubbed patricians (the 1310 **Tiepolo Conspiracy**) rose up against their disenfranchisement under the *Serrata*. Both were unsuccessful, but the latter threat was serious enough that a committee of public safety was formed to hunt down the conspirators, and in 1335 this committee became a permanent institution, the infamous **Council of Ten**. Because of its secrecy and speedy decisions, the Council of Ten (in later years it was streamlined into a Council of Three) was more truly executive than the figurehead Doge: it guarded Venice's internal security, looked after foreign policy and, with its sumptuary laws, kept tabs on the Venetians' moral conduct as well.

Away from home, the 14th century was marked by a fight to the death with Genoa over eastern trade routes. Each republic annihilated the other's fleet on more than one occasion before things came to a head in 1379, when the Genoese, fresh from a victory over the Venetian commander Vittor Pisani, captured Chioggia and waited for Venice to starve, boasting that they had come to 'bridle the horses of St Mark'. As was their custom, the Council of Ten had imprisoned Pisani for his defeat, but Venice was now in such a jam, with half of its fleet far away, that the people demanded his release to lead what remained of their navy. A brilliant commander, Pisani exploited his familiarity with the Lagoon and in turn blockaded the Genoese in Chioggia. When the other half of Venice's fleet came dramatically racing home, the Genoese surrendered (June 1380) and never recovered in the east.

Fresh Prey on the Mainland

Venice was determined never to feel hungry again, and set her sights on the mainland – not only for the sake of farmland, but to control her trade routes into the west that were being increasingly harried and taxed by the *signori* of the Veneto. Treviso came first, then opportunity knocked in 1402 with the sudden death of the Milanese duke Gian Galeazzo Visconti, whose conquests became the subject of a great land grab. Venice picked up Padua, Bassano, Verona and Belluno, and in 1454 added Ravenna, southern Trentino, Friuli, Crema and Bergamo. In 1489 the Republic's overseas empire reached its greatest extent when it was presented with Cyprus, a somewhat reluctant 'gift' from the king's widow, a Venetian noblewoman named Caterina Cornaro who received the hill town of Àsolo as compensation.

But just as Venice expanded, Fortune's wheel gave a creak and conspired to squeeze her back into her Lagoon. The Ottoman Turks captured Constantinople in 1453 and, although the Venetians tried to negotiate trading terms with the sultans (as they had previously done with the infidel Saracens, to the opprobrium of the west), they would be spending the next three centuries fighting a losing battle for their eastern territories. The discovery of the New World was another blow, but gravest to the merchants of Venice was Vasco da Gama's voyage around the Cape of Good Hope to India in 1497, blazing a cheaper and easier route to Venice's prime markets that broke her monopoly of oriental luxuries; Western European merchants no longer had to pay Venice for safe passage to the east. In just 44 years nearly everything that Venice had worked for for more than 500 years was undermined.

On the mainland, Venice's rapid expansion had excited the fear and envy of Pope Julius, who rallied Italy's potentates and their foreign allies to form the League of Cambrai to humble the proud Republic. They snatched her *terra firma* possessions after her defeat at Agnadello in 1509, but quarrelled amongst themselves afterwards, and before long all the territories they conquered voluntarily returned to Venice. Venice, however, never really recovered from this wound inflicted by the very people who should have rallied to her defence, and although her Arsenal produced a warship a day, and her captains helped to win a glorious victory over the Turks at Lepanto (1571), she was increasingly forced to retreat.

A Most Leisurely Collapse

The odds were stacked against her, but in her heyday Venice had accumulated enough wealth and verve to cushion her fall. Her noble families consoled themselves in the classical calm of Palladio's villas, while the city found solace in masterpieces of Venice's golden age of art. Carnival, ever longer, ever more licentious, was sanctioned by the state to bring in moneyed visitors, like Lord Byron, who dubbed it 'the revel of the earth, the masque of Italy'. In the 1600s the city had 20,000 courtesans, many of them dressed as men to whet the Venetians' passion. It didn't suit everyone: 'Venice is a stink pot, charged with every virus of hell,' fumed one Dr Warner, in the 18th century.

In 1797 **Napoleon**, declaring he would be 'an Attila for the Venetian state', took it with scarcely a whimper, ending the story of the world's longest-enduring republic, in the reign of its 120th doge. Napoleon took the horses of St Mark to Paris as his trophy, and replaced the old *Pax tibi, Marce, Evangelista Meus* inscribed in the book the lion holds up on Venice's coat-of-arms with 'The Rights of Men and Citizens'. While many patricians danced merrily around his Liberty trees, freed at last from responsiblity, the people wept. Napoleon gave Venice to Austria, whose rule was confirmed by the Congress of Vienna after the Emperor's defeat in 1815. The Austrians' main contribution was the railway causeway linking Venice irrevocably to the mainland (1846). Two years later, Venice gave its last gasp of independence, when a patriotic revolt led by Daniele Manin seized the city and re-established the Republic, only to fall to the Austrian army once again after a heroic one-year siege.

Modern Venice

The former Republic finally joined the new kingdom of Italy in 1866, after Prussia had conveniently defeated the Austrians. Already best known as a magnet to visitors, Venice played a quiet role in the new state. Things changed under Mussolini, the industrial zones of Mestre and Marghera were begun on the mainland, and a road was added to the railway causeway. The city escaped damage in the two World Wars, despite heavy fighting in the environs; according to legend, when the Allies finally occupied Venice in 1945 they arrived in a fleet of gondolas.

But Venice was soon to engage in its own private battle with the sea. From the beginning the city had manipulated nature's waterways for her own survival, diverting a major outlet of the Po, the Brenta, the Piave, the Adige, and the Sile rivers to keep her Lagoon from silting up. In 1782 Venice completed the famous *murazzi*, the 20ft-high sea walls to protect the Lagoon. But on 4 November 1966 a deadly combination of wind, torrential storms, high tides and giant waves breached the *murazzi*, wrecked the Lido and left Venice under record *acque alte* (high waters) for 20 hours, with disastrous results to the city's architecture and art. The catastrophe galvanized the international community's efforts to save Venice. Even the Italian state, notorious for its indifference to Venice (historical grudges die slowly in Italy), passed a law in 1973 to preserve the city, and contributed to the construction of a new flood barricade similar to the one on the Thames.

This giant sea gate, known as 'Moses', has now been completed, but arguments continue over whether it will ever be effective if needed, and what its ecological consequences might be. Venice today is perennially in crisis, permanently under restoration, and seemingly threatened by a myriad potential disasters – the growth of algae in the Lagoon, the effects of the outpourings of Mestre on its foundations, the ageing of its native population, and perhaps most of all the sheer number of its tourists. Proposals have been made to charge admissions at the causeway and limit the number who come in daily. Fears of an environmental catastrophe have, though, receded of late; somehow, the city contrives to survive, as unique as ever, and recent proposals to give it more of a function in the modern world as, for example, a base for international organizations, may serve to give it new life as well.

Architecture

At once isolated but linked to the traditions of east and west, Venice developed her own charmingly bastard architecture, especially in a style called Venetian Gothic, adopting only the most delightfully visual elements from each tradition. Ruskin's *The Stones of Venice* is the classic work on the city's buildings, which harsher critics – and Ruskin was one – disparage for being all artifice and show. The Venetians inherited the Byzantines' love of colour, mosaics, rare marbles and exotic effects, epitomized in the magnificently gaudy **St Mark's**. Venetian Gothic is only slightly less elaborate, and achieved its best products in the great palaces, most notably the **Palazzo Ducale** and the **Ca' d'Oro**, with their ogival windows and finely wrought façades.

The Renaissance arrived in Venice relatively late; its early phase is called Lombardesque, after the **Lombardo** family (Pietro and sons Tullio and Antonio), who designed the best of it, including **Santa Maria dei Miracoli** and the rich **Scuola di San Marco**. Later Renaissance architects brought Venice into the mainstream of the classical revival, and graced Venice with the arcaded **Piazza San Marco**, the **Libreria** of Sansovino, the **San Michele** of Mauro Codussi (or Coducci), and two of **Palladio**'s finest churches. Venice's best Baroque works are by **Longhena**, the spiritual heir of Palladio.

To support all this on the soft mud banks, the Venetians drove piles of Istrian pine 16½ft into the solid clay – more than a million posts hold up the church of Santa Maria della Salute alone. If Venice tends to lean and sink, it's due to erosion of these piles by the salty Adriatic, pollution, and the currents and wash caused by the deep channels dredged into the Lagoon for the large tankers sailing to Marghera. Or, as the Venetians explain, the city is a giant sponge.

Most Venetian houses are four to six storeys high. On the tops of some you can see the wooden rooftop loggias, or *altane*, where the Renaissance ladies of Venice were wont to idle, bleaching their hair in the sun; they wore broad-brimmed hats to protect their complexions, and spread their tresses through a hole cut in the crown.

Venetian Art

Venice may have been a Renaissance Johnny-come-lately, but the city and its hinterland are rivalled only by Tuscany when it comes to top-notch painting. Before the 14th century the Venetians excelled primarily in mosaic, an art they learned from the Byzantines, shown at their very best in St Mark's and Torcello. In 1306 **Giotto** painted his masterpiece in Padua's Cappella Scrovegni and gave local painters a revolutionary eyeful. His naturalism influenced a school of artists in Padua and **Paolo Veneziano**, the first great Venetian painter of note, although many artists would continue painting decorative Gothic pieces for a long time to come, notably **Jacobello del Fiore**, **Michele Giambono** and the **Vivarini** family.

Things began to change in the mid 15th century, with the advent of two great masters. **Andrea Mantegna** (1431–1506), trained in Padua, influenced generations with his strong interests in antiquity, perspective and powerful sculptured figures. His more lyrical and humane brother-in-law, **Giovanni Bellini** (1440?–1516) founded the Venetian school. Bellini learned the technique of oil painting from **Antonello da Messina** during his visit in 1475, and he never looked back: his use of luminous natural light and colour to create atmosphere ('tonalism') and sensuous beauty are characteristics all of his followers adopted, if few ever equalled. Meanwhile Giovanni's brother, **Gentile Bellini**, and **Vittore Carpaccio** (1470–1523) avoided tonalism altogether in their charming and precise narrative works.

The Cinquecento–Settecento

For the heavy hitters of Venice's 16th-century Golden Age, however, tonalism was a religion: while other Italians followed the Romans in learning drawing and anatomy, the Venetians went their own way, obsessed by the dramatic qualities of atmosphere. The short-lived **Giorgione di Castelfranco** (1475–1510) was the seminal figure in the new manner: his *Tempest* in the Accademia is a remarkable study in brooding tension. Giorgione also invented 'easel painting' – i.e. art that served neither Church nor State nor the vanity of the patron, but stood on its own for the pleasure of the viewer.

Giorgione's colleague, Tiziano Vecellio, or **Titian** (1485/90–1576), was the greatest master of the Venetian school. Known for his bold, spiralling compositions, his rich colours and his luscious mythologies, he was a revolutionary in his old age, using increasingly free brushstrokes and even applying paint with his fingers. **Tintoretto**

(1518–94), of the famously quick brushstrokes, took his Mannerist compositions to unforgettable extremes, while his contemporary, **Paolo Veronese** (1528–88), painted lavish *trompe l'œil* canvases and frescoes that are the culmination of Venice at her most decorative. This was also the period of **Palma Vecchio**, the sensuous painter of Venetian blonde goddesses, **Cima da Conegliano**, author of some of the loveliest landscapes, and **Lorenzo Lotto**, of the famous psychologically penetrating portraits, who was run out of Venice by Titian and his buddies.

Venetia enjoyed an artistic revival in the twilight years of the 18th century, when its art was in great demand at home and abroad. Much of the thanks for this goes to **Giambattista Tiepolo** (1697–1770), the first to cast aside Baroque gloominess to create an effervescent, light-filled, brilliantly coloured style; he was also the last great fresco-painter in Italy. His chief follower was his son Giandomenico, although his influence can also be seen in the luminous palettes of **Antonio Canaletto** (1697–1768) and **Francesco Guardi** (1712–93), who produced the countless views of Venice that were the rage among travellers on the Grand Tour; even now most of their works are in Britain and France. **Pietro Longhi**, their contemporary, devoted himself to genre scenes that offer a delightful insight into the Venice of 200 years ago.

Around the City

The Grand Canal

A ride down Venice's bustling and splendid main artery is most visitors' introduction to the city, and there's no finer one. The Grand Canal has always been Venice's status address, and along its looping banks the patricians of the Golden Book, or *Nobili Homini*, built a hundred marble palaces with their front doors giving onto the water, framed by peppermint-stick posts where they moored their watery carriages.

The highlights, from Piazzale Roma to Piazza San Marco, include the 12th-century **Fóndaco dei Turchi** (with rounded arches, on the right after the Station Bridge), which was the Ottoman merchants' headquarters until 1838 and is now the Natural History Museum. Nearly opposite it, Mauro Codussi's Renaissance **Palazzo Vendramin-Calergi**, where Richard Wagner died in 1883, is now the casino. Back on the right bank, just after the San Stae landing, the Baroque **Palazzo Pésaro** is adorned with masks by Longhena. And then comes the loveliest Venetian palace of all, the **Ca' d'Oro**, with a florid Venetian Gothic façade, formerly etched in gold, now housing the Galleria Franchetti (*see* p.354).

After the Ca' d'Oro Europe's most famous bridge, the **Ponte di Rialto**, swings into view. 'Rialto' recalls the days when the canal was the Rio Alto; originally it was spanned here by a bridge of boats, then by a 13th-century wooden bridge. When that was on the verge of collapse, the Republic held a competition for the design of a new stone structure. The winner, Antonio da Ponte, was the most audacious, proposing a single arch spanning 157ft; built in 1592, it has defied all the dire predictions of the day and still stands, even taking the additional weight of two rows of shops. The reliefs over the arch are of St Mark and St Theodore.

Signs and Directions

The Venetian language, Venetic or Venet, is still commonly heard; to the uninitiated it sounds like an Italian trying to speak Spanish with a numb mouth. It also turns up on the city's street signs: your map may read 'San Giovanni e Paolo', but you should inquire for 'San Zanipolo', while 'San Giovanni Decollato' (decapitated John) is better known as 'San Zan Degola'.

Despite the impossibility of giving comprehensible directions through the tangle of alleys (Venetians will invariably point you in the right direction, however, with a blithe *sempre diritto!* – straight ahead!), it's hard to get hopelessly lost in Venice. It only measures about one and a half by three kilometres, and there are yellow signs at major crossings, pointing the way to San Marco, Rialto and the Accademia, or Piazzale Roma and the Ferrovia if you despair and want to go home.

When hunting for an address, make sure you're in the correct *sestiere*, as some *calli* share names. Also, beware that houses in each *sestiere* are numbered consecutively in a system logical only to a postman from Mars; numbers up to 5,000 are not rare.

To the right stretch the extensive **Rialto Markets**, and on the left the **Fóndaco dei Tedeschi** (German Warehouse), once the busiest trading centre in Venice, where merchants from all over the north lived and traded. The building (now the post office) was remodelled in 1505 and adorned with exterior frescoes by Giorgione and Titian, of which only fragments survive (now in the Ca' d'Oro).

Beyond the Ponte di Rialto are two Renaissance masterpieces: across from the San Silvestro landing, Sanmicheli's 1556 **Palazzo Grimani**, now the Appeals Court, and Mauro Codussi's **Palazzo Corner-Spinelli** (1510), just before Sant'Angelo landing stage. Further along the left bank are the **Palazzi Mocenigo**, three palaces in one, where Byron lived for two years (*see* p.340). A little further, the wall of buildings gives way for the Campo San Samuele, dominated by the **Palazzo Grassi,** an 18th-century neoclassical residence, renovated by Fiat as a modern exhibition and cultural centre.

On the right bank, just after the bend in the canal, the lovely Gothic **Ca' Foscari** was built in 1437 for Doge Francesco Foscari; two doors down, by its own landing stage, is Longhena's 1667 **Ca' Rezzonico**, where Browning died. Further along, the canal is spanned by the wooden **Ponte dell'Accademia**, built in 1932 to replace the ungainly iron 'English bridge'. On the left bank, before Santa Maria del Giglio landing, the majestic Renaissance **Palazzo Corner** (Ca' Grande) was built by Sansovino in 1550. On the right bank, Longhena's Baroque masterpiece **Santa Maria della Salute** is followed by the Customs House, or **Dogana di Mare**, crowned by a golden globe and weather-vane of Fortune, guarding the entrance to the Grand Canal. The next stop is San Marco.

Piazza San Marco

Venice's self-proclaimed Attila, Napoleon himself, described this asymmetrical showpiece as 'Europe's finest drawing-room', and no matter how often you've seen it in pictures or in the flesh, its charm never fades. There are Venetians (not all of them purveyors of souvenirs) who prefer it in the height of summer at its liveliest, when

Venice Transport

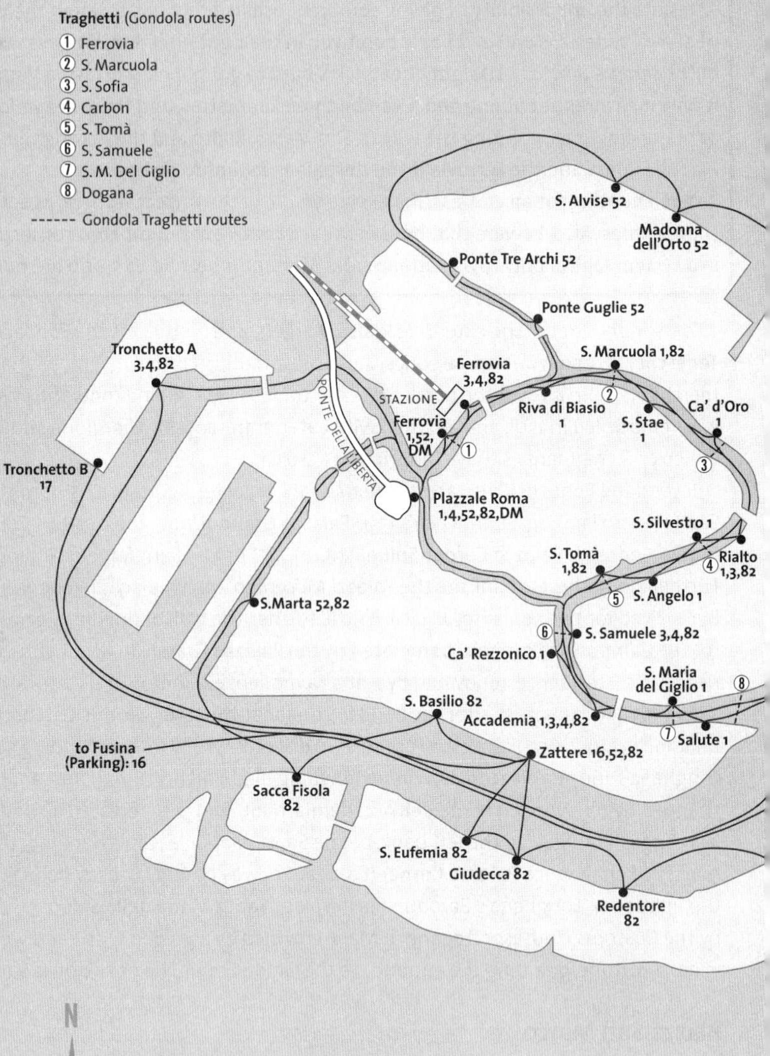
Traghetti (Gondola routes)
① Ferrovia
② S. Marcuola
③ S. Sofia
④ Carbon
⑤ S. Tomà
⑥ S. Samuele
⑦ S. M. Del Giglio
⑧ Dogana
------ Gondola Traghetti routes
S. Alvise 52
Madonna dell'Orto 52
Ponte Tre Archi 52
Ponte Guglie 52
Tronchetto A 3,4,82
Ferrovia 3,4,82
S. Marcuola 1,82
STAZIONE
PONTE DELLA LIBERTA
Riva di Biasio 1
S. Stae 1
Ca' d'Oro 1
Ferrovia 1,52, DM
Tronchetto B 17
Plazzale Roma 1,4,52,82,DM
S. Silvestro 1
Rialto 1,3,82
S. Tomà 1,82
S. Angelo 1
S.Marta 52,82
S. Samuele 3,4,82
Ca' Rezzonico 1
S. Maria del Giglio 1
S. Basilio 82
Accademia 1,3,4,82
Salute 1
to Fusina (Parking): 16
Zattere 16,52,82
Sacca Fisola 82
S. Eufemia 82
Giudecca 82
Redentore 82
N
1 km
1/2 mile

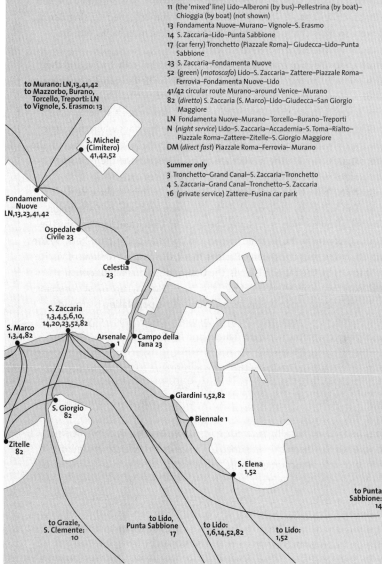

Regular Lines

1 (*accelerato*) Piazzale Roma–Ferrovia–Grand Canal–San Marco–Lido: stops everywhere
6 (*diretto motonave*) S. Zaccaria–Lido
10 S. Zaccaria–Lido
11 (the 'mixed' line) Lido–Alberoni (by bus)–Pellestrina (by boat)–Chioggia (by boat) (not shown)
13 Fondamenta Nuove–Murano– Vignole–S. Erasmo
14 S. Zaccaria–Lido–Punta Sabbione
17 (car ferry) Tronchetto (Piazzale Roma)– Giudecca–Lido–Punta Sabbione
23 S. Zaccaria–Fondamenta Nuove
52 (green) (*motoscafo*) Lido–S. Zaccaria– Zattere–Piazzale Roma–Ferrovia–Fondamenta Nuove–Lido
41/42 circular route Murano–around Venice– Murano
82 (*diretto*) S. Zaccaria (S. Marco)–Lido–Giudecca–San Giorgio Maggiore
LN Fondamenta Nuove–Murano– Torcello–Burano–Treporti
N (*night service*) Lido–S. Zaccaria–Accademia–S. Toma–Rialto–Piazzale Roma–Zattere–Zitelle–S. Giorgio Maggiore
DM (*direct fast*) Piazzale Roma–Ferrovia– Murano

Summer only

3 Tronchetto–Grand Canal–S. Zaccaria–Tronchetto
4 S. Zaccaria–Grand Canal–Tronchetto–S. Zaccaria
16 (private service) Zattere–Fusina car park

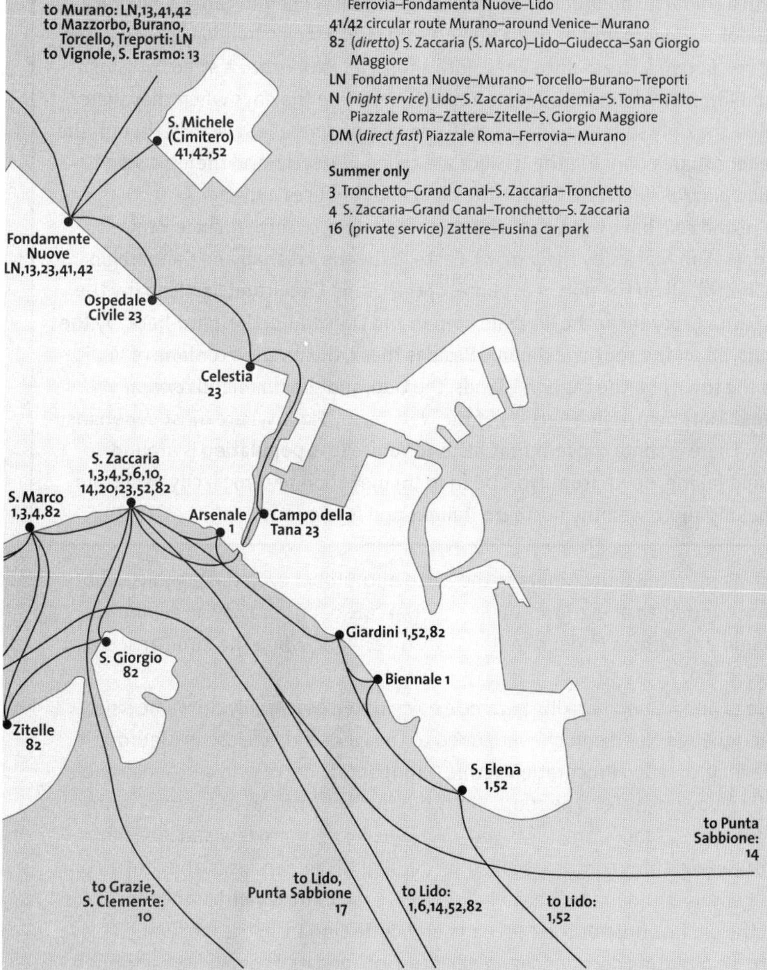

The Face of Venice

Venice stands on 117 islets, divided by more than 100 canals that are spanned by some 400 bridges. The longest bridges are the 4.2km rail and road causeways that link Venice to the mainland. The open sea is half that distance across the Lagoon, beyond the protective reefs or *lidi* formed by centuries of river silt and the Adriatic current. The Grand Canal, Venice's incomparable main street, was originally the bed of a river that fed the Lagoon; the other canals, its tributaries (called *rio*, singular, or *rii*, plural), were shallow channels meandering through the mud banks, and are nowhere as grand – some are merely glorified sewers.

A warren of 2,300 alleys, or *calli*, handle Venice's pedestrian-only traffic, and they come with a colourful bouquet of names – a *rio terrà* is a filled-in canal; a *piscina* a filled-in pool; a *fondamenta* or *riva* a quay; a *salizzada* a street that was paved in the 17th century; a *ruga* a street once lined with shops; a *sottoportico* a street passing under a building. A Venetian square is a *campo*, recalling the days when they were open fields; the only square dignified with the title of *piazza* is St Mark's, though the two smaller squares flanking the basilica are called *piazzette*, and there's a single fume-filled *piazzale* (Piazzale Roma), the dead end for buses and cars.

All the *rii* and *calli* have been divided into six quarters, or *sestieri*, since Venice's earliest days: San Marco (by the *piazza*), Castello (by the Arsenal) and Cannaregio (by the Ghetto), all on the northeast bank of the Grand Canal; and San Polo (by the church), Santa Croce (near the Piazzale Roma), and Dorsoduro, the 'hard-back' by the Accademia, all on the southwest bank. Besides these, the modern *comune* of Venice includes the towns on the Lagoon islands, the Lido, and the mainland *comuni* of Mestre and Marghera, Italy's version of the New Jersey Flats, where most Venetians live today. There is some concern that historic Venice (the population is around 60,000 and falling, down from 170,000 in 1946) may soon become a city of second homes belonging to wealthy northern Italians and foreigners.

Babylonians from the four corners of the earth outnumber even the pigeons, who swoop back and forth at eye level, while the rival café bands provide a Fellini-esque accompaniment. Others prefer it in the misty moonlight, when the familiar seems unreal under hazy, rosy streetlamps.

The piazza and its two flanking *piazzette* have looked essentially the same since 1810, when the 'Ala Napoleonica' was added to the west end, to close in Mauro Codussi's long, arcaded **Procuratie Vecchie** (1499) on the north side and Sansovino's **Procuratie Nuove** (1540) on the south. Both, originally the offices of the 'procurators' or caretakers of St Mark's, are now filled with jewellery, embroidery and lace shops. Two centuries ago they contained an equal number of coffeehouses, the centres of the 18th-century promenade. Only two survive – **Gran Caffè Quadri** in the Procuratie Vecchie, the old favourite of the Austrians, and **Caffè Florian**, in the Procuratie Nuove (for both, *see* p.324), its décor unchanged since it opened its doors in 1720, although with the price they charge for the espressos the proprietors could easily afford to remodel it in solid gold.

St Mark's Basilica

Open to visitors Mon–Sat 9.30–5, Sun and hols 2–4.30. No shorts; women must have their shoulders covered and a minimum of décolletage, or risk being peremptorily dismissed from the head of the queue, which can be diabolically long in season. Adm is free, but there are admission charges for many of the smaller chapels and individual attractions; different sections are frequently closed for restoration. There is disabled ramp access from Piazzetta dei Leoncini.

This is nothing less than the holy shrine of the Venetian state. An ancient law decreed that all merchants trading in the east had to bring back from each voyage a new embellishment for St Mark's. The result is a glittering robbers' den, the only church in Christendom that would not look out of place in Xanadu. Yet it was dismissed out of hand for centuries. 'Low, impenetrable to the light, in wretched taste both within and without,' wrote the Président de Brosses in the 18th century.

Until 1807, when it became Venice's cathedral, the basilica was the private chapel of the Doge, built to house the relics of St Mark after the 'pious theft' of his body from Alexandria in 828, a deed sanctioned by a tidy piece of apocrypha that had the good Evangelist mooring his ship on the Rialto on the way from Aquileia to Rome, when an angel hailed him with the famous '*Pax tibi*...' or 'Peace to you, Mark, my Evangelist. Here your body shall lie.'

The present structure, which was consecrated in 1094, was begun after a fire destroyed the original St Mark's in 976. Modelled after Constantinople's former Church of the Apostles, its exterior is characterized by five rounded doorways, five upper arches and five round Byzantine domes, all of which are frosted with a sheen of coloured marbles, ancient columns and sculpture ('As if in ecstasy,' wrote Ruskin, 'the crests of the arches break into marbly foam...'). The spandrils of the arches glitter with gaudy, Technicolor mosaics – the High Renaissance, dissatisfied with the 13th-century originals, saw fit to commission new painterly scenes, leaving intact only the *Translation of the Body of St Mark* on the extreme left, which includes the first historical depiction of the basilica itself. The three bands of 13th-century **reliefs** located around the central portal, which are among the finest Romanesque carvings in the entire country, show Venetian trades, the Labours of the Months, and Chaos in the inner band.

Front and centre, seemingly ready to prance off the façade, the controversial 1979 copies of the bronze **horses of St Mark** masquerade well enough – from a distance. The ancient originals (cast between the 3rd century BC and 2nd century AD, and now inside the basilica's Museo Marciano) were one of the most powerful symbols of the Venetian Republic. Originally a 'triumphal quadriga' taken by Constantine the Great from Chios to grace the Hippodrome of his new city, it was carried off in turn by the artful Doge Dandolo in the 1204 Sack of Constantinople. Another prize from Byzantium are the four porphyry 'Moors' huddled in the corner of the south façade near the Doge's Palace; according to legend, they were changed into stone for daring to break into St Mark's treasury, though scholars prefer to believe that they are four chummy 3rd-century Roman emperors, the Tetrarchs.

1 *Translation of the Body of St Mark* (1270)
2 *Venice Venerating the Relics of St Mark* (1718)
3 Central door, with magnificent 13th-century carvings in arches
4 *Venice Welcoming the Relics of St Mark* (1700s)
5 *Removal of St Mark's Relics from Alexandria* (1700s)
6 Pietra del Bando, stone from which the Signoria's decrees were read
7 *Scenes from the Book of Genesis* (1200) and 6th-century Byzantine door of S. Clemente
8 *Noah and the Flood* (1200s), tomb of Doge Vitale Falier (*d.* 1096)
9 *Madonna and Saints* (1060s); red marble slab where Emperor Barbarossa submitted to Pope Alexander III (1177); stair up to the Loggia and Museo Marciano
10 *Death of Noah and the Tower of Babel* (1200s)
11 *Story of Abraham* (1230s)
12 *Story of SS. Alipius and Simon;* and tondo with Justice (1200s)
14 Tomb of Doge Bartolomeo Gradenigo (*d.* 1342)
15 *Story of Joseph*, remade in 19th century
16 Porta dei Fiori (1200s); Manzù's bust of Pope John XXIII
17 *Christ with the Virgin and St Mark* (13th century, over the door)
18 Pentecost Dome (the earliest, 12th century)
19 On the wall: *Agony in the Garden* and *Madonna and Prophets* (13th century)
20 Baptistry, *Life of St John the Baptist* (14th century) and tomb of Doge Andrea Dandolo
21 Cappella Zen, by Tullio and Antonio Lombardo (1504–22)
22 On the wall: *Christ and Prophets* (13th century)
23 In arch: *Scenes of the Passion* (12th century)
24 Central Dome, the *Ascension* (12th century)
25 Tabernacle of the Madonna of the Kiss (12th century)
26 On wall: *Rediscovery of the Body of St Mark* (13th century)
27 Treasury
28 Dome of S. Leonardo; Gothic rose window (15th century)
29 In arch: *Scenes from the Life of Christ* (12th century)
30 Altar of the Sacrament; pilaster where St Mark's body was rediscovered, marked by marbles
31 Altar of St James (1462)
32 Pulpit where the newly elected doge was shown to the people; entrance to the sanctuary
33 Rood screen (1394) by Jacopo di Marco Benato and Jacobello and Pier Paolo Dalle Masegne
34 Singing Gallery and Cappella di S. Lorenzo, sculptures by the Dalle Masegnes (14th century)
35 Dome, *Prophets Foretell the Religion of Christ* (12th century); baldaquin, with Eastern alabaster columns (6th century?)
36 Pala d'Oro (10th–14th century)
37 Sacristy door, with reliefs by Sansovino (16th century)
38 Sacristy, with mosaics by Titian and Padovanino (16th century) and Church of St Theodore (15th century), once seat of the Inquisition, and now part of the sacristy: both are rarely open
39 Singing Gallery and Cappella di S. Pietro (14th century): note the Byzantine capitals
40 Two medieval pulpits stacked together
41 *Miracles of Christ* (16th century)
42 Dome, with *Life of St John the Evangelist* (12th century)
43 Cappella della Madonna di Nicopeia (miraculous 12th-century icon)
44 Cappella di S. Isidoro (14th-century mosaics and tomb of the Saint)
45 Cappella della Madonna dei Máscoli: *Life of the Virgin* by Andrea del Castagno, Michele Giambono, Jacopo Bellini
46 On wall: *Life of the Virgin* (13th century)
47 Finely carved Greek marble stoup (12th century)
48 *Virgin of the Gun* (13th century – rifle ex-voto from 1850s)
49 Il Capitello, altar topped with rare marble ciborium, with miraculous Byzantine Crucifixion panel

St Mark's Basilica

Note how crooked it is – in the Middle Ages symmetry was synonymous with death.

Captions in *italics* refer to mosaics.

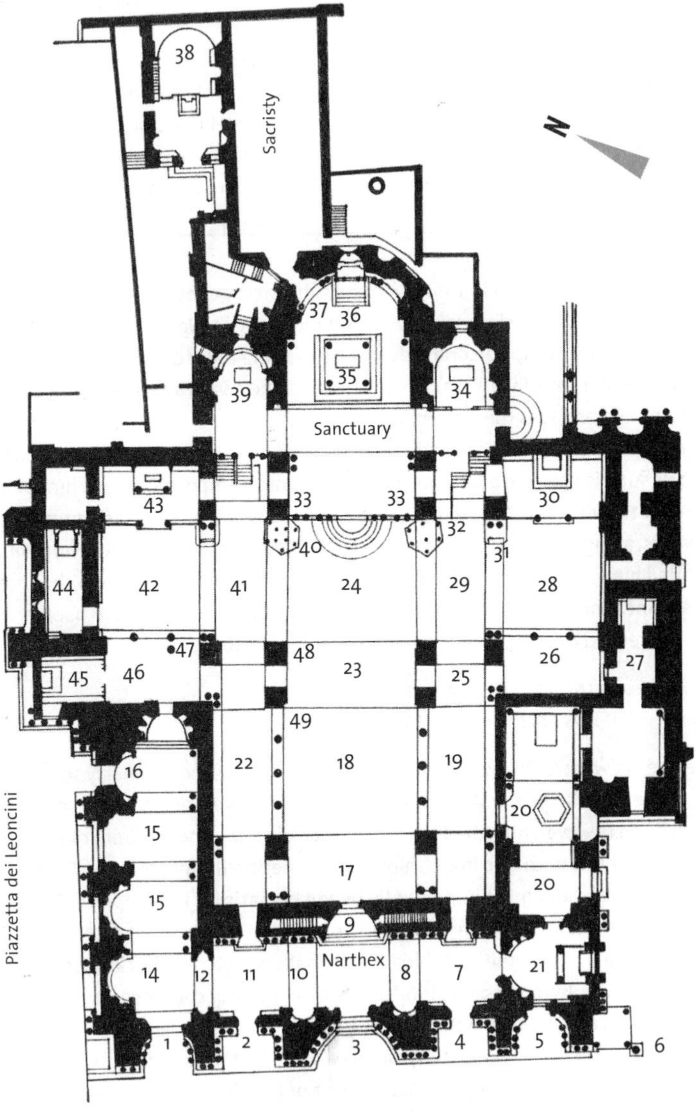

The Interior

The best mosaics, most of them from the 13th century, cover the six domes of the **atrium**, or narthex, their old gold glimmering in the permanent twilight. The oldest mosaic in St Mark's is that of the Madonna and Saints above the central door, a survivor of the original 11th-century decoration of the basilica. A slab of red marble in the pavement marks the spot where Emperor Barbarossa knelt and apologized to 'St Peter and his Pope' – Alexander III, in 1177. This is one of the few gold stars the Republic ever earned with the papacy; mistrust and acrimony were far more common.

The interior, in the form of a Greek cross, dazzles with its intricate splendour. The domes and upper vaults are adorned with golden mosaics on New Testament subjects, the oldest dating back to the 1090s. Ancient columns of rare marbles, alabaster, porphyry and verdantique, sawn into slices of rich colour, line the lower walls; the 12th-century pavement is a magnificent geometric mosaic of marble, glass and porphyry. Like a mosque, the nave is partially covered with carpets.

Byron Goes Swimming

Byron arrived in Venice in 1816, his heart full of romance as he rented a villa on the Brenta to compose the last canto of his *Childe Harold's Pilgrimage*. The city's canals at least afforded him the personal advantage of being able to swim anywhere (his club foot made him shy of walking); on one occasion he swam a race from the Lido to the Rialto bridge and was the only man to finish.

It wasn't long before the emotional polish of *Childe Harold* began to crack. To Byron's surprise, Venice didn't perfect his romantic temper, but cured him of it. He went to live in the Palazzo Mocenigo on the Grand Canal, in the company of 14 servants, a dog, a wolf, a fox, monkeys and a garlicky baker's wife, *La Fornarina*, who stabbed him in the hand with a fork – he ordered her out, whereupon she threw herself into the Grand Canal. Under such circumstances, all that had been breathless passion reeked of the ridiculous, as he himself admitted:

And the sad truth which hovers o'er my desk
Turns what was once romantic to burlesque

Venice, its women, its own ironic detachment and its love of liberty set Byron's mind free to write *Beppo: A Venetian Story*, spoofing Venice's *cavalieri serventi* (escort-lovers – even nuns had them) while celebrating the freedom of its people. He followed this with two bookish plays on Venetian themes, *Marino Faliero* and *The Two Foscari*, and most importantly began his satirical masterpiece, *Don Juan*.

Meanwhile debauchery was taking its toll: an English acquaintance wrote in 1818 that 'His face had become pale, bloated and sallow, and the knuckles on his hands were lost in fat'. Byron became infatuated with a young countess, Teresa Guiccioli, and left Venice to move in with her and her elderly husband in Ravenna. But, having tasted every freedom in Venice, Byron once more began to chafe; the *contessa* was 'taming' him. He bundled up the manuscript of *Don Juan* and left, only to die of fever at the age of 36 in the Greek War of Independence.

The first door on the right leads to the 14th-century **baptistry** (*currently closed*), much beloved by Ruskin and famous for its mosaics on the life of John the Baptist, with a lovely Salome in red who could probably have had just as many heads as she pleased. Attached to the baptistry, the **Cappella Zen** (*currently closed*) was designed by Tullio Lombardo in 1504 to house the tomb of one Cardinal Zen, who had left a fortune to the Republic on condition that he be buried in St Mark's. Further along the right transept is the **treasury** (*open Mon–Sat 9.30–5, Sun 1.30–5; adm*), containing the loot from Constantinople that Napoleon overlooked – golden bowls and crystal goblets studded with huge coloured gems, straight from the cavern of Ali Baba.

Near the Altar of the Sacrament, at the end of the right transept, a lamp burns 'eternally' next to one pillar: after the 976 fire, the body of St Mark was lost, but in 1094 (after Bari had beaten Venice to the relics of St Nicolaus) the good Evangelist staged a miraculous reappearance, popping his hand out of the pillar during Mass. St Mark is now safely in place in a crypt under the high altar, in the **sanctuary** (*open Mon–Sat 9–5, Sun 2–4; adm*). You can't visit his relics, but you can see the altar's retable, the fabulous, glowing **Pala d'Oro**, a masterpiece of medieval gold and jewel work. The upper section may originally have been in the Church of the Pantocrator in Constantinople, and the lower section was commissioned in that same city by Doge Pietro Orseolo I in 976. Over the years the Venetians added their own scenes, and the Pala took its present form in 1345.

In the left transept, the **Chapel of the Madonna of Nicopeia** shelters a 10th-century icon hijacked from Constantinople, the *Protectress of Venice*, formerly carried into battle by the Byzantine Emperors. More fine mosaics are further to the left in the Chapel of St Isidore (Venetian bodysnatchers kidnapped his relics from Chios – and in the mosaic he seems happy to go). In the **Chapel of the Madonna dei Máscoli**, the mosaics on the Life of the Virgin by Tuscan Andrea Castagno and Michele Giambono (1453) were among the first harbingers of the Renaissance in Venice.

Before leaving, climb the steep stone stair near the west door of the narthex, to the **Museo Marciano**, **Galleria** and **Loggia dei Cavalli** (*open daily 9.30–5; adm*) for a closer look at the dome mosaics from the women's gallery and a visit to the loggia, where you can inspect the replica horses and compare them with the excellently restored, gilded, almost-alive originals in the museum.

The Campanile

Open daily 9–7; adm.

St Mark's bell tower, to those uninitiated in the cult of Venice, seems like an alien presence, a Presbyterian brick sentinel in the otherwise delicately wrought piazza. But it has always been there, at least since 912; it was last altered in 1515, and when it gently collapsed into a pile of rubble on 14 July 1902 (the only casualty a cat) the Venetians felt its lack so acutely that they began to construct an exact replica, only a few hundred tons lighter and stronger, completed in 1912. It is 332ft tall; you can take the lift up for a bird's-eye vision of Venice and its Lagoon (from up here the city seems amazingly compact). Though you have to pay for the view, misbehaving priests had it for free: the Council of Ten would suspend them in cages from the windows. Under the campanile, Sansovino's elegant **loggetta** adds a graceful note to the brick belfry. Its marbles and sculptures glorifying Venice took it on the nose when the campanile fell on top of them, but they have been carefully restored.

The Correr Museum and Clock Tower

The Correr Museum incorporates the Archaeological Museum and Biblioteca Marciana, known collectively as the San Marco museums. Entrance to all except the Palazzo Ducale is via the Correr Museum. Open daily Apr–Oct 9–7; Nov–Mar 9–5; last tickets 90mins before closing; adm.

At the far end of the piazza, in the Procuratie Nuove, the **Museo Correr** contains an interesting collection of Venetian memorabilia – the robes, ducal bonnets and old-maidish nightcaps of the doges, the 20-inch-heeled *zoccoli*, once the rage among Venetian noblewomen, and a copy of the statue of Marco Polo from the Temple of 500 Genies in Canton. There are also musical instruments, arms and armour, some wonderful old globes and an interesting section called 'Venetian Civilization' with objects from Venetian domestic life: pots and pans, and other domestic artefacts. There are also some 18th-century games – a roulette wheel, playing cards, a draughts set, a jigsaw, children's games (a yo-yo), a bingo set, and dominoes.

Upstairs, the fine collection of Venetian paintings includes two great works by Carpaccio, *The Courtesans* (or Ladies – in Venice it was hard to tell) and *A Visitation*; Ferrarese/Bolognese's *Young Man in a Red Beret*, with his archetypal Venetian face; Antonello da Messina's damaged but luminous *Pietà*, and others by Cosme Turà and a young Giovanni Bellini; a lively early sculpture by Canova, *Daedalus and Icarus* (1779); and the Bosch-esque *Temptation of St Anthony* by Il Civetta ('the little owl').

At the head of the Procuratie Vecchie, two bronze wild men, the 'Moors', sound the hours at the top of the clock tower, the **Torre dell'Orologio** (*currently being restored, due to reopen in 2004; the innards of the clock are on display in the Ducal Palace*), built to a design by Mauro Codussi in 1499 above the entrance to Venice's main shopping street, the Mercerie. The old Italians were fond of elaborate astronomical clocks, but none is as beautiful as this, with its coloured enamel and gilt face, its Madonna and obligatory lion. The Council of Ten (which encouraged fearsome rumours about itself, to make its job easier) allegedly blinded the builders to prevent them creating such a marvel for any other city. Below, flanking the basilica's north façade in **Piazzetta Giovanni XXIII**, named after the Venetian patriarch who became pope in 1959, are a fountain and two porphyry lions.

Piazzetta San Marco

To the south of the basilica, the Piazzetta San Marco was the Republic's foyer, where ships would dock under the watchful eye of the Doge. The view towards the Lagoon is framed by two tall Egyptian granite **columns**, trophies brought to Venice in the 1170s. The Venetians had a knack for converting their booty into self-serving symbols: on one of the columns several Roman statues were pieced together to form their first patron saint, St Theodore with his crocodile (or dragon, or fish), while on the other stands an ancient Assyrian or Persian winged lion, under whose paw the Venetians slid a book, creating their symbol of St Mark.

Opposite the Doge's Palace stands the **Biblioteca** (*entry via Correr Museum*), built in 1536 by Sansovino and considered by Palladio the most beautiful building since antiquity, especially notable for the play of light and shadow in its sculpted arcades. Sansovino, trained as a sculptor, was notorious for paying scant attention to architectural details, and the library was scarcely completed when its ceiling collapsed. The goof-up cost him a trip to the Council of Ten's slammer, and he was only released on the pleading of Titian. Scholars with permission from the director can examine such treasures as the 1501 Grimani breviary, a masterwork of Flemish illuminators; Homeric *codices*, the 1459 world map of Fra Mauro, and Marco Polo's will. But not the famous library Petrarch willed to the Republic – the Venetians lost it.

Next to the library, at No.17, Venice's **Archaeological Museum** (*entry via Correr Museum*) is one of the few museums in the city that is heated in winter. It has an excellent collection of Greek sculpture, including a violent Leda and the Swan and ancient copies of the famous Gallic Warriors of Pergamon, all given to the city by collector Cardinal Grimani in 1523. On the other side of the Libreria, by the waterfront, is another fine building by Sansovino, the 1547 **Zecca**, or Old Mint, which once stamped out thousands of gold *zecchini*, and gave English a new word: 'sequin'.

The Palace of the Doges (Palazzo Ducale)

Open daily Apr–Oct 9–7; Nov–Mar 9–5; adm exp, includes entry to the Museo Correr. Entrance and tickets on Riva degli Schiavoni.

What St Mark's is to sacred architecture, the **Palace of the Doges** is to the secular – unique and audacious, dreamlike in a half-light, an illuminated storybook of Venetian history and legend. Like the basilica, it was founded shortly after the city's consolidation on the Rialto, though it didn't begin to take its present form until 1309 – with its delicate lower colonnade, its loggia of lacy Gothic tracery, and the top-heavy upper floor. Its weight is partly relieved by the diamond pattern of white Istrian stone and red Verona marble on the façade, which from a distance gives the palace its wholesome peaches-and-cream complexion. Less benign are the two reddish pillars in the loggia (on the Piazzetta façade) said to have been dyed by the blood of Venice's enemies, whose tortured corpses were strung out between them.

Some of Italy's finest medieval sculpture crowns the 36 columns of the lower colonnade, depicting a few sacred and many profane subjects – animals, guildsmen, Turks and Venetians. Beautiful sculptural groups adorn the corners, most notably the 13th-century Judgement of Solomon, near the grand entrance, the 1443 **Porta della Carta** (Paper Door), a Gothic symphony in stone by Giovanni and Bartolomeo Bon.

Fires in 1574 and 1577 destroyed much of the palace, and at the time there were serious plans afoot to knock it down and let Palladio start again *à la* Renaissance. Fortunately, however, you can't teach an old doge new tricks, and the palace was rebuilt as it was, with Renaissance touches in the interior.

A Doge's Life: Gormenghast with Canals

Senator in Senate and Citizen in City were his titles, as well as Prince of Clothes, because of his wardrobe of gold and silver damask robes and scarlet silks. Once the Doge was dressed, the rest of his procession would fall in line, bringing with them all the paraphernalia of Byzantine royalty: a naked sword, six silver trumpets, a damask parasol, a chair, a cushion, a candle and eight standards bearing the Lion of St Mark in four colours symbolizing peace, war, truth and loyalty.

Yet for all the pomp this was the only man in Venice not permitted to send a private note to his wife, or receive one from her, or from anyone else; nor could he accept any gift beyond flowers or rose-water, go to a café or theatre, or engage in any money-making activity, though he had to meet the expenses of his office out of his own pocket. Nor could he abdicate, unless requested to do so.

The office was respected, but often not the man. When a Doge died he was privately buried in his family tomb before the state funeral – which used a dummy corpse with a wax mask. An 'Inquisition of the Defunct Doge' was held over the dummy, to discover whether the Doge had kept to his *Promissione* (his oath of coronation), whether his family owed the state any money, and whether it were necessary to amend the *Promissione* to limit the powers of his successor still further. Then the dummy was taken to St Mark's to be hoisted in the air nine times by sailors, to the cry of '*Misericordia*!' (Mercy!), and then given a funeral service at the church of Santi Giovanni e Paolo.

Just within the Porta della Carta, don't miss Antonio Rizzo's delightful arcaded courtyard and his finely sculpted grand stairway, the **Scala dei Giganti**, named for its two Gargantuan statues of *Neptune* and *Mars* by Sansovino.

The new ticket office leads you straight into the big courtyard, designed by Antonio Rizzo and containing two of Venice's finest wellheads. First on the tour is the **Museo dell'Opera**, with its rooms full of vast bits of stone capitals, columns, chunks of stonework from the upper loggia, and models of the palace. Then you go back into the courtyard and begin the tour proper by ascending the **Scala dei Censori** to the first floor, or *primo piano nobile*, once the private apartments of the Doge, although its stripped-down, unfurnished state offers few clues as to how the Doge lived in this gilded cage of pomp and ritual.

Turn right, and Sansovino's **Scala d'Oro** continues up to the *secondo piano nobile*, from where the Venetian state was governed. After the fire that destroyed its great 15th-century frescoes, Veronese and Tintoretto painted the newly remodelled chambers with mythological themes and scores of allegories and apotheoses of Venice – a smug, fleshy blonde in the eyes of these two. These paintings are the palace's chief glory, and signboards in each room identify them. Visiting ambassadors and other foreign official guests would be required to wait in the first room, the **Anticollegio**, so the frescoes (Tintoretto's *Bacchus and Ariadne* and Veronese's *Rape of Europa*) had to be especially impressive; in the next room, the **Sala del Collegio**, with masterpieces by both artists, they would be presented to the hierarchy of the Venetian state.

Tintoretto's brush dominates in the **Sala del Senato** – which is less lavish, because only Venetians were admitted here – while the main work in the **Sala del Consiglio dei Dieci** is Veronese's ceiling, *Old Man in Eastern Costume with a Young Woman*. Under this the Council of Ten deliberated and pored over the accusations that were deposited in the *Bocche dei Leoni* – the lions' mouths spread over the Republic. To be considered, an accusation had to be signed and supported by two witnesses, and anyone found making a false accusation would suffer the punishment that would have been meted out to the accused had it been true. Adjacent to the Ten's chamber, the old **Armoury** (Sala d'Armi) houses a fine collection of medieval and Renaissance arms and armour.

From here the visit continues downstairs, to the vast and magnificent **Sala del Maggior Consiglio**, built in 1340 and capable of holding the 2,500 patricians of the Great Council. At the entrance hangs Tintoretto's crowded, and recently restored, *Paradiso* – the biggest oil painting in the world (23ft by 72ft), all the Blessed looking up at Veronese's magnificent *Apotheosis of Venice* on the ceiling. The frieze along the upper wall portrays the first 76 doges, except for the space that would have held the portrait of Marin Falier (1355) had he not led a conspiracy to take sole power; instead, a black veil bears a dry note that he was decapitated for treason. The portraits of the last 44 doges, each painted by a contemporary painter, continue around the **Sala dello Scrutinio**, where the votes for office were counted. Elections for Doge were Byzantine and elaborate – and frequent; the Maggior Consiglio preferred to choose doges who were old, and wouldn't last long enough to gain a following.

At the end of the tour the **Bridge of Sighs** (Ponte dei Sospiri) takes you to the 17th-century **Palazzo delle Prigioni**, mostly used for petty offenders. Those to whom the Republic took real exception were dumped into uncomfortable *pozzi*, or 'wells' in the lower part of the Palazzo Ducale, while celebrities like Casanova got to stay up in the *piombi* or 'leads' just under the roof.

The Secret Itinerary

In 1984 the section of the palace where the real nitty-gritty business of state took place, a maze of narrow corridors and tiny rooms, was restored and opened to the public. Because the rooms are so small the 1½-hour guided tour, the Itinerari Segreti ('Secret Itinerary') is limited to 20 people, and the reason why it's not better known is that it has previously only been available in Italian. It is now available in French and English too (*tours 10 and 12; adm includes state rooms; book at least a day in advance at the director's office on the first floor, or ring* ***t*** *041 522 4951*).

The tour begins at the top of the Scala d'Oro, with the snug wood-panelled offices of the **Chancellery** and the 18th-century **Hall of the Chancellors**, lined with cupboards for holding treaties, each bearing the arms of a Chancellor. In the justice department is the **Torture Chamber**, where the three Signori della Notte dei Criminali (judges of the night criminals) would 'put to the question' anyone who was suspected of treason, hanging them by the wrists on a rope that is still in place. This practice ended in the early 1700s, when Venice, along with Tuscany, became one of the first states in Europe to abolish torture.

Next is the ornate **Sala dei Tre Capi**, the chamber of the three magistrates of the Council of Ten, who had to be present at all state meetings. As this chamber might be visited by foreign dignitaries, it was lavishly decorated with works by Veronese, Antonello da Messina and Hieronymus Bosch.

From here it's up to the notorious **Piombi**, which despite their evil reputation appear downright cosy, as prisons go. Casanova's cell is pointed out, and there's an elaborate explanation of his famous escape through a hole in the roof. Near the end of the tour comes one of Venice's marvels: the **attic of the Sala del Maggior Consiglio**, where you can see how the Arsenale's shipwrights made a vast ceiling float unsupported over the room below; built in 1577, it has yet to need any repairs.

San Marco to Rialto

The streets between the piazza and the market district of the Rialto are the busiest in Venice, especially the **Mercerie**, which begin under the clock tower and are lined with some of the city's smartest shops. It was down the Mercerie that Baiamonte Tiepolo, miffed at being excluded from the Golden Book, led his rebel aristocrats in 1310, when an old lady cried 'Death to tyrants!' from her window and hurled a brick at his standard-bearer, killing him on the spot, and causing such disarray that Tiepolo was forced to give up his attempted coup. It was a close call that the Republic chose never to forget: the site, above the Sottoportego del Capello Nero, is marked by a stone relief of the heroine with her brick.

The Mercerie continue to the church of **San Zulian**, redesigned in 1553 by Sansovino, with a façade most notable for Sansovino's statue of its pompous and scholarly benefactor, Tommaso Rangone. Sansovino also had a hand in **San Salvatore** in the next *campo*, adding the finishing touches to its noble Renaissance interior and designing the monument to Doge Francesco Venier. An 89-year-old Titian painted one of his more unusual works for this church, the *Annunciation*, which he signed with double emphasis *Titianus Fecit* – '*Fecit*' because his patrons refused to believe that he had painted it. In a chapel north of the altar is the *Supper at the House of Emmaus*, by the school of Giovanni Bellini.

Humming, bustling **Campo San Bartolomeo**, next on the Mercerie, has for centuries been one of the social hubs of Venice, and still gets packed with after-work crowds every evening. Its centre is graced by the **statue of Goldoni**, whose comedies in Venetian dialect still make the Venetians laugh; and by the look on his jolly face he still finds their antics amusing. Follow the crowds up to the **Ponte di Rialto** (*see* 'The Grand Canal', p.332), the geographical heart of Venice, and the principal node of its pedestrian and water traffic.

The city's central markets have been just across the bridge for a millennium, divided into sections for vegetables and fish. Near the former you may pay your respects to Venice's oldest church, little **San Giacomo di Rialto**, founded perhaps as long ago as the 5th century and substantially reworked in 1071 and 1601. In the same *campo* stands a famous Venetian character, the 16th-century granite hunchback, **Gobbo di Rialto**, who supports a little stairway and marble podium from which the decrees of the Republic were proclaimed.

San Marco to the Accademia

If you follow the yellow signs 'To the Accademia' from Piazza San Marco (starting from the tourist office), the first *campo* you will come across belongs to Baroque **San Moisè** (1668), Italy's most grotesque church, with its grimy opera-buffa façade, rockpile and altarpiece. For more opera and less buffa, take a detour up Calle Veste (second right after Campo San Moisè) to monumental Campo San Fantin and the **Teatro La Fenice** (1792), the Republic's last hurrah and one of Italy's most renowned opera houses, which saw the premières of Verdi's *Rigoletto* and *La Traviata*. A fire set by a contractor during renovations ripped it apart in 1996, and rebuilding work was held up by endless bureaucratic and political wranglings, not to mention lack of money. Operas should finally be staged here again in autumn 2004. Venice has a venerable musical tradition, albeit one that had become more tradition than music by the time of the era of grand opera – although Mozart's great librettist, Lorenzo da Ponte, was a Venetian.

Back en route to the Accademia, in the next *campo* you'll find **Santa Maria Zobenigo** (or del Giglio), on which the Barbaro family stuck a fancy Baroque façade in 1680, not for God but for to glorify themselves; the façade is famous for its total lack of religious significance. The signs lead next to the Campo Francesco Morosini, named after the Doge who recaptured the Morea from the Turks but is remembered everywhere else as the man who blew the top off the Parthenon. Better known as **Campo Santo Stefano**, it's one of the most elegant squares in Venice, and a pleasant place to sit outside at a café table – particularly at **Paolin**, Venice's best *gelateria* (*see* p.324). At one end, built directly over a canal, the Gothic church of **Santo Stefano** has the most gravity-defying campanile of all the leaning towers in Venice (which is most alarmingly viewed from the adjacent Campo Sant'Angelo). The interior is also worth a look for its striking wood ceiling, soaring like a ship's keel, as well as for its wooden choir stalls (1488).

The Accademia

*Open Mon 9–2, Tues–Fri 9–9, Sat 9am–11pm, Sun 9–8; adm exp. It's a good idea to get there early, since only 300 visitors are allowed at a time, or to pre-book on **t** 041 520 0345 (small booking fee).*

Just over the bridge and Grand Canal from Campo Santo Stefano stands the Galleria dell'Accademia, the grand cathedral of Venetian art, ablaze with light and colour. The collection is arranged chronologically, beginning in the former refectory of the Scuola (**Room I**): among the works are 14th-century altarpieces by Paolo and Lorenzo Veneziano, whose half-Byzantine Madonnas look like fashion models for Venetian silks. Later altarpieces fill **Room II**, most importantly Giovanni Bellini's *Pala di San Giobbe*, one of the key works of the quattrocento: the architecture repeats its original setting in the church of San Giobbe, and on the left St Francis invites the viewer into a scene made timeless by the music of the angels at the Madonna's feet. Other beautiful altarpieces in the room are by Carpaccio, Basaiti and Cima da Conegliano (the subtle *Madonna of the Orange Tree*).

The next rooms are small but contain the best things: Mantegna's confidently aloof *St George*, the little allegories and a trio of Madonnas by Giovanni Bellini (including the lovely, softly coloured *Madonna of the Little Trees*) and Piero della Francesca's *St Jerome and Devotee*, a youthful study in perspective. In **Room V** you will find Giorgione's *La Vecchia*, with the warning '*Col Tempo*' ('With Time') in her hand, and the mysterious *The Tempest*, two of the few paintings scholars accept as being indisputably by Big George, but how strange they are! It is said that Giorgione invented easel painting for the pleasure of bored, purposeless courtiers in Caterina Cornaro's Àsolo, but these paintings seem to reflect rather than lighten their ennui and discontent.

Highlights of the next few rooms include Lorenzo Lotto's *Gentleman in his Study*, which catches its sitter off-guard before he could clear the nervously scattered scraps of paper from his table, and Paris Bordenone's masterpiece, *Fisherman Presenting St Mark's Ring to the Doge* (1554), celebrating a miracle of St Mark.

The climax of the Venetian High Renaissance comes in **Room X**, with Veronese's *Christ in the House of Levi* (1573), set in a Palladian loggia with a ghostly white imaginary background, in violent contrast to the rollicking feast of Turks, hounds, midgets, Germans and the artist himself (at the front, next to the pillar on the left). The painting was originally titled *The Last Supper*, and fell foul of the Inquisition, which took umbrage (especially at the Germans). Veronese was cross-examined, and was ordered to make pious changes at his own expense; the cunning artist saved himself both the trouble and the money by simply giving it the title by which it has been known ever since.

Room X also contains Veronese's fine *Annunciation*, and some early masterworks by Tintoretto – *Translation of the Body of St Mark*, and *St Mark Freeing a Slave*, in which the Evangelist, in true Tintoretto-esque fashion, nosedives from the top of the canvas. The last great painting in the room was also the last ever by Titian, the sombre *La Pietà*, which he was working on when he died in 1576, aged about 90, from the plague; he intended it for his tomb, and smeared the paint on with his fingers.

Alongside several more Tintorettos, the following few rooms mainly contain work from the 17th and 18th centuries (Tiepolo, Sebastiano and Marco Ricci, Piazzetta, Longhi, Rosalba Carriera). Canaletto and Guardi, whose scenes of 18th-century Venice were the picture postcards of the British aristocracy on their Grand Tour, are represented in **Room XVII**.

The final rooms of the Accademia were formerly part of the elegantly Gothic church of Santa Maria della Carità, and house more luminous 15th-century paintings by Alvise Vivarini, Giovanni and Gentile Bellini, Marco Basaiti and Crivelli. **Room XX** contains a fascinating series depicting the *Miracles of the True Cross* with Venetian backgrounds, painted by Gentile Bellini, Carpaccio and others. **Room XXI** has the dreamily compelling and utterly charming *Cycle of St Ursula* by Carpaccio, from the former Scuola di Sant'Orsola. The last room, **Room XXIV**, which was once the *albergo* of the church, contains two fine paintings that were originally made for it: Titian's striking *Presentation of the Virgin* (1538) and a triptych by Antonio Vivarini and Giovanni d'Alemagna (1446).

Dorsoduro

The *sestiere* of Dorsoduro boasts the second-most-visited art gallery in Venice, the **Peggy Guggenheim Collection** (*open Weds–Mon 10–6; 1 Apr–2 Nov also Sat 10–10; adm exp*), just down the Grand Canal from the Accademia in her 18th-century Venetian Palazzo Venier dei Leoni. In her 30 years as a collector, Guggenheim amassed an impressive quantity of 20th-century art – Bacon, Braque, Chagall, Duchamp, Max Ernst (her second husband), Giacometti, Kandinsky, Magritte, Picasso, Pollock and more. The collection can come as a breath of fresh air after so much high Italian art, and also sponsors temporary exhibitions, even in winter; look out for posters.

From here it's a five-minute stroll down to the serene octagonal basilica of **Santa Maria della Salute** ('of Health'; 1631–81; *open daily 9–12 and 3–5.30*), on the tip of Dorsoduro. One of five votive churches built after the passing of plagues (Venice, a busy international port, was particularly susceptible), La Salute is the masterpiece of Baldassare Longhena, its snow-white dome and marble jelly rolls dramatically set at the entrance of the Grand Canal. The interior is a relatively restrained white and grey Baroque, and the **sacristy** (*adm*) contains the *Marriage at Cana* by Tintoretto and several works by Titian, including his *St Mark Enthroned Between Saints*. Almost next to the basilica, on the point, stands the distinctive profile of the **Dogana di Mare**, the Customs House (*see* 'The Grand Canal', p.333).

The **Fondamenta delle Zattere**, facing the freighter-filled canal and island of Giudecca, leads around to the **Gesuati**, the only Venice church decorated by Umbrian artists. For a more elaborate feast, take the long stroll along the Fondamenta (or *vaporetto* Line 5 to San Basegio) to Veronese's parish church of **San Sebastiano** on Rio di San Basilio (*open Mon–Sat 10–5; adm*). Veronese, it is said, murdered a man in Verona and took refuge in this neighbourhood, and over the next 10 years he and his brother Benedetto Caliari embellished San Sebastiano – beginning in 1555 with the ceiling frescoes of the sacristy and ending with the magnificent ceiling, *The Story of Esther*, and illusionistic paintings in the choir (*the lights are always lit*).

From San Sebastiano head back towards the Grand Canal (Calle Avogaria and Calle Lunga San Barnaba); turn left up Calle Pazienza to visit the 14th-century church of the **Carmini** with its red campanile and lovely altars by Cima da Conegliano and Lorenzo Lotto. The **Scuola Grande dei Carmini** (*open Mon–Sat 9–6, until 4 in winter, Sun 9–1; adm; sometimes also open for concerts*), next door, was designed by Longhena in the 1660s, and contains one of Tiepolo's best and brightest ceilings, *The Virgin in Glory*.

The Carmini is on the corner of **Campo Santa Margherita**, traditionally the main marketplace of Dorsoduro, with its relatively inexpensive and untouristy restaurants and cafés. It is also close to **Ca' Rezzonico** (Rio Terrà Canal down to the Fondamenta Rezzonico), home to the **Museo de Settecento** (*open Weds–Mon 10–5; adm*), Venice's attic of 18th-century art, with bittersweet paintings by Giandomenico Tiepolo, wild rococo furniture by Andrea Brustolon, a pharmacy, genre scenes by Longhi (*The Lady and Hairdresser*), and a breathtaking view of the Grand Canal. The house was owned by Robert Browning's son, Pen, and the poet died there in 1889. One of the palaces opposite belonged to Doge Cristoforo Moro, whom the Venetians claim Shakespeare used as his model for Othello, confusing the Doge's name with his race.

San Polo and Santa Croce

From the Ponte di Rialto, follow the yellow signs to Piazzale Roma, passing the pretty **Campo** and church of **San Polo** (*open Mon–Sat 10–5, Sun 1–5; adm*), with Giandomenico Tiepolo's dramatic *Stations of the Cross* in the Oratory of the Crucifix. Signs then take you before a venerable Venetian institution: the huge brick Gothic church of **I Frari** (*open Mon–Sat 9–6, Sun and hols 1–6; adm*), one of the most severe medieval buildings in the city, built between 1330 and 1469. Monteverdi, one of the founding fathers of opera and choir director at St Mark's, is buried here, as is Titian, whose tomb follows the Italian rule – the greater the artist, the worse the tomb (see Michelangelo's in Florence). The strange pyramid with a half-open door was intended by Antonio Canova to be Titian's tomb but became the sculptor's own last resting place. The Frari is celebrated for its great art, and especially for the most overrated painting in Italy, Titian's *Assumption of the Virgin* (1516–18). Marvel at Titian's revolutionary Mannerist use of space and movement, but the big-eyed, heaven-gazing Virgin has as much artistic vision as a Sunday school holy card.

The same is not true of Giovanni Bellini's *Triptych of Madonna with Child and Saints* in the sacristy, or Donatello's rustic statue of *St John the Baptist* in the choir chapel. In the north aisle, Titian's less theatrical *Madonna di Ca' Pésaro*, modelled on his wife, had a greater influence on Venetian composition than the *Assumption*. Also note the beautiful 1476 Renaissance **Tomb of Doge Nicolò Tron** by Antonio Rizzo in the sanctuary,

The Scuola di San Rocco

Next to the Frari, the **Scuola di San Rocco** (*open summer 9–5.30, winter 10–4; adm*) was one of Venice's most important *scuole*. San Rocco, renowned for his juju against the Black Death, was so popular among the Venetians that they stole his body from Montpelier and canonized him before the pope did. The *scuola* has a beautiful, lively façade by Scarpagnino, and inside it contains one of the wonders of Venice – or rather, 54 wonders – all painted by Tintoretto, who worked on the project from 1562 to 1585 without any assistance.

Tintoretto always managed to look at conventional subjects from a fresh point of view; while other artists of the High Renaissance composed their subjects with the epic vision of a Cecil B. de Mille, Tintoretto had the eye of a 16th-century Orson Welles, creating audacious, dynamic 'sets', often working out his compositions in his little box-stages, with wax figures and unusual lighting effects. In the *scuola*, especially in the upper floor, he was at the peak of his career, and painted what is considered by some to be the finest painting cycle in existence, culminating in the *Crucifixion*, where the event is the central drama of a busy human world. Vertigo is not an uncommon response – for an antidote, look at the funny carvings along the walls by Francesco Pianta. In the same room there are several paintings on easels by Titian, and a *Christ* that some attribute to Titian, some to Giorgione.

Just north, beyond Campo San Stin, the **Scuola Grande di San Giovanni Evangelista** (*open on request, call* **t** *041 718 234*) deserves a look for its beautiful Renaissance courtyard and double-ramp stairway (1498), Mauro Codussi's masterpiece, noted for the rhythms of its domes and barrel vaults.

From Campo San Stin, if you start along Calle Donà and keep as straight as possible, you should end up at **Ca' Pésaro** on the Grand Canal, a huge 17th-century pile by Longhena that is occupied by the **Galleria d'Arte Moderna** (*currently closed*), with a collection principally of works exhibited in the Biennale exhibitions. Italian contemporary art, much of it unfamiliar to a foreign audience, is the mainstay, but some international figures are also represented, such as Gustav Klimt. Ca' Pésaro also houses a **Museum of Oriental Art** (*open Tues–Sun 8.15–2; adm*), with a higgledy-piggledy collection of Asian artefacts.

If you want to escape the crowds, head further up the canal to have a look at the stuffed Lagoon fowl in the **Natural History Museum** (*call* **t** *041 524 0885 for opening times*) in the Venetian–Byzantine **Fóndaco dei Turchi**.

San Marco to Castello

From Piazzetta San Marco, the gracefully curving, ever-thronged **Riva degli Schiavoni** took its name from the Slavs of Dalmatia; in 1782 Venice was doing so much business here that the quay had to be widened. A few steps beyond the Palazzo Ducale, one of the city's finest Gothic *palazzi* was converted in 1822 to the famous **Danieli** hotel (*see* p.319), the name of which is a corruption of that of the Dandolo family for whom it was built. The quay also has a robust **Memorial to Vittorio Emanuele II** (1887), where two of Venice's over 10,000 lions shelter – as often as not with members of Venice's equally numerous if smaller feline population between their paws.

From Riva degli Schiavoni, the Sottoportico San Zaccaria leads back to the lovely Gothic–Renaissance **San Zaccaria** (*open Mon–Sat 10–12 and 4–6, Sun 4–6*), begun by Antonio Gambello in 1444 and completed by Mauro Codussi in 1515. Inside, look for Bellini's recently restored and extraordinary *Madonna and Saints* in the second chapel to the right, and the refined Florentine frescoes by Andrea del Castagno in the chapel of San Tarasio.

Another church back on the Riva itself, **La Pietà** (*open only for concerts,* see *p.325*), served the girls' orphanage that the red-headed priest Vivaldi made famous during his years as its concert master and composer (1704–38). The church was rebuilt shortly afterwards by Giorgio Massari with a remarkable oval interior, in luscious cream and gold with G.B. Tiepolo's extravagant *Triumph of Faith* on top. It has particularly fine acoustics – Vivaldi helped design it.

Due north of La Pietà stands the city's Greek Orthodox church, the 16th-century **San Giorgio dei Greci**, with its tilting tower and *scuola*, next to the **Museo di Icone** (*open Mon–Sat 9–12.30 and 2–4.30, Sun 10–5; adm*), run by the Hellenic Centre for Byzantine and Post-Byzantine Studies. Many of its icons were painted in the 16th and 17th centuries by artists who fled the Turkish occupation. In Venice the Greeks came into contact with the Renaissance; the resulting Venetian–Cretan school nourished, most famously, El Greco.

Close by, another ethnic minority, the Dalmatians – present in Venice almost throughout the history of the Republic – began their tiny **Scuola di San Giorgio degli Schiavoni** in 1451 (*open Tues–Sat 9.30–12.30 and 3.30–6.30, Sun 9.30–12.30; adm*).

Its minute interior is decorated with the most beloved art in all Venice: Vittore Carpaccio's frescoes on the lives of the Dalmatian patron saints – Augustine writing, watched by his patient little white dog; Jerome bringing his lion into the monastery; George charging a petticoat-munching dragon in a landscape strewn with maidenly leftovers from lunch; and more. Some of the greatest paintings by Carpaccio's more serious contemporaries, the Vivarini and Cima da Conegliano, hold pride of place in **San Giovanni in Brágora** (between San Giorgio degli Schiavoni and the Riva); the best work, Cima's *Baptism of Christ*, is in the sanctuary.

The Arsenale

From the Riva degli Schiavoni, the Fondamenta dell'Arsenale leads to the twin towers guarding the **Arsenale**. Founded in 1104, this first of all arsenals derived its name from the Venetian pronunciation of the Arabic *darsina'a*, or workshop, and until the 17th century these were the greatest dockyards in the world, the foundation of the Republic's wealth and power. In its heyday the Arsenale had a payroll of 16,000, and produced a ship a day to fight the Turks. Dante visited this great industrial complex twice and, as Blake would later do with his 'dark satanic mills', found its imagery perfect for the *Inferno*. The Biennale has now taken over a vast section of its empty shipyards as a year-round space for exhibitions, arts events, music and the like.

The **Great Gateway** next to the towers was built in 1460, almost entirely from marble trophies nicked from Greece. Among the chorus line of lions is an ancient beast that Doge Francesco Morosini found in Piraeus, with 11th-century runes carved in its back in the name of Harold Hardrada, the member of the Byzantine Emperor's Varangian Guard who was later crowned king of Norway. Other very innocent-looking lions, since eroded into lambs, were taken from the island of Delos in 1718 when the Turks weren't looking.

Venice's glorious maritime history is the subject of the fascinating artefacts and models in the **Museo Storico Navale** (*open Mon–Fri 8.45–1.30, Sat 8.45–1; adm*). Most dazzling of all is the model of the Doge's barge, the *Bucintoro*. The museum is just past the gateway to the Arsenale, near the beginning of Via Garibaldi; in a neighbouring house lived two seafarers, originally from Genoa, who contributed more to the history of Britain than that of Venice, Giovanni and Sebastiano Caboto.

Via Garibaldi and Fondamenta Sant'Anna continue to the Isola di San Pietro, site of the unmemorable **San Pietro di Castello** (*open Mon–Sat 10–5, Sun 1–5; adm*), until 1807 Venice's cathedral, its lonely, distant site a comment on the Republic's attitude towards the papacy. The attractive, detached campanile is by Codussi, and inside there is a marble throne incorporating a Muslim tombstone with verses from the Koran, which for centuries was said to have been the Throne of St Peter in Antioch. To the south are the refreshing pines and planes of the **Public Gardens**, where the International Exhibition of Modern Art, or Biennale, takes place in odd-numbered years in the artsy pavilions. This, and the **Parco delle Rimembranze** further on, were a gift to this sometimes claustrophobic city of stone and water by Napoleon, who knocked down four extraneous churches to plant the trees. From here you can take Line 1 or 2 back to San Marco, or to the Lido.

San Marco to Santi Giovanni e Paolo

The *calli* that lead from the Piazzetta dei Leoncini around the back of San Marco and over the Rio di Palazzo take you to the Romanesque cloister of Sant'Apollonia and one of Venice's newest museums, the **Museo Diocesano** (*open Mon–Sat 10.30–12.30*), containing an exceptional collection of trappings and art salvaged from the city's churches. Through a web of alleys to the north there's more art in the 16th-century Palazzo Querini-Stampalia, home of the **Fondazione Querini-Stampalia** (*open Tues–Thurs and Sun 10–6, Fri and Sat 10–10; adm exp*), which has an endearing assortment of genre paintings – scenes of 18th-century Venetian convents, dinner parties, music lessons and the like by Pietro Longhi and Gabriel Bella, as well as works by Bellini, Palma il Vecchio, Vincenzo Catena (a 16th-century merchant and the first known amateur to dabble in painting) and G.B. Tiepolo – all in a suitably furnished 18th-century patrician's *palazzo*.

Santa Maria Formosa (*open Mon–Sat 10–5, Sun 1–5; adm*), in its charming *campo* just to the north, was rebuilt in 1492 by Codussi, who made creative use of its original Greek-cross plan. The head near the bottom of its campanile is notorious as being the most hideous thing in Venice, while inside, Palma il Vecchio's *Santa Barbara* is famed as the loveliest of all Venetian blondes, modelled on the artist's own daughter. Another celebrated work, Bartolomeo Vivarini's *Madonna della Misericordia* (1473), is in the first chapel on the right; the parishioners shown under the protection of the Virgin's mantle earned their exalted position by paying for the painting.

The next *campo* to the north is dominated by **Santi Giovanni e Paolo** (or San Zanipolo), which is after St Mark's the most important church on the right bank (*open Mon– Sat 8–12.30 and 3–6, Sun 3–5.30*). A vast Gothic brick barn commenced by the Dominicans in 1246, it was almost entirely rebuilt after 1333, and finally completed in 1430. No one could accuse it of being beautiful, despite its fine front doorway. San Zanipolo was the pantheon of the doges; all of their funerals were held here after the 1300s, and some 25 of them went no further, but remain here in their splendid Gothic and Renaissance tombs. Scattered among them are monuments to other honoured servants of the Venetian state, such as Marcantonio Bragadin, the commander who in 1571 was flayed alive by the Turks after he had surrendered Famagusta, in Cyprus, following a long siege; his bust sits on an urn containing his neatly folded skin.

The adjacent chapel contains Giovanni Bellini's polyptych of *St Vincent Ferrer*, a fire-eating subject portrayed by the gentlest of painters; nearby there's a buoyant Baroque ceiling by Piazzetta in St Dominic's chapel, and a small shrine containing the foot of St Catherine of Siena. The right transept has paintings by Alvise Vivarini, Cima da Conegliano and Lorenzo Lotto; the finest tomb is in the chancel, that of Doge Andrea Vendramin, by Tullio and Antonio Lombardo (1478), while the **Chapel of the Rosary** in the north transept, which was severely damaged by fire in the 19th century, has a ceiling by Veronese from the church of the Umilità, long demolished.

Adjacent to San Zanipolo, the **Scuola Grande di San Marco** boasts one of the loveliest Renaissance façades in the whole of Italy, the fascinating *trompe-l'œil* lower half by Pietro and Tullio Lombardo, and the upper floor by Mauro Codussi, finished in

1495. These days the *scuola* is used as Venice's municipal hospital, but it is possible to go in and see the lavish coffered ceiling in the library with the prior permission of the Direttore di Sanità.

Opposite is the dynamic **equestrian statue of Bartolomeo Colleoni**, the *condottiere* from Bergamo (1400–76) who served the Republic so well on the mainland. Proud of his emblem of *coglioni* (testicles – a play on his name), Colleoni envied Donatello's statue of his predecessor Gattamelata erected by the Venetians in Padua, and in his will left the Republic 100,000 ducats to erect a similar statue of him in front of St Mark's. Greedy for the money but unable to countenance a monument to an individual in their sacred Piazza, the Venetians put the statue up before the *scuola* of St Mark. Verrocchio, the master of Leonardo and Botticelli, had only finished the plaster moulds when he died in 1488, leaving Alessandro Leopardi to do the casting. Verrocchio never saw a portrait of his subject; all resemblances to Klaus Kinski are purely accidental.

Santa Maria dei Miracoli and the Ca' d'Oro

From Campo San Zanipolo, Calle Larga Giacinto Gallina leads to the perfect little Renaissance church of **Santa Maria dei Miracoli** (*open Mon–Sat 10–5, Sun 1–5; adm*), built by Pietro Lombardo in the 1480s and often compared to a jewel box, elegant, graceful and glowing with a soft marble sheen, inside and out. Just to the south are two enclosed courtyards, known as the **Corte Prima del Milion** and the **Corte Seconda del Milion**, where Marco Polo used to live. The latter in particular looks much as it did when the great traveller lived there; 'Million', his nickname in Venice, referred to the million tall tales he brought back with him from China. Nearby, Codussi's **San Giovanni Grisostomo** (1504) was his last work, a seminal piece of Renaissance architecture that contains Giovanni Bellini's last altar painting (*SS. Jerome, Christopher and Augustine*), as well as a beautiful high altarpiece by Sebastiano del Piombo.

Further towards the railway station up the Grand Canal, signposted off the Strada Nuova (Via 28 Aprile), stands the enchanting Gothic **Ca' d'Oro**, finished in 1440 and now housing the **Galleria Franchetti** (*open Mon 8.15–2, Tues–Sun 8.15am–9.15pm; adm*). In its collection are Mantegna's stern *St Sebastian*, Guardi's series of Venetian views, an excellent collection of Renaissance bronzes and medallions by Pisanello and Il Riccio, Tullio Lombardo's charming *Double Portrait*, and sadly faded fragments of the famous frescoes by Giorgione and Titian from the Fóndaco dei Tedeschi. Also present are minor works by Titian, including a voluptuous Venus. The building itself is famous for the intricate traceries of its façade, best appreciated from the Grand Canal, and the courtyard, with a beautifully carved wellhead by Bartolomeo Bon.

Due north, near the Fondamente Nuove, stands the church of the **Gesuiti** (*open daily 10–12 and 5–7; currently covered in scaffolding while undergoing restoration*), which was built by the Jesuits when the Republic relaxed its restrictions against them, in 1714–29: it's a Baroque extravaganza, full of *trompe l'œil* of white and green-grey marble draperies that would make a fitting memorial for Liberace. A previous church on this same site was the parish church of Titian, to which he contributed the *Martyrdom of St Lawrence* – the saint on a grill revered by Titian's patron, Philip II of Spain.

Cannaregio

Crumbling, piquant Cannaregio is the least visited *sestiere* in Venice. Here, perhaps, more than anywhere else in the city, you can begin to feel what everyday life is like behind the tourist glitz – children playing tag on the bridges, old men in shorts messing around in unglamorous, unpainted boats on murky canals, neighbourhood greasy spoons and bars, banners of laundry waving gaily overhead.

Northern Cannaregio was Tintoretto's home base, and he is buried in the beautiful Venetian Gothic **Madonna dell'Orto** (*open Mon–Sat 10–7, Sun 1–5; adm*). It also contains several of his jumbo masterpieces, such as the *Sacrifice of the Golden Calf*, in which Tintoretto painted himself bearing the idol – though he refrained from predicting his place in the *Last Judgement*, which hangs opposite it. He also painted the highly original *Presentation of the Virgin* in the south aisle, near one of Cima da Conegliano's greatest works, *St John the Baptist*. The first chapel by the door had a Madonna by Giovanni Bellini, stolen in 1993 and replaced by a photograph.

From the Campo Madonna dell'Orto, take a short walk down the Fondamenta Contarini, where, across the canal, in the wall of the eccentric **Palazzo Mastelli**, you can see one of Venice's curiosities: an old, stone relief of a Moor confronting a camel. There are three more 'Moors' in the **Campo dei Mori**, just in front of the Madonna dell'Orto. The original identities of these mysterious figures have long been forgotten, although a fourth, embedded in one corner of the square and with a metal nose like Tycho Brahe, is named Signor Antonio Rioba. He featured in many Venetian pranks of yore: anonymous satires or denunciations would be signed in his name, and new arrivals in the city would be sent off to meet him.

Also in the area little **Sant'Alvise** (*open Mon–Sat 10–5, Sun 1–5; adm*), which must be the loneliest church in Venice. Its main features are a forceful *Calvary* by Giambattista Tiepolo and a set of charming tempera paintings that Ruskin called the 'Baby Carpaccios', but which are now attributed to Carpaccio's master, Lazzaro Bastiani, as Carpaccio would only have been about eight years old when they were painted.

Three *rii* to the south of Sant'Alvise is the **Ghetto** – *the* Ghetto, for, as with the Arsenal, the Venetians invented it: *ghetto* derives from *getto*, meaning 'casting in metals', and there was an iron foundry here that preceded the establishment of a special quarter to which all Jews were ordered to move in 1516. The name is poignantly, coincidentally apt, for in Hebrew '*ghetto*' comes from the root for 'cut off'. And cut off its residents were in Venice, for the Ghetto is an island, surrounded by a moat-like canal, and at night all Jews had to be within its windowless walls. The cramped houses are tall with very low ceilings, which, as many people have noted, eerily presages ghetto tenements of centuries to come.

But the Venetians did not invent the mentality behind the Ghetto; Spanish Jews in the Middle Ages were segregated, as were the Jews of ancient Rome. In fact, Venetian law specifically protected Jewish citizens and forbade preachers from inciting mobs against them – a common enough practice in the 16th century. Jewish refugees came to Venice from all over Europe; here they were relatively safe, even if they had to pay for it with high taxes and rents. When Napoleon threw open the gates of the Ghetto in 1797, it is said that the impoverished residents who remained were too weak to leave. The island of the **Ghetto Nuovo**, the oldest section, is a melancholy place, its small *campo* often empty and forlorn. The **Scuola Grande Tedesca**, the oldest of Venice's five synagogues, built by German Jews in 1528, is in the same building as the small **Museo Comunità Israelitica/Ebraica** (*open Sun–Fri June–Sept 10–7; Oct–May 10–4.30; guided visits on the half-hour summer 10.30–5.30; winter 10.30–3.30; adm*). The informative tours (in English) visit this synagogue and two others, the **Scuola Spagnola** – an opulent building by Longhena – and the **Scuola Levantina**.

Light years from the Ghetto in temperament, the **Palazzo Labia** (next to the 1580 **Ponte delle Guglie**), has a ballroom with Giambattista Tiepolo's lavish, sensuous frescoes on the Life of Cleopatra. The *palazzo* is now owned by RAI, the Italian state broadcaster, and the ballroom is open for concerts (*call* **t** *041 781 277 well in advance to arrange free tickets or make an appointment to visit, 3–4 on Weds, Thurs and Fri*).

Away from the *palazzo* towards the railway station runs the garish **Lista di Spagna**, Venice's tourist highway, lined with restaurants, bars, hotels and souvenir stands.

San Giorgio Maggiore and the Giudecca

The little islet of San Giorgio Maggiore, which is crowned by Palladio's church of **San Giorgio Maggiore** (*open daily 9.30–12.30 and 2.30–6.30; adm to campanile*), dominates the view of the Lagoon from the Piazzetta San Marco (*vaporetto* Line 82). Built according to his theories on harmony, with a temple front, it seems to hang between the water and the sky, bathed by light with as many variations as Monet's series on the cathedral of Rouen. The austere white interior is relieved by Tintoretto's *Fall of Manna* and his celebrated *Last Supper* on the main altar, which is also notable for the fine carving on the Baroque choir stalls.

A lift can whisk you to the top of the **campanile** for a remarkable view over Venice and the Lagoon. The old monastery, partly designed by Palladio, now serves as the headquarters of the Giorgio Cini Foundation, dedicated to the arts and the sciences of the sea, and a venue for frequent exhibitions and conferences.

La Giudecca (*vaporetto* 82) actually consists of eight islands that curve gracefully like a Spanish *tilde* just south of Venice. Prominent among its buildings is a string of empty mills and factories – the product of a brief 19th-century flirtation with industry – and for the most part the atmosphere is relatively quiet and homely. Like Cannaregio, it's seldom visited, though a few people wander over to see Palladio's best church, **Il Redentore** (*open Mon–Sat 10–5, Sun 1–5; adm*). In 1576, during a plague that killed 46,000 Venetians, the Doge and the senate vowed that if the catastrophe ended they would build a church and visit it once a year until the end of time. Palladio completed the Redentore in 1592, and on the third Sunday of each July a bridge of boats was constructed to take the authorities across from the Zattere. This event, the Festa del Redentore, is still one of the most exciting events on the Venetian calendar (*see* p.324). The Redentore itself provides a fitting backdrop; Palladio's temple front, with its interlocking pediments, matches its basilican interior, with curving transepts and dome. The shadowy semi-circle of columns behind the altar adds a striking, mystical effect. It's all that survives of Palladio's desire to built a circular church, which he deemed most perfect to worship the essence of God.

The Lagoon and its Islands

Pearly and melting into the bright sky, iridescent blue or murky green, a sheet of glass yellow and pink in the dawn, or leaden, opaque grey, Venice's Lagoon is one of its wonders, a desolate, often melancholy and strange, often beautiful and seductive 'landscape' with a hundred different personalities. It is 56km long and averages 8km in width; half of it, the Laguna Morta ('Dead Lagoon'), where the tides never reach, consists of mud flats except during the spring, while the shallows of the Laguna Viva are always submerged, and cleansed by tides twice a day. In order to navigate this treacherous sea, the Venetians have developed an intricate network of channels, marked by *bricole* – wooden posts topped by orange lamps – that keep their craft from running aground. When threatened, the Venetians only had to pull out the *bricole* to confound their enemies; as such the Lagoon was always known as 'the sacred walls of the nation'. Keeping the Brenta and other rivers from silting it up kept engineers busy for centuries.

> *The city of the Venetians, by divine providence founded in the waters and protected by their environment, is defended by a wall of water. Therefore should anybody in any manner dare to infer damage to the public waters he shall be considered as an enemy of our country and shall be punished by no less pain than that committed to whomever violates the sacred border of the country. This act will be enforced forever.*
>
> 16th-century edict of the Maistrato alle Acque

'Forever' unfortunately ended in the 20th century. New islands were made of landfill that was dredged up to deepen the shipping canals, upsetting the delicate balance of lagoon life; outboards and *vaporetti* churn up the gook from the Lagoon and canal beds, and send corroding waves against Venice's fragile buildings. These affect the tide, and increase both the number of *acque alte* and the unnaturally low tides that embarrassingly expose Venice's underthings – and let air in where it was never supposed to go, accelerating the process of rot and the subsidence of its wooden piles and substructures.

Then there are the ingredients in the water itself. The Lagoon is a messy stew of 70 years' worth of organic waste, phosphates, agricultural and industrial by-products and sediments – a lethal mixture that ecologists warn will take a century to purify, even if by some miracle the pollution is stopped now. It's a sobering thought, especially when many Venetians in their fifties remember when even the Grand Canal was clean enough to swim in.

And in recent years the Lagoon has been sprouting the kind of blooms that break a girl's heart – algae, whole 'green pastures' of it, stinking and choking its fish. No one is sure that the algae epidemic isn't just part of a natural cycle; after all, there's an old church on one Lagoon island called San Giorgio in Alga (St George in Algae). Crops of algae are on record in the 1700s and 1800s and at the beginning of the 20th century, at times when water temperatures were abnormally high because of the weather. But other statistics are harder to reconcile with climatic cycles: since 1932, 78 species of algae have disappeared from the Lagoon, while 24 new ones have blossomed, these mostly micro-algae thriving off the surplus of phosphates. These chemicals have now been banned throughout the Lagoon communities, leading to a noticeable fall in recent algae counts.

Once the largest of the 39 Lagoon islands were densely inhabited, each occupied by a town or at least a monastery. Now all but a few have been abandoned, and many tiny ones have only a forlorn, vandalized shell of a building, overgrown with weeds. Occasionally one hears of plans to bring them back to life, only for them to wither on the vine of Italian bureaucracy. If you think you have a good idea for one, take it up with the Revenue Office (Intendenza di Finanza).

The Lido and South Lagoon

The Lido, one of the long spits of land that form the protective edge of the Lagoon, is by far the most glamorous of the islands, one that has given its name to countless bathing establishments, bars, amusement arcades and cinemas all over the world. On its 12 kilometres of beach, poets, potentates and plutocrats at the turn of the 19th century spent their holidays in palatial hotels and villas, making the Lido the pinnacle of *belle époque* fashion, so brilliantly evoked in Thomas Mann's *Death in Venice*, and Visconti's subsequent film. The story was set and filmed in the **Grand Hotel des Bains**, just north of the **Palazzo del Cinema**, where Venice now hosts its Film Festival.

The Lido is still the playground of Venetians and their visitors, with its bathing concessions, horse-riding clubs, tennis courts, golf courses and shooting ranges. The free beach, the **Spiaggia Comunale**, is situated on the northern part of the island, a 15-minute walk from the *vaporetto* stop at San Nicolò (go down the Gran Viale, and turn left on the Lungomare d'Annunzio). There you can hire a changing hut and have a frolic in the sand and sea.

Further north, beyond the private airfield, the **Porto di Lido** is maritime Venice's front door, the most important of the three entrances into the Lagoon, where you can watch the ships of the world sail by. This is where the Doge would sail to toss his ring into the waves, in the annual 'Marriage of the Sea'. It is stoutly defended by the mighty **Forte di Sant'Andrea** on the island of Le Vignole, built in 1543 by Venice's fortifications genius Sanmicheli. In times of danger, a great chain was extended from the fort across the channel.

One of the smaller Lagoon islands just off the Lido, with its landmark onion-domed campanile, is **San Lazzaro degli Armeni** (*vaporetto no.20 from San Zaccharia at 3.10; tours daily at 3.25; adm*). This was Venice's leper colony in the Middle Ages, but in 1715 the then-deserted island was given to the Mechitarist Fathers of the Armenian Catholic Church after they were expelled from Greece by the Turks. Today their monastery is still one of the world's major centres of Armenian culture, and its monks, noted linguists, run a famous polyglot press able to print in 32 languages, one of the last survivors in a city once renowned for its publishing. Tours of San Lazzaro take in a museum filled with relics of the ancient Christian history of Armenia, as well as memorabilia of Lord Byron, who spent a winter visiting the fathers and bruising his brain with Armenian. The fathers offer inexpensive prints of Venice for sale; alternatively, they appreciate donations.

Islands in the North Lagoon

Most Venetian itineraries take in Murano, Burano and Torcello, easily reached by inexpensive *vaporetti*. Lines 41 and 42 from Fondamente Nuove to Murano call at the cypress-studded cemetery island of **San Michele**, with its simple but elegant church of **San Michele in Isola** (*open daily 7.30–12 and 3–4*) by Mauro Codussi (1469), his first-known work and Venice's first taste of the Florentine Renaissance, albeit one with a Venetian twist in the tri-lobed front. It contains the tomb of Fra Paolo Sarpi, who led the ideological battle against the Pope when the Republic was placed under the Great Interdict of 1607. Venice, considering St Mark the equal of St Peter, refused to be cowed and won the battle of will after two years, thanks mainly to Sarpi, whose *Treatise on the Interdict* proved it was illegal. In return, he was jumped and knifed by an assassin: '*Agnosco stylum romanae curiae*,' he quipped ('I recognize the method or the "dagger" of the Roman court.'). His major work, the critical *History of the Council of Trent*, didn't improve his standing in Rome, but made him a hero in Venice. Sarpi's main interest, however, was science; he supported Copernicus and shared notes with Galileo, then lecturing at Padua, and 'discovered' the contraction of the iris.

The **cemetery** (*open Apr–Sept daily 7.30–6; Oct–Mar daily 7.30–4*) is entered through the cloister next to the church. The Protestant and Orthodox sections contain the tombs of some of the many foreigners who preferred to face eternity from Venice, among them Ezra Pound, Sergei Diaghilev, Frederick Rolfe (Baron Corvo) and Igor Stravinsky. The gatekeeper can provide a basic map.

Murano

This island (*vaporetti nos.41 and 42 from San Zaccaria or Fondamente Nuove, nos.12, 13 or 14 from Fondamente Nuove, or the DM, a fast route from Tronchetto, Piazzale Roma and Ferrovia*) is synonymous with glass, the most celebrated of the city's industries. The Venetians were the first in the Middle Ages to rediscover the secret of making crystal glass, especially mirrors, and it was a secret they kept a monopoly on for centuries, using the most drastic measures: if a glass-maker let himself be coaxed abroad, the Council of Ten sent their assassins after him in hot pursuit. Those who remained in Venice were treated with kid gloves. Because of the danger of fire, all the forges in Venice were relocated to Murano in 1291, and the little island became a kind of republic within a republic. It minted its own coins, policed itself, and even developed its own list of NHs (*Nobili Homini* – noblemen) in its own Golden Book – aristocrats of glass, who built solid palaces along Murano's own Grand Canal.

Glass-making declined like everything else in Venice, and it was only towards the end of the 19th century that the forges were once more stoked up on Murano. These days, after watching the glass itself being produced, you're treated to the inevitable tour of the 'Museum Showrooms' with their American funeral parlour atmosphere, all solicitude, carpets and hush-hush – this is not unfitting, as some of the blooming chandeliers, befruited mirrors and poison-coloured chalices begin to make Death look good. However, there is no admission charge, and there's not even too much pressure to buy.

It wasn't always so kitschy. The **Museo Vetrario** or Glass Museum (*open Thurs–Tues Apr–Oct 10–5; Nov–Mar 10–4; adm included with San Marco museums ticket*) in the 17th-century Palazzo Giustinian on Fondamenta Cavour has some simple pieces from Roman times, and a choice collection of 15th-century Murano glass.

Nearby stands another good reason to visit this rather dowdy island, the Veneto-Byzantine **Santi Maria e Donato** (*open daily 9.30–12 and 4–7; adm*), a contemporary of St Mark's basilica, with a beautiful arcaded apse. The floor is paved with a marvellous 12th-century mosaic, incorporating coloured pieces of ancient Murano glass, and on the wall there's a fine Byzantine mosaic of the Virgin. The relics of Bishop Donato of Euboea were nabbed by Venetian bodysnatchers; in this case they outdid themselves, bringing home not only San Donato's bones but those of the 'dragon' the good bishop slew with a gob of spit; you can see them hanging behind the altar.

Back on the Fondamenta dei Vetrai, the 15th-century **San Pietro Martire** (*open daily 9–12 and 3–6*) has one of Giovanni Bellini's best altarpieces, *Pala Barbarigo* (1484), a monumental Sacra Conversazione of the Madonna enthroned with saints Mark and Augustine, and Doge Barbarigo, with a rare serenity perfectly suited to the subject.

Burano

Burano (*vaporetto no.12 from Fondamente Nuove*) is the Legoland of the Lagoon, with everything in brightly coloured miniature – the canals, bridges, leaning tower and houses, painted with a Fauvist sensibility in the deepest colours. Traditionally the men fish and the women make Venetian point, 'the most Italian of all lace work' – beautiful, intricate and murder on the eyesight. All over Burano samples are sold (a great deal of them are machine-made or imported), and you can watch it being made at the **Scuola dei Merletti** in Piazza Galuppi (*open Wed–Mon Apr–Oct 10–5; Nov–Mar 10–4; adm*). '*Scuola*' in this case is misleading; when it was founded in 1872, traditional lacemaking was already in decline, and today no young woman in Burano wants to learn such an excruciating art. In the sacristy of the church of **San Martino** (with its tipsily leaning campanile) look for Giambattista Tiepolo's *Crucifixion*, which Mary McCarthy aptly described as 'a ghastly masquerade ball'.

From Burano hire a *sandolo* (small gondola) to **San Francesco del Deserto**, 20 minutes south. St Francis is said to have founded a chapel here in 1220, and the islet was then given to his order for a **monastery** (*open daily 9–11 and 3–5.30; donations welcome*). In true Franciscan fashion, it's not the buildings you'll remember (though there's a fine 14th-century cloister), but the love of nature evident in the beautiful gardens.

Torcello

Though fewer than 100 people remain, this small island (*vaporetto no.12 from Fondamente Nuove*) was once a serious rival to Venice herself. According to legend, its history began when God ordered the bishop of Roman *Altinum*, north of Mestre, to take his flock away from the heretical Lombards into the Lagoon. From a tower the bishop saw a star rise over Torcello, and so led the people of Altinum to this lonely island to set up their new home. It grew quickly, and for the first few centuries it seems to have been the real metropolis of the Lagoon, with 20,000 inhabitants, palaces, a mercantile fleet and five townships. However, malaria decimated the population, the *Sile* silted up Torcello's corner of the Lagoon, and the bigger rising star of Venice drew its citizens to the Rialto. Torcello is now a ghost island, its palaces either sunk into the marsh or quarried for their stone; narrow paths are all that remain of once-bustling thoroughfares. One of them follows a canal from the landing stage past the picturesque Ponte del Diavolo to the grassy piazza in front of the magnificent Veneto–Byzantine former cathedral of **Santa Maria Assunta** with its lofty campanile, founded in 639 and rebuilt in the same Ravenna basilica-style in 1008. The interior (*open daily Apr–Oct 10.30–5.30; Nov–Mar 10–5; adm*) has the finest mosaics in Venice, all by 11th- and 12th-century Greek artists, from the wonderful floor to the spectacular *Last Judgement* on the west wall and the heart-rending *Teotoco*, the stark, gold-ground mosaic of the thin, weeping Virgin portrayed as the 'bearer of God'.

Next to the cathedral is the restored 11th-century octagonal church of **Santa Fosca**, surrounded by an attractive portico, a beautiful and rare late Byzantine work. Near here stands an ancient stone throne called the **Chair of Attila**, though its connection with the Hunnish supremo is nebulous. Across the square, the two surviving secular buildings of Torcello, the Palazzo del Consiglio and Palazzo dell'Archivio, contain the small **Museo dell'Estuario** (*open Tues–Sun 10–12.30 and 2–5; adm*), with an interesting collection of archaeological finds and artefacts from Torcello's former churches.

The Veneto

Memories of Venice are strong in the Veneto, but each city has a distinct personality, formed in the rambunctious Middle Ages when each was an independent *comune*. **Padua**, the brain of the Veneto, has nearly as much fine art as Venice, as well as a saint who in modern polls beats Mark hands down. Petrarch practically invented villa life when he retired to the **Euganean Hills**. **Vicenza**, the city of Palladio, is full of architectural bravura, with a score of famous villas within an hour's drive; and **Verona**, the city of the Scaligeri, is a rose-tinted medieval beauty on the Adige. The minor art capital of **Rovigo** rules the Po flatlands; **Treviso** with its canals is a Venice in miniature; and **Belluno** enjoys a beautiful setting in the foothills of the Dolomites.

From Venice to Padua: Villas along the Brenta

In *The Merchant of Venice*, Portia, disguised as a young lawyer, leaves her villa of Belmont on the Brenta Canal and boats down to Venice to preserve Antonio's pound of flesh. Over the years, the River Brenta had made itself universally detested by flooding the surrounding farmland and choking the Lagoon with silt, and in the 14th century the Venetians decided to control its antics once and for all. They raised its banks and dug a canal to divert its waters, and when all the hydraulic labours were completed in the 16th century they realized that the new canal was the ideal place for their summer *villeggiatura*; their gondoliers could conveniently row them straight to their doors, or, as Goethe and thousands of other visitors have done, they could travel there on the *burchiello*, a water-bus propelled by oars or horses.

More than 70 villas and palaces sprouted up along this extension of the Grand Canal, famous for their summer parties. They were one of the choicest locations for Venetian patricians to go a-squiring in the country yet remain within easy communication of the city. Nowadays you just need a magic wand to make the traffic disappear. Follow the Brenta along the S11, either by car or by taking the half-hourly bus to Padua from Piazzale Roma. To reach La Malcontenta, there's a different hourly bus departing from Piazzale Roma.

Palladio's **Villa Foscari** or **La Malcontenta** (1560) is one of the first villas you reach, between Fusina and Oriago (***t** 041 520 3966; open Apr–Oct Tues and Sat 9–12 or by appointment; guided tours; adm exp*), named, they say, for Foscari's wife, the sad lady in one of the frescoes. La Malcontenta epitomizes the classical dream world of the

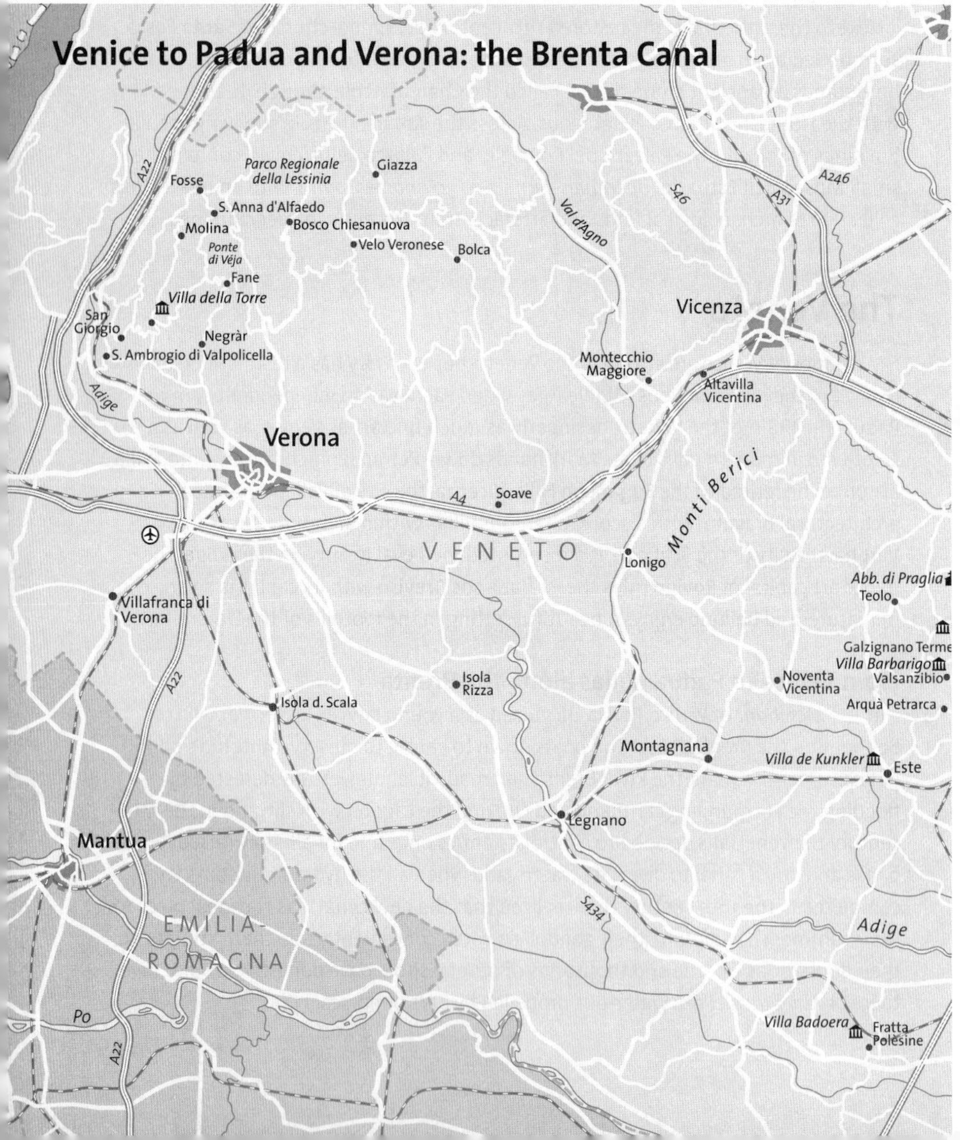

Renaissance and harmonic proportions that Palladio understood better than any other. Viewed from the canal, the villa is a vision begging for Scarlett O'Hara to sweep down the steps. This is no coincidence: Palladio's *Quattro Libri dell'Architettura* was the bible for 18th-century builders in America.

Further up the canal, **Mira Ponte** is the site of the 18th-century **Villa Widmann-Foscari** (*open for guided tours Apr–Sept daily 10–6, Oct daily 10–5, Nov–Mar Sat and Sun 10–5; adm exp*). If you only have time for one villa, don't make it this one, which was redone soon after its construction in the French Baroque style. It contains some of its original furniture and bright, gaudy murals by two of Tiepolo's pupils, but not much of real interest. Mira's post office occupies the **Palazzo Foscarini**, Byron's address from 1817 to 1819 while working on the fourth Canto of *Childe Harold*.

The grandest villa in the Veneto is further up at Strá: the **Villa Nazionale** (or **Pisani**), enlarged by Alvise Pisani to celebrate his election as Doge in 1735 (***t*** *049 502 074; open for 1hr guided tours Tues–Sun summer 8.30–7; winter 8.30–4; adm*). Modelled on Versailles, it was completed in 1760 and purchased by Napoleon in 1807 for his viceroy in Italy, Eugène de Beauharnais. In 1934 Mussolini chose it as a stage for his first meeting with Hitler. Inside, the villa has lost most of its decoration, but the ballroom has Giambattista Tiepolo's shimmering *Apotheosis of the Pisani Family*, a fresco as lovely as its subject matter is ridiculous. The park contains a fiendish garden maze.

Padua

Although only half an hour from Venice, Padua (Padova) refuses to be overshadowed by the old dowager by the sea, and can rightly claim its own place among Italy's most interesting and historic cities. Nicknamed *La Dotta*, 'The Learned', it is home to one of Europe's oldest universities, founded in 1221 and attended by Petrarch, Dante and Galileo. Padua's churches, under the brushes of Giotto, Altichiero, Giusto de' Menabuoi and Mantegna, were virtual laboratories in the evolution of fresco. But what the city attracts most of all are pilgrims of a more pious nature; its exotic landmark, a seven-domed mosque of a basilica, is the last resting place of St Anthony of Padua, who locals call simply *Il Santo*, 'The Saint'. The north of Padua was bombed in the Second World War, but some of the arcaded southern streets could still serve as a stage for *The Taming of the Shrew*, which Shakespeare set in this lively, student-filled city.

Giotto's Cappella degli Scrovegni and the Museo Civico Eremitani

Open daily 9–7, until 10 in summer, museum closed Mon; adm exp; book in advance for 15min chapel visits; ***t*** *049 201 0020.*

Padua deserves at least a day but, if you only have a couple of hours, take the short walk from the bus or railway station to the jewel in its crown: Giotto's extraordinary frescoes in the **Cappella degli Scrovegni** (or Madonna dell'Arena), sheltered by the crusty shell of Padua's Roman amphitheatre. The chapel was built by Enrico Scrovegni in 1303, in expiation for the sins of his father, Reginaldo the usurer. Fortunately, he left enough money behind for Enrico to commission Giotto, then at the height of his career, to fresco the interior with a New Testament cycle (1304–07). In sheer power and inspiration, Giotto's masterpiece was as revolutionary in its day as Michelangelo's Sistine Chapel would be 200 years later – a fresh, natural narrative composition, with three-dimensional figures solidly anchored in their setting. Dante visited Giotto while he worked, and as a compliment placed Reginaldo in the seventh ring of the *Inferno* (Canto XVII). Giotto, however, had no doubt where he was going in the end; you'll find him fourth from the left in the front row of the elect in the *Last Judgement*.

Padua's vast **Museo Civico** in the adjacent convent of the Eremitani combines archaeology (coins and vases from the Veneto, and 14 rare funerary *stelae* from the 6th to 1st centuries BC) and fine art, including Giotto's *Crucifixion* for the altar of the Cappella Scrovegni, works by his follower Guariento, founder of the medieval Paduan

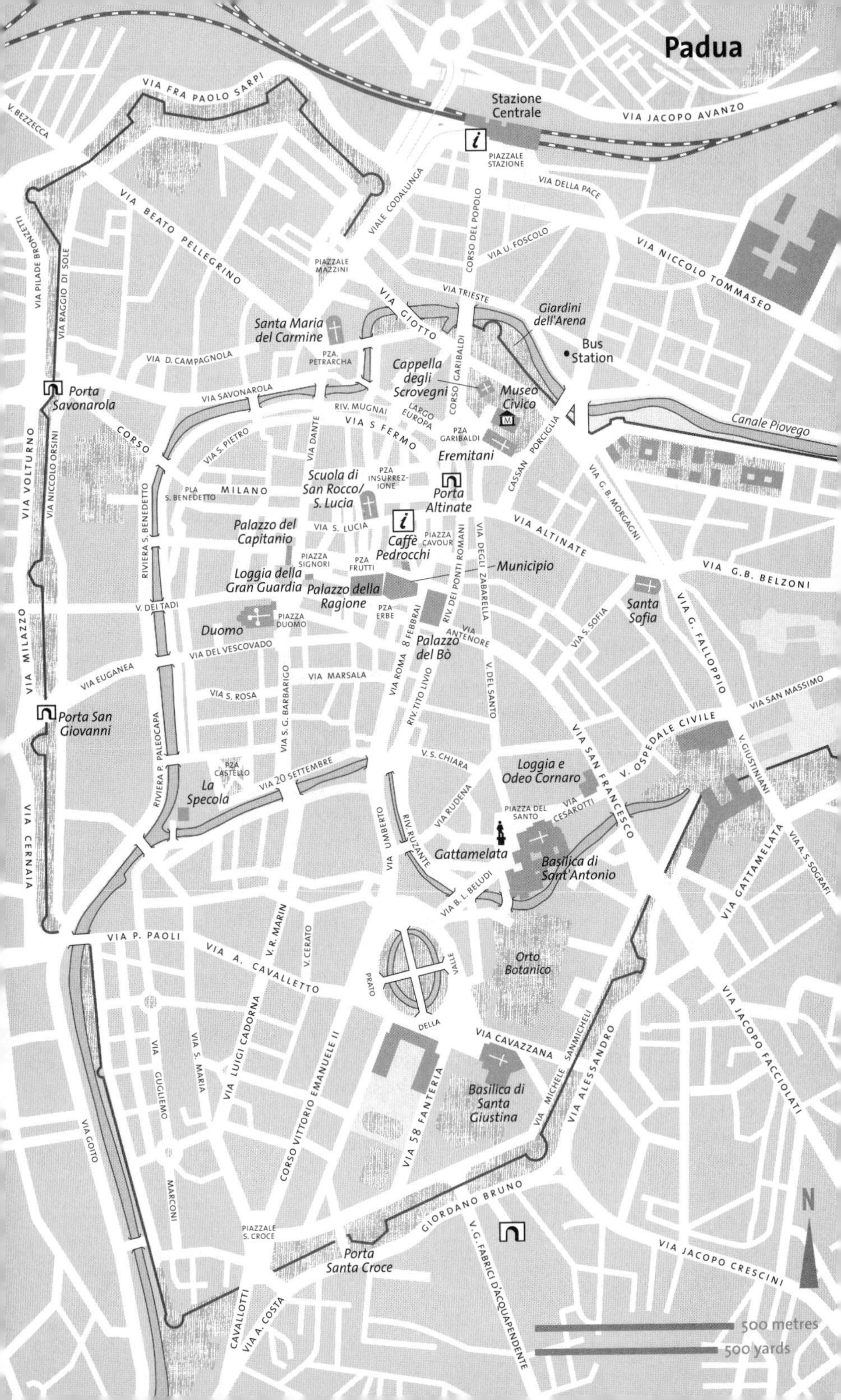
Padua
Stazione Centrale
Piazzale Stazione
Via Jacopo Avanzo
Via Fra Paolo Sarpi
V. Bezzecca
Via della Pace
Viale Codalunga
Corso del Popolo
Via U. Foscolo
Via Niccolo Tommaseo
Via Beato Pellegrino
Via Pilade Bronzetti
Via Raggio di Sole
Piazzale Mazzini
Via Trieste
Via Giotto
Santa Maria del Carmine
Giardini dell'Arena
Bus Station
Via D. Campagnola
Pza. Petrarcha
Cappella degli Scrovegni
Corso Garibaldi
Museo Civico
Porta Savonarola
Via Savonarola
Riv. Mugnai
Largo Europa
Canale Piovego
Corso
Via S. Pietro
Via Dante
Via S Fermo
Pza Garibaldi
Eremitani
Cassan Porciglia
Via Volturno
Via Niccolo Orsini
Pla S. Benedetto
Milano
Scuola di San Rocco/ S. Lucia
Pza Insurrezione
Porta Altinate
Via G. B. Morgagni
Riviera S. Benedetto
Palazzo del Capitanio
Via S. Lucia
Caffè Pedrocchi
Piazza Cavour
Via Altinate
Via degli Zabarella
Piazza Signori
Pza Frutti
Municipio
Via G.B. Belzoni
Loggia della Gran Guardia
Palazzo della Ragione
Riv. dei Ponti Romani
Santa Sofia
V. dei Tadi
Piazza Duomo
Pza Erbe
Via Roma
8 Febbraio
Via Antenore
Via S. Sofia
Duomo
Palazzo del Bò
Via G. Fallopio
Via Milazzo
Via del Vescovado
Via Euganea
Via S. G. Barbarigo
Via Marsala
Riv. Tito Livio
V. del Santo
Via S. Rosa
Via San Massimo
Porta San Giovanni
Via San Francesco
V. Ospedale Civile
V. S. Chiara
V. Giustiniani
Pza Castello
Via 20 Settembre
Loggia e Odeo Cornaro
La Specola
Riviera P. Paleocapa
Via Rudena
Piazza del Santo
Via Cesarotti
Via Cernaia
Via Umberto
Riv. Ruzante
Gattamelata
Basilica di Sant'Antonio
Via A. S. Sografi
Via Gattamelata
Via B. L. Beludi
Via P. Paoli
Via A. Cavalletto
V. R. Marin
V. Cerato
Prato
Valle
Della
Orto Botanico
Via Jacopo Facciolati
Via Luigi Cadorna
Via S. Maria
Via Guglielmo Marconi
Corso Vittorio Emanuele II
Via Cavazzana
Via Michele Sanmicheli
Via Alessandro
Via 58 Fanteria
Basilica di Santa Giustina
Via Goito
Giordano Bruno
N
Piazzale S. Croce
V. G. Fabrici d'Acquapendente
Via Jacopo Crescini
Porta Santa Croce
Cavallotti
Via A. Costa
500 metres
500 yards

Getting There

Padua is easily reached by **train** from Venice (40mins), Vicenza (45mins) and other cities on the Milan–Venice line. Outside the station is a booth with tickets and directions for city buses.

The **bus station**, a 10min walk away in Piazza Boschetti, Via Trieste 40, **t** 049 820 6844, has buses every half-hour to Venice, and good connections to Vicenza, Treviso, Este, Monsélice, Bassano and Rovigo; **ACAP** city buses (**t** 049 820 6811) from the station serve Àbano Terme, Montegrotto Terme and Torreglia. **Landomas**, **t** 049 860 1426, has direct connections to Marco Polo and Treviso airports from Padua and the Euganean hills – they'll pick you up at your door if you book a day in advance. **Radio taxi: t** 049 651 333.

Delta Tours, **t** 049 870 0232, offer **cruises** along the Brenta Canal, and mini-cruises aboard *La Padovanella* around Padua itself on the Piovego river.

Tourist Information

Railway station, **t** 049 875 2077 (*open Mon–Sat 9.15–7, Sun 9–12*); Galleria Pedrocchi, **t** 049 876 7927 (*open Mon–Sat 9–1.30 and 3–7*), *www.padovanet.it*.

The tourist office's *Padova Today* lists events, including summer concerts and exhibitions.

The Padova Card, valid for 48hrs, is worth investing in.

Where to Stay

Padua ✉ 35100

Expensive–Very Expensive

★★★★**Grande Italia**, Corso del Popolo 81, **t** 049 876 111, *www.hotelgranditalia.it*. A beautiful Liberty-style building opposite the railway station.

★★★★**Majestic Toscanelli**, Via dell'Arco 2, **t** 049 663 244, *www.toscanelli.com*. A comfortable option in the historic centre. There's no restaurant but light meals can be provided.

Moderate

★★★**Al Cason**, Via Paolo Sarpi 40, **t** 049 662 636, *www.hotelalcasson.com*. A friendly hotel near the station, with a restaurant serving all the classics. Some rooms are *expensive*.

★★**Al Fagiano**, Via Locatelli 45, **t** 049 875 0073, *www.alfagiano.it*. A welcoming spot close to Sant'Antonio, with en suite rooms and air-con.

★★**Arcella**, Via J. D'Avanzo 7, **t** 049 605 581. A decent option heading away from town but near the station, with congenial owners.

★★**Sant'Antonio**, Via S. Fermo 118, **t** 049 875 1393, *www.hotelsantantonio.it*. A family-friendly hotel 5 mins from Piazza della Frutta, with 3-star facilities, including air-con.

Cheap–Moderate

★**Junior**, Via L. Faggin 2, **t** 049 811 756. A homely hotel outside the centre (a 10-min walk from the station), with shared baths.

school, and others by nearly every Venetian who applied brush to canvas: Bellini, Tintoretto, Titian, Vivarini, Veronese, Tiepolo et al. Don't miss what must be the most camp portrait in all Italy: the 17th-century *Venetian Captain* by Sebastiano Mazzoni, framed among cupids, lions and a giant artichoke. The small Renaissance bronzes filling the halls were a speciality of Padua, especially those by Il Riccio (Andrea Briosco).

Next door, the church of the **Eremitani** (1306; *open Mon–Sat 8.30–12.30 and 3.30–6; Sun 4–6; same ticket as Cappella Scrovegni*) was shattered in an air raid in 1944. What could be salvaged of the frescoes has been painstakingly pieced together, including Andrea Mantegna's remarkable Ovetari chapel, frescoed in 1454–7 when he was in his early 20s; *The Martyrdom of St Christopher and St James* still astonishes, thanks to Mantegna's depiction of the cold might of Rome, and his wizardly use of perspective to foreshorten the action from below. Padua's oldest church, the 9th-century **Santa Sofia**, is to the east at the corner of Via Santa Sofia and Via Altinate. Rebuilt in the 11th century, it has a lovely Byzantine apse.

Eating Out

La cucina padovana is largely based around what are known here as 'courtyard meats' (*carni di cortile*) – chicken, duck, turkey, pheasant, capons, goose and pigeon – plus pork, rabbit and freshwater fish. Try one of the *risotti* for *primo*.

Very Expensive

Antico Brolo, Corso Milano 22, **t** 049 664 555. A restaurant located in an elegant 15th-century building not far from the historic centre, offering a range of Veneto and Emilian specialities: try *chateaubriand* with balsamic vinegar. There's a garden for outdoor dining and a good, much cheaper pizzeria in the old wine cellar. *Closed Sun lunch, Mon and part of Aug*.

Expensive

La Corte Dei Leoni, Via Pietro d'Abano 1, **t** 049 815 0083. A restaurant set in a walled courtyard in the historic centre of Padua, offering truly sumptious meals. There's a weekly-changing menu that combines all the best seasonal ingredients, and an extensive wine list featuring the very best vintages that Italy has to offer. Specialities that are worth trying include *lardo di colonata* (spiced and salted lard) and *scaloppa di rombo con finocchi gratinata* (fillet of turbot with fennel au gratin). *Closed Sun eve and Mon*.

Giovanni, Via Maroncelli 22 (bus no.9 from the train station), **t** 049 772 620. A restaurant offering classic Paduan home cooking, including boiled and roast meats. The home-made pasta is especially good, as are the locally raised capons. *Closed Sun, Mon lunch and Aug*.

Moderate

Antica Osteria dal Capo, Via degli Obizzi 2, **t** 049 663 105. A popular *osteria* by the cathedral, with simple, delicious fish and meat dishes. After *bigoli in salsa e olive* or *ravioli di zucca*, try baked lamb or grilled fish. Finish with an excellent house dessert, such as chestnut bavarese. *Closed Sun, Mon lunch and Aug*.

Bastioni del Moro, Via Bronzetti 18, **t** 049 871 0006. A restaurant rather off the beaten track, a 30-min walk from the centre (it's best to drive or take a taxi as the area is not particularly salubrious). Among the offerings is delicious gnocchi with scallops and *porcini* mushrooms. You can eat in the garden in summer. A *cheap* tourist menu is available; prices soar if you order fish. *Closed Sun*.

Godenda, Via F. Squarcione 4, **t** 049 877 4192. A stylish but informal winebar with a vast range of aperitifs, wines and delicacies. The fine foods on offer – funghi, cheese, salumi and the freshest scallops, oysters, prawns and snails – arrive daily from all over Italy and are prepared with flair. Desserts hail from Padua's best *pasticceria*, Graziati. *Closed Sun*.

Central Padua: The University and Palazzo della Ragione

A short walk from the Eremitani is Piazza Cavour, historic heart of Padua and site of what resembles an Egyptian-revival mausoleum with columned stone porches at either end. This is the **Caffè Pedrocchi**, built in 1831 by Giuseppe Jappelli, famous in its day for never closing (it had no doors), and for intellectuals and students who came here to debate the revolutionary politics of Mazzini; it still serves coffee. In Jappelli's adjacent neo-Gothic, bullet-scarred **Pedrocchino**, students turned words into deeds in 1848, clashing with the Austrian police.

Cater-corner on Via VIII Febbraio is the seat of the **university of Padua**, the 16th-century **Palazzo del Bò** ('of the ox'), a nickname derived from a 1221 tavern. Galileo lectured from its wooden pulpit; the Great Hall is coated with the arms of its alumni, and the **Anatomical Theatre** (1594) is believed to be the world's first permanent one, designed by Fabricius, who discovered the circulation of blood. Other professors included Gabriello Fallopio, discoverer of the Fallopian tubes.

Around the corner, **Piazza Antenore** has two sarcophagi for a centrepiece. The one on columns supposedly contains what remains of Antenor, hero of the Trojan War and founder of ancient *Patavium*, according to the great Roman historian Livy. Livy himself was born in the nearby Euganean Hills, and the other sarcophagus commemorates his 2,000th birthday. Perhaps he'll get something nicer for his 3,000th!

Opposite the Palazzo del Bò and behind the 16th-century **Municipio**, with its uncomfortable Fascist-era façade, the delightful **Piazza delle Erbe** and **Piazza della Frutta** still host bustling markets every morning. They're separated by the massive **Palazzo della Ragione** (*open Tues–Sun Feb–Oct 9–7; until 6 rest of year; adm*). Constructed as Padua's law courts in 1218 and rebuilt in 1306, its upper storey, *Il Salone*, is one of the largest medieval halls in existence, measuring 260ft by 88ft, the 85ft ceiling like a 'vaulting over a market square', as Goethe described it. Its great hull-shaped roof was rebuilt after a fire in 1756 – an earlier blaze, in 1420, destroyed the frescoes by Giotto, which were replaced a few years later with more than 300 biblical and astrological scenes by Niccolò Miretto. Exhibitions are frequently staged in the Salone, but two exhibits never change: the *pietra del vituperio*, a cold stone block where debtors were made to leave all their possessions and clothes, including the ones they were wearing, before going into permanent exile, and a giant **wooden horse** that was built for a joust in 1466, its fierce glance complemented by testicles the size of bowling balls.

Just to the west, Padua's stately **Piazza dei Signori** saw many a joust in its day, and can still boast Italy's oldest astronomical clock, built by Giovanni Dondi (1344) in the tower of the **Palazzo del Capitanio**. On the left is the fine Lombard-style **Loggia della Gran Guardia** (1523), while behind Dondi's clock you'll find the university's Arts Faculty, the **Liviano**, built in 1939 by Gio Ponti. The Da Carrara, Padua's medieval *signori*, lived here in the 1300s, and the Liviano incorporates their palace's **Sala dei Giganti** and its giant frescoes of ancient Romans, repainted by Domenico Campagnola in the 1530s; Altichiero added the more intimate 14th-century portrait of Petrarch sitting at his desk. Around the corner from the square stands Padua's rather neglected **Duomo**, begun in the 12th century but tampered with throughout the Renaissance – Michelangelo was only one of several cooks who spoiled the broth here before everyone lost interest. The **baptistry** (*open daily 10–6; adm*), however, was beautifully frescoed by Florentine Giusto de' Menabuoi in the 1370s. The dome, with its multitude of saints in the circles of paradise, is awesome but chilling.

St Anthony, Donatello and the Biggest Square in Italy

Below the commercial heart of Padua rise the exotic domes of the **Basilica di Sant'Antonio** (*open Mon–Fri 6.30am–7pm, Sat and Sun until 7.45*). St Anthony of Padua was a Portuguese missionary inspired by St Francis. He was shipwrecked in Italy en route to the heathen lands, but stayed, preached, and was canonized only 10 months after his death, in 1232. The basilica was begun in the same year and finished the following century. For pure fantasy it is comparable only to St Mark's, with its cluster of seven domes around a lofty, conical cupola, two octagonal *campanili* and two smaller minarets – a sign of the esteem in which he is held.

Inside, pilgrims queue patiently to press their palm against his tomb and to study the votive testimonials and photos (happy babies, wrecked cars) thanking the busy saint – who also runs Heaven's Lost Property Office. No one pays much attention to the 16th-century marble reliefs lining St Anthony's chapel, although they are exquisite works of the Venetian Renaissance: the fourth and fifth are by Sansovino, the sixth and seventh by Tullio Lombardo, and the last by Antonio Lombardo. Behind the chapel, the **Cappella di Conti** has rich frescoes by Giusto de' Menabuoi (1382).

The **high altar** by Donatello and his helpers (1445–50), much rearranged over the centuries, is crowned by a famous Crucifixion, with bronze statues of the Madonna and Six Patron Saints of Padua and reliefs of the Miracles of St Anthony below. The great **Paschal Candelabrum** is the masterpiece of Il Riccio, who, with his master Bellano, cast the 12 bronze reliefs of Old Testament scenes on the choir walls. Behind the high altar, in the ambulatory, is the **treasury** of gold reliquaries, one containing Anthony's tongue and larynx, found intact when his tomb was opened in 1981.

In the right transept, the **Cappella di San Felice** contains more beautiful frescoes and a remarkable Crucifixion, painted in the 1380s by Altichiero. The basilica complex includes several other exhibitions and museums: one, the **Museo Antoniano** (*open Tues–Sun 10–1 and 2.30–6.30; adm*), houses art made for the basilica over the centuries, including a lunette frescoed by Mantegna and a delightful 15th-century German reliquary in the shape of a ship.

Sharing the large piazza in front of the basilica, a bit lost among the pigeons and souvenir stands, is one of the key works of the Renaissance, Donatello's **statue of Gattamelata** (1453), the first large equestrian bronze since antiquity. The cool 'Honeyed Cat' *condottiere* from Narni in Umbria served Venice so well and honestly that the usually tightwadded Republic paid for this monument, which Donatello imbued with a serene humanistic spirit, in marked contrast to Verrocchio's arrogant Colleoni statue in Venice (*see* p.354).

Flanking the piazza opposite Gattamelata, the **Oratorio di San Giorgio** (*open daily 9–12.30 and 2.30–7; until 5 in winter; adm*) has beautiful frescoes by two heirs of Giotto: Altichiero and Jacopo Avanzi. The adjacent **Scuoletta del Santo** has paintings on the Life of St Anthony by various artists in the panelled upstairs room, including some – not his best – by a teenage Titian (*open Tues–Sat 9–12.30 and 2.30–7; adm*).

Very near the basilica, at Via Cesarotti 37, are the newly restored **Loggia e Odeo Cornaro** (*open Tues–Fri year round 10–1; Sat and Sun Nov–Jan 10–1 and 3–6, Feb–Oct 10–1 and 4–7; guided visits in Italian on the hour and half-past; adm*), built between 1524 and 1530 by Veronese architect Giovanni Maria Falconetto and all that remains of a complex of buildings owned (and co-designed) by Renaissance man Alvise Cornaro. It is here that he held court to the finest minds and artists of his day; inside are the lovely frescoed rooms where theatrical and musical performances were held.

A few streets south of Piazza del Santo, the **Orto Botanico** (*open Mon–Sat Apr–Sept, 9–1 and 3–6; Oct–Mar 9–1; adm*) is Europe's oldest botanical garden, established in 1545; it retains the original layout and a few original specimens. At 'Goethe's palm', planted in 1585 and still flourishing, the poet speculated on his Theory of the Ur-plant, that all plants evolved from one universal specimen.

Beyond, 'Italy's largest piazza', the **Prato della Valle** (1775), does service as car park and pantheon for 78 illustrious men and one woman associated with Padua. On one side stands the **Basilica of Santa Giustina** (*open daily 8.30–12 and 3–7*) by Il Riccio, its domes similar to St Anthony's but its façade unfinished and its interior still-born Baroque, if brightened by a Veronese altarpiece; off the right aisle, don't miss the 5th-century Sacellum di San Prosdocimo. On Saturdays the piazza hosts a large general market, and on the third Sunday of the month an antiques market.

South of Padua: the Euganean Hills and Around

The landscape south of Padua is as flat as any of the prairies of the Po, with the exception of the lush Euganean Hills, a retreat of poets and the jaded since Roman times. Dotted with villas, spas, walking trails and country restaurants, they remain Padua's favourite playground. South of the hills are a handsome trio of medieval towns: Monsélice, Este and Montagnana, all 'with pasts'.

The Euganean Hills

As soon as you leave Padua you'll spot the *Colli Euganei*, ancient volcanic islands now basking in the plain. Fertile, well-watered and defensible, they attracted the region's first settlers, the Paleoveneti, who made Este their chief stronghold. A few thousand years later, the Romans discovered the key secrets of the Euganean Hills: wine (now DOC Colli Euganei) and hot mud. Livy, Suetonius and Martial extolled the virtues of their springs, appreciated ever since: some 130 hotels built over thermal pools provide health or beauty cures at **Ábano Terme** and **Montegrotto Terme**, where the Roman spa has been excavated. At nearby **Torréglia**, the vast **Villa dei Vescovi** (*open mid-Mar–Nov Mon, Weds and Fri 10.30–12 and 2.30–6; adm*), designed by Giovanni Maria Falconetto (1579) for holidaying bishops, greatly influenced Palladio.

From Torréglia, there's a road west to **Teolo**, Livy's birthplace. Because of their unusual micro-climate, the hills are home to some interesting flora, now protected in a regional park; from Teolo you can join a 42-kilometre circular nature trail around the district or visit the Benedictine **Abbazia di Praglia**, founded in 1117 but given the full Renaissance treatment by Tullio Lombardo, Bartolomeo Montagna, Giambattista Zelotti and others (*open Tues–Sun summer 3.30–5.30 for tours every half-hour*).

South of Torréglia towards Galzignano Terme, the **Villa Barbarigo** at **Valsanzibio** (*open daily Mar–Nov 10–1 and 2–dusk; adm exp*) has the grandest gardens in the Veneto, laid out in the mid 1600s in the style of the Tivoli Gardens near Rome, with fountains, waterfalls, nymphaeums and a maze. Beyond, medieval **Arquà Petrarca** is the gem of the Euganean Hills, where the world-weary Petrarch, accompanied by his daughter Francesca and his stuffed cat, Laura II, retired in 1370. His charming villa, the **Casa del Petrarca** (***t*** *0429 718 294; open daily Feb–Sept 9–12 and 3–7; Oct–Jan 9–12.30 and 2.30–5.30; adm*), has retained many of its 14th-century furnishings; with the exception of a radio mast, the view from the poet's study remains the same. Petrarch died here in 1374, and now occupies a marble sarcophagus in front of the church.

Getting There and Around

The spas and towns in the **Euganean Hills** are easily reached by **bus** from the main station in Padua, at Piazza Boschetti.

There are also regular **trains** from Padua to Monsélice (23km), Este (32km), Montagnana (52km) and Rovigo (45km), which take about the same time as the buses (allow for the vagaries of the Italian train system). You may have to change trains at Monsélice. Buses from Monsélice go to Arquà Petrarca (10km) once a day except Sun.

Tourist Information

Ábano Terme: Via Pietro d'Abano 18, **t** 049 886 9055.

Montegrotto Terme: Viale della Stazione 60, **t** 049 793 384.

Monsélice: Piazza Mazzini, **t** 0429 783 026.

Este: Via G. Negri 9, **t** 042 600 462.

Montagnana: Castel S. Zino, **t** 042 981 320 (*closed Mon pm and Tues*).

Where to Stay and Eat

Ábano Terme ✉ 35031

★★★★**Quisisana**, Viale delle Terme 66, **t** 049 866 9111, *www.quisisana.it* (*expensive–very expensive*). A spa hotel in a class of its own, built by Giuseppe Jappelli in 1825. The large park and landscaped pools attract many who are seeking tranquillity rather than magic mud. *Closed Dec–Feb.*

★★★**Verdi**, Via F. Busonera 200, **t** 049 667 600, *www.abanoverdi.it* (*moderate*). A friendly hotel with pools and mud for half the price of the Quisisana.

Da Taparo, Via Castelletto 42, Torréglia, **t** 049 521 1060 (*expensive*). A restaurant with a beautiful terrace overlooking the hills and delicious Veneto cuisine. *Closed Mon.*

Antica Trattoria Ballotta, Via Carromatto 2, Torréglia, **t** 049 521 2970 (*moderate*). One of the oldest restaurants in Venetia, open since 1605 and offering fine dining inside or in its garden. *Closed Tues and Jan.*

Rifugio Monte Rua, Via Monte Rua 29, Torréglia, **t** 049 521 1049 (*moderate*). A restaurant in a panoramic location, with seasonal cuisine. *Closed Tues.*

Arquà Petrarca ✉ 35032

La Montanella, Via Costa 33, **t** 0429 718 200 (*expensive*). A place near the centre of Arquà, with a garden and lovely views. Try the *risotti* and the duck with fruit. There are special wine, olive oil and vinegar menus. *Closed Tues eve, Weds, 2wks Aug and Jan.*

Monsélice ✉ 35043

★★★**Ceffri Villa Corner**, Via Orti 7, **t** 0429 783 111, *www.ceffri.it* (*expensive*). A modern hotel with a pool, well-equipped rooms and a good restaurant.

Venetian Palace Hostel, 'Citta di Monsélice', Via Santo Stefano Superiore 33, **t** 0429 783 125 (*cheap*). A stylish hostel once used by the dukes of Padua as a guesthouse, offering comfortable dorms and en suite rooms.

La Torre, Piazza Mazzini 14, **t** 0429 73752 (*moderate, expensive for truffles*). An elegant place specializing in *funghi*. *Closed Sun eve, Mon, and part of July and Aug.*

Montagnana ✉ 35044

★★★**Aldo Moro**, Via G. Marconi 27, **t** 0429 81351, *www.hotelaldomoro.com* (*moderate*). Fine rooms beside the Duomo. The hotel restaurant serves local *prosciutto dolce del montagnanese*. *Closed Mon.*

Da Stona, Via Carrarese 51, **t** 0429 81532 (*cheap*). An excellent trattoria with tasty home cooking – *pasta e fagioli, prosciutto dolce* and so forth – and a good local wine list. *Closed Mon.*

Monsélice, Este and Montagnana

Spilling like an opera set down the southern slopes of the Euganean Hills, the natural citadel of **Monsélice** was first fortified by the Romans, and in 1239 by Ezzelino da Romano, the cruel tyrant of the Veneto. His beautifully restored Ca' Marcello is now part of the **Castello Monsélice** (*t 0429 72931; open for guided tours summer 9–12 and*

3–6; winter 9–12 and 2–5; some tours in English; adm) and houses a superb collection of medieval and Renaissance arms and antiques. The castle lies near the base of Vincenzo Scamozzi's striking **Via Sacra delle Sette Chiese** (1605), zigzagging up the hill, past the sumptuous **Villa Nani**, the Romanesque **Duomo**, seven **chapels** built by Scamozzi and frescoed by Palma di Giovane, and the elegant 16th-century **Villa Duodo** and **Esedra di San Francesco Saverio**, also by Scamozzi, now a university faculty. A path continues up to the **Mastio Federiciano** (**Rocca**), built over a Lombard fort by Frederick II, Ezzelino's boss (***t** 0429 72931; open Tues–Fri by appointment; Sat and Sun at 5pm*).

Monsélice's old rival, **Este** (ancient *Ateste*), is only nine kilometres to the west; its name was adopted by its 11th-century rulers, who moved on to greater glory in Ferrara. Like Monsélice, Este was a hotly contested piece of real estate, and bristles with the towers of the 1339 **Castello dei Carraresi,** now put out to pasture in a public garden. Abutting the garden, the 16th-century Palazzo Mocenigo houses the excellent **Museo Nazionale Atestino** (***t** 0429 2085; open daily 9–8; adm*), which covers the Paleoveneto civilization from the 10th century BC to Roman times. Don't miss the 7th-century BC *Situla Benvenuti*, a bronze vase decorated with warriors and fantastic animals. There is also a superb collection of 6th–5th-century BC bronzes, and – a bit out of place – a luscious red-dressed *Madonna and Child* by Cima da Conegliano.

Behind the castle, the **Villa De Kunkler** was Byron's residence from 1817 to 1818. Here Shelley, his guest, penned 'Lines written among the Euganean Hills', after the death of his little daughter, Clara. Don't miss the startlingly tilted 12th-century campanile of **San Martino**, just off Piazza Maggiore, and Giambattista Tiepolo's altarpiece of *Santa Tecla versus the Plague* in the **Duomo**.

Southwest is the newly restored **Abbazia Camaldolesi** (***t** 0429 619 777; open Sat and Sun 3–7*), a beautiful Augustinian abbey built in 1189 and enlarged in the Renaissance. In 1690 Pope Alexander VIII suppressed the abbey and auctioned it off to finance La Serenissima's war against the Turks. Bought by a Bergamo noble family, it was turned into a farm and summerhouse and now contains a small farming museum.

Montagnana, 15 kilometres west of Este, has some of Italy's best-preserved medieval fortifications, the work of Ezzelino da Romano and Padua's Carrara family. The two-kilometre walls were defended by 24 (still intact) towers, which were impressive but ineffective – Venice lost and regained the town 13 times in the War of the Cambrai. They now form a backdrop to Montagnana's colourful *palio* in September. In the main piazza, the **Duomo** has a portal by Sansovino, a Transfiguration by Veronese and a huge painting of *The Battle of Lepanto*. Palladio's **Palazzo Pisani** is by the Porto Padova.

Little Mesopotamia

About 20 kilometres south of Monsélice, Rovigo is the capital of the province wedged between the mighty Adige and the mightier Po, known as the Polésine or 'Little Mesopotamia'. Like ancient Mesopotamia it has been blessed and cursed by its rivers, which make it fertile but often spill over their banks, while miles of silt have left its ancient capital, Adria, high and dry.

Rovigo and Adria

Other inhabitants of the Veneto may sneer '*Rovigo no m'intrigo*', but this prosperous provincial capital doesn't give a damn. For a landmark, it can match Bologna with its odd leaning towers, the 11th-century **Torri Donà**, one tall, one stubby. Nearby (nothing is far), central Piazza Vittorio Emanuele II is a handsome trapezoid dotted with palaces, one containing the **Pinacoteca dell'Accademia dei Concordi** (*open Mon–Fri 9.30–12.30 and 3.30–6.30; Sat 9.30–12.30; Sun 10–12*), founded by scholars in 1580, with a fine collection of works by Giovanni Bellini, Lorenzo Lotto, Palma il Vecchio and others. From adjacent Piazza Garibaldi, follow Via Silvestri back to the octagonal **La Rotonda**, by Francesco Zamberlan, a pupil of Palladio, with a detached tower by Longhena and walls covered with 17th-century paintings glorifying Venetian bureaucrats.

From Rovigo it's 18 kilometres southwest to **Fratta Polésine**, where Palladio's pretty temple-fronted **Villa Badoera** (1570) has frescoes of pseudo-Roman grotesques by Giallo Fiortino (***t** 0425 21530; open mid-July–mid-Oct Sat and Sun 10–12 and 4.30–7.30; book ahead*). Buses and trains from Rovigo also head east for **Adria**, a dusty place dominated by a radio mast, founded by the Etruscans and colonized by the Greeks in the 6th century BC, when it stood on the shore of the sea that took its name. The Venice of its day, Adria has but one canal now, and a **Museo Archeologico Nazionale** at Piazzale degli Etruschi (***t** 0426 21612; open 9–7 daily, Thurs, Fri and Sat also 8.30–11pm; adm*), with lovely Roman glass and a 3rd-century BC iron chariot of Gaulish workmanship, found entombed with three tiny horses.

Getting There and Around

From Rovigo there are frequent **buses** to Adria and the Delta towns; **trains** also run from Rovigo to Adria and Chioggia (1hr 20mins), or south to Ferrara (30mins) and Bologna (1hr). The **bus station** is on Piazzale G. Di Vittorio, the **train station** is on Piazza Riconoscenza. Fratta Polèsine can be reached by bus from Rovigo.

Tourist Information

Rovigo: Via J.H. Dunant 10, t 0425 361 481, *www.provincia.rovigo.it*

Rosolina Mare: Via dei Ligustri 3, t 0426 68012.

Where to Stay and Eat

Rovigo ✉ 45100

********Villa Regina Margherita,** Viale Regina Margherita 6, **t** 0425 361 540, *www.hotelvillareginamargherita.it* (*moderate–expensive*). A Liberty-style villa situated just a few steps from the centre of town. The bedrooms are well equipped if lacking the stylishness of the public rooms.

*****Hotel Granatiere**, Corso del Popolo 235, **t** 0425 22301, *www.paginegialle.it/granatiere* (*moderate*). A small, comfortable option right in the centre.

Tenuta Castel Venezze, San Martino di Venezze, 8km from town, **t** 0425 99667, *www.tenutacastelvenezze.it* (*moderate*). A new *agriturismo* in a 15th-century building constructed from a ruined castle, with 12 rooms and 3 apartments, a restaurant, a swimming pool and extensive parkland. Rooms are furnished with antiques.

Degli Amici, Via Quirina 4, Arquà Polésine, 8km south of Rovigo, **t** 0425 91045 (*expensive*). Fresh- and salt-water fish and locally reared duck and goose cooked in an old wood-burning oven. *Closed Wed, and Sat and Sun lunch in summer.*

Tavernetta Dante dai Trevisani, Corso del Popolo 212, **t** 0425 26386 (*moderate*). A good place to try the medieval favourite, *pappardelle all'anatra* (broad flat noodles with duck sauce). *Closed Sun and Aug.*

The Po Delta

After travelling more than 652 kilometres, the Po splits into six major branches, creating a reed-filled delta, a marshy wonderland of a thousand islets, haven for waterfowl and migratory birds. Before it became the **Parco del Po**, a few resorts sprung up along the sandy, pine-shaded shores – **Rosolina Mare** and **Isola di Albarella**; they now try hard to be ecologically correct. There are several **boat cruises** exploring the delta, departing from **Porto Tolle** or **Taglio di Po**. Ask the tourist office for details.

North of Padua: up the Valley of the Brenta

Some of the Veneto's best-known sites are north of Padua, in the foothills of the Dolomites: Castelfranco, birthplace of Giorgione; Àsolo, where the Queen of Cyprus held her fabled Renaissance court; and several outstanding villas, including Masèr, where Palladio and Veronese collaborated to create a unique work of art.

Castelfranco and Cittadella

Piombino Dese, just off the main SS307 from Padua to Castelfranco, is a sprawling rural *comune*, and an essential detour for Palladiophiles. Its 1554 **Villa Cornaro**, a block from the Piombino Dese train station (***t** 0439 936 5017; garden open May–Sept Sat 3.30–6; interior by appointment*) is one of the master's most innovative and well-preserved structures, the first with a double loggia; it was frescoed in 1717 by Mattia Bortoloni with biblical scenes.

Castelfranco Véneto, further north, basks in the glory of having given the world Giorgione, in 1478. Big George in return gave Castelfranco a masterpiece: the **Duomo**'s *Castelfranco Madonna* (1504), a triangular composition of the Virgin, St Francis and the local soldier–saint Liberalis, their remote figures inhabiting the same ineffable, dreamlike world as his paintings in the Accademia in Venice. What you see is actually a copy – the original is being restored at the Accademia, where it will remain until a display case is created to protect it against the damp. Next to the Duomo, the **Casa del Giorgione** (*currently closed*) is being turned into a proper museum to Giorgione.

Castelfranco itself is a walled city, built by Treviso in 1199 to counter the ambitions of Padua. The Paduans, tit for tat, founded the egg-shaped **Cittadella** 15 kilometres west; one tower in its mighty 13th-century walls was Ezzelino's infamous torture chamber (*cf. Paradiso* IX, 54). The Venetians added the fine lion with a kinky tail in the square.

From Castelfranco you can also nip up to **Fanzolo**, five kilometres to the northeast, for another of Palladio's finest: **Villa Emo** (***t** 0423 476 334; open Apr–Oct Mon–Sat 3–7, Sun and hols 10–12.30 and 3–7; Nov–Mar Sat and Sun 2–6; adm exp*), and the only villa still owned by the family that commissioned it. Like most, this ranch was designed as a working farm, and was one of the first in Europe to grow maize (1536), used primarily to fatten pigeons before it was used for polenta to fatten Venetians. The main rooms were frescoed with brightly coloured mythologies by Giambattista Zelotti; the *barchesse* or storage wings are now a hotel. Palladio also designed the long rows of workers' cottages that are slowly being restored.

Villa Barbaro at Masèr

t 0423 923 004; open Mar–Oct Tues, Sat, Sun and hols 3–6; Nov–Feb Sat, Sun and hols 2.30–5; adm exp.

Montebelluna, which is also situated to the northeast of Castelfranco, was another favourite area for building summer villas, among them the lovely Villa Barbaro at Masèr. Commenced in 1568 for the brothers Daniele and Marcantonio Barbaro (the former was Patriarch of *Aquileia* and one of Venice's most distinguished humanistic scholars), Masèr is a unique synthesis of two great talents: that of Palladio and his friend Paolo Veronese.

Palladio taught Veronese about space and volume, and nowhere is this so evident as in these ravishing, architectonic *trompe l'œil* frescoes, populated by the original owners and their pets, who linger as if the villa lay under the same spell as Sleeping Beauty's castle – an effect heightened by the slippers passed out to visitors at the door (to protect the original floors). Signora Barbaro and her sons gaze down from painted balconies; a little girl opens a door; a dog waits in a corner; painted windows offer views of imaginary landscapes; the huntsman in the far bedroom is Veronese, gazing across the row of rooms at his mistress.

Behind the villa, the nymphaeum is guarded by giants sculpted by Marcantonio himself. The striking, if crumbling, **Tempietto**, just across the road, is a miniature pantheon designed by Palladio in 1580 and decorated by Alessandro Vittoria.

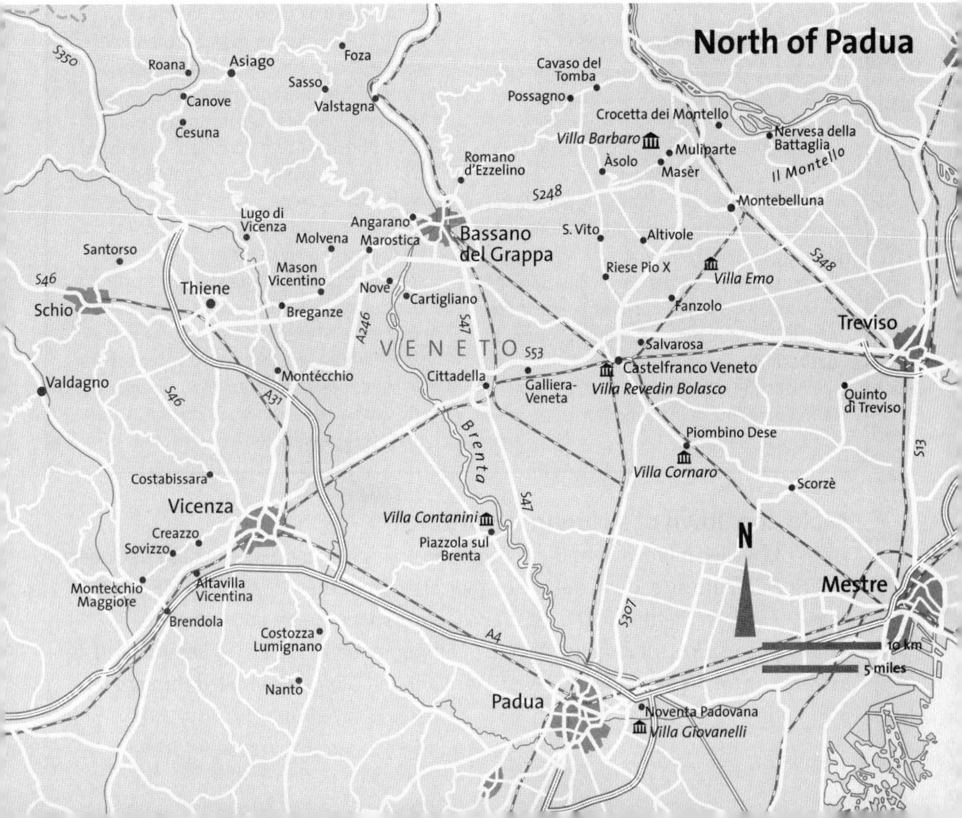

Getting There and Around

From Padua there are **buses** and **trains** to Bassano del Grappa via Castelfranco (40mins); from Vicenza change trains at Castelfranco, passing Cittadella on the way. From Venice, change in Treviso.

Bassano's **bus station** is in Piazzale Trento, near the tourist office, **t** 0424 30850; the **train station** is at the top of Via Chilesotti. Frequent buses from Montebelluna, Bassano or Treviso serve Àsolo (14km) and Masèr (6km further); others, from Bassano and Vicenza, run to Maròstica (20 buses daily), Lonedo di Lugo, Thiene (25km) and Asiago (36km).

Tourist Information

Castelfranco Veneto: Via Francesco Maria Preti 66, **t** 0423 495 000.

Àsolo: Piazza G. D'Annunzio 2, **t** 0423 529 046.

Where to Stay and Eat

Castelfranco Veneto ✉ 31033

****__Fior__, Via dei Carpani 18, **t** 0423 721 212, Salvarosa, *www.albergoroma.com* (*expensive*). An old villa and park with a pool.

***__Al Moretto__, Via S. Pio X 10, **t** 0423 721 313, *www.albergoalmoretto.it* (*moderate–expensive*). A 17th-century palace in the centre.

***__Roma__, Via Fabio Filzi 39, **t** 0423 721 616, *www.albergoroma.com* (*moderate*). A hotel and café-bar outside the fortifications but with a good view of them.

***__Ca' delle Rose__, on the Circonvallazione Est, Salvarosa, **t** 0423 420 374 (*cheap–moderate*). A little old hotel with a famous restaurant, **Barbesin**, **t** 0423 490 446. The setting is as idyllic as the seasonal cooking; the veal with apples melts in your mouth. *Closed Weds eve and Thurs.*

Al Palazzino, Via Roma 29, Galliera Vèneto, between Castelfranco and Cittadella, **t** 049 596 9224 (*very expensive*). A former hunting lodge offering Renaissance dishes such as pheasant stuffed with truffles. *Closed Tues eve, Weds and Aug.*

Alle Mura, Via Preti 69, **t** 0423 498 098 (*expensive*). A restaurant next to the walls, with well-prepared seafood dishes and a garden. *Closed Thurs and Aug.*

Masèr and Around ✉ 31010

Da Bastian, Via Cornuda, **t** 0423 565 400 (*expensive*). Enchanting surroundings up the road from Palladio's villa, with famous pâté, risotto, Venetian-style snails and desserts. *Closed Weds eve, Thurs and some of Aug.*

Àsolo ✉ 31011

****__Villa Cipriani__, Via Canova 298, **t** 0423 952 166, *www.starwood.com/italy* (*luxury*). One of Italy's most evocative hotels, in a 16th-century house that belonged to Robert Browning, decorated with Eleonora Duse's Persian carpets and boasting a lovely rose garden full of songbirds.

****__Al Sole__, Via Collegio 33, **t** 0423 528 111, *www.albergoalsole.com* (*very expensive–luxury*). A charming hotel in the historic centre, with a host of famous past guests.

***__Duse__, Via Browning 190, **t** 0423 55241, *www.hotelduse.com* (*moderate–expensive*). A hotel overlooking Àsolo's central piazza, with a little garden.

Osteria Ca' Derton, Piazza D'Annunzio 11, **t** 0423 52730 (*very expensive*). A restaurant set in one of Àsolo's oldest houses, offering traditional dishes. *Closed Sun eve and Mon.*

Ai Due Archi, Via Roma 55, **t** 0423 952 201 (*moderate*). A wood-panelled space serving delicious polenta. *Closed Weds eve and Thurs.*

Caffè Centrale, Via Roma 72. A historic café that every passing celeb calls in at for a drink.

Àsolo, the 'Town of a Hundred Horizons'

This old walled hilltown was the consolation prize given by Venice in 1489 to Queen Caterina Cornaro after demanding her abdication from the throne of Cyprus. It could have been worse: it's one of the most enchanting spots in Italy, and Caterina's Renaissance court lent it a high degree of refinement and art. Pietro Bembo used it as a setting for his dialogues on love, *Gli Asolani*, and Giorgione strolled through its rose gardens strumming his lute; the enforced idleness in Àsolo perhaps inspired his invention of art merely for the sake of pleasure. In the 19th century, Àsolo was also a beloved retreat of Robert Browning (his last volume of poems was entitled *Asolando*; 'Pippa Passes' was set here as well). Eleonora Duse and the great traveller Freya Stark lived and are buried here.

Some people never get beyond Àsolo's perfect piazza with its 16th-century **Fontana Maggiore**, but you can look at the **Castello** with its watch tower (in both senses of the word – it tells the time) and what little remains of the garden where Queen Caterina lived in 'lace and poetry'; the courtyard has a modern *bocce* court. In 1700 the great hall was replaced with a theatre, but in 1930 the John Deere tractor heir bought and rebuilt it in his villa in Sarasota, Florida.

Near the castle, the frescoed Loggia del Capitano contains the **Museo Civico** (*open Sat and Sun 10–12 and 3–7; adm*) dedicated to Queen Caterina, Browning and La Duse. The **Duomo** has works by Lotto, Jacopo da Bassano and Vivarini. For the famous view over Àsolo of 'a hundred horizons' climb (or drive – the road is halfway down the hill) up to the **Rocca**, built over a Roman fort (***t** 0497 710 977; open 10–dusk Sat, Sun or any day by appointment for groups, or ask in the tourist office; closed for bad weather; adm*).

Possagno, 10 kilometres north at the foot of Monte Grappa, was the birthplace of Antonio Canova (1757–1822), the ultimate neoclassical sculptor, the favourite of Napoleon and several popes. You can visit his house, and clay and plaster models, in the **Gypsoteca** (***t** 0423 544 323; open Tues–Sat 9–12 and 3–6; adm*).

Most artists leave a work or two in their home towns, but Canova left nothing less than a full-scale model of the Pantheon with the Parthenon stuck on front as his last resting place. The town itself describes the **Tempio** as 'one of the greatest monuments that man on earth has ever erected – in praise of God – to himself'. You can climb up the dome (*open Tues–Sun 9–12 and 2–5; until 6 in summer; adm*); or study the leaning bell tower, and try to figure out if it was built that way.

Bassano del Grappa, Maròstica and Asiago

Carry on west for more Veneto essentials: Bassano del Grappa with its covered bridge; Maròstica, where they play chess with human players; more villas by Palladio; and the mountains of Asiago.

Bassano del Grappa

Sprawled over the foothills of the Alps where the Brenta begins its flow down the plain, the colourful bustling town of Bassano celebrated its first millennium in 1998. Palladio gets credit for its pictureseque landmark, the **Ponte degli Alpini**, the unique covered wooden bridge. First constructed in 1599, the bridge has been rebuilt several times to the master's design – lastly in 1969, after it was swept away in the Brenta's flood. At one end, in the Palazzo Beltrame-Menarola, the grappa distillery Poli runs a **Museo della Grappa** where you can taste and buy the stuff (***t** 0424 524 426; open daily 9–7.30; adm for groups*).

Tourist Information

Bassano: Largo Corona d'Italia 35, **t** 0424 524 351.
Maròstica: Piazza Castello, **t** 0424 72127.
Asiago: Via Stazione 5, **t** 0424 462 661.

Where to Stay and Eat

Bassano del Grappa ✉ 36061

Dried mushrooms and honey as well as grappa are specialities of Bassano, but in the month of April it's yet another treat that attracts droves of hungry gourmets: Asparagi DOC di Bassano – long fat white asparagus, delicate, full of flavour, and perfect for spring-cleaning one's internal plumbing. Make sure that you sample it prepared the local way, *alla bassanese* (blanched and topped with a hollandaise-type sauce made with cooked eggs and olive oil), or simply *alla parmigiana*.

****__Villa Palma__, Via Chemin Palma 30, Mussolente, just east of town, **t** 0424 577 407, *www.villapalma.it* (*expensive–very expensive*). A lovely, award-winning hotel situated in an elegant 17th-century villa, with plush rooms full of hi-tech gizmos and a gourmet restaurant.

****__Belvedere__, Piazzale G. Giardino 14, **t** 0424 529 845, *www.bonotto.it* (*moderate–expensive*). A central 15th-century house with the best rooms in town (ask for one in the back to be sure of it being quiet). The hotel's elegant restaurant at Viale delle Fosse 1, **t** 0424 524 988, serves Bassano's finest food, in the form of Veneto and Italian classics. *Closed Sun*.

__Il Castello__, Via Bonamigo 19, **t 0424 228 665, *www.hotelilcastello.it* (*cheap–moderate*). A small, friendly, comfortable option right in the centre of town.

Al Sole-Da Tiziano, Via Vitorelli 41, **t** 0424 523 206 (*moderate*). A beautiful dining room that's presided over by the perfect host. Among the wonderful fare on offer are a faultless risotto, delicious duck, and a number of dishes featuring the town's favourite seasonal ingredients: mushrooms, white asparagus and radicchio. *Closed Mon and July*.

Maròstica ✉ 36063

Maròstica is famous both for its cherries and its *paetarosta col magaragno* – young turkey roasted on a spit and served with pomegranate sauce.

***__La Rosina__, Contrà Narchetti 4, Valle San Florian, 2km north of Maròstica, **t** 0424 75839, *www.larosina.it* (*moderate*). A hotel offering modern, comfortable rooms in a superb hilltop setting, together with a restaurant run by a talented chef. *Closed Aug*.

Ristorante al Castello, **t** 0424 73315 (*expensive*). A restaurant in a renovated castle, with lovely views and food based on fresh local ingredients. Top it off with a *caffè corretto*, 'corrected' with one of a score of grappas.

Asiago ✉ 36012

Asiago is synonymous with its low-fat cow's milk cheese with bite, one of the few in Italy to achieve DOC status, but surprisingly little known outside the country. There are two kinds: fresh *asiago pressato*, delicate and soft, often used in cooking, fried or in salads, and *asiago d'allevo*, sold *mezzano*, *vecchio* or *stravecchio* (middle-aged, old or extra old), becoming more intensely flavoured with age.

***__Da Barba__, Kaberlaba, 5km from Asiago, **t** 0424 463 363, *www.dabarba.it* (*moderate*). A little place not far from the pistes, with magnificent views, a warm welcome and good food. *Closed May and mid-Oct–Nov*.

Lepre Bianca da Pippo, Camona, in the *comune* of Gallio just northeast of town, **t** 0424 445 666 (*moderate*). Cosy rooms and an elegant English-style dining room (*expensive*) serving seasonal dishes, fantastically fresh seafood (rare up in these hills) and delicate desserts. *Closed Mon, Tues lunch in winter, and part of May and Nov*.

***__La Bocchetta__, Conco, midway between Bassano del Grappa and Asiago, **t** 0424 704 117, *www.labochetta.it* (*cheap–moderate*). A mountain inn and restaurant dating from the early 18th century, rebuilt in an OTT Tyrolean style, but with an indoor pool, a sauna and mountain bike hire.

***__Erica__, Via Garibaldi 55, **t** 0424 462 113, *www.hotelerica.it* (*cheap–moderate*). A long-established hotel that is a cosy bet for a summer or winter stay. *Closed 1st 2wks Oct*.

Bassano's centre is made up of a string of squares: first is medieval Piazzotto Montevecchio, where the old **Monte di Pietà** (municipal pawn shop) is covered with the coats of arms of 120 Venetian *podestà*. This is linked to piquant Piazza Libertà, hogged by the neoclassical façade of the mastodontic church of **San Giovanni**, while the next square, Piazza Garibaldi, is guarded, physically and spiritually, by a medieval **Torre Civica** and the Gothic church of **San Francesco**. Its cloister contains the **Museo Civico** (*open Tues–Sat 9–6.30, Sun 3.30–6.30; adm; same ticket as ceramics museum*), with an excellent archaeological section of finds from Magna Graecia, and paintings with an emphasis on the dark and/or stormy by the Bassano family, and especially Jacopo (his masterpiece, the twilit *Baptism of St Lucia*). Alessandro Magnasco weighs in with the uncanny *Burial of a Trappist Monk* and *Franciscan Banquet*, full of racing, wraith-like friars. There are calmer works too: Michele Giambono's *Madonna* and a beautiful Crucifix by Guariento.

In the mid 17th century Bassano and the nearby town of Nove became the Veneto's top ceramics manufacturers – a status they maintain to this day, boasting 56 firms. In the 18th-century Palazzo Sturm, just up Via Ferracina from the bridge, the **Museo della Ceramica** (*open Apr–Oct Tues–Sat 9–12.30 and 3.30–6.30, Sun 3.30–6.30; June–Sept also Sun 10–12.30; Nov–Mar Tues–Sat 9–12.30, Fri, Sat and Sun 3.30–6.30; same ticket as Museo Civico*) has a display of local ware and porcelain knick-knacks.

The 'Grappa' was added to Bassano's name in 1928 in memory of the terrible fighting in the First World War at Cima Grappa, where the Italians held the line after Caporetto. The road up to **Cima Grappa** (5,822ft), the Strada Cadorna, was built during the conflict and begins in Romano d'Ezzelino. On top, the **Galleria Vittorio Emanuele II** was the enormous trench dug by the Italian military to shelter its battery of guns; displays and a museum describe the conflict. The monumental cemetery holds the remains of 12,615 Italians; the slightly smaller Austro-Hungarian cemetery contains 10,590 dead (*open daily mid-May–Sept 10–12 and 2–5; Oct–mid-May 10–12 and 1–4*).

A Grappa Digression

Although a lot of grappa does come from Bassano del Grappa, its name doesn't derive from the town or its mountains but from *graspa*, the residue left at the bottom of the wine vat after the must is removed; it can be drunk unaged and white, or aged in oak barrels, where it takes on a rich, amber tone. First mentioned in a 12th-century chronicle, grappa, or aqua vitae ('the water of life'), was chugged down as a miracle-working concoction of earth and fire to dispel ill humours. In 1601 the Doge created a University Confraternity of Aqua Vitae to control quality; during the First World War Italy's Alpine soldiers adopted Bassano's enduring bridge as their symbol and its grappa to keep them on their feet. One of their captains described it perfectly:

> ***Grappa is like a mule; it has no ancestors and no hope of descendants; it zigzags through you like a mule zigzags through the mountains; if you're tired you can hang on to it; if they shoot you can use it as a shield; if it's too sunny you can sleep under it; you can speak to it and it'll answer, cry and be consoled. And if you really have decided to die, it will take you off happily.***

West of Bassano

More colourful ceramics wait in **Nove**, home to the national pottery school. Part of the complex includes the **Museo Istituto Statale d'Arte per la Ceramica**, Via Giove 1 (*open Mon–Sat 8–1; Tues, Thurs and Fri also 1.30–4*). The **Museo Civico della Ceramica** in the 19th-century Palazzo De Fabris (*open Tues–Sat 9–12.30, Sun 10–12.30; adm*) has works from the last 300 years by local masters and foreign artists, including Picasso.

Maròstica, seven kilometres west, is a striking town within 13th-century walls, its upper castle sprawled over the hill, its lower castle, abode of the Venetian lord and now the town hall, sitting like a giant rook in the main piazza. It's the perfect setting for the storybook event that put Maròstica on the map: the *Partita a Scacchi*, the human chess match that takes place in even-numbered years the second weekend in September. The game, played with its human (and horse) 'pieces' in medieval costume on a 72-sq ft board, commemorates the contest in 1454 for the hand of Lionora Parisio. Her father, the Venetian governor, refused to let her suitors fight a duel 'in sad memory of the unhappy lovers Madame Juliet Capuleti and Master Romeo Montecchio', and offered the loser his younger daughter. The level of play matches the gorgeous costumes; each game is a reproduction of a grand masters' duel, though things can go wrong when the pieces misunderstand the commands, announced in archaic Venet. At other times the Renaissance finery is on display in the castle's **Museo dei Costumi** (***t*** *0424 72127; open Mon–Sat 10–12 and 2.30–6; Sun 9–6; adm*).

Further west, in **Lonedo di Lugo**, near the town of Lugo (about six kilometres north of Breganze), are two important villas by Palladio. **Villa Godi Valmarana Malinverni**, Via Palladio 44 (*open Mar–May, Oct and Nov Tues, Sat, Sun and hols 2–6; June–Sept daily 3–7; adm*), built in 1540, was his first. The central portion, usually the most prominent and decorated part of his villas, is behind two large wings. The interior, frescoed by Padovano and assistants, has a fossil collection and rooms of Italian 19th-century painting. The later, more classically elegant **Villa Piovene Porto Godi** is a couple of doors down, in a neoclassical park (*gardens open daily summer 2.30–7, winter 2–5*).

In the centre of pleasant **Thiene**, 10 kilometres to the west, the quattrocento **Villa de Porta Colleoni** (***t*** *0445 366015; open for guided tours 16 Mar–16 Nov Sun at 3, 4 and 5; groups daily by appointment; adm*) is an attractive castle-villa with towers, battlements and Venetian Gothic windows; inside are frescoes, antique ceramics and jumbo paintings of the former residents of the 18th-century stables on the grounds. Opposite note the flamboyant little church of the **Natività**, its roofline studded with flames of curly kale. Thiene's slender **Torre Civica** dates from the 1600s.

North of Thiene you can climb into the cool, green, high plain of **Asiago** (3,257ft), which is known for its salubrious climate, cheese, pretty walks and skiing. Like all the villages, the main town of Asiago had to be completely rebuilt after its use as a battlefield in the war to end all wars. Its focal point is a massive pink stone **Municipio**, with an enormous tower and lion; in the park behind, a delightful **fountain** features Pan and all the animals of the forest. A ghastly number of war dead – 12,795 identified, 21,491 nameless, and 19,999 Austro-Hungarians – lie in the hilltop **Sacrario**, which also houses a small **Museo Storico** (*open daily mid-May–Sept 9–12 and 3–6; Oct–mid-May 9–12 and 2–5*).

Vicenza

'The city of Palladio', prettily situated below Monte Bérico, is an architectural pilgrimage shrine and knows it; where other Italians grouse about being a nation of museum curators, the prim Vicentini glory in their city, the intellectual product of a gentry immersed in humanistic and classical thought (a gentry, they gently remind you, that was far better educated than those merchants by the lagoon, who ruled Vicenza in its heyday). Their pride was vindicated when UNESCO placed Vicenza on its list of World Heritage Sites. Although it was heavily damaged during the Second World War, restorers have tidied up all the scars. Vicenza's other name now is the 'City of Gold', thanks to its gold-working industry, the most important in Europe; it is also the birthplace of Federico Faggin, inventor of the silicon chip. Add machine tools, textiles and shoes, and you have one of Italy's wealthiest cities.

Porta Castello to the Piazza dei Signori

From the station, Viale Roma enters the historic centre through the **Porta Castello**, with its powerful 11th-century tower. The palace with the columns the size of sequoias is the **Palazzo da Porto-Breganze,** designed by Palladio and partly built by his pupil Scamozzi, before the very monumentality of the design defeated him. Scamozzi also built the less exciting **Palazzo Bonin** at No.13, after his master's designs.

From Piazza Castello, Contrà Vescovado leads to the Gothic **Duomo**, which was carefully pieced back together after the war and houses a beautiful polyptych by Lorenzo Veneziano, painted in 1356, in the fifth chapel on the right. Excavations have revealed the Duomo's 8th-century ancestor and a stretch of Roman road and, under the square, a **Criptoportico**, a subterranean passage from a 1st-century AD palace. Down Contrà Porti, turn at Via Pigafetta for the fine eclectic **Casa Pigafetta** (1444), birthplace of Antonio Pigafetta, who happened to be in Spain in 1519 when Magellan was setting out for the first of all world tours. Pigafetta went along, and wrote the definitive account of the voyage three years later. Note his motto '*Il n'est rose sans espine*' by the door. Beyond, to the left, lies the Piazza dei Signori.

Piazza dei Signori

This kingly square is the heart and soul of Vicenza, its public forum from Roman times to this day. In the 1540s the Vicentines decided that the piazza's crumbling old medieval Palazzo della Ragione needed a facelift to match their Renaissance-humanist aspirations. Having rejected designs by such luminaries as Sansovino and Giulio Romano, they surprisingly hired a young unknown called Palladio to give it a facelift. The city would never be the same.

In 1549 Palladio began working on the building, since known as the **Basilica** – 'hall of justice', as in Latin (*open Tues–Sun 9–5, until 7 in July and Aug; adm*), and kept at it off and on until his death. Two tiers of rounded arches interspersed with Doric and Ionic columns give an appearance of Roman regularity, although Palladio had to vary the size of the arches to compensate for the irregularities in the Gothic structure. The roof is concealed behind a pediment lined with life-size statues; stare at them long

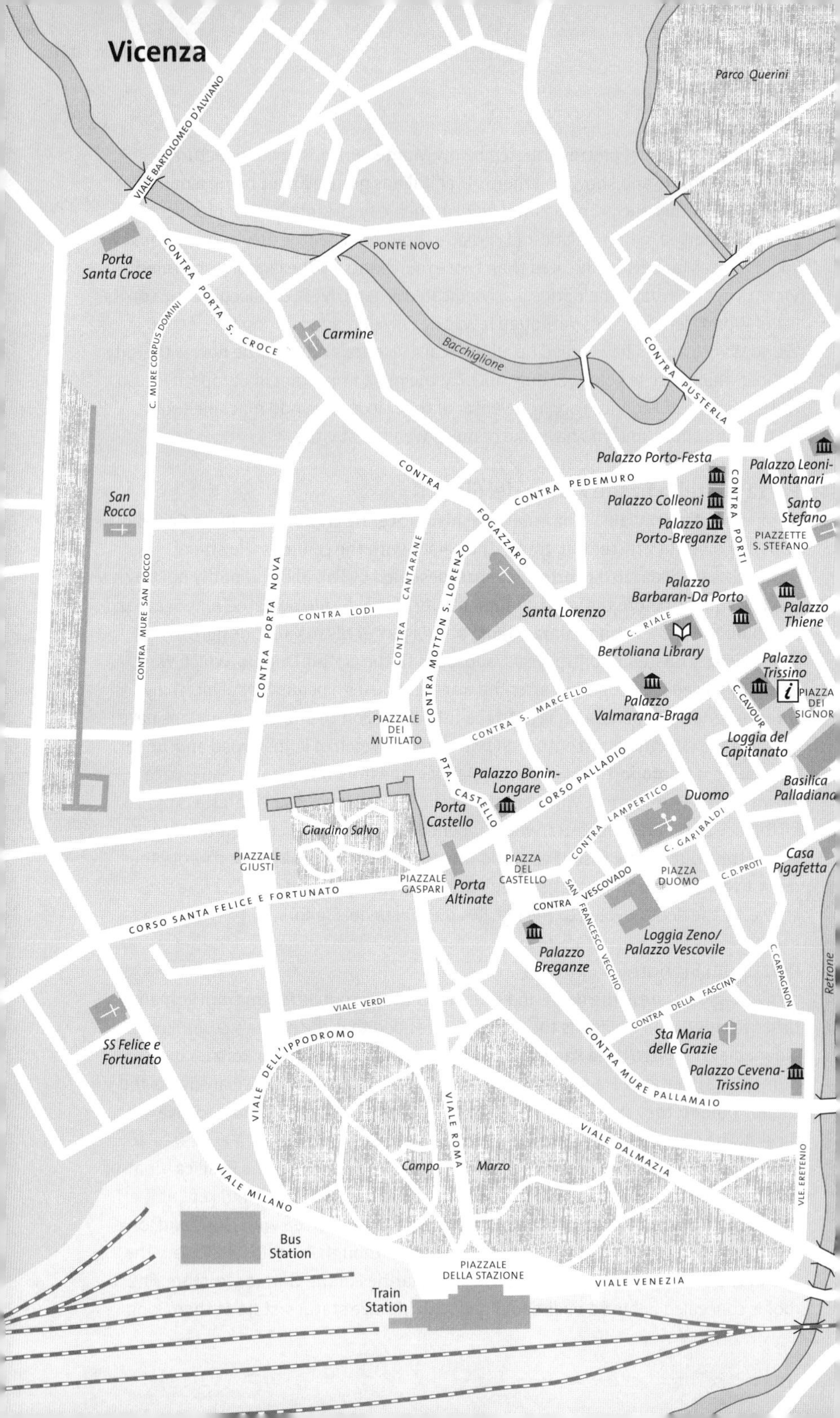

Vicenza
Parco Querini
Viale Bartolomeo d'Alviano
Ponte Novo
Porta Santa Croce
Contra Porta S. Croce
Carmine
Bacchiglione
C. Mure Corpus Domini
Contra Pusterla
Palazzo Porto-Festa
Palazzo Leoni-Montanari
Contra Pedemuro
Contra Fogazzaro
Palazzo Colleoni
Contra Porti
Santo Stefano
San Rocco
Palazzo Porto-Breganze
Piazzette S. Stefano
Contra Cantarane
Contra Motton S. Lorenzo
Contra Porta Nova
Contra Mure San Rocco
Palazzo Barbaran-Da Porto
Contra Lodi
Santa Lorenzo
Palazzo Thiene
C. Riale
Bertoliana Library
Palazzo Trissino
Piazza dei Signor
C. Cavour
Palazzo Valmarana-Braga
Contra S. Marcello
Piazzale dei Mutilato
Loggia del Capitanato
Pta. Castello
Palazzo Bonin-Longare
Corso Palladio
Basilica Palladiana
Porta Castello
Duomo
Contra Lampertico
Giardino Salvo
C. Garibaldi
Piazzale Giusti
Piazza del Castello
Casa Pigafetta
Piazzale Gaspari
Porta Altinate
Piazza Duomo
C. D. Proti
Corso Santa Felice e Fortunato
Contra Vescovado
San Francesco Vecchio
Loggia Zeno/ Palazzo Vescovile
Palazzo Breganze
C. Carpagnon
Retrone
Viale Verdi
Contra della Fascina
SS Felice e Fortunato
Viale dell'Ippodromo
Sta Maria delle Grazie
Contra Mure Pallamaio
Palazzo Cevena-Trissino
Viale Roma
Viale Dalmazia
Campo Marzo
Vle. Eretenio
Viale Milano
Bus Station
Piazzale della Stazione
Viale Venezia
Train Station

Borgo S. Lucia
Santa Maria Aracoeli
Viale Ferdinando Rodolfi
Borgo Santa Lucia
200 metres
200 yards
N
Contra Porta S. Lucia
Via Quattro Novembre
Via Legione Gallieno
Contra Vittorio Veneto
Contra della Canove
Palazzo Angaran
Palazzo Regaù
Contra S. Domenico
Piazza XX Settembre
Contra XX Settembre
Leva d'Angeli
Ponte dei Angeli
Teatro Olimpico
Museo Sta Corona
Contra S. Corona
Santa Corona
C. S. Stefano
Piazza Matteotti
Contra Porta Padova
San Pietro
Piazza S. Pietro
Corso Palladio
Palazzo Chiericati
C. S. Andrea
Corte di Roda
Corso Padova
Contra San Pietro
C. S. Barbara
Contra Cabianca
Via Nazaro Sauro
Viale Margherita
Torre di Piazza
Piazza della Biade
Contra delle Barche
Viale Giuriolo
Bacchiglione
Torre del Tormento
Piazza dell'Erbe
C. Paolo
Ponte S. Michele
C. Ptb. S. Michele
Oratorio di San Nicola
Ptta. S. Nicola
Viale Giangiorgio Trissino
Contra della Piarda
Piazzola Gualdi
Retrone
Viale dello Stadio
Viale Margherita
Santa Caterina
Contra S. Caterina
Piazzale T. Fraccoli
Viale X Giugno
Via Risorgimento Nazionale
Via Risorgimento Nazionale
Borgo Berga
V.A. Fusinato
Viale X Giugno
to Monte Berico
to Villa Valmarana & La Rotonda

Getting There

Vicenza is on the main **rail** line between Verona (45mins), Padua (35mins) and Venice (1hr); there is also a branch line up to Thiene. The station is on the south side of town, at the end of Viale Roma.

The FTV **bus** station, **t** 0444 223 115, is next to it: there are buses from here for Bassano and Maròstica as well as Asiago, Rovigo, Este, Lonigo and other destinations in the region.

You can hire a **bike** at the train station's *deposito bagagli*. There are attended **car** parks at the west end of town by the Mercato Ortofrutticolo, and to the east by the stadium. Both have buses to the centre every 5 mins.

Tourist Information

Piazza Matteotti 12; **t** 0444 320 854 (*open Mon–Sat 9–6.30*), *www.vicenzae.org*.

Where to Stay

Vicenza ✉ 36100

★★★★**Campo Marzio**, Viale Roma 21, **t** 0444 545 700, *www.hotelcampomarzio.com* (*very expensive–luxury*). Comfortable, characterful rooms near the railway station, in a range of styles from 'oriental' to 'traditional'.

★★★★**Genziana**, Via Mazzini 75, Selva, Altavilla, 6km west of town, **t** 0444 572 398, *www.hotelristorantegenziana.com* (*moderate–expensive*). A welcoming hotel full of art, with a pool and a restaurant. *Closed part of Aug*.

★★**Due Mori**, Contrà da Rode 26 (near Piazza dei Signori), **t** 0444 321 888 (*moderate*). A delightful hotel in the historic district.

★★★**Locanda Grego**, Via Roma 24, Bolzano Vicentino, above Vicenza Nord *autostrada* exit, **t** 0444 350 588, *www.ipiaceridellatavola.com* (*moderate*). An old postal relay station with well-furnished rooms and a good family-run restaurant. *Closed part of Aug*.

★★**San Raffaele**, Viale X Giugno 10 (through an arch in the Portici), **t** 0444 545 767 (*moderate*). A good-value, tranquil place on the slopes of Monte Bérico, with great views.

★**Vicenza**, **t** 0444 321 512 (*cheap–moderate*). A decent basic option.

Eating Out

This is hearty polenta and *baccalà* (salt cod) country. *Baccalà alla vicentina*, top-quality cod pummelled with a wooden hammer, soaked for 36hrs, sprinkled with cheese and browned in butter, oil, anchovies and onions, then cooked over a slow flame and seasoned with parsley, pepper and milk, is 'a whole refined civilization...simmering in the pot', according to writer Guido Piovene. A favourite way to eat polenta is sliced and grilled, with *sopressa* sausage from Valli del Pasubio and Recoaro, or pigeon roasted on embers.

Other specialities are gnocchi made with cinnamon and raisins, and *bigoli con l'arna* – fat spaghetti with duck sauce, delicious with a glass of red Tocai. Montecchio Maggiore is known for its *mostarda*, a spicy fruit condiment.

Nuovo Cinzia & Valerio, Piazzetta Porta Padova, **t** 0444 505 213 (*very expensive*). Perfectly prepared seafood, cuttlefish risotto, followed by home-made ice cream and crisp biscuits. *Closed Sun eve, Mon and Aug*.

Principe, Via S. Caboto 16, Arzignano, just east of Montecchio Maggiore, **t** 0444 675 131 (*very expensive*). Gastronomic fireworks by one of Italy's top young chefs, trained in France. Booking is obligatory. There are also 12 *moderate–expensive* rooms. *Closed Sat lunch, Sun, 10 days in Jan and Aug*.

Antica Decchio Trattoria Tre Visi, Corso Palladio 25, **t** 0444 324 868 (*expensive*). A charming 15th-century *palazzo* converted into an inn, offering high-quality Veneto cooking. *Closed Sun eve, Mon and July*.

Da Biasio 1848, Viale X Giugno 172, on the way to Monte Bérico, **t** 0444 323 363 (*expensive*). Unusual fare such as sole spring rolls with orange salad and walnut cream, and prawn ravioli with sweet pepper. The sweets are equally delicious. *Closed Mon, Oct and Nov*.

Antica Casa della Malvasia, Contrà delle Morette 5, near Piazza dei Signori, **t** 0444 543 704 (*cheap*). Excellent home cooking.

Righetti, Piazza Duomo (*cheap*). A bustling self-service canteen. *Closed Sat, Sun*.

Vecchia Guardia, Contrà Pescherie Vecchie 11, **t** 0444 321 231 (*cheap*). Pizza and other straightforward dishes. *Closed Thurs*.

Antica Offelleria della Meneghi, Contrà Cavour 18. A historic *pasticceria* near the basilica.

enough and the urge to shoot them off like ducks in a penny arcade becomes almost irresistible. To see what Palladio was disguising, go behind the basilica to the Piazza delle Erbe, home to a daily market and the Torre del Tormento, the medieval prison.

The basilica shares Piazza dei Signori with the needle-like **Torre di Piazza** (12th–15th century), and with Palladio's **Loggia del Capitaniato** (1571), built to celebrate the victory at Lepanto. If its grand columns and arches seem confined in too narrow a space, this is because the loggia was meant to extend over several more bays. The neighbouring 16th-century **Monte di Pietà**, built in two sections, was frescoed in the 1900s with Liberty-style pin-up girls, some of whom still faintly survive moral outrage, war damage and Father Time.

As in Venice, this piazza has two columns: of the Redeemer (1640) and of St Mark (1473). A right turn here down Via San Michele leads to the Retrone, one of Vicenza's two rivers, spanned here by the **Ponte San Michele** (1620). There are lovely views of the Retrone lapping the houses and, on the opposite bank, the **Oratorio di San Nicola** is remarkable for the creepiest altarpiece in Italy, *La Trinità* by the 17th-century Vicentine painter Francesco Maffei, whose feverish brush infected the Oratorio's walls as well, with the assistance of Giulio Caprioni.

Corso Palladio, Contrà Porti and Around

Returning to the Piazza dei Signori, step behind the Loggia del Capitaniato to get to **Corso Palladio**, which was once called 'the most elegant street in Europe, not counting the Grand Canal in incomparable Venice'. Just to your right you'll find Vincenzo Scamozzi's masterpiece, **Palazzo Trissino**, with an Ionic portico and a superb courtyard (begun in 1592, now the Municipio), the city's prettiest, and the late Gothic **Palazzo Da Schio** (1470s), or 'Ca' d'Oro'. Palladio himself is only dubiously linked to a couple of works on the street named after him; to find his work, you need to turn up **Contrà Porti**, another elegant street: **Palazzo Iseppo Da Porto**, at No.21, is one of his earlier works (1552), influenced by Raphael. Next door, the sombre Gothic **Palazzo Porto-Colleoni** (No. 19) hides an internal garden courtyard and an airy asymmetrical loggia; next to it, the late-Gothic **Palazzo da Porto-Breganze** (No.17) has a beautiful door and a precious mullioned window, the only one in Vicenza with Venetian reversed arches.

The vast medieval **Palazzo Thiene** (now the Banca Popolare; ***t*** *0444 544 519; open by appointment May, June and Sept Weds and Fri 9–12 and 3–6, Sat 9–12; Oct–Apr Tues and Weds 9–12 and 3–6*) was, like the basilica, a facelift project for Palladio, who was to make it the most imposing residence in all Vicenza; it was never completed – like many of Palladio's projects. The Contrà Porti side is a fine work by Lorenzo da Bologna. Around the corner is Palladio's work, with its weighty sculpted windows, rustication and Mannerist classicizing – his homage to Giulio Romano. Some of the interior retains its original and rather magnificent decoration, including the first-floor Rotonda with its domed vault and statues. Its neighbour on the corner of Contrà Riale, **Palazzo Barbaran-da Porto**, built from scratch by Palladio in 1570, now holds the **Museo Palladiano** (***t*** *0444 323 014, open Mar–Dec Tues–Sun 10–6; Jan and Feb Sat and Sun 12–6; other days by appointment; adm*).

Vicenza's Perfect Architect

A Paduan by birth, Andrea di Pietro della Gondola (1508–80) had worked in Vicenza as a stonemason from the age of 16. At 29, he met the great humanist Giangiorgio Trissino, who saw a spark in the young man, and gave him a Renaissance education, took him on a two-year tour of Rome, and endowed him with a new name: Palladio.

His first major commission, the Basilica, so captured the hearts of the Vicentines that they commissioned him to build their palaces and villas. He was, for them, the perfect architect, able to produce classical grandeur for very little money – mainly by using cheap brick coated with a marbly sheen of stucco. Towards the end of his career, he summed up everything he knew in *I Quattro Libri dell'Architettura*, of which Sir Reginald Blomfield, in his *Studies in Architecture*, wrote pointedly, 'With the touch of pedantry that suited the times and invested his writings with a fallacious air of scholarship, he was the very man to summarize and classify, and to save future generations of architects the labour of thinking for themselves.'

The book contributed greatly to the Palladian movement in Britain and America that began in 1603, when Inigo Jones visited Vicenza, and reached its peak in the 1700s under its 'high priest', Lord Burlington, and its great admirer, Thomas Jefferson.

Diagonally across the Contrà Zanella from the Palazzo Thiene, the church of **Santo Stefano** contains one of Palma il Vecchio's most beautiful paintings, *Madonna with SS. George and Lucy and Musical Angel*. More fine art waits just at the other end of the Contrà Santo Stefano in the chapels of the early Gothic **Santa Corona**, including Veronese's *Adoration of the Magi* (1573) and Giovanni Bellini's *Baptism of Christ*. Alongside the church, the **Museo Naturalistico Archeologico** (*open Fri–Sun 10–6; times may vary if an exhibition is on; adm*) contains natural history exhibits and Paleoveneti, Roman and Lombard relics discovered in the area.

At the north end of the Corso, Palladio's open, airy **Palazzo Chiericati** (1550–1650), one of his masterpieces, is home to the **Pinacoteca** (*open Tues–Sun 9–5, until 7 June–Aug; adm*). The ground floor retains its original frescoes, including a hilarious ceiling by Domenico Brusasorci, who took it upon himself to portray the sun god and his steeds from the viewpoint of earthlings at noon – all bums and bellies. Upstairs are 24 rooms of art dating from the 14th to the 20th centuries, by Paolo Veneziano, Memling, Bartolomeo Montagna, Cima da Conegliano, Lorenzo Lotto, Sansovino, Tintoretto, Van Dyck, Jan Brueghel the Elder, Bassano, Veronese, Tiepolo *père* and *fils*, and the irrepressible Francesco Maffei (*Glorification of the Inquisitor Alvise Foscarini*).

Teatro Olimpico

Open Tues–Sun 9–5, until 7 in July and Aug; ***t*** *0444 222 800; adm; tickets also cover the Basilica, Pinacoteca, Museo del Risorgimento and Museo Naturalistico.*

Across Piazza Matteotti from the museum, this was Palladio's swansong, one of his most original works, a unique masterpiece of the Italian Renaissance, and the oldest operational indoor theatre in the world (1580). Palladio himself was one of the 25 literati and dilettantes who formed the high-minded 'Olympic Academy' that built the theatre for their plays and lectures. For the seating and stage, Palladio as always went back to his Vitruvius and the Roman theatres he had seen during his sojourns. After his death Scamozzi added the stage set of a square and radiating streets in flawless, fake perspective – designed for the theatre's first production, Sophocles' *Oedipus Rex* in 1585, and meant to represent Thebes. But here Thebes has become a pure ideal, a Renaissance dream city so perfect that no one thought to change the set, or bothered, as the Council of Trent banned theatrical representations not long after. Now, however, it has been brought back to life, and is used for plays and ballets.

Outside the Historic Centre

Vicenza's oldest church, **SS. Felice e Fortunato** (a 10-minute walk from Piazza Castello), was built just after Constantine officialized Christianity. It has taken licks from barbarians and earthquakes, but has been un-restored as much as possible to its 4th-century appearance, revealings mosaics in the right aisle and a martyr's shrine. Two other churches full of art are north of the Duomo and Corso Palladio, up **Corso Fogazzaro**, an atmospheric street lined with porticoes. The 13th-century Franciscan **San Lorenzo** has a lovely marble portal, and, further on, Gothic **Santa Maria del Carmine** has 15th-century bas-reliefs and altars by Veronese and Jacopo Bassano.

Monte Bérico and the Villa Rotonda

Vicenza's holy hill, Monte Bérico, rises just to the south of the city. Buses make the ascent every half-hour from the bus station, or you can walk up under the kilometre-long **Portici**, built in the 18th century to shelter pilgrims climbing to the Baroque **Basilica di Monte Bérico** (*open Mon–Sat summer 6.15–12.30 and 2.30–7.30; winter 6–12.30 and 2.30–6; Sun and hols 6.15am–8pm*). This commemorates two 15th-century apparitions of the Virgin, and contains two first-class paintings: Bartolomeo Montagna's *La Pietà*, and the *Supper of St Gregory the Great* by Veronese, hung in the refectory (down the steps to the left), and carefully pieced together after Austrian soldiers sliced it up in 1848. Outside are superb views of the city and the Villa Rotonda.

From here, walk back down the Portici to Via Massimo d'Azeglio; not far down on the right is an alley to the **Villa Valmarana**, nicknamed 'dei Nani' after the stone dwarfs on the wall (*open 15 Mar–5 Nov Weds, Thurs, Sat and Sun 10–12 and Tues–Sun 2.30–5.30; adm exp*). Its sumptuous decoration is by Giambattista Tiepolo, who frescoed the *Palazzina* with scenes of love versus duty from the *Iliad*, *Aeneid*, *Orlando Furioso* and *Jerusalem Delivered*. Son Giandomenico's intimate, ironic scenes of rural life in the *Foresteria* (guest house) undermine his father's Grand Manner under his nose.

A further five-minute walk along the Stradella Valmarana (or bus no.8 from the railway station) is the **Villa Rotonda** (*open 15 Mar–14 Nov gardens Tues–Sun 10–12 and 3–6; interior Weds 10–12 and 3–6; adm for both, exp for interior*), designed by Palladio for Cardinal Capra in 1551 and completed after his death by Scamozzi. Unlike Palladio's other villas, which were farmhouses with outbuildings, Rotonda was built for sheer delight – and formed the perfect setting for Joseph Losey's film, *Don Giovanni*. One of the main interests of the Accademia Olimpica was mathematics, and the villa is an exercise in geometrical form – a circle in a cube, with four symmetrical porches.

Around Vicenza: More Villas

The tourist office publishes a map listing the most important of the hundreds of villas of Vicenza province. Only a handful are open, and the ones that are often have bizarre hours, so be sure to check before setting out. Most are in the north (*see* p.374) or south in the Colli Berici; otherwise, it's easy to take a bus from Vicenza out to **Montecchio Maggiore**, 13 kilometres west along the road to Verona, defended by two Scaliger castles that in Da Porto's 1529 *Romeo and Juliet* belonged to the Montagues and Cappelletti. Just before the village, the 18th-century **Villa Cordellina-Lombardi** (***t** 0444 696 085; open 1 Apr–15 Oct Tues–Fri 9–1; Sat, Sun and hols 9–12, 3–6; adm*), built in 1760 by Giorgio Massari, has colourful frescoes by a young Giambattista Tiepolo.

Verona

There is no world without Verona walls
But purgatory, torture, hell itself
Hence banished is banish'd from the world;
And world's exile is death.
Romeo and Juliet, Act III

Well, love leads one to extremes. When Cupid's pilgrims descend on Verona they sigh over 'Juliet's balcony' and other places concocted in response to a demand for shrines to the unlucky teenage lovers. But the gorgeous rose-pink city curling along the banks of the Adige has far more to offer than Romeo and Juliet and other star-crossed lovers singing their hearts out in its popular summer opera in the Roman Arena: evocative streets and romantic piazzas, sublime art, magnificent architecture, and all the gnocchi you can eat.

History

Blessed with a navigable river at the bottom of a busy alpine pass, Verona was favoured by the Romans from the time of its colonization in 89 BC, a period when it produced Vitruvius, the spiritual father of Palladio and Renaissance architecture, and the lyric poet Catullus. The city maintained its status as a regional capital under the Ostrogoths and Franks, and in 1107 it became a free *comune*. Freedom of government inaugurated the most violent era of Verona's history, when the city's nobility spiced Italy's Guelph and Ghibelline battles with a sideshow of purely domestic feuds and vendettas. Their notoriety inspired the story of *Romeo and Juliet* (first written by Luigi Da Porto in 1529), and led to the despairing *comune* actually inviting the 'son of Satan' himself, the tyrant Ezzelino da Romano, to take power, which he did until 1259, when the reins of the city were taken over by the Della Scala family.

The Della Scalas (or Scaligeri) were a typical late medieval Italian family of exquisite gangsters, combining a bloodthirsty passion for power with a taste for the arts. Their names were, however, uniquely canine: Cangrande I ('Big Dog'; 1311–29) both greatly expanded the family's claims in northern Italy and gave such generous hospitality to

Dante that the poet dedicated his *Paradiso* to him. Cangrande's heir, Mastino II ('the Mastiff'), consolidated his gains while his own successor, the fratricidal Cansignorio ('Lord Dog'; 1359–75), presided over the construction of the family's last great monuments. In 1387 the city was seized by the Milanese warlord Gian Galeazzo Visconti.

By the time of Visconti's death in 1402, Verona had had enough of *signori* and joined up with the Serenissima. After Venice's defeat in the Wars of the Cambrai, Verona opened its gates to the German army and didn't return to St Mark's fold until 1517. The jilted Venetians retaliated by making Verona foot the bill for a vast new system of walls designed by Sammicheli. However (and notably unlike Venice), Verona had the spunk to resist Napoleon in 1797 – only to be partly destroyed for its presumption. Bombed in the Second World War, Verona quickly rebuilt and remains a *città d'arte* of the first rank. It has also, since the war, become one of the economic boom towns of modern Italy.

Porta Nuova to the Arena

The first thing most people see of Verona, whether arriving by rail or road, is Sammicheli's Renaissance gate, the **Porta Nuova**, now stranded on a traffic island at the head of the Corso Porta Nuova. This avenue leads straight under the **Portoni della Brà**, built under Gian Galeazzo Visconti's tenure, and into the heart of tourist Verona: the large, irregular **Piazza Brà**, a favourite promenade of the Veronese and tourists, milling about a broad swathe of café-filled pavements (the Liston) and the **Arena** (*open Mon 1.45–7.30; Tues–Sun 8.30–7.30; during opera season 8.30–3.30; adm*). Built in the 1st century AD and, after the Colosseum, the best-preserved amphitheatre in Italy, the elliptical Arena measures 456ft by 364ft and seats 25,000, and has been kept in an excellent state of preservation since the 16th century. Earthquakes, however, have downed the original outer arcade except for the four arches of the wing, or '*ala*'. As amphitheatres go, the Arena is exceptionally lovely in its pink and white stone, enough to make one almost forget the brutal sports it was built to host; since 1913, the death and mayhem has been purely operatic, with sets in Karnak proportions.

Opposite rises the 17th-century **Palazzo della Gran Guardia**, with a Visconti tower peeking over its shoulder. The **Museo Lapidario Maffeiano**, on the corner of Via Roma, (*open Mon 1.45–7.30; Tues–Sun 8.30–2; adm*) was one of the first such museums in the world, established in 1714, with an important collection of ancient inscriptions.

Piazza delle Erbe and Piazza dei Signori

From Piazza Brà, **Via Mazzini** (the first street in Italy to ban cars) is the most direct route to the core of medieval and Roman Verona, **Piazza delle Erbe**, occupying the old forum and still fulfilling its original purpose, selling fast food, souvenirs and overpriced vegetables. Four old monuments on the piazza's spine poke their heads above the rainbow lake of parasols – a Lion of St Mark; a 1368 fountain built by Cansignorio topped by a Roman statue known as the 'Madonna Verona'; an elegant Gothic stone lantern; and a 16th-century loggia called the 'Berlina', where malefactors used to be tied and pelted with rotten produce.

Verona

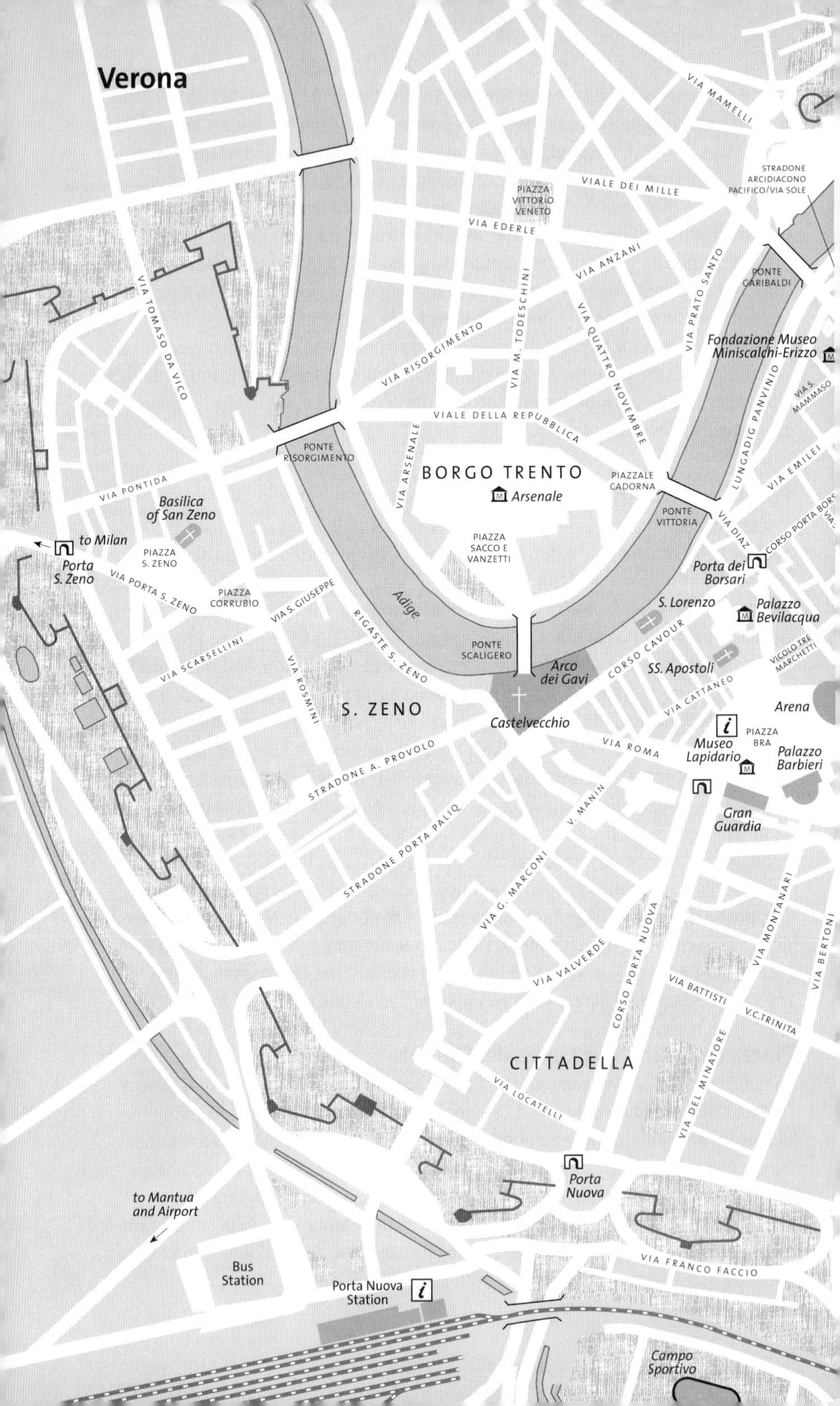

VIA MAMELLI
STRADONE ARCIDIACONO PACIFICO/VIA SOLE
PIAZZA VITTORIO VENETO
VIALE DEI MILLE
VIA EDERLE
VIA ANZANI
VIA PRATO SANTO
PONTE GARIBALDI
VIA TOMASO DA VICO
VIA M. TODESCHINI
VIA QUATTRO NOVEMBRE
VIA RISORGIMENTO
Fondazione Museo Miniscalchi-Erizzo
LUNGADIG PANVINIO
VIA S. MAMMASO
VIALE DELLA REPUBBLICA
VIA ARSENALE
PONTE RISORGIMENTO
BORGO TRENTO
Arsenale
PIAZZALE CADORNA
VIA EMILEI
VIA PONTIDA
Basilica of San Zeno
PONTE VITTORIA
VIA DIAZ
CORSO PORTA BORSARI
to Milan
Porta S. Zeno
PIAZZA S. ZENO
PIAZZA SACCO E VANZETTI
Porta dei Borsari
VIA PORTA S. ZENO
PIAZZA CORRUBIO
VIA S. GIUSEPPE
RIGASTE S. ZENO
Adige
S. Lorenzo
Palazzo Bevilacqua
CORSO CAVOUR
VIA SCARSELLINI
VIA ROSMINI
PONTE SCALIGERO
Arco dei Gavi
SS. Apostoli
VICOLO TRE MARCHETTI
VIA CATTANEO
S. ZENO
Castelvecchio
Arena
PIAZZA BRA
VIA ROMA
Museo Lapidario
Palazzo Barbieri
STRADONE A. PROVOLO
STRADONE PORTA PALIO
V. MANIN
Gran Guardia
VIA G. MARCONI
CORSO PORTA NUOVA
VIA MONTANARI
VIA BERTONI
VIA VALVERDE
VIA BATTISTI
V.C.TRINITA
CITTADELLA
VIA DEL MINATORE
VIA LOCATELLI
Porta Nuova
to Mantua and Airport
VIA FRANCO FACCIO
Bus Station
Porta Nuova Station
Campo Sportivo

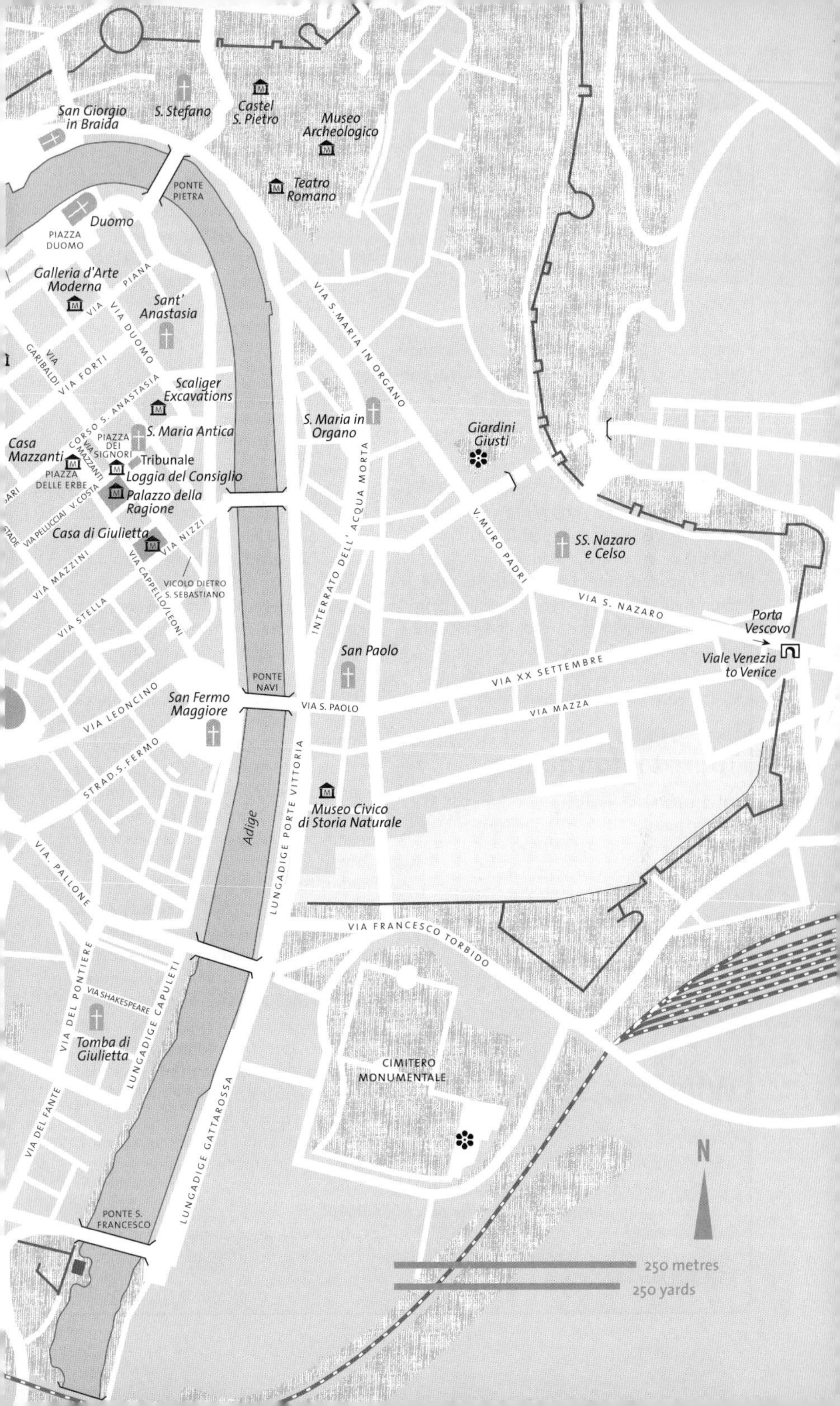
San Giorgio in Braida
S. Stefano
Castel S. Pietro
Museo Archeologico
Teatro Romano
PONTE PIETRA
Duomo
PIAZZA DUOMO
Galleria d'Arte Moderna
VIA PIANA
VIA DUOMO
Sant' Anastasia
VIA GARIBALDI
VIA FORTI
CORSO S. ANASTASIA
Scaliger Excavations
PIAZZA DEI SIGNORI
S. Maria Antica
Casa Mazzanti
VIA MAZZANTI
Tribunale
PIAZZA DELLE ERBE
Loggia del Consiglio
Palazzo della Ragione
V. COSTA
VIA PELLICCIAI
Casa di Giulietta
VIA NIZZI
VIA MAZZINI
VIA CAPPELLO/LEONI
VICOLO DIETRO S. SEBASTIANO
VIA STELLA
VIA LEONCINO
San Fermo Maggiore
STRAD.S.FERMO
PONTE NAVI
VIA S. PAOLO
Adige
LUNGADIGE PORTE VITTORIA
VIA. PALLONE
VIA DEL PONTIERE
VIA SHAKESPEARE
Tomba di Giulietta
LUNGADIGE CAPULETI
VIA DEL FANTE
LUNGADIGE GATTAROSSA
PONTE S. FRANCESCO
VIA S.MARIA IN ORGANO
S. Maria in Organo
INTERRATO DELL' ACQUA MORTA
Giardini Giusti
V.MURO PADRI
SS. Nazaro e Celso
VIA S. NAZARO
San Paolo
VIA XX SETTEMBRE
VIA MAZZA
Porta Vescovo
Viale Venezia to Venice
Museo Civico di Storia Naturale
VIA FRANCESCO TORBIDO
CIMITERO MONUMENTALE
N
250 metres
250 yards

Getting Around

Verona's **airport** Valerio Catullo, **t** 045 809 5666, southwest at Villafranca, has daily British Airways flights to London, and direct flights to Rome, Naples and Bari. There are buses every 20mins from the airport to Porta Nuova train station in Verona; there are also 3 buses daily to Brescia, Mantua and Trento.

Verona is the junction of major **rail** lines from Venice (1hr 45mins), Milan (2hrs), Bologna (1hr 40mins), Trento (1hr) and Bolzano (1hr 40mins). The station, **Porta Nuova**, is a 15min walk south of Piazza Brà, along Corso Porta Nuova; alternatively, city buses nos.11, 12 and 13 link the station with Piazza delle Erbe and Piazza Brà. A machine dispenses bus tickets opposite the station. The provincial APT **bus** station (**t** 045 805 7811) across the street has frequent departures to Lake Garda and the mountains, and Mantua (1hr).

The historic centre is closed to traffic 7.30–10am and 1.30–4.30pm (except for cars going directly to hotels). There are **car** parks near the train station, Arena and Corso Porta Nuova. **Bikes** can be hired on the southeast corner of Piazza Brà, **t** 045 504 901. **Taxis**: **t** 045 532 666.

Tourist Information

Palazzo Barbiera, Via Leoncino 61, **t** 045 806 8680 (next to the Arena); and Porta Nuova station, **t** 045 800 861 (*both closed Sun in winter*), *www.tourism.verona.it*.

Provincial office: Piazza delle Erbe 38, **t** 045 800 6997, *www.verona-apt.net*.

The **Verona Card** (1 or 3 days) allows access to various museums, churches and monuments, and public transport. On the first Sun of the month there's free admission to some sights.

Where to Stay

Verona ✉ 37100

Hotels are way overpriced here, with 3-stars very expensive and 2-stars almost universally bland and horribly furnished, with unfriendly staff. Even so, you need to book ahead for anything central in the opera season (July/Aug), and Mar, when there's a big agricultural fair. In high season many places will ask you to send a deposit or have your credit card debited to confirm the reservation.

Luxury

*******Due Torri Baglioni**, Piazza Sant' Anastasia 4, **t** 045 595 044, *www.baglionihotels.com*. Goethe and Mozart slept here and would still feel right at home today, at least in the rooms with 18th-century antiques.

Expensive

******Accademia**, Via Scala 12, **t** 045 596 222, *www.accademiavr.it*. An atmospheric 16th-century *palazzo* in the centre. Some rooms are *cheap*; others are *very expensive–luxury*.

******Colomba d'Oro**, Via C. Cattaneo 10, **t** 045 595 300, *www.colombahotel.com*. Very comfy rooms behind an old stone façade in a quiet, traffic-free street close to the Arena. Some rooms are *moderate*, some *very expensive*.

*****Giulietta e Romeo**, Vicolo Tre Marchetti 3, **t** 045 800 3554, *www.giuliettaeromeo.it*. A hotel on a quiet street by the Arena. Some rooms are *moderate*, some *very expensive*.

*****Italia**, Via Mameli 58, **t** 045 918 088, *www.hotelitalia.tv*. Tranquil, modern, comfy rooms over the Adige, near the Roman theatre.

*****Novo Hotel Rossi**, Via delle Coste 2, **t** 045 569 022, *www.novohotelrossi.it*. A *simpatico* option, convenient if you arrive by train. Some rooms are *moderate*, some *very expensive*.

Moderate

****Hotel Aurora**, Piazza delle Erbe, **t** 045 594 717, *www.hotelaurora.biz*. A well-priced hotel in the centre, with friendly staff and comfy if bland rooms. Some rooms are *expensive*.

****Sammicheli**, Via Valverde 2, **t** 045 800 3749. A convenient hotel for opera-goers. Some of the rooms are *cheap*, some *expensive*.

****Torcolo**, Vicolo Listone 3, **t** 045 800 7512, *www.torcolo.it*. An extremely welcoming hotel on a quiet little square handy for the Arena, with large, tastefully furnished rooms (some rooms are *cheap*, some *expensive*).

Cheap

***Catullo**, Via Valerio Catullo 1, **t** 045 800 2786. Central rooms, some with a bathroom and a balcony (*moderate*).

Eating Out

The Veronese have been fond of potato gnocchi (with melted butter and sage) since the 16th century, when the ingredients were distributed after a famine, and, like Parisians, attribute their liking for horsemeat to a siege when horses were all there was left to eat; it's served in a stew called *pastissada de caval*. In summer look for Italy's finest peaches.

Very Expensive

Arche, Via delle Arche Scaligere 6, **t** 045 800 7415. Long the classic place to go for a special meal in a plush setting, serving imaginatively prepared fish. *Closed Sun, Mon lunch.*

Bottega del Vino, Via Scudo di Francia 3 (off Via Mazzini), **t** 045 800 4535. Traditional recipes made using organic ingredients. *Closed Tues except in opera season.*

Il Desco, Via dietro San Sebastiano 7, **t** 045 595 358. A 15th-century palace with breathtakingly expensive seasonal dishes such as goose liver in a sauce of sweet wine and grapes. *Closed Sun, Mon lunch, July, Aug and Dec.*

I Dodici Apostoli, Corticella San Marco 3, **t** 045 596 999. An old favourite offering delicacies adapted from Roman or Renaissance recipes. *Closed Sun eve, Mon, 2wks June and July.*

Maffei, Piazza delle Erbe 38, **t** 045 801 0015. An ancient, elegant restaurant serving great risotto with pumpkin and Amarone. *Closed Sun, Mon in July and Aug.*

Expensive

Greppia, Vicolo Samaritana 3, **t** 045 800 4577. A restaurant in a quiet little square near Juliet's house, serving traditional and Veronese favourites. *Closed Mon, June.*

Moderate

All'Isolo, Piazza Isolo 5a, **t** 045 594 291. A simple trattoria away from the tourist hordes, with fettucine with duck, *baccalà* with polenta, soused pike and the like. *Closed Weds and Aug.*

Alla Pergola, Piazzetta Santa Maria in Solaro 10, **t** 045 800 4744. A reliable favourite in an old medieval church. *Closed Sun, Mon and Aug.*

Alla Strueta, Via Redentore 4 (over the Adige), **t** 045 803 2462. An old workers' *osteria* offering such delights as *pastissada de caval*. *Closed Mon and Tues lunch, and Aug.*

Cheap

Cordioli, Via Cappello 39. The best place in town for traditional Verona pastries. *Closed Weds.*

Osteria Morandin, Via XX Settembre 144 (over the Adige). An old standby, with good wines and a few dishes to go with them. *Closed Sun.*

Entertainment and Nightlife

The tourist office's free *Passport Verona*. *Siri-Sera*, fly-posted weekly in cafés and other venues around town, has information on club nights, films and casual artistic events.

Bars

The Veronese expression for pub-crawling is '*andar per goti*' (going Goth-ing), after a 5th century binge by Theodoric's gang. Bars in Piazza Brà and Piazza delle Erbe are the busiest.

Al Carro Armato, Via San Pietro Martire 2a, **t** 045 803 0175. An old-fashioned, atmospheric bar near Piazza dei Signori.

Cappa Cafè, Piazzetta Brà Molinari 1, **t** 045 800 4516. A bar at the far end of Via Forti, with outside tables and an Arab bazaar feel.

Le Vecete, Via Pellicciai 32, **t** 045 594 748. A popular wine bar. *Closed Sun.*

Opera Classical Music and Theatre

The **Stagione Lirica** opera and ballet festival has almost daily performances in the Arena in July and Aug. Tickets are sold next to the Arena at Via dietro Anfiteatro 6/b, **t** 045 800 5151. You can book in advance at *www.arena.it*. If you buy an unnumbered seat, arrive 2–3hrs before the start to get a place. Bring a cushion.

From Dec to Apr there's drama at the **Teatro Nuovo**. There's also a summer **Shakespeare festival** (in Italian) in the Roman theatre; tickets are available from Ente Lirico, Piazza Brà 28, **t** 045 805 1811.

Festivals and Carnivals

In spring the city hosts one of Italy's oldest carnivals, first recorded in 1530. The last Friday is the 'Bacchanal of Gnocchi', presided over by Papà del Gnocco, who walks about with a giant potato dumpling on a fork.

From mid-Dec to mid-Jan, the Arena arcades are used for a show of cribs (*presepi*).

A colourful variety of buildings encases the square, including the charming **Casa Mazzanti**, formerly part of a Scaligeri palace, brightened with 16th-century frescoes, and the 12th-century **Torre dei Lamberti**, 275ft high, with a lift to the top from the courtyard of the Palazzo della Ragione (*open Mon 1.30–7.30; Tues–Sun 9.30–7.30; adm*). The smaller **Torre del Gardello**, at the other end of the square, was another work of Cansignorio. Six ancient gods pose at the top of the adjacent Baroque **Palazzo Maffei**, while the battlemented red-brick palace, built in 1301 for a merchants' association, still does duty as Verona's Chamber of Commerce after 700 years.

From bustling Piazza delle Erbe, the **Arco della Costa** ('of the rib' – named after a whalebone hung in the arch) leads into stately **Piazza dei Signori**, the civic centre, presided over by a rather severe 1865 statue of Dante, and the striped **Palazzo della Ragione**, with a Romanesque–Gothic courtyard (Cortile del Mercato Vecchio) and striking grand staircase. Behind Dante, the **Loggia del Consiglio** (1493), with yellow and red frescoes and statues of five ancient citizens of Verona (including Pliny the Elder, pinched from Como), is the city's finest Renaissance building. The adjacent crenellated **tribunale** (law courts), formerly a Scaligeri palace, has a portal by Sammicheli; in the courtyard, and adjacent to Via Dante, you can peer down through glass into Verona's Roman streets, revealed in the **Scaligeri excavations**. The underground corridors are used for photo exhibitions (***t** 045 800 7490*).

The arch adjoining the Tribunale leads to the grandiose Gothic pantheon of the Della Scala, the **Scaligeri tombs** or Arche Scaligere. The three major tombs portray their occupants in warlike, equestrian poses on top and reposing in death below, although a copy has replaced the statue on the Tomb of Cangrande (*d.* 1329), built into the wall of the 12th-century church of **Santa Maria Antica**. Don't miss the crowned dogs next to Cangrande's effigy, holding up ladders, the family emblem. More ladder motifs can be seen in the fantastical pinnacles of the tomb of 'Lord Dog' Cansignorio (*d.* 1375), in the more sedate one of Mastino II (*d.* 1351), and in the web of their wrought-iron enclosure. The rather plain 14th-century house in the same Via delle Arche Scaligere belonged to the Montecchi family (Shakespeare's Montagues), and has been known ever since as the **Casa di Romeo**.

The tour groups, however, are all over at the **Casa di Giulietta**, Via Cappello 23, near Piazza delle Erbe (*open Mon 1.45–7.30; Tues–Sun 8.30–6.30; adm*). Although the association is slim (the 13th-century house was once an inn called 'Il Cappello', reminiscent of the Dal Cappello aka Capulet family), it was restored on the outside in 1935 to fit the bill, with lovely windows and *de rigueur* balcony; inside you can peruse lovelorn graffiti, ripe postcards and photos of Leonardo di Caprio.

Sant'Anastasia, Modern Art and the Duomo

North of the Scaligeri tombs, it's hard to miss Gothic **Sant'Anastasia**, Verona's largest church, begun in 1290 but never completed; of its woebegone façade, only the fine portal, with frescoes and reliefs of St Peter Martyr, gives an idea of what its builders intended. The interior is beautiful but, coming in from the sun, many people start at what appears in the dim light to be two men loitering under the holy water stoops; these are the *Gobbi*, or 'hunchbacks'. There are frescoes by Altichiero from 1390 in the

Cavalli Chapel (note how the horse-head helmets the worshippers wear on their backs are similar to the dragon head on Cangrande's statue); terracottas by Michele da Firenze; paintings by the school of Mantegna in the Pellegrini chapel; and, best of all, in the sacristry, a fresco of *St George at Trebizond* (1438) by Pisanello, Italy's unrivalled maestro of international Gothic; his watchful, calculating princess seems more formidable than any dragon.

Nearby, in Corso Sant'Anastasia, the medieval Palazzo Forti now houses the **Galleria d'Arte Moderna** (***t*** *045 800 1903; opening hours depend on exhibition*), where temporary exhibits share the walls with Italian masters (Hayez, Fattori, De Pisis, Boccioni, Birolli, Vedova and Manzù) of the 19th and 20th centuries.

A few streets down Via Duomo, almost at the tip of the river's meander, stands Verona's **Duomo**, consecrated in 1187 – it's Romanesque at the roots and Renaissance in the octagonal crown. The portal, supported on the backs of griffons, was carved by the 12th-century Master Nicolò of San Zeno. Look for the chivalric figures of Roland and Oliver by the west door, and on the south porch a relief of Jonah and the Whale.

Inside, in the Cappella Mazzanti, is the beautifully carved Tomb of St Agatha (1353), and in the first chapel on the left is an Assumption by Titian. Painted in 1540, it shows us a very different Virgin from the heaven-gazing goddess in Venice's Frari – this one looks down sympathetically at her friends on earth. The pretty cloister has a few remains of the Duomo's pre-Romanesque predecessor, and the ancient baptistry, **San Giovanni in Fonte**, has an eight-sided font big enough to swim in (1200), carved from a single piece of marble and decorated with beautiful reliefs. The chapter library, the **Biblioteca Capitolare**, Piazza del Duomo 10 (*open Mon–Weds, Fri and Sat 9.30–12.30; also Tues and Fri 4–6; closed July*), originated in the 5th century as a *scriptorium* and justifiably claims to be the oldest library still operating in Europe; it contains a magnificent collection of medieval manuscripts.

North of the Adige: Veronetta

The north bank of the Adige, 'Veronetta', is worth a morning to itself. Cross the Ponte Garibaldi, just down from the Duomo, and the large dome of **San Giorgio in Braida** (1477) looms to your right, sheltering a number of first-rate paintings, among them Paolo Veronese's *Martyrdom of St George*. Follow the Adige down to **Santo Stefano**, an important Paleo-Christian church pieced together in the 12th century from 5th–10th-century columns and capitals, brightened with 14th-century frescoes, some by Altichiero. In front, the Roman **Ponte Pietra** was blown up in World War II but partly reconstructed from its original stone dredged up from the Adige.

In ancient times the citizens of Verona would trot over this bridge to attend the latest plays at the **Teatro Romano** (*open summer Mon 1.30–7.30, Tues–Sun 8.30–7.30; winter Tues–Sun 9–3; adm*), carved out of the cypress-clad hill of San Pietro in the time of Augustus. They still do: the cavea and arches are in good enough nick to host Shakespeare in the summer. A lift goes up to the **Museo Archeologico** (*same hrs and ticket*), occupying a convent built on top of the theatre and containing small bronzes, portrait busts and a few mosaics. Above it, the **Castel San Pietro** was built by the Austrians over Roman fortifications, and has famous views over Verona at sunset.

South, on the Interato dell'Acqua Morta, **Santa Maria in Organo** has a façade (1533) by Fra Giovanni da Verona; the talented friar also made the charming *trompe l'œil* intarsia choir stalls, lectern and cupboards (in the sacristy) depicting scenes of old Verona, as well as birds, animals and flowers. Across the street that runs at the back of the church, behind the façade of the Palazzo Giusti, are the cool **Giardini Giusti** (*open summer 9–8, winter 9–7; adm*), described by Englishman Thomas Coryate as 'a second paradise'. That was in 1611, the date of the enormous cypresses, formal box hedge parterres, the fountains and grotto topped with a leering mask; the hillside was re-landscaped in the 19th century in the more romantic, informal English style.

Further south, **Santi Nazaro e Celso** (1484), on Via Muro Padri, contains 16th-century frescoes and a painting of the eponymous saints by Montagna, while **San Paolo** (rebuilt 1763), south on Via San Paolo, contains Veronese's beautiful *Madonna and Saints*, one of the few works he left in his home town before he had to move on to Venice, supposedly after committing a murder. On the river bank, at Lungadige Porta Vittoria 9, is the elegant Palazzo Pompei, built in 1530 by Sammicheli and now housing the **Museo Civico di Storia Naturale** (*open Mon–Thurs and Sat 9–7, Sun 2–7; adm*), with an excellent fossil collection.

San Fermo Maggiore and Juliet's Tomb

From Piazza delle Erbe, Via Cappello/Leoni leads past the picturesque ruins of the Roman **Porta dei Leoni** (incorporated in a building) to the splendid vertical apse of **San Fermo Maggiore**, an architectural club sandwich of two churches, one on top of the other. The Romanesque bottom was begun in the 11th century by the Benedictines, the upper Gothic church, with its attractive red and white patterns, was added by the Franciscans. The interior is covered with fine 14th-century frescoes, works by Caroto (*Madonna and Saints*), and a graceful Annunciation by Pisanello (1462).

The **Tomba di Giulietta** (*open Mon 1.30–7.30, Tues–Sun 8.30–7.30; adm*) is back by the river on Via del Pontiere, not far from Piazza Brà. Even the Veronese admit no plausible connection, but the Romanesque cloister and 14th-century red marble sarcophagus would make a fine set for the tragedy's last scene. A small **museum of frescoes** includes lovely 16th-century allegorical and mythological scenes by Paolo Farinati.

Piazza delle Erbe to Castelvecchio

From Piazza delle Erbe, Corso Porta Bórsari leads to an impressive Roman gate, **Porta dei Bórsari**, built in the 1st century AD and named after the *borsarii*, who collected duties on goods entering the city. Beyond the gate the street becomes Corso Cavour, embellished with palaces from various epochs, including Sammicheli's refined 1588 **Palazzo Bevilacqua** (No.19), noted for its ornate, rhythmic alternation of large and small windows, columns and pediments.

Opposite, the lovely Romanesque **San Lorenzo** (1117) preserves its upper women's gallery (*matroneum*), reached by way of its two cylindrical towers. Further down, Corso Cavour opens up into a small square with yet another Roman arch: the simple but elegant **Arco dei Gavi**, designed by Vitruvius in honour of a local family. The French demolished it in 1805, but in 1932 the local *Fascisti* put it back together again.

Castelvecchio and its Museum of Art

Next to the arch, Cangrande II's fortress of **Castelvecchio** (1355) has weathered centuries of use by other top dogs, from the Venetians to Napoleon and the Nazis, to become Verona's excellent and very well-arranged civic **museum of art** (***t** 045 594 734; open Mon 1.30–7.30, Tues–Sun 8.30–7.30; adm*). Among displays on the ground floor are a sarcophagus (1179) carved with vivid reliefs of saints Sergius and Bacchus, as well as some expressive 14th-century Veronese sculpture, especially a stark, painful Crucifixion. The museum is rich in lovely Madonnas, beginning with two straight out of fairy tales: the *Madonna of the Quail* by Pisanello, and the *Madonna of the Rose Garden* by Stefano da Verona; there are fine paintings by Crivelli and Mantegna, followed by another beautiful Madonna by Giovanni Bellini, and by Carpaccio's *SS. Caterina and Veneranda*.

Next comes Verona's mascot, the striking 14th-century equestrian **statue of Cangrande I** from the Arche Scaligere, displayed outside the first-floor window. The pyjama-clad steed, complete with an equine hood ornament and deathly eyes, and the moronically grinning 'Big Dog' himself, with his ghastly dragon-helmet slung over his back, make an unforgettable pair, straight out of a malevolent pantomime. Beyond Cangrande are paintings by Veronese, Tintoretto, Giovan Francesco Caroto (including his well-known *Child with Sketch*, a happy insight into Renaissance childhood), both Tiepolos, Guardi and Longhi.

Behind the castle, Cangrande II's **Ponte Scaligero**, spanning the Adige, repeats the attractive 'swallowtail' battlements of the Castelvecchio; like the Ponte Pietra, it was meticulously reconstructed from the original stones after the Second World War.

The Basilica of San Zeno Maggiore

A 15-minute walk west from the Castelvecchio, mostly along the riverbank (or bus nos.32 or 33 from Corso Porta Bórsari), will take you to the superb **Basilica di San Zeno** (*open Mon–Sat 8.30–6, Sun 1–6*), the belle of Verona's churches and one of the finest Romanesque buildings anywhere. First built in the 4th century, the church took its present form in the mid 14th century. Its magnificence demanded a legend: beneath its lofty campanile (finished in 1149) lies the tomb of a personage no less than the Frankish King Pepin the Short.

The rich façade of San Zeno has a perfect centrepiece: a 12th-century rose window of the *Wheel of Fortune* created by Maestro Brioloto. Below, the beautifully carved porch (1138) by Masters Nicolò and Guglielmo shows scenes from the months, the miracles of San Zeno, the Hunt of Theodoric and other allegories. The **bronze doors**, with their 48 panels, are a 'poor man's Bible' and constitute one of the wonders of 11th-century Italy. Even now, after a millennium has passed, they have retained an unmatched freshness and vitality: in the Annunciation scene Mary covers up her face in fear and anguish while the angel Gabriel does his utmost to comfort her; in the Descent into Hell, Christ and a large, leering Satan fight a tug-of-war for souls. Other scenes appear a bit strange to us, especially the one of two nursing mothers on the lower left-hand door, one of whom is suckling twin children, the other what look to be twin crocodiles.

The vast interior, divided into three naves by Roman columns and capitals, has a beautiful Gothic ceiling, 13th- and 14th-century frescoes and, on the altar, the magnificent triptych of the *Madonna col Bambino tra Angeli e Santi* (1459) by Andrea Mantegna, a work that brilliantly combines the master's love of classical architecture and luminous colouring. Although the French returned the painting after Napoleon took it, they kept the predella as a souvenir; the originals are in the Louvre. In the crypt below, the body of St Zeno glows in the dark.

Around Verona: Soave, Valpolicella and Lessinia

Verona's province is the sloshing cradle of four of Italy's best-known DOC wines: white Soave and Bianco di Custoza, and red Valpolicella and Bardolino. Each has at least one *strada del vino*, if you fancy spending a lazy hour or two touring and tasting. Bianco di Custoza and Bardolino grow on the shores of Lake Garda, while to the east along the Vicenza road (SS11), vines literally engulf the old town of **Soave**, distinguished by the well-preserved crenellated **Scaligeri castle** (*open Tues–Sun 9–12 and 3–6; adm*), which was first built in the 10th century. On Via Roma, you can try a Soave Classico or the sweet Recioto di Soave, a dessert wine made from raisins at the **Enoteca del Castello**.

Valpolicella, which lies to the northwest of Verona, has twin nuclei, **Negràr** and **Sant'Ambrogio**. The latter produces Verona's famous red marble – in addition to red wine. Nearby, in the lovely old hilltop hamlet of **San Giorgio**, the parish church was founded in the 7th century. The ciborium over the altar also dates from the 600s, and among the frescoes there's a fascinating 12th-century Last Judgement.

Northern Valpolicella melts seamlessly into **Lessinia**, the foothills of the Dolomites, which are famous for rocks – in formations, flintstones and fossils – and for falls, at Molina's Parco delle Cascate. To the north, beyond **Fosse**, the slopes of Corno d'Aquilio are pierced by the **Spluga della Preta**, one of the world's deepest chasms, its floor a staggering 2,906ft down. Lessinia's flint attracted the first people in *c*. 500,000 BC. Finds from the period can be found in the prehistory museum at **Sant'Anna d'Alfaedo**, along with a 20ft fossilized shark.

South of Sant'Anna, not far off the road to Fane, don't miss the **Ponte di Veja**, a spectacular, natural 170ft arch, the inspiration for the Malebolge bridge in Dante's *Inferno*. A winding road loops east to **Bosco Chiesanuova**, Lessinia's modest winter sports centre. From here follow the road to **Velo Veronese**, the starting point for a visit to the **Valley of the Sphinxes** (*Valle delle Sfingi*), named for its striking chasms and landforms, made of layers of red ammonite.

In 17th-century Lessinia, flintlocks were big business. Many of these were made by Bavarians who had settled here in the 13th century. Their roots are remembered in their language, costumes and the huge *tromboni* – a kind of arquebus that they blast on holidays. You can learn more about them at the museum in **Giazza**, one of Lessinia's prettiest villages with its medieval German houses. **Bolca**, southeast of Giazza, caused a sensation in the Renaissance when the discovery of a rich bed of fossilized fish was cited as scientific proof of Noah's Flood. Extremely beautiful and delicate, they are in the local fossil museum.

Treviso

Though famous for radicchio and Benetton, this is still one of the Veneto's best-kept secrets, laced with little canals (*canagi*) diverted from the River Sile, languorous with willows, water wheels, swans and mossy walls, yet humming with more than a little discreet prosperity. Like Verona, it formed its character in the century preceding its annexation by Venice (1389), when it was ruled by the Da Camino and embellished by one of Giotto's greatest pupils, Tommaso da Modena, who did little outside of Treviso.

Colours were an obsession in Treviso long before Benetton united them. Attractive building stone was scarce, so it became the custom to cover the humble brick walls with plaster and frescoes – in the 1300s with simple colours and patterns and, by the 1500s, with heroic mythologies and allegories. Although they're faded and fragmented – on Good Friday 1944 an air raid destroyed half of Treviso in five minutes – frescoes lurk delightfully under the eaves, or hidden in the shadows of an arcade.

Piazza dei Signori and the Duomo

From the bus or train station, it's a 10-minute walk over the Sile along the Corso del Popolo and Via XX Settembre to the Piazza dei Signori, the heart of Treviso. Here stands the city's only surviving *comunale* palace, the huge brick **Palazzo dei Trecento** ('of the Three Hundred'), built in the 1200s and rebuilt after wartime bombing; Treviso café society shelters below. The adjacent **Palazzo del Podestà** was rebuilt in 1877, along with the Torre Civica looming over its shoulder.

The arcaded main street, Calmaggiore, leads from the square to the **Duomo**, a Venetian Romanesque building with a cluster of domes (12th century); the adjacent baptistry gives an idea of what the cathedral looked like before its many alterations. Besides fine Renaissance tombs of local prelates, much of its best art is in the **Cappella Malchiostro**, just right of the altar, designed by Tullio and Antonio Lombardo, with works by Paris Bordone (*Adoration of the Shepherds*) and Girolamo da Treviso (*Madonna del Fiore*). The frescoes are by native son Pordenone, while his mortal enemy Titian contributed *The Annunciation* on the altar; Vasari wrote that Pordenone painted with his sword at his hip in case Titian showed up while he was working. Behind the cathedral, the **Museo Diocesano** (*open Mon–Thurs 9–12, Sat 9–12 and 3–6*) has one of Tommaso da Modena's masterpieces, the detached fresco *Cristo Passo*.

Museo Civico and San Nicolò

From Piazza Duomo, Via Canova leads past the 15th-century **Casa Trevigiana** (*open for special exhibitions*), a reliquary of the city's architecture. Via Canova meets Borgo Cavour near the **Museo Civico Luigi Bailo** (*closed for restoration*), with Bronze Age swords and 5th-century BC bronze discs from Montebelluna; and an excellent collection of masters from the Veneto: Giovanni Bellini, Titian, Lotto, Jacopo Bassano, Cima da Conegliano, the Tiepolos, Rosalba Carriera, Guardi, Longhi – and Joshua Reynolds. Borgo Cavour makes a grandiose exit through the great Venetian gate, **Porta dei Santi Quaranta** (1517), encompassed by an impressive stretch of the ramparts. However, if you turn instead down Via San Liberale and right in Via Absidi,

Getting Around

Treviso **airport** (**t** 0422 315 111) southwest of town has 3 daily Ryan Air flights from London Stansted; bus no.6 links it to the train station.

The train and bus stations (**t** 0422 577 311) are in Via Roma south of the centre. **Trains** run from Venice or Mestre to Treviso (30mins) and Belluno (2hrs), directly or with a change at Padua or Conegliano. One line to Belluno goes via Conegliano and Vittòrio Vèneto; the other, longer but more scenic, via Montebelluna (also a getting-off point for Masèr and Àsolo).

Don't try to take a **car** into Treviso: the traffic is mayhem. Many roads just outside town are one-way, so get a decent map.

Tourist Information

Piazza Monte di Pietà 8, **t** 0422 547 632, *www.provincia.treviso.it*.

Where to Stay

Treviso ✉ 31100

★★★★**Continental**, Via Roma 16, **t** 0422 411 662, *www.hcontinental.it* (*expensive–very expensive*). A modern hotel near the station.

★★★**Al Foghèr**, Viale della Repubblica 10, **t** 0422 432 950, *www.alfogher.com* (*expensive*). The pick of the bunch, outside the walls but within walking distance of the centre, with parking and a good restaurant.

★★★**Scala**, Viale Felissent 1, near the exit for Conegliano, **t** 0422 307 600, *www.hotelscala.com* (*expensive*). An attractive patrician hotel in a pretty park just north of town.

★★★**Locanda La Colonna**, Via Campana 27, **t** 0422 544 804, *www.ristorantelacolonna.it* (*moderate*). A small central *locanda* with 6 frescoed rooms, a restaurant and an *enoteca*.

★★★**La Fattoria**, Via Callalta 83, Silèa, near the Treviso Sud exchange on the A27, **t** 0422 361 770, *www.lafattoriahotel.com* (*moderate–expensive*). Cosy rooms in a restored farmhouse. *Closed part of Aug*.

★★**Campeol**, Piazza Ancilotto 8, **t** 0422 56601, *www.alcampeol.it* (*moderate*). A hospitable, long-established hotel in the historic centre.

Eating Out

Cichorium intybus or *radicchio trevigan* is a salad vegetable with the same DOC quality control as wine; it must have sprouted in one of eight *comuni* under organic conditions. It's best in Dec. Another speciality is *sopa coada*, casserole of baked pigeon.

Alfredo el Toulà, Via Collalto 26, **t** 0422 540 275 (*very expensive*). Treviso's most acclaimed restaurant, in a lovely *belle époque* setting. The imaginative menu has an emphasis on seafood, but it's also a good place to try *sopa coada*. Book ahead. *Closed Sun eve, Mon, Aug*.

Al Canevon, Piazza San Vito 13, **t** 0422 540 208 (*expensive*). An elegant restaurant in the heart of Treviso, with seating in the lovely square in summer and a menu of creative fare. *Closed Tues*.

Al Cavallino, Porta Santi Quaranta, Via Borgo Cavour 52, **t** 0422 412 801 (*expensive*). A restaurant and *enoteca* in the converted stables of the old house of patriot Daniele Manin, offering delicious Veneto staples. *Closed Tues, and Wed lunch*.

Beccherie, Piazza Ancilotto 10, **t** 0422 540 871 (*expensive*). One of Treviso's bastions of local atmosphere and cooking. Try *pasta e fagioli* with radicchio. *Closed Sun eve, Mon and July*.

Toni del Spin, Via Inferiore 7, **t** 0422 543 829 (*moderate*). An old favourite for its Veneto dishes (*bigoli, risi e bisi* and the like). *Closed Sun and Mon lunch*.

you'll come to Treviso's best church, Gothic **San Nicolò** with its polygonal apse. The interior is a treasure house of lovely frescoes – from a huge St Christopher on the south wall to the charming pages by Lorenzo Lotto by the d'Onigo tomb. Tommaso da Modena contributed the saints standing to attention on the columns, but even better are his perceptive portraits of 40 Dominicans (1352), some using medieval reading glasses, in the **Capitolo dei Domenicani**, in the adjacent Seminario (*open daily Apr–Sept 8–6; Oct–Mar 8–5.30; ring the bell at the porter's lodge*).

San Francesco

Treviso's east end is separated by one of its wider streams, the Cagnàn; on a little islet (take Via Trevisi–Via Pescheria from the Monte di Pietà), the lively and colourful **fish market** (1851) is open every morning except Sunday. San Nicolò's near twin, the tall brick, Romanesque–Gothic **San Francesco**, is just up Via S. Parisio, and has a fresco of the Madonna by Tommaso da Modena, as well as the tombs of Francesca Petrarch (*d.* 1384) and Pietro Alighieri (*d.* 1364), the children of Italy's two greatest poets, whose final meeting place here in Treviso was purely a coincidence.

Back along the walls to the east, Viale Burchiellati leads shortly to the city's other great gate, Guglielmo Bergamasco's exotic **Porta San Tommaso** (1518). From here follow Borgo Mazzini to the deconsecrated church of **Santa Caterina** (*open Tues–Sun 9–12.30 and 2.30–6*), now a museum with Tommaso da Modena's detached frescoes on *The Life of St Ursula*, a series that's just as delightful as Carpaccio's St Ursulas in the Accademia in Venice. It may also house items from the Museo Civico Luigi Bailo while that is being restored.

North of Treviso: the Marca Trevigiana

You can drive straight up to the Dolomites in less than two hours from Treviso, or spend a day exploring the fine towns of Marca Trevigiana province along the way.

Oderzo and Conegliano

A delightful town crisscrossed by canals and devoted to wine-making, **Oderzo** may not be a household name, but in its Roman heyday, as *Opitergium*, it was recorded as far away as Egypt. Piazza Vittorio Emanuele II marks the old forum, overlooked by the late Gothic **Duomo**; in Via Garibaldi, the **Museo Civico Archeologico** (***t*** *0422 713 333; open Weds–Sat 9–12 and 3.30–6.30, Sun 3.30–6.30*) has a good assortment of Roman finds and mosaics. Nearby, the **Pinacoteca Alberto Martini**, Via Garibaldi 63 (***t*** *0422 713 333; open Weds–Fri 9–12 and 3.30–6.30, and by appointment*) has works by the Oderzo-born surrealist painter Alberto Martini, as well as other contemporary Italian painters, mostly from Oderzo.

Make the short detour north of Oderzo to picturesque **Portobuffolè**, a village of frescoed buildings and three very funny Venetian lions (especially the spooked one with a pie pan face, sticking out its tongue on the 15th-century Monte della Pietà, now the Cassa Marca). The oldest house, 13th-century **Casa di Gaia da Camino**, currently houses a bicycle museum.

Conegliano, a town neatly divided into old and new, with the Accademia cinema and its giant sphinxes in the centre, was the birthplace of Giambattista Cima (1460–1518), 'the sweet shepherd among Venetian painters' as Mary McCarthy called him. The son of a seller of hides, he often painted his native countryside in his backgrounds. If you haven't seen the originals, reproductions are displayed at his birthplace, the **Casa di Cima**, on quiet Via Cima 24 (*call ahead,* ***t*** *0438 21660*). An original and beautiful Cima, a Sacra Conversazione in an architectural setting (1493), forms the altarpiece of the 14th-century **Duomo**. In the 16th century Ludovico Pozzoserrato and Francesco da Milano collaborated on the frescoes of Old and New Testament scenes in the adjacent **Sala dei Battuti**, the hall of a flagellants' confraternity (*open Sat 10–12, Sun and hols 3–6, other days by request;* **t** *0438 22606*).

Be sure to stroll down arcaded **Via XX Settembre**, which is lined with old frescoed palaces; the **castle** on the hill, begun in the 10th century, has a small **Museo Civico** with paintings and other odds and ends.

Conegliano produces a delightful Prosecco that you can taste along the pretty **Strada del Prosecco** – from the castle to **Valdobbiadene** to the west, then back east to Vittòrio Vèneto. On the way have a look at **San Pietro di Feletto**, its exterior frescoed in the 15th century by an unknown painter, who pictures Jesus in a unique fashion: lines from his wounds are connected to chickens, wine, people lying in bed, and farm tools.

Vittòrio Vèneto

The Venetian pre-Alps saw heavy action in the First World War, and the hills around Asiago, Monte Grappa and the Piave are often crowned with dispiritingly huge Italian, British or French war cemeteries. **Vittòrio Vèneto**, north of Conegliano, was the site of Italy's final victorious battle (October 1918). Vittòrio's name, however, is for Vittorio Emanuele II; in 1866, to celebrate the birth of Italy, the two rival towns of Cèneda and

Tourist Information

Oderzo: Piazza Castello 1, **t** 0422 815 251.
Conegliano: Via Colombo 145, **t** 0438 21230.
Vittòrio Vèneto: Piazza del Popolo 18, **t** 0438 57243.

Where to Stay and Eat

Oderzo ✉ 31046

*****Villa Revedin**, Via Palazzi 4, Gorgo al Monitcano, 5km east of town, **t** 0422 800 033, *www.villarevedin.it* (*moderate*). A 15th-century villa set in a park, with well-equipped rooms and superb breakfasts.

Gellius, Calle Pretoria 6, **t** 0422 713 577 (*very expensive*). An atmospheric former Roman prison in the centre. *Closed Sun eve, Mon, and 2wks Jan and Aug.*

Conegliano ✉ 31015

*****Canon d'Oro**, Via XX Settembre 129, **t** 0438 34246, *www.hotelcanondoro.it* (*moderate–expensive*). A welcoming hotel with an exterior frescoed in the 1500s.

*****Sporting Hotel Ragno d'Oro**, Via Diaz 37, **t** 0438 412 300, *www.hotelragnodoro.it* (*moderate*). A hotel set in parkland on Conegliano's outskirts, with a large pool.

Al Salisà, Via XX Settembre 2, **t** 0438 24288 (*expensive–very expensive*). An elegant restaurant in a 13th-century building, with snails (*lumache*) and game in season. There's a good local wine list, and lunch menus. *Closed Tues eve, Weds and Aug.*

Tre Panoce, Via Vecchia Trevigiana 50, just outside town (bus no.1 stops outside), **t** 0438 60071 (*expensive*). A lovely restaurant in a seicento farmhouse crowning a hill of vineyards, with outdoor tables in summer. The *menu veneto* offers lots of little dishes to try. *Closed Sun eve, Mon, 2wks Jan and Aug.*

Vittòrio Vèneto ✉ 31029

*****Hotel Terme**, Via delle Terme 4, **t** 0438 554 345, *www.hotelterme.tv* (*moderate*). Good, comfortable rooms near the station.

Il Capitello, Via S. Francesco, Corbanese, Tarzo, west of town, **t** 0485 564 279 (*expensive*). The best food in the area, cooked with modern flair. *Closed Weds, Thurs lunch, Jan and Aug.*

Postiglione, Via Cavour 39, **t** 0438 556 924 (*moderate*). A popular restaurant in an old posthouse, with hearty mountain specialities. *Closed Tues and 2wks in July–Aug.*

Serravalle were united. The **Castello di San Martino**, dating back to the Lombards, hovers over **Cèneda**, where the main Piazza Giovanni Paolo I holds the **Loggia del Cenedese**, designed by Sansovino in 1538, now home to a museum of the Battle of 1918 (***t*** *0438 57695; open Tues–Sun May–Sept 10–12 and 3.30–7; Oct–Apr 10–12 and 2–5; adm*); Albino Luciani (John Paul I) was a longtime bishop of Vittòrio Vèneto and founded the **Museo Diocesano** in the seminary, with works by Palma il Giovane and Titian (*open by request,* ***t*** *0438 948 411*). Another church, **Santa Maria del Meschio**, has a beautiful altarpiece of the Annunciation by Andrea Previtali.

Serravalle begins with a clock tower up the poetic street (Via Dante/Virgilio/Petrarca) which links the two halves of Vittòrio Vèneto. It's conserved its atmospheric old palaces and houses, especially in Piazza Flaminio, where the 15th-century **Loggia Serravallese** houses, confusingly, the **Museo del Cenedese** (*open Tues–Sun May–Sept 10–12.30 and 3.30–7; Oct–Apr 9.30–12.30 and 2–7; same ticket as Museo della Battaglia*), with a collection of Roman finds, sculpture and minor paintings. The **Duomo** has a fine altarpiece by Titian, *Madonna col Bambino* (1547). Vittòrio Vèneto's playground is the lovely **Bosco del Cansiglio**, a vast forest of fir, larch and beech on a lofty karstic plateau set aside by Venice in 1548 as its 'Forest of St Mark's Oars'; Monte Cansiglio itself offers the closest downhill skiing to Venice.

Towards the Dolomites: Belluno and Feltre

Belluno

A provincial capital at the junction of the Piave and Ardo rivers, Belluno is one of those small, perfectly proportioned Italian cities: urban, urbane and yet never far from magnificent views over the countryside – in this case of the Venetian Dolomites.

The old civic and religious centre of town, **Piazza del Duomo**, is home to two of Belluno's finest buildings, the ornate **Palazzo dei Rettori** (1491), which was the residence of the Venetian governors, and the **Duomo**. Founded in the 7th century, and last redesigned by Pietro Lombardo, the church was not finished until the 1600s, and tends to be overshadowed by the magnificent detached **Campanile**, designed by Filippo Juvarra in 1742 and offering bird's-eye views (***t*** *0437 943 464; open daily 3–5, mornings by arrangement*).

In Via Duomo, the **Museo Civico** (***t*** *0437 944 836; open mid-Apr–Sept Tues–Sat 10–12 and 4–7, Sun 10.30–12.30; Oct–mid-Apr Mon–Sat 10–12, also Tues and Fri 3–6; adm*) is a treat for fans of extrovert womanizing Baroque painter Sebastiano Ricci, with some of his greatest work; it also provides a chance to learn about some interesting if obscure local painters from the 1300s to the 1800s. Via Mezzaterra/Via Rialto follow the ancient Roman *castrum*, by way of atmospheric **Piazza del Mercato**, a picture-perfect little square with arcades and a fountain from 1410. To the south Via Mezzaterra ends at the 12th-century **Porta Ruga** and a postcard view of the Piave Valley and the mountains. Have a look at the Gothic church of **Santo Stefano** (1468) in Via Roma, where a 15th-century relief of the Madonna in her merciful umbrella pose guards the door, leading into a handsome striped interior.

Tourist Information

Belluno: Via Rodolfo Pesaro 21, **t** 0437 940 084, *www. infodolomiti.it.*

Feltre: Piazza Trento-Trieste 9, **t** 0439 2540.

National Park: Piazzale Zancanaro 1, Feltre, **t** 0439 3328, *www. dolomitipark.it.*

Where to Stay and Eat

Belluno ✉ 32100

*****Villa Carpenada**, Via Mier 158, **t** 0437 948 343, *www.paginegialle.it/villacarpenada* (*expensive*). A well-run hotel with quiet rooms in an 18th-century villa just to the west of the centre.

*****Astor**, Piazza dei Martiri 26-E, **t** 0437 942 094 (*moderate–expensive*). Comfortable, centrally located rooms.

*****Delle Alpi**, Via J. Tasso 13, **t** 0437 940 545, *www.dellealpi.it* (*moderate*). Welcoming rooms not far from the station, and one of the best restaurants in town, specializing in seafood. *Closed Sun and part of Aug.*

Al Borgo, Via Anconetta 8, **t** 0437 926 755 (*moderate*). A popular place serving traditional favourites in an 18th-century villa south of the Piave. *Closed Mon eve and Tues.*

Pieve d'Alpago ✉ 32010

Dolada, Via Dolada 9, Plois, just outside Pieve, **t** 0437 479 141 (*very expensive*). One of the top restaurants in Venetia, overlooking Lago di Santa Croce. The inspired dishes are in the best Italian tradition: home-made pasta, celebrated *zuppa dolada*, and superb fish, duck and lamb. There's an exceptional wine list too, and rooms are available. *Closed Mon and Tues lunch except July and Aug.*

If you don't have time for a foray into the Dolomites, take the bus to the **Alpi del Nevegàl**, 12 kilometres south of Belluno, for the chairlift to the Rifugio Brigata Alpina Cadore (5,248ft) with its Alpine garden. From there it's an easy three-hour walk up to the **Col Visentin**, where another refuge commands a unique panorama: north across the Dolomite peaks and south to the Venetian Lagoon. The hills of the **Alpago** are a popular weekend destination, especially the **Lago di Santa Croce**, the focal point for its small villages: aim for **Pieve d'Alpago** in a lovely setting, famous for its restaurant.

Feltre: the Dead Man and SS. Vittore e Corona

West from Belluno the SS50 skirts the Piave on its way to hilltop Feltre. Sacked by the troops of Emperor Maximilian in 1510 during the War of the Cambrai, Feltre was immediately rebuilt and has changed little since, especially the houses along **Via Mezzaterra**, with their faded frescoes and marble plaques hammered into illegibility. The jewel on Via Mezzaterra is the picturesque **Piazza Maggiore**, where a quizzical Lion of St Mark stands vigil over the castle; the church of San Rocco has a fountain by Tullio Lombardo, and the superb 16th-century **Palazzo dei Rettori** (now the Municipio) is decked out with a Palladian portico. Inside, a wooden theatre built in 1684 saw the production of Goldoni's first plays. In the centre of Piazza Maggiore, a statue honours the famous educator, Vittorino da Feltre (*see* Mantua, p.239).

The Palazzo Villabuono, by the east gate, houses the **Museo Civico** (***t*** *0439 885 242; open Tues–Fri 10.30–12.30 and 3–6, or 4–7 in summer*) which contains an altar to the *anna perrena* (the year), and paintings by Gentile Bellini, Cima da Conegliano and Feltre's own contribution to the Renaissance, Lorenzo Luzzo, better known by his punk nickname, *Il Morto da Feltre*, the 'Dead Man of Feltre', given to him because of his unusual pallor. The *Transfiguration*, the Dead Man's most acclaimed work, is nearby in the sacristry of the church of **Ognissanti**.

Five kilometres from Feltre, signposted off the Treviso road (SS473), the Romanesque **Santuario di SS. Vittore e Corona** (*t 0439 2540; open daily Apr–Sept 8–12 and 3–7; Oct–Mar 9–12 and 3–6*) is up a steep little road. Built in 1100 and unchanged, it has the remains of Vittore, a Roman soldier martyred in Syria in 171, and Corona who converted at the sight and was martyred too. The apse is filled with their elevated sarcophagus, decorated with windblown acanthus. Note the relief of Vittore on the underside, and behind, capitals inscribed with Kufic script, reading 'the Universe is God'. The frescoes are by the schools of Tommaso da Modena and Giotto, with figures copied directly from Padua's Scrovegni Chapel – Giotto sold the reproduction rights. Don't miss the *Last Supper*, in which the artist's prawns look like scorpions.

The Dolomites

...the most beautiful 'constructions' in the world.
Le Corbusier

There are mountains, and then there are the Dolomites. Born as massive corals in the primordial ocean, and heaved up from the seabed around 60 million years ago, they consist of dolomitic limestone and porphyry that has been whittled away at by countless storms and blizzards over the aeons to form an extraordinary landscape . The other-worldly, majestic peaks claw and scratch at the sky between the valleys of the Adige and the Piave rivers, each monumental range a petrified tempest of jagged needles, cloud-tickled pinnacles and sheer cliffs, dyed rose by the dawn and glowing red by the setting sun.

These most romantic and beautiful of mountains were named after a wandering French mineralogist with a fantastical and improbable name, Dieudonné Sylvain Guy Tancrède de Gratet de Dolomieu, who in 1789 became the first person to describe their mineral content. Marmolada (10,959ft), which is the highest peak in the range (there are 17 others topping 10,000ft) has glaciers even in summertime, but elsewhere the snowfields convert in July to a massive bouquet of wildflowers, streaked with blue gentians, yellow Alpine poppies and buttercups, edelweiss and pink rhododendron. The air and light during the autumn are so sharp and fine they can break your heart.

The Eastern Dolomites: the Cadore

Although mostly Italian-speaking, much of the Cadore, the district north of Belluno along the upper Piave, was incorporated into Italy only after the First World War. Its somewhat overripe, fashionable heart is the glossy resort of Cortina d'Ampezzo, host of the 1956 Winter Olympics, which did much to introduce the Dolomites to the world. The Alte Vie – the High Roads of the Dolomites – pass through this region as well, winding their way at high altitudes across some of the most renowned ridges and peaks in the range.

The Dolomites

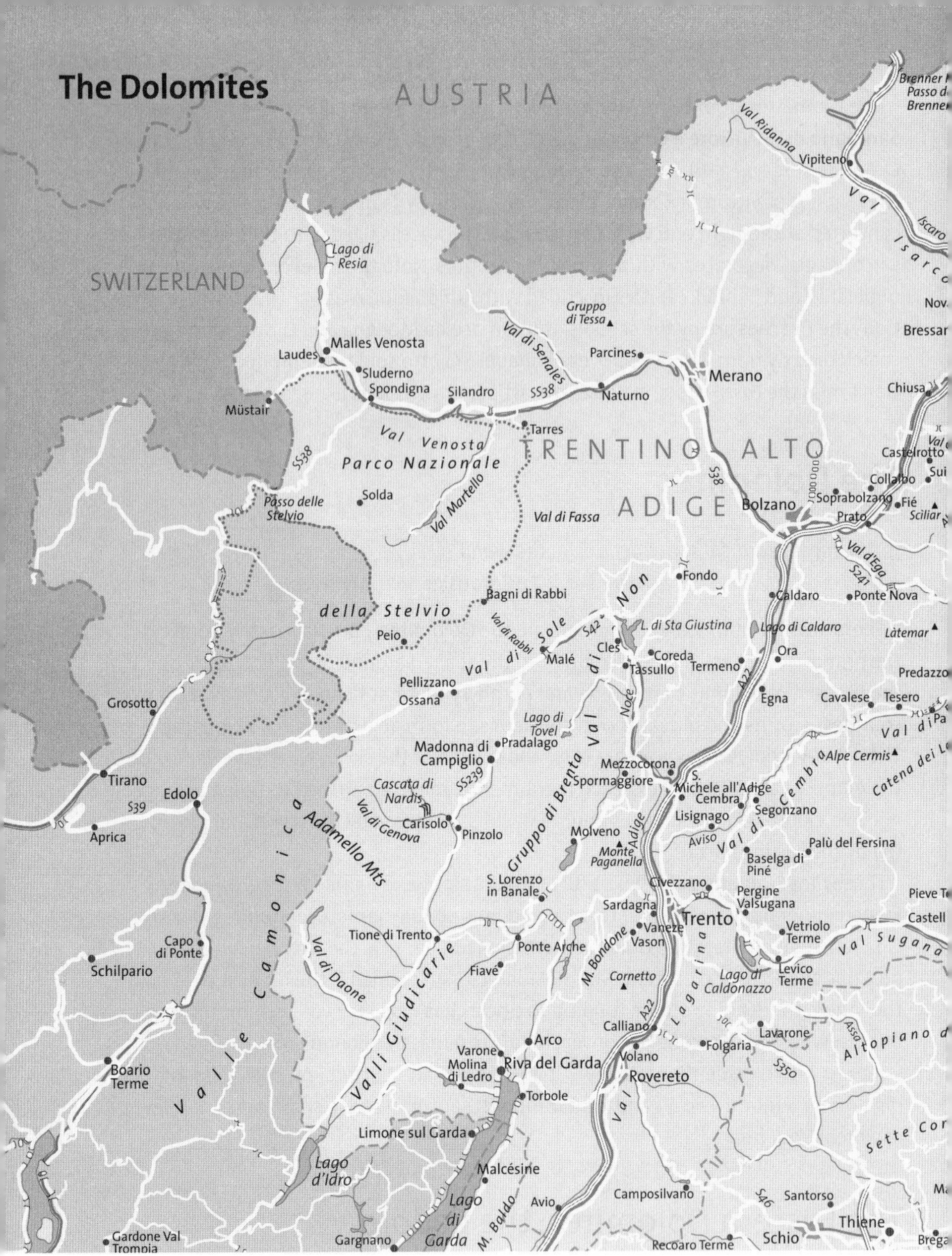

The Piave Valley

The roads north along the River Piave from Belluno (SS50) and Treviso (SS51) meet at the junction of Ponte nelle Alpi before continuing up through scenery marked by the steep pyramids of **Monte Dolada** and **Piz Gallina**. A less benign mountain, **Toc** (6,301ft), looms over the town of **Longarone**. In 1963 a landslide from its slopes crashed into the local reservoir, creating a tidal wave that killed 1,917 people in Longarone; a

memorial church documents the disaster and has a few poignant bits salvaged from the mud. A road runs along the path of the disaster, the lofty, narrow **Gola del Vaiont**, to the lake, six kilometres to the east. From Longarone you could also turn west on the SS251 for the **Val Zoldana**, a lovely valley lining the River Maè, with typical hamlets in wood and stone, the cradle of Italy's best *gelato* makers. The valley road passes the stunning peaks of Civetta and Pelmo on the way to Selva di Cadore (*see* p.413).

Getting Around the Dolomites

The **rail** line north from Venice, Treviso and Belluno passes through Pieve di Cadore before petering out in Calalzo di Cadore, 35km from Cortina d'Ampezzo (2½hrs from Venice). The western Dolomites are linked by the main line between Verona and Munich, by way of Trento (1½hrs) and Bolzano (2½hrs) to the Brenner Pass (4hrs). Branch lines run from Bolzano to Merano and Malles Venosta, to the west; from Fortezza, near Bressanone (both on the main line north) to Brunico, Dobbiaco (from where there's a bus service to Cortina) and San Candido to the east.

The Dolomites are exceptionally well served by 2 **bus** companies – Dolomiti-Bus in the east (including daily routes to Agordo, Arabba, Falcade, and Colle Santa Lucia from Venice) and SAD Buses in the west. In July and August they run scenic tours from the major centres.

When to Go

In June, early July and late Sept–Oct the refuges are open but not packed to the gills. Come straight after the New Year holidays for skiing, when everyone else has to go back to work and resorts offer big discounts.

Mountain Sports

The Dolomites are a candy shop for winter sports junkies. As the sunny side of the Alps, they enjoy good clear weather, and when it snows, it falls delightfully dry and powdery. As well as ski slopes, there are country trails, toboggan and bobsled runs, ice rinks and speed-skating courses.

Hiking

Hiking in the Dolomites is as close as some of us will ever get to heaven. There are routes for everyone from semi couch potatoes to rock-grappling daredevils, and eight **High Trails** (Alte Vie delle Dolomiti) designed for those 'vagabonds of the path' who fall between the two extremes. The trails range from 120 to 180km in length, and are designed to take average walkers 2 weeks.

Equipment

The High Trails keep you on top of mountains and plateaux for most of their length, but they do demand stout hiking boots with good rubber soles (80% of accidents are caused by slipping) and protection against sudden storms, even in summer. A telescopic walking stick for descents and a mobile phone in case of emergencies are also recommended.

Maps

Two good sets of maps include the Alte Vie and other paths, and the location of refuges: *Carta dei Sentieri e Rifugi*, Edizioni Tabacco Udine, and *Maps Kompass-Wanderkarten*, Edizioni Fleishmann-Starnberg. Both are scale 1:50,000, and are available at news-stands in the region. The relevant tourist offices have booklets on each trail in English with all the basic info, including phone numbers of the refuges and the level of difficulty. *See* also maps, Practical A–Z, p.84).

Refuges

For general information on *rifugi alpini*, *see* p.87. For information specific to this area, see *www.infodolomiti.it*, *www.trentino.to*, *www.suedtirol.info* and *www.guidecortina.com*, or try the **Italian Alpine Club** (CAI), Via Petrella 19, 20124 Milan, **t** 02 205 7231, *www.cai.it*.

Many of the 200 refuges in Trentino are run by the Società degli Alpinisti Tridentini (SAT), a branch of the CAI, at Via Manci 57, 38100 Trento, **t** 0461 982 804, *www.sat.tri.it*. In the Alto Adige, the address is CAI, Piazza dell'Erbe 46, 39100 Bolzano, **t** 0471 971 694.

Skiing

There are slopes of all levels of difficulty in the Dolomites. Other bonuses are ski schools in July, and heated indoor pools in midwinter.

Contact Belluno, Trento or Bolzano tourist offices, or book a *Settimana Bianca* package (a week's room and board at a hotel, ski-pass and instruction) from CIT (Citalia) or other travel offices in Italy.

If you want to try many resorts, the *Dolomiti Superski* pass gives unlimited access (for about €32 a day) to 464 lifts and 1,180km of ski runs for periods of 1, 2 or 3 weeks. For the latest information and prices, call **t** 04 7179 5350, or see *www.DolomitiSuperski.com*.

The main road from Longarone skirts the high banks of the Piave north into the foothills of the Antelao and Marmarole and **Pieve di Cadore**. *Pieve* means parish, and from Roman times on this was the most important one in the Cadore, a status that grew with the reputation of that mighty wielder of the brush, Tiziano Vecellio (Titian), born here *c.* 1483. His statue stands in the main piazza, just up from his birthplace, the pretty **Casa Natale di Tiziano** (***t*** *0435 32262; open daily 15 June–15 Sept 9.30–12.30 and 4–5; other times by appointment*), containing drawings, studies and some original furnishings. In the church of **Santa Maria Nascente**, the last chapel on the left holds his *Madonna with SS. Andrew and Titian*, starring his own family – his daughter as the Virgin, his son as Titian the Bishop, his brother as St Andrew and Titian himself looking in from the left. The most important building in Pieve doesn't leave room for any false modesty, calling itself the **Palazzo della Magnifica Comunità Cadorina** (*same hours as Casa Natale di Tiziano*). Built in 1525, it now houses the local historical museum, with pre-Roman weapons and 2nd-century BC bronze figurines.

Tourist Information

Calalzo di Cadore: Via Stazione 37, **t** 0435 32348.
Pieve di Cadore: Piazza Venezia 20, **t** 0437 31644.
Santo Stefano di Cadore: Via Venezia 40, **t** 0435 62230.
Sappada: Borgata Bach 9, **t** 0435 469 131.
San Vito di Cadore: Via Nazionale 9, **t** 0436 9119.
See also www.infodolomiti.it.

Where to Stay and Eat

Sappada ✉ 32047

*****Haus Michaela**, Borgata Fontana 40, **t** 0435 469 377, *www.hotelmichaela.com* (*moderate–expensive*). A little hotel with an indoor pool, sauna and gym. *Open mid-Dec–Easter and mid-May–Sept.*

*****Bellavista**, Via Cima, Cima Sappada, 4km from town, **t** 0435 469 175, *www.albergobellavista.com* (*moderate*). A hotel with lovely views and mountain bike hire. There are some *cheap* and some *expensive* rooms. *Open Dec–Easter and mid-June–Sept.*

*****Belvedere**, Piazza Cima 93, Cima Sappada, 4km from town, **t** 0435 469 112 (*moderate*). A 14-room hotel with a sauna and a good restaurant featuring mountain specialities. Some rooms are *cheap*, some *expensive*. *Open Dec–mid-Apr, mid-June–Sept.*

*****Siera Hof**, Borgata Soravia 110, **t** 0435 469 110, *www.sierahof.com* (*moderate*). A small place near the centre of the village.

****Corona Ferrea**, Borgata Kratten 11, **t** 0435 469 442, *www.corona-ferrea.it* (*cheap–moderate*). A hotel with comfortable en suite rooms. *Open mid-June–20 Sept and 20 Dec–31 Mar.*

Laite, Borgata Hoffe 10, **t** 0435 469 070 (*very expensive*). A lovely old wooden chalet offering delicious mountain specialities such as quail stuffed with foie gras and tarragon, ravioli with *camoscio* (roe deer), venison with wild thyme, and guinea fowl with mountain radicchio. *Closed Weds, Thurs lunch, Oct and June.*

Baita Mondschein, Via Bach 96, **t** 0435 469 585 (*expensive*). A pretty alpine chalet situated at the bottom of the slalom course, serving up really authentic cooking, including wonderful grills and interesting desserts, as well as home-made ice cream. *Closed Tues and Oct.*

San Vito di Cadore ✉ 32046

******Marcora**, Via Roma 28, **t** 0436 9101, *www.corahotel.it* (*very expensive*). A very comfortable hotel in a fine setting with a swimming pool. *Open mid-June–mid-Sept and mid-Dec–mid-Mar.*

*****Cima Belprá**, Via Calvi 1, Chiapuzza, **t** 0436 890 441, *www.hotelcimabelpra.com* (*moderate–expensive*). A welcoming place with the best restaurant in the area, **La Scaletta**, offering beautiful views, and traditional polenta and beef dishes. *Closed Mon out of season, and Nov.*

Towards Tai, at the crossroads, the **Museo degli Occhiali** (***t*** *0435 500 213; open Mon–Sat 1 June–10 Sept 8.30–12.30 and 4.30–7.30; 11 Sept–30 May 8.30–12.30; adm*) contains a collection of antique spectacles. But what Pieve is proudest of these days is Babbo Natale (the Italian Santa Claus), who has made the town his home, with a Christmas-letter-answering service for the *bambini*.

The road and the Piave continue north past the end of the rail line at **Calalzo**, where you can catch a bus for the resort of **Santo Stefano di Cadore**, in the lovely **Comelico valley**. From here continue northwest to Cortina, or take another beautiful road east towards the popular resort of **Sappada**, more Austrian in feel than Italian. From Pieve di Cadore there is also a direct road to Cortina d'Ampezzo, the SS51, winding through the **Valle del Boite** with its many rustic wooden chalets, between the Antelao massif, the 'King of Cadore' and **Pelmo**, one of the most unusual and striking peak clusters in the Dolomites. The road passes through **Borca di Cadore** and the more important resort of **San Vito di Cadore**, an excellent base for ascending Pelmo and nearby peaks.

Cortina d'Ampezzo

This is the sort of place where David Niven and Audrey Hepburn would sit on a café terrace in turtlenecks and sunglasses, but it also enjoys the best location in the Dolomites: a lofty (4,015ft–10,637ft) cross-shaped meadow at the junction of the Boite and Bigontina valleys, in the centre of a ring of extraordinary mountains – Tofane, the great mount 'owl' (scene of the 1997 World Cup); Cristallo; Sorapis, licked by stony flames; and the Cinque Torri, the 'five towers'.

Devoted heart and soul to fun and the sporting life, Cortina is well known for its night-time activities, when the *après-ski* crowd fills its clubs until dawn. But whatever worldly pleasure and delight this snowy fleshpot offers, it comes at a price, rating right up there with Capri, Portofino and Venice herself on the bottom line of the tab.

The Sporting Life

The 1956 Olympics endowed Cortina with superb winter sports facilities; you can ski-jump, speed-skate, fly down bobsled and luge runs, and cut figures of eight in the ice stadium, not to mention try out the thousand and one downhill and cross-country ski runs in the vicinity. In summer, it's an excellent base for hiking, rock climbing, delta-planing and more, while in town there's a riding school, tennis, summer and winter swimming pools, and activities such as the Ice Disco Dance.

Cortina has its share of trendy shops, and a museum of contemporary art, the **Museo Ciasa de Ra Regoles**, Via del Parco, on the corner of Corso d'Italia (*open daily mid-June–mid-Sept 10.30–12.30 and 4–7.30; until 8 Sat in July and Aug; Christmas–Easter 4–7.30; adm*), with works by De Pisis, Morandi, De Chirico and others, plus palaeontology and ethnography sections. Two cable cars (*closed from early/mid-Sept until start of ski season in Dec*) at the end of the town bus lines wait to whisk you up to the mountains: in the north, near the Olympic stadium, to **Tofana di Mezzo** (10,637ft) where there are privately run Alpine refuges, and in the west to **Tondi di Faloria** (7,685ft).

Excursions From Cortina

As a major crossroads, Cortina offers numerous forays into surrounding mountains. For the classic Great Dolomites Road between Cortina and Bolzano, *see* p.435.

Lake Misurina and Around

For a beautiful short trip from Cortina, take the SS48 and SS48b over the lofty **Tre Croci Pass** to **Lake Misurina**, shimmering below the jagged peaks of Sorapis and the remarkable triple-spired **Tre Cime di Lavaredo**, 15 kilometres northeast of Cortina. The colours of Misurina are so brilliant they look touched-up on the postcards; as a resort it makes a quiet alternative to Cortina, especially if ice-skating is your sport. From Misurina it's a magnificent seven-kilometre drive up to the **Rifugio Auronzo**, just beneath the Tre Cime di Lavaredo, where you can make the easy walk to the 1916 **Bersaglieri memorial**, honouring Italy's famous sharpshooters. More fine views await from **Monte Piana**, a lofty meadow six kilometres north of Misurina.

Getting Around

Cortina's **bus** station, situated just off Via Marconi, is served by SAD (**t** 800 846 047), which operates buses from Bolzano to Cortina via Dobbiaco, and from Cortina to Milan via Brescia and Bergamo on Sun in July and Aug. It is also served by Dolomiti-Bus (**t** 0437 941 167), which during the summer offers a daily service to Lido di Jesolo in Venice. There's one bus a day direct from Venice or Treviso (**t** 0436 867 921), and one to Venice airport (**t** 0421 5944).

The nearest **train** stations to Cortina are at Dobbiaco, 32km to the north (on the Bolzano–Linz line), and Calalzo di Cadore, 35km to the south; both have regular bus connections to Cortina.

Tourist Information

Piazzetta S. Francesco 8, near Piazza Venezia, **t** 0436 3231, *www.infodolomiti.it*.

Alpine guides (*open July, Aug and Sept*): Corso Italia 69, **t** 0436 868505, *www.guidecortina.com*.

Where to Stay

Cortina d'Ampezzo ✉ 32043

Visitors should expect to run up against the full- or half-board requirement just about everywhere in the resort during its high season.

Very Expensive–Luxury

★★★★★**Miramonti Majestic**, Via Peziè 103, **t** 0436 4201, *www.geturhotels.com*. A warm, traditional and rustic place with pretty wooden balconies affording truly magnificent views. The breathtakingly expensive rooms come complete with all imaginable creature comforts, and there's an indoor pool and sauna. *Open 22 June–8 Sept, 1 Dec–7 Apr.*

★★★★**De La Poste**, Piazza Roma 14, **t** 0436 4271, *www.hotels.cortina.it/delaposte*. A large, historic alpine chalet in the heart of the action, with classy rooms with balconies. The terrace and bar see much of Cortina's social round, especially in the evening.

Expensive

★★★★**Corona**, Via Val di Sotto 12, **t** 0436 3251. An alpine chalet 10mins from the centre, at the bottom of the valley beside the river and hence more convenient than most hotels for the ski lift. Its modern art collection is more extensive than that of the museum. Some rooms are *moderate*, others *very expensive*. *Open July–Sept and Dec–Apr.*

★★★**Da Beppe Sello**, Via Ronco 68, **t** 0436 3236, *www.beppesello.it*. An award-winning, welcoming hotel with a restaurant serving some of the best food in Cortina, including game in season. Some rooms are *moderate*, others *very expensive*. *Open Dec–Mar, mid-May–mid-Sept.*

★★★**Menardi**, Via Majon 110, **t** 0436 2400, *www.hotelmenardi.it*. A charming 800-year-old farmhouse run as an inn by the same family for the past century, furnished with antiques and bedecked with flowers. There are some *moderate* and some *very expensive rooms.Open June–20 Sept, 20 Dec–30 Mar.*

Moderate

★★★**Impero**, Via C. Battisti 66, **t** 0436 4246, *www.hotels-cortina.it/impero*. An unpretentious hotel with no restaurant but adequate en suite rooms (*some expensive*).

★★**Astoria**, Largo delle Poste 11, **t** 0436 2525. A charming, extremely friendly little hotel in the centre, with 7 rooms (some *cheap*, some *expensive*) and an excellent (*expensive*) restaurant, **Pontejel**, **t** 0436 863 828, where you can feast on the likes of *capellotti* (little hats) with figs and potato, steak, and peaches and *amaretti*.

Eating Out

Local cuisine is usually as *haute* as the price.

Tivoli, Via Lacedel 34, northeast of the centre, **t** 0436 866 400 (*very expensive*). A restaurant with lovely views and innovative, extremely refined cuisine. *Closed Mon.*

El Toulà, Via Ronco 123, near Pocol, **t** 0436 3339, (*expensive*). An elegant restaurant set in an old wooden farmhouse, specializing in grilled meats, roast lamb and Tyrolean desserts, and boasting a renowned wine list. *Open Christmas–Easter, and 15 July–30 Aug; closed Mon.*

Circular Routes from Misurina to Cortina

There are two possible circular routes from Misurina back to Cortina that make rewarding full-day excursions. Both begin to the east on the SS48 via **Auronzo di Cadore**, past a peak that is known as the **Corno del Doge** because of its resemblance to the Doge's bonnet. Auronzo, located on the shores of an artificial lake, surrounded by fragrant spruce forests, makes another fine base, and has a cable car and chairlifts up **Monte Agudo**. From Auronzo you can circle south around Pieve di Cadore and the Valle del Boite (161 kilometres; *see* p.410) or take the longer route around to the north (224 kilometres) through **Comelico** and the beautiful **Val di Sesto**. The route passes into the Alto Adige, through **San Candido/Innichen**, a resort on the River Drava; it has a Benedictine monastery and a Romanesque collegiate church, the 13th-century **SS. Candidus e Corbinian**, its altar decorated with a superb early 13th-century Crucifixion in polychrome wood.

The turn back to Cortina (SS51) is at **Dobbiaco/Toblach**, one of the original Dolomite resorts, thanks to its magnificent setting and lake, and a railway station built by the Habsburgs. The large **castle** in the old part of town was built for Emperor Maximilian in 1500. In July Dobbiaco holds a series of concerts in honour of Mahler, who spent his summers here; in summer, too, you can visit the little **Museo Gustav Mahler**, four kilometres from the centre at Casa Trenker (*ring the tourist office for hours*). From Dobbiaco the road heads south past wooded Lake Dobbiaco and enters the dramatic **Val di Landro**, where the Cristallo group looms over **Carbonin/Schluderbach**. Beyond are a pair of little lakes, and the lonely ruins of the **Castel Sant'Umberto**. The road then circles around castle-crowned **Podestagno**, before descending into the Ampezzo with the Tofane group storming up to the right.

Cortina to Colle Santa Lucia and Agordo

There are two routes to these mountains southwest of Cortina: the main one follows the Great Dolomites Road (*see* p.435) through the Falzarego Pass, before taking the SS203 south at Andraz; a lesser-known but equally pretty route takes the smaller SS638 road through the **Passo di Giau**, where in recent years some of the most important Mesolithic tombs in Europe (5000 BC) have been discovered.

The artefacts of 'Mondeval man' can now be seen down in **Selva di Cadore**, in the **Museo Storico** (*call* **t** *0437 720 243 for open times*). Selva is a growing resort in the lovely Val Fiorentina, where a road crosses into the Valle di Zoldana and ends up at Longarone (*see* p.406). Above Selva, **Colle Santa Lucia** is a pretty place with its old agricultural hamlets and a beautiful belvedere.

Continuing south from Colle, the road passes **Caprile** and the mighty north wall of Civetta en route to **Àlleghe** with its lovely lake, formed in 1771 by a landslide from Civetta. At **Cencenighe** you have the option of turning off for Falcade and San Martino di Castrozza (*see* p.424). **Àgordo** (45 kilometres is an attractive town and resort in the Val Cordévole, along one of the principal branches of the Piave.

The Passo Duran above Àgordo leads back to Cortina via the Valle di Zoldo and the village of **Dont** (another 21 kilometres) – there are splendid views of Civetta and Pelmo, and you can buy local woodcarvings.

Tourist Information

Veneto:

Auronzo: Via Roma 10, **t** 0435 9359.

Alleghe: Piazza Kennedy 17, **t** 0437 523 333.

Agordo: Via XXVII Aprile 5a, **t** 0437 62105.

Alto Adige:

Dobbiaco: Via delle Dolomiti 3, **t** 0474 972 132, *www.dobbiaco.info*.

San Candido: Piazza del Magistrato 1, **t** 0474 913 156, *www.tre-cime.info*.

Where to Stay and Eat

Misurina ✉ 32040

*****Lavaredo**, Via Monte Piana 11, **t** 0435 39227 (*moderate*). A hotel (some rooms *cheap*, some *expensive)* and good restaurant. *Closed Nov–mid-Dec.*

****Dolomiti des Alpes**, Via Monte Piana, **t** 0435 39031 (*cheap–moderate*). A hotel just above the lake, with a sauna. *Closed May, Oct and Nov.*

***Sport**, Via Monte Piana 18, **t** 043 39125 (*cheap–moderate*). Simple rooms with views of Lake Misurina. *Closed May, Oct and Nov.*

Auronzo di Cadore ✉ 32041

*****Auronzo**, Via Roma 30, **t** 0435 400 202, *www.dolomitihotel.com* (*moderate–expensive*). A cosy old place with tennis courts and lake-shore park. *Open Jan–Mar and May–Sept.*

****Vienna**, Via Verona 2, **t** 0435 9394 (*cheap*). An option near the lake, with mountain views.

Cavaliere, Cima Gogna, east of Auronzo, **t** 0435 9834 (*moderate*). A wood-panelled place offering suckling pig and more. *Closed Weds.*

San Candido/Innichen ✉ 39038

*****Orso Grigio**, Via Rainer 2, **t** 0474 913 115, *www.orsohotel.it* (*expensive*). Charming modern rooms in a handsome 18th-century building. *Open mid-June–Sept, Dec–Mar.*

*****Posthotel**, Via Sesto 1, **t** 0474 913 133, *www.posthotel.it* (*expensive*). A central, traditional choice with a games room for children, a Turkish bath, swimming pool and solarium, and excellent local and international cuisine. *Open mid-June–Sept, mid-Dec–Mar.*

Uhrmacher's Weinstübe, Via Tintori 1, **t** 0474 913 158 (*cheap*). A treat for wine or spirit lovers. You can visit the cellar and choose a bottle to go with a snack, or try a glass from one of the 30 or so bottles opened every day. *Closed Weds except in summer.*

Dobbiaco/Toblach ✉ 39034

******Cristallo**, Via S. Giovanni 37, **t** 0474 972 138, *www.hotelcristallo.com* (*expensive*). A fine resort hotel in a beautiful setting, with an indoor pool and sauna. *Open Christmas–Easter, June–mid-Oct.*

Winkelkeller, Via Conte Künigl 8, **t** 0474 972 022 (*moderate*). Refined mountain cuisine. *Closed Weds, Thurs and Oct.*

Selva di Cadore ✉ 32020

*****Giglio Rosso**, Pescul, **t** 0437 720 310, *www.lavalfiorentina.it* (*cheap–moderate*). A fine place to stay and to eat. The kitchen does great mulberry risotto, and turkey in beer.

Àlleghe/Caprile ✉ 32022

******Alla Posta**, Piazza Dogliani 19, Caprile **t** 0437 721 171, *www.hotelposta.com* (*moderate*). The most prestigious hotel in the area, with comfortable rooms (some *cheap* and some *expensive*), an indoor pool, a sauna and a good restaurant. *Open 20 Dec–15 Apr, 15 June–30 Sept.*

*****Coldai**, Via Coldai 13, **t** 0437 523 305 (*cheap–moderate*).Lovely lake views and pleasant rooms. *Closed May–mid-June, Oct, Nov.*

****Marmolada**, Corso Veneto 27, **t** 0437 721 107 (*cheap*). A simple but adequate option. *Closed May and Oct.*

The Western Dolomites: Trentino

The autonomous province of Trentino encompasses the western Dolomites, as beautiful as the eastern mountains, especially the Val di Fassa and the isolated but hauntingly majestic Brenta Group, west of the Adige. Unlike the Alto Adige/Süd Tirol further north, Trentino is mostly Italian in language and heritage, sprinkled with a Ladin minority in the valleys. Trento is a fine little art city, worth a day on its own.

From Verona to Trento: Val Lagarina and Rovereto

Following the Adige up from Verona, the A22 and SS12 enter Trentino near **Avio**, dominated by the proud 14th-century **Castello di Sabbionara** (*open Tues–Sun Feb–Sept 10–1 and 2–6; Oct and Dec 10–1 and 2–5; adm*). Its guardhouse preserves a wonderful fresco cycle of battling knights, while in the keep the frescoes depict scenes of courtly love. It also has a restaurant (***t** 0464 684 299*).

Further up the Adige, past a sea of vineyards, **Rovereto**, 'the Athens of the Trentino', is an evocative old place, the second city of the Trentino, built around an imposing Venetian castle; between 1416 and 1487 the city formed the northern extent of the Serenissima, before the Trentini, with the aid of the Tyroleans, shoved the Venetians back to Verona. This area was also hotly contested in the First World War, and the castle contains an extensive **war museum** devoted primarily to that conflict (*open Mar–Nov Tues–Sun 8.30–12.30 and 2–6; July–Sept Tues–Fri 10–6, Sat and Sun 9.30–6.30; adm*). Cannons from each of the 19 belligerents were melted down to make the largest ringing bell in the world, the **Campana dei Caduti**, located in the southern quarter of Rovereto; it rings in memory of the fallen every day at sundown.

The futurist Fortunato Depero (1892–1960) worked for many years in the town, and bequeathed it the **Museo Depero**, Via della Terra 53 (*closed for restoration, probably until 2007/8*), near the castle, a striking little museum designed by the artist as a showcase for his tapestries, puppets and paintings. It's under the auspices of the brand-new and very stylish **MART** museum (***t** 800 397 760*) at Corso Bettini 43, where much of Depero's work is on show, alongside a broad-based and frequently changing series of exhibitions.

Getting Around

Frequent **trains** and **buses** follow the Adige from Verona to Trento, stopping at main towns.

Tourist Information

Rovereto: Corso Rosmini 6/a, **t** 0464 430 363, *www.apt.rovereto.tn.it*.
Folgaria: Via Roma 62, **t** 0464 721 133.

Where to Stay and Eat

Rovereto ✉ 38068

*****Rovereto**, Corso Rosmini 82/d, **t** 0464 435 522, *www.hotelrovereto.it* (*expensive*). A fine central hotel, with comfortable rooms in a variety of styles, and an excellent restaurant, **Novecento**, featuring regional dishes and wonderful homemade pasta, and offering a vegetarian menu. *Closed Sun.*

Al Borgo, Via Garibaldi 13, **t** 0464 436 300 (*very expensive*). A surprisingly sophisticated little restaurant in the heart of town, offering delicious dishes such as ham and spinach in puff pastry, risotto with lemon, and turbot with artichokes, followed by fantastic desserts. There's piano music in the evening. *Closed Sun eve and Mon, part of Feb and July.*

Lavarone/Folgaria ✉ 38046

*****Hotel Al Lago**, Frazione Chiesa, Lavarone, **t** 0464 78322, *www.hotelallago.com* (*moderate*). A hotel in a pretty lakeside setting, with an indoor swimming pool. Freud once stayed here.

*****Caminetto**, near the Bertoldi chairlift, Lavarone, **t** 0464 783 214 (*moderate*). A charming, cosy hotel with lots of wood and flowers. *Open Dec–mid-Apr, mid-June–Sept.*

L'Antica Pineta, Via de Gasperi 66, Folgaria, **t** 0464 720 327 (*moderate*). A good place offering comforting dishes such as polenta with melted Asiago cheese.

The Western Dolomites

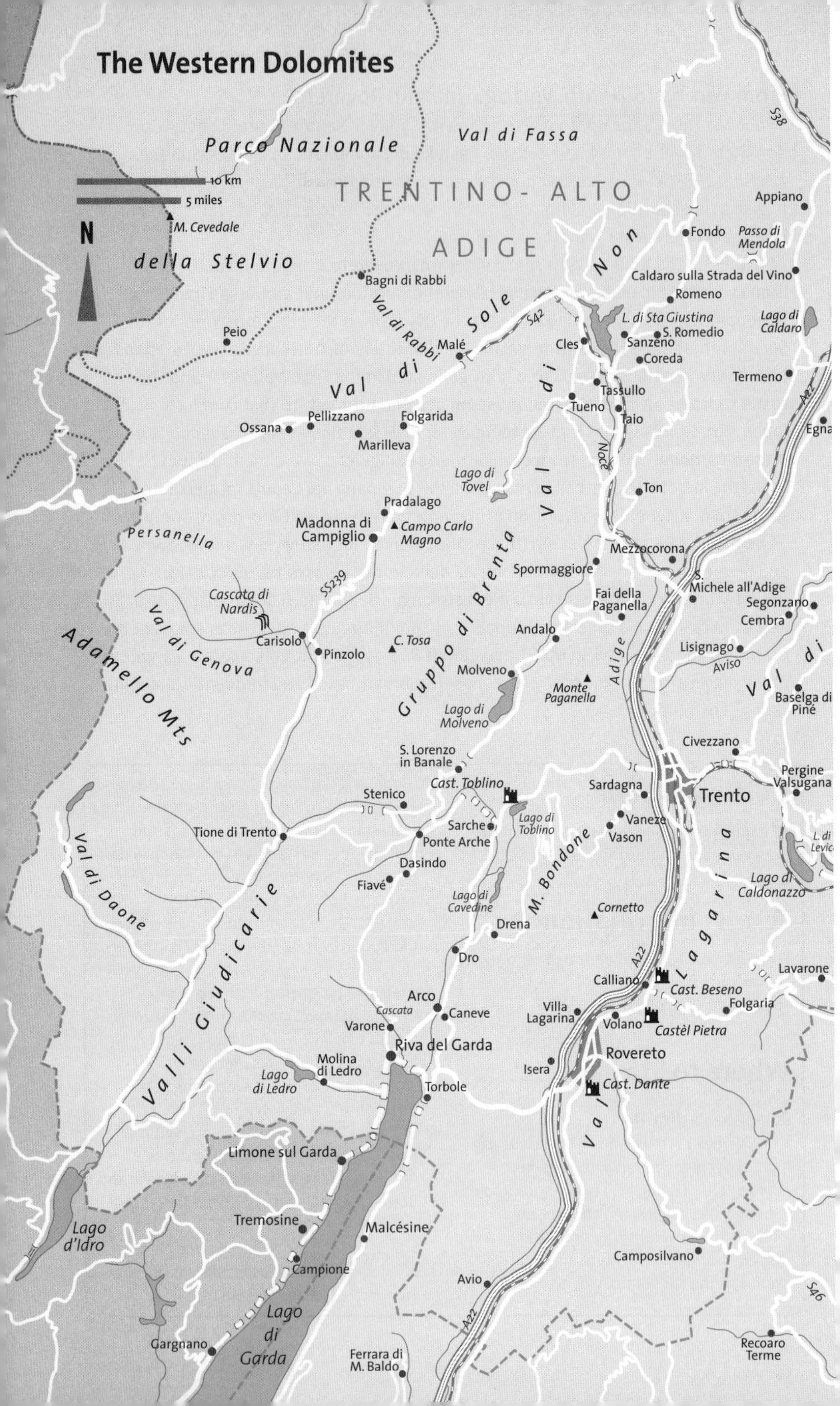

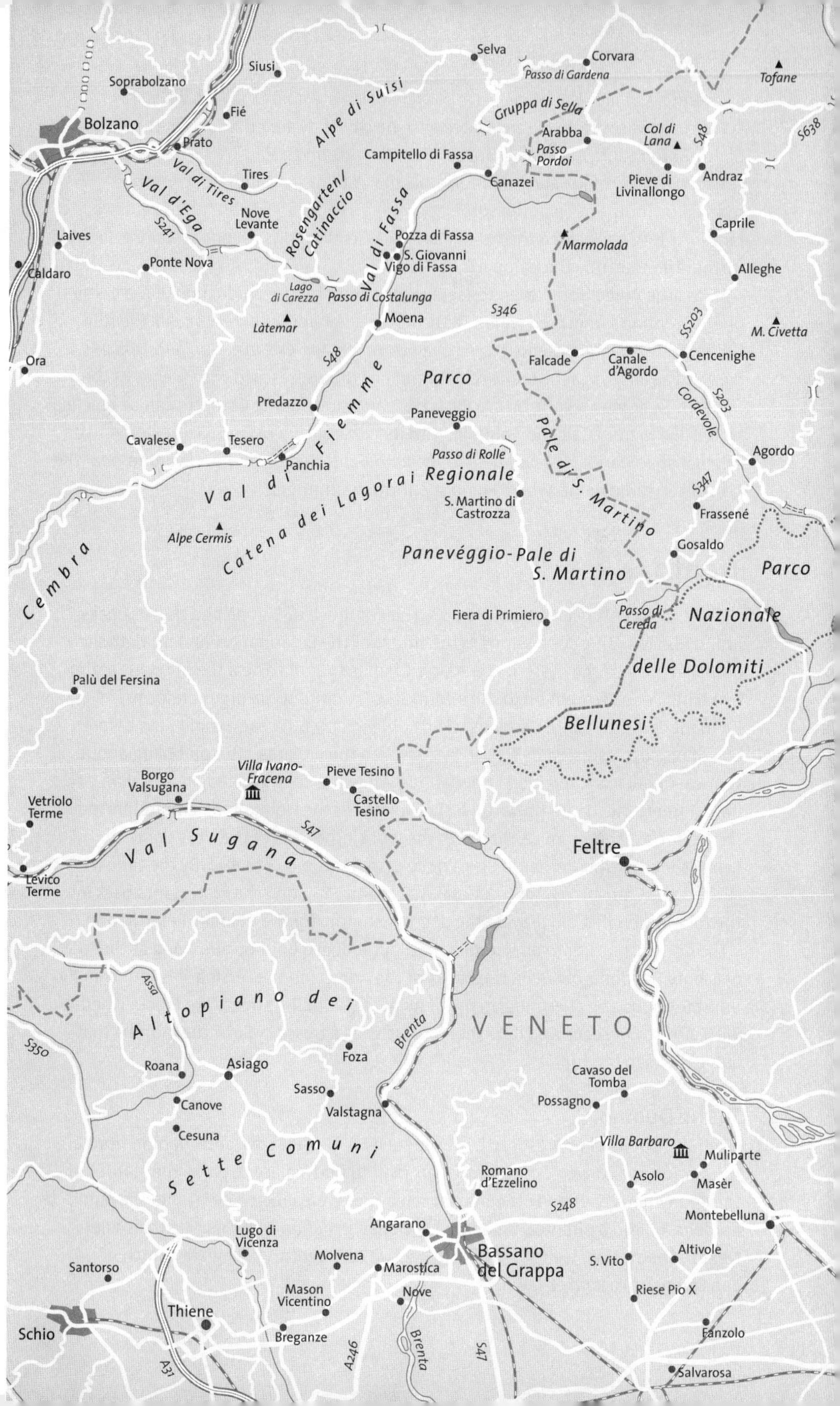
Selva
Corvara
Siusi
Soprabolzano
Passo di Gardena
Tofane
Fié
Gruppa di Sella
Bolzano
Alpe di Suisi
Col di Lana
S48
S638
Arabba
Prato
Passo Pordoi
Campitello di Fassa
Val di Tires
Canazei
Pieve di Livinallongo
Andraz
Tires
Val d'Ega
Rosengarten/ Catinaccio
Val di Fassa
S241
Nove Levante
Caprile
Marmolada
Pozza di Fassa
Laives
S. Giovanni
Vigo di Fassa
Ponte Nova
Alleghe
Caldaro
Lago di Carezza
Passo di Costalunga
S346
Làtemar
Moena
M. Civetta
SS203
S48
Ora
Falcade
Canale d'Agordo
Cencenighe
Parco
Cordevole
S203
Predazzo
Paneveggio
Pale di S. Martino
Val di Fiemme
Cavalese
Tesero
Agordo
Panchia
Passo di Rolle
Catena dei Lagorai
Regionale
S347
S. Martino di Castrozza
Frassené
Alpe Cermis
Cembra
Panevéggio-Pale di S. Martino
Gosaldo
Parco
Fiera di Primiero
Passo di Cereda
Nazionale
delle Dolomiti
Palù del Fersina
Bellunesi
Villa Ivano-Fracena
Borgo Valsugana
Pieve Tesino
Castello Tesino
Vetriolo Terme
S47
Val Sugana
Feltre
Levico Terme
Assa
Altopiano dei
Brenta
VENETO
S350
Foza
Roana
Asiago
Cavaso del Tomba
Sasso
Canove
Possagno
Valstagna
Cesuna
Sette Comuni
Villa Barbaro
Muliparte
Romano d'Ezzelino
Asolo
Masèr
S248
Montebelluna
Angarano
Lugo di Vicenza
Bassano del Grappa
Molvena
Altivole
Marostica
S. Vito
Santorso
Mason Vicentino
Nove
Riese Pio X
Thiene
Schio
Breganze
Fanzolo
A246
Brenta
S47
A31
Salvarosa

Rovereto was also the home town of archaeologist Paolo Orsi, who willed his statues and vases from Magna Graecia to the city. They are on display in the **Museo Civico**, Borgo Santa Caterina 43 (*open Tues–Sat 9–12 and 3–6*).

Just southeast of Rovereto, you can walk the 'Path of the Dinosaurs', which is marked by footprints planted some 200 million years ago. The 'Path of Peace', a long-distance walk along the front line of the First World War, ends at Mount Zugna, further the south, by the Campana dei Caduti.

Across the Adige from Rovereto, **Isera** is the centre for the production of Marzemino, one of Trentino's finest red wines. To the north, seen from the Trento road, the ruined but imposing **Castel Beseno** (***t*** *0464 834 600; open Apr–Oct Tues–Sun 9–12 and 2–5.30; adm*) is the largest castle in the region, and has rooms frescoed with scenes of the months. Two small resorts on a 3,280ft plateau below Monte Cornetto can be reached by the SS350 from Calliano: **Folgaria**, with its 17th-century Maso Spilzi, restored to its original appearance (***t*** *0464 721 133; open June–Sept*), and the larger **Lavarone**, near the lake of the same name, where Freud spent three summers.

Trento

In the 16th century Emperor Charles V, ruler of much of Europe and the Americas, found his Germanic possessions in the throes of the Reformation, and his Catholic domains braced for a hysterical reaction. Charles sought to heal the rift in his realm by asking Pope Clement VII to call a council to look into some urgent reforms. Clement demurred until Charles sacked Rome in 1527, but years would pass before one of his successors, Paul III, actually convoked the prelates, after quibbling about venue – Charles wanted it on Imperial turf, while the Pope insisted on an Italian city. Italian Trento, ruled by a powerful bishop-prince in the Holy Roman Empire, proved to be the perfect compromise, thanks to the lobbying efforts of the city's great Renaissance patron, Bernardo Cles, Prince-Bishop from 1514 to 1539. By the time it started, the Council of Trent (1545–63) was too late to bring the Protestants back into the fold, although it did provide the doctrinal ammo for the Counter-Reformation.

The Council put Trento on Europe's map, but it doesn't put on airs. Lying at the foot of Monte Bondone, between the banks of the Adige and the Fersina, it is refreshingly unpretentious and charming; many of its gently winding streets are embellished with alfresco frescoes, and its bishop's palace has a fresco cycle of the months that alone is worth the trip.

To the Duomo

Trento's points of interest can easily be seen on foot. **Piazza Dante**, right in front of the station, is a convenient place to start (and to find a place to park); the statues of the eponymous poet and other Italian celebrities were erected here amid the public gardens in 1896 by Trento's irredentist societies, in defiance of their Austrian rulers. Next to the station itself stands the attractive 12th-century collegiate church of **San Lorenzo** in a sunken lawn.

Getting Around

The **bus** station and FS **railway** station are on Piazza Dante. Atesina buses, **t** 0461 983 627, go up all the Trentino valleys. Trento-Malè station, with trains up the Val di Non to Cles and Marilleva, is 500m from the main station on Via Seconda da Trento 7, **t** 0461 238 350.

Tourist Information

Trento: Via Marici 2, on the corner with Via Belenzani, **t** 0461 983 880.

Trentino region: Via Romagnosi 3, **t** 0461 839 000, freephone **t** 1678 45034, UK information service, **t** 44 20 8879 1405, *www.trentino.to*.

Where to Stay

Expensive

********Accademia**, Vicolo Collico 4/6, near Santa Maria Maggiore, **t** 0461 233 600, *www.accademiahotel.it*. Comfortable wood-panelled rooms and an excellent restaurant with a monthly-changing menu.

********Buonconsiglio**, Via Romagnosi 16/18, **t** 0461 272 888, *www.hotelbuonconsiglio.it*. A fine place in the historic centre.

Moderate

******Aquila d'Oro**, Via Belenzani 76, **t** 0461 986 282, *www.aquiladoro.it*. Extremely comfy rooms right in the centre, and a café with tables spilling out into the street.

******America**, Via Torre Verde 50, **t** 0461 983 010, *www.hotelamerica.it*. A comfortable modern hotel near the train station.

******Villa Madruzzo**, Via Ponte Alto 26, Cognola, 3km east of town, **t** 0461 986 220, *www.villamadruzzo.it*. A 19th-century villa in a park, with modern, comfy rooms, fine views and a good traditional restaurant. One of the nicest places to stay if you have a car.

/Hotel Venezia/Albergo Garni**, Via Belenzani 70 and Piazza Duomo 45, **t** 0461 234 559, **t** 0461 234 144 *www.hotelveneziatn.it*. Adjoining hotels run by the same delightful family: the Via Belenzani side (2-star) has a lift, the Piazza Duomo side (1-star) is the older building, with stupendous views of the cathedral and nicer rooms. Both cost the same.

Eating Out

Trentino cuisine is basically alpine; popular dishes include *canederli*, gnocchi made from breadcrumbs, egg, cheese and bacon; *patao*, a minestrone of yellow flour and sauerkraut; and *osei scampadi*, veal 'birds' with sage.

Chiesa, Palazzo Wolkenstein, Parco San Marco (near Castello di Buonconsiglio), **t** 0461 238 766 (*very expensive*). Trento's most famous restaurant, with an 'Apple Party Menu' with Trentino's best-loved fruit in every course. There's also a 1500s menu based on the favourite dishes of Bernardo Cles, and a long wine list. Booking essential. *Closed Sun*.

Osteria a Le Due Spade, Via Don Rizzi 11, **t** 0461 234 343 (*very expensive*). A delightful 1545 dining room with mosaics, offering refined dishes. *Closed Sun, and Mon lunch*.

Al Vo', Vicolo del Vo' 11 (off Via Torre Verde) **t** 0461 985 374 (*moderate*). Good regional dishes and unusual specialities. *Closed Sun and 2wks July*.

Lo Scrigno del Duomo, Piazza Duomo 29, **t** 0461 220 030 (*moderate*). A stylish wine bar in a Renaissance *palazzo*, serving snacks to accompany its excellent vintages. The sumptuous cellar restaurant (*very expensive*) offers the likes of pigeon carpaccio with mountain honey and *porcini*. *Closed Mon*.

Forst, Oss Mazzurana 38, **t** 0461 235 590 (*cheap*). A popular place to drink beer and local wines in a 16th-century palace in the middle of town. Try pizza *tirolese* (with mushrooms and *speck*) or a *piatto trentino* (a plate of local specialities). *Closed Mon and July*.

From San Lorenzo, Via Andrea Pozzo and Via delle Orfane lead to the gracious pink **Santa Maria Maggiore** (1520), a simple and elegant Renaissance church with ornate portals, commissioned by Bernardo Cles. It was large enough to be used for several sittings of the Council of Trent, has a beautiful organ gallery by Vincenzo Grandi (1534) and *Dispute with the Doctors* by Giambattista Moroni from Bergamo.

One block east of Santa Maria Maggiore runs **Via Belenzani**, forced through the medieval quarters by Bernardo Cles who wanted a proper straight street to the cathedral. It is lined with fine palaces: the best, **Palazzo Pona Geremia**, is entirely covered with recently restored 16th-century frescoes of the locals receiving the Emperor Maximilian and mythological subjects. Via Belenzani ends with the handsome porticoed **Casa Cazuffi**, decorated with monochrome frescoes from the 1530s. These overlook **Piazza Duomo** and the 18th-century **Fountain of Neptune**, the region's sea god symbol – not an obvious mascot until you focus on the trident he wields and remember the city's Roman name, *Tridentum*. Recently restored remains of the Roman city can be viewed in the Piazza Cesare Battisti, below the Teatro Sociale in the heart of old Trento (***t** 0461 230 171; open Tues–Sun June–Aug 10–12 and 2.30–7; Sept–May 10–12 and 2–6; adm*). There you can see a 50-metre stretch of Roman road and several craft workshops.

The Duomo and Museo Diocesano Tridentino

Trento's beautifully cleaned and restored **Duomo** with its newly gleaming dome was designed in the 13th century and completed in 1515. Although it took 300 years to build, the style is all monumental Romanesque, richly decorated with galleries along its three apses and dome. The Council of Trent held its three major sessions here, and its decrees were blessed before the huge crucifix, which is still there in a right-hand chapel. The baldaquin over the high altar is a replica of St Peter's. Excavations unearthed a 6th-century basilica under the Duomo, the first home of the relics of Trento's patron, San Vigilio.

Next to the cathedral, the **Palazzo Pretorio**, crowned with swallowtail battlements, and a medieval **Torre Civica** house the excellent **Museo Diocesano Tridentino** (*open Weds–Mon 9–12.30 and 2.30–6; adm; includes access to excavations in cathedral*), renovated, and opened by John Paul II in 1995. There are paintings of the Council of Trent; a 16th-century portrayal of a Mass of St Gregory, its nonchalant congregation including a large band of pious skeletons; three 12th-century ivory caskets made by Islamic craftsmen; and four charming 15th-century wooden altarpieces from the Val di Non, portraying three local martyrs in scenes observed by a man in a beaver hat. The greatest prize, a cycle of six early 15th-century Flemish tapestries by Peter Van Aelst were brought to Trento by Bernardo Cles.

Castello di Buonconsiglio and its Museums

From Via Belenzani, Via Roma/Via Gian Antonio Manci leads to the magnificent residence of the bishop-princes, **Castello di Buonconsiglio** (***t** 0461 233 770; open Tues–Sun 10–6; adm exp*). Because of Trento's strategic location on the main highway to Rome, the medieval German emperors sought to keep the city's favour by granting its bishops a near-regal temporal status. Their castle consists of two buildings – the 13th-century Castelvecchio, with its Venetian Gothic loggia, and the Magno Palazzo, added by Bernardo Cles (1528–36). Today they house the provincial museum of art: medieval manuscripts, statues (especially fine wooden 15th- and 16th-century wooden sculptures) and paintings, although these are overshadowed by the castle's

Vigilio and the Ciusien-Gobj Masquerade

Vigilio was a Roman patrician who studied in Athens, then moved to Trento with his family, where he was made bishop. His persuasive powers were good enough to convert his diocese, but when he went further afield to the Val Rendena and tipped over a statue of Saturn he was stoned to death.

He is celebrated every 20–26 June with an enthusiastic *Palio dell'Oca*, in which teams from each of the city's districts don 17th-century costumes and race down the Adige on rafts, trying to slip a ring over the neck of a papier-mâché goose suspended over the river. The climactic moment comes on 26 June, commemorating the day back in the Middle Ages when Trento hired workers from Feltre to reinforce the town walls. Food supplies being low, Trento's bishop realized that the city could not afford to feed the workers and sent them home – only the Feltrese returned in the night to raid the stores. The ensuing battle is re-enacted in costume in Piazza Duomo – the *Ciusi* are from Feltre, and they have five chances to break the ranks of Trento's *Gobj* to make off with the prize: a pot of hot, bubbling polenta.

own 16th-century frescoes by Marcello Fogolino, Gerolamo Romanino and Dosso Dossi. Dossi painted the Olympian gods to conform to Counter-Reformation modesty levels – the gods model what look like turn-of-the-19th-century bathing costumes, and the goddesses resemble Tarzan's Jane.

Best of all are the ravishing, detailed **frescoes of the months** in the Torre dell'Aquila, painted around the year 1400. While the nobility sports and flirts in the foreground, peasants perform their month-by-month labours, tending their flocks, making cheese, planting and harvesting, and making wine. One scene has the oldest-known depiction of Trento, dominated by the castle itself.

Buonconsiglio also has an historical collection from the Napoleonic era to World War II; the idea was suggested in 1903 by local patriot Cesare Battisti, who, 13 years later, was executed for high treason in this same castle, by the Austrians. His and his companions' cells, the courtroom, and the ditch where they were shot and hanged, are shrines. Battisti's memorial is a marble circle of columns on the hill over the Adige. The present is illustrated by the **Galleria Civica d'Arte Contemporaneo** (*open Tues–Sun 10–12 and 4–7; adm*), which hosts temporary exhibitions.

More Museums: Art and Planes

Prince-Bishop Cristoforo Madruzzo did not feel quite at ease in the Castello di Buonconsiglio, and built a suburban residence on the Adige, the Palazzo delle Albere, ('of the poplars'), which now shelters **MART-Trento**, Via R. da Sanseverino 45 (***t** 0461 944 888)*, which has shows in parallel with MART in Rovereto (*see* p.415).

The **Museo dell'Aeronautica Gianni Caproni**, Via Lidorno 3, by Trento's airport (*open Tues–Fri 9–1 and 2–5, Sat and Sun 10–1 and 2–6; adm*) began in 1929 as the private collection of Gianni Caproni, one of Italy's leading aviation engineers in the 1910s and 20s, whose aviation factory in Trento only closed in the 1950s. It contains a number of unique specimens, as well as a model of Leonardo da Vinci's flying machine.

Around Trento: Monte Bondone and Lake Caldonazzo

The slopes of Trento's own mountain, Bondone, can be easily reached by road or cable car (*every 15–30mins daily 7am–10.30pm*), departing from Ponte di San Lorenzo in Trento (behind the bus station) and climbing as far as **Sardagna**. At least three buses a day continue on to **Vaneze** and **Vason**, both ski resorts; from Vason another cable car ascends to one of Bondone's three summits (6,881ft). Further on, **Viotte** has an Alpine refuge and **Botanical Garden** (*t 0461 948 050; open daily June and Sept 9–12 and 2–5, July and Aug until 6*), one of the richest in Europe, founded in 1938 on the banks of two artificial lakes and planted with more than 2,000 species of high-altitude flora.

Another popular excursion is east up the Val Sugana along the Brenta to warm **Lago di Caldonazzo**, 'Trento's Lido', ideal for swimming, sailing and windsurfing. From lakeside **Vetriolo Terme** you can hike up to the summit of Panarotta for splendid views over Caldonazzo and its equally warm neighbour, **Lake Levico**.

East of Trento

The magic mountains wait, whether you turn east, west or north of Trento. San Martino di Castrozza and Paneveggio National Park are the main attractions to the east, along with two lovely valleys and a score of lovely lakes.

Val di Fiemme and Val di Fassa

These two northeasternmost valleys of Trentino, running between the Pale di San Martino, Rosengarten and the western slopes of the Marmolada, are among the most stunning and well-known among the cross-country skiing fraternity. From Trento the road ascends the Val di Cembra, passing through a striking region of rocks eroded into spiky 'pyramids' near **Segonzano**. The once autonomous **Val di Fiemme** begins at **Cavalese**, where the elected *Regolani* held their parliament by the parish church; you can still see their stone benches, the **Banc de la Reson**. The *Magnifica Comunità* of Cavalese still has considerable say in local affairs, running the Val di Fiemme from the grand old frescoed **Palazzo della Comunità**, rebuilt in the 1500s by Bernardo Cles. Inside, a **museum** (*t 0462 340 365; open Mon–Sat July–mid-Sept 4.30–7.30*) documents Fiemme's proud past, and has works by the 17th–18th-century Fiemme school, a group of harmless painters who travelled about the smaller courts of Europe. A cable car from Cavalese ascends to **Mount Cermis** (7,311ft).

Other places to aim for in the Val di Fiemme include **Tesero**, a village with a 15th-century bridge, where furniture- and instrument-makers still ply their old trades, perhaps too well – the chapel of **San Rocco** (1528) is frescoed with a 'Sunday Christ', surrounded by all the tools that are taboo on the Sabbath. In **Predazzo** the **Civico Museo di Geologia** (*call t 0462 502 392 for open times*), which was founded in 1899, contains Dolomitic rocks and marine fossils; there are geological paths at Doss Cappèl, reached by the Predazzo chairlift. Predazzo is the turn-off for San Martino di Castrozza (*see* p.424).

Tourist Information

Cavalese: Via F.lli Bronzetti 60, **t** 0462 241 111, *www.aptfiemme.info*
Moena: Piazza C Battisti 33, **t** 0462 573 122, *www.fassa.com*
Canazei: Via Streda de Dolèda 105, **t** 0462 602 446, *www.fassa.com*
San Martino and Primiero: Via Passo Rolle 165, **t** 0439 768 867, *www.sanmartino.com*

Where to Stay and Eat

Cavalese ✉ 38033

★★★**San Valier**, **t** 0462 341 285, *www.italiaasc.it/az/sanvalier* (*moderate*). A hotel in a pretty setting, with an indoor pool and sauna. *Closed Nov.*

★★★**Sporting-Club Grand Chalet des Neiges**, **t** 0462 341 650 (*cheap–moderate*). A superbly positioned hotel on the pistes of Mt Cermis, at 6,562ft, with a pool and sauna. *Open mid-Dec–mid-Apr.*

★★★**Villa Trunka Lunka**, Via de Gasperi 4, **t** 0462 340 233 (*cheap–moderate*). A very pleasant 24-room hotel with a sauna and a solarium.

Cantuccio, Via Unterberger 14, **t** 0462 340 140 (*expensive*). A good place to try *caronzèi*, ravioli filled with potatoes, *puzzone* cheese, nutmeg and chives and topped with cheese, sage and poppyseeds. There's also a mean rabbit in garlic cream and artichokes. *Closed Mon eve and Tues out of season.*

Moena ✉ 38035

Moena is famous for its *puzzone* or 'stinky cheese', which is great with toasted polenta.

★★★★**Monzoni**, Passo di San Pellegrino above Moena, **t** 0462 573 352, *www.hotelmonzoni.it* (*expensive*). An old mountain refuge converted into a hotel, with an emphasis on nightlife and fun. *Open Christmas–mid-Apr and mid-July–Aug.*

★★★**Catinaccio Rosengarten**, Via Someda 6, **t** 0462 573 235, *www.hotelCR.com* (*moderate–expensive*). A hotel near the centre, with an indoor pool and plenty of mountain atmosphere. *Open Christmas–mid-Apr and July–mid-Sept.*

★★★**Post Hotel**, Piazza Italia, **t** 0462 573 760, *www.posthotelmoena.it* (*moderate*). A classy choice, with fine rooms and a good restaurant, **Tyrol**. *Open Dec–Easter and mid-June–mid-Sept.*

Malga Panna, Via Costalunga 29, **t** 0462 573 489 (*very expensive*). One of the best restaurants in the region, with various menus ranging from selections of local cheeses and cold meats to a *degustazione* of trout, rabbit, *tortelli ai porcini*, *speck*, venison and strawberries. *Open Dec–Apr and July–Sept; closed Mon.*

Canazei ✉ 38032

★★★**La Perla**, Via Pareda 103, **t** 0462 602 453, *www.hotellaperla.net* (*expensive*). A comfy hotel in a panoramic position near the ski slopes, with a pool and sauna. *Closed Nov.*

★★★**Bellevue**, Via Dolomiti 182, **t** 0462 601 104, *www.unionhotelscanazei.it* (*moderate–expensive*). Great mountain views and pleasant rooms.

★★**Dolomites Inn**, Via Arntersies 35, Penia, **t** 0462 602 212, *www.dolomitesinn.com* (*moderate–expensive*). A decent little place with two squash courts. *Open Dec–Apr and mid-June–mid-Sept.*

El Ciasel, Via Dolomiti 197, **t** 0462 62190 (*expensive*). A good restaurant specializing in *strangolapreti* ('priest-stranglers'), game dishes and polenta.

San Martino di Castrozza ✉ 38058

★★★★**Des Alpes**, Via Passo Rolle, **t** 0439 769 069, *www.hoteldesalpes.it* (*expensive–very expensive*). The place to soak up a turn-of-the-19th-century Dolomites atmosphere. *Open Christmas–Mar, July–mid Sept.*

★★★**San Martino**, Via Passo Rolle 277, **t** 0439 68011, *www.hotelsanmartino.it* (*expensive*). A decent hotel with an indoor swimming pool and a sauna.

★★★**Venezia**, Passo di Rolle, north of San Martino, **t** 0439 68315, *www.passorolle.it* (*moderate*). A great base for the National Park, with fantastic views across the valley.

★★**Suisse**, Via Dolomiti 1, **t** 0439 68087 (*cheap*). A simple but comfortable B&B 5mins walk up the hill from San Martino.

Malga Ces, Loc. Malga Ces, **t** 0439 68223 (*expensive*). *Canederli*, polenta with venison, village cheeses, fruits of the forest and more. *Open Dec–mid-Apr and mid-June–Sept.*

Otherwise, continue straight into the beautiful **Val di Fassa**; **Moena**, the largest town and winter sports centre, is the 'boundary'. It has two churches of note: the large 12th-century **San Vigilio**, with paintings by local artist Valentino Rovisi, a pupil of Tiepolo; and **San Volfango**, richly frescoed by one of the anonymous, itinerant artists who travelled around the Trentino in the 15th century.

Seven *comuni* in the Val di Fassa preserve their Ladin language (a cross between Celtic and Latin introduced by Roman settlers; *see* p.427) and culture, especially **Vigo di Fassa**, site of the Ladin Cultural Institute and several *tabià* – the Ladini's traditional wooden cabins. A 20-minute walk leads up to the Gothic church of **Santa Giuliana a Vigo.** Three chairlifts from nearby Pozzo di Fassa up the flanks of Rosengarten leave you at the path to the **Torri del Vaiolet**, a sheer triple pinnacle.

Campitello di Fassa, the next town up the valley, has a *funivia* to the **Col Rodella** (8,151ft), a famous viewpoint and winter sports centre. Further up the Val di Fassa, **Canazei**, rebuilt after a fire in 1912, is the base for exploring the other magnificent peaks in the area – Marmolada, Sassolungo and Sella. The passes above lead to Arabba and Cortina, or north into the Val Gardena (*see* p.433).

San Martino di Castrozza and Paneveggio National Park

Predazzo is the main turn-off for the pinnacle-crowned **Pale di San Martino** (Altars of St Martin; 10,466ft), the principal group of the southern Dolomites. **San Martino di Castrozza** at its feet is the biggest and best-equipped resort south of Cortina d'Ampezzo, but don't expect much character; the Austrians demolished the medieval town in the First World War, leaving only the ancient church. A popular excursion is the ascent by cable car and chairlift to the summit of **Rosetta** (8,997ft).

The best scenery around San Martino is within the **Parco Naturale Paneveggio–Pale di San Martino**, a wilderness of meadows, streams, wildflowers and wildlife. Access is from the visitors' centre in **Paneveggio**, north of San Martino, beyond the **Passo di Rolle**. Two paths take in tremendous vistas, not only of the Pale di San Martino, but also the distinctive peaks of **Marmolada**, **Pelmo** and **Civetta**. The forests here provided Stradivarius and co. with the wood for their fiddles until the Venetians replanted trees in straight lines for masts and punished tree-poachers with death. Rules are still strict: there are only a few campsites and no one may stay longer than 24 hours.

The Pale di San Martino are ringed by a scenic road. The southern route, via Agordo (SS347), climbs through the forests of Gosaldo to the **Passo di Cereda** and **Fiera di Primiero**, with a 15th-century centre and good skiing. From there it's an hour's walk up to sinister ruined **Castel di Pietra**, built, according to legend, by Attila the Hun.

West of Trento: the Brenta Dolomites

The Brenta Group, though a bit distant from the other Dolomites, is just as marvellous and strange, and a challenge for experienced alpinists, although there are numerous less demanding walks for ordinary folk. The Adamello–Brenta Park is the last refuge of brown bears in the Alps, but you'd have to be very lucky, if that's the word, to see one. The following section circles them, a round trip of 175 kilometres from Trento.

Around Monte Paganella

To reach Monte Paganella, the eastern flank of the Brenta group, head north to **San Michele all'Adige**, home to the **Museo degli Usi e Costumi della Gente Trentina**, a fascinating ethnographic collection in a former Augustinian monastery (*open Tues–Sun 9–12.30 and 2.30–6; adm*). Nearby **Mezzocorona** produces Teròldego; the 'prince of Trentino wines' and lies at the start of the Bolzano wine road (*see* p.433).

From there follow the signs to three well-equipped resorts, served by four buses a day from Trento: **Fai della Paganella**, **Andalo** (both with cable cars up Monte Paganella – 6,970ft) and **Molveno**, a good base for hiking. From Molveno the road goes south to **Ponte Arche** and **Fiavé**, where a 5,000-year-old settlement of lake dwellers was discovered. East of it is picture-postcard **Lake Toblino**, with its enchanting 12th-century castle on a tiny peninsula amid trees supposedly planted by Attila the Hun.

Tourist Information

Molveno: **t** 0461 586 924.
Pinzolo: **t** 0465 442 000.
Madonna di Campiglio: Via Pradalago 4, **t** 0465 442 000, *www.campiglio.net*.
Folgarida: **t** 0463 986 113, *www.valdisole.net*.
Malè: Viale Marconi 7, **t** 0463 901 280.

Where to Stay and Eat

San Michele all'Adige ✉ 38010

Da Silvio, Via Nazionale 1, Masetto de Faedo, **t** 0461 650 324 (*expensive*). An imaginative modern restaurant. Try *altamira* – mixed meats grilled at your table. *Closed Sun eve, Mon, and part of Jan and June.*

Molveno ✉ 38018

*****Belvedere**, Via Nazionale 9, **t** 0461 586 933, *www.belvedereonline.com* (*expensive*). Fine rooms (some *moderate*, some *very expensive*) with lovely views over the lake and mountains, plus an indoor pool and solarium. *Open Christmas, Feb and Apr–Oct.*

*****Miralago**, Piazza Scuole 3, **t** 0461 586 935, *www.miralagohotel.com* (*moderate*). An older hotel with a garden, an outdoor heated pool and a superb terrace.

Madonna di Campiglio ✉ 38084

This is the one resort in the Brenta Dolomites with accommodation and facilities to please the most demanding customers; prices are correspondingly high.

******Golf Hotel**, Passo Carlo Magno, **t** 0465 441 003, *www.golfhotelcampiglio.it* (*expensive–very expensive*). The one-time summer residence of the Habsburg emperors, now a beautiful hotel with a golf course. *Open mid-Dec–Mar and mid-June–mid-Sept.*

******Spinale Club Hotel**, Via Monte Spinale 39, **t** 0465 441 116, *www.effetravel.com* (*expensive–very expensive*). An elegantly appointed hotel with a large indoor pool. Children are very well catered for. *Open Dec–Apr and June–Sept.*

****Gianna**, Via Vallesinella 16, **t** 0465 41106, *www.hotelgianna.it* (*expensive*). A family-run hotel with a bus every half-hour into town and up to the ski lifts. *Open Dec–Easter and July–Sept.*

*****Palù**, Via Vallesinella 4, **t** 0465 441 695, *www.hotelpalu.com* (*moderate*). An older hotel with blazing fires in winter. *Open Dec–Easter and July–Sept.*

****Hermitage**, Via Castelletto 65, **t** 0465 441 558, *www.hotelchalethermitage.com* (*moderate*). A cosy little place with a fine panoramic terrace and good food. *Open Dec–mid-Apr and July–Sept.*

Artini, Via Cima Tosa 47, **t** 0465 440 122 (*expensive*). A bright modern restaurant specializing in wild mushroom dishes. *Open Dec–Apr and July–Sept.*

Malga Montagnoli, Spinale, **t** 0465 42141 (*expensive*). A restaurant serving up interesting local fare such as venison with redcurrant compote and risotto with mushrooms.

The Valli Giudicarie

The Brenta Group's southern flanks rise over the Giudicarie valleys, encompassing several rivers and torrents running from lake to lake, from Molveno down to Idro. Just south of Molveno, **San Lorenzo in Banale** has a road north up the **Val d'Ambiez** and the Rifugio al Cacciatore, providing a quick route for hikers to approach the highest peaks of the Brenta group. Further down, the Giudicarie is defended by the lovely 12th-century castle at **Stenico**, with some faded but good Renaissance frescoes. Part of it now houses the archaeological collections of the **Trentino Provincial Museum** (*open Tues–Sun Apr–Sept 9–12 and 2–5.30; Oct–Mar until 5; adm*).

One of the Giudicarie's rivers, the Sacra, feeds Lake Garda. The main road follows it up to **Pinzolo**, an attractive town with a cemetery church, **San Vigilio**, frescoed in 1539 by Simone Baschenis with an eerie medieval-style Dance of Death. Placid, businesslike skeletons conduct princes, popes, soldiers and others to their end, with a couplet of elegant poetry for each. More of Baschenis' precise work can be seen inside the church and at **Carisolo**, two kilometres away, where he painted another Danse Macabre on **Santo Stefano**. Frescoes within tell of an apocryphal visit by Charlemagne.

Carisolo is just in the **Val di Genova**, one of the most beautiful valleys in the Alps, once the haunt of ogres and witches, all of whom were turned to stone after the Council of Trent. Part of the **Parco Naturale Adamello–Brenta**, the Val di Genova is graced by the lofty **Cascate di Nardis**, a woodland waterfall flowing from the glacier on **Presanella** (10,673ft) – in Pinzolo you can find a guide to make the ascent. To the east a chairlift (the world's fastest, they claim, so hold on to your hat) rises to the lower slopes of **Cima Tosa**, the highest peak of the Brenta Dolomites.

Madonna di Campiglio

From Pinzolo the SS289 zigzags up to the most important resort in the Brenta Dolomites, the superbly sited **Madonna di Campiglio**, with a ski-jump, 31 lifts, speed-skating, a skating rink and an indoor pool. In summer it offers experienced climbers a chance to test their mettle on ice and a wild, rocky terrain; for walkers it has the most scenic trails. Even if you only get into a chairlift, you can enjoy splendid views from the **Passo del Grostè**, 7,413ft above Madonna to the east, or **Pradalago** to the west. Get the tourist office's map to take the classic walk through the beautiful Val di Brenta and Valsinella just to the south. A far more difficult path, the fabulous **Via Bocchette**, takes in the region's most bizarre naked pinnacles and fantastic cliffs. North of Madonna the road passes through **Passo Campo Carlo Magno**, named after Charlemagne, who stopped here on his way to Rome to receive the Emperor's crown.

Val di Sole

Still circling the Brenta Group, the **Val di Sole** occupies the upper reaches of the Noce River and the Trentino sector of the Stelvio National Park (*see* p.277). Italy's 'Sun Valley' is a cosy region of soft green meadows with lofty Monte Cevedale as a backdrop; valley churches have exterior frescoes by Simone Baschenis and kin; an Annunciation at Pellizzano and a St Christopher at Peio. The scenic roads up the

Val di Peio and **Val di Rabbi** lead into the Stelvio; there is a **park visitors' centre** in Bagni di Rabbi. **Malè** is the site of the **Museo della Civiltà Solandra** (*open daily mid-June–mid-Sept 10–12 and 4–7; call* **t** *0463 901 272 rest of year to arrange a visit*), which is in fact two museums – of handicrafts and agricultural implements. These days, the town is a woodworking centre, and has good skiing in winter.

Down the Val di Non: Lake Santa Giustina to Trento

The wooded Val di Non, the enchanting valley along the lower Noce, produces some of Italy's finest apples, especially Golden Delicious and 'Renetta del Canada', which look more like potatoes. The valley is especially lovely in the spring, when its apple blossoms, meadows and snow-clad mountains glow with colour.

Cles, the main town of the Val di Non (linked by local train to Trento), stands on the large artificial lake of Santa Giustina. Prince-Bishop Bernardo Cles was born in the 11th-century **Castello Cles**, but the most striking building is across the lake, six kilometres from **Sanzeno**: the **Santuario di San Romedio** (*open daily 7.30–6*), reached by a road up a narrow gorge (*bus no.6 from Cles, then a 2km walk*). The hermit Romedio lived as a kind of alpine St Jerome with his pet bear on the cliff; his sanctuary consists of chapels stacked one on top of another down the rock over the centuries. Don't miss the 11th-century barbaric reliefs on the portal, the disarming home-made ex-votos, or the ghastly souvenir shop.

South of Cles a 15-kilometre road leads to **Lago di Tovel** deep in the folds of the Brenta Dolomites. Unlike other mountain lakes celebrated for their sapphire hue, Tovel was until recently famous for its ruby redness at certain periods when a rare algae, *Glenodinium sanguineum*, covered its surface. Nowadays it is perhaps the only place in the world where one regrets that pollution has made the water turn blue.

From Lake Santa Giustina you can head east to Bolzano through the **Passo Mendola** (with a cable car up to the view), or continue down the Val di Non past its orchards and old castles to **Vigo di Ton**, where the **Castel Thun** was transformed into the most sumptuous palace of the Trentino. When restored, it will be a provincial museum; its paintings, long ignored, were recently found to be early 17th-century works by Crespi and the Bologna school. The road continues south to Trento via San Michele all'Adige.

Alto Adige/Süd Tirol

Everything has two names on the sunny side of the Alps. In isolated mountain valleys people speak German and little Italian, while others still converse in Ladin, a language that owes its origins to the days when Tiberius sent Roman soldiers to crush the Celts of the mountain valleys of Switzerland and the Tyrol. Some stayed, and their descendants became known as the Ladini, or Latins: the language they speak is a fusion of Latin and Celtic dialect. In the Middle Ages all were ruled by the bishop of Bressanone and the counts of Tyrol, based near Merano. In 1363 the region passed to the Habsburgs, so northern influence was much stronger here than in Trentino, and when Napoleon gave the Süd Tirol to Austria it had no objection – unlike Trentino.

After the First World War, however, Italy gained Trentino, and in the 1920s it absorbed the lands up to the Brenner Pass as the natural frontier. Mussolini, who was a dedicated cultural imperialist, immediately invented Italian names for all the towns in the Alto Adige and tried to ram the language of Dante down the throats of the inhabitants – until Hitler told him to lay off. Still, things were so bad that in 1939, when German citizenship was offered to anyone who didn't want to be Italian, most people left, leading to severe depopulation of the rural areas.

It was hardly an auspicious beginning, and if it weren't for the Italian vote from Trentino, the southern half of the autonomous region, separatism would have been a serious problem. As far as language goes, the figures are presently 69 per cent German-speaking, 27 per cent Italian and 4 per cent Ladin. Rome has done much to

mollify the region, granting it a great deal of autonomy, and enough economic perks to make it one of the country's wealthiest areas.

Its position at one of the great historical crossroads between north and south, its brilliant alpine scenery, its winter sports and its renowned climatic spa at Merano made the Süd Tirol a tourist destination long before the other Dolomite provinces. The region also has an exceptional collection of frescoes in its castles and churches, and produces fine wines, especially whites – there are some 40 different vines for every inhabitant. Try the light and smooth Riesling Renano, dry and snappy Gewürztraminer, Weissburgunder (Pinot Bianco), Welschriesling (Riesling Italico), Sylvaner (with a dry, delicate perfume) and Müller-Thurgau (light and fruity), all of which may be sampled along the wine road south of Bolzano.

Bolzano/Bozen

Bolzano, the lively, cultured capital of Alto Adige, with its narrow-gabled houses, beer cellars and arcaded streets, is an excellent base for visiting the mountains on either side. On the banks of the Isarco and Talvera, which merge just downstream to form the Adige, it has been an important market town since the Middle Ages.

Piazza Walther, the Duomo and Via dei Portici

Bolzano's cultural fusion manifests itself unexpectedly in its pretty parlour, **Piazza Walther**. In the centre stands a statue of the great *minnesinger* from these parts, Walther von der Vogelweide (1170–1230); at his feet slouch travellers munching on Big Macs. In front of Walther stands Bolzano's Gothic **Duomo**, with its green and yellow roof and pretty tower. The art, however, is a block behind the cathedral in the church of the **Domenicani** (*open Mon–Sat 9.45–5.30*), now the Music Conservatory, where the chapels of San Giovanni and Santa Caterina contain lovely 14th-century Giottoesque frescoes by artists from Padua, the best medieval work in the Alto Adige.

From here Via Goethe leads up to the jovial **Piazza delle Erbe**, the commercial hub, where Neptune and his trident (nicknamed *Gabelwirt* – 'Mine host with fork') watch over the daily fruit and veg market. On Via Argentieri, off Piazza delle Erbe, the 18th-century Palazzo Mercantile houses a **Museo Mercantile** (*open Mon–Sat 10–12.30; adm*), where period furniture and paintings attest to Bolzano's old flair for business.

This is still readily apparent if you return to Piazza delle Erbe to stroll up the main street, **Via dei Portici**, lined with smart shops. Via dei Portici passes the old heart of the city, Piazza del Grano (the former cornmarket) and ends in Piazza Municipio, with the ornate neo-Baroque town hall of 1907. Take Via dei Bottai, a street of beer cellars, to the Casa di Massimiliano (1512), the old Imperial customs house, now the **Museo Provinciale di Scienze Naturali** (*open Tues–Sun 10–6; adm*), with displays on glaciers and the first people to move into the valleys after they melted. From here Via Vintler leads around to Piazza della Madonna and Via dei Francescani, where the church of the **Francescani** (*open Mon–Sat 10–12 and 2.30–6*) has a pretty Gothic cloister, a 14th-century fresco of the Franciscan Doctors, and a beautiful altarpiece of the Nativity, by woodcarver Hans Klocker (1500). The street leads back to Piazza delle Erbe.

Museo Archaeologico dell'Alto Adige: the Ice Man Cometh

On Via Museo, around the corner from Piazza delle Erbe; open Tues–Sun 10–6, Thurs 10– 8; audio guides in English for a small fee.

In 1991 Erika and Helmut Simon were walking along the Similaun Glacier northwest of Merano when they chanced upon a body. There hadn't been an accident or murder there in years: the man they found mummified in the ice had died long before living memory – 5,300 years ago, at the start of the Copper Age. It was the first time that scientists had such an ancient body in such excellent condition, and after years of study and analysis, Ötzi, as he's been baptized, became the magnet of this museum, which opened in 1998. He was about 46 years old, they estimate, an experienced

Getting There and Around

There are **trains** for Trento to the south; Bressanone, Vipiteno, Brenner and Innsbruck to the north; Merano and Malles/Venosta to the northwest; and Brunico, Dobbiaco and Linz to the east, from the FS station, a short way from Piazza Walther down Viale Stazione.

The **bus station**, **t** 1678 46047, is across Via Garibaldi, with connections to Cortina and nearly every town in the Alto Adige.

Tourist Information

Bolzano: Piazza Walther 8, **t** 0471 307 0001/2/3.

Regional office: Piazza Parrochia 11, **t** 0471 993 808, *www.altoadige.com, www.suedtirol.info.*

Alpine information service: **t** 0471 993 809. The Club Alpino Italiano (CAI), Piazza delle Erbe 46, **t** 0471 971 694, *www.cai.it*, can provide information on mountaineering, hiking and organized day-trips.

Where to Stay and Eat

Bolzano/Bozen ✉ 39100

In summer Bolzano can be a sauna.

******Parkhotel Laurin**, Via 4 Laurino, **t** 0471 311 000, *www.laurin.it* (*very expensive–luxury*). A lavish hotel in the Viennese *Jugendstil*, set in a fine old park near the centre. It has a heated pool, a beautiful frescoed bar and the wonderful **Belle Epoque** restaurant.

******Luna-Mondschein**, Via Piave 15, **t** 0471 975 642, *www.hotel-luna.it* (*expensive*). A modern hotel next to a park in the centre, with a restaurant serving Tyrolean classics.

*****Eberle**, Passeggiata Sant'Osvaldo 1, **t** 0471 976 125, *www.hotel-eberle.com* (*moderate–expensive*). A peaceful 11-room hotel outside the centre, with a pool and sauna, and an excellent restaurant.

****Hotel Feichter**, Weintraubengasse 15, **t** 0471 978 768 (*moderate*). A wonderful place with fine rooms, all with balconies.

***Croce Bianca-Weisses Kreuz**, Piazza del Grano 3, **t** 0471 977 552 (*cheap*). A cheerful, welcoming budget option with a lobby café that opens on to the pavement. There are 3 en suite rooms; shared facilities for the rest are a little thin on the ground.

***Klaushof**, Colle 14 (cable car from opposite bank of the Isarco or bus no.11 from the train station), **t** 0471 329 999 (*cheap*). A tranquil old farmhouse with 10 rooms, some en suite.

The local cuisine is a bit more than half Austrian – instead of *prosciutto*, expect *speck* (smoked Tyrolean ham) on pizza. Other specialities are Wienerschnitzel, *sauerkraut, knödel* (breadcrumb dumplings), *Terlaner* (wine soup), apple, cheese, and poppyseed strudels, Sachertorte, and rich mousse.

Amadè, Vicolo Ca' de Bezzi 8 (off Via Cavour), **t** 0471 971 278 (*expensive*). Stylishly prepared Bolzano cuisine. *Closed Sun*.

Batzen Hausl, Andreas Hofer Strasse, **t** 0471 050 950 (*moderate*). A welcoming beer cellar and wine bar with excellent food and regular theatre, cabaret and music.

Cesare, Via Perathoner 15, **t** 0471 976 638 (*moderate*). A fine, central place to tuck into fresh pasta and succulent grilled meats.

Patscheiderhof, Signato, up the cable car (or road) in Renon, **t** 0471 365 267 (*moderate*). A favourite for Sunday lunch, though the traditional home-cooking is better when staff aren't so rushed. *Closed Tues and July*.

Cavallino Bianco/Weisses Rossel, Via dei Bottai 6, **t** 0471 973 267 (*cheap*). A popular and jovial 400-year-old place with an eclectic menu stretching from ham and eggs to *Bolognerschnitzel. Closed Sat eve and Sun*.

Appiano sulla Strada del Vino/ Eppan an der Weinstrasse ✉ 39057

******Schloss Korb**, Missiano, near Bolzano and the wine road, **t** 0471 636 000, *www. highlight-hotels.com/korb* (*expensive–very expensive*). An 11th-century castle surrounded by vines, with heated outdoor and indoor pools, tennis courts and a fine restaurant. *Open Easter–Nov*.

*****Schloss Aichberg**, San Michele, **t** 0471 662 247, *www.aichberg.com* (*expensive*). A hotel in a gorgeous setting amidst endless vineyards, with a pool and a *cantina* in the tower.

Zur Rose, San Michele, **t** 0471 662 249 (*expensive*). A gourmet restaurant in a 12th-century house. *Closed Sun, Mon lunch and July*.

Stroblhof, Via Piganò 25, San Michele, **t** 0471 662 250 (*moderate*). *Schlutzkrapfen* filled with seasonal treats and other regional specialities. *Closed Sun, part of Jan and June*.

mountaineer who got caught in a sudden storm. He had tattoos on his torso and legs, which might have served as a kind of acupuncture map. A room reproducing the cold and humidity of the glacier was built to house him, and a curious, rather poignant sensation it is, peering through the window at the body of a man who could be one's grandfather, 250 generations removed.

There's also a model of what he looked like, dressed in all his gear, which is spread out in the next cases. His clothing was designed for the weather, using the materials at hand in 3700 BC, from bearskin hat to goatskin underwear, and a mantle woven of grasses; he had a bow and arrows; and in his pouch he carried bone tools and lucky talismans. The museum's other exhibits – prehistoric to Roman – pale somewhat after the Ice Man, but don't miss the statue steles nor the cast of the Mithraic altar of Vipiteno (*see* p.437 for the real thing).

Museo Civico and Over the Talvera to Gries

Nearby, on the corner of Via Museo and Via Cassa di Risparmio, the **Museo Civico** (*open Tues–Sun 10–6; adm*) houses Gothic altarpieces by local masters Hans Klocker and Michael Pacher, Baroque art and ethnographic items. Via Museo ends at the bridge over the Talvera, a river lined with parks and promenades; to the right, in its own field, the stout-towered 13th-century **Castel Mareccio/Maretsch** (*open for guided tours Tues 11.30 and 4.30; adm*) no longer guards Bolzano, but hosts conventioneers. Just across the Talvera, the imposing fascist **Monumento alla Vittoria** celebrates Italy's victory in the First World War and was purposefully placed where the Austrian monument was slated to go; in 1978 Tyrolean nationalists attempted to blow it to smithereens. On Saturday morning it hosts an enormous market.

Corso Libertà leads through Mussolini's dreary industrial suburb (1937), purposely built as a contrast to old Bolzano and everything it stood for. The Corso ends in **Gries**, an old health resort. The old **parish church** of Gries (*open Mon–Fri Apr–Oct 10.30–12 and 2.30–4*) houses a beautifully carved Gothic wooden altar with doors by Michael Pacher (1475) and a masterful 13th-century Crucifix. (Bus no.10 returns to the centre.)

Around Bolzano

There are two fine walks around Bolzano. Beyond the Gries parish church, at the end of Via Knoller, begins the one-and-a-half-kilometre **Passeggiata del Guncina**, with an inn at the top for refreshments. A bit longer but more dramatic, the **Passeggiata Sant'Osvaldo** begins near the train station at Via Renico and descends by the head of the Lungotalvera promenade. Further up the Talvera, **Castel Roncolo** (***t*** *0471 329 808; open Tues–Sun 10–6*) has guarded the passage on its impregnable rock since 1237. The city gave it to Emperor Maximilian; it preserves 14th-century frescoes of chivalric knights, some of which were 'touched up' in 1508.

Three cable cars ascend from Bolzano, the most rewarding one from Via Renon, near the station, which climbs 4,005ft up the slopes of Bolzano's playground, Mt Renon/Ritten to **Soprabolzano/Oberbolzen** (*cable car daily 7am–8pm*). The views are splendid. Continue from here on the rack railway to **Collabo/Klobenstein**, and follow the path to the **Longomoso Pyramids** – rocks eroded to form a dense forest of needles and bizarre stone drapery. More fine views of the Dolomites can be had from **San Genesio/Jenesien**, a hamlet easiest reached by cable car from Via Sarentino (just before the Castel Roncolo).

La Strada del Vino/Die Weinstrasse

The inhabitants of the west bank of the Adige south of Bolzano have been making wine since before the Romans, and this lovely road through the vine-carpeted hills is so well known that the towns along it have taken its name. Specific places to aim for include **Castel d'Appiano**, one of 40 castles and manor houses in **Appiano sulla Strada del Vino/Eppen an der Weinstrasse**. In 1158, one of its lords, Federigo d'Appiano, had the cheek to hijack a precious treasure the Pope was sending to the Holy Roman Emperor, only to have his castle obliterated in response. It was rebuilt shortly after, but the holy armies left the original chapel, **Santa Caterina**, untouched, with its beautiful frescoes from the dawn of the 13th century (***t** 0471 662 206; open daily Apr–1 Nov; closed Tues in July*).

The winemaking capital, **Caldaro sulla Strada del Vino/Kaltern an der Weinstrasse**, overlooks Lago di Caldaro, which is warm enough for a dip from May to September. The **Museo Provinciale del Vino** in Castel Ringberg (***t** 0471 963 168; open Apr–mid-Nov Tues–Sat 9.30–12 and 2–6, Sun and hols 10–12; book for wine tastings*) is full of vinous lore and carved barrels. **Termeno sulla Strada del Vino/Tramin an der Weinstrasse** owes its fame to its blood-heating wine, Gewürztraminer Aromatico, of reputed aphrodisiac qualities; try it at the **Cantina Hofstätter**, in Piazza del Municipio, which claims to possess the largest wine cask in Europe. Termeno's neo-Gothic church conserves a quattrocento choir with elegant Renaissance frescoes. Just outside of town, rising out of a sea of vineyards, tiny **San Giacomo in Castelaz** has remarkable frescoes spanning the 13th to 15th centuries.

East of Bolzano: the Val Gardena and Rosengarten

Bolzano lies just to the west of the Süd Tirol's most celebrated Dolomite scenery, taking in the pinnacles of Pelmo, Civetta and Marmolada. Scores of alpine refuges, chairlifts and cable cars, and fast buses from Bolzano to the valleys, make access easy.

Val Gardena/Grödnertal

The most accessible, and certainly one of the most beautiful, excursions from Bolzano along the Brenner road north into the Ladin-speaking Val Gardena, lying between the jagged Odle group and **Alpe di Siusi**, a magnificent plateau noted for its sunny skiing and world-class ski schools, and for its endless meadows of flowers in late spring; there are numerous lifts up from the Val Gardena, or a road up from the resort town of **Siusi**. A classic but not strenuous hike from Siusi is the four-hour trek up **Monte Pez**, including a stay at one of the *grandes dames* of 19th-century alpine refuges, the **Rifugio Bolzano di Monte Pez**.

The SS242 enters the Val Gardena at **Ponte Gardena/Waidbrück**, in the shadow of medieval **Castel Trostburg** with its Gothic and late-Renaissance décor (*call* **t** *0471 654 401 for open hours and guided tours*). The valley's largest town, elegant **Ortisei/St Ulrich**, and the next two villages, **Santa Cristina** and **Selva di Val Gardena/Wölkenstein**, are well-equipped resorts with cable cars to the Alpe di Siusi; skiers should make time for the Saslonch-Ruacia piste passing right below the 17th-century **Castel Fischburg**. Santa Cristina has lifts into the Odle group and up to the foot of the most distinctive peak in the region, the spiralling, dream-like **Sassolungo** (10,430ft) to the south.

From the crossroads in Selva di Val Gardena there are spectacular routes over the **Passo di Sella** to Canazei in Trentino (*see* p.424), where you can pick up the Great Dolomites Road, and over the grand **Passo di Gardena** down into the **Alta Badia** to the

Tourist Information

www.valgardena.it.

Ortisei/Sankt Ulrich in Gröden: Via Rezia 1, **t** 0471 796 328.

Santa Cristina: Via Chemun 9, **t** 0471 793 046.

Selva di Val Gardena/Wölkenstein: Via Meisules 213, **t** 0471 795 122.

Corvara: Ciasa de Comun 198, **t** 0471 836 176.

Nova Levante/Welschnofen: Lago di Carezza, **t** 0471 613 126, *www.sudtirol.com/rosengarten*.

Where to Stay and Eat

Ortisei/Sankt Ulrich in Gröden ✉ 39046

★★★★**Adler**, Via Rezia 7, **t** 0471 796 203, *www.hotel-adler.com* (*luxury*). A glamorous hotel in a large park, with an indoor pool and beauty spa, and the best restaurant in town. *Open mid-Dec–mid-Apr and mid-May–Oct.*

★★★**La Perla**, Via Digon 1, **t** 0471 796 421, *www.laperlahotel.info* (*very expensive*). A lovely option just outside town, with a park and an indoor swimming pool. *Open mid-June–mid-Oct and mid-Dec–mid-Apr.*

★★★**Hotel Snaltnerhof**, Piazza S. Antonio 142, *www.snaltnerhof.it* (*moderate*). Modern rooms overlooking the central square.

Selva di Valgardena/ Wölkenstein in Gröden ✉ 39048

★★★★**Alpenroyal**, Via Meisules 43, **t** 0471 795 178, *www.alpenroyal.com* (*luxury*). A small, very comfortable hotel, with an indoor pool, whirlpool baths, a sauna, a solarium, a beauty centre and a fitness room. *Open mid-Dec–mid-Apr and June–Oct.*

★★**Freina**, Via Centro 403, **t** 0471 795 110, *www.hotelfreina.com* (*luxury*). A convenient hotel for the slopes, with 12 rooms. Half board or full board are required, but the food is excellent – stop here to eat if you're passing through.

★★**Europa**, Via Nives 50, **t** 0471 795 157, *www.europa-dolomiti.com* (*expensive–very expensive*). A typical little family-run mountain hotel. *Closed Mar and Nov.*

Santa Cristina in Valgardena/ Sankt Christina in Gröden ✉ 39047

★★★★**Diamant**, Via Skasa 1, **t** 0471 796 780, *www.hoteldiamant.it* (*expensive–very expensive*). A hotel in a quiet park, with lovely mountain views, an indoor pool and a sauna. *Open Dec–6 Mar and 15 June–7 Sept.*

★★★**Cendevaves**, Monte Pana, **t** 0471 792 062, *www.cendevaves.it* (*expensive*). A hotel with an indoor pool and good views. *Open early June–early Oct and early Dec–early Apr.*

Nova Levante/Welschnofen ✉ 39056

★★★★**Posta Cavallino Bianco/Weisses Roessel**, Strada Carezza 30, **t** 0471 613 113, *www.postcavallino.com* (*expensive–luxury*). The former postal relay station, with indoor and outdoor pools, tennis courts and much more. *Open mid-Dec–mid-Apr and mid-May–mid-Oct.*

★★★**Rosengarten**, Via Catinaccio 43, **t** 0471 613 262, *www.hotelrosengarten.it* (*moderate*). A pleasant place to stay, and the best place to eat in town, with cuisine based on the freshest local ingredients, garden herbs and home-made pasta. *Closed Mon, Tues lunch and Nov.*

The Woodcarvers of the Val Gardena

Ortisei farmers first took up carving to while away the winter evenings, using soft pine from the valley's slopes. In the 1640s some began to neglect their land to hike over the mountains and sell their carved toys, ornaments, furniture and implements. By 1820, 300 craftsmen were working in the valley, and a school was set up in 1872.

Today more than 3,000 woodcarvers whittle away in the Val Gardena. Ask the tourist office for a list of their workshops, and stop at Ortisei's parish church and museum to look at permanent exhibitions of their craft from the past 300 years.

east, a beautiful valley that has retained its Ladin culture. **Corvara in Badia** and **La Villa** are its main resorts. Another treat in the Alta Badia is the **Sella Ronda**, a circuit of the entire Sella group on skis, made possible by a series of refuges and lifts. North, the SS244 leads to San Lorenzo near Brunico; south the road descends to Arabba.

Catinaccio/Rosengarten

The name of the other main group accessible from Bolzano first appears in a 13th-century Tyrolean epic describing how when King Lauren of the Dwarves was dragged from his mountain realm, he put a curse on the roses that had betrayed him, to the effect that no one would see them again, by night or day. But he neglected to mention dawn or twilight, when they make the stony face of Rosengarten blush a deep red.

From Bolzano the road to Rosengarten (SS241) begins at Cardara/Kardaun and passes through the breathtaking deep red gorge of the **Val d'Ega**. As it nears **Nova Levante/Welschnofen**, the main resort, the peaks of the **Latemar** group loom to the right, while the massive wall of Rosengarten rises to the left. You can reach the slopes of Rosengarten from Nova Levante or the Passo di Costalunga near **Lake Carezza**, a popular stop on the road from Nova Levante. For an even more stunning approach, continue along the SS241, to **Pozza di Fassa** on the eastern slopes of Rosengarten.

The Great Dolomites Road: Bolzano to Cortina d'Ampezzo

The SS241 from Bolzano through the Val d'Ega to Rosengarten and Pozza is the first leg of the fabled 110-kilometre Great Dolomites Road, laid out in 1909. There are no buses, and it's torture to have to keep your eyes on the road. On the other hand, driving allows you to linger for as long as you like at the passes and other belvederes.

After Pozza di Fassa the road (now the SS48) continues up Trentino's Val di Fassa to Canazei (*see* p.424), the best base for the ascent of the Dolomites' mightiest peak, **Marmolada** (10,962ft). The road from Canazei climbs up to the **Passo Pordoi**, affording stupendous views of Sella and Marmolada, then writhes down towards **Arabba**, a resort, and **Pieve di Livinallongo**, below the odd-shaped **Col di Lana**, its summit blown off in the First World War. It then climbs again, to the **Sasso di Stria** (Witch's Rock) and the tunnel at **Passo di Falzarego**, where a cable car on threads ascends the vertiginous cliffs. From the pass the road begins the descent to Cortina, with views of the strange **Cinque Torri** (Five Towers) and nearly vertical slopes of Tofane, before reaching the top of the Valle del Boite, with beautiful views over Cortina (*see* p.410).

North Towards the Brenner Pass

North of Bolzano and Ponte Gardena lies the Val Isarco/Eisacktal, the main route to the Brenner Pass. Bressanone, Vitipeno and Novacella are the man-made highlights.

Val Isarco: Bressanone

On the way up from Bolzano the road passes the ancient town of **Chiusa/Klausen**, under the 4th-century **Monastero di Sabiona**, immortalized in Dürer's engraving, *The Great Fortune* (*Nemesis*) *c*. 1497. Its church, **Santa Croce** (*open daily 8–6; until 5 in winter*) has curious *trompe l'œil* frescoes of landscapes and architecture painted in 1679. A side road climbs to the 16th-century **Castel Velturno** (*t 0472 855 525; guided tours Tues–Sun Mar–Nov 10, 11, 2.30 and 3.30; adm*), summer residence of the bishop of Bressanone, decorated with frescoes and wood intarsio.

Tourist Information

Bressanone/Brixen: Viale Stazione 9, **t** 0472 836 401.
Brunico/Bruneck: Via Europa 22, **t** 0472 555 722.
Vipiteno/Sterzing: Piazza Città 3, **t** 0472 765 325, *www.infosterzing.it*.

Where to Stay and Eat

From Sept to late Nov, join locals in *Törggelen* – going from *maso* to *maso* to try unfermented grape juice (*Sußer*) and new wine (*Nuie*).

Bressanone ✉ 39042

******Elefant**, Via Rio Bianco 4, **t** 0472 832 750, *www.hotelelefant.com* (*very expensive*). A Renaissance inn bearing a fresco of the elephant sent to Emperor Maximilian by the King of Portugal in 1550, which spent a week in this building. It has lovely bedrooms, a pool, tennis courts, a pleasure garden, and a dairy and vegetable garden providing ingredients for the Tyrolean fare served in the restaurant. *Hotel open Mar–Nov and Christmas. Restaurant closed Mon out of season.*

******Dominik**, Via Terzo di Sotto 13, **t** 0472 830 144, *www.hoteldominik.com* (*expensive–very expensive*). A prestigious Relais & Châteaux hotel with spacious rooms boasting lovely views, and an indoor pool and sauna. The restaurant, one of the best in the region, serves regional and Italian specialities. *Hotel open Apr–mid-Nov, Christmas hols. Restaurant closed Tues.*

*****Hotel Cavallino d'Oro**, Via Brennero 3, **t** 0472 835 152 (*moderate–expensive*). A comfortable hotel (a hostelry for more than 350 years) with a swimming pool and wonderful views.

****Pension Mayrhof**, Via Tratten 17, **t** 0472 836 327, *www.mayrhofer.it* (*cheap–moderate*). A very cosy, charmingly furnished, central *pensione* with a quiet sunny garden.

Fink, Via Portici Minori 4, **t** 0472 834 883 (*moderate*). A century-old café situated by the old walls, with the downstairs **Arkade** serving simple dishes, and an upstairs restaurant (*expensive*) serving traditional Südtirolese cooking, including saddle of venison, *polenta nera* (made from buck-wheat) and a wide variety of cold meats and cheeses, plus vegetarian dishes. *Closed Tues eve, Weds and July.*

Vipiteno/Sterzing ✉ 39049

******Aquila Nera**, Piazza Città 1, **t** 0472 764 064, *www.schwarzeradler.it* (*expensive–very expensive*). A relaxing 16th-century hotel in the heart of town, with an indoor pool.

*****Albergo Post**, Città Nuova 14, **t** 0472 766 664, *www.highlight-hotels.com/post* (*moderate*). A comfortable hotel between the two towers on the main street, with wood-lined rooms with creaky floorboards.

Pretzhof, Tulve, 8km from town, **t** 0472 764 455 (*moderate*). A popular place offering a range of delicious traditional dishes made with ingredients from the family farm. *Closed Mon, Tues, and some of June and July.*

Bressanone/Brixen is the most charming city in the Alto Adige, capital of the region for a millennium and seat of a powerful prince-bishop, similar to Trento's. Though its Duomo became a dull Baroque church in the 18th century, the remodellers neglected the Romanesque cloister and its magnificent 14th-century frescoes, covering nearly every incident in the Bible. The bishops' palace with its lovely arcaded courtyard houses the **Museo Diocesano** (*open Tues–Sun 15 Mar–Oct 10–5; cribs only 1 Sept–31 Jan 2–5, closed 24 and 25 Dec; adm*), with the cathedral treasure and a fine collection of *presepi* (Christmas cribs). Beside the museum is a recently re-opened old kitchen garden, which gives on to a delightful café-restaurant, Kutscherhof.

Three kilometres north, the wine-making **Abbazia di Novacella** (***t*** *0472 836 189; open Mon–Sat 10–11 and 2–4*), begun in 1142, provides a fascinating study in the evolution of architecture, with its 12th-century tower, Baroque church, beautiful frescoed 14th-century cloister and the round, crenellated 12th–16th-century chapel of San Michele.

The Pusteria

The wide valley running east along the Rienza towards Dobbiaco/Toblach is dotted with typical Tyrolean villages and castles. Many of its churches contain works by the valley's 15th-century master woodcarver Michael Pacher, notably the 13th-century parish church of **San Lorenzo di Sebato**, with an ancient crypt (*closed Mon and Tues*). The capital of the Pusteria, medieval **Brunico/Bruneck**, has two lovely old gates and a 13th-century bishop's castle; along elegant Via di Città, even the pharmacy has frescoes. From here head up a wooded valley north to **Campo Tures/Taupers**, clustered under the baronial **Castel di Tures** guarding the entrance to the Val Aurina. Tours take in the hall of mirrors, two dozen rooms of tapestries, a chapel frescoed in 1482 by the school of Pacher and a beautiful library (*open for guided tours Tues, Fri and Sun mid-June–mid-July; mid-July–end Aug every 30mins 10–5; Sept–Oct 10, 11, 12, 2, 3.15, 4.30; 26 Dec–mid-June 3 and 4; adm*). Glacier alpinists come here for the **Vedrette Giganti** (or di Ríes), reached from Riva di Tures, and its waterfall. Extremists carry on north up the Val Aurina to **Casere** and its hamlet, **Pratomagno**, with the northernmost houses in Italy.

East of Brunico, **Monguelfo/Welsberg** is a resort under a 12th-century castle; a road turns south into the Val di Braies, with the **Lago di Braies**, celebrated for its stillness and intense green colour. East of Monguelfo the road continues to Dobbiaco (*see* p.413).

The Upper Val Isarco to the Brenner Pass

The main town between Bressanone and the pass, **Vipiteno/Sterzing**, belonged to the Fugger banking dynasty, who prized it for its mines, which enabled residents to build splendid battlemented houses after a devastating fire in 1443. The mines, closed since 1979, are remembered in the **Museo Provinciale delle Miniere Jöchlsthurn** (*open Tues–Sat Apr–Oct 10–12 and 2–5; adm*). The best houses are along Via Città Nuova; the courtyard of the Municipio has a Mithraic altar from the 3rd century BC. In Piazza Città, the **Museo Multscher** (*open Mon 2–5, Tues–Fri 10–12 and 2–5; adm*) displays elegant works by 15th-century painter Hans Multscher. Three kilometres southeast, the Counts Thurn und Taxis' 11th–14th-century frescoed **Castel Tasso** (*guided tours Mon–Thurs, Sat and Sun Easter–1 Nov 9.30, 10.30, 2 and 3; adm*) has Gothic decoration.

Further north, **Colle Isarco/Gossensass** offers skiing and hiking on Cima Bianca and in the Val di Fleres. Beyond this lies the **Brenner Pass** (4,510ft), the lowest of the alpine passes, and the route of countless invaders from the north, heavily bombed during the Second World War. From here it is 125 kilometres to Innsbruck.

Merano and the Upper Adige

A famous spa, vineyards and lots of castles follow the road and Adige up to the Resia Pass, near the Austrian and Swiss frontiers.

Merano

Just 28 kilometres up the Adige from Bolzano, Merano is an attractive town of gardens and flowers, and a favourite spa for central Europeans with respiratory complaints since the 1830s, basking in a balmy microclimate. The benefits of the waters, the clean air and the graded mountain walks are complemented by specific cures, such as the notorious grape cure in September and October – eating two pounds of Merano grapes a day, taking care to chew them well, apparently keeps the doctor away. Their juice usually works wonders for the rest of the year.

Apart from tackling digestive disorders, Merano has various other attractions: along the Adige, you'll find the striking Liberty-style casino and **Kursaal**, topped with dancing maidens and now used as a congress centre. Two streets back, the arcaded Via dei Portici was the main street in the medieval town; the stern 15th-century Gothic Duomo contains some International Gothic frescoes in the style of Trento's Castello di Buonconsiglio.

Tourist Information

Merano: Corso Libertà 35, **t** 0473 272 000, *www.meraninfo.it*.

Where to Stay and Eat

Merano ✉ 39021

Unsurprisingly for an old-world spa, there is little accommodation in the lower ranges.

*****__Palace__, Via Cavour 2, **t** 0473 211 300, *www.palace.it* (*very expensive–luxury*). An aristocratic hotel in beautifully maintained grounds in the heart of Merano, with a spa and beauty centre, and the best restaurant in town. Kafka once stayed here.

***__Castello Labers__, Via Labers 25, **t** 0473 234 484, *www.castellolabers.it* (*very expensive–luxury*). A 1200s castle-villa set among the vines above Merano, with a pool and views. *Open Apr–Nov.*

*****__Kurhotel Castel Rundegg__, Via Scena 2, **t** 0473 234 100, *www.rundegg.com* (*very expensive*). A picturesque 12th-century castle near the centre, with an indoor pool and fitness centre and a lovely park.

***__Westend__, Via Speckbacher 9, **t** 0473 447 654, www.westend.it (*moderate–expensive*) An atmospheric choice near the centre, with 22 lovely rooms in a 19th-century villa tucked away in its own garden.

*__Pension Tyrol__, Via 30 Aprile 8, **t** 0473 449 719 (*moderate*). A quiet hotel near the spa, with a big garden and free parking.

Sissi, Via Galilei 44, **t** 0473 231 062 (*expensive–very expensive*). One of the best restaurants in town, up by the Castello Principesco and offering delicious food with a Piemontese touch. *Closed Mon.*

Laubenkeller, Via dei Portici 118, **t** 0473 237 706 (*moderate*). A restaurant offering a range of reasonably priced *typische Südtiroler* dishes. *Closed Thurs.*

Via Cassa di Risparmio leads back to the 15th-century **Castello Principesco** (*open Tues–Sat 10–5, Sun 10–1; adm*), built by Archduke Sigismond and containing Gothic furnishings, arms and swords. Opposite, you can take a chairlift up to Tirolo or pick up the four-kilometre **Passeggiata Tappeiner**, a botanical wonderland overlooking the city. At Via delle Corse 42 the **Museo Civico** (*same hours as Castello*) has four Bronze-Age statue steles, Gothic sculptures and a Pietà by the school of Michael Pacher.

For centuries the valley landowners were generally left alone to defend their turf; as a result the area bristles with many of the Alto Adige's 350-plus castles. The big cheese lived just above Merano in **Tirolo**, at **Castel Tirol**, balanced on the precipice and home to the **Historical and Cultural Museum of the Province** (*open Tues–Fri Apr–Nov 10–5*). The castle gave its name to the region and remains a symbol of Tyrol identity, the headquarters of the independent Counts until 1363, when Margherita di Maultasch, the 'Ugly Duchess', ceded Tyrol to the Habsburgs. Adorned with medieval monsters and frescoes, it houses different exhibitions every year. Also in Tirolo, **Castel Fontana** (*open Weds–Sun Apr–early Nov 10–5; adm*), a rather fanciful reconstruction of a 12th-century castle, houses an agricultural museum and memorabilia related to poet Ezra Pound, who was found too crazy to stand trial for treason (he made pro-Mussolini radio broadcasts during the World War II) and retired here in 1958.

The Val Venosta

West of Merano, the Val Venosta follows the Adige west towards Austria. At **Naturno**, little **San Procolo** (*open Tues–Sun 9.30–12 and 2.30–5*) contains some 8th-century fresco fragments, the oldest in any German-speaking territory. Northwest, at Unser Frau in the Vale di Senales/Schnalstal, where the Ice Man's body was found (*see* p.430), a fascinating new **Archeoparc** (***t*** *0473 676 020; open Apr–Nov Tues–Sun 10–6 , 15 July–31 Aug also Mon; 28 Dec–31 Mar Tues–Sun 1–6; adm exp*) recreates his environment.

In the upper valley, an hour's drive from Merano, **Sluderno/Schludrens** was ruled by the Trapps, whose 13th/16th-century **Castel Coira/Churburg** (*open for guided tours Tues–Sun Mar–1 Nov 10–12 and 2–4.30; adm*) has gloriously painted Renaissance loggias and the largest private collection of armour in Europe. Nearby **Glorenza/Glurns**, the smallest walled city in Europe, looks much as it did in the 15th century.

At Sluderno the SS41 branches off west to Switzerland; the main road continues to ancient **Malles Venosta**, before turning north to Austria. Malles also has very old frescoes, colourful and Carolingian, in the chapel of **San Benedetto** (*open Mon–Sat 9–11.30 and 1.30–5; adm; key held at Via S. Bemedeo 31*). Just up in **Burgusio**, the beautiful 17th-century Benedictine **Abbazia di Monte Maria/Marienberg** (***t*** *0473 831 306*) has a gleaming white crown of towers and gables in a woodland setting; the crypt from the original church has rare, excellently preserved 12th-century frescoes of Jerusalem (*open for guided tours May–June and Sept Mon–Fri 10.45 and 3, Sat 10.45; July–Sept Mon–Fri 10, 11, 3 and 4, Sat 10 and 11; Nov–Mar by appointment; adm*). On the way to Austria the road passes the romantic ruins of **Lichtenburg** castle and the artificial **Lago di Resia**, with the church spire of a submerged village poking up.

If you leave the main valley road (the SS40) at Spondigna, just before Sluderno, and stay on the SS38, you'll enter the **Stelvio National Park** (*see* p.277).

Friuli-Venezia Giulia

For many British or American visitors, this elongated region east of Venice is *terra incognita*, a jumbly name that turns up on the wine list in Italian restaurants. Trieste, at the far end of Italy, evokes cloudy images of pre- and post-war intrigue, a kind of *Third Man* on the Mediterranean. From Trieste to Venice the imagination fails.

The region is burdened with a history as messy as its name. Roman *Aquileia* was the most important city and seat of the oldest patriarchate outside Rome. Its authority was gradually usurped by Cividale del Friuli, the Lombard capital, in the Dark Ages, then in the Middle Ages by Ùdine, before Venice took over in 1420. Trieste was Venice's bitter rival under the Counts of Gorizia and the Austrians. Napoleon threw the region in with the 'Kingdom of Illyria', a piece of real estate subsequently picked up by the

Wine in Friuli

The Friuli region has seven DOC regions. The best is the Collio (around Gorizia), famous for its whites, especially Pinot Bianco and Riesling. The Collio Orientale, a much larger region, also produces good whites and a brisk red, Refosco. Rochi di Cialla and Giovanni Dri are two of the best-known labels. The other DOC regions – Aquileia, Isonzo, Carso, Latisana and Grave del Friuli – produce good reds; look out for Schiopettino, Carso Terreno, and Riva Rossa.

To find out about *cantinas* and producers' tasting outlets, contact the Movimento Turismo del Vino, t 0432 289 540.

Austro-Hungarian Empire. In 1918 Italy inherited it, with all of Istria down to Fiume (modern Rijeka). After the Second World War, Tito took Trieste from the Germans; the western Allies then forced them to leave, occupying the city as a neutral free port until 1954, when it was readmitted into Italy, leaving the rest of Istria to Yugoslavia. The region's troubles were hardly over: two disastrous earthquakes in 1976 (6.5 and 6.1 on the Richter scale) shook Friuli to the core, killing 1,000 people, levelling entire towns, and leaving 70,000 buildings in need of major structural repair.

Weary of being marginal, Friuli-Venezia Giulia is now creating an identity of its own, but it's like trying to put together pieces from several jigsaw puzzles. The population in the east speaks Slovenian; the north has a sizeable German minority. In Trieste there are large Jewish, Greek and Serb minorities, and in the middle, around Ùdine, is a majority Friulian ethnic group who speak a language similar to the Swiss Rhaeto-Romansch. In the 1990s, with the reopening of central and eastern Europe, the region stopped being eastern Italy's dead end and became an important link to its future.

From Venice to Lignano-Sabbiadoro

Altino and Càorle

The SS14 from Venice passes first Marco Polo airport and then **Altino**, the modern name of Roman *Altinum*. Once renowned for its wealth, it was put to the sack by Attila the Hun – only the first of many hardships that led its inhabitants to give up and found a new city on the island of Torcello in the Venetian Lagoon. They took whatever Attila and the Lombards didn't wreck, so that all that remains in the **Museo Nazionale** (*open daily 9–8*) are mosaics and a few odds and ends.

The route continues over the Piave near **San Donà di Piave**, a town that had to be completely rebuilt after the First World War; it was here that Hemingway, then an ambulance driver for the Red Cross, was wounded in 1918, an experience that became the germ of *A Farewell to Arms*. From San Donà, a detour to the old fishing town and modern seaside resort of **Càorle** is tempting, for its isthmus, beaches and lagoon beloved of wildfowl, and its Duomo, built in 1038, with a charming cylindrical campanile and a splendid Venetian Pala d'Oro (12th–14th centuries). **Bibione**, to the east, is an even bigger resort, with a long strand.

Getting Around

Trains from Venice along the coast run about every 2hrs (taking 2hrs to Trieste). **Buses** are less frequent, though Càorle can most easily be reached by direct bus from Venice (or take the train to S. Donà di Piave and the local bus to Càorle from there). For Lignano-Sabbiadoro, take the train to Latisana, from where it's about 30mins by bus to the coast.

Tourist Information

Veneto:

Càorle: Calle delle Liburniche 16, **t** 0421 81085, *www.caorleturismo.it*.

Portogruaro: Via Martiri della Libertà 19, **t** 0421 73558, *www.bibionecaorle.it*.

Friuli-Venezia Giulia:

Lignano-Sabbiadoro: Via Latisana 42, **t** 0413 71821, *www.lignano.it*.

Where to Stay and Eat

In the beach resorts, high-season runs from mid-June to the end of Aug, with prices adjusted accordingly. Book ahead, especially for the first 3wks of Aug.

Squid ink, with which the docks are awash in the evenings, features heavily in local menus.

Càorle ✉ 30021

★★★**Garden**, Piazza Belvedere, **t** 0421 210 036, *www.hotelgardencaorle.com* (*expensive*). A hotel immersed in pines by the beach, with a pool and sauna. Nearly all rooms have balconies. *Open Apr–Sept.*

★★★**Diplomatic**, Via Strada Nuova 19, **t** 0421 81087, *www.promoservice.com* (*cheap–moderate*). A comfortable hotel on its own little port, with the area's best restaurant, **Duilio**, celebrated for its seafood *antipasti*, pasta and *secondi*. *Closed Mon, Jan.*

Lignano ✉ 33054

★★★★★**Greif**, Arco del Grecale 27, Lignano-Pineta, **t** 0431 422 261, *www.greifgroup.net* (*very expensive–luxury*). A large resort hotel near the pines. with a park, a pool, a sauna and a private beach.

★★★★**Miramare**, Via Aquileia 49/B, Lignano-Sabbiadoro, **t** 0431 71260, *www.miramare.com* (*very expensive*). A hotel with comfortable rooms, parking, a garden and its own beach. *Open mid-May–Sept.*

★★★★**Medusa Splendid**, Raggio dello Scirocco 33, **t** 0431 422 211, *www.hotelmedusa.it* (*expensive*). An intimate hotel with a pool, very good rooms and a garden. *Open mid-May–mid-Sept.*

★★★**Vittoria**, Lungomare Marin 28, Sabbiadoro, **t** 0431 71221 (*moderate–expensive*). A fine older hotel. *Open mid-May–Sept.*

★★★★**Eurotel**, Calle Mendelssohn 13, Lignano Riviera, **t** 0431 428 991, *www.eurotel-hotels.it* (*moderate*). A fashionable hotel enjoying perhaps the most beautiful setting in the area, with lovely rooms, a heated pool and more. *Open mid-May–mid-Sept.*

Al Bancut, Via Friuli 32, **t** 0431 71926 (*expensive*). A central place serving fine, traditional grilled fish. *Closed Tues eve and Weds.*

Bidin, Via Europa 1, **t** 0431 71988 (*expensive*). A convivial little place with a fish and a meat *menu degustazione*. *Closed Weds.*

Portogruaro and Around

Portogruaro is a seductive old town, dreaming away under its palm trees and its jauntily tilted 193ft campanile, built in the 12th century. The Duomo is a wallflower, but the neighbouring 14th-century **Loggia Comunale** is shaped like a mountain, the roofline crested with fantail Ghibelline battlements, which lend it a curiously organic appearance. The **Museo Nazionale Concordiese** in Via del Seminario (*open daily 9–8; adm*) is crowded with an assortment of bronzes and coins, among some other finds excavated in *Concordia Sagittaria*, just to the south. This was an arrow-manufacturing (*sagittae*) Roman colony, and has a Romanesque cathedral standing next to a ruined basilica (389) and a frescoed Byzantine baptistry of 1089.

In **Summaga**, three kilometres to the west of Portogruaro, the abbey of **Santa Maria Maggiore** (*call* **t** *0421 205 126 for open hours*) was built around a 6th-century votive chapel. The walls are covered with a fascinating cycle of restored 12th- and 13th-century frescoes; in the votive chapel, don't miss the fighting griffins and lions, chivalrous deeds, virtues and vices.

More fond old things await in **Sesto al Règhena**, nine kilometres north of Portogruaro, a quaint medieval village with a moat in the centre, originally part of the defences of **Santa Maria in Silvis** (**t** *0434 699 014; open daily 8–12 and 3–7*), a Lombard foundation that grew to become one of the most powerful abbeys in the area. The current basilica dates from the 12th century and is decorated with 14th-century frescoes, one showing Christ crucified on a voluptuous pomegranate tree. Among the bas-reliefs is a beautiful 13th-century Annunciation, while the crypt has an 8th-century Lombard–Byzantine sarcophagus of St Anastasia. Lastly, to the west near **Fossalta di Portogruaro**, by the little church of Sant'Antonio in Vilanova, grows one of the oldest oak trees in Europe, already 300 years old when they signed the Magna Carta.

Lignano-Sabbiadoro

From a few kilometres east of **Latisana**, where a new road (the SS354) branches off to the coast, you can follow the crowds south to the Laguna di Marano and the fastest-growing resort area on the Adriatic, **Lignano-Sabbiadoro**, the 'Austrian Riviera'. Set on the tip of the peninsula, with a lovely nine-kilometre sandy beach and scores of new hotels, apartments, bungalows and campsites, Lignano-Sabbiadoro and its two adjacent resorts of **Lignano-Pineta** (the prettiest section, under the pinewoods) and smart **Lignano Riviera** offer fun in the sun and Wienerschnitzel just like Mutti makes. Some of the smaller islands are dotted with *casoni*, steep thatched fisherman's cottages – some real, some recreated for visitors.

Pordenone and Around

There's not a lot to say about Pordenone, provincial capital and manufacturer of domestic appliances. Its name is only familiar thanks to the Renaissance artist G.A. Sacchiense, who adopted it and whose works may be seen in the **Museo Civico d'Arte**, housed in the pretty 15th-century Palazzo Richiere (**t** *0434 392 312; open Tues–Fri 9.30–12.30 and 3–6; adm*), and in the salmon-pink Duomo, where his odd masterpiece, the *Madonna della Misericordia* (1515), hangs.

The lofty campanile is Pordenone's landmark, a refined tower of Romanesque brickwork of 1347. The bijou **Palazzo Comunale**, the focal point of Pordenone's arcaded, palace-lined Corso Vittorio Emanuele, has a Venetian clock tower topped by two bell-ringing Moors, superimposed on a graceful 13th-century building. And that just about sums it up.

Hanging over the willowy banks of the Livenza, **Sacile** (west of Pordenone) is famous for its bird festival (the *Dei Osei*), held on the last Sunday in August ever since 1351. Thousands of songbirds are assembled in the main piazza, and prizes are awarded to the birds and the person who can best imitate their songs.

Tourist Information

Pordenone: Corso V. Emanuele II 38, **t** 0434 21912.
Spilimbergo: Piazza Castello, **t** 0427 2274.

Where to Stay and Eat

Pordenone ✉ 33170

★★★★**Villa Ottoboni**, Piazzetta Ottoboni 2, **t** 0434 208 891, *www.geturhotels.com* (*moderate–expensive*). An elegant hotel near the centre, with a restaurant going back as far as the late 1400s.

★★★**Park**, Via Mazzini 43, **t** 0434 27901, *www.bestwestern.it* (*moderate–expensive*). Modern, comfortable rooms in the centre.

★★★**Antica Trattoria La Primula**, Via San Rocco 47, San Quirino, 9km north of town, **t** 0434 910 005 (*moderate*). An 8-room hotel with a simple but elegant restaurant (*very expensive*) that has served up the best food in the province for six generations. Everything, from the *antipasti* through the seafood to the desserts, is simply prepared, classic and superb. *Restaurant closed Sun eve, Mon, 2wks Jan, and July.*

Gildo, Viale Marconi 17, Porcìa, 4km west of town, **t** 0434 921 212 (*very expensive*). An imposing Venetian palace in a large park, with a menu divided between meat and fish. Prices are considerably lower at lunch. *Closed Sun eve, Mon and Aug.*

Osteria Alle Nazioni, Via San Rocco, San Quirino, **t** 0434 910 005 (*expensive*). A frescoed osteria next to the Antica Trattoria, run by the same people, with good food. *Closed Sun eve, Mon, 2wks Jan, and July.*

Alla Cantina, Piazza Cavour 3, **t** 0434 520 358 (*moderate*). Classic Italian dishes in opulent surroundings in the centre. *Closed Tues.*

Da Zelina, Piazza San Marco, **t** 0434 27290 (*moderate*). A restaurant in an early Renaissance *palazzo*, offering good meat dishes, and pizzas in the evening. *Closed Sat lunch, Mon and part of Aug.*

Spilimbergo ✉ 33097

★★**Michielini**, Viale Barbacane 3, **t** 0427 50450 (*cheap*). An old family-run hotel in the centre of town, with a restaurant.

La Torre, Piazza Castello, **t** 0427 50555 (*expensive*). A restaurant in a castle, offering the likes of ravioli filled with pumpkin in mushroom sauce, and strudels. The wine cellar is superb. *Closed Sun eve, Mon and last 2wks Jan and Aug.*

Enoteca La Torre, Via di Mezzo 2, **t** 0427 2998, *cheap*). A wine bar in the castle gatehouse, offering San Daniele ham and a wonderful cellar of Friulian wines. Staff are friendly and helpful. *Closed Tues.*

Osteria Al Bacaro, Via Pilacorte 5, **t** 0427 2317 (*cheap*). Authentic Friulian dining, including *baccalà e trippe con polenta* (salted cod and tripe with polenta), around an open fire, amidst simple wooden furniture. *Closed Sun.*

Towards Ùdine: the Villa of the Last Doge, Spilimbergo and San Daniele

On the road to Ùdine, Codroipo is the site of the **Villa Manin** (1738), the biggest villa in all Venetia, the swan blast of a way of life (*open only for exhibitions; call **t** 0432 904 721*). When owner Ludovico Manin was elected doge in Venice, his chief rival declared, 'A Friulian as Doge! The republic is dead.' The prediction was no sooner proved correct than Napoleon himself stayed at this massive ranch as a guest, if not a welcome one. Visitors can see the church, the armoury and carriage museum and the park.

Spilimbergo, on the west bank of the Tagliamento, is a pretty 12th-century castle with exterior frescoes, a Gothic cathedral with a Romanesque portal and paintings by Pordenone, and a mosaic school (***t** 0427 2077; open Mon–Sat 8–12 and 1–4*). North of it, near Clauzetto, the **Grotte Verdi di Pradis** (***t** 0427 80323; open July and Aug daily during daylight hours if conditions allow; other months sunny Sun only; adm*) has walkways following the torrential Cosa up a high narrow gorge.

Surrounded by fields of maize and *prosciutterie*, **San Daniele del Friuli** is the 'Siena of Friuli', an ochre-tinted medieval market town famous for its sweet-cured hams. Don't miss the restored frescoes by Pellegrino di San Daniele (1498–1522) in the church of **Sant'Antonio**, his masterpiece, or the **Biblioteca Guarneriana**, Via Roma 1 (***t** 0432 940 765; open Tues–Sun 9–12*), founded in the 15th century by a canon of Aquileia, with lovely medieval manuscripts.

Palmanova, Aquileia and Grado

From north to south lie a planned military town, an ancient capital and a modern seaside resort – the only one in the Adriatic entirely facing south.

Palmanova

In the Renaissance, despite all Alberti's theories on town planning, only a handful of new towns were ever constructed. One of the most remarkable, **Palmanova**, was built in 1593 by the Venetians as a bulwark against the Austrians and Turks, and populated by 'volunteers'. Perhaps because it was never needed, it remains intact, a perfect example of 16th-century 'ideal' radial military planning and a geometric *tour de force*: the star formed by its walls has nine points. Most of the walls and moat are overgrown, their stone softly moulded into serpentine hills and gullies, but they are still defended by young conscripts. At the **Museo Storico**, Borgo Ùdine 4 (*open Thurs–Tues 9.30–12.30 and 3–6 except Sun am; adm*), ask about the Revocazione Istorica, a torchlight tour of the walkways within the walls on the second Sunday in July.

Aquileia

Aquileia, directly south, was the only major Roman city in Italy to die on the vine. While most other Roman metropolises are still notable towns, Aquileia has dwindled from an estimated 200,000 to 3,500 inhabitants, who now tend vineyards, plus the tourists who flock to see the most important archaeological site in northern Italy.

Founded as a Roman colony in 181 BC, *Aquileia* earned its name from the eagles that flew over town while plans were being laid for Augustus' German campaign. It proved a good augury. Augustus himself was in and out of Aquileia and received Herod the Great here. Christianity found an early foothold in the city; the Patriarchate of Aquileia was founded in 313, the year Constantine the Great issued the Edict of Milan, tolerating the religion, and its patriarch was given jurisdiction that extended to the Ukraine.

It didn't last long; after Aquileia was sacked by Attila (452) and the Lombards (568), the patriarch moved to a safer home in Grado, an island on its outer port. When Aquileia wanted the title back in the 7th century, Grado refused, and for 400 years rival patriarchs sat in Grado and Cividale del Friuli, the Lombard capital. When they were reconciled in 1019, Aquileia's great basilica was rebuilt, but it was the city's last hurrah. Its port on the Natissa silted up, malaria killed the people, and the patriarchate moved to Cividale, then to Ùdine, and was ultimately demoted to an archbishopric.

Getting Around

For Aquileia and Grado, take the **train** to Cervignano del Friuli then a **bus**; alternatively, there's a direct bus from Trieste. Local buses link Palmanova, Aquileia and Grado.

Tourist Information

Aquileia: Piazza Capitolo, **t** 0431 919 491 (*Apr–Nov*).

Grado: Viale Dante Alighieri 72, **t** 0431 877 111, *www.gradoturismo.info*.

Where to Stay and Eat

Aquileia ✉ 33051

******Patriarchi**, Via Giulia Augusta 12, **t** 0431 919 595, *www.hotelpatriarchi.it* (*moderate*). An air-conditioned hotel overlooking the Roman excavations.

***Aquila Nera**, Piazza Garibaldi 5, **t** 0431 91045 (*cheap*). A friendly, newly modernized hotel in the quiet main square, offering small en suite rooms with air-con. The restaurant is traditional and homely, with good gnocchi and fish dishes.

La Colombara, Via S. Zilli 34, 2km out of town on the Trieste road, **t** 0431 91513 (*moderate*). Fine cuisine, particularly seafood, and good wines from the Collio. *Closed Mon except high season, and Jan.*

Grado ✉ 34073

★★★★**Savoy**, Via Carducci 33, **t** 0431 897 111, *www.hotelsavoy-grado.it* (*expensive–very expensive*). An upmarket central option offering a swimming pool, a garden, parking facilities and comfortable rooms. *Open June–Oct.*

★★★**Antica Villa Bernt**, Via Colombo 5, **t** 0431 82516, *www.hotelbernt.it* (*expensive*). A refurbished 1920s villa in the centre of the town, with 22 lovely rooms (some of which are *moderate*, some *very expensive*). *Open Apr–Oct.*

★★★**Cristina**, Viale Martiri della Libertà 11, **t** 0431 80989, *www.hotelcristina-grado.it* (*moderate*). A hotel in a shady garden a short way from the sea. *Open May–Sept.*

★★★**Eden**, Via M. Polo 2, **t** 0431 80136, *www.hoteledengrado.it* (*moderate*). A typical holiday hotel by the beach. *Open Apr–mid-Oct.*

Albergo Ambriabella, Riva Slataper 2, **t** 0431 81479 (*moderate*). A hotel facing the Isola Della Schiusa, with a number of welcome personal touches.

All'Androna, Calle Porta Piccola 4, **t** 0431 80950 (*very expensive*). Fresh fish according to the day's catch, plus home-made bread and pasta. *Closed 1mth in winter.*

De Toni, Piazza Duca D'Aosta 37, **t** 0431 80104 (*moderate*). A restaurant overlooking the Roman excavations, offering fresh fish prepared in a variety of local styles and a long wine list. *Closed Weds.*

The Basilica

Aquileia's magnificent **Basilica** (*open daily Apr–Sept 8.30–7; Oct–Mar 8.30–12.30 and 2.30–5.30*) was founded in 313 by the first Patriarch Theodore. When Poppone rebuilt it in 1023 he covered Theodore's old-fashioned floor, which was rediscovered in 1909. The beautiful pavement, the largest Paleo-Christian mosaic in the west, combines the stories of Jonah and the whale and the good shepherd with scenes from nature . Original frescoes from 1031 survive in the apse, showing Patriarch Poppone dedicating the basilica, accompanied by Emperor Conrad II and Gisela of Swabia.

Set next to the wall, the 11th-century marble **Santo Sepolcro** is a reproduction of the Holy Sepulchre in Jerusalem. Next to this is the so-called **Cripta degli Scavi** (the excavations around the belltower), containing more mosaics from 313, sandwiched between pagan Roman mosaics and others from the 8th century. The **crypt** proper, under the altar, is adorned with colourful 12th-century Byzantine-style frescoes (*one adm for both crypts*).

The Museo Archeologico

Open Mon 8.30–2, Tues–Sun 8.30–7.30; adm; ring bell for access.

In an old palace on the same road, this houses one of the most impressive collections of everyday Roman items you're ever likely to see, including ancient gemstones, glass ornaments, and some highly individualized Republican portrait busts; unlike the Greeks, who idealized in marble, the Romans insisted that all their warts, cauliflower ears and crumpled noses be preserved for posterity. Among the bas-reliefs is a smith with his tools, amber and gold ornaments.

The Excavations

A circular walk from Via Sacra behind the basilica takes in most of Aquileia's excavations; proximity to that quarrying magpie Venice has shorn them of most of their grandeur. Via Sacra first passes by **Roman houses** and **Palaeo-Christian oratories** (some with mosaics intact), then continues up through the ruins of the ancient harbour, marked by cypresses: in the 1st century AD this was a bustling port. Continue straight and bear right after the crossroads on Via Gemina to the **Palaeo-Christian Museum** (*open daily 8.30–1.45*), with reliefs and sarcophagi, and a walkway over the undulating mossy mosaics of a huge 4th-century basilica. Return by way of Via Gemina to Via Giulia Augusta. To the right is the old Roman road, on the left the **Forum** with its re-erected columns. Just off a fork to the right, the **Grand Mausoleum** (1st century AD) was brought here from the distant suburbs. The meagre ruins of the amphitheatre, the baths and the **Sepolcreto** (five Roman family tombs) are on Via XXIV Maggio and Via Acidino, north of the village's central Piazza Garibaldi.

Grado: Up to Your Neck in Sand

Aquileia had an inner port and an outer port, or *grado*, on the island that still bears its name. Now linked by a causeway, this reigns as the queen of its own little lagoon and archipelago. The narrow alleys of the old town, the **Castrum Gradense**, are called *calli* as in Venice; most are traffic-free. In the 6th century the Patriarch of Nova Aquileia moved to the Duomo (Basilica of Sant'Eufemia). Here Corinthian capitals sit on exotic marble pillars, and the 11th-century domed pulpit is carved with four Evangelists; the painted baldaquin could easily be the tent of the sheikh of Araby.

The mosaic floor is from the 6th century; its scriptural adages and geometrical patterns may seem austere after the garden of delights in Aquileia's Basilica. One scene on the altar depicts *Castrum Gradense* and its islands; in the back glows a silver *pala* donated by Venice in 1372. An alley of sarcophagi separates Sant'Eufemia from the octagonal 5th-century baptistry, with an immersion font, and another smaller basilica, the 5th-century **Santa Maria delle Grazie**, with its original altar screens and mini-theatre for the clergy behind the altar – common in early-Byzantine basilicas.

Grado became a beach resort thanks to medicine. Keen to bring children with TB to the seaside, doctors sought a fresh-water spring on the peninsula of Grado. In 1892 one was discovered, and Franz Josef included Grado on his list of curative resorts.

A new town grew up to accommodate the nobility, since replaced by athletes, models and business people undergoing specific treatments, including the 'sand cure' – being buried up to one's neck in warm sand. If the free beaches are full, walk east to **Pineta**, or catch the boat to **Barbana**, a lagoon island with a religious community (*frequent boats daily in summer; Nov–May Sat and Sun only*). There are also daily boats to Trieste and the Istrian coast in summer, and the fishing village of **Porto Buso**.

Trieste

Once the main seaport of the Austro-Hungarian Empire, two world wars left Trieste the woebegone widow of the Adriatic. With the fall of the Berlin Wall, however, it became a very merry widow, quick to regain its cosmopolitan lustre. Streets and shops bubble with Slovene, Serbo-Croat, German, Hungarian and Czech, and a bewildering variety of car licence plates clog up the very central European 19th-century streets. Don't come here for art or beautiful buildings: the city's capitalist swag has been invested in banks, shipping lines and stocks. Come instead to sense the energy and excitement of a city shaking off decades of nostalgic sloth.

History

Founded as the Celtic port of *Tergeste*, Trieste first became an important city under Augustus. From the 9th to the 13th centuries it maintained precarious independence under its prince-bishops; in the 14th and 15th centuries it was Venice's chief rival in the Adriatic. Austria, always longing for a port, first offered the city its protection in 1382, and in 1719 Charles VI granted it free-port status, initiating a golden age. Trieste returned to Austrian rule after the fall of Napoleon in 1815, although bereft of free-port status. Their heavy-handed government turned the majority Italian population into ardent 'Irredentists' – unredeemed – turbulently desiring union with Italy.

Italian troops were welcomed in 1918, but the Italian government soon proved another disappointment, when Mussolini tried to force the heterogeneous population into a cultural straitjacket. Real disaster came in the aftermath of the Second World War, when Trieste found itself divorced from its Istrian hinterland in Slovenia and Croatia. Tito only gave up his claims to Trieste itself in 1954, and the border was not settled until 1975. In the mid-1960s, the city, lacking direction, decided to create a new role for itself as a scientific and research centre.

At the turn of the last century Trieste sparkled not with scientists, but literati. Sir Richard Burton, translator of the *Arabian Nights*, was consul here from 1870 until his death in 1890 – virtually in exile from his Middle Eastern interests. James Joyce, after eloping with Nora Barnacle, taught English in Trieste from 1904 to 1915 and 1919 to 1920; here he wrote *The Dubliners* and began *Ulysses* (fans can pick up a Joycean itinerary at the tourist office, marking all his old haunts). Joyce befriended and translated Ettore Schmitz (Italo Svevo), a member of Trieste's once-thriving Jewish community, and author of comedy neurosis novel *La coscienza di Zeno*. Unknown to either of them, Rainer Maria Rilke was living and working nearby at Duino.

Along the Port to Piazza dell'Unità d'Italia

From the station, Corso Cavour leads into the **Borgo Teresiano**, the neoclassical commercial centre laid out in 1750 by Maria Theresa's planners with a pair of rulers, planted with neoclassical architecture. The street passes over the **Canale Grande**, an inlet with moorings for small craft; adjacent Piazza Ponterosso has a daily **market**. At the head of the canal is the temple-fronted Roman Catholic church of **Sant'Antonio** and, near it, the exotic, blue-domed Serbian Orthodox **Santo Spiridone**. Just over the canal, overlooking the sea on Riva Tre Novembre, is Trieste's oldest coffee house, **Caffè Tommaseo** (1830), with *belle époque* furnishings.

Trieste's heart, **Piazza dell'Unità d'Italia**, is one of Italy's largest squares. It faces the harbour, framed by the **Palazzo del Comune**, topped by two Moors who ring the bell in the clock tower; on one side the **Palazzo del Governo** glows in its bright skin of neoclassical mosaics, on the other broods the **Palazzo di Lloyd Triestino**, now the seat of Friuli-Venezia Giulia's regional government. On one side, a pile of rocks and statuary purported to represent the *Four Continents* (1750) may send you staggering off for a drink at the **Caffè degli Specchi**, once an Irredentist meeting place.

Trieste keeps its art a few blocks south of Piazza dell'Unità d'Italia, around Piazza Venezia. The **Museo Revoltella**, Via Diaz 27 (*open Mon and Weds–Sat 9–2,Sun 9–1.30; longer hours for temporary exhibitions; guided tours 9, 10.30, 12, 3 and 6; adm*), was founded by Baron Pasquale Revoltella, one of the financiers of the Suez Canal (which was a big boon to Trieste's port). Full of original furnishings, it contains 18th- and 19th-century paintings by Triestine artists that evoke the city's golden days, as well as modern works by Morandi and De Chirico. Up a block, on Largo Papa Giovanni XXIII, the **Museo Sartorio** (*currently closed; call **t** 040 301 479 for information*), housed in an 18th-century villa, offers a glimpse into Triestine bourgeois life in the 19th century, along with a mix of new and old art, including a triptych by Paolo Veneziano.

Up the Capitoline Hill

Catch bus no.24 from the station or Piazza dell'Unità to ascend Trieste's very own Capitoline Hill, the nucleus of the Roman and medieval city. In the 5th century the Triestini raised the first of two basilicas here to their patron San Giusto. An adjacent basilica, built in the 11th century, was linked to the earlier church in the 14th century, giving the **Cathedral of San Giusto** (*closed 12–3*) its curious plan. The doorway, under a splendid Gothic rose window, is framed by the fragments of a Roman sarcophagus: six funerary busts gaze solemnly ahead like a corporate board of directors, while a Roman frieze embedded in the adjacent, squat campanile resembles a fashion plate for armour. The interior has some fine mosaics, especially the 13th-century Christ with SS. Giusto and Servulus, as well as good 12th-century frescoes. Buried on the right is Don Carlos, the Great Pretender of Spain's 19th-century Carlist Wars, who died as an exile in Trieste in 1855.

Next to San Giusto are fragments of the Roman forum and a 1st-century basilica, of which two columns have been re-erected. The excellent view over Trieste from here is marred by a 1933 **Monument to the Fallen**, which extols the principal Fascist virtues of

Getting There

By Air

Trieste's **airport**, with daily flights from Rome, Milan and London (on Ryanair), and weekly British Airways flights from London , is 30km north at Ronchi dei Legionari, **t** 0481 773 224. There's a bus to the main bus station. Alitalia is at Piazza Sant'Antonio 1, **t** 040 631 100.

By Rail

There are frequent trains to Venice, Gorizia and Ùdine, as well as to Austria, Slovenia and other destinations in eastern Europe, from the **Stazione Centrale** at Piazza della Libertà 8.

By Long-distance Bus

The main **bus station** at Piazzale Libertà, **t** 040 425 001, has services to Venice, Treviso, Padua, Belluno, Trento, and Cortina and Sappada in the Dolomites; long-distance coaches to Milan, Mantua and Genoa; and international services to Ljubljana, Rijeka, Zagreb, Athens, Istria and more.

By Sea

The *Marconi* links Trieste Weds–Sun late May–Sept with Grado (**t** 040 303 540) and Lignano, Piran (Slovenia) and Umag, Porec, Rovinj and Pula (Croatia). Take a passport for Slovenia and Croatia. Tickets are available from the Stazione Marittima, **t** 040 303 540.

In summer, Anek, Via Rossini 2, runs 4 weekly **ferries** to Greece (Igoumenitsa, Patras and Corfu), **t** 040 322 0561. Sem Ferries, Via Milano 4, sail to Split once weekly, **t** 040 760 033.

Getting Around

Finding one's way around on foot is relatively simple, though use the crossings carefully – these streets make Rome's seem pedestrian. City **buses, t** 800 016 675, are frequent; most routes run from or by the central bus station.

A **funicular railway** (*tranvia*) runs every 22mins from Piazza Oberdan to Villa Opicina.

Cars are banished from the centre and parking can be diabolical; there are garages/car parks near Piazza della Libertà and Piazza Unità d'Italia. Radio **taxi**, **t** 040 307 730.

Tourist Information

Trieste: Via San Nicoló 20, **t** 040 67961, and Riva III Novembre 9, **t** 040 347 8312.

Friuli regional tourist office: Via G. Rossini 6, **t** 040 363 952, *www.triestetourism.it*.

Where to Stay

Trieste ✉ 34100

Very Expensive–Luxury

****__Duchi d'Aosta__, Piazza dell'Unità d'Italia 2, **t** 040 760 0011, *www.majesta.com*. The city's finest hotel, in an 1873 palace on its finest square. The luxurious rooms have all modern comforts, and there's a superb restaurant, **Harry's Grill.**

Expensive

***__Duino Park__, along the coast at Duino, near the old citadel, **t** 040 208184, *www.duinoparkhotel.it*. A modern hotel with a pool and private spot of beach.

***__Milano__, Via Ghega 17, **t** 040 369 680, *www.hotel-milano.com*. A comfy place by the station.

***__Novo Hotel Impero__, Via S. Anastasia 1, **t** 040 364 242, *www.fenicehotels.it*. A good option near the station. Some rooms are *moderate*.

***__Nuovo Hotel Daneu__, Strada per Vienna 55, Opicina, **t** 040 214 241, *www.hoteldaneu.com*. A hotel with a good restaurant and indoor pool, above the hurly-burly of the big city.

***__San Giusto__, Via C. Belli 3, **t** 040 762 661, *www.hotelsangiusto.it*. A modern, well-equipped hotel by the historic hill. Some rooms are in the *moderate* bracket.

strength and vulgarity. The 15th-century **Castello di San Giusto**, which was started by the Venetians and finished by the Austrians, offers more views from its ramparts and a small **Museo Civico** (*currently closed*) full of armour and weapons. Located just down the lane from the cathedral is the **Civico Museo di Storia ed Arte e Orto Lapidario** (***t** 040 308 686; open Tues–Sun 9–1, Weds until 7; adm*), housing finds from

Moderate

★★**Hotel James Joyce**, Via dei Cavazzeni 7, **t** 040 311 023. A newly opened, cosy and popular hotel with 12 rooms a couple of minutes' walk from Piazza dell'Unità.

★★★**Lido**, Via Battista 22, Muggia, **t** 040 273 338, *www.hotellido.com* (*moderate*). A modern hotel on the edge of town and the sea, with a restaurant serving local seafood.

Cheap

Look around Via Roma, Via della Geppa or Via XXX Ottobre for budget options.

★★**Belvedere**, Via Sistiana 50, Duino Aurisina, **t** 040 299 256, *www.hotelbelvedere.ts.it* (*cheap*). A reasonable hotel with a garden and sea views.

★**Alabarda-Flora**, Via Valdirivo 22, **t** 040 630 269, *www.alabarda.it*. A clean, cosy and comfortable hotel offering a warm welcome. En suite rooms are *moderate*.

Eating Out

Slovenian and Hungarian influences are strong in the kitchen. *Jota* is a bean, potato and sauerkraut soup, *kaiserknödel* are bread dumplings with grated cheese, ham and parsley. For *secondo*, there's a wide variety of tasty, cheap fish such as *sardoni* (big sardines), fried or marinated. Goulash, roast pork and *stinco* (veal knuckle) are also popular. The middle-European influence is especially noticeable in desserts: strudels, *gnocchi di susine* (plums) and *zavate*, a custard puff pastry.

Very expensive

Al Cantuccio, Via Cadorna 14a, **t** 040 300 131. A haven for lovers of creative food, located right by the seafront. Try the scallops with pinenuts and balsalmic vinegar, the risotto with prawns and prosecco, or the chicken with black grapes, then delicious zabaglione with bitter chocolate.

Expensive

Antica Trattoria Suban, Via Comici 2, **t** 040 54368. A wonderful old inn in the suburb of San Giovanni (take a taxi – it's hard to find), with fine views over Trieste. The *cucina Triestina* on offer includes a famous *jota* and *sevapcici* (Slovenian grilled meat fritters). *Closed Mon lunch, Tues, part of Jan, and Aug.*

Città di Cherso, Via Cadorna 6, **t** 040 366 044. Delicious seafood Friuli-style. *Closed Tues, and end-July–end-Aug.*

Moderate

Scabar, Via dell'Istria at Erta di S. Anna 63, **t** 040 810 368. Gourmet fish and mushroom dishes; the day's special is usually fantastic. *Closed Mon, Tues, Feb, and mid-July–Aug.*

Cheap

Birreria Forst, Via Galatti 11 (near Piazza Oberdan), **t** 040 365 276. An old favourite for goulash and beer. *Closed Sun.*

Buffet da Pepi, Via Cassa di Risparmo 3, **t** 040 366 858. A thriving restaurant founded in 1903, offering Trieste specialities. *Closed Sun and half of July.*

Re di Coppe, Via Geppa 11, **t** 040 370 330. A place where the waiters still write orders on the tablecloths. Try the classic *jota*. *Closed Sat, Sun and mid-July–mid-Aug.*

Entertainment

The **opera** season at the Teatro Comunale Verdi runs from Nov to March; in summer the theatre and the Sala Tripcovich in Piazza della Libertà play host to an International Operetta Festival (**t** 040 672 2500, *www.teatroverdi-trieste.com*).

Carnival is celebrated with Venetian flair in the fishing port of Muggia, with a lavish parade. In early Oct Trieste puts on a splendid regatta and festival, the Coppa d'Autunno Barcolana, with concerts and markets.

ancient Tergeste, and a famous 5th-century deer's head rhyton from ancient *Tarentum*. The Orto Lapidario contains a red granite Egyptian sarcophagus and the tomb of J. J. Winckelmann, the famous art historian who was murdered in Trieste in 1768 by a cook. On the way down to the centre, make sure to have a look at the 1st-century **Roman theatre** on Via Teatro Romano.

More Cafés and Museums

The Grand Cafés, once filled with fervent conversation and spies, have mostly vanished, or deal primarily in nostalgia. Joyce was an habitué of **Caffè Pirona**, Largo Barriera Vecchia 12, north of the castle hill; locals say he conceived *Ulysses* over its *pinzas* and *putizzas*. On the other side of Piazza Goldoni, **Caffè San Marco**, Via Cesare Battisti 18, was rebuilt after it was blown up in the First World War, with Venetian murals that betrayed the owner's pro-Italian sentiments. A street away, on Via San Francesco, is Italy's most beautiful **synagogue**, built in 1910 on ancient Syriac models.

At Via Romagna 6 the **Ipanema Rovis** (*call **t** 040 308 686 for open hours*) is a real treasure trove of minerals and fossils, the personal collection of a former coffee importer from Istria. Items on display include enormous amethyst druses and geodes and a giant petrified tree trunk. In sombre counterpoint, Trieste had Italy's only concentration camp used for mass exterminations, the **Risiera di San Sabba** at the southern extreme of the city (Ratto della Pileria 1; *bus nos.20, 21, 23 or 19, or no.8 from the station*). The building now houses a small **museum** (*open Tues–Sun 9–1*).

Excursions from Trieste

You can't go far without running into Slovenia. For a short jaunt, take the **Opicina Tranvia** up the cliffs from Piazza Oberdan for the fine panorama from the **Vedetta d'Opicina**. Another popular excursion is to **Miramare**, seven kilometres up the beach-lined Riviera di Barcola (bus no.36 from Piazza Oberdan or Stazione Centrale). On the way the **Faro della Vittoria** is a lofty lighthouse and 1927 war memorial to sailors.

Miramare: Habsburg Folly by the Sea

*Open daily Mar–Oct 9–6; Nov–Feb 9–6.30; adm. Park open daily summer 9–sunset, winter 8–5. To do sub aqua or look round the visitors' centre of the marine park, call **t** 040 224 147.*

Set on its own promontory by the sea, the castle of Miramare hides a dark history behind its charming 19th-century façade. It was built by the Habsburg Archduke Maximilian and his Belgian wife Carlotta, and visitors are greeted by a stone sphinx with a cryptic smile that seems to ask, 'Why did Maximilian leave this pleasure palace and let Napoleon III's financiers con him into becoming Mexico's puppet emperor in 1864, and why did he linger around there to face a firing squad three years later? Was he an idealist as his apologists claim, or too much of a Habsburg to know any better?'

Carlotta, after desperately trying to rally European support for her husband, went mad after his execution and survived him for another 50 years in Belgium; while Miramare acquired the ominous reputation of laying a curse on anyone who slept within its walls, when another Habsburg – the Archduke Ferdinand – stayed here on his way to assassination in Sarajevo. When the Americans occupied the palace in 1946, their superstitious commander insisted on sleeping out in the park in a tent.

The charming park was designed by Maximilian, who made a better botanist than emperor of Mexico; the gardens and coastal waters are now managed by the Worldwide Fund for Nature and shelter the rare Stella's otter and marsh harriers.

The Carso

Most of Trieste's slender province lies within the Carso, named for its karst or pliable limestone, easily eroded by the rain into remarkable shapes – and here, pale cliffs that form Italy's most dramatic Adriatic coastline north of Monte Cònero. Inland the karst has been buffeted into petrified waves of rock dotted with *dolinas* (swallow holes), and underground, aeons of dripping water have formed vast caverns, ravines and subterranean lakes and rivers. Elsewhere the landscape is dominated by sumach, which autumn ignites into a hundred shades of scarlet.

Between Miramare and the industrial shipbuilding town of Monfalcone lies the fishing village of Duino, with its 15th-century **Castello Nuovo** (*t 040 208 120; open Mar–Sept Weds–Sun 9.30–5.30; Oct and Nov Weds–Sun 9.30–4; Dec–Feb by appointment*) on a promontory over the sea. Castello Nuovo has long been owned by the Princes von Thurn und Taxis, one of whom played host to Rilke here from 1910 to 1911. There's a beautiful two-kilometre **Rilke walk** along the promontory, beginning in nearby **Sistiana**, a pretty resort with a yacht harbour. In summer the castle hosts a sound and light show, 'Miramare's Imperial Dream' (*Fri and Sat mid-July–Aug 9.30 and 11pm; adm; call* **t** *040 679 6111 for possible performances in English*).

The main attraction in the Carso is the **Grotta Gigante** (*t 040 327 312; bus no.42 every 30mins from Piazza Oberdan; guided tours Tues–Sun Mar–Oct 10–4, also Mon in July and Aug; Nov–Feb 10–12; adm exp*), the largest cavern in the world open to visitors. A 346ft pair of stalactites are the biggest anywhere. A belvedere overlooks a sheer 360ft drop. The cave is in Sgonico, also the site of a beautiful botanical garden, the **Carsiana** (*open 25 Apr–15 Oct Tues–Fri 10–12, Sat, Sun and hols 10–1 and 3–7*).

The Duino Elegies

When Princess Marie von Thurn und Taxis left Rilke alone in the castle in the winter of 1910–11, the poet was restless. One day he received a nasty business letter, and despite the blustery winds went for a walk along the bastions to sort out his thoughts. In the wind and waves crashing far below he heard a voice: 'Who, if I cried, would hear me among the angelic orders?' It was the muse he had been waiting for; he jotted the words down, and by evening the first of his 10 'Duino Elegies' was written. Another followed, but 11 years and the war intervened before his 'voice' returned and he completed them.

As the expression of Rilke's very personal and prophetic vision of reality, the Elegies were as difficult to write as they are to read. Rilke felt that in the 20th century it was impossible to find external symbols to express our inner lives and, like Blake, he used angels in a highly personal way. On one level, as he wrote to his Polish translator, he felt a responsibility and foreboding that many Europeans of his time dimly understood:

'Now there comes crowding over from America empty, indifferent things, pseudo-things, dummy life... The animated, experienced things that share our lives are coming to an end and cannot be replaced. We are perhaps the last to have still known such things. On us rests the responsibility of preserving not merely their memory (that would be little and unreliable), but their human and laral worth...'

Gorizia and Around

The frontier town of Gorizia was for centuries ruled by a powerful dynasty of counts, who were always ready to stir up trouble against Venice, with the approval of the kings of Hungary. When the last count died in 1500, the city was briefly controlled by Venice before being taken over by the Habsburgs. As in Trieste, the Austrians gave Gorizia broad, straight boulevards and parks.

The city saw fierce fighting in the First World War, but it was after the Second World War that it became Italy's Berlin, thoughtlessly divided between Italy and Slovenia. Things improved in 1979, when residents were granted a 16-kilometre zone around the city to transact their affairs freely. In 1991 Gorizia saw the first shots of the Balkan War, when Slovenia declared independence and the Yugoslav army was sent in to wrest back the lucrative border posts. Today, as independent Slovenia prospers, it has flashy boutiques catering for cross-border traffic.

Borgo Castello

This is a little medieval village within the city, enveloped by a Venetian fortress of 1509. In the centre the **Castle of the Counts of Gorizia**, first mentioned in 1001 but rebuilt after the First World War, houses the **Museo del Medioevo Goriziano** (*closed for restoration*), with a display dedicated to Gorizia's complicated history. Just below is the pretty church of **Santo Spirito** (1386) and the **Museo Provinciale** (*open Tues–Sun summer 10–7, winter 10–1 and 2–7; adm*), featuring local artists, especially Giuseppe Tominz, painter of the bourgeoisie of Gorizia and Trieste (*d*. 1866). Best of all are the basement rooms, dedicated to the Isonzo front and its trenches.

Tourist Information

Gorizia: Via Roma 5, **t** 0481 386 222/5/4, *www.comune.gorizia.it*.

Where to Stay and Eat

Gorizia ✉ 34170

★★★★**Golf Hotel**, Via Oslavia 2, San Floriano del Collio, just north of town, **t** 0481 884 051, *www.romantikgolfhotel.it* (*very expensive*). A 17th-century manor house with 15 rooms, a pool, tennis courts and golf facilities.

★★★**Euro Diplomat**, Corso d'Italia 63, **t** 0481 82166, *www.eurodiplomathotel.it* (*cheap–moderate*). The best place to stay in town, with modern rooms on the main street.

Lanterna d'Oro al Castello, Borgo Castello, **t** 0481 82007 (*expensive*). Splendid medieval surroundings where you can feast on Friuli specialities such as *prosciutto di San Daniele*, and good game. *Closed Sun eve and Mon.*

Cormòns ✉ 34071

★★★**Felcaro**, Via S. Giovanni 45, **t** 0481 60214, *www.hotelfelcaro.it* (*moderate–expensive*). The best place to sleep in the Collio – an old Austrian villa spread out over several buildings, with a pool and a fine restaurant specializing in game dishes.

★★★**La Subida**, Monte 22, **t** 048 60531, *www.lasubida.it* (*moderate–expensive*). A handful of rooms, some sleeping up to 5, in a charming rural setting, with an outdoor pool and riding facilities. The restaurant, **Il Cacciatore** (*very expensive*), serves excellent regional dishes, with extensive borrowings from Slovenia. Cold breast of pheasant in mushroom cream is a popular summer dish. *Restaurant closed at lunch except Sat and Sun.*

Al Giardinetto, Via Matteotti 54, **t** 0481 60257, (*very expensive*). Innovative Friulian dishes such as *millefoglie di polenta* and gnocchi with crinkly cabbage and game sauce. *Closed Mon eve, Tues and July.*

Wine Around Gorizia

The hills around Gorizia, the Collio, have produced wonderful white wines since the Middle Ages. You can taste all the Friulian wines at the Enoteca Regionale Serenissima (*open Tues–Sun 10–1 and 4–11*) at Gradisca d'Isonzo. Cormòns, another major wine town, is home to the Cantina Prodottori Vini del Collio e Isonzo, t 0481 61798 (*closed Sun*), which produces a Vino della Pace, made from vines gathered from around the globe, and sent out annually to the world's heads of state.

In 1990 Guglielmo Coronini, last count of Gorizia, died. You can wander through the English park of his home, the **Villa Coronini Cronberg** (1594), Viale XX Settembre 14 (*open Tues–Sat 10–1 and 4–8, Sun 10–12 and 4–8*); the villa is only open for special exhibitions.

In modern Gorizia, at Via Ascoli 19, is a **synagogue** (*open Tues and Thurs 6–8pm, winter 5–7pm, also 10–1 on 2nd Sun of month*) housing a museum of the former Jewish community of Gorizia and the personal art collection of Jewish philosopher Carlo Michelstaedter, who committed suicide at the age of 23.

Ùdine

Ùdine is something of a well-kept secret, scorned even by Italians from further south, who don't know what they're missing. Artistically, you'll see much that looks Venetian and much by lagoonland's greatest 18th-century painter, Giambattista Tiepolo, thanks to his first important patron, Patriarch Dionisio Delfino, who kept him here with commissions between 1726 to 1730. The city itself took Aquileia's place as seat of the patriarchate from 1238 to 1751. In 1420 its leading family gave it to the Serenissima. In the Second World War it was the last city in Italy to be liberated.

Piazza della Libertà

This has been called 'the most beautiful Venetian square on *terra firma*'. Its most striking building, the candy-striped **Loggia del Lionello**, a mini doge's palace, was built by a goldsmith in 1448 and faithfully reconstructed after a fire in 1876. A second loggia, the **Loggia di San Giovanni** (1533), supports a clock tower and a bell rung by two Venetian-inspired 'Moors'. There is the usual Venetian column topped by a Lion of St Mark, accompanied by statues of Heracles and Justice, with unusual Bette Davis eyes. The **Municipio**, all in white Istrian stone, is a fine piece of Art Deco by Raimondo D'Aronco (1910–31) that blends right in.

Palladio's rugged **Arco Bollani** (1556) forms the gateway to the sweeping **portico**, which was built in 1487 to shelter visitors to the **Castello**, former seat of the Patriarch and the Venetian governor. Rebuilt in 1517, and restored after the earthquake, it now houses the **Civici Musei** (*open Tues–Sat 9.30–12.30 and 3–6; Sun and hols 9.30–12.30; adm, free Sun am*); sections include prints and a large and excellent collection of paintings, with especially good works by Carpaccio, Giambattista Tiepolo and a painter who is little known outside his hometown but well worth looking at, Luca Carlefarijs of Ùdine (1662–1730).

Getting Around

Ùdine's **railway station** (from which there are services to Venice, Trieste and Gorizia) is on Viale Europa Unità; a private local railway links the station with Cividale (20mins). The **bus station** is on the other side of the same street, **t** 0432 504 012.

Tourist Information

Ùdine: Piazza 1 Maggio 7, **t** 0432 295 972.
Cividale del Friuli: Corso Paolino d'Aquileia 10, **t** 0432 731 461.

Where to Stay and Eat

Ùdine ✉ 33100

★★★★**Astoria Hotel Italia**, Piazza XX Settembre 24, **t** 0432 505 091, *www.hotelastoria.udine.it* (*expensive–very expensive*). The *grande dame* of Ùdine hotels, in the heart of town, with air-conditioning, a garage, rooms with all mod cons, and a fine restaurant specializing in Venetian meat and fish dishes. The frescoed conference room is by Japelli.

★★★**Al Bue**, Pracchiuso 75, **t** 0432 299 070, *www.locandaalbue.it* (*moderate–expensive*). A hotel-restaurant with 12 clean and comfortable rooms and a small garden close to Piazza 1 Maggio.

★★★**La' di Moret**, Viale Tricesimo 276, just north of centre, **t** 0432 545 096, *www.ladimoret.it* (*moderate–expensive*). An elegant turn-of-the-19th-century hotel with award-winning rooms. The restaurant, which is one of the best in the region, serves Friuli-style seafood. *Restaurant closed Sun eve and Mon.*

★★★**Hotel Cristallo**, Piazzale D'Annunzio 43, **t** 0432 501 919, *www.cristallohotel.com* (*moderate*). A well-priced, very comfortable option between the station and the centre, with secure parking.

★**Al Vecchio Tram**, Brenari 32, **t** 0432 502516, (*cheap*). A good budget option right in the centre, with shared bathrooms.

Vitello d'Oro, Via Valvason 4, **t** 0432 508 982 (*very expensive*). A historic inn offering traditional specialities, with an emphasis on fish. *Closed Weds and 3wks July.*

Osteria di Villafredda, Via Liuti 7, Loc. Loneriacco, between Udine and Tarcento, **t** 0432 792 153, (*expensive*). A popular *osteria* with delicious local specialities such as vegetable and basil soup, and veal with sage. Try the blueberry strudel with cinnamon ice cream for dessert. *Closed Sun eve and Mon.*

Caffè Contarena, Piazza Libertà, **t** 0432 512741 (*cheap*). A beautiful Stilo Liberty bar owned by the Enoteca Regionale La Serenissima, with local beer and fine wines, delicious nibbles and knowledgeable staff.

Vecchio Stallo, Via Viola 7, **t** 0432 21296 (*cheap*) A charming, excellent-value restaurant, offering a selection of good food and wines by the glass. *Closed Weds.*

Cividale del Friuli ✉ 33043

★★★**Locanda al Castello**, Via del Castello 20, suburb of Fortino, **t** 0432 733 242, *www.alcastello.net* (*moderate–expensive*). An ivy-covered hotel in a former fortified Jesuit seminary, with Cividale's most atmospheric rooms, and a fine restaurant with views from its balcony. *Closed Nov and Feb.*

★★★**Roma**, Via G. Gallina, **t** 0432 731 871, *www.hotelroma-cividale.it* (*moderate*). A central modern hotel with parking.

★★**Locanda Pomo d'Oro**, Piazza S. Giovanni 20, **t** 0432 734 189, *www.alpomodoro.com* (*moderate*). A romantic hotel set in an 11th-century hostel.

Alla Frasca, Via de Rebeis 8a, **t** 0432 731 270 (*expensive*). A restaurant with a charming Renaissance atmosphere and tasty Friulian dishes, including a *menu di funghi* featuring truffles and mushrooms in every dish. *Closed Mon, Jan and Feb.*

Al Fortino, Via Carlo Alberto 46, **t** 0432 731 217 (*expensive*). A pleasant place offering typical Friuli fare and home-made pasta. *Closed Mon lunch and Tues.*

Il Cantiniere Romano, Via Ristori 31, **t** 043 273 2033 (*moderate*). A restaurant offering a fine array of *salumi*, cheese, desserts and wines, plus excellent cooked food, including asparagus flan, steamed sea bass, chicory soup, and couscous with fish. *Closed Sun, and Mon eve.*

Trattoria Al Paradiso, Via Cavour 21, **t** 0432 732 438 (*cheap*). A good trattoria that's always packed with locals. *Closed Mon.*

Down in the City

Just east of Piazza Libertà, the oft-altered **Duomo** has a charming 14th-century lunette over the door with figures so weathered they look like gingerbread. The inside, a dignified Baroque symphony of grey and gold, has two frescoes by Tiepolo. In the campanile, the small **Museo del Duomo** has excellent 1349 frescoes of the *Funeral of St Nicolas* by Vitale da Bologna, and a 14th-century sarcophagus. In 1759, when he was at the height of his powers, Tiepolo returned to fresco the **Oratorio della Purità** (*ask at the sacristy if they'll let you in*), added to the cathedral in 1680; he also painted the altarpiece of the *Immaculate Conception*; the chiaroscuro frescoes on the walls are by his son Giandomenico.

There's more on the Tiepolo trail: from Piazza Libertà take Via Manin to Piazza Patriarcato and the **Museo Diocesano** (*open Weds–Sun 10–12 and 3.30–6.30; adm*), with a gallery of Old Testament scenes frescoed by G.B. in the 1720s. There's more recent art (Severini, Carrà, De Chirico, De Kooning, Lichtenstein, Dufy, and the brothers Afro, Mirko and Dino Basaldell of Ùdine) in the **Galleria d'Arte Moderna** (*open Tues–Sat 9.30–12.30 and 3–6, Sun 9.30–12.30; adm, free Sun am*): take bus no.2 from the station.

Cividale del Friuli

A hop and skip from Ùdine in the valley of the Natisone, this is a fine old town founded by Caesar in 50 BC and named for his family, *Forum Iulii*, condensed over the centuries into 'Friuli'. The Lombards invaded in 568 and made Cividale the capital of their first duchy. The Patriarch of Aquileia moved here in 737, initiating a magnificent period documented by Paulus Diaconus, the Lombard historian born in Cividale.

The town centre is a series of squares around the old forum. In the most important, **Piazza Duomo**, is the 13th–15th-century **Palazzo Comunale**, a statue of Caesar and the **Duomo** (*open 9.30–12 and 3–7, till 6 in winter*), begun in 1453 and given its plain Renaissance façade by Pietro Lombardo. It contains a 12th-century silver altarpiece, the *Pala di Pellegrino II*, with 25 saints and two archangels; a fine gilded equestrian monument (1617); and the Renaissance sarcophagus of Patriarch Nicolò Donato. Off the right aisle, the **Museo Cristiano** (***t*** *0432 731 144; open daily 9.30–12 and 3–7, until 6 in winter*) contains the octagonal Baptistry of Callisto and the Altar of Ratchis, dating back to 749, when there was still considerable confusion about lion anatomy and how hands and arms are attached to the human body. In the scene of the Magi, Mary and baby Jesus frown as if they didn't like their presents.

Next to the Duomo, the **Museo Archeologico Nazionale** (***t*** *0432 700 700; open Mon 9–2, Tues–Fri 8.30–7.30; adm*), housed in Palladio's Palazzo Pretorio, is a vast treasure of Roman items, especially the unique Zuglio bronzes – an enormous shield with a man's portrait in the centre – as well as objects from Lombard tombs of the 6th and 7th centuries: crosses, *fibulae*, swords and shield-holders (*ambone*). There are ivory pieces for a game called *ad tabulam*, the 8th-century Carolingian *Pax del Duca Orso*, adorned with an ivory crucifix and studded with jewels; a 5th-century Evangelical of St Mark, autographed by Lombard nobles who thought it was written in the apostle's hand; and architectural bits and bobs from the Romanesque Duomo – mermaids, monsters and a man in a funny hat.

Just up from the Ponte del Diavolo is the mysterious **Ipogeo Celtico**, Via Monastero 6 (*Bar All'Ipogeo on Via Paolino d'Aquileia*, **t** *0432 701 211, has the key*), a creepy pit that may have served as a funeral chamber in the 3rd century BC. The Romans and Lombards used it as a prison, where unfortunates would have had to look at the three monstrous carved heads that peer out of the walls, seemingly since the dawn of time.

Follow the Natisone river up to the happier **Tempietto Longobardo**, or Santa Maria in Valle (*open Apr–Sept Mon–Sat 9.30–12.30 and 3–6.30, Sun 9.30–1 and 3–7.30; Oct–Mar 9.30–12.30 and 3–5, Sun and hols 9.30–12.30 and 2.30–6; adm*), the finest 8th-century work in Italy, restored in the 13th century after an earthquake shattered most of its ornamentation and all of its mosaics. The stuccoes that remain are a love letter from the Dark Ages: ravishing, uncanny and perhaps even miraculous: gently smiling saints and princesses in high relief, standing at either side of a beautiful, intricately carved window, all positioned over an even more intricate arch with a vine motif.

North of Ùdine: the Julian and Carnia Alps

The mountainous north of Ùdine is linked to the city by an *autostrada* that has yet to bring in the crowds. The Julian Alps are Slovene-speaking, their church towers crowned with colourful garlic domes. If the peaks lack the romance of their Dolomite neighbours, they also lack their crowds and lofty prices.

Into Friuli's Mountains

Just off the *autostrada*, **Gemona** and **Venzone** were the epicentre of the 1976 earthquake. Residents rebuilt them meticulously, in a labour of love that is almost completed. Set in the Julian foothills, Gemona del Friuli's gem is a 13th-century cathedral with a façade featuring a remarkable St Christopher, sculpted by a Nordic artist in 1331. Nearby Venzone, a smaller, double-walled town, began as a crossroads stop on the Julia Augusta road. A display under the painted ceiling of the loggia has astonishing 'before and after' photographs of the earthquake zone.

The *autostrada* continues northeast into the Julian Alps. The mountains south of **Tarvisio** (near the Austrian and Slovenian borders) cradle an up-and-coming resort, **Sella Nevea**, near two pretty lakes. Tri-national ski passes are available.

The Carnia Mountains rise to the west, next to the Dolomites. **Tolmezzo**, an 18th-century producer of damasks and taffetas, is the main town and transport hub of the mountains. In a 16th-century palace in Via della Vittoria, the **Museo Carnico Delle Arti Popolari** (**t** *0433 43233; open Tues–Sun 9–1 and 3–6, also Mon in Aug and hols*) has a fine ethnographic collection covering mountain life in the 14th–19th centuries. Beyond Tolmezzo the scenery grows increasingly delightful. From **Comeglians** there is a scenic road up to **Sappada** in the Cadore (*see* p.410). West of Tolmezzo, at **Ampezzo**, pick up the road to isolated **Sauris** with its beautiful lake. The road west to Pieve di Cadore (*see* p.409) passes **Forni di Sotto**, a village rebuilt after the Nazis burnt it down in reprisal for partisan activities, and **Forni di Sopra**, in a beautiful setting, with a fine 15th-century triptych in the Romanesque church of San Floriano.

Emilia-Romagna

13

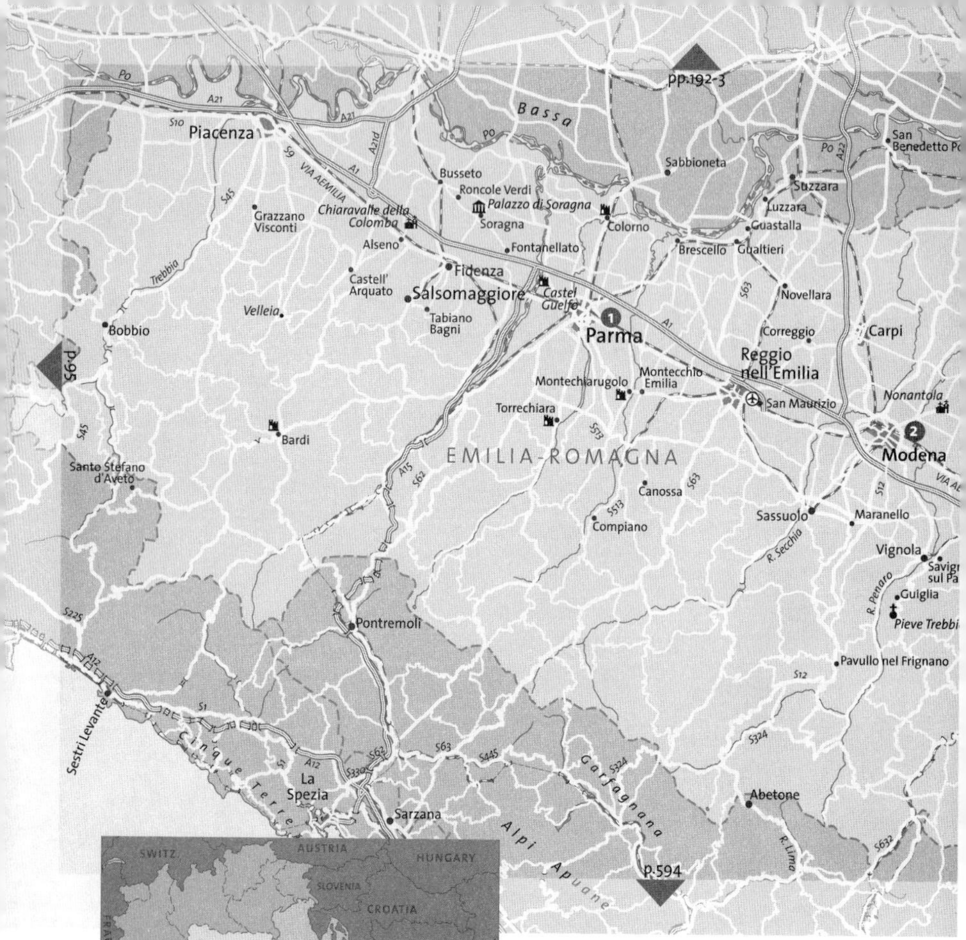

Highlights

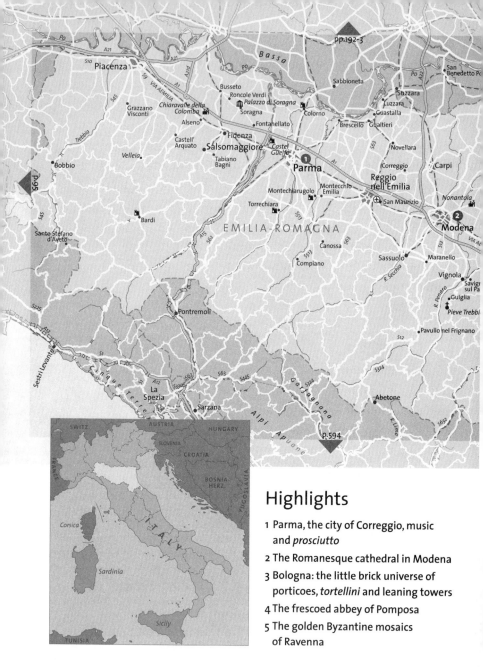

1 Parma, the city of Correggio, music and *prosciutto*
2 The Romanesque cathedral in Modena
3 Bologna: the little brick universe of porticoes, *tortellini* and leaning towers
4 The frescoed abbey of Pomposa
5 The golden Byzantine mosaics of Ravenna

Between the sparkling wines of Lombardy, the elegant Soave of the Veneto and the full-bodied Chianti of Tuscany, Emilia-Romagna seems like a glass of warm beer. It is mostly flat, on the southern plain of the Po, hot and humid in summer and cold and fog-bound in the winter. Most tourists see it only from the train window when they're chugging between Venice and Florence.

But for anyone interested in cracking the surface of this glossiest and most complex of nations, Emilia-Romagna is an essential region to know. For this is Middle Italy: agricultural, wealthy, progressive, a barometer of Italian highs and lows – the birthplace of the country's socialist movement, but also of Mussolini and Fascism. In Emilia-Romagna hard-working cities such as Modena, Parma and Bologna share space with Rimini, Italy's vast, madcap international resort, with Ravenna, the artistic jewel of the region with its stupendous Byzantine mosaics, and with traditional Apennine villages. Emilia-Romagna is the cradle of innovative film directors – Fellini, Bertolucci and Antonioni; of musical giants such as Verdi, Toscanini, Pavarotti, Tebaldi and Bergonzi; and of such diverse talents as Marconi, Correggio, Savonarola, Ariosto, Pavarotti, Parmigianino and Ferrari.

As a united region, Emilia-Romagna is a child of the Risorgimento. Emilia, to the west of Bologna, was named after the Via Aemilia, built by Marcus Aemilius Lepidus in 187 BC between Piacenza and Rimini, running almost dead straight for hundreds of kilometres along the course of the Apennines. Nearly all of Emilia's cities grew up at intervals along the road, like beads on a string. Romagna, east of Bologna, recalls the period from the 5th century to 751 when this was 'Rome', when Ravenna was the last

The Gourmet in Emilia-Romagna

Nothing sums up this area so well as food, and, beside the wonderful experiences awaiting you in restaurants, it's easy to find treats to take home. Cheese, meat, wine, liqueurs and sweets travel well. Most Parmesan cheese, called *Grana* on account of its grainy quality, is actually *Parmigiano-Reggiano*, and is produced around Parma, Modena and Reggio Emilia. A true Parma ham is left to dry in the sweet air of the Magra valley, to lose its excessive saltiness and gain the scent of pine and olives, then taken down the Cisa Pass to take the chestnutty air of the Apennines. Even more revered is *culatello*, a sausage made from a pig's buttocks, which can be prepared only in the humid lowlands of the Po valley.

Nocino is a liqueur that tradition states must come from Sassuolo, near Modena, and be made from unripe walnuts picked on St John's Day, 24 June. Alcohol is poured over the crushed nuts, then sugar, cinnamon, cloves and lemon rind are added; the mixture is left for 40 days before being sieved through cotton. The other great specialities of Modena are balsamic vinegar – the finest of which is as prized and precisely regulated as any DOC wine – and cherries, from Vignola.

In Bologna, the delicatessens sell fresh tortellini, stuffed with any combination of ricotta cheese, minced beef or veal, bread, chicken, nutmeg and fresh herbs. The city is also famous for its desserts and patisserie, the most specialized of which is *torta di riso*, a sweet, thick rice pudding. It is also the home of Lambrusco, which, if it's the right stuff, should foam like a beer when it's first poured, to reveal a sparkling, elegant and full-bodied wine below.

enclave of the Roman Empire in the west, ruled by the exarchs of the Eastern Roman Empire in Byzantium. By the Middle Ages these cities had gone their own way, controlled by dukes or *signori* – the Farnese, Este, Malatesta, Bentivoglio and Da Polenta – who claimed allegiance to the pope, and held the front line between the Papal States and the Venetians and Milanese.

In Emilia-Romagna you'll find, besides the remarkable art of the Byzantines and Ostrogoths in Ravenna, exceptional Romanesque churches (Parma and Modena), two of Italy's crookedest towers (Bologna), beautiful Renaissance art (Parma, Bologna and Ferrara) and the Renaissance's strangest building, the Malatesta Temple in Rimini. You can ski, hike, ride or hang-glide in the Apennines, sunbathe in style on the Adriatic, visit the ancient Republic of San Marino or Italy's ceramics capital at Faenza, or attend grand opera in Parma, Reggio, Bologna or Modena. You'll also find Italy's best food (*see* above), although this is not the place if you want good seafood.

Piacenza

Competing with the more famous charms of nearby Parma and Cremona, Piacenza is the unassuming wallflower of Renaissance cities. Nevertheless, it can boast two of the most gallant horses in Italy, a Botticelli, and an amazing bronze liver. A Roman colony established in 218 BC at the conjunction of the Via Aemilia and the Po, Piacenza was an important *comune* in the 12th and 13th centuries, and a member of the Lombard League in 1314. It spent much of its history under the Farnese thumb, as part of the Duchy of Parma. In 1848, after a plebiscite, Piacenza became the first city to unite with Piemonte in the new nation of Italy, earning itself the nickname of *Primogenita* or 'first-born'.

Piazza Cavalli

Piacenza's excellent Piazza Cavalli (to get there from the station, cut across the park to Via Giulio Alberoni and Via Roma, then turn left on Via Carducci) takes its name from its two bronze horses with flowing manes, masterpieces of the early Baroque, cast in the 1620s by Francesco Mochi. Riding them are two members of the Farnese clan: Alessandro, the 'Prince of Parma', one of the key figures of the 1500s, who was Philip II

Getting Around

The **train** station, on Piazzale Marconi, a 10-min walk from the centre, has frequent connections to Milan, Parma and Cremona. The **bus** station, **t** 0523 390 637, in Piazza Cittadella, near the Palazzo Farnese, has buses to Cremona, Bobbio (10 a day), Grazzano Visconti, Castell'Arquato and other towns in the province. Buses to the Velleia excavations are infrequent; if you go make sure you don't get stranded. STAT Turismo will take you long-distance to Genoa and the Riviera, Bolzano or Trento, **t** 0142 781 660.

Tourist Information

IAT, Piazza Cavalli 7, **t** 0523 329 324 (*closed Mon*), *www.provincia.piacenza.it/turismo*.

Where to Stay

Piacenza ✉ 29100

★★★★**Grande Albergo Roma**, Via Cittadella 14, **t** 0523 323 201 *www.grandealbergoroma.it* (*very expensive*). Piacenza's most prestigious hotel, just off Piazza Cavalli, with soberly elegant woodwork and furnishings, old-fashioned service and the good **Ristorante Panoramico**, with pretty views over the city.

★★★**Hotel City**, Via Emilia Parmense 54, southeast of town on the Parma road, **t** 0523 579 752, *www.hotelcitypc.it* (*expensive*). A modern hotel with 60 quiet rooms.

Ostello Don Zermani, Via Zoni 38/40, **t** 0523 712 319, *www.ostellodipiacenza.it* (*cheap*). A very good youth hostel, with single, double and family rooms, reached from the station by bus nos.3 or 7.

Eating Out

Antica Osteria del Teatro, Via Verdi 16, near Sant'Antonino, **t** 0523 384 639 (*very expensive*). One of Italy's best restaurants, combining local recipes with French *nouvelle cuisine*. The *tortelli del Farnese* with butter and sage are light as a summer breeze; *secondi* include *foie gras* in pastry, layered with honey and Calvados, and roast suckling pig perfumed with myrtle; and for dessert you can splurge on various heavenly chocolate concoctions. Book well in advance. *Closed Sun, Mon and Aug.*

Vecchia Piacenza, San Bernardo 1, **t** 0523 305 462 (*very expensive*). Tasty *antipasti* (try *porcini* if they're on the menu) and *primi* and *secondi* based on the market and the chef's whim. There are two set menus (including wine). *Closed Sun and end June–end July.*

La Pireina, Via Borghetto 137, **t** 0523 338 578 (*cheap*). A traditional trattoria close to the old city walls, serving up typical local and regional dishes cooked in a simple, unpretentious way: *tortelli d'erbetta* (stuffed with spinach and ricotta), *tagliolini al ragù*, and *faldia* (a type of schnitzel made with horse steak). *Closed Sun, Mon eve, and first half of Aug.*

of Spain's governor in the Low Countries during the Dutch War of Independence (not a position that won him any popularity contests, despite the fine statue, his lack of religious fanaticism and his aversion to gratuitous violence and massacres), and his son Ranuccio, a bad Duke and a paranoid waster. The piazza also contains the Gothic Palazzo del Comune, better known to the Piacentini as **Il Gotico** for its pointed arches (*open for temporary exhibitions*), built in 1280, with swallowtail crenellations, mullioned windows and a rose window, and the 13th-century church of San Francesco, noted for its Gothic interior.

Rising up at the end of the main Via XX Settembre, the Lombard–Romanesque **Duomo** (1122–1233) is an imposing pile begun four years before the *comune*; a picturesque confusion of columns, caryatids and galleries in the shadow of an octagonal cupola and campanile (1333). Its façade is undergoing restoration work. The transitional interior (Romanesque to Gothic) has a striking striped marble floor and good 15th-century frescoes. The relics of the city's patron, obscure 4th-century martyr Santa Giustina, are in the impressive crypt, with its 108 columns.

From here Via Chiapponi leads to **Sant'Antonino**, Piacenza's oldest church, with an 11th-century octagonal lantern believed to be the first built in Italy, and a lofty Gothic porch called the Paradiso. Just southwest on Via San Siro and Via Santa Franca, opposite a picturesque but derelict Art Nouveau theatre, is the Ricci–Oddi Gallery (*open Tues–Sun 10–12 and 3–6; adm*), a huge collection that shows a keen eye for what Italian artists were up to between 1800 and 1930.

The Palazzo Farnese

From Piazza Cavalli, Corso Cavour leads to the pachydermic, uncompleted Palazzo Farnese, local headquarters of the ducal family (begun in 1558 by Vignola). Inside is the **Museo Civico** (*open Tues–Thurs 8.30–1, Fri and Sat 8.30–1 and 3–6.30, Sun 9.30–1 and 3–6.30; guided tours mid-Sept–June Tues–Thurs 9.30, Fri 9.30 and 3.30, Sat and Sun 9.30, 11, 3 and 4.30; July–mid-Sept weekday tours start 30mins later; adm*). Botticelli's lovely tondo from the 1480s, when he was trading in mythological fancies for Christian piety, is the highlight of the paintings; you can also see the most famous Etruscan bronze of all: the *fegato di Piacenza*, a model of a sheep's (or some say human) liver, designed for apprentice haruspices, or augurs, diagrammed and inscribed with the names of the Etruscan deities. The Etruscans regarded the liver as a microcosm of the sky, ruled over by the gods, and looked in it for blemishes to see which deity had anything to communicate. The carriage museum contains a wonderful piece of folk art, a Sicilian cart painted with scenes from the operas of Verdi.

Across the courtyard stands the scanty remains of the 14th-century **Cittadella**. The Farnese pulled most of it down, as no doubt the place was an embarrassment to them: Pier Luigi, the first duke, met his end here in 1547 when rebellious Piacentini nobles murdered him and threw his corpse out of a window into the moat.

About two kilometres southwest of the city, the **Collegio Alberoni** (*group visits by appointment,* **t** *0523 455 402*), dedicated to San Lazzaro, has a fine collection of Flemish tapestries and a rare work by Sicilian Antonello da Messina, Italy's first oil painter: his *Ecce Homo* is an unusual composition and the Renaissance's most sorrowful Christ.

Environs of Piacenza

The rarely visited hills and mountains south of Piacenza offer possibilities for excursions or road stops. The main SS45 to Genoa follows the Trebbia valley to **Bobbio** (46 kilometres), where St Columbanus founded a monastery in 612. Columbanus, one of several scholarly Irishmen who came to the illiterate continent as missionaries in the Dark Ages, had also founded the great abbey of Luxeuil (Vosges), but been forced to leave because of his views of the Frankish barons and his Celtic observances. Another, later abbot became Pope Sylvester II in 999 – despite being accused of sorcery for constructing planetary spheres and mechanical clocks.

Bobbio began to decline in the 1400s, and the abbey was largely rebuilt, but the **Basilica** (*open Mon–Sat 8–7; Sun 8–12.30 and 2.30–7*) retains traces of its medieval splendours – a 9th-century campanile and apse; 12th-century mosaics of mythological beasts in the crypt, labelled for the perplexed, including a dragon and a 'quimera' (chimera); and an intricate wrought-iron screen – as well as Columbanus' Renaissance sarcophagus. The **Museo dell'Abbazia** (*open July and Aug daily 3–6, Sat and Sun also 11–12; Sept–June Sat 3–4.30, Sun 11–12 and 3–5*) contains a famous 4th-century *teca*, an ivory urn with reliefs, and Romanesque statuary and painting; in the town of Bobbio, clustered around the monastery and castle, there are many fine old stone houses.

Emilia's best-preserved Roman town, prettily situated on a hillside, is ***Velleia***, 33 kilometres south of Piacenza between Bobbio and Salsomaggiore. It was never very large, but it retains its forum, temple, amphitheatre and strange large carved stones resembling bathplugs. Most of the finds are now in Parma, but bits and pieces remain in the *antiquarium* on the site (*open daily 1 Mar–4 Nov 8–7.30; 5 Nov–28 Feb 8–3*).

If you're driving, cut over the hills from here to Lugagnano and **Castell'Arquato**, a lovely walled hill town built around an asymmetrical Palazzo del Podestà (1293), a picturesque Romanesque church of the same period with a Paradiso portico and some barbaric carved capitals, and its Rocca. Just as picturesque, closer to Piacenza but not as authentic, **Grazzano Visconti** was recently rebuilt in the medieval style. The village is a good place to purchase ornamental wrought iron. Just north of Castell'Arquato, **Vigolo Marchese** has a Romanesque church and a rare 11th-century circular baptistry; inside it are some rare bits of frescoes from the same period.

Piacenza to Parma

North of the Via Aemilia between Piacenza and Parma lies the flat Po valley known as the **Bassa**, a favourite in Italian films. Down the Via Aemilia itself, the Cistercian abbey of **Chiaravalle della Colomba** (*open Mon–Sat 8.30–11.30 and 2.30–5.30; Sun and hols 8.30–12 and 2–6; last entry 30mins before closing time*), four kilometres north of Alseno, has a Romanesque church, Giottesque frescoes and a beautiful brick cloister. More of the same awaits at **Fidenza**, Roman *Fidentia Iulia*, owned by the Pallavicini for 600 years and known for centuries as Borgo San Donnino – until Mussolini resurrected its more imperial-sounding name. It has an interesting 13th-century **Duomo**, with a very lovely porch by the followers of Antelami, the master of Parma's baptistry.

Where to Stay and Eat

Salsomaggiore ✉ 43039

★★★★★**Grand Hotel et de Milan**, Via Dante 1, **t** 0524 572 241, *www.demilan.it* (*very expensive*). The plushest of the scores of hotels to take the waters at, in a large 19th-century country villa once owned by the dukes of Parma. The public rooms have retained their old-fashioned charm. Many bedrooms have private spas, and there's a heated pool in a pretty garden; a solarium and beauty farm; and a restaurant serving both regional cuisine and meals for guests on special diets. *Open April–mid-Dec.*

★★★★**Grand Hotel Porro**, Viale Porro 10, **t** 0524 578 221, *www.grandhotel-porro.it* (*very expensive*). A Liberty-style building in a 12-acre park, dedicated to life in the slow lane, with comfortable rooms to relax in after visits to the spa and sauna. It offers menus for special diets, and is one of the few places in Salsomaggiore open all year.

★★★★**Valentini**, Viale Porro 10, **t** 0524 578 251, *www.hotel-valentini.it* (*moderate–expensive*). An old hotel with its own spa and swimming pool in a tranquil park setting. *Closed 10 Nov–20 Dec.*

Osteria Bellaria, Via Bellaria 14, west of town on the Piacenza road, **t** 0524 573 600 (*expensive*) A restaurant featuring *porcini* and truffles in most of its simply prepared and delicious dishes – *sott'olio* as an *antipasto*, in *tortelli*, in *tortino*, on the grill, next to steak. *Closed Mon, most of Jan, and late July–mid-Aug.*

Busseto ✉ 43011

★★★**Palazzo Calvi**, Frazione Samboseto 26, **t** 0524 90211, *www.palazzocalvi.it* (*very expensive*) The guesthouse of an 18th-century villa just outside the centre, in a lovely garden with a pool. There's also an excellent restaurant and an *enoteca* for Verdian wine-tastings. *Closed Aug.*

★★★**I Due Foscari**, Piazza Carlo Rossi 15, **t** 0524 930 031/039 (*moderate*). The best place to stay in Busseto, named after one of Verdi's operas and owned by the family of a tenor who often performs in them. Neo-Gothic and neo-Moorish, it's small, very comfortable (the public rooms have lovely ceilings and furnishings) and usually full. It also has one of Busseto's best restaurants, offering solid, traditional Parmigiano cooking. *Closed in Jan and Aug.*

South of Fidenza, **Salsomaggiore** ('Big Salt'), with its 109 hotels, is the largest and best-known of a cluster of saline water spas specializing in arthritic and rheumatic cures. It was very popular among members of the Italian royal family at the turn of the 19th century, and is now favoured by opera singers. Its baths, the Terme Berzieri, are concentrated in a half-baked Liberty-style palace, while the Palazzo dei Congressi on Viale Romagnosi was once the grand hotel, owned by César Ritz; past clients included Caruso, Toscanini and Queen Margherita of Italy. The lobby is still one of the grandest in the whole of Italy – it's a Liberty-arabesque fantasy with fabulously colourful frescoes by Galileo Chini. Another important spa nearby is **Tabiano Bagni**, with stinky sulphur springs.

Busseto and its Swan

Some 15 kilometres north of Fidenza on the road to Cremona, Busseto is the attractive, neatly rectangular walled town that gave the world Joe Green – Giuseppe Verdi. To Italians Verdi is not just another great composer, but the genius who expressed the national spirit of the Risorgimento in music: Italy's answer to Richard Wagner. In the 1850s, crowds at the opera screamed 'Viva Verdi!' – but not just as a tribute to the composer: everybody knew it was also a not-too-subtle demand for **V**ittorio **E**manuele, **R**e **D**'**I**talia!

Campanini, Via Roncole Verdi 136, just outside Busseto at Madonna Prati, **t** 0524 92569 (*moderate*). A restaurant that's been in the same family for generations, specializing in *culatello*; the humid environment that is essential for curing it is supplied in spades by the winter fogs here (the famously misty, moist *culatello* capital, Zibello, is located just up the road). Try it, and other cold meats made by the family, as well as their wonderful pasta. In spring they offer sturgeon in parchment, at other times *bolliti* and roast duck. *Closed Tues, Weds and mid-July–mid-Aug.*

Soragna ✉ 43019

****Locando del Lupo**, Via Garibaldi 66, **t** 0524 597 100, *www.locandadellupo@com* (*expensive*). The charming 18th-century coach house and outbuildings of Meli Lupi princes' castle, beautifully restored from their terracotta floors to their oak beams. Baroque paintings adorn the walls, and special pride is taken in the wrought-iron beds, with their dreamy mattresses and linen sheets. The excellent restaurant serves regional and international dishes. Bikes are available for hire.

Antica Osteria Ardenga, Via Maestra 6, Diolo, **t** 0524 598 289 (*expensive*). Another atmospheric one-time property of the Meli Lupi (Bertolucci shot several scenes of his film *La Luna* here), offering *salumi* made *in casa*, *agnolini* in capon broth, *bomba di riso*, and roast duck or goose. *Closed Tues and Weds, and half of July.*

Fontanellato ✉ 43012

Locanda Nazionale, Via A. Costa 7, **t** 0521 822 602 (*moderate*). An excellent restaurant offering Parmigiano home-cooking. All the pasta is home-made (try *maltagliati* with asparagus); hearty second courses include roast duck, *stracotto* (beef braised in red wine and stewed) and *tagliata* (steak) cooked with balsamic vinegar.

Sacca di Colorno ✉ 43052

Stendhal-Da Bruno, Via Sacco 80, **t** 0521 815 493 (*expensive*). The perfect, wonderfully serene gastronomic complement to a visit to the Farnese palace, specializing in fish (eels and small fry from the Po, and sea fish brought in daily from Chioggia). There's also great charcuterie and home-made desserts. *Closed Tues.*

Opera buffs can take in the complete 'Swan of Busseto' tour (*a combined ticket is available for all venues*), beginning in the house at **Roncole** (***t** 0524 97450; open Tues–Sun summer 9.30–12.30 and 3–7; winter 9.30–12.30 and 2.30–5.30; adm*), nine kilometres southeast of Busseto, where the composer was born in 1813 (the same year as Wagner), son of a grocer and tavern-keeper. While in Roncole, you can also visit the parish church where little Giuseppe was baptized and where he played the organ.

In Busseto proper a statue of Verdi relaxes in an armchair near the medieval castle, or **Rocca**, built by Pallavicini lord Oberto, who became the subject of Verdi's first and seldom-heard opera, *Oberto*. The Rocca contains the **Teatro Verdi**, which was modelled after La Scala and built in the composer's honour in 1845; Verdi frequently attended performances. The Rocca's Palazzo Pallavicino is now the **Museo Civico** (***t** 0524 92487; currently undergoing restoration; Sat and Sun 9.30–12 and 3–6.30 a slideshow in the courtyard shows you what you're missing*), full of Verdian memorabilia.

With the proceeds from *Rigoletto*, Verdi built the **Villa Verdi** in Sant'Agata di Villanova, three kilometres to the north of Busseto (***t** 0523 830 000; open Mar–Sept Tues–Sun 9–12 and 3–7; Oct and Nov Tues–Sun 9.30–11.30 and 2.30–5.30; Dec Tues–Fri 10–11.30 and 2.30–4.30, Sat and Sun 9.30–11.30 and 2.30–4.30; Jan Sat and Sun 9.30–11.30 and 2.30–4.30; adm*); it boasts a replica of the hotel room in Milan where Verdi died in 1901.

The Castles of Parma

The province of Parma is known for its beautiful castles, some of which lie between Busseto and Parma. The **Palazzo di Soragna** (*open for guided tours Mar–Oct Tues–Sun 9, 11, 2.30 and 5; Nov–Feb Tues–Sun 9, 11, 3 and 6; adm*), which was begun in the 8th century as a castle, was converted into a palace ten centuries later by its current owners, the princes of Meli Lupi, and was frescoed by the likes of Parmigianino and Gentile da Fabriano.

In Fontanellato the moated Renaissance **Rocca San Vitale** (*open for guided tours 1 Jan–7 Feb Tues–Sat 9.30, 11.30, 3 and 5, Sun and hols 9.30, 12, 2.30 and 5; 8 Feb–15 May daily 9.30–6, also Fri 8.30pm–11; 16 May–31 Oct Tues–Sat 9.30, 11.30, 3 and 6, Sun and hols 9.30, 12, 2.30 and 6; adm*) is much more of a fairy-tale castle. It is adorned inside with frescoes; the rich, sensuous Diana and Actaeon in the boudoir was painted by Parmigianino, hiding here on the run from the police after a spat with some monks in Parma. Another imposing fortress nearby, **Castel Guelfo** (*can only be viewed from the outside*), once belonged to the Ghibelline Pallavicini family of Busseto, but was renamed as an insult by its Guelph captors in 1407.

In **Colorno**, just north of Parma on the road to Mantua, one of the Farnese dukes, Ranuccio II, converted an old castle, **Reggia**, into a 'miniature Versailles' in 1660 (*open for guided tours Apr–Oct Tues–Sun 11 and 4; Mar and Nov Sat, Sun and hols 10, 11, 3, 4 and 5; Dec and Jan Tues–Fri 11 and 3, Sat, Sun and hols 10, 11, 3, 4 and 5*). It has beautiful gardens, with canals, an orangery, and tunnels: the later Bourbon rulers – who spent much time here – must have been nervous, for they installed escape hatches leading all over the countryside, one supposedly running all the way to Parma. Nearby **Castelnuovo Fogliani** (*open by appointment, **t** 0523 947 112*) is a medieval stronghold that was reshaped into an up-to-date palace with sumptuously decorated rooms and a large park by Luigi Vanvitelli, 18th-century court architect to the King of Naples and builder of the 'Italian Versailles' at Caserta.

One other must-see castle in these parts is the **Rocca dei Rossi** at San Secondo Parmense (***t** 0521 873 214; guided tours Tues–Sun 10, 11, 3, 4, 5 and 6, also open Mon pm in Aug; costumed tours 9.30pm last Sat of month; adm*). Troilo Rossi I of the Rossi family made it into an elegant pleasure dome, commissioning the frescoes of the 'Wolf Room', and an original cycle on *The Golden Ass* of Apuleius. Troilo Rossi II added 12 scenes on the glory of the Rossi family.

Parma

Le Monde rates Parma as the best of all Italian cities to live in. Besides its general air of well-being and contentment, Parma's many admirers can cite her splendid churches and elegant lanes, her art and antiquities, the lyrical strains of grand opera that waft from her Teatro Regio – a house that honed the talents of the young Arturo Toscanini – and the glories of its famous cheese and ham at table as reasons not only to visit, but to return again and again. Parma is the place to see the masterpieces of Benedetto Antelami (1177–1233), the great sculptor trained in Provence whose

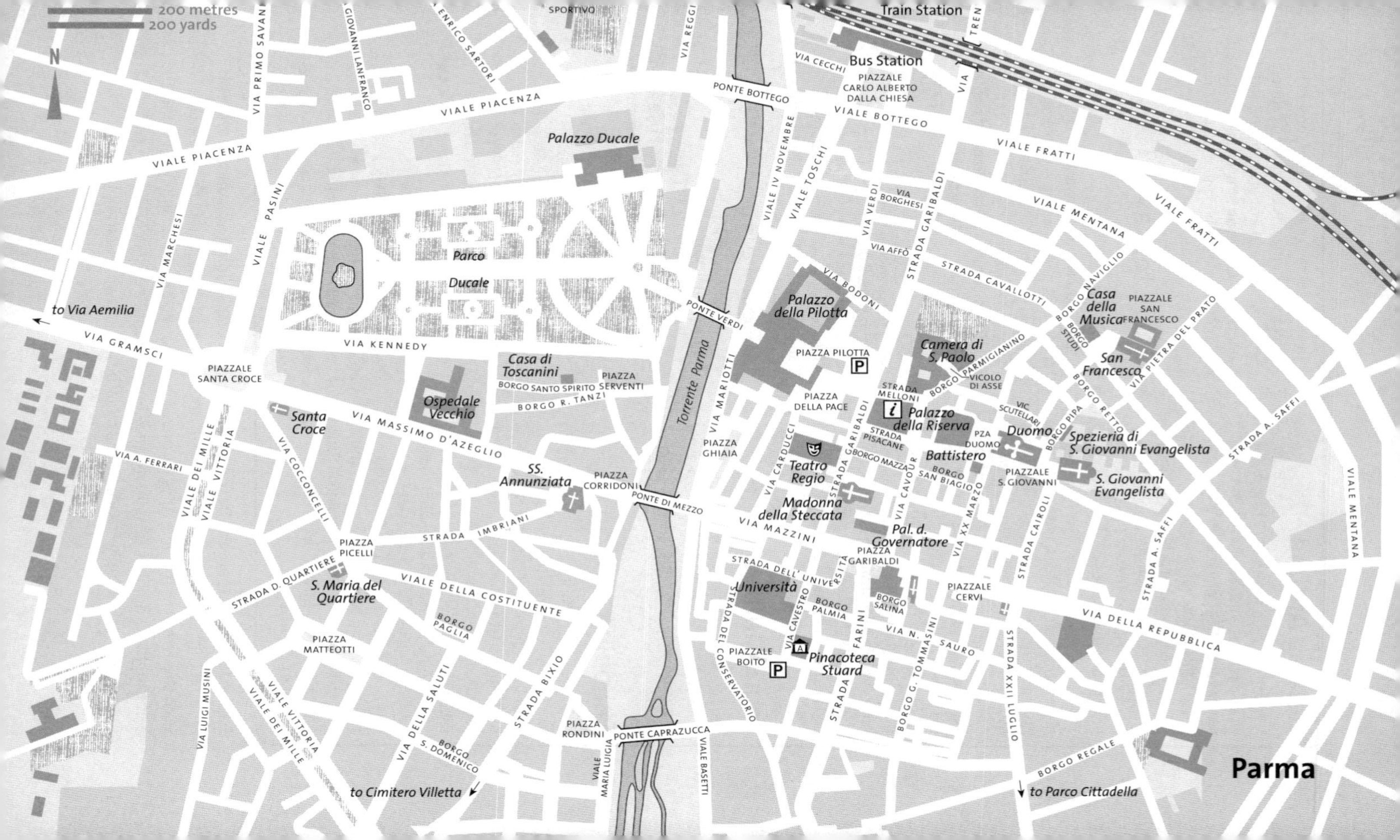
Parma
200 metres
200 yards
N
Train Station
Bus Station
Piazzale Carlo Alberto dalla Chiesa
Via Cecchi
Viale Bottego
Ponte Bottego
Viale Piacenza
Palazzo Ducale
Parco Ducale
Via Kennedy
Via Gramsci
to Via Aemilia
Piazzale Santa Croce
Santa Croce
Casa di Toscanini
Borgo Santo Spirito
Piazza Serventi
Borgo R. Tanzi
Ospedale Vecchio
Via Massimo d'Azeglio
SS. Annunziata
Piazza Corridoni
Ponte di Mezzo
Torrente Parma
Ponte Verdi
Via Mariotti
Piazza Ghiaia
Palazzo della Pilotta
Piazza Pilotta
Piazza della Pace
Via Bodoni
Camera di S. Paolo
Borgo Parmigianino
Vicolo di Asse
Strada Melloni
Palazzo della Riserva
Teatro Regio
Madonna della Steccata
Battistero
Pza Duomo
Duomo
Piazzale S. Giovanni
S. Giovanni Evangelista
Spezieria di S. Giovanni Evangelista
Casa della Musica
Piazzale San Francesco
San Francesco
Borgo Studi
Borgo Naviglio
Via Pietra del Prato
Borgo Retto
Borgo Pipa
Vic Scutellari
Strada A. Saffi
Viale Mentana
Viale Fratti
Strada Cavallotti
Strada Garibaldi
Via Verdi
Via Borghesi
Via Affò
Viale Toschi
Viale IV Novembre
Via Reggi
Sportivo
Via Primo Savani
Giovanni Lanfranco
Enrico Sartori
Viale Pasini
Via Marchesi
Via Carducci
Strada Pisacane
Borgo Mazza
Borgo San Biagio
Via Cavour
Via XX Marzo
Pal. d. Governatore
Piazza Garibaldi
Via Mazzini
Strada dell'Università
Università
Via Cavestro
Borgo Palmia
Borgo Salina
Piazzale Cervi
Strada Cairoli
Via della Repubblica
Via N. Sauro
Strada Farini
Borgo G. Tommasini
Strada XXII Luglio
Piazzale Boito
Pinacoteca Stuard
Strada del Conservatorio
Viale Basetti
Ponte Caprazucca
Viale Maria Luigia
Piazza Rondini
Strada Bixio
Borgo S. Domenico
Via della Saluti
to Cimitero Villetta
Borgo Regale
to Parco Cittadella
Strada Imbriani
Piazza Picelli
S. Maria del Quartiere
Strada D. Quartiere
Viale della Costituente
Borgo Paglia
Piazza Matteotti
Via Cocconcelli
Viale dei Mille
Viale Vittoria
Via A. Ferrari
Via Luigi Musini

Getting Around

Parma has a small **airport** northwest of the city, **t** 0521 9515, with services to Rome and a few other destinations, mostly within Italy (plus flights to London in summer).

The city is easy to reach by **rail**, on the main lines from Turin and Milan via Bologna to Florence and Rome. There are also lines to Brescia, and to La Spezia on the Ligurian coast, and Rimini on the Adriatic. The station is north of the centre, on Piazzale Carlo Alberto Dalla Chiesa, at the end of Via Verdi; buses no.1 and no.8 link it to the centre (it's a 10min walk).

The **bus** station, **t** 0521 273 251, is also on Piazzale dalla Chiesa (often referred to by its old name, Piazzale della Stazione). TEP buses serve villages of the province (the office is on the west side of the piazza); Zani Autoservizi serves Venice, Rimini and the other resorts (**t** 0521 242 645); Autolinee Lorenzini, Viareggio and the Ligurian coast (**t** 0521 273 251).

Tourist Information

Strada Melloni 1/a, just off the main Strada Garibaldi, **t** 0521 218 889 (*open Mon 9–1 and 3–7, Tues–Sat 9–7, Sun and hols 9–1*).

Shopping

There are lots of antique shops around Via Nazario Sauro, and on the third Sun of the month a huge antiques fair, the **Mercatino dell'Antiquariato**, takes place at Fontanellato. **Fashion shops** are clustered around Borgo Angelo Mazza, along with perfume shops selling **Violetti di Parma** and Marie Louise's hairdresser Borsari's 300 other scents.

The main market in Piazza Ghiaia, by the river, is a good place to stock up for a picnic or pick up local produce. Try **Specialità di Parma**, Strada Farini 9/c, a magnificent emporium of regional delicacies.

To join weekday group tours of some of the producers of Parma's *prosciutto* and Parmesan cheese, ask at the tourist office or one of the cooperatives: **Consorzio Prosciutto**, **t** 0521 243 987, or **Consorzio Parmigiano**, **t** 0521 292 700.

Where to Stay

Parma ✉ 43100

Parma's trade fair grounds are busy in May and Sept (high season in all of Emilia-Romagna's trade fair cities); reserve a couple of months in advance. If a hotel has a set room rate, the price range will be stable; if not, it can go from moderate to very expensive from one week to the next if there's a fair on.

Luxury

****Star Hotel du Parc**, Viale Piacenza 12/c, **t** 0521 292 929, *www.starhotels.com*. A hotel overlooking the Parco Ducale, slightly outside the centre. The Liberty-style public rooms are full of lovely furniture; the bedrooms are quiet.

Very Expensive

****Hotel Villa Ducale**, Via Moletolo 53a, Moletolo, 2km from the centre, **t** 0521 272 727, *www.villaducale.com*. A quiet 18th-century country villa that belonged to Marie Louise, set in its own park of lawns and century trees and deftly combining old and new.

****Park Hotel Stendhal**, Via Bodoni 3, **t** 0521 208 057, *www.hotelstendhal.it*. An older hotel with good facilities, in the heart of town alongside Piazza Pilotta. Prices can reach *luxury* levels in high season.

Expensive

***Torino**, Via Angelo Mazza 7, **t** 0521 281 046, *www.hotel-torino.it*. A centrally located option with ample, comfortable rooms, a Liberty-style breakfast room and a courtyard filled with flowers.

baptistry here introduced the Italians to the idea of a building as a unified work of architecture and sculpture. Parma's distinctive school of art began relatively late, with the arrival of Antonio Allegri Correggio (1494–1534), whose highly personal and self-taught techniques of *sfumato* and sensuous subtlety deeply influenced his many followers, most notably Francesco Mazzola, better known as Parmigianino.

Moderate

*****Brenta**, Via Giambattista Borghesi 12, **t** 0521 208 093, *www.hotelbrenta.it*. A little family-run place close to the station, simple and fairly quiet.

*****Button**, Borgo della Salina 7, **t** 0521 208 039. A cute hotel in the knot of small streets behind the Palazzo del Comune. Rooms are small but very comfortable. *Closed in July*.

Cheap

***Lazzaro**, Via XX Marzo 14, **t** 0521 208 944. A tiny old-fashioned *locanda* close to the cathedral and baptistry, with well-kept rooms upstairs (hot in summer – there's no air-con) and a good solid trattoria offering *tortelli* and the usual favourites, plus light lunches of big salads (*insalatone*) and crêpes.

Eating Out

The pig is like the music of Verdi;
nothing in it of waste.
old Parma saying

Music and food are the Parmigiani's ruling passions; a perfect dish of pasta, dusted with freshly grated Parmesan, is greeted with the same rapt silence as a perfect aria. Besides the famous ham and cheese, look out for *stracotto* (stewed beef), *carpaccio* (raw beef, or sometimes horse), *carciofi* (artichokes), in fritters, pasta dishes and crêpes, and the famous pasta dishes: *tortelli d'erbetta* (stuffed with ricotta and spinach and served with melted butter and Parmesan), *di zucca* (with pumpkin), or with potato. Note that few restaurants open on Sun in summer.

Very Expensive

Angiol d'Or, Vicolo Scutellari 1, **t** 0521 282 632. A restaurant near the Duomo, with outside seating that allows you to contemplate the Baptistry while enjoying a steaming plate of *tortelli d'erbetta*, potato and truffle tortellini, sturgeon risotto, or tripe with *parmigiano*. For dessert, try peach mousse with raspberry juice. *Closed Sun, and part of Aug*.

La Greppia, Strada Garibaldi 39, **t** 0521 233 686. Housed in a former stable, 'The Manger' offers some of Parma's most modern, innovative cuisine, based on local traditions. There's a delicious selection of *pasta di verdure* (made with spinach or tomatoes) and other original vegetable dishes, and good *secondi*, all prepared before your eyes in the glass-walled kitchen. *Closed Mon, Tues and mid-July–mid-Aug*.

Al Tramezzo, Via del Bono 51/b, on the east side of town, at San Lazzaro Parmense, **t** 0521 487906. One of Parma's most popular eateries, serving some of its most creative cuisine, with an emphasis on seafood. The wines and spirits list is excellent. *Closed Mon, and first half of July*.

Il Trovatore, near the station, Via Affò 2/a, **t** 0521 236 905. An elegant restaurant offering both classics and less traditional dishes, such as pork with figs, or turbot with lemon and vanilla stew. There's a good-value four-course menu with wine, and dessert wines by the glass. *Closed Sun and Aug*.

Expensive

Cocchi, Via Gramsci 16, **t** 0521 981 990. An elegant but unfussy establishment dedicated to bringing out the finest in Parma ingredients, in dishes such as *culatello di Zibello* and *prosciutto*, rich *minestrone*, various *bolliti*, delicately stewed *baccalà* and stuffed veal. Don't miss the old-fashioned home-made ice cream. *Closed Sat, Sun in June and July; and all Aug*.

Il Cortile, Borgo Paglia 3, **t** 0521 285 779. A stylish, intimate venue in a covered courtyard, offering traditional and modern dishes – risotto with asparagus tips or pistachios, pigeon with pine nuts, sea bass cooked in salt, and sturgeon grilled with chives. *Closed Sun and Aug*.

History

Parma provides a fine example of how Italians can adapt and even prosper in the face of continual political uncertainty. After starting out life as a small Roman way-station on the Via Aemilia, the fledgling medieval town of Parma found itself insecurely poised on the edge of the spheres of influence of pope and emperor,

Trattoria del Ducato, Via N. Paganini 5, **t** 0521 486 730. A good trattoria offering delicious dishes made from the finest ingredients, including potato tortelli with mushroom *sugo*, *taglierini* with black truffle, and veal in balsamic vinegar. Try semifreddo San Marzano and plums soaked in port for dessert. *Closed Tues, hols and July.*

Trattoria del Tribunale, Vicolo Politi 5 (corner of Strada Farini), **t** 0521 285 527. Typical *cucina parmigiana*, including fresh tortellini, beef in balsamic vinegar, and tripe and duck. There are also some excellent house wines, friendly, efficient staff, and outside tables. Unusually, it's open on Sundays in summer.

Moderate

Antica Cereria, Borgo Rodolfo Tanzi 5, **t** 0521 207 387. An old candle factory near the Parco Ducale, serving one of the region's famous dishes, *bomba di riso con il piccione* (a moulded round of rice around boned pigeon in mushroom sauce, baked in the oven), and delicious home-made desserts. *Closed Mon and Aug.*

Bottiglia Azzurra, Borgo Felino 63, **t** 0521 285 842. Long narrow dining rooms crammed with tables, drawing a young, lively crowd. The weekly-changing menu offers good fare, including a wide choice of Italian and French cheeses and other things that go well with bottles on the extensive wine list. It stays open until late. *Closed lunchtimes, Sun, July and Aug.*

Trattoria dei Corrieri, Via Conservatorio 1, **t** 0521 234 426. A trattoria serving traditional Parma cuisine at very reasonable prices, in an old postal relay station close to the university. The walls are a museum of old Parma photos and relics. The menu usually features salami and ham *antipasti*, *carpaccio* with rocket, *risotto alla parmigiana*, quail, and a filling *bollito misto*. Get in early for a seat at lunch. *Closed Sun.*

Cheap

Antica Osteria Fontana, Strada Farini 24a, **t** 0521 286 037. A long-standing *enoteca* with a small menu of typical dishes at lunchtime, and a good choice of sandwiches and charcuterie to make up a light meal around a bottle in the evening (until 9pm). *Closed Sun, Mon and most of Aug.*

Entertainment and Nightlife

Opera mobilizes an extremely enthusiastic local audience in Parma. The main season at the **Teatro Regio**, with its new Auditorium Niccolò Paganini designed by Renzo Piano, runs from Dec to Mar, although there are some concerts the rest of the year: **t** 0521 218 678, *www.teatroregioparma.org* (*box office open weekdays 10–2 and 5–7, Sat 9.30–12.30 and 4–7*). There are also occasional performances at the **Teatro Farnese**.

Parma also hosts two **music competitions**, one for conductors at the end of Aug, and another for opera singers in Oct. In Sept there's also the **Verdi Festival**; for information, contact Fondazione Verdi Festival, Strada Farini 34, **t** 0521 289 028. Throughout **summer**, concerts are also held in surrounding **castles** – the tourist office can provide a full list of forthcoming events.

Also of interest to music lovers is the new **Casa della Musica** in the restored Renaissance Palazzo Cusani in Piazzale San Francesco 1, **t** 052 031 170, *www.lacasadellamusica.it*, an international research centre for music periodicals with a multimedia music library, the archive of the Teatro Regio, a Verdi research centre, and a concert hall.

Nearby **Busseto**, Verdi's home, has its own **philharmonic** and chorus, and puts on its own small opera season in Dec and Jan; for information and tickets contact the tourist office, Piazzale Verdi 10, **t** 0524 92487.

a conflict that was echoed internally by the factions of the Da Correggio and Rossi families. The *popolo* began to assert itself in 1250 with the aid of a tailor called Barisello, and commoners ran the town for a whole nine years. From then on various *signori* – the Visconti, Della Scala, Este, Sforza and others – ruled the city until its incorporation in the Papal States in 1521. Even this state of affairs endured only until

1545, when Pope Paul III (who was otherwise known as Alessandro Farnese) required a tax farm for his natural son, Pier Luigi Farnese, and created the Duchy of Parma and Piacenza to fit the bill.

Pier Luigi's own ambitions led shortly to his assassination by a Spanish-led conspiracy, but all in all the Farnese duchy gave Parma a measure of stability. In 1748, with the extinction of the male Farnese line, it passed to a branch of the French Bourbons, who ruled it until the Napoleonic era. The year 1815 saw the arrival of Parma's best-loved ruler, Napoleon's estranged Empress Marie Louise, who was given the duchy by the Congress of Vienna. In 1859 mass unrest forced her to abdicate; a year later, after a plebiscite, the city was incorporated into the Kingdom of Italy.

Palazzo della Pilotta

If you arrive in Parma by train or bus, one of the first buildings you notice is the **Museo Archeologico Nazionale** (*open Tues–Sun 8.30–2; adm*). It's also, sadly, the most pathetic. The Palazzo della Pilotta, built for the Farnese, begun in 1602 by gloomy Duke Ranuccio and named after *pelote*, a ball game once played in its courtyard, is ungainly, unfinished and, since 1944, bomb-mutilated. But looks are deceiving, for within this patched-together shell are Parma's greatest treasures.

A grand staircase leads to the museum, founded in 1760 and containing finds from the excavations at Roman Velleia (*see* p.465). The single most important exhibit is the *Tabula Alimentaria*, a large bronze tablet that records private citizens' dole contributions in Trajan's time, as well as Egyptian sarcophagi, Greek vases from Etruscan tombs, and Roman statues including one of Nero as a boy.

On the second floor, the **Galleria Nazionale** (*open Tues–Sun 8.30–1.45; adm*) was founded even earlier, in 1752. To reach it, you pass through the fine wooden **Teatro Farnese**, which was built in a hurry in 1618–19 by Palladio's pupil, Giambattista Aleotti to honour Duke Cosimo of Florence – who never showed up. In 1944 a bomb tore the theatre into splinters and sawdust, but it has since been restored according to the motto of Italian restorers: '*dov'era, com'era*'. Most of the gallery's paintings are from Emilia-Romagna and Tuscany. Early Renaissance works are by the Tuscans Gaddi, Giovanni di Paolo and Fra Angelico, and the Emilians Simone de' Crocefissi and Loschi – top dog of the Parma quattrocento (his St Jerome holds a toddler of a lion paternally by the paw). Further along there's a lovely portrait sketch by Leonardo, *La Scapigliata*, paintings by Venetian Cima da Conegliano, and Sebastiano del Piombo's portrait of the handsome if calamitous Medici pope, Clement VII.

Some of Correggio's most celebrated works are here – the tender *Madonna di San Gerolamo* and the *Madonna della Scodella* – as well as Parmigianino's *Marriage of St Catherine* and the flirtatious *Turkish Slave*; Sebastiano Ricci's huge mythological *Rape of Helen* came here after two centuries entertaining the nurses of Parma's Foundlings' Hospital. Non-Italians include El Greco's *Guarigione del Cieco*, Peter Brueghel the Younger, Van Dyck, and Holbein with his portrait of the sharp-featured Erasmus. Alongside gigantic classical statues of Hercules and Bacchus – looted by the Farnese clan from the Palatine in Rome – are portraits of the looters, and Canova's statue of Marie Louise on her throne.

On the same floor as the gallery, the **Palatine Library** (*open Mon–Sat 8.15–2*) has a vast array of incunabula, codices, manuscripts and editions published by city printer, Bodoni, who gave his name to the popular type he invented. The Palazzo Pilotta also has a small museum about Bodoni (***t** 0521 220 411; open daily 9–12 by appointment*).

Piazza della Pace and Around

Once a car park, the piazza facing Palazzo della Pilotta provided Parma with an interminable soap opera for most of the 1990s while politicians argued over various plans and counter-plans for its redevelopment. More complications were added when the builders – inevitably – uncovered some important archaeological remains, and the piazza spent years closed off behind an ugly board fence. Now completed, it is a pleasant park with shady trees and fountains.

In the meantime, the fat and not-so-fat ladies still sing at the celebrated **Teatro Regio** (*entrance in Strada Garibaldi; guided tours Mon–Sat 10.30–12, except in opera season*), built by Marie Louise in 1829. This is one of operatic Italy's holy-of-holies, and the best place to hear Parma's favourite son, Verdi. Its audiences are contentious and demanding, and each year tenors and sopranos from all over the world submit either to avalanches of flowers or catcalls from the famous upper balconies, the *loggioni*. Toscanini began his career playing in its orchestra, since re-named in his honour.

Across Strada Garibaldi stands one of Parma's grand churches, the **Madonna della Steccata,** begun in 1521 though not entirely completed until 1730; inside are some hyper-elegant frescoes by Parmigianino, including the *Wise and Foolish Virgins, Adam and Eve, Aaron* and *Moses*. He never finished his commission, and the church canons briefly had him jailed for breach of contract; gossips said the artist's obsession with his alchemical experiments was taking up all his time.

Just north, the huge Riserva palace, once used for entertainments and to house the dukes' guests, is shared by the post office, some shops and the **Museo Glauco Lombardi** (*open Tues–Sat 9.30–3.30, Sun 9–6.30; Sun only to 1.30 in July and Aug; adm*). Few museums are so successful in summoning up the spirit of a distant age. Its grand Empire-style salons are filled with art and the personal possessions of Marie Louise from the days when Napoleon was still on top and she was empress of most of Europe.

Just off the piazza on Via Melloni is one of the most remarkable sights of Parma: the **Camera di San Paolo** (*open Tues–Sun 8.30–1.45; adm*), in the ex-convent of San Paolo. In 1519 its worldly abbess, Giovanna Piacenza, hired Correggio to fresco her refectory with mythological scenes representing the theme of 'the conquest of moral virtue', along lines discussed by her learned circle of humanist friends; he portrayed the abbess herself as a sensuous goddess Diana over the fireplace, with the enigmatic inscription *Ignem Gladio ne Fodias*, 'Do not use the sword to poke the fire' – leading the pope to cloister the nuns in 1524.

The decorative scheme in the vault is unique, with 16 putti set over 16 emblems, which are of mysterious import. The abbess wasn't the only woman in the Renaissance to conceal her meaning in secret code: Isabella d'Este did the same in Mantua. Another room contains equally mysterious allegorical frescoes and grotesques by Araldi (1514).

Piazza Duomo

Strada Pisacane connects Piazza della Pace to Piazza Duomo, the heart of medieval Parma and the site of its superb cathedral and baptistry. The **Duomo** (*open daily 9–12.30 and 3–7*) is ambitious, angular Romanesque, embellished with rows of shallow arches; three tiers cross the façade, creating an illusion of depth around the central arched window. The pattern continues in the rich decoration of the apses and dome, but the campanile is Gothic. Frescoes cover every inch of the interior, which has two masterpieces: a relief of the *Deposition from the Cross* by Antelami and, in the dome, Correggio's *Assumption* (1526–30), celebrated since Vasari wrote of its three-dimensional portrayal of clouds, angels and saints – one of the first illusionistic dome frescoes, anticipating the Baroque. Come on a sunny morning to get the full effect.

The octagonal **Baptistry** (*open daily 9–12.30 and 3–6.30; adm*), built of pale rose-coloured marble from Verona, is one of the jewels of the Italian Romanesque (it may be familiar from *panettone* boxes), designed in 1196 by Antelami, who also carved the remarkable ribbon frieze of animals and allegories encircling it. Its architect planned the mystic octagon with a decorative *summa theologica* meant to represent everything on earth and in the heavens, but the meaning behind all the winged cats, archers, griffons and sea serpents is as elusive as Correggio's ceiling at San Paolo; the Tale of Barlaam, portrayed over the south door, was a popular medieval legend that migrated from India – based on a moral fable told by Buddha. Antelami also carved the doorways dedicated to the Virgin Mary and the Last Judgement, and the statues in the niches. Inside are his famous reliefs of the months, with the labours and zodiacal signs, spring and winter. The 16-sided interior is almost entirely covered with paintings, one of the most complete ensembles of Italian medieval art: those in the upper portion, from the 1200s, are tempera, not true fresco. The vault is divided into six zones with a starry heaven; below is a grab-bag of biblical figures.

San Giovanni Evangelista, the church just behind the cathedral (*open daily 8–12 and 3.30–6*), shelters a key work of the High Renaissance under its Baroque skin: Correggio's fresco in the dome of the *Vision of St John*. This is one of the most carefully planned ceiling frescoes ever: starting from the door, the composition gradually reveals itself as you walk down the nave. Sadly, when the church was remodelled in 1587 Correggio's reputation was at a low, and the rest of his ceiling was destroyed, though a fresco of St John survives over the door north of the altar. Some of the other frescoes are by Parmigianino.

Near the church you can visit the historic **Spezieria di San Giovanni** on Borgo Pipa (*open Tues–Sun 8.30–1.45; adm*), which dispensed drugs non-stop from 1298 until 1881; its grand Renaissance–Baroque interior contains alembics, medieval pharmaceutical instruments and paintings of great doctors of antiquity – real and mythological – from Apollo to Hippocrates.

Piazza Garibaldi

In company with the other old gents of Parma, Garibaldi and Correggio, or at least their statues, spend the day in the modern centre of the city, Piazza Garibaldi. Here, too, stands the yellow 17th-century **Palazzo del Governatore**, with its intricate sundials telling you when noon reaches towns from Quebec to Constantinople. South of the piazza on Via Cavestro, the **Pinacoteca Giuseppe Stuard** (*open Mon–Sat 9–6.30, Sun until 6; adm*) contains a small collection that ranges from trecento Tuscans to 19th-century Parma salon painters. East of the piazza, on Via della Repubblica, **Sant'Antonio Abate** (*currently closed for restoration*) has some bizarre late Baroque vaulting and a false ceiling – the architect, Ferdinando Bibiena, was also a stage designer.

South of the city centre, the **Cittadella** was Alessandro Farnese's only gift to Parma. Most of this huge fortress has been demolished, and the ground converted into a park, though some of the ornate Baroque gates survive.

Paganini, Toscanini and Stendhal

Parma's west end across the river, the Oltratorrente, is home to some interesting churches, notably the proto-Baroque **SS. Annunziata** (1561), just over the Ponte di Mezzo on Via d'Azeglio, and **Santa Maria del Quartiere** (1604) in Piazza Picelli. Here too is the **Parco Ducale**, built by the Farnese.

Of the various musical and literary pilgrimages to make in Parma, two are in the Oltratorrente. The first is to the **tomb of Paganini**, the embalmed wizard of catgut and bow, who lies decked out in virtuoso splendour in Villetta cemetery, after the rest of Europe, suspecting his talents were diabolic, refused him Christian burial (*open daily 7.45–12.30; May–Sept also 4–7; Feb–Apr and Oct also 2.30–5.30; Nov–Jan also 2–5*). It's a good 15-minute walk from the centre.

The **birthplace of Arturo Toscanini** (1867–1957) is a modest house at Borgo Rudolfo Tanzi 13 (*open Tues–Sun 9–1 and 2–6; adm*), between the Ponte di Mezzo and the Parco Ducale; it contains memorabilia and a copy of every record he ever made. He became an enthusiastic Fascist in 1919, but later turned against the movement's violent *squadre* and Mussolini's dictatorship, and was beaten up for refusing to play the Fascist anthem at a concert in Bologna.

Stendhal aficionados will be glad to know that there really is a **Charterhouse of Parma**, the Certosa (*open Mon–Fri 9–12 and 2–4, Sat 8–12, Sun 8–10*), although it bears no resemblance to the novelist's invention. Four kilometres east of town (take bus no.10), it was founded in 1281 but rebuilt in the 17th century, and now serves as a military school. The cloister is out of bounds, but you can visit the church's frescoed interior.

Four More Castles

Further afield are Parma's famous castles, each reachable by bus from the city. In the foothills to the south – where Parma hams and Parmigiano cheeses are produced aplenty – and visible from miles around (on the Langhirano road), towers **Torrechiara** (*open Apr–Sept Tues–Sun 8.30–7; Oct–Mar Tues–Fri 8.30–4, Sat and Sun 9–5; adm*), a castle of brick and fantasy almost unchanged since the 15th century, and defended by four mighty towers. Inside is an elegant courtyard with ornate terracotta tiles; frescoes of acrobats performing impossible feats with hoops on the backs of lions; and a fresco cycle by Bembo in the 'Golden Bedchamber', depicting the tragic tale of the original owner and his young lover Bianca, who died in his arms in this room.

Southwest of Parma, the 15th-century **Bardi** castle (*open Mar–May and Oct Sat 2–6, Sun 10–6; June and Sept Mon–Sat 2–7, Sun 10–7; July daily 10–7; Aug Mon–Sat 10–7, Sun 10–8; Nov Sat 2–5, Sun 10–5; Dec Sat and Sun 2–5; adm*), has lovely beamed ceilings. On the local road to Reggio Emilia via Montecchio, **Montechiarugolo** (*open Mar–Nov Sun 10–12.30 and 3–6.30*), built by the Visconti in 1313, has a Torrechiara-style tower and a lavish bedchamber with frescoed scenes of farming, study, navigation and war.

Compiano (*open July and Aug Mon–Sat 3–6; also Apr–Oct Sun and hols 3–6.30; rest of year by appointment, **t** 0525 825 541; adm*), in the mountains on the SS513, claims to have something rare in Italy – ghosts – and a curious museum of English freemasonry. Part of it is now open for overnight stays.

Reggio Emilia

A bright, prosperous agricultural city, Reggio Emilia was the Roman *Regium Lepidi*. In the Middle Ages it was known for its violent factionalism, and from 1409 to 1796 was ruled by the Este family of Ferrara, during which time its most famous son, Ludovico Ariosto (1474–1533), author of *Orlando Furioso*, was born. Nowadays it is noted for its ballet schools, balsamic vinegar and Parmesan cheese, Parmigiano-Reggiano, which tastes exactly the same as Parma's to any sane person.

Piazza Prampolini

Reggio grew up on the Via Aemilia, which now divides its old and new parts. In the older, southern half is Piazza Prampolini, the city's civic and ecclesiastical heart, with its peculiar **Duomo** topped by a single octagonal tower. Most of its Romanesque features were remodelled away in the 16th century, though fine statues of Adam and Eve were added to the façade, and in the tower niche is a copper Madonna flanked by the cathedral donors. On the same piazza, **Palazzo del Monte di Pietà** has a lofty Torre dell'Orologio. The **Palazzo Comunale** is where the Tricolore was first proclaimed the Italian national flag in 1797, during the second congress of Napoleon's Cispadane Republic – a short-lived entity that covered the area between Reggio, Mantua, Ferrara and Bologna. The **Broletto**, a covered arcade where the bishops used to grow their cabbages, leads behind the cathedral to **Piazza San Prospero**, the main market square and a wonderful place to see and stock up on local produce. The 16th-century **Basilica di San Prospero** is noted for its fine choir, with frescoes and inlaid stalls.

North of the Via Aemilia

Via Aemilia is Reggio's main shopping street, passing through **Piazza Cesare Battisti**, roughly the site of the Roman forum. To its north, Piazza Cavour has the 19th-century **Teatro Municipale**, the opera house. Crowned by a surplus of musing statuary, it is one of Italy's most lavish theatres, built to upstage the Regio in Parma. It largely succeeds: performances of opera, concerts and plays (*Sept–Apr; www.iteatri.re.it*) are of a high quality, if not quite as prestigious as Parma's. Nearby, the **Palazzo Magnani** (**t** *0522 454437 for open times*) hosts internationally acclaimed modern art exhibitions.

Tourist Information

Piazza Prampolini 5, by the cathedral: **t** 0522 451 152; *www.municipio.re.it/turismo.*

Where to Stay and Eat

Reggio Emilia ✉ 42100

★★★★**Delle Notarie**, Via Palazzolo 5, **t** 0522 453 500, *www.albergonotarie.it* (*very expensive*). Discreet luxury, spacious bedrooms and lovely old wooden floors in a palace close to the cathedral. *Closed Aug.*

★★★★**Posta**, Piazza del Monte, **t** 0522 432 944, *www.hotelposta@re.it* (*very expensive*). The 14th-century Palazzo del Capitano del Popolo, later home to Francesco d'Este, in the heart of Reggio. The public rooms still have frescoes. Bike hire is available.

★★★ **Albergo Reggio**, Piazza del Monte, **t** 0522 451 533, *www.albergoreggio.it@re.it* (*moderate*). The new annexe of the Posta, with 16 rooms and cooking facilities.

★★★**Park**, Via de Ruggiero 1, **t** 0522 292 141, *www.parkhotel.it* (*moderate*). A delightful little hotel, comfortable and friendly, 4km from the centre of town in a tranquil setting, with a garden and a restaurant. There's a minibus service into town.

Like Parma, Reggio is a major producer of Parmesan cheese (Parmigiano-Reggiano), and like Modena it distils *aceto balsamico.*

5 Pini da Pelati, Viale Martiri di Cervarolo 46c, **t** 0522 553 663 (*very expensive*). The finest dining space in town, with excellent set menus featuring dishes such as prawns with pancetta and balsamic vinegar, guinea fowl with Reggiano cheese, and apple tart with Calvados. The wine list is encyclopaedic. *Closed Tues eve, Weds and Aug.*

Canossa, Via Roma 37, **t** 0522 454 196 (*expensive*). A fine, old-fashioned, friendly place where you can try *antipasto* of local hams and *tortelli* made on the premises. *Closed Weds and 3wks Aug.*

Trattoria della Ghiara, Vicolo Folletto 1/c, **t** 0522 435 755 (*moderate*). A bastion of tradition near Piazza Roversi, though heavier dishes such as *salumi* and delicious *cappelletti in brodo* are given a light modern touch, so you can walk rather than waddle out. There's a small but good selection of regional wines. *Closed Sun, last 2wks June and most of Aug.*

Sotto Broletto, Via Broletto 1, **t** 0522 439 676 (*cheap–moderate*). A thriving *pizzeria-ristorante* in the arcade leading off Piazza Prampolini. *Closed Thurs.*

Forno Katia, Via Terrachini 35/c (*cheap*). A good place to pick up an *erbazzone*, a local vegetable tart ideal for picnic lunches.

Correggio ✉ 42015

★★★★**Dei Medaglioni**, Corso Mazzini 8, **t** 0522 632 233, *www.bestwestern.it/deimedaglioni* (*very expensive*). A converted palace with stylish rooms. *Closed much of Aug and Christmas.*

Brescello ✉ 42041

★★★**La Tavernetta del Lupo**, Piazza M. Pallini, Loc. Sorbolo Levante, **t** 0522 680 509 (*moderate*). A reasonably priced hotel with a restaurant (*expensive*) serving skilful Italian *cucina nuova* such as gnocchi made from carrots with basil and pine nuts, and salmon with raspberry vinegar and poppyseeds. *Closed Mon, early Jan and Aug.*

Guastalla ✉ 42016

★★★**Old River**, Viale Po 2, **t** 0522 838 401, *www.paginegialle.it/albergooldriver* (*moderate*). The best place to stay north of Reggio, with excellent rooms in a pleasant green setting.

Rigoletto, Piazza Martiri 29, Reggiolo, east of town, **t** 0522 973 520 (*very expensive*). The best restaurant in these parts, in a late 18th-century villa with a pretty garden. The fare embraces raisin and gorgonzola bread, *tortelli* with catfish in a buttery dill sauce, stuffed baby squid in a salad of toasted almonds and crispy bacon, and crayfish and shellfish *zuppa*. There are sublime desserts and a superb wine list. Two special menus are offered, seafood and land food. *Closed Sun, Mon, Jan and Aug.*

Canossa ✉ 42026

La Cueva, Loc. Giarretta 7, Currada, just south of town, **t** 0522 876 316 (*expensive*). An old country mill on the banks of the Enza, offering the beloved *gnocco frito* with *salumi, tortellini* and grilled meats. *Closed Mon, Tues and Jan.*

The **Musei Civici** (*open Tues–Sun 9–12; 28 June–7 Sept also 9pm–midnight*), a block east on Via Secchi (near a powerful monument to the Martyrs of the Resistance), is a charmingly old-fashioned museum containing everything from Roman mosaics of the two-faced god Janus to stuffed crocodiles, from the buxom Neolithic *Chiozza Venus* to the works of obscure Emilian painters; one room is dedicated to the humorous socialist 'painter of the Resistance' Mazzacurati. In Reggio's **Giardino Pubblico**, site of an Este castle, is the imposing 1st-century AD funerary monument of a Roman family, the **Tomb of the Concordii**. Near here is the very eclectic **Galleria Parmeggiani** (*same hours as Musei Civici*), with a 16th-century Moresco doorway brought over from Valencia.

In San Maurizio, three kilometres east of Reggio, **Villa Il Mauriziano** was the summer home of Ariosto's family. Some rooms have been restored to the appearance they had when the poet came to visit from Ferrara, featuring charming frescoes of love scenes and literati (*open Mon–Sat 9–12; for visits outside these hours, call* **t** *0522 456 527*).

Around Reggio

Some 15 kilometres northeast of Reggio, **Correggio** is a pretty town with old arcaded streets that suffered an earthquake in 1996; all the damage seems to have been repaired. It is the birthplace of the painter Antonio Allegri, better known as Correggio (*d.* 1534); his home on Borgo Vecchio was reconstructed in 1755. The brick Renaissance Palazzo dei Principi contains the **Museo Civico** (*open 1st and 3rd Sat and Sun of month 10.30–1 and 3–7; closed Aug*), with a Christ by Mantegna and some lovely cinquecento Flemish tapestries. The Renaissance church of **San Quirino** is attributed to the Farnese's favourite architect, Vignola.

To the north in **Novellara**, the Gonzaga dukes of Mantua built a fine 14th-century castle, now the town hall and **Museo Gonzaga**, with frescoes and faïence chemists' jars of crabs' eyes and ground stag horn. On the banks of the Po, **Gualtieri**, once Lombard *Castrum Walterii*, has the grand arcaded Piazza Bentivoglio and the 16th-century brickwork Palazzo Bentivoglio. The palace (*open Sun 10–12 and 3–6.30; closed Jan, Feb and Aug*) has some fine frescoes in its Sala dei Giganti, depicting scenes from Tasso's *Gerusalemme Liberata*.

Another old Lombard town, **Guastalla** (originally *Warstal*) – much sought after for its strategic position on the Po – was subsequently held by the Canossa, Visconti, Da Coreggio and Gonzaga dynasties. It conserves many Gonzaga mementos: the grid of streets centred on the 'noble street', Via Gonzaga; the sad, abandoned ducal palace; and a bronze statue of the *condottiere*, Ferrante Gonzaga, who shaped the town. Outside Guastalla is a fine 10th-century Romanesque church, the Basilica della Pieve.

Further down the Po, on the outskirts of Luzzara, the former convent is now the charming **Museo Nazionale delle Arti Naïf**, with a permanent collection of naïf art, including copies of the paintings and theatre costumes of Antonio Ligabue of Gualtieri (*open 15 June–15 Dec Tues–Sat 10–12.30 and 3–7, Sun 3–7; adm*).

Back west along the Po, **Brescello** is famous in Italian popular culture as the home town of Giovanni Guareschi's Don Camillo, the priest of the post-war era, eternally, fraternally at war with the Communist mayor Peppone. The pair are immortalized in Fernandel's films – gentle parables that perfectly captured the mood of a recovering postwar Italy, which had seen enough of the bleakness of *cinema verità*. For fans, there is a **Museo Don Camillo e Peppone** (*open daily 10–12 and 3–6*).

All of these villages are accessible by bus or train from Reggio; for **Canossa**, south of Reggio, you'll have to drive, or alternatively walk seven kilometres from the nearest bus stop. Its name will ring a bell with anyone who ever studied medieval history: this is the spot where an emperor once humbled himself before a pope, kneeling in the snow for three days begging forgiveness. It all started in 951, when a knight named Atto Adalbert gave Queen Adelaide refuge here from a usurper, Berengar of Ivrea. German King Otto I came over the Alps to defeat Berengar, married Adelaide, and had them crowned Holy Roman Emperor and Empress – this was the birth of the post-Charlemagne empire that was the mainspring of Italian history for the following seven centuries.

Meanwhile, Atto's descendants, the Di Canossa dynasty, were gaining their own fame: the most powerful was the charismatic and warlike Countess Matilda. In 1077, Emperor Henry IV deposed Pope Gregory VII; when the pope in turn excommunicated the emperor, Matilda was instrumental in bringing Henry to Canossa on his knees in the snow to apologize. Gregory later saw Rome sacked by imperial forces, and died in exile, but Canossa was a turning point – for the next two centuries, the popes held the moral high ground over the kings and barons of Europe. Today the impregnable eyrie of the **Castello di Canossa** (*open Tues–Sun 9–3*) is a scenic and tranquil ruin; historic pageants are sometimes staged inside.

Modena

Modena puts on a class act – 'Mink City' they call it. It's the city with Italy's highest per capita income, a city with 'a psychological need for racing cars' according to the late Enzo Ferrari, whose famous flame-red chariots compete with the shiny beasts churned out by cross-town rival Maserati. Sleek and speedy, Modena also has a lyrical side of larger-than-life proportions: Luciano Pavarotti was born here, and its scenographic streets take on an air of mystery and romance when enveloped in the winter mists rising from the Po.

Known in Roman days as *Mutina*, Modena first came to note in the 11th-12th centuries under Countess Matilda, powerful ally of the pope (*see* above); under her rule the city began its great cathedral (1099). When it became an independent *comune*, however, Modena's Ghibelline party dominated in response to the Guelph policies of arch rival, Bologna. In 1288 the city came under the control of Obizzo II d'Este, Duke of Ferrara, and the Este Duchy of Modena endured until 1796; with the building of the Ducal Palace, the Corso Canalgrande and other projects under Francesco I (1629–58) and his successors, Modena was transformed into a model Baroque city. A feebly independent duchy was recreated by the Vienna Congress in 1815, only for Modena, like Parma, to be swept into the Kingdom of Italy by the wave of nationalistic feeling in 1859–60.

Duomo di San Geminiano

Via Aemilia is Modena's main thoroughfare, and it is in the centre of this city that the old Roman highway picks up one of its loveliest gems, the cobbled and partially porticoed Piazza Grande, site of Modena's celebrated Romanesque **Duomo di San Geminiano**. Begun with funds from Countess Matilda in 1099, the cathedral was designed by a master-builder named Lanfranco and completed in the 13th century. Curiously, its main features are Ghibelline–Lombard; Lanfranco followed the bidding of Modena's burghers to show their independence both from Matilda and from the powerful abbey of Nonántola. Complementing the Duomo's fine proportions are magnificent carvings by the 12th-century sculptor Wiligelmo above the three main entrances and elsewhere. His followers, and after them the anonymous Lombard sculptors and architects known as the Campionese masters, carried on the work, making this cathedral a living museum of medieval sculpture.

Wiligelmo's friezes on either side of the main **Lion Portal** illustrate scenes from the medieval mystery play on the Book of Genesis, the *Jeu d'Adam*. His **South Portal** depicts the life of Modena's 4th-century patron, St Geminiano. The weights and measures carved into the façade, where a Medusa hides amid the foliage, recall the days when the daily market was held in the square.

Another contemporary, the 'Master of the Metopes', executed the eight fascinating relief panels of mythological creatures and allegorical subjects on top of the buttresses: an upside-down inhabitant of the antipodes, a hermaphrodite and a nude woman with a dragon, a three-armed woman, a bearded crouching man, a giantess with an ibis and a sphinx, and a fork-tailed siren. These are copies; the originals, which deserve a much closer look, are in the adjacent **Museo Lapidario** on Via Lanfranco (*open Tues–Sun 9.30–12.30 and 3.30–6.30*). Yet another 12th-century sculptor put King Arthur in the lunette over the **Porta della Pescheria**.

Later 12th-century work, including the rose window, was done by the Campionese masters of Lake Lugano, who also added the final touches to Lanfranco's charming interior, with its rhythm of arches supported by slender columns and ponderous piers. To decorate the wall the masters created the great Pontile, carved with lion pillars and polychromed reliefs of the life of Christ, and incorporating the ambone, a pulpit with pillars with excellent capitals. Underneath is a crypt of 32 columns with capitals carved by Wiligelmo and his followers, with more lions and a chimera. San Geminiano is buried here, in a Roman sarcophagus.

The mighty if slightly askew campanile, the **Ghirlandina**, houses a famous trophy – an ancient wooden bucket stolen during a raid on Bologna in 1325, and the subject of a 17th-century mock-heroic epic, *La Secchia Rapita*. The Bolognese make periodic attempts to steal it back; according to rumour, they have it now and the one you see is only a replica. It *is*, in fact, a replica: behind the Duomo, Modena's **Palazzo Comunale** (*open Mon–Sat 8.30–7, Sun and hols 3–7*) contains the real one, along with some fascinating Baroque frescoes on the history of the city. Outside, the enormous slab of red Verona marble in the angle of the Palazzo Comunale's façade is the *Preda Ringadora*, a speakers' platform in use since the 1200s (an *arringadore* meant an orator; that's where we get our word 'harangue').

Getting Around

There are frequent **rail** connections with Bologna, Parma and Milan, and with Mantua via Carpi. The station is on Piazza Dante, a 10min walk from the centre (bus nos.1 or 3).

The **bus** station (**t** 059 308 801) on Viale Monte Kosica, 1km west of the train station (city buses no.1, 2, 9, 10 and 11 go between them), has frequent connections to Bologna, Ferrara and destinations in Modena province (Vignola, Sestola and Fiumalbo).

There are 9 daily shuttles to Bologna **airport**, taking about 1hr, and **bike rental** at Parco Novi Sad, near the bus station.

Tourist Information

Via Scudari 12, **t** 059 206 660 (*open Mon 3–6, Tues–Sat 9–1 and 3–6, Sun 9–1*), *www.comunemodena.it*.

Modenatur, Via Scudari 8, **t** 059 206 686, *www.modenatur.net*, books hotels, restaurants, shows, events and visits to wine/cheese makers.

Where to Stay

July and Aug are low season for many Emilia-Romagna hotels, so rates then are often considerably lower, especially in Modena, Bologna and Ferrara. Often a four-star hotel becomes highly affordable; ask hotels to quote for specific dates.

Modena ✉ 41100

Expensive–Very Expensive

★★★★**Canalgrande**, Corso Canalgrande 6, **t** 059 217 160, *www.canalgrandehotel.it*. Named after Modena's long-gone medieval canal, the one-time *palazzo* of the Marchesi Schedoni has richly decorated and stuccoed 18th-century public rooms, with crystal chandeliers and ceiling frescoes, and plush bedrooms. Ancient trees grace its pretty inner garden.

Moderate

★★★**Centrale**, Via Rismondo 55, **t** 059 218 808, *www.hotelcentrale.com*. A very central, cosy, friendly option with spotless modern bathrooms. There's a new suite with a whirlpool bath. Some of the rooms without bathrooms are in the *cheap* bracket. Mention Cadogan for special rates.

★★★**Principe**, Corso Vittorio Emanuele 94, **t** 059 218 670. A good hotel near the station and the Giardini Pubblici. Staff are extremely friendly and helpful.

Cheap

★**Sole**, Via Malatesta 45, **t** 059 214 245. A clean, old-fashioned *locanda* in a small ancient street, offering 7 basic but spacious rooms without bathrooms.

San Filippo Neri, Via S. Orsola 48, **t** 059 234 598. *www.ostellioonline.org/modena*. A simple youth hostel between the station and the historic centre, with family rooms and dorm beds.

Eating Out

Modena is nearly as mad about its food as Parma: there are *consorzi dei prodotti tipici* for *aceto balsamico* (of which there is a festival in late May and early June), cherries, cheese and hams that are quite as tasty as Parma's. Situated in the heart of Emilia's pig country, the city prides itself on its variety of *salumeria*. Minced pork fills its *tortellini*, and its famous main course is *zampone* (pig's trotter, boiled and sliced).

Palazzo dei Musei

The other main sight in Modena is the **Palazzo dei Musei** (with your back to the cathedral, turn left along Via Aemilia). Upstairs, the **Galleria Estense** (*open Tues–Sun 8.30–7.30; adm*) was founded by Francesco I d'Este, whose excellent bust by Bernini greets visitors at the entrance. His taste and budget weren't quite as elevated as that of some other dukes, but here's your chance to see works by Modena's greatest medieval painter, Tommaso da Modena, as well as other good early Emilian works,

This is also the best place to taste true Lambrusco (of which there's a festival in May), which must be drunk young to be perfectly lively and sparkling; the test is to see if the foam vanishes instantly when it's poured.

At weekends, the Modenesi embark on gastronomic voyages into the Apennines, where roadside restaurants (choose those with the most cars outside) offer simple meals of smoked meats, cheeses, raw vegetables, *tigelle* (flat, baked muffins) and *crescente* (thin dough fried in fat). If you go during the week you won't have to wait for a table.

Modena ✉ 41100

Very Expensive

Fini, Rua Frati Minori 54, **t** 059 223 314. The cathedral of Modenese cuisine, offering a hearty and delicious regional pasta (the *pasticcio di tortellini* is exceptional) and meat dishes (*zampone* and *bollito misto*). *Closed Mon, Tues and mid-July–mid-Aug.*

Hosteria Giosti, Vicolo Squallore 46, **t** 059 22253. The world's oldest *salumeria*, first documented in the late 1600s. The local fare includes fried gnocchi, capon, *tagliatelline* with lamb, and, naturally, the finest local cheese and hams. It's wise to book. *Closed Sun, Mon, Aug and part of Dec and Jan.*

Osteria la Francescana, Via Stella 22, **t** 059 210 118. One of Modena's more innovative places, offering arty décor, a great wine list and delicious food, including *mousseline di carciofi*. *Closed Sat lunch, Sun and Aug.*

Expensive

Osteria Ruggera, Via Ruggera 18, **t** 059 211 129. A tiny, 150-year-old place near the cathedral, with delicious daily specials such as gnocchi with gorgonzola and walnuts, fusilli with ricotta, and the famous *cotoletta alla Ruggera*. *Closed Tues and Aug.*

Moderate

Stallo del Pomodoro, Largo Hannover 63, **t** 059 214 664. The 'Tomato Stall', named after the tomato market once held here, with outdoor tables. Spring specialities include smoked goose breast with asparagus. There's a wide choice of wine, cheese and desserts. *Closed Sat lunch except by arrangement and Sun.*

Cheap

Aldina, Via Albinelli 40, **t** 059 236 106. A resolutely old-fashioned but good lunch venue, hidden away on the first floor of a building opposite the Mercato Coperto, serving plates of fresh pasta and roast meat, desserts and bottles of Lambrusco to a wide range of customers. *Closed lunchtimes, Sun and Aug.*

Caffè Concerto, Piazza Grande, **t** 059 222 232. A trendy hangout with modernist décor, offering snacks, meals, wine, cocktails and live music (usually jazz).

Compagnia del Taglio, Via Taglio 12, **t** 059 210 377. A classy wine bar in the *centro storico*.

Ermes, Via Ganaceto 89 (no phone). A simple family-run place that offers a fixed-price lunch menu (2–3 choices per course) consisting of home-made pasta, a main course (*bollito misto* on Saturdays), a side dish, Lambrusco and coffee. *Closed eves, Sun, Sat in July, and Aug.*

Entertainment

The concert, ballet and opera season at the **Teatro Comunale** on Corso Canalgrande (**t** 059 206 993) runs from Sept to May. **Pavarotti** gives a **concert** in Piazza Grande at the end of May; crowds sit in neighbouring bars and listen to the music while watching the show on TV. The Pavarotti **singing competition** also takes place in in May.

bronzes by Il Riccio of Padua, a good Flemish collection, works by the Venetians Palma il Vecchio, Cima da Conegliano, Veronese and Tintoretto (a set of ceiling paintings by Tintoretto called the *Ottagoni*, depicting energetic scenes from Ovid's *Metamorphoses*, was brought here from Venice in 1658), and Velázquez's portrait of Francesco I d'Este. The Florentines really steal the show, especially Botticelli's ripe Technicolor *Madonna con il Bambino*, but for all that, the painting you can't stop staring at will be the masterpiece and last known work of the great quattrocento eccentric Cosmè Tura, the cadaverous, beautiful, horrific *St Anthony of Padua* (1484), a life-sized vision of spiritual and anatomical deformity, captured in a garish pink sunset, which will send any good Catholic out in search of a stiff drink.

Besides the museum, the *palazzo* houses the **Biblioteca Estense** (*open Mon–Sat 9–1*). Among its famous collection of illuminated manuscripts is one of the most fabulous anywhere, the *Bible of Borso d'Este*, made for the Duke of Modena, a gorgeously coloured 1,200-page marvel illustrated in the 15th century by Emilians Taddeo Crivelli and Franco Rossi. On the way back to Piazza Grande, stop by to see the terracotta *Deposition* by Guido Mazzoni (1476) in **San Giovanni Battista**.

From Piazza Grande, Via Cesare Battisti leads to the huge Baroque **Palazzo Ducale**, once the home of the Este dukes and now the **National Military Academy**; some surviving frescoes and 18th-century rooms are accessible via guided tour (*call **t** 059 220 022*). The dukes' gardens have a botanical garden with a greenhouse of tropical plants. Between this behemoth and the station the main landmark is the neo-Romanesque Tempio Monumentale, erected in 1923.

The streets south of the Piazza Grande, around porticoed Corso Canal Chiaro and Via Canalino, are some of Modena's oldest and loveliest. The 'canal' street names recall that Modena was once a city full of canals, built by the medieval *comuni* to drain water from the marshy land, via the Canale Naviglio, into the Po. Modena's dukes started bricking over the canals in the 1600s, and the last of them was gone by 1800. In this neighbourhood too you'll find the city markets, including the delightful glass and iron **Mercato Coperto**, on Piazza XX Settembre just south of Piazza Grande.

North of Modena: Carpi and Nonántola

North of Modena buses and trains run to Carpi, a wealthy, workaholic town dominated by the oceanic **Piazza dei Martiri**; formerly called the Borgogioioso, this is the third largest piazza in Italy. Beside it stands the equally remarkable 16th-century **Palazzo Pio**, which holds the **Museo Civico Giulio Ferrari** (*closed for restoration until 2006*), including some brilliant High Renaissance frescoes, a tribute to Ugo da Carpi, inventor of the *chiaroscuro* tinted woodcut (which made possible mass reproductions of paintings), and a **museum** (*open Thurs, Sat, Sun and hols 10–12.30 and 3.30–7*) remembering the Italian Jews deported to Germany from a Nazi camp here. Carpi's real treasure is hidden behind the *castello*'s bulk: **Santa Maria in Castello** (1120), one of the many churches built by Countess Matilda of Canossa; among the medieval and quattrocento frescoes inside is a lovely cycle on the *Life of St Catherine* by followers of Giovanni da Modena.

Eleven kilometres northeast of Modena, the important abbey of **Nonántola** (*open daily 7.30am–8pm*) was founded in 752 by the Lombard abbot Anselmo, rebuilt in the 12th century and later given the Baroque one-two. The portal, however, retains its beautiful carving by the workshop of Wiligelmo. The church contains relics of the 4th-century St Sylvester, pope under Constantine, while the crypt contains 64 columns with carved capitals, and the tomb of another pope, St Adrian III, who died here in 885 en route to the Diet of Worms. The abbey has two cloisters, as well as a refectory with frescoes from the 11th and 12th centuries.

Where to Stay and Eat

Nonántola ✉ **41015**

Osteria di Rubbiara, Via Risaia 2, near Nonántola at Rubbiara, **t** 059 549 019 (*expensive*). A hostelry that's been in the same family since 1861, offering generous portions of home cooking. There's no menu: you get whatever's on offer, including at least one dish with the family's balsamic vinegar. They also make a huge variety of liqueurs. *Open lunch only except Fri and Sat eves; closed Tues and Aug.*

Sestola ✉ **41029**

********San Marco****, Via delle Rose 2, **t** 0536 62330, *www.albergosanmarco.it* (*expensive–very expensive*). A large 19th-century villa with a panoramic terrace and a pine wood for a backdrop. *Closed Oct.*

*****Tirolo**, Via delle Rose 9, **t** 0536 62523 (*cheap–moderate*). Very comfortable rooms. *Open June–Sept and mid-Dec–Mar.*

****Sport Hotel**, Via delle Ville 58, **t** 0536 62502 (*cheap*). A pleasant little hotel that's open year round, offering double rooms with or without bath.

San Rocco, Corso Umberto I 47, **t** 0536 62382 (*very expensive*). A restaurant offering lavish vegetable and pasta dishes (try the *pecorino* cheese with onions and balsamic vinegar, or tagliatelle with pine nuts), and tender roast meats. There are 11 rooms to stay in. *Closed Mon, May and Oct.*

South of Modena

At Montale Rangone just south of Modena, the major **Parco Archeologico di Montale** museum site (***t*** *059 532 020*) was due to open as we went to press, dedicated to Bronze Age civilizations in the area.

From Modena you can make a break away from the flatlands of the Po by heading southwards into the Apennines, which achieve majestic proportions on the Tuscan border. The region has perfect updraughts for hang-gliding and sailplanes, especially around **Pavullo** and **Montecreto**. In April the foothills of **Vignola** and **Savignano** are covered with the lacy blossoms of Vignola's famous cherry trees; these are celebrated in a Cherry Blossom Festival held in April each year, with horse races and medieval costumes (you can get there from Bologna on the free seasonal Cherry Train, the 'Treno dei Ciliegi'). From here you can continue further south to **Guiglia** and the peculiar pinnacles of **Rocca Malatina** in the **Parco Naturale di Sassi.** Just to the south of Guiglia, don't miss the 11th-century church at **Pieve Trebbio**, with primitive capitals inside.

Motorheads won't want to miss **Maranello**, where the **Galleria Ferrari** (*daily 9.30–6; adm exp*) is dedicated to the legendary marque, with scale models, trophies, vintage cars and a reconstruction of Enzo Ferrari's office. **Sassuolo**, to the southwest of Modena, is the centre of Italy's ceramic tile industry, which has been booming since Italian designers discovered that people spend as much money decorating their bathrooms and kitchens as on themselves. Under the rule of the Este family, however, the tiles produced were more artistic.

The most striking scenery to be had in the vicinity is up at **Sestola**, a winter and summer resort close to the highest peak of the Northern Apennines, the 7,100ft **Monte Cimone** (*call* ***t*** *0536 62350 for a ski report*). From Sestola you can visit the pretty glacial Lago della Ninfa and the **Giardino Esperia** at the Passo del Lupo, a botanical frontier where alpine and Apennine species grow side by side (*open mid-June–mid-Sept Tues–Sun 9.30–12.30 and 2–6, also open Mon mid-July–mid-Aug;*

adm). Another excursion that can be made from Sestola is to **Pian Cavallaro**, and from there to the summit of Monte Cimone for a unique view – on a clear day you can see both the Tyrrhenian and Adriatic seas, and all the way north to the Julian Alps and Mont Blanc. You can also make the ascent from **Fiumalbo**, just below the **Passo Abetone** that separates Emilia from Tuscany. There is an unusual mountain lake in the meadows south of Fanano, a little east of Sestola: the small **Lago Pratignano.** In spring its banks are strewn with wild flowers and carnivorous plants – bring your waders.

Bologna

'You must write all the beautiful things of Italy,' said the Venetian on the train, but the man from Bologna vehemently shook his finger. 'No, no,' he insisted. 'You must write the truth!' And it is precisely that – a fervent insistence on the plain truth as opposed to the typical Italian *bella figura* – that sets Bologna apart. A homespun realism and attention to the detail of the visible, material world are the characteristics of the Bolognese school of art (recall Petrarch's comment that while only an educated man is amazed by a Giotto, anyone can understand a Bolognese picture).

The city's handsome, harmonic and well-preserved centre disdains imported marble or ornate stucco, preferring honest red brick. Bologna's municipal government, long in the hands of the Italian Communist Party (now the PDS), was long considered the least corrupt and most efficient of any large city in the whole country. In the 11th century it was the desire for truth and law that led to the founding of the university of Bologna, whose first scholars occupied themselves with the task of interpreting the law codes of Justinian in settling disputes over investitures between pope and emperor. And it is Bolognese sincerity and honest ingredients in the kitchen that has made *la cucina bolognese* one of Italy's finest.

La Dotta, La Grassa and *La Rossa* (the Learned, the Fat and the Red) are Bologna's sobriquets. It may be full of socialist virtue, but the city is also very wealthy and cosy, with a quality of life often compared to that of Sweden. The casual observer could come away with the impression that the reddest things about Bologna are its phone booths and street names such as Via Stalingrado, Via Yuri Gagarin and Viale Lenin. But Bologna is hardly a stolid place – its bars, cafés and squares brim with youth and life, and there's a full calendar of concerts from rap to jazz to Renaissance madrigals, as well as avant-garde ballet, theatre and art exhibitions. In July and August, it can be as exciting as the cheap supermarket salami that bears its name, though like most 'art cities' it has a series of concerts,. and, in the main square, old Italian movies shown 'under the stars'.

History

Born as the prosperous Etruscan outpost of *Felsina*, and renamed *Bononia* by the Gauls, Bologna grew up at the junction of the Via Aemilia and the main road over the Apennines from Florence. Dominated by Ravenna for centuries, it emerged from the Dark Ages around 1000 AD to start the new millennium with a bang, founding one of

Italy's first free *comuni* and starting what became Europe's first university. By the 1100s it was a hemp-, wool- and linen-trading boom town on an American scale, with tower-fortresses of the urban nobility zooming up like modern skyscrapers – some 180 of them, more than any city outside Florence. With 50,000 inhabitants by 1200, it was one of the great cities of Europe; thanks to its university it became the intellectual centre of Italy, and was the first city where books were copied for sale.

Bologna's golden age continued through the 12th and 13th centuries, when it was one of the Guelph leaders of the Lombard League. As such it warred with Ghibelline Modena, and defeated that city in the Battle of Fossalta in 1249, capturing the talented Enzo, King of Sardinia and natural son of Emperor Frederick II. Defying custom, Bologna refused to ransom him and kept him in a castle until he died in 1272.

Bologna became part of the Papal States in 1278, though for the next few centuries real power was held by 'first citizens', most famously the Bentivoglio ('wish-you-well') family (1401–1506), who gained control after a brief period of reform. They heralded a flowering of local culture, despite a sensational family saga of assassination, high living and questionable legitimacy – the paternity of Annibale, father of the great art patron Giovanni II, was decided by a throw of the dice. Giovanni II ruled for 43 years until ousted by Pope Julius II (patron of Michelangelo), after which Bologna was ruled directly by a papal legate, putting an end to its independence once and for all.

Bologna witnessed one of the key turning points in Italian history in 1530 when Charles V insisted on being crowned Holy Roman Emperor in its basilica of San Petronio instead of in Rome, which his troops had sacked three years previously. Charles felt that going to Rome would seem like an act of contrition, and such was the low standing of papal authority that when he told Pope Clement VII that he 'did not need to seek crowns, but that crowns ran after him', the humbled pope could only agree. Charles' coronation, both as emperor and king of Italy, was celebrated with tremendous pomp, but marked the death knell for the Renaissance and the beginning of three centuries of foreign domination for Italy. Luigi Barzini notes that from then on the Italians put away their bright clothes and began to wear black in the Spanish style, as if they were in mourning – just as the *Fascisti* donned black shirts under Mussolini. A great age of post-Bentivoglio palace-building rapidly gave way to the totalitarian Church of the Counter-Reformation – although it also gave expression to Bologna's local artistic talent, such as the Carracci and Guido Reni.

Modern Bologna

In the 19th century Bologna was the birthplace of Marconi, who carried out his first experiments with radio at the Villa Grifone. It was also at this time that the city took the lead in the Italian socialist movement; in the 20th century it endured the brunt of the Fascist reaction. It was on the Germans' 'Gothic Line' (1944–5), and the scene of fervent partisan activity – leading to brutal Nazi reprisals such as the massacre at Marzabotto – but emerged from the Second World War relatively unscathed. After the war, Bologna's Communists got their chance to run the city, and made the most of it, making it a showcase for the Italian brand of Communism.

Bologna

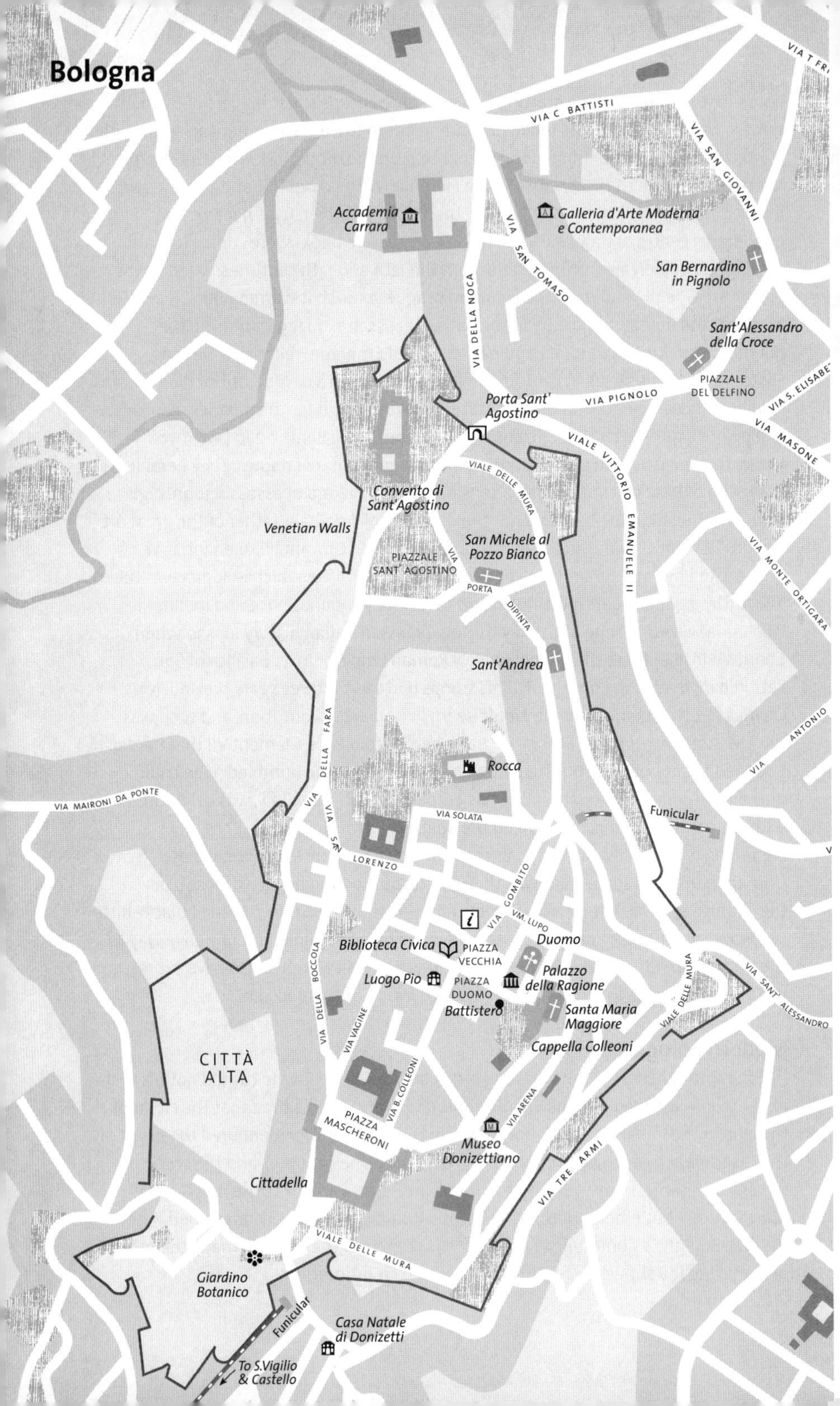

Bologna
VIA T FR
VIA C BATTISTI
VIA SAN GIOVANNI
Accademia Carrara
Galleria d'Arte Moderna e Contemporanea
VIA SAN TOMASO
VIA DELLA NOCA
San Bernardino in Pignolo
Sant'Alessandro della Croce
PIAZZALE DEL DELFINO
VIA S. ELISABE
VIA PIGNOLO
Porta Sant' Agostino
VIA MASONE
VIALE VITTORIO EMANUELE II
VIALE DELLE MURA
Convento di Sant'Agostino
Venetian Walls
San Michele al Pozzo Bianco
PIAZZALE SANT' AGOSTINO
VIA PORTA DIPINTA
VIA MONTE ORTIGARA
Sant'Andrea
VIA ANTONIO
VIA DELLA FARA
Rocca
VIA MAIRONI DA PONTE
VIA SOLATA
Funicular
VIA SAN LORENZO
VIA GOMBITO
VM. LUPO
Duomo
Biblioteca Civica
PIAZZA VECCHIA
Luogo Pio
PIAZZA DUOMO
Palazzo della Ragione
VIA DELLA BOCCOLA
VIALE DELLE MURA
VIA SANT' ALESSANDRO
Battistero
Santa Maria Maggiore
VIA VAGINE
Cappella Colleoni
CITTÀ ALTA
VIA B. COLLEONI
PIAZZA MASCHERONI
VIA ARENA
Museo Donizettiano
VIA TRE ARMI
Cittadella
VIALE DELLE MURA
Giardino Botanico
Funicular
Casa Natale di Donizetti
To S.Vigilio & Castello

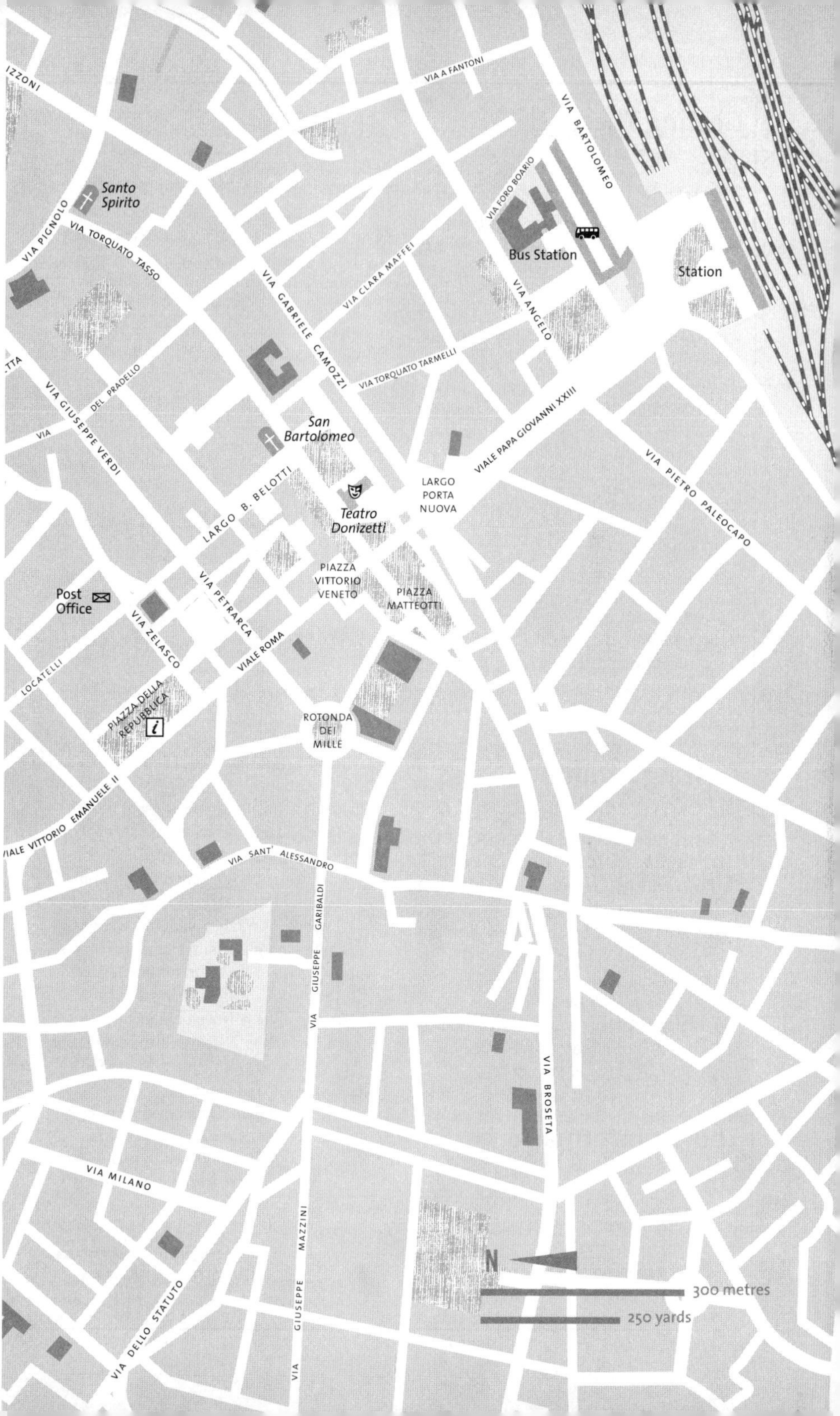

IZZONI
VIA A FANTONI
VIA BARTOLOMEO
VIA FORO BOARIO
Santo Spirito
VIA PIGNOLO
VIA TORQUATO TASSO
Bus Station
Station
VIA CLARA MAFFEI
VIA GABRIELE CAMOZZI
VIA ANGELO
VIA TORQUATO TARMELLI
VIA DEL PRADELLO
VIA GIUSEPPE VERDI
San Bartolomeo
VIALE PAPA GIOVANNI XXIII
LARGO PORTA NUOVA
VIA PIETRO PALEOCAPO
LARGO B. BELOTTI
Teatro Donizetti
PIAZZA VITTORIO VENETO
PIAZZA MATTEOTTI
Post Office
VIA PETRARCA
VIA ZELASCO
VIALE ROMA
LOCATELLI
PIAZZA DELLA REPUBBLICA
ROTONDA DEI MILLE
VIALE VITTORIO EMANUELE II
VIA SANT' ALESSANDRO
VIA GIUSEPPE GARIBALDI
VIA BROSETA
VIA MILANO
VIA GIUSEPPE MAZZINI
VIA DELLO STATUTO
N
300 metres
250 yards

Getting There

By Air

Guglielmo Marconi **airport**, northwest in the Borgo Panigale, **t** 051 647 9615, has links with major Italian and European cities. The **Aerobus** (**t** 051 290 290) runs to the train station every 15mins 8am–8pm but can take 1hr in traffic. There is also a direct bus from the airport to the Fiera district during trade shows (30mins).

By Rail

Bologna is one of the prime nodes of the FS network, with frequent fast trains to Venice, Florence, Milan, Ravenna, Rimini, Rome and almost everywhere else from the **Stazione Centrale**, **t** 1478 88088, in Piazza Medaglia d'Oro on the north side of the city centre, about a 10–15-min walk from Piazza Maggiore (bus nos.11 and 27 go straight there).

By Bus

The **bus** station, near the rail station at Piazza XX Settembre (**t** 051 247 354), has services every hour for Ferrara, Imola, Modena and Ravenna.

Getting Around

Most of Bologna's sights are within easy walking distance, but there's also an efficient **local bus** system (ATC), with offices dispensing tickets, bus maps and information at the main bus station, at a booth outside the railway station, and in the centre at Via IV Novembre 16, **t** 051 290 290. Tickets must be bought before boarding and are also available from *tabacchi* and news kiosks.

You can hire bicycles near the Porta Galliera, at Piazza XX Settembre 7, **t** 051 630 2015. For a taxi, call **t** 051 372 727, or **t** 051 534 141.

Tourist Information

Piazza Maggiore 6, **t** 051 246 541 (*open Mon–Sun 9–8*); branches at the railway station and the airport; *www.iat.comune.bologna.it*.

A one- or three-day *Carta Bologna di Musei*, available at museums and the tourist office, gets you in free or cheap at some places.

Shopping

Via Rizzoli and Via dell'Indipendenza are the main centres for **chic boutiques** and **fashion chains**, but Bologna's best buy is **food**: there are **markets** at Via Ugo Bassi 2 and Via Clavature, just off Piazza Maggiore (Mon–Sat mornings).

There's a string of general food stores in the streets around Piazza Maggiore, particularly towards the Due Torri. **Paolo Atti & Figli**, Via Caprarie 7 and Via Drapperie 6, in business since 1880, sells excellent home-made pasta and pastries. For perfect cheeses, try **Al Regno della Forma**, Via Oberdan 45a. **Tamburini**, Via Caprarie 1, is famous for its *salumeria*.

Where to Stay

Prices vary hugely according to the room, time of year, and events at Bologna Fiera. Avoid nasty surprises by confirming prices when booking, or try Accommodation Service (**t** 051 648 7607). July and Aug are low season.

Very Expensive–Luxury

★★★★**Dei Commercianti**, Via Pignattari 11, **t** 051 233 052, *www.bolognahotel.net*. A little hotel within spitting distance of San Petronio and the best shopping streets. Most rooms have balconies; the nicest, with ancient beams and the odd piece of fresco, are at the top.

★★★★**Grand Hotel Baglioni**, Via dell'Indipendenza 8, **t** 051 225 445, *www.baglionihotels.com*. The central 16th-century Palazzo Ghisleri-Fava, where Morandi's paintings were first exhibited in 1914, offering luxurious rooms and a wonderful restaurant frescoed by the Carracci, specializing in Bolognese cuisine.

★★★**Orologio**, Via IV Novembre 10, **t** 051 231 253, *www.bolognahotel.net*. An atmospheric old *palazzo* in a pleasant square beside San Petronio, with cosy rooms

★★★★**San Donato**, Via Zamboni 16, **t** 051 235 395, *www.hotelsandonato.it*. A 17th-century palace near the Due Torri, with a loyal clientele, comfy rooms and lovely summer terrace.

Expensive

★★★**Palace**, Via Montegrappa 9/2, **t** 051 237 442, *www.hotelpalacebologna.com*. A central, genteelly faded old *palazzo*. The best rooms are big and haven't changed much since the early 1900s. There are some *moderate* and some *very expensive* rooms. *Closed Aug.*

*****Roma**, Via D'Azeglio 9, **t** 051 226 322, *www.hotelroma.biz*. One of Bologna's all-round nicest, friendliest hotels, offering large rooms in the medieval *centro storico*.

*****Touring**, Via Mattuiani 1/2 (corner of Piazza Tribunali), **t** 051 584 305, *www.hoteltouring.it*. A central but tranquil option with a roof terrace. Some rooms are *very expensive*.

Moderate

****Albergo delle Drapperie**, Via Drapperie 5, **t** 051 223 955. Newly restored rooms just off Piazza Maggiore; the market outside starts up early, but you couldn't be better placed. All rooms are en suite; some are *expensive*.

****Centrale**, Via della Zecca 2, **t** 051 225 114. A hotel on the third floor (with lift) of an old *palazzo* in the centre, with air-con.

****Rossini**, Via Bibiena 11, **t** 051 237 716. Clean, comfortable rooms in the university quarter, and friendly staff. Some of the rooms without bath are *cheap*; some of the en suite rooms are *expensive*.

Cheap

***Hotel Giardinetto**, Via Massarenti 76, **t** 051 343 793, *www.goldengroup.net*. A cheerful option with air-conditioned en suite rooms, part of a small chain offering good summer rates; you could also try the 3-star **Holiday** at Via Bertiera 13, **t** 051 235 326, and **University** at Via Mentana 7, **t** 051 229 713.

Eating Out

Cucina petroniana rarely disappoints. Besides famous pasta dishes, the city is known for the best pâtés in Italy, for veal dishes and, of late, for its culinary innovations.

Even on weeknights in winter you might find it hard to walk into a good restaurant in the centre and get a table without a booking.

Very Expensive

Antica Trattoria del Cacciatore, Via Caduti di Casteldebole 25, **t** 051 564 203. A restaurant founded in the 19th century for hunters, who would wade here through the river, and known for its carts of delicious *antipasti*, side dishes and desserts. In summer you can dine on the verandah. Booking essential. *Closed Sun eve and Mon.*

Godot Wine Bar, Via Cartoleria 12, **t** 051 226 315. Delicious cuisine and the finest wines by the glass or bottle, in the heart of the *centro storico*. Try rabbit fillet with herbs and balsamic vinegar, and orange semifreddo. There are delicious nibbles, both in the wine bar and the restaurant. *Closed Sun and Aug.*

Pappagallo, Piazza della Mercanzia 3, **t** 051 232 807. The most famous restaurant in town, set in a quattrocento *palazzo* and beloved of celebs. The Italian food with French influences includes *antipasto* of prawns with red risotto; fresh pasta; a wide range of seafood *secondi*; and meat dishes such as Chateaubriand. The wine list is vast. *Closed Sun.*

Re Enzo, Via Riva di Reno 77, **t** 051 281498. Emilian cooking with a touch of Umbria, in dishes such as *gramigna alla quattro bianchi* (pasta with four white meats) and rabbit with capers. *Closed Sun.*

Torre de' Galluzzi, Corte Galluzzi 5/a, **t** 051 267 638. An atmospheric place in a tiny square behind the cathedral, with outside tables. The fine original dishes include plenty of *tortelloni* and roast rabbit glazed in sweet Albana. *Closed Sun and most of Aug.*

Expensive

Caminetto d'Oro, Via de' Falegnami 4, just off Via dell'Indipendenza, **t** 051 263 494. Unusual Emilia-Romagna specialities: try *rigatoni con formaggio di fossa* and *spaghetti alla chitarra* in lamb sauce. *Closed Tues eve, Weds, 1wk Jan and Aug.*

Da Cesari, Via de' Carbonesi 8, **t** 051 237 710. A long-standing restaurant serving Bologna standards such as tripe *alla parmigiana*, sometimes with innovative twists. *Closed Sun and Sat in June and July.*

Da Leonida, Vicolo Alemagna 2, **t** 0512 39742. A popular trattoria near the Due Torri, with endless variations on tortellini and tagliatelle, plus roast pheasant, rabbit with polenta and home-made desserts. *Closed Sun and end-July-end-Aug.*

Rosteria Luciano, Via N. Sauro 19 (north of Via Ugo Bassi), **t** 051 231 249. An old-fashioned place serving snails, smoked goose breast, and the like. *Closed Weds, late July–late Aug.*

Serghei, Via Piella 12, **t** 051 233 533. A rustic little family-run trattoria not far from the university, with home-made pasta, pork cooked in milk, *ossobuco*, and a wonderful ricotta tart. *Closed Sat eve, Sun and Aug.*

Moderate

Belle Arti, Via Belle Arti 14, **t** 051 267 648. A lively place near the university, with local and Mediterranean fare, including pasta with *cozze* (mussels) or *bottarghe* (fish roe). Various menus are available.

Gigina, Via Stendhal 1b (north of the centre), **t** 051 322 300. A classic Bolognese trattoria offering favourites such as lasagne, roast guinea fowl and *bollito misto*, plus famous old-fashioned desserts such as *torta di riso, zuppa inglese* and *crema fritta*. Book a couple of days in advance. *Closed Sat, most of Aug.*

Cheap

La Farfalla, Via Bertiera 12 (near the church of San Martino), **t** 051 225 656. Authentic, rustic food, including delicious *tortellini in brodo*, aubergine *parmigiana*, stuffed courgettes, *bollito misto* and donkey with *polenta*, all accompanied by jugs of house wine. Arrive early for a seat. No credit cards. *Closed Sun.*

Osteria del Sole, Vicolo Ranocchi, just off Piazza Maggiore. An institution, founded in 1468, with long wooden tables where you can eat food bought at the surrounding market and sample the excellent wine. *Open until 9pm; closed Sat, Sun and Aug.*

Trattoria-Pizzeria La Mela, Via de' Fusari, **t** 051 234 654. Neapolitan pizzas and seafood in a cosy, friendly place tucked away behind Piazza Maggiore and very popular with locals. *Closed Mon.*

Cafés

Pasticceria Impero, Via dell'Indipendenza 39. A good place to come for breakfast. The speciality is *certosini* – cakes with pine nuts, candied fruit, almonds and honey. *Closed Thurs pm and Sun.*

Pasticceria Majani, Via dei Carbonesi 5. A 'laboratory of sweet things' since 1796, famous for its *cioccolata scorza*. *Closed end-June–end-Aug.*

La Torinese, Piazza Re Enzo 1. A century-old café famous for its hot chocolate and pastries.

Entertainment and Nightlife

People here eat late – around 10pm – and there are plenty of bars and cafés open until 3am. See posters in student bars to find out about concerts, films, exhibitions and clubs; or check the listings in Bologna's local paper, *Il Resto del Carlino*.

Opera, Classical, Theatre and Cinema

The drama season at the **Teatro Duse,** Via Cartoleria 42, **t** 051 231 836, runs from Nov to May. Operas are performed at the **Teatro Comunale, t** 051 529 011, from Dec to May. Other classical music venues are the **Basilica di Santa Maria dei Servi,** and the **Accademia Filarmonica,** Via Guerrazzi 13, **t** 051 648 6261.

In July and Aug, the **Bologna Sogna festival** features open-air theatre and films; and dance and concerts are held in Piazza Maggiore.

In winter, *versione originale* **films** are shown at Tiffany, Piazza di Porta Saragozza 5, **t** 051 585 253. Cinema Lumière, Via Pietralata 55, **t** 051 523 539, shows undubbed art-house movies.

Live Jazz, Blues, Rock, Alternative

The city's traditional *osterie* serve food, host live music and stay open late.

Cantina Bentivoglio, Via Mascarella 4, **t** 051 265 416. A smart cellar bar with live acoustic jazz some nights (cover charge), snacks and full meals. *Closed Sun in summer.*

Osteria dell'Orsa, Via Mentana 1, **t** 051 231 576. A beer cellar/restaurant near the university, with outside tables and jazz twice weekly.

Officina Estragon, Via Calzoni 6, **t** 051 365 825. Ska, hip-hop and reggae.

Le Stanze, Via del Borgo di San Pietro 1, **t** 051 228 767. A bar housed in a Bentivoglio chapel of 1500, offering occasional live music.

Clubs and Discos

Many clubs are outside the centre. In summer the council sponsors cheap open-air raves.

Corte degli Aranzi, Via Dozza Giuseppe 26, **t** 051 451 541.

Forte Jola, Via M. Donato 17, *www.fortejola.com*.

Link Project, Via Fioravanti, *www.linkproject.org*.

Sottotetto Sound Club, Viale Zagabria 1, *www.nott.it*.

Like the rest of Italy, Bologna in the late 1960s and the 1970s had more than its fair share of troubles. Italy was making a sharp left turn, and a new generation sought radical alternatives to the PCI. In the so-called '*anni di piombo*' (leaden years), shadowy rightist groups within the security police and the army infiltrated the 'Red Brigades' and fomented terrorism: Bologna's Communists and the city itself were prime targets. In 1980 the rightist terrorists made their bloodiest strike ever – a bomb in the city's Stazione Centrale that killed 85 people and wounded more than 200 others. Things gradually calmed down after that, but by the 1990s a sharp increase in crime and drug addiction made many Bolognesi highly discontented with their city government.

The 'catastrophe', as the local leftists like to call it, came in the mayoral election of 1998, when a conservative squeaked in, Giorgio Guazzaloca. The right crowed and cackled across Italy: the great Red bastion had capitulated. Drama occurred again in March 2002, when Marco Biagi, the advisor to the labour ministry on controversial new legislation, was gunned down in Bologna while he was cycling home. The Red Brigades claimed responsibility, but there are various theories about the real identity of the killers, with Italy, as ever, caught up in political power struggles between far-left and far-right factions.

As for Guazzaloca, his most controversial move has been to allow cars back into the city's *centro storico*. This historic centre is one of the best preserved and maintained in the whole of Italy, to the credit of the city's policy of 'active preservation' since the 1970s – old houses in the centre are gutted and renovated for municipal public housing, maintaining the character and diversity of the old quarters. Nor is this the first time that Bologna has found a creative solution to its housing needs: you will soon notice that every street is lined with arcades, or *portici*; the original ones date back to the 12th century, when the *comune*, faced with a housing shortage caused by its 2,000 students, allowed rooms to be built on to existing buildings over the streets. Over time the Bolognese became attached to these overhanging additons and the shelter they provided from the weather. Now it claims 70 kilometres of *portici* – more than in any other city in the world.

Piazza Maggiore

The centre stage of Bolognese public life is Piazza Maggiore and its antechamber, Piazza Nettuno, graced with the virile and vaguely outrageous **Fountain of Neptune**, 'who has abandoned the fishes to make friends with the pigeons', designed in the 16th century by Tommaso Laureti of Palermo and embellished with the statue by Giambologna. Adjacent, and occupying part of both squares, are the **Palazzo di Re Enzo** of 1244 (where Frederick II's son was kept prisoner in some luxury, writing love poetry), and the **Palazzo del Podestà**, begun in 1212 and remodelled in 1484 by Aristotele Fioravanti, who went on to design parts of the Kremlin. The corners of the **Voltone** (the big *portico*) contain 16th-century statues of Bologna's four patron saints.

Filling the western side of Piazza Maggiore, the crenellated **Palazzo Comunale** (*open Tues–Sat 9–6.30, Sun and hols 10–6.30; adm*) incorporates the **Casa Accursio** of 1287 (the arcaded section), and the 1425 annexe by Fioravante Fioravanti, father of

Aristotele. Over the door there is a bronze statue of Pope Gregory XIII, the creator of the Gregorian calendar and a native of Bologna. Under a canopy to the left you'll see a beautiful terracotta Madonna by Nicolò dell'Arca, a Renaissance sculptor from Puglia whose best work is in Bologna.

Inside are two museums: the **Collezioni Comunali d'Arte**, reached via Bramante's grand staircase and containing works by the Bolognese school, and the **Museo Morandi**, devoted to Bologna's greatest modern painter, Giorgio Morandi (1890–1964). The latter rarely left the city and, although a friend of Futurists and Metaphysicists in Ferrara, kept to himself, quietly producing some of the 20th century's best paintings. The subject matter – jars and jugs – is mundane, but Morandi's fierce gaze transforms it; as Umberto Eco put it, he 'made the dust sing'. There are also landscapes of Grizzana, where Morandi spent his summers.

Opposite the Palazzo del Podestà, the **Basilica di San Petronio** by Antonio da Vicenza (1390) is the largest structure on the square. Had the Bolognese had their way, this temple to their top patron would have been even larger than St Peter's in Rome. However, Pope Pius IV in 1565 ordered them to spend their money on the university's Archiginnasio instead, leaving even the façade unfinished; the white and red marble stripes recalling the city's heraldic emblem only made it up to the portals – perhaps sparing the city the embarrassment of another 'cathedral wearing pyjamas', like the one in Florence. The remarkable main door has reliefs by Jacopo della Quercia of Siena, begun in 1425. Like Ghiberti's doors to the baptistry in Florence (for which Della Quercia was an unsuccessful candidate), they are landmarks in the visual evolution of the early Renaissance, and seem strangely modern – almost Art Deco in sensibility.

Missing from the front of San Petronio, however, is Michelangelo's colossal bronze statue of Pope Julius II, commissioned by him in 1506 after he regained the city for the Papal States. Julius also built a large castle in the centre of Bologna. Both were torn to bits by the population as soon as the Pope's luck changed; and to rub salt into his wounded pride the bronze was sold as scrap to his arch-enemy, Alfonso I of Ferrara, who melted it down to cast an enormous cannon – which he fondly named 'Julius'.

The lofty interior saw the crowning of Charles V and, according to tradition, the conversion of a visiting monk named Martin Luther who became so sickened by papal pomp and pageantry that he decided to start the Reformation. In 1655 astronomer Cassini designed the huge astronomical clock, which tells the time with a shaft of light through an *oculus* in the roof. Two of the chapels (third and fourth on the left) are noteworthy – one with 15th-century frescoes of Heaven and Hell, the other containing Lorenzo Costa's *Madonna and Saints*. In the **museum** at the end of the aisle are models of Bologna's basilican pipe dreams (*open Weds–Mon 10–12.30, Sat and Sun also 4–5.30; closed July and Aug*).

Via dell'Archiginnasio

The eastern side of Piazza Maggiore is closed by the **Palazzo dei Banchi**, with its long, elegant façade designed by Vignola (1568). Beyond is Bologna's excellent **Museo Civico Archeologico** at Via dell'Archiginnasio 3 (*open Tues–Sat 9–6.30, Sun and hols 10–6.30; adm*). Into its dim and dusty wooden cases is crammed one of Italy's best collections of antiquities – beautifully wrought items from the Iron Age Villanova culture, native Italics who were eventually conquered by the Etruscans, and artefacts from Bologna's beginnings as Etruscan Felsina. Felsina may have been a frontier town, but it is richly represented here with tomb art, circular gravestones 10ft in diameter carved with proud warriors and ships, and an embossed bronze urn, the *Situla di Certosa*, similar to others found in Tuscany. The Etruscans traded extensively with the Greeks, whose Attic vases are one of the highlights of the museum. There are a few items from Gallic *Bononia*, Roman artefacts (a lovely copy of Phidias' bust of Athena Lemnia), and an excellent Egyptian collection.

The next long porticoed façade is the seat of the old university, the **Palazzo dell'Archiginnasio** (*open Mon–Sat 9–1*), its walls covered with the escutcheons and memorials of famous alumni. Bologna's university is the oldest in Europe, but was not provided with a central building until 1565 – at the expense of San Petronio. After 1803 this became the **Biblioteca Comunale**. Upstairs is the ornate old **anatomical theatre** (*open Mon–Sat 9–1 and occasional afternoons*), shattered by a bomb in the Second World War and painstakingly rebuilt in 1950. The monument in the piazza in front commemorates Luigi Galvani, the 18th-century Bolognese discoverer of electrical currents in animals, who gave his life and name ('galvanize') to physics. Just off Piazza Maggiore on Via Clavature, stop in **Santa Maria della Vita** to see the terracotta *Lament over the Dead Christ* by Nicolò dell'Arca, a work harrowing in its grief and terror, a 15th-century version of Edvard Munch's *Scream*.

Two Leaning Towers

In the passage under Via Rizzoli, you can see remains of the Via Aemilia. The end of Via Rizzoli is framed by **Piazza Porta Ravegnana** and a pair of towers that might have wandered off the set of *The Cabinet of Dr Caligari*. After the initial shock wears off, however, fondness invariably sets in for this odd couple, the Laurel and Hardy of architecture. The taller one looks respectable only because the other is so hilarious.

Dante's mention of the Garisenda tower comes in Canto XXXI of the *Inferno*, when he and Virgil encounter the giant Antaeus frozen in ice at the bottom of Hell:

Qual pare a riguardar la Garisenda
Sotto 'l chinato, quando un nuvol vada
Sovr'essa si, che ella incontro penda

Tal parve Anteo a me, che stava a bada
Di vederlo chinare, e fu tal ora
Ch'i' avrei voluto ir per altra strada.

('...like looking at the Garisenda, under the leaning side, when a cloud comes; so seemed Antaeus to me, about to fall – to see him leaning so, I wished I had taken another path.'). He is referring to an optical illusion that every child in Bologna knows – stand under the lean of the tower when clouds are moving in the opposite direction, and you'll see it.

The **Due Torri** were built in 1119 in a competition between two families. The winner, the svelte 318ft **Torre degli Asinelli** (*open daily summer 9–6, winter 9–5; adm*), is still the tallest building in Bologna. It tilts about three feet out of true, though the 500 steps that lead to the top are more likely to make your head spin than the tilt. The view over Bologna is worth the trouble, however. Its sidekick, the **Torre Garisenda**, sways tipsily to the south, 10ft out of true; the Garisenda contingent failed to prepare a solid foundation and, when they saw their tower pitching precariously, they threw in the towel. In 1360 it became such a threat to public safety that its top was lopped off, leaving only a squat 157ft stump; inscribed in its base you can read what Dante wrote about it in the *Inferno* (*see* p.495).

Beyond the towers, five streets fan out to gates in the eastern walls of the old city. One of these, the palace-lined Strada Maggiore, follows the route of the Via Aemilia, passing by **San Bartolomeo**, a church that is notable for housing two works by Bolognese masters: Albani's *Annunciation*, which is kept in a chapel on the south aisle, and Guido Reni's *Madonna*. In the 19th century Italians considered the 'Divine Guido' their greatest artist; since then he has taken a precipitous and admittedly deserved fall from fashion.

At Strada Maggiore 13, the **Casa Isolani**, home of the British Council, is one of the best-preserved 13th-century houses left in Bologna; at No.44 the 18th-century **Palazzo dei Giganti** (or Davia) (*open Tues–Sat 9–2, Sun 9–1*) contains the **Galleria Davia-Bargelli**, housing Vitale da Bologna's famous *Madonna with Teeth*, the patroness of dentists and perhaps the most characteristic and earnest work of the earnest Bolognese school, and the **Museum of Industrial Art**. At this point the *portici* of the street intermingle with those of the arcades of the city's Gothic jewel, **Santa Maria dei Servi**, which contains among its works of art a rare Madonna by Cimabue (in the apse), which you'll need to illuminate to see.

Santo Stefano

Via Santo Stefano, another street radiating from the two towers, may also be reached from Santa Maria dei Servi via Via Guerrazzi (where, at No.13, the 14-year-old Mozart was elected to the Accademia Filarmonica). The street has a curious quartet of churches, with a cloister and two chapels thrown in (*all open daily 9–12.15 and 3.30–6, hols 9–12 and 3.30–7*). They are all part of the monastery of Santo Stefano that was founded by St Petronius, who reproduced here the seven holy sites of Jerusalem (over a temple of the Egyptian goddess Isis) and dedicated the ensemble to the first Christian martyr. Three of the churches of this unique and harmonious 8th–12th century Romanesque ensemble face Piazza Santo Stefano – the largest is the **Crocefisso**, which was begun in the 11th century and boasts an altar in its façade and an ancient crypt situated below its raised choir. To the left is polygonal **San Sepolcro**, modelled on the Holy Sepulchre and containing the **Edicola di San Petronio**, a large pulpit adorned with reliefs and encircled by the columns of Isis's circular temple. **SS. Vitale e Agricola**, further to the left, is Bologna's oldest church, built in the 5th century, incorporating bits and pieces of old Roman buildings, and alabaster windows.

Beyond it is the **Cortile di Pilato**, containing an 8th-century Lombard bathtub that somehow gained the sinister reputation of being the basin in which Pontius Pilate washed his hands. From here you can enter the fourth church, the 13th-century **Trinità**, which has a lovely 10th-century cloister and contains works by Simone de' Crocefissi. Up Via Santo Stefano towards the Due Torri you'll find the lovely Gothic **Palazzo della Mercanzia** (1384); it has an ornate loggia by the architect of San Petronio, Antonio da Vincenzo.

Via Zamboni

Again from the towers, Via Zamboni leads shortly to **Piazza Rossini**. Rossini, composer of *The Barber of Seville* and *William Tell*, studied from 1806 to 1810 at the **Conservatorio G.B. Martini** (*open Mon–Sat 9–1; closed Aug*), and spent much of his life in a nearby *palazzo*. The conservatory houses original scores by Mozart, Monteverdi and Rossini and, oddly enough, a portrait by Thomas Gainsborough.

Also on the square is **San Giacomo Maggiore**, which was begun in 1267. This was the parish church of the Bentivoglio, one of whom, Giovanni II, hired Lorenzo Costa to paint the frescoes in the Cappella Bentivoglio – the *Triumph of Death*, the *Apocalypse* and *Madonna Enthroned* – with himself and family in their midst. In these pictures the Bentivoglio seem benign enough, but the Bolognese reviled them so much that they tore their palace apart brick by brick when they were deposed. The fresco itself was commissioned in thanksgiving for the thuggish Giovanni's escape from hired assassins. The fine altarpiece in the chapel is by Francesco Francia, a native of Bologna, while the high-mounted tomb opposite, of Anton Galeazzo Bentivoglio (1435), is by della Quercia.

The **Oratory of Santa Cecilia** (*open daily 10–1 and 2–6*), entered from Via Zamboni, was frescoed by Costa and Francia. The **Teatro Comunale**, further up in Piazza Verdi, was built by Antonio Bibiena in 1763 over the Bentivoglio palace. The Bibiena clan of theatre and stage designers were in demand all over Europe in the 17th and 18th centuries, and did much to popularize the typical Baroque tiers of boxes, which the Teatro Comunale preserves behind its 1933 façade.

The University

Beyond the theatre is the university, which was moved in 1803 from the too-central Archiginnasio (where the students could cause trouble) into Pellegrino Tibaldi's Mannerist **Palazzo Poggi**, topped by the eclectic astronomers' observation tower, the **Torre della Specola** – part of Luigi Ferdinando Marsigli's attempt to bring new empirical sciences to Bologna in 1720 – and adorned with Tibaldi's frescoes of Ulysses, an influential Mannerist illusionistic *quadratura* painting. Famed for medicine and astronomy (Copernicus studied here), Bologna has been known best for jurisprudence, ever since its founding by the *glossatori* (who 'glossed' or annotated Justinian's codes). One student, Vacarius, went on to found the law school at Oxford in 1144.

There are a number of small museums connected with the university in the Palazzo Poggi (*open Tues–Fri 9–5.30, Sat and Sun 10–6.30*), including the **Museo Aldovrandi**, housing the collections of the great Renaissance naturalist who established botany, zoology and entomology; the **Museo di Astronomia**; and the quirky **Museum of the Toy Soldier**. Further north on Via Irnerio is the **Orto Botanico**, one of the world's oldest botanical gardens, the **Museo di Anatomia Umana Normale** (*open Mon–Fri 9–1*), one of the most popular oddball attractions in Bologna, housing wax anatomical models made by the most talented artists of the 18th century as medical teaching aids. For a sobering look at Fido sans skin, there's also the **Museo Anatomico di Animali Domestici** (*visits by request, call* **t** *051 792 999*).

Pinacoteca Nazionale

Via Belle Arti 56, **t** *051 243 222; open Tues–Sun 9–7; adm.*

Across from the university, Bologna's most important art is stored here. You'll find works by both 14th-century Bolognese artists – of whom Vitale da Bologna emerges as the star, with his intense *St George and the Dragon* – and 'foreigners', with pride of place going to a Giotto polyptych. There are fine Renaissance works by the Vivarini brothers and Cima da Conegliano of Venice; works by the Ferrara school; and later Bolognese paintings. The most famous painting in the entire museum is Raphael's *Ecstasy of St Cecilia*, which the artist sent from Rome to his friend Il Francia. Parmigianino represents Emilia-Romagna's Mannerist decades, sharing space with Perugino and Titian. The Carracci brothers, who initiated Bologna's move into the forefront of Italian art, and the perfect little world of Guido Reni, Bologna's favourite son, each earn a room of their own.

Via Belle Arti, heading back towards the centre, passes several fine palaces before ending at the intersection of Via Mentana. Turn left for **San Martino**; Paolo Uccello painted a fresco here that was believed lost until 1981, when a *Nativity* fragment was found. The church also contains fine works by Francia, Costa and the Carraccis.

North and West of Piazza Maggiore

Via dell'Indipendenza links Piazza Maggiore to the station; on it is Bologna's 10th-century cathedral, **San Pietro**, rebuilt in the Baroque era. As with Venice's San Pietro di Castello, this symbol of the papacy received scant affection – the basilica of the city's patron saint was far more important. Hence San Pietro is not too interesting, unless you are a devotee of St Anne, whose skull is the chief treasure, a gift from Henry VI of England. The Romanesque campanile is a survivor of the original church. For a taste of medieval Bologna with all its towers stroll down Via Altabella and its adjacent lanes.

Opposite the cathedral, Via Manzoni leads to the **Palazzo Fava**, site of the **Museo Civico Medioevale e del Rinascimento** (*open Tues–Sat 9–6.30; from 10 Sun and hols; adm*), one of the unmissable sights of the city, containing tombs of medieval scholars carved with life-like images of professors expounding to perplexed, earnest, daydreaming students; a colossal bronze propaganda statue of the most grasping and arrogant of popes, Boniface VIII; a collection of armour, ceramics, majolica, ivory and glass, and a 13th-century English cope. In several rooms you can see where Annibale Carracci and other Bolognese painters frescoed scenes from the *Aeneid* and classical mythology (*Jason and the Argonauts*).

Via Ugo Bassi, the westerly section of the Via Aemilia, leads to narrow and lively **Piazza Malpighi**, home to some odd little pavilions with pyramidal roofs raised off the ground on slender columns – the 13th-century **Tombs of the Glossatori**, tombs of noted doctors of the Law. The apse and rare flying buttresses of the lovely Gothic **San Francesco** back on to the piazza; begun in the saint's lifetime in 1236, the church has a striking, lofty interior, all white with brick piers and vaulting, and a beautiful 14th-century sculpted marble ancona. Back towards the centre, Via Cesare Battisti runs south from Via Ugo Bassi to the 17th-century San Salvatore, with a striking Mannerist Marriage of St Catherine (1534), the masterpiece of Girolamo da Carpi.

South of Piazza Maggiore

From the Archiginnasio, Via Garibaldi leads south to **San Domenico**, built in 1251 to house the relics of St Dominic, founder of the Dominican order of preaching friars. He built a convent on this site and died here in 1221; his tomb, the **Arca di San Domenico**, is a masterwork. Many chisels contributed to it, including those of Nicola Pisano and his school, who executed the beautiful reliefs of the saint's life, and Nicolò dell'Arca, who gained his name from it – adding the eight patron saints of Bologna on top; when he died mid-work, a 20-year-old refugee from Florence called Michelangelo finished them off, sculpting SS. Petronius and Proculus and an angel holding a candle.

From San Domenico, Via Marsili leads to Via D'Azeglio, with the **Palazzo Bevilacqua**, a 15th-century Tuscan-style palace where the Council of Trent took refuge from a plague in Trent in 1547. Just north at Via Val D'Aposa 6 is the lovely brick and terracotta façade of **Spirito Santo**. Via Marsili, now Via Urbana, continues to the **Collegio di Spagna** (*visits by appointment, **t** 051 330 408*), the Spanish college founded in 1365 by Cardinal Albornoz, the papacy's top man in Italy while the popes were hiding out in Avignon. In the Middle Ages Bologna had many such colleges, but this one (an official corner of Spanish territory) is the only one to survive. Cervantes studied here, as did St Ignatius. From here Via Saragozza wends down to the **Porta Saragozza**, starting point for the portico to beat all porticoes – winding four kilometres up the hill to the **Santuario della Madonna di San Luca**. The church was built to house an icon attributed to St Luke, and the 666-arch portico added between 1674 and 1793.

There are fantastic views of the Apennines from the sanctuary (if you can't face the hike, bus no.20 from Via dell'Indipendenza covers some of the route). Other famous viewpoints in the hills south of Bologna are from **San Michele in Bosco**, a hospital in a former convent (bus no.30), and from **Villa Aldini** (bus no.52A), built on the site where Napoleon admired the panorama of the city. From this villa you can walk down towards the Porta San Mamolo and the fine 15th-century church of the Annunziata.

East of Bologna

Between Bologna and the Adriatic are a hotchpotch of attractions – Italy's most important trotting course and the Imola motor-racing course; the fine medieval town of Brisighella; Italy's top ceramics town, Faenza; and Forlì, decorated by Mussolini.

Imola

Nearest to Bologna, Imola is synonymous with the San Marino Grand Prix, which is held on the race track here, and for a restaurant, the San Domenico, a pilgrimage shrine for grand gourmets (*see* p.502). Otherwise, in the cathedral you can pay your respects at the tomb of Imola's patron, San Cassiano, a schoolteacher whose martyrdom was particularly unpleasant: he was stabbed with the pens of his students. The **Rocca Sforzesca** (*open weekends only; adm*), which is situated to the south of the Via Aemilia, was defended by Caterina Sforza from the time of her husband Girolamo Riario's assassination in 1488 (for his role in the unsuccessful Pazzi conspiracy against Lorenzo de' Medici) until its capture by Cesare Borgia in 1499. As Caterina rallied her supporters to help defend the castle, they pointed out that her six children were still in the hands of the enemy, leaving the family with no heirs; she reportedly hoisted up her skirts and told the crowd she could still make plenty more. However, the final, losing battle may have been a little unbalanced: the Borgia side had a renowned expert on fortifications to assist their siege, a certain Leonardo da Vinci – who later drew a town plan of Imola, made for improving the defences, that is now held at Windsor Castle. Caterina's life came full circle: she ended it married to a Medici.

Her other castle, at **Dozza**, a few kilometres back towards Bologna, houses the **Enoteca Regionale Emilia-Romagna** (***t*** *0542 678 089; open Tues–Sun 9.30–1 and 2.30–6.30*), a treasure trove where you can sample 600 wines of the region. Dozza is also famous for its biannual September festival, the 'Painted Wall' (Muro Dipinto), in which the walls of the houses become canvases for large murals.

Faenza

'Faïence ware' was born in the 16th century in Faenza with the invention of a new style of majolica: a piece was given a solid white glaze then very rapidly, almost impressionistically, decorated with two tones of yellow and blue. It caused an absolute sensation, and was in such demand throughout Europe that Faenza became a household name. Today, though rather a shabby place, it has regained much of its 16th-century lustre as a ceramics centre. There are 500 students enrolled in its Istituto d'Arte per la Ceramica, and some 60 artists from around the world run workshops in the town. The **Associati Ente Ceramica**, Voltone della Molinella 2, **t** 0546 22308, issues a list of studios that you may visit and buy from. Among several buildings and palaces adorned with majolica, the most splendid is the Liberty-style **Palazzo Matteucci** in Corso Mazzini. Every year from September to October Faenza hosts an international ceramics exhibition; the theme is contemporary in odd years, and antique in even.

The **Museo Internazionale delle Ceramiche** at Viale Baccarini 19 (***t*** *0546 25231; open Apr–Oct Tues–Sat 9–7, Sun 9.30–1 and 3–7; Nov–Mar Tues–Fri 9–1.30, Sat 9–1.30 and 3–6, Sun 9.30–1 and 3–6; adm; if you're going to Ravenna, purchase a* biglietto cumulativo, *which includes the main monuments there*) was founded in 1908 and restored after bombing in the war. It houses a magnificent collection, centred on 16th- and 17th-century Italian ceramics; pieces from Faenza adorned with giraffe-necked

Renaissance ladies were typical nuptial gifts. There are fine Liberty-style pieces by Domenico Baccarini and Francesco Nonni, and downstairs you'll find pieces by Picasso, Matisse, Chagall and Rouault.

Nobody knows how **Bagnacavallo**, located to the north of Faenza, came by its name, which means 'horse-bath', but it has the distinction of having been the property of Sir John Hawkwood, the English mercenary captain of the 1300s whose monument you can see in Florence's Duomo.

Some 12 kilometres south of Faenza on the Florence road, **Brisighella** is a charming village and thermal spa in the Lamone valley. The sharp cliffs overhead are crowned by the splendid towers of the 12th-century Rocca and the Torre dell'Orologio, the latter originally a respectable guard tower (1290) with a clock slapped on its front in the 18th century. Brisighella produces much of the clay that is fired in Faenza's kilns – next to the village you can see the gashes left in the hills by the old quarries. So precious was this cargo borne by mule caravans that a special protected, elevated passageway, the Via degli Asini (Mule Road), was built. Several ceramics workshops still operate in Brisighella; from the end of June into the first week of July the city hosts an elaborate medieval festival, complete with music, games, feasts, plays and locals dressed up in gorgeous costumes.

Forlì

The *Forum Livii* on the Via Aemilia was elided over the years into Forlì, a city split between an attractive old town and the architectural legacy of Mussolini, who was born in nearby Predappio. The old centrepiece of old Forlì is the striking 12th-century **Basilica di San Mercuriale**, with a good campanile (1180), a fine lunette of the Magi by the school of Antelami, and an interesting interior. The **Duomo** on Corso Garibaldi has a temple façade; inside, note the painting of 15th-century firemen.

On Corso della Repubblica, the **Pinacoteca Saffi** (*open Tues–Sat 9–1.30, Tues and Thurs also 5–5.30, Sun 9–1; closed Aug*) has works by local artist Marco Palmezzano, Fra Angelico, and Canova's marble *Hebe*, a rarefied neoclassical fantasy. Nearby, **Santa Maria dei Servi** contains the finely sculpted tomb of Luffo Namai (1502). South of the centre, Forlì's castle, the highly picturesque 15th-century **Rocca di Ravaldino**, also belonged to Caterina Sforza, and was the birthplace in 1498 of her son Giovanni de' Medici ('Giovanni delle Bande Nere', a famous *condottiere* and father of Cosimo I, the first Duke of Tuscany). It is now a prison.

At the eastern edge of the centre, on and around Piazza della Vittoria, is the centre of an entire district that was laid out between 1925 and 1932, called the **Città del Duce.** Plenty of nonsense has been written about architecture and design under the Fascist regime; but for the inscriptions and pasted-on fasces and slogans, Mussolini's architecture was no more 'authoritarian' than that of Paris in the 1930s. A little Bauhaus and a discreet touch of travertine Roman monumentalism are the main ingredients, with recurring conceits such as the open porticos of tall square columns, which are seen all over Italy. The entire ensemble is a reminder of how much Fascism, like the Baroque, depended on mass spectacles in appropriate settings. Appearance was everything.

Getting Around

Between Bologna and Rimini, **trains** are fast, frequent and sometimes packed, particularly in Aug. A slow local train from Faenza to Florence stops at Brisighella; to carry on to Florence you may have to change trains at Borgo San Lorenzo.

Bagno di Romagna and other towns near the Tuscan frontier can best be reached by **bus** from Forlì or Florence.

Tourist Information

Imola: Via Mazzini 14, **t** 0542 602 207, *www.comune.imola.bo.it*.
Faenza: Piazza del Popolo 1, **t** 0546 25231.
Brisighella: Piazzetta Porta Gabolo 5, **t** 0546 81166 (*summer only*).
Forlì: Corso della Repubblica 23, **t** 0543 712 435, *www.turismoforlivese.it*.

Where to Stay and Eat

Imola ✉ 40026

San Domenico, Via G. Sacchi 1, **t** 0542 29000 (*very expensive*). A place of veneration for gastronomes from around the world for the past 35 years, offering a daily-changing menu of sublime traditional dishes in a rather 1970s dining room. Several set menus are available, from an expensive lunch to the extremely expensive *menu degustazione*. The wine list is superb. *Closed Mon, Sun eve and Aug.*

Osteria del Vicolo Nuovo, Vicolo Codronchi 6, **t** 0542 32552 (*expensive*). A restaurant situated in a 17th-century cellar, serving delicious modern dishes based on local traditions, including cheese soufflé with *porcini* mushrooms, home-made pasta (including gnocchi with *porcini*, and tortellini with asparagus), rabbit roasted in Sangiovese wine, tongue with *salsa verde*, and an variety of vegetarian dishes. There's also an assortment of delicious cheeses. *Closed Sun, Mon and Aug.*

È Parlaminté, Via G. Mameli 33, **t** 0542 30144 (*expensive*). A cheerful family-run favourite where the whole of Imola comes to feast on the likes of *passatelli in brodo* or *baccalà*, and discuss the affairs of the day. *Closed Sun eve and Mon.*

Faenza ✉ 48018

There are many *affittacamere* (rooms for rent) in private houses; ask at the tourist office.

*******Hotel Vittoria**, Corso Garibaldi 23, **t** 0546 21508, *www.hotel-vittoria.com* (*moderate–very expensive*). An attractive hotel in the centre, with 19th-century furnishings and the occasional frescoed ceiling. Rooms are large and a laundry service is available.

Le Volte, Corso Mazzini 54, **t** 0546 661 600 (*expensive*). A restaurant hidden away in the old wine cellars under the Galleria Gessi arcade, near the Pinacoteca, and filled with antique furniture. Try *tortelloni al radicchio*, duck breast roast with cabbage and pepper, or rack of lamb in a herb crust. *Closed Sun.*

Brisighella ✉ 48013

*******Gigiolè**, Piazza Carducci 5, **t** 0546 81209, *www.gigiole.it* (*expensive*). Five-star-standard rooms in the centre of Brisighella, and an excellent restaurant that has long been a mecca for foodies, with dishes based on

Into the Apennines

South of Forlì three principal routes lead into Tuscany. Some of the best scenery is in the **Montone Valley**, the main route to Florence (along the SS67) passing the Renaissance planned village of **Terra del Sole**, begun in 1564 in the form of a perfect rectangle. Ruined medieval castles haunt the next towns of **Dovadola** and **Rocca San Casciano**. Dante's Beatrice spent several summers in the pretty old medieval town of **Portico di Romagna**; the Portinari house where she stayed is in the main street. Near the Tuscan frontier the 9th-century abbey at **San Benedetto in Alpe** sheltered Dante after his unsuccessful bid to return to Florence from exile (*Inferno*, Canto XVI, 94–105).

Romagna's medieval culinary traditions. Try the classic *borlonga*, filled with greens and cheese; ravioli stuffed with rabbit and mint; veal with wild fennel; or chestnut-flour pasta with *porcini* mushrooms. There's also a rich dessert cart. *Closed mid-Feb–mid-Mar; restaurant also closed Mon.*

★★★**Valverde**, Via Lamone 14, **t** 0546 81388, *www.hotelvalverde.com* (*moderate*). A good choice in a garden setting.

Trattoria di Strada Casale, Fraz. Strada Casale, **t** 0546 88054 (*very expensive*). Superb creative food based on the finest ingredients. There's a daily-changing menu, as well as a fabulous five-course, *moderate menu degustazione* (and a more expensive one with 3 different wines). *Closed lunch except Sat and Sun, dinner Weds, Sat and Sun.*

Cantina del Bonsignore, Via Recupeati 4a, **t** 0546 81889 (*expensive*). The atmospheric wine cellar of the *monsignore*'s palace, in the *centro storico*. Delicacies include poppyseed ravioli, and *tortino di polenta* with *porcini* mushrooms. *Closed for lunch except Thurs, 2wks in Jan and 2wks in Aug.*

Forlì ✉ 47100

★★★**Vittorino**, Via Baratti 4, **t** 0543 21526 (*moderate*). Central, small, simple rooms.

La Casa Rusticale dei Cavalieri Templari, Via Bologna 275, **t** 0543 701 888 (*very expensive*). A house built as a Templar lodge in the 13th century, subsequently a church and a farmhouse, and now the place to come for delicious *piadine*, home-made pasta dishes and classic Romagnoli *secondi*. A selection of cheap and moderate lunchtime *menu degustazione* are available. *Closed Sun, Mon and Aug.*

La Volpe e l'Uva, Via G. Saffi 76, **t** 0543 33600 (*expensive*). A good restaurant located close to the Pinacoteca, serving a range of traditional dishes such as *tigelle*, green *garganelli*, fish and salads. *Closed Mon and July–Aug.*

Bagno di Romagna ✉ 47021

★★★★**Hotel Tosco Romagnolo**, Piazza Dante Alighieri 2, **t** 0543 911 260, *www.paoloteverini.com* (*moderate–expensive*). A charming, modern and very relaxing place to stay, with a garden on the banks of a *torrente*, a swimming pool, and one of Italy's most enchanting restaurants, **Paolo Teverini** (*very expensive*). The menu is based on Tuscan and Romagnolo country traditions, cooked with a very special touch: Teverini, considered the top vegetable chef in the country, is capable of making a gastronomic Mona Lisa from an onion. There are four *menu degustazione*, fabulous desserts and dessert wines served by the glass. *Closed Mon and Tues.*

Cesena ✉ 47023

★★★★**Casali**, Via B. Croce 81, **t** 0547 22745, *www.hotelcasalicesena.it* (*expensive*). The nicest hotel in town, traditional and luxurious but only really convenient if you're driving.

Osteria Michiletta, Via Fantaguzzi 26, **t** 0547 24691 (*moderate*). A popular, charming place offering such delights as pumpkin with gorgonzola, *spaghettini* with goats' cheese and mint, rabbit baked in pancetta, and poppyseed tart with honey and pannacotta. Service is friendly and attentive. *Closed Sun and Aug.*

In San Benedetto you can hire horses to explore the region's valleys, especially the lovely **Valle dell'Acquacheta** with its bucolic, stepped waterfall. The rapid Brusia river is popular with canoeists, and this is a marvellous area for hill walking.

The route just east (SS9 ter) passes through the **Sangiovese** wine country around **Predappio**, where Mussolini was born in 1883 and to the cemetery of which his remains were transferred in 1957. Mussolini made Predappio the seat of the local *comune*, and embellished it with public buildings, leaving the old *comune*, Predappio Alta, alone beneath its overgrown castle. In Predappio Alta, you can taste the local Sangiovese or 'blood of Jove' at the **Cà de Sanvèz** (*open Weds–Mon 12–12*).

The Local *Palio*

Siena's *palio* (traditional horse race) may be the most famous, but it's neither unique in Italy, nor the only one to claim the longest history. However, whereas Siena's *palio* has continued virtually uninterrupted for centuries, the others, particularly those in Emilia-Romagna, have resurrected themselves over the past few decades, and as a result lack the pomp, vast crowds and deep emotional response of that gallop around the Campo.

Yet though the *palii* in Montagnana, Ferrara, Faenza (last two Sundays in July) and Forlimpopoli may be less vital, violent, cosmopolitan and crooked, they do have other charms: no tourists, few police, small crowds, and a chance to see an Italian community expressing its self-love. Older traditions do remain (the tug of war to decide placings at the race's start), but the lack of formality and crowds allow for a relaxed atmosphere; kids in medieval finery spend the afternoon tearing round the streets, beating on drums.

Siena provides the framework that lesser *palii* copy. The day begins with a procession in medieval costume, probably led by the town's standard, followed by a delegation from each district: 'landowners' on horseback, young married couples holding hands, a matron in the middle of a crowd of urchins, a criminal in the stocks, massed ranks of young men clasping spears and pushing a catapult, a cart piled with geese, and troupes of teenage *sbandierati* twirling long, silken flags from one hand to the other, tossing them into the air and, as they unfurl, catching them again.

By comparison, the race itself is chaotic. Bales of hay line wooden barriers that shield the crowds from the thundering horses. Each bareback rider carries a *nerbo*, a whip with which he may hit any horse or opponent, and wears a small coat named *giacchetto*, from which we derive the English word 'jockey' (and 'jacket'). The horses, fired up, take several minutes to form a regular starting-line. The race is brief and furious. Its aftermath depends on where you are: in Montagnana, near Rovigo, the victor will be carried home for a beer and barbecue. In Siena supporters will try to kill the losers for having lost and the victor for having won; the entire city weeps for joy or shame at the outcome; casks of wine are splintered open on the pavement and goblets handed out to any passer-by.

From **Forlimpopoli**, with its well-preserved medieval castle, a third road heads south for **Bertinoro**, an old town famous for its wine and hospitality. Such were the squabbles over guests that a column was erected in front of the 14th-century Palazzo Comunale and hung with rings, one belonging to each family. The ring a stranger tethered his horse to decided which family got to be his host. Nearby **Polenta** has a fine 9th-century Byzantine–„Romanesque temple.

The main SS310 from Forlì continues into the scenic, heavily forested Upper Bidenta valley. There are ski facilities at Monte Campigna, near the old Tuscan town of Santa Sofia. Much further south, near Balze, there's more skiing at Monte Fumaiolo, on the slopes of which the Tiber begins its 418-kilometre journey to Rome. San Piero in Bagno and Bagno di Romagna, with thermal and mud baths, are popular summer resorts.

Cesena and the Crossing of the Rubicon

In the 14th and 15th centuries, Cesena, site of the European Trotting Championships in August, was one of the jewels of the Malatesta clan. Their castle still dominates the town, while a 1452 basilica built for Domenico Malatesta Novello is the main sight, housing the **Biblioteca Malatestiana** (***t*** *0547 610 892; open Mon–Sat 8.30–12.30 and 3–5.30, Sun 10–12.30; closes dusk in winter; adm*), with a priceless collection of manuscripts. Between Cesena and Rimini at Savignano, the road crosses an excuse for a stream that most authorities accept as the shadowy Rubicon, which divided what was then Gaul from Roman Italy, and which Caesar crossed with his army in 49 BC, thereby defying the Senate and declaring his intention to take over the Roman state. Today it separates respectable Emilia-Romagna from the beach Babylon of Rimini.

Ferrara

There's been a certain mystique attached to Ferrara ever since Jacob Burckhardt called it 'the first modern city in Europe' in his classic *Civilization of the Renaissance in Italy*. Whether or not Burckhardt was right can be debated endlessly; what is certain is that the famous 'additions' to the medieval city in the Renaissance were far too ambitious. Ferrara, even in the most brilliant days of the Este family, never mustered more than 30,000 citizens – not enough to fill the long, straight, rational streets laid out within the nine-kilometre circuit of the walls.

But what was a failure in the Renaissance is a happy success today; if Italian art cities can be said to come and go in fashion, Ferrara is definitely in, popularized by a well-received international campaign to save its unique walls, and a rebirth of interest in its great quattrocento painters. Thanks to the tyrannical Este, the charming city they enclose was one of the brightest stars of the Renaissance, with its own fine school of art led by Cosmè Tura, Ercole de' Roberti, Lorenzo Costa and Francesco del Cossa. Poets patronized by the Este produced three great Italian Renaissance epics – Boiardo's *Orlando Innamorato* (1483), Ariosto's continuation of the story, *Orlando Furioso* (1532), and Tasso's *Gerusalemme Liberata* (1581), all praising the ducal family.

History

Ferrara grew up on a formerly navigable branch of the Po river, and until the 17th century based its economy on river tolls, the salt pans of the Comacchio and the rich agricultural land of the Delta. It was always ruled by one family or the other, but it was the rise of the Este in 1250 that made it a great city, an outpost of papal power in the north. The Este clan produced and married some of the most interesting characters of the Renaissance: there was Nicolò II (1361–88), 'the Lame', a friend of Petrarch; Alberto (1388–93), who founded the University of Ferrara; Nicolò III (1393–1441), reputedly the father of hundreds of children on both banks of the Po, as well as being the villain who perpetrated one of the tragic love stories of his day – he found that his young wife Parisina and his son by another woman, Ugo, were lovers, and had both of them executed.

Getting Around

Ferrara's **train** station is a 15min walk west of the centre along Viale Cavour (local buses no.1, 2, 3c or 5), just outside the city walls, There are frequent trains to Bologna, Venice and Ravenna.

The **bus** station is near the corner of the Rampari di San Paolo and Corso Isonzo; a network of lines (ACFT Punto Bus, **t** 0532 599 490) serves the coast, Bologna, Modena, Ravenna and local destinations.

Pancake-flat Ferrara has the second-largest ratio of **bicycles** to people in Europe (after Copenhagen). You can hire one at the *deposito* just outside the train station, **t** 0532 772 190.

Tourist Information

Castello Estense, **t** 0532 299 303, *www.ferraraterraeacqua.it*.

A Civic Museums card is available (excluding the Casa Romei).

Activities

Ferrara has its own annual **Palio** or traditional horse race (*www.palliodiferrara.it*) on the last Sun in May. There's also a **Buskers' Festival** in the last week of Aug, with performers from all over the world, and the **Ferrara Musica**, an international season of **concerts** and **opera** from Sept to May. Venues include the stunning Teatro Comunale, which can also be visited (*t 0532 218 3302; open 10–11am; adm*).

Where to Stay

Ferrara ✉ 44100

Very Expensive

*******Duchessa Isabella**, Via Palestro 70, **t** 0532 202 121, *www.duchessaisabella.it*. A magnificent Renaissance palace with a private park in the heart of the city, with antiques, linens and crystals in the old rooms, some of which still have frescoes by the Ferrara school and coffered ceilings. Guests can use the hotel's bicycles or horse-drawn carriage to visit the city. Some rooms are *expensive*, others *luxury*. Staff can be snooty. *Closed Aug*.

******Annunziata**, Piazza della Repubblica 5, **t** 0532 201 111, *www.annunziata.it*. Casanova's favourite inn, with big windows overlooking the Castello Estenese, charming staff, extremely comfortable rooms (some *expensive*), and free bikes for guests. The hotel also has some independent apartments, the **Prisciani Artsuite**, in a nearby palazzo at Via Garibaldi 70, containing specially commissioned paintings and sculptures and 300-year-old frescoes. Some have kitchens and washing machines.

******Astra**, Viale Cavour 55, **t** 0532 206 088, *www.astrahotel.com*. A sturdy, well-furnished hotel on the main street to the station, with a fine restaurant. Some rooms are *expensive*.

******Ripagrande**, Via Ripagrande 2, **t** 0532 765 250, *www.ripagrandehotel.it*. Ferrara's most memorable accommodation, in the Renaissance Beccari-Freguglia palace in the medieval quarter. The ground floor has the original décor of old brick walls, marble stairs and heavy-beamed ceiling, and there is a pleasant inner courtyard. It's worth asking about the junior suites, which are only marginally more expensive than doubles; some have beautiful big balconies, wooden beams and mezzanines. Bicycle hire is available.

Expensive

*****Europa**, Corso Giovecca 49, **t** 0532 205 456, *www.hoteleuropaferrara.com*. A 17th-century palace designed by Rossetti, where Verdi spent time with a lady friend who lived in Ferrara (Room 4). The bedrooms are simple but well appointed; no.32 has frescoes. The lobby is full of 18th-century antiques and there's a pretty garden courtyard. Some rooms are *moderate*. Flats are also available.

The legitimate sons of Nicolò III – Leonello, Borso and Ercole I (1471–1505) – met happier fates, and were responsible for the city's great cultural flowering. Ercole I had the first addition to the city (known as the Herculean Addition) designed by his architect Rossetti; his offspring, Isabella (wife of Francesco Gonzaga), Beatrice

Moderate

******Villa Regina**, Via Comacchio 402, Cocomaro di Cona, **t** 0532 740 222, *www.villaregina.it*. A beautiful converted villa in a park outside the city but within easy reach of it. Some rooms are *expensive*.

*****Hotel de Prati**, Via Padiglioni 5, **t** 0532 241 905, *www.hoteldeprati.com*. A friendly, peaceful option with 15 rooms, full of family heirlooms and hosting changing exhibitions by contemporary local artists.

****San Paolo**, Via Baluardi 9, **t** 0532 762 040, *www.hotelsanpaolo.it*. A pleasantly situated hotel near the city walls by Piazza Travaglio, with tasteful décor, spotless rooms and very friendly and helpful staff. There are bikes for hire, and adjacent free parking.

Cheap

***Casa Degli Artisti**, Via Vittoria 66, **t** 0532 761 038. A friendly, clean, central option on a quiet sidestreet near the Duomo.

Eating Out

Ferrara's most famous dish (Lucrezia Borgia's favourite) is *salama da sugo* – a spicy sausage cured for a year then gently boiled for about four hours and eaten with a spoon. Little caps of pasta, *cappelletti*, filled with pumpkin, are another speciality. Ferrara's bakers are famous for their X-shaped bread, *ciupèta*.

Renée of France brought her own vines to Ferrara; this is the origin of the local viticulture and the delicious Vino di Bosco.

Very Expensive

Il Don Giovanni, Via del Primaro 86, Loc. Marrara, 17km south of Ferrara, **t** 0532 421 064. A weekly-changing menu taking advantage of seasonal produce and the day's catch. The imaginative combinations might include ravioli filled with sea bass and coriander in an onion sauce. The desserts, cheeses and wine list are great. Book ahead. *Closed Mon eve, Sun, Jan and July.*

Expensive

L'Oca Giuliva, Via Boccacanale di Santo Stefano, **t** 0532 207 628. A traditional menu featuring the likes of *pasticcio di maccheroni alla ferrarese*, and another menu changing every two weeks. There are 250 wines to choose from, many by the glass. *Closed Mon, Tues lunch, and last 2wks Sept.*

Quel Fantastico Giovedì, Via Castelnuovo 9 (corner of Via Camaleonte), **t** 0532 760 570. Creative dishes with a light touch – salmon marinated in herbs, squid stuffed with aubergines in a yellow pepper sauce, and game dishes in season. The name, 'What a Wonderful Thursday', comes from a story by John Steinbeck. Reservations are essential. *Closed Wed, late Jan and mid-July–mid-Aug.*

Il Testamento del Porco, Via Mulinetto 109–11, **t** 0532 760 460. A popular place outside the walls by the hippodrome, with wonderful minestrone, home-made tagliatelle with *porcini*, ostrich and fillet of beef with balsamic vinegar. *Closed Sat lunch, Sun and Aug.*

Moderate

Antica Trattoria Il Cucco, Via Voltacasotto 3, off Via C. Mayr, **t** 0532 760 026. Local classics such as wild boar ham, smoked goose, *cappellacci di zucca* and, if you book ahead, *salama da sugo* or *pasticcio alla ferrarese*. Follow your meal with traditional *ciambella* and sweet wine. *Closed Wed.*

Cheap

Al Brindisi, Via Adelardi. A convivial wood-panelled *enoteca* offering fine cheeses, *salama da sugo* and other treats. *Closed Mon and last 2wks July.*

Enotria, 41 Via Saraceno. A central *enoteca* with a fine selection of wines, plus *bruschetta* and *crostini*. *Closed Sun in summer.*

La Zirudela, Via Saraceno 85–7, **t** 0532 204 903. Typical Ferrarese cuisine, plus seafood, amid delightful décor, including a frescoed ceiling. The tempting à la carte dishes are *moderate–expensive*. *Closed Tues.*

(married to Lodovico Sforza, Il Moro), and Cardinal Ippolito, were among the most cultured and influential people of their day. His heir, Alfonso I (1505–34), married the beautiful and unjustly maligned Lucrezia Borgia, who ran a brilliant and fashionable court, patronizing Ariosto and Titian, while her husband spent his days casting huge cannons. With the guns, and with some carefully crafted marriages, Alfonso's skilful diplomacy helped Ferrara to avoid invasion and to emerge from the Wars of Italy with its independence intact. The couple's son, Ercole II (1534–59), married Renée, the daughter of Louis XII of France, and a Calvinist, who sheltered John Calvin in Ferrara under an assumed name; eventually relations with Rome became so touchy that she had to be sent away.

The last Duke, Alfonso II (1559–97), who was the patron of the unstable Tasso, was considered the best-educated and most courtly ruler of his day, but at the expense of his people. When he died without issue, Ferrara, which was sick and tired of paying the bills, was glad to see the last of the Este, and be ruled by a papal legate. The city soon became a backwater, and its population declined. In the 20th century, however, the modern 'Metaphysical School' of painting (which included De Chirico, Carrà, De Pisis, Morandi and others) had its origins in the city, inspired at least in part by the great frescoes in the Palazzo Schifanoia.

The Castle and the Cathedral

At the very centre of Ferrara towers the imposing **Castello Estense** (*open daily 9.30–5.30; adm*), which would look like a Victorian factory building were it not for its moat and drawbridges. It was begun as a fortress in 1385 by Nicolò II after a tax revolt, but later the Este transformed it into their chief residence, its crenellations replaced by white marble balustrades, and its great halls adorned with art. A few of its decorated rooms survive: the *Salone*, the *Saletta dei Giochi* (the games room, belonging to the children) and the fine *Sala dell'Aurora* (Ercole II's study) and *Camerina dei Baccanali* are the most interesting. The guided tour includes a look at Renée's Calvinist chapel, as well as the Torre dei Leoni, where Ugo and Parisina languished prior to their beheading, and Giulio and Ferrante, brothers of Alfonso I, spent their lives after attempting a coup. The dukes weren't the forgiving kind: Ferrante died after 34 years in the tower, while Giulio came out with a pardon after 53 years, aged 81.

From the *castello*, Corso dei Martiri leads first to the **Palazzo Comunale,** built in 1243 and adorned with statues of Nicolò III and Borso; next to it in Piazza della Repubblica stands a statue of Savonarola, a native of Ferrara. Opposite the *palazzo* is the handsome rose-coloured **Duomo**, begun in 1135 by Wiligelmo of Modena fame and his follower Nicolò, and finished by 1300. Its glory is a marble portico: Nicolò executed the relief on the tympanum of *St George* and various Old Testament scenes; the pediment above the loggia on top is carved with a magnificent 13th-century Last Judgement. The candy-striped campanile is said to be Alberti's work. The upper loggia on the south side is a bit of show-offish Romanesque bravura, with twisted columns; the picturesque portico below, flanking the Duomo, was added in 1473.

The interior was catastrophically remodelled in the 17th century, but you can see the best art in the **Museo della Cattedrale** on Via San Martino (*open Tues–Sun 9–1 and 3–6; adm*), including the marble *Madonna of the Pomegranate* by Jacopo della Quercia and two painted organ shutters by Cosmè Tura that rank among his greatest works: a naturalistic Annunciation and a surreal St George.

Renaissance Palaces

From behind the cathedral in Via Voltapaletto, Via Savonarola takes you to the **Casa Romei** (*open Tues–Sun 8.30–7.30; adm*), a fine example of the typical Renaissance palace, built for a banker who won the sweepstakes by marrying an Este in 1445. As well as its charming frescoes, terracotta fireplaces and elegant courtyards, there are expressive detached frescoes that were transferred here from Sant'Andrea and other disused churches.

To the south on Via Pergolato, behind the church of San Girolamo, the church of **Corpus Domini** (*open Mon–Fri 9.30–11.30 and 3.30–5.30*) contains the austere tombs of Alfonso I, Alfonso II and Lucrezia Borgia. North of Via Savonarola, up Via Ugo Bassi, the late-Renaissance **Palazzina di Marfisa d'Este** is in a garden at Corso della Giovecca 170 (*open daily 9–1 and 3–6; adm*). Marfisa, a friend of Tasso, was beautiful and eccentric, and the subject of several ghost stories; it seems that she enjoyed post-mortem midnight rides through Ferrara in a wolf-drawn carriage. The interior of her little palace has unusual *grotteschi* frescoes on the ceiling. Outside is a loggia with frescoes of two little girls: one is Marfisa.

Palazzo Schifanoia

Ferrara's most famous palace, but not its most beautiful, is the 1385 Palazzo Schifanoia (*open Tues–Sun 9–6; adm*), a couple of streets away at Via Scandiana 23 (follow Via Ugo Bassi to Via Madama). Schifanoia means 'disgust with boredom', but it would be hard to stay bored in the utterly delightful **Salone dei Mesi**, frescoed for Borso d'Este *c.* 1475 by Ferrara's finest – Cosmè Tura, Ercole de' Roberti and Francesco del Cossa. The mythological and allegorical scenes (*currently being restored, though some will be visible at any given time*), peopled by amiable aristocrats, are believed to have been inspired by Petrarch's Triumphs – in each month a different god is seen to triumph, most famously the Triumph of Venus for the month of April, with a rare Renaissance kiss. Another inspiration comes from the occult astrology that shaped so much of Renaissance thought and life. The palace has several other rooms with beautiful ceilings, and houses an eclectic collection of medieval art (note the alabaster *Passion of Christ* from Nottingham) and ancient art.

Palazzo di Lodovico il Moro

Turn right at the walls at the end of Via Scandiana and continue to Via XX Settembre for No.124, the elegant Palazzo di Lodovico il Moro designed by Biagio Rossetti and named after Beatrice d'Este's Milanese husband, although it never belonged to him. It has frescoes on the ground floor by Raphael's pupil, Garofalo, and upstairs an excellent **Museo Archeologico Nazionale** (*open Tues–Sun 9–2; adm*), with artefacts from the necropolis of the Graeco-Etruscan seaport of Spina, including Attic vases, a splendid gold diadem and two pirogues carved from tree trunks in the later Roman period. Nearby in Via Beatrice d'Este, the convent of **Sant'Antonio in Polèsine** has fine frescoes dating back to the 13th century and inlaid choir stalls. Just outside the walls (through the Porta Romana), **San Giorgio**, Ferrara's cathedral until the 12th century, is worth a look for the sumptuous 1475 tomb of Lorenzo Roverella, who was Pope Julius

II's physician. Back towards the centre, on Via delle Scienze, the 13th-century **Palazzo Paradiso** was the former seat of the university and is now the Ariosto library, with the complete manuscript of *Orlando Furioso* and Ariosto's tomb.

Just north of here you'll find a labyrinth of narrow, cobbled streets, brick arches and alleyways that comprise Ferrara's former ghetto. There's a **Jewish Museum** (*open for guided tours Sun–Thurs 10, 11 and 12; closed Jewish hols; adm*) in Via Mazzini, where there used to be three synagogues. The building has been the focus of Jewish life in Ferrara since 1485, when it was purchased by a rich financier from Rome employed at the Estense court: he left it in his will 'forever for the common use of the Jews'. Jewish refugees from Spain and the Papal State were subsequently welcomed in Ferrara, and made up a thriving community until the popes locked them up in a ghetto from 1627 to 1859. Most of Ferrara's Jews were deported late in the Second World War; only five came back.

The Herculean Addition

North of the Castello Estense stretches the Herculean Addition, which was laid out by Biagio Rossetti for Ercole I and which more than doubled the size of 15th-century Ferrara. Not long after the fall of the Este dynasty, travellers noted that many of the streets here were rather abandoned and overgrown, and even today they feel somewhat melancholy and quiet. Corso Ercole I was intended as the new district's 'noble street' and it attracted many to build their palaces in the area, including the new home of the Este dukes, Rossetti's showpiece **Palazzo dei Diamanti**. In the very centre of the Addition, it takes its name from the 8,500 pointed, diamond-shaped stones that stud the façade – diamonds being an emblem of the Este.

It houses the **Pinacoteca Nazionale** (*open Tues, Weds, Fri and Sat 9–2, Thurs 9–7, Sun 9–1; adm*), which has a fine collection by the Ferrara school – Tura, Cossa, Costa, Roberti, the sweet Raphaelesque Garofalo (a favourite of the 18th century) and Dossi – and detached frescoes from churches and palaces. There's also Carpaccio's *Death of the Virgin*, and works by two local artists known only as the 'Maestro degli Occhi Spalancati' (Master of the Wide-open Eyes) and a 'Maestro degli Occhi Ammicanti' (Master of the Winking Eyes). On the ground floor is a **Galleria Civica d'Arte Moderna** (*currently closed for restoration*) and the **Museo Michelangelo Antonioni** (*open daily 9–1 and 3–6; adm*), containing a multimedia fantasy by the famous director, the 'Enchanted Mountain'.

The palace lies at the junction of two main streets; Via Ariosto leads off Corso Biagio Rossetti to the right, to the **Casa di Ariosto** (*open Tues–Sat 10–1 and 3–6, Sun 10–1*), which the poet built for himself. 'Small,' he described it modestly, 'but suited to me.' To the east, the **Palazzo Massari** at Corso Porta Mare 9 (*open Tues–Sun 9–1 and 3–6; adm*) houses two more museums, the first of which is the **Museo Civico d'Arte Moderna e Contemporanea**, dedicated to Ferrara's Metaphysical School. Pass through the courtyard to reach the **Palazzina dei Cavalieri di Malta**, formerly the seat of the Knights of Malta 1826–34, now home to the fascinating **Museo Giovanni Boldini**, a shrine to a flagrant and very fashionable salon painter of the mauve decades, a man born to paint society ladies in evening gowns. Verdi dedicated an opera to him.

Ferrara's well-preserved nine-kilometre circuit of red-brick walls is most easily seen by bicycle. They date from the 15th and 16th centuries, and were one of the prototypes for the new model fortifications of the Renaissance. The best stretch is between the Porta Mare and the former Porta degli Angeli, which was built by Rossetti on the north side of the city. Cycle paths run along their length, linking up with routes out to the Po.

Around Ferrara

The region around Ferrara is flat and somewhat dreary. **Argenta**, to the southeast of the city, has an attractive quattrocento church of **San Domenico** (*open Sat and Sun 3–6.30*), which houses a small art gallery, with works by Garofalo and others. Between Ferrara and Modena, **Cento**, under its 14th-century castle, was the birthplace of Disraeli's ancestors and painter Giovanni Francesco Barbieri, better known by his nickname Guercino or 'Squinty' (1591–1666); a collection of his work is in the **Pinacoteca Civica**, Via Matteotti 10 (*open weekends only during exhibitions*).

The Coast: from the Po to Ravenna

For most people the main attractions along this coast are the Po Delta and the magnificent Romanesque abbey of Pomposa, though there are plenty of family lidos in the vicinity if you're tempted to join the summer ice-cream and parasol brigades.

The Southern Po Delta

Alfonso II d'Este was the first to start draining the marshes south of the Po Delta. Much of the land was planted with rice; a large part of the rest now belongs to the **Parco del Delta del Po**, one of Italy's most important wetlands, and a birdwatcher's paradise. Part of the primordial coastal pine forest survives intact in the **Bosco di Mésola**, now a nature reserve (*open Mar–Oct 8–6, or sunset if earlier*). Not far to the west, near Italba, this varied and ever-changing coastline offers something completely different – a marooned 100-acre patch of dunes, once part of the coast, called the '**Moraro**'. Excursion boats ply the narrow canals between the reeds and explore the mouth of the Po di Goro and the Valle di Gorino, departing from the picturesque fishing hamlets of Gorino, Goro, Cannevie or Porto Garibaldi. A full list of companies and excursions is available from the tourist office.

The Abbey of Pomposa

The main coast road from the north, SS309, follows the old Roman coastal road, the Via Romea. Just south of the Po di Goro it passes through **Mésola**, with its old hunting lodge, the 'Delizia Estense' of Alfonso I d'Este, then continues down to the haunting and serene **abbey of Pomposa** (*open daily 8.30–7*), an 8th-century Benedictine foundation that was formerly on its own islet; in this atmosphere of total tranquillity the monk Guido d'Arezzo invented the modern musical scale in the early 11th century. Uninhabited since the 17th century, the abbey is dwarfed by its campanile (1063), adorned with mullioned windows, which progress tier by tier from a narrow slit on the bottom to a grand *quadrifore* (four arches) on top; the colourful ceramic plaques are replacements for the originals, made by monks in Egypt. The church (7th–11th centuries) has a lovely Byzantine atrium, done in patterned bricks and relief panels. Inside is a magnificent pavement, in maze-like patterns of stone and mosaics, and above it walls covered with the entire Old and New Testaments in colourful 14th-century frescoes. Some of the best (*Life of Sant'Eustachio*) are by the charming Vitale da Bologna; there are other frescoes by his school in the monks' Chapter House. The abbot governed from the beautifully austere 11th-century Palazzo della Ragione.

The resorts along the sandy **Lidi di Comacchio** begin at the Lido di Volano on the other side of the wetlands of the Valle Bertuzzi, where the setting sun ignites the waters in a thousand colours. Of the resorts, the **Lido delle Nazioni** and **Porto Garibaldi** are the most interesting. The name of the latter recalls the defeated hero's attempt to escape from here after the collapse of the Roman Republic in 1849, in a desperate guerrilla movement that cost the life of his pregnant wife Anita. The most important town is **Comacchio,** the Romagna's 'Little Venice', with its monumental triple bridge, the Trepponti, spanning three of the town's many canals. Comacchio used to make its living on salt but is now famed for its eels, farmed in the Valli di Comacchio – if you're in the area between September and December you can watch the fishermen scoop them up. On the Canale Maggiore, the old hospital of San Camilo has been restored to house the **Museo delle Culture Umane nel Delta del Po**. Just west of Comacchio stood the Graeco-Etruscan Spina, for centuries the main port of Felsina (Bologna), but now miles from the sea. Almost nothing remains of it.

Ravenna

Innocently tucked away among the art towns of Emilia-Romagna is one famous city that has nothing to do with Renaissance popes and potentates, Guelphs or Ghibellines, sports cars or socialists. Little, in fact, has been heard from Ravenna in the last thousand years. Before that time, however, this city's career was simply astounding – it was heir to Rome itself, and the leading city of western Europe for centuries. For anyone interested in Italy's shadowy progress through the Dark Ages, this is the place to visit.

There's a certain magic in three-digit years; history guards their secrets closely, giving us only occasional glimpses of battling barbarians, careful monks 'keeping alive the flame of knowledge' and local Byzantine dukes and counts doing their best to hold things together. In Italy, the Dark Ages were never quite so dark. This can be seen in Rome, but much more clearly here, in the only Italian city that not only survived but prospered all through those troubled times. In Ravenna's churches, adorned with the finest mosaics ever made, such an interruption as the Dark Ages seems to disappear, and you experience the development of Italian history and art from ancient to medieval times as a continuous and logical process.

History

On an important route to Dalmatia and the Danube, Ravenna and its port of Classe became prominent during the reign of Augustus. With their nearly impregnable site, surrounded by marshes, their military advantage was clear, and Classe became Rome's biggest naval base on the Adriatic. As conditions in Italy grew unsettled in the 5th century, Ravenna's relative safety began to look very inviting to scared emperors.

Honorius moved the capital of the Western Empire here in AD 402 – just in time, what with Alaric's sack of Rome coming eight years later. Honorius' sister, Galla Placidia, ruled the city in the emperor's absence, and began to embellish it with churches and monuments befitting its new status. When the Visigoths attacked Ravenna, Galla Placidia was taken hostage, and married the Visigothic king Ataulf. They got on well together in Toulouse, and before his assassination she rode at his side everywhere, even in battle. She returned eventually to Ravenna, however, and ruled it until she died in 450.

By the 6th century, with sheep grazing in the Roman forum, Ravenna had become accepted as the metropolis of Italy. The Ostrogothic kings, Odoacer and Theodoric, made it their capital; during the reign of the latter the last flowering of Latin letters took place, under the influence of his famous councillors: Boethius, Symmachus and Cassiodorus. Boethius, one of the Fathers of the Church, wrote The *Consolation of Philosophy* in Theodoric's dungeon, where the king had consigned him after suspecting the philosopher of intrigues with Constantinople.

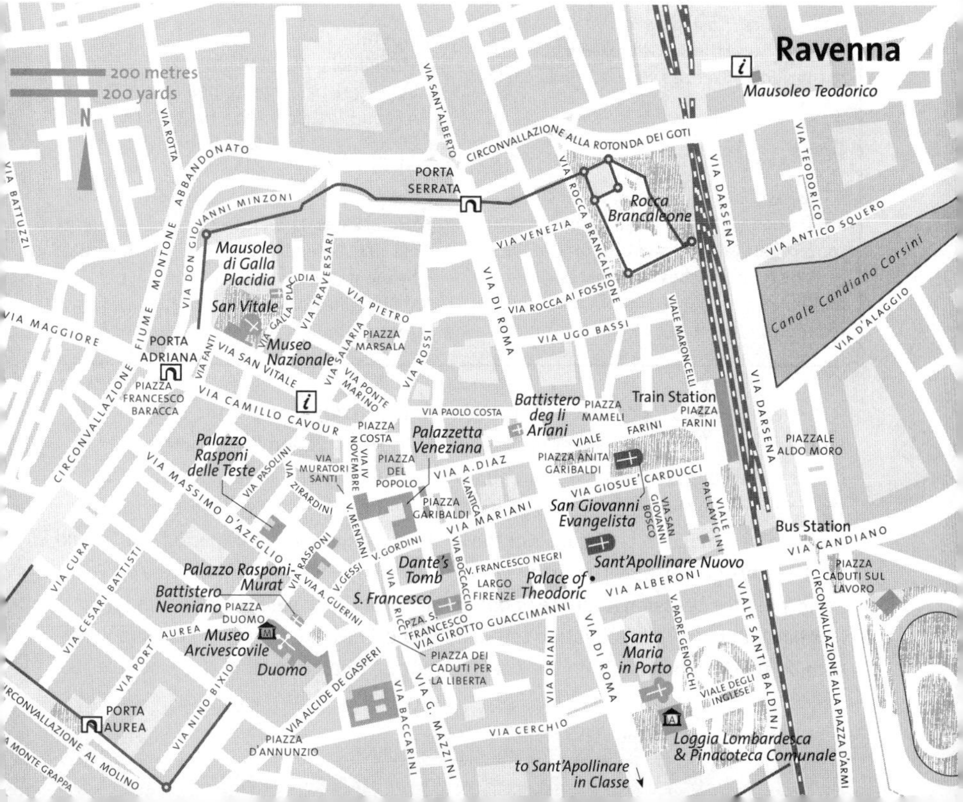

Getting There and Around

There are several **trains** a day from Florence, Venice, Ancona and Bologna (change at Faenza, Ferrara or Rimini from other cities). The station is in Piazza Farini, east of the old town next to the ship channel. The **bus station** is just across the tracks on Via Darsena.

Bus no.2 from the train station or Piazza del Popolo goes past Theodoric's Mausoleum, otherwise a 30-min walk from the centre. Buses no.1 and 70 go to Marina di Ravenna. Buses no.4 and 44 from the station or Piazza del Popolo go to S. Apollinare in Classe. Other buses from the train station or Piazza dei Caduti will take you to Classe or any of Ravenna's nearby lidos. You can hire **bicycles** in Piazza Farini in front of the station, and in the ACI car park near San Vitale.

Tourist Information

Via Salaria 8, **t** 0544 35404, and at the Mausoleo Teodorico; *www.turismo.ravenna.it*.

A *Biglietto Cumulativo* will get you into combinations of sights for a discount; there's a ticket including San Vitale, Sant' Apollinare and the Battistero Neoniano, and one including Faenza's ceramics museum too.

Festivals

The Ravenna Festival, during which internationally renowned musicians perform concerts, recitals and opera in some of the city's historic churches and palaces, runs from mid-June to mid-July. For information contact the tourist office or see its website.

Where to Stay

Ravenna ☒ 48100

Expensive

*****Cappello**, Via IV Novembre 41, **t** 0544 219 813, *www.albergocappello.it*. One of the smartest and most central options, with seven rooms in a 14th-century *palazzo* reputed to have been the home of Francesca da Rimini. There are frescoes, wood-panelled ceilings and antique fireplaces, and a romantic little restaurant. *Restaurant closed Sun eve and Mon.*

Moderate–Expensive

*****Centrale Byron**, Via IV Novembre 14, **t** 0544 33479, *www.hotelbyron.com*. A gracefully ageing favourite situated just off Piazza del Popolo, with some very nice rooms and some very plain ones.

*****Diana**, Via G. Rossi 4, **t** 0544 39164, *www.hoteldiana.ra.it*. A delightful and comfortable hotel in an 18th-century palace near the tomb of Galla Placidia, with a charming Baroque lobby and bike loan.

Moderate

*****Columbia**, Viale Italia 70, Marina Romea, **t** 0544 446 038, *www.columbiahotel.it*. A beautiful modern hotel a little way north of the city, a 10min walk from the beach.

Cheap

****Hotel Ravenna**, Viale P. Maroncelli 12, **t** 0544 212 204. A friendly, comfortable option right by the station. All rooms are en suite.

***Al Giaciglio**, Via Rocca Brancaleone 42, **t** 0544 39403. A budget option with fans and TVs in

The terrible wars for control of Italy, between the Ostrogoths and the Eastern Emperor, were beginning. Ravenna was spared the destruction the Byzantine generals Belisarius and Narses spread through the rest of Italy; after their victory the city became the seat of the exarchs, the Byzantine viceroys who were to rule increasingly smaller bits of Italy over the next 500 years. It was this period that would see the city's golden age. The Greek exarchs, never popular among their new subjects, performed the occasional service of obtaining Constantinople's aid in keeping the Lombards at bay. While tolerating the exarch's presence, the people of Ravenna were coming to rely increasingly on their own resources; when help from the east failed to all bedrooms. The restaurant offers good home cooking, a daily-changing cheap lunch menu and pizzas.

Eating Out

Very Expensive

Taverna San Romualdo, Via Sant' Alberto 364, **t** 0544 483 447. A typical rustic Romagnolo *osteria* not far from San Vitale, serving hearty dishes. The seasonal *antipasti* may include *tortellacci* stuffed with nettles and served with mascarpone and pine nuts, or octopus stewed with balsamic vinegar and served tepid with rocket and cannellini beans. There's a good choice of game in winter. Try nougat *semifreddo* with chocolate sauce for dessert. *Closed Tues.*

Tre Spade, Via Faentina 136, **t** 0544 500 522. An innovative place in the western suburbs. Most locals come for the seafood, but there are also adventurous vegetable/pastry concoctions, stuffed pigeon and original pasta combinations. *Moderate* seafood and meat menus are available. *Closed Sun eve, Mon and Aug.*

Expensive

Saporetti Trattoria al Pescatore, Via N. Zen 13, Marina di Ravenna, **t** 0544 530 208. A trattoria run by a very *simpatico* family, serving delicious seafood. In summer you can dine in the garden. *Closed Tues.*

Moderate

La Gardela, Via Ponte Marino 3, **t** 0544 217 147. A central place serving home-made tortelloni, plus dishes such as *scaloppine* with *taleggio* and rocket. There's a daily-changing set menu and a wide choice of grappa. *Closed Thurs.*

Locanda del Melarancio, entrances at Via Mentana 33 and Via Gessi 9, **t** 0544 213 684. A friendly restaurant situated in a beautiful 16th-century building complete with painted ceilings, offering the likes of *ravioli di piselli* (stuffed with peas), rabbit in *porchetta*, pigeon, and almond milk pudding. There are three *cheap* menus, and the *locanda* also offers four B&B rooms (*cheap*). *Closed Weds and 4–25 Aug.*

La Rustica, Via Alberoni 55, **t** 0544 28128. A restaurant close to the station, offering a range of traditional Romagnolo dishes, including especially good pasta, served amidst a décor of old country kitchen gear. *Closed Fri.*

Cheap

Ca' de Ven, Via Corrado Ricci 24, **t** 0544 30163. An *enoteca* with a huge selection of Emilia-Romagna wines, and snacks made from local cheeses, hams and sausages. Set in a cinquecento grocers-*locanda*, it's suitably calm and dark, and a great local favourite – the perfect place to while away an afternoon after a morning with the Byzantines. *Closed Mon, 10 days in Jan and 3wks in Aug.*

Ristorante-Cantina Cappello, Via IV Novembre 41, **t** 0544 219 876. A *cantina* and wine bar situated next to but separate from the hotel of the same name, serving a range of summer salads, winter soups, salami and fresh pasta. There's also an *expensive* adjoining restaurant serving fancier fare, and offering two *moderate* daily menus. The wine list is extensive.

appear, it was their own militia that defended the city against invaders. So, in the worst times, the city survived as a sort of cultural time capsule, protected by its own efforts – and its swamps – still maintaining trade and cultural relations with the east, and carrying on the best traditions of classical culture single-handedly.

In 751 the Lombards finally succeeded in taking Ravenna, chasing out the last exarch. Only six years later, however, Pepin the Short's Frankish army snatched it back, and the city was placed under the rule of the popes. Ravenna declined slowly and gracefully in the following centuries. Venice took over its role as leading port of the Adriatic as Classe silted up and was abandoned. The newer cities of Romagna, such as Ferrara and Faenza, assumed a larger role in the region's economy, and even Ravenna's ancient school of Roman law was transferred to Bologna, there to become the foundation of Europe's first university.

Despite its declining fortunes, Ravenna still managed to rouse itself in 1177, becoming a free *comune*. During the 13th century, government fell into the hands of the Da Polenta family, famous for offering refuge to Dante in his exile from Florence. Dante finished the *Divine Comedy* in Ravenna, and died here in 1321. In 1441 Ravenna came under the rule of Venice, and enjoyed a brief period of renewed prosperity that lasted until the popes came back in 1509; the economic decadence brought by papal rule has been reversed only since the 1940s. Parts of the city were heavily damaged in the Second World War, but in the last few decades, with the construction of a ship channel and new port, the discovery of offshore gas deposits and the introduction of large chemical industries, Ravenna has become a booming modern city – just coincidentally one with a medieval centre full of Byzantine mosaics.

San Vitale

Via San Vitale, near Porta Adriana, the western gate of the centro storico. *Open daily summer 9–7, winter 9–4.30, Mar and Oct 9–5.30.*

At first this dark old church may not seem like much, but as soon as the lights come on, the 1,400-year-old mosaics ignite into an explosion of colour: the mosaics of San Vitale, Ravenna's best, are one of the last great works of art of the ancient world.

The octagonal church, begun in AD 525 during the reign of Theodoric, is itself a fine example of the surprisingly sophisticated architecture of a troubled age. By the time the church was finished, in AD 548, the city was in the hands of Belisarius' Byzantine army; portraits of Justinian and Theodora represent the traditional imperial style of political propaganda. But far from being the sorry recapitulation of old forms and styles you might expect, San Vitale was a breathtakingly original departure in architecture. While the world was falling around their ears, late-Roman architects were making advances, using complex geometry and new vaulting techniques.

Take some time to admire the exterior, with its beautiful interplay of octagons, arches, gables and *exedrae* – pure proportional geometry done in plain solid brick. Inside, the curious double capitals on the columns are no design conceit, but an important 5th-century invention; the trapezoidal impost block on top is a capital specially designed to support the weight of arches. Holding up the second-floor galleries and large octagonal cupola was an unusual design problem; these capitals and the eight stout piers around the dome were the solution.

We do not know whether San Vitale's architects were Latins or Greeks, but the year after it was begun work commenced on the similar church of SS. Sergius and Bacchus in Constantinople, the prototype for the Hagia Sophia 10 years later. In its structure the great dome in Constantinople owes everything to the little dome of Ravenna: the innovation of the galleries, for example, in which the women were segregated, and the elongated apse cleverly combining the central plan favoured by eastern Christians with the basilica form needed for a court's religious ceremonies.

Mosaics

Either light was born here,
or reigns here imprisoned.

Latin inscription, Sant'Andrea chapel

In Byzantine times the greatest gift that an emperor could bestow on a dependent town was a few tons of gold and enamel *tesserae* and an artist. From Justinian's time the art became almost a trademark of Byzantine civilization. Before Christianity, mosaics were a favourite Roman medium, usually reserved for the decoration of villas, in particular floors. Some reached the level of fine art (of which there are examples in the Naples museum), but more often the productions were on the level of the famous 'beware of the dog' mosaic in Pompeii, or prophylactic images of Priapus. It was the early Christians, with a desire to build for the ages and a body of scriptures that are best related pictorially, who made mosaics the new medium of public art in the 6th century. Mostly it was the Greeks who still had the talent and resources for it; we don't know for certain, but it's most likely that Greek artists from the court of Constantinople created the celebrated mosaics in the churches and baptistries of Ravenna.

Western Christian art was born here, developing from simple images – the Good Shepherd and the Cross and Stars – to the iconic Christ in Sant'Apollinare Nuovo and the scriptural scenes in San Vitale. Never, though, did early mosaicists turn their back on the idea of art; with the ideals of the ancient world still in their minds, they thought of art and religion as going hand in hand, and had no problem serving the cause of both. Using a new vocabulary of images and the new techniques, they strove to duplicate, and surpass, the sense of awe and mystery half-remembered from the interiors of pagan temples.

Try to imagine a church like San Vitale in its original state, with lamps and candles flickering below the gold ground and gorgeous colours. You may see that same light that enchanted the Byzantines – the light of the Gospels, the light from beyond the stars. Alternatively, try to visit San Vitale, the mausoleum of Galla Placidia or the Domus dei Tappeti di Pietra on a Friday evening from mid-June to late-August, when the mosaics are floodlit from 9 to 11.

Nowhere in Constantinople, however, or anywhere in the east for that matter, will you find anything as brilliant as the mosaics in San Vitale. A great deal was undoubtedly lost elsewhere during the iconoclastic troubles of the 8th century, but iconoclasm was fiercely resisted in Italy – it was one of the first causes of the rupture between the Roman and Greek churches – and most of Ravenna's art was fortunately left in peace.

The colours are utterly startling. Almost all the other surviving Byzantine mosaics, in Sicily, Greece and Turkey, are simple figures on a bright gold ground, dazzling at first but somewhat monotonous. There is plenty of gold on the walls of San Vitale, but the best mosaics, in the **choir,** have deep blue skies and rich green meadows for backgrounds, highlighted by brightly coloured birds and flowers. (The usual nomenclature is misleading here: the 'choir' is the site of the main altar, while the clergy sat on a bench around the apse.)

The two **lunettes** positioned over the arches flanking the choir, each of them a masterpiece, show the two events in the Old Testament that prefigure the Transfiguration of Christ: the hospitality of Abraham and the sacrifice of Isaac, and the offerings of Abel and Melchizedek, set under fiery clouds with hands of benediction extended from Heaven. Around the two lunettes are scenes of Moses and Jeremiah; note, above the lunettes, the delicately posed pairs of angels holding golden crosses – almost identical to the fanciful figures from earlier Roman art displaying the civic crown of the Caesars.

In front of the choir the **triumphal arch** has mosaic portraits of the Apostles supported by a pair of dolphins; the galleries have portraits of the four evangelists. The **apse** is dominated by the famous mosaic portraits of Justinian and Theodora – mostly, of course, of Theodora, the dancing girl from Constantinople who used her many talents to become an empress, eventually coming to wear poor Justinian like a charm on her bracelet. Here she is wearing a rich crown, with long strings of fat diamonds and real pearls. Justinian, like Theodora, appears among his retinue offering a gift to the new church; here he has the air of a hung-over saxophone player, badly in need of a shave and a cup of coffee. His cute daisy slipper steps on the foot (a convention of Byzantine art to show who's boss) of his general Belisarius, to his left. The likenesses are good – very like those in Constantinople – suggesting that the artist may have come from there, or at least have copied closely imperial portraits on display at Ravenna.

It can easily be imagined how expensive it was in the 5th century to make mosaics like these. It is said that the Hagia Sophia in Constantinople had more than four acres of them, and even the treasury of Justinian was not bottomless; consequently most of San Vitale remained undecorated until the 17th-century bishops did the rest in a not-too-discordant Baroque. The bishops' floor has been pulled up to reveal the original, of inlaid marble in floral and geometric patterns, the direct ancestor of medieval pavements in the churches of Tuscany and the south.

Mausoleo di Galla Placidia

Open same hours as San Vitale.

This small chapel, set in the grounds of San Vitale and originally attached to the neighbouring church of Santa Croce, never really held the tomb of Ravenna's great patroness – she is buried near St Peter's in Rome, and it's anyone's guess who occupies the three huge stone sarcophagi, traditionally the resting places of Galla Placidia and two emperors, her second husband Constantius III and her son Valentinian. Galla Placidia did construct the chapel, however – a small, gabled and cross-shaped building that looks shorter than when it was built; the ground level has risen seven feet in 1,400 years. This allows a better view of the mosaics and gives a much more intimate experience.

The simplicity of the brick exterior, as in San Vitale, makes the brilliant mosaics within that much more of a surprise. The only natural light inside comes from a few tiny slits of windows, made of thin sheets of alabaster. The two important mosaics, on **lunettes** at opposite ends of the chapel, are coloured as richly as San Vitale. One represents St Lawrence, with his flaming gridiron; the other is a beautiful and typical early Christian portrait of Jesus as the Good Shepherd, a beardless, classical-looking figure in a fine cloak and sandals, stroking one of the flock. On the lunettes of the cross-axis, pairs of stags come to drink at the fountain of life; around all four lunettes, floral arabesques and maze patterns (strikingly modern to our eyes) in bright colours cover the arches and ceilings. Everything in the design betrays as much of the classical Roman style as the nascent Christian, and the unusual figures on the **arches** holding up the central vault seem hardly out of place. They are SS. Peter and Paul, dressed in togas and standing with outstretched hands in the conventional pose of Roman senators.

The **vault** itself, a deep blue firmament glowing with hundreds of dazzling golden stars set within concentric circles, is the mausoleum's most remarkable feature. In the centre, at the top of the vault, a golden cross represents the unimaginable, transcendent God above the heavens. At the corners, symbols of the four evangelists provide an insight into the origins of Christian iconography. Mark's lion, Luke's ox and Matthew's man occupy the places in this sky where you would expect the constellations of Leo, Taurus and Aquarius, 90 degrees apart along the zodiac. For the fourth corner, instead of the objectionable Scorpio (or serpent, as it often appeared in ancient times), the early Christians placed the eagle of St John.

The Museo Nazionale

The medieval and Baroque **cloisters** attached to San Vitale now house the large collection of antiquities found in Ravenna and Classe (*open Tues–Sun 8.30–7.30; adm*). There's a little bit of everything: good Roman plumbing, a boy's linen shirt from the 6th century, Byzantine forks (they invented them) and no end of coins and broken pots. The well-labelled coin collection is interesting even to the non-specialist, providing a picture history of Italy from classical times into the early Middle Ages. Exceptional works of art include the 6th-century Byzantine carved screens, and a possibly unique sculpture of Hercules capturing the Cerynean hind. This, too, is from the 6th century; perhaps the last piece of art made in ancient times with a classical subject, it's possibly a copy of an earlier Greek work. Lovely, intricately carved ivory chests and plaques from the Middle Ages and Renaissance, with charming tableaux of medieval scenes such as tournaments and banquets, fill an entire room.

Domus dei Tappeti di Pietra

Open Tues–Sun 1 Mar–4 Nov 10–6.30; 5 Nov–28 Feb 10–4.30; adm.

One of the most significant recent discoveries in Italy, inside the church of Sant' Eufemia on Via Barbiani 100 metres from San Vitale, was this mosaic floor, once part of a magnificent *c.* 6th-century Byzantine palace. Only unveiled to the public in late

2002, it boasts geometric, floral and figurative patterns, and is as enchanting as the mosaics in the Basilica at Aquileia. The unique *Dance of the Geniuses of the Seasons* and *Good Shepherd* diverge markedly from the conventional Christian representation.

Ravenna's Centre

Piazza del Popolo was built by the Venetians during their brief period of rule, along with the twin columns bearing statues of Ravenna's patrons, San Vitale and Sant' Apollinare. Just south, off porticoed Piazza San Francesco, is a modest neoclassical pavilion built in the 18th century over the tomb of Dante. Ravenna is proud of having sheltered the storm-tossed poet in his last years, and the city gently reminds you of it in its street names, tourist brochures, Teatro Alighieri and frequent artistic competitions based on themes from the *Divina Commedia*. Coming here may help you understand what Dante means to Italy; in all the country's more recent wars, for example, soldiers have come here for little rituals to 'dedicate their sacrifice' to the poet's memory.

Today there are always wreaths or bouquets from organizations and people from all over Italy. Beside the tomb is the **Museo Dantesco** (*open daily 9–12 and 3.30–6; adm*), with a collection of paintings, sculptures and books connected with the poet. Behind it, the church of **San Francesco** was founded in the 5th century but rebuilt in the 11th and thoroughly Baroqued in the 1700s. Greek marble columns and a 4th-century altar survive, and there are some fine Renaissance tombs. Some of the beautiful original mosaic pavement is visible through a hole in the floor – under eight feet of water, kept company by a handful of goldfish. In the church itself and the Braccioforte oratory (behind the iron gate, by Dante's tomb) are fine early Christian sarcophagi, one familiarly called the 'Tomb of Elijah'.

North of Piazza del Popolo, Ravenna has a fine example of a medieval leaning tower: the tall, 12th-century **Torre Pubblica**, now supported by steel struts. This one seems good evidence for those who believe such things to be intentional. Despite the angle of the tower, the windows near the top were built perfectly level. Byron lived in nearby Via Cavour during his affair with Countess Teresa Guiccioli; his home now houses the Carabinieri.

In a little square between Via Paolo Costa and Via Armando Diaz, the **Battistero degli Ariani** or Arian Baptistry (*open daily Apr–Sept 9.30–12.30 and 3–6; Mar and Oct 9.30–12.30 and 3–5; Nov–Feb 10–12 and 2–4; adm*), also known as Santo Spirito, recalls church struggles of the 5th century. Theodoric and his Ostrogoths, like most of the Germanic peoples, adhered to the Arian heresy, a doctrine that mixed in elements of pagan religion and was condemned by more orthodox Christians as denying the absolute divinity of Christ. Like all heresies, this one is really the story of a political struggle, between the Gothic kings and the emperor in Constantinople. Unlike Justinian, a great persecutor, the Goths tolerated both faiths; the baptistry belonged to the adjacent Santo Spirito church (rebuilt in the 16th century), once the Arians' cathedral, while the Athenasians (orthodox) worshipped at what is now the cathedral of Ravenna. The baptistry preserves a fine mosaic ceiling, with the 12 apostles arranged around a scene of the Baptism of Jesus. The old man with the palm branch, across from John the Baptist, represents the River Jordan.

There is another leaning tower – an even tipsier one – nearby on Viale Farini, two streets up from the railway station. It is the 12th-century campanile of **San Giovanni Evangelista**, a much-altered church that was begun by Galla Placidia in 425. Bombings in the last war destroyed the apse, with its original mosaics, but some parts of the 13th-century mosaic floor, with scenes of the Fourth Crusade and some fantastical monsters, can be seen in the aisles.

Sant'Apollinare Nuovo

Open daily Apr–Sept 9.30–7; Mar and Oct 9.30–5.30; Nov–Feb 9.30–4.30; adm.

After those of San Vitale, the mosaics of this 6th-century church are the finest in Ravenna. Theodoric built it, and after the Byzantine conquest and the suppression of Arianism it was re-dedicated to St Martin, another famous persecutor of heretics. The present name dates from the 9th century, when the remains of Sant'Apollinare were moved here from the old Sant'Apollinare in Classe. The tall, cylindrical campanile, a trademark of Ravenna's churches, was added in the 10th century.

Unlike San Vitale, Sant'Apollinare was built in the basilican form, with a long nave and side aisles. The two rows of Greek marble columns were probably recycled from an ancient temple. Above them are the mosaics on panels that stretch the length of the church. On the left, just by the door, you see the city of Classe (*undergoing restoration work until the end of 2004*), with ships in the protected harbour between twin beacons, and the monuments of the city rearing up behind its walls. On the right, among the monuments of Ravenna, is the Palatium, Theodoric's royal palace. The curtains in the archways of the palace cover painted-over Gothic notables and probably Theodoric himself, effaced by the Byzantines.

Beyond these two urban scenes are processions of martyrs bearing crowns: 22 women on the left side, 26 men on the right. The female procession is led by colourful, remarkable portraits of the Magi (officially enrolled as Saints of the Church, according to the inscription above), offering their gifts to the enthroned Virgin Mary. One of the best times to come is around 6pm in summer, when the sun casts its golden light on to the golden roses of the saints.

Above these panels, more mosaics portray Old Testament prophets, doctors of the Church, and scenes from the life of Jesus. These mosaics, smaller and not as well executed, are from Theodoric's time. Next door are the remains of the 6th-century building that is known as the **Palace of Theodoric** (*open daily 8.30–1.30*); more likely it was a governmental building of some sort – it may in fact have been the palace of the Byzantine exarchs.

The Battistero Neoniano and the Museo Arcivescovile

Open daily Apr–Sept 9–7, Mar and Oct 9.30–5.30, Nov–Feb 9.30–4.30; adm.

An earthquake in 1733 wrecked Ravenna's cathedral, west of Piazza del Popolo, and there's little to see in the replacement but another round medieval tower. Somehow the disaster spared the 'Orthodox' or **Neonian Baptistry**, named after the 5th-century bishop Neon who commissioned its splendid mosaics.

Unlike in the Arian Baptistry, here almost the entire decoration has survived: a scene of the baptism of Jesus and portraits of the 12 apostles on the ceiling under the dome, while below the eight walls bear four altars and four empty thrones. The *etimasia*, the preparing of the throne for Jesus for the Last Judgement, is an odd bit of Byzantine mysticism; interestingly enough, classical Greek art often depicts an empty throne as a symbol for Zeus, only with a pair of thunderbolts instead of a cross. In the 1,500 years since its construction, the ground level here has risen more than 10ft – and so has the baptistry's floor. In the side niches are a 6th-century Byzantine altar and a huge, thoroughly pagan marble vase. The 13th-century marble font is big enough for the immersion baptism of adults.

The **Archiepiscopal Museum**, behind the cathedral, comes as a real surprise. Its little-known treasures include the ivory throne of Bishop Maximian, a masterpiece of 6th-century sculpture thought to have been a gift from Emperor Justinian, and an 11th-century reliquary, the silver 'Cross of Sant'Agnello'. Among the fragments of sculpture and mosaics are works saved from the original cathedral. The large marble disc by the wall, divided into 19 sections, is an episcopal calendar, regulated to the 19-year Julian cycle to allow Ravenna's medieval bishops to calculate the date of Easter and other holy days.

The biggest surprise, however, comes when you discover that the nondescript archbishop's palace in which the museum is located is, in certain parts, as old as anything in Ravenna. A little door at the back leads to a small chapel called the **Oratorio di Sant'Andrea** (*closed for restoration until 2005*), built *c.* 500 during the reign of Theodoric. The mosaics that adorn the vaults are among the best in the city: in the antechamber there's a fanciful scene of multicoloured birds and flowers, and an unusual warrior Christ kitted out in full Roman armour and wielding the cross like a sword, treading a lion and snake underfoot. In the chapel itself, four angels and the four evangelists' symbols surround Christ's monogram on the dome, and the apse bears a beautiful starry sky around a golden cross, resembling the one at the Galla Placidia mausoleum.

The best mosaics, however, are the excellent portraits of saints decorating the arches. Early Christian representations of the saints are often much stronger than the pale, conventional figures of later art. Such portraits as these betray a fascination with the personalities and the psychology of saints; such figures as St Felicitas or St Ursicinus may be forgotten today, but to the early Christians they were not mere holy myths, but near contemporaries, the spiritual heroes and heroines who were responsible for the miraculous growth of Christianity, the exemplars of a new age and a new way of life.

Mausoleo Teodorico

Via Cimitero, near the industrial zone; open daily 8.30–7; adm.

For the real flavour of the days of the Roman twilight, nothing can beat this compellingly strange, sophisticated yet half-barbaric building outside the old city. To reach it, walk north from the railway station, past the new port and the Venetian fortress called the **Rocca di Brancaleone,** which now has a park inside. Theodoric's tomb, which is perhaps the only regular 10-sided building in Italy, is situated in another small park. Downstairs is a cross-shaped chamber of unknown purpose. The second storey, also decagonal but smaller, contains the porphyry sarcophagus, which is now empty. It is a comment on the times that scholars believe that this is a recycled bathtub from a Roman palace. Theodoric was hardly broke, though; he could afford to bring the stone for his tomb over from Istria – and note the roof, a single slab of stone weighing more than 300 tons. No one has explained how the Goths brought it here and raised it – or why.

Sant'Apollinare in Classe

Open daily 9–5; adm.

There is another important monument to Ravenna's golden age to be seen at the site of Classe, five kilometres from town; any local train towards Rimini or the regular bus service (most no.4 and 44 buses, and bus no.176 from the train station) can take you there. Sant'Apollinare in Classe, in fact, is literally all that remains of what was once the leading port of the northern Adriatic. The little River Uniti began to silt up Classe's harbour in classical times; when the port ceased to be a Roman military base and the funds for yearly dredging were no longer there, the city's fate was sealed. By the 9th century Classe was abandoned. The people of Ravenna carted away most of its stone and encroaching forests and swamps erased the rest. Today the former port is good farmland, six kilometres from the sea.

Sant'Apollinare, a huge basilica-form church that was completed in 549, survives solely because of its importance as the burial place of Ravenna's patron. The plain brick exterior is another finely proportioned example of Ravenna's pre-Romanesque, with another tall cylindrical campanile. Inside it's almost empty, with only a few early-Christian sarcophagi lining the walls. The Greek marble columns have well-carved capitals in a unique style. Above them are some 18th-century portraits of Ravenna's bishops – important to this city in which for centuries the bishops defended local autonomy against emperors, exarchs and popes. But the real attraction is the mosaics in the apse, an impressive green-and-gold-ground allegorical vision of the Transfiguration of Christ, set in a flower-strewn Mediterranean landscape, with Sant'Apollinare in attendance and three sheep representing Peter, James and John, who were with Christ on Mount Tabor. As at San Vitale, there are scenes of the sacrifices of Abel, Melchizedek and Abraham, opposite a mosaic of the Byzantine emperor Constantine IV bestowing privileges on Ravenna's independent church. Archangels Gabriel and Michael appear in Byzantine court dress, under a pair of palm trees, the 'tree of life'.

Elsewhere around Classe there's little to see; bits of Roman road, pine groves, some foundations. Excavations began only in 1961, and continue today (*visiting hours Mon–Sat 9–7, or dusk in winter, Sun 8–2; adm*). Sant'Apollinare is near the centre of an immense necropolis with some half-million burials. Some interesting things could turn up here in coming years.

The Adriatic Riviera

From Ravenna and Classe the long stretch of small resorts that began at Comacchio straggles on towards the beach-Babylon of Rimini – 40 miles long and a few blocks deep, a mass of compacted (and mostly quite attractive) urbanity, with the SS16 on one side and a solid line of beach on the other. It's the place where Italians come because their grandparents did, where Germans come to look for Italians, the British come to fill shopping trolleys with British gin, and Russians finally get a chance to wear their designer sunglasses.

The fall of the Iron Curtain made it possible for Czechs, Poles, Russians, Hungarians and everyone else in eastern Europe to get out for a holiday again, and only one place was close, friendly and relatively inexpensive. They only add to the charm of the biggest, funkiest, most unpretentious and most cosmopolitan lido in Europe. On any given night in August, more than 100,000 people will be sitting down to *tagliatelle al ragù* in their *pensioni* and thinking that life is pretty damn sweet.

The beaches nearest Ravenna suffer somewhat from industrial pollution, but there has been a big effort to clean them up. Marina Romea, a spit of land with a broad beach and a pine forest, is perhaps the nicest; all are an easy day's outing from Ravenna. The first big centre on the coast is **Cervia-Milano Marittima**, which earned its living with 'white gold' or salt from the time of the ancient Greeks.

The next, **Cesenatico**, was built around a pretty, canal-like harbour designed for Cesare Borgia in 1502 by Leonardo da Vinci. The Museo della Mariniera in the harbour itself is a floating maritime museum, a display of the traditional fishing and trading boats used in the northern Adriatic; colourful sails are raised in summer.

Rimini

At first glance Italy's biggest resort may strike you as strictly cold potatoes, a full 15 kilometres of peeling skin and pizza, serenaded by the portable radios of 10,000 teenagers and the eternal whines and giggles of their little brothers and sisters. To many Italians, however, Rimini means pure sweaty-palmed excitement. In the 1960s, following the grand old Italian pastime of *caccia alle svedesi*, a staple of the national film industry was the Rimini holiday movie, in which a bumbling protagonist with glasses was swept off his feet by some incredible Nordic goddess, who was as bouncy as she was adventurous. After many complications, embarrassing both for the audience and the actors, it all led to true love.

For the bumbling protagonists of real life, whether from Milan or from Munich, all this may only be wishful thinking, but they still come in their millions each year. As a resort Rimini has its advantages. Noisy as it is, it's a respectable family place, relatively cheap for northern Italy, convenient and well organized.

Also, tucked away behind the beachfront is a genuine old city, dishevelled, damaged during the Second World War, but inviting nonetheless, and offering one first-rate Renaissance attraction.

Getting There and Around

In summer there are regular **flights** from Milan and London Stansted to Rimini's airport (**t** 0541 715 711) behind the beaches at Miramare, plus a stream of foreign charters.

On this stretch of coast, the FS Adriatic **rail** line works like a tram service, with lots of trains and stops near the beaches in all the resorts. The railway station is on Piazzale Cesare Battisti; from it **buses** run to most nearby towns, including San Marino.

Regular **city buses** run up and down the beach strip in summer. A 24hr or 8-day 'Orange Ticket' gives unlimited travel within Rimini and to the beach at Riccione; you can also buy carnets of 6 or 12, and family and weekend tickets.

At the height of summer, arrivals at the station are often met by police with dogs, checking for drugs. The road between the station and the beach is not safe after dark; always take bus no.11 or a taxi (**t** 0541 50020).

Cultural day-trippers who shudder at all the beach madness can dip in easily – the Tempio Malatestiano and the rest of the lovely old town are only a 10min walk from the station.

Tourist Information

In summer Rimini and its suburbs have as many information offices as ice-cream stands. The main ones are at Piazzale C. Battisti, next to the station, **t** 0541 51331, and on the beach at Piazza Fellini 3, **t** 0541 56902. There are five information desks along the 15km beach. See *www.turismo.provincia.rimini.it.*

Where to Stay

Rimini ✉ 47900

Rimini hotels usually offer pleasant modern rooms with balconies. The places listed here are close to the beach and the town. The **Promozione Alberghiera** booking service is at Piazzale Fellini 3, by the train station, **t** 0541 53399. There are four other well-marked offices around town, plus one each in Bellaria, **t** 0541 340 060, and Riccione, **t** 0541 693 628.

Expensive–Luxury

*******Grand Hotel**, Via Ramusio 1, **t** 0541 56000, *www.grandhotelrimini.com.* An imposing turn-of-the-19th-century dream palace that helped to make Rimini what it is today. The young Federico Fellini was fascinated with it, and it gets a starring role in his *Amarcord* (though a hotel nearer Rome actually played it). The bedrooms are almost indecently luxurious, with well-polished brass and enormous crystal chandeliers. It has its own dance orchestra, a pool and a private beach.

******Hotel Ambassador,** Via Regina Elena 86, **t** 0541 387 207, *www.ambassadorrimini.com.* An early 1900s building just in from the sea, with a nice shady garden and a pool. In low season some rooms are *moderate*. There's a minimum 3-night stay.

******Milton**, Via Cristoforo Colombo 2, **t** 0541 54600, *www.hotelmilton.com*. A hotel set right on the beach in a residential area, with elegant rooms, a good restaurant, a garden bar, a pool and bicycles for guests. *Closed mid-Dec–mid-Jan.*

******Le Meridien**, Lungomare Murri 13, **t** 0541 393 322, *www.lemeridienrimini.com.* A splashy building by celebrated architect Paolo Portoghesi, capturing the elegance of a bygone era with a modern twist. In the centre of the action, it has a private beach, a pool and a solarium.

Cheap–Moderate

*****Esedra**, Viale Caio Duilio 3, **t** 0541 23421, *www.esedrahotel.com*. A handsome remodelled 1890s seaside villa with 42 spacious up-to-date rooms, a garden and a pool. *Closed Nov and Dec.*

*****Napoleon**, Piazza C. Battisti 22, **t** 0541 27501. A pleasant 1970s hotel near the station, with big bathrooms, bicycles and a laundry service.

*****Saxon**, Via Cirene 36, **t** 0541 391 400. A cheaper option one street behind the main drag by the sea.

****Card**, Via Dante 50, **t** 0541 26412, *www.hotelcard.com*. A extremely friendly, clean and efficient option located near the station and the Tempio Malatestiano, and open 24 hours.

Eating Out

Very Expensive

Acero Rosso, Viale Tiberio 11, San Giuliano, **t** 0541 53577. One of the most elegant places in Rimini, just outside the historic centre, with three *menu degustazione* (fish, meat and vegetarian). *Closed Sun eve and Mon, late July–mid-Aug.*

Dallo Zio, Via S. Chiara 16, **t** 0541 786 741. An excellent seafood palace in the old town, popular with both locals and tourists. *Closed Mon, Tues–Fri lunch, and July–end-Aug.*

Taverna degli Artisti, Viale Vespucci 1, **t** 0541 28519. A place best known for its seafood but also offering imaginative light pasta dishes and whisky tastings. *Closed Weds.*

Expensive

Il Quartino, Via Coriano 161, **t** 0541 731 215. An old farmhouse on the edge of Rimini (take the Via Flaminia), serving very good *carpaccio* with *formaggio di fossa* and other regional delights. *Closed Tues.*

Osteria de Borg, Via Forzieri 12, San Giuliano, **t** 0541 56074. An imaginative menu that may include *strozzapreti* with broccoli and spicy sausage. *Open eves only except Sun and hols; closed Mon, half of Jan and half of July.*

Saraghina's, Via Poletti 32, **t** 0541 783 794. A popular spot for seasonal dishes in the heart of town. *Open eves only; closed Mon.*

Moderate

Osteria di Santa Colomba, Via Agostino di Duccio 2, **t** 0541 780 048. An old favourite in a campanile near the market, with simple traditional fare such as pasta with chickpeas. No credit cards. *Closed lunch Mon–Fri.*

Cheap

Rimini is famous for its cheap, filling and delicious *piadina calda* (cornbread).

Caffè della Rose, Viale Vespucci 1, **t** 0541 23038. A café-bar dominated by a huge settecento crystal chandelier, open from early till late and offering a 'free' buffet with its cocktails,

4 Moschetteri, Via S. Maria al Mare, just off Piazza Ferrari, **t** 0541 5649. A trattoria in the old centre, with good pizza and pasta, and a daily-changing menu of local favourites.

Entertainment and Nightlife

Music, Theatre and Cinema

The tourist office's *Instantaneo* listings guide has detailed info on what's on in the area.

Fellini's city has 14 cinemas and hosts a fairly continual series of **film events** centred on the semi-official **Film Festival** in Sept.

In late summer and autumn there's the **Sagra Musicale Malatestiana** classical music festival, **t** 0541 26239. In July nearby Santarcangelo holds a **theatre festival** of dynamic, innovative work (**t** 0541 626 185).

Clubs and Discos

Rimini and its trendy neighbour Riccione are a magnet for ravers from Italy and abroad. On summer weekends crowds descend from all cities within a 200km radius, and the following mornings the road back to Bologna is often scattered with their battered cars.

For listings and information on clubs, one-nighters and anything else coming up, check *Il Resto del Carlino* and the magazine *Chiamami Città*, or look out for posters.

Most clubs are along the seafront and get going from about 10pm; there's also another little knot of activity in Rimini away from the beach in Covignano. A night bus, the 'Blue Line' (tickets can be purchased on board), runs the length of the seafront between Riccione and Bellaria, and to Covignano.

For bars in the old town, look around Piazza Cavour and Via Pisacane.

Paradiso, Via Covignano 260, *www.paradisoclub.it*. The most fashionable club, situated in Rimini itself, with a regular diet of Euro-dance and weekly special events. The entrance fee is astronomical.

Pascià, Via Sardegna 30, Riccione. One of the best-established clubs on the Riviera, a large, stylish venue offering house, techno and Euro-dance.

Rock Island, Piazzale Boscovich, Molo di Levante, **t** 0541 50178, *www.rockislandrimini.com*. A young, noisy, trendy but unpretentious bar, club and fish restaurant on a pier (it's the only venue right on the sea – ideal for watching sunsets and the moonlight dance on the sea). *Closed Mon.*

The Tempio Malatestiano

Open Mon–Fri 7.50–12.30 and 3.30–7, Sat and Sun 9–1 and 3.30–7.

Sigismondo Malatesta ('Headache'), the tyrant of Rimini, went down in the history books as one seriously bad hombre. According to author Jakob Burckhardt, 'the verdict of history...convicts him of murder, rape, adultery, incest, sacrilege, perjury, and treason, committed not once, but often.' Burckhardt adds that Malatesta's frequent attempts on the virtue of his children, both male and female, may have been the result of 'some astrological superstition'. In 1462 Pope Pius II accorded Malatesta a unique honour – a canonization to Hell. The Pope, who was behind most of the accusations, can be excused for indulging in a little exaggeration – he wanted Sigismondo's land, and resorted to invoking supernatural aid when he couldn't vanquish him at war.

Modern historians give Sigismondo better reviews, finding him on the whole no more pagan and perverse than the average Renaissance duke, and less so than many popes. The family had ruled at Rimini since the 1300s – ironically, it was a pope who first put them in business. Early dukes, such as Malatesta 'Guastafamiglia' ('Destroyer of Families'), were hard men, and good role models for Sigismondo, but they succeeded for a time in spreading their rule as far as Cesena and Fano. By Sigismondo's time, money and allies were suddenly lacking, and the family was deposed by the unspeakable Alexander VI in 1500.

The shortage of funds (along with Sigismondo's excommunication) was also responsible for the abandonment in 1461 of Sigismondo's personal monument, the eclectic and thoroughly mysterious work that has come to be known as the Malatesta Temple. Whatever Sigismondo's personal habits, he was a learned man and a good judge of art. To transform this unfinished 13th-century Franciscan church into his temple he called in Leon Battista Alberti to redesign the exterior and Agostino di Duccio for the reliefs inside.

Scholars have been scratching their heads for centuries over what Sigismondo's intentions were. Although the temple has been Rimini's cathedral since 1809, it is hardly a Christian building at all, being full of undecipherable sculptural allegories, with everywhere the entwined monograms of Sigismondo and his wife Isotta degli Atti. In part the building seems a tribute to this famous lady, who is buried here together with her husband. Court scholar Roberto Volturio wrote that the entire temple was full of symbols that would proclaim the doctrines of arcane philosophy to the learned while remaining hidden to vulgar folk. Unfortunately, that includes all of us; whatever secret neo-Platonic philosophy was current at Sigismondo's court is probably now lost for ever.

Alberti's unfinished exterior, on which Roman arcades and pilasters are grafted on to the plain Franciscan building, grievously feels the lack of the planned cupola that might have tied it all together. Alberti's intentions can be perceived in a medal that was minted at the beginning of its construction:a second-storey arch was to have been built over the portal; the gable-like pediment around it would have been rounded, and the entire work was to be dominated by a great dome, as wide as the building itself and more than doubling it in height. The big arches on the sides were meant to hold the sarcophagi of Rimini's notable men; only a few were ever used. Inside these arches, four pairs of chapels hold the **sculptural reliefs** that were created by Agostino – they count among the very greatest works of the Renaissance. These low reliefs, on blue backgrounds similar to those of Della Robbia cameos, depict angels and child musicians, the Arts and Sciences, St Michael, putti, Sigismondo himself and the Triumph of Scipio. Some of the best are allegorical panels of the planets and signs of the zodiac; note in particular the enchanting Moon, Cynthia in her silver car, and a scene of 15th-century Rimini captured beneath the claws of the Crab.

Among the other works in the Temple are a fresco by Piero della Francesca of Sigismondo and his patron, St Sigismund of Burgundy, and a painted crucifix by Giotto. The tombs of Sigismondo and Isotta, with their strange device (the omnipresent monograms S and I together like a dollar sign) and elephants (the Malatesta heraldic symbol) are also fine works.

Old Rimini was the home town of the late film director Federico Fellini (he was born in the San Giuliano district), and you may recognize some of the street scenes here from *Amarcord*, though the streets themselves were actually reconstructed in Cinecittà for the movie. The **Fondazione Fellini** in the director's sister Maddalena's former house at Via Oberdan 1 (***t*** *0541 50303*), which until now has been a study centre housing Fellini's personal library, various drawings of him and a selection of other effects, was in the process of being transformed into a proper museum as we went to press. His favourite cinema is also currently being restored as a university cinematography faculty.

Some ruins in old Rimini survive as reminders of Roman *Arminium*, a thriving Adriatic port and a rival to Classe: the foundation of a 15,000-capacity amphitheatre near the southern walls in the 2nd century AD (*guided tours once daily in summer, bookable via the tourist office; adm*), and the **Arco di Augusto** in the southern gate near the post office. This arch marked the meeting of the Via Aemilia and the Via Flaminia. The Roman high street, the *cardo*, is now Corso di Augusto; from here it passes through central Piazza Tre Martiri – which retains arcades in the shop fronts from the days when it was the Roman forum – and continues on to the north gate and the five-arched **Bridge of Tiberius** (AD 21), badly patched up after damage in the Greek–Gothic wars.

A few streets further over the bridge, the church of San Giuliano contains a painting of that saint's martyrdom, Paolo Veronese's last work. From here towards the sea, along the riverbank, stretches Rimini's colourful fishing port. Back at the centre, a lovely marble fountain of 1543 and a glowering statue of Pope Paul V grace **Piazza Cavour**, site of the Wednesday and Saturday morning markets. The **Palazzo de l'Arengo** on the piazza has been Rimini's town hall since 1207; it is joined by an arch to the 1300s **Palazzo del Podestà,** and faces the bulky castle of the Malatesta, the **Rocca Sigismondo**, over the piazza; you can see how it originally looked in Piero's painting in the Tempio. The *rocca* did time as a prison until 1964, sat empty for years and is now an exhibition space.

Some Beach Statistics

Rimini is not the place for those who want to be alone.

tourist brochure

It's a subject that makes the town's holiday barons and the hotel consortium mildly uneasy. 'There's room for everybody,' they say, and in a way they're right. The resort has 15 kilometres of broad beaches, and roughly 1,200 hotels offering some 40,000 rooms in total. At the usual resort ratio, that computes to about 62,000 beds. That could be a problem in the really busy season. If all the beds are full – and then you add a further 25,000 day-trippers, campers and holiday apartment tenants – it makes nearly 90,000 souls, or approximately 6,500 per kilometre of beach front.

With only 5½ inches of shore per behind, if everyone hit the water at the same time the results could be truly catastrophic. Luckily this really need never happen. Many of these people at any given time will be at one of Rimini's 751 bars, 343 restaurants, 70 dance halls and discos, 49 cinemas, 14 miniature golf courses, seven luna parks (fun fairs) and three bowling alleys, or at one of the many sailing and wind-surfing schools, or one of three dolphin shows. If all else fails to amuse you, there is Fiabilandia, an amusement park with a genuine King Kong, or the long water-slides at Riccione.

Not many of the works that were created by the trecento 'school of Rimini' can still be seen in the city, but some of the best are housed in the church of **Sant'Agostino**, on Via Cairoli just off Piazza Cavour. An old Jesuit monastery on Piazza Ferrara houses the **Museo della Città** (*open 18 June–16 Sept Tues–Sat 10–12.30 and 4.30–7.30, Sun 4.30–7.30, Fri in July and Aug also 9pm–11; 17 Sept–17 June Tues–Sat 8.30–12.30 and 5–7, Sun 4–7; adm*), which is home to Roman mosaics, two Guercinos and paintings by Ghirlandaio and Giovanni Bellini.

More Beaches

Holiday madness continues through the string of resorts that lie south of Rimini. **Riccione**, **Misano Adriatico**, **Cattòlica** and **Gabicce Mare** are all huge places, and in the summer they can be as crowded and intense as Rimini itself. None of them has any particular charm, and it's hard to tell one from another – they're really more or less suburban extensions of Rimini; Riccione has the aura of fashion, if you want to try to keep up with the Italians.

The Adriatic Riviera begins to fade when the wide beaches of the Romagna give way to the more rugged coast of the Marche, but it soon picks up again when the hills recede once more at Pesaro and beyond. The only real curiosity in this area is the village of **San Giovanni in Marignano**, situated just inland from Cattòlica. The inhabitants here have borne the nickname *Mangiatedeschi* ('German-eaters') since the year 539, when two women who were living in these parts lured in and wolfed down 17 Goths.

San Marino

Just 23 kilometres inland of Rimini you will find the world's only sovereign and independent roadside attraction, which forms the perfect counterpart to the sand-strewn funfair of the resort. Before Rimini became the Italian Miami Beach, the 26,000 citizens of San Marino scraped together a living peddling postage stamps. Now, with their medieval streets crowded with day-trippers, the San Marinesi have been unable to resist the temptation to order some bright medieval costumes, polish up their picturesque mountain villages, and open up some souvenir stands and 'duty free' shops.

Their famous stamps, though nothing like the engraved numbers of half a century ago, are still prized by collectors, and recently the country has begun to mint its own coins again after a lapse of 39 years; nevertheless the citizens of San Marino, who may just have the highest average income in Europe, still make their living almost entirely from tourism.

The World's Smallest Republic

San Marino lays claim to being both the world's smallest and the world's oldest republic. According to legend, it was founded as a Christian settlement on the slopes of Monte Titano by a stonecutter by the name of Marinus, who was fleeing from the persecutions of Diocletian in the early 4th century. 'Overlooked', as the San Marinesi charmingly put it, by the empire and various states that followed it, the little community had the peace and quiet in which to evolve its medieval democratic institutions; its constitution in its present form dates from 1243, when the first pair of

Getting There

There are frequent bus services to San Marino from Rimini's train station, run by Bonelli, **t** 0541 372 432, and Benedettini, **t** 0549 903 854.

Tourist Information

San Marino town: Contrada Omagnano 20, **t** 0549 882 412; *www.omniway.sm*. There are also offices in the villages.

The tourist office also offers a hotel booking service on **t** 0549 885 431, *www.sanmarino2000.sm*.

Where to Stay and Eat

San Marino ✉ 47031

★★★★**Titano**, Contrada del Collegio 21, **t** 0549 991 006, *www.hoteltitano.com* (*moderate*). A good option set in a restored century-old building on San Marino's citadel, right in the middle of the old town. Half of the bedrooms have great views over the surrounding countryside.

★★★**La Rocca**, Salita alla Rocca, **t** 0549 991 166 (*moderate*). A reasonably priced choice offering 10 rooms with balconies with a view, plus a pool.

Buca San Francesco, **t** 0549 991 462, Piazzetta Placito Feretrano (*expensive*). A pretty restaurant, the best in the centre. The food is nothing out of the ordinary, but there are good soups, tortellini and *scallopine alla sanmarinese*.

Locanda dell'Artista, Via del Dragone 18, Loc. Montegiardino, **t** 0549 996 024 (*moderate*). A restaurant serving traditional dishes of the little republic, some vegetarian, accompanied by home-baked bread and sweets. There's a good *menu degustazione*, and rooms are available. *Closed lunchtimes, Mon and Nov.*

'consuls' was elected by a popular assembly. The consuls are now called Captains Regent, but little else has changed in 700 years.

Twice, in 1503 and 1739, the republic was invaded by papal forces, and its independence was preserved only by a little good luck. Napoleon, who was passing through in 1797, found San Marino rather amusing and half-seriously offered to enlarge its boundaries – a proposal that was politely declined. In 1849 San Marino offered shelter to Garibaldi, his wife Anita and approximately 1,500 of his followers, who were fleeing Rome after the fall of the republic with an Austrian army in hot pursuit; Garibaldi dissolved his army during the night and made a run for the coast at Cesenatico before dawn the next morning. Since then, the republic has taken on the role of an island of peace, providing a haven for thousands of refugees during the Second World War.

When you enter San Marino from Rimini at the hamlet called **Dogana** (although there are no border formalities these days), you pass through a series of villages strung along a ferociously built-up main road that cuts a swathe through some green and pretty countryside. San Marino, no midget like the Vatican City, is all of 12 kilometres long at its widest extent.

At the foot of Monte Titano, rising dramatically above the plain, is **Borgomaggiore**, San Marino's largest town, from which there is a cable car up to the capital and citadel of the republic, also called **San Marino**. This is a steep medieval hill town carefully preserved in aspic, with wonderful views over Rimini and the coast. Not everything here is as old as it looks, however; the Palazzo del Governo, which is full of Ruritanian guardsmen, is a reconstruction dating from 1894, with a fairly recent restoration by Gae Aulenti. Here the Grand Council meets and the Captains Regent have their offices.

Aside from that, there's a somewhat cheesy batch of private museums that have been conjured up to extract euros from tourists – museums on Medieval Criminals, Torture, Reptiles, Curiosities and Waxworks – but you'd be well advised to avoid them like the plague. A much better idea is to take a pleasant walk through Monte Titano's forests to the three (rebuilt) medieval tower fortresses occupying the three peaks that give San Marino its famous silhouette – famous to philatelists anyhow, and long the symbol of the republic.

Around San Marino

There are two other mountain towns close to San Marino that are most easily visited from Rimini. The first is **Verucchio**, a pleasant medieval village that retains some of its gates and churches, as well as a 10th-century fortress that became the stronghold of the tyrants of Rimini, the Rocca Malatesta. There is also a small Museo Archeologico at the lower end of town, with displays including some unusual ceramics from the 1400 BC Villanova culture.

The second town is **San Leo** on the western side of San Marino (actually in the Marches), which boasts a perfect Renaissance castle that is awesomely sited on a sheer cliff; *see* p.542.

Montefiore Conca in the Valconca has another Rocca Malatestiana. This one is highly impressive in its sobriety, with its sheer naked walls that were built in the form of a single massive tower during the early 14th century; Bellini used it in at least two of his backgrounds.

Finally, it's worth visiting **Montegridolfo**, a handsome medieval fortified village located right on the border with the Marche, which was perfectly restored after decades of total abandonment, and **Mondaino**, a picturesque medieval burg wrapped in its walls and focused around the pretty semicircular piazza.

The Marches

14

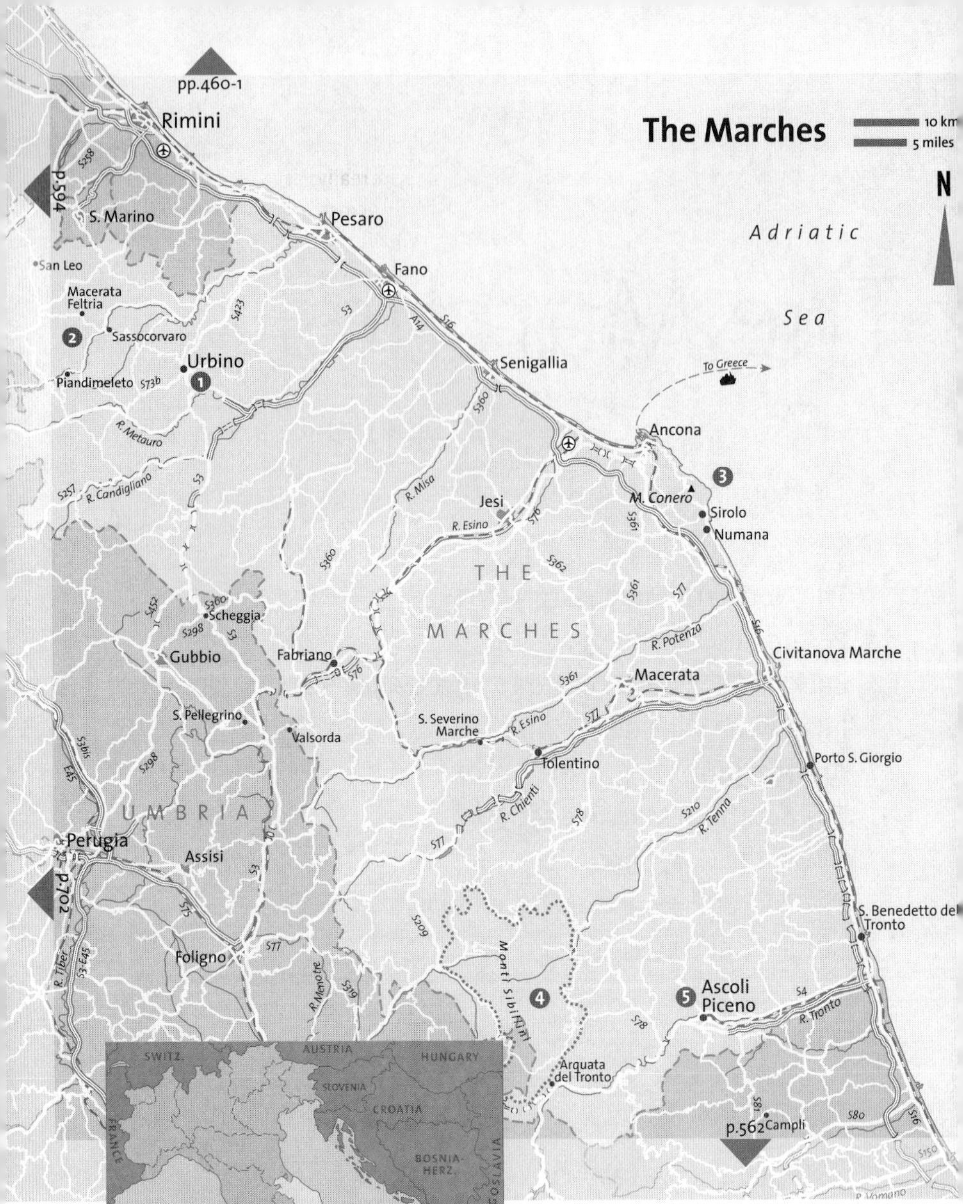

Highlights

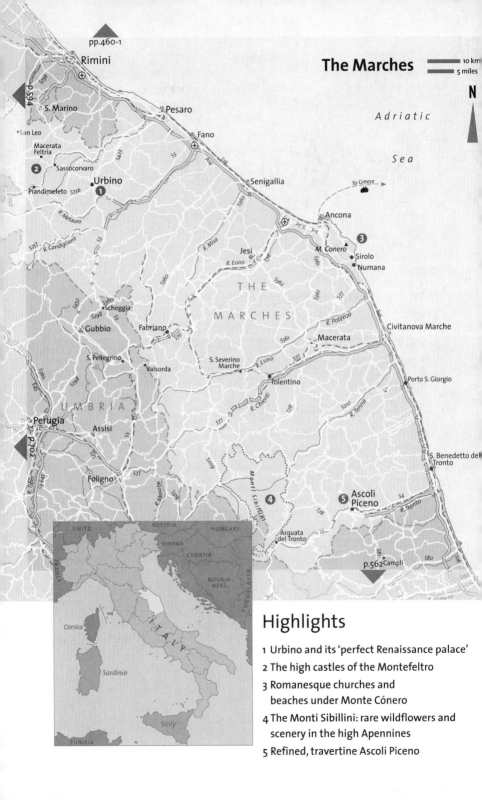

1 Urbino and its 'perfect Renaissance palace'
2 The high castles of the Montefeltro
3 Romanesque churches and beaches under Monte Cónero
4 The Monti Sibillini: rare wildflowers and scenery in the high Apennines
5 Refined, travertine Ascoli Piceno

'Better a corpse in the house than a man from the Marches at the door.'

old Italian saying

The inhabitants of this placid little region aren't so bad, really; the saying comes from the old days when many of the Marchigiani served across the Papal States as the popes' tax collectors. Since then, their neighbours have more often ignored than insulted this obscure patch of territory along the Adriatic. A *march*, or *mark*, in the Middle Ages meant a border province of the Holy Roman Empire, usually an unsettled frontier held by one of the Emperor's fighting barons. With no better name than that, one might expect this Italian region to be somewhat lacking in personality. In fact, this has always been the odd bit of central Italy. In ancient times, too, it was a border zone, shared by Umbrii, Gauls, Sabines and the Piceni. Today, the Marchigiani still have a little identity problem, but it doesn't keep them awake at night. Their land, tucked between the Apennines and the sea, is one of the greenest, prettiest and most civilized corners of Italy, with two lovely Renaissance art towns in Urbino and Ascoli Piceno, lots of beaches, and scores of fine old rosy-brick towns in the valleys that lead up to the impressive snowy peaks of the Sibilline Mountains.

The Northern Marches

Pesaro and Urbino

Just across the border from Emilia-Romagna, the impressive 11th–14th-century **Rocca di Gradara** (***t*** *0541 964 181; open Mon 8.30–2, Tues–Sun 8.30–7.15; adm*) marks the entrance to the Marches. Tradition says this was the scene of the story of Francesca da Rimini and Paolo Malatesta, the tragic lovers consigned to hell by the heartless Dante in the fifth canto of the *Inferno* – a story exploited to the hilt, as it's within easy tour bus distance of Rimini. Beyond, the road soon arrives at provincial capital Pesaro.

Pesaro

Under the Byzantines, the five big ports of the central Adriatic – Rimini, Fano, Senigallia, Ancona and Pesaro – were known as the Pentapolis. Pesaro is the nicest, with a handsome little historic centre. The Sforzas of Milan ruled Pesaro until they sold it to the Della Rovere family of Julius II in 1512, two years after completing the crenellated **Palazzo Ducale** in Piazza del Popolo. In the Sforza years Pesaro rivalled Faenza as a producer of ceramics; see examples in the nearby **Pinacoteca e Museo delle Ceramiche**, Piazza Toschi Mosca 29 (***t*** *0721 387 541; open July and Aug Tues and Thurs 9.30–12.30 and 5–11, Weds and Fri–Sun 9.30–12.30 and 5–8; Sept–June Tues and Weds 9.30–12.30, Thurs–Sun 9.20–12.30 and 4–7; adm*), plus majolica from Urbino, Deruta and Gubbio. There are also a few good pictures and one great one, Giovanni Bellini's *Coronation of the Virgin* (1474). The **Museo Archeologico Oliveriano** at Via Mazza 97 (*Sept–June Mon–Sat 9–12 on request; July and Aug Mon–Sat 4–7;* ***t*** *0721 33344*) displays remains left by the Romans and some of the peoples they quashed.

Getting Around

Pesaro's **railway** station (all trains on the main Adriatic north–south line stop) is on Viale Roma, about ½km south of the centre.

At least 10 **buses** a day go to Urbino, some via Fano and (usually) Fermignano. There are several companies, all of which leave from or stop at Pesaro station; SAPUM buses (**t** 0721 21724) are the most frequent.

In Urbino, the bus depot is Piazzale Mercatale, at the town's southern gate, with connections to most of the inland villages and towns in Pesaro province; all arrivals and departures are listed on a board under the loggia in Piazza della Repubblica.

Tourist Information

Pesaro: Piazzale Libertà 11, **t** 0721 69341; Via Rossini 1, **t** 0721 359 501; also freephone (from within Italy) **t** 800 563 800.

Urbino: Piazza Rinascimento 1, **t** 0722 2613.

Where to Stay and Eat

Pesaro ✉ 61100

At first sight Pesaro looks a refined, perhaps exclusive resort; it comes as a pleasant surprise to find that prices aren't over the top. The town's speciality is the modern, understated 3-star hotel; it's difficult to recommend one over the other. There is also a selection of 1- and 2-star places along the beach and sidestreets.

****Vittoria**, Via Vespucci 2, **t** 0721 34343, *www.viphotels.it* (*luxury*). At the top of the list and one of the 'Hundred Historic Hotels of Italy', set in a renovated century-old *belle époque* villa at the centre of the beach strip. Rooms are furnished with period beds, mirrors and wardrobes; there's also a pool and a billiards room.

****Savoy**, Viale Repubblica 22, **t** 0721 67440, *www.viphotels.it* (*very expensive*). A modern hotel, run by the same team as the Vittoria, set in an attractive shady place with a pool.

***Villa Serena**, Via San Nicola 6, **t** 0721 55211, *www.villa-serena.it* (*expensive*). A 17th-century palace in a serene scenic park just south of Pesaro, with fireplaces and antique furniture in every room. *Closed 2wks in Jan.*

***Principe**, Viale Trieste 180, **t** 0721 30222, (*cheap*). A hotel that stands out for its excellent, popular restaurant **Teresa** (*moderate*), offering enticing dishes such as risotto made with wild herbs picked locally, and fried calamari with sage.

The fishy local cuisine includes ravioli with sole fillets, *garagoli in aorchetta* (shellfish tossed with olive oil, garlic, rosemary and wild fennel), stuffed cuttlefish and red mullet with *prosciutto*.

Alceo, Strada Panoramica Ardizio 101, **t** 0721 51360 (*very expensive*). Fresh fish and home-made pasta and desserts, served in a friendly atmosphere with tables outside offering sea views. *Closed Sun eve and Mon.*

Lo Scudiero, Via Baldassini 2, **t** 0721 64107 (*expensive*). A restaurant in the cellar of a 17th-century palace, offering imaginative seafood and pasta dishes, including ravioli

Pesaro is also proud to have given the world composer Gioacchino Rossini, who was born here in 1792; visitors can have a look at mementos of the *maestro* in his **Casa Natale** at Via Rossini 34 (*open same hours as the Pinacoteca,* ***t*** *0721 387 357*). You can also see his piano and manuscripts at the **conservatory** he founded, in Piazza Olivieri (*call* ***t*** *0721 33671 for an appointment*), and take in an opera at the grand, five-tiered **Teatro Rossini** in Piazza Lazzarini (***t*** *072 69359; currently closed for restoration*), during the festival in late summer.

It's a lovely town to walk through, both its older quarters and arcaded streets and the new streets by the beach, which are full of trees and villas from the 19th century in the Liberty style, including the small but outrageous **Villino Ruggeri**, its cornice supported by terracotta lobsters, designed by Giovanni Brega in 1907. Pesaro's castle, the **Rocca Costanza**, was built in 1478 by Laurana, designer of the palace at Urbino.

with sole, and *tagliatelle marine*, as well as good roast lamb. *Closed Sun and July.*

Antica Osteria La Guercia, Via Baviera 33, on corner of Piazza del Popolo, **t** 0721 33463 (*cheap*). The oldest eatery in town, serving all the classics. *Closed Sun.*

Il Cantuccio di Leo, Via Perfetti 18, **t** 0721 68088 (*cheap*). A central *enoteca* in the centre, serving boar terrines, cheeses, pasta and meat dishes to go with its wines. It stays open until 2am. *Closed Tues and July.*

La Tana del Lupo, in Montefabbri, by Colbordolo **t** 0721 495721 (*cheap*). A good lunch stop about midway along the road from Pesaro to Urbino. *Closed June–Sept.*

Urbino ✉ 61029

The few hotels in Urbino can be crowded in the summer, and even spring, so book ahead.

★★★★**Albergo San Domenico**, Piazza Rinascimento 3, **t** 0722 2626, *www.viphotels.it* (*very expensive*). A plush hotel in an old convent opposite the Palazzo Ducale.

★★★★**Bonconte**, Via delle Mura 28, **t** 0722 2463, *www.viphotels.it* (*expensive*). A luxurious place on the city walls, with lovely views.

★★★**Italia**, Corso Garibaldi 32, **t** 0722 2701 (*expensive*). A good central option a block from the ducal palace.

★★★**Raffaello**, Via S. Margherita 40, **t** 0722 4784, *www.albergoraffaello.com* (*moderate–expensive*). Nicely furnished rooms in an 18th-century house, on a quiet lane just north of Raphael's birthplace.

★★★**Tortorina**, Via Tortorina 4, northeast of the centre, **t** 0722 308 100, *www.hoteltortorina.it* (*cheap–moderate*). A hotel with a large terrace and rooms furnished with antiques.

★★**San Giovanni**, Via Barocci 13, **t** 0722 2827 (*cheap*). A hotel in an old *palazzo*, with a good restaurant. *Closed Jan.*

★**Locanda La Brombolona**, Via S. Andrea in Primicilio 22, Canavàccio, 10km down the Fossombrone road, **t** 0722 53501 (*cheap*). Rooms in a former church in a pretty setting.

★**Pensione Fosca**, Via Raffaello 67, **t** 0722 2542 (*cheap*). The only central budget option.

There are also several student and religious institutions in town that have space in the summer: ask at the tourist office.

Taverna degli Artisti, Via Bramante 52, **t** 0722 2676 (*moderate*). Great food (including pizza) at excellent prices, until 2am most evenings. Arrive early or book to get a table. *Closed Tues.*

Vecchia Urbino, Via Vasari 3/5, **t** 0722 4447 (*moderate*). An elegant option with *tartufi* and *porcini* feasts in the autumn–winter season. *Closed Tues.*

Franco, Via del Poggiol, **t** 0722 2492 (*moderate–cheap*). A place just off the top of the main square, with a self-service area (lunch only) and a proper restaurant with slightly fancier dishes, such as *ravioli ai carciofi*. *Closed Sun.*

Osteria l'Angolo Divino, Via Sant'Andrea 14 (off Via Cesare Battisti), **t** 0722 327559 (*cheap*). A pretty room in an old palace, offering old Urbino specialities – pasta with chickpeas, bacon, lamb or bread-crumbs, and tasty *secondi* from the grill. There are also some vegetarian dishes. *Closed Sun eve and Mon lunch.*

Urbino

From Pesaro – and almost nowhere else – it is easy to reach the isolated mountain town of Urbino. With its celebrated **Palazzo Ducale**, and the memory of the refined Duke Federico da Montefeltro who built it, Urbino is one of the monuments of the Italian Renaissance. Today its boosters go perhaps a little too far, calling it 'the ideal city of the Renaissance' and 'the most beautiful palace in the world', in doing so showing a lack of modesty that wasn't at all Federico's style.

But despite the hype, Urbino does represent more clearly than any other Italian town a certain facet of the Renaissance: elegance, learning and intelligent patronage combined in a relatively small place. The town's golden age may not have lasted a long time but, as an example of what a community can be, it still exerts a certain fascination.

The Court of Montefeltro

Beginning in 1234, Urbino's fortunes were attached to those of the house of Montefeltro – mountain warlords from around San Leo who gradually extended their influence in the northern Marches. Most of them were *condottieri* working throughout Italy, serving various masters. In 1443, Oddantonio da Montefeltro earned the title of duke for his services, and was then assassinated. His half-brother and successor, Federico (who reigned from 1444 to 1482), was the most successful of all the family, a crafty and respected warrior who earned the money for his famous palace serving the cause of Alfonso of Naples and the Pope.

In later years, with more of a chance to stay at home, Federico became one of the quattrocento's most celebrated patrons of art and literature, as well as a slow but close student of the classics and the new humanities; he learned Greek and Latin, and the library he assembled was one of the best in Europe. Federico ruled Urbino paternally and well, and was always liberal to those of his subjects in need, peering into every detail of his little state's economy and social life, and educating the sons of the poor. It is also said that he banished gambling and cursing, and made the people of Urbino exert themselves mightily to keep the place clean. His admirable wife, Battista Sforza, was a duchess beloved by her subjects, and a lady capable of delivering an impromptu speech in impeccable Latin; both were immortalized in Piero della Francesca's warts-and-all portraits, now in the Uffizi.

Their son, Guidobaldo I (1472–1508), was as enlightened a ruler as his father, married to the cultivated Elisabetta Gonzaga, and maintaining a court idealized as the height of civilized existence in Baldassare Castiglione's *The Courtier* (1528), one of the most widely read books of the century. He was also clever enough to survive and prevail after an occupation of Urbino by Cesare Borgia's Papal army in 1497; however when he died without an heir, the duchy fell to a Della Rovere nephew and relative of Pope Julius II. Urbino was willed to the papacy in 1626, and declined rapidly.

Urbino had a moment of high drama in 1944. Many of the works of art of central Italy had been brought here for safekeeping near the end of the war. During the retreat in August, a German commander planted enough explosives under the town walls to blow the whole place to kingdom-come. Only a small number went off, and the rest were defused by the British after the liberation – a job that took a week.

The Palazzo Ducale

Open Tues–Sun 8.30–7.15, Mon 8.30–2; visits every 15mins in winter; adm; **t** *0722 2760 (group bookings* **t** *0722 322 625).*

So many architects helped Federico build his dream house, it is difficult to divide the credit. Alberti may have been an original adviser; the Dalmatian Luciano Laurana generally gets credit for most of the work and the elegant arcaded courtyard. The region's favourite architect, Francesco di Giorgio Martini, may have designed its two internal squares; while the finest part of it, the twin-turreted façade, is by Ambrogio Barocci. That Italian schoolchildren all know this to be 'the most beautiful palace in the world' is an interesting reflection both on the Italians and on the quattrocento. Federico's palace is not finished, not symmetrical, and not really even very grand; its aesthetic is utterly foreign to the tastes of the centuries that followed.

For all that, it is a great building, and a test of one's faith in the genuine Renaissance – the 15th-century high noon of life and art, as opposed to the cinquecento of Spaniardism and neurotic excess. Many critics have regarded it as the culmination of Renaissance architecture, not yet entirely enslaved to perspectivism or imitation of the ancients, but a creation of freedom and delight. The palace was comfortable for the Montefeltro to live in, and a delightful decoration for the city of Urbino.

The palace façade, overlooking the hills on the edge of town, consists of three levels of balconies between two slender towers; the decorative trim is done in a fine Dalmatian limestone that eventually hardens to look like marble. To enter the palace today, you'll need to go round the back through the Cortile d'Onore, a prototype for so many other courtyards around the western Mediterranean.

Inside, much of the palace is occupied by the **Galleria Nazionale delle Marche**, a splendid collection whose finest works were originally the property of Duke Federico. Piero della Francesca's amazing *Flagellation* is perhaps the best-known work in Urbino, an endlessly disturbing image that has troubled art scholars for centuries. Standing before a pavilion of fantasy classical architecture, three gentlemen in contemporary dress hold a serious discussion, indifferent to the scourging of Christ going on behind them – a bloodless scourging, for that matter. Piero, one of the luminaries of Federico's court, had already written one of the great Renaissance treatises on theoretical perspective; a complex system of foreshortening here is the major feature of the work. The combination of a surreal, dream-like scene and a drily scientific visual presentation gives the painting its enigmatic quality – as critics have often noted, this is one of the places where art crosses the line into sorcery.

The same room contains Piero's *Madonna di Senigallia*, another superb work; the Virgin looks as if she has just stepped into a grey room, holding her baby; everyday things sit on the shelves, and even the angels look like a pair of homeowners – yet the domestic scene is rendered timeless, meditative and almost hypnotic through Piero's sorcery. Almost as strange a display of perspectivist wizardry is the *Ideal City*, often attributed to Laurana. The scene is a broad, paved square, lined with buildings in the new style, dominated by a large circular temple in the centre. Disturbingly, there are no people present – no living things at all in this display of vanishing-point virtuosity.

Not to be outdone, Paolo Uccello offers a similarly mysterious (and newly restored) *Miracle of the Profaned Host*, while Piero's student Luca Signorelli is represented by two dark and inspired paintings, the *Crucifixion* and *Pentecost*. Other works not to miss include a Crucifixion by Antonio Alberti de Ferrara, showing off contemporary fashions in armour as well as court dress; the *Annunciation* of Vicenzo Pagani (a very pagan-looking work); *La Muta*, a lovely portrait of a lady by Raphael, and his *St Catherine of Alexandria*; plus fine works by Luca della Robbia, Giovanni Santi (Raphael's dad), Carlo Crivelli, Verrocchio and the Venetian Alvise Vivarini. The Spanish artist Pedro Berruguete contributes the other famous *Portrait of Duke Federico*: the tough old warrior, with his broken nose, symbolically still wears his armour as he pores over a heavy book, with his little son Guidobaldo at his knee; note the badge of the Order of the Garter, which was conferred on Federico by King Edward IV of England.

Some of the surviving interior decoration of the palace is wonderful too – carved mantelpieces and window frames, intarsia doors, cornices and stuccoes, carved and painted ceilings, all bearing the monogram FE DUX and family emblems. Best of all is the intimate intarsia **Studiolo of Duke Federico**, which looks as if the scholarly *condottiere* might wander in at any moment. The inlaid wood designs are by Botticelli, Bramante and Francesco di Giorgio Martini, and they portray the 'Life of a Scholar' with mesmerizing *trompe l'œil* effects. The paintings above, representing philosophers and illustrious men, are by Berruguete and Giusto di Gand, although only half of the 28 are original – the rest are in the Louvre.

Reached by a spiral staircase inside one of the façade's towers are the **Cappella del Perdono**, boasting an ornate ceiling of hundreds of angel heads in stucco, and an equally fancy chamber called the **Tempietto delle Muse**. A Last Supper by Titian hangs in the duchess's bedroom, while the huge throne room, where Federico liked to entertain on a grand scale, has seven tapestries on the Acts of the Apostles from Raphael's cartoons.

The palace's upper floor, the **Appartamento Roveresco**, has rooms full of 16th- and 17th-century paintings, and many portraits of the poor Italians dressed in black like their Spanish overlords. On the ground floor is an **archaeology museum** with Greek and Roman funeral inscriptions and some early Christian reliefs and symbols. The basement contains the laundry, kitchens, ice rooms, storage, the 'duchess's bath' and plumbing, with graffiti scrawled here and there on the walls.

The Town and Walls

Urbino is above all a university town, and, despite its small size, is a lively place. Its streets and roads are often steep, but the town and surrounding hills make an enchanting spot for walks. Next to the ducal palace, in long Piazza Rinascimento, the **cathedral** (*open daily 8–12 and 3.30–6*) was rebuilt as a dull neoclassical church after an earthquake in 1789 caused its dome to collapse. Its detached trecento frescoes and religious artefacts are in the **Museo Albani** (***t*** *0722 2850; open daily summer 9–12 and 2.30–6; winter 9–12 and 3–6*). The oldest thing in the piazza is the little Egyptian **obelisk** from 580 BC, in front of the original Montefeltro palace, now Palazzo dell'Università, and the handsome 1451 portal of Gothic San Domenico.

On Via Barocci, off Via Mazzini, the street leading up from the main gate, the little 14th-century **Oratorio di San Giovanni Battista** (***t*** *347 671 1181; open Mon–Sat 10–12.30 and 3–5.30; Sun 10–12.30 and 3.30–6; closed Feb*) has strikingly colourful frescoes of the Crucifixion, the Madonna, and the Life of John the Baptist by brothers Iacopo and Lorenzo Salimbeni (1416), artists from San Severino Marche, near Macerata, who show a distinctive approach to early-Renaissance painting, still heavily under the influence of Giotto. On the same street, the **Oratorio di San Giuseppe** (***t*** *0722 350025; open daily 10–12.30 and 3.30–6;*) has an exquisite stucco *presepio* (crib) by a 16th-century artist from Urbino, Federico Brandani.

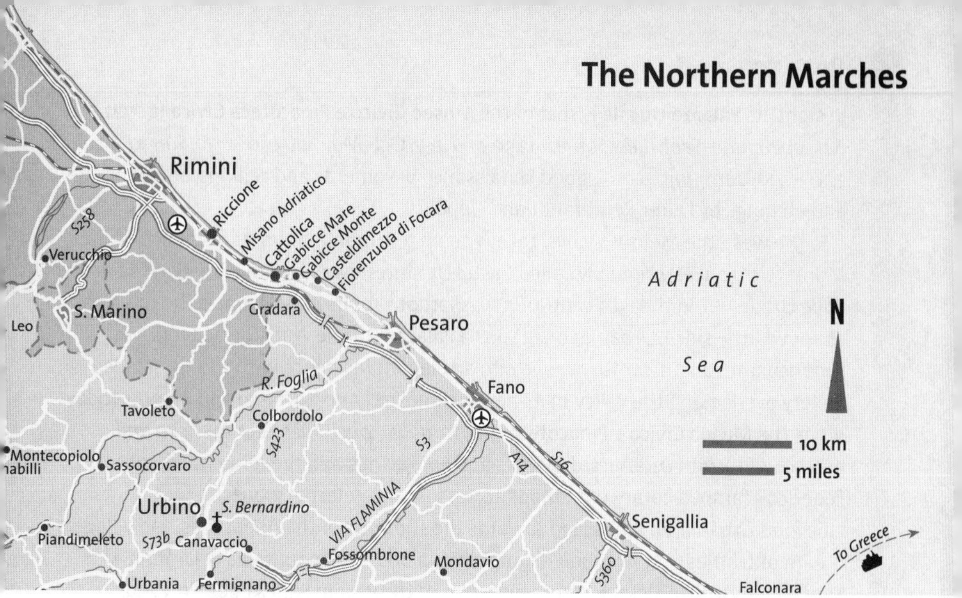

Urbino's most famous son was Raphael (Raffaello Sanzio), born here in 1483. Now a museum, the **Casa di Raffaello** (*t 0722 320 105; open Mar–Oct Mon–Sat 9–1 and 3–7, Sun and hols 10–1; Nov–Feb Mon–Sat 9–2, Sun and hols 10–1; adm*) has little to see – a Madonna by the artist as a child, and works by his father, Giovanni Santi, who taught him the basics of painting and humanist thought.

All of Urbino's 16th-century walls are intact, and the garden enclosed by one of the corner bastions, the **Fortezza Albornoz** (*open daily 9–6*), has a fine view of the palace and town. A pleasant half-hour walk from the west end of town takes you to the pretty church of **San Bernardino degli Zoccolanti** (*t 0722 320539; open daily 8–6*) by Francesco di Giorgio Martini (1491); inside are the starkly impressive black marble tombs of the Montefeltro Dukes.

Towns and Villages Around Urbino

Urbino can be used as a base for excursions to the towns and villages in the rolling hills and mountains of the northern Marches – towns that are as serene and lovely as those in Tuscany but much less known. Some of the most enchanting landscapes lie in the ancient fief of the Montefeltro; the rolling hills are studded with remarkable bare rocky crags, each crowned by a castle from the days when the dukes of Urbino and the Malatesta of Rimini clobbered each other for control of the turf. It's a lovely region, just being discovered by the outside world (Umberto Eco has a house here).

Fermignano, where Bramante may have been born in 1444 (that honour is also claimed by Urbánia), is one of the most conveniently located towns, about nine kilometres south of Urbino. At its centre, under a graceful medieval tower and bridge, is a little waterfall on the Metauro river. From Fermignano, follow the Metauro valley east through a rocky ravine called the **Gola del Furlo**. The Romans, under Vespasian, dug the tunnel to reach **Fossombrone**, then known as *Forum Sempronii*, after the reformer Sempronius Gracchus. Scenographically built on tiers under a Montefeltro palace, Fossombrone is full of tattered palaces and churches, but with nary a tourist in sight. Its **Palazzo Ducale** is seat of the **Museo Civico e Pinacoteca Civica** (***t** 0722 714 645; open June–Sept Tues–Sun 10–12.30 and 4–7; Oct–May Sat 3.30–6.30, Sun 10–12 and 3.30–6.30; adm*), with some good Renaissance pavements and ceilings, and paintings and etchings by Dürer, Rembrandt and Tiepolo.

To the west, the Metauro valley takes you on to **Urbánia**, another residence of the Montefeltro dukes; originally called Castel Durante, it was renamed in 1636 to flatter Pope Urban VIII. In the 15th century, it was famous for its majolica, and the town has changed little since. Urbánia too retains a **Palazzo Ducale**, transformed for Duke Federico from a 13th-century castle into an elegant residence with a long, arcaded gallery overlooking the valley. In its heyday it hosted Ariosto, Tasso and Bembo; today it has the **Museo Civico e Pinacoteca** (***t** 0722 313 151; open Tues–Sun 10–12.30 and 3–6.30; adm*) with ceramics, drawings and engravings and the remains of Duke Federico's famous library, with maps, terrestrial and celestial globes.

Beyond Urbánia, all roads lead towards the summits of the Apennines, and villagers dream of truffles, just like their counterparts across the mountains in Umbria. The *Sagra del Tartufo* in October is the big event of the year in **Sant'Angelo in Vado**, another exceptionally pretty town on the Metauro; it was the home of the Zuccari brothers, late Renaissance painters whose best works are in Rome. The octagonal church of San Filippo has a wooden statue attributed to Lorenzo Ghiberti, who wandered the Marches until the great Florentine baptistry door contest changed his life. From here the road begins the climb over the mountains to Arezzo and Perugia.

To the north **Piandimeleto**, **Sassocorvaro** and **Tavoleto** are three villages built around genteel Renaissance castle-palaces; Sassocorvaro's striking 15th-century **Rocca Ubaldinesca** (***t** 0722 76177; open for guided tours Apr–Sept daily 9.30–12.30 and 3–7; Oct–Mar Sat and Sun 9.30–12.30 and 2.30–6; adm; call ahead to reserve a tour in English*) is an unusual round citadel built by Francesco di Giorgio Martini.

A narrow mountain road runs north via Pennabilli to **Sant'Agata Féltria**, protected by the **Rocca Fregoso**, another fantastical castle balancing precariously on its rock. Inside (***t** 0541 929 111; open daily summer 10–1 and 3–7.30; until 6.30 in winter; adm*) there's a collection of Renaissance frescoes. Sant'Agata really comes into its own in the autumn, when it holds a white truffle market on four consecutive Sundays, beginning with the second Sunday in October.

In the northernmost corner of the Marches, **San Leo** was according to legend founded by a companion of Marinus, but it lost its independence long ago. The rough-walled, 9th-century church called the Pieve is worth a look, but the real attraction is the castle (*open daily 9–7, also 20 July–31 Aug 9pm–10.30; adm*), built for the Montefeltro dukes in the 15th century. Like their palace at Urbino, this is a perfect representative building of the Renaissance: balanced, finely proportioned in its lines, a building of intelligence and style – impregnably hung on a breathtakingly sheer cliff. Once this mountain held a temple of Jupiter; as Mons Feretrius (referring to Jove's lightning) it gave its name to the Montefeltro family. A later fortress on this site was briefly 'capital of Italy' in the 960s, during the reign of King Berengar II. Now there is a small picture gallery in the castle and the dismal cell where the popes kept one of their most famous prisoners, Count Cagliostro, until he went raving mad and died.

Tourist Information

Fano: Viale Cesare Battisti 10, **t** 0721 803 534.
Senigállia: Piazza Morandi 2, **t** 071 792 2725.

Where To Stay and Eat

Fano and Senigállia have only standard beach hotels, all less than 30 years old. The former, however, offers the cheapest, tastiest seafood in the Marches.

Fano ✉ 61032

****__Augustus__, Via Puccini 2, **t** 0721 809 781, *www.hotelaugustus.it* (*moderate*). A central, family-run hotel. *Restaurant closed Mon.*

***__Astoria__, Viale Cairoli 86, **t** 0721 803 474 (*moderate*). A pleasant hotel on the best part of the beach. *Open Easter–Oct.*

__Mare__, Viale C. Colombo 20, **t 0721 805 667 (*cheap*). If you're feeling nostalgic for the *pensioni* of 20 years ago, try this place off the beach, where mamma Anna cooks some of the best and most affordable seafood (*cheap*) in town. *Restaurant closed Sun eve.*

Ristorantino Giulio, Viale Adriatico 100, **t** 0721 805 680 (*expensive*). A reliable favourite serving seafood *marchigiano*-style: try *fusilli con le canocchie* (a local shrimp). *Closed Tues and Nov.*

Pesce Azzurro, Viale Adriatico 48, near the port **t** 0721 803 165 (*cheap*). A unique self-service restaurant set up by the local fishermen's cooperative to promote the glories of 'blue fish' – sardines, anchovies, mackerel and other small fish. The degradation of the Adriatic makes them harder to find each year, but here you can try them in 3 courses, with the local white wine, Bianchello del Metauro. *Closed Mon, and Oct–Mar.*

Senigállia ✉ 60019

****__Duchi della Rovere__, Via Corridoni 3, **t** 071 792 7623, *www.hotelduchidellarovere.it* (*expensive*). A modern, fairly stylish hotel situated by the park, just a couple of blocks from the beach.

***__Cristallo__, Lungomare Alighieri 2, right by the rotunda, **t** 071 792 5767 (*moderate*). A typical resort hotel with balconies and a roof terrace. *Open June–Sept.*

***__La Vela__, Piazzale N. Bixio 35, **t** 071 792 7444 (*moderate*). A nice place near the port with a garden; the furthest hotel from the rail line.

Madonnina del Pescatore, Lungomare Italia 11, Marzocca, 7km south of town , **t** 071 698 267 (*very expensive*). A restaurant that's always packed with happy clients feasting on its brilliant and creative seafood dishes, and some of the best desserts in the Marches. Book ahead. *Closed Mon, 2wks mid-Jan, 1wk Easter and 1wk Sept.*

Riccardone's, Via Rieti 69, **t** 071 64762 (*expensive*). An excellent restaurant with tables on a garden terrace and dishes made from the freshest ingredients; try squid with artichokes, or the mixed seafood grill. *Closed Tues Sept–June.*

Osteria del Tempo Perso, Via Mastai 53, **t** 071 60345 (*moderate*). A restaurant offering seasonal vegetarian dishes right in the *centro storico. Closed Thurs.*

Back on the Coast: Pesaro to Ancona

South of Pesaro, the string of Adriatic resorts continues through Fano and Senigallia – fine old towns, both members of the Pentapolis.

Fano

Older even than the Romans, Fano takes its name – *Fanum Fortunae* – from a famous temple of the goddess Fortuna. Under Roman rule it became the most important of the Marches' coastal cities, the terminus of the Via Flaminia from Rome, and it still looks uncannily like the perfect provincial Roman town. Today, in the central Piazza XX Settembre, a replica Fortuna smiles on Fano from the 16th-century **Fontana della Fortuna.** Behind it, the Palazzo della Ragione (1299) is an austere Romanesque Gothic hall, linked by an arch with the **Palazzo Malatestiano** (*t 0721 828 362; open Tues–Sun 9.30–12.30 and 4–7; 15 June–15 Sept also 9pm–11; adm*), built in the 1420s, when Fano was ruled by the tyrants of Rimini. It has a lovely courtyard with crenellations, mullioned windows and a portico; the elegant loggia on the right, attributed to Iacopo Sansovino, was added in 1544. The picture gallery stars works by Michele Giambono, Guercino and the real Fortuna.

The church of **Santa Maria Nuova**, two blocks south on Via dei Pili, is decorated with stuccoes and altarpieces by Perugino and Giovanni Santi, one with a small predella panel attributed to Santi's young son Raphael. From Roman times, Fano preserves a stately gate built in AD 2, the **Arco di Augusto**. The church of **San Michele** has a relief carved on its façade showing how the arch looked before having its block knocked off with artillery in 1463. The eventually successful besieger was none other than Duke Federico of Urbino, working for the pope; the defender was Sigismondo Malatesta of Rimini. The portico of San Francesco's ruined basilica holds the **Arche Malatestiane**, the Renaissance tomb of Pandolfo III Malatesta (1460) attributed to Alberti. Fano's Lido, modern and overbuilt, is one of the nicer resorts on the Adriatic.

Senigallia

Senigallia, next down the coast, was best known for its duty free port, the site of an important trade fair that attracted some 500 ships from the 12th to the 18th century. Besides its long 'velvet beach', its landmark is an elegant fortress, the **Rocca Roveresca** (*t 071 63258; open daily 8.30–7.30; adm*), built for Duke Federico's son-in-law in 1480.

Inland: the Valle dell'Esino

The mountain valleys, stretching in parallel down to the sea, neatly divide the Marches' geography. South of the Metauro, the Esino is the next important valley, most easily reached from Falconara, south of Senigallia. The first town is Jesi (Roman *Aesis*), set on a narrow ridge between crumbling Renaissance walls with houses built on and over their tops, overlooking the industry that's made Jesi the 'little Milan of the Marches'.

In 1194, **Jesi** was the birthplace of Emperor Frederick II *Stupor Mundi*. Constance de Hauteville, at the age of 40 and after nine years of marriage to Emperor Henry VI of Hohenstaufen, was on her way home to Sicily when she was assailed by labour pains. She pitched her tent in the piazza and invited the town's matrons and 19 churchmen to witness the birth and testify to the legitimacy of her son. Near the adjacent **Palazzo del Comune** is the engraved text of a letter from Frederick to Jesi confirming the town's privileges. In the next square, the 16th-century **Palazzo Ricci** has a waffle-iron façade like the Gesù Nuovo's in Naples. The town's real treasure, however, is the lavishly stuccoed rococo gallery and a set of paintings by Lorenzo Lotto, including the strange, beautifully lit *Annunciation* (1526) in the **Pinacoteca e Musei Civici** (*t 0731 538 343; open Tues–Sun 10–1 and 4–7; adm*), in the Palazzo Pianetti on Via XX Settembre. Outside the walls, **San Marco** (*ring bell of Clarisse's convent to right of church*) has some exceptional 14th-century Giottesque frescoes.

Beyond Jesi, the Valle dell'Esino is squeezed into another limestone gorge, the **Gola di Rossa**; a road off to the right leads to the village of **Genga** and the **Grotte di Frasassi** (**t** *0732 97211; open Nov–Feb Mon–Fri 11–3, Sat 11–4.30, Sun and hols 9.30–6; Mar–July and Sept daily 9.30–6; Aug daily 8–6.30; 20 July–25 Aug also open nightly 8–10.30; closed 4 Dec, 25 Dec, 1 Jan and 10–30 Jan; tours last 70mins; adm exp*), the largest karstic complex in Italy, extending over 18 kilometres (the tour takes in a small section). The massive **Grotta Grande del Vento** ('Cave of the Wind') is a spectacular display of glistening pastel stalactites reflected in calcareous pools. Uphill from Genga station the **Grotta del Santuario** (*open daily dawn–sunset*) is named for its octagonal domed church by Valadier (1828), with a Canova Madonna. Nearby is the 10th-century church of **San Vittore delle Chiese**. A difficult road winds 17 kilometres up to the medieval village of **Arcévia**, the impregnable 'Pearl of the Mountains' on its crag, with a fortified gate, Palazzo Comunale and nine towers. The church of San Medardo (*closed for renovation*) has a Baptism of Christ by Luca Signorelli.

Fabriano, further up the valley near the border with Umbria and a stop on the Rome–Ancona railway, was famous in Renaissance times for paper-making; the watermark (*filigrana*) was invented here, and Fabriano still makes its living from the stuff, using modern methods as well as artisan techniques. On the edge of the *centro storico*, the convent of San Domenico houses the **Museo della Carta e della Filigrana** (*open Tues–Sat 10–6, Sun 10–12 and 2–5; adm*) to tell you how they did and do it. The museum holds the key for the church of San Domenico (*closed for restoration; only ever open on the Festa di Santa Lucia, 13 Dec*), with frescoes from the 1300s.

The centre of town is a beautiful stage set that was badly damaged in the 1997 earthquake and, unlike its Umbrian equivalents, has yet to be restored, with several palazzi and churches under scaffolding. The arcaded **Piazza del Comune**, with a crenellated Palazzo del Podestà (1250), a Palazzo Comunale and Fontana Sturinalto (1281–1351), is strangely reminiscent of those in Perugia. Fabriano was the home of a school of painting that produced one of Italy's most influential International Gothic artists, Gentile da Fabriano (*c.* 1370–1427), master of the famous *Adoration of the Magi* in the Uffizi. Works by the school are held by the the **Pinacoteca Civica**, which is *closed indefinitely for restoration*, though many of its pieces are on display in the Museo della Carta or at the special **Deposito Attrezzato Opere d'Arte** at via Fontanelle (*open Sat and Sun 10–12.30 and 3–7; other days by appointment, call* **t** *0732 709 230*), which also houses works from earthquake-damaged churches.

For a detour off the beaten track, press on south to **Matelica**, a fine town with a pretty main square; a civic palace, the Palazzo Pretorio, with Roman ruins inside and a clock tower from 1270; and a fine picture gallery, the **Museo Piersanti**, at Via Umberto I 11 (**t** *0737 84445; open Aug daily 10–12 and 5–7; Easter–July, Sept and Oct Tues–Sun 10–12 and 5–7; Nov–Easter Sat and Sun 10–12 and 4–6; adm*) with an exceptional Crucifixion *Crucifixion* by Antonio da Fabriano (1452). The Palazzo Ottoni houses a **Museo Archeologico** (*open Weds–Mon 11–1 and 5–7; adm*), the prize exhibit of which is a 2,000-year-old Greek marble globe thought to have been a 'solar clock' for calculating time and the movements of the Sun, planet and stars. **Cerreto d'Esi**, nearby, has the remains of a Byzantine gate and a leaning tower, built in the time of Justinian.

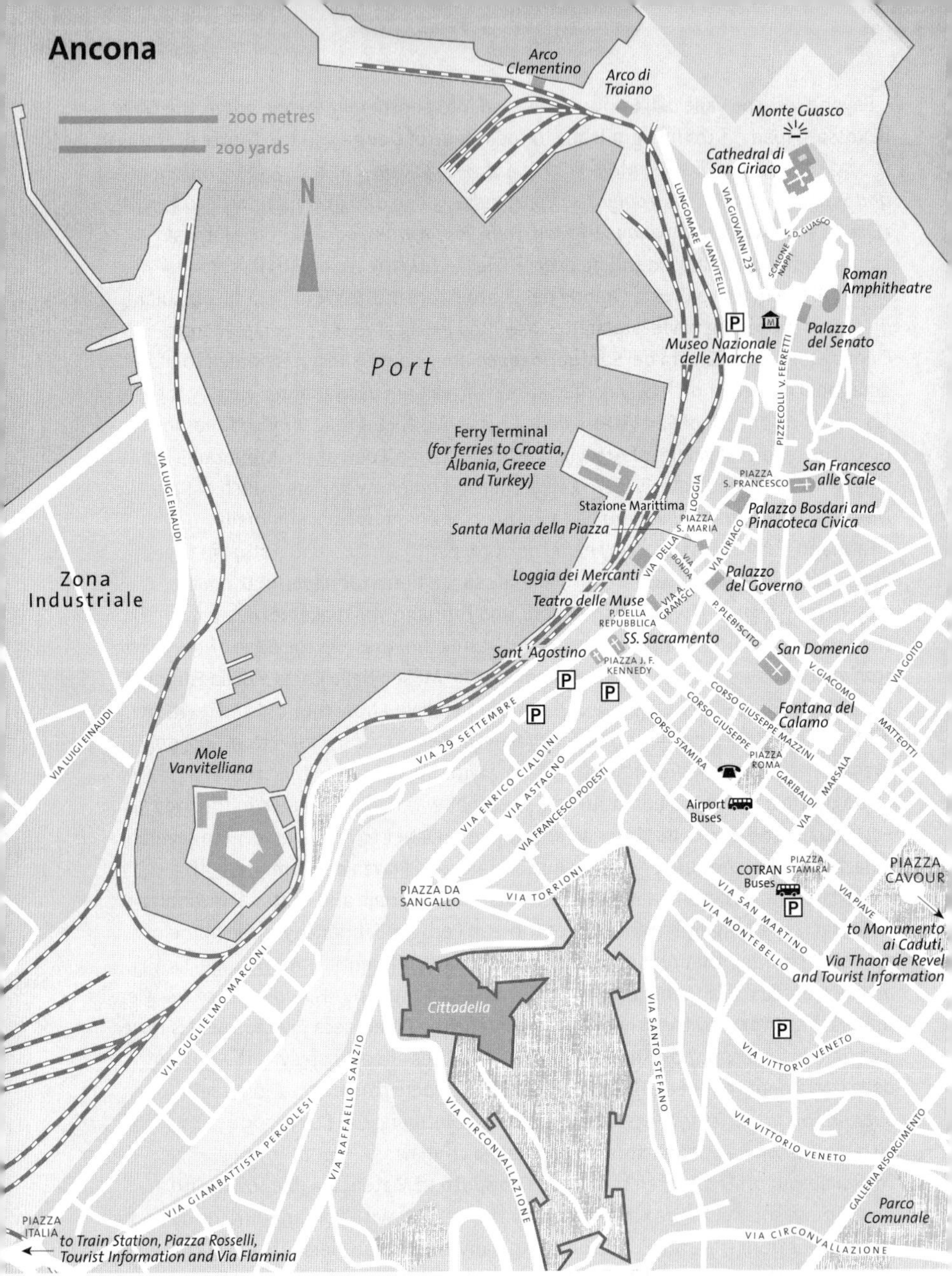

Ancona

Filthy hole: like rotten Cabbage. Thrice swindled. James Joyce

Just before the city, the mountains once more reach the sea, giving the mid-Adriatic's biggest port a splendid setting, a crescent-shaped harbour beneath the steep promontory of Monte Guasco; here colonists from Syracuse founded the city in the

5th century BC. It was the furthest north the ancient Greeks ever went in the Adriatic, and the colony was never a great success until it was built up by Roman emperors, notably Trajan, who hired Apollodoro of Damascus to lay out the port and town. Ancona later became the leading city of the Byzantine Pentapolis, and was given to the Church by Charlemagne. It recovered from the bad centuries to make a living trading with Dalmatia and the east – and battling with Venice on the seas, and the emperors, as well as the lords of Jesi, Rimini and Macerata, on land. In 1532, Medici pope Clement VII reasserted the authority of the Church, moving in a papal army and constructing a citadel to house them.

The 20th century was murderous to Ancona. The Austrians bombarded it in 1915, an earthquake damaged it in 1930, and the British and Americans bombed it again in 1944. Then came a major flood, a serious earthquake in 1972, and a landslide that caused the abandonment of parts of the old town. For all its troubles, Ancona has come up smiling. The port is prospering, and even though most of the population now live in newer districts to the south and west, the city is devoting its attention to the restoration of the historic centre.

Around the Port

It's surprising that anything is left at all of Ancona, but the majority of the city's monuments have survived the recent misfortunes, even if many are a little the worse for wear. The business centre has gravitated a few streets inland and is focused around broad Piazza Cavour; from there Corso Garibaldi leads down to the sea. At its western end, the long curve of the port is anchored by the **Mole Vanvitelliana**, a pentagonal building that resembles a fortress but served as Ancona's *lazzaretto* or quarantine station. At the other end the tall, graceful **Arco di Traiano** was built in AD 115, in honour of Ancona's imperial benefactor; even though the sculptural reliefs have disappeared, it is one of the better preserved Roman arches in Italy. Nearby, Pope Clement XII imitated Roman glory by having an arch put up to himself; the **Arco Clementino**, like the *lazzaretto*, was the work of Vanvitelli, the court architect of the Bourbons at Naples and best known for his palace at Caserta. The elegant 15th-century Venetian Gothic **Loggia dei Mercanti**, the merchants' exchange, is the best souvenir of Ancona's heyday as a free maritime city.

If you want to have a peek at the oldest quarters of Ancona you'll have to climb a little, starting up Via Gramsci and passing under the Renaissance decorative arch of the **Piazza del Governo**. Off in a little square to the left, **Santa Maria della Piazza** (***t*** *071 202 778; open daily 7.30–7*) has a fine late Romanesque façade, with figures of musicians, soldiers and odd animals carved by a 'Master Philippus'. Another two cross-streets up take you to **San Francesco dalle Scale**, with another Gothic portal, and a late Renaissance palace that houses the **Pinacoteca Civica** (***t*** *071 222 5041; open Tues–Sat 9–7, Mon 9–1, Sun 3–7; adm*). It contains a masterpiece by the eccentric but endearing Carlo Crivelli, the tidiest of all Renaissance painters – a Madonna col Bambino, with his trademark apples and cucumbers hanging overhead. There is also a good Madonna by Lotto, formerly in the Santa Maria church, and yet another by Titian, floating smugly on a cloud.

Getting There and Around

By Air

Ancona's Raffaello Sanzio **airport** (**t** 071 28271 or **t** 071 282 7233), 10km to the north at Falconara, has daily flights from Rome, Milan, London and Munich, as well as several flights a week from Bucharest and Moscow.

Airport buses run to Piazza Cavour. Trains run from the airport to Ancona, Jesi, Fabriano and Foligno. For airport taxis, call **t** 0171 918 221.

By Rail

Ancona lies at the intersection of two major railway lines – the **Adriatic coast route** and the **Ancona–Rome** line, with no long waits for trains in either direction. For information call **t** 848 888 088 or **t** 071 592 3447.

The station is west of the port on Piazza Roselli (take buses no.1 or 3 to or from Piazza Repubblica near the port). A few trains carry on to Ancona Marittima station on the port.

By Bus

RENI **buses** to the Cónero Riviera via Camerano depart from Piazza Cavour in the centre, **t** 071 286 8409. For towns in the province (Jesi, Recanati, Ósimo, Castelfidardo, Loreto, Senigállia, and in summer, Portonovo), CONERO buses leave from Piazza Cavour, freephone from within Italy **t** 800 218 820, or **t** 071 280 2092; many buses also stop at the railway station.

By Sea

There are plenty of **ferries**, ready to bustle you off to Greece, Albania, Croatia and Turkey. If you're heading to Greece and coming from Rome or anywhere north, taking the ferry from here is a moderately better bet than making the long train trip down to Brindisi, Bari or Otranto. Fares are only slightly higher, and in both cases it will be an overnight trip. Book well in advance through a tourist office or travel agent for summer crossings.

Ferry lines to Greece include: **Minoan Lines**, Via Astagno 1, **t** 071 201 708, *www.minoan.it*; **Anek Lines**, Via Cialdini 57, **t** 071 202 223; **Strintzis Lines**, Corso Garibaldi 28, **t** 071 206 725; **Superfast**, Via XXIX Settembre 2/o, **t** 071 202 033, *www.superfast.com*; and **Marlines** (also to Turkey), Via di Vittorio 8, **t** 071 286 6713.

All the ferry companies have ticket booths at the Stazione Marittima, which may only be open at sailing times.

Tourist Information

Via Thaon de Revel 4, **t** 071 358 991. There are summer branch offices in the railway station and in the port, **t** 071 201 183.

Where to Stay and Eat

Ancona ✉ 60100

★★★★**Grand Hotel Palace**, Lungomare Vanvitelli 24, **t** 071 201 813, *www.hotelancona.it* (*expensive*). The finest hotel in the city, a comfortable little place set in a 17th-century palace and boasting a roof garden with magnificent views over the bustling port.

★★★★**Grand Hotel Passetto**, Via Thaon de Revel 1, **t** 071 31307, *www.hotelpassetto.it* (*expensive*). A central option with an outdoor pool.

★★★**Fortuna**, Piazza Rosselli 15, **t** 071 42663 (*moderate*). A comfortable choice close to the station.

★★**Viale**, Viale della Vittoria 23, **t** 071 201 861, (*moderate*). Tranquillity and lower prices nearly a kilometre out of the centre.

★★**Gino**, Via Flaminia 4, **t** 071 42179 (*cheap*). A hotel with an assuming-looking restaurant (*moderate*) that serves excellent fresh seafood. *Closed Sun*.

★★**Dorico**, Via Flaminia 8, **t** 071 42761 (*cheap*). An option near the station, with simple rooms with or without bath.

The dish to try in Ancona is *stoccafisso all'anconetana*, dried cod casserole with tomatoes, potatoes and marjoram. Nearly every port city in Italy developed a taste for dried cod in the Middle Ages, when barrel-loads from England and the Baltic passed through in exchange for wine; in Ancona it's preferred even to the day's catch from the Adriatic. Another local speciality is *brodetto*, a tasty fish soup. Like any self-respecting port, Ancona has dozens of simple *trattorie* in which you can put away a range of less grandiose marine delights at inconceivably low prices.

Passetto, Piazzale IV Novembre, **t** 071 33214 (*expensive*). An excellent seafood place with a seaside terrace, offering both a *menu degustazione*, and a less pricey set menu featuring meat dishes, both including wine. *Closed Sun eve, Mon, and last 2wks Aug.*

La Moretta, Piazza Plebiscito 52, **t** 071 202 317 (*expensive*). A restaurant in a handsome 19th-century building, long a favourite with townspeople for its excellent *stoccafisso all'anconetana* and *spaghetti agli scampi*. *Closed Sun.*

Corte, Via della Loggia 5, **t** 071 200 806 (*moderate*). A restaurant situated in an elegant 18th-century palace close to the port, with a very pretty summer garden and excellent gourmet dishes. *Closed Sun and Jan.*

Carloni, Via Flaminia 247, Torrette, north of town, **t** 071 888 239 (*moderate*). A seafood hot spot situated between the rail tracks and the sea – expect your mussels to rattle when trains pass. *Closed Mon.*

Osteria del Pozzo, Via Bonda 2, **t** 071 207 3996 (*cheap*). An elegant but absurdly cheap option at the centre of the port; try the mixed fry or seafood pasta of the day. *Closed Sun and Aug.*

La Cantinetta, Via Gramsci, **t** 071 201 107 (*cheap*). A restaurant offering a foretaste of Greece if you're hopping on a ferry, complete with Greek seamen fingering worry beads. It's one of the most popular places in town – not for its décor, but for its *stoccafisso*, served every Friday, its nightly fish fry, its traditional *vincisgrassi* (*see* p.555) and, oddly, its lemon sorbet. *Closed Sun.*

Portonovo ✉ 60020

★★★★**Fortino Napoleonico**, Via Poggio 166, **t** 071 801 450, *www.hotelfortino.it* (*very expensive*). An award-winning hotel incorporating part of a fortress built in the Napoleonic Wars; set apart, quiet and modern, it has its own beach and a swimming pool. Big spenders book the 'Josephine suite'. This is also one of the finest places to dine in the Marches, with two beautiful dining rooms and immaculate service. The eight superb courses include stuffed olives and scampi, sole stuffed with spinach, cream and smoked salmon, shrimps with fennel and orange, and gnocchi with caviar.

★★★★**Emilia**, Collina di Portonovo, **t** 071 801145, *www.hotelemilia.com* (*expensive*). Luxurious accommodation in a lovely setting. Artists stay free in exchange for a painting, and the place is covered with pictures, including one by Graham Sutherland.

★★★**Internazionale**, Via Portonovo 149, **t** 071 801 001 (*moderate*). A sturdy stone building set in the trees, with ravishing views above the bay, its own beach and a good restaurant.

Il Laghetto, near Portonovo's little lake, **t** 071 801 183 (*moderate*). A great little place to feast on fish and *frutti di mare*, prepared in unusual ways. *Closed Mon and mid-Jan–mid-Mar.*

Sirolo ✉ 60020

★★★**Locanda Rocco**, Via Torrione I, **t** 071 933 0558, *www.locandarocco.it* (*expensive*). A charming, stylishly decorated inn that's been on this site since 1300. The restaurant serves modern Italian cuisine on the piazza in front. *Closed Tues and winter.*

★★★**Monte Cónero**, built around the Badia di San Pietro, **t** 071 933 0592 (*expensive*). A great get-away-from-it-all place, enjoying a quiet, sublime setting near the very top of the headland, with a pool and restaurant (*moderate*). *Closed mid-Nov–mid Mar.*

Numana ✉ 60026

★★★**Gigli Eden**, Via Morelli 11, **t** 071 933 0652, *www.conerohotels.it* (*moderate*). An option at the pricier end of this range, but one that's worth the bill, bearing in mind the number of dismal spots that have been thrown up as part of the recent building boom. This has nice bedrooms with views, 2 pools, and acres of ground with plenty of trees. There's a secluded private beach, but it's a bit of a climb to get back from it.

★★**Teresa a Mare**, Via del Golfo 26, **t** 071 933 0623 (*moderate*). A slightly cheaper and more basic option.

On Monte Guasco

Further up, the street changes its name to Via del Guasco, and bits of decorative brickwork from Roman Ancona's theatre peek out from in between and from under buildings. This was the area that was hardest hit by the earthquake and landslide, and only in 1988 did the **Museo Archeologico Nazionale delle Marche** re-open, in the ripe interiors of a 16th-century palace in Via Feretti 6 (*t 071 202 602; open Tues–Sun 8.30–7.30; adm*). It has an exceptional archaeological collection, including some superb Greek vases, some beautiful Etruscan bronzes, gold and amber from Gaulish and Piceni tombs, and extensive Roman finds. Also damaged in 1972 was the 13th-century **Palazzo del Senato**, around the corner, Ancona's capital when it was a self-governing *comune*.

Ancona's pink and white **Cattedrale di San Ciriaco** (*t 071 52689; open daily summer 8–12 and 3–7, until 6 in winter; adm*) crowns Monte Guasco, the ancient Greek acropolis, a site that in antiquity held a famous temple of Venus. To reach it, climb the long garden stairway, the **Scalone Nappi**, or catch the no.11 bus from Piazza Cavour. Unusually for a church this far north, the 11th-century cathedral shows a strong influence from the Puglian Romanesque, and but for the long, rounded transepts the building would not look out of place in any of the cathedral towns around Bari.

The fancy Gothic porch is by Margaritone d'Arezzo – Big Daisy's only known foray into architecture – and the sculpted portals and detached campanile were added about 1200. The marble columns inside came originally from the Temple of Venus, some crowned with Byzantine capitals. The cathedral is dedicated to St Cyriacus, the converted Jew who revealed the whereabouts of the True Cross to St Helen and, in a clever piece of 4th-century propaganda, was said to have been martyred by the virtuous but non-Christian Emperor Julian the Apostate.

The Conero Riviera

The same arm of the Apennines that stretches down to shelter Ancona's port also creates a short but uniquely beautiful stretch of Adriatic coast. South of Ancona, the cliffs of Monte Conero plunge steeply into the sea, forcing the railway and coastal highway to bend inland, and isolating a number of beautiful beaches and coves only a few kilometres from the centre of Ancona; it's now a national park.

The little resort town of **Portonovo**, on the northern slopes of Conero, can be reached by bus from Ancona in half an hour. Tucked under the cliffs, it's the most beautiful place for a swim in these parts, with a clean pebble beach, and a lovely church of the 1030s in the same style as Ancona cathedral. **Santa Maria di Portonovo**, with the same blind arcading around the roofline and a distinctive cupola in the centre, is one of the better Romanesque churches in the north; Dante mentions it – 'the House of Our Lady on the Adriatic coast' – in the 21st canto of *Paradiso*.

The southern end of Conero is marked by the attractive but often very crowded resorts of **Sirolo** and **Numana**. Both have beaches nearby, but the best in the area are in places that can only be reached by small boat, such as the **Due Sorelle**, or the stretch of jagged white cliffs called the **Sassi Bianchi**.

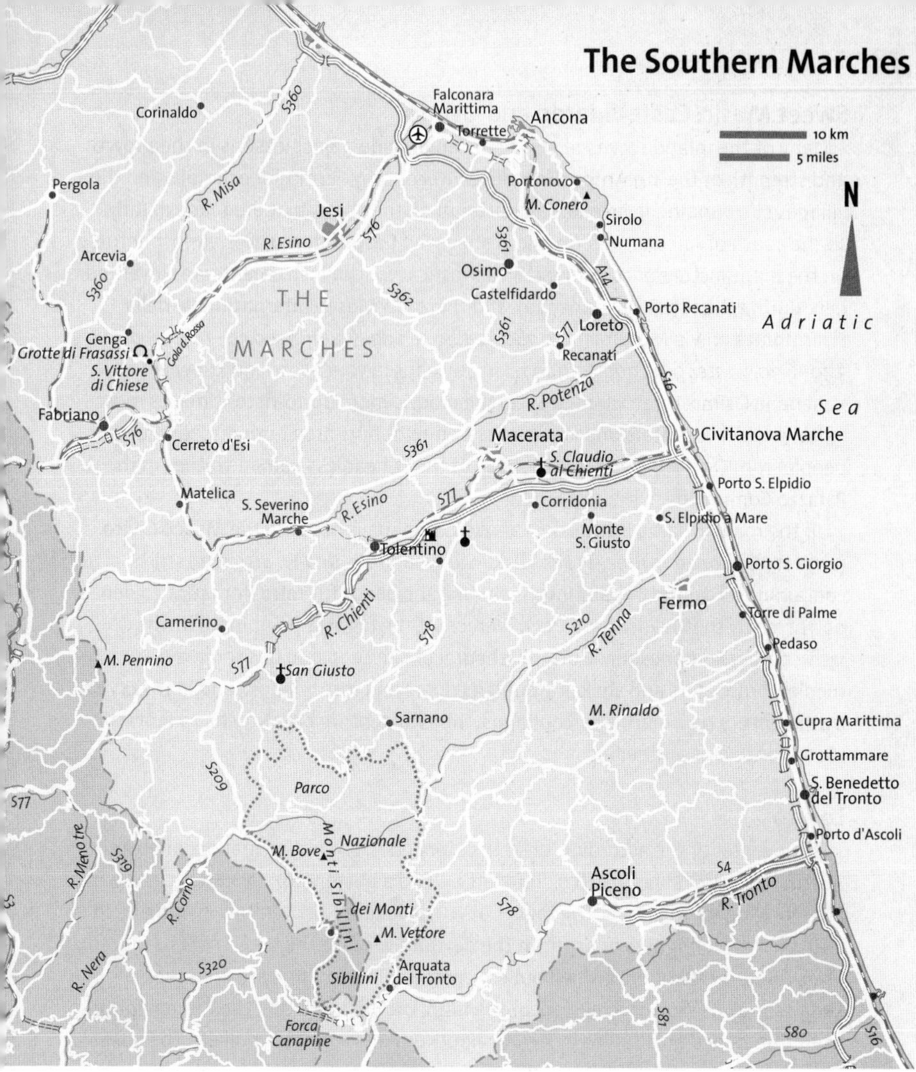

The Southern Marches

Down the Coast

After Monte Conero, the Adriatic won't show you another stretch of beautiful coastline until you reach the dramatic Gargano Peninsula in Puglia. All through the southern Marches the seaside is dotted with humble but growing resort towns, all pleasant enough but nothing special: **Porto Recanati**, **Civitanova Marche**, **Porto Sant'Elpidio**, **Porto San Giorgio** and **Pedaso**. If you're looking for a chance to dip inland, the best places to visit are the pilgrimage shrine of Loreto – home of the Holy House – and the fine old town of Fermo, six kilometres west of Porto San Giorgio.

Sweet Music: Castelfidardo and Ósimo

Many of the inland towns of this area can provide object lessons in the growth and strength of the 'new model' small-scale economy. Fermo, for example, and the villages surrounding it, produce a quarter of all the shoes that are made in Italy. To the south of Ancona, meanwhile, dishevelled **Castelfidardo** lives almost entirely on the manufacture of accordions. This most catholic of instruments was invented here during the 1870s, or so they say, and there is a **Museo Internazionale della Fisarmonica** on Via Mordini (***t*** *071 780 8288; open daily summer 9.30–12.30 and 3.30–6.30; winter 9–12 and 3–6*) to fill in any gaps in your accordion knowledge. Venerable **Ósimo**, three kilometres up the road, is more up-to-date; it makes most of Italy's electric guitars and keyboards. Its neighbours aren't impressed; they call people from Ósimo '*senza teste*' because of the 12 headless Roman statues in the **Palazzo Comunale**.

Up the road in Piazza Dante, the Palazzo Campana is home to the **Museo Civico** (***t*** *071 714 621; open 15 June–15 Sept Tues–Sun 5–8, Thurs and Fri also 9pm–11*), containing a handful of paintings, including the beautiful, retro (for 1464) golden polyptych by the Vivarini brothers of Venice. At the highest point in town, the 13th-century Romanesque–Gothic **cathedral** of San Leopardo has some quirky medieval monsters and snakes around its doors and rose window, and in the crypt, a 4th-century Luni marble sarcophagus; the 12th-century baptistry has a fantastic 1629 bronze font and ceiling.

Loreto

The inventor of the accordion, or so the story goes, got his inspiration when an Austrian pilgrim on his way to Loreto left behind a button-box concertina as a gift after lodging for the night. The town puts up billboards all over Italy inviting us to visit, but few foreigners apart from the devout ever take the hint. That is a pity, for, like Urbino, Loreto offers a small but concentrated dose of fine art from the Renaissance. Its story is a mystery of the faith. During the 1200s, the Church found itself threatened on all sides by heretical movements and free-thinkers. The popes responded in various subtle ways to assimilate and control them; creating the Franciscan movement was one approach, encouraging the cult of the Virgin Mary another. Conveniently, a legend of a miracle in the Marches gained currency. Mary's house in Nazareth was transported by a band of angels to a hill in Istria on 10 May 1291, then flew off again on 9 December 1294, this time landing in these laurel woods (*loreti*) south of Ancona. Supposedly the house had bestirred itself in protest over Muslim reoccupation of the Holy Land; the popes were thumping the tub for a new Crusade, and Loreto was just coincidentally located on the route to the Crusader ports on the Adriatic.

Recent research has indicated that the Holy House did indeed come from Nazareth, but it seems that angels had little to do with its removal: it was in fact a dowry that was given by the Nikeforos Angelo, king of Epirus, to his daughter on her wedding to Philip of Taranto. When the Crusaders lost Palestine in 1291, Nikeforos had the house dismantled and took the stones with him. They ended up at Loreto.

Getting There and Around

There are frequent **trains** along the coast between Ancona and Pescara. Loreto is also on this line – the station (**t** 0171 978 668) is outside the town, but there is a regular connecting bus service. There is also a line that cuts inland from Civitanova Marche to Macerata, and meets the Ancona–Rome line near Fabriano.

COTRAN **buses** (**t** 0171 202 766) from Ancona have frequent services to Loreto and Recanati by way of Ósimo and Castelfidardo; CONTRAM buses (**t** 0171 970 327) run down the coast linking Porto Recanati to Loreto, Recanati and Macerata, and there's a bus a day linking Loreto to Camerino, Tolentino and Sarnano. Three daily START buses from Fermo run down the coast to Porta d'Ascoli, then head inland to Ascoli Piceno and Rome (freephone within Italy **t** 800 443 040, or **t** 0734 229 903).

Tourist Information

Loreto: Via Solari 3, **t** 071 970 276.
Fermo: Piazza del Popolo 6, **t** 0734 228 738.

Where To Stay and Eat

Loreto ✉ 60025

The best places are outside the centre.

****__Villa Tetlameya__, Via Villa Costantina 187, Loreto Archi, **t** 071 978 863, *www.loretoitaly.com* (*expensive*). An elegant 19th-century villa with the most comfortable rooms and one of the best restaurants in the area, **Zi Nene**, specializing in classic seafood and historical *marchigiano* recipes. *Closed Mon.*

***__La Vecchia Fattoria__, Via Manzoni 19, **t** 071 978 976 (*moderate*). A hotel with a restaurant that's a local favourite for weddings and banquets. *Closed Mon.*

***__Blu Hotel__, Via Villa Costantina 89, **t** 071 978 501, *www.cssg.it* (*cheap*). Simple but pleasant rooms. *Closed over Christmas.*

In the centre of town, hotels are invariably clean, quiet and respectable, and have a crucifix above every bed. Many are run by religious orders – Ursulines, Franciscan Sisters and the Holy Family Institute of Piedmont – as accommodation for pilgrims.

***__Casa del Clero Madonna di Loreto__, Via Asdrubali 104, **t** 071 970 298 (*cheap*). A typical example, with 32 rooms with bath.

__Centrale__, Via Solari 7, **t 071 970 173 (*cheap*). A slightly cheaper with a more secular atmosphere. *Closed Jan.*

Andreina, Via Buffolareccia 14, **t** 071 970 124 (*moderate*). A restaurant that has been here for donkey's years, serving wonderful grilled meats and *marchigiano* specialities. *Closed Tues and part of July.*

Fermo ✉ 63023

Both the hotel restaurants are okay (rare for central Fermo), but there are pizzerias too.

***__Astoria__, Viale Veneto 8, **t** 0734 228 601 (*moderate*). A modern, comfortable choice in the centre, with a restaurant.

***__Casina delle Rose,__ Piazzale Girfalco 16, **t** 0734 228 932 (*moderate*). An older, slightly cheaper hotel facing the cathedral and town park, with a restaurant.

The Santuario della Santa Casa

***t** 071 970 107; basilica open daily 6.45am–7pm (8 in summer); Santa Casa closed 12.30–2.30.*

From 1468, the simple church built to house the Santa Casa was reconstructed and embellished in a building programme that took well over a century. Corso Boccalini, lined with souvenir stands, leads from the town centre up to the sanctuary, which materializes in all its glory when you enter the enclosed **Piazza della Madonna**, with the church, a great fountain by Carlo Maderno, the Palazzo Apostolico and an elegant loggia by Bramante. The piazza is often filled with the 'white train' loads of sick people hoping Loreto's Madonna succeeds where modern medicine has fallen short.

The sanctuary's understated façade is typical early Roman Baroque, if a little ahead of its time (1587); no one is sure to whom to ascribe it, since so many architects had a hand in the work. Giuliano da Sangallo built the cupola (a copy of Brunelleschi's dome in Florence), Bramante did the side chapels, and Sansovino and Sangallo the Younger also contributed. One of the best features is the circle of radiating brick apses on the east end, turreted like a Renaissance castle. The only unfortunate element in the ensemble is the ungainly neoclassical campanile, topped with a bronze-plated garlic bulb, designed by Vanvitelli in the 1750s. Don't blame the architect: it had to be squat and strong to hold the 15-ton bell, which makes itself heard once it gets going.

Chapels line the walls inside, embellished by the faithful from nations around the world, including recent ones from the United States (with an aeroplane). The English chapel holds a memorial of lyric poet Richard Crashaw, a refugee from Protestant intolerance. A good deal of Loreto's art was swiped by Napoleon; but the two sacristies on the right aisle have fine frescoes by Luca Signorelli and Melozzo da Forlì. Under the dome you'll see the object of the pilgrims' attention; the Santa Casa, a simple brick room with traces of medieval frescoes, contains the venerated black Madonna of Loreto, sculpted out of cedar in 1921; the original was destroyed in a fire. The house was sheathed in marble by Bramante to become one of the largest and most expensive sculptural ensembles ever – the better to make the flying house stay put. Its decoration includes reliefs by Sangallo and others, showing scenes from the Life of Mary. The upper floor of the Apostolic palace houses what the crooks missed in the **Museo-Pinacoteca** (***t*** *071 977 759; open Apr–Oct Tues–Sun 9–1 and 4–7, mid-June–mid-Sept also Thurs and Fri 9pm–11; Nov–Mar Sat and Sun 10–1 and 3–6; adm*), especially the excellent, dramatic late paintings by Lorenzo Lotto.

Fermo

The Sabine town of *Firmum*, later a close ally of Rome, has gained importance and lost it several times; in the 10th century it was the capital of a duchy that included all the southern Marches. Fermo's handsome, brick-arcaded **Piazza del Popolo** has always been its drawing room and is now the lounge area for the more pretentious visitors to the coast. From 1398 to 1826 it was also the seat of its university, whose building, the Baroque **Palazzo degli Studi**, is still there at the end of the square, holding the university's superb library. Another corner of the piazza is closed by the 15th-century **Palazzo Comunale**, adorned with a bronze statue of Pope Sixtus V – by a 16th-century sculptor with a great name, Accursio Baldi – inviting you in to the art collection of the **Pinacoteca Civica** (***t*** *0734 284 327; open mid-June–Sept 10–1 and 3.30–7.30, Thurs until 10.30; Oct–mid-June 9.30–1 and 3.30–6.30; adm; joint ticket available with Piscina*). Works include a very moving and intense Nativity by a young Rubens; local records recall a Fermo priest commissioning it in 1608 for the grand sum of 1700 *scudi*.

A singular relic of Roman times can be visited under the Via degli Aceti: the **Piscina Epuratoria** (*same hours as the Pinacoteca; adm*), an enormous underground reservoir built in AD 41–61 to hold and clarify rain- and spring-water. Behind the Palazzo Comunale, Via Perpenti leads down to the Gothic church of **San Francesco**, with 15th-century frescoes and a tomb by Andrea Sansovino.

Getting Around

Macerata's suburban **train** station is linked to Piazza della Libertà by city buses no.2, 2a and 6. **Buses** to the province leave from the Giardini Diaz, west of the centre, off Viale Puccinotti.

Tourist Information

Macerata: Piazza della Libertà 12, **t** 0733 234 807.
Recanati: Piazza G. Leopardi, **t** 071 981 471.
Tolentino: Piazza Libertà 18, **t** 0733 972 937.
Camerino: Piazza Cavour 2, **t** 0737 632 534.

Where To Stay and Eat

Macerata ✉ 62100

★★★★**Claudiani**, Via Ulissi 8, **t** 0733 261 400, *www.hotelclaudiani.com* (*moderate*). A modern hotel in an old palace in the historic centre.

★★★**Da Rosa**, Via Armaroli 94, **t** 0733 232 670 (*moderate*). A pleasant option in the centre very close to Piazza della Libertà.

★★**Arena**, Vicolo Sferisterio 16, **t** 0733 230 931 (*cheap*). A small but good option right next to the Sferisterio.

Macerata is the place to try *vincisgrassi*, a kind of lasagne with a rich sauce of chicken livers, gizzards and brains, mushrooms, minced meat and wine, topped with béchamel sauce.

Da Rosa, Via Armaroli 17, **t** 0733 260 124 (*moderate*). A good trattoria with a daily-changing menu. *Closed Sun and Christmas.*

Da Secondo, Via Pescheria Vecchia, **t** 0733 260 912 (*moderate*). Macerata's best restaurant, in the centre, offering *vincisgrassi* and a famous *fritto misto* of lamb and vegetables. There are lovely views too, and a terrace. Reserve, because it's always crowded. *Closed Mon, and part of Aug.*

Osteria dei Fiori, Via Lauro Rossi 61, **t** 0733 260 142 (*moderate*). A good, busy choice between the Sferisterio and Piazza della Libertà, with *vincisgrassi*, stuffed deboned pigeon, *fritto misto* and other hearty favourites. *Closed Sun and mid-Aug–mid-Sept.*

Tolentino ✉ 62029

★★★★**Hotel 77**, Viale B. Buozzi 90, **t** 0733 967 400, *www.hotel77.com* (*moderate*). A cosy hotel just outside the centre, with an open-air pool.

★★Milano, Via Roma 13, **t** 0733 973 014 (*cheap*). An older, more modest choice, in the centre.

Re Gioacchino, Contrada Cisterna 55, **t** 0733 969 347 (*cheap*). The town's best restaurant, situated in an 18th-century villa named for Napoleon's general Joachim Murat, hidden away down in Tolentino's urban sprawl. The good classics are accompanied by pitchers of Verdicchio. There are 6 small but comfy bedrooms, some with frescoed ceilings. *Restaurant closed Mon.*

Camerino ✉ 62032

★★★**I Duchi**, Via V. Favorino 72, **t** 0737 630 440 (*cheap*). A modern, family-run place in the *centro storico*.

★★**Roma**, Piazza Garibaldi 6, **t** 0737 632 592 (*cheap*). A simple, central, cheaper option (some rooms share bathrooms).

Osteria dell'Arte, Via Arco della Luna 7, **t** 0737 633 558, (*moderate*). One of the oldest restaurants in town, with unusual pasta (with wild fennel, for instance), and good rabbit and trout. *Closed Fri and 2 wks Jan.*

The Pocket Province of Macerata

You won't find a more out-of-the-way corner in central Italy. This hilly enclave lacks great attractions but its towns put up a good front, with stout medieval walls or a gay Romanesque tower to lure you in for a short stop. Many of its villages and towns also have fine works of art in their little museums.

Macerata, Recanati and Tolentino

Macerata is a pleasant medieval-looking town of 43,000 people. About one-sixth of them can fit into the town's major landmark, a huge colonnaded hemicycle and outdoor theatre called the **Arena Sferisterio**, built in the 1820s by local subscription for a game similar to Basque pelota, *pallone al bracciale*, which required a long wall on one side. The builders of the Sferisterio endowed it with excellent acoustics, making for one of the grandest settings for opera south of Verona; the **Macerata Opera Festival** (*t 0733 230 735, box office at Piazza Mazzini 10*) from mid-July to mid-August is a popular event.

Nearly as many people could fit into Macerata's central Piazza della Libertà, which is decorated with Macerata's proudest monuments: a Tuscan **Loggia dei Mercanti** (1505), built by Papal Legate Alessandro Farnese, the future Pope Paul III; the 17th-century **Palazzo del Comune** with an atrium decorated with statues and inscriptions from *Helvia Ricina*; and an elegant 18th-century **Teatro Rossi**, designed by the great Bibbiena family of theatre designers.

On Piazza Vittorio Veneto, the **Museo Civico e Pinacoteca** (*t 0733 256 361; open Tues–Sat 9–1 and 4–7.30, Sun 9–1*) has a Madonna by Crivelli (there are no cucumbers, but it's a lovely work just the same), and works by Sassoferrato and Parmigiano. If you're fond of Christmas cribs, Macerata has a **Museo Tipologico del Presepio**, at Via Maffeo Pantaleoni 4, near the Sferisterio (*open by request, t 0733 234 035*), with 4,000 figures from the 17th century to the present. There's an excellent collection of modern Italian painters and sculptors (Manzu, De Chirico, Carrà, Messina, De Pisis, Morandi, Balla) in the **Palazzo Ricci Gallery,** Via D. Ricci 1 (*t 0733 232 802; open Tues and Thurs 4–6, Sat 10–12*). Two kilometres outside the Porta Picena, Macerata has a domed Renaissance church in the form of a Greek cross, **Santa Maria delle Vergini** (1582), with a rich stucco interior, a fine Nativity by Tintoretto (1587), and a stuffed crocodile.

Recanati, between Macerata and Loreto, was the birthplace of Italy's greatest modern poet, Giacomo Leopardi (1798–1837), and the town has made a discreet cottage industry out of this melancholy soul. His family, still residing in the **Casa Leopardi e Biblioteca** in Piazzuola Sabato del Villaggio, permits visits to the library where Giacomo spent much of his dismal stifled childhood (*t 071 757 3380; open daily 9–12.30 and 2.30–5.30; summer 9–7; adm*). Really keen fans can study the poet's death mask and first editions in the neighbouring **Centro Nazionale di Studi Leopardiani** (*t 071 757 0604; open summer Mon–Fri 9–12.30 and 3.30–6.30, Sat 9–12.30; winter Mon–Fri 9–12.30 and 4.30–6, Sat 9.30–12.30*). Below, the gardens take in the never-ending panorama of hills of Leopardi's famous poem, the *Colle dell'Infinito*. The Cappuccin church by the palace contains the unusual *Our Lady of the Salad*, while relics of another favourite son, tenor Beniamino Gigli, fill the **Pinacoteca** (*t 071 757 0410; open summer Tues–Sun 9–1 and 3–10; winter Tues–Fri 9–12 and 3–7, Sat and Sun 9–1 and 3–8; adm*); other highlights are works by Lorenzo Lotto, including what may be the silliest ever Annunciation (1528).

South of Macerata, the valley of the Chienti carries you deeper into the province, towards the Monti Sibillini. At Corridonia, four kilometres south, is an interesting 7th-century Byzantine church, **San Claudio al Chienti**, built over the ruins of an ancient Roman villa, with a pair of round campanili. The **Pinacoteca** (*open by request; call t 0733 431 832*) has another remarkable Madonna by Carlo Crivelli, enclosed in a wreath of angels. Ten kilometres east of Corridonia, Monte San Giusto's church of **Santa Maria Telusiano** has a dramatic Crucifixion by Lorenzo Lotto (1531).

Tolentino, further up the Chienti valley on the SS77, is one of the larger hilltowns in the Marches, prosperous and modern on the outside and not much to look at until you reach the walled medieval centre and its **Santuario di San Nicola** (***t*** *0733 969 996; open daily 7–12 and 3.30–7.30*). San Nicola da Tolentino (1245–1305) was a miracle-working Augustan preacher whose special concern was souls in Purgatory. The impressive **portal** (1430s), set in a restrained Baroque façade, was designed by the Florentine Nanni di Bartolo. An artist known only as the 'Maestro di Tolentino' left a beautiful series of Giottesque frescoes in the **Cappellone**: intense, inspired work that bears comparison with the best trecento painting in Tuscany. Around the attractive cloister, wreathed in wisteria, are a series of **museums** (*open daily 9.30–12 and 4–7*) containing silverwork, ceramics, a giant *presepio*, a spooky diorama of the life of San Nicola, and ex-votos testifying to the saint's spiritual prowess. **Piazza della Libertà** (with a fine assortment of palaces) has a fascinating clock tower that will tell you the phases of the moon, the canonical hour and the day.

Camerino and the Monti Sibillini

Camerino, upriver on its ridge, passed the time during the Midle Ages in endless fighting with arch-enemy Fabriano just to the north. Home to a small university since the 1300s, it has two picture galleries, the **Museo Diocesano** (***t*** *0737 630 444; closed indefinitely for restoration*) and the **Pinacoteca** (***t*** *0737 402 310; open Tues–Sun Apr–Sept 10–1 and 4–7; Oct–Mar 10–1 and 3–6; adm*); the best works are by local quattrocento painter Girolamo di Giovanni. In the main piazza, Da Varano's elegant Renaissance **Palazzo Ducale** has an Urbino-style courtyard and frescoed halls (now a law faculty).

Beyond Camerino, narrow mountain roads lead over the Apennines to Foligno and Spoleto in Umbria. The **Alte Valli del Fiastrone**, the mountainous region to the south, is peppered with castles, towers and fortresses; the most striking is the ruined white castle east of Camerino, the **Rocca di Varano**, from the 1200s. Three kilometres away is a lovely, isolated duecento church, **San Giusto**.

Further south, the mountains grow higher, reaching a climax in the dark, dramatic legendary range of the **Monti Sibillini**, the most striking mountains in the Apennines, the habitat of wolves and scores of rare wildflowers and orchids, all now protected in a national park. No one is quite sure how the 'Mountains of the Sibyls' got their name; ancient writers record no such oracular priestesses in these parts. Italy, though, is full of stories about them, and supposedly these mountains gave birth to the legend of Wagner's *Tannhäuser*. The Sibillini's highest peak is **Monte Vettore** (8,123ft); its uncanny Lago di Pilato is associated with Pontius Pilate, who is said to have thrown himself into its waters to drown in remorse, turning the lake red as blood.

Arquata del Tronto is a lovely village under a 13th-century Rocca, a *comune* that borders on four regions: the Marches, Umbria, Lazio and Abruzzo. In one of its *frazioni*, Capodacqua, is a little octagonal church, Madonna del Sole, attributed to Cola dell'Amatrice, who may also have painted the frescoes within. Just beyond Arquata you can take a slow but often spectacular, twisting road over the 1,500m pass, the **Forca Canapine**, and continue through the spectacular mountain meadow called the Piano Grande, or take the dull new tunnel into Umbria.

Ascoli Piceno

Urbino, at the northern end of the Marches, and Ascoli at the southern, are almost polar opposites. Unlike the northern town, led by its enlightened, aesthetic dukes, Ascoli with its long heritage as a free *comune* has always had to do for itself. It's a beautiful city, but beautiful in a gritty, workaday manner like Florence. The hard knocks that it has taken in its 2,500 years have helped make it a city of character.

History

Ascoli, as its name implies, began with the Piceni, and probably served as the centre of their confederation, united under the sign of their totem woodpecker. To the Romans, *Asculum Picenum* was an early ally after its conquest in 286 BC but later proved a big headache. Asculum fought Rome in the Samnite Wars, and initiated the pan-Italian revolt of the Social Wars. The Romans took the city in 89 BC and razed it to the ground, refounding it with a colony of veterans. The street plan has hardly changed since then; it is one of the most perfect examples in Italy of a rectilinear Roman *castrum*.

In the Dark Ages, Ascoli's defensible position between steep ravines helped avert trouble. Its citizens, too, showed admirable determination, defeating Odoacer's Goths on one occasion, and the Byzantines and Saracens on several others. Despite periods under the rule of others, it emerged by the 1100s as a strong free *comune*. Reminders of this glorious period are everywhere – in the 13th-century Palazzo del Popolo, the clutch of tall, noble towers like those of San Gimignano, and in the famous Quintana jousting contest held the first weekend in August. With the coming of papal rule in the 15th century, Ascoli lost its freedom immediately, and its prosperity gradually, only recovering some of its wealth and importance in the last 100 years.

Piazza del Popolo

Like Rome, Ascoli is built of travertine, and like Rome, it has more traffic than it can handle, so your first impression may be of a grey, sooty town that shows its age. It's more wonder, then, that the central **Piazza del Popolo** can be so nonchalantly, so effortlessly, one of the most beautiful squares in Italy. This is no grand architectural ensemble, not monumental, not even symmetrical, and it's a real town square, with children riding bikes and playing football. But the travertine paving shines almost like marble; the low brick arcades around it give it architectural unity, and a setting for two fine buildings bearing statues of popes who keep an eye on the bustle.

The 13th-century **Palazzo dei Capitani del Popolo** was begun in the 1200s and redone in the late 16th century, after its papal governor set it on fire to discomfit his enemies. It has a façade by Ascoli's best-known architect and artist, Cola dell'Amatrice, and a statue of Paul III over its huge portal. At the narrow end of the piazza, the 1260 church of **San Francesco** (*open daily 9.30–12.30 and 4–7.30*) turns its back on the square, but the apse and transepts are the best part of the building – a classic, austere ascent of Gothic bays and towers under a low dome added in the late 15th century. Over the south door is a statue of Pope Julius II. The façade, around the corner, is a strange, flat square of travertine with a tiny plain rose window and a good sculpted portal,

Getting Around

The only **train** service to Ascoli is on a dead-end branch off the Adriatic coastline, from San Benedetto del Tronto. The station (trains roughly once an hour; **t** 0736 341 004) is on Viale Marconi in the new town. **Buses**, for Fermo, Ancona and Rome, leave from Viale Alcide de Gasperi behind the cathedral. Info on trains and buses can be obtained from the Brunozzi travel agency, Corso Trento e Trieste, near Piazza del Popolo, **t** 0736 262 128.

Tourist Information

Piazza del Popolo 1, **t** 0736 253 045.

Where to Stay and Eat

Ascoli Piceno ✉ 63100

One of Ascoli's attractions is that it is largely undiscovered, but that also means choices for accommodation are few.

*******Gioli**, Via Alcide De Gasperi 14, **t** 0736 255 550 (*moderate*). A pleasant hotel near the cathedral, with a small garden.

*******Marche**, Viale Kennedy 34, **t** 0736 45475 (*moderate*). A modern, comfortable choice about 1.5km east of the centre.

******Pennile**, Via Spalvieri, **t** 0736 41645 (*moderate*). A modern place in the same area, quiet and set amidst the pines.

***Pavoni**, Via Navicella 135, **t** 0736 342 575 (*cheap*). Ten simple rooms in the centre.

Cantina dell'Arte, Rua della Lupa 8, **t** 0736 255 620 (*cheap*). An old palace in the centre, with hearty local specialities and pitchers of wine, plus a handful of rooms to stay in.

To most Italians Ascoli means wonderful *olive ascolane*, stuffed, breaded and fried. It's one of the most tedious dishes to prepare, so you won't often find them outside Ascoli.

Tornasacco, Piazza del Popolo 36, off Piazza Arringo, **t** 0736 254 151 (*moderate*). Olives and many other specialities *all'ascolana*, alongside tagliatelle with lamb sauce, very good local cheeses and charcuterie. *Closed Fri, part of July and Christmas–New Year.*

Gallo d'Oro, Corso Vittorio Emanuele 13, **t** 0736 253 520 (*moderate*). A restaurant that's been doing business for 30 years, offering good food (fresh seafood on Weds and Fri) in its three dining rooms, including a tourist menu featuring the famous olives, *funghi porcini* and *tartufi*. *Closed Mon, Aug and Christmas–New Year.*

C'era Una Volta, Via Piagge 336, 6km south of town on the Colle San Marco road, **t** 0736 261 826 (*cheap*). A restaurant offering hearty soups, stuffed gnocchi, and olives fried with lamb. *Closed Tues.*

Gastronomia Enoteca Migliori, Piazza Arringo 2. One of the best places in town to sample the famous olives.

guarded by sarcastic-looking lions. Inside are some grand and simple Gothic vaults. The southern end of the façade adjoins the **Loggia dei Mercanti**, built by the Wool Corporation – a medieval-style manufacturers' guild – in the early 1500s. On the north side, one of two Franciscan cloisters has become Ascoli's busy and colourful market.

Via del Trivio, in front of San Francesco, is the centre of activity in Ascoli; follow it northwards to Ascoli's oldest and prettiest neighbourhoods, on the cliffs above the Tronto river, where you'll find most of the city's surviving towers. Ascoli has as many of these medieval family-fortresses as San Gimignano in Tuscany, but they are not as well known; the tallest is the **Torre degli Ercolani** on Via Soderini. Piazza Ventidio Basso, the medieval commercial centre, has two good churches. One is 11th-century **SS. Vincenzo ed Anastasio**, with an unfinished Renaissance façade divided into 64 squares that once framed frescoes, and some Romanesque carvings around the portal; there is a miraculous well in the crypt that used to cure leprosy, until the waters were diverted. The second is gloomy Gothic 13th-century **San Pietro Martire**, with a portal from 1523 by Cola dell'Amatrice.

From here, picturesque Via di Solestà leads to the northern tip of Ascoli; a doughty single-arch Roman bridge, the **Ponte di Solestà**, still carries traffic across to the suburbs without a creak or groan. If you cross it and walk along the river bank to the east, you'll see signs for **Sant'Emidio alle Grotte**, on the street of the same name, an elegant 1623 Baroque façade that closes off the front of a cave; here St Emidio, Ascoli's patron, was martyred, and the site became the city's earliest place of Christian worship.

Around the northern edge of Ascoli, the lovely Tronto valley is a perfect picnic spot. Parts of Ascoli's walls show the characteristic diamond-shaped Roman brickwork (*opus reticulatum*). At the western entrance to the town, the **Porta Gemina**, a little Roman gate, spans the Via Salaria. Finally there's **San Gregorio Magno**, built over a Roman temple of Vesta, with two columns and more *opus reticulatum*.

Piazza Arringo

Ascoli's oldest square, monumental Piazza Arringo, is home to the **cathedral** (***t*** *0736 259 774; open daily 8–12.30 and 4–7.30*), a 12th-century building similar to San Francesco but with a façade from the 1530s, also by Cola dell'Amatrice. In a chapel on the south side there's an inevitable cucumber in the beautiful restored polyptych by Carlo Crivelli; in the crypt, there's a Gothic tomb of a knight; another curious tomb left of the altar shows the deceased leaning forwards on his books, as if lazily attending Mass. The **Museo Diocesano** (***t*** *0736 259 901; open Tues–Thurs and Sun 9–12*), in the adjacent bishop's palace, has two rare statues in travertine, of Adam and Eve (1300) from a pulpit; works by Cola dell'Amatrice (whose style changed tremendously after he went to Rome to see the Raphaels); and a Carlo Crivelli (three apples).

The 10th-century octagonal **baptistry,** to the side of the cathedral, stands resolutely in the middle of one of Ascoli's busiest streets. Facing the cathedral, behind the fierce dragons and seahorses in the twin Renaissance fountains, is the **Palazzo Arringo**, the 13th-century town hall hidden behind an imposing Baroque façade. It houses the **Pinacoteca Civica** (***t*** *0736 298 213; open summer daily 9–7; winter Tues and Thurs 9.30–1 and 3–6.30, Weds, Fri and Sat 1.30–6.45, Sun 2.30–7; adm*), with more paintings by Cola dell'Amatrice and other local artists, as well as Titian, Van Dyck and, of course, Crivelli, plus ceramics and musical instruments, and a superb 13th-century English-made cope that Pope Nicolas IV (a native of Ascoli) donated to the cathedral in 1288.

Across the square, in Palazzo Panichi ('Panicky Palace'), the **Museo Archeologico** (***t*** *0736 253 562; open daily 8.30–7; adm*) has some good bronzes of the ancient Piceni, some of the stones they hurled at the Romans, engraved with curses, and a plan of the city in Roman times. A walk north of Piazza Arringo takes you past some of the palaces of medieval Ascoli, with strange carvings and morally uplifting inscriptions on the old houses; one, the **Palazzo Bonaparte** on Via Bonaparte, was built by a prominent 1500s family that local legend claims as the ancestors of the famous Bonapartes; Napoleon himself said he didn't know if it were true or not. The 16th-century Palazzo Malaspina at Corso Mazzini 224, one of the fancier buildings, houses the **Civica Galleria d'Arte Contemporanea** (***t*** *0736 248 633; open Tues–Sun 9–1 and 4–7; adm*), providing a good introduction to Italian modern art, from Futurist Gino Severini to Lucio Fontana, a central figure of Arte Povera.

Abruzzo and Molise

15

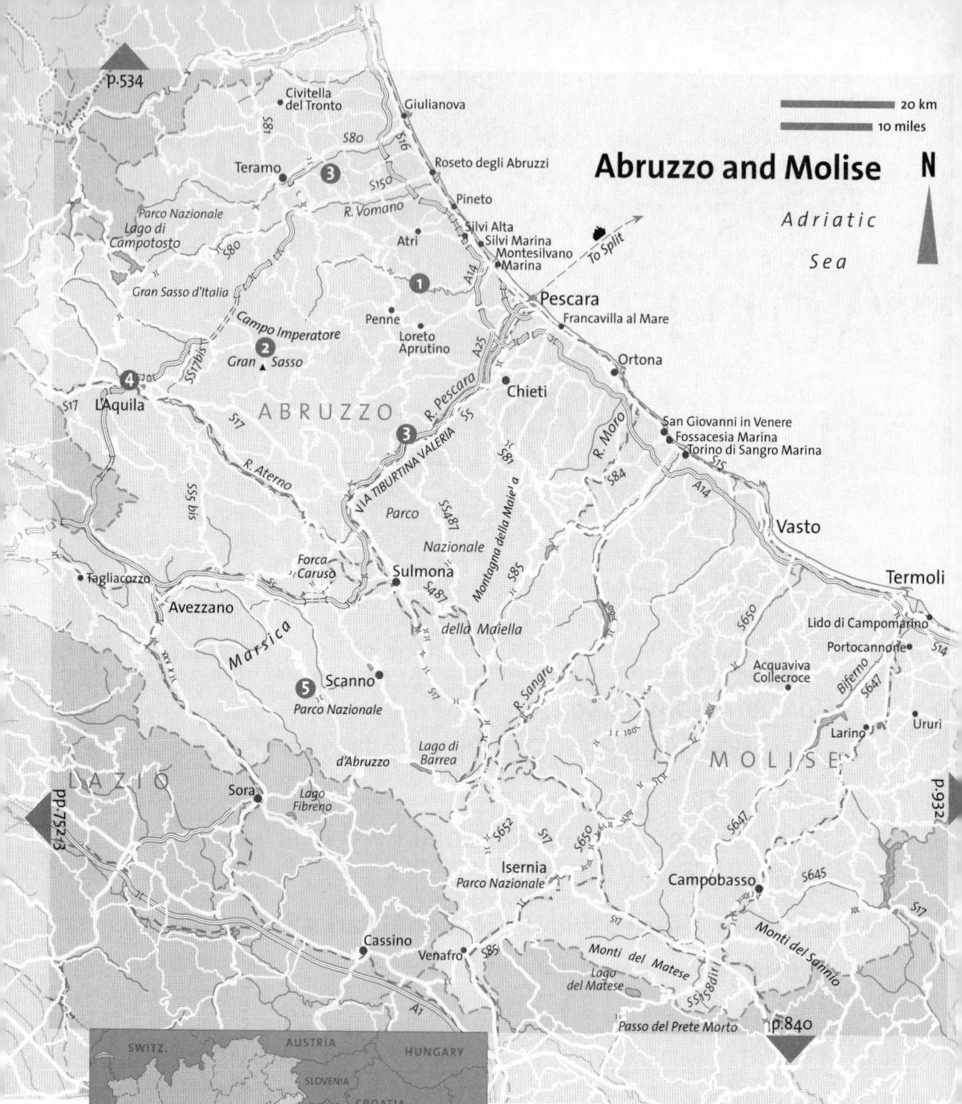

Highlights

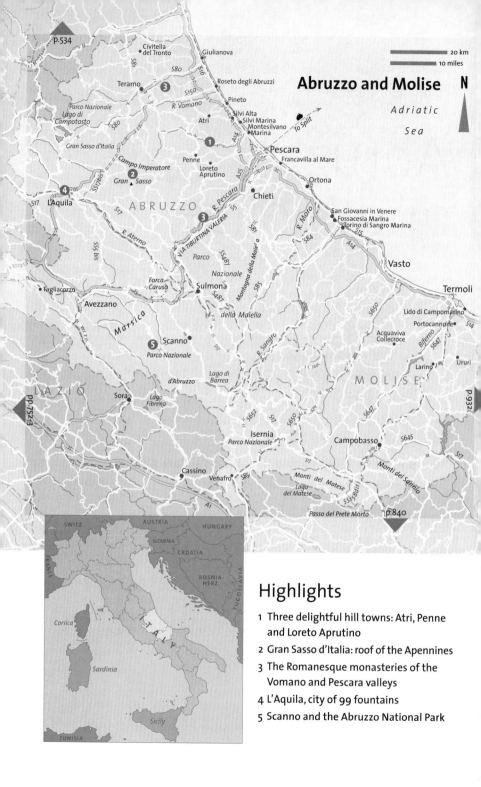

1 Three delightful hill towns: Atri, Penne and Loreto Aprutino
2 Gran Sasso d'Italia: roof of the Apennines
3 The Romanesque monasteries of the Vomano and Pescara valleys
4 L'Aquila, city of 99 fountains
5 Scanno and the Abruzzo National Park

In Italy's long and narrow peninsula, dense with ruins, cities and art, packed with *autostrade*, pizzerias and sultry sunglassed signorinas, Abruzzo and Molise come as a breath of fresh air. Sparsely populated and marginal to the great affairs of state, these two regions stand out for their majestic natural beauty; vast tracts of unspoiled wilderness encompass the highest peaks of the Apennines, the habitat of Italy's unique species of bear. With its four national or regional parks, three of them recently established, Abruzzo has fully one-third of its land reserved for nature: the most, the Abruzzesi claim, of any region in Europe.

Because of the harsh and rugged terrain, of which only small pockets are suitable for agriculture, the region's economy has traditionally been pastoral, but with an emphasis on crafts: ceramics; wood, gold and iron-work; weaving and lace-making. And though many towns wear the proud badge of modernity, the Abruzzese have little care to compete with Milan and Rome – like Candide, they tend their own garden. Yet from this mountain-bound land of country tradition came two of Italy's most urbane, sophisticated and passionate poets, Ovid and Gabriele D'Annunzio, and its greatest modern philosopher, Benedetto Croce. It is also the region most enthusiastic about rugby: L'Aquila has been Italy's national champion several times.

History

In prehistoric times the coast of **Abruzzo** formed part of a little-known Bronze Age culture, the Middle Adriatic, that produced the enigmatic *Warrior* in Chieti's archaeology museum (*see* p.569). Culture was less advanced up in the hills, but the different Italic tribes who gathered here – the Praetutii, the Vestini, the Paeligni and others, of whom next to nothing is known beyond their names – provided a formidable challenge to Roman expansion before being overwhelmed by the legions in the Social Wars of 91–82 BC.

After the fall of Rome, the Lombards ruled what is now the Abruzzo as part of their Duchy of Spoleto, while Molise went to the Duchy of Benevento. The Normans under King William I of Sicily picked up the region from the English pope Adrian IV, and Emperor Frederick II – who inherited the Norman possessions in Italy – made the Abruzzo an independent province. Frederick had grand plans for the region, but they died with him as the Abruzzo was swallowed up by the Angevins, then kings of Naples. Like Umbria, Lazio and most of the Marche, Abruzzo and Molise then began to stagnate – the only difference being that these regions stagnated under the kings of Naples, rather than under the popes. It was the Bourbons who divided the Abruzzo into four territories – Abruzzo Citeriore, Ulteriore Primo, Ulteriore Secondo and Molise – which is why you'll often see the region's name in the plural (the Abruzzi).

But if Abruzzo was neglected and sucked dry by the Neapolitans, its lot under the kings of Italy was scarcely better, and thousands migrated to North America, Britain and other parts of Europe – among them the father of Dante Gabriel Rossetti and the ancestors of Madonna. Only since the Second World War, with the small boom of its compact seaside resorts, the development of small-scale industries and the building of new roads by the Cassa per il Mezzogiorno, as well as the growing interest in the unsullied charms of its landscape, has the tide of emigration been stemmed.

Food and Wine

Abruzzo pasta and saffron are sold all over Italy, but the great local speciality is *maccheroni alla chitarra*, square spaghetti named after the ingenious implement that is used to cut it: a wooden frame with metal strings called a guitar, which you can buy in most markets. Inland Abruzzo is mountainous, and well-suited to sheep-rearing; lamb dishes (especially grilled or roasted) are popular here, along with pork, rabbit and game dishes. The local variant of *pecorino* cheese, made from sheep's milk, is often served with pasta, while another favourite, *scamorza* (a bit like mozzarella), often apppears grilled as a main course. As in all coastal areas of Italy, the coastal areas of Abruzzo have their own favourite fish stews, and a squid speciality – squid stuffed with anchovies, breadcrumbs and garlic.

The food of the Molise uses many of the same basic ingredients as Abruzzo cooking, except that here you're likely to come across more tripe and offal, and virtually everything tends to be flavoured with little hot red peppers, called *diavolini* ('little devils') by the Molisani – they are increasingly popular in the Abruzzo too. Serious heat, long relegated to home cooking, is making a comeback in restaurants. The hand-made pasta here is *cavatelli*, shaped like tiny shells usually in a lamb sauce. Montepulciano d'Abruzzo is the best-known wine of the area. It's a smooth, dry red that, like many Italian wines, is best drunk within three years.

Belted with mountains, **Molise** is an atavistic, introspective backwoods, designated its own region not so much for historical as for cultural reasons. This rather charming patch of the Abruzzi that got away has its own customs and dialect – a result of its impossible geography and the large Slav and Albanian settlements established in the 15th and 16th centuries. Molise is one of the last regions in Italy where women still don traditional costumes to please themselves and not the shutter-happy hordes.

Northern Abruzzo

Down the Coast: from Giulianova to Termoli

Small, inexpensive seaside resorts packed with Italian families in summer, and some beautiful works of art and churches of the Romanesque era, are the main attractions along the Adriatic Coast and its hinterland. If you're not into Italian-style seaside holidays – where everyone pays for a beach chair, umbrella and changing facilities laid out in neat rows, in order to watch everyone else do the same thing – you may have difficulty finding stretches of beach where you can just relax on the sand under the pines.

Giulianova, Roseto and the Lower Vomano Valley

Between the Marche and Pescara, the Adriatic is lined with the same kind of small Italian family resorts that are found south of Ancona; places such as Alba Adriatica, Giulianova, Roseto degli Abruzzi, Silvi and Pineto all offer big beaches, modern hotels, amusement arcades and playgrounds. The most interesting is **Giulianova**, with its medieval old town set back behind the beachfront sprawl. Within the old walls stands the town's best monument, the Romanesque **Santa Maria a Mare**, with unusual bas-reliefs on its façade (*normally closed to the public, but you may be able to make an appointment with Don Ennio to visit,* ***t*** *085 800 7044*), and the Renaissance cathedral. The SS80 turns inland here for Téramo (*see* p.571).

Roseto degli Abruzzi, another resort out of the same mould, lies near the mouth of the Vomano, one of the principal rivers coming down from the Gran Sasso, and has fine views up the valley to the naked limestone peaks of the Corno Grande. From Roseto you can head up the valley (on the SS150) to see two Romanesque gems. One is the 11th-century **San Clemente a Guardia Vomano**, near Notaresco (*currently closed for restoration*), whose builders made good use of Roman ruins, fitting them together like a jigsaw. The church houses an unusual and lovely 12th-century *ciborium*.

The other is the abbey of **Santa Maria di Propezzano**, near Morro d'Oro (*to visit contact Signora Pompeo, owner of the bar next to the church,* ***t*** *085 895 8318*), where the Abruzzese fondness for simple forms has created a handsome asymmetrical façade and a charming two-storey cloister. The interior is embellished with 12th- and 13th-century frescoes, the cloister with scenes by the 17th-century Polish artist Sebastiano Majewski. A side road to the north leads to Canzano, famous for its *tacchino alla canzanese* – turkey in aspic.

Atri and Penne

Pineto, another little resort with a pretty pine-lined beach, has for its landmark the **Torre di Cerrano**, built by Charles V against the Ottoman threat and now a merchant marine research station. Pineto is a starting point for visiting **Atri** (10 kilometres inland), a lovely natural balcony eight kilometres from the sea and 1,400ft above it by car or ARPA bus (*15 times a day Mon–Sat on the Pescara–Pineto route*). Atri stands on the site of the ancient Sabine city and Roman colony of *Hatriaticum*, founded under the sign of the woodpecker, the bird of Mars. Atri disputes with Adria in the Veneto the honour of having lent its name to the Adriatic Sea – a controversy that raged among ancient scholars such as Pliny, Livy and Strabo. Atri tried to boost its claim by engraving the fact on its singular coins – the heaviest ever minted in western Europe, guaranteed to put a hole in the pocket of any toga.

Roman sites in town include the remains of ancient baths, which are located in the crypt of Atri's majestic 13th-century **cathedral**. This building has an austerely elegant square façade and matching campanile, and in the choir there are some excellent quattrocento frescoes by Andrea de Litio, the Piero della Francesca of the Abruzzo, who gave his scenes of The Life of the Virgin surreal landscapes of knobbly hills and imaginary towers. In the **cathedral museum** (***t*** *085 879 8140; open June–Sept Mon, Tues, Thurs–Sun 10–12 and 4–8; Oct–May Thurs–Tues 10–12 and 3–5; adm*) there are ivories, polyptychs and statues, majolica by Grue of Castelli (*see* p.575), and mosaics and fragments dating from the 9th-century church that preceded the cathedral. During the Middle Ages and Renaissance, Atri was controlled by the Acquaviva dukes, whose frowning 14th-century **Palazzo Ducale** (now the town hall and post

Getting There and Around

Pescara airport (**t** 085 432 421) has daily **flights** to Milan and Turin with Air One (**t** 085 421 3022) and direct flights to London Stansted and Frankfurt with Ryanair (**t** 0871 246 0000, *www.ryanair.com*).

In summer, **boats** and hydrofoils link Ortona to Vasto, and Vasto to Términoli, the Tremiti Islands and Rodi Garganico in Puglia. Térmoli is the main port for the Tremiti (*see* Puglia, p.943), with **hydrofoils** and motorboats daily.

Coastal **train** and **bus** services are good. There is a direct rail line from Rome to Chieti and Pescara, via Sulmona, and between Bologna and Lecce, the length of the coast. ARPA (**t** 06 4423 3928), the Abruzzo bus company, links Chieti with Pescara (3 times a day).

Tourist Information

Loreto Aprutino: Via dei Normanni 8, **t** 085 829 0484.
Montesilvano: Via Romagna 6, **t** 085 445 8859, freephone from within Italy **t** 800 656 256.
Pescara: Via Paolucci 3, **t** 085 421 9981, and Piazza I Maggio 3, freephone within Italy **t** 800 502 520, *www.regione.abruzzo.it*
Chieti: Palazzo INAIL, Via B. Spaventa 29, **t** 0871 63640.
Ortona: Piazza della Repubblica 9, **t** 085 906 3841.
Vasto: Piazza del Popolo 18, **t** 0873 367 312.
Térmoli: Piazza Bega, **t** 0875 706 754.

Where to Stay and Eat

Most of the hotels in the region are fairly modern. Some prices have rocketed, but they are a bargain compared with the rest of Italy.

Giulianova ✉ 64022

****Grand Hotel Don Juan**, Lungomare Zara 97, **t** 085 800 8341 (*very expensive*). The smartest hotel on this stretch of coast, with its own beach, a pool, tennis courts and a garden. There's a minimum 3-night stay. *Closed Oct–mid-May.*

***Promenade**, Lungomare Zara 119, **t** 085 800 3338 (*moderate*), *www.hotelpromenade.com*. A smaller and less stylish option with similar amenities. *Closed Oct–mid-May.*

Beccaceci, Via Zola 28, **t** 085 800 3550 (*expensive*). The Abruzzo's most celebrated seafood restaurant, with long-established fish and pasta dishes such as squid stuffed with prawns and *linguine alla giuliese*. *Closed Sun eve, Mon and 27 Dec–10 Jan.*

Osteria della Stracciavocc', Via Trieste 124, **t** 085 800 5326 (*moderate*). Traditional cuisine, including outstanding pasta and seafood. *Closed Mon, Tues lunch and 2wks Oct.*

Pescara ✉ 65100

Pescara has by far the most hotels and restaurants on the coast, but tranquillity is a rare commodity in summer, and full board is usually required in July and Aug.

****Carlton**, Viale Riviera 35, **t** 085 373 125 (*expensive*). A very comfortable resort palace with a private beach.

****Esplanade**, Piazza I Maggio 46, **t** 085 292141, *www.esplanade.net* (*expensive*). The fanciest hotel in town, in a *belle époque* mansion facing the sea.

***Bellariva**, Viale Riviera 213, **t** 085 471 2641 (*moderate*). An unpretentious, friendly place to stay, good for families.

***Salus**, Lungomare Matteotti 13/1, **t** 085 374 196 (*moderate*). Good standard rooms and a private beach. *Closed Christmas.*

Guerino, Viale della Riviera 4, **t** 085 421 2065 (*expensive*). The city's best seafood restaurant, elegantly furnished and boasting a seafront terrace. The Adriatic speciality of fillets of John Dory (*pesce San Pietro*) with *prosciutto* go down especially well. *Closed Tues (except July and Aug) and 22 Dec–5 Jan.*

office) contains a cheerful courtyard. The outskirts of Atri boast some strange geology in the form of once-inhabited caves, eroded rock formations – *calanchi* – and 'Dantesque pits'.

The pale pink town of **Penne**, further to the south, was an important town of the Vestini and preserves a rare if eclectic urban harmony, its narrow winding streets

Duilio, Via Regina Margherita 11, **t** 085 378 278 (*moderate*). Delicately prepared dishes, most of which feature seafood. *Closed Sun eve, Mon and Aug.*

La Terrazza Verde, Via Tiberi 4–8, **t** 085 413 239 (*moderate*). One of the very restaurants in the area that doesn't serve any fish dishes. Located in a panoramic setting high up in the hills and boasting a beautiful garden terrace, it offers delicious gnocchi and duck, a popular dish in Abruzzo, prepared in a variety of different ways. *Closed Weds and 10 days July.*

Trattoria Roma, Via Trento 86, **t** 085 295 374 (*cheap*). A secluded spot offering hearty Abruzzese cooking, featuring at least one very good fish choice on the daily-changing menu. It's very popular among the locals so try to reserve in advance. *Closed Sun and 1wk July.*

Montesilvano Marina ✉ 65016

****__Serena Majestic__, Viale Kennedy 12, **t** 085 83699, *www.serenamajestic.it* (*moderate*). A large, modern, comfortable hotel on the beach, with gardens, tennis courts and two pools.

***__Piccolo Mondo__, Via Marinelli 86, **t** 085 445 2647, *www.hotelpiccolomondo.com* (*cheap*). One of the best-value hotels on the coast, with 20 rooms, a roof terrace and a garden. A good choice for a family holiday. Full board is obligatory in July and Aug.

Chieti ✉ 66100

Venturini, Via De Lollis 10, **t** 0871 330 663 (*moderate*). A local institution offering fairly priced, well-cooked meals, including mushroom risotto with mozzarella, a speciality. *Closed Tues.*

Nonna Elisa, Via Per Popoli 265, Loc. Brecciarola (near the freeway exit), **t** 0871 684 152 (*moderate*). A strictly Abruzzese experience, offering delicious food. *Closed Mon, 1wk July and 1wk Sept.*

Guardiagrele

****__Villa Maiella__, Via Sette Dolori 30, **t** 0871 809 362, *http://villamaiella.it* (*moderate*). One of the most popular hotel-restaurants in the area, with 14 comfortable rooms, traditional but imaginative cooking, enthusiastic service and excellent wine. *Closed Mon and 2wks July.*

Lanciano

La Ruota, Via Per Fossacesia 62, **t** 0872 44590 (*expensive*). A popular restaurant among locals, offering some lovely seafood dishes and a handful of meat dishes. *Closed Sun and 2wks July.*

Vasto

Vasto is somewhat of a gastronomic capital on the coast.

All'Hostaria del Pavone, Via Barbarotta 15, **t** 0873 60227 (*moderate*). Great *brodetto* – local soup that has nourished generations of sailors – and other fish specialities. *Closed Tues Oct–May, and several wks Jan and Feb.*

Térmoli ✉ 86039

****__Corona__, Corso M. Milano 2/a, **t** 0875 84043 (*moderate*). A medium-sized, traditional hotel located in the town centre, with good food. *Closed Sun.*

Z'Bass, Via Oberdan 8, **t** 0875 706703 (*expensive*). A tempting fish menu in a lively atmosphere. There are tables outdoors in summer. *Closed Mon Oct–May.*

Da Noi Tre, Via Ruffini 47, **t** 0875 703 639 (*moderate*). A modest, old-fashioned trattoria with a blaring TV, serving good fish. *Closed Mon in winter.*

Torre Saracena, SS16 Adriatica Highway, 3km north of the town centre, **t** 0875 703 318 (*moderate*). A restaurant in an old Saracen watchtower on the beach, serving the freshest fish prepared in surprising ways. The moderate set menu includes wine. *Closed Mon and Nov.*

dotted with Renaissance mansions. Its sights include the ancient crypt of the cathedral, itself destroyed in the Second World War and rebuilt; the crypt houses the **Museo Civico** (*open daily 10–1 and 3–6; adm*), with some eccentric, fascinating medieval sculpture. **Santa Maria in Colleromano** (*ring the bell if closed; church museum open Sun 9–12*), a 15-minute walk from the centre, has good 14th–15th-century statues.

South of Pineto, the SS16bis heads inland from Montesilvano Marina, a satellite resort of Silvi, towards another clutch of interesting villages. In **Loreto Aprutino**, the church of **Santa Maria in Piano** (*open daily in summer 9–7; winter 9–4*) contains some 14th–15th-century frescoes – the *Life of St Thomas Aquinas* and the spectacular *'Particular Judgement'*, portraying Heaven's elect marching to the pearly gates on a bridge the width of a hair. Loreto also has the **Museo Civico della Civiltà Contadina**, a collection of tools, traditional craft work and naïve tableaux of peasant life; the **Museo delle Ceramiche** of local ceramics; an **archaeological museum**; and the little **Museo dell'Olivo** devoted to the region's fine extra-virgin olive oil (***t*** *0339 441 1319 for all four; all open Sat and Sun 10.30–12.30 and 3.30–5.30; combined adm*). In nearby Moscufo, a village devoted to the mandolin (nearly everyone plays one), **Santa Maria del Lago** merits a visit for its unique 12th-century pulpit adorned with painted reliefs.

Pescara

Pescara is Abruzzo's biggest resort, most prosperous town, a fishing port and a provincial capital. In ancient times its port was shared by several Italic tribes and later by the Romans, who made it the terminus of the Via Valeria–Via Tiburtina (the modern SS5). In 1864 Gabriele D'Annunzio was born here; partly due to his influence, Mussolini poured lots of money into what had become a sleepy fishing village, and a new city was born. D'Annunzio's birthplace, or **Casa Natale** at Corso Manthonè 101 (***t*** *085 60391; open daily 9–1.30; adm*), has a charming little courtyard. The town also has an outdoor theatre built in his honour, the venue for a jazz festival in the first half of July.

The **Museo delle Genti d'Abruzzo** at Via delle Caserme 22 (***t*** *085 451 0026; open summer Mon–Fri 9–1 and 9–midnight, afternoons and weekends by request; winter Mon, Weds and Sun 9–1, Tues and Thurs 9–5 and 2.30–5; adm*) is dedicated to everyday life and popular traditions in the Abruzzo over the centuries. But Pescara's golden egg is its 16-kilometre **sandy beach**, almost solid with hotels, cafés and fish restaurants between the Pescara river and Montesilvano; its old buildings were decimated in the Second World War. Still, this is no Rimini; families bake together in the day, and stroll about eating ice cream in the evening. There are riding stables, go-karts, tennis courts and the pescatorial **Museo delle Meraviglie Marine** (*open Tues and Fri 8.30–1 and 3.30–5.30, Weds, Thurs and Sat 8.30–1; adm*), in Pescara's bustling **fish market** on Lungofiume Paolucci. Close by and facing the sea, the new **Museo d'Arte Moderna 'Vittoria Colonna'** (*opening times vary; call tourist office for details*) hosts temporary exhibitions of modern and contemporary art.

Chieti

For something a bit weightier than gills and beachballs, head up to **Chieti**, about 13 kilometres up the Pescara river. Another provincial capital, Chieti was the Roman *Theate Marrucinorum*, a name that its bishop, Pietro Carafa, made use of when founding the Theatine Order in 1524. Carafa went on to become Paul IV, the most vicious and intolerant of popes, but it's no reflection on Chieti; he was a Neapolitan.

The **Museo Nazionale Archeologico di Antichità** (*open daily 9–6.30; adm*), in the Villa Comunale, is Chieti's star attraction, and one of the region's most important museums: it's the chief repository of pre-Roman and Roman artworks unearthed in the Abruzzo, including the shapely 6th-century BC **Warrior of Capestrano**, dressed like a Mexican bandit and accompanied by an inscription in the language of the Middle Adriatic Bronze Age culture. There is a room of other items found in Bronze Age tombs, and rooms containing Hellenistic and Roman sculptures, tombs, portraits, coins, jewellery and votive offerings, many discovered in *Alba Fucens*, in the Parco Nazionale d'Abruzzo, and at *Amiternum*, near L'Aquila. The documentation of material from Abruzzo's many Upper Palaeolithic caves is displayed with ancient ceramics and artefacts from Italic necropolises.

Out of doors, Chieti retains a dramatic 12th–14th-century Gothic **cathedral**, begun by Charles of Anjou, and a couple of traces of Theate Marrucinorum – the remains of three little temples on Via Spaventa, near the post office. In the eastern residential quarters stand the **Terme Romane** or baths (***t*** *0871 331 668; open daily 9–3*), of which a mighty cistern is the most impressive feature. Best of all are the lovely views, stretching from the sea to the Gran Sasso and Maiella Mountains.

The Via Valeria: Chieti to Pópoli

Inland from Chieti, the old Roman Via Valeria–Via Tiburtina accompanies the A25 up the Pescara valley. There is certainly no shortage of Romanesque churches along the way. In the 10th and 11th centuries there was plenty of empty land in these parts for hard-working Benedictines to put to use. The Lombard dukes were favourable, and this valley developed one of the biggest concentrations of monasteries in Italy, mostly founded from the great Benedictine motherhouse of Montecassino.

At Manoppello Scalo you'll see a steep, prominent hill overlooking the river that once bore a sanctuary and altar (*ara*) to *Dea Bona*, the 'Good Goddess'. In its place stands the delightful 13th-century **Santa Maria Arabona**, a Cistercian Gothic church (founded from Fossanova in Lazio) that owes much of its charm to the big glass wall that now closes off the unfinished nave. Up the hill in **Manoppello** town, is something you can't see anywhere else – the face of Jesus. Manoppello's holy icon, the *Volto Santo*, mysteriously appeared here about 1600, about the same time that one of the greatest relics of St Peter's in Rome dropped out of sight: the veil of Veronica, on which the image of Jesus was impressed when he stopped to wipe his face on it during the carrying of the cross. Large numbers of pilgrims come to see it, at the impressive **Santuario del Volto Santo** on the heights overlooking the village.

Beyond Manoppello, on the tortuous SS539 that skirts the northern edge of the Montagna della Maiella, stands perhaps the finest of all the Benedictine churches in the Abruzzo, in one of the loveliest settings — **San Liberatore a Maiella**, above the village of Serramonacesca (*open usual church hours*). The church, which was begun in 1080, shows influences from both Puglia and Lombardy; inside is an excellent carved pulpit and pavement, and fragments of frescoes that include a portrait of Charlemagne. There are some beautiful walks from the church, including an easy botanical walk along the river bank.

Near the village of **Torre de' Passeri**, more Romanesque awaits at **San Clemente a Casauria**, founded by Emperor Louis II (Charlemagne's great-grandson) in 871. The Cistercians took over and rebuilt the church in the 12th century, endowing it with a magnificent three-arched porch and intricately carved capitals, and a stunning portal with reliefs that form a fitting frame for the ornate bronze doors. The same sculptors may also have carved the baldaquin and pulpit in the Romanesque interior. Louis II's original crypt, preserved during reconstruction, is reached by steps from the aisles.

Ortona and Lanciano

Back on the coast, south of Pescara, beyond the pleasant resort of Francavilla al Mare, lies Abruzzo's largest port, **Ortona**. Over the years the town has taken more than its share of damage from earthquakes and warfare, particularly in autumn 1943, when the Germans were well entrenched along a line north of the Sangro river, and thousands of lives were lost in the six-week Battle of the Sangro and Moro rivers before the Germans were routed. There are two large **British military cemeteries** in the vicinity, one near the Moro river, about three kilometres south of Ortona, and the other just south of Torino di Sangro Marina, between Ortona and Vasto.

From Ortona you can take a narrow-gauge local train for an inland loop (though admittedly the bus is much faster), seeing Guardiagrele and Lanciano on the way. The sweet hill town of **Guardiagrele** was a famous goldsmiths' centre in the Renaissance, the birthplace of the renowned Nicola da Guardiagrele in the 15th century; he made the silver crucifix in the treasury of **Santa Maria Maggiore** (***t** 0871 82117 or **t** 0348 414 5800; open mid-July–Aug daily 10–12.30 and 4–7.30; other times call ahead*). This church has a huge exterior fresco of St Christopher by Andrea de Litio, which was believed to bring good luck to any traveller who saw it.

Lanciano, a medieval market town that attracted merchants from all over the Med to its wool and cloth fairs, retains some fine grey stone monuments, such as the **cathedral**, built on top of a Roman bridge. Pilgrims have long come to nearby **San Francesco** for its relics of an 8th-century miracle – some drops of blood and a piece of human heart. According to legend the bread and wine of the Mass really did transubstantiate into flesh and blood for a sceptical monk.

At the northern end of town is **Porta San Biagio**, the only surviving medieval gate. In the medieval quarter, Cittanova, the fine French Gothic church of **Santa Maria Maggiore** holds another work of Nicola da Guardiagrele. Above Cittanova is the 11th-century fortress of **Torri Montanare**, which has great views of the hills and mountains further inland. Lanciano is also the starting point for one of the most spectacular drives in the Abruzzo – the SS84 to Roccaraso, near the Parco Nazionale d'Abruzzo.

San Giovanni in Venere and Vasto

Back on the coast, above the railway station of the small resort of Fossacesia Marina, stands one of Abruzzo's most remarkable monuments, **San Giovanni in Venere** (***t** 0872 60132; open daily 8–8*). 'Venere' refers to Venus, over whose temple this church was erected: temples to the love goddess were often placed in similar spots, high above the sea. Begun as early as the 8th century, the church was rebuilt in 1015 and converted into a Cistercian abbey in 1165. There are several Puglian–Sicilian touches here, perhaps introduced by Frederick II's architects – in the decoration of the narrow windows, the robust figures of the bas-reliefs, and the design of the magnificent marble **Portale della Luna**, the 'Portal of the Moon' (1230). Be sure to walk around the church to see the beautiful apses. Inside, the ceiling is supported by cruciform piers, and there are some old, if not very interesting, frescoes dating back to the 12th century. The large crypt, entered from the aisles, contains ancient columns from the temple of Venus and 12th-century frescoes of a Madonna with St Nicholas and St Michael, resplendent in fine Byzantine court dress.

Further south is **Vasto**, one of the most attractive towns on the Adriatic and the home of Gabriele Rossetti, poet and father of Dante Gabriel and Christina Rossetti. It stands on a low natural terrace above its beach and port, the former attracting large numbers of French as well as Italian tourists. Its narrow streets end at the weathered but distinctive 13th-century castle, with a cylindrical tower. Vasto is proud of its painter, Filippo Palizzi (1818–99), whose works can be seen in the church of **San Pietro**, and in the local **Museo Civico** (*open daily June and Sept 10.30–12.30 and 6.30–10.30; July and Aug 10.30–12.30 and 6.30–midnight; Oct–May 9.30–12.30 and 4.30–8; adm*).

Termoli

Crossing the Trigno river, you enter Molise, which is, in the main, even more rural and unspoiled than Abruzzo, though this may not be immediately apparent from the busy beaches. Termoli gets top billing here – a bright little fishing town with a long sandy beach, palms and oleanders. The diva of the old town, or at least the part that survived a Turkish raid in 1566, is the exotic 13th-century **cathedral**, with its blind Puglian-style arcades; inside is a marble floor of mythological beasts.

Termoli also boasts a **castle** and walls from the same period, both built by Emperor Frederick II. After enjoying the view from the castle, there's nothing more demanding to do than relax on the beach and decide which seafood restaurant to try in the evening. Termoli is also a summer ferry port for the Tremiti Islands (*see* p.943). If Termoli's too crowded, there's another modest resort down the coast, Campomarino. A little further south, the road enters Puglia.

Téramo

From Giulianova the SS80 heads 20 kilometres inland to **Téramo**, midway between the coast and the Gran Sasso. Originally a Roman city, Téramo knew its happiest days in the 14th century under the Angevins, and though it wears mostly 20th-century fashions today, it preserves several fine monuments. The **cathedral** stands out, with its remarkable Cosmati-decorated portal and Romanesque saints; around them a miscellany of lions, collected from here and there, lend feline elegance to the façade, which is as simple, square and ungabled as any in Abruzzo. The cathedral's Ghibelline crenellations recall the days when Téramo was the fief of its bishop, who still possesses the title 'Prince of Téramo', although he no longer makes much use of a special papal dispensation from more rough-and-ready days that allows him to wear armour under his robes and keep his sword handy by the altar. The campanile is from the 15th century. Inside is a silver altar frontal with 30 biblical scenes, a masterpiece by Nicola da Guardiagrele (1448), who also made the silver statues of Mary and Gabriel by the door. The 15th-century polyptych is by the Venetian Jacobello del Fiore.

Near the cathedral lie the ruins of the **Teatro Romano** and, a short distance further on, the original cathedral, **Santa Maria Aprutiensis** (6th–12th century), its name recalling the Italic tribe of the Praetutii who gave their name to *Aprutium* (and hence to Abruzzo). Santa Maria (also called Sant'Anna), built of bits of Roman columns and other ancient fragments, is Téramo's attic of odds and ends – Lombard carvings, a 6th-century *triforium* and ancient angelic frescoes.

In the Franciscan convent of **Madonna delle Grazie** (*open Tues–Sun 10–12 and 3–5; longer afternoon hours in summer*), to the east by Piazza della Libertà, is a painted wooden statue of the Madonna and Child by one of the Abruzzo's best sculptors, Silvestro dell'Aquila (15th century). More quattrocento Abruzzese art is on display in the **Pinacoteca** on Viale Bovio, while the **Museo Archeologico** on Via Delfico displays local finds (***t** 0861 250 873; both open Tues–Sun 9–1 and 3–7; combined ticket for the two museums and convent sold at Museo Archeologico,* see *below; adm*).

Around Téramo

Heading north from Téramo towards Ascoli Piceno on the SS81, the road passes **Campli**, just to the east, a small town with Romanesque and Gothic monuments. The formidable **Palazzo del Comune** was built in the 14th century but much altered in 1520. Romanesque **San Francesco** is a fine embodiment of the Abruzzese ideal that less is more; inside are some 14th-century frescoes. Its former convent houses a **Museo Archeologico** (***t** 0861 569 158; open daily 9–8; adm*), containing artefacts from

Getting Around

Téramo is fairly easily reached by **train**, on a spur from the coastal line at Giulianova. ARPA **buses** (**t** 06 442 33928) also quickly link Téramo to the coast, to Ascoli Piceno and to L'Aquila.

Tourist Information

Via del Castello 10, **t** 0861 244 222, *www.provincia.teramo.it* (*open Mon–Sat 9–1 and Mon–Fri 3.30–6*).

Where to Stay and Eat

Téramo ✉ 64100

******Sporting**, Via De Gasperi 41, **t** 0861 414 723/412 661 (*moderate*). Téramo's most attractive hotel because of its garden, located on the outskirts of town.

***Castello**, Via del Castello 62, **t**0861 247 582 (*cheap*). A basic but adequate option, with 7 rooms and shared bathrooms.

Il Duomo, Via Stazio 9, **t** 0861 242 991 (*moderate*). A restaurant serving local specialities such as *maccheroni alla chitarra*, and a variety of meat dishes, including grilled kid. *Closed Sun eve, Mon, 2nd and 3rd wks Aug and 2wks Jan.*

Osteria al Bottaccio, Via Piano d'Accio 10 (off the Giulianova road), **t** 0861 558 335 (*cheap*). Strictly local cuisine served up in an informal atmosphere. *Closed Sun, 2wks Jan and 3wks Aug.*

Sotto le Stelle, Via dei Mille 59, **t** 0861 247 126. (*cheap*). An informal local hangout. *Closed Sun and 2wks Jan.*

The *Virtù* of Téramo

Téramo has its own culinary speciality, *virtù*, customarily cooked on the first of May. Judging from its ingredients, it began as a way of using up winter stocks and adding the first of the new season's goodies – traditionally, local women each contributed an ingredient. It's a cross between a soup and a stew – a type of minestrone, in fact – based on a stock to which are added 12 kinds of dried peas, beans and lentils, along with celery, sausage and different bits and pieces of pig, such as trotters and ears, all well salted and seasoned with herbs.

the 6th–3rd-century BC Italic necropolis at Campovalano, a kilometre away. Nearby is the abbey and church of **San Pietro**, founded in the 8th century and rebuilt in the 13th; the frescoed figures on the piers inside were designed to be part of the congregation (*to visit the necropolis and San Pietro, call Signore Pietro d'Amalio, owner of the Alimentari store in Campovalano's main square,* **t** *0861 56306, during shop hours*).

A few kilometres north of Campli rises the superbly positioned Renaissance town of **Civitella del Tronto**, crowned by an impregnable castle that the Bourbons managed to hold right to the bitter end in 1861. First built around the year 1000, it has half a kilometre of travertine-walled terrace, lending it its distinctive crew-cut skyline.

The Gran Sasso: 'The Big Rock of Italy'

The Gran Sasso offers alpine grandeur only an hour by motorway from Rome, and as such is an immensely popular ski and hiking resort. There are plans to designate it a nature park, but until then environmentalists and developers will continue to disagree about its future.

Approaching the Gran Sasso from the East, and Castelli

South of Téramo the SS150 divides into two arms embracing the **Gran Sasso**: the main road that joins up with the SS80 from Téramo and continues up the narrow upper **Val di Vomano** to the north – the most scenic road in the region (*see* p.575) – and another that follows the higher **Valle di Mavone** to the south. The latter (SS491) is an excellent approach to the mountains, with the highest peak of the Apennines, the Corno Grande (9,551ft) looming ahead. Several curiosities along the SS491 offer tempting detours – near Castel Castagna there's **Santa Maria di Ronzano** (*opening hours irregular; call* **t** *0861 697 250 mornings only*), a three-nave church embellished with frescoes dated 1181 and among the finest examples of Lombard art in central Italy. Between Montorio al Vomano and Isola del Gran Sasso you can take in the village of **Tossicìa**, with a pretty medieval nucleus lying between two mountain streams; the tiny church of **Sant'Antonio Abate** has a grand 1471 Renaissance portal by the Venetian Antonio Lombardo.

The scenery is stunning as the road reaches **Isola del Gran Sasso**, a fine stone village and a good base for hikes up to the Campo Imperatore (*see* p.576); it has another Romanesque church, **San Giovanni ad Insulam**, as well as a more recent shrine to the

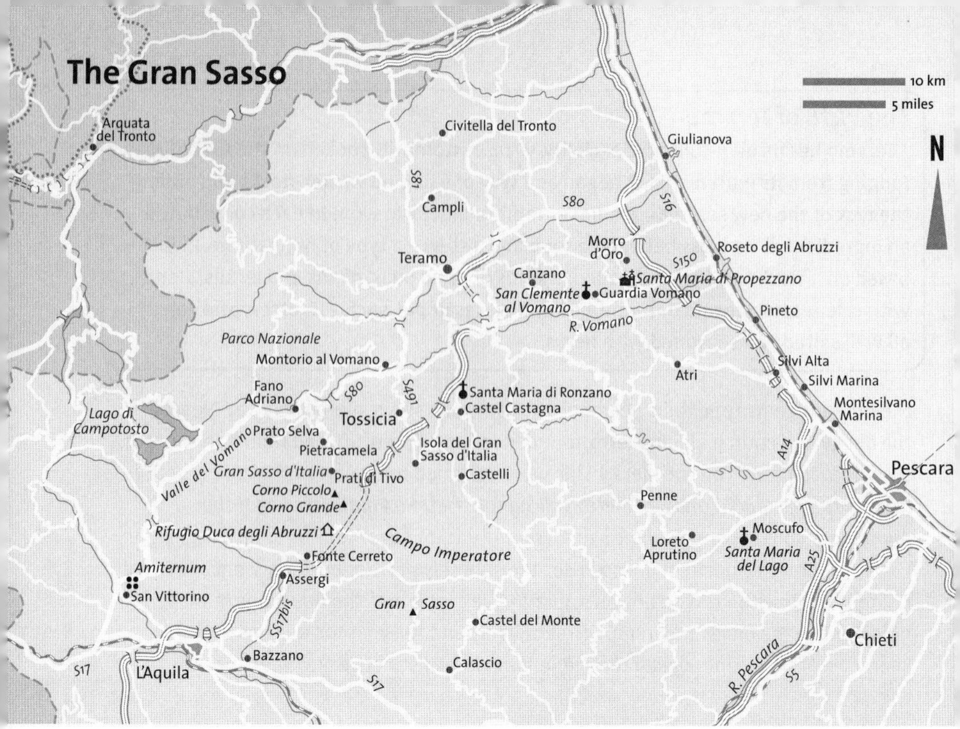

modern patron saint of Abruzzo–Molise, San Gabriele dell'Addolorata, a young Franciscan monk from Assisi who died in the monastery here in 1862. His relics draw pilgrims by the busload – processed through a huge, disconcerting steel-and-concrete basilica designed in shopping mall modern.

To the southeast of Isola, dramatically positioned at the foot of the great wall of Monte Camicia, is **Castelli**, which forms another good mountain base. Castelli is the great centre in the Abruzzo for ceramics – an industry that achieved art and glory in the 17th-century workshops of the Grue and Gentili families. The ceramic tradition is still continued in various workshops throughout the town and during the August ceramics fair, where part of the fun consists in tossing reject plates over the river. Castelli's **Chiesa Madre** contains a majolica *pala* by Francesco Grue, as well as some 12th-century wooden statues.

More of the Grues' work (as well as that of other local craftspeople) may be seen in the **Museo della Ceramica Abruzzese** (***t*** *0861 979 398; open Tues–Sun June–Sept 10–1 and 3–7; Oct–May 9–1; adm*). The museum also serves as a tourist office, which organizes guided tours around Castelli.

Most splendiferous of all is the rural church of **San Donato**, which Carlo Levi quite rightfully dubbed 'The Sistine Chapel of Italian Majolica', for its ceiling (visible from the outside through a grate) of a thousand ceramic tiles – the only ceiling like it in Italy, an impressive 360 square feet covered with a colourful patchwork of folk motifs, including plenty of rabbits, skulls, portraits, notices of various kinds, geometric patterns and so on (1615–17). Also on the outskirts is the derelict Romanesque church of **San Salvatore**, with a charming medieval pulpit.

The Upper Vomano Valley: Téramo to L'Aquila

At **Montorio al Vomano** the SS150 joins the main SS80, the scenic road that, like the more efficent but inevitably less panoramic *autostrada*, links Téramo with L'Aquila. Montorio, which is topped by its grand but never-completed Spanish castle, has an eclectic church, the **Collegiata di San Rocco**, with a façade that has been added to whenever funds were handy; within, the carved wooden Baroque altar and tapestries are the main attraction.

Further up the valley the twin, blunt, snow-shrouded peaks of the **Due Corni del Gran Sasso** look over the shoulder of **Fano Adriano**, an old town and now a small winter and summer resort, with skiing and hiking at Pratoselva. The village's name means 'Hadrian's Temple', although none of this remains; the 12th-century **San Pietro** is modern Fano's finest church, with a Renaissance façade from 1550.

Pietracamela, even higher up in the lap of the Gran Sasso (3,296ft), is a base for hikes over the **Sella dei Due Corni** to the Campo Imperatore (*see* p.576), and for skiing at the Gran Sasso's biggest resort, **Prati di Tivo**, a fine lofty meadow of beech forests.

The SS80 towards L'Aquila continues past the Lago di Campotosto, then winds around the western flank of the Gran Sasso. About 10 kilometres before L'Aquila it comes to **Amiternum**, the ruins of a Sabine city that was mentioned in Virgil's *Aeneid*. Later a Roman colony, this was the birthplace of the poet Sallust. A small theatre, an amphitheatre, houses with mosaics and frescoes, and other relics were brought to light in 1978 (*open daily; can be seen well from outside when closed*).

Nearby, medieval **San Vittorino** has, under the 12th–16th-century church of **San Michele** (*call* **t** *0862 461 695 to arrange a visit*), something out of the ordinary for this part of the world – catacombs. Unlike the great ones in Rome, however, these have been embellished with 15th-century frescoes. A procession is held through them on the last Sunday in May.

Tourist Information

Centro Turistico del Gran Sasso, Corso Vittorio Emanuele 49, L'Aquila, **t** 0862 22146. A helpful travel agency with information on outdoor activities in the region's mountains.

Club Alpino Italiano, Vicolo Fassa 34 (near Piazza Duomo), L'Aquila, **t** 0862 24342 (*open Mon–Sat 6pm–8*). An association providing useful maps and hiking information.

Where to Stay and Eat

The Gran Sasso ✉ 67100

★★★★**Hotel Campo Imperatore**, **t** 0862 400 000 (*moderate*). Mussolini's least favourite hotel (*see* p.576), situated at the top of the cable-car route and very comfortable – there's no reason to escape.

★★★★**Miramonti**, up in Prati di Tivo, **t** 0861 959 621 (*moderate*). A comfortable, modern resort hotel with a garden, pool and tennis courts. *Closed Oct.*

★★**La Villetta**, Fonte Cerreto, by the lower funicular station, **t** 0862 606 171 (*moderate–cheap*). Another hotel that was used to hold Mussolini in 1943. It's a pretty, friendly place that makes a good base for visiting the mountains.

Il Mandrone, Frazione San Pietro, Isola del Gran Sasso d'Italia (about 20km north of Campo Imperatore), **t** 0861 976 152 (*cheap*). Genuine mountain cuisine, including *strongole alla barcarola* – a home-made pasta dressed with 20 different wild herbs from the Gran Sasso – soups, lamb and ricotta-based specialities. *Closed Tues and Weds except in Aug, 10 days Nov–Dec and 10 days Jan–Feb.*

Mussolini's Least Favourite Hotel

Near the upper funicular station, the **Hotel Campo Imperatore** once sheltered a real would-be emperor. After the ad hoc Italian government of Marshal Badoglio deposed Mussolini and began to seek peace with the Allies, there remained the delicate question of what to do with the former Duce. After being shuttled off to a Tyrrhenian island, he was brought to this hotel, at the time inaccessible by road.

On 12 September 1943 came SS Commando Otto Skorzeny's daring rescue, when German paratroopers slipped in and out by flying in a Fieseler Storch – an aeroplane the size of the average bedroom – into which Skorzeny somehow squeezed the portly Mussolini. Hitler then set up a new headquarters for his associate on Lake Garda, the capital of the ill-fated Italian Social Republic.

This episode fooled the Allies, and has fooled historians for decades. Only recently has it been established that Skorzeny's exploit was all a publicity stunt – part of Hitler's campaign to glorify the SS at the expense of the regular German army, which was getting beaten on all fronts, and whose political loyalty was already suspect.

Many of the trails that wind their way through the Gran Sasso begin at the Hotel Campo Imperatore, including one that goes up past the Duca degli Abruzzi refuge as far as the **Corno Grande** (9,551ft), affording a spectacular eight-hour walk. If you want to take it a bit easier, there are also three ski lifts in the Campo Imperatore, and four nearby at **Monte Cristo**.

South of L'Aquila there is more good skiing to be had, as well as bobsledding. at **Campo Felice**, above the pretty village of **Rocca di Cambio**, which is the highest in Abruzzo at 4,700ft.

Approaches from L'Aquila and the West

If you're coming from L'Aquila, catch buses no.6 or 6/d from Via Castello to the *funivia* at **Fonte Cerreto**, near Assergi, the village at the mouth of the Gran Sasso Tunnel (*it's a 2km walk from the bus stop to the funicular, which usually closes during spring for maintenance, so call in advance,* ***t*** *0862 22147*).

Alternatively, if you have a car and the roads are clear, drive up the SS17bis by way of **Bazzano**, the site of an interesting 12th-century church, **Santa Giusta**. Both the funicular and the road will bring you to the **Campo Imperatore** (6,973ft), a beautiful, gentle upland basin that is filled with flowers in the late springtime and with ski bunnies in the winter.

L'Aquila

L'Aquila, which is the regional capital, is an intriguing town in its own right, as well as forming an excellent base for travelling around the rest of the Abruzzo region. The name means 'the eagle', which is the symbol of empire, and it comes as no surprise to discover that the city was founded by Emperor Frederick II in 1240 in order to form a bulwark against the popes.

L'Aquila is one of the few Italian cities of any importance not to have ancient precedents: to populate his new town, Frederick relocated the inhabitants of surrounding castles and hamlets – 99 of them, according to tradition – who each built their own church. But what made L'Aquila's fortune was its loyalty to Queen Giovanna II in 1423, when the city was besieged for more than a year by the Aragonese. The queen thanked the city for its steadfastness by granting it privileges that helped it to become, for several centuries, the second city in the Kingdom of Naples, a wool and livestock market town and a producer of silk and saffron. It attracted Adamo di Rottweil, a student of Gutenberg, who founded a printing press here in 1482, one of the first in Italy.

L'Aquila's good fortune made it cocky, and in 1529 it rose up against its rulers in Naples. The Spanish viceroy quickly put an end to its pretensions and punished the Aquilani by forcing them to pay for a huge new citadel to discourage any further revolts. Much of what the Spaniards didn't destroy in their reprisal fell down in the earthquake of 1703. However, in spite of its many vicissitudes, L'Aquila has managed to retain a considerable portion of its labyrinthine old quarter, its walls and even some of its exceptional 13th-century monuments.

Tourist Information

Via S. Maria de Paganica 5, **t** 0862 410 808.

Getting Around

Trains connect L'Aquila (with no great hurry or frequency) to Rieti in Lazio and Terni in Umbria, as well as to Pescara by way of Sulmona, the main junction for rail routes in the central Abruzzo.

L'Aquila is also less than 2hrs from Rome by ARPA **bus** (Rome, **t** 06 442 33928, L'Aquila, **t** 0862 412 808, Pescara, **t** 085 421 5099, Téramo, **t** 0861 245 857), with 18 departures a day (11 on Sun) from outside Stazione Tiburtina; in Rome you must buy tickets before boarding at Via Teodorico 28 (*open Mon–Sat 5.30am–9.30pm, Sun 6.30am–10.15pm*).

Where to Stay and Eat

L'Aquila ✉ 67100

As elsewhere in the Abruzzo, prices are low compared to the Italian norm. The region's eating establishments are more original than its hotels, especially if you come in early May when the locals are cooking up pots of *virtù*, Téramo's speciality (*see* p.573).

★★★**Castello**, Piazza Battaglione Alpini, **t** 0862 419 147 (*moderate*). A classy hotel opposite the castle.

★★★**Duomo**, Via Dragonetti 6, **t** 0862 410 893 (*moderate*). A 17th-century palace with 28 slightly cramped rooms.

★★★**Duca degli Abruzzi**, Viale Papa Giovanni XXIII 10, **t** 0862 28341 (*moderate*). Comfy rooms in a quirky modernist building.

★**Orazi**, Via Roma 175, **t** 0862 412 889 (*cheap*). Ten good-value rooms, two with bathrooms, a little way from the centre.

Antiche Mura, Via XXV Aprile 2, **t** 0862 62422 (*moderate*). Traditional Abruzzese cuisine, including rabbit with peppers and saffron, and *ferratelle*, a waffle dessert. *Closed Sun.*

L'Antico Borgo, Piazza San Vito 1, **t** 0862 22005 (*cheap*). Delicious vegetarian *ravioli* and, in season, 'truffled' treats. *Closed Tues Oct–May.*

La Cantina del Boss, Via Castello 3, **t** 0862 413 393 (*cheap*). A renovated cellar offering snacks of stuffed pizza or *frittata*. *Closed Sat lunch, Sun and 15 July–15 Aug.*

Elodìa, Camarda, on the SS17bis (10km north of town), **t** 0862 606 024 (*cheap*). Abruzzese cuisine at its best. *Closed Sun eve, Mon and 2wks July.*

Osteria Nudo e Crudo, Via F. Cannella 9, **t** 0862 404990 (*cheap*). Tasty daily specials, an excellent house wine and charming service.

A 99-headed Fountain

L'Aquila's famous **Fontana delle 99 Cannelle**, built in 1272, stands in a pink-and-white chequered courtyard in a corner of the walls near the **Porta Rivera**, not far from the railway station on the western side of the old city. The fountain's water flows through the mouths of 93 mouldering grotesque heads (and six unadorned spouts), each representing one of the hamlets that were brought together to form the city of L'Aquila. The fountain has three sides (the one to the left is a more recent addition, built in the 16th century). While you're there, try to figure out how the two sundials work on the façade of the little church opposite.

From the fountain, Via San Jacopo ascends to join Via XX Settembre, which is the main entry point into the city if you're approaching from Rome. If you follow Via XX Settembre straight into a small piazza laid out as a park, turn right at the next street and then left onto the Viale di Collemaggio, you'll reach L'Aquila's greatest Romanesque church, **Santa Maria di Collemaggio**, founded in 1270 by the hermit Pietro Morrone. The church has one of the most sumptuous and attractive façades of any in Abruzzo, its three rounded portals decorated with spiral mouldings and niches for saints, who have mostly vanished. Above the portals runs a pretty ribbon frieze, and above that are three rose windows of different patterns, the centre one a masterpiece of the stonecarver's art.

The elegant interior has been stripped of several centuries' accumulation of art and debris, leaving the fancy Renaissance **tomb of Celestine V** as its chief decoration. Pietro Morrone was an utterly holy man but a rather naïve one, and, in 1294, to his surprise, he was crowned pope here by cardinals who hoped to use him as their instrument. After a few months it became evident that the new Pope Celestine V wasn't quite turning out as expected and he was subtly 'encouraged' in Naples' Egg Castle (*see* p.857) to resign St Peter's throne – he was the only pope ever to do so voluntarily. Soon after his death, however, one of his successors canonized him, and here he rests as St Peter Celestine. He gained an additional somewhat humiliating claim to fame in 1988 when his relics were stolen and held to ransom, only to be returned without further ado when it became clear to the bodysnatchers that no one thought that Celestine was worth the asking price. A privilege Celestine V granted the church during his brief office is a Holy Door, an uncommon feature, which is opened annually on 28 August for the faithful to pass through and receive the still-distributed papal indulgence.

Around Piazza Duomo

From Via XX Settembre and the park, Corso Federico II leads into **Piazza Duomo**, L'Aquila's main market square since 1304, when Charles of Anjou granted the town the right to hold one here; you'll find produce and handicrafts on sale from dawn to 1pm (except on Sundays). Frequently shattered by earthquakes, the Duomo itself is dressed in a dull neoclassical façade, making it a wallflower next to the piazza's 18th-century Baroque **Santuario del Suffragio**, with opulent curves and a death's head above the entrance. The neighbourhood around Piazza del Duomo is one of L'Aquila's most attractive. On Via Santa Giusta, the 13th-century church of **Santa Giusta** has a good portal and rose window embellished with 12 droll figures, while all around it the streets are full of Baroque palaces. On Via Sassa, the church of **San Giuseppe** (*usually closed to the public*) contains a 15th-century equestrian tomb by Ludovico d'Alemagna, while **Palazzo Franchi**, at No.56, has a lovely Renaissance courtyard with a double *loggia*. From Piazza Duomo, Corso Vittorio Emanuele leads to the **Quattro Cantoni**, the 'Four Corners', the city's main crossroads. To the left, on Corso Umberto, lies Piazza del Palazzo, the *palazzo* in question being the **Palazzo di Giustizia**, from where Margherita of Austria, a daughter of Charles V born on the wrong side of the blanket, ruled as Governess of Abruzzo. The bell in the palace's tower sounds 99 strokes every day at dusk.

San Bernardino

On the other side of the Quattro Cantoni, Via San Bernardino leads to the masterpiece of Abruzzese Renaissance – the church of San Bernardino. The great revivalist preacher, San Bernardino da Siena, spent several years in the Franciscan convent in L'Aquila before he died, whereupon one of his disciples, St John of Capestrano, founded this church as his memorial. Work began in 1452, but the perfectly balanced, elegant façade was only finished by Cola dell'Amatrice in 1542. It is best seen from the bottom of the stair in front of the church; we are in Abruzzo, so the roof is gable-less. The 1703 earthquake smashed the vast interior, which was rebuilt in flagrant Baroque; the magnificent gilt wood ceiling, incorporating San Bernardino's IHS monogram, is by Ferdinando Mosca. San Bernardino's mausoleum and the tomb of Maria Pereira are both by Silvestro dell'Aquila, who was a pupil of Donatello. The second chapel on the right contains a *pala* by Andrea della Robbia, the grandson of the more famous Luca.

The Castello and Museo Nazionale d'Abruzzo

To the north, the Corso Vittorio Emanuele runs out into the shady Parco del Castello and, above it, the grand, moated **castello**. Built in 1535 by Pier Luigi Escribà, it is a showpiece of military architecture unwillingly financed by the citizens of L'Aquila, with a grand doorway crowned by Charles V's two-headed eagle. The castle contains the **Museo Nazionale d'Abruzzo** (***t*** *0862 6331; open Tues–Sun 9–8; adm*), the region's finest, with a well-arranged collection of art salvaged from abandoned local churches and archaeological treasures. The biggest exhibit is on the ground floor, to the right of the entrance: the *Elephas Meridionalis*, a reconstructed prehistoric pachyderm, discovered near L'Aquila in 1954. Here too are Roman portraits, statues, tombs, tympanums, reliefs, tools and more.

On the first floor, the medieval section has a vast collection of religious art: superb polychrome wooden statues, including a St Sebastian and a Madonna and Child by Silvestro dell'Aquila, and a fine 15th-century panel painting of St John of Capestrano. Other fine triptychs show a Sienese–Umbrian influence. On the next floor you'll find works by Andrea Vaccaro, Calabrian painter Mattia Preti and Abruzzese artists such as Pompeo Cesari. The third and final floor contains 20th-century works, mainly by local artists. Concerts are held regularly in the castle's auditorium.

From L'Aquila to Pópoli

The SS17 runs southeast from L'Aquila along the southern flanks of the Gran Sasso, passing quiet villages such as **Calascio**, with its impressive ruined citadel 4,920ft up, and **Castel del Monte**, further up still, and boasting an interesting medieval core. On the other side of the SS17, **Fossa** has some 12th-century frescoes of the Day of Judgement in its church of **Santa Maria ad Cryptas** (*irregular opening hours*), said to have inspired Dante.

Tiny **Bominaco** (near Caporciano) is the site of the most celebrated monuments in this corner of Abruzzo – two churches that belonged to a fortified **Benedictine abbey** (*call the custodian, Signor Cassiani, on* **t** *0862 93604, to arrange a visit*). The monastery dates from some shadowy three-digit year; **San Pellegrino** is said to have been founded by Charlemagne, though it was rebuilt in 1263. The interior, rectangular with an ogival vault, is covered with the colourful, stylized frescoes of the period: a pictorial calendar of the months and major feast days, scenes from the New Testament, saints and geometrical patterns. The sanctuary is set apart by a marble transenna carved with a griffon with a cup, and another with a fearsome dragon – not your ordinary church fare. The saint is buried under the sanctuary and it is said that you can hear his heart beating through a hole by the altar. **Santa Maria Assunta** has none of the ancient strangeness of San Pellegrino, but is a 12th-century gem, beautifully endowed with carved doors, windows, capitals and a pulpit.

Just to the west of Bominaco are the caves of the **Grotte di Stiffe** (***t*** *0862 861 000; 50-min guided tours daily 10–1 and 3–6; adm exp; includes visit to speleological museum in town; call ahead to arrange a tour in English*), where a long illuminated walkway takes you past an underground river beneath eerie stalactites.

From Navelli the road makes a dramatic writhing descent to Pópoli (*see* below), on the Via Valeria and the Rome–Pescara *autostrada*, or you can turn eastwards to **Capestrano**, birthplace of San Bernardino's saintly follower, St John of Capestrano (1386–1456). The swallows come back here, too, if not on the same tight schedule as their Californian cousins (who famously return each year to the Spanish mission of San Juan Capestrano on the so-called 'missions road' between LA and San Francisco – giving rise to the expression 'as sure as the swallows returning to Capestrano').

Pópoli stands at the confluence of the Aterno and the Sagittario, where they meet to form the Pescara. The town's largest church, Romanesque **San Francesco**, is topped with statues and pierced by an unusual rose window. The 14th-century **Taverna Ducale**, decorated with escutcheons, was not where Pópoli's Cantelmi dukes drank, but where they stored the tithes from their subjects. It has survived in better shape than their castle, which looms over Pópoli.

Corfinio, to the west, was called Pentima until Mussolini gave it back its ancient name – for here stood the Paeligni capital *Corfinium*, famous in history as the united headquarters of the Italic tribes in the Social Wars of the 1st century BC. They renamed the city *Italia*, the first instance in history that the name signified a union of the peninsula's peoples, hoping it would soon take over from Rome as capital. Now even its ruins are meagre: there's a small **archaeology museum** in the convent of Sant'Alessandro (*for admission, ask at the church*).

Southern Abruzzo and the National Park

For many people the highlight of the region is the **Parco Nazionale d'Abruzzo**, Italy's second largest national park, with its rare fauna and flora. For mountain-lovers the **Montagna della Maiella** range is nearly as impressive as the Gran Sasso and much less touristy. Man-made sights here include Alba Fucens, Abruzzo's best archaeological site, and intriguing old towns such as **Sulmona**, **Scanno**, **Pescocostanzo** and **Tagliacozzo**.

The Marsica

The region southwest of Pópoli, towards the Lazio border, is known as the **Marsica**, after its ancient inhabitants, the Marsi. The 'people of Mars' were among the most determined foes of Rome in ancient times, and they took a prominent part in the Social War in 90 BC. They also had such a talent for medicine, using the local herbs, that the Romans accused them of witchcraft. Their snake goddess Angizia seems to still haunt the region today, most famously at the annual 'Procession of the Serpents' in **Cocullo**, where floats, townspeople and children parade covered in writhing snakes.

Celano, just off the A25, is a charming hill town spread out beneath the skirts of its four-square **Piccolomini castle**, home to the excellent **Museo Nazionale della Marsica** (*open summer Tues–Sun 9–8, some Sats until midnight; winter Tues–Fri 9–1.30, Sat and Sun 9–8; adm*), displaying a wealth of medieval art ranging from the eccentric to the downright strange: a Byzantine triptych covered in tiny pearls, a relief of a whale, and the church doors from San Pietro, with a series of mystical images. Celano was the birthplace of the Blessed Tommaso da Celano, St Francis's first biographer; he also composed the *Dies Irae*, the eerie medieval hymn of the dead most often heard now in the finale of Berlioz's *Symphonie Fantastique*. Nearby you can visit the **Gole di Celano**, a stunningly steep and narrow gorge, or head north on the SS5bis towards L'Aquila, by way of the mountain resort towns of **Ovindoli** and **Rocca di Cambio**.

Avezzano and Alba Fucens

Marsica's modern capital, **Avezzano**, has little to commend it, having been toppled by an earthquake in 1915 and bombed in the Second World War. Its one monument, the **Castello Orsini**, has a portal with a relief celebrating the victory of Lepanto over the Turks in 1571. In the **Palazzo Comunale** is a small **museum** of inscriptions and architectural fragments from the cities of the Marsica, with a little *pinacoteca* (***t** 0863 43251; open daily 8–8; adm*). In the squat fortified former arsenal at the entrance to the town, the **Museo della Civiltà Contadina e Pastorale** (***t** 0863 5021; open on request*) has earnest exhibits relating the history of the Fucino plain. Avezzano is a departure point for the Parco Nazionale d'Abruzzo.

If the ancient Marsi were to return to their homeland today, they'd be amazed to find their lake – once the largest in central Italy – replaced by the fertile basin called the **Piana del Fucino**. But they would also tell you that their *Lacus Fucinus* had been a mess, with an inadequate outlet, and prone to flooding. To drain it, Emperor Claudius ordered what became the greatest underground engineering work of antiquity (AD 54): a six-kilometre tunnel intended to spill the lake's waters into the River Liri.

However, for all the skill that went into the work, the tunnel didn't work well and was eventually blocked up. In 1240 Frederick II tried but failed to have it unblocked, and only in 1875 did British, Italian, French and Swiss engineers finally drain the lake, reclaiming thousands of hectares. Now it's one of the most surreal landscapes in Italy, a large expanse of straight canals and roads numbered like the streets in an American city. Over it loom the radio dishes of Italy's biggest space research installation, the **Centro Telespaziale**.

Of all the ancient cities of the Marsi, the only one to leave behind many traces is **Alba Fucens** (***t*** *0863 23561; open daily 8 until dusk*), near modern Albe, eight kilometres from Avezzano (*linked by ARPA buses,* ***t*** *0863 26561*) and rebuilt after the 1915 quake. Alba was founded as a Roman colony in 300 BC to keep an eye on the area's tribes – hence the mighty walls. Ancient Alba occupies three hills, and its ruins intermingle with the ruins of medieval Alba. Much has been excavated, including the amphitheatre, the forum, the basilica, the weedy theatre, the baths and a section of the original Via Valeria. Near the amphitheatre is the well-preserved Romanesque church of **San Pietro** (*if no one's there, ask about key at bar near entrance*), adorned with Cosmati work. The church was originally a temple of Diana, which the Romans once used as a prison – prisoners' graffiti can still be read on the walls.

Getting Around

As a major **rail** junction, and with bus services to most of the area, Sulmona is the best base for exploring the area, but bus and train connections are infrequent so you need to be well organized.

Buses run fairly frequently from L'Aquila to Avezzano, and from there to Pescasséroli, the administrative centre of the Abruzzo National Park. There's a direct early morning ARPA bus to Pescasséroli from Rome, which returns to Rome in the evening (mid-June–mid-Sept).

Spectacular **roads** include the SS5bis from L'Aquila to Celano, the SS84 from Lanciano to Roccaraso, and the SS83 from Pescina, near Celano, through the National Park.

Tourist Information

Tagliacozzo: Via Vittorio Veneto 6, **t** 0863 610 318.
Sulmona: Corso Ovidio 208, **t** 0864 53276.
Scanno: Piazza Santa Maria della Valle 12, **t** 0864 7431.
Roccaraso: Via Claudio Mori 1, **t** 0864 62210 (*open daily 9–1 and 4.30–6.30*).

Where to Stay and Eat

Most hotels here only open in summer and winter. Avezzano has the largest choice, many of them along the SS5.

Avezzano ✉ 67051

Dei Marsi, Via Cavour 79/b, **t** 0863 4601, (*moderate*). The best-value option in town, with modern, comfy rooms.

Vecchi Sapori, Via Montello 3, **t** 0863 416 626 (*cheap*). A good, fairly priced restaurant serving up local specialities, including pasta and lamb dishes.

Tagliacozzo ✉ 67069

******Albergo Bocconcino***, Via V. Veneto 25, **t** 0863 66866 (*cheap*). A reasonably priced central option offering bright, modern bedrooms with private baths.

*****Miramonti**, Via Variante 87, **t** 0863 6581 (*cheap*). A decent choice with 21 comfortable rooms and a garden.

Sulmona ✉ 67039

*****Europa Park**, on the SS17 (off Bivio Badia), just north of town, **t** 0864 251 260 (*moderate*). Sulmona's largest and comfiest hotel, with a bar and a good restaurant.

***Italia**, Piazza San Tommaso 3, **t** 0864 52308 (*cheap*). A comfortable, atmospheric hotel with antique-filled rooms, run by a charming family. Highly recommended.

Italia, Piazza XX Settembre 22, **t** 0864 33070 (*moderate*). Winning variations on traditional local cuisine, including home-made pasta and lamb with rosemary. *Closed Mon.*

Clemente, Vico della Quercia 5, **t** 0864 52284 (*moderate*). Home-made sausages, delicious local dishes such as roast kid, and good desserts. *Closed Thurs, Christmas and 10 days July.*

Ristorante Frangio, Via Ercole Ciofano 51, **t** 0864 212773 (*moderate*). One of Abruzzo's best restaurants, with exquisite regional specialities, a fine wine list, sunny décor, a huge shady terrace and impeccable service.

Roccaraso ✉ 67037

*****Excelsior**, Via Roma 28, **t** 0864 602 351 (*moderate*). One of the classier hotels in the area. *Open mid-Dec–mid-Jan and Apr–Aug.*

Scanno ✉ 67038

*****Del Lago**, Viale del Lago 202, **t** 0864 74343, (*moderate*). A small, tranquil hotel with a garden in a lovely setting on the lake. *Open mid-Dec–mid-Jan and Mar–Oct.*

*****Margherita**, Via D. Tanturri 100, **t** 0864 74353 (*cheap*). A good-value hotel (rare for Scanno).

Agli Archetti, Via Silla 8, **t** 0864 74645 (*moderate*). A refined place offering dishes made from home-grown ingredients; try grilled lamb with pears. *Closed Tues Oct–May.*

Pescasséroli ✉ 67032

******Grand Hotel del Parco**, **t** 0863 912 745, (*expensive*). The grandest hotel in the area, with a beautiful setting, a garden and an outdoor pool for summer. *Open Christmas–Easter and June–Sept.*

*****Il Pinguino**, Via Collacchi 2, **t** 0863 912 580, (*moderate*). A good choice in the national park, with rooms that are far too snug for a real penguin. Full or half board are compulsory in July and Aug.

Tagliacozzo

West of Albe, **Tagliacozzo** is a pretty, ancient town on the slopes of Monte Bove, less than two hours by train from Rome on the Rome–Pescara route. Named after Thalia, the muse of theatre, it is known for the battle of 12 August 1268, which ended the reign of the Swabians and heirs of Frederick II – as described by Dante. The site is marked by the ruined church of **Santa Maria della Vittoria**, at **Scurcola Marsicana**, east of Tagliacozzo. In the town itself, the church of **San Francesco**, with a fine rose window and portal, contains the relics of Tommaso da Celano. The secular architecture is more interesting than the churches: the 14th-century **Palazzo Ducale**, a grand building on a grand piazza, has a *loggia* on the first floor with fine but damaged frescoes by Lorenzo da Viterbo. The quarter around genteel old **Piazza dell'Obelisco**, with its Renaissance obelisk, has picturesque houses and peeling palaces from the 14th and 15th centuries.

Sulmona

South of the Via Valeria, **Sulmona**, in a green basin surrounded by mountains, was the capital of another obscure Italic tribe, the Paeligni, but is best remembered as the birthplace of Ovid (43 BC–AD 17), commemorated with a large 20th-century statue in Piazza XX Settembre. Much later, Sulmona was made capital of the province created by Frederick II. It became a minor centre of learning and religion, home of the Celestine Order's main abbey, and of Pietro Angeleri, who lived in the hermitage of Monte Morrone before being brought down to L'Aquila and crowned Pope Celestine V (*see* p.578). In the early Renaissance its craftsmen were celebrated for their gold-work, although they have since learned a sweeter skill – what the Italians call *confetti*.

The main street, Corso Ovidio, holds Sulmona's loveliest monument, the church and palace of **Santa Maria Annunziata**, a Gothic and Renaissance ensemble begun in 1320. The three portals on the **palace** façade were done at different periods, but the result is as harmoniously sweet as *confetti*: the left one is finely carved florid Gothic, crowned by a statue of St Michael, while the middle portal is pure symmetrical Renaissance; the plain portal on the right was built last, in 1522. Doctors of the Church and saints stand sentry along the façade; above them runs an intricate ribbon frieze, and above that are three lacy Gothic windows. Within the palace, the **Museo Civico** (*open Tues–Sun 9–1, Sat–Sun also 4–6.30*) contains traditional Abruzzese costumes, work by the goldsmiths of Renaissance Sulmona, and sculpture and paintings dating from

Confetti Nuts

To Italians *confetti* means the sweets covered in sugar in all kinds of colours that are given out to guests at a wedding. They have been a speciality of the Abruzzo since the Middle Ages and, although the original *confetti* were sugared almonds, today they come with a variety of fillings that include chocolate or hazelnuts. The capital of *confetti* is Sulmona, where any number of shops in the historic centre sell confectionery made up to look like flowers or ornate gold and silver ornaments, and have lavish window displays to match. William di Carlo, which has its showroom near the station, claims to be the oldest *confetti*-manufacturer in town.

the 16th to the 18th century; and the **Pinoteca Civica d'Arte Moderno** (**t** *0864 210 216, open by request*) is dedicated to modern art. The Baroque **church** façade, which was rebuilt after the 1703 earthquake, complements the adjacent palace, where summer concerts are held.

Running through the centre of Sulmona is an unusual Gothic **aqueduct** (1256); it can be seen in huge Piazza Garibaldi, site of the 1474 **Fontana del Vecchio**, named after the jovial old man on top. Over the road stands the carved Romanesque portal of **San Francesco delle Scarpe** ('with shoes' – these Franciscans wore shoes instead of sandals); the rest tumbled during an earthquake. Outside town, five kilometres towards Monte Morrone, are Roman ruins (a mosaic pavement), part of a **Temple of Hercules**, which locals refer to as 'Ovid's villa', though links with the poet have been disproved.

Around Sulmona

There are picturesque hill towns near Sulmona, such as **Pacentro**, nine kilometres to the east, its lanes winding around the battlemented towers of the ruined **Castello Cantelmo**. Beyond Pacentro the SS487 heads up into the rugged Maiella mountains; a few winding kilometres east, near Passo San Leonardo, it reaches a T-junction where you can turn north to **Caramanico Terme** (a hill town spa) and the Via Valeria, or south past the **Campo di Giove**, a winter sports centre with a cable car up the slopes of the Round Table (7,885ft), towards the dramatic SS84 and the Sangro Valley.

Pescocostanzo, Rivisondoli and Roccaraso (stops on the Sulmona–Isernia railway) are well endowed with sports facilities. Charming **Pescocostanzo** once owed allegiance to Vittoria Colonna, poet and friend of Michelangelo, and made lace before it became a ski resort; its lovely **Collegiata di Santa Maria del Colle** (*open daily for services*), has excellent wood carvings dating back to the 11th century.

On the SS84 between Roccaraso and Lanciano (accessible by bus from either end) is **Taranta Peligna**, with a cable car that rises to central Italy's most spectacular cave, the **Grotta del Cavallone** (*open for hourly guided visits Apr–Sept Mon–Sat 9–1 and 4–6.30; contact the Lama dei Peligni tourist office,* **t** *0872 916120; cable car and adm exp*), used as a setting in D'Annunzio's play *La Figlia di Jorio*. The cave's name, the 'Big Horse', comes from the profile carved by nature on the wall at the grandiose entrance of the grotto: other rooms are adorned with stone flowers or lace, alabaster streaks that remind Italians of ham (in the 'Sala del Prosciutto') and fairies.

Scanno

From Cocullo or Anversa degli Abruzzi, just west of Sulmona, the SS479 ascends the **Valle del Sagittario**, passing through the steep **Gole del Sagittario** and along the Lago di Scanno. High above the lake, **Scanno** is a picturesque place that fascinated 18th-century travellers, who wondered at its customs and costumes, which are more reminiscent of those of Asia Minor than Italy. Even today its women sometimes wear their traditional dress, with their turban-like head-dresses; the best time to see the costumes is on 14 August, when the folkloric Matrimonio di Scanno is celebrated.

For magnificent views of the sunset, drive up the zigzagging road from here to Frattura, or take the chairlift up to **Monte Rotondo.**

Parco Nazionale d'Abruzzo

West of Cocullo is the SS83 for the **Parco Nazionale d'Abruzzo**. Founded in 1923 and enlarged in 1976, the park covers 400 square kilometres of some of the loveliest scenery in the Apennines. It is a paradise of flowery meadows and forests of beech, pine, oak, ash, maple and yew, and the last home of *Ursus arctos marsicanus*, the brown Abruzzo bear, and the Abruzzo chamois; here too are Apennine lynxes, boars, wolves, badgers, red squirrels, eagles, falcons, woodpeckers, owls and many unusual species of songbirds, all protected by law from enthusiastic Italian hunters.

After passing through the beautiful **Passo del Diavolo** ('Devil's Pass'), the road reaches the largest village in the park, **Pescasséroli**, birthplace of Benedetto Croce (1866–1952), the greatest Italian philosopher of the past two centuries. The **national park visitors' centre** has trail maps and information on flora and fauna; there's also a small **museum** on Viale Colli dell'Oro (*open daily 10–1 and 3–7; adm*).

A pleasant excursion from here even for non-committed hikers is the two-hour walk up to the **Valico di Monte Tranquillo**. In mid-summer and winter you can also ride Pescasséroli's cable car up to the summit of **Monte Vitelle**. Further south are **Opi** and **Barrea**, near the **Lago di Barrea** and the **Camosciara**, where the graceful chamois live.

Just outside the park the fine scenery continues around **Alfedena**, on the site of the Samnite town of *Aufidena* – across the river are the ancient walls and necropolis. A three-kilometre track leads up from here to the lake of **Montagna Spaccata**.

Molise

Isolated, mountainous and even more sparsely populated than Abruzzo, **Molise** is one of the least-known regions of Italy. It belonged to the tenacious Samnites of old, and Italians still sometimes call it *Sanno*; at some point in the murky early Middle Ages it became the county of Molise, and then it was joined to the Kingdom of Naples. In the 14th and 15th centuries Slav and Albanian refugees from the Turkish invasion found homes here; their languages contributed to the great variety of regional dialects; there are still villages unable to understand one another.

Though an improved road network has ended most of Molise's isolation, the terrain makes the going slow however you travel. This is just as well – this is a region to drink in slowly. It is very much backwoods Italy; the biggest local events are village rodeos, and the most famous attractions are ancient remains. In its freshness, this is one of Italy's last frontiers.

Isernia

Down the SS17 from Sulmona and Castel di Sangro, the dismal little capital of **Isernia** was the Samnite town of *Aesernium*, where the Italic tribes either first united against Rome, or fled after the Romans captured their capital of Corfinium in the Social Wars. At any rate the town modestly claims to have been 'the first capital of

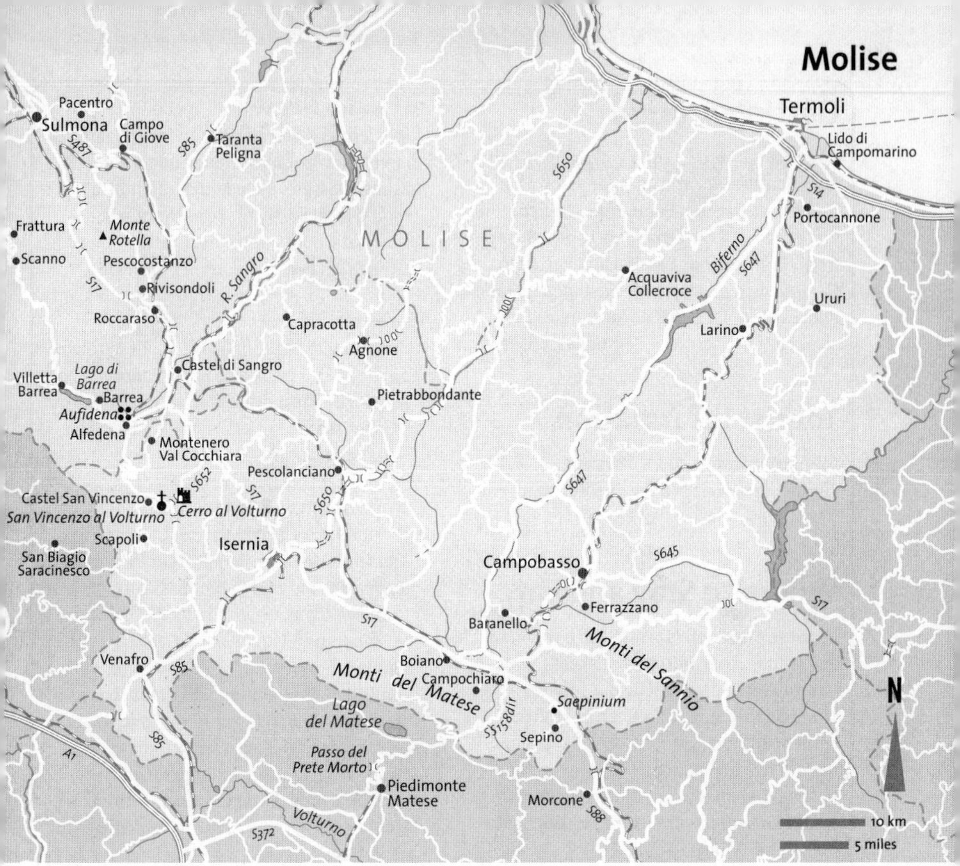

Italy'. Yet even that boast pales before the fame of its onions (fêted every 28–29 June) and its lace. Isernia has been severely damaged by quakes – the last in 1984 – and was badly bombed in 1943, so there is little to see of its old town other than the 14th-century **Fontana Fraterna**, built using Roman masonry and bearing the inscription AE PONT, which led to a popular belief that Aesernium gave the world Pontius Pilate.

Today the main attraction is much much older – a Palaeolithic village uncovered in 1979. At a million years old, this is the most ancient evidence of human life found in Europe. No human remains were discovered, but there are relics such as weapons and face paint, and the remains of elephant, deer, rhinoceros, bison, bear and hippo ancestors. They are well presented in the **Museo Nazionale Santa Maria delle Monache** on Corso Marcello 48 (***t*** *0865 415 179; open daily 8.30–7.30; adm*). Excavations continue at the site itself (***t*** *0865 413 526; open Mon–Fri 9–sunset*).

North of Isernia

The *comuni* in the high altitudes north of Isernia have been compared to the isolated villages of Tibet, each perched on its lonely hilltop. Highest in all the Apennines, at 4,661ft, is **Capracotta**, a village immersed in mountain pastures, often buried under banks of snow in winter; residents sometimes have to use their upper-floor windows as doors. It's a fitting place for the first Italian ski club, founded in 1914.

Getting Around

Isernia is linked by **train** with Naples, Rome, Sulmona, Pescara and Campobasso; other trains pass through Benevento, then continue on to the coast at Térmoli, via Larino. **Buses** – from Naples, Rome, Cassino and Vasto to Campobasso and Isernia – are much quicker and less aggravating. The **bus** service for villages, from Isernia or Campobasso, is fair.

Tourist Information

Isernia: Via Farinacci 9, **t** 0865 3992.
Campobasso: Piazza della Vittoria 14, **t** 0874 415 662.

Where to Stay and Eat

Molise's few hotels tend to be either new and sterile or old and down-at-heel.

At table, the Molisani favour solidly old-fashioned, spicy fare such as stuffed lamb heads (*testine d'agnello*), kid tripe, *pizza con le foglie* topped with greens and boiled pork, smelly mountain cheese, and *polenta maritata* with red beans, olive oil, hot peppers and garlic.

Isernia ✉ 86170

*****La Tequila**, Via G. Tedeschi 85, **t** 0865 412 345 (*moderate*). A good option outside the centre, in the new San Lazzaro neighbourhood.

Taverna Maresca, Corso Marcelli 186, **t** 0865 3976 (*cheap*). A fine old restaurant in the old quarter. *Closed Sun, 2wks Aug, 1wk at Christmas, and Easter Mon.*

Capracotta ✉ 86082

***Montecampo**, Contrada Santa Lucia, **t** 0865 949 128 (*cheap*). A basic but pleasant 13-room hotel up in the mountains and out of the way, with a restaurant.

Agnone ✉ 86061

*****Sammartino**, Largo P. Micca 44, **t** 0865 78239 (*cheap*). A hotel with comfortable bedrooms and an excellent restaurant (*moderate*), **t** 0865 77577, serving first-rate grilled meat, including Molise's succulent baby lamb.

Da Casciano, Viale Marconi 29, **t** 0865 77511 (*moderate*). A restaurant serving the rare lamb *sotto la coppa* (cooked under the ashes). Desserts include the unforgettable *ostie*, a local pastry made with walnuts, chocolate, honey and wine must. *Closed Tues except in summer, and Nov.*

Venafro

Il Quadrifoglio, Madonnella, just out of town on the SS85, **t** 0865 909 886 (*cheap*). A place serving the freshest seafood (Venafro is a stop for seafood trucks travelling from the Adriatic to Rome).

Campobasso ✉ 86100

******Hotel Roxy**, Piazza Savoia 7, **t** 0874 411 541 (*moderate*). A plush, modern choice with a disco for those wild Campobassani nights. *Disco closed July–Sept.*

*****Skanderbeg**, Via Novelli 3, **t** 0874 413 341 (*moderate*). A hotel combining modern comforts with traditional local touches.

****Tricolore**, Via San Giovanni in Golfo 112, **t** 0874 63190 (*cheap*). A small family-run hotel in one of the prettier parts of town.

Vecchia Trattoria da Tonino, Corso Vittorio Emanuele II 8, **t** 0874 415 200 (*expensive–moderate*). A refined, less strictly local restaurant, with a wine list including some of the finest Molise labels. *Closed Sun and Mon, and last wk July.*

Da Emilio, Piazza Spenzieri 18, **t** 0874 416 576 (*moderate*). One of the best restaurants in the area, offering dishes with a delightful Emilia-Romagna touch. There's a terrace for summer dining. *Closed Tues, last 2wks Jan and 1st 2wks July.*

Aciniello, Via Torino 4, **t** 0874 94001 (*cheap*). A simple place with genuine atmosphere and cuisine, offering dishes such as *pizza rustica* and rabbit. *Closed Sun and 2wks Aug.*

Larino

*****Campitelli Due**, Via San Benedetto 1, **t** 0874 823 541 (*moderate*). A functional modern choice with good service.

*****Campitelli Uno**, Via Mazzini 9 (near the amphitheatre), **t** 0874 822 666 (*cheap*). The cheaper sister hotel of the Due, with a good restaurant, **t** 0874 822 339. *Hotel closed Oct–May.*

Nearby **Agnone**, the 'Athens of the Samnites', is famous for its bells: the one surviving factory, the **Marinelli Pontifical Foundry**, Italy's oldest, supplies the Vatican. Bells are cast according to an ancient formula; as the bronze is poured into the mould a priest chants medieval litanies guaranteeing clear tones. You can see the foundry at work and visit its small museum at Via d'Onofrio 14 (***t** 0865 78235; guided tours weekdays July and Aug 11–6, Sept–June 11–4; at other times by prior request; adm*). Agnone is also known for its coppersmiths, whose workshops line the main streets. Note also the cathedral's Romanesque portal.

South of Agnone, **Pietrabbondante** has extensive **Samnite ruins** (***t** 0865 76130; open Mar–Oct Mon–Tues 9–sunset, Weds–Sun 9–1; adm*). The site was a religious sanctuary and includes a Greek theatre and a couple of temples, built in the 2nd century BC. **Pescolanciano**, on the way back towards Isernia, is dominated by its picturesque **Castello d'Alessandro**, founded in the 13th century and later topped by a pretty arcade.

West of Isernia

In mid-August Spaghetti Western fans can whoop it up at the 'rodeo' at **Montenero Val Cocchiara**, northwest of Isernia; as usual in Italy, food is as much of an attraction as the events. In this case it's barbecues. In the pre-cowboy days of the Lombards, the Benedictines built the abbey of **San Vincenzo al Volturno** to the south near **Castel San Vincenzo**. Much altered, damaged and rebuilt, it was last restored in the 1950s; the crypt of **San Lorenzo**, which escaped the disasters, has some 11th-century frescoes (***t** 0328 342 2393 or **t** 0865 955 246; open 7.30–dusk; crypt by appointment*).

The most impressive castle in Molise, **Cerro al Volturno** (*occasionally open to the public; call town hall on **t** 0865 953 104*) was built by the same Benedictines in the 10th century but rebuilt at the end of the 15th century. Appearing to grow organically out of a massive rock, it is inaccessible except by a narrow path; the cement bulwarks on the hill were added in the 1920s. Further south, in **Scapoli**, there's a *zampogna* (bagpipe) market in the last week of July. The bagpipe has a long tradition among the shepherds of the Molise; they still take them down to play in the streets of Rome and Naples for Christmas. You can also explore the world of bagpipes at the **Museo della Zampogna** on the edge of town (***t** 0865 954 143; open by request*).

On the road south towards Campania, **Venafro** was made famous by Horace for its olive oil. A little run down, it is one of the most interesting towns in Molise. Cyclopean walls run along the road into town, and in the Middle Ages the Roman amphitheatre was turned into an oval piazza and the arcades into the front doors of the houses. Portable remains of Roman *Venafrum* are now in the **Museo Archeologico** (***t** 0865 900 742; open daily 8.15–7.40; adm*) in the former convent of Santa Chiara. The **Annunziata** church has preserved its Romanesque interior and contains 15th-century English alabasters. The recently restored interior of Venafro's 14th–16th-century **castle** *(open Tues–Fri am)* boasts some life-sized relief horse frescoes. The 15th-century fortified ducal **Palazzo Caracciolo** is under restoration.

Venafro has a couple of curiosities, too: La Portella, probably once a secret passage, is the world's shortest street, at just over 16ft; while the romantic ruins of the turret on a crag above the town are said to guard the devil's treasure.

The Matese

South of Isernia and Campobasso is a curve of snow-swept peaks and forests called the **Matese**, of which the southern half lies in Campania. Few Italians, much less foreigners, penetrate its quiet villages, where women in traditional dress sit out in the streets over their round *tomboli* making delicate lace. The lakes of the Matese are full of waterfowl, its streams brim with fish, and its forests are home to wildcats, wolves and other creatures seldom seen in Italy; its glens produce *funghi porcini* by the ton.

The scenery is spectacular, especially around the largest of the lakes, the **Lago del Matese**, with its resort of **Piedimonte Matese**, both in Campania. The road back to Molise (SS158dir) runs through the **Passo del Prete Morto** ('Dead Priest Pass'). The northern slopes of the Matese are equally lovely, with a quality of light that gives **Campochiaro** its name. This medieval village retains its walls and tower, and a huge Samnite temple complex has been unearthed nearby. Just to the west is the lofty little town of **Boiano**, the former Samnite stronghold of *Bovianum*. The upper part of town, Cività, retains Megalithic-era walls and the ruins of a Lombard castle. The views are great – especially if you're up to a stiff two-hour climb to the summit of **Monte la Gallinola** (6,307ft) – and on a clear day you can see as far as the Bay of Naples.

Saepinum

In 295 BC the Samnite city of *Saipins* was laid waste by the Romans. The inhabitants were either killed or taken into slavery, and Saipins was rebuilt as a Roman colony called *Saepinum*. As a quiet provincial town it managed to avoid most of history until the 9th century, when the Saracens destroyed it. Later in the Middle Ages, when times were surer, the site was resettled, two and a a half kilometres uphill from the ruins – now modern **Sepino** – and old Saepinum was slowly covered by the dust of the ages and quarried here and there for its stone. Dilettantes began excavating the ancient town in the 18th century, and nowadays groups of archaeologists come to uncover more of it every summer. A bus runs from Campobasso to Sepino roughly every two hours, but only one bus a day stops at the *area archeologica*, and you'll have to walk back to modern Sepino to catch the return bus to Campobasso (***t** 0874 790 848*).

The charm of Saepinum comes partly from its remote and lovely setting in the Matese, making it one of the most evocative Roman sites in all Italy – the best example of a small provincial city, in fact. In Saepinum there is very little marble, no plush villas as in Pompeii and Herculaneum, but neither are there any modern intrusions beyond a few farmhouses making use of a column here, an architrave there.

The defensive walls encompassing Saepinum, built in diamond-patterned *opus reticulatum*, are more than a kilometre long and defended by 27 bastions – the best preserved of which, more than 35ft high, stands near the theatre. Four gates lead into the central axis of the city. From the car park at **Porta di Terravecchia** you pass through the walls on the *cardus maximus*. This street retains its original paving stones as you approach the central crossroads with the *decumanus*, the main street. Here you'll find the forum and civic buildings. The slender Ionic columns on one corner belonged to the basilica, the main meeting place and law courts of a Roman city, with its podium for orators and lawyers. Just off it is an octagonal atrium, surrounded by the foundations of shop counters – Saepinum's central market. Across from the forum itself on the *decumanus* are, first, on the corner, the *comitium* (elections office), the *curia* (town hall), a temple, believed to have been dedicated to the cult of an emperor, the *terme* (baths) and the well-preserved Griffon fountain.

The *decumanus* continues past a house called the **Casa dell'Impluvio Sannitico** – the atrium of which contains a fountain and Samnite-style *impluvium* (a container to collect rainwater) with an inscription in Oscan, the pre-Roman language of the region – to the **Porta di Benevento**, marked by a figure of Mars. Beyond the gate stands a funeral monument, with its inscriptions lauding the virtues of the deceased Caius Ennius Marso, one of the town's leading citizens.

In the opposite direction the *decumanus* passes through Saepinum's main commercial district, lined with shops, taverns and private residences. It ends at the most complete gate, the impressive **Porta Boiano**, with steps to the top for an excellent view of the excavations. Figures of prisoners or slaves stand on plinths on either side, and its inscription informs us that Emperor Tiberius and his brother Drusus paid for the walls. Beyond this gate is a monumental **mausoleum of Numisio Ligure**. Along the walls are the remains of a private bath complex; beyond is the well-preserved **theatre** (*open daily 8–sunset*), with a crescent of medieval farmhouses that were built into the upper *cavea*; in its heyday the theatre seated 3,000 spectators. The stage is now occupied by another farmhouse, which contains an interesting **museum** (***t*** *0874 790 207; open summer daily 8–8; call for times the rest of the year*).

Campobasso

The capital of the county of Molise, **Campobasso** and the surrounding region hit the news in late 2002, when earthquakes rocked the area. Worst hit was the little village of San Giuliano de Puglia (near Larino; *see* p.592), where 29 people were killed, including 26 six-year-olds who were at a school Hallowe'en party. Around 3,000 people in towns and villages across the region were made homeless as buildings collapsed or began to crack, and many of the older houses are still propped up by elaborate scaffolding.

In the past, Campobasso was famous for its engraved cutlery – its knives, scissors and razors are still highly regarded – but is now better known as the site of the National School for Carabinieri and for its June procession, the *Sagra dei Misteri di Corpus Domini*. In the 17th century, Campobasso's old Corpus Domini processions were banned by the bishop for making spectators laugh, and remained so until 1740, when local sculptor Di Zinno came up with the idea of building metal contraptions to support real people in the soaring Baroque postures of the angels and saints he carved for churches. The bishop accepted these as serious augmenters of the faith, and indeed they are, for it seems as if faith alone is holding up the bevy of six-year-old angels and saints suspended on the 13 floats or 'Mysteries' that are solemnly paraded through the streets to the accompaniment of local bands. The **museum of Samnite antiquities** at Via Chiarizia 12 (*t 0874 412 265; open daily 9–1 and 3–7*) is well worth a look, and the older, upper part of town has a couple of Romanesque churches, **San Giorgio** and **San Leonardo**, and the **Castello Monforte** (now a weather station).

From Campobasso, buses head out to scenic villages nearby, including **Ferrazzano**, with its castle and belvedere, and **Baranello**, an ancient town, the heir of the Samnite *Vairanum*. Baranello has a little **Museo Civico** (*open Mon–Sat 8–2; call* comune *office, t 0874 460 406, to arrange a visit*) containing Samnite artefacts, 18th-century Neapolitan kitsch paintings and other *objets d'art*. Nearby, on the Biferno river, you can watch a water wheel grind the grains that go into Molise's folksy cuisine.

Larino

Between Campobasso and Termoli, the small town of Larino – the Samnite *Larinum* – is prettily located amid hills of olive groves. During and after the 2002 earthquakes, it became the centre of operations for relief workers. Its most important monument, the **cathedral**, was built in 1319 and embellished with an ornate portal in its Puglian-style façade; the nearby **church of San Francesco** has some good 18th-century frescoes. Near the cathedral, the **museum** of **Palazzo Comunale** (*open Mon–Fri 9–1*) has some beautiful Roman polychrome mosaics from the 2nd and 3rd centuries.

The *Ara Frentana*, a cylindrical Roman altar, is visible by the road leading to the train station. This was once the centre of the ancient Samnite town; its ruined amphitheatre hosts concerts, plays and other events in summer. From 25 to 27 May, Larino holds a religious festival, the *Festa di San Pardo*. On the first evening there's a procession of 150 decorated ox carts from the cathedral to a Palaeo-Christian basilica dedicated to the three martyrs Primiano, Siriano and Cassio, to bring the statue of Primiano back to the cathedral for a late-night mass. The spectacle is at its best during the two-kilometre return trip, when the carts are escorted by thousands of people bearing torches.

Albanian and Slavic Villages

In the district around Larino are several diehard communities of Albanians and Slavs who maintain their language, traditions and festivals. **Ururi**, west of Larino, is an Albanian town, as is **Portocannone**, which conserves in its Romanesque church an icon of the Madonna of Constantinople, brought over by settlers. The most interesting of the Slavic villages is **Acquaviva Collecroce**, where a dialect called 'Stokavo' is spoken. In the campanile of the church of **Santa Maria Esther** there is a medieval curiosity: a stone carved with the palindromic magic square with a bastard-Latin inscription, an ancient charm.

Tuscany

16

Tuscany

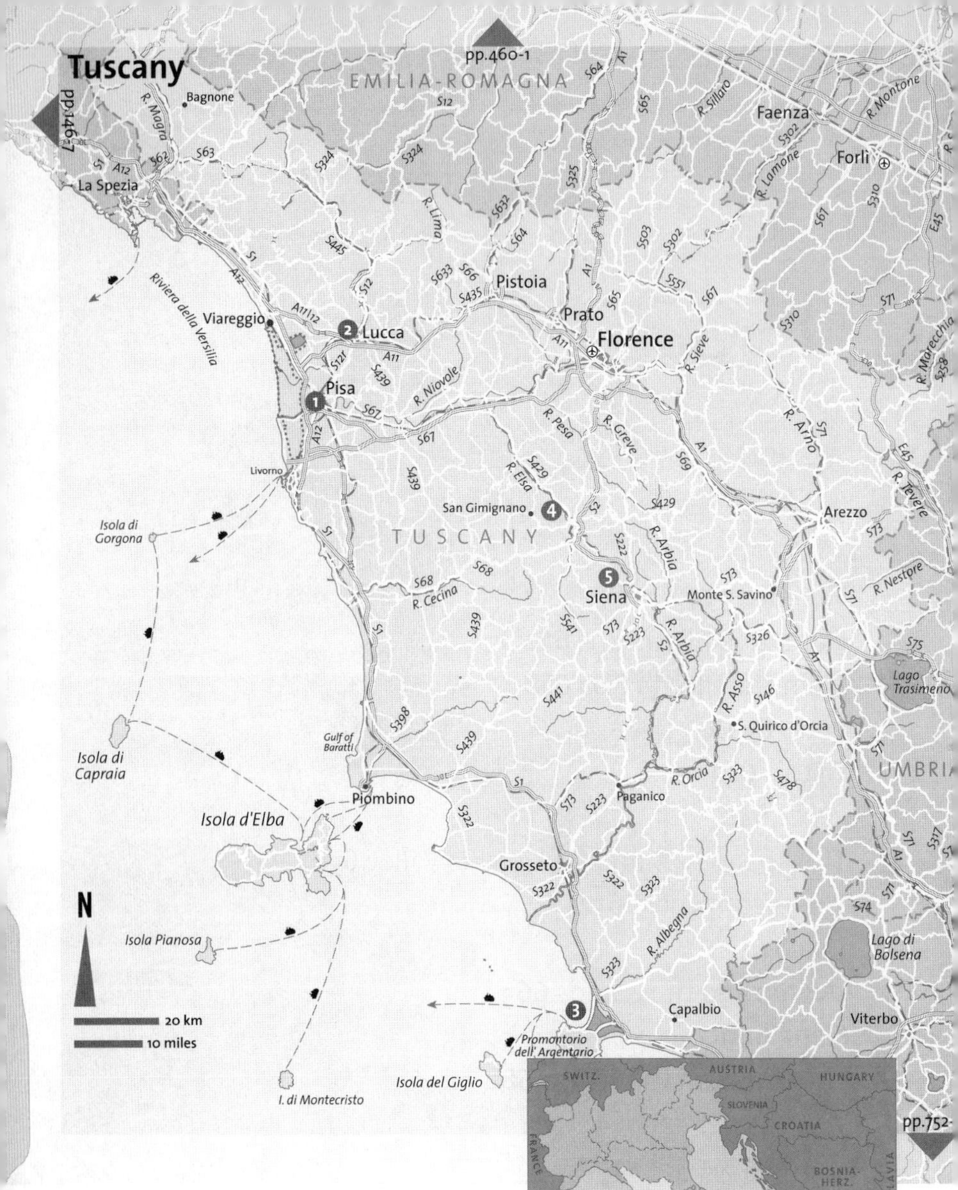

Highlights

1 Pisa's Field of Miracles
2 Lucca's brick walls and marble churches
3 Monte Argentario: Spanish forts and posh resorts
4 San Gimignano's skyline of medieval skyscrapers
5 The Palazzo Pubblico and Siena's Campo

No region could be more essentially Italian: its Renaissance culture and art became the whole of Italy's, and its dialect, as refined by Dante, cast 100 other dialects into the shadows to become the Italian language. Nevertheless, Tuscany seems to stand a bit aloof from the rest of the nation; it keeps its own counsel, never changes its ways, and faces the world with a Mona Lisa smile that has proved irresistible to northerners since the days of Shelley and Browning.

Today Britons, Dutch, Germans and Americans jostle each year for the privilege of forking out for a month in a classic Tuscan farmhouse, with a view over a charmed, civilized landscape of cypresses and parasol pines, orderly rows of vines and olives, and a chapel on the hill with a quattrocento fresco. In Florence and the other cities, they stand in queues like refugees, waiting to enter the churches and museums that are the shrines of Tuscan art.

For a province that has contributed so much to western civilization since the Middle Ages, Tuscany's career remains slightly mysterious. Some have attempted to credit its cultural prominence to an inheritance from the ancient Etruscans, but most of modern Tuscany was never more than provincial throughout Etruscan and Roman times. Out of the Dark Ages, inexplicably, new centres of learning and art appeared, first in Pisa and Florence, then in a dozen other towns, inaugurating a cultural Renaissance that really began as early as the 1100s.

As abruptly as it began, this brilliant age was extinguished in the 16th century, but it left behind a new province of Europe, finished, solid and well formed. Tuscany can be excused a little complacency. Though prosperous and enlightened, fully a part of modern Italy today, the region for centuries has seemed perfectly content to let the currents of culture and innovation flow elsewhere. There's no sense in painting when anything new would have to hang next to Da Vincis and Botticellis, no incentive to build in a city full of churches and palaces by the medieval masters. After the wave of bad taste that brought the Renaissance to a close, Tuscany was shamed into an introspection and cultural conservatism of almost Chinese proportions.

Of course these centuries, during which Tuscany has quietly cultivated its own garden, have not been without some advantages. Its cities and their art treasures have been preserved with loving care. So has the countryside; if anything the last few hundred years have emphasized the frugal, hard-working side of the Tuscan character, the side that longs for the rural life, counts its pennies, and finds tripe with chickpeas a perfectly satisfying repast. All this at times makes a striking contrast with the motorways, the new industry around the cities, and the hordes of tourists descending on Florence, Pisa and Siena.

Florence

Venice, they say, moves one to dream a bit; Rome inspires you to contemplate the endless panorama of popes and Caesars; Naples convinces you that all is vanity. Florence (Firenze) on the other hand, a town long famed for good common sense and healthy scepticism, is different. It will not tempt you to easy conclusions. It is as romantic as a reference library. Florence, they say, moves one to *argue*.

Most writers have assumed a certain point of view. You may think Florence is a museum city, they'll tell you, but you'll be wrong: Florence is a thriving, progressive town that refuses to live in the past, insisting on earning its own way in the 20th century. Once it made Galileo's telescope; today it still exports precision optical instruments. In the 1400s, it led Europe in fashion as well as art; today its industrious backstreet seamstresses do much of the work for the designers in Milan.

This argument is nice, but untrue; despite its noise, ice cream, light industry and horrendous traffic, Florence *is* a museum city, and if you don't care to look at pictures, you'd do better just to stay on the train. But what a museum city it is! Florence's collections easily surpass those of any other Italian city, and just from the odd bits in the back rooms its curators are able to mount a score of blockbuster special exhibitions each year. Most impressive of all is the fact that nearly all the art in them was made by the Florentines themselves – testimony to the city's position during two centuries as the great innovator of Western culture.

History

The Etruscans, who founded Florence, perhaps as early as 1000 BC, were typically coy about providing any further details; the city's early history remains a puzzle. Like so many cities, however, Florence seems to begin with a bridge. Dante and many other writers commonly invoke the *marzocco*, the battered ancient icon that sat in the middle of the Ponte Vecchio and any number of bridges that preceded it, until a flood swept it away in the 14th century. Often pictured as a lion (like the replacement for the original made by Donatello, on display in the Bargello Museum), the *marzocco* may really have been a cult image of the god Mars. Nothing could be more fitting, for in the centuries of its greatness Florence was a town full of trouble.

The city's apprenticeship in strife came during the Italian wars of the 4th–2nd centuries BC, when Rome was consolidating its hold on the peninsula. Florence seems to have chosen the wrong side. Sulla razed it to the ground during the Social Wars, and the town struggled back only gradually. Julius Caesar helped by planting a colony of veterans here in 59 BC. Roman Florence prospered, trading in the whole Empire. Its street plan survives in the neat rectangle of roads at the city's core. The town had an impressive forum right in the middle, at what is now Piazza della Repubblica.

If almost nothing remains from Roman times, it is only because Florence has been continuously occupied ever since, its centre constantly replanned and rebuilt. There were some hard times, especially during the Greek–Gothic wars of the 6th century and the Lombard occupation, but the city regained importance in the time of Charlemagne, becoming for a while the seat of the 'march' of Tuscany. Here, in what must have been one of the most fascinating eras of the city's history, we are once again left without much information. Florence, for whatever reason, was one of the first inland cities to regain its balance after the fall of the empire. In the Dark Ages the city was already beginning to develop the free institutions of the later republic, and establishing the trading connections that were later to make it the merchant capital of Europe. About 1115, on the death of the famous Countess Matilda of Tuscany, Florence became a self-governing *comune*.

The Florentine Republic

From the beginning, circumstances forced the city into an aggressive posture against enemies within and outside its walls. Florence waged constant war against the extortionist petty nobles of the hinterlands, razing their castles and forcing them to live in the city. As an important Guelph stronghold, Florence constantly got itself into trouble with the emperors, as well as with Ghibelline Pisa, Pistoia and Siena – towns that were to become its sworn enemies. In its darkest hour, after the crushing defeat at Montaperti in 1260, the Sienese almost succeeded in convincing their allies to bury Florence. A good sack would have been fun; Florence by the mid 13th century was possibly the richest banking and trading centre anywhere, and its gold florin had become a recognized currency across Europe.

In truth, Florence had no need of outside enemies. All through its history, the city did its level best to destroy itself. Guelph fought Ghibelline with impressive rancour, and when there were no Ghibellines left, the Guelphs split into factions called the Blacks and Whites and began murdering each other. In a different dimension, the city found different causes of civil strife in the class struggles between the *popolo grosso* – the 'fat commons' or wealthy merchant class – and the members of the poorer guilds. Playing one side against the other was the newly urbanized nobility. They brought their gangster habits to town with them, turning Florence into a forest of tall brick tower-fortresses and carrying on bloody feuds in the streets that the city officials were helpless to stop. No historian has ever been able to explain how medieval Florence avoided committing suicide altogether. But despite the troubles, this was the era of Dante (*d.* 1321, in political exile in Ravenna) and Giotto (*d.* 1337), and the beginning of Florence's cultural golden age. Banking and the manufacture of wool (the leading commodity in the pre-industrial economy) were booming, and the florins kept rolling in no matter which faction was on top.

In 1282, and again in 1293, Florence tried to clean up its violent and corrupt government by a series of reforms; the Ordinamenti della Giustizia finally excluded the nobles from politics. It didn't work for long. Political strife continued through the 14th century, along with eternal wars with Lucca, Pisa and Siena, and novel catastrophes. In 1339 Edward III of England repudiated his enormous foreign debt and Florence's largest banks, the Bardi and Peruzzi, went bust. Plagues and famines dominated the 1340s; the plague of 1348, the Black Death, killed three-fifths of the population (and provided the frame story for Boccaccio's *Decameron*). The nobles and merchants took advantage of the situation to establish tight boss rule. Their Guelph Party building is on Via Porta Rossa, where the spoils were divided – the original Tammany Hall. A genuine revolution in 1378 among the *ciompi*, the wool trade proletariat, might have succeeded if its leaders had been half as devious and ruthless as their opponents.

Florence's continuing good luck again saw it through, however, and prosperity gradually returned after 1400. In 1406 Pisa was finally conquered, giving Florence a sea port. Florentine armies bested the Visconti of Milan twice, and once (1410) even occupied Rome. At the dawn of the Renaissance not only Florence's artists, scholars and scientists were making innovations – the city government in the 1420s and 1430s invented the progressive income tax and the national debt.

The Rise of the Medici

Although they are said to have begun as pharmacists (*medici*), by 1400 the House of Medici was the biggest merchant concern in Florence. With the resources of the Medici Bank behind him, Cosimo de' Medici installed himself as the city's political godfather, coercing or buying off the various interests and factions. In 1469 his grandson Lorenzo inherited the job, presiding over the greatest days of the Renaissance and a sustained stretch of peace and prosperity. Opposition, squashed originally by Cosimo, stayed squashed under Lorenzo. His military campaigns proved successful on the whole, and his impressive propaganda machine gave him an exaggerated reputation as a philosopher-king and patron of the arts. Lorenzo almost ruined the Medici Bank through neglect, but then made up his losses from public funds. His personal tastes in art seem to have been limited to knick-knacks, big jewels and antique bronzes, but his real hobby was nepotism. His son Giovanni, later to be made Pope Leo X at the age of 38, became a cardinal at 14.

Two years after Lorenzo's death, the wealthy classes of Florence ended Medici rule when they exiled his weak son and successor, Piero, in 1494. The republic was restored, but soon came under the influence of a remarkable Dominican demagogue, Girolamo Savonarola. His fierce fundamentalist preaching resulted in the famous 1497 'Bonfire of Vanities' on Piazza della Signoria, when the people collected their paintings, fancy clothes, carnival masks and books and put them to the flame (a Venetian merchant offered to buy the whole lot from them, but the Florentines sketched a portrait of him too, and threw it on the pyre). But Savonarola was more than a ridiculous prude. His idealistic republicanism resulted in some real democratic reforms for the new government, and his emphasis on morals provided a much-needed purgative after the depravity of the previous 200 years. The friar reserved his strongest blasts for the corruption of the Church; not a bad idea in the time of Alexander VI, the Borgia pope. When Savonarola's opponents, the Arrabbiati ('Infuriated'), beat his supporters, the Piagnoni ('snivellers'), in the 1498 elections, the way was clear for Alexander to order the friar's execution. Savonarola burned on 22 May 1498, on the same spot where the 'Bonfire of Vanities' had been held, and his ashes were thrown in the Arno.

The Medici returned in 1512, thanks to Pope Julius II and his Spanish troops. The Spaniards' sack of Prato, with remarkable atrocities, was meant as a lesson. It had the desired effect, and Lorenzo's nephew Giuliano de' Medici re-entered the city. When Giuliano was elected Pope Clement VII in 1523 he tried to continue running the city at a distance, but another Medici expulsion took place after his humiliation in the sack of Rome in 1527, followed by the founding of the last Florentine republic.

By now Florentine politics had become a death struggle between an entire city and a single family; in the end the Medici proved to have the stronger will. The last republic lived nervously in an atmosphere of revolutionary apocalypse; meanwhile Clement intrigued with the Spaniards for his return. An imperial army arrived in 1530 to besiege the city and, despite heroic last-ditch resistance, Florence had to capitulate when its commander sold out to the Pope and turned his guns on the city itself. In 1532 the Medici broke the terms of the surrender agreement by abolishing all self-government, obtaining the title of Grand Dukes of Tuscany from Emperor Charles V.

To all intents and purposes Florentine history ends here. Cosimo I Medici (*d.* 1574) ruled over a state that declined rapidly into a provincial backwater. When the last Medici, fat Gian Gastone, died in 1737, the powers of Europe gave the duchy to the House of Lorraine. With the rest of Tuscany, Florence was annexed to Piedmont-Sardinia in 1859, and from 1865 to 1870 it served as the capital of united Italy.

Today, despite repeated attempts to diversify the local economy through the creation of new industrial areas on the outskirts, Florence largely lives on the sheer weight of its past creativity. It suffered badly in the Second World War, when the retreating German army blew up all the bridges over the Arno except the Ponte Vecchio, and destroyed many medieval buildings along the river's edge. Still worse damage was caused by the great floods of 1966, which left several people dead and many buildings and artworks in need of restoration work that continues today. The most recent damage to be inflicted on the city came in 1993, when a bomb planted by the Mafia exploded near the Uffizi, killing the family of a caretaker, destroying a Renaissance library and substantially damaging parts of the Uffizi itself, particularly the Vasari corridor. The perpetrators were tried in 1998 and 14 life sentences were given, including the conviction of Toto Riina, the 'Boss of Bosses'.

Florentine Art

Under the assault of historians and critics over the last two centuries, 'Renaissance' has become such a vague and controversial word as to be nearly useless. Yet however you interpret this rebirth of the arts, and whatever dates you assign it, Florence takes the credit for initiating it. This is no small claim. Combining art, science and humanist scholarship into a visual revolution that often seemed pure sorcery to their contemporaries, a handful of Florentine geniuses taught the western eye a new way of seeing. Perspective seems a simple enough trick now, but its discovery determined everything that followed, not only in art but in science and philosophy as well.

Florence in its centuries of brilliance accomplished more than any city, ever – far more than Athens in its classical age. The city's talents showed early, with the construction of the famous Baptistry, perhaps as early as 700. From the start Florence showed a remarkable adherence to the traditions of antiquity. New directions in architecture – the Romanesque after the year 1000 – had little effect; what passed for it in Florence was a unique style, evolved by a self-confident city that probably believed it was accurately restoring the grand manner of the Roman world. This new architecture (*see* the Baptistry, San Miniato, Santa Maria Novella), based on elegantly simple geometry with richly inlaid marble façades and pavements, was utterly unlike even the creations of nearby Pisa and Siena, and began a continuity of style that reached its climax with the work of **Brunelleschi** and **Alberti** in the 15th century.

Likewise in painting and sculpture, Florentines made an early departure from Byzantine-influenced forms, and avoided the International Gothic style that thrived so well in Siena. Vasari's famous *Lives of the Artists* (1547) lays down the canon of Florentine artists, the foundation of all subsequent art criticism. It begins with **Cimabue** (*c.* 1240–1302), who according to Vasari first began to draw away from Byzantine stylization towards a more 'natural' way of painting. Cimabue found his greatest pupil **Giotto** (1266–1337) as a young shepherd boy, chalk-sketching sheep on slate. Brought to Florence, Giotto soon eclipsed his master's fame (artistic celebrity being another recent Florentine invention) and achieved the greatest advances on the road to the new painting, a plain, idiosyncratic approach that avoided Gothic prettiness while exploring new ideas in composition and expressing psychological depth in his subjects. Even more importantly Giotto, through his intuitive grasp of perspective, was able to go further than any previous artist in representing his subjects as actual figures in space. In a sense Giotto invented space; it was this, despite his often awkward and graceless draughtsmanship, that so astounded his contemporaries.

Vasari, for reasons of his own, neglected the artists of the Florentine trecento, and many critics have tended to follow slavishly – a great affront to the master artist and architect **Andrea Orcagna** (*d.* 1368; works include the Loggia dei Lanzi and the Orsanmichele tabernacle) and others, including **Taddeo** and **Agnolo Gaddi** (*d.* 1366 and 1396), whose frescoes at Santa Croce can be compared to Giotto's.

The Quattrocento

The next turn in the story, what scholars self-assuredly called the 'Early Renaissance', comes with the careers of two geniuses who were good friends. **Donatello** (1386–1466), the greatest sculptor since the ancient Greeks, inspired a new generation of sculptors and painters to explore new horizons in portraiture and 3D representation. **Brunelleschi** (1377–1446), neglecting his considerable talents in sculpture for architecture and science, not only built the majestic cathedral dome, but threw the Pandora's box of perspective wide open by mathematically codifying the principles of foreshortening.

The new science of painting occasioned an explosion of talent unequalled before or since, as a score of masters, most of them Florentine by birth, each followed the dictates of his own genius to create a range of themes and styles hardly believable for one single city in a few short decades of its life. Among the most prominent were **Lorenzo Ghiberti** (*d.* 1455), famous for the bronze doors of the Baptistry; **Masaccio** (*d.* 1428), the eccentric prodigy much copied by later artists, best represented by his naturalistic frescoes in Santa Maria del Carmine and Santa Maria Novella; **Domenico Ghirlandaio** (*d.* 1494), Michelangelo's teacher and another master of detailed frescoes; **Fra Angelico** (*d.* 1455), the most spiritual and visionary of them all, the painter of the Annunciation at San Marco; **Paolo Uccello** (*d.* 1475), one of the most provocative of all artists, who according to Vasari drove himself bats with too-long contemplation of perspective and the newly discovered vacuum of empty space; **Benozzo Gozzoli** (*d.* 1497), a happier soul, best known for the springtime *Procession of the Magi* in the Medici Palace; **Luca Della Robbia** (*d.* 1482), greatest of a family of sculptors, famous for the cantoria of the cathedral museum and exquisite blue and white terracottas all over Tuscany; **Antonio Pollaiuolo** (*d.* 1498), an engraver and sculptor with a nervously perfect line; **Fra Filippo Lippi** (*d.* 1469), who ran off with a brown-eyed nun to produce **Filippino Lippi** (*d.* 1504), a similarly exceptional painter and stickler for detail; and finally **Sandro Botticelli** (*d.* 1510), whose progress from his astounding early mythological pictures to conventional holy pictures, done after he fell under the sway of Savonarola, marks the first failure of nerve in the Florentine imagination.

Leonardo, Michelangelo and the Cinquecento

With equal self-assurance, the critics used to refer to the early 1500s as the beginning of the 'High Renaissance'. **Leonardo da Vinci**, perhaps the incarnation of Florentine achievement in both painting and scientific speculation, lived until 1519 but spent much of his time in Milan and France. **Michelangelo Buonarroti** (*d.* 1564) liked to identify himself with Florentine republicanism, but finally abandoned the city during the siege of 1530 (even though he was a member of the committee overseeing Florence's defence). His departure left Florence with no important artists except the incredibly strange **Jacopo Pontormo** (*d.* 1556) and **Rosso Fiorentino** (*d.* 1540). These two, along with Michelangelo, were key figures in the bold, neurotic, avant-garde art art can be seen as a last fling amid the growing intellectual and spiritual exhaustion of 1530s Florence, conquered once and for all by the Medici. The Mannerists' calculated exoticism and exaggerated, tortured poses, together with the brooding self-absorption of Michelangelo and many others, are the prelude to Florentine art's remarkably abrupt downturn into decadence, and prophesy its final extinction.

There was another strain to Mannerism in Florence, following the cold classicism of Raphael of Urbino – less disturbed, less intense and challenging than Michelangelo or Pontormo. With artists such as **Agnolo Bronzino** (*d.* 1572), sculptor **Bartolomeo Ammannati** (*d.* 1592), **Andrea del Sarto** (*d.* 1531), and **Giorgio Vasari** himself (*d.* 1574), Florentine art loses imaginative and intellectual content, becoming a virtuoso style of interior decoration adaptable to saccharine holy pictures, portraits of dukes, or absurd mythological fountains and ballroom ceilings. In the cinquecento, when there was plenty of money to spend and a long Medici tradition of patronage to uphold, this got out of hand. Under the reign of Cosimo I, indefatigable collector of *pietra dura* tables, gold gimcracks, and exotic stuffed animals, Florence gave birth to kitsch.

In the cinquecento, Florence taught vulgarity to the Romans, degeneracy to the Venetians, and preciosity to the French – oddly enough, having as great an influence in its age of decay as in its age of greatness. The cute, well-educated Florentine pranced across Europe, finding himself praised as the paragon of culture and refinement, even in England – though that honest nation soon found him out:

A little Apish hatte, couched fast to the Pate, like an Oyster,
French Camarick Ruffes, deepe with a witnesse, starched to the purpose,
Delicate in speach, queynte in arraye: conceited in all poyntes:
In Courtly guyles, a passing singular odde man...

Mirror of Tuscanism, Gabriel Harvey, 1580

It's almost disconcerting to learn that Florence gave us not only much of the best of our civilization, but even a lot of the worst. Somehow the later world of powdered wigs and chubby winged putti is unthinkable without 1500s Florence. Then again, so is all of the last 500 years of art unthinkable without Florence, not to mention modern medicine (the anatomical studies of the artists set it on its way) or technology (the endless speculations and gadgets of Leonardo) or political science (from Machiavelli). The Florentines of course found the time to invent opera too, and give music a poke into the modern world. And without that discovery of the painters,

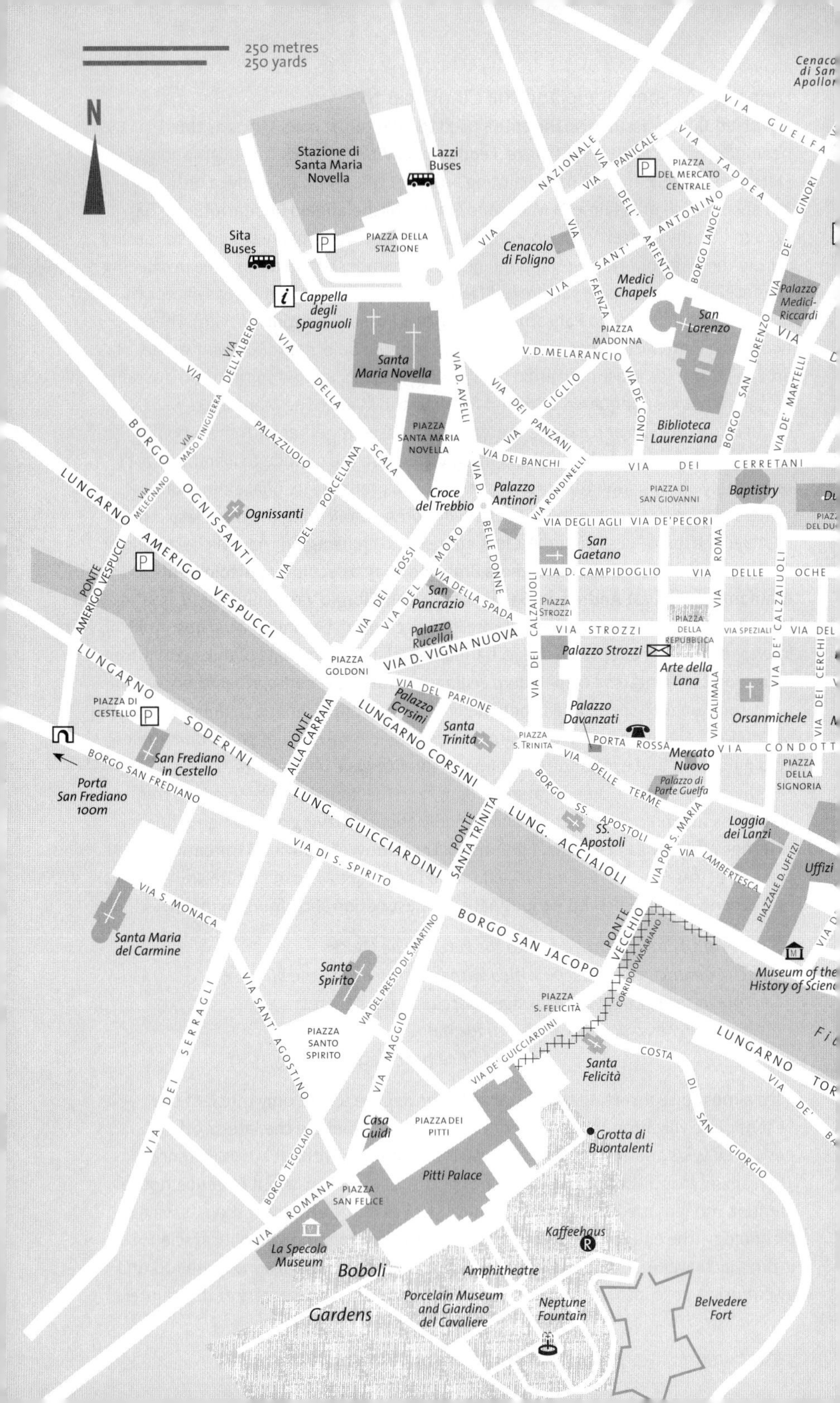
250 metres
250 yards
N
Stazione di Santa Maria Novella
Lazzi Buses
Sita Buses
PIAZZA DELLA STAZIONE
Cappella degli Spagnuoli
Santa Maria Novella
PIAZZA SANTA MARIA NOVELLA
Croce del Trebbio
Palazzo Antinori
Ognissanti
San Pancrazio
Palazzo Rucellai
PIAZZA GOLDONI
Palazzo Corsini
Santa Trìnita
PIAZZA S. TRINITA
San Frediano in Cestello
PIAZZA DI CESTELLO
Porta San Frediano 100m
Santa Maria del Carmine
Santo Spirito
PIAZZA SANTO SPIRITO
Casa Guidi
PIAZZA DEI PITTI
Pitti Palace
PIAZZA SAN FELICE
La Specola Museum
Boboli Gardens
Amphitheatre
Kaffeehaus
Porcelain Museum and Giardino del Cavaliere
Neptune Fountain
Belvedere Fort
Grotta di Buontalenti
Santa Felicità
PIAZZA S. FELICITÀ
Cenacolo di Foligno
Medici Chapels
San Lorenzo
Biblioteca Laurenziana
Palazzo Medici-Riccardi
PIAZZA DEL MERCATO CENTRALE
PIAZZA MADONNA
Cenacolo di San Apollonia
PIAZZA DI SAN GIOVANNI
Baptistry
Duomo
PIAZZA DEL DUOMO
San Gaetano
PIAZZA STROZZI
PIAZZA DELLA REPUBBLICA
Palazzo Strozzi
Arte della Lana
Orsanmichele
Palazzo Davanzati
Mercato Nuovo
Palazzo di Parte Guelfa
PIAZZA DELLA SIGNORIA
SS. Apostoli
Loggia dei Lanzi
Uffizi
Museum of the History of Science
VIA NAZIONALE
VIA PANICALE
VIA GUELFA
VIA TADDEA
VIA GINORI
VIA SANT' ANTONINO
VIA DELL' ARIENTO
BORGO LANOCE
VIA FAENZA
V.D.MELARANCIO
VIA DE' CONTI
BORGO SAN LORENZO
VIA DE' MARTELLI
VIA DEI CERRETANI
VIA DEI BANCHI
VIA DEI PANZANI
VIA DEL GIGLIO
VIA RONDINELLI
VIA D. AVELLI
VIA D. BELLE DONNE
VIA DEGLI AGLI
VIA DE' PECORI
VIA D. CAMPIDOGLIO
VIA DELLE OCHE
VIA ROMA
VIA STROZZI
VIA SPEZIALI
VIA DEL CORSO
VIA DEI CALZAIUOLI
VIA DE' CERCHI
VIA CALIMALA
PORTA ROSSA
VIA CONDOTTA
VIA DELLE TERME
BORGO SS. APOSTOLI
VIA POR S. MARIA
VIA LAMBERTESCA
PIAZZALE D. UFFIZI
VIA DELLA SCALA
VIA DEL PALAZZUOLO
VIA DELL'ALBERO
VIA MASO FINIGUERRA
VIA MELEGNANO
BORGO OGNISSANTI
VIA DEL PORCELLANA
VIA DEI FOSSI
VIA DEL MORO
VIA DELLA SPADA
VIA D. VIGNA NUOVA
VIA DEL PARIONE
LUNGARNO AMERIGO VESPUCCI
PONTE AMERIGO VESPUCCI
LUNGARNO SODERINI
BORGO SAN FREDIANO
PONTE ALLA CARRAIA
LUNGARNO CORSINI
LUNG. GUICCIARDINI
PONTE SANTA TRINITA
LUNG. ACCIAIOLI
PONTE VECCHIO
CORRIDOIO VASARIANO
VIA DI S. SPIRITO
BORGO SAN JACOPO
VIA S. MONACA
VIA DEI SERRAGLI
VIA SANT' AGOSTINO
VIA DEL PRESTO DI S. MARTINO
VIA MAGGIO
VIA DE' GUICCIARDINI
COSTA DI SAN GIORGIO
VIA DE' BARDI
LUNGARNO TORRIGIANI
BORGO TEGOLAIO
VIA ROMANA
Fiume Arno

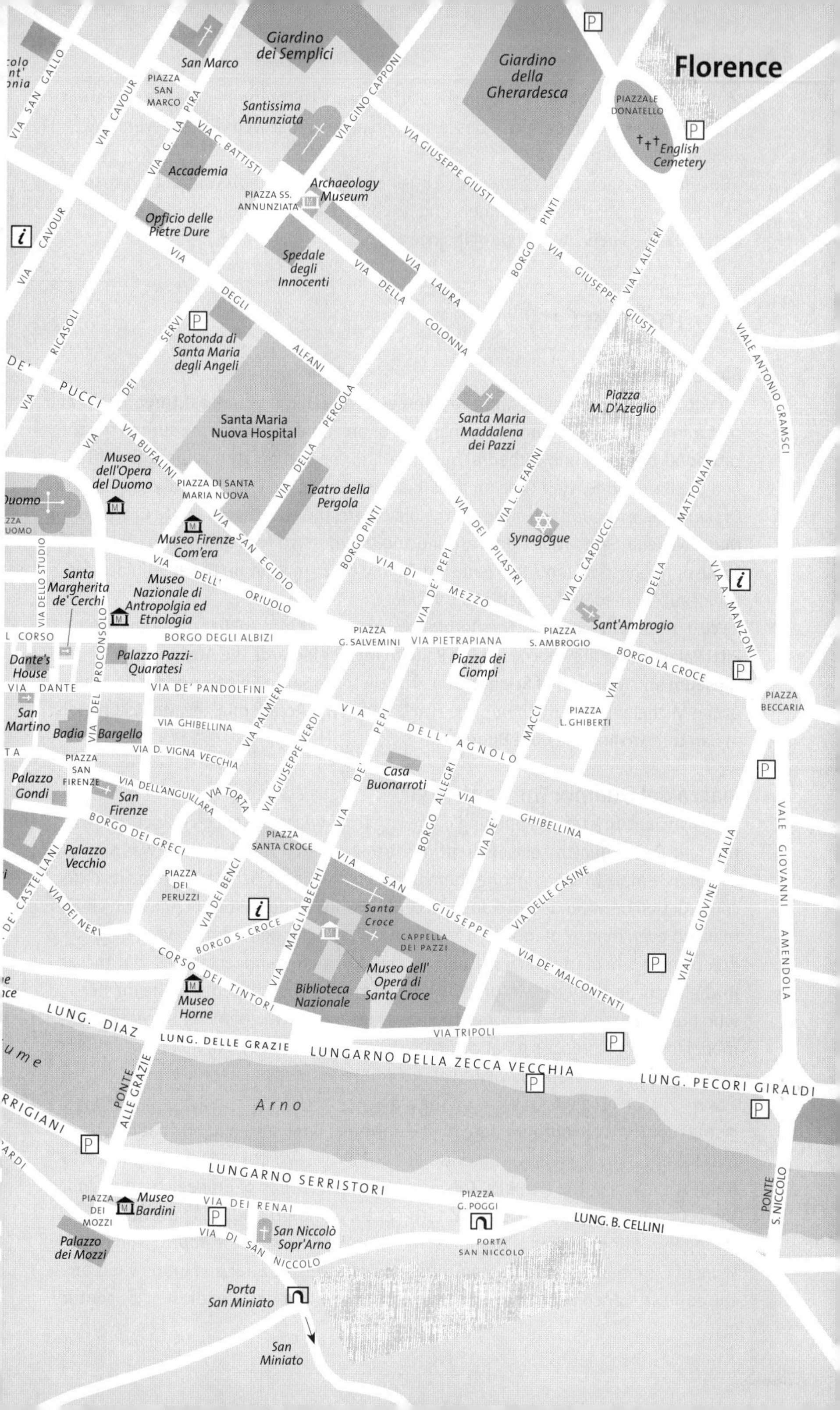
Florence
Giardino dei Semplici
San Marco
Giardino della Gherardesca
Piazzale Donatello
English Cemetery
Piazza San Marco
Via San Gallo
Via Cavour
Via G. La Pira
Via C. Battisti
Santissima Annunziata
Via Gino Capponi
Via Giuseppe Giusti
Accademia
Piazza SS. Annunziata
Archaeology Museum
Opficio delle Pietre Dure
Spedale degli Innocenti
Via della Colonna
Via Laura
Borgo Pinti
Via Giuseppe Giusti
Via V. Alfieri
Via degli Alfani
Via dei Servi
Via Ricasoli
Rotonda di Santa Maria degli Angeli
Viale Antonio Gramsci
Piazza M. D'Azeglio
Via de' Pucci
Santa Maria Nuova Hospital
Via della Pergola
Santa Maria Maddalena dei Pazzi
Via Bufalini
Museo dell'Opera del Duomo
Piazza di Santa Maria Nuova
Teatro della Pergola
Via L. C. Farini
Via Mattonaia
Duomo
Piazza Duomo
Museo Firenze Com'era
Via San Egidio
Via dei Pilastri
Synagogue
Via G. Carducci
Via dello Studio
Santa Margherita de' Cerchi
Museo Nazionale di Antropolgia ed Etnologia
Via dell'Oriuolo
Via di Mezzo
Via de' Pepi
Via della Mattonaia
Via A. Manzoni
Via del Proconsolo
Sant'Ambrogio
Via del Corso
Borgo degli Albizi
Piazza G. Salvemini
Via Pietrapiana
Piazza S. Ambrogio
Borgo la Croce
Dante's House
Palazzo Pazzi-Quaratesi
Piazza dei Ciompi
Via Dante
Via de' Pandolfini
Piazza Beccaria
Piazza L. Ghiberti
Via Macci
San Martino
Badia
Bargello
Via Ghibellina
Via Palmieri
Via dell'Agnolo
Via D. Vigna Vecchia
Via Giuseppe Verdi
Piazza San Firenze
Casa Buonarroti
Palazzo Gondi
San Firenze
Via dell'Anguillara
Via Torta
Borgo Allegri
Via Ghibellina
Viale Giovanni Amendola
Borgo dei Greci
Piazza Santa Croce
Via de' Macci
Palazzo Vecchio
Via de' Castellani
Piazza dei Peruzzi
Via dei Benci
Via San Giuseppe
Via delle Casine
Viale Italia
Via dei Neri
Santa Croce
Cappella dei Pazzi
Viale Giovine Italia
Borgo S. Croce
Via Magliabechi
Museo dell' Opera di Santa Croce
Via de' Malcontenti
Corso dei Tintori
Biblioteca Nazionale
Museo Horne
Lung. Diaz
Lung. delle Grazie
Via Tripoli
Lungarno della Zecca Vecchia
Lung. Pecori Giraldi
Fiume
Ponte alle Grazie
Arno
Lung. Torrigiani
Lungarno Serristori
Ponte S. Niccolo
Piazza dei Mozzi
Museo Bardini
Via dei Renai
Piazza G. Poggi
Lung. B. Cellini
Palazzo dei Mozzi
Via di San Niccolo
San Niccolò Sopr'Arno
Porta San Niccolo
Porta San Miniato
San Miniato

so simple though so hard for us in the 20th century to comprehend – the invention of space – Newton, Copernicus, Descartes and all who followed would never have discovered anything.

But Florence soon tired of the whole business. The city withdrew into itself, made a modest living, polished its manners and its conceit, and generally avoided trouble. Not a peep has been heard out of it since 1600.

Around the City

Florence Highlights

If you wanted to see everything worth seeing, it would take at least three weeks and cost a small fortune in admission charges. For an abbreviated tour, be sure to see the **cathedral, baptistry** and **cathedral museum**, and the two great museums, the **Uffizi** and the **Bargello**, leaving time for a walk around the Ponte Vecchio and a stop at **Orsanmichele**. Around the edges of the old centre, the churches of **Santa Croce, Santa Maria Novella, Santa Maria del Carmine** and the monastery of **San Marco** contain some of the best of Florentine painting. Finally, try to make it up to **San Miniato**, for the beautiful medieval church and the view over the city.

With more time, consider the florid 16th-century art in the **Palazzo Vecchio** and **Pitti Palace**, Gozzoli's frescoes in the **Palazzo Medici-Riccardi**, the **Archaeology Museum** and **Museum of Science**, and Brunelleschi's **Santo Spirito**. And for devotees of the Michelangelo cult, there's the real David in the **Accademia**, the **Medici Chapels** at San Lorenzo and the **Casa Buonarroti**.

Piazza del Duomo: The Baptistry

This ancient, mysterious building is the egg from which Florence's golden age was hatched. By the quattrocento, Florentines firmly believed their baptistry was originally a Roman temple to Mars, linking them to a legendary past. Scholarship sets its date of construction between the 6th and 9th centuries, in the darkest Dark Ages, which makes it even more remarkable; it may as well have dropped from heaven. Its dark green and white marble facing, the tidily classical arches and rectangles that tricked Brunelleschi and Alberti, was probably added around the 11th century. The masters who built it remain unknown, but their original exercise in geometry provided the model for all of Florence's great church façades. When it was new, there was nothing remotely like it in Europe; to visitors it must have seemed almost miraculous.

Every 21 March, New Year's Day on the old Florentine calendar, children born in the last 12 months were brought here for a communal baptism – a habit that helped make it not merely a religious monument but a civic symbol, in fact the oldest and fondest symbol of the republic. The Florentines never tired of embellishing it. Under the octagonal cupola, the 13th- and 14th-century gold-ground mosaics show a strong Byzantine influence, though some (*The Life of St John the Baptist*) may be the work of Cimabue. The equally beautiful mosaics over the altar and in the vault are the earliest, signed by a monk named Iacopo in the first decades of the 13th century.

Getting There

Florence is the central transport node for Tuscany and harder to avoid than to reach.

By Air

Vespucci **airport** 6km away at Peretola, **t** 055 373 498 or **t** 055 306 1702 (recorded flight message in Italian and English), has regular buses to Santa Maria Novella station (15mins). A taxi to the centre is about €15.50 plus surcharges (baggage and so on).

To get to Florence from Pisa airport, take the special train service to Santa Maria Novella, taking 1hr and leaving every hour or so.

By Train

The central station is **Santa Maria Novella**, **t** 8488 88088. Many long-distance trains arriving at night use **Campo di Marte** station (buses no.10, 12 or 13).

By Bus

You can reach nearly every city, town and village in Tuscany from Florence once you know which bus company to use. The tourist office has a full list of destinations; these are some of the most popular:

SITA: (near station, Via S. Caterina da Siena 15, freephone within Italy **t** 800 373 760, or **t** 055 294 955): towns in the Val d'Elsa, Chianti, Val di Pesa, Mugello and Casentino; Arezzo, Bibbiena, Castelfiorentino, Certaldo, Consuma, Figline Valdarno, Firenzuola, Marina di Grosseto, Montevarchi, Poggibonsi (for Volterra and San Gimignano), Pontassieve, Poppi, Pratovecchio, Scarperia, Siena, Stia, Vallombrosa.

LAZZI: (Piazza Stazione 47r, **t** 055 351 061 Mon–Fri, or 24hr recorded info **t** 166 845 010): along the Arno to the coast, including Calenzano, Cerreto Guidi, Empoli, Forte dei Marmi, Livorno, Lucca, Marina di Carrara, Marina di Massa, Montecatini Terme, Montelupo, Montevarchi, Pescia, Pisa, Pistoia, Pontedera, Prato, Signa, Tirrenia, Torre del Lago, Viareggio.

CAP: (Via Nazionale 13, **t** 055 214 637): Borgo S. Lorenzo, Impruneta, Incisa Valdarno, Prato.

COPIT: (Piazza S. Maria Novella, **t** 055 214 637: Abetone, Cerreto Guidi, Pistoia, Poggio a Caiano, Vinci.

RAMA: (Lazzi Station, **t** 055 239 8840): Grosseto.

By Car

All roads into the city meet an inner ring of roads, the *Viali* around the historic centre, much of which is closed to traffic. There are large car parks all around the *Viali*, particularly around **Fortezza da Basso** and **Piazza Libertà** at the 'Parterre'; they are quite expensive but not as much as those in the centre.

Getting Around

Nearly everything you'll want to see is within easy walking distance, large areas in the centre are pedestrian zones; there are no hills, and it's hard to lose your way for long.

There are two sets of **address numbers** on every street – red ones for business, blue or black for residences; your hotel might be either. However, recent years have seen some improvement in the signage department: every major piazza, landmark or monument has a plaque with background information, and maps have been posted around the city.

By Bus

City buses (ATAF) are an excellent means of reaching sights on the periphery. Most lines begin at Santa Maria Novella station. ATAF supplies a comprehensive booklet with a clear map and details of all routes, available at the info/ticket booth at the station, tourist offices, some bars, and ATAF's central office in Piazza della Stazione, **t** 055 565 0222.

A fleet of Lilliputian electric buses, routes A, B and D, mainly serve the centre, often taking circuitous routes 'round the houses', and are a good way of seeing some of the sights if you've had enough walking. Details of routes can be found on the ATAF maps.

By Taxi

Taxis in Florence don't cruise; you'll find them in ranks at the station and in the *piazze*, or ring for a radio taxi: **t** 055 4798 or 4390.

Bicycle, Scooter and Car Hire

Hiring a bike can save you tramping time, but watch out for cars and pedestrians. You can hire bikes and motorbikes at:

Alinari, Via Guelfa 85r, **t** 055 280 500.

Florence by Bike, Via S. Zanobi 120/122r, **t** 055 488 992.

Tourist Information

Florence

There are central **tourist offices** at Via Cavour 1r, **t** 055 290 832 (*open Mon–Sat 8.15–7.15, Sun 8.30–1.30*), Borgo Santa Croce 29r, **t** 055 234 0444 (*open Mon–Sat 9–7, Sun 9–2*) and Piazza Stazione, **t** 055 212 245 (*open Mon–Sat 8.30–7, Sun 8.30–1.30*). See *www.turismofirenze.it* and *www.comune.firenze.it*.

In summer, look out for the mobile 'Tourist Help Points' set up in the centre of town.

Fiesole

Via Portigiani 3, **t** 055 598 720 (*open Mon–Sat 8.30–7.30, Sun 10–7*).

APT tourist service: *www.firenze.turismo.toscana.it*.

Shopping

Markets and Antiques

Florence's famous, boisterous street markets are usually open every day. The big **San Lorenzo market**, which has spread all over the neighbourhood around San Lorenzo church, is where ordinary Florentines buy most of their clothes. In this little bit of Naples transplanted to Tuscany, the range of choice is equal to that of 3 department stores; you'll see plenty of fake designer labels, and even some real ones.

Further west in Santa Croce, in **Piazza dei Ciompi**, the daily *mercato delle pulci* (flea market) offers a wide array of desirable junk, beneath Vasari's fish loggia; the shopkeepers, being Florentines, are a little smug and not inclined to bargain. More serious **antiques shops** are clustered in the streets between Via Tornabuoni and the Ognissanti, and on Via Maggio.

The **Mercato Nuovo**, or *Mercato del Porcellino*, right in the centre of town, still performs its age-old function of selling Florentine straw goods – hats and bags. There is a bustling **food market** at Sant'Ambrogio.

Fashion and Jewellery

Florence has shaken off its one-time staidness in terms of shopping: Prada, Gucci, Armani and the like all now have mega-stores here. The big fashion names and the chain stores are well represented in smart **Via Tornabuoni**, **Via Calzaiuoli** and the streets around the Duomo.

Have a look around **Via della Vigna Nuova**, **Via del Parione** and **Piazza S. Croce** for choice leather goods.

The jewellery shops lining the **Ponte Vecchio** are forced into competition by their location, and you can get good prices for Florentine brushed gold, cameos and antique jewellery (much of it now made in Arezzo). They're not here just to exploit tourists – they've been on the bridge for more than 300 years.

Marbled Paper

Florence is one of the few places where marbled paper, an art brought over from the Orient by Venice in the 12th century, is made. Marbled-paper-covered stationery and sheets of marbled paper are available at **Giulio Giannini e Figlio**, Piazza Pitti 37r, the oldest manufacturer in the city, **Il Papiro**, Via Cavour 55r, Piazza del Duomo 24r and Lungarno Acciaiuoli 42r, **La Bottega Artigiana del Libro**, Lungarno Corsini 40r, and **Il Torchio**, Via de' Bardi 17, a shop/workshop where you can see the artisans in action.

Where to Stay

Florence ✉ 50100

You should count on paying around 25 per cent more for a room here than anywhere else in Italy. Historic old palace-hotels are the rule rather than the exception; the ones we've listed are some of the more atmospheric and charming, but few are secrets, so book well in advance. Nearly every hotel with a restaurant will require half-board, and many will also try to lay down a heavy breakfast charge as well.

There are almost 400 hotels in Florence, but this is not enough for everyone who arrives in July and Aug without a reservation. However, there are several agencies that can help you find a room in nearly any price range for a small commission.

ITA: Santa Maria Novella station, **t** 055 282 893, *open 9–8*. No phone bookings.

Florence Promhotels: Viale A. Volta 72, **t** 055 553 941. A free booking service.

For **agriturismo** (farmhouse) accommodation in the countryside, self-catering or otherwise, contact: Agriturist Toscana, Via degli Alfeni 67, **t** 055 287 838, *www.agriturist.it*; or Turismo Verde Toscana, Via Verdi 5, **t** 055 234 4925.

Luxury

★★★★★**Excelsior**, Piazza Ognissanti 3, **t** 055 2715, *www.westin.com*. Napoleon's sister Caroline's one-time address, with lots of marble and plants and decadent bedrooms, many with river views (for a price).

★★★★★**Gallery**, Hotel Art, Vicolo dell'Oro 2, **t** 055 27263, *www.lungarnohotels.com*. Florence's only design hotel, East-meets-West in style yet far from minimalist. The smart bar serves fusion food.

★★★★★**Helvetia & Bristol**, Via dei Pescioni 2, **t** 055 287 814, *www.charminghotels.it*. Fifty-two lovely bedrooms, each different, with rich fabrics adorning windows, walls and beds. Stravinsky, D'Annunzio, Bertrand Russell and Pirandello stayed here; added pluses are the restaurant (one of the finest in town) and the delightful winter garden.

★★★★★**The Savoy**, Piazza Repubblica 7, **t** 055 283 313, *www.rfhotels.com*. A once-crumbling hotel now striking a minimalist tone with its cream, beige and grey décor. It has a bar and restaurant on the piazza.

★★★★**Lungarno**, Borgo San Jacopo 14, **t** 055 27261, *www.lungarnohotels.com*. A discreet hotel on the river, a 2min walk from the Ponte Vecchio. The ground-floor restaurant has picture windows over the water. The modern building incorporates a medieval tower. The small-ish bedrooms are decorated in smart blue and cream; the best have balconies with 'The View' (book way ahead for these).

Expensive

★★★**Beacci Tornabuoni**, Via Tornabuoni 3, **t** 055 212 645, *www.bthotel.it*. An excellent small hotel in the centre of fashionable Florence, situated on the top three floors of an elegant Renaissance palace. The rooms are comfortable, and you can enjoy drinks on the panoramic roof terrace.

★★★**Hermitage**, Vicolo Marzio 1, **t** 055 287 216, *www.hermitagehotel.com*. A little hotel tucked away behind the Ponte Vecchio on the north side of the river. The reception and elegant sitting room are on the fifth floor, together with a ravishing roof garden. The bedrooms below are on the small side but charmingly furnished with antiques and tasteful fabrics; some have river views.

Moderate

★★★★**Villa Belvedere**, Via Benedetto Castelli 3, 1km above Porta Romana, **t** 055 222 501, *www.villa-belvedere.com*. A pleasant alternative to central accommodation, with a beautiful garden, a nice pool and good views. Rooms are modern, spacious and comfortable, with lots of wood. Light meals are served in the restaurant, and there's a nearby bus into town.

★★★**Casci**, Via Cavour 13, **t** 055 211 686, *www.hotelcasci.com*. A relaxed and cheerful hotel in a 15th-century *palazzo* that was once home to Rossini. The reception area is full of helpful information, the breakfast room has a frescoed ceiling, and the rooms are bright and modern (some look on to a garden at the back).

★★★**Classic Hotel**, Viale Machiavelli 25, **t** 055 229 351, *www.classichotel.it*. A pink-washed villa in a shady garden (a welcome respite from the heat of the city) in a very pleasant location just above Porta Romana on the way to Piazzale Michelangelo, a 5min walk from a bus stop to the centre. Breakfast is served in a conservatory in summer.

★★★**Mario's**, Via Faenza 89, **t** 055 216 801, *www.hotelmarios.com*. A haven in a street with more than its fair share of hotels, many dubious, convenient for the station and a block or two from the central market. The atmosphere is friendly, the décor rustic Florentine, the breakfasts generous. Guests are pampered with fresh flowers and fruit on arrival. Rooms at the front can be noisy.

★★**Residenza Johanna Uno**, Via Bonifacio Lupi 14, **t** 055 481 896, *www.johanna.it*. A 'non hotel' a short way from the centre of town, with no phones or TVs in the pretty, mainly en suite rooms, though furnishings are comfortable, there are DIY breakfast trays in the rooms and kettles in the corridor, and lots of reading matter is supplied. Johanna Due is at Via Cinque Giornate 12, near the Fortezza da Basso (**t** 055 473 377).

★★★**Silla**, Via dei Renai 5, **t** 055 234 2888, *www.hotelsilla.it*. An old-fashioned *pensione* situated in a quiet and relatively green neighbourhood a 10min walk east of the Ponte Vecchio on the south bank of the river. Set on the first floor of a 16th-century *palazzo*, it boasts a very spacious breakfast terrace affording wonderful views over the Arno and beyond.

Cheap

★★**Belletini**, Via de' Conti 7, **t** 055 213 561, *www.firenze.net*. A friendly place located near the Medici chapels and decorated in traditional Florentine style; a couple of the bedrooms offer stunning views of the nearby domes.

★**Azzi**, Via Faenza 56, **t** 055 213 806. A friendly, homely *pensione* situated in a street full of cheap options near the station, aimed at students and budget travellers. Three of the bedrooms have en suite facilities, and there is a big terrace.

★**Maxim**, Via dei Medici 4, **t** 055 217 474, *www.firenzealbergo.it/home/hotelmaxim*. A centrally located budget hotel with a bright, elegant reception room and well-furnished modern bedrooms, all en suite, one with a jacuzzi.

★**Orchidea**, Borgo degli Albizi 11, **t** 055 248 0346. A hotel run by an Anglo-Italian family, set in a 12th-century building where Dante's in-laws once lived. There are 7 cheerful rooms, one with a private shower; the best look on to a garden at the back.

★**Scoti**, Via Tournabuoni 7, **t** 055 292 128. A simple *pensione* in an upmarket location – ideal if you would rather splurge on clothes in the surrounding shops. It has basic, large rooms of up to four beds with shared baths but there's bags of atmosphere, starting with the wall frescoes in the sitting room.

★**Sorelle Bandini**, Piazza Santo Spirito 9, **t** 055 215 308. A popular place despite its state of disrepair and relatively high prices – partly because of the romantic loggia along one side of the fourth-storey hotel, partly because of its location on Piazza Santo Spirito, bustling by day and lively (and noisy) at night. Expect uncomfortable beds, cavernous rooms, heavy Florentine furniture and a certain shabby charm.

Fiesole ✉ 50014

Fiesole is cooler and quieter than Florence itself, and at night the city far below twinkles as if made of fairy lights.

★★★★★**Villa San Michele**, Via Doccia 4, **t** 055 567 8200, *www.orient-expresshotels.com* (*luxury*). A 14th-century monastery boasting a breathtaking location just below Fiesole, with a façade and loggia that were reputedly designed by Michelangelo. One of the most beautiful hotels in Italy, it is set in a lovely Tuscan garden with a pool. The 29 bedrooms are elegantly furnished and air-conditioned; suites have jacuzzis. The food is superb.

★★★**Villa Fiesole**, Via Beato Angelico 35, **t** 055 597 252, *www.villafiesole.it* (*luxury*). Once part of the San Michele convent, this newish hotel has smart, neoclassical interiors and 4-star facilities. Light meals are served in a sunny dining room or on the adjacent terrace, and there is a pool. It's fully wheelchair-accessible.

★★★**Pensione Bencistà**, Via Benedetto di Maiano 4, **t** 055 59163 (*moderate*). A former monastery with wonderful views from its flower-decked terrace and friendly service. Bedrooms are comfortably furnished with solid antique pieces. Half-board is obligatory but prices are reasonable.

★★**Le Cannelle**, Via Gramsci 52, **t** 055 597 8336, *www.lecannelle.com* (*moderate*). A friendly B&B run by 2 sisters on the main street. Rooms are comfortably rustic and there is a pretty breakfast room.

★**Villa Sorriso**, Via Gramsci 21, **t** 055 59027, (*cheap*). An unpretentious, comfortable hotel in the centre of Fiesole, with a terrace overlooking Florence.

Eating Out

Even in the cheaper restaurants standards are high, and there's always lots of good red Chianti to accompany your meal. The city centre is full of *tavole calde*, pizzerias and snack bars where you can grab a sandwich or a salad instead of a full sit-down meal.

Many of the best places close for all or part of Aug; you would also be wise to call ahead and reserve for the others.

Florentine food is simple: a typical *primo* could be *pappardelle*, a wide egg-pasta served with a meat sauce, or game such as wild boar, rabbit and duck. Soups are also popular: try *ribollita*, a thick, hearty soup unique to the region, made with left-over bread, beans, black cabbage and other vegetables; or *pappa al pomodoro*, a bread-based soup with tomatoes, basil and sludgy local olive oil.

The most famous main course is *bistecca alla fiorentina*, a thick steak on the bone, cut from loin of beef, cooked on charcoal and simply seasoned with salt and pepper. As for vegetables, try *piselli alla fiorentina*, peas with oil, parsley and diced bacon; *tortino di carciofi*, omelette with fried artichokes; *fagioli all'uccelletto*, cannellini beans stewed with tomatoes, garlic and sage; and *spinaci saltati*, spinach sauteed with garlic and olive oil.

Real Florentine soul food rarely turns up on restaurant menus, and unless you make an effort to find it you'll never learn what a Florentine cook can do with cockscombs, intestines, calves' feet and tripe.

Desserts tend to be sweet and fattening: *bomboloni alla crema* are vanilla-filled dough-nuts and *le fritelle di San Giuseppe* bits of deep-fried batter covered in sugar. If you prefer cheese, try the sturdy *pecorino toscano*.

Very Expensive

Enoteca Pinchiorri, Via Ghibellina 87, near the Casa Buonarroti, **t** 055 242 777. One of the finest gourmet restaurants in Italy, with two Michelin stars. The food, a mixture of *nouvelle cuisine* and traditional Tuscan recipes, wins prizes every year, though Italians tend to complain about the minute portions. The cellars contain some 80,000 bottles of the best that Italy and France have to offer. Meals are served in a garden court in summer. *Closed Sun, Mon and Weds lunch.*

Expensive

Caffè Concerto, Lungarno C. Colombo 7, **t** 055 677 377. A beautifully located place on the north bank of the Arno east of the centre, with a warm wood and glass interior with lots of greenery. Traditional ingredients are given a new twist, and portions are hearty. *Closed Sun and 3wks Aug.*

Cibreo, Via dei Macci 118r, **t** 055 234 1100. One of the most Florentine of Florentine restaurants, overlooking Sant'Ambrogio market. Either go native and order tripe *antipasto*, cockscombs and kidneys, or play it safe with *prosciutto* from the Casentino, a fragrant soup of tomatoes, mussels and bell-pepper, and leg of lamb stuffed with artichokes, topped off with delicious lemon *crostata*, cheesecake or chocolate cake. *Closed Sun, Mon and Aug.*

Don Chisciotte, Via C. Ridolfi 4r, **t** 055 475 430. A small place between the Fortezza Basso and Piazza dell'Indipendenza, serving inventive Italian food with an emphasis on fish and vegetables, including baked baby squid, delicate warm vegetable and fish salad, and green tagliatelle with scampi and zucchini. *Closed Sun, and Mon lunch.*

Moderate

Buca Lapi, Via del Trebbio 1r, **t** 055 213 768. The old wine cellar of the lovely Palazzo Antinori, offering traditional favourites ranging from *pappardelle al cinghiale* (wide pasta with boar) to a *bistecca fiorentina con fagioli* that is hard to beat, plus Tuscan wines. *Closed Sun, and Mon lunch.*

Baldovino, Via Giuseppe 22r (Piazza S. Croce), **t** 055 241 773. An excellent trattoria/pizzeria run by a young Scotsman, where you can eat anything from a filled focaccia, a big salad and pizzas (from a wood-burning oven) to pasta, fish and steaks from the Val di Chiana. *Closed Mon.*

Beccofino, Piazza degli Scarlatti, **t** 055 290 076. A trendy restaurant on the river and beneath the British Institute library, with creative, elegantly presented dishes such as octopus salad, pasta flavoured with zucchini and saffron, sea bass on truffle mash, steak fillet with caramelized shallots, and a fabulous *bistecca alla Fiorentina*. You can eat a light meal in the wine bar, where prices are a good deal lower. *Closed Mon and lunchtimes.*

Il Latini, Via dei Palchetti 6r (by Palazzo Rucellai), **t** 055 210 916. A noisy, fun Florence institution (be prepared to queue; they don't accept bookings) where you eat huge portions of Florentine classics at long tables. The *primi* aren't great; go for the *bistecca* or the *gran pezzo* – a vast rib-roast of beef. The house wine is good; try a *riserva*. *Closed Mon and Aug*.

Sostanza, Via della Porcellana 25r, **t** 055 212 691. One of the last authentic Florentine trattorias, and a good place to eat *bistecca*, as well as the simple but delectable *petto di pollo al burro* (chicken breast sautéed in butter). *Closed Sat and Sun*.

Alla Vecchia Bettola, Viale Ariosto 32–34r, **t** 055 224 158. A noisy trattoria to the west of the Carmine, offering great food. The menu changes daily, but you can nearly always find *tagliolini con funghi porcini*. The grilled meats are tasty and succulent, and the ice cream comes from Vivoli. *Closed Sun and Mon*.

Cheap

Aquacotta, Via dei Pilastri 51r, **t** 055 242 907. A restaurant named after the simple but delicious bread soup, a speciality. Follow it with deep-fried rabbit with crisply fried zucchini flowers. *Closed Tues eve and Weds*.

La Casalinga, Via Michelozzi 9r, **t** 055 218 624. A family-run trattoria near Piazza Santo Spirito, always busy because of its simple home cooking and low prices. The *ribollita* is excellent. *Closed Sun*.

Centro Vegetariano Fiorentino, Via delle Ruote 30r, **t** 055 475 030. A self-service place west of San Marco, with a big choice of excellent soups, salads and more substantial dishes. *Closed Sun lunch and Mon*.

Ruth's,Via Farini 2a, **t** 055 248 0888. A bright, modern kosher vegetarian restaurant next to the synagogue, serving fish and Middle Eastern dishes. Try *brik*, a savoury pastry filled with fish, potatoes or cheese. *Closed Fri eve and Sat lunch*.

Santa Lucia, Via Ponte alle Mosse 102r, **t** 055 353 255. A noisy, steamy, unromantic Neapolitan-style pizzeria north of the Cascine, with possibly the best pizza in Florence. *Closed Weds*.

Trattoria del Carmine, Piazza del Carmine 18s, **t** 055 218 601. A bustling trattoria in the San Frediano district, with a long menu featuring *ribollita*, *pasta e fagioli* and roast pork, plus seasonal dishes such as risotto with asparagus or mushrooms, pasta with wild boar sauce and *ossobuco*. *Closed Sun*.

Trattoria Cibreo, Via de' Macci 122r, **t** 055 234 1100. A little annexe to smart Cibreo (*see* p.609), offering one of the best deals in town – the food is the same (excluding the odd more extravagant dish) but is served in a rustic setting on cheaper porcelain, and you pay a third what those dining next door pay. *Closed Sun and Mon*.

Cafés and *Gelaterie*

Caffè Ricchi, Piazza Santo Spirito. A local institution serving excellent, good-value light lunches and wonderful ice cream. The outside tables are on one of the most beautiful piazzas in Florence.

Dolci e Dolcezze, Piazza Cesare Beccaria 8r, east of Sant'Ambrogio market, **t** 055 234 5458. The most delicious cakes, pastries and marmalades in the city. The *crostate*, *torte* and *bavarese* are worth the splurge. *Closed Mon*.

Gelateria de' Ciompi, Via dell'Agnolo 121r. A traditional Florentine ice-cream parlour, tucked around the corner from Santa Croce and priding itself on its authentic home-made recipes, some of which are more than 50 years old.

Gilli, Piazza della Repubblica 13–14r. The oldest of Florence's grand old cafés, dating back to 1733, when the Mercato Vecchio still occupied this area. Its two panelled back rooms are especially pleasant during the winter.

Hemingway, near Piazza Carmine, **t** 055 284 781. A lovely café serving cocktails, a range of interesting light meals, excellent Sunday brunches and a selection of dreamy hand-made chocs and puddings (make sure to try the *sette veli* chocolate cake). Reservations are advised.

Rivoire, Piazza della Signoria 5r. An elegant, classy watering hole, with a marble-detailed interior as lovely as the piazza itself.

Vivoli, Via Isola delle Stinche 7r, between the Bargello and S. Croce. Decadently delicious ice-cream confections and rich *semifreddi*. *Closed Mon*.

Wine Bars

Fuori Porta, San Niccolo. Possibly the most famous *enoteca* of all, with 600 labels on the wine list and dozens of whiskeys and grappas. Snacks and hot dishes include *crostoni*, slabs of local bread topped with something delicious and grilled. *Closed Sun.*

Vini, Via dei Cimatori 38r. One of the last wine bars of its kind in Florence; join the locals standing on the street, glass and *crostino* in hand. *Closed Sun.*

Le Volpi e L'Uva, Piazza dei Rossi. A place just south of the Ponte Vecchio, specializing in relatively unknown labels. Snacks on offer include a marvellous array of French and Italian cheeses.

Entertainment and Nightlife

Slowly, slowly, Florence by night is beginning to mean more than the old *passeggiata* over the Ponte Vecchio and an ice cream, and perhaps a late trip up to Fiesole to contemplate the lights. Look for listings of concerts and events in Florence's daily, *La Nazione*. The tourist office's free *Florence Today* contains bilingual monthly information and a calendar, as does called *Florence Concierge Information*, a booklet available in hotels and tourist offices. **Box office**, Via Alamanni 39, **t** 055 210 804, is a central ticket agency for all major events in Tuscany and beyond, including classical, rock and jazz concerts.

Performance Arts and Music

The opera and ballet season runs from Sept to Christmas; performances also take place from Jan to Apr at the **Teatro del Maggio**, Corso Italia 16, **t** 055 211 158, and during the **Maggio Musicale** festival from mid-Apr until the end of June. There is usually more opera in July.

Classical concerts are held mainly at the **Teatro del Maggio**, **Teatro della Pergola**, Via della Pergola 12–32, **t** 055 226 4316; and **Teatro Verdi**, Via Ghibellina 99–101, **t** 055 212 320. Many smaller events take place year round in churches, cloisters and villas, with plenty of outdoor concerts in summer. Look out for posters: they are not always well publicized.

Rock and jazz concerts are held all year round. One of the best venues for live music is **Auditorium Flog**, Via M. Mercati 24b, **t** 055 490 437. Look out for the Musica dei Popoli festival in Nov. In summer there are lots of rock and jazz venues all over the city, many free, for when people move outdoors to cool off.

Cinemas

English-language **films** are shown on Mon and Tues at the Odeon, Via Sassetti 1, **t** 055 214 068, and on Thurs at **Fulgor**, Via Masi Finiguerra, **t** 055 238 1881.

From mid-June to mid-Sept, open-air screens in several venues show 2 films in Italian nightly. Details appear in newspapers.

Clubs and Discos

Many clubs have themed evenings; keep an eye out for posters or handouts or buy the listings magazine *Firenze Spettacolo*. Places are somewhat seasonal as well.

Central Park, Parco delle Cascine. Possibly the trendiest place in Florence in summer, full of serious clubbers dancing to live music on three dance floors.

Du Monde, Via San Niccolò 103r. A cocktail bar offering food, drink and music for elegant Florentines until 5am.

Ex-Mood, Corso dei Tintori 4. A young, energetic, underground venue with a good mix of music. *Closed Mon.*

Jackie O, Via Erta Canina 24. An old favourite amongst the 30-something crowd. *Closed Mon–Weds.*

Jazz Club, Via Nuova de' Caccini 3. A pleasant but smoky venue with live jazz on Fri and Sat nights, and a free jam session on Tues. *Closed Sun and Mon.*

Mago Merlino, Via dei Pilastri 31r. A relaxed tearoom/bar with live music, theatre, shows and games.

Maracanà, Via Faenza 4. Live samba, mambo and bossanova.

Piccolo Café, Borgo Santa Croce 23r. A tiny, friendly, arty gay bar.

Space Electronic, Via Palazzuolo 37. A high-tech noise box.

Tabasco, Piazza Santa Cecilia 3r. Italy's first gay bar, opened in the 1970s.

Universale, Via Pisana 77r. A vast ex-cinema boasting a giant cinema screen, designer décor, live music performances, a restaurant, several bars and a pizzeria. Chic, sleek surroundings for a chic, sleek crowd. *Closed Mon.*

To match the mosaics there is a beautiful inlaid marble floor decorated with the signs of the zodiac. Even more than the exterior, the patterned green and white marble of the interior walls is remarkable, combining influences from the ancient world and modern inspiration for something entirely new. It isn't cluttered inside; only a 13th-century Pisan-style baptismal font and the tomb of Anti-pope John XXIII, by Donatello and Michelozzo, stand out.

Art historians used to date the coming of the 'Renaissance' to 1401, with the famous competition for the baptistry's **bronze doors**, when Lorenzo Ghiberti defeated Brunelleschi and others for the commission. The south door had already been completed by Andrea Pisano, with scenes from the life of John the Baptist in Gothic quatrefoil frames, and in his north door Ghiberti attempted no new departures. After 1425, however, he began the great east doors (the ones with tourists piled up in front), which were to occupy much of his time for the next 27 years. These are the doors Michelangelo is said to have called 'worthy to be the Gates of Paradise', and undoubtedly they made a tremendous impression on all the artists of the quattrocento, using the same advances in composition and perspective and the same wealth of detail as the painters. The doors (they're copies – some of the original panels, restored after flood damage, are on display in the Museo dell' Opera del Duomo) have been cleaned and stand in gleaming contrast to the others.

The Old Testament scenes begin with the creation of Adam and Eve in the upper left corner, finishing with Solomon and Sheba in the Temple on the lower right-hand panel. On the frames, busts of contemporary Florentine artists peer out from tiny circles. It is a typical exhibition of Florentine pride that Ghiberti should put his friends among the prophets and sibyls that adorn the rest of the frames. Near the centre, the balding figure with arched eyebrows is Ghiberti himself.

The Duomo

Open Mon–Weds and Fri 10–5, Thurs 10–3.30, Sat 10–4.45, Sun 1.30–4.45.

For all its prosperity, Florence was one of the last cities to plan a great cathedral. Work began in the 1290s, with the sculptor Arnolfo di Cambio in charge, and the Florentines attempted to make up for their delay with audacity and size. Arnolfo laid the foundations for an octagonal crossing 146ft in diameter, then died before working out a way to cover it, leaving future architects the job of designing the biggest dome in the world. Surprisingly, the Duomo was built with little regard for innovation or for the prevailing styles; a visitor from France or England in the 1400s would have found it drab and architecturally primitive. Visitors today often do not know what to think; they confusedly circle its grimy, ponderous bulk (this is one of very few cathedrals in Italy you can walk around completely). Instead of the striped bravura of Siena or the elegant colonnades of Pisa, they behold an eccentric pattern of marble rectangles and flowers – like Victorian wallpaper or, as one critic said, a 'cathedral wearing pyjamas'.

The west front can't be blamed on Arnolfo; his original design, only quarter finished, was taken down in the late 16th century in a Medici rebuilding programme that never got off the ground. The Duomo turned a blank face to the world until 1888, when the present neo-Gothic extravaganza was added. After this façade, the austerity of the interior is almost startling. There is plenty of room; contemporary writers mention 10,000 souls packed inside to hear the brimstone and hell-fire sermons of Savonarola. Even so, the Duomo hardly seems a religious building – more of a *Florentine* building, with simple arches and the counterpoint of grey stone and white plaster, full of old familiar Florentine things. Near the entrance are busts of Brunelleschi and Giotto along the right side. For building the great dome, Brunelleschi was accorded a great honour – he is the only Florentine buried in the cathedral.

On the left wall are the two most conspicuous monuments to private individuals ever commissioned by the Florentine republic. The older one, on the right, is to Sir John Hawkwood, the English *condottiere* whose name the Italians mangled to Giovanni Acuto, a legendary commander who served Florence for many years. All along he had the promise of the Florentines to build him an equestrian monument after his death. It was a typical Florentine trick to cheat a dead man – but still they hired the master of perspective, Paolo Uccello, to make a picture that looked like a statue. Twenty years later they pulled the same trick again, commissioning another great illusionist, Andrea del Castagno, to paint the non-existent equestrian statue of another *condottiere* named Nicolò da Tolentino.

A little further down, near the entrance to the dome, Florence commemorates its own secular scripture with a fresco of Dante by Michelino, a vision of the poet and his *Paradiso* outside the walls of Florence. Two singular icons of Florence's fascination with science stand at opposite ends of the building: behind the west front a bizarre clock, also painted by Uccello, and in the pavement of the left apse a gnomon fixed by the astronomer Toscanelli in 1475. A beam of sunlight strikes it every year on the summer solstice.

There is surprisingly little religious art – most of it has been carted off to the Museo dell'Opera del Duomo (*see* p.615). Luca della Robbia contributed terracotta lunettes above the doors to the sacristies; the scene of the Resurrection over the north sacristy is one of his earliest and best works. He also did the bronze doors beneath it, with tiny portraits on the handles of Lorenzo il Magnifico and his brother Giuliano de' Medici, targets of the Pazzi conspiracy in 1478. In this ill-fated attempt to dispose of the Medici, Giuliano was stabbed during Mass, but Lorenzo escaped, taking refuge in this sacristy. In the middle apse is a beautiful bronze urn by Ghiberti containing relics of the Florentine St Zenobius. The only really conventional religious decorations are the frescoes in the dome, high overhead – mostly the work of Vasari.

Brunelleschi's Dome

Open Mon–Fri 8.30–7, Sat 8.30–5.40; adm.

Losing the competition for the baptistry doors was a bitter disappointment to Brunelleschi but a piece of luck for Florence. His reaction was typically Florentine: not content with being the second-best sculptor, he began to devote all his talents to a field where he thought no one could beat him. He launched himself into an intense study of architecture and engineering, visiting Rome and probably Ravenna to snatch secrets from the ancients. When proposals were solicited for the cathedral's dome he was ready with a *tour de force*. Not only would he build the biggest dome of that era, and the most beautiful, but he would do it without any need for expensive supports while work was in progress, making use of a cantilevered system of bricks that could support itself while it ascended. Even today architects marvel at Brunelleschi's systematic way of tackling the job. Problems with weather and air pressure were foreseen and managed; hooks were inserted to hold up scaffolding for future cleaning or repairs.

Not only had Brunelleschi recaptured the technique of the ancients, he had surpassed them, with a system simpler and better than that of the Pantheon or Hagia Sophia. To the Florentines it must have come as a revelation; the most logical way of covering the space turned out to be a work of perfect beauty. Brunelleschi, in building his dome, put a crown on the achievements of Florence – after 500 years it is still the city's pride and its symbol. To climb it, take the door on the left aisle near the Dante fresco; the complex network of stairs and walks between the inner and outer domes provides a thorough lesson on how Brunelleschi did it, and the views from the top are priceless.

Giotto's Campanile

Open daily 8.30–7.30; adm.

There's no doubt about it: the dome steals the show on Piazza del Duomo, putting one of Italy's most beautiful bell towers in the shade both figuratively and literally. The dome's great size – 366ft to the gold ball on top of the lantern – makes the campanile look small, though 280ft is not exactly tiny. Giotto was made director of the cathedral works in 1334, and his basic design was completed after his death (1337) by Andrea Pisano and Francesco Talenti. It is difficult to say whether they were entirely faithful to the plan. Giotto was an artist, not an engineer; after he died his successors realized the thing was about to topple – a problem they overcame by doubling the thickness of the walls.

Besides its lovely form, the campanile's major fame rests with Pisano and Talenti's sculptural relief – a veritable encyclopaedia of the medieval world-view, with prophets, saints and sibyls, allegories of the planets, virtues and sacraments, the liberal arts and industries (the artist's craft is fittingly symbolized by a figure of Daedalus). All these are copies; the originals can be seen in the cathedral museum (*see* p.615). If after climbing the dome you can manage another 400 steps or so, the terrace on top offers a slightly different view of Florence.

Some lesser-known monuments line the southern edge of the Piazza del Duomo. The 14th-century **Loggia del Bigallo** was built for one of Florence's great charitable confraternities, the Misericordia. It originally served as a lost and found office, although instead of umbrellas it dealt in children; if unclaimed after three days they were sent to foster homes. A little way to the east, **Dante's Seat** is the ancient stone bench where, according to local legend, the poet would take the air, observing his fellow citizens and the building of the Duomo.

Museo dell'Opera del Duomo

Piazza del Duomo 9, near the central apse; open Mon–Sat 9–6.30, Sun 9–1.40; adm.

The cathedral museum is one of Florence's finest, housing both relics from the actual construction of the cathedral and the masterpieces that once adorned it. It reopened in early 2000 after major restructuring to improve the layout and make it more visitor friendly: there is now full disabled access, better information, a more logical layout, in a more or less chronological order, and greatly increased floor space. There are long-term plans to incorporate two neighbouring buildings into the museum, doubling its size.

Arnolfo di Cambio's sculpture from the original façade is here, along with drawings that show how it would have looked. There are a dozen large models of proposed reconstructions from the 1580s in various hack Mannerist styles – the façade could have been much, much worse. Florentines were never enthusiastic about the worship of relics, and long ago they shipped San Girolamo's jawbone, John the Baptist's index finger and St Philip's arm across the street to this museum.

In the 1980s Michelangelo's last Pietà joined the company – a strange, unfinished work that so exasperated the artist that he finally took a hammer to it, breaking Christ's left arm and leg. The tall, hooded figure supporting Christ – Nicodemus – dominates the composition; according to Vasari its face is that of Michelangelo himself. The finished, polished sections of the work, Mary Magdalen and part of the body of Jesus, are not Michelangelo's work at all, but that of a student, who also did his best to patch the arm.

In the 1430s Donatello and Luca della Robbia were commissioned to create a matching pair of *cantorie* or marble choir balconies. Both works, in exquisite low relief, rank among the greatest productions of the Renaissance: Donatello's features dancing *putti* in a setting of quattrocento decorative motifs, while Della Robbia's contains a delightful horde of children dancing, singing and playing instruments – a truly angelic choir. From the campanile, besides the reliefs of Pisano, there are some fine Old Testament figures by Donatello, as well as his gruesome wooden statue of Mary Magdalen, which was something that the Florentines no longer wished to see in their baptistry.

The new part contains fascinating relics of the Duomo's past (brick moulds, tools, and a block and tackle from the original construction), models of the dome, and even Brunelleschi's death mask.

Orsanmichele

Florence likes things neat and in their place. To balance Piazza del Duomo, the religious centre, there is Piazza della Signoria, the civic centre, with an equally formidable array of architecture and art, directly to the south at the other end of Via dei Calzaiuoli, long the city's main artery. On your way there, through the crowds navigating their way past the via's fashionable jewellery shops and knick-knack sellers, you pass the unusual church of Orsanmichele.

This stately square building, built up to the street, is easy to miss; it doesn't look anything like a church, and in fact began its life as a grain market, with an open loggia at street level and emergency storehouses above where grain was kept against a siege. The loggia was originally used by the city's powerful guilds, the *Arti*, as a trade and meeting hall. In 1380, when the market relocated, Simone Talenti was hired to close in the arches of the loggia and make the 'Oratory of St Michael' (as the building was familiarly known because of the ancient chapel that had preceded it) into a church, although throughout the following century it continued to be closely associated with the guilds, the leaders of each of which strove to outdo the other by commissioning sculptures from the finest artists of the day.

All around the exterior the guilds erected statues of their patron saints: it's a remarkable collection that includes Donatello's famed *St George* (a copy; the original is in the Bargello) and *St Mark*, a work much admired by Michelangelo. *St Stephen* and *St Matthew* are by Ghiberti. *Doubting Thomas* is by Verrocchio. The dim interior (*open Mon–Fri 9–12 and 4–6, Sat and Sun 9–1 and 4–6; closed 1st and last Mon of month*), full of stained glass and painted vaults, is ornate and cosy, with more of the air of a guildhall than a church. It makes a picturebook medieval setting for the wonderful **tabernacle**, a free-standing chapel with fine reliefs and sculpted angels by Andrea Orcagna (1350), precious stones and metalwork (every guild contributed something if it could), and a Madonna by Bernardo Daddi.

Piazza della Signoria

Now the city has finally chased the cars out of this big medieval piazza, it serves as a great corral for tourists, endlessly snapping pictures of the Palazzo Vecchio. In the old days it would be full of Florentines, the stage set for the tempestuous life of their republic. The public assemblies met here, and at times of danger the bells would ring and the piazza quickly fill with citizen militia, assembling under the banners of their quarters and guilds. Savonarola held his 'Bonfire of Vanities' here, and only a few years later the disenchanted Florentines ignited their Bonfire of Savonarola on the same spot (you can see a painting of the event at San Marco). Today the piazza is still the favoured spot for political rallies.

The three graceful arches of the **Loggia dei Lanzi**, next to the Palazzo Vecchio, were the reviewing stand for city officials during assemblies and celebrations. Florentines often call it the Loggia dell'Orcagna, after the architect who designed it in the 1370s. In its simple classicism the Loggia anticipates the architecture of Brunelleschi and all those who came after him. The city has made it an outdoor sculpture gallery, with some of the best-known works in Florence: Cellini's triumphant Perseus (*currently being restored*) and Giambologna's *Rape of the Sabines*, his bronze equestrian statue of Cosimo – standing imperiously at the centre of the piazza – as well as some of his other works, and a chorus of Roman-era Vestal Virgins.

All the statues in the piazza are dear to the Florentines for one reason or another. Some are fine works of art; others have only historical associations. Michelangelo's *David*, a copy of which stands in front of the Palazzo near the spot the artist intended for it, was meant as a symbol of republican virtue and Florentine excellence. At the opposite extreme, Florentines are taught almost from birth to ridicule the **Neptune fountain**, a pompous monstrosity with a giant marble figure of the god. The sculptor, Ammannati, thought he would upstage Michelangelo, though the result is derisively known as *Il Biancone* ('Big Whitey'). Bandinelli's statue of *Hercules and Cacus* is almost as big and just as awful; Cellini called it a 'sack of melons'.

Palazzo Vecchio

Open Mon–Weds and Fri–Sun 9–7, Thurs 9–2.

Florence's republican government was never perfect. In the better times chronic factionalism was barely kept in check, usually by the utter destruction or exile of one side or the other. Typically, however, the Florentines managed to give their aspirations a perfect symbol. The proud republic would accept nothing less than the most imposing 'Palazzo del Popolo' (as it was originally called), and Arnolfo di Cambio was able to give it to them. Even though the 308ft tower was for a long time Florence's tallest, Arnolfo avoided the sort of theatrical façade he was planning for the Duomo. The **Palazzo Vecchio** is part council hall, part fortress and part prison, and looks to fit all three roles well. Its rugged façade, copied in so many Florentine palaces, is not quite as frank and plain as it looks; all its proportions are based on the Golden Section of the ancient Greeks, rediscovered by medieval mathematicians. You may also accuse it of politically playing both sides, with square Guelph crenellations on the cornice and the swallowtail Ghibelline style on the tower.

The palace is often called the Palazzo della Signoria, the name it had under the rule of the Medici. After the final consolidation of their new government, the Duchy of Tuscany, the Medici turned the Palazzo Vecchio upside down. The house where Guelphs and Ghibellines once brawled in the council hall, and where lions were kept in the basement as a totem animal for the state, became a florid Mannerist bower fit for a duke. Cosimo de' Medici's pet architect, Giorgio Vasari, oversaw the work in the 1550s and 1560s. Though the Medici did not reside there for long, the Palazzo was always used for state functions.

Today the Palazzo has somewhat recovered its old purpose – it serves as Florence's city hall, and the council holds its meetings in the **Salone dei Cinquecento**, built by the republic in 1495. At that time Leonardo da Vinci and Michelangelo were commissioned to fresco the two longer sides – a contest of talents that everyone in Florence looked forward to. For a number of reasons it never came off; only a small part of Leonardo's fresco was ever completed, and Vasari painted over it 60 years later. Even the designs for both men's concepts have been lost. Michelangelo's statue of Victory, originally intended for the tomb of Pope Julius II in Rome, was installed here by Vasari in the 1560s.

Despite the Palazzo's functional role as a base for the city administration, nearly all the more historic rooms are open to the public, so you can have a look around the ferociously over-decorated **Cortile**, or courtyard, redone by Vasari. Inside, on the first floor, is the fascinating **Studiolo di Francesco I**, a little retreat created for Duke Cosimo's son, who liked to dabble in poisons, where Vasari and his assistants painted a vast allegory of mythology, science and alchemy; more Vasari in the chambers of Leo X and Clement VII (including a famous scene of the 1527 siege); and even more Vasari in the Quartiere degli Elementi upstairs. Rooms with frescoes glorifying the Medici go on and on; try not to miss the rooms of Eleanor of Toledo (Cosimo I's consort) done by Bronzino, or the **Sala dei Gigli**, with a fine ceiling by the Da Maiano brothers and *Judith and Holofernes* by Donatello.

Museo Nazionale del Bargello

Open daily 8.15–1.50; closed alternate Sun and Mon; adm.

For centuries this medieval fortress-palace on the Via del Proconsolo, behind the Palazzo Vecchio, was Florence's prison; today the inmates are men of marble – the country's finest collection of sculpture, a fitting complement to the paintings in the Uffizi. When it was begun, about 1250, the Bargello was the Palazzo del Popolo, though by 1271 it was home to the foreign *podestà* installed by Charles of Anjou. When the republic was reconstructed under the *Ordinamenti*, the decision was made to erect a bigger and grander seat of government – the Palazzo Vecchio. Just as that structure served as the model for so many Florentine palaces, so the Bargello was the model for the Palazzo, a rugged, austere work with a solid air of civic virtue about it. The Medici made a jail of it, but a thorough – and perhaps somewhat imaginative – restoration of the interior in the 19th century got it ready for its current job of housing the **Museo Nazionale**.

After the plain façade, the delightful arcaded courtyard comes as a surprise, full of interesting architectural fragments, plaques and coats of arms in a wild vocabulary of symbols. In the ground-floor galleries are some early works of Michelangelo, including the Bacchus, and Giambologna's *Mercury* – a work so popular it has entered everyone's consciousness as the way Mercury should look. There are also a number of works by Cellini, including his preliminary model for *Perseus* and his bust of *Cosimo I*. Upstairs, passing through the **Loggia**, now an 'aviary' for Giambologna's charming bronze birds, you come to the **Salone del Consiglio**. This 14th-century hall contains many of the greatest works of Donatello: the fascinatingly androgynous *David*, the *St George* from Orsanmichele and the enigmatic Cupid or *Amor Atys*. These three alone make up a powerful case for considering Donatello the greatest of Renaissance sculptors. The alert watchfulness of *St George* created new possibilities in expressing movement, emotion and depth of character in stone – a revolution in art that was obvious even to Donatello's contemporaries. The *David*, obviously from a different planet from Michelangelo's *David*, explores depths of the Florentine psyche the Florentines probably didn't know they had. The same could be said of the dangerous-looking little boy Cupid. No one knows for whom Donatello made it, or who it is really meant to represent. With its poppies, serpents and winged sandals, it could easily be the ancient idol people in the 18th century mistook it for. Like Botticelli's mythological paintings, it reflects the artistic and intellectual undercurrents of the quattrocento, full of pagan philosophy and eroticism – a possibility rooted out in the terror of the Counter-Reformation and quite forgotten soon after.

Among the other artists represented in the hall are Luca della Robbia, Verrocchio, Bernini, Michelozzo and Di Duccio. The two bronze panels made by Brunelleschi and Ghiberti for the baptistry doors competition are preserved here; judge for yourself which is the better. Above, on the second floor, the collection continues with works mainly by Antonio Pollaiuolo and Verrocchio.

The Bargello also houses an important collection of the decorative arts – rooms full of pretty bric-à-brac, such as combs, mirrors, jewel caskets, reliquaries, Turkish helmets, vases and silks, wax anatomical figures and majolica from Urbino. Some of the most beautiful pieces are in a collection of medieval French ivory – intricately carved scenes such as the *Assault on the Castle of Love* and other medieval fancies. The Bargello's **chapel** has frescoes by an unknown follower of Giotto.

Dante's Florence

Dante contemplated his Beatrice, the story goes, at Mass in the **Badia Fiorentina** (*open Mon 3–6*), a Benedictine church on Via del Proconsolo (entrance on Via Dante Alighieri) across from the Bargello, with a lovely Gothic spire to grace this corner of the Florentine skyline. The church has undergone many rebuildings since Willa, widow of a Margrave of Tuscany, began it in around 990, but there is still a monument to Ugo, the 'Good Margrave' mentioned in Dante, and a painting of the Madonna Appearing to St Bernard by Filippino Lippi.

Between the Badia and Via dei Calzaiuoli is a little corner of medieval Florence that has survived the changes of centuries. In these quiet, narrow streets you will find the **Casa di Dante** (*open summer Weds–Mon 9–6; winter Mon and Weds–Sat 10–4, Sun 10–2; adm*), which was actually built in 1911 over the ruins of an amputated tower house, although scholars agree that the Alighieri lived somewhere in the vicinity. Nearby, the stoutly medieval *Torre della Castagna* is the last extant part of the original Palazzo del Popolo, predecessor to the Bargello and Palazzo Vecchio. After giving up on Beatrice, Dante married his second choice, Gemma Donati, in **Santa Margherita** church on the same block. Another church nearby, **San Martino del Vescovo**, has a fine set of frescoes from the workshop of Ghirlandaio – it's worth a look inside if it's open.

Florence As It Was

If, tramping the long and tired streets of this city, you still haven't discovered the Florence you came to find, stop in at the **Museo di Firenze Com'Era** ('Museum of Florence As It Was') at Via dell'Oriuolo 24 (*open Fri–Weds 9–2; adm*), north of the Bargello and not far from the Duomo. In the first room, almost covering the entire wall, is the *Pianta della Catena*, the most famous and beautiful of the early views of Florence. Made in 1490 by an unknown artist (the handsome fellow pictured in the lower right corner), it is really a copy of the original, which was lost during the Second World War in a Berlin museum. This fascinating painting captures Florence at the height of the Renaissance. Not much has changed – the great churches are without their façades, the Uffizi and Medici chapels have not yet appeared, and the Medici and Pitti palaces are shown without their later extensions.

This museum is not large – it has only a selection of plans and maps, plus some watercolours of Florence's sights from the last century. One surprising fact that becomes clear from a visit is that today's fussy, staid Florentines are much less interested in Renaissance Florence than in the city of their grandparents. For further evidence , check around the corner on Via Sant'Egidio, where remodelling uncovered posters from 1925 announcing plans for paying the war debt and a forthcoming visit of the Folies Bergère – they have been restored and put under glass.

The Uffizi Gallery

***t** 055 294 883 (pre-booking); open Tues–Sun 8.15–6.50; adm exp; queues common in summer; try to arrive early.*

Giorgio Vasari's roosterish boastfulness and conviction that his was the best of all possible artistic worlds, set next to his very modest talents, have made him almost a comic figure in some art criticism. Even the Florentines don't like him. But on one of the rare occasions when he tried his hand as an architect he gave the city something to be proud of. The Uffizi ('offices') were meant as Cosimo's secretariat, incorporating the old mint and archive buildings, with plenty of room for the bureaucrats needed to run the efficient, modern state Cosimo was building. The matched pair of arcaded buildings with restrained, elegant façades conceals a revolutionary but little-known innovation. Iron reinforcements inside the façades make the huge window areas possible, and keep the building stable on the soft ground below; it was a trick almost be forgotten until the building of the Crystal Palace and the first US skyscrapers. The Uffizi is also a noteworthy piece of Renaissance urban design, an intelligent conception that unites the Piazza della Signoria with the Arno.

The Uffizi underwent a major **reorganization** a few years back. Some of this involved the restoration of remaining damage after the bomb (all but a very few paintings are back on display), but improvements were also made on a practical level. The most significant changes involved the ground floor, where major restoration resulted in a vastly improved space; there are now three entrances (for individuals, groups and those with pre-paid tickets), bookshops, cloakrooms, video and computer facilities, and information desks. If you are keen on seeing a certain painting, note that rooms may be temporarily closed when you visit; this seems to depend on staff availability. There is a list of closures at the ticket counters.

Almost from the start, the Medici began to store their enormous art collections in parts of the Uffizi. The last of the Medici, Duchess Anna Maria Lodovica, willed the entire hoard to the people of Florence in 1737. Give yourself a day or two to spend in the most important picture gallery in Italy. The size of the collection itself is not overwhelming, but every work here is choice. All of the Florentine masters are represented, and the Medici even deigned to purchase a few foreigners.

Room 2 has some fine trecento works by **Duccio di Buoninsegna** and **Cimabue**. If you can't make it to Siena this trip, be sure to see the works of that city's school, especially those by the **Lorenzetti brothers** and **Simone Martini**. From the early quattrocento Florentine painters there is **Uccello's** *Battle of San Romano*; even with only a third of the original present this is one of the most provocative of all paintings, a surreal vision of war with pink, white and blue toy horses. **Piero della Francesca** contributes a portrait of Federico da Montefeltro with his famous nose (*see* Urbino, p.537); **Filippo Lippi** is also here. **Botticelli** gets one big room to himself, in which are displayed his uncanny, erotic masterpieces, including *The Birth of Venus*, *Primavera* and *Pallas and the Centaur* (another subtle allegory of the Medici triumph – the rings on Athena's gown were a family symbol), as well as some of his religious paintings and the disturbing *Calumny*, an introduction to the dark side of the quattrocento psyche.

Be sure to visit Room 15 and **Leonardo**'s *Annunciation* – an intellectual revelation that is one of the foremost achievements of Florentine art. Nearby is a formidable sea monster in **Piero di Cosimo**'s *Perseus and Andromeda*. In the Tribuna, a gaudy chamber designed by Bernardo Buontalenti, the Medici kept a valuable collection of Hellenistic and Roman sculpture, as well as portraits of Cosimo and Eleanor of Toledo by **Bronzino**. There's a surprising amount of German and Flemish painting, including **Dürer**'s *Adoration of the Magi* and *Adam and Eve*, both looking as much like Italian painting as he could make them, and **Cranach**'s *Portraits of Luther and Melanchthon*, spying on the Catholics. Venetians aren't as well represented, but there is the *Judgement of Solomon* by **Giorgione** and a Sacred Allegory by **Giovanni Bellini**.

Michelangelo always maintained that sculpture and fresco were the only arts fit for a man; oil painting he disdained, and just coincidentally he wasn't very good at it. The *Doni Tondi* here is the only canvas he ever finished. Next come some portraits by **Raphael, Rosso Fiorentino** and **Pontormo**; and the brightly coloured paintings of **Andrea del Sarto**. **Titian**'s overdressed Spaniards and well-upholstered girls get a room to themselves. The collections continue through painters of the 17th and 18th centuries – works of **Rembrandt** (two self-portraits), **Rubens, Van Dyck**, and even **Goya**; the one exceptional picture here is the *Boy Playing at Cards* by **Chardin**.

In 1565 Francesco I commissioned Vasari to link the Palazzo Vecchio and the Uffizi to the Pitti Palace across the river, so he could pass through without rubbing elbows with his subjects. After 400 years, Florence just wouldn't look right without this covered passageway, the **Corridoio Vasariano**, which contains a unique collection of ' self-portraits, by Vasari, Velázquez, Rembrandt, Hogarth and many French artists (*only open certain times of year; check with tourist office and book a visit early if possible*.)

Given the amount that Florence and the rest of Tuscany contributed to the birth of science, it is only fitting to have the **Museo di Storia della Scienza** (Museum of the History of Science) in the heart of the city, just behind the Uffizi on Via Castellani (*open summer Mon and Weds–Fri 9.30–5, Tues and Sat 9.30–1; winter Mon and Weds–Sat 9.30–5, Tues 9.30–1, also 2nd Sun of month 10–1; adm exp*). Even in the dark centuries, Florence never abandoned its scientific interests; the collection began with an institute that was founded by the Medici in the 1730s, the Accademia del Cimento, whose motto was 'Try and try again'. Pride of place goes to Galileo's instruments, including his first telescope, in addition to a large number of astrolobes, early microscopes, models of the planets, and armillary spheres, many of which are beautiful works of art in their own right. The last rooms contain wax anatomical models – a 15th-century Medici fetish.

Ponte Vecchio and Ponte Santa Trinità

No one knows how long the Arno has been spanned at this point. The present bridge, built in 1345, replaced a wooden construction from the 970s, which in turn was the successor to a span that may have dated back to the Romans. Like medieval bridges in London and many other European cities, the new 14th-century bridge had shops and houses built all along it. By the 16th century it had become the street of the butchers; after Vasari built Cosimo's secret passage over the top the duke evicted the butchers (he didn't like the pong) and gave their places to the goldsmiths. They have kept their spot ever since, and hordes of shoppers from around the world descend on it each year to scrutinize the Florentine talent for jewellery. This is the most prestigious shopping location in Florence, and the jewellers are happy to stay – they could not be deterred even by the 1966 flood, when a fortune in gold was washed down the Arno.

In the summer of 1944 the river briefly became a German defensive line during the slow painful retreat across central Italy. Before they left Florence, the Germans blew up every one of the city's bridges, saving only the Ponte Vecchio. Somehow the city managed to talk them out of it, and instead buildings on both sides were destroyed and the rubble piled up to block the approaches. Florence's most beautiful span, the **Ponte Santa Trinità**, had to go, however. The Florentines like their city just as it is, and immediately after the war they set about replacing the bridges exactly as they were. In the case of Santa Trinità it was quite a task – old quarries had to be reopened to duplicate the stone, and old methods used to cut it (modern power saws would have done it too cleanly). The graceful curve of the three arches was a problem; they cannot be constructed geometrically and considerable speculation went on over how the architect (Ammannati, in 1567) had done it. Finally, remembering that Michelangelo had advised Ammannati on the project, someone discovered that the same form of arch could be seen on the decoration of Michelangelo's Medici Chapels, constructed most likely not by mathematics and common engineering, but by pure artistic imagination. Fortune lent a hand in the reconstruction; of the original statues of the *Four Seasons*, almost all the pieces were fished out of the Arno and reconstructed. Spring's head was missing, however, and controversy raged for a decade over whether to replace it or leave it as it was, until some divers found it, completely by accident, in 1961.

Around Piazza della Repubblica

On the map it is easy to pick out the small rectangle of narrow, straight streets at the heart of Florence; these remain unchanged from the little *castrum* of Roman days. At its centre the old forum deteriorated through the Dark Ages into a shabby market square, surrounded by the Jewish ghetto. So it remained until Florence, during a fit of post-Risorgimento ambition, decided to make it a symbol of the city's reawakening. The square was given a new design and a thorough facelift, and a grand arch was built, with a big inscription: THE ANCIENT CITY CENTRE RESTORED TO NEW LIFE FROM THE SQUALOR OF CENTURIES. Unfortunately, the results were the same as in the new façade for the Duomo; Piazza della Repubblica is one of the ghastliest squares in Italy.

Just the same, it is a popular place with tourists and natives alike, full of cafés with outside tables, and providing something of an oasis among the severe, unwelcoming streets of old Florence.

Those streets are worth walking: however dreary they may look at first sight, they are part of the very soul of Florence. Also, they are full of surprises; walk down Calimala, an important shopping street south of the Piazza, and you will encounter the **Arte della Lana**, behind Orsanmichele and connected to it by an overhead passageway. The 'Wool Corporation', the richest of the guilds save that of the bankers, was really a sort of manufacturers' co-operative; its headquarters, which was built in 1308, was restored in 1905 in a delightful William Morris style of medieval picturesque. Nearby, further towards the river, is one of Florence's oldest marketplaces, covered by a beautiful loggia built in the 1500s. The **Mercato Nuovo**, where vendors hawk purses, toys and every sort of trinket, was in medieval times a merchants' exchange; it was also the place where the *carroccio*, the decorated wagon that served as a rallying point for the citizen armies during battles, was kept in times of peace. Florentines often call this the *Loggia del Porcellino*, after the drooling bronze boar put up as a decoration in 1612, a copy of a Greek sculpture in the Uffizi (it was replaced by another copy in 1999).

Between Via delle Terme and Via Porta Rossa, the 14th-century **Palazzo Davanzati** recreates the atmosphere of a wealthy merchant's house of the 15th century in the form of the **Museo della Casa Fiorentina Antica** (*currently closed for restoration; ground-floor exhibition open 8.30–1.50; closed alternate Sun and Mon*). Some of the furnishings date from a century or two later, but the late medieval atmosphere is present and, if historically accurate, a tribute to the taste of the honest burghers of the time. Some of Florence's most typical old townhouses lie between here and the river. Off Via Pellicceria, behind the Mercato Nuovo, is the 14th-century Guelph Party Building, often the real seat of power in the city, built with money confiscated from exiled Ghibellines.

Closer to the Arno stands the 11th-century **SS. Apostoli**, with a tabernacle by Andrea della Robbia; in the narrow streets around it is the Piazzetta del Limbo, where unbaptized babies were buried in the Middle Ages. Further along the river, Gothic **Santa Trinità** has a dull façade added in the 1590s. One of the chapels has colourful frescoes by Lorenzo Monaco, who also did the altarpiece; another, the Sassetti Chapel, was decorated by Ghirlandaio. Ostensibly a series on the life of St Francis, the frescoes are commented on by scholars as a document of Florence's social history. All the Medici, Sassetti and their friends are present in finely detailed portraits, subtly arranged to show the city's new hierarchy of political and economic power.

For more Ghirlandaio, continue on to the 13th-century **Ognissanti** (All Saints' church), which has another heavy façade added later. The man who named a continent, Amerigo Vespucci, is buried by the second altar on the right. Botticelli and Ghirlandaio both contributed versions of St Jerome for the cloister (*open daily 8–12 and 4–7*), and the latter's *Cenacolo* in the refectory (*open Mon, Tues and Sat 9–12*) is one of his better known works, a Last Supper that is more a garden party, with lemon trees and exotic birds, as well as a sulky Judas, third from the right.

Conspicuous Consumption *alla Fiorentina*

The streets west of Piazza della Repubblica have always been the choicest district of Florence. Via Tornabuoni, the fanciest shopping street, is as well known in fashion as Via Montenapoleone in Milan or Via dei Condotti in Rome. In the 15th century this was the area most of the new merchant élite chose for their palaces. Today's bankers build great skyscrapers for the firm and settle for modest mansions themselves; in medieval Florence, things were reversed. The bankers and wool tycoons really owned their businesses, and in absolute terms probably had more money than anyone had ever had before. While their places of business were usually quite simple, for themselves they built imposing city palaces; all in the same conservative style, and competing with each other in size like a Millionaires' Row of Victorian-era America.

The style, derived from the Palazzo Vecchio, began at the **Palazzo Rucellai** on Via della Vigna Nuova, designed by Alberti in 1446 for a prominent manufacturer and patron of learning. Much has been made of it as a turning point in architecture; its real innovation is a consistent and skilful use of the classical 'orders', the system of proportion learned from Vitruvius. Of the other palaces in the neighbourhood north of Piazza Santa Trinità, two stand out – the 1465 **Palazzo Antinori**, at the northern end of Tornabuoni, and the **Palazzo Strozzi**, two streets south. The Strozzi is the daddy of them all, the accustomed design blown up to heroic proportions; though it has three storeys like the rest, here each floor is as tall as three or four normal ones. Filippo Strozzi, head of a family of bankers who often felt strong enough to challenge the leadership of the Medici, built it in 1489 at the height of the clan's fortunes. Fifty years later his grandchildren were all exiles, bankers and advisers to the king of France. Both the Antinori and Strozzi palaces were the work of Benedetto da Maiano; the Strozzi often hosts art exhibitions.

Santa Maria Novella

Open Mon–Thurs and Sat 9.30–5, Fri and Sun 1–5; adm.

Santa Maria Novella, begun by the Dominicans in 1246, was always associated with the great families; in the 1600s the wealthy families of the neighbourhood held an annual carriage race around the two fat obelisks in the piazza. Between them they bestowed so much money to embellish it that by the 1500s the church was a museum, with important works by many late medieval and Renaissance artists. The brilliant black and white patterned façade, still the finest in Florence, shows the continuity of the city's style from medieval times. The lower half is part of the original work, finished before 1360; the rest had to wait for one of the Rucellai family to commission Alberti to finish the job. It's his best work in Florence, a synthesis of classical architecture and medieval Florentine tradition, with volutes and arabesques that seem already to prefigure the Baroque. The sun at the apex is the only image or symbol in Alberti's plan. Lower down, Cosimo I added the unusual sundials over the left and right arches.

Inside, Giotto's recently restored crucifix (*c.* 1300), one of the artist's first works, now hangs dramatically in mid nave. Above the portal is a Nativity by Botticelli. From there, proceeding clockwise around the church, are a pulpit with reliefs by Brunelleschi;

Santa Maria Novella

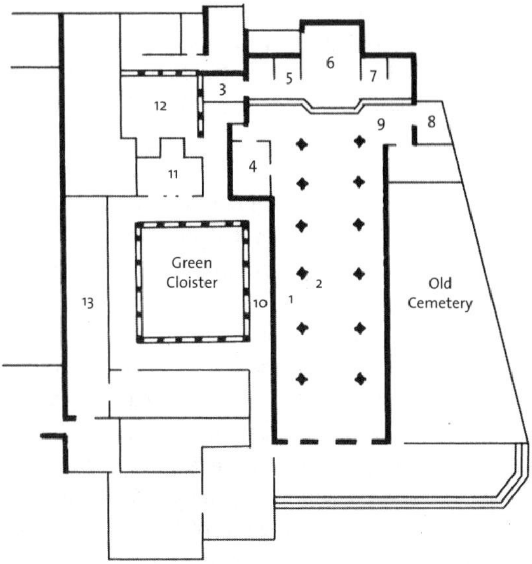

1 Masaccio's *Trinità*
2 Brunelleschi's Pulpit
3 Cappella Strozzi
4 Sacristy
5 Cappella Gondi
6 Sanctuary
7 Filippo Strozzi Chapel
8 Rucellai Chapel
9 Gothic Tombs
10 *Universal Deluge*
11 Spanish Chapel
12 Chiostrino dei Morti
13 Refectory

Masaccio's *Trinità* fresco, one of the earliest works with the temerity to depict God the Father; and a Resurrection by Vasari. In the left transept, the Gondi Chapel has Brunelleschi's only wood sculpture, a crucifix – Vasari tells how he made it to show Donatello a Christ with proper dignity, as his friend's crucifix (now in Santa Croce) made the Redeemer 'look like a peasant'. A great series of frescoes of the Lives of St John and the Virgin by Ghirlandaio surrounds the main altar. All his students helped him complete it, little Michelangelo included. Some equally fine frescoes by Filippino Lippi adorn the Filippo Strozzi Chapel in the right transept, where Strozzi is buried; the architect who designed his palace, Da Maiano, also carved his tomb.

There's little of interest in the right chapels, but just outside the left transept are some of the best parts of this surprisingly large monastic complex. Another Strozzi chapel, this one from the 1360s, has a fine early fresco series of the Last Judgement by Nardo di Cione, brother of Orcagna. The Spanish Chapel, commissioned by Cosimo I's Spanish wife Eleanor of Toledo, offers a chilling touch of Counter-Reformation with frescoes detailing the history of the Dominicans: the *domini canes* ('dogs of the Lord') sit at the pope's feet, symbolizing the order that ran the Inquisition and sniffed out heretics and freethinkers. In the background a view of the Duomo as a fairly pink confection may represent the original plans of Arnolfo di Cambio. Best of all, however, is the famous **Green Cloister** (*entrance just to left of the church; open Mon–Thurs 9–2, Sat and Sun 8–1; adm*), decorated with the most important frescoes by Paolo Uccello, a mysterious interpretation of the story of Noah that has stoked controversy for centuries. The frescoes are much deteriorated, but the best-preserved one, the *Universal Deluge*, is uncanny enough to haunt your imagination for years.

San Lorenzo and the Medici Chapels

Just behind Santa Maria, another large, amorphous square will detract from your appreciation of one of Italy's finest modern buildings – the railway station, designed by Michelucci in 1935. Adorned only by a glass block canopy at the entrance (and an early model of that great Italian invention, the digital clock), the station is remarkable for its clean lines and impeccable practicality – form follows function in a way even Brunelleschi would have appreciated.

Around the railway station beats the true heart of tourist Florence – dozens of streets around the Via Nazionale packed with hotels, restaurants and bars. There's an almost Neapolitan air about the boisterous street market that surrounds the **Mercato Centrale**, built in the 1890s to replace the old market evicted from the Piazza della Repubblica and known locally as 'Shanghai'.

The market *bancarelle* extend all the way to **San Lorenzo**, a church always associated with the Medici, and a shrine to the art of Brunelleschi and Michelangelo. The former built it in the 1420s; Michelangelo designed a façade that was never realized, leaving the odd-shaped church as charming as a huge dreadnought docked in the piazza. The interior, however, is essential Brunelleschi, a contemplative repetition of arches and columns in grey and white. Nothing else in Florence prepares you for the two pulpits in the nave, the last violent, near-impressionistic works of Donatello. Off the left transept, the **old sacristy** is a beautiful vaulted chamber with calmer sculptural decoration by Donatello.

Outside, a separate entrance on Piazza Madonna degli Aldobrandini leads to the **Medici Chapels** (*open daily 8.15–5; closed alternate Sun and Mon; adm exp*) and their celebrated sculptures by Michelangelo. First you have to pass through the Prince's Chapel, under a huge eight-sided dome that dwarfs the rest of San Lorenzo, begun in 1604 following a design by a dilettante architect member of the Medici family. Several Medici dukes are buried in this dreary rotunda, the true monument of the ducal period and a sobering demonstration of how soon Florence's great age of art declined into provincialism and preciosity. It certainly cost enough – the lower walls and floor are done in *pietra dura* with rich marbles from around the world, a job still not completed.

From here a corridor to the left leads to the **new sacristy**, designed by Michelangelo in a severe style to match the Old Sacristy on the other side. The two tombs, of Giuliano Medici, Duke of Nemours, and Lorenzo, Duke of Urbino, the ruler to whom Machiavelli dedicated *The Prince*, are decorated with an allegorical sculptural scheme that has caused much discussion over the centuries. Giuliano is portrayed as a soldier representing the Active Life, with figures representing Day and Night reclining on his sarcophagus below. Lorenzo, as the Contemplative Life, sits and contemplates, overlooking figures of Dawn and Dusk (true to life in one respect; the passive Lorenzo was a disappointment to Machiavelli and everyone else). The male figures, at least, are among Michelangelo's triumphs. The women, Dawn and Night, come off less well. Michelangelo never had much use for the ladies – he wouldn't even use female models – and, whatever role they played in his personal mythology, he portrays them here as imperfect men, male forms with flabbier musculature and breasts stuck on like superfluous appendages.

In front of San Lorenzo is a separate entrance to the **Biblioteca Laurenziana** (*open Mon–Sat 8.30–1.30*), designed for the Medici by Michelangelo and built by Ammannati. A landmark in architecture, it was Michelangelo's first commission (along with the Medici Chapels), and one of the first steps on the slippery slope to Mannerism.

Palazzo Medici Riccardi

San Lorenzo became the Medici's church because it stood just round the corner from the family palace – a huge, stately building on Via Cavour constructed by Alberti and Michelozzo about the same time as the Palazzo Rucellai. The family's coat-of-arms, which you've probably noticed everywhere in Florence, is prominently displayed in the corners. The seven (sometimes six) red boluses probably come from the family's origin as pharmacists. Opponents called them 'the pills', but Medici supporters made them their battle cry in street fights: 'Balls! Balls!'

The main reason for visiting is one of Florence's hidden delights: the **chapel** (*open Thurs–Tues 9–7; adm; only a few people allowed in at a time; in summer book on* **t** *055 276 0340*), with extravagantly colourful frescoes by Benozzo Gozzoli. The *Procession of the Magi* is hardly a religious painting – it's a merry scene full of portraits of the Medici and others among the crowd following the Three Kings. The artist included himself, with his name on his hat. In the foreground of one of the panels, note the black man carrying a bow. Blacks (and Turks, Circassians, Tartars and other non-Europeans) were common enough in Renaissance Florence. Though originally brought as slaves, not all were still servants by the 1400s. Contemporary writers mention them as artisans, fencing masters, soldiers and, in one famous case, as an archery instructor, who may be the man pictured here. For an extraordinary contrast pop into the **gallery** with its 17th-century ceiling by Neapolitan Luca Giordano, showing the last, unspeakable Medici floating around in marshmallow clouds.

San Marco

Convent open Mon–Fri and Sun 8.15–1.50, Sat 8.15–6.50; closed 1st and 3rd Sun of month and 2nd and 4th Mon of month; adm. Church open daily 7–12 and 4–7.

Despite all the others who contributed to this Dominican monastery and church, it has always been best known for the work of its most famous resident. Fra Angelico lived here from 1436 until his death in 1455, spending the time turning Michelozzo's simple **cloister** into a complete exposition of his own deep faith, expressed in bright playroom colours and angelic pastels. Fra Angelico painted the frescoes in the corners of the cloister, and on the first floor is a small museum of his work, collected from various Florentine churches, as well as a number of early 15th-century portraits by Fra Bartolomeo, capturing some of the most sincere spirituality of that age. The Last Supper in the refectory is by Ghirlandaio.

Other Fra Angelico works include the series on the Life of Christ, telling the story sweetly and succinctly, and a serenely confident Last Judgement in which the saved are well-dressed Italians, holding hands. They keep their clothes in heaven, while the bad (mostly princes and prelates) are stripped to receive their interesting tortures.

When you turn right at the top of the stairs to the monks' dormitory, your eyes meet the angelic Friar's masterpiece, a miraculous Annunciation that offers an intriguing comparison with Leonardo's Annunciation in the Uffizi. The subject was a favourite among Florentine artists, not only because it was a severe test – that of expressing a divine revelation with a composition of strict economy – but because the Annunciation, falling near the spring equinox, was New Year's Day for Florence until the Medici adopted the papal calendar in the 17th century.

In each of the monks' cells, Fra Angelico and students painted the Crucifixion, always the same except for some slight differences in pose; walking down the corridor and glancing in the cells successively gives you the impression of a cartoon. One of the cells belonged to Savonarola, who was the prior here during his period of dominance in Florence; it has simple furniture of the period and a portrait of Savonarola by Fra Bartolomeo. Michelozzo's Library, off the main corridor, is as light and airy as the cloisters below; in it is displayed a collection of choir books, including one illuminated by Fra Angelico.

If you liked Andrea del Castagno's work in the Uffizi, just around the corner from San Marco is a work many consider to be his best, the *Last Supper*, in the convent of **Sant'Apollonia** on Via XXVII Aprile 1 (*open daily 8.30–1.30; closed alternate Sun and Mon*).

Piazza Santissima Annunziata

This square, which represents the only Renaissance attempt at a unified ensemble in Florence, is surrounded by arcades on three sides. The earliest of its buildings, one of Brunelleschi's most famous works, is also a monument to Renaissance Italy's long, hard and ultimately unsuccessful struggle towards some kind of social consciousness. Even during the best of times, Florence's poor were treated like dirt; if any enlightened soul had been so bold as to propose even a modern conservative 'trickle down' theory to the Medici and the banking élite, their first thought would have been how to stop the leaks. Babies, at least, had it a little better. The **Spedale degli Innocenti** (*open Thurs–Tues 8.30–2; adm*), which was built in the 1420s, was Florence's foundling hospital, and still functions as an orphanage today. Brunelleschi's beautiful arcade, decorated with the famous tondi of infants in swaddling clothes by Luca della Robbia, was one of the early classicizing experiments in architecture. There's a small picture gallery containing Ghirlandaio's *Adoration of the Magi* and a number of other works.

To complement Brunelleschi's arches, the old church of **Santissima Annunziata** was rebuilt, Michelozzo giving it a broad arcaded portico facing the street. Behind the portico, the architect added the *Chiostrino dei Voti*, a porch decorated with a collection of early 16th-century frescoes, including two by Andrea del Sarto. The best of these, faded as it is, is a finely detailed *Nativity* by Alessio Baldovinetti, one of the quattrocento's under-appreciated masters. It's the gaudiest church in Florence; its gilded elliptical dome, its unusual polygonal tribune around the sanctuary, and mega-tons of *pietra dura* have helped it become the city's high-society parish, where even funerals are major social events. The **Tempietta**, the candlelit chapel in the rear, also by Michelozzo, shelters a miraculous painting of The Annunciation.

The Accademia

Just off Piazza Santissima Annunziata; open Tues–Sun 8.15–6.50; adm exp.

This may not be Florence's most interesting museum, but in summer the queues here are often as long as those at the Uffizi. What people are most anxious to get a look at is Michelangelo's *David*, ccompleted for the city in 1504, when the artist was 29. It was the work that established the reputation he had in his own time. Just over 100 years ago, Florence decided to take this symbol of republican liberty in out of the rain. Looking contented with his own perfection, he stands in a classical exedra built for him (behind protective glass). As the political symbol the republic commissioned he may be excessive – the irony of a David the size of Goliath is disconcerting – but as a symbol of the intellectual aspirations of the Renaissance he is unsurpassed. Other Michelangelos include the famous *non finiti*: the *Prisoners* and *St Matthew*, tortured forms waiting for the artist to finish liberating them from the stone.

There is plenty of indifferent painting in the Accademia, but persevere for such works as the *Deposition from the Cross* by Perugino, the sweet and small *Madonna del Mare* by Botticelli; and *Thebaid* by a follower of Uccello. Some of the best pieces are in a room of lesser-known masters of the quattrocento, especially Mariotto di Cristoforo and the 'Maestro del Casione Adimare', the latter known only for the painted chest displayed here, a delightful scene of a marriage in Florence in the 1450s that has been reproduced in half the books ever written about the Renaissance. There is also a collection of musical instruments.

Museo Archeologico

Via della Colonna 36; open Mon 2–7, Tues and Thurs 8.30–7, Weds and Fri–Sun 8.30–2; adm.

One of the tricks of the Florentine museum torture is to hold your interest by changing the subject; just when you can't take another transcendent Renaissance painting, they offer you the chance to see Tuscany's greatest collection of Etruscan art. Nor is that all; the Egyptian collection here is also exceptional. Again, the Medici are responsible; the museum began with purchases by Cosimo and Lorenzo il Magnifico.

The Etruscans fill room after room, but the star attractions are two lovely bronzes: the *Arringatore*, or Orator, a civic-minded, civilized-looking gent whom the inscription tells us was named Aurus Metellus; and the *Chimera*, a remarkable beast with three heads – of a lion, a goat and a snake. This 5th-century BC Etruscan work, dug up near Arezzo in 1555 and snatched by the Medici, had a great influence on Mannerist artists.

Greek art is also represented; Etruscan and Roman noble families were wont to buy up all they could afford. There is an excellent *kouros*, a young man in the archaic style from 6th-century BC Sicily, an almost complete ancient chariot, some good vases, and an unusual 4th-century BC silver urn called the *Baratti Amphora*, made in Antioch and covered with scores of small medallions showing mythological figures. Scholars believe that the images and their arrangement may encode an entire system of belief, the secret teaching of one of the mystic-philosophical cults common in Hellenistic times, and they hope some day to decipher it.

Santa Croce

Open Mon–Sat 9.30–5.30, Sun 1–5.30; adm.

Santa Maria Novella was the Dominicans' church, and the Franciscans had to have one just as big and grand. The original church, said to have been founded by St Francis himself, went by the board in Florence's colossal building programme of the 1290s. Arnolfo di Cambio planned its successor, which was largely completed by the 1450s, though a 'restoration' job by Vasari in the 1560s ruined much of the original interior. The façade, in the accustomed Florentine black and white marble, nevertheless has something of the Victorian Gothic about it – just as it should, since it was only added in the 1850s, a gift from Sir Francis Sloane. No one has succeeded in doing anything with the vast, hideous piazza in front, though it is the venue each June for *Calcio in Costume*, a ball game similar to rugby, believed to be descended from a Roman sport with origins in the exercises of the citizen militias of the Florentine republic. It's fun to watch the immaculate Florentines in their Renaissance duds mixing it up in the dirt.

Like Santa Maria Novella, the interior is a museum in itself. On the left near the door is the **tomb of Galileo**, whose remains were moved here after the Church grudgingly allowed him a Christian burial in 1737. For a while it was the custom to bury great Italians here, and you'll see plenty of tombs along both sides, mostly of forgotten men of the 19th century. Continuing clockwise, two chapels down is the Monument to Carlo Marsuppini, a mine of good quattrocento sculpture, mostly by Verrocchio and Desiderio da Settignano. Look in the Bardi chapel in the left transept for the Crucifix by Donatello (the one Brunelleschi said looked like a peasant). Many of the small vaulted chapels that flank the high altar contain important late (1330s) works by Giotto, his assistants and followers. In the second Bardi chapel are frescoes on the Life of St Francis that can be compared with the more famous frescoes of his life at Assisi.

The **Peruzzi Chapel** frescoes detail the Lives of St John the Evangelist and St John the Baptist. These works had a huge influence on all the later Florentine artists, but by the 18th century they were considered eyesores and whitewashed for 150 years – hence their fragmentary state. Two of Giotto's artistic heirs, the Gaddi, also contributed much to Santa Croce. Agnolo did the stained glass around the high altar, as well as the fascinating frescoes on the Legend of the Cross – how Seth received a branch from St Michael and planted it over Adam's grave, how the tree that grew from it was shaped into a beam for a bridge, then buried by Solomon when his guest the Queen of Sheba prophesied it would some day bring about the end of the Jews. The beam was dug up and shaped into Christ's Cross, later found by St Helena, Constantine's mother, then stolen by a Persian king and finally recovered by Emperor Heraclius. In the **sacristy**, to the right, are more fine frescoes by Agnolo Gaddi's father Taddeo, and yet more Gaddis in the Castellani Chapel (Agnolo) and Baroncelli Chapel (Taddeo).

Back down the right side of the church, Donatello's **tabernacle** has a beautiful relief of the Annunciation. Then come more **tombs**: those of Rossini, Machiavelli, Michelangelo and Dante (not buried here). Michelangelo's is the work of Vasari, who thought himself just the fellow for the job. Vasari's vandalism ruined most of the chapels on this side, once embellished with frescoes by Orcagna and other trecento painters.

Santa Croce

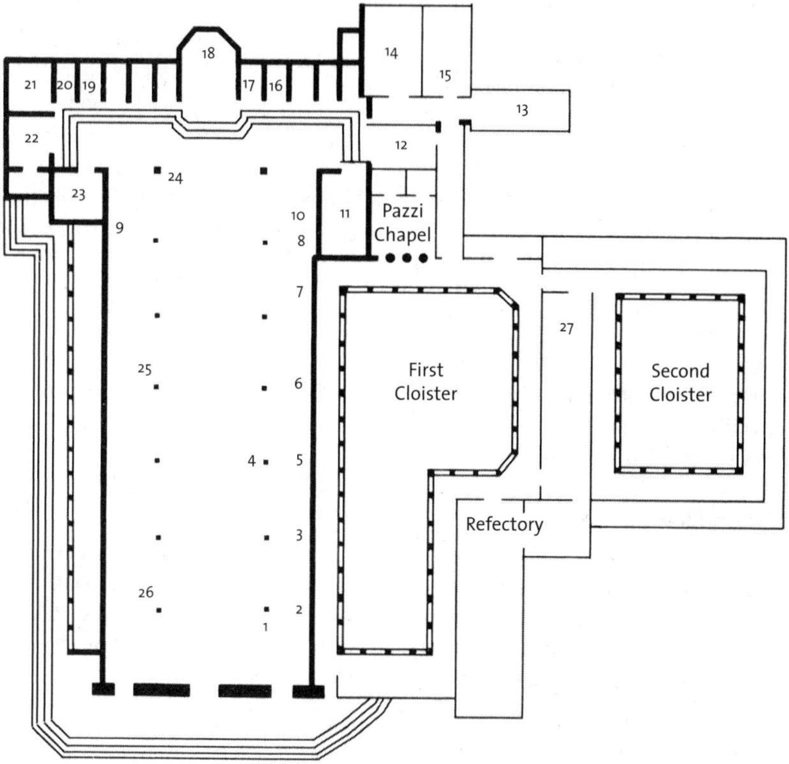

1 Madonna del Latte
2 Tomb of Michelangelo
3 Monument to Dante
4 Benedetto da Maiano's Pulpit
5 Vittorio Alfieri's Tomb
6 Tomb of Machiavelli
7 Donatello's *Annunciation*
8 Tomb of Leonardo Bruni
9 Tomb of Carlo Marsuppini
10 Tomb of Rossini
11 Castellani Chapel
12 Baroncelli Chapel
13 Medici Chapel
14 Sacristy
15 Rinuccini Chapel
16 Peruzzi Chapel
17 Bardi Chapel
18 Sanctuary
19 Bardi di Libertà Chapel
20 Bardi di Vernio Chapel
21 Niccolini Chapel
22 Bardi Chapel
23 Salviati Chapel
24 Monument to Alberti
25 Tomb of Lorenzo Ghiberti
26 Galileo's Tomb
27 Museo dell'Opera di Santa Croce

The Pazzi Chapel

Open Thurs–Tues 10–5, later opening hours in summer; adm.

This Santa Croce chapel is well worth its entrance fee. Brunelleschi saved some of his best work for small places, but if you don't know the architect and something about the austere religious tendencies of the Florentines, the chapel is inexplicable: it's a Protestant reformation in architecture unlike anything that was ever built before. The 'vocabulary' is essential Brunelleschi: simple pilasters, arches and rosettes in grey stone and white plaster. The only decoration is a set of modest terracotta Apostles by Luca della Robbia, coloured roundels of the Evangelists by Donatello, and a small stained-glass window by Alessio Baldovinetti. Even so, this is enough. The contemplative repetition of elements makes for an aesthetic that posed a direct challenge to the International Gothic of the time.

Across the broad cloister, the monks' refectory and several adjoining rooms house the **Museo dell'Opera di Santa Croce**, with more works by Della Robbia, bits from a large fresco by Orcagna wrecked by Vasari's remodelling, one of Donatello's statues from Orsanmichele – the gilded bronze *St Louis of Toulouse* – and a famous, mournful **Crucifix** by Cimabue, one of the early landmarks of Florentine painting, which it was only possible to partially restore after damage in the 1966 flood.

Around Santa Croce

The east end of Florence, packed with artisans and small manufacturers, was the artists' quarter in Renaissance times. Close to the river, it has never quite recovered from the 1966 floods. Few things around this district are very old, but just west of Piazza Santa Croce is a series of streets – Via Bentacorti, Via Torta and Piazza Peruzzi – making an almost complete ellipse. These mark the course of the inner arcade of Roman Florence's amphitheatre; some stones can still be seen among the foundations of the old palaces. To the south, on Via dei Benci near the Arno, is a collection that Herbert Horne (1844–1916), an English art historian and Florentinophile, bequeathed to Italy as the **Museo Horne** (*open Mon–Sat 9–1; adm*), with odds and ends, ceramics, and works by Giotto, Gozzoli and Desiderio da Settignano.

Michelangelo never actually lived in the **Casa Buonarroti** at Via Ghibellina 70 (*open Weds–Mon 9.30–2; adm exp*). The artist's fascination with real estate has given critics since Vasari something to gossip about; he picked this property up for some of his relatives, and later generations made it into a Michelangelo museum. Besides some drawings and models, the collection contains some of the artist's early works, the *Battle of the Centaurs* and a beautiful bas-relief called the *Madonna of the Stairs*.

Three blocks north along Via Buonarroti is the city's most colourful corner, Sant'Ambrogio market and the *mercatino* in **Piazza dei Ciompi**. This is Florence's famous flea market, where dozens of vendors wait to sell you endearing junk in all shapes and sizes behind the typically Florentine 'Fish Loggia', designed by Vasari and moved here when the old market in Piazza della Repubblica was demolished. Just to the east is the church of **Sant'Ambrogio**, which has been thoroughly Baroqued inside, though you can seek out good frescoes by Orcagna and Baldovinetti.

Across the Arno: the Palazzo Pitti

Across the Ponte Vecchio, a different Florence reveals itself: greener, quieter and less burdened with traffic. The **Oltrarno** is not a large district. A chain of hills squeezes it against the river, and their summits afford the best views over the city. Across the bridge, the Medici's catwalk passes almost over the top of **Santa Felicità**, best known as a monument to quirky Mannerist painter Jacopo Pontormo. This artist, a recluse who lived at the top of a tower he built for himself, often pulling up the ladder to keep his friends at bay, frequently got himself into trouble with his neighbours for keeping the place full of dead animals and even human bodies, from which he studied form and anatomy. His work in Santa Felicità includes his acknowledged masterpiece, the *Deposition*, with its luminous, distorted figures and exaggerated expressions, as well as frescoes of the Annunciation and the Evangelists.

As the Medici consolidated their power in Florence, they made a point of buying up all the important properties of their former rivals, especially their proud family palaces. The most spectacular example of this ducal eminent domain was the acquisition by Cosimo I of the **Pitti Palace**, built in 1457 by a powerful banker named Luca Pitti. The palace and its extensive grounds, now the Boboli Gardens, were purchased by Cosimo in the 1540s; he and his wife, Eleanor of Toledo, liked it much better than the medieval Palazzo Vecchio, and soon moved in for good. The palace remained the residence of the Medici, and later the House of Lorraine, until 1868.

The original building, said to have been designed by Brunelleschi, was only as wide as the seven central windows of the façade. Succeeding generations found it too small for their burgeoning collections of bric-à-brac, and several stages of symmetrical additions resulted in a long bulky profile resembling some sort of Stalinist ministry. Piazza Pitti was a prized address in the old days – the greatest of all Florence fans, the Brownings, lived across from the palace, and so for a time did Dostoevsky.

There are eight separate **museums** in the Pitti, including collections dedicated to clothes, ceramics, carriages and paintings (by the likes of Titian, Raphael and Botticelli). They form a tribute to Medici acquisitiveness in the centuries of decadence, a period from which, in the words of Mary McCarthy, 'flowed a torrent of bad taste that has not yet dried up… if there had been Toby jugs and Swiss weather clocks available, the Grand Dukes would certainly have collected them.' For the diligent visitor, the Pitti is pitiless; it is impossible to see all in one day.

Boboli Gardens

Open daily 9–1hr before sunset; adm.

This is the loveliest park in the centre of Florence, the only park in the centre of Florence, and if you're visiting in summer, the sooner you become acquainted with it the better. The Boboli is the only escape from the sun, humidity and crowds of July and August. Cosimo I began the planning and landscaping in the 1550s. The tone for what was to be the first Mannerist park was set early on by the incredible **Grotta del Buontalenti** (*currently under restoration; work is likely to continue for some time*), near the entrance behind the Pitti Palace. This artificial grotto is sheer madness, all

Gaudíesque dripping stone with peculiar creatures seeming to grow out of it. Inside are some fantastic painted landscapes, surrounded by leopards, bears, satyrs and other creatures harder to define.

There's a **museum of porcelain** (*open daily 9–4.30; later in summer; closed 1st and last Mon of month*) in a little palace called the Casino del Cavaliere, and the groves and walks of the Boboli are haunted by platoons of statuary, some Roman and some absurd Mannerist work, such as the fat baby Bacchus riding a turtle. There's a genuine obelisk, in the centre of a miniature Roman circus, and a fountain from the Baths of Caracalla. Some of the best parts of the gardens are the furthest away: shady paths and flower beds towards the south, near Florence's southern gate, the Porta Romana.

Santo Spirito and Santa Maria del Carmine

The centre of the Oltrarno district, Piazza Santo Spirito, usually has a small market under its plane trees, as well as restaurants and a quiet café or two. The church, **Santo Spirito**, has a severe 18th-century façade that conceals one of Brunelleschi's triumphs: a characteristic, contemplative interior of grey and white surrounded by ranks of semi-circular chapels. Though later architects tinkered grievously with the plan, many consider this to be one of his best churches. Among paintings in the chapels are works by Filippino Lippi (south transept, a Madonna and Child) and Orcagna (a fresco of the Crucifixion).

With its walls of rough stone – the projected façade was never completed – **Santa Maria del Carmine** looks more like a country farmhouse than a church. Most of it was destroyed in a fire and reconstructed in the 1700s, but the **Brancacci Chapel** (*open Mon and Weds–Sat 10–5, Sun and hols 1–5; adm; only 30 people admitted at a time, for 15mins*), another landmark of Florentine art, somehow survived and has been restored. Three artists worked on the chapel frescoes: Masolino, beginning in 1424, his pupil Masaccio, working alone from 1428, and Filippino Lippi, who completed the work in the 1480s. Scholars never tire of disputing the attributions of the various scenes, especially those that could be either Masolino's or Masaccio's. It doesn't matter; 'Little Tom' and 'Shabby Tom' both contributed greatly to the visual revolution of quattrocento painting. Both were revolutionary in their understanding of light and space, though art historians these days make more of a fuss over the precocious Shabby Tom, who died aged 27 shortly after his work here. Some scenes – the *Expulsion of Adam and Eve*, the *Tribute Money*, and scenes from the life of St Peter – are among Masaccio's masterpieces. Almost every artist of the later 1400s and 1500s came here to study how Shabby Tom did it; some of Michelangelo's sketches after Masaccio survive.

A City with a View: the Forte di Belvedere

For the best views over Florence and the best chance to get away from the dust and noise, climb up to the heights around Oltrarno, either up Costa San Giorgio and through the old city walls, or via a longer route towards Piazzale Michelangelo. This leads through an interesting, little-known corner of the city around Via dei Bardi and San Niccolò – two fine old streets with a scattering of Renaissance *palazzi*, and frescoes by Alessandro Baldovinetti in **San Niccolò sopr'Arno**.

At the top of a winding road and a long set of steps, Piazzale Michelangelo is a popular lookout point adorned with another full-size copy of the *David*. Beneath it, Via del Belvedere leads between the walls and some country villas to the **Belvedere Fort** (*closed for restoration*), dating from 1590 and dominating the city's defences along the southern heights. The fort and adjacent walls replaced the earlier ones (those Michelangelo helped design) that survived the siege of 1529. The view alone makes the climb worthwhile.

San Miniato

Although the lovely Romanesque façade of this church can be glimpsed from almost anywhere in Florence, few visitors see it up close, so you may have one of the city's finest churches to yourself. Built in 1015 over an earlier church, on the spot where the head of obscure St Minias bounced after the Romans decapitated him, it has an exterior that echoes the black and white geometric style of the Baptistry.

Despite its distance from the city centre, this has always been dear to the hearts of the Florentines. At the top of the façade is the gold eagle symbol of the Calimala, the medieval cloth merchants' guild. These rich businessmen had the church in their care, and over the centuries bestowed on it many lovely things. The playful patterns are continued inside, framing a richly coloured 13th-century mosaic of Christ Pantocrator in the apse. Be sure to see the wonderful marble floor, inlaid with signs of the zodiac and fantastical animals, and the **Cappella del Crocifisso**, a joint effort by Michelozzo and Luca della Robbia. The fine pulpit and choir screen date from the early 1200s, and the chapel of the Cardinal of Portugal contains work by Baldovinetti (who restored the apse mosaic), Della Robbia, the Pollaiuoli and Rossellino.

Fiesole

No ordinary suburb, **Fiesole** can claim to be the mother city of Florence itself. The town is of Etruscan origin, the northernmost member of the federation of city-states called the Dodecapolis. *Faesulae* dwindled in the heyday of Roman Florence, but in the Dark Ages its secure hilltop site ensured its survival. When times became a little safer, its families began moving back down to the Arno to rebuild Florence. For centuries, Fiesole has played the role of Florence's aristocratic suburb; its cool breezes and views make it the perfect retreat from the torrid Florentine summers.

There's no escaping the tourists, however; we foreigners have been tramping up and down Fiesole's hill since the days of Shelley. They're used to us by now, and a day-trip here is for many visitors an obligatory part of a stay in Florence. The no.7 city bus from the Piazza della Stazione will have you here in less than half an hour, stopping in Piazza Mino da Fiesole, the centre.

Mino da Fiesole is a favourite local son, a quattrocento sculptor whose best work can be viewd in the early 11th-century **Duomo** on the piazza; the tomb of Bishop Salutati off the right aisle contains his altarpiece with the Madonna and saints. Behind the cathedral on Via Dupré is the **Museo Bandini** (*open summer daily 10–7,* *winter Weds–Mon 10–5; adm*), a must for anybody who loves the iridescent Della Robbia terracottas on Tuscany's churches and would appreciate a chance to see some up close. The museum has an entire roomful of them, along with a collection of 14th- and 15th-century Tuscan paintings.

Not much is left of Etruscan or Roman Fiesole, but you can pay a visit to the small **Teatro Romano** (*open Weds–Mon summer 9.30–7, winter until 5; adm*), which was excavated in 1911 and is often used as a venue for plays and concerts in the summer; the archaeological area, situated on the hillside near the Bandini Museum on Via Partigiani, also includes some scanty remains of baths and temples, and a small museum (*same hours*).

Perhaps the best sights that Fiesole has to offer, though, are the perfect views over Florence and the surrounding area from old streets such as Via Francesco on the edge of town. Walks around the outskirts reveal some lovely countryside and a few surprises: the church of **San Domenico** at San Domenico di Fiesole, a couple of kilometres from town, has three paintings by Fra Angelico, who lived for a while in the adjoining monastery. Nearby on Via di Badia, the **Badia Fiesolana** (*open Mon–Fri 9–5, Sat 9–12*), Fiesole's original cathedral, has an unfinished 11th-century geometric façade reminiscent of that of San Miniato or Santa Maria Novella, and an interior in the manner of Brunelleschi.

Florentine Excursions

The countryside surrounding Fiesole presents a civilized landscape of villas and gardens, cypresses and parasol pines. Outside **Settignano** you'll pass the Villa Poggio Gherardo, which Florentines claim was the rendezvous for the genteel storytellers of the *Decameron*, and also the church of **San Martino a Mensola**, parts of which date back as far as the 9th century, containing paintings by Agnolo and Taddeo Gaddi. Settignano itself (bus no.10 from the station or Piazza San Marco) has fine views over Florence and its valley.

South of Florence is one of the typically grand fortress-monasteries of the Carthusian order, begun in the 1340s. The **Certosa di Galluzzo** (*open Tues–Sun 9–12 and 3–6; buses no.36 or 37 from the station*), near the SS2 highway to Siena, contains works by the Della Robbias and Pontormo. A few monks look after the place, and they also keep up the tradition of cooking up bottles of potent chartreuse; they will be glad to sell you one in their old pharmacy.

Like their Bourbon cousins in France, the Medici dukes liked to pass the time by constructing new palaces for themselves. In their case, however, the reason was less self-exaltation than pure and simple speculation – the Medici always thought several generations ahead. As a result, the countryside around Florence is littered with Medici villas, most of them privately owned but some open to the public. **Villa la Petraia** (*open daily 8.15–6, later hours in summer; closed 2nd and 3rd Mon of month; adm*), in the northern suburbs near Via Gramsci, has beautiful gardens and a fountain statue of Venus of Giambologna.

The Wine of the Iron Baron

What we know as Chianti was born in the 19th century, of a husband's jealousy. The 'Iron Baron' Bettino Ricasoli was extremely wealthy but not very good looking. After serving as the second prime minister of unified Italy, he married and took his lovely bride to a ball in Florence. A young man asked her to dance. The baron at once ordered her into their carriage and drove straight to the ancient family seat in Brolio in the Monti dei Chianti – an isolated castle that the poor woman would rarely leave for the rest of her life.

To pass the time the baron experimented in his vineyards, and over the years evolved a joyful, pleasing blend of Sangiovese and Caniolo grapes, with a touch of Malvasia. At the same time the famous dark green flask clad in straw (the *strapeso*) was invented. The Baron's Chianti and its distinctive bottle took the Paris Exposition of 1878 completely by storm. As imitators flooded the market, the boundaries of Chianti Classico were drawn in 1924, and the black cockerel, the symbol of the Lega dei Chianti in 1385, was made its trademark, distinguishing it from Tuscany's six other Chianti-growing districts.

If you take the Via Chiantigiana (SS222) between Florence and Siena, you'll find many vineyards to explore and places to taste wine, especially at Greve, midway down the SS222, or at the Castello di Brolio itself, 10 kilometres south of Gaiole on the N484 (*open daily 9–12 and 3–sunset*).

Nearby are more lovely gardens, typical of late Renaissance landscaping, at the **Villa di Castello** (*open daily 8.15–6, later hours summer; closed 2nd and 3rd Mon of month; adm*) in the suburb of Castello. Here there's a fascinating example of the Medici's penchant for the offbeat and excessive – an artificial cavern, the Grotta degli Animali, filled by Ammannati and Giambologna with statues of animals and fish and mosaics made of seashells. It's a great example of kitsch in the best Medici tradition.

Perhaps the best known of all Medici villas is the **Villa Careggi** (*open Mon–Fri 9–6, Sat 9–12; you can stroll freely through*), which began as a fortified farmhouse and was enlarged for Cosimo il Vecchio by Michelozzo in 1434. In the 1460s the villa became synonymous with the birth of humanism: the greatest Latin and Greek scholars of the day, Ficino, Poliziano, Pico della Mirandola and Argyropoulos, would meet here with Lorenzo il Magnifico and hold philosophical discussions in imitation of the Platonic symposium, calling their society the Platonic Academy and inspiring the early works of Botticelli with their ideas. When Lorenzo felt his end was near he had himself carried out to the villa to die.

The people of **Impruneta**, which forms the gateway to Chianti from Florence, prefer making bricks and terracotta to growing grapes, but the place is worth a stop for its **Collegiata**, which has some beautiful works by Michelozzo and Andrea della Robbia in two of its chapels. Up in the mountains to the east, San Polo is famous for the cultivation of irises. **Greve**, the unofficial capital of the Chianti, has an unusual arcaded triangular piazza, and attracts big crowds for the Chianti Classico Market Show every September.

North of Florence

The lush green valley of the **Mugello** and the hills around it border four provinces; it's a little-known corner of Tuscany, though its villages have their share of summer holiday homes. **Vicchio**, a humble town, was the birthplace of Fra Angelico, and Giotto came from nearby Vespignano. To the west, past Borgo San Lorenzo, **San Piero a Sieve** sits beneath the mouldering pentagonal San Martino fortress, built by Buontalenti for the Medici; its church has a lovely baptismal font by Luca della Robbia. Michelozzo designed a pretty Medici villa (1451) on the site of an earlier fortress at nearby **Caffagiolo**.

Up in the mountains to the north, **Scarperia**'s interesting Palazzo Pretoria was a governors' palace built by the Florentines in the early 14th century, its façade covered with the coats of arms of all the town's many governors. This is an important centre for the manufacture of cutting tools; you can buy beautifully crafted knives in the many workshops in the town. The church of the **Madonna dei Terremoti** ('Our Lady of the Earthquakes') has frescoes attributed to Filippo Lippi. Lovely **Firenzuola** with its narrow, arcaded streets is a good place to stop for a break on the way to Bologna.

From Florence to Pisa

There are two routes, whether you're going by train or car: the valley of the Arno has always been the less populated and less busy route. Trade and traffic prefer to follow a northern route through the large towns of Prato, Pistoia and Lucca.

Empoli and the Arno Valley

Montelupo, with its castle overlooking the Arno, is a pretty town given over to the manufacture of delicately painted ceramics, famous throughout Tuscany. Further down the valley comes **Empoli**, known for its Collegiata on central Piazza Farinata degli Uberti, with a green and white geometrical façade in the best medieval Florentine style. The adjacent Collegiata Museum (*open Tues–Sun 9–12 and 4–7; adm*) contains a famous Pietà fresco by Masolino, a pair of saints by Pontormo, and works by Botticini, Rossellino and Della Robbia.

There are a couple of possible detours from Empoli: south to **Castelfiorentino** up in the hills, with its crumbling castle and **Museo di Arte Sacra Santa Verdiana** (*open Sat 4–7, Sun and hols 10–12 and 4–7; to visit at other times, call* **t** *0571 686 1338*), with some excellent trecento paintings; or north to **Vinci**, a village in a lovely quattrocento landscape, where fans of Leonardo can visit his birthplace, and lovers of gadgets can have a good time with the intricate models of the master's inventions in the Museo Leonardiano (*open daily 9.30–7; winter until 6; adm*), including the bicycle, tank and helicopter. The museum is housed in the 13th-century Guidi Castle, which also has a small art collection.

Closer to the main Pisa and Livorno road, **San Miniato**, which is home to the national kite-flying festival (held on the first Sunday after Easter), is a fine town in some of the fairest Tuscan countryside. It has a good picture gallery in the Museo Diocesano (*open Tues–Sun 10–12.30 and 3–6.30; adm*).

Prato

Living in Florence's shadow for 1,000 years has not dampened Prato's spirit as much as you'd expect. A town of almost 150,000 people, with a textile industry that was important in Europe for 600 years, Prato could certainly express some weariness at having seen its wealth and talent constantly drained off to glorify its imperious neighbour. Twice Florence conquered the city, and on one occasion the Florentines simply bought it. Twice, in 1470 and 1512, the Pratese rebelled, but both times they were crushed. The sack of the city in 1514, an atrocity with which the Spaniards and the Medici Pope Leo X meant to intimidate all Italy, quietened Prato considerably. Now, almost 500 years later, its industries are thriving again, and the town makes a point of showing that it, too, has culture. If you come in by rail (the station, with its park and bridges over the Bisenzio, is a blissful introduction), one of the first things you see is a big puffy sculpture by Henry Moore in the middle of a roundabout.

Santa Maria delle Carceri

The defiantly swallowtail crenellations of the **Castello dell'Imperatore** as you enter old Prato by Viale Piave mark a strange Ghibelline interlude in Prato's history. Frederick II built it in 1237 – his only such castle in northern Italy. Its clean lines must have seemed very sharp and modern in the 13th century, but its location inside the walls hints that the purpose was less to protect Prato from the Florentines than to protect imperial officials from the Pratese. There isn't much inside, but the city often uses it for special exhibitions.

Behind is the unfinished black and white marble façade (*currently undergoing restoration*) of **Santa Maria delle Carceri**, begun in 1485 by Giuliano de Sangallo. Brunelleschian architecture was always a fragile blossom, as shown clearly by the failure of this sole serious attempt to transplant it outside of Florence. It was an audacious enterprise: Sangallo, a diligent student of Vitruvius and Alberti, attempted a building based entirely on philosophical principles. Order, simplicity and correct proportion, as in Brunelleschi's churches, were to be manifest, with no frills allowed. Sangallo, favourite of Lorenzo il Magnifico, proved a better theorist than architect; Santa Maria came out tedious and clumsy. The interior is better than the outside – a plain Greek cross in the Brunelleschi manner, with a frieze and tondos by Andrea della Robbia. The name – *carceri* means prisons – refers to a miracle, a speaking image of the Virgin painted on a nearby prison wall, that led to the church's construction.

The Duomo

North of the church, Via Pugliesi and Via Garibaldi pass several medieval towers on their way to Piazza del Duomo. Prato's **cathedral of St Stephen**, in flagrant green and white stripes like the Duomo at Siena, was begun in the 13th century and finished in bits and pieces over the next 200 years. Its best features are an exotic, almost Moorish-looking campanile, an Andrea della Robbia lunette of the Madonna with St Stephen over the door, a big clock where the rose window ought to be, and the **pulpit of the Sacred Girdle** (*Pulpito del Sacro Cingolo*), a perfectly felicitous ornament,

something beautiful and special the Pratese can look at every day as they cross the piazza. Michelozzo designed it (1428) and Donatello added the delightful reliefs of dancing children, along the lines of his *cantoria* in the cathedral museum in Florence. Mary's girdle came to Prato during the First Crusade; the outdoor pulpit was built so that it could be displayed to the people, five times a year on major church holidays.

In the cathedral, the prime attraction is in the choir: two series of lucent, precise **frescoes** (*currently undergoing lengthy restoration, though it's possible to see the chapel and observe work in progress by guided tour; enquire at the tourist office*) by Filippo

Lippi illustrating the stories of St Stephen and John the Baptist (the nun who later ran off with Lippi is said to have been the model for Salome). A separate entrance on the side leads to the **Museo dell'Opera del Duomo** (*open Mon and Weds–Sat 9.30–12.30 and 3–6.30, Sun 9.30–12.30; adm*), where you can see the original Donatello reliefs from the pulpit – copies had to be made to face the weather – plus works by Filippino Lippi, an early Uccello and a sophisticated Madonna by the quattrocento 'Master of the Nativity of Castello'. Outside the museum, stop for a look at the Romanesque cloister, done in patterns of the same green and white stone as the exterior.

Getting There and Around

The fastest **train** line between Florence and Pisa is via Empoli, but there is also a frequent service through Prato, Pistoia and Lucca and then to Pisa or Viareggio.

Prato has two train stations, Stazione Centrale, and Stazione Porta al Serraglio closer to the centre (not all trains stop here).

Buses depart from Piazza Ciardi, north of the Duomo, or the Stazione Centrale.

Tourist Information

Prato: Piazza Santa Maria delle Carceri 15, **t** 0574 24112, *www.prato.turismo.toscana.it*.

Shopping

Prato still makes its living from fine fabrics and clothing, including **cashmere**. Design houses such as Calvin Klein, Donna Karan and Armani buy their fabrics from Prato's 'lanifici', and people flock here from all over Tuscany for the discount **factory outlets**.

Where to Stay

Prato ✉ 50047

Prato's hotels are mostly of the business variety but can be a good bet in summer, when Florence is packed. Low season here is Aug and Christmas, and weekends are cheaper than during the week.

*****Villa Santa Cristina**, Via Poggio Secco 58, **t** 0574 595 951 (*expensive*). A relaxing spot with a garden, pool and most other comforts, over the river in the hills to the east.

*****Hotel Giardino**, Via Magnolfi 2, **t** 0574 26189 (*expensive*). A smartly modernized and very friendly hotel off Piazza del Duomo, boasting a good bar, a reading room and a private garage.

*****San Marco**, Piazza San Marco 48, **t** 0574 21321, *www.hotel-sanmarco.com (moderate)*. A pleasant place between the Stazione Centrale and the Castello, convenient if you're arriving by train.

****Toscana**, Piazza Ciardi 3, **t** 0574 28096, (*moderate*). One of the cheapest options in town, situated on a quiet square on the far side of the Stazione Porta al Serraglio. Some rooms have air-conditioning.

Villa Rucellai, Via di Canneto, 16km northeast of town, **t** 0574 460 392 (*moderate*). A delightful bed and breakfast set in a Renaissance villa, with formal gardens and a swimming pool. It's very good value.

Eating Out

Osvaldo Baroncelli, Via Fra Bartolomeo 13, **t** 0574 23810 (*very expensive*). A small, unpretentious establishment outside the city walls, offering innovative dishes such as fricasée of salt cod, Tuscan bean and spelt soup with fish and frizzled leeks, pasta with fish and artichoke hearts, and fish couscous, as well as more traditional Tuscan favourites. There's an excellent-value set menu and a fabulous array of Italian and French cheeses. *Closed Sat lunch and Sun.*

Il Pirana, Via Valentini 110 (south of Viale Vittorio Veneto, the main street between Stazione Centrale and Piazza San Marco), **t** 0574 25746 (*very expensive*). A restaurant offering some of the best seafood in inland Tuscany; the *gnocchetti* with scampi and zucchini flowers, the fish ravioli in lobster sauce, and the sea bass baked in a salt crust are all worth trying. *Closed Sat lunch and Sun.*

Osteria Cibbé, Piazza Mercatale 49, **t** 0574 607509 (*cheap*). A small, family-run *osteria* in a brick-vaulted room with marble-topped tables. The delicious rustic dishes include *pappa al pomodoro*, *garganelli* with aubergine and wild mushrooms, stock fish *in inzimino* (spicy sauce with Swiss chard), and meatballs with ricotta. *Closed Sun.*

La Vecchia Cucina di Soldano, Via Pomeria 23, **t** 0574 34665 (*cheap*). A satisfying trattoria serving uncomplicated fare such as *ribollita*, *pasta e fagioli*, stuffed celery and other old-fashioned soups and stews, including a hearty beef and onion stew known as *francesina*, the house speciality. *Closed Sun.*

Maffei, Via Ricasoli 22 (*cheap*). A *biscotteria* and bar selling the best *biscotti* or *cantucci di Prato* around, displayed in distinctive bright blue bags in the window.

More Museums

The sleepy streets of old Prato bear only a few reminders of the city's businesslike past. **Piazza del Mercatale**, by the river, is an attractive, huge, very Tuscan square, full of peeling yellow paint and flowers. Near the centre of town, on Via Rinaldesca, is the house of Renaissance Prato's most flamboyant tycoon, Francesco di Marco Datini. If there were an accountants' hall of fame, Datini would be one of the stars. He helped invent that dismal science, and also gets credit, according to the Pratese, for the 'invention of the promissory note'. Datini put his talents to good use, piling up an indecent fortune, fooling about in politics, and giving vast sums to charity. His **Palazzo Datini** (*c.* 1350) shows bits of the frescoes that covered the façade – scenes from his life.

Two streets to the north, the rugged, four-square **Palazzo Pretorio**, Prato's seat of government in the days of independence, is home to the **Galleria Comunale** (*currently closed*), a rich collection with works by the Lippis, Bernardo Daddi and many lesser-known Renaissance artists. From here, Via Cesare Guasti takes you four blocks to the big 13th-century church of **San Domenico**, the cloister of which houses the **Museo di Pittura Murale** (*open Mon and Weds–Fri 10.30–6.30, Sat 10.30–2.30, Sun 4–7; adm*), with a small collection of frescoes from local churches and *palazzi*, plus an ongoing exhibition, 'Tesori della Città', that includes important works moved from the Galleria Comunale and Museo dell'Opera del Duomo because of closure or reorganization.

Lastly, Prato celebrates its medieval and modern textile industry in the **Museo del Tessuto** in an old textile mill at Via Santa Chiara 24 outside the city walls (*call tourist office for opening hours*), housing fabrics and looms dating back to the 5th century AD.

Pistoia

Many people have found this a gloomy town, and indeed, Pistoia does seem to get more than its share of fog and clouds. Laughter in its plain, narrow streets seems a bit out of place. The city has been around since Roman times, as *Pistoria*, and it has usually been bad luck for somebody. The Catiline conspiracy, the famous attempted coup against the Roman Republic in 62 BC, ended when the legions tracked down the escaped Catiline and his henchmen near Pistoia. In the Middle Ages, Pistoia had a dark reputation among its neighbours for violence and treachery. The Black versus White Guelph struggles that obsessed Florence for so long began here. Dante, a victim of that feud, never let a chance go by in the *Divine Comedy* to condemn the fateful city. In 1329 Florence captured Pistoia once and for all. The city carried on, living well off its old speciality, iron-working. True to its reputation, it supplied the warriors and conspirators of Europe with fine daggers. Later, keeping up with technology, the city gave its name to the pistol.

Today Pistoia, the centre of a plain full of gardens, is better known for its flowers. Its people laugh at their odd history; bring it up and they'll be ready to blame it all on those obnoxious Florentines. Pistoia's somnolence over the last six centuries has left it with a historic centre that is almost entirely intact, a good many fine buildings, and a wealth of art.

Piazza del Duomo

Old Pistoia is almost perfectly diamond-shaped, surrounded by 16th-century walls with the old moats preserved on the north and east sides. In the middle, the L-shaped **Piazza del Duomo** is an excellent example of medieval urban design. The façade of the **Duomo**, with its Pisan arcades and stripes over a Florentine tympanum by Andrea della Robbia, strikes an uneasy balance between the two traditions. The impressive campanile tips the balance towards Pisa, with a touch of the exotic in its Moorish-inspired arches. Inside, the real attraction is the enormous **altar of St James**, about a ton of solid silver, begun in 1287 and added to over the next two centuries.

Directly across is the striped, octagonal **baptistry** of 1350 (*open Tues–Sun 10–12.30 and 3–6*), credited to Andrea Pisano. One of Tuscany's outstanding Gothic buildings, it has a fine sculptural trim on the exterior and a conical dome under the roof. The 12th-century Palazzo dei Vescovi contains Etruscan and Roman finds in an **archaeological itinerary**, and the old cathedral is included in the **Museo San Zeno**, with paintings and a reliquary by Ghiberti (*guided tours of both Tues, Thurs and Fri 10–1 and 3–5; call first to check,* ***t*** *0573 369 272; joint adm*).

On the façade of the **Palazzo Comunale** is a head in black marble set into the wall – the face of a Moorish king captured on a freebooting expedition to Mallorca. Besides the mayor, the building houses the **Museo Civico**, which provides an introduction to the often weird 13th- and 14th-century 'Pistoian School' and much else; don't miss the hallucinatory battle scenes by Francesco Graziani.

From behind the cathedral, Via F. Pacini takes you north to another surprise – the refined, arcaded façade of the **Ospedale del Ceppo**, done in the manner of the famous Ospedale degli Innocenti in Florence. As in Florence, the Della Robbias provided the decoration, but besides the simple terracotta medallions there is a unique terracotta frieze across the entire façade, in Renaissance Technicolor; created by Giovanni della Robbia and later artists in the 1510s and 1580s, it portrays the works of the hospital and allegorical virtues. Just to the west, the 12th-century **Sant'Andrea** (*open daily 8–12.30 and 3.30–6*) contains a lovely pulpit by Giovanni Pisano, lifted on columns over figures of the four Evangelists and surrounded with reliefs full of intricately carved figures – a fitting introduction to the more famous works of the Pisano family in Pisa.

Two other churches on the northern side of town are worth a look. **San Francesco al Prato**, on the piazza of the same name, has an exceptional collection of 14th-century frescoes, and the **Madonna dell'Umiltà**, on central Via della Madonna, is a curious, octagonal High Renaissance building. In the 1560s Giorgio Vasari was called upon to complete this long-unfinished church; he added a dome so heavy that the church has been threatening to collapse ever since.

More Stripes

One block south and another east from Piazza del Duomo is Piazza San Leone; its stubby tower once belonged to perhaps the rottenest of all Pistoians, a 13th-century noble thug and sworn enemy of the Church named Vanni Fucci; Dante found him in one of the lower circles of Hell, cursing and making obscene gestures up at God. **San Giovanni Fuoricivitas**, just around the corner of Via Cavour, must be the stripiest

Getting There and Around

The **train** station, which has connections to Florence, Pisa and occasionally Bologna, is on the southern edge of town, two blocks from the town walls on Via XX Settembre.

Most **buses** to other Tuscan cities leave from Piazza San Francesco, at the west end of town, inside the walls off Corso Gramsci.

Cars are banned from most of the centre of Pistoia (in theory), but there's lots of parking around the Fortezza di Santa Barbara.

Tourist Information

Pistoia: Piazza Duomo, in the bishop's palace, **t** 0573 21622, *www.provincia.pistoia.it*.

Montecatini Terme: Viale Verdi 66, **t** 0572 772 244.

Where to Stay and Eat

Pistoia ✉ 51110

Pistoia is used to lodging and feeding more business than leisure travellers.

★★★**Il Convento**, Via S. Quirico 33, Pontenuovo, 5km east of town, **t** 0573 452 651 (*moderate*). A former convent that has preserved its exterior, if not all of its interior. The setting is quiet, with views over Pistoia. It has a pool and one of the city's better restaurants.

★★★**Leon Bianco**, Via Panciatichi 2, **t** 0573 26675 (*moderate*). A comfortable if slightly dated option with views over the campanile.

Tenuta di Pieve a Celle, Via Pieve a Celle, **t** 0573 913 087 (*expensive*). A new *agriturismo* in a lovely setting next to the zoo (from which you'll hear the odd roar), with five stylish guest rooms. There's a fine pool, and dinner is provided by prior arrangement.

La Bottegaia, Via del Lastrone 17, **t** 0573 265 602 (*moderate*). A wine bar/restaurant tucked away behind the baptistry, with a beautiful vaulted room and lovely terrace. The short but ever-changing menu includes snacks (cheeses, meats, *bruschette* and salads) and full meals. The excellent-value *menu degustazione* includes the likes of celery soup with *pecorino*, leek flan, pesto lasagne, and guinea fowl cooked with Moscato wine. There are some 600 wines to choose from. *Closed Sun lunch and Mon.*

Rafanelli, Via Sant'Agostino 47, Sant'Agostino, **t** 0573 532 046 (*moderate*). A pretty country villa offering Tuscan home cooking, including *maccheroni* with duck, game and lamb. *Closed Sun eve, Mon and Aug.*

San Jacopo, Via Crispi 15, **t** 0573 27786 (*cheap*). A pleasant trattoria serving top-quality traditional fish and meat dishes, including Tuscan soups, spaghetti with clams, tripe, *baccalà* and rabbit with olives. *Closed Tues lunch and Mon.*

Trattoria dell' Abbondanza, Via dell' Abbondanza 10, **t** 0573 368037 (*cheap*). A cheerful trattoria near the Duomo, serving delicious rustic food such as *porcini* soup, *gnocchi all'Abbondanza* (with tomatoes, pesto and *pecorino*), octopus and potato stew, and roast pork with rosemary and garlic. *Closed Thurs lunch and Weds.*

Montecatini Terme ✉ 51016

★★★★★**Grand Hotel & La Pace**, Corso Roma 12, **t** 0572 75801, *www.grandhotellapace.it* (*luxury*). A hotel renowned throughout Europe for its genuine *belle époque* charm, with an elegant restaurant. *Closed Nov–Mar.*

★★★★★**Grand Hotel Bellavista**, Viale Fedeli 2, **t** 0572 78122, *www.panciolihotels.it* (*luxury*). One of the grandest hotels in the area, with luxurious rooms, an indoor pool, a sauna, a health club and other opportunities for self-indulgence. *Open Apr–Nov.*

★★★**Corallo**, Viale Cavallotti 116, **t** 0572 78288, *www.golfhotelcorallo.it* (*moderate*). A small, refined hotel on a quiet sidestreet near the park, with a pool and garden.

Il Salotto di Gea, Via Talenti 2, **t** 0572 904318 (*moderate*). A delightful and good-value alternative to the some of the overblown hotels here. The 8 rooms are unfussy and tasteful. The restaurant serves the likes of warm octopus salad, aubergine ravioli with pesto, and fillet of beef with Chianti sauce. Breakfast is taken in the piazza in summer.

Enoteca da Giovanni, Via Garibaldi 25, **t** 0572 71695 (*very expensive*). A unique, much-lauded place with imaginative, impeccable *haute cuisine* based on game and fish. *Closed Mon.* The **Cucina da Giovanni** next door offers simple fare at more modest prices (try the *antipasti* and the fabulous *maccheroncini* with duck sauce).

church in Christendom. Turning its side to the street, and bristling with lozenge windows and blind arches, the 12th-century work looks more Pisan than anything you'll see in Pisa. Inside (if it's open) is another fine pulpit, by a pupil of Pisano, and a Della Robbia plaque of the Visitation.

San Domenico, nearby on Corso Silvano, is less flamboyant on the outside, but the church and adjacent convent have some good frescoes, as does the **Cappella del Tau** (*open Mon–Sat 9–2*) across the street. Some of the pictures here, scenes from the story of Adam and Eve, are little-known works by Masolino.

There is another good Gothic façade on **San Paulo**, a block east. The best stripes of all, however, are on the zebras in **Pistoia Zoo** (*open daily Apr–Sept 9–7; Oct–Mar 9–5; adm exp*), four kilometres northwest of town on Via Pieve a Celle and one of the best in the country.

Montecatini Terme

Only 15 kilometres west of Pistoia, this is perhaps Italy's best-known thermal spa – a party centre for crowned heads and their sycophants in the 1890s and popular ever since. The waters, said to be good for just about anything, are the town's reason for being. In the 19th century, to please its elevated clientele, Montecatini built itself into quite an elegant place, with a large park at the centre and imposing establishments such as the Versailles-like **Tettuccio**, where string quartets serenaded those who came to take the waters. Even if you prefer stronger stuff than mineral water for your cures, come for the florid 1890s architecture and genteel atmosphere. The other favourite recreation of visitors is taking the **cable car** up to pretty Montecatini Alto.

Further west towards Lucca, **Pescia** is a gardening area with a famous wholesale flower market. Its church of San Francesco has a painting of St Francis done shortly after his death and believed to be an accurate portrayal by an artist who knew him. In **Collodi** you'll see a park with a monument to Pinocchio; his creator, Carlo Collodi, took his pen name from his family's native town.

Lucca

The famous walls – 'much like the walls of Berwick-on-Tweed', the Lucchese like to say – seem more like a garden wall than something that would keep the Florentines at bay. Behind them you can see only pine trees and neat stucco buildings with green shutters. The walls and the surrounding areas, once the outworks of the fortifications, are now full of lawns and trees, making a sort of green belt. The Lucchese ride their bikes and walk their dogs around the ramparts, and often stop to admire the view.

Lucca at first glance may seem too bijou and tidy to be true. It is a dream city – not like Venice, but in a quiet, very domestic sort of way. After its long and brave history, it has certainly earned the right to a little quietude. The annual hordes of Tuscan tourists leave Lucca alone for the most part, though there seems to be a small number of discreet visitors who come back every year. They don't spread the word, apparently trying to keep one of Italy's most beautiful cities to themselves.

Getting There and Around

The **train** station (**t** 0583 892 021) is just south of the walls on Piazza Ricasoli. Lots of trains on the Pisa–Florence line stop here.

Buses leave from Piazzale G. Verdi, just inside the walls at the western end of the city: LAZZI buses run to Florence, Pistoia, Pisa, Prato and Viareggio; CLAP buses (**t** 166 845 010) go to towns in Lucca province, including the upper Serchio Valley in the Apuan Alps.

You can hire a **bicycle** from the tourist office or Barbetti, Via Anfiteatro 23 (**t** 0583 954 444).

Tourist Information

Lucca: Vecchia Porta San Donato, Piazzale Verdi, **t** 0583 583 150.

Where to Stay

Lucca and Around ✉ 55100

There aren't enough rooms (especially cheap ones) to meet demand, so book ahead.

*******Locanda l'Elisa**, Via Nova per Pisa, Massa Pisana, **t** 0583 379 737, *www.locandalelisa.com* (*luxury*). An 18th-century villa in a glorious garden, with luxurious public rooms and bedrooms, the latter with canopied beds. There is a conservatory restaurant (*expensive*) and a pool. *Closed Jan.*

******Ilaria**, Via del Fosso 20, **t** 0583 47558, *www.hotelilaria.com* (*expensive*). Fourteen smart, comfortable rooms with contemporary décor, plus parking.

*****Universo**, Piazza Puccini, **t** 0583 493 678, *www.hoteluniverso.it* (*moderate*). A frayed but delightful hotel in the centre; Ruskin and nearly everyone who followed him to Lucca slept here. Its restaurant, **Il Giglio**, **t** 0583 494 058 (*expensive*), serves Lucca's best seafood, with river trout a speciality. *Restaurant closed Tues eve and Weds.*

****Diana** Via del Molinetto 11, **t** 0583 492 202, *www.albergodiana.com* (*moderate*). A friendly, well-run place near the cathedral, with some en suite rooms and a more upmarket annexe nearby.

Eating Out

Il Buca di Sant'Antonio, Via della Cervia 3, **t** 0583 55881 (*expensive*). A 1782 inn offering old recipes such kid on a spit, and newer dishes such as ravioli with ricotta and sage. *Closed Sun eve and Mon.*

La Mora, Via Sesto di Moriano 104, Ponte a Moriano (north of town), **t** 0583 406 402 (*expensive*). An old posthouse with a pergola for summer dining. Seasonal goodies include delicious ravioli with asparagus or truffles, and gourmet roast lamb.

Puccini, Via della Cervia 3, **t** 0583 55881 (*expensive*). One of the best restaurants in Lucca, opposite the Casa Puccini. Modern and elegant, it serves mainly fish. *Closed Tues in winter.*

Vipore, in nearby Pieve Santo Stefano, **t** 0583 394065 (*expensive*). An old farmhouse with views over the fertile plain of Lucca, offering top-quality fresh pasta and meat dishes. *Closed Mon.*

Buatino, Corte S. Lorenzo 1–3, **t** 0583 316 116 (*moderate*). Excellent meals in lively surroundings, including *zuppa di farro* (spelt), delicious roast pork, and salt cod with leeks. *Closed Sun.*

Da Leo, Via Tegrini 1, **t** 0583 492 236 (*cheap*). A chaotic place rammed with locals and tourists, offering the likes of rabbit stewed with olives, and veal with green peppers. On Fridays there's exclusively fish. *Closed Sun.*

Gli Orti di Via Elisa, Via Elisa 17, **t** 0583 491 241 (*cheap*). A great trattoria for a cheap and cheerful meal, with pizzas, salads and good pasta dishes. *Closed Weds and Thurs.*

Lucca's rigid grid of streets betrays its Roman origins. The town survived the bad centuries, and emerged in the age of the *comuni* one of the leading trading towns of Tuscany, specializing in the production of silk. In the early 1300s, perhaps the height of its wealth and power, a remarkable adventurer named Castruccio Castracani appeared in the spotlight. Castracani, who for years had lived in exile – part of it in England – returned in 1314 when Pisan and Ghibelline troops captured Lucca. Within a year he had chased the Pisans out and seized power for himself, and by 1325 he had built for Lucca a little empire that included both Pisa and Pistoia. After routing the Florentines at Altopascio in that year he was making plans to snatch Florence too, but died of malaria just before the siege was to begin – another example of Florentine good luck. Internal bickering between the powerful families put an end to Lucca's glory days almost immediately, and it barely escaped being gobbled up by one or other of its neighbours. As a competently functioning republic Lucca used tact and tenacity to survive even after the arrival of the Spaniards. After the Treaty of Cateau-Cambresis, Lucca amazingly found itself standing with Venice as the only truly independent Italian states. Like Venice the city was an island of relative tolerance and enlightenment during the Counter-Reformation, and it shared Venice's fate in 1805 when Napoleon arrived, and ordered its political extinction.

The Walls

Lucca's walls owe their considerable charm to Renaissance advances in military technology. The city began them in 1500, urged to the effort by the beginning of the Wars of Italy. The councillors wanted fortifications entirely up to date, to counter advances in artillery, and their (unknown) architects gave them the state of the art, a model for the new style of fortification that would soon be transforming the cities of Europe. Being Renaissance Tuscans, they also made them a little more elegant than perhaps was necessary.

The walls were never severely tested. Today, with the outer ravelins, fosses and salients cleared away (such earthworks usually took up as much space as the city itself), Lucca's walls are just for decoration, with a double row of shady trees planted on top to make an elevated garden boulevard that extends clear around the city. St Peter's Gate, near the station, still has its portcullis, and Lucca's proud motto LIBERTAS is inscribed over the entrance.

San Martino

Lucca's **Duomo**, perhaps the outstanding work of the Pisan style outside Pisa itself, was begun in the 11th century and only completed in the 15th. A porch with three arches, each a different size, makes the façade somewhat unusual. Above is a typical Pisan design of three levels of colonnades, and behind the arches are exquisite 12th- and 13th-century reliefs and sculpture – the best work Lucca has to offer. See especially the *Adoration of the Magi* by Nicolà Pisano, and a host of fantastical animals and hunting scenes, the 12 months and their occupations, even *Roland at Roncevalles*, all by unknown masters.

Inside, a large marble tabernacle in the left aisle contains the *Volto Santo* ('Holy Image'), a painted wooden crucifix brought from Byzantium to Italy in 782 during the Iconoclast movement. According to legend the crucifix was carved by Nicodemus and accurately represents the face of Jesus. The image takes part in a candlelit procession each 13 September. A door from the right aisle leads to the sacristy (*adm*), where you can see Lucca's real icon, Jacopo Della Quercia's remarkable **tomb of Ilaria del Carretto** (1408), a tranquil effigy complete with family dog.

Next to the cathedral is the **Museo della Cattedrale** (*open daily 10–6; adm*), with a second work by della Quercia, *St John the Evangelist*, as well as other treasures from the cathedral and the adjoining church of San Giovanni.

From the cathedral, in a quiet corner of town close to the southern wall, Via Duomo takes you to twin *piazze* full of trees, the focus of Lucca's evening *passeggiata*, **Piazza del Giglio** and **Piazza Napoleone**. After Napoleon seized Lucca, he gave it to his sister Elisa Baciocchi. This queen for a day occupied the old seat of the republican council on Piazza Napoleone and, after Waterloo, when Lucca was given to a branch of the Bourbons, the 16th-century building became the **Palazzo Ducale**, which is the name that it still bears.

San Michele in Foro

Many people mistake this church, set on a piazza right in the centre of Lucca, for the cathedral. Built about the same time, and with a similar Pisan façade, it is almost as impressive. The name comes from its location on what was Roman Lucca's forum. The ambitious façade rises high above the level of the roof, like the false fronts on buildings in wild-west towns of the 1880s. Every column in the Pisan arcading is different; some are doubled, some twisted like corkscrews, others inlaid with mosaic Cosmati work, or carved into medieval monsters. The graceful, rectangular campanile is Lucca's tallest and best.

West of San Michele, in a neighbourhood perfumed by the big tobacco factory near Porta Vittorio Emanuele, the 17th-century Palazzo Mansi contains the **Pinacoteca Nazionale** (*open Tues–Sat 8.30–7, Sun 8,30–1; adm*), with mostly 16th–17th-century paintings, works by Bronzino, Pontormo and Veronese. East of the church, **Via Fillungo** and its surrounding streets make up Lucca's busy shopping area, a tidy nest of straight and narrow alleys where the contented cheerfulness that distinguishes Lucca from many of its neighbouring cities seems somehow magnified. Near Via Fillungo's northern end, the 12th-century church of **San Frediano** stands out thanks to the big mosaic panel on its façade, showing Christ and the Apostles in an elegant, flowing style. Inside is a beautiful covered baptismal font and a terracotta of the Annunciation by Andrea della Robbia.

Across Via Fillungo, narrow arches lead to the **Anfiteatro Romano**. Not a stone of it remains – the marble was probably carted off for San Michele and the cathedral – but Lucca is a place that changes so gradually and organically that the outline of the amphitheatre was perfectly preserved. Where the grandstands were you now see a complete ellipse of medieval houses, with a piazza where the gladiators slugged it out. Down Via Sant'Andrea you'll pass a number of resolutely medieval palaces, including that of the Guinigi family; long the leading powerbrokers of Lucca, the Guinigi once even went so far as to imitate the Visconti and Medici and seize power for themselves from 1400 to 1430. Their stronghold, the **Torre Guinigi** (*open summer 9–7.30, winter 10–5.30; adm*), next to their palace, is one of Lucca's landmarks, the best example of the odd Italian fancy of towers with big trees growing out of the top. One of the most elaborate of the medieval family fortresses, it's well worth the climb up for the view over the city and the Apuan Alps.

Continuing eastwards you pass the Via del Fosso; the canal running down the middle was the moat (*fosso*) of Lucca's oldest fortifications. Another Guinigi house, a suburban villa before the extension of the walls, contains the **Museo Guinigi** (*open Tues–Sat 8.30–7, Sun 8.30–1; adm*), which contains a good selection of painting and sculpture from this side of Tuscany. Sculptures from the 9th to the 15th century demonstrate the logical development of the Pisan–Luccan style, along with some original columns from the façade of San Michele, and an inspired Annunciation and other works by a sculptor named Matteo Civitali, who deserves to be better known. Lucchese Renaissance painting, with a fond reluctance to give up the Middle Ages, is also well represented.

North of the city are two showy but refined 16th-century villas, both with extensive 'English' gardens: **Villa Mansi** at Segromigno (*open daily summer 10–1 and 3–6, winter 10–12.30 and 3–5; adm*); and the **Villa Pecci-Blunt ex-Villa Reale**, nearby at Marlia, the country home of Elisa Bonaparte Baciocchi during her reign. Only the park and the Giardino Orsetti are open (*guided tours Mar–Nov Tues–Sun at 10, 11, 12, 3, 4, 5 and 6 by appointment, call* **t** *0583 30108; Dec–Feb call in advance; adm*), but they are lovely.

The Apuan Alps and the Serchio Valley

All across northern Tuscany the mountains have never been far away. In the region's northwest corner they stretch to the very edge of the sea itself. These are no piddling foothills: two peaks within 45km of Lucca are 6,560ft high. Not many tourists find their way up the Serchio – it may be the only corner of Tuscany that hasn't been overrun. But if you simply can't look at another cathedral or picture gallery, and would like a spell in some striking yet civilized mountain scenery, this is the place.

Lucca to Bagni di Lucca

North of Lucca you quickly arrive at **Diécimo** – a name that has survived from Roman times – ten Roman miles from the city. Its fine Renaissance campanile stands out starkly among the surrounding hills. Next, **Borgo a Mozzano** is famous for its beautiful little hog-back bridge, the Ponte Maddalena, with arches in five different sizes, and a legend attached to it of how the devil built it in one night. The credit really goes to Countess Matilda of Tuscany who, besides the bridge, endowed the villages around Borgo with a set of solid Romanesque churches.

A little further up river beyond the turn, still on the SS12, **Bagni di Lucca** has an interesting 19th-century suspension bridge (1840) hung on iron chains, the Ponte alle Catene. Bagni, a spa that enjoyed a brief spell of high society's favour during the 19th century and was then quietly forgotten, is well worth visiting, with its elegant old establishments in which to take the waters (one resembling a miniature Roman pantheon), a pretty riverside situation, charming villas and gardens, and even a Victorian–Gothic–Alhambresque Anglican church; among the many English visitors in the old days were Shelley, Byron and Browning. Bagni's casino (1837) invented roulette to clean them out.

Getting Around

There are **buses** to most destinations in the valley from Lucca, but some services are slow.

Tourist Information

Bagni di Lucca: Viale Umberto I, 139, **t** 0583 805 745 (*summer only*).
Barga: Piazza Angelio, **t** 0583 724 733.
Fivizzano: Via Roma, **t** 0585 92017.
Pontrémoli: Piazza della Repubblica, **t** 0187 833 278.

Where to Stay and Eat

Bagni di Lucca or Barga are pleasant places to stay a few days to recharge your batteries.

Bagni di Lucca ✉ 55022

Bagni di Lucca is wonderfully genteel, with a score of quiet, modest Victorian-era hotels.

*****Regina Park Hotel**, Viale Umberto I 157, **t** 0583 805508 (*expensive*). A comfortable, smart hotel in a Renaissance *palazzo* in the centre of Bagni, with all mod cons. A lovely loggia overlooks the ample grounds, which back onto the Lima river.

*****Corona**, Via Serraglia 78, **t** 0583 805151, *www.coronaregina.it* (*moderate*). A very comfortable place under the same ownership as the Regina. The restaurant serves zucchini, *taleggio* and truffle timbale, gnocchi with baby squid and chickpeas, duck breast with blackcurrants and other imaginative dishes.

***Roma**, Via Umberto I 110, Villa di Bagni, **t** 0583 87278 (*cheap*). A small, old-fashioned place with a shady garden in a pretty suburb a couple of kilometres up the river. Toscanini stayed here.

Circolo dei Forestieri, Loc. Ville, **t** 0583 86038 (*moderate*). A quite smart place offering the likes of *filetto al pepe verde* and *crespelle ai funghi*. *Closed Mon.*

Da Vinicio, Via del Casino, **t** 0583 87250 (*cheap*). A chaotic and popular pizzeria just west of the bridge, also serving good roast pigeon and seafood.

Barga ✉ 55051

******Il Ciocco in Castelvecchio**, Pascoli, 6km north of town, **t** 0583 7191, *www.ciocco.it* (*expensive*). A huge resort hotel with the full works, including tennis courts.

*****Villa Libano**, Via del Sasso 6, **t** 0583 723 774, *www.villalibano.com* (*moderate*). A lovely place in a courtyard, next to the city park. The restaurant has tables out in the garden.

Terrazza, Albiano, 5km north of town, **t** 0583 766 155 (*cheap–moderate*). Very good specialities of the region. *Closed Weds.*

Fivizzano ✉ 54013

****Il Giardinetto**, Via Roma 151, **t** 0585 92060 (*cheap*). A delightful place overlooking Piazza Medicea, with comfortable rooms and a little garden for lounging it. The lovely restaurant (*moderate*) has tempting *antipasti*, pasta, game and a flan with spinach and cheese, made from a Renaissance recipe. *Closed Oct.*

Pontrémoli ✉ 54027

*****Golf Hotel**, Via Pineta, **t** 0187 831 573, (*moderate*). Ninety very comfortable rooms, all with bath, outside town in a pine wood.

Osteria Caveau del Teatro, Piazza Santa Cristina, **t** 0187 833328 (*moderate*). An elegant but cosy cellar restaurant offering such dishes as pâté of foie gras with port, potato *tortelli* with parmesan cream,and roast pork with orange. The adjoining 17th-century tower houses 7 delightful bedrooms, beautifully furnished with antiques.

Da Bussé, Piazza del Duomo 31, **t** 0187 831 371 (*moderate*). An age-old restaurant offering Pontrémoli's special *testaroli* wih pesto, roast meats, stuffed vegetables and other local dishes. *Closed Mon–Thurs eves and Fri.*

Up in the mountains above Bagni, **San Cassiano** has a picturesque medieval bridge and a little-known 13th-century Pisan-style church, with a delicate carved façade. From Bagni, you have a choice of continuing along the SS12 towards **Abetone**, Tuscany's only big ski resort, under Monte Cimone (the highest peak in the area), or turning back to head up the Serchio, into the Garfagnana region.

The Garfagnana and the Lunigiana

Barga, the main town along the Serchio Valley, is a little mountain *comune* that retained independence until 1341. It has an unusual 13th-century cathedral, begun in 1000 and set high on a terrace, with a plain, squarish façade that makes it look more like a medieval Palazzo del Popolo. Step in and see the 13th-century pulpit, by a Como sculptor named Guido Bigarelli. The pillars that support it, resting on a pair of lions devouring some poor fellows, are in the Pisan style, but the reliefs around the pulpit itself are unique, startling naïve–sophisticated versions of familiar scriptural scenes.

From Barga it's 17 kilometres to the **Grotta del Vento** (***t*** *0583 722 024, open for 1hr guided tours daily 10, 11, 12, 2, 3, 4, 5 and 6; 2hr tours Apr–Oct daily 11, 3, 4 and 5; 3hr tours Apr–Oct daily 10 and 2, Nov–Mar Sun and hols only; at certain times of year only part of cave is visited; adm exp*), up in the mountains, a long cavern with fat stalactites in a barren, eerie landscape of eroded limestone. It's less crowded in the mornings.

The castle at **Castelnuovo Garfagnana**, further up the valley, properly decorative in the best 14th-century manner, was once commanded by the poet Ariosto, then in the service of the Estes of Ferrara. Further north, past **Piazza al Serchio**, the road leaves the Serchio and crosses over a pass into the **Lunigiana**, the mountain hinterlands of the long-disappeared Roman port town of Luni. This rugged territory covered with chestnut forests has often given its governors fits; at the turn of the 19th century it was a stronghold of rural anarchy, and in 1944 the partisans made it one of the bigger free zones in the north. It must always have been like this, for these mountains are full of castles: **Monti, Fivizzano, Bagnone** and **Fosdinovo** have the best ones, and on the back roads are a number of tiny mountain lakes and Romanesque country churches.

This hidden corner conceals a genuine prehistoric mystery. Up in **Pontrémoli**, the northernmost town in Tuscany, the restored stout grey 14th-century Castello del Piagnaro is now a museum (*open Tues–Sun 9–12 and 3–6; adm*) containing more than a score of large, carved 'statue-steles' of an unknown culture that flourished in Lunigiana about 2000–100 BC. The steles – sort of menhirs with personality – include some that have been shaped into stylized warriors with daggers or axes; others are women with little knobby breasts. Dozens have been discovered in the Lunigiana, all in isolated areas. Similar things turn up in southern Corsica and in Languedoc. Interestingly, the records say Christianity only began to make headway here after AD 700. Most of the steles at Pontrémoli have their heads knocked off – a sure sign that the Pope's missionaries were here.

The Tuscan Coast

The ancient Etruscans weren't shy; these early free traders happily accepted goods, art and ideas from all over the Mediterranean world. For the last 1,000 years, however, for all its accomplishments, modern Tuscany has been a moody, introspective region, and is usually a little dismissive towards what goes on in the rest of the world. The Tuscan coastline somehow reflects this: there is one big port, and a few little resorts, but on the whole Tuscany turns a blank face to the sea.

Carrara and Massa

Carrara owes its living and its fame to the marble masses of the Apuan Alps that surround it. Carrara marble has added the lustre to ancient Rome, Renaissance Rome and art museums and banks the world over. The town is still busy, with scores of marble sawmills and 'artistic workshops' turning out everything from sculptures for new churches to reproductions of famous statues. Some Carraran marble went into its distinctive **cathedral**, with its lovely 14th-century rose window. The quarries in the surrounding hills are an unforgettable sight; usually they extend almost to the peaks, a shining white scar on the mountains with a narrow access road zigzagging to the top. This part of the Apuan Alps is haunted by Michelangelo, in old clothes and smelly goatskin boots, taking his horse into inaccessible corners to discover new veins of perfect white stone. Michelangelo loved spending time here with his rock, and he claimed with his usual modesty to have 'introduced the art of quarrying' to the area. Carrara's quarries are in little danger of running out; you wonder if they're joking when they mention that there are only a few cubic kilometres of good stone left.

Massa, the small city to the south that shares the honour of provincial capital with Carrara, was the seat of a duchy during the Renaissance. The only things to see are its 17th-century Palazzo Cybo-Malaspina, with a beautiful ornate courtyard, and its 11th-century **castle** (*open July and Aug Tues–Sun 9.30–12.30 and 5–11.30; Sept–June Sat 9–12 and Sun 3.30–6*) with Renaissance additions. Pietrasanta, an attractive town about 10 kilometres further south, has a Renaissance cathedral and many marble works. The villages inland from Carrara, Massa and **Pietrasanta** have some of the best scenery in the Apuan Alps; mountain hiking is popular, and there are marked trails.

Viareggio

From the Ligurian border almost as far as the mouth of the Arno, the coast is dotted with small resorts. **Forte dei Marmi**, built under a fortress of the Tuscan grand dukes, is the most interesting, a posh resort that had its moment of fashion in the 1860s. The others, very popular with people from Milan and other big Italian cities, are as polluted as the Riviera to the north, but less so than the beaches around the Arno and Livorno. In summer, all are very crowded. **Viareggio**, the largest, is a town that goes back to Roman times. On top of tourism it tries to make an honest living for itself from fishing and a dockyard. Everyone in Italy knows Viareggio for its big carnival, with its parade of grandiose floats. Though it only began in the 1890s, it rivals Venice and Rome as the most popular place to be around Shrove Tuesday. The 1890s bequeathed to Viareggio a number of Art Nouveau hotels and beachfront pavilions. These, plus the two shore promenades and the large pine groves that surround the town, make it one of the more pleasant resorts on the Tyrrhenian Sea.

A few kilometres south, **Torre del Lago Puccini** is a beauty spot around a small lake. The Villa Puccini, where the composer (for whom they renamed the town) wrote most of his operas, is now the **Museo Pucciniano** (*open Tues–Sun Mar and Apr 10–12.30 and 3–5.30; May–Oct 10–12.30 and 2.30–6.30; Jan and Feb 10–12.30 and 2.30–5; adm*). Every summer there's also a small Festival Pucciniano, with opera performances in an open-air theatre built out on to the lake – the stage is actually on the water.

The Tuscan Coast

Getting Around

The main Rome–Genoa **rail** line runs a few kilometres inland all along the coast, making transport easy. **Buses** to smaller destinations run from Massa or Viareggio.

Tourist Information

Marina di Carrara: Viale G. Galilei, **t** 0585 632 519.
Marina di Massa: Viale Vespucci 24, **t** 0585 240 063, *www.aptmassacarrara.it*.
Viareggio: Viale Carducci 10, **t** 0584 962 233. There's a summer office in the train station.
Torre del Lago: Viale Kennedy 1, **t** 0584 359 893.
Forte dei Marmi: Via Franceschi 8b, **t** 0584 80081.

Where to Stay and Eat

Carrara ✉ 54033

★★★**Michelangelo**, Corso F. Rosselli 3, **t** 0585 777 161 (*moderate*). Decent modern rooms.

Da Venanzio, Colonnata, **t** 0585 758 062 (*expensive*). A good place to try the local speciality, *lardo* (a delicately-flavoured pork fat lard preserved in salt and rosemary in large marble vats). *Closed Thurs, and Sun eve.*

Roma, Piazza Battisti, **t** 0585 70632 (*cheap*). Simple Tuscan cooking, plus stuffed mussels and a good *fritto misto* of fish. *Closed Sat.*

Forte dei Marmi ✉ 55042

There's nothing cheap but many places slash their prices in June and September.

★★★★★**Augustus**, Viale A. Morin 169, **t** 0584 787 200, *www.versilia.toscana.it/augustus* (*very expensive*). An elegant old villa set back from the sea, with a pool and a chic private beach.

★★★**Hotel Mignon**, Via G. Carducci 58, **t** 0584 787 495, *www.hotelmignon.it* (*very expensive*). A pleasant hotel just back from the sea, with airy rooms, a pool and a private beach.

★★★**Hotel Franceschi**, Via XX Settembre 19, **t** 0584 787 114, *www.hotelfranceschi.it* (*very expensive–expensive*). A villa in a shady garden, with comfy rooms, many with balconies. The restaurant (*expensive*) is excellent. Prices almost halve out of season.

Da Lorenzo, Via Carducci 61, **t** 0585 89671 (*very expensive*). Beautifully and imaginatively prepared seafood. Book ahead. *Closed Mon.*

Pietrasanta

★★★★**Albergo Pietrasanta**, Via Garibaldi 35, **t** 0584 793 727, *www.albergopietrasanta.com* (*luxury*). A 17th-century *palazzo* in the old town, with a conservatory and a pretty courtyard, and contemporary Italian artworks in public rooms and bedrooms.

★★★**Palagi**, Piazza Carducci 23, **t** 0584 70249 (*expensive*). Comfortable rooms just outside the old town walls.

Enoteca Marcucci, Via Garibaldi 40, **t** 0584 791 962 (*moderate*). A restaurant with a fabulous wine list, frequented by the rich and famous. The grilled duck breast with herbs is delicious. Book ahead. *Closed lunch and Mon.*

Da Sci, Vicolo Porta a Lucca 3, **t** 0584 790 983 (*cheap*). A traditional trattoria serving the likes of vegetable flan, spinach and ricotta gnocchi and stewed rabbit. *Closed Sun.*

Viareggio ✉ 55049

★★★★**Grand Hotel Excelsior**, Viale Carducci 88, **t** 0584 50726 (*very expensive*). A 1923 Chini-Belluomini confection, with original décor in the public rooms. *Open Apr–Oct.*

★★★★**Plaza e de Russie**, Piazza d'Azeglio 1, **t** 0584 44449, *www. plazaederussie.com* (*very expensive*). Tasteful bedrooms and a stunning rooftop breakfast room and restaurant.

★★**Apollo**, Viale Carducci 76, **t** 0584 407 2823 (*moderate*). *Belle époque* features, spartan bedrooms, a garden and a restaurant (*cheap*).

★★**Al Piccolo Hotel**, Via Duilio 16, **t** 0584 51014 (*cheap*). A modest Liberty-style villa a few blocks from the sea. *Closed winter.*

Al Porto, Via Coppino 118, **t** 0584 383 878 (*very expensive*). A fabulously situated restaurant overlooking the port with its chic yachts, with a huge roof terrace. It's known for its *carpaccio di mare* and other seafood. *Closed Sun eve, Mon.*

Romano, Via Mazzini 122, **t** 0584 31382 (*very expensive*). Creative cooking, including delicious seafood *à la toscana*. Book in advance. *Closed Mon.*

La Darsena, Via Virgilio 154, **t** 0584 392 785 (*moderate*). A trattoria popular with local dockworkers at lunchtimes (it's more expensive in the evening). *Closed Sun.*

Osteria Numero Uno, Via Pisano 140, south of the harbour, **t** 0584 388 967 (*cheap*). Seafood that won't break the bank. *Closed Mon.*

Pisa

Unless you spend all your time in the narrow streets around the market and the university, Pisa may strike you as an uncannily quiet, almost empty place. But this is no museum city; it has 100,000 inhabitants who do not choose just to live in the past. Still, the city itself seems somehow too big for them. There are no ruins, but there's definitely an air of unfulfilled ambitions, of a past greatness nipped in the bud.

Change the scene to about 1100, when, according to chroniclers, Pisa, the 'city of marvels', the 'city of ten thousand towers', had a population of some 300,000. The medieval writers are to be excused for their extravagance. Excepting Venice, nothing like this enormous, exotically cosmopolitan city had been seen in Christian Europe since the fall of Rome. Its merchants made themselves at home in every corner of the Mediterranean, bringing back new ideas and new styles in art in addition to their fat bags of profit. Pisa in the early Middle Ages made good use of these cultural exchanges, contributing as much as any city to the rebirth of western culture.

History

In the Middle Ages Pisa liked to claim that it began as a Greek city, founded by colonists from Elis. Most historians, however, won't give them credit for anything earlier than about 100 BC, when a Roman veterans' colony was settled here. Records on what followed are scarce, but Pisa, like Amalfi and Venice, must have had an early start building a navy and establishing trade connections. By the 11th century, the effort had blossomed into opulence; Pisa had built itself a small empire, including Corsica, Sardinia and, for a while, the Balearics. In about 1060, work began on the great cathedral complex and other buildings, inaugurating the Pisan Romanesque.

The First Crusade, when Pisa's archbishop led the entire fleet in support of the Christian knights, was an economic windfall for the city, but when the Pisans weren't battling the Muslims of Spain and Africa they were learning from them. Influences from Andalucían mosques turn up in most Pisan Romanesque work, and a steady exchange of ideas brought much of medieval Arab science and philosophy into Europe through Pisa's port. The influence of Pisan architecture, the highest development of the Romanesque in Italy, spread from Sardinia to Puglia; in addition, when Gothic arrived in Italy, Pisa was among the few cities to take it seriously. In science, Pisa contributed a great if shadowy figure, mathematician Niccolò Fibonacci, who either rediscovered the principle of the Golden Section or learned it from the Arabs, and also introduced Arabic numerals to Europe. Pisa's scholarly tradition over the centuries was crowned in the 1600s by its most famous son, Galileo Galilei.

Pisa was always a Ghibelline city, the greatest ally of the Emperors in Tuscany if only for expediency's sake. When a real threat came, however, it was not from Florence or the other Tuscan cities but from the rising mercantile port of Genoa. After years of constant struggle, the Genoese devastated the Pisan navy at the Battle of Meloria (an islet off Livorno) in 1284. It meant the end of Pisan supremacy, and all chance of recovery was quashed by an even more implacable enemy: the Arno. Pisa's port was gradually silting up, and when the cost of dredging became greater than the traffic

Getting There and Around

Pisa's Galileo Galilei **airport** (**t** 050 500 707) has its own railway station with direct links to Florence and other cities; trains also stop at Pisa's Stazione Centrale (a 5min journey). City bus no.5 also links the airport to the centre.

Pisa's **Stazione Centrale, t** 050 892 021, is south of the Arno on Piazza della Stazione, about a 20min walk from the centre; city bus no.1 goes from outside the station to the Field of Miracles and city centre. Some coastal lines also stop at Stazione San Rossore, near the cathedral and Leaning Tower.

All Intercity **buses** leave from near Piazza Vittorio Emanuele II, the roundabout north of the Stazione Centrale: CPT buses to Volterra, Livorno and the coastal resorts (to the left on Via Nino Bixio, **t** 050 505 511); and LAZZI to Florence, Lucca and La Spezia (on Via d'Azeglio, **t** 050 42688). Many long-distance and local buses also stop at Piazza Manin, just outside the walls by the Leaning Tower.

Tourist Information

Via Cammeo, near the Baptistry, **t** 050 560 464; and outside Stazione Centrale, **t** 050 42291.

Where to Stay

Pisa ✉ 56100

★★★**Giardino**, Piazza Manin, **t** 050 562 101, *www.csinfo.it/giardino* (*expensive*). A smart place with modern, stylish rooms.

★★★**Royal Victoria**, Lungarno Pacinotti, **t** 050 940 111 (*expensive*). An atmospheric 1839 place overlooking the Arno, with large 1930s-style rooms. Dickens and Ruskin stayed here.

★★★**Di Stefano**, Via Sant'Apollonia 35–7, **t** 050 553 559, *www.hoteldistefano.pisa.it* (*moderate*). A friendly little hotel behind Piazza dei Cavallieri, with modern rooms, some en suite.

★★★**Verdi**, Piazza Repubblica 5, **t** 050 598 947 (*moderate*). A good choice in this range, in a well-restored historic palace in the centre.

The cheap places are often full of students, so try to call first.

★**Gronchi**, in Piazza Arcivescovado 1, **t** 050 561 823 (*cheap*). The best budget option in town.

Eating Out

Walks on the wild side of the Tuscan kitchen are more common here than in other towns – you'll find eels, tripe, 'twice-boiled soup' and dishes waiters can't explain. There are many unpretentious *trattorie*, many around the university. Most places are closed Sun nights.

Expensive

Ristoro dei Vecchi Macelli, Via Volturno 49, **t** 050 20424. A gourmet stronghold on the north bank of the Arno, with imaginative dishes based on coastal Tuscan traditions. *Closed Sun lunch and Weds.*

Moderate

Cagliostro, Via del Castelletto 26/30, **t** 050 575 413. A restaurant/*caffè*/*enoteca*/art gallery/nightclub and general trendy hangout. The cooking is 'Tuscan Creative' with other Italian dishes thrown in. *Closed Sun and Sat lunch.*

Osteria dei Cavalieri, Via San Frediano 16, **t** 050 580 858. Creative food, including good game dishes such as rabbit with thyme. Fixed-price menus are available. *Closed Sun.*

Osteria La Grotta, Via San Francesco 103, **t** 050 578 105. A cosy place with traditional but imaginative food. *Closed Sun.*

La Mescita, Via D. Cavalca 2, **t** 050 544 294. An attractive trattoria in the Vettovaglie market area, with dishes such as gnocchi with zucchini flowers and goats' cheese. *Closed Mon and lunch Tues–Thurs.*

Il Nuraghe, Via Mazzini 58, **t** 050 443 68. Tuscan and Sardinian specialities, including ricotta ravioli and snails. *Closed Mon.*

Re di Puglia, Via Aurelia Sud 7, Loc. Mortellini, 1km from the Pisa Sud *autostrada* exit, **t** 050 960 157. An eatery in a converted farmhouse using fresh farm produce. *Open Weds–Sun eves and Sun lunch.*

Cheap

Trattoria S. Omobono, Piazza Sant'Omobono, **t** 050 540 847. A simple, rustic trattoria off the main market place, offering wonderful fish *fritto misto* and more. *Closed Sun.*

Vineria di Piazza, Piazza delle Vettovaglie 13. Simple, tasty food such as risotto with radicchio and gorgonzola, served on tables in the market. *Closed Sun.*

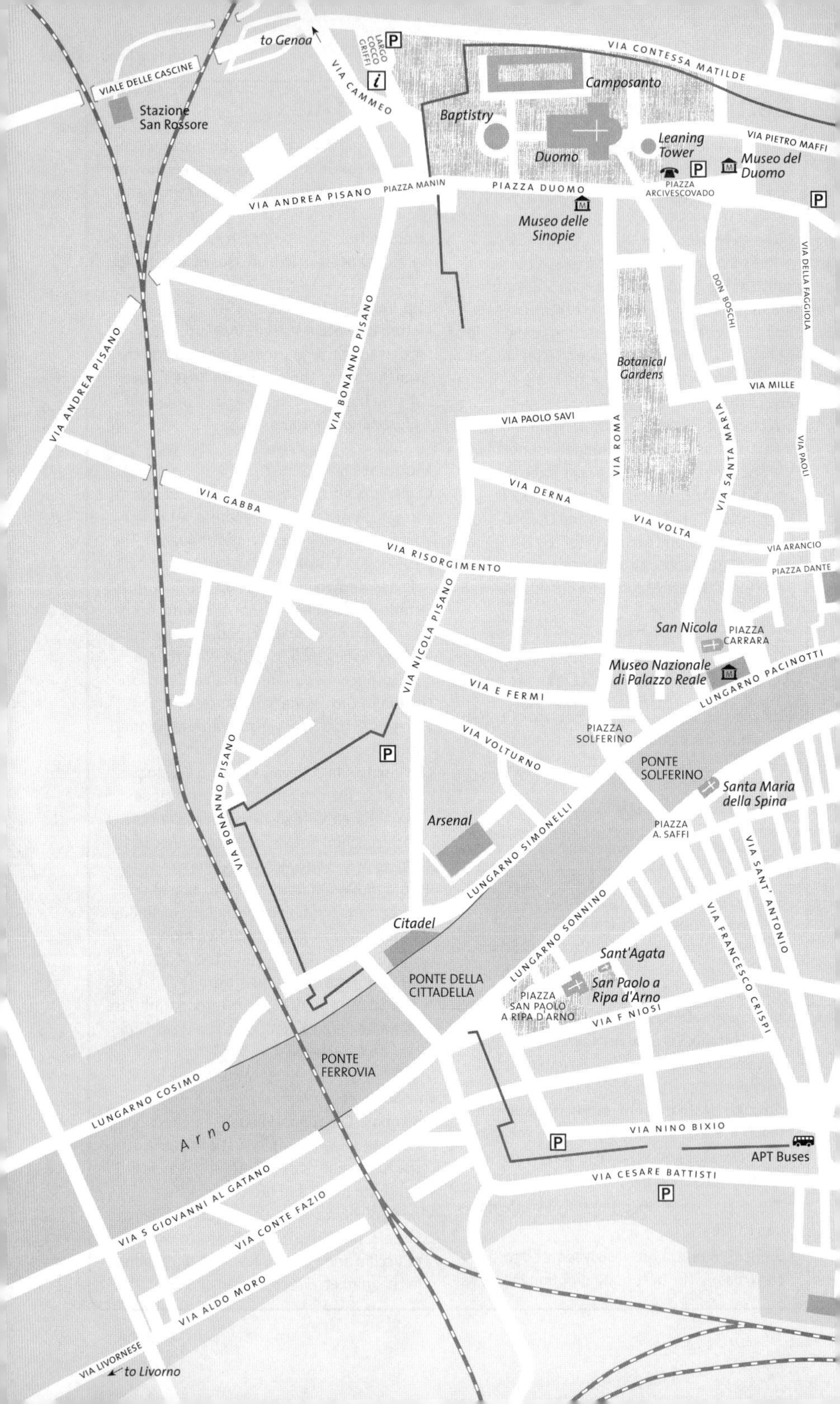

to Genoa
LARGO COCCO GRIFFI
VIA CONTESSA MATILDE
VIALE DELLE CASCINE
Stazione San Rossore
VIA CAMMEO
Camposanto
Baptistry
Leaning Tower
Duomo
Museo del Duomo
VIA PIETRO MAFFI
VIA ANDREA PISANO
PIAZZA MANIN
PIAZZA DUOMO
PIAZZA ARCIVESCOVADO
Museo delle Sinopie
DON BOSCHI
VIA DELLA FAGGIOLA
VIA ANDREA PISANO
VIA BONANNO PISANO
Botanical Gardens
VIA MILLE
VIA PAOLO SAVI
VIA ROMA
VIA SANTA MARIA
VIA PAOLI
VIA DERNA
VIA GABBA
VIA VOLTA
VIA ARANCIO
VIA RISORGIMENTO
PIAZZA DANTE
VIA NICOLA PISANO
San Nicola
PIAZZA CARRARA
Museo Nazionale di Palazzo Reale
VIA E FERMI
LUNGARNO PACINOTTI
PIAZZA SOLFERINO
VIA VOLTURNO
VIA BONANNO PISANO
PONTE SOLFERINO
Santa Maria della Spina
Arsenal
PIAZZA A. SAFFI
LUNGARNO SIMONELLI
VIA SANT' ANTONIO
LUNGARNO SONNINO
VIA FRANCESCO CRISPI
Citadel
Sant'Agata
PONTE DELLA CITTADELLA
San Paolo a Ripa d'Arno
PIAZZA SAN PAOLO A RIPA D'ARNO
VIA F NIOSI
PONTE FERROVIA
LUNGARNO COSIMO
Arno
VIA NINO BIXIO
APT Buses
VIA CESARE BATTISTI
VIA S GIOVANNI AL GATANO
VIA CONTE FAZIO
VIA ALDO MORO
VIA LIVORNESE
to Livorno

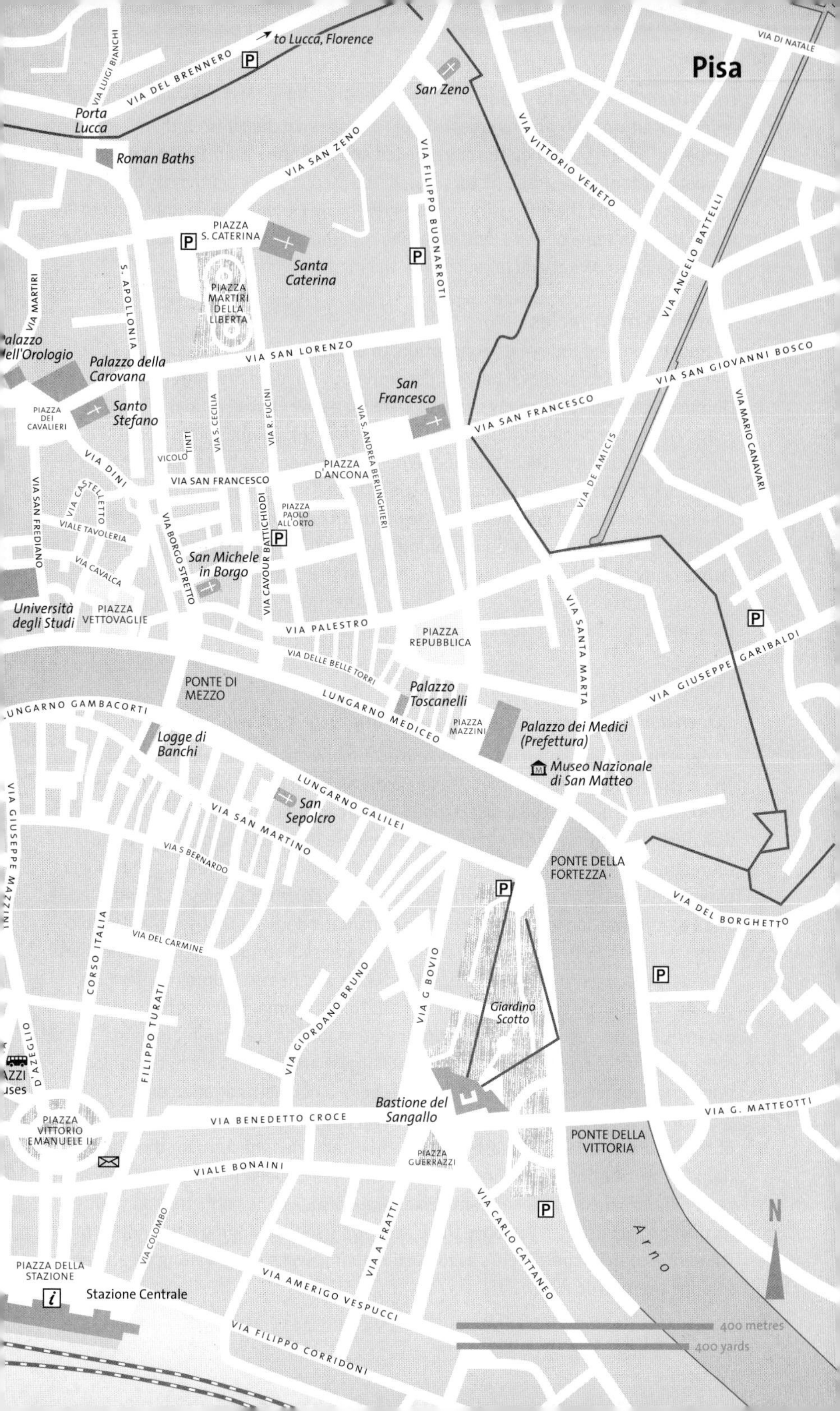
Pisa
to Lucca, Florence
Via del Brennero
Via Luigi Bianchi
Porta Lucca
Roman Baths
San Zeno
Via San Zeno
Via Filippo Buonarroti
Via di Natale
Via Vittorio Veneto
Via Angelo Battelli
Piazza S. Caterina
Santa Caterina
Piazza Martiri della Libertà
Via Martiri
S. Apollonia
Palazzo dell'Orologio
Palazzo della Carovana
Via San Lorenzo
Via San Giovanni Bosco
Piazza dei Cavalieri
Santo Stefano
San Francesco
Via San Francesco
Via Mario Canavari
Via de Amicis
Vicolo Tinti
Via S. Cecilia
Via R. Fucini
Via S. Andrea Berlinghieri
Piazza d'Ancona
Via Dini
Via San Francesco
Via San Frediano
Via Castelletto
Viale Tavoleria
Via Cavalca
Via Borgo Stretto
Piazza Paolo all'Orto
Via Cavour Battichiodi
San Michele in Borgo
Università degli Studi
Piazza Vettovaglie
Via Palestro
Piazza Repubblica
Via Santa Marta
Via delle Belle Torri
Via Giuseppe Garibaldi
Ponte di Mezzo
Palazzo Toscanelli
Lungarno Gambacorti
Lungarno Mediceo
Piazza Mazzini
Palazzo dei Medici (Prefettura)
Logge di Banchi
Museo Nazionale di San Matteo
Via Giuseppe Mazzini
Lungarno Galilei
San Sepolcro
Via San Martino
Via S Bernardo
Ponte della Fortezza
Via del Borghetto
Corso Italia
Via del Carmine
Via Filippo Turati
Via Giordano Bruno
Via G Bovio
Giardino Scotto
D'Azeglio
Piazza Vittorio Emanuele II
Via Benedetto Croce
Bastione del Sangallo
Via G. Matteotti
Ponte della Vittoria
Viale Bonaini
Piazza Guerrazzi
Via Colombo
Via A Fratti
Via Carlo Cattaneo
Arno
N
Piazza della Stazione
Stazione Centrale
Via Amerigo Vespucci
Via Filippo Corridoni
400 metres
400 yards

could bear, the city's fate was sealed. The Visconti of Milan seized the economically enfeebled city in 1396, and nine years later Florence snatched it from them. Excepting the period 1494–1505, when the city rebelled and kept the Florentines out despite an almost constant siege, Pisa's history ended. The Medici dukes did the city one big favour, supporting the university and even removing Florence's own university to Pisa. In the last 500 years of Pisa's long, pleasant twilight, this institution has helped the city stay alive and vital, and in touch with the modern world.

The Field of Miracles

Almost from the time of its conception, this title, *Campo dei Miracoli*, was the nickname given to medieval Italy's most ambitious building programme. As with Florence's cathedral, too many changes were made over two centuries of work to tell exactly what the original intentions were. But of all the unique things about this complex, the location strikes one first. Whether their reasons had to do with aesthetics or land values – probably a little of both – the Pisans built their cathedral on a broad expanse of green lawn at the northern edge of town, just inside the walls. It was begun in 1063; the famous Leaning Tower and the baptistry came in the mid 12th century, at the height of Pisa's fortunes, and the Campo Santo in 1278.

If you plan to visit all three monuments and the museums here, it's worth getting the joint ticket, the *biglietto cumulativo*.

The Baptistry

Open daily summer 8–7.40, spring and autumn 9–5.40, winter 9–4.40.

This is the biggest baptistry in Italy; those of many other cities would fit inside it. The architect, felicitously named Master Diotisalvi ('God save you'), saw the lower half of the building done in the typical stripes-and-arcades Pisan style. A second colonnade was meant to go over the first, but as the Genoese muscled Pisa out of its trade routes, funds ran short. In the 1260s, Nicolà and Giovanni Pisano redesigned and completed the upper half in a harmonious Gothic crown of gables and pinnacles. The Pisanos also added the dome over the prismatic dome of Diotisalvi, still visible from the inside. Both domes were among the largest attempted in the Middle Ages.

Inside, the austerity of the simple, striped walls and heavy columns of grey Elban granite is broken by two superb works of art. The **baptismal font** was by Guido Bigarelli, the 13th-century Como sculptor who made the crazy pulpit in Barga. There is little figurative sculpture on it, but the 16 large marble panels are finely carved in floral and geometrical patterns of inlaid stones – a northern variation on the Cosmati work of medieval Rome and Campania. Nicolà Pisano's **pulpit**, made *c.* 1260, was one of the first of that family's masterpieces, and established the form for their later pulpits, the columns resting on fierce lions, the relief panels crowded with intricately carved figures in impassioned New Testament episodes. The baptistry is famous for its uncanny acoustics; if you have the place to yourself, try singing a few notes from the centre of the floor. If there's a crowd, the guards will be just waiting for someone to bribe them to do it.

The Cathedral

Open Mon–Sat 10–7.40, Sun 1–7.40.

One of the first and finest works of the Pisan Romanesque, the cathedral has a façade that came out a little more ornate than architect Buscheto planned in 1063, with four levels of colonnades. These columns, with the similar colonnades around the apse and the Gothic frills later added around the unique elliptical dome, are the only showy features on the calm, restrained exterior. On the south transept, the late 12th-century **Porte San Ranieri** has a fine pair of bronze doors by Bonanno, one of the architects of the Leaning Tower. The biblical scenes are enacted under real palms and acacias; the well-travelled Pisans would have known what they looked like.

In the interior, little of the original art survived a fire in 1595. The roof went, as well as the Cosmati pavement, of which a few spots remain. But some fine work survives, including the great mosaic of Christ Pantocrator in the apse by Cimabue. The **pulpit**, done *c.* 1300 by Giovanni Pisano, is the acknowledged masterpiece of that family. The 1595 fire was used as an opportunity to get rid of this medieval relic, and the greatest work of Pisan sculpture sat disassembled in crates, forgotten until this century. It is startling, mixing classical and Christian elements with a fluency never seen before his time. St Michael, as a *telamon*, shares the honour of supporting the pulpit with Hercules and the Fates, while prophets, saints and sibyls look on from their appointed places. The relief panels, jammed with expressive faces, diffuse an electric immediacy equal to the best work of the Renaissance. Notice particularly the Nativity, the Massacre of the Innocents, the Flight into Egypt and the Last Judgement.

The Leaning Tower

Open daily summer 8–7.40, winter 9–4.40; adm v exp; 30 people admitted on each 30min tour, of which there are 10–12 a day. Online advance booking at www.duomo.pisa.it. *No children under 8. There are 300 steps to the top.*

Most likely, the stories claiming the tilt was accidental were tales woven by Pisans to account for what, before mass tourism, must have seemed a civic embarrassment. That the tower would start to lean when only 328ft tall seems hard to believe; half the weight would still be in the foundations. Even less credible would be that they kept building it after the lean commenced. The architects who measured the stones in the last century to get to the bottom of the mystery concluded that the tower's state was absolutely intentional. Just try telling that to someone from Pisa, though.

The leaning campanile is hardly the only strange thing in the Field of Miracles. The more time you spend here, the more you will notice: little monster-griffins, dragons and such, peeking out of every corner of the oldest sculptural work, skilfully hidden where you have to look twice to see them; or the big bronze griffin on a column at the top of the apse (a copy), the Muslim arabesques in the Campo Santo, and the perfect classical Corinthian capitals in the cathedral nave, next to the pagan images on the pulpit. The elliptical cathedral dome, in its time the only one in Europe, shows that the Pisans had the mathematical skills to back up their audacity. You may have noticed that the baptistry too is leaning – about 5ft in the opposite direction. And the cathedral façade leans outwards about an inch and a half – it's hard to notice but disconcerting if you see it from the right angle. So much in the Field of Miracles gives evidence of a very sophisticated, strangely modern taste for the outlandish, it may well have been that the medieval master masons in charge here simply thought that plain perpendicular buildings were becoming just a little trite.

Whatever, the campanile is a beautiful building and something unique in the world, as well as a very expensive bit of whimsy, with some 190 marble and granite columns. At the moment, 16½ft off perpendicular, it's also proving expensive to the local and national governments as they try to shore it up. The first phase was completed a few years ago, when counterweights (800 tonnes of lead ingots) were stacked at the base of its leaning side, stopping the tilt. The next stage was trickier: replacing the lead ingots with an underground support, laying a ring of cement around the foundations, and anchoring it to 10 steel cables attached to the bedrock 164ft underground. In 1998 it was given a rather unsightly girdle of plastic-coated steel braces, attached by a pair of 72ft steel cables to a counterweight system hidden among buildings on the north end of the Campo dei Miracoli. The last project involved removing soil from under the north, east and west sides from a depth of about six metres, thereby decreasing the difference in depth between the north and south side. This seems to have worked; the tower is not only stable but has actually righted itself about 40cm.

The Campo Santo and the Museums

Open daily summer 8–7.40, winter 9–4.40; adm.

If one more marvel in the Campo dei Miracoli is not excessive, there is a remarkable cloister–cemetery, a rectangle of gleaming white marble, unadorned save the blind arcading around the façade and the beautiful Gothic tabernacle of the enthroned Virgin over the entrance. With its uncluttered lines, the Campo Santo seems more a work of our own century than of the 14th. The cemetery began, according to legend, when battling Archbishop Lanfranc, who led the Pisan fleet into the Crusades, came back with boatloads of soil from the Holy Land, in which prominent citizens could be given extra-blessed burials. The building around the site was constructed about a century later, in the 1270s. Over the centuries an exceptional hoard of painting and sculpture accumulated here. Much went up in flames in July 1944, when an Allied bomb set the roof on fire. Many priceless works of art were destroyed and others, including most of the frescoes, damaged beyond hope of being perfectly restored.

The biggest loss, perhaps, was the set of frescoes by Benozzo Gozzoli – the *Tower of Babel, Solomon and Sheba, Life of Moses, Grape Harvest* and others; in their original state they must have been as fresh and colourful as his famous frescoes in Florence's Medici Palace. Even better known, and better preserved, are two 14th-century frescoes of the *Triumph of Death* and the *Last Judgement* by an unknown artist (perhaps Andrea Orcagna of Florence), whose failure to leave his name unfortunately put him down to posterity as the 'Master of the Triumph of Death'. In this memento of the century of plagues and trouble, the damned are variously cooked, wrapped up in snakes, poked, disembowelled, banged up and chewed on; still, these are some of the best paintings of the trecento, and somehow seem less gruesome and paranoid than similar works of centuries to come (though they are good enough to have inspired that pop classic, Lizst's *Totentanz*).

Another curiosity is the **Theological Cosmography** of Piero di Puccio, a diagram of the 22 spheres of the planets and stars, angels, archangels, thrones and dominations, cherubim and seraphim, and so on; in the centre, the small circle that is trisected by a T-shape was a common medieval map pattern for the known earth. The three sides represent Asia, Europe and Africa, and the three lines the Mediterranean, the Black Sea and the Nile. Among the sculptures in the Campo Santo are sarcophagi and Roman bath tubs, and, in the gallery of pre-war photographs of the lost frescoes, a famous Hellenistic marble vase with bas-reliefs.

The collection of the **Museo del Duomo** (*same hours; adm*) is in the chapterhouse, in the southeast corner of the Campo dei Miracoli, near the Leaning Tower. The first rooms contain the oldest works, including two strange Islamic pieces, the 11th-century **griffin** originally on the top of the cathedral, believed to have first come from Egypt, and a bronze basin. Most of the statues by the Pisanos exhibited here were brought in from the elements only when they were so worn and bleached as to be barely recognizable, and resemble a convention of mummies. However, in Room 5 there is Giovanni Pisano's superb *Madonna del Colloquio*, one of the finest of the family's sculptures, and in Room 10 his lovely ivory *Madonna and Child*. The museum carries on upstairs with intarsia, Roman and Etruscan odds and ends, some rare illuminated scrolls, and the Pisan Cross carried by the Pisan soldiers on the First Crusade.

Many of the damaged frescoes from the Campo Santo were moved to the **Museo delle Sinopie** (*same hours; adm exp*), across the piazza from the cathedral, along with the *sinopie* discovered underneath when they were removed from the walls. Many of these simple sketches are works of art in their own right, and together with drawings and photos made before the bombing help give an idea of how the frescoes looked.

North Pisa

With the cathedral on the edge of town, Pisa has no real centre. Still, Pisans are very conscious of the division made by the Arno; every year on 27 June the two sides fight it out on the Ponte di Mezzo in the *Gioco del Ponte*, a medieval tug-of-war where the opponents try to push a big decorated cart over each other. From the Field of Miracles, Via Cardinale Maffi leads east to some ruins of **Roman baths** near the Lucca gate; two interesting churches here are **San Zeno**, in a corner of the walls, with parts dating back to the 5th century; and **Santa Caterina**, a Dominican church with a beautiful, typically Pisan façade. Inside is an Annunciation and a sculpted tomb by Nino Pisano, as well as a large 1340s painting of the Apotheosis of St Thomas Aquinas, with Plato and Aristotle in attendance and defeated infidel philosopher Averroes below.

The long street that begins near the Campo dei Miracoli as Via Carducci and changes its name along its route, becoming the old, arcaded **Borgo Largo** and **Borgo Stretto**, is Pisa's traditional main artery, the most fashionable shopping street and the centre for the evening *passeggiata*. The twisting alleys of the lively market area are just off to the west, along with the **university**, still one of Italy's most important, and the **Piazza dei Cavalieri**. In 1562 Duke Cosimo I started what was probably the last crusading order of knights, the Cavalieri di Santo Stefano. The crusading urge had ended long before, but the Duke found this useful for indulging the anachronistic fantasies of the Tuscan nobility – most of them newly titled bankers – and licensing out freebooting expeditions against the Turks. Cosimo had Vasari build the **Palazzo della Carovana** for the order, demolishing the old Palazzo del Popolo, symbol of Pisa's lost independence. Vasari gave the Palazzo an outlandish sgraffito façade; it's now a college of the university. Next to it, the **Palazzo dell'Orologio** was built around the 'Hunger Tower' (left of the big clock), famous from Dante's story in the *Inferno* of Ugolino della Gherardesca, the Pisan commander walled in here with his two young sons after his fickle city suspected him of intriguing with the Genoese.

Santo Stefano, the order's church, is also by Vasari, though the façade is by a young dilettante of the Medici family; inside are some long, fantastical war pennants that the order's pirates captured from the Muslims in North Africa.

Museo Nazionale di San Matteo

Open Tues–Sat 9–7, Sun 9–2; adm.

Much of the best Pisan art from the Middle Ages and Renaissance is in this old convent and one-time prison. Most came from Pisan churches, so there's a lot of straightforward religious subjects. The Pisano family is well represented, including one magically beautiful Madonna in medieval Pisan dress, a wooden sculpture by Andrea Pisano. Besides the Pisan statues, reliefs, ivory work and sarcophagi, there are paintings by such artists as Masaccio (*St Paul*), Fra Angelico, Ghirlandaio, Simone Martini, Gozzoli and Brueghel.

South of the Arno

Pisa's stretch of the Arno is an exercise in Tuscan gravity – two mirror-image lines of blank-faced yellow and tan buildings all the same height. Only one landmark breaks the monotony – near the Solferino bridge, **Santa Maria della Spina** sits on the bank like a tiny Gothic jewel box. Though a rare outstanding achievement of Italian Gothic, originally it wasn't Gothic at all. Partially rebuilt in 1323, it was transformed by its new architect – perhaps one of the Pisanos – into an extravaganza of pointy gables and blooming pinnacles. All of the sculptural work is first class, especially the figures of Christ and the Apostles in the 13 niches facing the streets. The chapel takes its name from a thorn of Christ's crown of thorns, a relic brought back from the Crusades.

Not far west, near the walls where the famous 'Golden Gate' – Pisa's door to the sea – stood, remains of the old Citadel and Arsenal are visible across the river. On the southern side, **San Paolo a Ripa d'Arno** has a 12th-century façade similar to that of the cathedral. In a small park, it is believed to have been built over the site of Pisa's original cathedral: perhaps building cathedrals in open fields was an old custom. Behind it, the unusual little 12th-century chapel of **Sant'Agata** has eight sides and an eight-sided prismatic roof. A similar building is at the other end of south Pisa, the octagonal **San Sepolcro** off Lungarno Galilei, built originally for the Knights Templar.

Around Pisa

Just outside Pisa are good Romanesque Pisan churches in the villages of Calci, Vicopisano and San Casciano. The **Certosa di Pisa** (*open Tues–Sat 8.30–6.30, Sun 8.30–12.30; adm*), a typically lavish 18th-century charterhouse, has a prominent site north of the Arno and a huge low building in some sort of 1920s Spanish–Californian exhibition style. West of the city at **Gombo** is a small beach where in 1822 Shelley was brought ashore after being drowned when a storm struck his small boat on the way to Livorno. His body was burned here, as Trelawney, Leigh Hunt and Byron looked on.

Livorno and the Islands

Livorno

A few kilometres out to sea beyond Livorno's harbour, a medieval stone tower marks Meloria, the tiny islet where the Genoese navy put an end to Pisa's importance as a Mediterranean power in 1284. And when the silting up of its river harbour put an end to Pisa as a great port, fate had this spot in mind to replace her. Livorno was founded in 1571 by Cosimo d'Medici; over the next 200 years, while nearly all of peninsular Italy was in economic decline, it thrived as the nation's third port, after Genoa and Naples. It was an interesting town: after Duke Ferdinand decreed religious liberty for it, persecuted Jews, Greeks, English Catholics and Spanish Moors settled here, along with political refugees from all over Europe. From the beginning there was a strong connection with England: an English engineer, son of the Duke of Leicester, designed the port, and trade links were strong. Englishmen became so familiar with Livorno in the 17th century that they bestowed on it the bizarre anglicization of Leghorn.

Livorno, though the home town of artist Modigliani, hasn't much to show for its 400 years, but its modern, ambitious outlook has earned it an important role in sea container traffic. The city has plenty of ferries you can leap on to get to Mediterranean islands, and a reputation for seafood that is wholly deserved (*see* p.668).

While you're waiting at the port, have a look at Livorno's landmark, the **monument to Ferdinand I**, better known as the 'Quattro Mori' for the four bronze Moors in chains around the pedestal – exceptional sculptures by a 17th-century artist named Pietro Tacca (four Moors' heads are the symbol of Sardinia).

The best part of Livorno is the 'Venice' neighbourhood near the port, sliced through by small canals. Otherwise, the city wears a strangely blank look, pure north-Tuscan taciturnity undiluted by medieval or Renaissance charm. It's pleasant enough, and the people are on the whole good cheerful communists, but even when the streets are crowded Livorno can seem like a city seen in a dream.

The Tuscan Archipelago

Mostly this means Elba, one of Italy's top holiday playgrounds, though there are also six smaller islands, tracing a broad arc along the coast from Livorno to Orbetello. Some of them might also have been desirable holiday destinations, but for the Italian government's bad habit of using them as prisons.

Elba, reached by ferry from Piombino or Livorno, attracts more than two million visitors each year, who spend unspectacular, family-style holidays on its miles of beaches. The scenery, reminiscent of nearby Corsica, is often impressive; pink granite, green *macchia* and forests, and a severely mountainous coast. In ancient times, Elba was best known for its iron ore, and more recently for the brief sojourn of Napoleon (1814–15). Everyone visits his thoroughly depressing palace in the otherwise lovely island capital of **Portoferraio.** Other sights are few, but you can enjoy the mountains and beaches and have a fish dinner accompanied by Elban *Aleatico* or *Moscato*, two of Tuscany's best wines.

As for the other islands, the northernmost, **Gorgona**, once had villas of wealthy Romans but now is just a gloomy prison. The larger **Capraia**, formerly a penal colony, has more Roman ruins, cliffs, and five hotels. Below Elba are **Pianosa**, another prison (and the rather improbable setting for the US base in *Catch 22*); **Montecristo**, a beautiful, uninhabited nature reserve, accessible only by day-trip from Elba; and **Giglio**, the only real resort island, which boasts superb scenery and bird life, several hotels, three little villages, one of them medieval – Giglio Castello – and fine small beaches. Finally, there's **Giannutri**, a pretty, tiny island without roads, just big enough to hold some villas and one holiday village.

Gorgona and Capraia can be reached by a regular ferry service from Livorno and Elba; Giglio and Giannutri from Porto Santo Stefano, near Orbetello.

South of Livorno

The rugged coast to the south of Livorno is dotted with small beaches that can get tremendously crowded all through the summer: around **Castiglioncello**, which is a pretty spot when things are slow, then Rosignano Solvay, Marina di Cecina, San Vincenzo, Follonica and Punta Ala, all along the coastal plain. There are some Etruscan tombs, not especially interesting, at **Populonia**, one of the big Etruscan cities of which few traces remain. It stands on a mountainous promontory, at the other end of which is **Piombino**, a town full of steelworks that is also the most convenient ferry port for Elba.

Getting Around

Livorno's **train** station, from which there are plenty of trains to Pisa, Florence and all points along the Tyrrhenian coast, is on the edge of the city; there are regular **city buses** from there to the port and Piazza Grande in the centre.

Buses for all villages in Livorno province (the strip of coast down as far as Follonica) leave from Piazza Grande. LAZZI buses for Florence depart from Scali A. Saffi, on the Fosse Reale, just off Piazza Cavour.

Ferries go from Livorno to the islands of Elba, Gorgona and Capraia (Toremar, usually at least twice daily, **t** 0586 896 113), to Bastia in Corsica (Corsica Ferries, **t** 0586 881 380, and Corsica Marittima, **t** 0586 210 507) and to Olbia in Sardinia (Sarda Navigazione, **t** 0586 409 925, and Moby Lines, **t** 0586 826 847). All offices are in the Stazione Marittima in the port. Ferries to Elba get heavily booked up in mid-summer and it can be easier to get the boat from Piombino, closer to Elba.

Tourist Information

Livorno: Piazza Cavour 6, **t** 0586 898 111; summer offices at Porto Mediceo and Terminal Calata Carrara; *www.livorno.turismo.toscana.it*

Elba: Grattacielo building, Calata Italia 26, Portoferraio, **t** 0565 914 671/2.

Grosseto: Via Monterosa 206, **t** 0564 462 611.

Porto Santo Stefano: Corso Umberto 55, **t** 0564 814 208.

Where to Stay

Livorno ✉ 57100

******La Vedetta di Montenero**, Via della Lecceta 5, Montenero, **t** 0586 579 957, *www.hotellavedetta.it* (*very expensive*). A good alternative to the rather grim hotels in the centre, with comfy rooms (many with a sea view) and a restaurant.

*****Gran Duca**, Piazza Micheli 16, **t** 0586 891 024, *www.granduca.it* (*expensive*). Livorno's most interesting hotel, built into a section of the walls right on the piazza at the entrance to the harbour area (the interior is modern).

****Giardino**, Piazza Mazzini 85, **t** 0586 806 330 (*moderate*). A decent option near the port.

There are lots of cheap hotels across the piazza from the train station, and around the port and Via Grande; some are dives, but Corso Mazzini, a few blocks south of the Fosso Reale, has some nice ones.

***Hotel Marina**, Corso Mazzini 148, **t** 0586 834 278 (*cheap*). A good old-fashioned budget choice.

Elba ✉ 57037

This is a package-tour destination, so despite the scores of lodgings, book ahead.

******Villa Ottone**, Ottone, **t** 0565 933 042 (*luxury*). A 19th-century villa right on the beach, with a shady garden.

****L'Ape Elbana**, Salita de' Medici 2, Portoferraio, **t** 0565 914 245 (*moderate*). The island's oldest hotel, where Napoleon's visitors stayed.

****Andreina**, Cala, **t** 0565 908 150 (*moderate*). Reasonable rooms blissfully out of the way, west of Marciana Marina.

****La Conchiglia**, Cavoli, **t** 0565 987 010 (*moderate*). A small hotel on Elba's best beach.

Orbetello ✉ 58035

***Piccolo Parigi**, Corso Italia 169, **t** 0564 867 233 (*cheap*). A friendly, very Mediterranean establishment in the middle of town, ideal if you're travelling on a budget and just want to pass through for a look at the Argentario.

Porto Ercole ✉ 58018

******Il Pellicano**, Cala dei Santi, **t** 0564 858 111, *www.pellicanohotel.com* (*luxury*). A Relais & Châteaux hotel popular with yachtsmen and Italian TV stars, providing every imaginable amenity, including a beach, a pool, watersports facilities, tennis courts and a first-class restaurant.

Grosseto, a fair-sized provincial capital, has no ancient memories, having been underwater until late-Roman times. It does have Medici fortifications and a small archaeological museum (***t*** *0564 488 752; open summer Tues–Sun 10–1 and 5–8; winter Tues–Fri 9–1, Sat and Sun 9–1 and 4–6; adm*). Its plain, reclaimed from swamps and made into rich farmland, marks the beginning of the **Maremma**, a low-lying region

Porto Santo Stefano ✉ 58019

★★★**La Caletta**, Via Civinini 10, **t** 0564 812 939 (*expensive*). A hotel with pleasant rooms overlooking the sea.

★★★**Filippo II**, close to the beaches at Poggio Calvello, **t** 0564 811 611 (*expensive*). The best accommodation in town.

★★**Alfiero**, Via Cuniberti 12, **t** 0564 814 067 (*moderate*). A simple hotel by the harbour.

Eating Out

Livorno

The Livornese ways of preparing seafood are much copied up and down the Tuscan coast, but restaurants here are easier on your pocket than elsewhere. Lobster, grilled fish and pasta with seafood figure on all local menus, as does *cacciucco*, the famous fish stew.

After a rich meal try a *bomba livornese*, the local answer to Irish coffee, made with rum.

Ciglieri, Via Franchini 38, in the seaside suburb of Ardenza to the south, **t** 0586 508 194 (*very expensive*). A highly regarded, elegant restaurant serving high-quality fish dishes such as scampi ravioli. The wine list is comprehensive. *Closed Weds.*

La Chiave, Scali delle Cantine 52, **t** 0586 888 609 (*expensive*). A seafood place considered by many the best restaurant in Livorno. Be sure to try one of the seafood pasta *primi. Closed lunchtimes and Weds.*

L'Antico Moro, Via Bartelli 59, **t** 0586 884 659 (*moderate*). A seafood favourite since the 1920s, near the market. *Closed Weds.*

Da Oscar, Via Franchini 78, Ardenza, **t** 0586 501 258 (*moderate*). A decades-old favourite with a good selection of wines to accompany linguini and clams, excellent *risotti* and grilled *triglie* and *orate*. *Closed Mon.*

Cantina Nardi, Via L. Cambini 6, **t** 0586 808 006 (*cheap*). A wine bar serving excellent food at a few tables at lunchtime. *Closed eves and Sun.*

Elba

Elba's DOC wines can hold their own with any in Tuscany.

La Ferrigna, Piazza della Repubblica 22, Portoferraio, **t** 0565 914 129 (*moderate*). One of the most popular places in Portoferraio, offering extravagant seafood *antipasti*, stuffed roast fish, and an Elban version of *cacciucco*. There are tables on the convivial piazza. *Closed Tues.*

Orbetello

Osteria del Lupacante, Corso Italia 103, **t** 0564 867 618 (*moderate*). Dishes made with the freshest of fish, from salad of octopus and potato to spaghetti with sea urchin, or zucchini flowers stuffed with baby squid. *Closed Tues in winter.*

Porto Ercole

Gambero Rosso, Lungomare Andrea Doria, **t** 0564 832 650 (*expensive*). Fancy seafood, such as spaghetti with lobster sauce, at fancy prices, plus *zuppa di pesce* at weekends.

La Grotta del Pescatore, Via delle Fonti, **t** 0564 835 265 (*moderate*). A cheaper alternative where you can try a bowl of steaming *zuppa di scampi con patate* – more stew than soup.

Porto Santo Stefano

Dal Greco, Via del Molo 1, **t** 0564 814 885 (*expensive*). An elegant place on the yacht harbour. *Terrina di pesce* with vegetables is the star dish. *Closed Tues.*

I Due Pini, Loc. La Soda, **t** 0564 814 012 (*expensive*). A wood-panelled restaurant with a stunning beachside setting on the coast road into Porto Santo Stefano. The good food includes a fabulous array of *antipasti*, pasta with lobster or clams, and fish and crustacea.

Orlando, Via Breschi 3, **t** 0564 812 788 (*expensive*). One of the few genuine places left in town, specializing in grilled fish. It's popular and lively. *Closed Thurs in winter.*

that extends almost as far as Rome. Once one of the centres of Etruscan civilization, it was almost completely abandoned as a result of malaria and Roman misrule. For centuries it remained a ghostly, disease-ridden marsh, but modern drainage and reclamation projects much like those in the Pontine Marshes to the south have made good farmland of it once more. Parts have been maintained in their original state as a nature park, including the **Monti dell'Uccellina**, a range of ragged hills among parasol pine forests on the coast south of Grosseto. This is a favourite rest stop for migratory birds going to and from Africa – hence the name (*uccello* is Italian for 'bird'). Nine walks have been laid out, and there are tours in English in summer (*call visitors' centre at Alberese,* **t** *0564 407 098; open 8–1hr before sunset; adm*). There are no roads, but you can explore the coast by boat from **Talamone**, a fishing port at its southern tip.

Near the end of Tuscany's coast is a geographical curiosity, **Monte Argentario**. Once, perhaps thousands of years ago, Argentario was an island, the member of the Tuscan archipelago closest to the shore. It gradually became joined to the mainland by two narrow sand bars, now solid and covered with trees. There's a story that sailors gave the Argentario its name in classical times, noticing the flashes of silver from the olive leaves that still cover the mountain slopes. The placid lagoons between the sand bars make up another renowned nature and bird reserve, and those who are prepared to walk out along the southernmost strip are also rewarded by remarkably unspoilt beaches. **Orbetello**, on the central strip, was a fashionable resort, but today this charming town makes way for trendy **Porto Ercole** and **Porto Santo Stefano**, pretty fishing villages that in summer become overburdened with Florentines and Romans.

Siena

Understanding Florence, Siena's arch-enemy and artistic rival over the centuries, requires some work – a few bulky tomes of history and art criticism for starters, and an effort of the imagination beyond that. For Siena, on the other hand, you need only come to the city and look around. Draped on its hills, Siena is a flamboyant ensemble of medieval buildings in honest brown (*siena*-coloured) brick; on the lower slopes, gardens and olive groves fill almost half the space within the old city wall, and above it all Tuscany's tallest tower and its gayest, most dazzling cathedral compete like beauties at the fair. Medieval Siena created beauty almost effortlessly, and its fierce civic pride tolerated nothing less than the building of a city that in itself is a single great work of art.

History

A Roman foundation, Siena emerged in the age of the *comuni* as one of the leading powers of central Italy, achieving total independence in 1125. Like Florence, it lived on wool and banking; the clothing industry was never very large, but the bankers managed to make themselves indispensable to kings and princes all over Europe.

Ghibelline by convenience, Siena found itself almost constantly at war with Guelph Florence. The greatest moment in its history came in 1260, when news arrived of a huge army raised by Florence and other Tuscan cities coming to demand Siena's surrender. The city militias – reinforced by about 5,000 Florentine political exiles – marched out and met the Florentines at Monteaperti, beating them so badly that Florence was entirely at their mercy; only the attitude of the Florentine exiles prevented the Sienese from razing Florence to the ground (a famous story told by

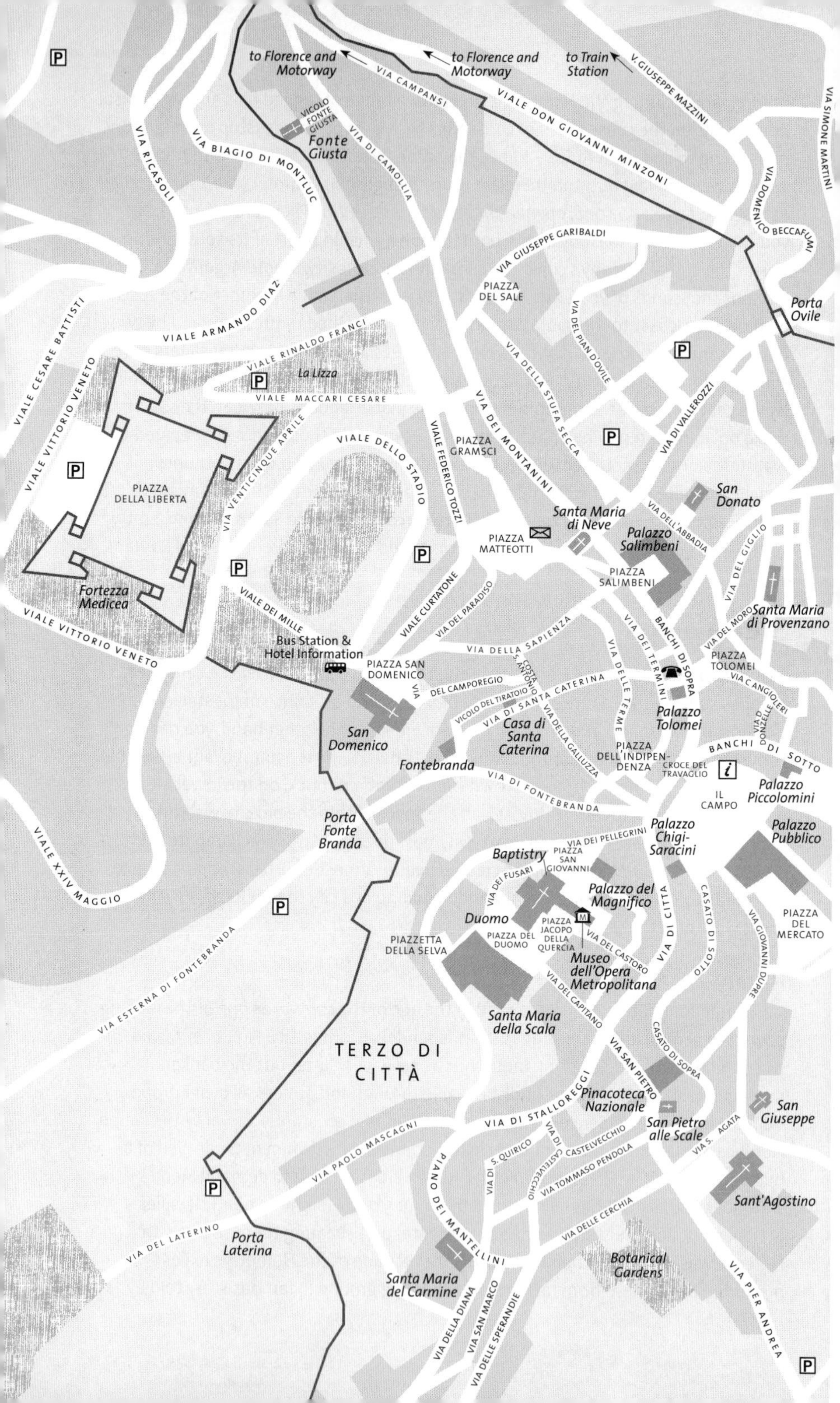
to Florence and Motorway
to Florence and Motorway
to Train Station
V. GIUSEPPE MAZZINI
VIA CAMPANSI
VIALE DON GIOVANNI MINZONI
VIA SIMONE MARTINI
VICOLO FONTE GIUSTA
Fonte Giusta
VIA DI CAMOLLIA
VIA BIAGIO DI MONTLUC
VIA RICASOLI
VIA DOMENICO BECCAFUMI
VIA GIUSEPPE GARIBALDI
PIAZZA DEL SALE
Porta Ovile
VIA DEL PIAN D'OVILE
VIALE ARMANDO DIAZ
VIALE CESARE BATTISTI
VIALE RINALDO FRANCI
La Lizza
VIALE MACCARI CESARE
VIA DELLA STUFA SECCA
VIA DI VALLEROZZI
VIALE VITTORIO VENETO
VIA VENTICINQUE APRILE
VIALE DELLO STADIO
VIALE FEDERICO TOZZI
PIAZZA GRAMSCI
VIA DEI MONTANINI
PIAZZA DELLA LIBERTA
San Donato
VIA DELL'ABBADIA
Santa Maria di Neve
Palazzo Salimbeni
PIAZZA MATTEOTTI
PIAZZA SALIMBENI
VIA DEL GIGLIO
Fortezza Medicea
VIALE DEI MILLE
VIALE CURTATONE
VIA DEL PARADISO
Santa Maria di Provenzano
VIA DEL MORO
VIALE VITTORIO VENETO
Bus Station & Hotel Information
VIA DELLA SAPIENZA
VIA DEI TERMINI
BANCHI DI SOPRA
PIAZZA TOLOMEI
PIAZZA SAN DOMENICO
COSTA S. ANTONIO
VIA DELLE TERME
VIA C ANGIOLIERI
VIA DEL CAMPOREGIO
VIA DI SANTA CATERINA
VICOLO DEL TIRATOIO
Palazzo Tolomei
VIA D. DONZELLE
Casa di Santa Caterina
VIA DELLA GALLUZZA
San Domenico
PIAZZA DELL'INDIPENDENZA
BANCHI DI SOTTO
Fontebranda
CROCE DEL TRAVAGLIO
VIA DI FONTEBRANDA
IL CAMPO
Palazzo Piccolomini
Porta Fonte Branda
Palazzo Chigi-Saracini
Palazzo Pubblico
VIA DEI PELLEGRINI
Baptistry
PIAZZA SAN GIOVANNI
VIALE XXIV MAGGIO
VIA DEI FUSARI
Palazzo del Magnifico
CASATO DI SOTTO
VIA DI CITTÀ
Duomo
PIAZZA JACOPO DELLA QUERCIA
VIA GIOVANNI DUPRÉ
PIAZZA DEL MERCATO
PIAZZETTA DELLA SELVA
PIAZZA DEL DUOMO
VIA DEL CASTORO
Museo dell'Opera Metropolitana
VIA ESTERNA DI FONTEBRANDA
VIA DEL CAPITANO
Santa Maria della Scala
TERZO DI CITTÀ
VIA SAN PIETRO
CASATO DI SOPRA
Pinacoteca Nazionale
San Giuseppe
VIA DI STALLOREGGI
San Pietro alle Scale
VIA PAOLO MASCAGNI
VIA DI S. QUIRICO
VIA DI CASTELVECCHIO
CASTELVECCHIO
VIA S. AGATA
VIA TOMMASO PENDOLA
PIANO DEI MANTELLINI
Sant'Agostino
VIA DEL LATERINO
Porta Laterina
VIA DELLE CERCHIA
Botanical Gardens
Santa Maria del Carmine
VIA DELLA DIANA
VIA SAN MARCO
VIA DELLE SPERANDIE
VIA PIER ANDREA

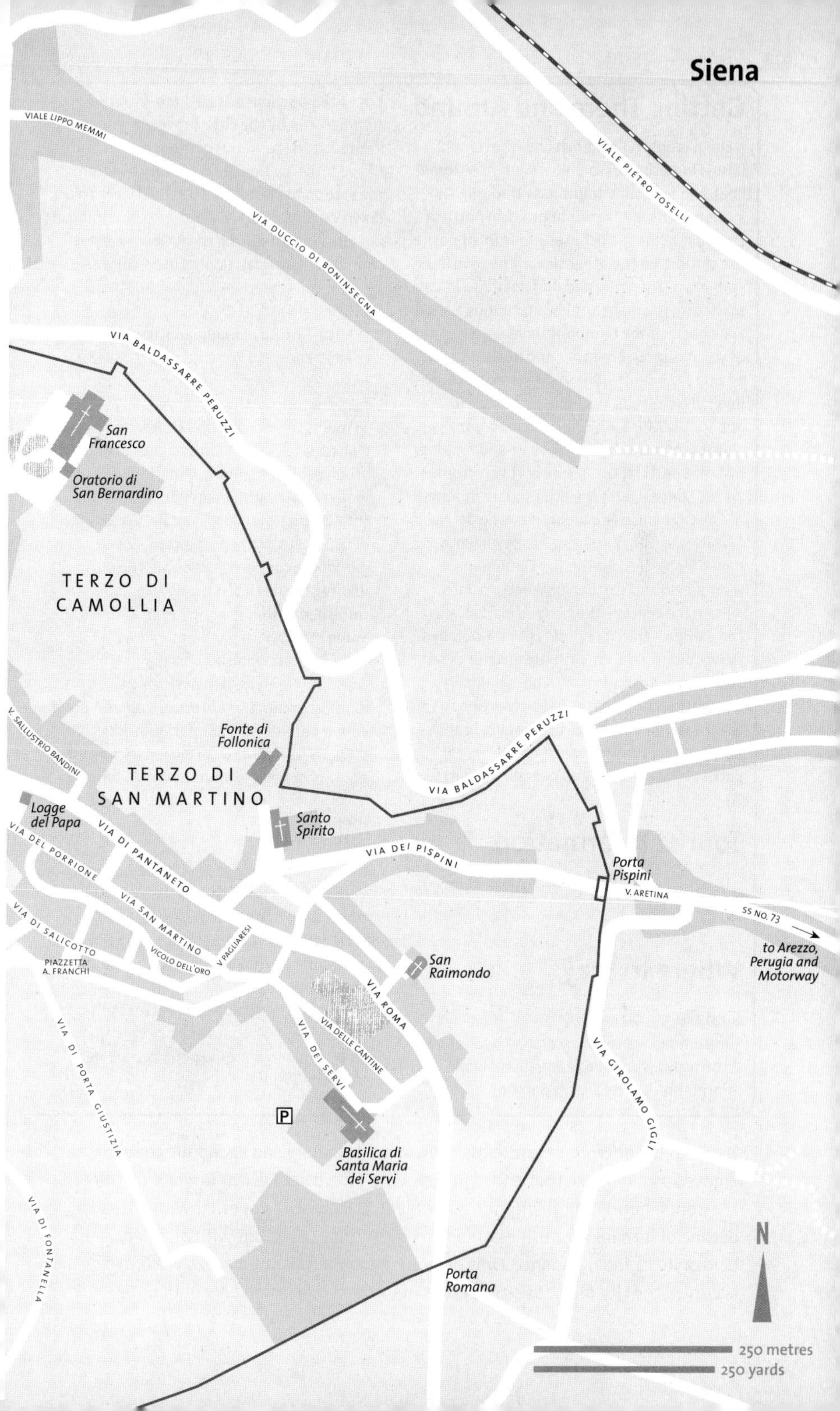
Siena
VIALE LIPPO MEMMI
VIALE PIETRO TOSELLI
VIA DUCCIO DI BONINSEGNA
VIA BALDASSARRE PERUZZI
San Francesco
Oratorio di San Bernardino
TERZO DI CAMOLLIA
Fonte di Follonica
TERZO DI SAN MARTINO
V. SALLUSTRIO BANDINI
Logge del Papa
Santo Spirito
VIA BALDASSARRE PERUZZI
VIA DEI PISPINI
Porta Pispini
V. ARETINA
SS NO. 73
to Arezzo, Perugia and Motorway
VIA DI PANTANETO
VIA DEL PORRIONE
VIA SAN MARTINO
VIA DI SALICOTTO
VICOLO DELL'ORO
V PAGLIARESI
PIAZZETTA A. FRANCHI
San Raimondo
VIA ROMA
VIA DELLE CANTINE
VIA DEI SERVI
VIA DI PORTA GIUSTIZIA
VIA GIROLAMO GIGLI
P
Basilica di Santa Maria dei Servi
VIA DI FONTANELLA
Porta Romana
N
250 metres
250 yards

Getting There and Around

Siena is only on a branch line from Empoli (Pisa–Florence line) to Chiusi (Florence–Rome line), and not many **trains** pass through. The station is on Via Mazzini, about 2km north of the old city; most city **buses** run from opposite the station (on the other side of the road – the stop has a large map and info board) to Piazza Matteotti, the main local bus terminus a short walk north of the Campo. If there are 4 or more of you it is probably easier and quicker to take a **taxi** to the centre. Bus and rail information and rail tickets are available at Il Caroccio agency, Via Montanini 73, **t** 0577 226 964.

Stops for **buses** to the province and for long-distance destinations are a short way from Piazza Matteotti, on the little square in front of San Domenico and along the Viale dei Mille. TRA-IN (*sic*), **t** 0577 204 245, has several buses a day to Florence, Volterra, San Gimignano, Montalcino and smaller local destinations.

From the centre – the famous piazza called the **Campo** – the city unfolds like a 3-petalled flower along 3 ridges, with the quarter called the **Terzo di Città**, including the cathedral, to the southwest; the **Terzo di San Martino** to the southeast; and the **Terzo di Camollia** to the north. No cars are allowed in; there are **car parks** at the Fortezza and outside the gates.

Tourist Information

Il Campo 56, **t** 0577 280 551, *www.siena.turismo.toscana.it*.

Where to Stay

Siena ✉ 53100

In summer, rooms are scarce so book ahead. If you arrive without a reservation, **Hotel Information Centre**, Piazza San Domenico, **t** 0577 288 084 (*open Mon–Sat 9–7, until 8 in summer*), run by the city's innkeepers and located at the terminus of intercity bus routes (if you arrive by train, take the city bus from the station to Piazza Matteotti and walk a block down Via Curtatone) will find you something at any time except during the Palio, when you should book several months in advance.

Luxury

*****__La Certosa di Maggiano__, 1km southeast of city near Porta Romana, **t** 0577 288 180, *www.certosadimaggiano.it*. A restored 14th-century Carthusian monastery with 18 rooms, a heated pool, a chapel and cloister, a backgammon and chess salon, an excellent restaurant, and a library that would be an antiquarian's dream.

*****__Grand Hotel Continentale__, Via Bianchi di Sopra 85, **t** 0577 56011/44204, *www.grandhotelcontinentalesiena.it*. The only luxury hotel in the centre, with 51 rooms furnished with fine antiques and fabrics. Some rooms have panoramic views.

****__Villa Scacciapensieri__, Strada Scacciapensieri 10, 3km north of city, **t** 0577 41441, *www.tin.it/villascacciapensieri*. A quiet country house with 28 spacious rooms and glorious sunset views over Siena. There's a pool and a good restaurant with a terrace.

Expensive

***__Antica Torre__, Via di Fieravecchia 7, **t** 0577 222 255. Siena's most popular small hotel, with 8 rooms in a restored 16th-century tower with marble floors and beams.

***__Duomo__, Via Stalloreggi 38, **t** 0577 289 088. A comfortably old-fashioned place south of the Duomo.

__Il Giardino__, Via Baldassare Peruzzi 35, **t 0577 285 290. A well-regarded place with good views and a swimming pool, located near the Porta Pispini.

Dante in the *Inferno*. Nevertheless, as Florence's military and economic equal, Siena enjoyed a golden age that ended in 1348, when the Black Death carried off a third of the population. Political infighting as violent as Florence's, together with a steady decline of its banking business, made recovery impossible, but with difficulty Siena held on to its independence. Only once, in 1399, when Gian Galeazzo Visconti of Milan occupied the city, did it lose its liberty, but Visconti rule lasted only until 1404.

★★★**Palazzo Ravizza**, Piani dei Mantellini 34, just inside the walls near the Porta Laterina, **t** 0577 280 462, *www.palazzoravizza.it*. An elegant 19th-century *palazzo* with upmarket rooms furnished with antiques, a lovely back garden and a restaurant. Half board is obligatory in season.

Moderate

★★**Canon d'Oro**, Via Montanini 28, **t** 0577 44321. A well-run bargain near the bus station.

★★**Piccolo Hotel Etruria**, Via delle Donzelle 3, **t** 0577 283 685. A friendly place with good amenities, well located off Via Banchi di Sotto near the Campo.

Cheap

Inexpensive places are hard to find, especially before term time when they're full of students looking for digs.

★**Tre Donzelle**, Via delle Donzelle, **t** 0577 280 358. A good budget option with a midnight curfew.

Eating Out

Siena is between three of Italy's great wine-producing areas, the Chianti, the Brunello of Montalcino and the Vino Nobile of Montepulciano, so there's always something good to wash down the simple Sienese dishes.

Siena is a university town, and snacks and fast food are common: a *cioccina* is a local variation on pizza, while *pici* (thick south Tuscan spaghetti with a sauce prepared from ground fresh pork, *pancetta*, sausages and chicken breasts, added to tomatoes cooked with Brunello wine) is a favourite pasta dish.

The city's real speciality is sweets, and many visitors find they have no room for lunch or dinner after visits to pastry shops for slices of *panforte*, a heavy cake laced with fruits, nuts, orange peel and secret ingredients, or *panpepato*, a similar cake containing pepper.

Expensive

Da Enzo, Via Camollia 49, **t** 0577 281 277. A traditional restaurant with a long and varied menu, including a good classic spaghetti with baby clams. *Closed Mon.*

Ai Marsili, Via del Castoro 3, **t** 0577 47154. An elegant place just off Piazza del Duomo, with excellent Sienese dishes, including Catherine de' Medici's famous *faraona alla Medici*, guinea fowl roasted with pine nuts, almonds and plums. *Closed Mon.*

Osteria Le Logge, Via del Porrione 33, off the Campo, **t** 0577 48013. Good *risotti* and pasta dishes, exotic second courses such as stuffed guinea fowl, and a fine wine list. *Closed Sun.*

Moderate

Guido, Vicolo Pier Pettinato 7, **t** 0577 280 042. A central, traditional place with excellent grilled lamb, veal and *bistecca*.

Osteria di Castelvecchio, Via Castelvecchio 65, **t** 0577 49586. The former stable block of one of Siena's oldest *palazzi*, with modern décor. The traditional menu has a vegetarian emphasis; try herby risotto. *Closed Tues.*

Osteria di Ficomezzo, Via dei Termini 71, **t** 0577 222 384. Simple lunches and more inventive evening fare, including guinea fowl with tarragon. *Closed Sun.*

Tullio ai Tre Cristi, Vicolo Provenzano, **t** 0577 280 608. An authentic local restaurant, set up *c.* 1830, offering the likes of tripe with sausage and roast Maremma boar. *Closed Mon.*

Cheap

Il Grattacielo, Via dei Pontani 8, **t** 0577 289 326. A popular student hangout, especially at lunchtime. The roast pork and other simple dishes are good, and the wine flows freely.

Osteria La Chiacchiera, Costa di Sant'Antonio 4, **t** 0577 280 631. A friendly little trattoria with outdoor tables, serving excellent *pici*, *ribollita*, kidneys, cockscombs (*cibreo*) and more.

In art, if the quattrocento was the high noon of Florence's Renaissance, the 13th and 14th centuries belonged to Siena. With palaces, churches and public buildings far grander than those of Florence at this time, Siena also led in painting. Giorgio Vasari, because he was a Florentine, gave all the credit for advances in painting to Cimabue and Giotto, but Sienese artists such as Duccio di Buoninsegna, Simone Martini, Matteo di Giovanni, and Pietro and Ambrogio Lorenzetti often surpassed their

Florentine counterparts in many ways – they were less innovative, perhaps, but they brought the 'International Gothic' style of art to its highest form in Italy. Even as its economic decline continued, Siena remained an important artistic centre.

Throughout the 15th century factionalism kept Siena paralysed. Like Florence, the city eventually found some peace with the accession of a powerful political boss, Pandolfo Petrucci, called 'il Magnifico' like Lorenzo de' Medici. He and his successors ruled the city from 1487 to 1524. By that time Siena was only a pawn in Italian politics. In a nine-year war, starting with a popular revolt against Charles V's garrison in the city in 1552, combined Florentine and Spanish forces conquered the republic, eventually starving the city into submission in a protracted siege.

With its independence lost and its economy irrevocably ruined, Siena withdrew into itself. For centuries there was to be no recovery, little art or scholarship, and no movements towards reform. This does much to explain why medieval and Renaissance Siena is so well preserved – for better or worse, nothing happened to change it. It was not until the 1830s that Siena was rediscovered, with the help of literati such as the Brownings, who spent several summers here, and later that truly Gothic American, Henry James. The Sienese were not far behind in rediscovering it themselves. The old civic pride that had lain dormant for centuries yawned and stretched like Sleeping Beauty and went diligently back to work.

Before the century was out, everything that could still be salvaged of the city's ancient glory was refurbished and restored. More than ever fascinated by its own image and eccentricities, and more than ever without any kind of an economic base, Siena was ready for its present career as a cultural attraction, a tourist town.

The Campo and the Corsa del Palio

It is hard to imagine a lovelier square, or one more beloved by the people who live and work around it. Laid out on the site of the Roman forum of *Sena Julia*, the unique, semicircular Campo was paved in brick in the 1340s. Today, lined with pavement cafés all along its steep northern arc, it is still the centre of everything.

Twice a year, on 2 July and 16 August, Siena puts on the noisiest medieval blowout in Italy – the horse race around the Campo called the **Palio**. Though its origins go back to the days of the *comune*, the Palio in its present form began in the 1600s. Riders from 10 of the city's 17 quarters (each *contrada* known by its totem animal: elephant, snail, unicorn, giraffe, owl, caterpillar, and so on) careen recklessly around the edge of the piazza while thousands of spectators jam the centre and any available open space. The riders mean business; losers have a year of insults and rotten tomatoes to look forward to in their home district.

With no rules (not even against bribery!), they crowd and push frantically. Especially at the two right angles that they have to navigate, the sight of not only jockeys but horses flying through the air is not uncommon. Often less then half actually finish. The post-Palio carousing, while not up to medieval standards, is impressive; in the winning *contrada* the parties go on for days. Siena's tranquil beauty today conceals its true character – in addition to the Palio, there was once also a festival called *Gioca del Pugno*, a general fistfight in the Campo involving 300 men on each side.

On the curved north end of the Campo, the **Fonte Gaia** is a large rectangular fountain with mythological reliefs by Jacopo della Quercia (copies; the eroded originals are in the Palazzo Publico). In the 14th century the Sienese dug up a beautiful Greek statue of Venus by Lysippus and built a pedestal for her on the fountain. After the plague, the priests convinced the people that the pagan statue had called down God's wrath. It was smashed, and a band of Sienese dressed as peasants smuggled the pieces over the border with Florence and buried them, to transfer the bad luck to their enemies.

Palazzo Pubblico

This is the civic pride of Siena expressed in brick and marble, a huge building that still serves as the seat of the city council, as well as being the repository of much of the best Sienese art. Above it rises the tallest secular tower of medieval Italy, the graceful, needle-like construction that Henry James called Siena's 'Declaration of Independence'. The **Torre del Mangia** (*see* p.676) takes its odd name from a legendary glutton (and relative of the artist Duccio) whose job it was to ring the bell – there's a little statue of him in one of the courtyards. At the foot of the tower, the equally graceful marble loggia leads to the **Cappella di Piazza**, built to give thanks for Siena's deliverance from the Black Death.

Most of the Palazzo was built in the early 14th century. At the top you'll notice the familiar Christian symbol of the letters IHS inside a radiant sun. This was the mark of 14th-century religious reformer San Bernardino, who often preached before huge crowds in the Campo. San Bernardino wanted to persuade the constantly warring nobles to replace their own heraldic devices with this holy sign – without much success. Around the façade are other devices from Siena's history: the city's black and white coat of arms, the wolf (according to legend Siena was founded by a son of Remus), and Medici dukes' balls. Inside, the ground floor is all city offices; you'll need to climb the long stairs to see the rooms open to the public (*open daily July and Aug 10am–11pm; mid-Mar–Oct 10–7; Nov–mid-Mar 10–6.30; adm*).

Among the old municipal chambers are the **Sala di Risorgimento**, with florid late 19th-century frescoes of Garibaldi and Vittorio Emanuele II in action, and an 'allegory of Italian liberty'; a **Sala del Concistoro** (Council Room), with Gobelin tapestries and figures of political virtue from antiquity by an interesting 15th-century Sienese painter named Beccafumi; and more of the same – classical gods, Caesar, Pompey and Judas Maccabaeus – around the pretty **chapel**, frescoed with a giant St Christopher (before setting out on a journey it was good luck to glimpse this saint, and in Italy and Spain he is often painted as large as possible so no one could miss him).

The **Sala del Mappamondo**, named after a lost cosmographical fresco, has a number of 13th-century frescoes, including the famous scene of the resolute *condottiere* Guidoriccio da Fogliano, off to besiege a castle. It has traditionally been attributed to Simone Martini (*c.* 1330), the greatest of Sienese fresco artists, though this has been called into question. Unquestionably his is the fabulous *Maestà* in the same room – a dignified Madonna surrounded by saints, believed to be his earliest work (1315). The Palazzo's greatest treasure, however, is the unique series of frescoes by Ambrogio Lorenzetti in the **Sala della Pace**, the *Effects of Good and Bad Government*.

Here, medieval allegory is applied to politics; two rival princes sit in state, one with Justice, Wisdom and Compassion for his counsellors, the other with such characters as Pride, Wrath and Avarice. On the long walls of the chamber two mirror-image cities are portrayed, the well-governed one (with Siena's cathedral discreetly painted in) is clean, orderly and happy, with smiling shopkeepers who look to be making nice profits; the other, with urban blight, crime, oppression, corruption, housing problems and slipshod municipal services, is the very picture of a 14th-century South Bronx.

Climb more stairs up to the **loggia**, where the original reliefs from the Fonte Gaia are kept, or still further stairs up the 328ft Torre del Mangia (*open daily July and Aug 10am–11pm; mid-Mar–June, Sept and Oct 10–7; Nov–mid-Mar 10–4; adm*), for a view over Siena that is definitely worth the slight risk of cardiac arrest and the long queues (only 20 people are allowed in at a time).

Behind the Palazzo, steps lead down to the **Piazza del Mercato**, Siena's cheerful marketplace. At the opposite end of the Campo, narrow stairs under arches lead up to the **Croce del Travaglio**, the meeting place for the main streets from the three corners of the city. Here stands the 15th-century arcade known as the **Loggia della Mercanzia**, where guilds transacted business and Italy's most respected commercial tribunal once sat in judgement.

Terzo di Città and the Cathedral

From Via di Città, winding behind the Campo, a narrow street off to the right called Via dei Pellegrini leads to what seems at first to be a huge striped bastion in the wall. Siena's glorious **cathedral** sits on the highest point in the city. The apse spills down the slope, its crypt at the street level of the rest of the city. Perhaps to save space and money, the architects tucked their **baptistry** (*open daily summer 9–7.30, Oct 9–6, winter 10–1 and 2.30–5; adm*) under here. It contains some of the best art in Siena, though it's dim and hard to see even when the lighting machine is working. The baptismal font, one of Siena's crown jewels, has some relief panels by Donatello (*Herod's Banquet*), Ghiberti (*Baptism of Christ*) and Jacopo della Quercia (*Birth of John the Baptist*). Donatello also contributed the six bronze angels and some of the other statuary. Across the street from the baptistry, the **Palazzo del Magnifico** was home to Siena's 15th-century power brokers, the Petrucci.

A flight of steps leads up to the Piazza del Duomo, but at the top you must first pass through a portal in a huge, freestanding wall of striped marble arches. Siena's cathedral, 289ft long, might have seemed big enough, but the news that Florence was beginning a bigger one came as an insult to the city's pride. In 1339 the Council adopted an incredible plan to rebuild the cathedral; the old one was to be preserved as a transept, and a new nave, almost double the length of the old one, would be built out from the southern end. Had it ever been completed, it would have surpassed even St Peter's in Rome, the biggest in the world. Only nine years later, however, the Black Death struck, and Siena soon found itself without the means to continue. The northern wall and façade still stand, their arches bricked in and incorporated into other buildings. What was to be a cathedral nave is now a piazza, and a symbol for the end of a city's ambitions.

Even after all the other grand Tuscan cathedrals, Siena's comes as a revelation. It may not be a transcendent expression of faith, and it may not be an important landmark in architecture, but it certainly is one of the most delightful ornaments in Christendom. One suspects that even sober-minded art critics are tempted to buy one of the illuminated plastic models in the souvenir shops, to take home and put on top of their TV sets. The tall campanile stands striped like an ice-cream parfait, its stripes darker and bolder than in Pisa or Lucca. The façade, even more confectionery-like, was largely the work of Giovanni Pisano, who added many of the statues of saints, prophets and pagan philosophers on the three great portals. The upper half was completed later, in the 1390s, and the glittering mosaics in the gables were added by artists from Venice only in the 19th century.

Inside, one hardly knows where to look first. Above the striped columns and walls the ornate Gothic vaulting is painted as a blue firmament with golden stars and angels – note the long rows of finely detailed heads of saints, running all along the nave. The most spectacular feature, however, is under your feet. Beginning in the 1360s, and continuing over the next two centuries, Siena's finest artists were commissioned to create inlaid marble scenes for the **pavement**, nearly an acre of them covering the entire cathedral floor. The subjects are fascinating. Entering from the west door, for example, you see a portrait of Hermes Trismegistus, the legendary patron of alchemists whose 'works', brought from Byzantium, caused such a stir in medieval Europe. Further down come the 10 Sibyls of antiquity, and a few images straight out of a deck of tarot cards: snakes and newts, a wheel of fortune, Socrates and Crates, and other symbols too arcane to think about. Many of the best have become somewhat fragile, and are now covered up for most of the year.

The **stained glass**, some of it from designs by Duccio, is also not to be missed, along with a **pulpit** by Nicolà Pisano, with reliefs of philosophers and allegories of the Liberal Arts. Also, in the left aisle, there is the **Altare Piccolomini**, with some early work by Michelangelo (the statues of four saints on the lower level), and in the transept on the same side of the church are two beautiful Renaissance sculptural ensembles, that of Bishop Giovanni Pecci, by Donatello, and another, of a cardinal, by Tino di Camaino.

The Piccolomini family, prominent in Siena for centuries, eventually attained European renown. Some were famous generals for the emperor in the Thirty Years' War (Schiller wrote a trilogy of plays about them), and during the Renaissance two of them made it to the Vatican – Popes Pius II and Pius III. The latter, in 1495, created the **Biblioteca Piccolomini** (*open summer Mon–Sat 9–7.30, Sun and hols 2.30–7.30; winter Mon–Sat 10–1 and 2.30–5, Sun and hols 2.30–5; adm*), just off the left aisle of the cathedral, to hold the library of the former, who was his uncle. Pius II, Aeneas Silvius Piccolomini, was a genuine Renaissance man: a poet, diplomat, historian, antiquarian, religious reformer and great geographer; Columbus studied his works closely.

Pius III hired Pinturicchio to cover the library walls with frescoes of his famous uncle's life. We see Aeneas Silvius in the courts of James II of Scotland and Emperor Frederick III, proclaiming a crusade and canonizing Catherine of Siena, among others. Pinturicchio's frescoes are spectacularly colourful, incorporating dozens of careful portraits of the famous and not-so-famous of the age, with loving attention paid to current court fashions in dress and coiffure. No better image of *la dolce vita* at the height of the Renaissance could be imagined. Aeneas Silvius' books have been carted off somewhere, but one of his favourite things still holds pride of place in the centre of the library: a beautiful marble vase with the Three Graces, a Roman copy of a work by Praxiteles that was studied closely by a good number of Renaissance artists.

Museo dell'Opera Metropolitana

Open daily 16 Mar–30 Oct 9–7.30, Nov–15 Mar 9–1.30; adm.

For a close-up look at the façade of the cathedral, the only place to go is the cathedral museum, where most of the original sculptural work has been preserved. Some of these rank among the best Italian Gothic and Renaissance sculpture, especially statues of saints by Nicolà Pisano and Jacopo della Quercia, remarkable for their kinetic possibilities – they seem ready to hop down from their pedestals and start declaiming if they suspect for a minute you've been skipping Sunday Mass. Besides them, there are some original bits of the cathedral's pavement that had to be replaced, as well as some leftover pinnacles and other architectural details.

Upstairs, the collection of Sienese paintings includes Duccio di Buoninsegna's masterpiece, the former cathedral altarpiece called the *Maestà*, with an enthroned Virgin on one side and scenes from the Passion on the other. Duccio's animated composition and expressive faces here clearly surpass the work of his more celebrated contemporary, Giotto. The cathedral treasure contains lavish golden monstrances and reliquaries, and in one corner a simple, exquisite bouquet of gold flowers – the kind of gift that popes sent along with their ambassadors in the 13th and 14th centuries. Part of the museum is built into the unfinished 14th-century cathedral. From the top floor you can climb to the **Facciatone** ('big façade') for a view over the cathedral and the city.

Ospedale di Santa Maria della Scala

Open daily Mar–Oct 10–6, Nov–Feb 10.30–4.30; adm.

The neighbourhood around the cathedral is rhinoceros country. To be specific, you're in the neighbourhood of the *Selva* (forest); that beast is its symbol. Opposite the old cathedral façade, one entire side of the piazza is occupied by the great **Ospedale di Santa Maria della Scala**, believed to have been founded in the 9th century and for centuries one of the largest and finest hospitals in the world. Slowly, the hospital functions have been moved out (one of the last patients to die here was Italo Calvino) and they're converting it into a museum, dedicated to all the arts and to the city's history, destined to be one of the largest in the world. Don't ask when it will be finished; as a *cantiere didattico*, part of the point is that the process of museum building itself is part of the attraction.

For now, go inside to see the **Sala del Pellegrinaio**, with some 15th-century frescoes of everyday hospital activities (Santa Maria was the seat of many revolutionary advances, such as doctors washing their hands, back in the 1300s). Other original features of the hospital include the **Cappella del Sacro Chiodo**, with some damaged frescoes by Vecchietta, the elaborate **Cappella SS. Annunziata**, and the thoroughly spooky **Cappella di Santa Caterina**, which begins with a leering skull and ends with an altarpiece by Taddeo di Bartolo. Old views and relics of the hospital are displayed in many of the long hallways; in some of the oldest, you can see how the façade was originally covered with frescoes (by Pietro and Ambrogio Lorenzetti), forming a colourful counterpoint to the cathedral façade across the way. Another part of the complex houses the **Museo Archeologico** (*open daily summer 10–6, winter 10.30–4.30; adm with Santa Maria della Scala)* with its Etruscan and Roman collection.

If you take the little stairs just west of the cathedral you'll find yourself in **Piazza della Selva**, where a bronze rhinoceros commemorates some past Palio victory. South of the cathedral on Via San Pietro, Siena's **Pinacoteca** (*open Mon 8.30–1.30, Tues–Sat 8.15–7.15, Sun 8.15–1.15; adm*) occupies the restored 14th-century Palazzo Buonsignori, and has an excellent collection of Sienese art from its beginnings to the 17th century. The earliest works, on the top floor, include fine pieces by Guido di Siena, often called the founder of Sienese painting, and his followers. Most were brought here from churches around the city. As always, the works of Pietro and Ambrogio Lorenzetti stand out, for their dramatic faces and poses, and for their original approach to colour.

On the other floors, Madonnas and saints line up in room after room. Very few are without interest, though; the serious spirituality of all its painters, paradoxically expressed in rich settings and gorgeous colours, is a constant feature of the Siena school. Something else readily apparent is Sienese civic pride: almost all the painters have a fondness for painting their town in the background, even in a Nativity. Among later Sienese painters, Beccafumi is well represented, along with Il Sodoma, who initiated the Mannerist tradition in Siena, as well as acquiring his name from a still-popular vice. More Sodoma (an Epiphany) and some other fine paintings can sometimes be seen in the Piccolomini Chapel of **Sant'Agostino**, a 13th-century church two blocks south of the Pinacoteca, on Via della Cerchia.

Terzo di San Martino

Beginning again at the Loggia della Mercanzia, Via Banchi di Sotto leads down into the southeast 'third' of Siena, through the quarters of the unicorn and the elephant. Just off the Campo, the 1460 **Palazzo Piccolomini** (*closed for restoration; call* **t** *0577 280 551 for an update*) has for centuries been the home of Siena's archives. The surprise attraction here is old Siena's **account books**. From the 1200s it became a tradition to have the city's best artists paint the covers, resulting in fascinating scenes of such prosaic subjects as medieval citizens coming to pay their tax, city workers receiving their pay, and honest monks at tables trying to make the figures square.

Another elegant loggia, the **Loggia del Papa** built by Aeneas Silvius (Pius II), stands on the next small piazza on the Banchi di Sotto. In the narrow lanes leading down to the Piazza del Mercato is yet another Palio victory statuette – an elephant, for the Torre district – in pretty little Piazzetta Franchi on Via Salicotto. The **Basilica Servi di Maria** is this *terzo's* biggest church, with some good frescoes in the right transept by Pietro Lorenzetti.

Terzo di Camollia

The biggest and busiest of the *terzi* runs northwards along Via Banchi di Sopra, Siena's fashionable shopping street and for centuries the town's main drag, where the entire population appears to make an evening *passeggiata* down to the Campo and back. Along it are some of the palaces of the great medieval banking families. **Palazzo Tolomei** (1200–50) is the oldest, but much larger is the **Palazzo Salimbeni**, around a small piazza of the same name further up the street. The latter is the head office of Siena's bank, the Monte dei Paschi di Siena, which was founded in 1472. At the bottom of the hill behind it is the large church of **San Francesco**, with more frescoes by the Lorenzettis.

The quarter of the goose, west of Banchi di Sopra, is a warren of narrow streets associated with the tortured life of St Catherine of Siena, co-patron of Italy and one of medieval Italy's great mystics and religious reformers. Caterina Benincasa, born in 1347, the 24th of 25 children in a poor family, began having visions at an early age and, like St Francis, received the stigmata. Besides her devotional writings, for which she has been proclaimed a Doctor of the Church, she kept a busy interest in the affairs of her day; as a woman she was able to constantly insult the popes over the crooked Church they ran without coming to any harm. The **Santuario e Casa di Santa Caterina** (*open daily 9–12.30 and 3.30–6*) still stands, on Costa Sant'Antonio just below San Domenico, and has been restored as a shrine and museum.

San Domenico itself, a lofty 13th-century church at the end of Viale Curtatone, has St Catherine's head in a golden reliquary, with some wonderfully hysterical frescoes of her life by the aforementioned Sodoma. San Domenico may seem plain from the outside, but you'll have a good view of its Sienese Gothic subtleties from below, at the **Fonte Branda**, a medieval fountain that was once the city's only source of water.

On the western edge of the city, the triumphant Duke Cosimo I of Florence built a fortress in 1560 to keep watch over the conquered city. The **Fortezza Medicea**, however, has nothing threatening about it; this most genteel of fortifications seems less a military work than a nobleman's villa and garden. The Sienese, who have long memories, have turned the grounds into a park called Piazza della Libertà.

Sienese Pastimes

If you have more time to spend in Siena, there are plenty of ways to do it enjoyably. Just walking around the city is a treat. Nearly any old church you find open will be worth a look inside; more than most cities, Siena has preserved its medieval interiors and their art intact. South of the cathedral, you can take a walk in the country without leaving town, in the valleys between the *terzi*. Most of the medieval walls, and eight of the gates, survive.

If you want to learn more about the *contrade* and the Palio, each of the 17 local neighbourhood organizations (which are really legally chartered communities, a fascinating survival of the 'tribes' into which Roman and pre-Roman cities were organized) maintains its own museum. Staff are happy to show you around with some advance warning; the tourist office can give you a list of addresses and phone numbers, and will sometimes arrange visits for you.

Just outside the city, with fine views over Siena and its countryside, the monastery of **L'Osservanza** was founded by San Bernardino in the 1420s. Severely damaged in 1944, the church and cloister have been restored according to the original plans; it has works by Sano di Pietro and other Sienese painters, as well as Andrea della Robbia.

The Southern Hill Towns

Southern Tuscany may not be exactly what you think. There is plenty of carefully tended Tuscan farmland, arranged as if by an artist, with every garden, orchard, wood and vineyard in its proper place, but among the variety of landscapes in this small corner of Italy are marshland and rugged hills, and even lonely, deserted corners such as the half-eroded heaths the Tuscans call the *crete*. Some of the hill towns in this region go back to the Etruscans, and many can show you fine buildings and works of art from the age of the *comuni* or the Renaissance. Any number of them would make memorable day-trips from Siena on the way to Rome or further down the coast.

West of Siena

Colle di Val d'Elsa

This lovely village, set along a steep ridge, is a perfect introduction to the hill towns. Though it only has around 16,000 people, it boasts a wall with a grand Renaissance gate by Giuliano da Sangallo on the Volterra road, a 16th-century **cathedral** and three museums, including the **Museo d'Arte Sacra** (*open Oct–Apr Tues–Fri 3.30–5.30, Sat, Sun and hols 10–12 and 3.30–6.30; May–Sept Tues–Fri 4–6, Sat, Sun and hols 10–12 and 4.30–7.30; adm*) in the old episcopal palace, with a few Sienese and Florentine paintings plus frescoes commissioned by a jolly 14th-century bishop – not martyrs, but scenes of the hunt and from the Crusades, believed to be the work of Ambrogio Lorenzetti.

The Collegiani will never allow the world to forget that their town was the birthplace of Arnolfo di Cambio, the architect who built Florence's Palazzo Vecchio and began its cathedral; his house is marked with a plaque. On the way to the town from Siena, the road passes **Monteriggioni**, an old Sienese castle with huge towers mentioned by Dante, and **Abbadia a Isola** up in the hills, with frescoes from the 1400s.

San Gimignano

In many smaller towns of Italy you can sense a false start, a free, self-reliant *comune* of the Middle Ages that could build a wall and defend itself, yet lacked the money or will to turn itself into a Florence or a Siena. When they ceased to grow, many crystallized into their medieval form. None did this more completely than San Gimignano. The startling skyline pokes out from the surrounding hills from miles away: the dozen lofty square towers, some more than 148ft tall, are haphazardly arranged like the boxy skyscrapers of a Dallas or Calgary. The main museums and attractions of San Gimignano offer a *biglietto cumulativo* giving admission to all of them.

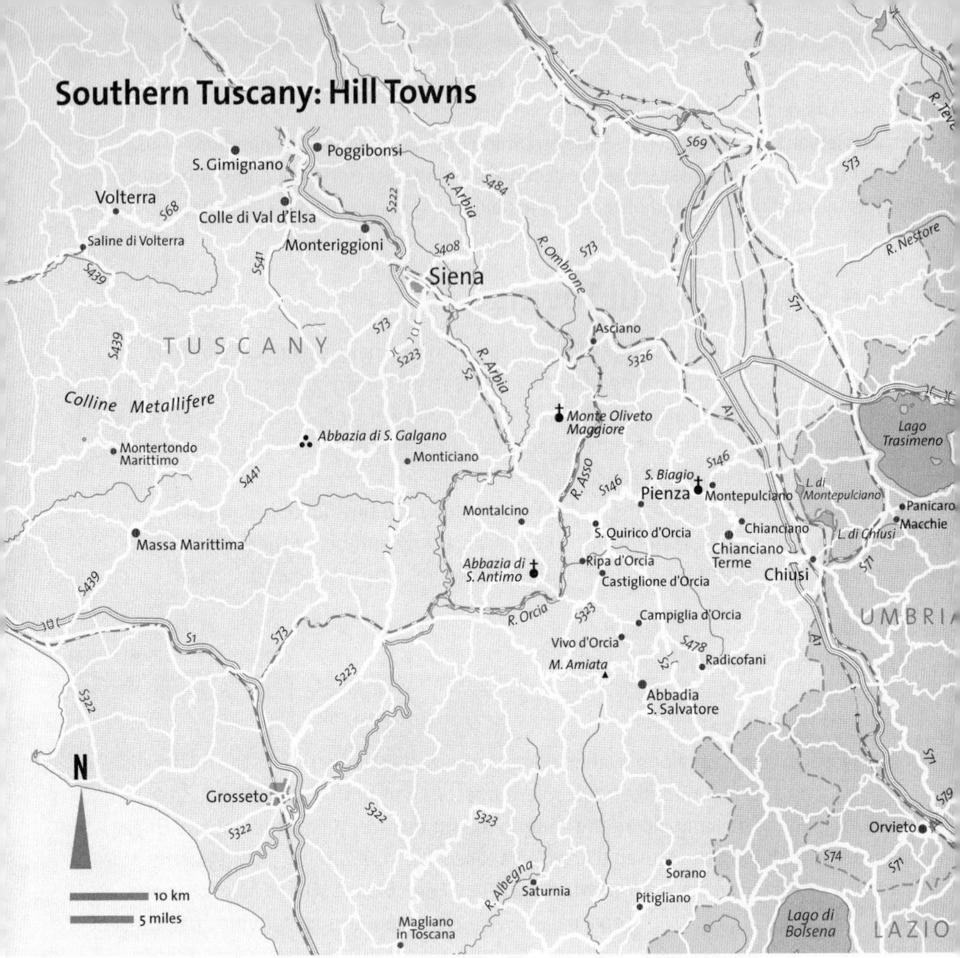

The Palazzo del Popolo

Unlike its 20th-century imitators, San Gimignano is an utterly charming town. Since the Middle Ages its population has dwindled to less than 8,000, and those who are left are kept busy feeding day-trippers from Florence. Its medieval beauty and serenity have made it perhaps the trendiest tourist destination in Tuscany (it has seven hotels, all three-star) but it wears its strange fate well.

The usual entrance is the southern **Porta San Giovanni**, at Piazza Martiri di Montemaggio, where you can park your car. Going up through the walls into the old town, Via San Giovanni leads you past another ancient gate, the Arco dei Bacci, to San Giovanni, a Pisan-style church that was constructed for the Knights Templar, and then to the triangular Piazza della Cisterna, with the town's well and a few of its medieval towers. If you can imagine it, San Gimignano in the 13th century was said to have had 76 of these family fortresses. Pisa's and Florence's numbered in the hundreds. Most cities eventually made regulations against them, or demolished them. For whatever reason, San Gimignano was a special case; even in the 1400s it was known as the 'city of towers'.

By city ordinance none could be taller than the 167ft **Torre della Rognosa**, part of the **Palazzo del Podestà** on adjacent Piazza del Duomo. This was a Ghibelline tower; Frederick II built it and the *palazzo* as the seat of the imperial officials. Civic pride, however, dictated an even taller one be built for the **Palazzo del Popolo**, designed perhaps by Arnolfo di Cambio in about 1300.

The tower remains San Gimignano's tallest at 177ft, and the only one you can climb; the *palazzo* also has a beautiful, rustic-looking courtyard with bits of frescoes surviving around its walls, and upstairs the **Museo Civico** (*open daily Mar–Oct 9.30–7.30, Nov–Feb 10.30–5.50; same hours for tower; adm*), with an Annunciation by Filippo Lippi and other works by Florentine and Sienese artists.

Other rooms of the *palazzo* have interesting frescoes, including the Sala di Dante, an audience hall so called because Dante once spoke here, as a Florentine ambassador attempting to talk the citizens into joining the Guelph League. Dante wasn't the only Florentine to pay a call; in the quattrocento San Gimignano seems to have been almost a kind of resort for the big city; besides the artists who left behind so many fine works, Savonarola, Machiavelli and others all spent time here.

The Collegiata

This is San Gimignano's biggest church (1466–70), plain on the outside but a delightful, smaller version of Siena's cathedral within: it has the same striped arches and starry vaults, and a superb collection of frescoes on its walls, including a Crucifixion by Barna di Siena full of angels, devils, evil Romans and fainting women, among other New and Old Testament scenes, and a Last Judgement by Taddeo di Bartolo.

A ticket from the Museo Civico will get you into the **Capella di Santa Fina** (*open Mar–Oct Mon–Fri 9.30–7.30, Sat 9.30–5, Sun 1–5; Nov–20 Jan Mon–Sat 9.30–5, Sun 1–5; Feb Mon–Sat 9.30–5, Sun 1–5; 21 Jan–Feb only open for mass; adm*), with an introduction to Italy's most moronic saint story. There are many competitors for this honour, but consider little Fina going to the well for water, and accepting an orange from a young swain. When she returned home, her mother told her how wicked she was to take it, and the poor girl became so mortified that she lay down on the table and prayed for forgiveness for five years. After this, St Anthony appeared to call her soul to heaven, and the table burst into bloom with violets. Domenico Ghirlandaio got the commission to paint all this; he pocketed the money and did a splendid job, with sweet faces and springtime colours. Note San Gimignano's famous towers in the background.

In a courtyard to the left of the Collegiata, the **baptistry** has another work of Ghirlandaio, an Annunciation. The **Museo d'Arte Sacra** and **Museo Etrusco** (*open daily Apr–Oct 9.30–7.30; Mar, Nov and Dec 9.30–5; adm*) occupy two sides of the courtyard; one has more 13th–15th-century sculpture, painting and illuminated choir books, the other finds from Etruscan tombs excavated in the area.

Behind the Collegiata, you can walk around the half-ruined fortress, the **Rocca**, or continue north to Piazza Sant'Agostino and the church of **Sant'Agostino**, famous for a series of frescoes by Benozzo Gozzoli on the life of St Augustine. The merriest of all Renaissance painters has a good time with this one, as in the charming panel where the master of grammar comes to drag sullen little Augustine off to school.

Getting Around

Buses run to most villages in the region from Piazza San Domenico in Siena (*see* p.672). To get to San Gimignano it's possible to take a train to Poggibonsi (on the Empoli–Siena line) then a bus from there, but it can be quicker just to take a bus direct from Siena.

There's no **rail** service to Volterra, but an infrequent branch line service runs from Cecina on the coast to Saline di Volterra, 10km away. There are also frequent bus services to Florence, Pisa, Siena and Massa Marittima, all from Piazza XX Settembre in Volterra.

Parking is difficult in most of these towns but there are usually car parks on perimeter roads around the *centro storico*, and you can walk in from there.

Tourist Information

San Gimignano: Piazza del Duomo 1, **t** 0577 940 008, *www.sangimignano.com*.

Volterra: Palazzo dei Priori, Via Turazza 2, **t** 0588 86150, *www.provolterra.it*.

Where to Stay and Eat

San Gimignano ✉ 53037

In summer you may need some help in finding a place: try the **Hotel Association**, just inside the gate on Via S. Giovanni, **t** 0577 940 809. Ask there about low-cost rooms let out by locals.

*****Antico Pozzo**, Via San Matteo 87, **t** 0577 942 014, *www.lanticopozzo.com* (*expensive*). A stylish option in a 1500s building right next to the main square. Several rooms have delicately frescoed ceilings.

*****Le Renaie**, Loc. Pancole, about 7km towards Certaldo, **t** 0577 955 044, *www.hotellerenaie.com* (*expensive*). An attractive modern building with a garden and pool in a lovely patch of Tuscan countryside north of town.

*****La Cisterna**, Piazza della Cisterna, **t** 0577 940 328, *www.hotelcisterna.it* (*moderate–expensive*). A highly recommended option. Its restaurant, **Le Terrazze** (*moderate*), is one of the most popular places in town, both for its panoramic views and its cuisine. Try old house specialities such as *zuppa sangimignese* and *pappardelle alla lepre* (wide noodles with hare sauce), then *medaglione al vin santo* or *ossobuco alla toscana. Restaurant closed Tues and Weds lunchtime.*

*****Leon Bianco**, Piazza della Cisterna, **t** 0577 941 294, *www.leonbianco.com* (*moderate*). A very good hotel with modern rooms.

Dorando, Vicolo del Oro 2, **t** 0577 941 862 (*very expensive*). Adventurous re-creations of authentic Etruscan cuisine, including *cibreo* (a chicken liver pâté so rich Catherine de' Medici nearly died from a surfeit of it), *pici* with mint-leaf pesto, and crème caramel with coriander. *Closed Mon.*

Osteria delle Catene, Via Mainardi 18, **t** 0577 941 966 (*moderate*). Good regional food such as *ribollita alla sangimignese. Closed Weds.*

Osteria del Carcere, Via del Castello 13, **t** 0577 941905 (*cheap–moderate*). A tiny restaurant serving unusual cold cuts and terrines, a delicious saffron-flavoured goats' cheese

Volterra

Volterra has a talent for making visitors a bit uneasy. Its situation, among bleak, windy hills, could be the scene for some medieval Tuscan *Wuthering Heights*, and the city seems taciturn and grey, brooding on ancient memories. *Velathri* was a powerful city, the northwestern corner of the Etruscan Dodecapolis. Its five-and-a-half kilometre circuit of walls encloses an area three times the size of the present town.

Volterra's periphery is as interesting as the town itself; besides the **Etruscan walls**, traceable for most of their length, there are the *balze* – barren, eroded ravines that probably began as Etruscan mining cuts. They have already swallowed up medieval churches and exposed some ancient ruins, and they are still growing. It was this erosion that led to the discovery of the Etruscan necropoli around Volterra.

mousse, soups, roast guinea fowl with chestnuts and lamb with *pecorino*. No credit cards. *Closed Weds, and Thurs lunch.*

Volterra ✉ 56048

Inexpensive rooms are as hard to find here as in San Gimignano.

****San Lino**, Via San Lino 26, near Porta San Francesco, **t** 0588 85250, *www.hotelsanlino.com* (*expensive*). Tasteful rooms in an old cloister. This is the only option with parking.

***Nazionale**, Via dei Marchesi 11, **t** 0588 86284, *www.albergonazionalevolterra.it* (*moderate*). A pleasant old hotel within the walls.

***Sant' Elisa**, about 3km from town on the SS68, **t** 0588 80034 (*moderate*). A hotel with a swimming pool and one of the most popular restaurants (*cheap*) among locals. The country setting is plain, but the simple home-cooked food is superb. There's lots of game, including *pappardelle* with wild boar or deer sauce. *Closed Mon.*

***Villa Nencini**, Borgo S. Stefano, **t** 0588 86386, *www.villanencini.it* (*moderate*). A 16th-century house just north of the centre, with lovely views.

Many restaurants in Volterra specialize in roast boar and the like – good medieval cuisine in keeping with the spirit of the place.

Del Duca, Via di Castello 2, **t** 0588 81510 (*expensive*). A newish place with a good-value *menu degustazione*, plus pork cooked with tarragon, wild boar flavoured with myrtle, and delicious chocolate soufflé. *Closed Tues.*

Il Sacco Fiorentino, Piazza XX Settembre 18, **t** 0588 88537 (*moderate*). An imaginative menu that changes with the seasons. There's a vast assortment of *crostini*, wonderful gnocchi with baby vegetables, penne with Tuscan cheeses, roast pork with black olives, rabbit cooked in garlic and Vin Santo, and lamb with mint and sultanas .

Il Porcellino, Vicollo delle Prigioni 18, **t** 0588 86392 (*cheap–moderate*). Seafood, familiar Tuscan favourites and local treats such as roast pigeon and boar with olives. A good bargain. *Closed Oct–Mar.*

Massa Marittima ✉ 58024

Massa is increasingly popular, and its capacity of 38 rooms is often stretched to the limit.

****Duca del Mare**, Piazza D. Alighieri 1/2, **t** 0566 902 284, *www.ducadelmare.it* (*moderate*). A modern building with a simple trattoria just to the south of the town centre , in a lovely setting with a garden and views over the countryside.

****Girifalco**, Via Massetana, **t** 0566 902 177 (*moderate*). A similar option to the Duca del Mare, with the same amenities and views but lower rates.

Da Bracali, Loc. Ghirlanda, **t** 0566 902 318 (*very expensive*). *Haute cuisine* variations on local cooking and a formidable wine list, in an elegant setting. *Closed Tues.*

Taverna del Vecchio Borgo, Loc. Ghirlanda, **t** 0566 903 950 (*expensive*). An ambitious, highly recommended restaurant, both for its game dishes, including pheasant, boar and venison, and its extensive list of grappas. *Closed Sun eve and Mon.*

Pizzeria Le Mura, Via Norma Parenti, behind Duomo (*cheap*). Good pizza and inexpensive dishes such as grilled swordfish.

You can see the remains of a **Roman theatre** and **baths** just outside the northern wall by the Porta Fiorentina, and some ruins in the 'archaeological park' near the **Fortezza Medicea**, a big castle built on what was the Etruscan acropolis in the 1470s. Just north of it, at Via Don Minzoni, the **Museo Etrusco Guarnacci** (*open daily 16 Mar–4 Nov 9–7; rest of year 9–2; adm exp; joint ticket with other museums*) has a huge collection of funerary urns found in the *balze* tombs since the 1700s.

Volterra's most conspicuous ancient relic, however, is the **Etruscan arch** in the south wall, over Via Porta all'Arco. Much rebuilt in Roman times, the gate has three black stone protuberances, once probably images of the Etruscan versions of Jupiter, Juno and Minerva, now worn away. Near the other end of Via Porta all'Arco, Piazza dei Priori is the medieval centre, with the 1208 **Palazzo dei Priori**, Tuscany's oldest town hall.

The imperial **Palazzo Pretorio** is nearly as old. Around the corner on Via Sarti, the **Pinacoteca Comunale** (*same hours as Museo Etrusco; adm exp; joint ticket with other museums*) has a small collection of very fine 15th-century paintings, including a great Annunciation by Luca Signorelli, though the prize of the collection is the precise, intense and unforgettable Deposition (1521) by Rosso Fiorentino, a seminal work on the threshold between the late Renaissance and early Mannerism.

Behind Piazza dei Priori is the 15th-century **cathedral**, with a large octagonal baptistry from the 1280s. Inside the Duomo, in a chapel off the left aisle, is a fresco of the Three Kings by Gozzoli and a tabernacle over the high altar by Mino da Fiesole. In the **Museo d'Arte Sacra** (*open daily 16 Mar–4 Nov 9–1 and 3–6; 5 Nov–15 Mar 9–1 ; adm exp*), you can see a Della Robbia bust of Volterra's patron, San Lino (Linus), successor to Peter as bishop of Rome – the first pope.

Etruscan and Roman Volterra made its living by mining, and alabaster is still one of the mainstays of the local economy. Volterra is full of workshops where artists turn this luminous stone into vases and figurines (just look for the coating of fine white dust on the buildings), or stop at the artists' co-operative on Via Turazza.

Massa Marittima and the Abbazia di San Galgano

South of Volterra, along the SS439, you'll pass over one of the loneliest corners of Italy. The **Colline Metallifere**, as the name implies, have been attractive to miners (and nobody else) since Etruscan times. The iron the Etruscans found here and on nearby Elba made them rich; today the ore is mostly worked out, but there is plenty of borax and other minerals. After the pass called **Ala dei Diavoli** ('Devils' wing'), make a detour west on to the SS398 to see the real kingdom of borax at **Lago Boracifero**, near Monterotondo Marittimo. It's a bizarre landscape, and it smells bad too; miniature geysers and steamy pits bubble up boric salts amid grey and yellow slag piles. In places the ground is covered with webs of steampipes, since the *comune* discovered its geothermal resources could power everything in town almost for free.

The Sword in the Stone

On some altarpieces in churches and museums in Siena you may have noticed the odd figure of a saint in what appears to be a scene from *Morte d'Arthur*. This is San Galgano, a dissolute young soldier who received a vision of St Michael and thrust his sword into a stone, leaving his old ways to become a holy hermit. As Michael directed, after Galgano's death a circular chapel was built around the sword.

This is the **Cappella di Montesiepi**, on a hill above San Galgano abbey, and here you will find the sword still in its stone, sticking up from the pavement in the centre of the chapel. Whatever role this legend had in someone's religious secret agenda, like all the sites associated with St Michael it is exceedingly strange – a relic from the great age of western mysticism. There are some frescoes by Ambrogio Lorenzetti on the saint's life, but note also the strange shallow dome, done in 22 concentric stripes of brick and stone and probably representing the heavenly spheres of the medieval cosmology, as in the famous fresco in Pisa's Campo Santo.

Across the metal hills, **Massa Marittima** is the unlikely setting for one of Tuscany's finest cathedrals, a big 13th-century Pisan Romanesque building on a stepped pedestal at the end of a broad piazza. There is a beautiful altarpiece in one of the chapels, a Madonna delle Grazie attributed to Duccio; the tomb of San Cerbone, Massa's patron, is down in the crypt, with 14th-century reliefs of the saint's life.

The **Museo di Arte e Storia della Miniera** on Piazza Matteotti has a only small mining collection; there's a bigger one at the **Museo della Miniera** on Via Corridoni (*__t__ 0566 902 289; open for guided tours Tues–Sun summer 10.15–5.45; winter 10.15–4.15; adm*), which has nearly a kilometre of old mine tunnels, with exhibits to show how the job was done from medieval days to the present. The well-organized but not especially interesting **Museo Archeologico** and the small **Pinacoteca** are in the 1230 Palazzo del Podestà (*open Tues–Sun Apr–Oct 10–12.30 and 3.30–7; Nov–Mar 10–12.30 and 3–5; adm*); the latter has a notable Maestà by Ambrogio Lorenzetti.

If you take the SS441/SS73 between Massa Marittima and Siena, be sure not to miss the ruined abbey of **San Galgano** (*open daily 8am–11pm*) about halfway between, near the village of Monticiano. A Cistercian community from France settled here in the 1100s, and work commenced in 1218 on what must have been the grandest purely French Gothic building in Italy. The monastery was dissolved in the 1600s, and since then the roof and marble façade have gone, leaving as romantic a ruin as you could ask for: beautiful pointed arches and stone columns, with grass for a pavement and the sky for a roof. Parts of the vaulting remain, and San Galgano affords a rare opportunity to look at the bare structure of a Gothic building, which will increase your appreciation of the 13th century.

South of Siena

Monte Oliveto Maggiore and Montalcino

As the SS2 rolls towards Rome, it passes through another empty region of chalk hills and cliffs called the *crete*; like the *balze* of Volterra, these are uncanny monuments to the power of erosion, often appearing in the backgrounds of 14th- and 15th-century Sienese and Florentine paintings. East of the main road, **Asciano** is a medieval walled village with a small collection by Sienese artists in its Museo d'Arte Sacra (*open daily 8–12 and 3–6*), next to the Collegiata church.

Some nine kilometres to the south, the **Monte Oliveto Maggiore** monastery complex (*open daily 9.15–12 and 3.15–5; until 5.45 in summer*) was founded by Giovanni Tolomei, a member of one of Siena's leading families who abandoned banking and civic strife for the life of a hermit. With such backing, it comes as no surprise that it became one of the most elegant retreats in Tuscany. A few fortunate monks – artisans who specialize in the restoration of old books – still keep the place going. Set in a striking grove of cypresses that is something of an oasis among the bare chalk hills, the monastery has a lovely fortress-gate decorated with Della Robbia terracottas, a simple, exceptionally well-proportioned early 15th-century church, and a library with some skilful wooden intarsia pictures by Giovanni da Verona.

The real prize, though, is the **great cloister**, with a cycle of 36 frescoes (*currently undergoing restoration*) from the life of St Benedict, whose monastic rule Giovanni Tolomei and his new Olivetan order were attempting to restore in all its purity. Nine of them are by Luca Signorelli; they show the artist's usual perfection of line and characteristic colouring. The rest are the work of Sodoma, seemingly attempting to work in the style of Signorelli, but with a Mannerist tendency to more excited poses and expressions, extravagant architectural backgrounds, and the inclusion of his badger and other pets in the scenes.

To the south of the monastery, **Montalcino**, an easy day-trip from Siena by bus, has a strong castle, the Rocca (*open daily summer 9–8, winter 9–6; adm to go up on the walls*), that was the last word in 14th-century military architecture. It defended the town well. After the siege of Siena in 1552, a party of bitter-enders escaped here to found the 'Republic of Siena at Montalcino' – in doing so forming perhaps the first ever republican government-in-exile. With the help of the Rocca, they held out for a period of several years against the minions of Spain and the Medici, and were one of the last strongholds of Italian liberty. Today the town is better known for its red wines, which are some of Tuscany's best – the dark, pungent Brunello and the slightly less prestigious but also very good Rosso di Montalcino. There is a good collection of Sienese painting in Piazza Cavour, in the **Museo Civico e Diocesano** (*open Tues–Sun 10–1 and 2–5.40; adm*).

Just south of the town is another abandoned monastery, the 12th-century **Abbazia di Sant'Antimo** (*open Mon–Sat 10.30–12.30 and 3–6.30, Sun 9–10.30 and 3–6*). It has left behind an especially beautiful Romanesque church, with a luminous interior partially done in alabaster. Another good Romanesque church, from the 1080s, can be seen in the nearby village of **San Quirico d'Orcia**, back on the main road.

Pienza

Italians like to carry on, more perhaps than is necessary, about Pienza, a small town in the sheep country east of Montalcino that became one of the most characteristic early Renaissance experiments in architecture and design. Before 1460, it was just the humble little village of Corsignano, but in that year Pope Pius II (Aeneas Sylvius Piccolomini) decreed that the town of his birth was to be glorified into a city of art, which he modestly renamed after himself.

The new city got off to a flying start with Pius' commissioning of Bernardo Rossellino to design a cathedral and palace around a central piazza. The **cathedral** has a simple three-arched entrance, decorated only with the Piccolomini arms and the keys of St Peter; ironically the best features are pure Gothic in inspiration – the high pointed vaulting and some pretty traceried windows. They chose a bad spot for it; the cathedral has been settling and threatening to collapse since it was built, and occasionally sulphur fumes seep out of the floor. Around the cathedral square (Piazza Pio II), Rossellino's newly restored **Palazzo Piccolomini** (*open Tues–Sun summer 10–12.30 and 3–6; winter 10–12.30 and 4–7; adm*) is nearly a copy of Alberti's design for the Rucellai Palace in Florence, which Rossellino helped build. The best part is around the back – a three-storey loggia and a garden.

Getting Around

There are regular **buses** from Siena to most places in the area. The only town directly accessible by **train** is Chiusi, on the Florence–Rome line, which also has good bus links with Chianciano and Montepulciano. Montepulciano train station is 10km north-east of town, and only very local trains stop.

Tourist Information

Montalcino: Costa del Municipio 8, **t** 0577 849 331.
Pienza: Pro Loco, Piazza Pio II, **t** 0578 749 071.
Montepulciano: Via Gracciano nel Corso 59a, off Piazza Grande, **t** 0578 757 341.
Chianciano: Piazza Italia 67, **t** 0578 671 122.
Chiusi: Piazza Duomo 1, **t** 0578 227 667.
Abbadia San Salvatore: Via Adua 25, **t** 0577 775 811.

Where to Stay and Eat

Montalcino ✉ 53024

★★★★**La Vecchia Oliviera**, Porta Cerbaia, **t** 0577 846 028, *www.vecchiaoliviera.com* (*very expensive*). A former olive press by the old gate into town, with 13 comfy, elegant rooms and a swimming pool with a jacuzzi.

★★★**Dei Capitani**, Via Lapini 6, **t** 0577 847 227 (*expensive*). An old *palazzo* in the centre, with great views, a small pool and a car park.

★★★**Bellaria**, Via Osticcio 19, **t** 0577 849 326 (*moderate*). A farmhouse hotel a short walk through a pine wood from town. Some rooms, and the pool, have fabulous views.

Boccon Divino, Loc. Colombaio Tozzi, **t** 0577 848 233 (*expensive*). Some of the best food in the area, including *gnocchetti* with truffles and meat roasted *sotto sale* (in a salt crust). *Closed Tues.*

Il Pozzo, Piazza del Pozzo, Loc. S. Angelo in Colle, **t** 0577 844 015 (*moderate*). A restaurant offering reasonably priced traditional meals. *Closed Tues.*

Osteria Osticcio, Via Matteotti 23, **t** 0577 848 271 (*moderate–cheap*). A pleasant wine bar with magnificent views, serving good snacks such as cheeses, meats, *crostini* and salads. *Closed Sun.*

Locanda Sant'Antimo, near the church in Sant'Antimo (*cheap*). A good pizzeria that also has a few rooms.

Pienza ✉ 53026

★★★**Il Chiostro**, Corso Il Rossellino 26, **t** 0578 748 400, *www.relaisilchiostrodipienza.com* (*very expensive*). An old cloister in the centre, with stylishly modernized rooms with all the amenities, lovely gardens, and a restaurant.

★★★**Corsignano**, Via della Madonnina 9, **t** 0578 748 501(*moderate*). A comfy modern option.

Ristorante del Falco, Piazza Dante 3, **t** 0578 748 551 (*moderate*). Spartan rooms near the bus stop. *Closed Fri.*

Il Prato, Viale S. Caterina 1/3, **t** 0578 749 924 (*moderate*). The best place to stop for a bite, with tables in a little garden and local dishes such as home-made *pici* and *crespelle* filled with ricotta. *Closed Weds.*

Montepulciano ✉ 53045

If you can't find a room, try Sant'Albano, 3km from Montepulciano.

★★★**Marzocco**, Via G. Savonarola 18, **t** 0578 757 262 (*moderate*). An airy, tranquil, family-run establishment just inside the main gate.

★★★**Borghetto**, Borgo Buio, **t** 0578 757 535, *www.ilborghetto.it* (*moderate*). Pleasant rooms, some with great views over the edge of town.

★★★**Il Riccio**, Via Talosa 21, **t** 0578 757 713 (*moderate*). A very comfortable, very central hotel with tastefully furnished rooms.

La Grotta, next to San Biagio, **t** 0578 757 607 (*expensive*). Traditional dishes with a creative twist, including smoked goose breast, and duck breast with juniper berries and orange peel. *Closed Weds and mid-Jan–Mar.*

Osteria Borgo Buio, Via di Borgo Buio 10, **t** 0578 71749 (*moderate*). An excellent *osteria* offering local cuisine plus historical dishes such as *pepposo*, a peppery beef stew cooked in *vino nobile*. *Closed Thurs.*

Montefollonico ✉ 53040

La Chiusa, Via Madonnina, **t** 0578 669 668 (*very expensive*). An old olive press acclaimed as the best restaurant in southern Tuscany, offering an incredible seven-course *menu degustazione* and an extensive wine list. There are also some luxurious suites and rooms. *Closed Tues.*

The Piccolomini had large estates around Pienza; Aeneas Silvius was born here only because the family had temporarily exiled itself from Siena, after a revolt that excluded nobles from public office. Several other palaces went up in the wake of the Piccolomini, including the Palazzo dei Canonici; most of its contents are in the **Museo Diocesano** on Corso Rossellini (*open Weds–Mon 10–1 and 3–6.30*), which also has an important collection of paintings, sculptures and tapestries. Pienza never fulfilled the ambitions of its founder; today it is just another Tuscan village known for its piazza and its *cacio*: the 'Capital of Sheep Cheese' has been making it since the days of the Etruscans.

Montepulciano

Inhabitants of this town, the Roman *Mons Politianus*, are called *Poliziani*, and that is the name by which we know its most famous son. Angelo Ambrogini, as Poliziano, was a favourite at the court of Lorenzo the Magnificent and one of the greatest classical scholars of his day, as well as a playwright and poet (Botticelli's mythological paintings may have been inspired by his *Stanze per la Giostra*).

Like Pienza, Montepulciano has its share of Renaissance monuments, most notably Antonio da Sangallo's church of **San Biagio** (1518), a kilometre south of town. This superb though unfinished building captures some of the highest aspirations of Renaissance architecture. The graceful loggia of the adjacent **Canonica** (parish house), also by Sangallo, makes a fitting architectural complement.

In the town, the also unfinished **Duomo** has a beautiful altarpiece by Taddeo di Bartolo, and other works by Florentine and Sienese artists. The two cities fought over Montepulciano for centuries. Florence finally prevailed in both politics and art; the **Palazzo Comunale** (begun *c.* 1360), facing the Duomo, is a smaller copy of Florence's Palazzo Vecchio, with a façade by the Florentine Michelozzo, who also contributed a fine Renaissance façade for **Sant'Agostino** on Via Sangallo.

In the 16th century, the town became something like Florence's southern outpost, and was equipped by the city's favoured architects, Sangallo the Younger and Vignola, with a set of walls, public buildings and *palazzi*. Today they seem out of proportion for a small town. There are plenty of good palaces, several by Sangallo, along the Corso. Note his **Palazzo Bucelli** at No.73, with a foundation made entirely of carved Etruscan burial urns, filled with cement and stacked. Montepulciano is also much visited today for its powerful red wine, Vino Nobile di Montepulciano, sold at *enoteche* around town.

South of Montepulciano, **Chianciano Terme** is a large, bright and busy spa, whose motto. *Chianciano – fegato sano* ('Chianciano for a healthy liver'), draws in many an imbibing Tuscan for an annual flush. It's not only the perfect cure for too much *Vino Nobile*, but usually has overnight accommodation in a pinch.

Chiusi

If anyone ever read you Lord Macaulay's rouser *Horatio at the Bridge* when you were a child, you will remember the fateful name Lars Porsena of Clusium, leading the Etruscan confederation to besiege Rome in the brave days of old. Thanks to Horatio, Rome survived and made a name for itself; you can come here to see what happened to Clusium – or *Camars* as the Etruscans actually called it.

Modern Chiusi has a market on Mondays and a first-class archaeological museum, the newly restored **Museo Nazionale Etrusco** (*open Mon–Fri 9–2, Sat and Sun 9–1; adm*), with lots of burial urns – many decorated with scenes from Homer – and examples of the black pottery called *bucchero* that was an Etruscan speciality. Several tombs can be visited off the road to Chianciano Terme (ask the museum guards); the **Tomba della Scimmia**, which has some wall paintings, is the most interesting.

From Chiusi, the SS478 takes you back to the southern end of Siena province, passing **Radicofani**, a startling sight with its tall castle on top of a weirdly eroded barren hill. Further south is the region of **Monte Amiata**, Tuscany's highest peak (5,649ft), with Europe's second largest mercury mine; Amiata is an extinct volcano full of unusual minerals. There is a small ski resort at **Abbadia San Salvatore**, and the remains of a 12th-century Cistercian abbey that was the predecessor to San Galgano.

The southernmost corner of Tuscany is a strange and empty quarter, thriving in the days of the Etruscans but at no time since. Some ruins of Etruscan tombs and walls can be seen at **Saturnia** and **Pitigliano** (*open Sun 10–1, with a tour that takes in other Jewish relics of the town*); the synagogue in Pitigliano is also worth a visit. **Sorano**, north of Pitigliano, is the natural conclusion to this somewhat disturbing region; it is almost a ghost town, most of it abandoned after landslides in the 1920s.

From Florence to Arezzo

Like all the northern part of Arezzo province, the routes along the Arno are lined with typically Tuscan small towns that managed not to be left behind in the Middle Ages. On the contrary, it is a highly industrialized region; lignite and felt hats are important, but new factories and power lines seem to be going up all the time. At **Incisa Val d'Arno** the cliffs close in towards the river; from here you have the choice of the fast route, the A1 *autostrada* direct to Arezzo, or of dallying through the pretty villages in the hills above either bank of the Arno along the SS69.

San Giovanni Valdarno, birthplace of Masaccio and a long-time Florentine fortress on the border with hostile Arezzo, is the largest and most interesting town in this area, with its arcaded piazza around the Palazzo Comunale, a building thought to be by Florence's Arnolfo di Cambio. The loggias that surround it are covered with the coats of arms of its Florentine governors. In the museum adjacent to the 15th-century **Basilica di Santa Maria delle Grazie** (*open summer Mon, Tues and Thurs–Sat 10.30–12.30 and 4–7, Sun 4–7; winter Mon, Tues and Thurs–Sat 10.30–12.30 and 3.30–6.30, Sun 3.30–6.30; adm*) is a priceless Annunciation by Fra Angelico – an early work that seems like a study for his famous Annunciation at San Marco in Florence.

In **Montevarchi** there is a little museum where you can see a mastodon skeleton, a relic of the area's prehistory. **Terranuova Bracciolini** is an old Aretine fortress town, its walls still standing. In the hills north of the Arno, **Grópina**, near Loro Ciuffenna, has a Romanesque church with a truly bizarre relic of the Dark Ages – a stone pulpit carved with wolves, eagles and unusual patterns, which may date back to the time of the Lombards or even earlier.

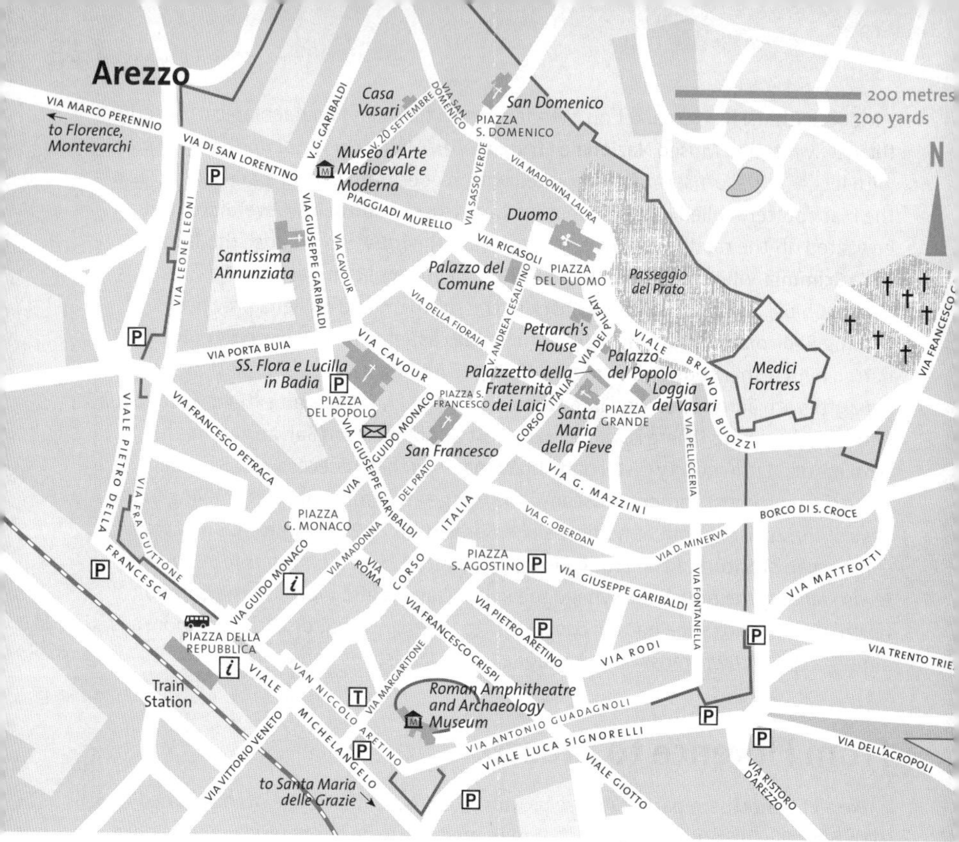

Arezzo

Compared with the other cities of Tuscany, Arezzo looks a little down-at-heel and rustic, as if the art and sophistication of the Renaissance had somehow passed it by. The medieval air is part of its charm, however, and is easily explainable: the city lost its prosperity along with its independence when Florence annexed it in 1384. And the lack of fine buildings here conceals a mildly glorious past – Arezzo was one of the richest cities of the Etruscan Dodecapolis (the famous bronze chimera in the Florence archaeology museum was found here).

The long list of famous Aretini begins back in Roman times with Maecenas, the fabulously wealthy friend of Augustus and the patron of Horace and Virgil. In the Middle Ages, Arezzo was a typical free *comune*, a rival to Florence and a city of great cultural distinction. Guido d'Arezzo, the inventor of musical notation and the scale, was born here, as was Petrarch. Later came Giorgio Vasari and Pietro Aretino, the uninhibited writer and poet whose celebrated poison pen allowed him to make a fortune by *not* writing about contemporary princes and popes, making him undoubtedly the most genteel extortionist of all time. In the game of Tuscan power politics Arezzo was at its strongest during the early 14th century, under the rule of a remarkable series of warrior-bishops, of whom the best remembered is the fierce Guido Tarlati (*d.* 1327).

Today Arezzo is a very prosperous place. It should be, having what is perhaps the biggest jewellery industry of any city in Europe, with hundreds of firms stamping out chains and rings, and bank vaults heaving with gold ingots. The old centre, however, hasn't really shared in this prosperity. Most people have moved out, and more and more shop fronts are given over to the city's other industry – antiques. Arezzo has become a curiosity shop, especially during the **antiques fairs** that are held on the first Sunday of every month in Piazza Grande. It has also found a new role as a film set, providing a picturesque setting for, for instance, Roberto Benigni's Oscar-winning *La Vita è Bella* (*Life Is Beautiful*).

The Piazza Grande

The medieval-looking houses around **Piazza Grande** make a perfect setting for Arezzo's annual medieval festival, the *Giostra del Saracino*, in early September, where the colourful old costumes are dusted off and the town sports tilt at a wooden figure called the 'King of the Indies'. The antiques fairs are also held here. Giorgio Vasari built

Getting There and Around

From Florence, Perugia and Cortona, the **train** is the easiest way to reach Arezzo. The station is at the southern end of town, where Via Guido Monaco crosses Viale Piero della Francesca and the old city walls. Many smaller towns, such as San Giovanni Valdarno, Poppi, Bibbiena, Sansepolcro and Castiglion Fiorentino, can also be easily reached by train.

Buses for Cortona and other towns in Arezzo province, as well as for Siena, leave from the bus station, opposite the railway station on Viale Piero della Francesca. Schedules are posted for all lines.

Tourist Information

Piazza della Repubblica, in front of the train station, **t** 0575 377 678.

Piazza Risorgimento 116, **t** 0575 239 523.

Where to Stay and Eat

Arezzo ✉ 52100

****__Minerva__, Via Fiorentina 4, **t** 0575 370 390, *www.hotel-minerva.it* (*expensive*). A hotel offering pleasant rooms a few blocks west of the city walls (it's probably the most convenient option if you're travelling by car), and containing an excellent, unpretentious restaurant (*moderate*).

***__Continentale__, Piazza Guido Monaco 7, **t** 0575 20251, *www.hotelcontinentale.com* (*expensive*). A fine, older hotel with a roof terrace. The restaurant fare includes *zuppa del Tarlati* – chicken soup prepared according to a 12th-century recipe. *Closed Mon.*

__Truciolini__, Via G. Ferraris 29, **t 0575 984 104, (*moderate*). A decent reasonably priced option.

La Foresteria, Via Bicchieraia 32, **t** 0575 370 474, (*cheap*). Twelve simple rooms in a 14th-century Benedictine convent, approached through a marvellous cloister. Most have beautiful frescoes and, although simple, they are not without style. Meals are served

Buca di San Francesco, Via S. Francesco 1, **t** 0575 23271 (*expensive*). A long-established tourist haunt right opposite Piero's frescoes, with an honest-to-goodness medieval atmosphere and tasty Tuscan cooking. *Closed Mon eve, Tues and July.*

Osteria La Capannaccia, Loc. Campriano 51c, **t** 0575 361 759 (*moderate*). One of the best places around Arezzo for a meal in the countryside. The rural Aretine specialities include simple dishes such as *minestra di pane* (bread soup) and roast meats, and there are wines from the Colli Aretini. *Closed Sun eve and Mon.*

Antica Osteria Agania, Via Mazzini 10, **t** 0575 295 381 (*cheap*). A popular, rustic, excellent-value place offering the likes of tripe, *baccalà*, rabbit, duck, and fried eggs topped with truffle shavings.

the long **Loggia** in the manner of an ancient Greek stoa, and contributed the clock tower to the **Palazzo della Fraternità dei Laici**, an odd building, half-Gothic and half by Bernardo Rossellino. If you thought this was the town hall, you've been fooled: the *palazzo* is the home of a lay brotherhood founded in the 1200s, and Arezzo's old Palazzo del Popolo exists only in ruins, behind Vasari's Loggia on Via dei Pileati. Like Pisa's, it was destroyed by the Florentines after they captured the city.

Also on Via dei Pileati, the **Casa di Petrarca** (*open Mon–Sat 10–12 and 3–5*) is a replacement for the original, which was destroyed during the Second World War; it stands near the 14th-century **Palazzo Pretorio**, decked with the coats of arms of imperial and Florentine governors. One block south you'll see the singular façade of Arezzo's finest church, **Santa Maria della Pieve**, which turns its back on Piazza Grande, showing only a graceful arched apse. In the front, a distinctive irregular campanile and four levels of columns make a unique mountaineer's version of the Pisan–Luccan Romanesque style, done in rough-hewn stone with hardly any two columns or capitals alike. Under the arch at the front portal, note the interesting, newly restored early medieval reliefs of the 12 months: April with its flowers, February with its pruning hook, and the pagan two-headed god Janus for January. The interior is dim and stark, but there is a good altarpiece by Pietro Lorenzetti, with a Madonna and saints modelling Tuscan fashions of the 14th century.

The Cathedral and Art Museum

Narrow streets from Piazza Grande lead up to the **Passeggio del Prato**, a big, English-style park with lawns and monuments. All of Arezzo slopes gradually upwards from the railway station, ending abruptly here; from the cliffs on the edge of the Prato there is a memorable view over the mountains, extending towards Florence and Urbino. Overlooking the park is a half-ruined Medici fortress dating from the 16th century; at the other end, you'll see the back of the **cathedral** with its lovely Gothic belltower (19th century). This Duomo, which was built in bits and pieces over the centuries, is worth a look inside for the 16th-century stained-glass windows, done by a French master named Guillaume de Marcillat, whose work resembles illuminated frescoes by a Gozzoli or Luca Signorelli. In the north aisle the 1327 **tomb of Bishop Guido Tarlati** is a fascinating early predecessor of the heroic sculptural tombs of the Renaissance, perhaps designed by Giotto; 16 relief panels tell the story of his life, his battles and his good works – all under a big Ghibelline eagle, like a party badge. The Duomo also has terracottas by Andrea della Robbia and a fresco by Piero della Francesca.

From here Via Ricasoli leads west towards the **Museo d'Arte Medioevale e Moderna** (*open Tues–Sun 8.30–7.30; adm*), where you can get to know some good local artists who are not often seen elsewhere, such as Spinello Aretino, his son, Parri di Spinello, and Bartolomeo della Gatta. Renaissance ceramics from Urbino, Deruta and Montelupo are also well represented. Around the corner on Via XX Settembre you can swallow a heavy load of Mannerist excess at the **Casa di Vasari** (*open Mon and Weds–Sat 9–7, Sun 9–1*). In the frescoes for his own house the indefatigable Vasari and his workshop went far beyond anything they ever did for Duke Cosimo.

San Francesco

For many, the real allure of Arezzo is inside this dowdy, barnlike, typically Franciscan church (*visits to see the restored frescoes by appointment only; call* **t** *0575 900 404 or see* www.pierodellafrancesca.it). From 1452, Piero della Francesca created here one of the greatest of all Renaissance fresco cycles, the *Legend of the Cross*. As with Giotto's cycle at Santa Croce in Florence, the story is from Jacopo da Voragine's *Golden Legend*. The restored work shows Piero's use of glowing colours and complex perspectives, especially in such virtuoso achievements, novel in his day, as grimly lifelike battles and night scenes. Even Vasari was impressed, though the best compliment he can manage in *Lives of the Artists* is that the horses were 'almost too excellent for those times'.

Out on the southern edge of Arezzo, near the station on Via Margaritone, are the remains of a **Roman amphitheatre**, made into a quiet park. A former monastery, built on a curve over the amphitheatre's foundations, has been restored to house the **Museo Archeologico** (*open daily 8.30–7.30; adm*). Not much has survived from the thriving Etruscan and Roman city of *Arretium*, but there are some mosaics and sarcophagi, Greek vases and Etruscan funerary urns.

Finally, a 15-minute walk from Via Mecanate out through Arezzo's southern suburbs is the simple but exceptionally pretty Renaissance church of **Santa Maria delle Grazie**, built by Benedetto di Maiano in 1444 and boasting a Florentine-style loggia for a porch in front, and a Della Robbia tabernacle.

Around Arezzo

North of Arezzo: the Casentino and the Valtiberina

If you're going to or coming from Florence by car, the SS70 and SS7171 make an attractive alternative route to the *autostrada* up the Arno valley. This route follows the Arno too, but up to its source and then over the Consuma pass to Florence. It traverses the **Casentino**, a hard-working, backwoods corner of Tuscany full of grapes, olives, small family businesses, chestnut groves, cattle and monasteries.

Starting from Arezzo, the first important town is **Bibbiena**, a typical hill town from which you can make a detour to **Chiusi della Verna**, up in a range of hills that bravely calls itself the 'Alpe di Catenaia'. St Francis lived here for many years, as a hermit on the wooded slopes of Monte Penna, and it was here in 1224 that he received the stigmata, an event recorded in the frescoes of the basilica at Assisi and scores of other churches around Italy. **La Verna**, an unusual rocky outcrop three kilometres above Chiusi della Verna, was the site of his hermitage. A Franciscan sanctuary still occupies the rock. They are always happy to receive visitors; in the Chiesa Maggiore and two smaller chapels is one of the largest collections of Andrea della Robbia terracottas – some of his best work, including a brilliant Annunciation. From the monastery there's an easy walk through pine groves up to the summit of Monte Penna.

North of Bibbiena, the valley road divides. The SS71 northeastwards takes you to another famous monastic retreat, **Camaldoli**, set in thick forests over 3,608ft up the mountains, the home of an order founded by San Romualdo in the early 11th century.

The monks still live in separate cottages, sworn to complete isolation. The narrower SS70 carries on up the Arno Valley. **Poppi**, eight kilometres, up from Bibbiena, is the real attraction of this route: a beautiful little town of arcaded streets and squares with a stalwart, erect Palazzo Pretorio modelled after the Palazzo Vecchio in Florence.

From Bibbiena, the road past Chiusi della Verna leads east over the mountains to the next valley, that of the Tiber. Both the Tiber and Arno are near their sources here, and in places they flow less than 15 kilometres apart. A few bumpy kilometres south of Chiusi della Verna, **Caprese Michelangelo** does not let any opportunity go by to remind you of its famous son. Besides changing its name, the hamlet has restored the artist's purported birthplace, the old town hall where his father was a Florentine governor. Now a museum, the Casa del Podestà (*open summer daily 9.30–7, winter Tues–Sun 9.30–5.30*), it has some full-size reproductions of Michelangelo's works, memorabilia, and dubious tributes from modern sculptors.

Further down the Tiber valley, the town **Sansepolcro** lives on as a shrine to *its* favourite son, Piero della Francesca; there are two of his most famous paintings in the town hall's Museo Civico (*open daily 9.30–1 and 2.30–6; until 7.30 in summer; adm exp*). *The Resurrection*, an intense, almost eerie depiction of the triumphant Christ rising over his tomb and the sleeping soldiers guarding it, shares pride of place here with the *Misericordia Polyptych*, a gold-ground altarpiece that is dominated by a giant Madonna, sheltering under her cloak members of the confraternity who commissioned the picture. Other works present are from Luca Signorelli, Pontormo and Matteo di Giovanni; more Renaissance painting, by both Sienese and Florentine artists, can be seen in Sansepolcro's Romanesque **cathedral**.

For yet another Piero della Francesca, stop at the cemetery chapel on the SS221 just to the west of **Monterchi**, south of Sansepolcro near the border with Umbria: his *Madonna del Parto*, a rare portrayal of a weary, pregnant Virgin, is a popular icon for expectant mothers, and the drive there is spectacular, especially when the sunflowers are in bloom.

South of Arezzo: the Valdichiana

Much of this area consists of a broad plain called the Valdichiana, which was all swamps and lakes before a 19th-century reclamation plan and is now filled with prosperous farms. On both sides you'll find some of the most beautiful villages in this part of Tuscany – none of them have much history of their own, but they are comfortable, essentially Tuscan towns that are worth a stop and a walk around if you're on your way to Rome or Perugia.

Monte San Savino, the home town of the architect Sansovino, is one such; he designed the market loggia and other buildings around the town. Nearby **Lucignano** will literally run you in circles – the village has a unique plan of concentric ellipses, with four picturesque piazzas in the centre. The Palazzo Comunale, now the Museo Civico, has a number of interesting frescoes. Just as distinctive is **Marciano della Chiana**, an old fortress town of gates and towers.

Across the Valdichiana, **Castiglion Fiorentino** was known as Castiglion Aretino until the Florentines snatched it in 1384. It, too, has a museum in its Palazzo Comunale, with 15th- and 16th-century works of art, and some good frescoes in the Collegiata church. The town takes its name from the large castle of **Montecchio** on the opposite hill, a landmark visible all over the Valdichiana, now abandoned. For a while in the 1400s it was the stronghold of the *condottiere* Sir John Hawkwood, he of the famous 'monument' in Florence cathedral.

Cortona

Cortona may not be entirely undiscovered, but it is still one of the real jewels among the Tuscan hill towns. Set amidst terraced slopes covered with olives and vines, almost a kilometre above sea level, it's a web of crooked streets that climb precipitously to the old fortress – even halfway up, if there's a space between the houses, you will be able to see Lake Trasimeno below. Cortona was an Etruscan city, one of the Dodecapolis, and ragged, monolithic Etruscan stonework can still be seen

Tourist Information

Bibbiena: Via Berni 25, **t** 0575 593 098.
Sansepolcro: Piazza Garibaldi 2, **t** 0575 740 536.
Cortona: Via Nazionale 42, **t** 0575 630 352.

Where to Stay and Eat

Sansepolcro ✉ 52037

★★★★**La Balestra**, Via del Montefeltro 29, **t** 0575 735 151, *www.labalestra.it* (*moderate*). Modern, comfortable rooms and a good restaurant with delicious home-made pasta and *secondi* such as lamb chops with zucchini flowers.

★★★**Fiorentino**, Via L. Pacioli 60, **t** 0575 740 350, (*moderate*). The town inn since the 1820s, situated near the main gate and containing basic rooms and Sansepolcro's best restaurant. Try Italian onion soup, well-prepared local specialities and the wide choice of local cheese. *Closed Fri.*

Il Convivio, Via Traversari 1, **t** 0575 736 543 (*moderate*). A restaurant in a Renaissance *palazzo*, offering interesting dishes from the Valtiberina. Try tortelloni flavoured with lemon peel, onion soup, saddle of lamb, veal with tarragon, and *porcini* mushrooms and truffles. *Closed Tues.*

Enoteca Guidi, Via Pacioli 44, **t** 0575 736 587 (*cheap*). A cosy wine bar with a small front room lined with bottles and a larger dining room at the back. Choose between various kinds of ravioli or *carpacci*, and a selection of cheeses, salads and desserts. *Closed Sun lunch, Weds and Sat.*

Locanda La Pergola, Via Tiberina, Pieve Santo Stefano, 16km north of town on the La Verna road, **t** 0575 797 053 (*cheap*). A classy country inn serving superb rustic food, including fresh ravioli with local ricotta.

Caprese Michelangelo ✉ 52033

★★★**Il Faggeto**, in the Alpe Faggeto above town, **t** 0575 793 925 (*moderate*). A pleasant little mountain hotel and restaurant in a lovely forested landscape, offering simple rooms and delicious food based on local ingredients – chestnuts, wild mushrooms, truffles, game and mountain hams. The pasta is excellent, as are the home-made *semifreddi*. *Closed Mon, Tues, and weekdays in winter.*

Monte San Savino ✉ 52048

★★★★**Castello di Gargonza**, 8km from town, just off the SS73, **t** 0575 847 021, *www.gargonza.it* (*expensive*). The top place in the Valdichiana for peace and quiet, and for

at the foundations of its wall. As a medieval *comune*, it held its own against Siena, Arezzo and Perugia until 1490, when the mercenary King Ladislas of Naples captured the city and sold it at a good price to the Florentines.

As in Arezzo, Florentine rule meant a long decline for Cortona, and consequently much that is genuinely medieval has survived. Some old streets, such as Via del Gesù, have brick or stuccoed houses with the upper floors propped out over the street on timbers – the very picture of an old Italian town from any quattrocento painting. Cortona also retains one superb medieval square, the **Piazza della Repubblica** – an asymmetrical masterpiece of urban design in a very small space. The building with the clock is the 13th-century **Palazzo Comunale**.

Directly behind it, facing the adjacent Piazza Signorelli, the Palazzo Pretorio houses the fascinating **Museo dell'Accademia Etrusca** (*open Tues–Sun 10–7; closed Mon; adm*). Not everything here is Etruscan – the fine Greek vases and Egyptian artefacts testify to the city's wealth and trade contacts long ago. Among the Etruscan art, the star exhibit is an odd bronze lamp that looks for all the world like an Aztec calendar stone. There are paintings, too, by Lorenzetti of Siena, Pinturicchio and Luca Signorelli, who was born in Cortona.

a medieval atmosphere. A walled village, it has 7 double rooms in the main house and 25 restored houses/self-catering apartments. There's also a pool, forests all around, and a popular restaurant (*moderate*) offering local specialities and a choice wine list. *Closed Tues.*

***Sangallo**, Piazza Vittorio Veneto 16, **t** 0575 810 049, *www.hotelsangallo.it* (*moderate*). A fine provincial hotel in the centre of town.

Cortona ✉ 52044

Lodgings here can be in short supply, especially beween June and Oct.

****Il Falconiere**, Loc. San Martino 370, 3km from town, **t** 0575 612 679, *www.ilfalconiere.com* (*luxury*). A refined option, frescoed and furnished with antiques and canopied beds. There a pool and a first-class restaurant (*very expensive*). *Closed Weds in winter.*

****San Michele**, Via Guelfa 15, **t** 0575 604 348 (*expensive*). An elegant, comfortable hotel in a Renaissance palace, with antiques and a private garage.

***Oasi Neumann**, Via Contesse 1, **t** 0575 630 354, *www.oasineumann.com* (*moderate*). One of the nicest places to stay, with rooms in a fine old mansion, lovely gardens and a very warm welcome. *Open Apr–Oct.*

***San Luca**, Piazza Garibaldi 2, **t** 0575 630 460, *www.sanlucacortona.com* (*moderate*). A simple but comfortable choice. Many of the bedrooms have wonderful views out over the surrounding countryside.

*Athens**, Via S. Antonio 12, **t** 0575 630 508 (*cheap*). A good budget choice situated high up in the old town, offering spacious rooms in an old building. *Closed Dec–May.*

Cortona's unpretentious restaurants make a point of employing local ingredients – home-made pasta, *salumeria* and beefsteaks from the Valdichiana, and *porcini* mushrooms and truffles from the wooded hillsides. To accompany it are the local white wines, the *bianchi vergini* (white virgins).

Tonino, Piazza Garibaldi, **t** 0575 630 500 (*expensive*). The most elegant restaurant in town, offering a range of wonderful hot and cold *antipasti*, followed by traditional pasta dishes and the Valdichiana's tender beef. *Closed Mon eve and Tues.*

Osteria del Teatro, Via Maffei 2, **t** 0575 630 556 (*moderate*). A restaurant where you can feast on a selection of seasonal treats; in summer don't miss ravioli with zucchini flowers. *Closed Weds.*

La Grotta, Piazzetta Baldelli 3, **t** 0575 630 271 (*moderate*). A friendly but intimate place that the Cortonese would like to keep a secret, tucked away off the main squar e. *Closed Tues.*

Behind the museum, yet another tiny piazza leads to the **Duomo**, which was rebuilt to an uninteresting design in the 1560s. The **Museo Diocesano** (*open Tues–Sun Apr–Sept 9.30–1 and 3.30–7; Oct–Mar 10–1 and 3–5; adm*), however, has a number of excellent paintings, including an Annunciation by Beato Angelico, who spent 10 years in Cortona, and a famous Deposition and other works by Luca Signorelli. There are also some pieces by Duccio di Buoninsegna and Pietro Lorenzetti, and a Roman sarcophagus with reliefs of the Battle of Lapiths and Centaurs that was closely studied by, and served as inspiration for, Donatello and Brunelleschi.

Up and Down Cortona

If you have the urge to do a little climbing, it's well worthing visiting **San Francesco** (1245), where both Luca Signorelli and Brother Elias, St Francis' businesslike successor, are buried. From here you can carry on up to the medieval neighbourhood around **San Nicolò**. This handsome little Romanesque church, built by an anachronistic architect in the 1440s, was the seat of San Bernardino da Siena's Company of St Nicholas, for whom Luca Signorelli painted a magnificent standard of the Deposition that is still hanging by the altar.

The town's four gates are set at the four points of the compass. The northern **Porte Colonia** has an Etruscan–Roman arch; the southern gate, on Via Nazionale, has a little terrace with the best view over Lake Trasimeno. Climb higher to reach an area within the walls devoted to olives and vegetable gardens; there are even better views from the 19th-century **Basilica Santa Margherita.** The original church was built by Santa Margherita (1247–97), a beautiful farmer's daughter and mistress of a young nobleman; upon his sudden death she got religion, became a Franciscan tertiary and founded a convent and hospital where she cared for the sick. Her remains are in a silver urn on the altar. The overgrown **Medici Fortress** at the top of Cortona's hill, built on the site of the ancient Etruscan acropolis, is a great place for a picnic.

Outside Cortona, down on the plain near the city's modern suburb of Camucia, is **Maria del Calcinaio** (1485), with elegant Renaissance symmetry by Giorgio Martini, on a simple central plan with an octagonal drum and dome. The stained glass is by Guillaume de Marcillat, who worked at Arezzo cathedral. Unfortunately it's rarely open; ask at the tourist office. Nearby are some Etruscan tombs, the intriguingly named, circular **Tanella of Pythagoras** and the **Tanella Angori**.

Umbria

17

Highlights

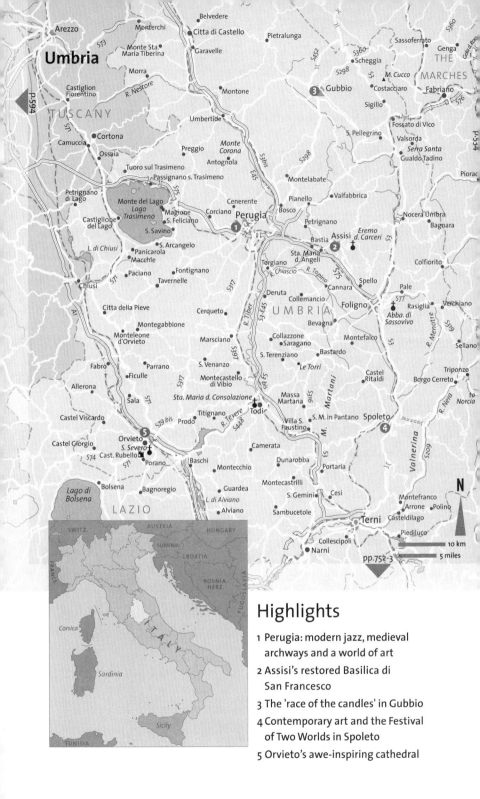

1 Perugia: modern jazz, medieval archways and a world of art
2 Assisi's restored Basilica di San Francesco
3 The 'race of the candles' in Gubbio
4 Contemporary art and the Festival of Two Worlds in Spoleto
5 Orvieto's awe-inspiring cathedral

Umbrians tell it this way: in the centre of the world there is a sea, in the centre of the sea lies a peninsula, in the centre of the peninsula there is a region, in the centre of the region there is a town, in the centre of the town there is a bar, in the centre of the bar stands a billiard table, in the centre of the billiard table there are four markers, and in the centre of these markers lies the centre of all creation.

The town is Foligno, and the Umbrians, as unabashedly parochial as only Italians can be, are only partly in jest. Their rural little city-region, the 'Green Heart of Italy', is also her introspective soul, scarcely touched by the onrush of contemporary events. There are exceptions; in September 1997, fate unkindly sent an earthquake centred on – of all places – the very centre of the universe, Foligno. The damage to the famous Basilica of St Francis in Assisi, now largely repaired, captured most of the world's attention, but towns and villages across the region suffered greatly, and in many places you'll find the Umbrians are still calmly and determinedly putting the pieces back together just the way they were.

Outside of earthquakes, Umbria is rarely in the news; it bowed out of time long ago, a medieval backwater that stagnated for centuries under papal rule. As Americans say of North Carolina, it is 'a vale of humility between two mountains of conceit', and Tuscany and Rome are veritable Everests of conceit, casting long shadows even back in the days of the Umbrii, an Italic tribe that gave the region its name. The Umbrii were best known for their pacifism in a bossy peninsula. Rather than fight the Etruscans, they assimilated their ways, and used their alphabet whenever they had something to say (which, as far as anybody knows, was only once). Later, in the Etruscan twilight, the Umbrii were one of the few tribes passive (or smart) enough to accept the Romans without spilling buckets of blood.

Mild-tempered and isolated from outside influences – Umbria is the only Italian region that neither touches the sea nor shares a frontier with another country – the Umbrians tend to be complacent in their cocoon and conservative in their ways,

Getting Around

The FS state **railways** Umbrian train routes are as follows:

Florence–Terontola–Passignano–Perugia–Assisi–Spello–Foligno–Spoleto–Terni–Orte–Rome

Florence–Rome via Chiusi–Orvieto–Attigliano

Ancona–Fossato di Vico (Gubbio)–Foligno –Spoleto–Terni (or Foligno–Assisi–Perugia)

Umbria also has a private line, the humble FCU (Ferrovia Centrale Umbra), from Sansepolcro in Tuscany to Città di Castello, Umbertide, Perugia, Todi and Terni. The main FS Rome–Ancona line reaches Terni, Spoleto and Foligno; at Foligno you can change for the branch line to Perugia. From Terni trains head south for Rieti and L'Aquila in Abruzzo. Trains between Rome and Florence stop at Orte (where you can change for Terni), Orvieto and Terontola (junction for Perugia).

Towns not reached by train, like Gubbio, are served by **buses**, though services aren't frequent, especially at weekends. This is one region where you should seriously consider hiring a **car** (*see* p.75).

Tourist Information

General information on Umbria is available at *www.umbria2000.it*. For details of many of the region's museums, log on to *www.sistemamuseo.it*.

refusing even to improve the recipe for the medieval paving stones they call bread. But for many this basic lack of interest in the outside world, combined with Umbria's gentle beauty, makes the region an ideal retreat for the spirit. St Francis of Assisi's doctrine of mystical love for all creation seems to come out of the soft bluish-green hills of Umbria, which has proved a fertile land for saints, producing a bumper crop – not only St Francis and St Clare, but also St Benedict, the founder of monasticism, St Rita, the saint of impossibilities, and St Valentine, the patron of lovers. Umbrians visit their relics the way we would call on a fond uncle or aunt.

Umbria is lush and green, even in the middle of its blistering summer. Its medieval towns, hilltop tiaras of pinkish-grey stone, are evocative and lovely, and their churches and museums contain artworks that rival those of big sister Tuscany. But perhaps the greatest gift Umbria has to offer to the modern visitor is its stillness. You can see it in the soulful, introspective works of the Umbrian school of painting, in early Peruginos and gilded Pinturicchios – but especially in the paintings of Piero della Francesca, born on the Tuscan–Umbrian frontier, whose figures, having achieved mathematical perfection, are beyond all time. 'Umbria,' as the friendly nun said on the bus, 'speaks in silences.'

Lake Trasimeno

Approaching Umbria from Tuscany, the first stop is Lake Trasimeno, easily reached by train from Cortona. The fourth-largest lake in Italy after Lombardy's big three, it has a subtle charm: it's sleepy, placid and shallow, kissed by gently rolling hills covered with olives and vineyards. Special flat-bottomed boats skim its waters, fishing for eels; the lake is doing its darnedest to become a peat bog. Of late, the villages around Trasimeno have become popular with English expatriates, searching for new pastures away from the crowded hillsides of Chiantishire, but this is not a lake for idyllic bathing and picnic spots.

The Lake Towns

In 217 BC the peace of Trasimeno's north shore at **Tuoro** was shattered when Hannibal ambushed the pursuing Romans, a battle that ended with the dismal destruction of two legions of the SPQR. It is said that 15,000 legionaries perished – their rivers of blood are commemorated in the name of the hamlet **Sanguineto**, and their whitened bones in **Ossaia** (from *ossa*, bones). After its defeat at Trasimeno the Roman military machine grimly threw even more legions to their death against Hannibal at Cannae, before giving the Carthaginians the run of the peninsula, defeating them by refusing to fight.

Passignano sul Trasimeno, nearby, the lake's busiest resort, is set on its own promontory and has a walled old quarter. From here a road ascends to **Castel Rigone**, a restful little town with a fine Renaissance church, the Tricine.

On the west bank of Trasimeno, **Castiglione del Lago**, with its picturesque promontory, is the biggest town on the lake, with a castle and beaches. Boats sail from here or Passignano to pretty **Isola Maggiore**, home of fishermen and lace-making

Getting Around

Train travel to Lake Trasimeno and the lake towns can be awkward: Castiglione del Lago is a stop on the Florence–Rome line, but only on slower trains. Most do stop at Terontola, the junction for Perugia, Tuoro and Passignano; from Siena change at Chiusi for Castiglione or Città della Pieve.

Perugia is the main **bus** terminus for the area (*see* p.708). Connections from Cortona and Siena are less frequent. Fairly frequent APM services (freephone within Italy **t** 800 512 141, or **t** 075 506 781) run round the north shore (Tuoro–Passignano–Magione–San Feliciano–San Savino–Perugia) and around the southern shore (Perugia–Magione–Sant'Arcangelo–Panicarola–Macchie–Castiglione del Lago). Tourist offices have timetables.

On the lake APM **boats** (**t** 075 827 157) link Castiglione, Tuoro and Passignano with each other and with Isola Maggiore. Connections are frequent in summer, but there are only one or two boats a day in winter.

Trasimeno's flat shoreline makes it a good place to get around by **bicycle**; bike hire is available in Castiglione, Passignano and Tuoro.

Tourist Information

Castiglione del Lago: Piazza Mazzini 10, **t** 075 965 2484, *www.lagotrasimeno.net*

Città della Pieve: Piazza del Plebiscito 1, **t** 0578 299 375.

There are also summer offices at Passignano and Tuoro, and on Isola Maggiore.

Where to Stay and Eat

Medieval Perugians were so fond of Trasimeno fish that Nicola Pisano sculpted some on his fountain in front of their cathedral. Today the catch isn't big enough to send far outside the lake area, but you can try some of the muddy fish at the little restaurants around the lake, most of them unpretentious.

Passignano sul Trasimeno ✉ 06065

★★★**Villa Paradiso**, Via Fratelli Rosselli 5, **t** 075 829 191 (*moderate–expensive*). A large, comfy hotel with a rustic feel and a pool.

★★★**Lido**, Via Roma 1, **t** 075 827 219 (*moderate*). A slightly cheaper option right on the water, with well-equipped rooms, and a garden in which to sit and watch the ferries sailing to and fro. *Open Apr–Nov.*

★**Del Pescatore**, Via San Bernardino 5, **t** 075 829 6063 (*cheap*). Basic rooms and an attractive trattoria (*moderate*) serving lake fish and more. *Closed Tues.*

Il Fischio del Merlo, Loc. San Donato, **t** 075 829 283 (*expensive*). Creative cuisine based on sea fish and Chianina meat. *Closed Tues and 3wks Nov.*

Castiglione del Lago ✉ 06061

★★★**Duca della Corgna**, Via Buozzi 143, **t** 075 953 238 (*moderate*). A comfortable and relaxing option in a quiet wood, with a restaurant. *Restaurant closed winter.*

★★★**Trasimeno**, Via Roma 174, **t** 075 965 2494 (*cheap*). A hotel with a swimming pool to make up for the lake's indifferent waters. *Open July and Aug.*

L'Acquario, Via Vittorio Emanuele 69, **t** 075 965 2432 (*moderate*). A reliable option in the historic centre, serving delicately smoked eel fillets, risotto of lake fish, and carp wrapped in *porchetta* (a typical Trasimeno dish). *Closed Wed, and Tues in winter.*

Isola Maggiore

★★★**Da Sauro**, Via Guglielmi, **t** 075 826 168 (*moderate*). Perhaps the most unusual place to stay in the area, and certainly the best place in Umbria to get away from it all. Gracious and uncomplicated, with just 12 rooms, it's the only hotel on the island. It has a brilliant restaurant, specializing in fish from the lake – eel, carp and more – along with traditional Umbrian dishes. It's altogether excellent value.

Città della Pieve ✉ 06062

★★**Vannucci**, Via Icilio Vanni 1, **t** 0578 299 572 (*cheap*). An adequate hotel in which to spend a night or two.

Da Bruno, Via Pietro Vannucci 90, **t** 0578 298 108 (*moderate*). Fine, unpretentious fare. *Closed Mon.*

Trattoria Serenella, Via Fiorenzuola 28, **t** 0578 299 683 (*moderate*). Good simple food. *Closed Mon.*

women. In 1211, while visiting the island, St Francis threw back a pike a fisherman had given him, only to be followed across the lake by his grateful 'brother fish' until the saint blessed him – the events are commemorated in the island church of San Michele. St Francis survived the 40 days of Lent on half a loaf of bread, to the fisherman's astonishment. A pretty path encircles the island, a good spot for a picnic.

Castiglione is also a good base for visiting Etruscan Chiusi in Tuscany and handsome red-brick **Città della Pieve**, the latter the home town of Pietro Vannucci (1446–1523), better known as Il Perugino. He left several works in his home town: a lovely fresco of The Adoration of the Magi in Santa Maria dei Bianchi (*open June–Sept daily 10.30–12.30 and 4–7; Oct–May Fri–Sun 10–12.30 and 3.30–6*) and some paintings in the Duomo (*open daily 9.30–7*). Although a forerunner of the High Renaissance, the teacher of Raphael and a master of technique, Perugino became – if there is any truth in the rather unflattering biography in Vasari's *Lives of the Artists* (to Vasari, Perugino committed the unpardonable sin of not being born in Tuscany) – the most bitter of Renaissance artists. Born into a desperately poor family, he 'would have gone to any lengths for money', it was said, and success made him a miser, riding from job to job with saddlebags full of cash. Midpoint in his career he became an atheist; even so, he cranked out two more decades of richly rewarded but vacuous religious scenes before dying, stubbornly unconfessed on his deathbed (extremely rare in the 16th century), rejecting any future with the sweet-faced angels he depicted for others.

Perugia

What a town for assassinations!

H.V. Morton

Balanced on a commanding hill high above the Tiber, Perugia is a fascinating medieval acrobat adroitly able to juggle several roles at the same time: those of an ancient hill town, a magnificent *città d'arte*, and a slick, cosmopolitan modern city, famous for its two universities and its chocolates. Perugians themselves have the knack of dressing more sharply than the Florentines for half the money and effort.

It is a fit capital for Umbria, with splendid monuments from the Etruscan era to the late Renaissance, artistically stacked side by side; its gallery contains the region's finest paintings, but in its medieval alleyways cats sleep undisturbed.

History

An ancient Umbrian centre, conquered or assimilated by the Etruscans relatively late (around 500 BC), *Pieresa* grew to become the easternmost of the 12 cities of the Etruscan Federation, and was integrated into the Roman world in 310 BC. After Caesar's assassination, it chose the wrong side in one of the civil wars, with catastrophic results. Octavian's troops besieged it for seven months, until an Etruscan diehard committed suicide rather than surrender. His funeral pyre burned the city to the ground. Some years later Octavian, by then Emperor Augustus, had the city rebuilt and renamed *Augusta Perusia*.

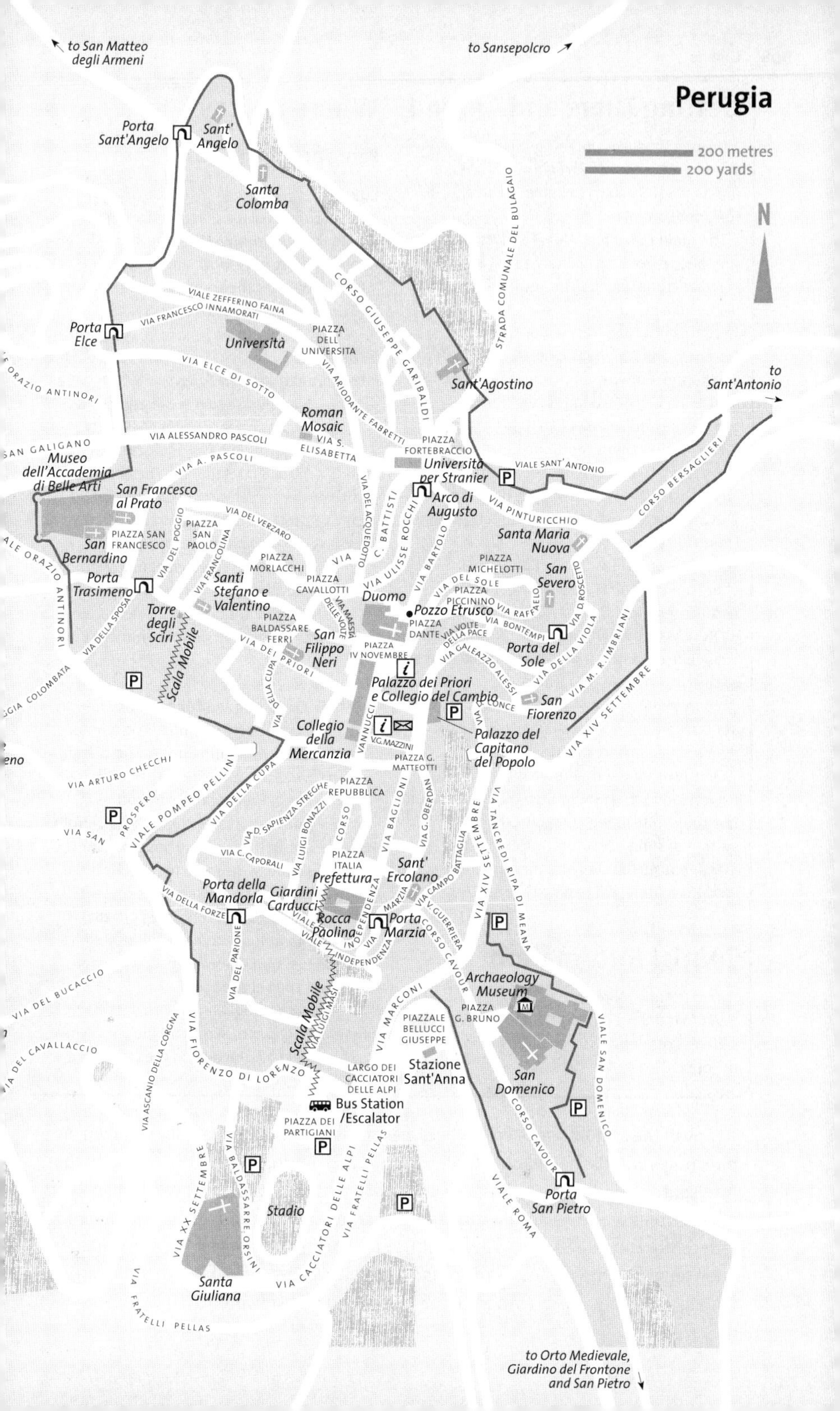
Perugia
200 metres
200 yards
N
to San Matteo degli Armeni
to Sansepolcro
to Sant'Antonio
to Orto Medievale, Giardino del Frontone and San Pietro
Porta Sant'Angelo
Sant' Angelo
Santa Colomba
Porta Elce
Università
PIAZZA DELL' UNIVERSITA
VIALE ZEFFERINO FAINA
VIA FRANCESCO INNAMORATI
VIA ELCE DI SOTTO
CORSO GIUSEPPE GARIBALDI
STRADA COMUNALE DEL BULAGAIO
Sant'Agostino
VIA ARIODANTE FABRETTI
Roman Mosaic
VIA S. ELISABETTA
VIA ALESSANDRO PASCOLI
VIA A. PASCOLI
PIAZZA FORTEBRACCIO
Università per Stranier
VIALE SANT' ANTONIO
CORSO BERSAGLIERI
Museo dell'Accademia di Belle Arti
San Francesco al Prato
PIAZZA SAN FRANCESCO
San Bernardino
Porta Trasimeno
VIA DEL POGGIO
PIAZZA SAN PAOLO
VIA DEL VERZARO
VIA FRANCOLINA
PIAZZA MORLACCHI
Santi Stefano e Valentino
PIAZZA CAVALLOTTI
VIA DELL'ACQUEDOTTO
C. BATTISTI
VIA ULISSE ROCCHI
Arco di Augusto
VIA PINTURICCHIO
Santa Maria Nuova
VIA BARTOLO
PIAZZA MICHELOTTI
San Severo
VIA DEL SOLE
PIAZZA PICCININO
VIA RAFFAELO
VIA D. ROSCETTO
Duomo
Pozzo Etrusco
PIAZZA DANTE
VIA VOLTE DELLA PACE
VIA BONTEMPI
Porta del Sole
VIA DELLA VIOLA
VIA M. R. IMBRIANI
Torre degli Sciri
Scala Mobile
VIA DELLA SPOSA
PIAZZA BALDASSARE FERRI
San Filippo Neri
VIA MAESTÀ DELLE VOLTE
VIA DEI PRIORI
PIAZZA IV NOVEMBRE
VIA GALEAZZO ALESSI
Palazzo dei Priori e Collegio del Cambio
San Fiorenzo
VIA XIV SETTEMBRE
VIA DELLA CUPA
Collegio della Mercanzia
VANNUCCI
V.G. MAZZINI
Palazzo del Capitano del Popolo
PIAZZA G. MATTEOTTI
VIA ARTURO CHECCHI
VIALE POMPEO PELLINI
VIA SAN PROSPERO
PIAZZA REPUBBLICA
VIA D. SAPIENZA STREGHE
VIA LUIGI BONAZZI
CORSO
VIA BAGLIONI
VIA G. OBERDAN
VIA TANCREDI RIPA DI MEANA
VIA C. CAPORALI
PIAZZA ITALIA
Prefettura
Sant' Ercolano
VIA CAMPO BATTAGLIA
Porta della Mandorla
Giardini Carducci
VIA DELLA FORZE
VIALE INDEPENDENZA
Rocca Paolina
Porta Marzia
V. GUERRIERA
CORSO CAVOUR
VIA DEL PARIONE
Archaeology Museum
PIAZZA G. BRUNO
PIAZZALE BELLUCCI GIUSEPPE
VIA MARCONI
Scala Mobile
VIA LUIGI MASI
VIA DEL BUCACCIO
VIA DEL CAVALLACCIO
VIA ASCANIO DELLA CORGNA
VIA FIORENZO DI LORENZO
LARGO DEI CACCIATORI DELLE ALPI
Stazione Sant'Anna
San Domenico
VIALE SAN DOMENICO
Bus Station /Escalator
PIAZZA DEI PARTIGIANI
VIA XX SETTEMBRE
VIA BALDASSARE ORSINI
Stadio
VIA CACCIATORI DELLE ALPI
VIA FRATELLI PELLAS
Porta San Pietro
VIALE ROMA
Santa Giuliana
VIA FRATELLI PELLAS

Getting There and Around

Umbria's main **airport** is Sant'Egidio (**t** 075 592 141), 12km east of Perugia. It has Alitalia flights (**t** 8488 65641) to Rome, Milan and, in summer, Sardinia.

The main FS **train** station, Fontivegge (freephone from within Italy, **t** 1478 88088) in Piazza Vittorio Veneto 3km south of the centre (accessible by bus or escalator), has links to Terontola (for Lake Trasimeno, Arezzo and Florence) and Foligno (for Assisi, Spoleto, Terni and Rome). Halfway up the hill, Stazione Sant'Anna is the FCU rail station for Todi, Umbertide and Sansepolcro (**t** 075 575 401).

The provincial **bus** terminus (**t** 075 572 3947) in Piazza dei Partigiani has services to Gubbio, Norcia, Spoleto and the villages of Perugia province (APM **t** 075 573 1707), as well as Rome, Fiumicino airport and Florence (SULGA, **t** 075 500 9641) and Siena (SENA, **t** 075 500 4888). There are also the Freccia dell'Appennino, to Ascoli Piceno and the coast of the Marches (CONTRAM, **t** 0737 632 402).

If you're **driving**, parking is a headache: most of the city is closed to traffic, and garages and car parks (in Piazza Italia, Piazza Piccinino, and at Piazza Pellini, Mercato Coperto and Piazza dei Partigiani) charge by the hour.

On the other hand, Perugia is a delight to explore **on foot**; its steep topography has been mastered with some ingenuity, though a system of stairs, elevators and escalators (*scala mobile*) that link the train and bus stations and the car parks to the centre.

Tourist Information

Piazza IV Novembre 3, **t** 075 573 6458, and Via Mazzini 6, **t** 075 572 8937.

Unless otherwise stated, **churches** in Perugia are open 8–12 and 4–sunset.

Where to Stay

Perugia ✉ 06100

Luxury

*******Brufani Palace**, Piazza Italia 12, **t** 075 573 2541, *www.sinahotels.it*. A renovated 19th-century hotel with about 80 rooms, fine views over the countryside, luxurious fittings and an attractive courtyard.

Expensive

******Perugia Plaza**, Via Palermo 88, **t** 075 34643, *www.umbriahotels.com*. A prestigious hotel in a green setting at the foot of the city. Large and comfy, it has a pool and sauna, and an excellent restaurant, **Fortebraccio**, with *moderate* set menus. *Closed Mon.*

******La Rosetta**, Piazza Italia 19, **t** 075 572 0841, *www.perugiaonline.com/rosetta*. An older hotel, deservedly popular, with cosy, quiet rooms, some modern, others furnished with antiques. The celebrated restaurant has a garden for summer dining.

Moderate

******Giò Arte e Vini**, Via Ruggero d'Andreotto 19, **t** 075 573 1100, *www.hotelgio.it*. A hotel dedicated to wine-drinking, a short drive from town. Each room, furnished with rustic pieces, has a display case with bottles of wine – guests can taste them and buy from the cellars. In the evening, the *sommelier* chooses three wines and, for a modest fee, diners can quaff to their heart's content.

*****Fortuna**, Via Bonazzi 19, **t** 075 572 2845, *www.umbriahotels.com*. A well-located option just off Corso Vannucci, with more comfort than charm.

****Priori**, Via Vermiglioli 3, **t** 075 572 3378, *www.perugia.com*. A reasonable option in a refurbished old building in the city centre.

Early in the Middle Ages, Perugia became an autonomous and rascally city keen on punch-ups with its neighbours. Strife, external and internal, was a constant until the 19th century, and if the city was well fortified against assaults, the towers and palaces of its citizens were well fortified against one another. The leading family from the 13th century on, the Baglioni, were kept from power by their chief rivals, the Oddi. Their feud was interrupted by the *condottiere* Braccio Fortebraccio ('Arm Strongarm'), who took the city in 1414 with the pope's army, and ruled it well.

Cheap

★★Aurora, Viale Indipendenza 21, **t** 075 572 4819. A hotel on the main road from the station, with spartan rooms but friendly service.

★Etruria, Via della Luna 21, **t** 075 572 3730. A simple place just off Corso Vannucci.

★Paola, Via della Canapina 5, **t** 075 572 3816. A basic but clean, comfortable, central choice.

Torgiano ✉ 06089

Expensive–Very Expensive

★★★★★Le Tre Vaselle, Corso Garibaldi 48, between Perugia and Deruta, **t** 075 988 0447, *www.3vaselle.it*. A luxurious hotel in an old *palazzo* and adjoining houses amid vineyards and olive groves. It has a baby-sitting service, pool, sauna and fitness suite. The *expensive* restaurant is ranked among the best in Umbria, but standards are inconsistent.

Eating Out

Some of Perugia's best restaurants are in the hotels listed opposite.

Very Expensive

Osteria del Bartolo, Via Bartolo 30, **t** 075 573 1561. Inventive dishes created from ancient Umbrian recipes. *Closed Sun and Weds lunch.*

Moderate–Expensive

Aladino, Via delle Prome 11 (extension of Via del Sole), **t** 075 572 0938. One of the most popular restaurants in the city, specializing in Sardinian and other Mediterranean dishes. *Closed lunchtimes and Mon.*

Il Falchetto, Via Bartolo 20, **t** 075 573 1775. A restaurant near the cathedral, with a medieval atmosphere and good, filling Umbrian mountain specialities and great desserts. *Closed Mon and 15–30 Jan.*

Ubu Re, Via Baldeschi 17, **t** 075 573 5461. A quattrocento *palazzo* with good variations on the hearty Umbrian theme, including *coscio di agnello alle olive* (thigh of lamb with olives). *Closed lunchtimes, Mon and part of July and Aug.*

La Bocca Mia, Via U. Rocchi 36, **t** 075 572 3873. Some of the best seafood in town, near the Etruscan arch, plus good desserts. *Closed Sun, Mon lunch, 1–7 Jan and 1–25 Aug.*

Cheap

Il Cantinone, Via Ritorto 6, **t** 075 573 4430. A place just left of the cathedral, with simple offerings such as *spaghetti all'amatriciana*, and beans and sausage. *Closed Tues.*

Il Paiolo, Via Augusta 11, **t** 075 572 5611. Good-value meals and delicious pizzas, served in a Renaissance *palazzo*. *Closed Weds, and part of Aug.*

Osteria del Gufo, Via della Viola 18 (by San Fiorenzo), **t** 075 573 4126. A seasonal menu with specialities such as foie gras terrine, and duck breast in red wine, thyme and honey sauce. *Closed lunchtimes, Sun and Mon.*

Ceccarani, Piazza Matteotti 16. Perugia's best bread, baked in some 30 ways.

Sandri, Corso Vannucci. One of the prettiest pastry shops in Italy, with a frescoed ceiling and divinely artistic confections.

Entertainment

The main Perugian occupation is the evening *passeggiata* down Corso Vannucci, with a stop for a bite or a drink at Bar Ferrari, perhaps, before hanging out in Piazza IV Novembre.

Other activities include July's **Umbria Jazz** festival (*www.umbriajazz.com*), which has drawn the likes of Wynton Marsalis. In Sept the **Sacra Musicale Umbra** features sacred music in Perugia's churches.

After Fortebraccio's enforced peace, the Oddi and Baglioni were at it again. Even in the murderous Renaissance, the Baglioni were notorious for their audacious liquidations of Oddi and rivals within their own family. One Baglioni gangster even tried to assassinate Pope Julius II when he came to visit Perugia – a failed attempt that was regretted by Machiavelli because it would have made the family immortal, for its iniquity. But the Baglioni had more immediate concerns than fame; as the Renaissance papacy became powerful, the popes' legates were eroding their old privileges. When Pope

Paul III raised the price of salt in 1540, it was the excuse that Perugia needed to revolt in what is known as the Salt War. While the city vainly awaited assistance from Florence, the papal army captured it. To add still more salt to the wound, Paul III used the Baglioni palaces as the foundation for his fortress, the Rocca Paolina. As a protest, to this day, Perugians, and indeed all Umbrians, eat bread made without salt (they swear it tastes better!).

From then on, until the Risorgimento, Perugia, like the rest of Umbria, was firmly held in the unnourishing bosom of the Papal States, states that were, as Goethe remarked, kept 'alive only because the earth refuses to swallow them'.

Up to Piazza Italia

Most people ascend into Perugia from the west on Via XX Settembre. Between the FS and Sant'Anna stations, Largo Cacciatori delle Alpi gives on to Piazza dei Partigiani, from where elevators ascend to Piazza Italia, fully inside the city. On the way you can stroll through a surreal, shadowy medieval quarter, all of it underground. These streets were vaulted over to support the **Rocca Paolina**, the popes' fortress, designed after the Salt War by Sangallo, and a much-hated symbol of papal authority that was joyfully ripped apart in 1860 when Perugia joined the new Italian Kingdom.

Only a bulwark remains of the handsome but useless structure, pierced by the lovely Etruscan gate called the **Porta Marzia**, dating from the 3rd century BC; Sangallo liked it enough to take it apart and reconstruct it. Porta Marzia leads into **Via Baglioni Sotteranea** (*open daily 8–7*), the main underground street. By literally burying the Baglioni palaces, Pope Paul III effectively put a halt to that murderous family's influence; today, this silent, sunless land of good medieval brick is their memorial.

On top of the Baglioni palaces lie the **Giardini Carducci**, a terraced public garden with a view of the Umbrian countryside. Next to the gardens stand the dignified public buildings and hotels of **Piazza Italia** that replaced the Rocca Paolina; the proud griffon, emblazoned on the **Prefettura**, is the symbol of both the old and new *comune*.

Corso Vannucci

Two of Perugia's principal streets radiate from Piazza Italia: Via Baglioni and pedestrian-only **Corso Vannucci**, a splendid curve lined with the fortified palaces of Perugia's no-account nobility. Their forbidding residences are now elegant cafés and shops; their street has been renamed after Perugino (Pietro Vannucci), who, in 1499, was commissioned to fresco the hall and chapel of the **Collegio del Cambio**, or Bankers' Guild (***t** 075 572 8599; open 1 Mar–31 Oct and 20 Dec–6 Jan Mon–Sat 9–12.30 and 2.30–5.30, Sun 9–12.30; 1 Nov–19 Dec and 7 Jan–28 Feb Tues–Sat 8–2, Sun 9–12.30; adm*). The hall is adorned with fashionably clothed allegorical figures. Perugino painted a self-portrait in the middle of the left wall, and his pupil, Raphael, then a mere pup of 17, painted the figure of Fortitude. The same ticket is good for the **Collegio della Mercanzia** (***t** 075 573 0366; open 1 Mar–31 Oct and 20 Dec–6 Jan Mon–Sat 9–1 and 2.30–5.30, Sun 9–1; 1 Nov–19 Dec and 7 Jan–28 Feb Tues, Thurs and Fri 8–2, Weds and Sat 8–4.30, Sun 9–1; adm*), decorated with almost Moorish style 15th-century carvings and inlays, located at the far end of the Palazzo dei Priori.

Palazzo dei Priori

Next to the Collegio del Cambio, this huge, magnificent complex, crowned with toothsome crenellations and pierced by narrow mullioned windows, has been the civic centre of Perugia since 1297. The façade on the Corso Vannucci was added in 1443, and wears a beautiful portal; enter here for the lift to the third-floor **Galleria Nazionale dell'Umbria**, the finest and largest ensemble of Umbrian paintings, with many Florentines to keep them company (***t** 075 574 1400; open mid-June–mid-Sept daily 8.30–7.30, until 11pm on Sat; closed 1st Mon of month; adm exp*).

The pious Umbrians never painted anything secular, and the gallery's Madonnas and saints may give you holy vertigo after a while. The first rooms contain a number of striking early works: fountain sculptures by Arnolfo di Cambio (1281) and the originals from the Fontana Maggiore by Nicola and Giovanni Pisano. If you do feel vertigo coming on, save your eyes for the masterpieces: a sweet Madonna by Duccio di Buoninsegna; Fra Angelico's Guidalotti polyptych; and Piero della Francesca's *Sant'Antonio* polyptych. In the Annunciation at the top, Piero creates an eerie stillness with his mathematical purity – on either side of the angel and Virgin rows of arches recede into a blank wall.

From the International Gothic wizard of the Marches, Gentile da Fabriano, comes a Virgin and Child (1408) – notice how the wood of the Virgin's throne is alive and budding. The *Madonna dell'Orchestra* by another *marchigiano*, Giovanni Boccati da Camerino, is a lovely, musical work. His *Madonna del Pergdato* shows his mastery of angelic choirs, putti, flowers and perspective.

There are also paintings by Perugino and Pinturicchio, who both worked on the *Miracles of San Bernardino of Siena*. At his best Perugino eschews drama and tension, preferring simplicity, gentle lines and static compositions that are often filled with a 'sweetness' that Raphael mastered, which gives sugar-shock to people who cut their teeth on Michelangelo. The second Perugian, Pinturicchio (Bernardino di Betto; 1454–1513), was called the 'rich painter' because of his use of gold and gorgeous colours. Though Pinturicchio refused to participate in the High Renaissance, his most interesting works here are his small experiments in perspective. Near the end of the gallery are some good 16th-century views of Perugia, bristling with now mostly vanished towers; other city scenes, by Benedetto Bonfigli, are in the Cappella dei Priori.

Piazza Quattro Novembre

Harmonious Corso Vannucci ends with melodic rapture in this lovely square, a fine example of the subtle art of medieval town planning. Built long ago over a 1st-century AD Roman reservoir, the sloping piazza is adorned with the most beautiful Gothic fountain in Italy, the circular **Fontana Maggiore**, designed by Fra Bevignate in 1280, with bas-relief panels executed by Nicola and Giovanni Pisano. The 48 panels on the lower basin show the labours of the months, each with their zodiacal sign, sciences and arts, Aesop's fables, Roman legends and saints' lives – a complete circular image of the medieval world. The upper basin has 24 saints; on the topmost basin pose three water nymphs. Facing the fountain is the 13th-century principal façade of the Palazzo dei Priori, with stairs leading up to its main door.

Above the portal you'll find Perugia's original griffon (perhaps crafted from an Etruscan creature) and the lion of the Guelph party; the scrap iron dangling beneath it is said to be chains and bolts from the gates of Siena, captured after a famous victory at Torrita in 1358 (this isn't true – the real war trophies, whatever they were, disappeared two centuries ago; these chains simply held them up). The doorway below leads to the **Sala dei Notari**, a monumental vaulted council hall covered with fine 13th-century frescoes by an anonymous painter (*open Tues–Sun 9–1 and 3–7; also Mon June–Sept*).

Across the piazza stands the Gothic 15th-century **cathedral of San Lorenzo** (*open Mon–Sat 9–12.45 and 4–5.15, Sun 4–5.45*). The Perugians never seemed much interested in their cathedral. Its finest hour came in a fit of civic strife in 1488, when the warring Baglioni, fighting the Oddi, turned it into a fortress. So much blood was spilled, it had to be washed out with wine and reconsecrated. Its best exterior feature is the **Loggia di Braccio Fortebraccio**, added by the *condottiere* in 1423. The stylized bronze pope in front is Julius III: the pulpit behind him was constructed for the charismatic San Bernardino of Siena to preach to the crowd in the piazza. The sombre interior contains the 'wedding ring' of the Virgin, which the Perugini pinched from Chiusi. The onyx stone ring, size XXXL and said to change colour according to the moral character of the wearer, is kept in a reliquary with 15 locks (in case the Chiusini try to steal it back) in the **Cappella del Santo Anello**, and displayed only on 30 July. It inspired Raphael's *Betrothal of the Virgin*. On the same side of the church look for the bas-reliefs by Agostino di Duccio. In the Cappella del Sacramento hangs Luca Signorelli's luminous *Pala di Sant'Onofrio* (1484), one of his earliest and best works, showing the Madonna enthroned with saints and a pot-bellied angel tuning a lute. Much of the cathedral's other art is in the **Museo Capitolare della Cattedrale** (***t** 075 572 3832; open Mon–Fri 10–1, Sat, Sun and hols 10–1 and 4–6; adm*).

Oratorio di San Bernardino

Flanking the Palazzo dei Priori, medieval Via dei Priori leads down past Perugia's tallest surviving tower-fortress, the 13th-century **Torre degli Sciri** (many fell victim to the city's internal warfare), and an Etruscan arch remodelled as the medieval **Porta della Mandorla**. Turn at the Renaissance church of **Madonna della Luce** for Piazza San Francesco. Perugia was never a lucky city for St Francis: as a young rake he spent a year in prison after a Perugian raid on Assisi, and became ill (events that led to his conversion). His 13th-century church, **San Francesco al Prato**, with its lovely Cosmatesque work, was partly ruined in a landslide in 1737, then looted by Napoleon's soldiers. Next to it stands a Renaissance gem, the **Oratorio di San Bernardino** (1461), its façade rich with colourful marbles and Agostino di Duccio's exquisite bas-reliefs. They are in the same almost Art Deco spirit as his famous ones on the Malatesta Temple in Rimini, with especially good angels. One of the panels on the lower frieze portrays the original 'Bonfire of the Vanities'; seven bales of women's hair went up in smoke after a rousing sermon by Bernardino in front of the cathedral. Go in to see the 3rd-century AD sarcophagus used as the altar and Benedetto Bonfigli's gonfalon, showing the Madonna sheltering Perugia from the plague (1464), from the church of San Francesco.

An alternative route back to Piazza IV Novembre, by Via del Poggio, Via Tartuga and Via Aquilone, takes you past the beautiful **Teatro Morlacchi**, designed in 1788 by Alessio Lerenzini. After Piazza Cavallotti you can walk through a medieval architectural triumph of interwoven arches and asymmetrical vaults, **Via Maestà delle Volte**.

North Perugia

From Piazza Dante, next to the cathedral, Via del Sole leads up to fine old **Piazza Michelotti**, the highest point in the city, with good views. This was Augusta Perusia's acropolis. The arched lane of Via dell'Aquila descends to **San Severo** (***t** 075 573 3864; open Apr and Oct daily 10–1 and 2.30–6.30; May–Sept Tues–Sun 10–1 and 2.30–6.30; Nov–Mar Mon–Fri 10.30–1.30 and 2.30–4.30, Sat and Sun until 5.30; adm*), an ancient church built over the ruins of a Sun temple. Baroqued in the 18th century, it preserves intact a Renaissance chapel containing Raphael's first important solo commission, a fresco of the Holy Trinity and Saints painted in 1505.

Via Ulisse Rocchi, also beginning in Piazza Dante, heads down to what has become Perugia's symbol, the **Arco di Augusto**, a magnificent gate built over a span of 2,000 years – the lowest section is by the Etruscans, the upper part is by the Romans, after the siege by Augustus (the name Augusta Perusia is still legible over the arch), and on top of it all is a pretty loggia added in the 16th century.

Beyond the gate lies Piazza Fortebraccio and the 18th-century Palazzo Gallenga Stuart, home of the **University for Foreigners** (Università per Stranieri), founded in 1921 as a centre for studies in Italian language and culture. Behind the university, steps lead down to Via Sant'Elisabetta and the Istituto di Chimica, built around a beautiful 2nd-century AD **Roman mosaic** portraying the myth of Orpheus (*open Mon–Fri 8–7*). To the north, in a former Olivetan monastery, is the main **University of Perugia**, founded in 1307 in the medieval proletarian quarter of Borgo Sant'Angelo.

At the northernmost edge of Perugia (take Via Garibaldi or Via Z. Faina) stands a tower built by Fortebraccio and a remarkable, 5th-century round church, **Sant'Angelo** (***t** 075 572 2624; open Tues–Sun 9.30–12 and 3.30–sunset*), dedicated to St Michael and standing on the site of an ancient temple, of which 24 columns were re-used in the building of the church. Another church located at the other end of Via Garibaldi, **Sant'Agostino** (*same phone no. and hours as Sant'Angelo*), contains lovely inlaid choir stalls by Baccio d'Agnolo and frescoes from the 14th–16th centuries.

South Perugia

Perugia's second main street, Via Baglioni, widens below Piazza IV Novembre to form Piazza Matteotti, which was built over the Etruscan walls and lined with early Renaissance palaces. From here, Via Oberdan descends to Perugia's oddest church, **Sant'Ercolano** (1326), a tall octagon with a railway station clock and lace curtains in the upstairs window. The Porta Marzia (*see* p.710) is right nearby, while Corso Cavour descends to Piazza Giordano Bruno and the huge church of **San Domenico**, which was founded in 1305 and rebuilt in 1632, with an immense 15th-century stained-glass window, the beautiful 14th-century **tomb of Pope Benedict XI**, poisoned by figs, and terracottas by Agostino di Duccio.

San Domenico's monastery contains the excellent **Museo Archeologico Nazionale dell'Umbria** (*t 075 572 7141; open daily 8.30–7.30 except Mon am; adm*), with material from prehistoric and Etruscan Umbria, especially the Iron Age settlement at Belverde sul Monte Cetona. Much comes from Etruscan cemeteries – a lovely 3rd-century BC incised bronze mirror, gold filigree jewellery, sarcophagi, a stone slab with one of the longest Etruscan inscriptions found (the famous *Cippus Perusinus*), funerary urns, vases (one showing a hero who looks just like a dentist about to examine a monster's teeth), bronzes, armour, and a *kottabos*, thought to have been used in Etruscan party games. The Romans contribute busts, statues and tombs.

Further down, Corso Cavour passes through **Porta San Pietro**, a 15th-century gate by Agostino di Duccio, then, as Borgo XX Giugno, continues to **San Pietro**, begun by the monks of Montecassino in 926 and remodelled, but maintaining its ancient basilican form inside. This is the most gloriously decorated church in Perugia; nearly every square inch is covered with frescoes and canvases. It has a colourful ceiling and works by Perugino (in the nave and sacristy), beautiful inlaid choir stalls from the 1520s and stone pulpits; an inlaid door leads out to a terrace with a stunning view towards Assisi. Across the street take a breather in the 18th-century **Giardini del Frontone**.

Around Perugia

Near Ponte San Giovanni, west of Perugia, signs lead to its finest Etruscan tomb, the 2nd-century BC **Ipogeo dei Volumni**, in a modern yellow shelter (*freephone **t** 199 101 330, or **t** 075 393 329; open daily July and Aug 9–12.30 and 4.30–7; Sept–June 9–12.30 and 3.30–6.30; adm; 7 people at a time for 5 mins each*). The hypogeum is shaped like an Etruscan house, with an underground atrium (under a high gabled roof). The main room holds travertine urns containing the ashes of four generations of the family. The oldest, that of Arnth, is a typical Etruscan tomb with a representation of the deceased on the lid; that of his 1st-century AD descendant, Publius Voluminius, shows a rapid Romanization, decorated with unusual stucco high-reliefs rather than flat paintings.

Deruta

About 10 kilometres south of Perugia, Deruta is Umbria's most famous ceramics centre, having produced its colourful majolica since the Middle Ages. Shops in its streets are adorned with contemporary examples of the art, while pieces from the past may be seen in the **Museo della Ceramica** (*t 075 971 1000; open Apr–June daily 10.30–1 and 3–6; July–Sept daily 10–1 and 3.30–7; Oct–Mar Weds–Mon 10.30–1 and 2.30–5; adm*), along with detached frescoes from local churches.

Assisi

Rome may be the Eternal City, capital of an empire and whore of Babylon; Florence the birthplace of the Renaissance, of modern western culture and the Italian language; and Foligno's billiard table the centre of the cosmos; but Assisi is the gentle soul of Italy, imbued with the spirit of the country's patron saint, known affectionately as *Il Poverello*, the Little Poor One. The importance of St Francis (1182–1226) in the history of Christianity cannot be overestimated; he was the first to crack the strict hierarchy of the established Church, a democrat who preached a natural, everyday religion of love, and who had a simple, humble faith without dogma that had such a deep, mass appeal that the Church quickly institutionalized his teachings. Francis's own life, as an imitation of Christ, became part of the new iconography of the great religious revival he initiated.

Born to a wealthy cloth merchant named Pietro Bernardone, he was baptized Giovanni but was always called Francesco by his Francophile father. He grew up speaking Provençal, the language of his Occitan mother, and spent a merry, wild youth as a troubadour. He was captured in Assisi's war against Perugia, and spent a year in prison reflecting on the vanity of the world. When released, he gave everything he owned to the poor, tended lepers and preached his message of poverty, humility and joy, attracting a band of followers. Although he refused to take priestly orders, he received authorization for his community from Innocent III in 1209.

Francis spent much of his career preaching and wandering, travelling through Spain to Morocco, accompanying the Crusaders to Egypt and the Holy Land. His songs and canticles, drawing on his troubadour days, were among the first vernacular verses composed in Italy, and the foundation for a 13th-century literary movement, of which the most famous work was the *Fioretti*, 'The Little Flowers', believed to be in part written by Francis himself. In 1221 the Franciscan Rule of poverty, chastity and obedience was sanctioned by Honorius III. Francis subsequently received the stigmata, and died two years later.

More than any other saint, Francis crosses ecumenical boundaries; in 1987, when Pope John Paul II invited representatives of all the world's religions to pray together, he chose Assisi as the host city. But Assisi is not only Italy's greatest pilgrimage shrine after Rome – it's a beautiful medieval town as well, built high on a spur of Monte Subasio overlooking the velvet green Umbrian countryside.

Don't get too distracted by the crowds or souvenir shops peddling toy monks, child-size crossbows and other baubles (no Italian shrine would seem right without them). For a taste of Assisi as Francesco and Chiara (*see* p.721) would recognize it, stroll through the city's steep, dimly lit lanes at midnight, when all is silent and still.

There are two periods when Assisi is anything but silent or still: Easter week, when its processions and mystery plays bring thousands of people to the city; and the *Calendimaggio* (first 10 days in May), a medieval celebration that commemorates Francis's troubadour past with songs, dances, torchlit processions and competitions between Upper and Lower Assisi.

Tragically, an earthquake in September 1997 brought the roof of the Basilica di San Francesco down, killing two friars and two journalists who were examining the damage caused by the first shock of the day. The upper church reopened in November 1999 after extensive restoration and structural reinforcements. The two arches that collapsed have been repaired, but are blank. Technicians are still working on the incredibly painstaking task of piecing the frescoes back together; much of what they

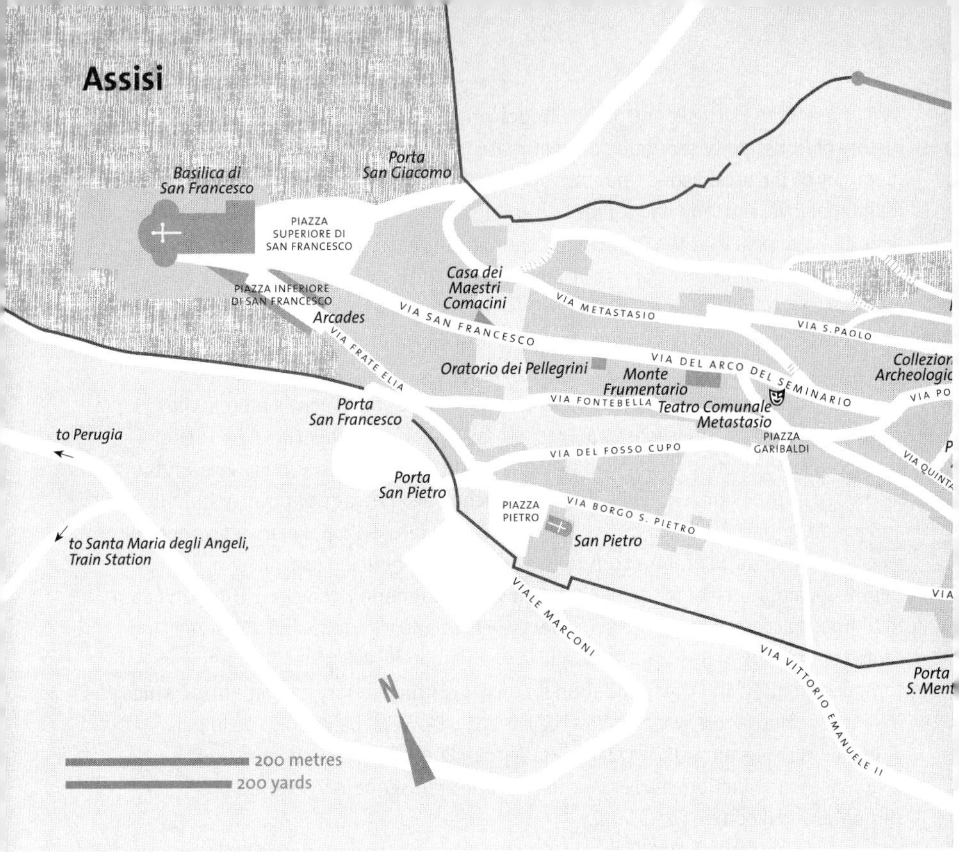

are working with is little more than fine rubble. However, the other frescoes in the nave were virtually unscathed and the façade has been beautifully restored. The *palazzi* on the east side of Piazza del Comune were all badly damaged, as were many other buildings around town. Most of the scaffolding came down in time to reveal pristine façades for the big Jubilee celebrations of 2000, and all of the churches have reopened. However, consolidation work continues. Some buildings on Piazza del Comune are again clad in scaffolding, as are many in other parts of town. Piazza San Rufino and around are practically invisible beneath scaffold and nets. The Rocca, too, is still undergoing restoration, and the Assisi skyline is dotted with cranes.

The Basilica di San Francesco

__t__ 075 819 001, __w__ www.sanfrancescoassisi.org; information office Piazza San Francesco (__t__ 075 819 0084). Open daily Easter–Nov Mon–Sat 6.30am–7pm (Sun until 7.30); Nov–Easter 6.30–6; upper basilica daily 8.30–6. No shorts or bare shoulders.

Before Francis died, he asked to be buried with the criminals on 'Infernal Hill' outside the city walls. His lieutenant, Brother Elias, was not about to go against his wishes, but he waited until Francis was canonized in April 1228, and the next day began work

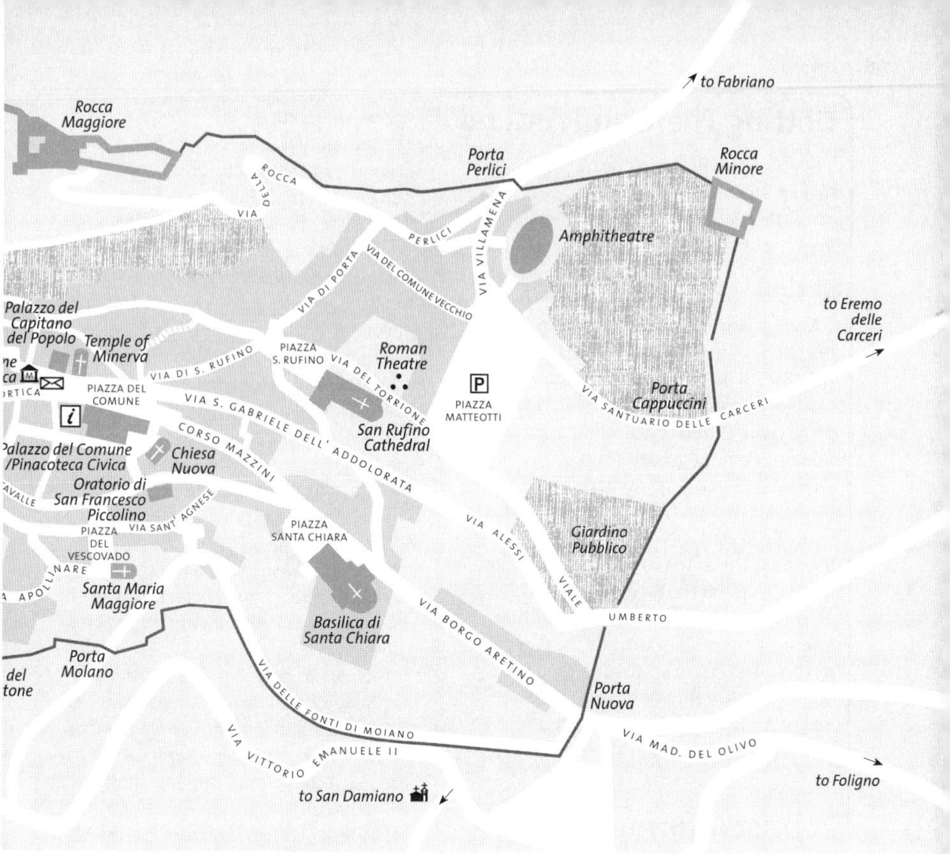

on an ambitious two-storey basilica on the hill, now re-christened the Hill of Paradise. Not all of the order agreed that such a project was fitting for a holy man wedded to poverty, but brother Elias and Pope Gregory IX, who laid the cornerstone, won the day, creating not only the chief Franciscan memorial, but a rare work of art as well.

The two churches that make up the basilica are believed to have been designed by Brother Elias himself, who created here what was to become a model for numerous other Franciscan churches, especially in the simple lines of the Gothic upper church.

The Lower Church

The lower church most resembles a crypt with its low dark vaults, though once your eyes adjust to the dim light you can see that they are covered with beautiful frescoes by the masters of the 13th and 14th centuries (bring plenty of coins to illuminate them). The first chapel to the left of the frescoed nave contains magnificent frescoes on the Life of St Martin by Simone Martini, painted around 1322, while the third chapel on the right contains frescoes on the Life of Mary Magdalene, attributed to Giotto (1314). The frescoes attributed in Assisi to Giotto (from 1295) constitute one of the longest-raging controversies in art history. The Italian faction is convinced that the frescoes in the lower and upper churches are the climax of Giotto's early career, while most foreign scholars believe Giotto didn't paint them at all. In any case, Martini's

Getting There and Around

Assisi is a 30-min **train** ride from Perugia or Foligno, where you'll have to change if you've come from Rome or Terni. The station is 5km from the centre, in Santa Maria degli Angeli; regular connecting buses will take you up to Piazzale Unità d'Italia, just below the Basilica.

Assisi is also linked by **bus** (APM/SSIT, freephone within Italy **t** 800 512 141, or **t** 075 506 781; SULGA **t** 075 500 9641) from Piazza Matteotti, Largo Properzio and Piazzale Unità d'Italia with Perugia, Foligno, Ascoli Piceno, Florence, Rome and local villages.

There are three large **car parks** around the fringes of the old city, most of which is closed to traffic: in Piazzale Unità d'Italia, south of the Basilica; near the Porta Nuova, south of Santa Chiara, off the Foligno road; and at Piazza Matteotti, within the walls, by the Duomo. A series of little buses, the A and B, run between Piazza del Comune and Piazza Matteotti every 20mins or so (tickets from news stands, bars and tobacconists); Assisi isn't really that big, but it's steep in places.

Tourist Information

Piazza del Comune 12, **t** 075 812 534/450; and Largo Properzio, **t** 075 812 315 (*Easter–Oct*), *www.umbria2000.it*.

Unless otherwise stated, **churches** are open daily 7–12 and 2–sunset.

Where to Stay

Assisi ✉ 06081

There are a lot of rooms here, but not enough for *Calendimaggio*, Easter, July and Aug, when you should reserve ahead. There is a booking service at Via Cristofani, **t** 075 816 566.

Expensive–Luxury

*******Subasio**, Via Frate Elia 2, **t** 075 812 206, *www.umbria.org/hotel/subasio/ita/*. Long Assisi's top hotel, the traditional, formal Subasio is linked to the Basilica by a portico. Many rooms have views over the famous mystical countryside from vine-shaded terraces, and there's an attractive medieval-vaulted restaurant. The King of Belgium and Charlie Chaplin stayed here.

******Fontebella**, Via Fontebella 25, **t** 075 812 883, *www.fontebella.com*. A 17th-century *palazzo* a bit closer to the centre. Bedrooms are comfortable, public rooms elegant; the garden is an added attraction.

Moderate

******Dei Priori**, Corso Mazzini 15, **t** 075 812 237. A gracious 18th-century *palazzo* just off the main piazza. Some rooms are *cheap*, some are *expensive*.

******Giotto**, Via Fontebella 41, **t** 075 812 209. Pleasant modern rooms (some *expensive*) by the Basilica, plus relaxing garden terraces.

******Hermitage**, Via G. Degli Aromatari 1, **t** 075 812 764. A comfortable option a short walk from the Basilica.

******Il Palazzo**, Via San Francesco 8, **t** 075 816 841 (some rooms *expensive*). Twelve rooms simply but tastefully furnished with antiques in a 13th-century building in the centre, between San Francesco and Piazza del Comune.

******Umbra**, Via degli Archi 6, **t** 075 812 240. A charming little family-run inn at the end of a narrow alley near Piazza del Comune, quiet, sunny and friendly. Rooms can be a bit small but many have balconies overlooking the countryside (some are *expensive*). The restaurant is one of Assisi's most attractive, featuring variations on the best of regional cuisine, such as risotto with white truffles

International Gothic style poses a serious artistic challenge to the great precursor of the Renaissance. This master of line and colour, whom Berenson called 'the most lovable painter of the pre-Renaissance', creates a wonderful narrative of St Martin's life, a perfect foreshadowing of that of St Francis.

Giotto is credited with the four beautiful allegorical frescoes over the high altar: *Poverty*, *Chastity*, *Obedience* and the *Glory of St Francis*. Note the striking *Marriage of St Francis with Lady Poverty*. In the left transept are some fine works by Pietro Lorenzetti of Siena, among the best in the basilica, especially the lovely *Madonna* from Gubbio, and a cellar full of excellent wine; in good weather meals are served in the little walled garden. *Closed Sun.*

****Country House**, Via di Valecchie 41, **t** 075 816 363. An old stone building in a pretty country setting a 10-min walk from the west gate of Assisi, with lovely rooms furnished with items from the owner's antiques shop on the ground floor. The *signora* prepares substantial, reasonably priced evening meals for guests; book in the morning.

****Ideale per Turisti**, Piazza Matteotti 1, **t** 075 813 570. A fine, small hotel with a garden and views, near the amphitheatre.

Cheap

***Anfiteatro Romano**, Via Anfiteatro Romano 4, **t** 075 813 025. A good quiet choice near Piazza Matteotti, with seven rooms, some with private bath.

****Pallotta**, Via S. Rufino 4, **t** 075 812 307. A few simple rooms attached to a good, traditional eatery.

If everything is full, try the large pilgrimage houses in Santa Maria degli Angeli, but be prepared to be on best behaviour: unmarried couples may be separated, and some dorms have curfews. The tourist office has a list of smaller religious houses and rooms in private houses, of which there are dozens, catering to pilgrims but happy to house tourists too.

****Cenacolo Francescano**, Via Piazza d'Italia 70, **t** 075 804 1083. One of the best, with 130 basic rooms, all with private bath, a short walk from the train station.

Della Pace, at Via di Valecchie 177, **t** 075 816 767. A newish dorm 1km from Porta San Pietro.

Sant'Antonio's Guest House, Via G. Alessi 10, **t** 075 812 542. One of most pleasant private houses, run by American sisters in a 12th-century villa. Good cheap lunches are served but no dinner. Beware the early curfew.

Eating Out

See also Umbra, opposite.

Moderate

Buca di San Francesco, Via Brizi 1, **t** 075 812 204. A well-known restaurant in a medieval cellar, with delicious cannelloni, home-made pasta with meat and *porcini* mushrooms, and *filet al Rubesco* (fillet of steak cooked in red Umbrian wine), plus good wines. *Closed Mon, 10 Jan–Feb and most of July.*

Il Medio Evo, Via dell'Arco dei Priori 4, **t** 075 813 068. A venerable choice with an elegant medieval atmosphere, serving delicious *antipasti* with Umbrian *prosciutto*, pasta with truffles in season, and *faraone all'uva* (guinea fowl with grapes). *Closed Weds, Sun eve, most of Jan and middle 2wks of July.*

San Francesco, Via S. Francesco 52, **t** 075 812 329. Defying the old Italian rule that places with views serve food for dogs, this combines good Umbrian cuisine, an *enoteca* wine list and a verandah overlooking the Basilica. *Closed Weds and 1–15 July.*

Cheap

Piazzetta dell'Erba, Via S. Gabriele dell' Addolorata 15b, **t** 075 815 352. Delicious daily specials at kind prices near the Temple of Minerva. *Closed Mon.*

La Stalla, Via Eremo delle Carceri, Fontemaggio, **t** 075 812 317. A country trattoria converted from an old barn, making a lovely stop on the road up to the sanctuary of Eremo delle Carceri. The hearty fare is accompanied by flagons of local wine. *Closed Mon.*

La Bottega del Pasticcera, Via Portica 9. Rich strudels and chocolate and nut breads – good for sustenance as you follow the pilgrim routes up and down windy streets, lanes and alleyways around the old town.

della Tramontana with *St Francis and St John*, a badly damaged Crucifixion and a Descent from the Cross. In the right transept is Cimabue's *Madonna and Saints*, with a famous portrait of St Francis (1280), believed to be an accurate likeness; a female saint nearby, by Simone Martini, is believed to be St Clare.

In the **crypt** lie the tombs of Francis and four of his closest followers, which were rediscovered in 1818 after being secretly sealed off in the 15th century to protect them from Assisi's devious, relic-snatching enemy, Perugia, who even tried to kidnap Francis as he returned home to die. From the transepts stairs lead up to a terrace and the **Museo-Tesoro della Basilica** (*open Apr–Oct Mon–Sat 9.30–12 and 2.30–6.30; adm*), containing whatever wasn't pillaged over the centuries, including a lovely Venetian cross, a French ivory Madonna from the 13th century, a Flemish tapestry of St Francis, and the contents of the former 'secret sacristy' – Pope Honorius III's Bull approving the Order's Rule (1223), the saint's tunic, cowl, girdle and sandals, an ivory horn given to Francis by the Sultan of Egypt, which he would blow to assemble his followers, the Laud to the Creator and Benediction of Brother Leone on parchment, in the saint's own hand, and a chalice and paten used by Francis and his Franciscan followers.

The Upper Church

In comparison with the lower church, the upper church, facing its emerald-green lawn, is strikingly bright and airy, and dazzles with its colour. It contains two major series of medieval frescoes; the earthquake left them cracked in places, but more or less intact. Restoration work continues a little at a time on the fragmented sections. The lower set on the Life of St Francis is by Giotto or his school, and the upper, with Old and New Testament scenes, is attributed to Pietro Cavallini. What makes most Italian scholars attribute the St Francis frescoes to Giotto is the artist's mastery of composition: Giotto amazed his contemporaries by his ability to illustrate the physical and spiritual essentials of a scene with simplicity and drama, cutting directly to the core. The scenes begin with *St Francis Honoured by a Simple Man*, who lays down his cloak and foretells his destiny; he returns his clothes to his father, who in his anger and disappointment has to be restrained; Pope Innocent III has a dream of Francis supporting the falling Lateran; the demons are expelled from Arezzo by Brother Sylvester; Francis meets the Sultan of Egypt, and creates the first Christmas crib, or *presepio*, at Greccio; he preaches to the attentive birds, then to Pope Honorius III; he appears in two places at the same time, and receives the stigmata from a six-winged cherub. Finally he dies, bewailed by the Poor Clares, and is canonized.

The transepts were painted in 1277 by Giotto's master, Cimabue, though these had deteriorated into shadows of their former selves even before the earthquake turned them to crumbs; they are very patchy now, but what can be salvaged will be, and by hook or by crook some kind of Cimabue clones will eventually refill the rebuilt transepts, good enough to give most of us non-experts a feeling for what was lost, perhaps even of the great *Crucifixion*, a faded masterpiece of 1277. Behind the Basilica, propped on huge arches, the enormous convent is now used as a missionary college.

To the Piazza del Comune

From the Basilica, Via San Francesco leads up past many fine medieval houses to the centre of Assisi. On the way are several buildings of note: No.14, the Mason's Guild or **Casa dei Maestri Comacini** (most of the Basilica's builders came from Como); at No.11, the pretty, frescoed **Oratorio dei Pellegrini** (***t*** *075 812 267; open Mon–Sat 9–7*), a 15th-century gem surviving from a hospice built for pilgrims; and at No.3, the portico of **Monte Frumentario**, a 13th-century hospital, converted into a granary. Next to it a 16th-century fountain still bears the warning that the penalty for washing clothes here is one *scudo* and confiscation of the laundry. Near here at Via Portica 1 is the

Museo e Foro Romano (***t*** *075 813 053; open daily mid-Mar–mid-Oct 10–1 and 2–6, until 5 rest of year; adm*), in the crypt of a now-vanished church, with a few Etruscan urns and Roman frescoes. A passage from the museum leads into the **Roman forum** under the piazza. Here are bases of statues, a platform that may have been an altar, an inscription to the Dioscuri, steps to the Temple of Minerva, and remains of a fountain.

The long, attractive **Piazza del Comune** was built up after the barbarians destroyed the forum. It has always been the main axis of Assisi, and is embellished with the 13th-century buildings of the old *comune* (the **Torre del Popolo**, **Palazzo del Comune** and **Palazzo del Capitano del Popolo**), and what looks like a decrepit bank building but is in fact a Roman **Temple of Minerva**, its Corinthian columns and travertine steps incorporated into the church of **Santa Maria della Minerva** (***t*** *075 812 268; open Mon, Weds, Thurs and Sat 7.15–12 and 5.15–7, Sun 8.30–7*). When Herr 'anti-Gothic' Goethe came to Assisi, it was to see this façade. Left of the palazzo, the **Chiesa Nuova** (***t*** *075 812 339; open daily summer 6.30–12 and 2.30–5; until 6 in winter*) was built by Philip III of Spain on property owned by Francis's father. In an adjacent alley, the **Oratorio di San Francesco Piccolino** (of 'little baby St Francis') is believed to mark the saint's birthplace.

Upper Assisi: the Cathedral and the Castle

From the piazza, Via San Rufino leads up to the **Cattedrale di San Rufino** (***t*** *075 812 283; open daily summer and Holy Week 7–7; winter 8–1 and 2–6*) , with its huge campanile and beautiful Romanesque façade, designed by Giovanni da Gubbio in 1140 and adorned with three fine rose windows and the kind of robust medieval carvings of animals and saints that Goethe disdained. The interior was redone in the 16th century and is of little interest, but if it is open you can see the porphyry font where saints Francis and Clare were baptized, as well as Emperor Frederick II, who was born in Jesi in the Marches (*see* p.544). It is an amazing coincidence that two leading figures of the 13th century should have been baptized in the same place; the holy water must have had a special essence in it, as both Francis and Frederick were profoundly influenced by the East and were among the very first poets to write in vernacular Italian, rather than Latin.

From the cathedral a stepped lane leads up to the **Rocca Maggiore** (***t*** *075 815 292; open daily 10–sunset; from 9 in Aug; adm*), Assisi's well-preserved castle, built in 1174 and used by Corrado di Lutzen (who cared for the little orphan Emperor Frederick II), then destroyed and rebuilt on several occasions. It offers excellent views of Assisi and the countryside. From the Rocca you can visit more of Roman *Asisium* – the remains of the **amphitheatre** in the public gardens, and the **theatre** in Via del Torrione, flanking the cathedral. The **Porta Perlici** near the amphitheatre dates from 1199, and there are some well-preserved 13th-century houses on Via del Comune Vecchio.

Basilica di Santa Chiara

Chiara Offreduccio (St Clare, 1194–1253) ran away from her wealthy and noble family at 17 to become a disciple of St Francis, and later head of the Franciscan Order for women, the Poor Clares. Rumours were never lacking that there was more to her relationship with Francis than practical piety. Gentle, humble and well-loved, she once had a vision of a Christmas service in the Basilica of St Francis while at the monastery of San Damiano, more than a kilometre away – a feat that led Pope Pius XII in 1958 to declare her the patron saint of television. Her **basilica**, built in 1265, below Piazza del Comune (by way of Corso Mazzini), is a pink and white striped beauty with a lovely rose window, made memorable by the huge flying buttresses that support its outward side, masterpieces of medieval abstract art. It was built on the site of old San Giorgio, where Francis attended school and where his body lay for two years.

The basilica was badly damaged by the earthquake but has been fully restored. The interior was decorated with fine frescoes by followers of Giotto, although they are damaged and hard to see. The chapel on the right contains the famous San Damiano Crucifix that spoke to St Francis, commanding him to 'rebuild my church', while the adjacent chapel of the Holy Sacrament has fine Sienese frescoes. By the altar, the portrait of St Clare, with scenes from her life, is by the Byzantine-ish 13th-century Maestro di Santa Chiara. St Clare's body, darkened with age, lies like Sleeping Beauty in a crystal coffin in the neo-Gothic crypt.

From Santa Chiara, Via Sant'Agnese leads to the very simple church of **Santa Maria Maggiore** (***t*** *075 813 085; open daily Easter–Nov 8–7, until 5 rest of year*), built in 1163 on the site of a temple of Apollo, traces of which are still visible in the crypt. Near here was the **house of Sextus Propertius**, the Roman poet of love (46 BC–AD 14), complete with wall paintings, which may open to the public some fine day. Between here and the Piazzale Unità d'Italia, stroll along Via Cristofani and Via Fontebella, the latter adorned with wrought-iron dragons and another old fountain.

On the Outskirts of Assisi

The seminal events of Francis's life all took place in the countryside around Assisi. From Santa Chiara it's a gentle two-kilometre walk down to **San Damiano** (***t*** *075 812 273; open daily summer 10–12 and 2–6; winter until 4.30*), a small, simple, asymmetrical church, where, in 1205, the crucifix commanded Francis to 'rebuild my church', setting him on the path of poverty (he sold his father's horse and clothes to raise money, and rebuilt the church with his own hands). Here he composed his masterful *Canticle of All Things Created*, and brought Clare to live with her sisters in frugal contemplation.

Another Franciscan shrine, the peaceful **Eremo delle Carceri** (***t*** *075 812 301; open daily Easter–Nov 6.30am–7.15pm, until sunset the rest of the year*), lies along the scenic road up Monte Subasio four kilometres east of Assisi. This was Francis's forest hermitage, where he would walk through the woods, and preach to the birds from a simple stone altar; here you can see his humble bed hollowed from the rock. The handful of Franciscans here live a traditional Franciscan existence off the alms they receive.

Santa Maria degli Angeli (***t*** *075 80911; open daily 6.15am–8pm, also 9pm–11 in Aug*), near the railway station, is a large unwieldy nutshell of a basilica built in 1569 to protect a sacred kernel – the tiny Porziuncola, an ancient chapel belonging to the Benedictines in the 6th century, where angels were wont to appear. The chapel was given by the Benedictines to St Francis in return for a yearly basket of carp from the Tescio river, still faithfully paid by the Franciscans, and St Francis founded his first friary here, the remains of which have been partially excavated under the high altar.

Where to Stay and Eat

Bettona ✉ 06084

★★★**Hotel S. Andrea**, Via Caterina 2, **t** 075 987 114, *www.hotelsantandrea.it* (*expensive–moderate*). An unexpected corner of contemporary style in sleepy Bettona. Situated in an old stone building that has been a hospital, an *oratorio* and a *frantoio* (oil press), the 19 rooms are beautifully furnished in simple good taste. The good restaurant, **Opera Prima** (*moderate*), serves Umbrian dishes with the odd twist.

Spello ✉ 06038

★★★★**La Bastiglia**, Via dei Molini 17, **t** 0742 651 277, *www.labastiglia.com* (*expensive*). A charming restored mill with pleasant rooms, a beautiful terrace, lovely views and a good restaurant.

★★★★**Palazzo Bocci**, Via Cavour 17, **t** 0742 301 021, *www.palazzobocci.com* (*expensive*). An elegant, frescoed 17th-century building with beautiful rooms and a hanging garden. Dining is under the vaulted ceiling of the hotel's restaurant, **Il Molino**, **t** 0742 651 305, just opposite, in Piazza Matteotti – try the home-made pasta or tender Umbrian meats cooked over the flames with some of Spello's own wines. *Closed Tues and 10–24 Jan.*

★★★**Altavilla**, Via Mancinelli 2, **t** 0742 301 515 (*moderate*). Twenty-four well-furnished rooms and a pleasant terrace.

★★**Il Cacciatore**, Via Giulia 42, **t** 0742 651 141, (*moderate*). Staying here saves you a walk to its very popular restaurant, where you can enjoy beautifully prepared home-made pasta and other dishes at decent prices. *Closed Mon and Nov.*

La Cantina, Via Cavour 2, **t** 0742 651 775 (*moderate*). A seasonal menu that might feature *oca al sagrantino e castagne* (goose braised with chestnuts in Sagrantino wine), *agnello al limone* (lamb cooked with lemon) or, in summer, lighter dishes such as fresh grilled trout. *Closed Weds.*

Here St Clare took her vows of poverty as the spiritual daughter of Francis; here Francis died, 'naked on the bare earth', in the infirmary, now the **Cappella del Transito**, with a statue of St Francis by Andrea della Robbia.

The garden contains the roses that St Francis threw himself on while wrestling with temptation, staining their leaves red with blood, only to find that they lost their thorns on contact with his body. Still thornless, they bloom every May. Francis's cave has been covered with the frescoed Cappella del Roseto, and there's an old pharmacy and **museum** (***t*** *075 805 1430; open daily Apr–Oct 9–12 and 3–6*), with a portrait of St Francis by an unknown 13th-century master, another sometimes attributed to Cimabue and a Crucifix by Giunta Pisano.

The big feast day in the basilica, the Festa del Perdono, was initiated by Francis after he had a vision of Christ at the Porziuncola, who asked what would be most helpful for the soul. Francis asked for forgiveness for any who crossed the threshold; and indulgences are still given out on the 1st and 2nd of August.

Towns Around Assisi: Bettona and Spello

There are a couple of pretty towns easily reached from Assisi. **Bettona**, an almost elliptical hill town to the southwest, retains much of its Etruscan walls. In its stern Palazzo del Podestà is a small **Pinacoteca Comunale** (***t*** *075 987 306; open Mar–May and Sept daily 10.30–1 and 2–6; June and July daily 10.30–1 and 3–7; Aug daily 10.30–1 and 3–7.30; Nov–Feb Tues–Sun 10.30–1 and 2.30–5*), with two minor Peruginos, as well as works by Dono Doni and Andrea della Robbia. At the Pinacoteca, ask to visit the Oratorio di Sant'Andrea, decorated with a fresco of the Passion by Giotto's school.

Rosy-tinted **Spello**, an outstanding medieval hill town towards Foligno, was Roman *Hispellum* and retains its republican-era main gate, the **Porta Consolare**. Its main claim to fame is its frescoes by Pinturicchio (1501) in the Cappella Baglioni in Romanesque **Santa Maria Maggiore** (*t 0742 301 792; open daily summer 8.30–12.30 and 2.30–6*), painted with the same brilliant palette that he used in Siena's Piccolomini Library; the *Annunciation* is especially lovely. Even the floor, made of Deruta majolica tiles, is bright and colourful. Pinturicchio also painted the altarpiece in **Sant'Andrea** (*open Mon–Sat 8–12.30 and 3–7, Sun 3–7*), up the street, famous for its 13th-century Umbrian crucifix. Between the churches, the **Pinacoteca Civica** (*t 0742 301 497; open Tues–Sun Apr–Sept 10.30–1 and 3–6.30, Oct–Mar 10.30–12.30 and 3–5*) is a repository of works from Spello's churches; there's a fine carved wooden Madonna and Child of 1240.

Further up, there are excellent views from the **Belvedere**, near the scant remains of the Roman acropolis and the medieval castle. Around Spello are two other Roman gates in the walls: the **Porta Urbica** and the **Porta Venere**, a beautiful, almost perfectly preserved monumental gate from the time of Augustus, flanked by a pair of tall cylindrical towers, a relic even more remarkable than the Arco di Augusto in Perugia.

North of Perugia

The two attractions north of Perugia are artsy Città di Castello and medieval Gubbio, the former linked by train with Perugia, the latter by bus. There is little worth stopping for between – typical Umbrian countryside, low hills, tobacco fields and sheep.

Città di Castello

An ancient Umbrian settlement on the upper Tiber, once called *Tifernum Tiberinum*, this is a major tobacco, textile and printing town retaining its 1300s civic monuments – the **Palazzo del Podestà** and **Palazzo Comunale**, with a lofty vaulted hall. The part-Romanesque, part-Renaissance **Duomo** has a tilted Ravenna-style campanile, a Rosso Fiorentino, the 6th-century Treasure of Canoscio and an enamelled and gilded 12th-century silver altarpiece in its **museum** (*t 075 855 4705; open Tues–Sun Apr–Sept 9.30–1 and 2.30–7, Oct–Mar 10–1 and 2.30–6.30; adm*). **San Domenico** has ruined frescoes and a copy of Raphael's *Crucifixion* (the original is now in the National Gallery, London).

Città di Castello's best pictures are in the **Pinacoteca** of the Palazzo Vitelli alla Cannoniera (*t 075 852 0656; open Tues–Sun Apr–Oct 10–1 and 2.30–6.30, Nov–Mar 10–12.30 and 3–5.30; adm*), a harmonious Renaissance palace by Antonio da Sangallo the Younger, with exterior sgraffito by Vasari. The gallery holds fine Renaissance works, including a half-mined processional standard by Raphael, a San Sebastiano by Signorelli, a Ghirlandaio Coronation of the Virgin and sculptural works by Ghiberti and the Della Robbia family. The 16th-century frescoes are by Cola dell'Amatrice and Doceno. The **Collezioni Burri** (*t 075 855 4649; open Tues–Sat 9–12.30 and 2.30–6, Sun 10.30–12.30 and 3–6; adm*), in the Palazzo Albizzini and Ex-Seccatoi del Tabacco, has paintings by Alberto Burri, one of Italy's best-known late 20th-century artists.

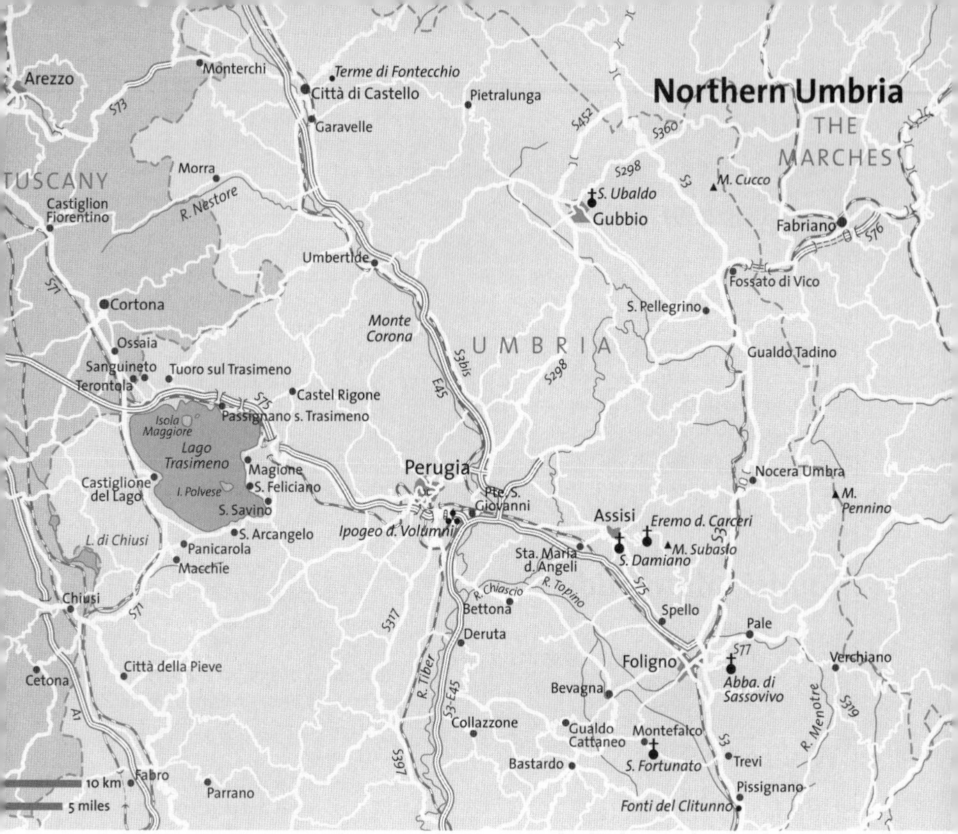

Gubbio

It's hard to think of any other town in Italy that is as resolutely medieval as good grey Gubbio, the sombre stone 'City of Silence', with its orderly Roman street plan draped over the steep, lower slopes of Monte Ingino. As one of the most visited hill towns in Umbria, its dark magic has become grist for the tourist mill. Like many other towns in the area, it is also a ceramics centre, having inherited the tradition – if not the secrets – of the 16th-century Mastro Giorgio, who discovered a beautiful ruby lustre to add to his majolica. Mastro Giorgio's recipe died with him, but Gubbio's potters continue to produce fine ware, black like that of the Etruscans, or in lovely muted colours.

Gubbio was an important town of the ancient Umbrii, known as *Eugubium*. Long an independent *comune*, it was plagued in the Middle Ages by wolves, one of which terrorized the populace. St Francis heard about it and, ignoring the townspeople's pleas for his safety, brought it to the town, and made a public agreement that in exchange for regular meals it would stop preying on Gubbio – an agreement that was sealed with a shake of the paw. The wolf kept its part of the bargain, and is immortalized in a bas-relief over the door of a little church in Via Mastro Giorgio. Gubbio was captured by Urbino in 1384, and from that time on its fortunes followed those of the Marches. It has retained two exceedingly medieval festivals, however,

Getting Around

Città di Castello is on the FCU local **rail** line from Perugia and the FS line to Arezzo. It is linked by daily SITA **buses** to Gubbio, Perugia and Urbino.

There are no trains to Gubbio but some 10 APM **buses** a day along the beautiful SS298 from Perugia, stopping at Piazza Quaranta Martiri in Gubbio, where schedules are posted. There are also buses from here to Fossato di Vico, 20km south, the closest train station, on the Foligno–Ancona line to Rome, and to Città di Castello, Arezzo, Florence and Rome. There is a **bus and train information office** in Gubbio, at Via della Repubblica 13, **t** 075 922 0066.

Tourist Information

Città di Castello: Via Sant'Antonio 1, **t** 075 855 4817; and Piazza Matteotti, **t** 075 855 4922.
Gubbio: Piazza Oderisi, **t** 075 922 0693.

Where to Stay

Città di Castello ✉ 06012

******Tiferno**, Piazza R. Sanzio 13, **t** 075 855 0331, *www.hoteltiferno.it* (*expensive*). The best place to stay and dine in central Città di Castello, in a 17th-century palace with good, comfortable rooms and one of the best restaurants in the area, offering dishes such as ravioli with shrimp in orange sauce, and pigeon with white grapes.

*****Hotel delle Terme**, Fontecchio, a few km east of town, **t** 075 852 0614, *www.termedifontecchio.it* (*cheap*). A large, pleasant hotel offering thermal treatments and a fine open-air pool.

****Europa**, Via V.E. Orlando 2, **t** 075 855 0551, (*cheap*). A good, clean if uninspiring hotel.

****Umbria**, Via dei Galanti, **t** 075 855 4925 (*cheap*). A similar option to the Europa.

Gubbio ✉ 06024

Booking is essential for July and Aug.

******Park Hotel ai Cappuccini**, Via Tifernate, 3km from town, **t** 075 9234, *www.parkhotelaicappuccini.it* (*expensive*). A beautifully restored, award-winning Franciscan monastery in its own grounds, with a cloister, chapel, pool and sauna.

******Relais Ducale**, Via Galeotti, **t** 075 922 0157, *www.mencarelligroup.com* (*expensive*). Three historic buildings in the heart of medieval Gubbio, sumptuously furnished with antiques.

*****Beniamino Ubaldi**, Via Perugina 74, **t** 075 927 7773 (*moderate*). A former seminarians' college just outside the walls, with a bar and restaurant.

*****Bosone**, Via XX Settembre 22, **t** 075 922 0688 (*moderate*). A picturesque old *palazzo* just off Piazza Grande, with comfy rooms.

*****Gattapone**, Via G. Ansidei 6, **t** 075 927 2489, *www.mencarelligroup.com* (*moderate*). A pleasant locale in the medieval centre.

*****San Marco**, Via Perugina 5, **t** 075 922 0234, *www.hotelsanmarcogubbio.com* (*moderate*). Modern comforts in a former convent, with a pretty garden terrace. All rooms have bath.

****Dei Consoli**, Via dei Consoli 59, **t** 075 927 3335 (*cheap*). A simple little hotel excellently

which fill the solemn streets with colour and exuberance, most tumultuously the festival of the *Corsa dei Ceri* on 15 May in honour of Sant'Ubaldo, Gubbio's patron, who persuaded Frederick Barbarossa not to attack the town in 1155; the *festa* itself is first documented a couple of years later, although it may have borrowed something from a lost pagan rite. The *ceri* (or 'candles') are tall, wooden, phallic towers, each topped by a wax saint representing a clan – Sant'Ubaldo, San Giorgio and Sant'Antonio Abate. The *ceri* are baptized with a jug of water, then carried on supports by teams of 10 men. The climax of the day comes when the teams race pell-mell through the crowds up to the mountaintop church of Sant'Ubaldo, a steep race that the saint invariably wins. On the last Sunday in May, crossbowmen from Sansepolcro come to compete in the *Palio dei Balestrieri*, a contest dating back to 1461.

located near Piazza Grande, with a good restaurant in a medieval cellar, offering tasty *spiedini* (meat on a spit).

★**Galletti**, Via Ambrogio Piccardi 1, **t** 075 927 7753 (*cheap*). A hotel overlooking the river, with simple rooms, some of which are en suite. The restaurant, which serves roast duck and lamb, has outdoor tables in a pretty setting.

Eating Out

Città di Castello

Città di Castello is one place in Umbria where you can find good bread, especially *pane nociato*, with walnuts.

Il Bersaglio, Via V.E. Orlando 14, just outside the city walls, **t** 075 855 5534 (*moderate*). The place to come for a wealth of pasta dishes, well-prepared meat and game, and especially good truffles and wild mushrooms, many gathered by the owner himself. Make sure to the local Colli Altotiberini wines. *Closed Weds.*

Amici Miei, Via del Monte 2, **t** 075 855 9904 (*cheap*). Wonderful home cooking using seasonal ingredients, including *strangozzi* (fat spaghetti) with goose sauce, calves' kidneys, roast lamb and duck. *Closed Weds.*

Da Meo, SS Adriatica, Fraccano, on the SS257 10km east of town, **t** 075 855 3870 (*cheap*). A small restaurant of the kind that is fast disappearing, with a limited but excellent menu of the day – usually a good pasta dish followed by meat grilled over the fire in front of you. *Closed Weds.*

Gubbio

Gubbio has no good wines, but there are local herbal poisons like Amaro Iguvium and Liquore Ingieno to round off a meal.

Taverna del Lupo, Via Ansidei 21a, **t** 075 927 4368 (*expensive*). Excellent, traditional fare served up in an atmospheric medieval setting, including boar sausage, game during the autumn, and *tartufi passatelli* (Gubbio, like Piedmont, is a land of white truffles), as well as delicious pasta dishes such as lasagne with *prosciutto* and truffles, and *frico*, a local speciality of mixed meats with cress. *Closed Mon except public hols, Aug and Sept.*

La Fornace di Mastro Giorgio, Via Mastro Giorgio, **t** 075 922 1836 (*expensive*). A classic local restaurant situated in the workshop where the master ceramicist once created his famous ruby glaze. The unusual menu includes some of Umbria's more esoteric specialities. *Closed Tues and Weds lunch and 10–31 Jan.*

Alla Balestra, Via della Repubblica 41, **t** 075 927 3810 (*moderate*). Unusual *antipasti* (*aringa*), dishes such as *fondutina con tartufo*, home-made pasta and a good selection of meats. *Closed Tues.*

S. Francesco e Il Lupo, Via Cairoli 24, **t** 075 927 2344 (*moderate*). Local products, *porcini* mushrooms, truffles and pizza. *Closed Tues.*

Funivia, on Monte Ingino, **t** 075 922 1259 (*cheap*). A place combining great views (on clear days) with delicious pasta with truffles or *porcini*, and tasty *secondi* such as grilled lamb or stuffed pigeon. There are also good desserts and local wines. *Closed Weds.*

Gubbio, from the Bottom Up

Approaching Gubbio from the west, you'll see the large, well-preserved 1st-century AD **Roman theatre** (***t*** *075 922 0992; open daily Apr–Sept 8.30–7.30, Oct–Mar 8–1.30*), now used for summer performances of classical plays and Shakespeare. Lower Gubbio proper is entered by way of green **Piazza dei Quaranta Martiri**, named in memory of 40 citizens executed by Nazis in reprisals for partisan activities. To the right, mid 13th-century **San Francesco** (***t*** *075 927 3460; call ahead to visit*) has a fine triple apse and some good, if damaged, frescoes, especially the series on the Life of the Virgin (1408–13) in the left apse by Gubbio's International Gothic master Ottaviano Nelli. On the other side of the piazza is the **Loggia dei Tiratori**, Weavers' Loggia, a 14th-century arcade under which newly woven textiles could be stretched to shrink evenly.

From the piazza, picturesque medieval lanes line the banks of the rushing Camignano river. Many of the houses and modest *palazzi* here date back to the 13th century, and are here and there adorned with carved doors or windows, or an extra door called the *Porta del Morto*, which was used solely to remove the dead. The main street, Via dei Consoli, passes by one of Gubbio's finest buildings, the 14th-century **bargello**, the police station and governor's office; its fountain used to be Gubbio's main water source. Further up, the street widens to form magnificent **Piazza della Signoria**, occupying a ledge of the hill over a steep drop and a stunning view of the town below.

The king of the piazza is the beautiful **Palazzo dei Consoli**, a lofty, graceful town hall that was begun in 1332 by Gubbio's master architect, Gattapone. Supported on the hill by a mighty substructure of arches, the *palazzo* is graced with an elegant loggia, a slender campanile, Guelph crenellations, and asymmetrically arranged windows and arches. Inside it houses three museums (***t** 075 927 4298; open daily Apr–Sept 10–1 and 3–6; Oct–Mar 10–1 and 2–5; closed 13–15 May, 25 Dec and 1 Jan; adm*). The **Museo Archeologico** has an Etruscan and Roman collection, while the **Museo Civico** has a variety of archaeological odds and ends and a unique treasure, the bronze Eugubine Tablets, which were discovered in the 15th century near the Roman theatre. These are the only extant records ever found in the Umbrian language, five written in Etruscan characters, the other two in Latin letters – they concern priestly rites and auguries. A stiff climb up the stairs leads to the **Pinacoteca**, containing some of Gubbio's ceramics and a collection of art spanning the centuries. Most memorable, however, is the grand view from the loggia.

Further up stands Gubbio's simple **Duomo**, built in the 13th century and most notable for the pattern of its stone vaulting and its 12th-century stained-glass windows. Local talent is well represented in the side chapels, and in the presbytery there's a Nativity attributed to Pinturicchio's talented student Eusebio di San Giorgio. The high altar is a Roman sarcophagus. Opposite, the **Palazzo Ducale** (***t** 075 927 5872; open Thurs–Tues 8.30–7; adm in summer*) was designed for Federico da Montefeltro by Luciano Laurana, as a more compact version of the ducal palace in Urbino. The courtyard is well worth a look.

From the Duomo you can make the stiff climb up Monte Ingino to the sanctuary of **Sant'Ubaldo**, but it's much easier to take the funicular (***t** 075 927 3881; open summer 9–7; winter 10–1 and 2.30–5*) up from the Porta Romana on the southeast side of town. In Sant'Ubaldo you can examine the three *ceri*, and see that it's no wonder that the Gubbites need considerable Dutch courage to run up the mountain lugging these towers on their shoulders. There's a café where you can while away the afternoon, or you can walk further up for even more spectacular views from the **Rocca** (2,913ft).

Two churches near Porta Romana and the lower funicular station contain some of the finest works by Gubbio's Ottaviano Nelli. In **Santa Maria Nuova** is the lovely, joyous *Madonna del Belvedere*, Nelli's masterpiece from 1403 (*visitors need permission from the Sovrintendenza di Perugia,* ***t*** *075 57411, or try asking at the tourist office*). The 13th-century **Sant'Agostino**, just outside the gate, has some more fine frescoes by Nelli and his students in the apse.

Via Flaminia: Gualdo Tadino to Spoleto

Whether you're travelling by car, bus or train, the eastern Umbrian towns along the ancient Via Flaminia (SS3) offer both lovely scenery and monuments, including some unexpected artistic treasures. Admittedly, most people don't know about Foligno's cosmic billiard table, but many have heard of Spoleto's **Two Worlds Festival**, the concept of which has given birth to a twin Spoleto festival in Charleston, North Carolina. Spoleto is also one of Umbria's loveliest hill towns, while Nocera Umbra, Trevi, Montefalco and Clitunno are small but worthy destinations in between.

Gualdo Tadino and Nocera Umbra

Gualdo Tadino is a lofty little town in which the Byzantine eunuch general Narses defeated the Goths in 552 – a battle essential in preserving the Marches for the Eastern Church. It has taken some big blows from earthquakes: the one in 1751 felled many public buildings, and the 1997–8 ones were pretty bad too. Some paintings by native Matteo da Gualdo (15th century) are displayed in the Rocca Flea's **Museo Civico**, along with ceramics. The town's latest project is the **Museum of Emigration** in the Palazzo del Podestà (***t** 075 914 2445; call for opening hours*); the earthquakes are reason enough to leave the area, and many people have.

From Gualdo the road descends the Valle del Topino (Little Mouse Valley) to **Nocera Umbra**, famous for its sparkling mineral water. It was at the epicentre of the 1997–8 quakes, and it's still a mess – virtually a ghost town, in fact. The *centro storico* is cordoned off, with access only during the day. Inside the barrier, every other building seems to be propped up with heavy scaffolding or steel girders. Some 6,000 people, as well as offices and banks, are still accommodated in containers and prefab housing. The surrounding hills are dotted with cranes and abandoned buildings.

Foligno

Foligno is an ancient and important town, once Roman *Fulginia*, and subsequently one of the earliest printing centres in Italy, producing copies of the first book in Italian (Dante's *Divina Commedia*) in 1470. But the 20th century was rough on Foligno, which was bombed to smithereens in the Second World War. Some of the old quarter survived, including central Piazza della Repubblica, but this took a walloping in September 1997, when Foligno, the centre of the cosmos, became the epicentre of the quake. Thousands around the world watched as its medieval Torre Comunale collapsed in one of the aftershocks. It is still being restored, and the town has a dreary, defeated feel, with many *palazzi* under scaffolding.

The 14th-century Palazzo dei Signori, the Trinci, is now a **Pinacoteca** (***t** 0742 357 989; open Tues–Sun 10–7; adm*); in its chapel are more works by Gubbio's Ottaviano Nelli. The nearby **Duomo** has retained an impressive south front of 1201, which rates as one of the most unorthodox in Italy: among the zodiac, monsters and medieval bestiary is a portrait of Emperor Frederick II, arch-enemy of the popes, and even a little Islamic star and crescent. The oldest thing in Foligno is the Romanesque **Santa Maria Infraportas**, with 12th-century frescoes in the Byzantine style.

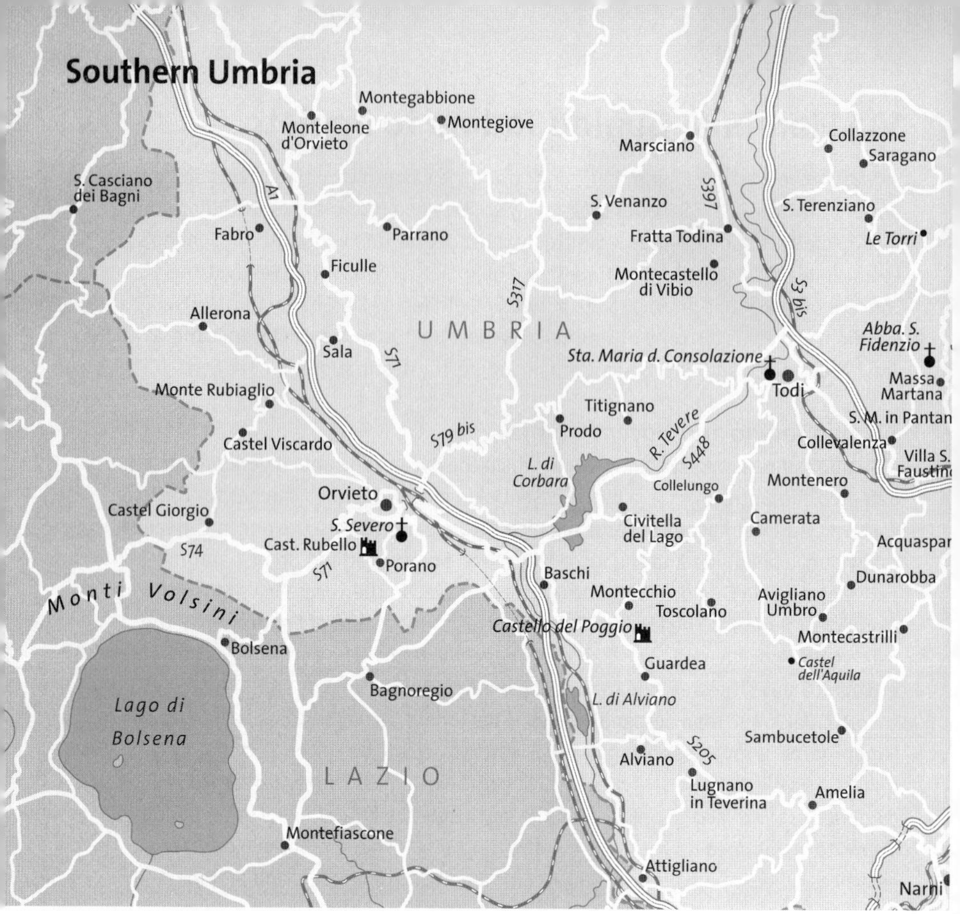

Foligno takes its Giostra della Quintana on 14–15 June very seriously: 'knights' from 10 rival districts of the town, dressed in medieval costumes, compete in jousting matches, the streets are decked in flags, and there are other games, a fair, parades and outdoor taverns. On 14–15 Sept the teams return for a rematch. The **Museo dei Tornei, delle Giostre e dei Giochi** at Porta Romana (***t*** *0742 354 694; open Tues–Sun summer 10–1 and 4–8, winter 10–1 and 3–7*) has displays about the town's tradition of medieval pageantry, as well as similar jousts and tournaments around the world.

More interesting than Foligno itself are the sites that surround it, all linked to the city by bus, with the exception of the 13th-century **Abbazia di Sassovivo** (*closed for restoration*) an hour's walk to the east (or a five-minute drive over the Via Flaminia towards Casale), with its serene cloister. The area beyond, up the Menotre valley, was hit especially hard by the earthquakes: while collapsed buildings have been cleared, scaffolding and cranes are still everywhere.

Southwest lie three charming hill towns. **Bevagna** has two Romanesque churches, San Silvestro (*open daily 9.30–12 and 3–7*) and San Michele Arcangelo (*closed*), in Piazza Silvestri, a medieval and theatrical pièce de résistance that also contains a Corinthian column, a fountain and the Gothic Palazzo Comunale of 1270, housing a theatre. At its highest point, the 13th-century church of San Francesco holds the stone on which St

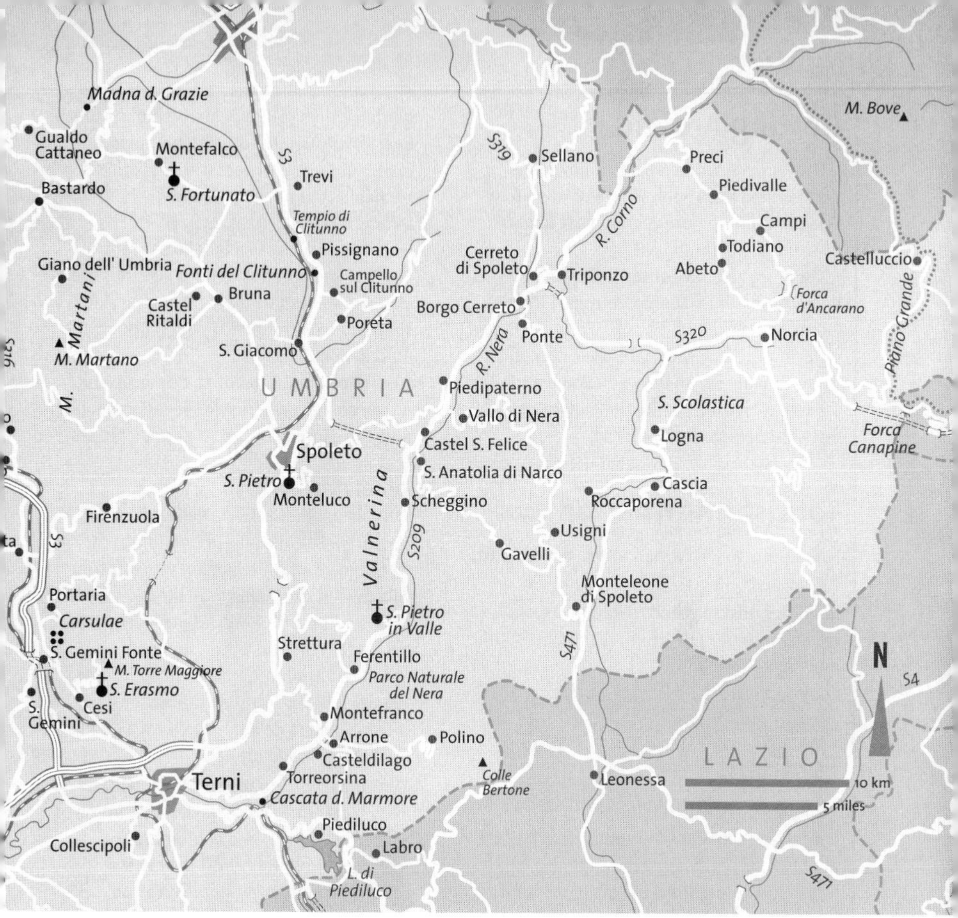

Francis stood when he preached to the birds. The other towns are tiny medieval **Gualdo Cattaneo** and old **Montefalco**, called the 'Balcony Rail (*Ringhiera*) of Umbria' because of its commanding position. The pride of Montefalco is its rich 15th-century fresco cycle on the Life of St Francis by Benozzo Gozzoli, painted in the apse of the church-museum of **San Francesco** (***t*** *0742 379 598; open Mar–May, Sept and Oct daily 10.30–1 and 2–6; June and July daily 10.30–1 and 3–7; Aug daily 10.30–1 and 3–7.30; Nov–Feb Tues–Sun 10.30–1 and 2.30–5*). Above the church the attractive, round **Piazza della Repubblica** affords excellent views of the countryside, especially from the tower of the Palazzo Comunale. Most of Montefalco's other churches contain good frescoes as well, especially **Sant'Agostino**, near the frescoed main gate **Porta Sant'Agostino**, and **San Fortunato**, beyond the Porta Spoleto, which boasts a few Gozzolis of its own.

Trevi, just on the eastern side of the main road, is another charming hill town, wrapped in olive groves that produce Umbria's rich green oil (buses link the train station with the town up above). Its name, like that of the famous fountain in Rome, is derived from *Tre Via*, or Three Roads. Its tight, narrow streets contain the medieval buildings dating from its time as a free *comune*, while just south is the 15th-century church of **Madonna delle Lacrime** (*closed for restoration*), sheltering a fresco of the Adoration of the Magi by the ever-sceptical 76-year-old Perugino. In town, the Palazzo

Getting Around

The Rome–Ancona **railway** follows the Via Flaminia from Spoleto all the way up to Gualdo Tadino, before veering east towards Jesi and Ancona.

There are also SSIT **buses** (**t** 0743 212 208) linking Spoleto to Gualdo, Perugia, Città di Castello and Gubbio.

During the **Due Mondi** festival, special trains and buses run between Rome and Spoleto to accommodate the crowds of festival-goers from the capital.

Tourist Information

Foligno: Corso Cavour 126, **t** 0742 354 459/165.

The earthquake left many of Foligno's buildings unstable, and restoration work is still in progress, despite what the tourist office may say to the contrary.

Spoleto: Piazza della Libertà 7, **t** 0743 220 311.

Festivals

Spoleto's Festival dei Due Mondi is a world-renowned feast of music, theatre and dance held over 3wks between mid-June and mid-July. Contact the Associazione Festival dei Due Mondi, Piazza del Duomo, freephone within Italy **t** 800 565 600, or **t** 0743 44700, *www.spoletofestival.net* for information, programmes and tickets.

Where to Stay and Eat

Foligno ✉ 06034

***** **Villa Roncalli**, Viale Roma 25, just south of the centre, **t** 0742 391 091 (*moderate*). A fashionable 17th-century villa hotel with a shady garden and a swimming pool, as well as the city's finest restaurant (*expensive*), serving gourmet Umbrian dishes. *Closed Mon and 2wks Aug.*

**** **Belvedere**, Via F. Ottaviani 19, **t** 0742 353 990 (*cheap*). A family-run place near the station, with pleasant rooms.

Osteria del Teatro, Via Petrucci 8, **t** 0742 350 745 (*expensive*). A delightful restaurant with a vaulted ceiling, theatre posters and a garden where you can eat zucchini fritters, deep-fried sage, ravioli with pumpkin, and excellent lamb and beef (the *tagliata* is particularly good). *Closed Weds.*

Da Remo, Via F. Filzi 10, **t** 0742 340 522 (*moderate*). A classic place to eat for the last four generations, set in a Liberty-style villa and serving *strangozzi* and roast kid simmered in Montefalco's Sagrantino wine. *Closed Mon.*

Bacco Felice, Via Garibaldi 73, **t** 0742 341 019. A cosy *enoteca* where wine-lovers can while away an evening over bottles and cheeses.

Montefalco ✉ 06036

****** **Villa Pambuffetti**, Via della Vittoria 20, **t** 0742 378 823, *www.villapambuffetti.com* (*very expensive*). A delightful 19th-century villa owned by a noble local family, with 15 rooms, some with antiques. Its lovely park has huge trees and an outdoor pool.

**** **Ringhiera Umbra**, Corso G. Mameli, **t** 0742 379 166 (*cheap*). A comfortable choice just south of Piazza del Comune, with a good restaurant (*moderate*).

Montefalco is perhaps best known for its red wines, Sagrantino – with its delicate aroma of blackberries – and Rosso di Montefalco.

Coccorone, Vicolo Fabbri, off the central square, **t** 0742 379 535 (*moderate*). An elegant, understated place with tempting crêpes and *tagliatelle al tartufo* as starters and *faraona in salmì* (braised woodcock) and grilled pigeon as main dishes. *Closed Weds.*

Il Falisco, Via XX Settembre 14, **t** 0742 379 185 (*cheap*). Local specialities such as *filetto al Sagrantino* (beef fillet cooked in Sagrantino wine). *Closed Mon.*

Trevi ✉ 06039

If you come to Trevi in Oct, try its famous *sedano nero* (black celery).

**** **Il Pescatore**, Via Chiesa Tonda 50, **t** 0742 381 711 (*cheap*). A peaceful *pensione* with 9 pleasant rooms, near a brook. Its excellent restaurant, **Taverna del Pescatore**, **t** 0742 780 920 (*moderate*), has imaginative menus based on meat or fish, both very good value and beautifully prepared. *Closed Weds.*

*** **Il Terziere**, Via Salerno 1, **t** 0742 78359 (*cheap*). A budget option with attractive views and good dinners.

Campello sul Clitunno ✉ 06042

This town provides a quiet alternative to Spoleto if you've come for the festival.

★★★**Vecchio Molino**, Via del Tempio 34, Loc. Pissignano, **t** 0743 521 122 (*expensive*). An old mill with two streams running through the garden. *Closed Nov–Mar.*

★★**Fontanelle**, Via d'Elci 1, Loc. Fontanelle, **t** 0743 521 091 (*cheap*). A hotel and restaurant (*moderate*) surrounded by greenery. The Umbrian specialities include country *prosciutto*, *strangozzi* ,and platters of tender lamb, chicken and pigeon.

★★**Ravale**, Via Virgilio, Fonti del Clitunno, **t** 0743 521 320 (*cheap*). Simple rooms, and a modest *ristorante-pizzeria* (*moderate*).

Spoleto ✉ 06049

During the festival accommodation is tight in Spoleto and the area from Foligno to Terni, so reserve months in advance. The tourist office in Spoleto has a list of private rooms and *agriturismo*, or try Con-Spoleto (**t** 0743 220 773, *www.conspoleto.com*).

★★★★**Gattapone**, Via del Ponte 6, **t** 0743 223 447 (*very expensive*). A serene stone house clinging to the slope near the Rocca and the Ponte delle Torri, with fabulous views.

★★★★**Albornoz Palace**, Viale Matteotti 10, **t** 0743 221 221, *www.albornozpalace.com* (*moderate–very expensive*). A refined and stylish option with its own contemporary art collection and a pool, just outside the historic centre near Piazza della Libertà.

★★★★**Dei Duchi**, Viale Matteotti 4, **t** 0743 44541, *www.deiduchi.com* (*moderate–expensive*). An attractive modern hotel, popular with festival performers.

★★★**Charleston**, Piazza Collicola 10, **t** 0743 220 052 (*cheap–moderate*). A pretty 17th-century *palazzo* in the *centro storico*, with 18 comfortably furnished rooms.

★★★**Clarici**, Piazza della Vittoria 32, **t** 0743 223 311 (*cheap–moderate*). A newer option in the lower part of town, decorated with style.

★★★**La Macchia**, Loc. Licina 11, **t** 0743 49059 (*cheap–moderate*). A quiet hotel just north of the centre, off Via Flaminia. The modern furniture in the 12 bedrooms is made by local craftspeople. The restaurant specializes in *cucina spoletana*, and there's a lovely garden that you can sit in.

★★**Dell'Angelo**, Via Arco di Druso 25, **t** 0743 222 385 (*cheap*). A decent choice in the centre of town, offering 7 double rooms.

★★**Il Panciolle**, Via Duomo 4, **t** 0743 45677 (*cheap*). A hotel that's worth bearing in mind for its good restaurant (*moderate*), where meat is grilled over an open fire. *Closed Weds.*

Apollinare, Via S. Agata 14, **t** 0743 223 256 (*expensive*). A series of romantic dining rooms set in a 12th-century Franciscan convent, serving elaborate concoctions such as fillet of suckling pig with *pecorino* sauce. There are a few rooms to stay in too. *Closed Tues.*

Il Tartufo, Piazza Garibaldi 24, **t** 0743 40236 (*moderate–expensive*). A restaurant where the black diamonds of the Valnerina (*tartufi*) appear in various forms: the duck breast with potatoes and truffles is well worth trying. Other dishes include grilled lamb, kid and veal. Prices depend on your level of indulgence. *Closed Sun eve, Mon and last 2wks Jan and July.*

Il Pentagramma, Via Martani 4, **t** 0743 223 141 (*moderate*). A welcoming festival favourite situated in a former stable close to Piazza della Libertà, owned by the daughter of Arturo Toscanini. The local dishes include *garbanzo* soup, *strangozzi di Spoleto* (pasta with olive oil, garlic, tomato and basil), truffles, lamb and trout. *Closed Mon and part of Jan and Aug.*

Trattoria Pecchiarda, Vicolo San Giovanni, **t** 0743 221 009 (*moderate*). A good place tucked away off Via Porta Fuga, serving delicious dishes prepared with olive oil from the owner's grove, plus his own white and red Colli Spoletini wine. *Closed Thurs except summer.*

Monteluco ✉ 06049

★★★**Michelangelo**, **t** 0743 40289 (*cheap*). A hotel with large rooms and very friendly staff, near the top of town. *Closed Nov–Mar.*

★★★**Paradiso**, **t** 0743 223 427 (*cheap*). A hotel offering a garden, great views, and peace and quiet.

★★**Ferretti**, **t** 0743 49849 (*cheap–moderate*). A *pensione* with plenty of charm. Some rooms have balconies looking out on to the pretty tree-shaded piazza.

Lucarini now hosts the **Trevi Flash Art Museum** (*t 0742 381 818; open Weds–Fri 3–7, Sat and Sun 10–1 and 3–7 during exhibitions; adm*), a joint endeavour of *Flash Art* magazine and the *comune*, offering a permanent collection of contemporary Umbrian, Italian and foreign artists, as well as changing exhibitions.

The convent of the church of San Francesco – on the site where Francis's preaching was drowned out by the braying of an 'indomitable ass' that he subdued with his words – houses the **Museo Civico** (*t 0742 381 628; open Apr, May and Sept Tues–Sun 10.30–1 and 2.30–6; June and July Tues–Sun 10.30–1 and 3.30–7; Aug daily 10.30–1 and 3–7.30; Oct–Mar Fri–Sun 10.30–1 and 2.30–5; adm*) and its paintings: a Madonna by Pinturicchio, a Deposition by the school of Sodoma, and a fine Incoronazione di Maria by Lo Spagna.

Further south, just off the Via Flaminia, the **Fonti del Clitunno** (*t 0743 521 141; call for opening times*), ancient *Clitumnus*, is famous for its snow-cold clear spring and pool, though it's now a bit of a coach-tour paradise. The ancient Romans built villas on the surrounding hillside, and bred pure white oxen on its dark green banks. The Roman villas and temples that stood here are long gone, but bits were reassembled in a mysterious little building, the **Tempietto del Clitunno**, just north of the Fonti (*t 0743 275 085; open Tues–Sun summer 8.45–7.45; winter until 6; adm*). Two centuries ago, this was believed to be a pagan temple converted to Christian use. Goethe thought it an original Christian work, and for once this most misinformed of geniuses got it right. The most recent studies put it somewhere in the 6th century, or even as late as the 8th, making the obscure, lovely building in a way the last work of classical antiquity, Christian enough, but an architectural throwback to a world that was already lost.

Spoleto

Set among thickly wooded hills, ancient Spoleto is one of the most attractive towns in Italy, providing, in its well-preserved monuments, a nearly complete history of the peninsula. At night, when its landmarks are illuminated and its lights twinkle, it's magical, a setting fit for the dynamic **Festival dei Due Mondi** (Two Worlds Festival), founded by composer Gian Carlo Menotti and the late Thomas Schippers in 1958, now Italy's most important performing arts festival. The annual influx of international culture has left a mark on this once drowsy hill town: monuments have been restored, art galleries and trendy shops line the medieval streets, and prices, during the three weeks of the festival (between mid-June and mid-July) get knocked way out of line.

Ancient Umbrian *Spoletium* was settled by the Romans in 242 BC, a few decades before an over-confident Hannibal came knocking at the gates, expecting an easy victory after his rout at Lake Trasimeno. But Spoletium held firm and repulsed him, and Hannibal, who intended to move on to Rome from there, took his elephants to graze in the Marches instead. The Goths under Totila wrecked the city, while the Lombards, slowly piecing it back together, made it a powerful duchy – so powerful that in 890 Duke Guido III made an armed play for the imperial crown against the heirs of Charlemagne; later the duchy became a fief of Countess Matilda of Tuscany, the Guelphest of Guelphs, and in the 13th century it was incorporated into the Papal

States. In 1499 it was ruled by Lucrezia Borgia, a 19-year-old recently married to the second of her three husbands by her intriguing father. By all accounts Lucrezia did well, but she was sent off two years later to marry Alfonso d'Este of Ferrara.

If you arrive by train you're greeted by a huge iron sculpture by Alexander Calder, a relic of the 1962 festival now shading a taxi stand. Buses every 10 minutes link the station to central **Piazza della Libertà**, with the tourist office and the nearby **Roman theatre** (*open daily 8.30–7.30; adm*), some 380ft in diameter, built in the 1st century AD and restored for festival performances. The stage structure was removed in the Middle Ages and replaced by the Convent of Sant'Agata, which houses the **Museo Archeologico** (***t*** *0743 223 277; open daily 8.30–7.30; adm*), with inscriptions and architectural fragments, and busts of Caesar, Augustus and other distinguished Romans. More Roman memories are nearby, beyond Piazza Fontana: the **Arco di Druso e Germanico**, built in AD 23 to celebrate a victory over the barbarians. This marked the entrance to the Roman forum, now Piazza del Mercato, but before you get there take the steps down to the 12th-century crypt of **San Isacco**, with its rare Byzantine-style frescoes. The church above, **Sant'Ansano** (***t*** *0743 40305; open daily Apr–Oct 7.30–12 amd 3–5.30, until 6.30 Nov–Mar; adm*), was built into a Roman temple, remains of which may be seen near the altar. In Piazza del Mercato the landmark is an 18th-century fountain incorporating Carlo Maderno's 1626 monument to Urban VII.

The next square, pretty Piazza Municipio, contains a **Roman house** believed to have once been that of Emperor Vespasian's mother, with an atrium, bedrooms and baths, some with mosaics. The **Pinacoteca** (***t*** *0743 43707; open daily mid-Mar–mid-Oct 10–8; rest of year 10.30–1 and 3–6.30; adm*), with works by Giovanni di Pietro (Lo Spagna), L'Alunno and other Umbriani, is in the Palazzo Rosari-Spada on Corso Mazzini.

The Rocca and Ponte delle Torri

From the Piazza del Municipio, Via Saffi climbs up to Piazza Campello, which has a 17th-century fountain called the **Mascherone** because of its grotesque face. Above this looms the **Rocca** (***t*** *0743 43707; call for opening times*), the impressive six-towered castle that was built by Gattapone for the 14th-century papal legate, Cardinal Albornoz. It is built of third-hand stone, first used in the Roman amphitheatre and later cannibalized by the Goth supremo Totila for his own fortress.

The Rocca was a popular papal resort frequented by Julius II, accompanied on occasion by Michelangelo, who loved the peace of the surrounding hills. Until 1983 it was used as a prison; now that its long restoration is nearing completion, there are plans to install a museum dedicated to the Duchy of Spoleto, a lab for the restoration of books and art, an exhibition and conference area, and an open-air theatre.

For now, the best thing to do is stroll along the garden walk that encircles the Rocca, with great views of Spoleto below. The **Porta della Rocca** leads down to Master Gattapone's masterpiece, and one of the great engineering works of the trecento, the **Ponte delle Torri**, a bridge and aqueduct of 10 towering arches linking Spoleto with the slopes of Monteluco, spanning a 260ft ravine and the Tessino river far below. Gattapone built the bridge on a Roman foundation; it leads to the towers that gave it its name, and to the road for San Pietro and San Francesco (*see* p.737).

Sant'Eufemia and the Duomo

Below the Rocca on Via Saffi stands the pure and lovely 12th-century **Sant'Eufemia** (*t 0743 231 041; open Apr–Sept Mon and Weds–Sat 10–1 and 4–7, Sun 10.30–1 and 3–6; Oct–Mar Mon and Weds–Sat 10–12.30 and 3–6, Sun 11–5; adm*), with a dignified façade and beautiful Romanesque interior of ancient capitals and columns, a *matroneum* (women's gallery) and picturesque vaults. Next door is the dramatic **Via dell'Arringo**, a grand stairway descending to **Piazza del Duomo**, which must have been what sold Menotti when he travelled about seeking a venue for the Two Worlds Festival: it doubles perfectly as an outdoor auditorium for concerts, with the cathedral and Umbrian hills as a backdrop. Thomas Schippers, co-founder of the festival, was so fond of the concerts and piazza that he asked to be buried here when he died, in 1977.

The elegant **Duomo** (*t 0743 44307; open daily Mar–Oct 7.30–12.30 and 3–6; Nov–Feb until 5*) was consecrated in 1198 by the most powerful of medieval popes, Innocent III, having been rebuilt after Emperor Frederick Barbarossa – the greatest of papal enemies – had razed its predecessor. It has several unusual features: four rose windows and four circular emblems of the Evangelists of varying sizes, like buttons, adorn its horizontally divided façade, surrounding a gold-ground Byzantine-style mosaic of 1207. Its campanile is built out of Roman odds and ends, and some very un-Italian flying buttresses help to hold it up.

Though the interior was re-done in the 17th century, it contains several treasures, most piously the 12th century *Santissimo Icone*, with a picture of the Madonna, brought to Spoleto from Constantinople. Pinturicchio painted the frescoes in the first chapel, the Eroli, and the apse contains lovely frescoes on the Life of the Virgin by Fra Filippo Lippi, who portrayed himself among the mourners in the scene of the Virgin's death. The fun-loving monk from Florence died in Spoleto while working on the project, and it was finished by his chief helper, Fra Diamanti; when Lorenzo de' Medici asked that Lippi's body be returned to Florence, the Spoletini refused, and Lorenzo had to be content with ordering a fine Florentine tomb for him, now in the right transept.

Lower Spoleto

On the opposite side of town (Via del Duomo to Via Filitteria) there's another grand theatre, the **Teatro Nuovo**, headquarters of the Two Worlds Festival and the even older September Festival of Experimental Opera. Nearby, the colourful church of **San Domenico** (*closed for restoration*), built in the 1200s, contains some interesting if fragmentary frescoes. From San Domenico you can walk down to the tall-towered 13th-century **Porta Fuga**, then along Via Cecili, to take in an excellent stretch of Spoleto's **walls**, an intriguing record of the town's history, beginning at their 6th-century BC 'Cyclopean' base of huge polygonal rough blocks built by the ancient Umbrii, and going all the way up to the 15th-century additions on the top.

The street ends at Piazza Cairoli; from here Via dell'Anfiteatro descends past the ruined **amphitheatre**, now part of a barracks, to Piazza Garibaldi, with the fine 12th-century church of **San Gregorio** (*t 0743 44140; open daily 9–12 and 3.30–6*) and the Roman **Ponte Sanguinario** ('bloody bridge'), supposedly named after the Christians martyred in the amphitheatre. From the bridge, signs point the way to the cemetery church of **San Salvatore** (*t 0743 49606; open daily Mar, Apr, Sept and Oct 7–6; May–Aug 7–7; Nov–Feb 7–5*), a 15-minute walk. Built in the 4th century, it has an unusual façade, and preserves many of its original vertical lines and its simplicity, despite subsequent rebuildings. The elegant, fluted Corinthian columns inside were incorporated from a Roman temple.

Monteluco

Beautiful, forested Monteluco is Spoleto's holy mountain, lying just to the east of town, connected by bus from the Piazza della Libertà, or by walking from the Ponte delle Torri. If you're walking, take the right-hand fork for the Romanesque church of **San Pietro** (*t 0743 44882; open daily 9–11 and 3.30–6.30; in the afternoon ring the custodian's bell near the church*), only a few minutes away, with a romp of a façade dating back to the dukes of Spoleto. If you've visited the medieval cathedrals of the north you'll recognize the animals, real and imaginary, that the Lombards delighted in portraying: here is a fox playing dead to capture some too-curious chickens, battles with lions, oxen, eagles, a wolf in monk's clothing, and the rest.

The other (left) fork in the road demands vigorous walking through holm oak forests to reach the 12th-century church of **San Giuliano** (*call Padre Bonaventura Vergari on **t** 0743 40711, or ask at San Francesco*), with a façade incorporating some 6th-century elements of its predecessor. Anchorites and hermits, refugees from the wars in the Holy Land, settled here in the 7th century; in the 13th century St Francis and San Bernardino of Siena came to meditate here, and St Francis founded the tiny monastery of **San Francesco** near Monteluco's summit, a serene spot with a lovely view of the surrounding countryside. Monteluco now has more summer villas and hotels than hermitages, but it's still a cool and tranquil place to spend an afternoon, and a good place to look for accommodation.

The Valnerina

The Nera, one of the main tributaries of the Tiber, flows from the mighty Monti Sibillini along the southern edge of Umbria. Many of its sights are still Italian secrets; its black truffles, waterfalls and saints enjoy a national reputation, but the rest is touristically *terra incognita*.

Norcia and Cascia

Little Norcia gave the world St Benedict (480–543), the father of monasticism, and his twin sister St Scolastica. It has also been known at times for its witches, barber surgeons (who, in the 16th century, were the only ones capable of properly castrating a boy with operatic potential), cheeses and boar hams (in Umbria, a *norcineria* is a cheese and ham shop). An ancient place, mentioned by Virgil, it looks more Spanish than Italian, and, although earthquakes have slapped it around, old Norcia survives around central Piazza San Benedetto. It has a stern statue of St Benedict for a

Getting Around

Terni and Narni are the only Valnerina towns served by **rail**. Both are on the Rome–Ancona line, and from Terni there are also trains to Rieti in Lazio and L'Aquila in Abruzzo.

Frequent SSIT **buses** (*see* p.732) leave Spoleto's Piazza della Repubblica for Cascia and Norcia; others go to Scheggino, where you can catch a Terni provincial bus down the rest of the valley to Terni, Narni or Orvieto. From Terni, ATC buses, **t** 0744 492 711, go to Narni, Piediluco, Arrone, Ferentillo and Scheggino, and also to Orvieto. However, this valley is one where you're best off with a **car**.

Tourist Information

Terni (regional office): Viale C. Battisti 7/a, **t** 0744 423 047, *open Mon–Fri 9–1, Tues and Thurs also 3–6*.
Norcia: in the Municipio, **t** 0743 828 173.
Cascia: Piazza Garibaldi, **t** 0743 71147.
Narni: Piazza dei Priori 3, **t** 0744 715 362
Amelia: Via Orvieto 1, **t** 0744 981 453.

Where to Stay and Eat

Norcia ✉ 06046

*****Nuovo Hotel Posta**, Via C. Battisti 10, **t** 0743 817 434 (*moderate*). A fine establishment with pleasant rooms. The restaurant serves robust fare: Castelluccio lentils, boar salami and the like, topped off by tumblers of local grappa flavoured with black truffles.

*****Grotta Azzurra**, Via Alfieri, **t** 0743 816 513 (*moderate*). A good stopover with a restaurant in which the mandatory truffled dishes compete with a tasty risotto with crayfish from the Nera, fettuccine with trout, and delicious grilled mushrooms. *Closed Tues.*

Dal Francese, Via Riguardati 16, **t** 0743 816 290 (*moderate*). Bumper meals of smoked turkey and home-made salami *antipasto*, pasta medleys of *tris al tartufo*, *gnocchi al tartufo* and *tortellini con crema di tordi* (thrushes) *e tartufi*; trout, tender grilled lamb; and the unusual *braciola in agrodolce con tartufi* (sweet-and-sour chop with truffles). The wine list is good. *Closed Fri except summer.*

Cascia ✉ 06043

*****Cursula**, Via Cavour 3, **t** 0743 76206 (*moderate*). Extremely pleasant rooms and good Umbrian home cooking.

****Mini Hotel La Tavernetta**, Via Palombi, **t** 0743 76303 (*cheap*). A family-run place offering clean comfortable rooms and a good restaurant (*moderate*) where you can feast on well-cooked local dishes based on wild mushrooms, salami, trout and lamb. *Closed Tues.*

Scheggino ✉ 06040

****Del Ponte**, Via Borgo 15, **t** 0743 61253 (*cheap*). A charming little hotel on the Nera river, offering 12 rooms with bath, and delicious meals in the restaurant (*moderate*), based on crayfish and truffles (try the fettucine with a sauce of both). *Closed Mon.*

Ferentillo ✉ 05034

******Abbazia San Pietro in Valle**, Loc. Macenaro, **t** 0744 780 129, *www.sanpietroinvalle.com* (*expensive*). A very peaceful hotel and restaurant in the old abbey (*see* p.740), with elegantly furnished rooms in the old monks' quarters, some of them frescoed. *Open 22 Mar–27 Oct.*

*****Fontegaia**, Montefranco, on SS209 towards Ferentillo, **t** 0744 388 621 (*moderate*). Very comfy rooms, a children's playground and beautiful gardens for alfresco dining. The

centrepiece, the 14th-century church of **San Benedetto**, built over the late Roman house where the famous twins were born, and the handsome **Palazzo Comunale**, with a 13th-century campanile, next door to shops decked with bristling hams. The other side of the square is occupied by the **Castellina** (*t 0743 817 030; June, July and Sept daily 10–1 and 4–7; 1–20 Aug daily 9.30am–11pm; rest of Aug daily 10–1 and 4–7.30; Oct–Apr Tues–Sun 10–1 and 3–5*), designed in 1554 by Vignola for Pope Julius III, now housing a modest museum of Umbrian art.

restaurant is a favourite with locals on special occasions, though the creamy sauces can be a bit overwhelming.

★★★**Monterivoso**, Via Case Sparse 5, Loc. Monterivoso, **t** 0744 780 772 (*cheap*). An old mill with antiques-furnished rooms looking out over a lawn and an excellent restaurant serving the unusual *struzzo* (ostrich) *al marsala* and more. *Restaurant closed Mon, and Tues–Thurs lunch.*

Piermarini, Via della Vittoria 53, **t** 0744 780 714 (*moderate*). A wonderful restaurant serving local dishes as 'la nonna' (granny) would make them, including *coratina di agnello* (lamb's innards) with wild asparagus, lamb cutlets *scottadita* ('burn your fingers') served with olive focaccia, fresh-water trout and river crayfish. In autumn there are mushrooms and chestnuts.

Arrone ✉ 05031

★★**Rossi**, on the SS209, **t** 0744 388 372 (*cheap*). Sixteen modern en suite rooms, and one of the best restaurants in the area (*moderate*), serving excellent *crostini*, spaghetti with truffles, grilled meats and a variety of trout dishes. In summer you can eat in the pretty garden. Book ahead for the popular and overwhelming seafood feast. *Closed Fri.*

Rema, up the Polino road, by the aqueduct, **t** 0744 389 292 (*cheap*). A fine little trattoria with an outdoor grill and utterly authentic home cooking at old-fashioned prices; make sure to try *ciriole* (home-made spaghetti) with mushrooms and grilled lamb *scottadita*. *Closed Mon.*

Terni ✉ 05100

Terni is a good base for visiting the Valnerina if you're dependent on public transport; it's also worth looking for lodgings here if Spoleto is filled up for the Two Worlds Festival.

★★★★**Valentino**, Via Plinio il Giovane 3, **t** 0744 402 550, *www.hotelvalentinoterni.com* (*expensive*). A central option with comfy modern rooms and one of Terni's classiest restaurants, **La Fontanella**.

★★★★**Garden**, Viale Bramante 6, **t** 0744 300 041, *www.gardenhotelterni.it* (*expensive*). Terni's prettiest hotel, with plant-filled balconies, a pool and all mod cons.

★★★**Hotel de Paris**, Viale Stazione 52, **t** 0744 58047 (*moderate*). A convenient option for the station.

Villa Graziani, Papigno, 4km from town, **t** 0744 67138 (*moderate*). An 18th-century establishment that was once graced by Byron, where you can dine well and fashionably on Umbrian specialities and Italian classics. *Closed Sun eve and Mon.*

Lu Somaru, Viale Cesare Battisti 106, **t** 0744 300 486 (*moderate*). A popular choice on the western edge of the centre, offering Umbrian specialities and dining in the garden in summer. *Closed Fri.*

Narni ✉ 05035

★★★**Dei Priori**, Vicolo del Comune 4, **t** 0744 726 843 (*moderate*). The finest hotel in the centre, in a medieval palace on a narrow lane, with comfy rooms. Its restaurant, **La Loggia**, **t** 0744 722 744, has long been on the maps of visiting gourmets, though its reputation has slipped of late. *Closed Mon.*

★★★**Il Minareto**, Via Cappuccini Nuovi 32, **t** 0744 726 343 (*cheap*). A Moorish-style villa on the outskirts of town, with 8 rooms, a tiny lake and a garden.

Cavallino, Via Flaminia Romana 220, towards Terni, **t** 0744 761 020 (*cheap*). A good old-fashioned inn, with solid Umbrian cookery that has kept folk coming back for more than 30 years, and a few inexpensive rooms. *Closed Tues, and part of July.*

Eighteen kilometres from Norcia lies the beautiful **Piano Grande**, an unusual flat meadow measuring 16 square kilometres and surrounded by rolling hills and mountains that seem covered with huge swathes of coloured velvet in May and June. It is a rarefied landscape (used by Zeffirelli in his 'Franciscan film' *Brother Sun, Sister Moon*), where herds graze and fields produce the famous tiny lentils of **Castelluccio**, the old village in an upper corner of the plain. Castelluccio had 700 permanent inhabitants in 1951, and now has around 40; winter conditions are so bad that the village is often cut off. In summer it attracts plenty of hanggliders and tourists. From the summit of Monte Vettore (8,121ft), the tallest peak in the area, you can see both the Adriatic and Tyrrhenian seas on clear days. In winter there's skiing at Forca Canapine, on the south side of Piano Grande.

Cascia, in the Corno valley south of Norcia, is an even more popular pilgrimage destination, thanks to Santa Rita, the 'Saint of Impossibilities', who was born near here in 1381, and suffered a rotten husband (hence all the tired Italian housewives you see) and a smelly wound in the middle of her forehead, but had to wait until the Fascist era to get a (hideous) sanctuary.

Down the Valnerina: Crayfish and Mummies

Back in the main valley on the SS209, **Scheggino** is a pretty little town on the Nera river, laced with tiny canals full of trout and a rare species of crayfish (*gamberettini*) imported from Turkey. It is also the fief of Italy's truffle tycoons, the Urbanis. Further down the valley is a sign for the abbey of **San Pietro in Valle** (*t 0744 780 316; open daily 10.30–1 and 2.30–6; if the church is locked, the custodian's house is marked on the road up to the abbey*), founded in the 8th century by Faroaldo II, duke of Spoleto. Set far above the road, with views across the valley to an abandoned citadel, it has a lovely 12th-century campanile embedded with Roman bits, and a two-storey cloister with a Roman sacrificial altar in the centre. Inside, the nave is covered with frescoes from 1190 – an unusual example of the Italian response to the Byzantine style. The altar is a rare example of Lombard work, sculpted on both the front and back; one of their early saints is interred to the right in a 3rd-century Roman sarcophagus. On either side of the altar are 13th-century frescoes by the school of Giotto. In the back the cylindrical Etruscan altar is used for monetary rather than animal offerings. Among the stone fragments on the wall is a real rarity – a bas-relief of a monk with oriental features, believed to depict one of two Syrian monks who set up a hermitage here in the 7th century. Their quarters have been coverted into a hotel and restaurant (*see* p.738).

The abbey is in the *comune* of **Ferentillo**, defended by two 14th-century fortresses. In Precetto, the oldest part of town, the crypt of **Santo Stefano** (*t 0743 54395, open daily Apr–Sept 9–12.30 and 2.30–7.30; Mar and Oct 9.30–12.30 and 2.30–6.30; Nov–Feb 10–12.30 and 2.30–5; knock on door marked 'custode' opposite church*) has something you don't expect to find in Umbria: **mummies**. Accidentally preserved by the soil and ventilation, they were Chinese newlyweds who came here on honeymoon in the 18th century and got cholera instead. There are also two gruesome French prisoners hanged in the Napoleonic era, and a grinning pyramid of skulls. A desiccated vulture mummy points the way inside with its wing.

Picturesque **Arrone**, spilling over its rock, was once run by feudal lordlings, the bitter enemies of the abbots of Ferentillo. Their tower, sprouting a tree, is the local landmark. From Arrone, the road leads up to Piediluco and **Polino**, also endowed with a feudal tower and a monumental fountain; above Polino the Colle Bertone affords panoramic picnicking sites.

Cascata delle Marmore and Lake Piediluco

Between Arrone and Terni the road passes below another pretty hill townlet, **Torreorsini**, before reaching the 416ft, green and misty **Cascata delle Marmore**, one of Europe's tallest waterfalls. Surprisingly, this is an artificial but antique creation; in 271 BC Curius Dentatus, conqueror of the Sabines, dug the channel to drain the marshlands of Rieti, diverting the Velino river into the Nera. The falls are usually swallowed up by hydroelectric turbines, but the big waters are let down at regular – though ever-changing – times; after dark they are brilliantly illuminated (***16 Mar–30 Apr:*** *Mon–Fri 12–1 and 4–5, Sat 11–1 and 4–9, Sun 10–1 and 4–9;* ***May:*** *Mon–Fri 12–1 and 4–5, Sat 11–1 and 4–10, Sun 10–1 and 3–10;* ***June:*** *Mon–Fri 4–5 and 9–10, Sat 11–1 and 3–10, Sun 10–1 and 3–10;* ***July–Aug:*** *12–1, 5–6 and 9–10, Sat 11–1 and 3–10, Sun 10–1 and 3–10;* ***Sept:*** *12–1, 4–5 and 9–10, Sat 11–1 and 4–9, Sun 10–1 and 3–9;* ***Oct:*** *Sat 11–1 and 4–8, Sun 10–1 and 3–8;* ***Nov–15 Mar****: Sun and hols only 3pm–4pm*).

There are two places from which to view the falls – from down below on the SS209, or from the belvedere on top, in the village of Marmore. A path through the woods connects the two, though it's steep, prone to be muddy, and much nicer to walk down than up (the path at the bottom begins just downstream from the falls). There are some pleasant places to swim near the bottom, but you can't use them when the falls are on – a siren goes off 15 minutes before the falls are turned on to warn swimmers not to linger. Both places are easily reached by bus from Terni, six kilometres away.

Above Marmore, **Lake Piediluco** zigzags in and out of the wooded hills, one of which is crowned by a 12th-century fortress. There are a couple of beaches, but the water is cold and dangerous. Perched high above the east shore of the lake is the pale old village of **Labro**, former nest of noblemen on the run, now largely taken over by Belgian expats. Just below the lake the Arrone road passes **Villalago**, which has an outdoor theatre used during the Easter instalment of the Umbria Jazz Festival and summertime events, and lovely gardens for picnicking.

Terni

Because doves mate on his day (so they say), the first bishop of Terni, San Valentino, became the special patron of lovers and the greetings-card industry. Curiously, the stodgy Terni-ites have only recently picked up on the notoriety of their old bishop, but every 14 February the town is now taken over, not only by a traditional market and fireworks, but by a full range of international chocs and schlock. An 'Act of Love' prize is solemnly awarded to the city, person or organization that has performed the best one (in 1996 it was given in memory of Israeli prime minister Yitzhak Rabin).

Terni has little else to offer, besides trains and buses to other places, and shots of viper juice (*Viparo*, an *aperitivo* with all the qualities of flat rum and cola). As one of Italy's chief steel and armaments manufacturers, the city was condensed into rubble by air raids during the Second World War. It was during the original building of the steelworks that bulldozers uncovered one of the largest and richest Etruscan necropolises, though all the finds have been carted off to Rome's Villa Giulia Museum. The ancient Romans called it *Interamna Nahars* and it was traditionally considered the birthplace of the historian Tacitus, though scholars now quibble that Terni produced a more meagre Tacitus, Claudius Tacitus, emperor for a day. These days the city makes the most of its industrial heritage, with tours on such educational themes as 'The Culture and Conditions of a Worker's Life'. Its proletarian past has kept it ardently Communist, the heart of red Umbria and a fun place to be on 1 May. As Italian film-makers grow estranged from costly Cinecittà, Terni has stepped into the breach; some of Italy's best special-effects wizards are concentrated in the Centro Multimediale di Terni. This, and cheap space, drew Roberto Benigni here for the production of *Life Is Beautiful* and *Pinocchio*.

Of Roman Terni only part of the **amphitheatre** (AD 32) remains, in the city's prettiest area, off the main Corso del Popolo. Visible from the Corso and Piazza Europa, tiny round **San Salvatore**, known locally as the Sun Temple, was built in the 5th century, with a nave added in the 12th. The nearby **Palazzo Spada** (1546) by Antonio Sangallo the Younger is the best of Terni's surviving palaces. Palazzo Gazzoli, on Via del Teatro Romano, houses the **Pinacoteca Comunale**, with Umbrian paintings, a Marriage of St Catherine by Gozzoli and, best of all, a large collection of works by Terni's own Orneore Metelli (1872–1938), a shoemaker and great naïve artist.

San Gemini Fonte, 13 kilometres north of Terni, is known for its mineral springs in a pretty park. Four kilometres on are the ruins of the Roman city of ***Carsulae***, destroyed by the Goths. Lying unfenced out in the open, Carsulae is made lovely by its environs: you can stroll along the original Via Flaminia, past the ruins of a theatre, a mausoleum, an amphitheatre, temples and an arch dedicated to Trajan. Further north, **Acquasparta**, within its medieval walls, has more locally famous curative waters (though it's suffering from a shortage); in summer it hosts a German *lieder*-singing contest.

Narni

Narni, on a cliff over the Nera, is a picturesque hill town, tumbling in a jumble under its well-preserved castle, built in the 1370s by the ubiquitous Cardinal Albornoz. It was a Roman colony, and birthplace of Emperor Nerva, who lasted somewhat longer than Terni's emperor. Narni has several gems – in its **Duomo**, founded in the 12th century, there's a lovely early medieval screen of marble and Cosmati work. In the attractive 13th-century **Palazzo del Podestà** hang a Ghirlandaio, a Gozzoli, and other paintings; with the nearby **Loggia dei Priori** by Gattapone it forms a fine setting for Narni's springtime medieval pageant, the *Corso dell'Anello* – the Tournament of the Ring – in which the various quarters of the town compete in a festival traditionally held on the second Sunday in May, one of the most spectacular and evocative *feste* in Umbria.

Narni has several other interesting churches, including the pretty 12th-century **Santa Maria in Pensole** and the 15th-century **Sant'Agostino**, on the other side of town. Down by the river and Narni's train station are the romantic ruins of the **Ponte d'Augusto**, the 1st-century bridge that carried the Via Flaminia over the Nera.

Amelia

North of Narni, halfway between the Nera and the Tiber, is the ancient agricultural town of Amelia. Both Cato and Pliny wrote that *Ameria* was centuries older than Rome; as towering evidence of the fact stand its ancient **Pelasgian–Umbrian Walls**, dating back to the 5th century BC, built from polygonal blocks 12ft thick and 25ft high. Near the Porta Romana, at Piazza Augusta Vera 10, the **Museo Archeologico** (***t*** *0744 978 120; open Apr–June and Sept Tues–Sun 10.30–1 and 3–6; July and Aug daily 10.30–1 and 4–7; Oct–Mar 10.30–1 and 3–5.30*) recently reopened to great fanfare after it won a years-long tug-of-love with Perugia for the bronze statue of Germanicus, father of Caligula, found near the town in 1963. The **Duomo**, built in 1050, with its original campanile, contains two Turkish banners captured at the Battle of Lepanto. On the first Sunday in October, wine is miraculously made to pour from Amelia's fountains.

Near the Tiber, **Lugnano in Teverina** has a 12th-century church, **Santa Maria Assunta**, a Romanesque gem with a curious porch and bas-reliefs, topped by an eagle instead of a cross; inside there's a good triptych by L'Alunno.

Penna in Teverina, near Orte, is an old fortified town with a castle much disputed by Rome's eternal Punch and Judy factions, the Colonna and Orsini families, until the Colonna simply sold it to the Orsini. Some members of the family liked the area so much that they constructed a **Palazzo Orsini** with a fine 19th-century Italian garden attached. Other relics of that century are the *Mammalocchi*, allegorical figures in travertine standing at the entrance to another estate.

Todi and Orvieto

Two of Umbria's best-known hill towns are easily accessible from Rome; Orvieto especially, with its stupendous cathedral and wine, is a popular destination among day-trippers. Todi is a bit further and a bit more sombre, more mysteriously Umbrian, and a good foil to Orvieto. For a memorable dose of beauty and culture take in both towns and the lovely scenery in between, with a stop at Baschi for an amazing meal at one of the jewels in Italy's gastronomic crown (*see* Vissani, p.746).

Todi: the World's Most Liveable Town

Despite a name that suggests an Italian *Wind in the Willows*, this is a serious-minded place, perched on its high and lonely hill, with more affinity with eagles than with amphibians – it was the former who showed the ancient Umbrians where to plant the city they called *Tuter*, high up on what is now the Rocca. Later, the Etruscans built their city lower down, around Piazza del Popolo, and, according to legend, one day they went nasty, slaughtering their Umbrian neighbours and making the rest slaves.

In Todi's plump and prosperous Middle Ages the eagle struck again, this time swooping down on Amelia and Terni (symbolized by the two eaglets on Todi's coat of arms); yet at the same time it produced one of Italy's great uncanonized saints, Jacopone dei Benedetti (1228–1306), the master of the *Laudesi* – medieval Franciscan poets – who, like St Francis, sang songs of praise to cheer the people. Jacopone, before becoming 'Christ's clown', was a wealthy lawyer, married to a noble lady. Like any true Italian he loved to see her dressed up to the nines and, although she gently protested, she let him have his way. Then came the day, at a public festival, when the platform she stood on collapsed; as she lay there, Jacopone ripped aside her garments to examine her injuries, only to discover that under her silks she wore a rough hair shirt. She died, and he became a convert – but such an eccentric one that the Franciscans at first refused him admission. In the end, however, he found his niche with the Spirituals, the most unworldly branch of the order, living in a monastery at Collazzone, near Perugia, where he is believed to have composed the famous Latin *Stabat Mater Dolorosa* and the *Stabat Mater Speciosa*.

Modern Todi is a sophisticated little place that is famous for its carpentry and woodwork. Over the past few years it has, believe it or not, consistently been voted the world's most liveable town by the University of Kentucky – an accolade that has brought American tycoons and the sort of New Yorkers who used to summer in the Hamptons rushing to snap up its villas. In April it hosts one of Italy's major antiques fairs, and in August and September there's the *Mostra Nazionale dell'Artigianato*, a national crafts fair.

Tempio di Santa Maria della Consolazione

The best way to approach Todi is from the southwest, where the road, winding its way to the clouds, passes by way of one of the most perfect of Renaissance churches, the ivory-coloured Tempio della Consolazione, designed by Cola da Caprorola in 1508, and completed 99 years later. Its serene purity of form, geometrically harmonious lines and lovely proportions are the hallmarks of Bramante, who may well have had a hand in the design. The Tempio's lonely setting lends it a special charm; it's best viewed from Todi's citadel. The white classical interior (*open Weds–Mon Apr–Oct 9–1 and 2.30–6; Nov–Mar 10–12.30 and 2.30–6*), in the symmetrical form of a Greek cross, contains Baroque statues of the apostles.

Piazza del Popolo

Todi's streets converge on its magnificent Piazza del Popolo, the centre of civic life since the days of the Etruscans. The piazza is a medieval pageant in grey stone; sternest of them all, the **Palazzo dei Priori** (1293–1337) has square battlements with a chunky tower, while the **Palazzo del Popolo** (1213), with the swallowtail crenellations, and its adjacent **Palazzo del Capitano** (1290) manage to drum up more charm, with a grand Gothic stairway and attractive mullioned windows. Up on the fourth floor there's a **Pinacoteca** you can take in if it rains (***t*** *075 894 4148; open Mar and Sept Tues–Sun 10.30–1 and 2–5; Apr daily 10.30–1 and 2.30–6; Oct–Feb Tues–Sun 10.30–1 and 2–4.30; adm*), with various odds and ends.

On the far side of the piazza, the squarish **Duomo** (*open daily Apr–Oct 8.30–12.30 and 2.30–6.30; Nov–Mar 8.30–4.30*) is enthroned at the top of another distinguished flight of steps. Begun in the 12th century, the façade has a fine rose window and a delicately decorated portal, while the interior is embellished with some good Gothic capitals and a Gothic arcade with a 14th-century altarpiece; parishioners who turned around to gossip during Mass were confronted by a not-too-terrifying 16th-century vision of the Last Judgement by Farraù da Faenza. Before leaving the piazza, be sure to take a look from its belvedere.

Getting There and Around

Todi is linked by **bus** with Terni (ATC), Perugia (APM) and Rome, and by the FCU's little **trains** with Perugia and Terni. Trains arrive at the Stazione Ponte Rio, **t** 075 894 2092, from which there are municipal buses up to town.

One bus (SULGA) a day runs between Todi and Orvieto, passing through the lovely scenery above the Tiber valley.

Tourist Information

Todi: Piazza Umberto I 6, **t** 075 894 3395.

Where to Stay

Todi ✉ 06059

★★★★★**Relais Todini**, on the road to Collevalenza di Todi, **t** 075 887521, *www.relaistodini.com* (*very expensive*). A 14th-century *palazzo* with antiques, a heated pool, tennis courts, an elegant restaurant and beautiful views up to Todi. The 750-acre park has camels, kangaroos, zebras and penguins; horses and carriages to ride; and four boating lakes.

★★★★**Fonte Cesia**, Via L. Leoni 3, **t** 075 894 3737, *www.fontecesia.it* (*expensive*). An 18th-century building near Piazza Jacopone in the historic centre, offering stylish accommodation.

★★★★**San Lorenzo Tre**, Via S. Lorenzo, **t** 075 894 4555 *www.todi.net/lorenzo* (*moderate*). A 'Residenza d'Epoca' in a listed *palazzo* in town, with everything, from the furniture to the linen, as it would have been in the late 19th century, and no TVS or telephones in the bedrooms.

★★★**Villa Luisa**, Via A. Cortesi 147, **t** 075 894 8571, *www.villaluisa.it* (*cheap*). A pleasant place near the centre, with a large garden.

There are no cheap hotels to be found in Todi, but there are a number of seasonal *agriturismo* nearby:

L'Arco, Cardigliano, **t** 075 894 7534.

Poponi, Via delle Piagge 26, **t** 075 894 8233.

Castello di Porchiano, Porchiano, **t** 075 885 3127.

Eating Out

Local specialities include pigeon, lamb and *porchetta*, and home-made fat spaghetti called *ombricelli*, served by preference *alla boscaiola* (with tomatoes, piquant black olives and hot peppers). The dry white Grechetto di Todi dates back to Roman days.

Umbria, Via S. Bonaventura 13, just off Piazza del Popolo, **t** 075 894 2390 (*expensive*). Fine Umbrian cuisine and an enchanting Umbrian view. Meals begin with a delicious variety of *antipasti*, followed perhaps by *spaghetti alla tudertina*. Book for a table with an unobstructed view. *Closed Tues.*

Lucaroni, Via Cortesi 57, **t** 075 894 2694 (*moderate*). Sophisticated cuisine, including delicious risotto with pigeon, black truffles and port, and excellent *linguini* with crab. *Closed Tues.*

Italia, Via del Monte 27, **t** 075 894 2643 (*moderate*). An unpretentious trattoria down a narrow alley off the main piazza, with cheerful red tablecloths and a rustic feel. Specialities include *capriccio*, an oven-baked pasta dish. *Closed Mon.*

Antica Hosteria de la Valle, Via Ciufelli 19, **t** 075 894 4848 (*moderate*). An atmospheric osteria offering a menu of creative dishes, including *antipasto della casa* (cheese fondue with truffles, rustic pâté and *bruschette*), which is highly recommended. Book ahead. *Closed Mon.*

San Fortunato and the Rocca

Todi's medieval lanes invite roaming, but if you're in a hurry head for Franciscan **San Fortunato** (*open Apr–mid-Oct Mon 8.30–12.30, Tues–Sun 8.30–12.30 and 3–7; mid-Oct–Mar Tues–Sun 9.30–12.30 and 3–5*), built in 1292. The locally revered tomb of Jacopone is in its crypt. The unfinished façade has three recessed Romanesque portals; inside is Todi's greatest work of art, a fresco by Masolino of the Madonna and Child. Above San Fortunato is the **Rocca**, Todi's ruined 14th-century citadel and public park, offering an unforgettable view of the valley of the Tiber and the Tempio della Consolazione.

Getting There and Around

Orvieto Scalo, below the old city, is on the main **rail** line between Florence (2hrs) and Rome (2hrs) and an hour from Perugia.

It is also linked by ATC **bus**, t 0763 301 224, with Amelia, Narni and Terni; there is one bus a day on the scenic SS79 to Todi. All buses stop at the railway station, from where bus no.1 takes you up to the top, or there's a *funivia* every 10–15mins until 8.30pm. At the top, shuttle bus A takes you to the cathedral, and bus B takes you around the *centro storico*.

There are well-marked **car** parks linked by bus, lift or *funivia* to the centre. Ask there about combined parking/bus/museum tickets.

Tourist Information

Piazza del Duomo 24, **t** 0763 341 772, *www.comune.orvieto.tr.it*.

Where to Stay

Orvieto ✉ 05018

★★★★**Palazzo Piccolomini**, Piazza dei Ranieri 36, **t** 0763 341 743, *www.hotelpiccolomini.it* (*expensive*). A superbly restored medieval palace in the historic town centre, with light modern décor.

★★★★**Villa Ciconia**, Orbetello Scalo, Via dei Tigli 69, **t** 0763 305 582, *villaciconia.hotel–italia.biz* (*expensive*). A 16th-century villa in a green oasis amid the ugly sprawl of Orbetello Scalo, with well-equipped rooms and a fine frescoed restaurant.

★★★★**Aquila Bianca**, Via Garibaldi 13, **t** 0763 341 246, *www.argoweb.it/hotel_aquilabianca* (*moderate*). An old-fashioned, central option with a wine cellar for Orvieto tastings.

★★★**Virgilio**, Piazza Duomo 56, **t** 0763 341 882, (*moderate*). A refurbished trecento building across from the cathedral.

★★★**Valentino**, Via Angelo da Orvieto 30–32, **t** 0763 342 464 (*moderate*). A 16th-century house with all mod cons and a garage.

★★**Duomo**, Via di Maurizio 7, **t** 0763 341 887 (*cheap*). Refurbished rooms by the cathedral.

★★**Posta**, Via Luca Signorelli 18, **t** 0763 341 909 (*cheap*). A hotel right off Corso Cavour in the historic centre, with a small garden to sit in.

Eating Out

The busloads of day-trippers from Rome have helped keep some mediocre, often overpriced venues in business, so choose with care. Aside the town's famous wine, local specialities are *cinghiale in agrodolce* (sweet-and-sour boar) and *gallina ubriaca* ('drunken chicken').

I Sette Consoli, Piazza Sant'Angelo, **t** 0763 343 911 (*very expensive*). The best local ingredients, imaginatively employed in dishes such as *pappardelle* with duck sauce, and gnocchi with zucchini and mint. There's outside dining in summer, a good *menu degustazione* with three wines, and a fine wine list. *Closed Sun eve, and Weds Nov–Mar.*

Vissani, on the SS448 towards Civitella del Lago, **t** 0744 950 206 (*very expensive*). An almost religious inner sanctum of *cucina altissima*, with such marvels as oyster lasagne with basil, and peppers with black truffles, Parmesan and foie gras. Each dish is accompanied by a special bread. There's a fabulous array of Italian and French cheeses, and exquisite wines. Reserve in advance. *Closed Weds, Thurs lunch and Sun eve.*

Le Grotte del Funaro, Via Ripa Serancia 41, **t** 0763 343 276 (*expensive*). An elegant restaurant in a set of tufa caves with a terrace, serving solid Umbrian cuisine, plus pizza at night. *Closed Mon except July and Aug, and 1wk in Jan and July.*

Osteria dell'Angelo, Piazza 29 Marzo 8A, **t** 0763 341 805 (*expensive*). Local ingredients cooked with flair, in dishes such as goose liver and red turnip in puff pastry with raspberry vinegar, and ravioli with *pecorino* and nettle sauce. The wine list is excellent. *Closed Mon, Tues lunch and 1–15 Aug.*

La Taverna de' Mercanti, Via Loggia dei Mercanti 34, **t** 0763 393 327 (*expensive*). Creative regional *cucina* in the stylish cellars of the Palazzo Piccolomini. *Closed Tues.*

L'Asino d'Oro, Vicolo del Popolo 9, **t** 0763 344 406 (*moderate*). The best place to eat in Orvieto, with a daily-changing menu of simple but innovative dishes such as boar *prosciutto* with rocket and *pecorino*.

Etrusca, Via Lorenzo Maitani 10, **t** 0763 344 016 (*moderate*). The best trattoria, serving lovely traditional food in a cinquecento building by the cathedral. *Closed Mon and 6 Jan–8 Feb.*

Orvieto

Orvieto owes much of its success to an ancient volcano. First it created the city's magnificent pedestal – a 1,066ft sheer-cliffed mesa straight out of the American southwest – then it enriched the hillsides below with a mixture of volcanic minerals that form part of the alchemy of Orvieto's famous white wine. Though new buildings crowd the outskirts of Orvieto's unique crag, the medieval town on top, crowned by its stupendous cathedral, looks much the same as it has for the last 500 years.

Attracted by Orvieto's incomparable natural defences, the Etruscans settled it early and named it *Velzna* (or *Volsinium* as the Romans pronounced it). It was one of the 12 cities of the Etruscan confederation, and one that fought frequently with the Romans until those upstarts laid it waste in 280 BC. The Etruscans departed in a huff and founded a new Volsinium on the shores of Lake Bolsena, leaving behind their old city (*Urbs Vetus*, hence 'Orvieto'). Orvieto in the Middle Ages was a stronghold of the Papal States – important primarily for popes who could take refuge here when their polls went down with the fickle Romans.

The Duomo

***t** 0763 342 477: open daily Mar and Oct 7.30–12.45 and 2.30–6.15; Apr–Sept 7.30–12.45 and 2.30–7.15; Nov–Feb 7.30–12.45 and 2.30–5.15. For Cappella di San Brizio,* see *below.*

It was during one of Orvieto's papal visitations, in the 1260s (Urban IV), that the Miracle of Bolsena occurred. A Bohemian priest named Peter, passing through on his way to Rome, was asked to celebrate Mass in the town of Bolsena, just to the south. Father Peter had long been secretly sceptical about the doctrine of transubstantiation (that the Host in truth becomes the body of Christ), but during this Mass the Host answered his doubts by dripping blood on the altar linen. Peter took the linen to the pope in Orvieto, who declared it a miracle and instituted the feast of Corpus Christi. St Thomas Aquinas, also in Orvieto at the time, was instructed to compose a suitable office for the new holy day, while the pope promised Orvieto (a bit unfairly for Bolsena!) a magnificent new cathedral to enshrine the relic. The cornerstone was laid in 1290 and, though begun in the Romanesque style, the cathedral's plan was transformed into Gothic by master architect Lorenzo Maitani of Siena in 1310. Subsequent master architects included Andrea Pisano, Orcagna and Sammicheli, but even then the mighty edifice, visible for miles around, wasn't completed until 1617.

The end result is one of Italy's greatest cathedrals, with a stunning façade like a giant triptych. This is Maitani's masterpiece, and the reason the church is called the 'Golden Lily of Cathedrals'. You're struck first by the dazzling, Technicolor hues of its mosaics, then by the elaborate prickly spires and tracery, and the richness and beauty of the sculptural detail. It is said that 152 sculptors worked on the cathedral, but it was Maitani who contributed the best work – the remarkable design and execution of the **bas-reliefs** on the lower pilasters that recount the Christian story from the Creation to the Last Judgement, a Bible in stone that captures the essence of the stories with vivid drama and detail. The Madonna and the three sculptures from the Porta del Corporale are being restored by the Opera del Duomo, which has yet to decide whether to display them in its renovated museum or replace them in their original positions. Maitani also cast the four bronze figures of the Evangelists' symbols, all ready to step right off the façade, and sculpted the angels in the lunette over the central portal, who pay homage to a Madonna by Andrea Pisano (*removed for restoration*). The great rose window is by Orcagna, and the controversial bronze doors, portraying Works of Mercy, are by Emilio Greco, finished in 1965.

In contrast with the verticality of the façade, the sides and interior are banded with horizontal stripes; inside, in the muted light filtered through alabaster windows, they merge into shadows. The lack of clutter does much to reveal the cathedral's fine proportions and height. The columns of the nave support rounded arches, and above them runs a pretty clerestory. In the nave note Gentile da Fabriano's 1426 fresco of the Madonna and Child, and the 1579 *Pietà* by Ippolito Scalza, a native of Orvieto.

The greatest treasures are in the chapels, especially the **Cappella della Madonna di San Brizio** (***t** 0763 342 477; open Mon–Sat Apr–Sept 10–12.45 and 2.30–7.15; Mar and Oct 10–12.45 and 2.30–6.15; Nov–Feb 10–12.45 and 2.30–5.15; Sun July–Sept 2.30–6.45, Oct–June 2.30–5.45; buy tickets at the tourist office or souvenir shops in Piazza del Duomo; only 25 people admitted at a time*), embellished with one of the finest fresco cycles of the Renaissance. The project was begun in 1447 by Fra Angelico, with the aid of Benozzo Gozzoli. The Angelic One finished two sections – the serene *Christ in Judgement*, with the prophets – while Gozzoli contributed the hierarchies of angels. Before he could finish, Fra Angelico was summoned to Rome. Orvieto commissioned Perugino to complete the work, but he never got around to it, and finally, in 1499, the city hired Luca Signorelli, who finished the vaults according to Fra Angelico's design.

The walls, however, are Signorelli's own masterpiece; his awesome compositions of the Last Judgement, the Preaching of the Antichrist (a very unusual subject) and the Resurrection of the Dead are generally acclaimed as the forerunners of Michelangelo's *Last Judgement* in the Sistine Chapel. Yet it's hard to say that Michelangelo surpassed them; Signorelli's remarkable foreshortening skills, draughtsmanship and ability to simplify nature and architecture into their essential geometrical forms give the frescoes tremendous power. To the left of the figure of the preaching Antichrist, Signorelli has portrayed himself and Fra Angelico listening solemnly, as does Dante amid the crowd, while in the background chaos and catastrophe are busy at work. Then the world ends, a darkened sky is shot with streaks of fire, the earth shakes, and in literal detail the dead re-emerge from the earth, skeletons pulling themselves out of the ground forming new coats of flesh. Some are met by Charon, who rows them across to an overcrowded Renaissance Hell, to keep company with Signorelli's faithless mistress. Below the frescoes Signorelli painted medallions of the great poets and the pre-Socratic philosopher Empedocles, and some scenes from the *Divine Comedy*.

The **Cappella del Corporale** has frescoes: the *Miracle of Bolsena* by Ugolino of Siena (1360s), and the 1339 *Madonna dei Raccomandati* by Lippo Memmi. The silver and enamel Reliquary of the Corporale on the altar is by another Sienese, Ugolino di Vieri; the blood-stained cloth it holds is shown only on major religious holidays.

The Piazza del Duomo

The cathedral square is a fitting setting for the Golden Lily. On one side a row of old houses includes a couple of *enoteche* where you can try local vintages and *salumeria*, while on top of the square clock tower a 14th-century figure named Maurizio strikes the hours. Opposite, in Palazzo Faina, the **Museo Archeologico Claudio Faina e Museo Civico** (***t*** *0763 341 511; open Apr–Sept daily 9.30–6; Oct–Mar Tues–Sun 10–5; adm*) hosts one of Italy's top private archaeological collections and the town's excellent Etruscan collection from local tombs. The ground floor has the civic collection of decorations from the Belevedere temple and the *Venus of Cannicella*; the two upper floors house the private collection. The top floor enjoys one of the best views of the cathedral.

On the south side of the cathedral the **Palazzo Papale**, begun by Boniface VIII in 1297 and finished in the 1500s, contains the **Museo dell'Opera del Duomo** (***t*** *0763 342 477*), with art that once filled the cathedral – statues by grand masters such as Arnolfo di Cambio and the Pisanos, and grand statues by little-known hands. The best work is a richly coloured polyptych by Simone Martini. The adjacent Palazzo Apostolico (1304) holds the **Museo Archaeologico** (***t*** *0763 341 069; open daily 8.30–7.30, Sat until 11pm Aug–mid-Sept; adm*), with another excellent collection.

Smaller Churches

The rest of Orvieto is unpretentious and worldly, a solid, bourgeois, medieval town. On Via del Duomo stands the **Torre del Moro**, a medieval tower you can climb, and further on the pretty 13th-century **Palazzo del Popolo** is a tufa palace with mullioned windows and arches; the little piazza in front hosts a colourful vegetable market. From here Via della Pace leads back to the narrow church of **San Domenico**, built in 1233 just after St Dominic's canonization. The most scholarly Dominican of all, St Thomas Aquinas, taught here at the former monastery, but this did not spare the church from a savage amputation of its naves in 1934 to make room for a barracks.

From Via del Duomo, Orvieto's main drag, Corso Cavour, continues west to the main square, Piazza della Repubblica. On the corner 12th-century **Sant'Andrea** has a very rare 12-sided campanile, pierced by mullioned windows and topped by bellicose crenellations. A 6th-century church was discovered beneath, and underneath that an Etruscan street and buildings were found (*the sacristan has a key to the excavations*). Sant'Andrea basks in the memory of great events that took place within its walls: here Innocent III proclaimed the Fourth Crusade, and here, in 1281, Charles of Anjou and his glittering retinue attended the coronation of Pope Martin IV.

Beyond Piazza della Repubblica are ancient streets lined with tufa houses; follow them back to the northwestern corner of town, site of **San Giovenale**, first built in 916, rebuilt in 1687 and crammed full of frescoes from the 12th–15th centuries.

San Lorenzo di Arari, reached by Via Maitani from Piazza Duomo, was built in the 14th century and shelters a cylindrical Etruscan altar under its high altar, protected by a lovely 12th-century stone canopy. Byzantine-style frescoes cover the walls, with elongated figures and staring eyes; another set of frescoes depict the life of St Lawrence, who retained his sense of humour even while being literally grilled ('Turn me over, I'm done on this side,' he said).

The Vine of Life

Refined over the centuries, Umbria's most famous wine is grown in 16 designated areas in the provinces of Terni and Viterbo, and consists of a careful mixture of grapes, with Tuscan Trebbiano and Verdello dominant. Light straw-coloured Orvieto DOC comes in four different varieties. Dry (Orvieto *secco*) now predominates because of the market, but you can still find the more authentic moderately dry (*abboccato*, often served with appetizers), medium sweet (*amabile*) and sweet (*dolce*), made like a sauterne from noble rot (*muffa nobile*). If it's made in the oldest growing zone, right near Orvieto, it's called Classico.

The tourist office has a list of local vineyards that welcome visitors.

Pozzo di San Patrizio

Orvieto's northeastern end (near the upper station of the funicular) is dominated by a **citadel** built in 1364 by the great papal legate, Cardinal Albornoz. Only the walls, a gate and a tower survive, encompassing a pretty little garden of parasol pines. There are lovely views from the ramparts, stretching from the shallow Paglia river to the Tiber valley.

Next to the citadel lie the foundations of an **Etruscan temple** and the **Pozzo di San Patrizio**, or St Patrick's Well (***t** 0763 343 768; open daily summer 10–7, winter 10–6; adm*), designed in the 1530s by Antonio da Sangallo the Younger on the orders of the calamitous Pope Clement VII. It is a unique work of engineering, meant to supply Orvieto in times of siege; to reach the spring below, Sangallo had to dig down the equivalent of seven storeys. To haul the water to the surface he designed two spiral staircases of 248 steps, one for the water-carriers and their donkeys going down, another for going up. Clement, having just fled the sack of Rome, was perhaps justified in the paranoia that made him desire such a monumental drinking hole, but it was never needed. The stairs are dimly lit by windows on to the central shaft, but beware if you descend; you have to get back up again. Bring a sweater, too.

Below Orvieto's northern cliffs, along the road to the railway station, are several **Etruscan tombs** worth a look if you don't get chance to see any of the more elaborate models. The most impressive is the 6th-century BC **Crocifisso del Tufo** (***t** 0763 343 611; open daily Apr–Sept 8.30–7; Oct–Mar 8.30–5.30; adm*), on the SS71 north of town.

Villages Around Orvieto

Between Orvieto and Todi, **Baschi** is a harmonious hill town set above the Tiber valley, near where the river widens to form the **Lago di Corbara**; the area has many *agriturismi* amid the vineyards. **Porano**, south of Orvieto, is a pretty town with a castle, set in the rolling hills.

Walled **Ficulle**, north of Orvieto on SS71, was the birthplace of Rome's tragic hero of the Middle Ages, Cola di Rienzo, and its castle of the Marchese Antinori (*call **t** 0763 86051 to arrange a visit*) produces some of Orvieto's finest wine.

Lazio

18

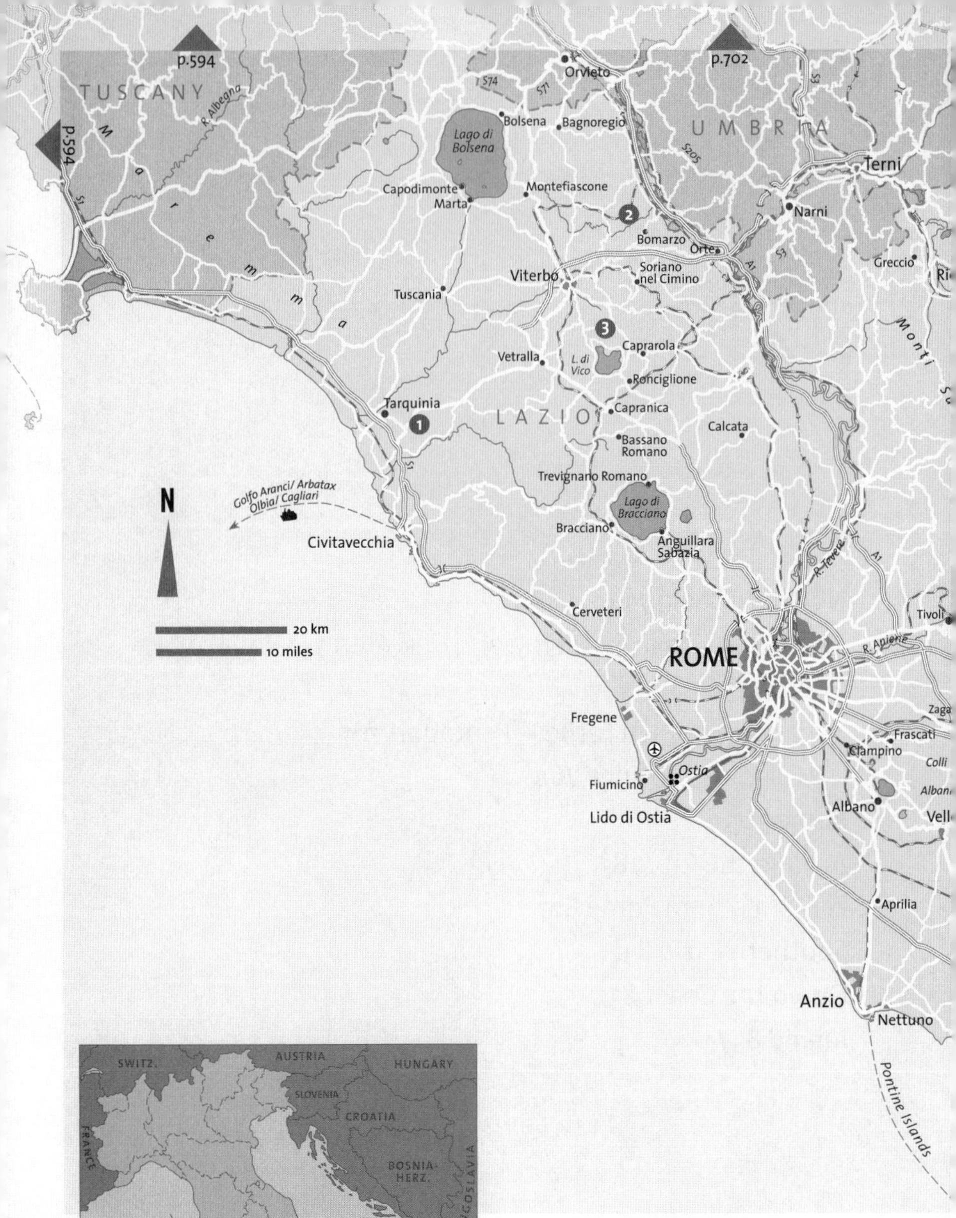

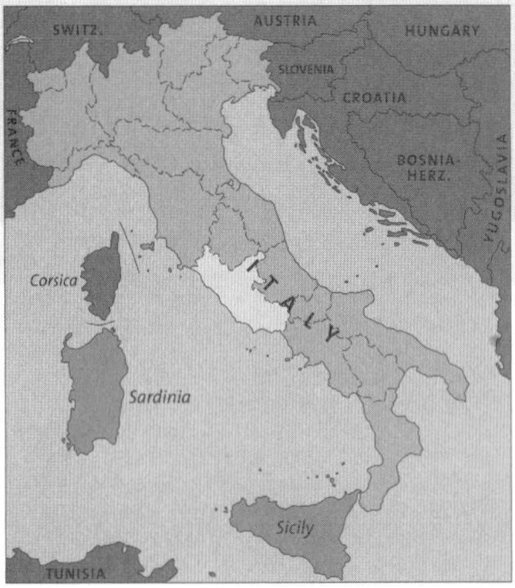

Highlights

1 The painted Etruscan tombs at Tarquínia
2 Bomarzo's Renaissance folly, the Monster Park
3 Lake Vico, and Caprarola's Farnese Palace
4 The 'Medieval Sistine Chapel', Anagni cathedral

On a Saturday-night variety show, the television host discusses the founding of Rome with two comedians dressed up as Romulus and Remus; turning to Remus, the sillier-looking of the pair, he asks: 'What did you ever do?' Remus gets a big laugh from the audience by proudly claiming, 'Well, I founded Lazio.'

Despite being the location of the capital city, Lazio does not get much respect from the average Italian, who thinks of it as a sort of vacuum consisting of swamps and poor mountain villages that need to be crossed to get to Rome. Northerners often lump it in with Campania and Calabria as part of the backward south. To an extent it is, although great changes have come in the last 60 years with land reclamation and new industry. Lazio's problem is a simple one: Rome, that most parasitic of all cities. Before there was a Rome, this was probably the wealthiest and most densely populated part of non-Greek Italy, the homeland of the Etruscans as well as the rapidly civilizing nations of Sabines, Aequi, Hernici, Volscii and the Latins themselves, from whom Lazio (*Latium*) takes its name.

After the Roman triumph the Etruscan and the Italic cities shrivelled and died; those Romans who proved such good governors elsewhere caused ruin to their own back yard. A revival came in the Middle Ages, when Rome was only one of a score of squabbling feudal towns, but once again, when the popes restored Rome, Lazio's fortunes declined. To finance their grandiose building projects, Renaissance popes taxed Lazio into extinction; whole villages and large stretches of countryside were abandoned and given over to bandits, and land that was drained in medieval times reverted to malarial swamps. Modern Rome, at least since Mussolini's day, has begun to mend its ways; the government still considers Lazio a development area, and pumps money into it.

Northern Lazio

The North Coast: Tarquinia and Cerveteri

It's hard to believe that this bare stretch of coast north of Rome was the richest and most heavily populated part of Etruria, including the only two sites worth visiting for non-archaeology fiends: the museums and necropoli at Tarquinia and Cerveteri.

Tarquinia and Vulci

From the Tuscan border on the coastal highway (the Roman Via Aurelia), dedicated Etruscophiles may wish to make a detour into the hills to **Vulci**, an important town in the 9th–1st centuries BC, and a renowned bronze-working centre. There are scanty ruins of the city, a small museum in modern Vulci's 13th-century **Castello dell'Abbadia** (**t** *0761 437 787*), and a large if unexciting necropolis with something like 15,000 tombs (*open Apr–Sept Tues–Sun 9–7; Oct–Mar Tues–Sun 9–4; adm*).

Getting Around

There are frequent COTRAL **buses** to Cerveteri and Tarquínia from Lepanto bus terminus in Rome.

Tourist Information

Tarquínia: Piazza Cavour 1, **t** 0766 856 384 (*open Mon–Sat 8–2*).

Where to Stay and Eat

Tarquínia ✉ **01016**

*****San Marco**, Piazza Cavour 18, **t** 0766 842 234, *www.san-marco.com* (*moderate*). A well-run hotel with a good restaurant. *Closed Tues.*

Due Orfanelle, Vicolo Breve 4 (off Via di Porta Tarquínia), **t** 0766 856 307 (*moderate–cheap*). Local dishes, and especially good grilled meat. *Closed Tues.*

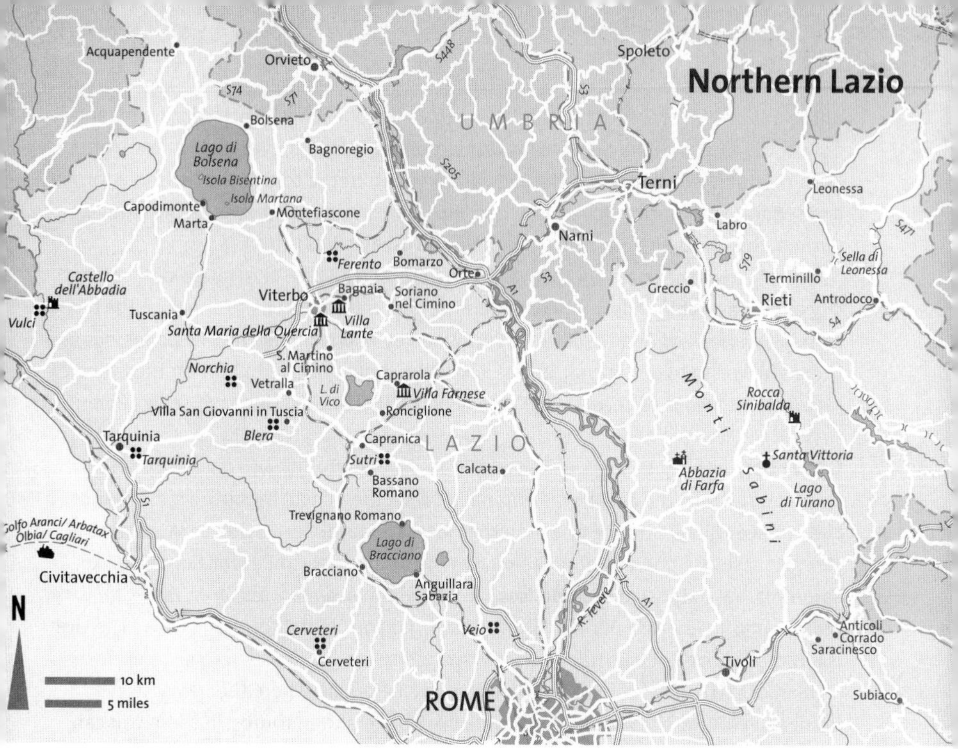

After the turn-off for Vulci, as you continue southwards, the next Etruscan site is at the large, modern town of **Tarquinia**, which is of interest in its own right, with **Santa Maria di Castello**, a Cosmatesque 12th-century church, at the top of the town, and the elegant rococo façade of the **Chiesa del Suffragio** in the centre. Near this, in the 15th-century Palazzo Vitelleschi on Piazza Cavour, many of the finest discoveries from the Etruscan city and its necropolis have been assembled in the **Museo Nazionale Tarquiniense** (*t 0766 856 036; open Tues–Sun 8.30–7.30; adm*). The stars of the collection are the famous winged horses from the 'Altar of the Queen' temple on the acropolis: beautiful beasts, but ones made of clay like most Etruscan temple decorations, which explains why so few have survived. Well-carved sarcophagi are present in abundance, and Greek vases by some of the greatest 6th–5th-century BC Attic painters. The Etruscans were talented at ceramics, too, as is evidenced by the large amount of fine *bucchero* ware – their black pottery incised or painted with the usual puzzling Etruscan images. Some of the paintings from the tombs have been relocated here for their protection, including scenes of chariot-riding and athletics – almost any subject is likely to turn up on Etruscan tomb walls.

There are not enough staff to keep all the hundreds of tombs open at Tarquinia's **Monterozzi necropolis,** a 15-minute walk from Via Porta Tarquinia (*open Tues–Sun Apr–Oct 8.30–7.30, Nov–Mar 8.30–4.30; adm, cheaper joint ticket with museum*), all that remains of the city that dominated southern Etruria for centuries and enforced on Rome its early dynasty of Etruscan kings. The few you can see on any given day, however, rank among the finest products of Etruscan art. Tombs like that of 'the Lionesses', with their beautiful 'Ionic style' paintings, seem remarkably close to the art of the ancient Minoans. These paintings began to appear in the 6th century BC, and only in the tombs of the richest Etruscans; more typical of the rest is the 'Tomb of the Warrior', hung with arms and trophies, all carved from the tufa. There are more tombs in a separate excavation across the road, including images of the *Vanth* and the *Caronti*, the spirits that came to carry away Etruscan souls.

Further down the coast, on the way to Cerveteri, you'll pass the not-so-old-looking city of **Civitavecchia**, a port for Rome and the gateway for ferries to Sardinia. The big fortress overlooking the harbour was designed by Michelangelo for the popes, but there's little else to detain you, unless you feel a sudden desire to bolt for the island of *nuraghi* and *malloreddus*, in which case head for the Tirrenia Line or FS ferry offices.

Cerveteri

Cerveteri, down the coast, was originally *Caere*, the richest if not the strongest of the Etruscan cities, and the one with the closest cultural ties to Greece. According to Herodotus it was the only non-Greek city with a sanctuary at Delphi. Cerveteri, like Tarquinia, has extensive **necropolises** (*2km from town, signposted; open Tues–Sun May–Sept 8.30–sunset, Oct–Apr 8.30–4; adm*), laid out in the form of a town. The site is large; study one of the maps before walking too far.

The most striking section is the Banditaccia Necropolis, where the heavy stone domes, set low to the ground, look more like bunkers than tombs. In them you can see the forerunners of all the round tombs in Rome, such as the Mausolea of Augustus and Hadrian. Make sure to see the 'Tomb of the Capitals', carved from tufa to resemble the interior of an Etruscan house (the Etruscans built all their homes, public buildings and even temples out of wood, plaster and terracotta, which explains why only tombs are left).

The 'Tomb of Shields and Chairs' has unusual military decoration; another, even stranger, is covered with stone reliefs of cooking utensils and other household objects. In town, the Castello Orsini houses the **Museo Nazionale** (***t*** *06 994 1354; open Tues–Sun 9–7; adm*), which has finds dug out from the Banditaccia, although the best pieces are now in the Villa Giulia and Vatican museums in Rome.

Viterbo

Ah, Viterbo. Where else can one rest in a café on Death Square, or stroll over to the Piazza of the Fallen to pay one's respects to Our Lady of the Plague? Although it's surrounded by grey, forbidding walls and ghastly modern districts, the city is actually rather cute at the centre, full of grand churches and palaces, and medieval streets brightened with fountains and flowers. The population seems evenly divided between teenagers on scooters, as bejewelled and trendy as their counterparts in Rome, and blasé soldiers from Italy's biggest army base. Like the rest of Lazio, Viterbo has had more than its share of troubles, most of them traceable to the proximity of Rome. That geographical necessity, however, also gave Viterbo its greatest period of glory. For much of the 13th century, Viterbo, and not Rome, was the seat of the popes.

Getting Around

Viterbo has three **train stations** just outside the city walls. Regular **FS** trains to Orvieto and Florence stop at **Stazione Porta Fiorentina**, north of the walls on Viale Trento. Most trains for Rome leave from here too, stopping at **Stazione Porta Romana** on Viale Raniero Capocci, east of the walls. There's also a local line run by Lazio transport authority **COTRAL**, with a separate route from its station next to Porta Fiorentina, via Bagnaia, Soriano nel Cimino and Civita Castellana, to Piazzale Flaminio (Roma-Nord) station in Rome.

However, the fastest way to reach Viterbo from Rome is by COTRAL **buses** (freephone within Italy, **t** 800 431 784), which leave roughly every 30 mins from Stazione Saxa Rubra in Rome. More buses for Tarquinia, Bolsena, Civitavecchia and other provincial towns leave from Piazza Martiri d'Ungheria, next to Piazza dei Caduti in the town centre.

Tourist Information

Piazza San Carluccio 5, **t** 0761 304 795.

Where to Stay

Viterbo ✉ 01100

★★★★**Terme dei Papi**, Strada Bagni 12, **t** 0761 3501, *www.termedeipapi.it* (*very expensive*). A well-run spa hotel, with a naturally heated outdoor pool open to non-guests at certain times (for a fee).

★★★**Milano Due**, Via San Luca 17, **t** 0761 303 367 (*moderate*). A spick and span hotel with modern décor.

★★★**Leon d'Oro**, Via della Cava 36, **t** 0761 344 444 (*moderate*). A quiet if slightly staid place to stay.

★★**Roma**, Via della Cava 26, **t** 0761 226 474, (*cheap*). A basic option with parking.

Eating Out

Restaurants here serve traditional Viterban cuisine: slender fettuccine called *fieno* (hay), roast baby lamb, eels, and fish from the lakes, including *lattarini, coregone* (lake whitefish) and *persico* (perch).

Enoteca La Torre, Via della Torre 5, **t** 0761 226467 (*expensive–moderate*). A smart restaurant in a stone palace, serving immaculate Viterban dishes and fine regional wines. The wine bar has delicious local cheese and ham snacks.

Il Richiastro, Via della Marrocca 18, **t** 0761 228 009 (*moderate*). The courtyard and cellars of a medieval palace near Piazza Dante, offering smoked trout, roast lamb, polenta and unusual home-made desserts, all seasonal, at good prices. *Open Thurs–Sat and Sun lunch only; closed July and Aug.*

Scaletta, Via Marconi 45, **t** 0761 340 003 (*cheap*). Another old favourite, with traditional cooking, and pizza in the evening. *Closed Mon.*

Tre Re, Via Marcel Gattesco 3, **t** 0761 304 619 (*cheap*). An excellent budget dinner spot north of Piazza del Plebiscito. *Closed Thurs and 2wks Aug.*

History

Viterbo was a small city in Etruscan and Roman times; its modern history began with fortification by the Lombards in the 8th century. By 1100, it was one of the few cities in this part of Italy strong enough to have become a free *comune*. It was usually an enemy of Rome and when Arnold of Brescia's revolution made Pope Eugenius III a refugee in 1145, he came here. Frederick I Barbarossa soon restored the popes to Rome, but again in 1257 Martin V found hospitality here when the Guelph–Ghibelline wars made Rome too hot for him. In this confusing period of Italian history, more than a dozen popes were crowned, died or spent time here on their way to or from France, Tivoli, or even Rome. In 1309, when the 'Babylonian Captivity' carted the papacy off to Avignon, Viterbo could only decline, and when the popes returned, the city that had been Rome's strongest rival found itself a provincial town of the Papal State.

Piazza del Plebiscito

In Viterbo's centre, two not-so-fierce-looking lions, the city's ancient symbol, gaze out over the typical pair of buildings representing the often conflicting imperial and local powers: the 13th-century **Palazzo dei Priori** (or **Palazzo Comunale**, now home to the town hall) and its clock tower, and **Palazzo del Podestà** dating from the 1460s. The politicians won't mind you looking around the former and its fine Renaissance courtyard; ask to see the **Sala Regia** (*t 0761 304 643; open Mon, Weds, Fri and Sat 9.30–1.30, Tues and Thurs 9.30–1.30 and 3–6*) with its fanciful Mannerist frescoes on the history of Viterbo from Etruscan times. Across the square is the church of **Sant'Angelo**, the façade of which has for centuries incorporated a Roman sarcophagus (now replaced by a mere photograph) containing the body of a medieval lady of incomparable virtue named Galiena; accounts of her fatal charm and sad demise vary from one Viterban to another.

There are any number of directions you can take from here. Via Ascenzi, under the arch, leads to Piazza dei Caduti and the **Madonna della Peste** (*usually closed*), an octagonal Renaissance church next to the tourist office. Beyond that, by the walls, is the **Rocca**, which was built by Cardinal Albornoz in 1354 to keep watch on the Viterbans when the pope returned to Rome. This squat palace-fortress how houses the small **Museo Archeologico** (*t 0761 325 929, open Tues–Sun 8.30–7.30; adm*), with reconstructions of Etruscan houses (not tombs, for once!) and finds from the Roman theatre in Fèrento and Musarna.

Two of Viterbo's 13th-century popes are buried in the church of **San Francesco**, near Porta Murata at the northern end of the walls. Nearby, off Piazza Verdi, the late 19th-century church of **Santa Rosa** houses the considerable remains of Viterbo's 13th-century patroness, too holy to decompose and usually on display for all to see. Santa Rosa's preaching helped the Viterbans defy a siege by the heretical Emperor Frederick II in 1243 and, to commemorate her, each year on 3 September the men of the town carry a 99ft illuminated wooden steeple called the *macchina* – which is always in danger of toppling – through the streets, surmounted by an image of Rosa. Money permitting, local artists create a new *macchina* every five years.

East from Piazza del Plebiscito, Via Cavour takes you past the **Casa Poscia**, a rare 13th-century house on a stairway to the left of the **Fontana Grande**, the best of Viterbo's many fountains. Via Garibaldi leads on further east to the Roman gate and the church of **San Sisto**, parts of which date back to the 9th century, and which boasts an altar made of ancient sculptural fragments. Outside the walls and across Viale Capocci, 13th-century **Santa Maria della Verità** was vandalized by 18th-century redecorators; the plaster frosting is gone now, but fragments have survived of the Renaissance frescoes by Melozzo da Forlì. The **Cappella Mazzatosta**, behind an iron grille, has the best painting Viterbo can offer: frescoes of the Marriage of the Virgin by Renaissance artist Lorenzo da Viterbo (1469), strongly influenced by Piero della Francesca. The adjacent cloisters house the **Museo Civico** (*t 0761 325 462; open Tues–Sun summer 9–7, until 6 in winter; adm*) with an archaeological section and a good picture gallery. The most fascinating items on display, however, are the fake ancient monuments created in the 15th century by a mad monk who called himself

Annius of Viterbo. They were meant to support the equally fantastical histories Annius wrote to boost his home town – stories of how Viterbo was founded by Hercules and refounded by Noah, and enjoyed a visit from the Egyptian god Osiris when it was the 'capital of the Etruscans'.

San Pellegrino and the Palazzo Papale

From Piazza del Plebiscito the best route of all is down Via San Lorenzo into the heart of Viterbo's oldest quarter. Three streets down and off to the left, **Santa Maria Nuova** is the best preserved of the city's medieval churches. An ancient image of Jupiter is set into the portal, and St Thomas Aquinas once preached from the small outdoor pulpit in the corner. On the other side of Via San Lorenzo, Viterbo's old market square faces the 11th-century church of the **Gesù**, a medieval tower-fortress, one of several left in the city, and a palazzo that long ago was the town hall. To the south, trailing down from the aforementioned **Piazza della Morte** – ironically one of the lovelier squares in Viterbo – the San Pellegrino quarter hangs its web of alleys, arches and stairs along Via San Pellegrino with a romantic and thoroughly medieval air, though in fact few of the buildings are quite that old. The **Museo della Macchina di Santa Rosa** at Via San Pellegrino 60 (***t*** *0761 345 157; open Fri 3–5.30, Sat and Sun 10–1 and 3–5.30*) chronicles Viterbo's famous *festa*.

In the opposite direction from San Pellegrino, a bridge on Roman and Etruscan foundations, the **Ponte del Duomo**, carries you over to Piazza San Lorenzo and the **Palazzo Papale**, begun in 1266. This squarish, battlemented building, very much in the style of a medieval city hall, is a finer building than the pope's present address in Rome, though admittedly much smaller. On the best part, the open Gothic loggia, you will see lions (for Viterbo) interspersed with the striped coat of arms of the French pope Clement V, who completed the building. Three popes were elected at conclaves in the palace's Great Hall.

Popes and cardinals did not always have an easy time in Viterbo. When Clement IV died – just two weeks after he arrived – arguments between the French and Italian cardinals led to a two-year deadlock. Eventually the exasperated people of Viterbo tried to speed up the conclave by locking them in the palace and tearing off the roof; somehow the prelates got around this by making tents in the Great Hall. Finally the Viterbans decided to starve them out, and before long the Church was blessed with the undistinguished compromise choice of Gregory X. He had the roof fixed, but should have repaired the floor as well, since it collapsed six years later, killing his successor, John XXI. He is buried next door in the plain Romanesque **cathedral**, which has a small and rather dull museum (*open Tues–Sun 9–12; adm*).

Around Viterbo: Hot Mud and Tombs

West of the city, some of the Etruscans' and Romans' favourite thermal springs still do whatever it is they do that makes Italians so happy. At the ancient **Springs of Bullicame** you can stop by the roadside for a dip in a sulphurous pool, check into a hotel spa, and have an aerosol inhalation to help your sinuses or an icing of hot mineral mud to calm your nerves.

Further west, **Tuscània** stands alone at the centre of one of the emptiest, eeriest corners of Italy, a region of low green hills where you will find Etruscan ruins, old castles and religious shrines, but no people. Tuscània was a leading Etruscan city around the 4th century BC and regained its importance for a short while in the early Middle Ages. Today the city has nearly recovered from a bad earthquake in 1971, and its lovely medieval centre has a fine ensemble of buildings around **Piazza Basile**, including a fountain that has been flowing since Etruscan times (though this incarnation of the **Fontane delle Sette Canelle** is 13th-century). Etruscan sarcophagi are on display at the **Museo Nazionale Archeologico** (***t*** *0761 436 209; open Tues–Sun 8.30–7.30*) in the former Santa Maria del Riposo convent. The real attraction in Tuscània are the two unique early churches situated on the hill above the town: **San Pietro** and **Santa Maria Maggiore** (*both open daily summer 9–1 and 3–7, winter 9–1 and 2–5*), both begun in the 8th century, with additions in the 11th and 12th centuries. Besides their carved altars, pulpits and painting from the 8th–14th centuries, both have unusual sculpted façades – San Pietro especially, which has colourful Cosmati work, fragments of ancient sculpture and outlandish grotesques. Perhaps some of the churches of Rome looked like this before their Renaissance and Baroque rebuildings. Santa Maria Maggiore has a wonderful medieval Last Judgement frescoed inside.

Another road east from Viterbo – this one an eight-kilometre dead end – leads to the site of **Fèrento**, a rival city that Viterbo destroyed in the Middle Ages. Little is left save a well-preserved **Teatro Romano**, where concerts are sometimes held in summer (*open Tues–Sun 9–1.30; longer hours Sat and in summer*). East of Viterbo, the road for Orte enters the old suburb of La Quercia, passing in front of a landmark of Renaissance architecture: **Santa Maria della Quercia**, built in the late 1470s. The distinctive 1509 façade has a carved oak tree (*quercia*) and lions, and lunettes by Andrea della Robbia over the doors. Inside, the beautiful marble tabernacle contains a miraculous painting of the Virgin, and there is also a fine Gothic cloister; ask the custodian (***t*** *0761 303430*) to let you into the fascinating **Museo degli Ex-Voto**, filled with plaques painted over the centuries with scenes of the Madonna's miracles.

Bagnaia, six kilometres east, was a hill village expanded by Viterban bishops into a summer resort. In the 1570s Cardinal de Gambara commissioned Vignola to create **Villa Lante** (***t*** *0761 288 008; gardens open Tues–Sun 9–1hr before sunset; guided tours every 30mins; adm*), with one of the most striking Renaissance palace complexes: two villas sharing a large park and classic geometric Italian garden, full of groves and statuary, with water rising from fountains then cascading back down decorative stairs and terraces aligned on a long axis towards the incredible Grand Fountain. De Gambara was a relative of the Farnese, and Lante was his attempt to upstage their flashy palace at Caprarola; note the carved reliefs of prawns (*gamberi*), the family symbol.

This road continues into the beech forests of the Cimino Hills, meeting **Soriano nel Cimino**, with its medieval castle and an extinct volcano, Monte Cimino, for a neighbour. South of Viterbo as you head for Lake Vico (*see* p.762), you'll pass through lovely **San Martino al Cimino**, built around a fine 13th-century French Gothic Cistercian abbey; the town itself is an unusual example of Baroque planning, full of trees and half-surrounded by a single curving lane of terraced houses.

The Monster Park (Parco dei Mostri)

***t** 0761 924 029; open daily 8–sunset; adm exp/*

Some of the same sculptors who worked on St Peter's in Rome made this bizarre nightmare hidden away in the Lazio hills, just outside the village of Bomarzo. The two works seem somehow related, as opposite sides of the coin that may help in explaining the tragic, neurotic atmosphere of late 16th-century Italy. One of the Orsini, that ancient and powerful Roman family, commissioned this collection of huge, strange sculptures; he called it his *Sacro Bosco* – Sacred Wood – but in its present shabby state it is impossible to tell whether it was indeed a complex allegory or just a joke.

Long neglected and almost forgotten, the park has been restored over the last few decades by its owners, Giovanni Bettini and his family. Near the entrance you come upon the impressive though dilapidated Tempietto, a domed temple of unknown purpose attributed to Vignola. From there you wander the ill-kept grounds, encountering at every turn colossal monuments and eroded illegible inscriptions: a 20ft-tall screaming face, where you can walk inside the mouth, under an inscription that reads 'every thought flees', and find a small table and benches, apparently waiting for a dinner party; a life-size elephant, perhaps one of Hannibal's, crushing a terrified Roman soldier in its trunk; a giant wrestler, in the act of ripping a defeated opponent in two from the legs; and a leaning tower, just for fun. In every corner decayed Madonnas, mermaids, sphinxes, nymphs and harpies wait to spook you. All are done in a distorted, almost primitive style. The Monster Park will make you feel like an archaeologist, discovering some peculiar lost civilization.

Three Lakes, and a Farnese Pentagon

All of the lakes of northern Lazio are volcanic craters; long ago they must have been similar to the famous Phlegraean Fields outside Naples. They are also the most appealing features in the Lazio landscape: they're not exactly off the main tourist track, but for swimming purposes they are often more pleasant than the coastal beach resorts near Rome.

Lake Bolsena

Pristine, lovely and full of fish, this is the largest and northernmost of the three lakes. **Bolsena** town, at the northern end, was Etruscan *Velzna*, founded by refugees after the Romans destroyed the original Velzna (Orvieto, in nearby Umbria), in 264 BC. In the centre are narrow beaches and resort hotels, and behind them the 15th-century church of **Santa Cristina**, with a holy grotto and catacombs underneath. It's a stiff climb under medieval arches up to the **Castello Monaldeschi** (***t** 0761 798 630; open summer Tues–Sun 9.30–1.30 and 4–8; winter Weds–Fri 10–1, Sat and Sun 10–1 and 3–6; adm*), which has a good archaeological collection. Just above the castle, excavations of the ruins of old Velzna are currently underway (*open Tues–Sun 9–1.30*). Boat tours (***t** 0761 798 033*) are available from Bolsena to the lake's two islands: the pretty rock of

Est! Est!! Est!!!

In the year 1111, a German abbot, Giovanni Defuc, and his servant Martin were on their way to Rome for the coronation of Emperor Henry V. The good abbot liked his wine, and Martin's job was to keep ahead of him and act as a roving *sommelier*, testing the plonk in each cellar. If it was good, he would write *Est* ('there is') on the door; if it was exceptional, he would write *Est, Est*. When he tried the muscatel at Montefiascone, he was overwhelmed. *Est! Est!! Est!!!* he wrote. His master agreed, and after the coronation he and Martin returned and drank until Defuc dropped dead, leaving Martin to write his epitaph '*per il troppo Est qui morì il mio signore*' – 'my master died of excess here' – which still graces his tomb in San Flaviano.

Martana, with its steep granite cliffs and woods above, and **Isola Bisentina**, a favourite retreat of the Farnese in the 1500s, when the family was just beginning its spectacular career, and still a private residence (boat trips include guided tours). The Farnese commissioned Antonio da Sangallo the Younger to build them a palace and a large domed church, **SS. Giacomo e Cristoforo**, which is now in decay. The island's hill also has a string of Calvary chapels. At the southern end of the lake, **Capodimonte** on its small promontory offers more beaches and boat excursions.

Towns around Lake Bolsena include **Acquapendente**, situated at the northern extremity of Lazio, with an ancient crypt under its cathedral, built as a copy of the Holy Sepulchre in Jerusalem, and a nature reserve on nearby Monte Rufeno. **Bagnoregio**, to the east of Bolsena town, is worth a visit for the bizarre ghost town of **Civitá di Bagnoregio**, a one-kilometre walk over a pedestrian bridge from the town. Set in a weirdly eroded landscape, Cività dates back to the Etruscans, and its walls retain one of the few surviving Etruscan gates. It was gradually abandoned after an 18th-century earthquake made it nearly inaccessible; a few adventurous folk are fixing up some of the houses now.

Montefiascone, just south of the lake, has been famous for its wine since a medieval German bishop did himself in by drinking too much of it (*see* above). His tomb is in the 12th-century church of **San Flaviano**. Montefiascone makes a good living from its wine, and the embroidered legend that goes with it.

Lake Vico and Caprarola

The smallest and perhaps loveliest of the lakes, Vico is ringed by rugged hills. Unspoiled marshes line some of its shore – which is now a wildlife reserve – and its ancient crater has a younger volcano (also extinct) poking up inside it, known as **Monte Venere**. Just over the hills from the lake, in Caprarola, is one of Italy's most arrogantly ambitious late Renaissance palaces, the **Villa Farnese** (***t** 0761 646 052; villa open Tues–Sun 8.30–6.45; visits to the gardens at 10, 11, 12, 2 and 3, also 4 and 5 May–Aug; adm*).

When Alessandro Farnese, member of an obscure Lazio noble family, set his sister Giulia up as mistress to Pope Alexander VI, his fortune was made. Alessandro later became Pope Paul III – both a great pope who called the Council of Trent, rebuilt Rome, and kept Michelangelo busy, and a rotten pope who oppressed his people, reinvigorated the Inquisition, and became the most successful grafter in papal history. Before long the Farnese family ruled Parma, Piacenza and most of northern Lazio. With the fantastic wealth that Alessandro had accumulated, his grandson, who was also named Alessandro, built this family headquarters. Vignola, the family architect, turned the entire town of Caprarola into a setting for the palace, ploughing a new avenue through the town as an axis that led to a grand stairway, then a set of gardens (now disappeared), and then another stairway up to the huge pentagonal villa, built over the massive foundations of an earlier, uncompleted fortress.

The palace is empty today; the Farnese lost everything in later papal intrigues, and someone, some time, probably had to sell the furniture. Nevertheless it is still an impressive place; the tour includes Vignola's elegant courtyard, a room with uncanny acoustic tricks that the guides love to demonstrate, frescoes of the Labours of Hercules, another with a wonderful ceiling painted with the figures of the constellations, and Vignola's decorative masterpiece – an incredible **spiral staircase** of stone columns and frescoes. The best part of the visit, however, is the 'secret garden', a park filled with azaleas and rhododendrons leading up to a sculpture garden of grotesques and fantastical *telemones* that recall the Bomarzo Monster Park (there is a connection – one of the Orsini was Alessandro Farnese's secretary), and finally to a delightful, smaller villa, the **Palazzina del Piacere**.

The hills between Lake Vico and the coast conceal no fewer than 12 minor Etruscan sites; all you'll see of these vanished cities, however, are the usual rock-cut tombs, some with temple-like carved façades, as at **Blera** and **Norchia**. Also at Norchia is a strange avenue stretching more than 1,200ft cut deeply into the easily worked tufa.

Getting Around

Bracciano town is on the FS **rail** line between Rome and Viterbo, but the way to get to the lakes is by COTRAL **buses**. There are frequent services from Lepanto and Agnanina termini in Rome to Bracciano and Vico respectively, and from Viterbo to Lake Bolsena.

Where to Stay and Eat

******Villa Clementina**, Via Traversa Quarto del Largo 12, **t** 06 998 6268, *www.charmerelax.it/villaclementina* (*expensive*) Bracciano's most sumptuous hotel, situated in a whitewashed country house with beautiful gardens and 7 quirkily decorated rooms. There's also a swimming pool, tennis courts and an excellent restaurant. *Closed Nov–Feb except 2wks over Christmas and New Year.*

*****Albergo Nuovo Torrione**, Viale Garibaldi 127, **t** 06 999 9046 (*moderate*). A family-run hotel with large comfy rooms, some with huge terraces with lake views, plus a little garden and a pizzeria (*cheap*).

*****Bella Venere**, Loc. Scardenato, Caprarola, **t** 0761 612 342 (*moderate*). A little gem on Lake Vico, with gardens, a beach, tennis courts and a restaurant (*cheap*). *Closed Nov.*

*****Sans Soucis sul Lago**, Via dei Noccioleti 18, Punta del Lago, near the road to Ronciglione **t** 0761 612 052 (*cheap*). A hotel with a beach and garden, and views over the Lake Vico.

Gino al Miralago, Lungolago Marconi 58, Marta, on the south side of Lake Bolsena, **t** 0761 870 910 (*cheap*). A lovely waterfront trattoria. *Closed Tues.*

Osteria La Cantinella, Piazza V. Emmanuele III, **t** 06 999 9580 (*cheap*). Typical local dishes, including very tasty grilled lamb, served in a stone-vaulted dining room or on a tiny terrace in summer. *Closed Thurs.*

Sutri and Cìvita Castellana

Between Lake Vico and Lake Bracciano, **Sutri** is famously old, perhaps dating back as far as 1000 BC. It was a strategic spot for the Etruscans and again in the Middle Ages, when it was rebuilt on a safer height and became a proper hill town. Remains can be seen in the **Parco Archeologico Preistorico-Paesaggistico** (*open summer Mon–Fri 4–7, Sat and Sun 10–1 and 4–7; winter 10–1 and 3–6.30*), including tombs and a cave church that was once a temple of Mithras.

Cìvita Castellana, in the hills to the east, was home to the Faliscans, a small people related to the Latins who were conquered by Rome in 395 BC. People around here still call themselves *Falisci*, and the faces on the street do often bear striking resemblances to ancient portrait busts in the **Museo Archeologico dell'Agro Falisco** (*open Tues–Sun 8–7; adm*), housed in one of the most elegant of all Renaissance fortresses, the **Rocca** built by Giuliano and Antonio da Sangallo for the popes. This lovely and distinguished town also has a **cathedral** with a gorgeous, completely preserved Cosmati façade (1210), all glittering gold mosaic work and reliefs. The Faliscan lands lie in the shadow of **Monte Soratte** (Mount Soracte), which was a holy site for pagans and Christians (the 5th-century chapel at its summit was reconstructed from a temple of Apollo), and a favourite subject for Romantic-era painters. South of Cìvita, **Calcata** is central Italy's improbable New Age village, colonized by artists and alternative folk.

Lake Bracciano

This broad sheet of water is one of Rome's most popular swimming holes, yet it's still remarkably clean and beautiful. A good view of it can be gained from the grim 1470s castle of the Orsini family, the **Castello Orsini-Odescalchi** (***t*** *06 9980 4348; open Tues–Sun Apr–Sept 10–12 and 3–6.30, Oct–Mar 10–12 and 3–5, daily in Aug; adm exp*), in the town of Bracciano. Boats run from there around the lake in summer. The pretty lakeside villages of Trevignano and Anguillara have medieval centres and places to eat.

Rieti and its Province

This comes as something of a digression, but this strip of land reaching over the Apennines to the borders of the Marche is also a part of Lazio. Before Roman conquest it was the land of the Sabines, often fierce enemies of Rome. The Romans pushed their Via Salaria through here on its way to the Adriatic, generally following the route of the modern SS4 to Ascoli Piceno, and made it an important staging post.

Lazio's Least-known Towns

Rieti, the capital, has a 12th-century cathedral, a small picture collection in its Museo Civico (***t*** *0746 287 456; open Tues–Thurs 8.30–1.30, Fri and Sat 8.30–1.30 and 3–6, Sun 10–1.30 and 3–6; adm*), and well-preserved and very medieval-looking walls. The territory around it, once swamps, was drained by the Romans when they built the Marmore Falls in Terni; now it's a fertile plain with views of some of the highest peaks of the Apennines – the Gran Sasso is just over the border in Abruzzo (*see* p.573).

Getting Around

Rieti is on the Terni–L'Aquila **rail** line but trains are infrequent. There are several **buses** a day to Rome (from Stazione Tiburtina), Terni and L'Aquila (**t** 0746 256 740).

Tourist Information

Rieti: Piazza Vittorio Emanuele II, **t** 0746 203 330, *www.apt.rieti.it*.
Terminillo: Via dei Villini 33, Pian de'Valli, **t** 0746 261 121.

Where to Stay and Eat

Rieti ✉ **02100**

****Quattro Stagioni**, Piazza C. Battisti 14, **t** 0746 271 071 (*moderate*). An elegant and comfortable choice.

Bistrot, Piazza San Rufo 25, **t** 0746 498 798 (*cheap*). A family-run eatery offering an adventurous menu that draws in local foodies. Booking is essential. *Closed Sun, and Mon lunch.*

Il Grottino, Piazza C. Battisti 4, **t** 0746 497 683 (*cheap*). Good traditional meals. *Closed Tues.*

There is plenty of lovely scenery and good walking country in the province, most of it in rather remote areas. South of Rieti there are the hills around the artificial lakes of **Salto** and **Turano**; on the way to the latter you will see an impressive medieval castle, the Rocca Sinibalda. North of Rieti, **Monte Terminillo** has a modest ski resort on the slopes of its 6,993ft peak; in summer the road around it makes a panoramic drive to **Leonessa**, an attractive medieval town that is one of the quietest and most out-of-the-way places in Italy. St Francis spent much time in these mountains; among the humble sanctuaries where he preached, **Greccio**, on its lovely mountaintop site west of Rieti, is said to be where the saint made the first Christmas crib; the event is celebrated with a real-life nativity scene on 24 and 26 December and 6 January.

Rome

To know what Rome is, visit the little church of San Clemente, hidden away on the backstreets behind the Colosseum. The Baroque façade conceals a 12th-century basilica with a beautiful marble choir screen 600 years older. In 1857 a cardinal from Boston discovered the original church of 313, one of the first great Christian basilicas, just underneath. And beneath that are two buildings and a Temple of Mithras from the time of Augustus; from it you can walk out into a Roman alley that looks exactly as it did 2,000 years ago, now some 28ft below ground level. There are some commemorative plaques in San Clemente, placed there by a Medici duke, a bishop of New York, and the last chairman of the Bulgarian Communist Party.

You are not going to get to the bottom of this city, whether your stay is for three days or a month. With its legions of headless statues, acres of paintings, 913 churches and megatons of artistic sediment, this metropolis of aching feet will wear down even the most resolute of travellers (and travel writers). The name Rome passed out of the plane of reality into legend some 2,200 years ago, when princes as far away as China first began to hear of the faraway city and its invincible armies. At the same time the Romans were cooking up a personified goddess, the Divine Rome, and beginning the strange myth of their destiny to conquer and pacify the world – a myth that would still haunt Europe 1,000 years later.

Museo Nazionale di Villa Giulia
Galleria Nazionale d'Arte Moderna
V. D. BELLE ARTI
VIA FLAMINIA
LUNG. DELLE NAVI
LUNG. DELLE ARMI
MAZZINI
PIAZZA G. MAZZINI
VIALE GIUSEPPE
VLE. ANGELICO
PIAZZALE CLODIO
CLODIA
CIRCONVAL.
VIA TRIONFALE
CIRC. TRIONFALE
VIA DELLA GIULIANA
STAZIONE ROMA-VITERBO
PIAZZALE FLAMINIO
VIALE DEL MURO TORTO
Monte Pincio
V.L.DI SAVOIA
S. Maria del Popolo
PZA. DEL POPOLO
VIALE DELLA MILIZIA
LUNG. MICHELANGELO
VIALE GIULIO CESARE
LARGO TRIONFALE
VIA A. DORIA
PIAZZALE DEGLI EROI
V.LEONE IV
VIA OTTAVIANO
VIA COLA DI RIENZO
LUNG. IN AUGUSTA
LUNG. MELLINI
VIA RIPETTA
VIA BABUINO
Villa Medici
Spanish Steps
Mausoleum of Augustus
V.B. DI LEONE
V. D. MACELLI
Trinità del Monte
Ara Pacis
V. DEL CONDOTTI
VIA ANGELO EMO
VATICANO
PIAZZA DEL RISORGIMENTO
VIA CRESCENZIO
PIAZZA CAVOUR
Musei Vaticani
CITTÁ DEL VATICANO
Giardino del Vaticano
VIALE VATICANO
Castel S.Angelo
V. FRATTINA
V.DI MERCEDE
VIA DEL CORSO
PZA SILVESTRO
Palazzo di Montecitorio
V. DELLA SCROFA
LUNG. CASTELLO
(Tiber)
Tévere
LUNG. TOR DI NONA
Basilica di San Pietro
PIAZZA S. PIETRO
Ospedale di S. Spirito
VIA AURELIA
Palazzo Madama
PIAZZA DELLA ROTONDA
PIAZZA COLONNA
Fontana di Trevi
VIA DEI CORONARI
Borsa
Chiesa Nuova
PIAZZA NAVONA
C. RINASCIMENTO
Pantheon
S. Ignazio
Palazzo Doria Pamphili
S. Onofrio
LUNG. GIANICOLENSE
VIA DELLA LUNGARA
VIA GIULIA
LUNGOTEVERE
CORSO VITTORIO EMANUELE II
Chiesa del Gesù
PIAZZA VENEZIA
Vittoriano
VIA GREGORIO VII
VIA DELLE FORNACI
VIALE DELLE MURA
PIAZZA FARNESE
VIA DEI FARNESI
PIAZZA CAMPO DE FIORI
VIA DEI GIUBBONARI
Teatro di Pompeo
Palazzo Venezia
S. Maria in Aracoeli
Monte Gianicolo
VIA ARENULA
VIA DEL TEATRO MARCELLO
Galleria Corsini
Palazzo Farnese
Palazzo Spada
S. Maria d. Quercia
LUNG. FARNESINA
TEBALDI
Villa Farnesina
Sinagoga
LUNG. CENCI
Villa Abamelek
AURELIO
VIA GARIBALDI
LUNG. R. SANZIO
Teatro di Marcello
Monte Capitolino
ISOLA TIBERINA
PIAZZALE GIUSEPPE GARIBALDI
PZA. S. MARIA IN TRAST.
PZA. G. BELLI
Torre di Anguillara
S. Pietro in Montorio
VIA AURELIA ANTICA
S.Maria in Trastevere
V.S. FRANCESCO A RIPA
V. DELLA LUNGARETTA
VIA DEL CERCHI
Villa Doria Pamphili
Villa Aurelia
S. Crisogano
V. DEL GENOVESI
PIAZZA BOCCA DELLA VERITÀ
VIA DEL CIRCO MASSIMO
PZA. S. COSIMATO
V. NICOLA FABRIZI
VIALE GLORIOSO
VIA DI S. PANCRAZIO
VIA GIACINTO CARINI
S. Cecilia
VIA ANICIA
V.D.S. MICHELE
LUNG. RIPA
LUNG. AVENTINO
S. Sabina
VIALE DI TRASTEVERE
Ponte Sublicio
S. Prisca
S. Alessio
VIA DI S. SABINA
GIANICOLENSI
VIA VITELLIA
Priorio delle Cav. di Malta
VIA S. ALESSIO
VIA MARMORATA
V. DI S. ANSELMO
Monte Aventino
VIA FONTEIANA
VIALE DEI QUATTRO VENTI
VIA A.G. BARRILI
VIA ALESSANDRO POERIO
VIA PORTUENSE
LUNGOTEVERE TESTACCIO
PIAZZA ALBANIA
V. PIR CESTIA
N
VIA N. ZABAGLIA
VIA GALVANI
PIAZZA PORTA S. PAOLO
Porto S. Paolo
Piramide
VIALE MARCO POLO
METROPOLITANA
500 m
1/4 mile
Monte Testaccio
VIA E. ROLLI
Cimitero Protestante
VLE. DEL CAMPO BOARIO
STAZIONE ROMA-LIDO DI OSTIA
AIRPORT BUS STOP
Stazione Trastevere (100 metres)

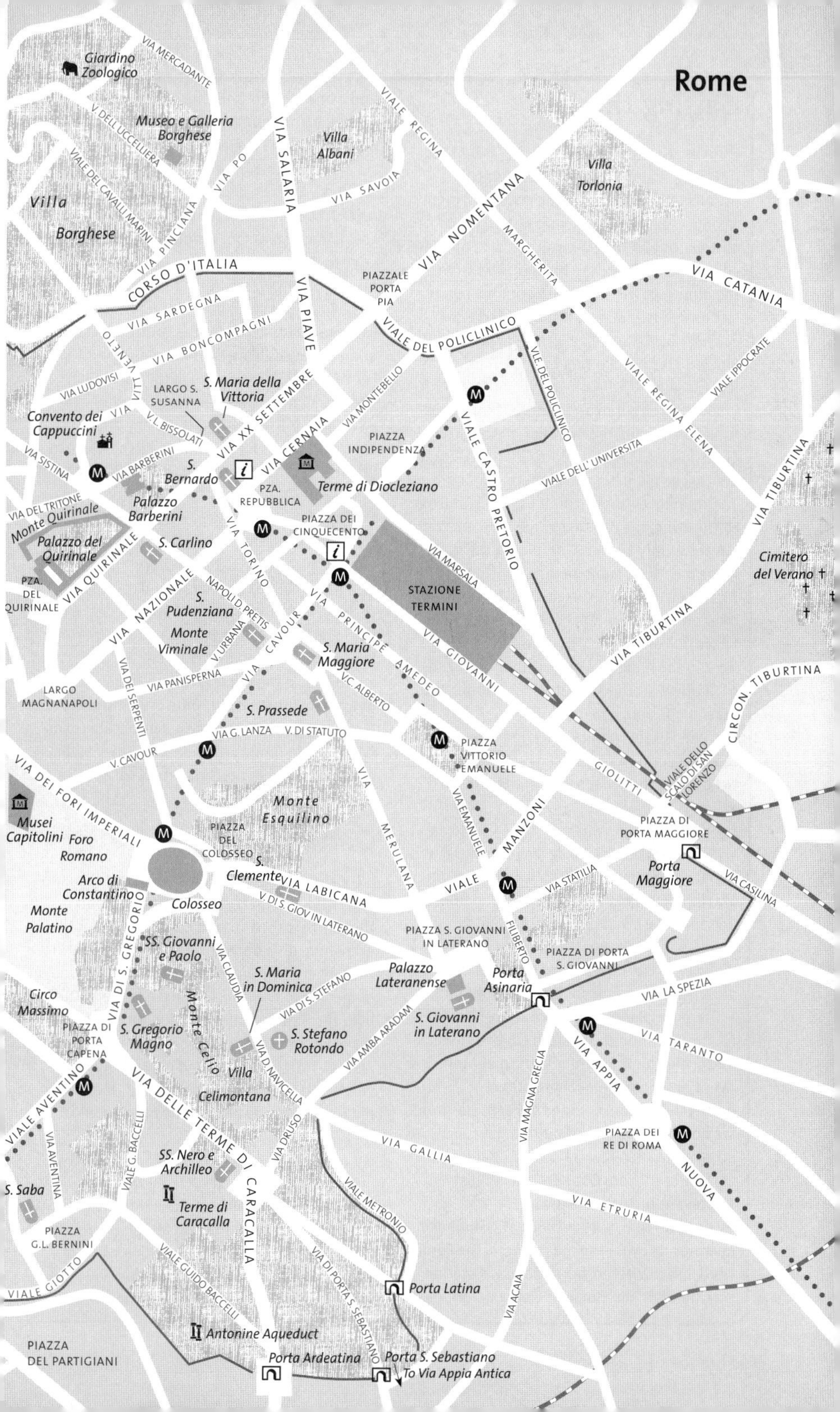
Rome
Giardino Zoologico
Museo e Galleria Borghese
Villa Borghese
Villa Albani
Villa Torlonia
VIA MERCADANTE
V. DELL'UCCELLIERA
VIALE DEL CAVALLI MARINI
VIA PINCIANA
VIA PO
VIA SALARIA
VIALE REGINA
VIA SAVOIA
VIA NOMENTANA
MARGHERITA
CORSO D'ITALIA
VIA SARDEGNA
VIA BONCOMPAGNI
VIA PIAVE
PIAZZALE PORTA PIA
VIA CATANIA
VIALE DEL POLICLINICO
VLE. DEL POLICLINICO
VIALE REGINA ELENA
VIALE IPPOCRATE
VIA VENETO
VIA LUDOVISI
LARGO S. SUSANNA
S. Maria della Vittoria
VIA XX SETTEMBRE
VIA MONTEBELLO
PIAZZA INDIPENDENZA
VIALE CASTRO PRETORIO
VIALE DELL' UNIVERSITÀ
VIA TIBURTINA
Convento dei Cappuccini
V. L. BISSOLATI
VIA SISTINA
VIA BARBERINI
S. Bernardo
VIA CERNAIA
Terme di Diocleziano
PZA. REPUBBLICA
Palazzo Barberini
VIA DEL TRITONE
Monte Quirinale
Palazzo del Quirinale
S. Carlino
PIAZZA DEI CINQUECENTO
VIA MARSALA
STAZIONE TERMINI
Cimitero del Verano
PZA. DEL QUIRINALE
VIA QUIRINALE
VIA NAZIONALE
VIA TORINO
NAPOLI D. PRETIS
S. Pudenziana
Monte Viminale
V. URBANA
VIA CAVOUR
VIA PRINCIPE AMEDEO
VIA GIOVANNI GIOLITTI
S. Maria Maggiore
V.C. ALBERTO
VIA PANISPERNA
LARGO MAGNANAPOLI
VIA DEI SERPENTI
S. Prassede
CIRCON. TIBURTINA
VIA G. LANZA
V. DI STATUTO
V. CAVOUR
PIAZZA VITTORIO EMANUELE
VIALE DELLO SCALO DI SAN LORENZO
VIA DEI FORI IMPERIALI
Monte Esquilino
VIA MERULANA
VIA EMANUELE
Musei Capitolini
Foro Romano
PIAZZA DEL COLOSSEO
VIALE MANZONI
PIAZZA DI PORTA MAGGIORE
Porta Maggiore
Arco di Constantino
S. Clemente
VIA LABICANA
VIA STATILIA
VIA CASILINA
Colosseo
Monte Palatino
V. DI S. GIOV IN LATERANO
PIAZZA S. GIOVANNI IN LATERANO
FILIBERTO
SS. Giovanni e Paolo
VIA CLAUDIA
VIA DI S. GREGORIO
PIAZZA DI PORTA S. GIOVANNI
Palazzo Lateranense
Porta Asinaria
S. Maria in Dominica
VIA DI S. STEFANO
VIA LA SPEZIA
Circo Massimo
Monte Celio
S. Giovanni in Laterano
PIAZZA DI PORTA CAPENA
S. Gregorio Magno
S. Stefano Rotondo
VIA AMBA ARADAM
VIA TARANTO
VIA APPIA NUOVA
Villa Celimontana
VIA D. NAVICELLA
VIALE AVENTINO
VIA DELLE TERME DI CARACALLA
VIA MAGNA GRECIA
PIAZZA DEI RE DI ROMA
VIA GALLIA
VIA DRUSO
VIA AVENTINA
VIALE G. BACCELLI
SS. Nero e Archilleo
S. Saba
Terme di Caracalla
VIA ETRURIA
VIALE METRONIO
PIAZZA G.L. BERNINI
VIALE GIOTTO
VIALE GUIDO BACCELLI
VIA DI PORTA S. SEBASTIANO
Porta Latina
VIA ACAIA
PIAZZA DEL PARTIGIANI
Antonine Aqueduct
Porta Ardeatina
Porta S. Sebastiano
To Via Appia Antica

Getting There

By Air

The main airport, **Leonardo da Vinci**, is usually referred to as **Fiumicino** (**t** 06 65951). Taking a **taxi** from there into Rome should cost about €40, including airport and luggage supplements. There are two **rail** links from the airport to the city: to Stazioni Trastevere, Ostiense, Tuscolana and Tiburtina (*every 20mins;* €4.70) and an express service to Stazione Termini, Rome's main rail station (*every 30mins;* €8.80 one way).

Between 10.20pm and 7am, COTRAL **buses** run from outside the Arrivals hall to Stazione Tiburtina, via Ostiense (both Ⓜ Line B). Tickets are €5; cheaper if you buy before you board. The train takes about 30mins from Fiumicino to Tiburtina; the bus takes at least 50mins.

A secondary airport, **Ciampino** (**t** 06 794 941) is the base for a few scheduled and charter flights, including those with Ryanair, who offer an expensive (€8) but hassle-free shuttle to central Rome. A COTRAL **bus** runs from here to the Anagnina stop at the south end of Ⓜ Line A, from where it's about 20mins to Stazione Termini (*daily 6.50am–11.40pm*); you need exact change (€0.77) for the machine; otherwise you can purchase a ticket from the tobacconist in the airport.

By Rail

Almost all long-distance trains arrive at and depart from the huge, chaotic but efficient **Stazione Termini**. The information and ticket windows are often terribly crowded, so allow plenty of time. There is a taxi stand in front, along with city buses to most points in Rome, and the main metro station is underneath.

There are plenty of other stations: **Tiburtina** (Ⓜ Tiburtina), on the eastern edge of town, and **Ostiense** (Ⓜ Piramide), south of Monte Aventino, serve some long-distance north–south lines. During the night (*12–5am*), Stazione Termini is shut and trains stop at the other stations. A few trains to Tuscany and Umbria start from **Ostiense** and stop at **Trastevere**, on Viale Trastevere.

The Lazio transport authority, COTRAL, also operates its own little rail network: the Roma-Nord line to **Viterbo**, from their own station on Piazzale Flaminio, north of Piazza del Popolo, and a line to **Ostia** and the Lido, from Porta San Paolo (next to the main Stazione Ostiense FS) and Ⓜ Magliana (Line B).

By Bus

COTRAL buses serve almost every town in Lazio. They leave from various locations on the edge of Rome, depending on the destination: buses heading north-northwest leave from Saxa Rubra (on the Roma-Nord rail line) and Lepanto (Ⓜ Lepanto); for the south, southwest and east, buses leave from Ⓜ Anagnina, Ⓜ EUR Fermi and Ⓜ Tiburtina. For details (in Italian) about schedules and fares, call freephone **t** 800 150 008 (*Mon–Fri 8–6*). Many different companies offer long-distance bus services to and from Rome; check with the tourist office.

By Road

All the *autostrade* converging on Rome run into the giant ring road, the *Grande Raccordo Anulare* or *GRA*. From there, good routes into the city are the Via Aurelia (SS1) from the west, the local SS201 *autostrada* from the airport in the southwest, and the A24 from the east. Rome is, as it has been for 2,000 years, the hub of a network of ancient routes serving every direction, now transmogrified into state roads (SS) but retaining their old names; they still provide the most direct means of escape.

Getting Around

Looking at the map, Rome seems to be made for getting around on foot. This may be so in the *centro storico* around Piazza Navona, but elsewhere it's a different story – city blocks in the newer areas are huge, and it will take you longer than you think to walk anywhere. The hills, the outsize scale and the traffic also make Rome a tiring place, but there is some pleasant strolling to be had in the old districts west of the Corso, around the Isola Tiberina, in old Trastevere and around the Monte Celio.

By Metro

Rome's underground system is not particularly convenient, as it seems to avoid the historic parts of the city; imagine trying to dig any sort of hole in Rome, with legions of archaeologists ready to pounce. The two lines, A and B, cross at Stazione Termini and will take you to the Colosseum, around the Monte Aventino, to Piazza di Spagna, San Giovanni in Laterano, San Paolo Fuori le Mura, Piazza del Popolo, or within eight blocks of St Peter's.

Single tickets (€0.77), also good for city buses – valid for 75mins from when you punch them in the turnstile – are available from machines in metro stations, tobacconists, bars and kiosks. Daily and weekly tickets are also available from tobacconists (*see* below).

By Bus and Tram

Buses are by far the best way to get around. Pick up a map of routes from the **ATAC** (city bus company) booth outside Stazione Termini. Tickets (€0.77) are good for travel on any ATAC bus or tram and one metro ride – within 75mins of the first use of the ticket – which must be stamped in the machines in the back entrance of buses or trams. There are also day tickets called BIG (which include the metro) for €3, plus weekly passes (CIS, €12.40) and monthly passes available from tobacconists.

Some useful bus routes:

3 (tram) Villa Borghese–Viale Regina Margherita–San Lorenzo–San Giovanni in Laterano– Colosseum–Viale Aventino–Porta San Paolo.

19 (tram) Piazza Risorgimento (near the Vatican)–Viale delle Milizie–Villa Borghese–Viale Regina Margherita–Porta Maggiore –San Lorenzo and Via Prenestina.

23 Musei Vaticani–Castel Sant'Angelo–Tiber banks–Porta San Paolo–San Paolo.

36 Termini–Via Nomentana (Sant'Agnese).

46 Piazza Venezia–Corso V. Emanuele– Vatican.

63 Largo Argentina–Via del Corso–Via del Tritone–Via Vittorio Veneto.

64 Termini–Via Nazionale–Corso Vittorio Emanuele–Vatican (the main bus route from the *centro storico* to the Vatican and famous for its pickpockets, so be extra careful).

116T Piazza della Repubblica–Via Nazionale – Via del Tritone–Via del Corso–Piazza Venezia–Largo Argentina–Mausoleo di Augusto (*8pm–1.30am*).

116 Via Veneto–Piazza Barberini–Via del Tritone–Piazza del Parlamento–Corso Rinascimento–Corso Vittorio Emanuele –Campo de' Fiori–Piazza Farnese–Via Giulia (a circular minibus, *weekdays 8am–9pm, Sat 8am–midnight*).

119 Piazza del Popolo–Via del Babuino–Piazza di Spagna–Piazza Barberini–Via Veneto– Porta Pinciano (and back).

218 San Giovanni in Laterano–Porta San Sebastiano–Via Appia Antica–Via Ardeatina (passing the catacombs and tombs).

By Taxi

Official taxis (painted white) are plentiful, and easier to get at a rank in one of the main piazzas than to flag down. They are quite expensive, with surcharges for luggage, on Sundays and after 10.30pm. Fares are clearly explained in English inside every taxi. Don't expect to find one when it's raining. To phone for a taxi, call **t** 06 3570, or **t** 06 4994.

By Car

This is absolutely not recommended – Rome is nearly as chaotic as Naples, parking is expensive and difficult to find, and many areas in the centre are closed to traffic.

Tourist Information

Azienda di Promozione Turistica (APT), Via Parigi 11, 00185, **t** 06 488 991 (*open Mon–Fri 9.30–12.30, Mon and Thurs also 2.30–4.30*). There's also a useful branch office at Fiumicino airport, **t** 06 6595 6074 (*open Mon–Sat 8.15–7*). The APT offices are the best source of information about what's on in Rome and its province.

Comune di Roma Tourist Information Office, Termini Station (*open daily 8–8*). A good place for free city maps and brochures in English, plus free, very useful ATAC public transport maps.

Comune di Roma helpline, **t** 06 3600 4399, select 2 for an English-speaking operator. (*open daily 9–7.30*), *www.romaturismo.com*.

Enjoy Rome, Via Varese 39, **t** 06 445 1843. An English-speaking information service near Stazione Termini.

In addition, there are tourist kiosks (*all open daily 9.30–7.30*) at Largo Goldoni, Piazza Pia, Piazza del Tempio della Pace, Piazza delle Cinque Lune, Via Marco Minghetti, Via Nazionale, Piazza Sonnino, Piazza San Giovanni in Laterano, Via dell'Olmata and Stazione Termini.

To make the most of the sights, you should purchase a cumulative ticket called the **Roma Archeologia Card**, which is valid for 7 days and includes entry to the Palatino, Colosseum, Crypta Balbi, Palazzo Massimo, Palazzo Altemps, Terme di Diocleziano, Baths of Caracalla, Tomb of Cecilia Metella and Villa dei Quintili. It can be acquired at any of these sites and costs €20.

Shopping

Rome isn't as exciting for big-game shoppers as Milan, though when it comes to clothing you will find all the major designers and labels. Serious shoppers should check out the website *www.made-in-italy.com*.

There is no shortage of shops selling **antiques**; many are between the Tiber and Piazza Navona (look especially off Via Monserrato, Via dei Coronari and Via dell'Anima). For **old prints**, which are generally inexpensive, try Casali, Piazza Rotonda 81A. Alinari, Via Alibert 16/a, is a good address for artistic black and white pictures of old Rome. **L'Art Nouveau**, Via dei Coronari 221, offers just what its name implies. Antiques can also be had in the celebrated Sunday morning **flea market** at Porta Portese, along with anything else you can imagine (*open dawn–1*).

The most **fashionable shopping** is between Piazza di Spagna and the Corso, with Via Condotti still the designer shopping street *par excellence*. Massoni, Largo Goldoni 48, near Via Condotti, much frequented by film stars, sells some of Rome's finest **jewellery**; for **menswear**, try Testa, Via Borgognona 13 and Via Frattina 42, or Valentino Uomo, Via Condotti 12; for **custom tailoring**, go to Battistoni, Via Condotti 61/a.

Designer **women's clothes** in the same area include Missoni, Via del Babuino 96, Giorgio Armani, Via Condotti 76–7 and Via del Babuino 140, Mila Schöen, Via Condotti 51, and Fendi, Via Borgognona 36/e. For **leather**, there's Gucci at Via Condotti 8 and Fausto Santini, Via Frattina 120. **Discounted designer fashion** may be had at Il Discount dell'Alta Moda, Via Gesù e Maria 16/a; **high-fashion shoes** at Barrilà, Via Condotti 29 and Via del Babuino 33. For **Borsalino hats** try Troncarelli, Via della Cuccagna 15, near Piazza Navona.

For a special bottle of **wine**, see the wide selection at Enoteca Costantini, Piazza Cavour 16. If you wish to stock up on Italian **coffee**, Tazza d'Oro, Via degli Orfani 84, has special bags of the city's best, the 'Aroma di Roma'.

If you need a good **book**, there's the Anglo-American Book Co., Via della Vite 27, the Lion Bookshop, Via dei Greci 36, the Economy Book Center, Via Torino 135/a, near Via Nazionale, and Feltrinelli International at Via Orlando 84–6 (this also stocks a range of guides and maps).

For an amazing selection of **fancy kitchen gear**, try C.U.C.I.N.A., Via Mario dei Fiori 65; for serious, professional **pans, pots and tools** head to Zucchi, Via Sant'Antonio all'Esquilino 15, near Santa Maria Maggiore. Image, Via della Scrofa 67, has **posters, postcards and photos**.

Sports and Activities

Rome's two first-division **football** clubs, AS Roma and Lazio, both play on Sat or Sun afternoons at the Stadio Olimpico, Viale dei Gladiatori 2 (Ⓜ Linea A to Ottaviano, then bus no.32) during the season (Sept–May).

Tickets (€18–110) go on sale 10–14 days ahead; contact Lazio Point, Via Farini 34, **t** 06 6482 6688; or *Orbis*, Piazza Esquilino 37, **t** 06 474 4776.

Where to Stay

Rome ✉ 00100

When it comes to hotels, prices are higher and service and quality lower than elsewhere in Italy, and places with a history, a view or quiet gardens are rare. That said, the city went into overdrive building, renovating and sprucing up its hotels for 2000.

Much of the city's accommodation is to be found around the Stazione Termini district, but it is overbuilt, dingy and down-at-heel, and inconvenient for most of the sights, although it's handy for the newly trendy San Lorenzo district.

Rooms can be difficult to find at short notice, but the **Hotel Reservation Service, t** 06 699 1000 (*daily 8am–10.45pm*) and the private **Enjoy Rome** (*see* p.769) both make commission-free hotel bookings.

Luxury

★★★★★**Art**, Via Margutta 56, 00187, **t** 06 421 281, *www.hotelart.it*. A sleek boutique hotel successfully combining antiques and contemporary design within a former *palazzetto* close to the Spanish Steps. Added attractions include a Turkish bath, a sauna and a Jacuzzi.

★★★★★**Excelsior**, Via Veneto 125, 00187, **t** 06 47081, *www.westin.com/excelsiorroma*. A plush hotel in a choice area, though it's lacking the aura it had in the 1950s. The reception areas have thicker carpets, bigger chandeliers and more gilded plaster than any other hotel in Italy. The rooms are all as good, so don't let them try to give you a modernized one. There's a famous bar and a minuscule cinema.

★★★★★**Hassler-Villa Medici**, Piazza Trinità dei Monti 6, 00187, **t** 06 699 340, *www.hotelhasslerroma.com*. One of Rome's best, with a fine location at the top of the Spanish Steps, wonderful views over the city, a beautiful courtyard, a rooftop terrace and excellent service.

★★★★**D'Inghilterra**, Via Bocca di Leone 14, 00187, **t** 06 699 811, *www.hoteldinghilterraroma.it*. Another favourite near Piazza di Spagna, parts of which date from a 15th-century prince's guesthouse. As a hotel (since 1850), it has played host to many of Europe and America's literati and artists. Don't miss the beautiful roof garden.

★★★★**Columbus**, Via della Conciliazione 33, 00193, **t** 06 686 5435 or **t** 06 6819 9360, *www.hotelcolumbus.net*. A staid but very reliable option that's slightly geared towards business travellers, with a number of well-equipped rooms, some boasting views over St Peter's.

★★★★**Forum**, Via Tor de' Conti 25, 00184, **t** 06 679 2446, *www.hotelforum.com*. The only fancy establishment near the ancient Forum. It's somewhat worn these days, but offers unbeatable views from its roof terrace.

★★★★**Raphael**, Largo di Febo 2, 00186, **t** 06 682 831, *www.raphaelhotel.com*. A vine-covered charmer decorated with antiques, situated very near to Piazza Navona. Rooms have TV, air-conditioning and business facilities. Breakfast is extra.

Very Expensive

★★★★**La Residenza**, Via Emilia 22, 00187, **t** 06 488 0789, **w** *www.venere.it/roma/laresidenza*. Beautifully appointed rooms situated in an old townhouse close to Via Veneto, with some luxuries that are more common to the most expensive hotels. It's a no-smoking establishment.

★★★**Carriage**, Via delle Carrozze 36, 00187, **t** 06 699 0124, *www.hotelcarriage.net*. A sleepy but charming spot almost at the foot of the Spanish Steps, with tastefully refurbished rooms and welcoming staff. Book well in advance.

★★★**Celio**, Via del Santio Quattro 35c, **t** 06 7049 5333, 00184, *www.hotelcelio.com*. A welcoming, idiosyncratic hotel close to the Colosseum. The bedrooms bear the names of opera singers and the bathrooms have mosaic-style floors. Some of the room rates fall into the *luxury* category, others into *expensive*.

★★★**Due Torri**, Vicolo del Leonetto 23, 00186, **t** 06 687 6983, *www.hotelduetorri.roma.it*. An attractive little hotel on a quiet street, once the home of a famous prelate, with comfortable, if slightly small, rooms (try to get one with rooftop views).

★★★**Fontana**, Piazza di Trevi 96, 00187, **t** 06 678 6113, *www.fontanahotel.com*. A hotel that would be good anywhere – the fact that it is right across the street from the Trevi Fountain guarantees nice dreams. Prices can reach *luxury* levels.

★★★**Fontanella Borghese**, Largo Fontanello Borghese 84, 00186, **t** 06 6880 9504, *www.fontanellaborghese.com*. An atmospheric little hotel in a 15th-century palazzo, with tasteful rooms and large bathrooms.

★★★**Locarno**, Via della Penna 22, **t** 06 361 0841, 00186, *www.hotellocarno.com*. A welcoming Art Nouveau-style hotel close to Piazza del Popolo, with elegant, well-equipped rooms (some with hi-fi, video players and modem connections) and a lovely roof terrace. Book in advance.

★★★**Portoghesi**, Via dei Portoghesi 1, 00186, **t** 06 686 4231, *www.hotelportoghesi.roma.com*. A small, well-kept hotel located inside a former mansion on a quiet street to the north of Piazza Navona, offering antiques-filled rooms.

***Hotel Sant'Anselmo, Piazza Sant'Anselmo 2, 00153, t 06 574 8119, *www.aventinohotels.com*. A peaceful hotel on the Monte Aventino, with a garden and individually decorated rooms (some with city views).

***Villa San Pio, Via Santa Melania 19, 00153, t 06 574 8119, *www.aventinohotels.com*. A glorious Aventine villa with a secluded statue-studded garden. The refurbished bedrooms are quietly elegant; some lead out onto the garden.

Expensive

***Lancelot, Via Capo d'Africa 47, t 06 7045 0615, 00184, *www.lancelothotel.com*. A charming, family-run hotel close to the Colosseum, with refurbished rooms.

***Hotel Scalinata di Spagna, Piazza Trinità dei Monti 17, t 06 679 3006, 00187. A 15-room hotel at the top of the Spanish Steps. The room rates are worth it for the views from the breakfast terrace alone, though they soar to *luxury* category in high season.

***Teatro di Pompeo, Largo del Pallaro 8, 00186, t 06 6830 0170, *web.tiscali.it/hotelteatrodipompeo*. A small, welcoming hotel with plain rooms, built on the Teatro di Pompeo close to Campo de' Fiori and perfect if you want peace and quiet.

**Campo de' Fiori, Via del Biscione 6, 00186 t 06 6880 6865, *www.campodefiori.com*. A revamped, ivy-covered hotel boasting a hall-of-mirrors corridor, theme-park bedrooms and vertiginous views from the roof garden. Some cheaper rooms are available. Breakfast is extra.

**Sole, Via del Biscione 76, 00186, t 06 687 9446. A family-run favourite near Campo de' Fiori. The best rooms face the pretty garden overlooked by a church. *Moderate* rooms without bathrooms are available. Book in advance. Breakfast isn't provided.

Moderate

**Abruzzi, Piazza della Rotonda 69, 00186, t 06 679 2021. A slightly ragged but amenable option across from the Pantheon, with TV, a bar, air-con and showers in the hall.

**Hotel Boccaccio, Via del Boccaccio 25, t 06 488 5962, 00187, *www.hotelboccaccio.com*. A charming 8-room hotel near Piazza di Spagna, with a pretty plant-filled courtyard.

The City Guesthouse, Viale Opita Oppio 78, 00174, t 06 7698 3140, *www.cityguesthouse.com*. A friendly option a 20-min metro ride from Termini or the Spanish Steps, with trendy bold prints and slick, minimalist furniture. There are plenty of really good restaurants in the neighbourhood.

**Nardizzi Americana, Via Firenze 38, t 06 488 035, 00184, *www.hotelnardizzi.it*. A well-priced, simple option near Termini, with friendly staff, well-equipped rooms (with air-con) and a roof garden.

Inexpensive

The area around **Stazione Termini** offers a wide choice of inexpensive hotels, which range from plain, family-run establishments to bizarre dives.

Accommodation Planet 29, Via Gaeta 29, t 06 486 520, 00185, *www.mclink.it/com/travel*. A friendly place with 15 simple rooms, some with cupboard kitchenettes.

Colors Hotel and Hostel, Via Boezio 31, t 06 687 4030, 00192, *www.colorshotel.com*. A popular, bright hotel and hostel close to the Vatican (making it one of the few budget places outside the Termini area), with dorms (€19pp) and doubles (*c*. €75). There's a kitchen, terrace, TV lounge and laundry facilities.

Freedom Traveller, Via Gaeta 25, t 06 4782 3862, 00185, *www.freedom-traveller.it*. A big, brash backpacker hostel close to Termini, with an Internet café, kitchen facilities, a common room, a terrace and organized pub crawls. Dorm beds start at €18; double rooms at €50. Breakfast is included in the rates.

**Pensione Primavera, Piazza San Pantaleo 3, 00186, t 06 6880 3109. A little-known *pensione* with 8 simple rooms, a 2-min walk from Campo de' Fiori and Piazza Navona.

*Restivo, Via Palestro 55, t 06 446 2172, 00185. An immaculate *pensione* run by a very sweet Sicilian lady.

Bed and Breakfast

The APT tourist office publishes a comprehensive list of B&B establishments in Rome, and the Rome Chamber of Commerce has a free booking service for establishments that have been given its quality award (t 06 679 5937, *www.hotelreservation.it*).

Eating Out

Unlike many other Italians, Romans aren't afraid when it comes to trying out new things, and as well as many Chinese restaurants, you'll find everything from Arab cuisine to macrobiotic cooking. The city also attracts talented chefs from all over Italy, resulting in a microcosm of Italian cuisine that you'll find nowhere else.

This is not to be taken as a reflection on local cuisine, however, which includes *saltimbocca* (paper-thin slices of veal cooked with prosciutto), *stracciatella* (soup with eggs, Parmesan cheese and parsley), *carciofi alla giudia* (fried artichokes) and veal *involtini*. In less expensive places, you're likely to encounter favourites such as *baccalà* (salt cod), *bucatini all'amatriciana* (in a tomato and bacon sauce), tripe and gnocchi.

Much of the wine on lists will originate from the Castelli Romani – these are light, fruity whites, of which the best come from Frascati and Velletri.

You could spend as much as €150 on a meal (without wine) if you followed the politicians and the TV crowd, but most prices here follow the Italian average. However, be wary of tourist traps near major sights, with their 'tourist menus'.

Very Expensive

Alberto Ciarla, Piazza San Cosimato 40, Trastevere, **t** 06 581 8668. A restaurant located some way south of Santa Maria, with a French-trained owner. The perfectly prepared and graciously served fare includes oysters, seafood ravioli and *pesce crudo* (raw fish). *Closed lunchtimes, and 2wks Jan and 1wk Aug*.

Checchino dal 1887, Via di Monte Testaccio 30, **t** 06 574 3816. The acknowledged temple of old Roman cooking, owned by the same family for more than a century. Both the fancy and humble sides of Roman food are represented, meaning that there's plenty of the powerful offal dishes that Romans have been eating since ancient times, and the setting is unique – on the edge of Monte Testaccio, with one of Rome's best cellars excavated under the hill. *Closed Mon, Aug and Christmas*.

Il Convivio, Vicolo dei Soldati 31, **t** 06 686 9432. A restaurant offering some of the most innovative cuisine in Rome, including unbeatable chilled fruit soups, baked zucchini flowers and exquisite pastries. Reserve ahead. *Closed Mon lunchtime and 1wk in Aug*.

La Pergola dell'Hotel Hilton, Via Cadlolo 101, **t** 06 3509 2152. One of the city's best restaurants for *alta cucina*, served in elegant surroundings. There's a roof terrace from which diners have all of Rome at their feet. Reserve well in advance. *Closed lunchtimes, Mon and Jan*.

La Rosetta, Via della Rosetta 8, near the Pantheon, **t** 06 686 1002. The best fish restaurant in the city, with heaps of shiny fish, oysters and sea-urchins arranged on a marble slab in the hall. Reserve well ahead. *Closed lunchtimes except Thurs and Fri, Sun and Aug*.

Expensive

Dal Bolognese, Piazza del Popolo 1, **t** 06 361 1426. *The* place for those in search of Emilian specialities – don't miss the tortellini or the *fruttini* (real fruit shells filled with sorbet). There are tables on the grand piazza and a view of the Pincio. *Closed Mon, Tues lunchtime, Aug and Christmas*.

Camponeschi, Piazza Farnese, **t** 06 687 4927. A fine restaurant with views of the elegant Palazzo Farnese, popular with celebs. Service is charming and knowledgeable. *Closed 10–24 Aug*.

Al Ceppo, Via Panama 2, **t** 06 841 9696. A place situated in the heart of the Parioli neighbourhood, boasting an open grill, traditional Italian cuisine (including specialities from the Marches), warm décor that's rather reminiscent of a bourgeois drawing room and tables outside in summer. Reserve for Sunday lunch. *Closed Mon and 3wks in Aug*.

Margutta Vegetariano, Via Margutta 119, **t** 06 3600 1805. One of Rome's few vegetarian restaurants, chic and overpriced but offering a plant-filled terrace on a quiet square. *Closed Sun*.

Papà Giovanni, Via dei Sediari 4, **t** 06 686 5308. An intimate setting for some of the most heavenly food in Rome, with menus based on old Roman recipes and market availability. *Closed Sun and 1st 2 wks of Aug.*

Da Paris, Piazza San Calisto 7/a, Trastevere, **t** 06 581 5378. A restaurant beyond Piazza Santa Maria serving classic Roman–Jewish cuisine such as *minestra di arzilla* (skate soup) and *tagliolini con scampi e fiori di zucca* ('little cut' pasta with prawns and pumpkin flowers). *Closed Sun eve, Mon and Aug.*

Piperno, Via Monte de' Cenci 9, **t** 06 6880 6629. The best place to try *carciofi alla giudia*, right on the edge of the old ghetto at the city's most famous purveyor of Roman–Jewish cooking. The mainly simple dishes are very well prepared. *Closed Sun eve, Mon and Aug.*

Il Toscano, Via Germanico 58, **t** 06 3972 5717. A family-run place that's popular with Roman families – it's perhaps the best option in the tourist-trap Vatican area. Among the well-prepared Tuscan specialities on offer are *pici* (rough, fresh spaghetti rolled by hand) in game sauce, and *fiorentina* steak. Reserve in advance. *Closed Sun, Mon and last wk of Dec.*

Vecchia Roma, Piazza di Campitelli 18, **t** 06 686 4604. A restaurant in a lovely quiet setting not far from Piazza Venezia, with outdoor tables, an imaginative seasonal menu and a fine wine list. *Closed Weds and Aug.*

Moderate

Less expensive places are not difficult to find in the *centro storico*, though you won't find many places offering anything other than Roman cuisine.

Albistrò, Via dei Banchi Vecchi 140, **t** 06 686 5274. A family-run restaurant offering the likes of lamb with honey sauce and chicken with leeks. Arrive early for a table in the courtyard. Tapas are served 5.30–7.15 Mon and Thurs–Sat. *Closed lunchtimes except Sun, Mon, and mid-July–mid-Aug.*

Armando al Pantheon, Salita dei Crescenzi 31, **t** 06 6880 3034. An authentic trattoria famous for its *spaghetti cacio e pepe* (with pecorino cheese and black pepper), *saltimbocca* and ricotta tart. *Closed Sat eve, Sun and Aug.*

Checco er Carettiere, Via Benedetta 10, Trastevere, **t** 06 580 0985. One of the oldest inns in Trastevere, offering well-prepared versions of Roman specialities, including *coda alla vaccinara*, and good seafood. *Closed Sun eve and May.*

La Cantina Tirolese, Via Vitelleschi 23, **t** 06 686 9994. A cheerful cellar decorated in the Tyrolese style, offering a selection of hearty, delicious recipes originating from the alpine region. *Closed Mon lunch and 2wks in Aug.*

Ditirambo, Piazza della Cancelleria, **t** 06 687 1626. A noisy favourite among young Romans, offering a range of home-made pasta and vegetarian dishes. *Closed Mon lunch and 2wks in Aug.*

L'Eau Vive, Via Monterone 85, **t** 06 6880 1095. A good French restaurant run by a Catholic lay missionary society, offering nourishing meals (the likes of *sole meunière* and onion soup) in a scrubbed and rather righteous atmosphere near the Pantheon. The fixed lunch menu is a great bargain. *Closed Sun and Aug.*

Grappolo d'Oro, Piazza della Cancelleria 80, **t** 06 689 7080. Good-value traditional Roman cooking near Campo de' Fiori. This is one of the best places to sit outside at night. *Closed Sun and Aug.*

Café Romana de l'Hotel d'Inghilterra, Via Bocca di Leone 14, **t** 06 6998 1500. An elegant retreat right in the heart of the shopping district, at the foot of the Spanish Steps. Dinner is *expensive*.

Cheap

Africa, Via Gaeta 26, **t** 06 494 1077. A wonderful Ethiopian/Eritrean restaurant offering spicy fare, including breakfasts. *Closed Mon.*

Acchiappafantasmi, Via del Capillari 66, **t** 06 687 3462. A rustically decorated trattoria located close to the Campo de' Fiori, with delicious home cooking at reasonable prices. *Closed Tues and 2wks in Aug.*

Enoteca Corsi, Via del Gesù 87, **t** 06 679 0821. A buzzy, down-to-earth and extremely popular trattoria in the heart of the city, with a short but regularly changing menu. *Closed Aug.*

Tram Tram, Via dei Reti 44, **t** 06 490 416. A crowded and trendy restaurant in the arty San Lorenzo neighbourhood east of Termini. *Closed Mon.*

Pizzerias

Roman pizza is crisp and thin, as opposed to the softer, thicker Neapolitan-style pizza, which has recently won a fat slice of the market in the city.

Most pizzerias have tables outside and are open only for dinner, often until 2am.

Blu, Via de Sabelli 193, San Lorenzo, **t** 06 494 0863. A mellow, candlelit bistro serving good pizza and pasta dishes. *Closed Mon lunch and 2wks Aug.*

Dar Poeta, Via del Bologna 46, Trastevere, **t** 06 588 0516. An enormously popular pizzeria that also serves good *bruschette*, salads, and a famous *calzone* with ricotta and Nutella. *Closed Tues lunch and Sept.*

Frontoni, Viale Trastevere 52, **t** 06 3630 7865. A low-key place offering 'pizza sandwiches' with a large choice of fillings, and staying open until late

La Montecarlo, Vicolo Savelli 12, **t** 06 686 1877. A tightly packed space where you have to duck as brilliant pizzas, chairs and tables are whipped over your head by manic waiters. *Closed Mon Nov–Apr, and 2 wks in Aug.*

Pizzaré, Via di Rapetta 14, **t** 06 321 1468. A nice selection of Neapolitan-style pizzas, including 'pizza sostanziosa' (with everything on it). There's another branch, **Pizzaré 2**, at Via Oslavia 39, Prati, **t** 06 372 1173. *Closed 2wks in Aug .*

Supplì e Pizza al Taglio, Via San Francesco a Ripa, **t** 06 588 0516. A place serving up slices of pizza and roasted chicken, plus famous *supplì* – deep-fried rice balls with melted mozzarella in the middle.

Wine Bars/*Enoteche*

At lunchtime, many of Rome's wine bars offer good selections of cured meat and cheese, soups, salads and occasional quiches and flans. Desserts are usually made in house, and you can choose from about 20 wines served *in mescita* (by the glass) and hundreds by the bottle.

Semidivino, Via Alessandria 230, **t** 06 4425 0795. A classy wine bar that's run by an Iranian expatriate, serving up first-rate meals of excellent salads, interesting cheeses, cured meats and comforting soups. *Closed Sun and Aug.*

Trimani, Via Cernaia 37/b, not far from Termini, **t** 06 446 9630. A haven of sanity that's very popular among business types and intellectuals. *Closed Sat lunch, Sun and 2wks in Aug.*

Cul de Sac, Piazza Pasquino 73, **t** 06 6880 1094. A tiny, crammed bar with a few tables outside, serving light meals (cured meats, cheeses and salads) to gastronomes, plus home-cooked lasagne and a selection of other dishes. *Closed May.*

Cavour 313, Via Cavour 313, **t** 06 678 5496. A wood-beamed bar offering a range of delicious snacks, light lunches and evening meals, plus 500 wines. *Closed Sun except eves Oct–May.*

Il Cantinere de Santa Dorotea, Via Santa Dorotea, Trastevere, **t** 06 581 9025. A welcoming *enoteca* with delicious soups, pastas and cured meats to accompany its excellent selection of wines.

Cafés and Bars

Babington's Tea Rooms, Piazza di Spagna 23. The place to come for scones and tea, or for a full lunch, all served up in a proper Victorian atmosphere.

Forno del Ghetto, Via del Portico d'Ottavia 2 (*closed Sat*). The Jewish bakery, serving a range of breads and pastries.

Il Gelato di San Crispino, Via della Panetteria 42, near the Trevi Fountain. The best *gelato* in Rome.

Caffè Greco, Via Condotti 86, **t** 06 679 1700. The oldest café in the city, dating back to 1760. It's here that Keats and Casanova came to sip their java.

Bar della Pace, Via della Pace 5. An ultra-hip establishment that's much frequented by Italian celebrities.

Rosati, Piazza del Popolo 4, **t** 06 322 5859. An elegant place that was founded way back in 1922 and is popular among the Roman intelligentsia. Make sure to try one of the extravagant ice-cream confections for which it's known.

Sant'Eustachio, Piazza Sant'Eustachio 82, near Piazza Navona. The trendy home of Rome's most famous coffee.

Vineria Reggio, Campo de' Fiori 15. A funky, friendly, traditional wine bar/shop with tables outside.

Entertainment and Nightlife

The best entertainment on offer is often in the cosmopolitan spectacle of Rome's streets – as nightlife goes, it can be a bit of a snoozer compared with other European cities.

If you're determined, the backstreets around Piazza Navona or Campo de' Fiori swarm with people in the evenings, and these are the places to come to plan your night ahead, as leaflets and free tickets (often to newly opened places) are always being handed out. The current hip neighbourhoods for going out are San Lorenzo, east of Termini station, and Testaccio.

Other sources are *Romac'e'* (which can be bought at newsstands; or see *www.romace.it*), which has comprehensive listings and a small section in English, and the weekly *Time Out*, which has listings and articles in Italian.

Rome can be an uncomfortable, sticky place in Aug but there's plenty going on to take your mind off the heat. The *Estate Romana* ('Roman Summer', **t** 06 3600 4399, *www.estateromana.caltanet.it*) is a three-month festival of outdoor events, live music, theatrical performances and film (shown on outdoor screens around the city), and most museums are open for longer hours.

A far older Roman party is the traditional **Festa de' Noantri**, held inTrastevere (16–31 July), where you may well find a gust of old Roman spontaneity, along with live music performances from across the spectrum, acrobats, dancing and stall upon stall down Viale Trastevere.

Opera, Classical Music, Theatre, Film

Orbis, Piazza Esquilino 37 (**t** 06 474 4776, *www.ticketone.it; open Mon–Sat 9.30–1 and 4–7.30*), is a reliable agency from which to purchase concert, opera and theatre tickets.

From Nov until May you can take in operatic performances at the **Teatro dell'Opera di Roma**, Piazza B. Gigli, off Via del Viminale, **t** 800 016665, *www.opera.roma.it*.

Other classical concerts are performed at and by the **Accademia Nazionale di Santa Cecilia**, in its auditorium on Via della Conciliazione 4, **t** 06 361 1044, and by the **Accademia Filarmonica Romana**, Via Flaminia 118, **t** 06 6880 9222. Medieval, Baroque, chamber and choral music concerts are performed at the **Oratorio del Gonfalone**, Via del Gonfalone 32/a, **t** 06 687 5952.

There's traditionally a range of special seasons thoughout the summer. Evening concerts are held outside in the **Teatro di Marcello**, **t** 06 481 4800, or **t** 06 780 4314 (mid-June–Sept), and concerts are performed by the Accademia di Santa Cecilia and visiting international orchestras at **Villa Giulia** (July). The opera moves outside in the summer – to the **Villa Borghese** and the **soccer stadium**.

You can watch films in *versione originale* at:

Alcazar, Via Cardinal Merry del Val 14, Trastevere, **t** 06 588 0099 (*Mon*).

Nuovo Sacher, Largo Ascianghi 1, Trastevere, **t** 06 5811 8116 (*Mon and Tues*). This is one of the best places to see new cinema in Rome.

Pasquino, Piazza Sant'Egidio, near Santa Maria in Trastevere, **t** 06 580 3622 (*daily*).

Quirinetta, Via M. Minghetti 4, **t** 06 679 0012.

Rock, Jazz and Nightclubs

Il Locale, Vicolo del Fico 3, **t** 06 687 9075. A venue hosting concerts by various hip Italian bands.

Big Mamma, Vicolo San Francesco a Ripa 18, Trastevere, **t** 06 581 2451, *www.bigmamma.it*. A rock-oriented venue.

Alpheus, Via del Commercio, 36, Ostiense, **t** 06 574 7826. A blues club.

Caffè Latino, Via de Monte Testaccio 96, **t** 06 5728 8556. A dance club where you can hear live Latin music.

Jazz has a strong local following. Try the following venues.

Alexanderplatz, Via Ostia 9, **t** 06 3974 2171.

Gregory's, Via Gregoriana 54, **t** 06 679 6386, *www.gregorysjazzclub.it*.

For serious **dancing**, the following clubs are *di tendenza* (keep up with UK/US trends). Most are closed in late July and Aug.

Akab Cave, Via Monte Testaccio 69, **t** 06 578 2390. Hip live music and DJ sessions.

Alien, Via Velletri 13, near Piazza Fiume, **t** 06 841 2212.

Alpheus, Via del Commercio 36, off Via Ostiense, **t** 06 574 7826.

Gilda, Via Mario de' Fiori 97, **t** 06 678 4838. A venue that's popular with an older crowd (jackets are required).

In our prosaic times, though, you may find it requires a considerable effort of the imagination to break through to the past Romes of the caesars and popes. They exist, but first you need to peel away the increasingly thick veneer of the 'Third Rome', the burgeoning, thoroughly up-to-date creation of post-Reunification Italy. Ancient Rome at the height of its glory had perhaps a million and a half people; today there are four million, and at any given time at least half of them will be pushing their way into the metro train while you are trying to get off. The popes, for all their centuries of experience in spectacle and ceremony, cannot often steal the show in this new Rome, and have to share the stage with a deplorable overabundance of preposterous politicians, with Cinecittà and the rest of the cultural apparatus of a great nation, and of course with the tourists, who sometimes put on the best show in town.

The old guard Romani, now a minority in a city swollen with new arrivals, bewail the loss of Rome's slow and easy pace, its vintage brand of *dolce vita* that once impressed other Italians, not to mention foreigners. Lots of money, lots of traffic and an endless caravan of tour buses have a way of compromising even the most beautiful of cities. Don't concern yourself; the present is only one snapshot from a 2,600-year history, and no one has ever left Rome disappointed.

History

The beginnings are obscure enough. Historians believe the settlement of the Tiber valley began some time about 1000 BC, when an outbreak of volcanic eruptions in the Alban Hills to the south forced the Latin tribes down into the lowlands. Beyond that there are few clues for the archaeologists to follow. But remembering that every ancient legend conceals a kernel of truth – perhaps more poetic than scientific – it would be best to follow the accounts of Virgil, the poet of the Empire, and Livy, the great 1st-century chronicler and mythographer.

When Virgil wrote, in the reign of Augustus, Greek culture was an irresistible force in all the recently civilized lands of the Mediterranean. For Rome, Virgil concocted the story of Aeneas, fleeing from Troy after the Homeric sack and finding his way to Latium. Descent from the Trojans, however specious, connected Rome to the Greek world and made it seem less of an upstart. As Virgil tells it, Aeneas' son Ascanius founded Alba Longa, a city that by the 800s was leader of the Latin Confederation. Livy takes up the tale with Numitor, a descendant of Ascanius and rightful king of Alba Longa, tossed off the throne by his usurping brother Amulius. In order that Numitor should have no heirs, Amulius forced Numitor's daughter Rhea Silvia into service as a Vestal Virgin. Here Rome's destiny begins, with an appearance in the Vestals' chambers of the god Mars, staying just long enough to leave Rhea Silvia pregnant with the precocious twins **Romulus and Remus**.

When Amulius found out he packed them away in a little boat, which the gods then directed up the Tiber to a spot close to today's Piazza Bocca della Verità. The famous she-wolf looked after the babies, until they were found by a shepherd, who subsequently brought them up. When Mars revealed to the grown twins their origin, they returned to Alba Longa to sort out Amulius, and then returned (in 753 BC, traditionally) to found the city that the gods had ordained. Romulus soon found himself constrained to kill Remus, who would not believe the auguries that declared that his brother should become king, and thus set the pattern for the bloody millennium of Rome's history to come.

The legends portray early Rome as a glorified pirates' camp, and the historians are only too glad to agree. Finding themselves short of women, the Romans stole some from the Sabines. Not especially interested in farming or learning a trade, they adopted the hobby of subjugating their neighbours and soon polished it to an art.

Seven Kings of Rome

Romulus was the first, followed by Numa Pompilius, who laid down the forms for Rome's cults and priesthoods, its auguries and College of Vestals. Tullius Hostilius, the next, made Rome ruler of all Latium, and Ancus Martius founded the port of Ostia. The next king, **Tarquinius Priscus**, was an Etruscan, and probably gained his throne thanks to a conquest by one of the Etruscan city-states. Tarquin made a city of Rome, building the first real temples, the Cloaca Maxima or Great Drain, and the first Circus Maximus. His successor, **Servius Tullius**, restored Latin rule, inaugurated the division between patricians (the senatorial class) and plebeians, and built a great wall to keep the Etruscans out. It apparently did not work, for as next king we find the Etruscan **Tarquinius Superbus** (*c.* 534 BC), another great builder. His misfortune was to have a hot-headed son like **Tarquinius Sextus**, who imposed himself on a noble and virtuous Roman maiden named Lucretia (cf. Shakespeare's *Rape of Lucrece*). She committed public suicide; the enraged Roman patricians, under the leadership of **Lucius Junius Brutus**, chased out proud Tarquin and the Etruscan dynasty for ever. The republic was established before the day was out, with Brutus as first consul, or chief magistrate.

The Invincible Republic

Taking an oath never to allow another king in Rome, the patricians designed a novel form of government, a **republic** (*res publica* – public thing) governed by the two consuls elected by the Senate, the assembly of the patricians themselves; later innovations in the Roman constitution included a tribune, an official with inviolable powers elected by the plebeians to protect their interests. The two classes fought at home but joined forces with impressive resolve in their foreign wars: Etruscans, Aequi, Hernici, Volscii, Samnites and Sabines were defeated by Rome's citizen armies. Some of Livy's best stories come from this period, such as the taking of Rome by Gauls in 390 BC, when the cackling of geese woke the Romans and saved the citadel on the Capitoline Hill.

By 270 BC Rome had eliminated all its rivals to become master of Italy. It had taken about 200 years, and in the next 200 Roman rule would be established from Spain to Egypt. The first stage had proved more difficult. In Rome's final victory over the other Italians, the city digested its rivals: whole cities and tribes simply disappeared, their peoples joining the mushrooming population of Rome. After 270 it was the same story, but on a wider scale. In the three **Punic Wars** against Carthage (264–146 BC), Rome gained almost the whole of the western Mediterranean; Greece, North Africa and Asia Minor were absorbed in small bites over the next 100 years. Rome's history was now the history of the western world.

Imperial Rome

The old pirates' nest had never really changed its ways. Rome, like old Assyria, makes a fine example of that species of carnivore that can only live by continuous conquest. When the Romans took Greece they first met Culture, and it had the effect on them that puberty has on little boys. After some bizarre behaviour, evidenced in the continuous civil wars (**Sulla**, **Marius**, **Pompey**, **Julius Caesar**), the Romans began tarting up their city in the worst way, vacuuming all the gold, paintings, statues, cooks, poets and architects out of the civilized East. Beginning perhaps with Pompey, every contender for control of the now constitutionally deranged republic added some great work to the city centre: Pompey's theatre, the Julian Basilica, and something from almost every emperor up to Constantine. Julius Caesar and Augustus were perhaps Rome's greatest benefactors, initiating every sort of progressive legislation, turning dirt lanes into paved streets and erecting new forums, temples and the vast network of aqueducts. In their time Rome's population probably reached the million mark, surpassing Antioch and Alexandria as the largest city in the western world.

It was **Augustus** who effectively ended the Republic in 27 BC, by establishing his personal rule and reducing the old constitution to formalities. During the imperial era that followed his reign, Rome's position as administrative and judicial centre of the empire kept it growing, drawing in a new cosmopolitan population of provincials from Britain to Mesopotamia. The city became the unquestioned capital of banking and finance – and religion; Rome's policy was always to induct everyone's local god as an honorary Roman, and every important cult image and relic was abducted to the Capitoline Temple. The emperor himself was *Pontifex Maximus*, head priest of Rome, whose title derives from the early Roman veneration of bridges (*pontifex* means keeper of bridges). **St Peter**, of course, arrived, and was duly martyred in AD 67. His successor, Linus, became the first **pope** (or *pontiff*) – the first in the long line of hierophants who would inherit Rome's long-standing religious tradition.

For all its glitter, Rome was still the complete predator, producing nothing and consuming everything. No one with any spare *denarii* would be foolish enough to go into business with them, when the only real money was to be made from government, speculation or real estate. At times almost half the population of Roman citizens (as opposed to slaves) was on the dole. Naturally, when things went sour they really went sour. Uncertain times made **Aurelian** give Rome a real defensive wall in AD 275. By AD 330 the necessity of staying near the armies at the front led the western emperors to spend most of their time at army headquarters in Milan. Rome became a bloated backwater, and after three sackings (Alaric the Goth in 410, Gaiseric the Vandal in 455 and Odoacer the Goth in 476), there was no reason to stay. The sources disagree: perhaps 100,000 inhabitants were left by the year 500, perhaps 10,000.

Rome in the Shadows

Contrary to what most people think, Rome did not ever quite go down the drain in the Dark Ages. Its lowest point in prestige undoubtedly came in the 14th century, when the popes were at Avignon. The number of important churches built in the Dark Ages (most, unfortunately, later Baroqued) and the mosaics that embellished them, equal in number if not in quality to those of Ravenna, testify to the city's importance. There was certainly enough to attract a few more sacks (Goths and Greeks in the 6th-century wars, Saracens from Africa in 746).

As in many other Western cities, but on a larger scale, the bishops of Rome – the popes – picked up some of the pieces when civil administration disintegrated and extended their power to temporal offices. Chroniclers report fights between them and the local barons, self-proclaimed heirs of the Roman Senate, as early as 741. It must have been a fascinating place, much too big for its population though still, thanks to the popes, thinking of itself as the centre of the western world. The forum was abandoned, as were the gigantic baths, rendered useless as the aqueducts decayed. Almost all the temples and basilicas survived, converted to churches. **Hadrian**'s massive tomb on the banks of the Tiber was converted into a fortress, the Castel Sant'Angelo, which was an impregnable haven for the popes in troubled times.

The popes deserve the credit for keeping Rome alive, but the tithe money trickling in from across Europe confirmed the city in its parasitical behaviour. With two outrageous forgeries, the 'Donation of Constantine' and the 'Donation of Pepin', the popes staked their claim to temporal power in Italy. **Charlemagne** visited the city after driving the Lombards out in 800; during a prayer vigil in St Peter's on Christmas Eve, Pope Leo III sneaked up behind the Frankish king and set an imperial crown on his head. The surprise coronation, which the outraged Charlemagne could not or would not undo, established the precedent of Holy Roman Emperors having to cross over the Alps to receive their crown from the pope.

Arnold of Brescia and Cola di Rienzo

Not that Rome ever spoke with one voice; over the next 500 years it was only the idea of Rome, as the spiritual centre of the universal Christian community, that kept the actual city from disappearing altogether. Down to some 20,000–30,000 people in this era, Rome evolved a sort of stable anarchy, in which the major contenders for power were the popes and noble families. First among the latter were the Orsini and the Colonna, racketeer clans who built fortresses for themselves among the ruins and fought like gangs in 1920s Chicago. Very often outsiders would get into the game. A remarkable woman of obscure birth named **Theodora** took the Castel Sant'Angelo in the 880s; with the title of Senatrix she and her daughter Marozia ruled Rome for decades. Various German emperors seized the city, but were never able to hold it.

In the 10th century, things got even more complicated as the Roman people began to assert themselves. Caught between the people and the barons, nine of the 24 popes in that century managed to get themselves murdered. The 1140s was a characteristic period of this convoluted history. A Jewish family, the Pierleoni, held power, and a Jewish antipope sat enthroned in St Peter's. Mighty Rome occupied itself with a series of wars against its neighbouring village of Tivoli, and usually lost. A sincere monkish reformer appeared, the Christian and democrat **Arnold of Brescia**; he recreated the Senate and almost succeeded in establishing Rome as a free *comune*, but in 1155 he fell into the hands of the German emperor Frederick Barbarossa, who sold him to the English pope (Adrian IV) for hanging.

Too many centuries of this made Rome uncomfortable for the popes, who frequently removed themselves to Viterbo. The final indignity came when, under French pressure, the papacy decamped entirely to Avignon in 1309. Pulling strings from a distance, the popes only made life more complicated. Into the vacuum they created stepped one of the noblest Romans of them all, later to be the subject of Wagner's first opera. **Cola di Rienzo** was the son of an innkeeper, but he had a good enough education to read the Latin inscriptions that lay on ruins all around him, and Livy, Cicero and Tacitus wherever he could find them. Obsessed by the idea of re-establishing Roman glory, he talked at the bewildered inhabitants until they caught the fever too. With Rienzo as Tribune of the People, the Roman Republic was reborn in 1347. Power does corrupt, however, in Rome more than any spot on the globe, and an increasingly fat and ridiculous Rienzo was hustled out of Rome by the united nobles before the year was out. His return to power, in 1354, ended with his murder by a mob after only two months. Rome was now at its lowest ebb, with only some 15,000 people, and prosperity and influence were not completely restored until the reign of Pope Nicholas V after 1447.

The New Rome

The old papacy, before Avignon, had largely been a tool of the Roman nobles; periods when it was able to achieve real independence were the exception rather than the rule. In the more settled conditions of the 15th century, a new papacy emerged, richer and more sophisticated. Political power, as a guarantee of stability, was its goal, and a series of talented Renaissance popes saw their best hopes for achieving this by rebuilding Rome. By the 1500s this process was in full swing. Under **Julius II** (1503–13) the papal domains for the first time were run like a modern state; Julius also laid plans for the reconstruction of St Peter's, beginning the great building programme that transformed the city. New streets were laid out, especially Via Giulia and the grand avenues radiating from Piazza del Popolo; Julius' architect, Bramante, knocked down medieval Rome with such abandon that Raphael nicknamed him 'Ruinante'.

Over the course of the next two centuries, the work continued at a frenetic pace. Besides St Peter's, hundreds of churches were either built or rebuilt, and cardinals and noble families lined the streets with new palaces, which were imposing if not beautiful. A new departure in urban design was developed in the 1580s, under **Sixtus V**, recreating some of the monumentality of ancient Rome. Piazzas linked by a network of straight boulevards were cleared in front of the major religious sites, each with an Egyptian obelisk.

The New Rome, symbol of the Counter-Reformation and the majesty of the popes, was, however, bought at a terrible price. Besides the destruction of Bramante, buildings that had survived substantially intact for 1,500 years were cannibalized for their marble; the popes wantonly destroyed more of ancient Rome than Goths or Saracens had ever managed. To pay for their programme, they taxed the economy of the Papal States out of existence. Areas of Lazio turned into wastelands as exasperated farmers simply abandoned them; the other cities of Lazio and Umbria were set back centuries in their development. The New Rome was proving as voracious a predator as the old. Worst of all, the new papacy in the 16th century instituted terror as an instrument of public policy. In the course of the previous century the last vestiges of Roman liberty had been gradually extinguished. The popes tried to extend their power by playing a game of high-stakes diplomacy between Emperor Charles V of Spain and King Francis I of France, but reaped a bitter harvest in the 1527 Sack of Rome. An out-of-control imperial army occupied the city for almost a year, causing tremendous destruction, while the disastrous Pope Clement VII looked on helplessly from the Castel Sant'Angelo. Afterwards, the popes were happy to become part of the Imperial–Spanish system. Political repression was fiercer than anywhere else in Italy; the **Inquisition** was refounded in 1542 by Paul III, and book burnings, torture of freethinkers and executions became even more common than in Spain itself.

The End of Papal Rule

By about 1610 there was no Roman foolish enough to get burned at the stake; at the same time workmen were adding the last stones to the cupola of St Peter's. It was the end of an era, but the building continued. A thick accretion of Baroque collected, like coral, over Rome. Bernini did his Piazza Navona fountain in 1650, and the Colonnade for St Peter's 15 years later. The political importance of the popes, however, disappeared with surprising finality. As Joseph Stalin was later to note, the popes had plenty of Bulls but few army divisions, and they drifted into irrelevance in the power politics of modern Europe during the Thirty Years' War.

Rome was left to enjoy a decadent but pleasant twilight. A brief interruption came when revolutionaries in 1798 again proclaimed the Roman Republic, and a French army sent the pope packing. Rome later became part of **Napoleon**'s empire, but papal rule was restored in 1815. Another republic appeared in 1848, on the crest of that romantic year's revolutionary wave, but this time a French army besieged the city and had the pope propped back on his throne by July 1849. **Garibaldi**, the republic's military commander, barely escaped with his life.

For 20 years **Napoleon III** maintained a garrison in Rome to look after the pope, and consequently Rome became the last part of Italy to join the new Italian kingdom. After the French defeat in the war of 1870, Italian troops blew a hole in the old Aurelian wall near the Porta Pia and marched in. Pius IX, who ironically had decreed papal infallibility just the year before, locked himself in the Vatican and pouted; the popes were to be 'prisoners' until Mussolini's Concordat of 1929, by which they agreed to recognize the Italian state.

As the capital of the new state, Rome underwent another building boom. New streets such as Via Vittorio Veneto and Via Nazionale made circulation easier; villas and gardens disappeared under blocks of speculative building (everything around Stazione Termini, for example); long-needed projects such as the Tiber embankments were constructed; and the new kingdom strove to impress the world with gigantic, absurd public buildings and monuments, including the Altar of the Nation (Il Vittoriano) and the Finance Ministry on Via XX Settembre, as big as two Colosseums. Growth has been steady; from some 200,000 people in 1879, Rome has since increased twentyfold.

The Twentieth Century

In 1922 the city was the objective of **Mussolini**'s 'March on Rome', when the Fascist leader used his blackshirt squads to demand, and win, complete power in the Italian government, though he himself famously made the journey into town by train, and in his best suit. Mussolini was one more figure who wanted to create a 'New Roman Empire' for Italy. For 20 years Piazza Venezia was the chosen theatre for his oratorical performances. He also had big ideas for the city itself: it was under Fascism that many of the relics of ancient Rome were first opened up as public monuments in order to remind Italians of their heritage, and Via dei Fori Imperiali was driven past the Forum, destroying some of the archaeological sites in the process. His greatest legacy was the EUR suburb, the projected site of a world exhibition for 1942, and a showcase of his preferred Fascist–classical architecture. At the end of the war it was only half built, but the Italians, not wishing to waste anything, decided to finish the project, and it now houses a few of Rome's museums and sports venues.

Since the war Rome has continued to grow fat as the capital of the often ramshackle, notoriously corrupt political system thrown up by the Italian Republic, and the headquarters of the smug *classe politica* that ran it. Rome has been accused by Lombard regionalists of drawing off wealth from the productive areas of Italy in much the same way that it once demanded to be fed by the Empire; nevertheless, Romans have joined in Italy's 'Moral Revolution' of the last few years, abusing the old-style political bosses, despite the fact that a great many in this city of civil servants themselves benefited from the system.

Today's visitors enjoy the benefits of improvements that were carried out for the Holy Year 2000, including more than 700 public works projects (restorations, refurbished museums, upgraded transportation and additional car parks). Among the highlights for those who have not been to Rome for a few years are the Domus Aurea, Musei Capitolini, façade of Saint Peter's, Vittoriano monument on Piazza Venezia, and Trajan's Markets.

Around the City

Piazza Venezia and the Monte Capitolino

This traffic-crazed piazza may be a poor introduction to Rome, but it does make a good place to start, with the ruins of old Rome on one side and the boutiques and bureaucracies of the new city on the other. It takes its name from the **Palazzo Venezia**, built for the Venetian Cardinal Pietro Barbo (later Pope Paul II) in 1455, but long the embassy of the Venetian Republic. Mussolini made it his residence, leaving a light on all night to make the Italians think he was working. His balcony, from which he declaimed to the 'oceanic' crowds in the square (renamed the Forum of the Fascist Empire in those days), still holds its prominent place. Nowadays the *palazzo* holds a rather dull **museum of Renaissance and Baroque decorative arts** (***t** 06 679 8865; open Tues–Sun 8.30–7.30; adm*), though it's worth going inside to look at the palace's vast gloomy stone staircase and carved wooden ceilings. The palace

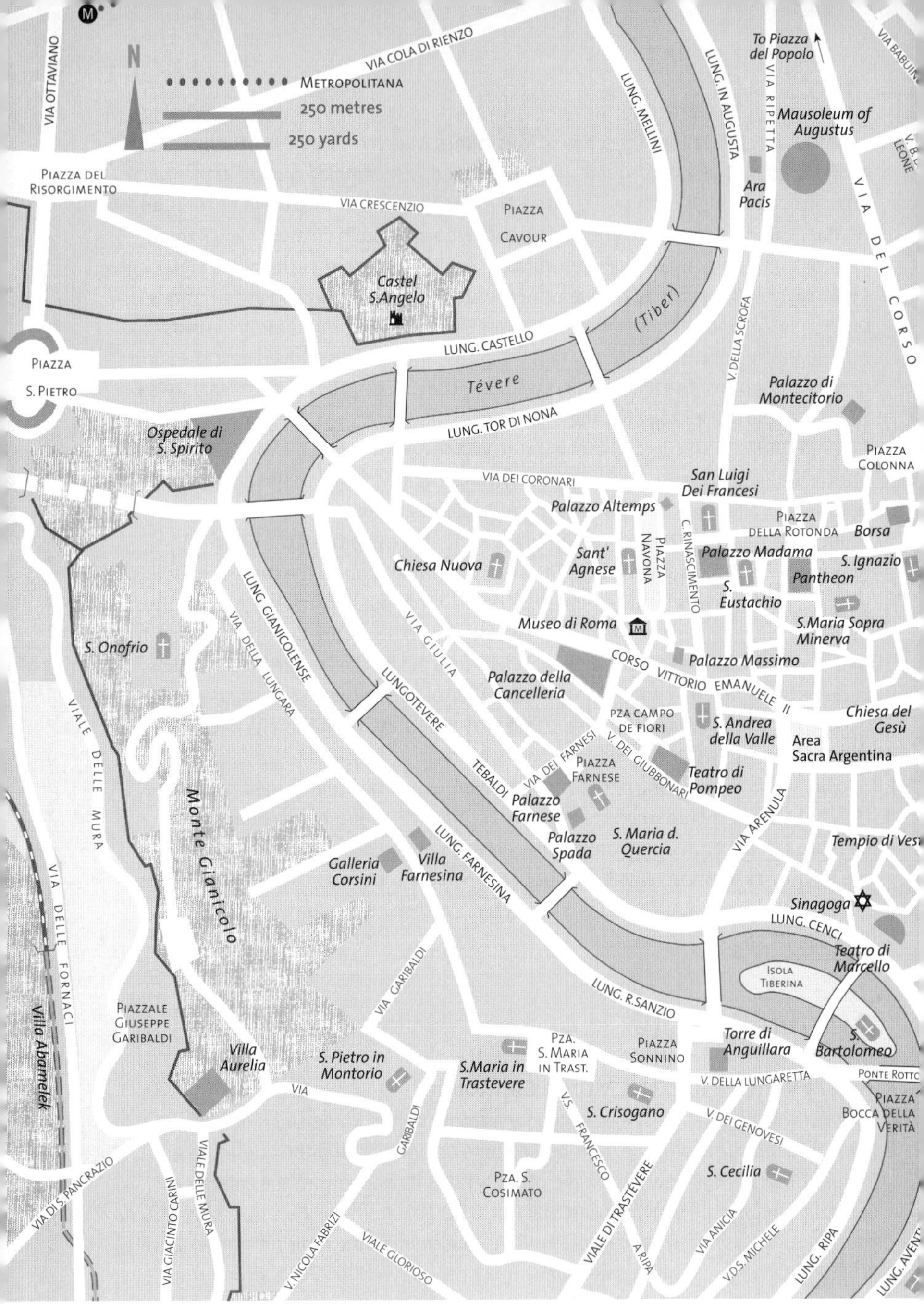

complex was built around the ancient church of **San Marco** (***t*** *06 679 5305; open 9,30–1 and 4.30–6.45; no entrance during services*), with a 9th-century mosaic in the apse. Parts of the building are as old as AD 400, and the Renaissance façade is by Benedetto di Maiano.

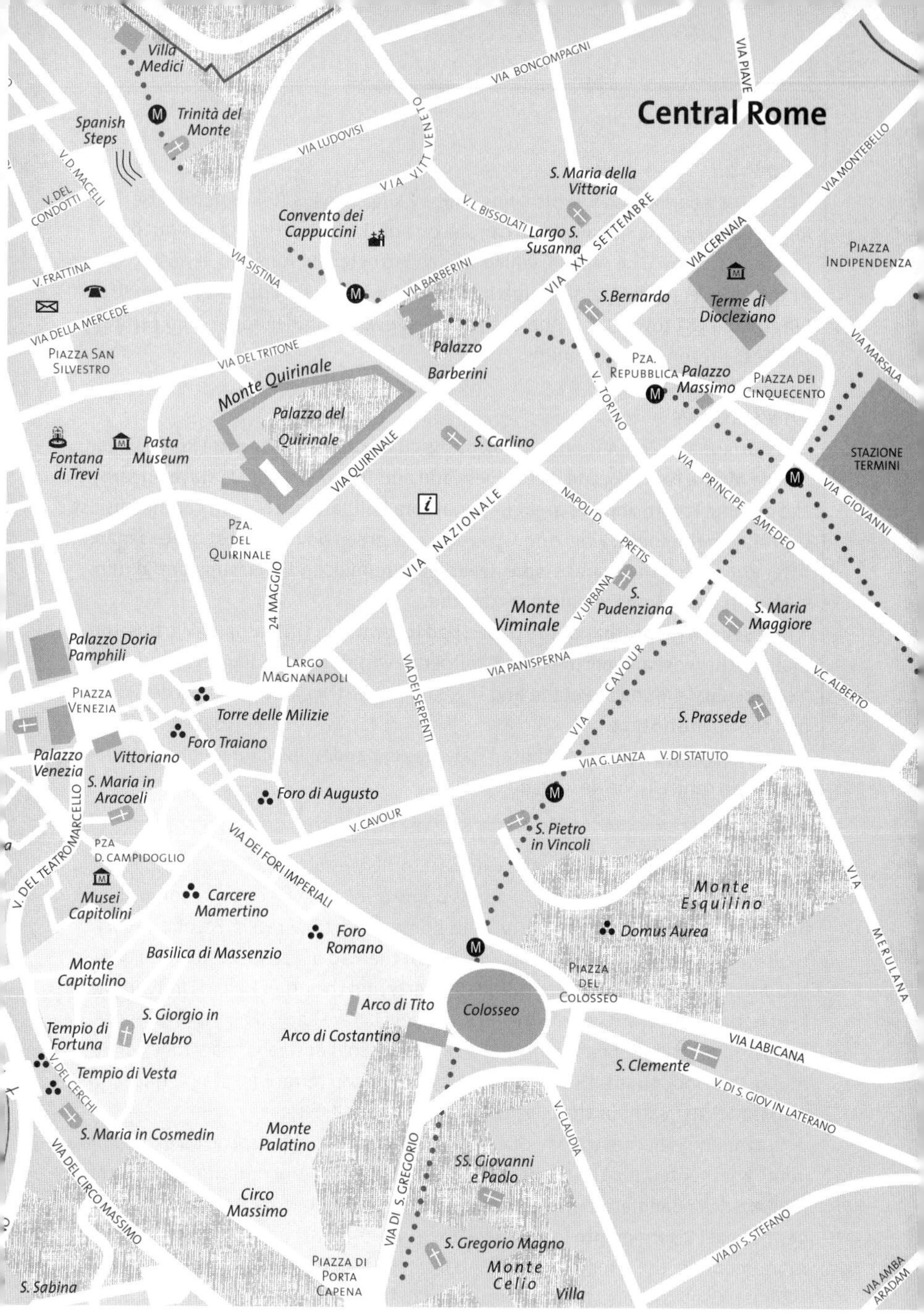

Long ago the southern edge of this piazza had approaches up to the Monte Capitolino. The hill is still there, though it's now entirely blocked out by the **Altar of the Nation**, also known as **Il Vittoriano**, the 'Wedding Cake' or the 'Typewriter' (***t*** *06 699 1718; open Tues–Sun 10.30–6.30, last adm 5.30; adm free*), Risorgimento Italy's own

A Little Orientation

Two Walls

Of Rome's earliest wall, which was built by king Servius Tullius before the Republic, very little remains; you can see one of the last surviving bits outside Stazione Termini. The second, which was constructed by Aurelian in AD 275, is one of the wonders of Rome, although it is taken for granted. With its 19-kilometre length and 383 towers, it is one of the largest ever built in Europe – and certainly the best-preserved of antiquity.

Three Romes

Historians and Romans often think of the city in this way. **Classical Rome** began on the Monte Palatino, and its business and administrative centre stayed nearby, in the original Forum and the great Imperial Fora built around it. Many of the busiest parts lay to the south, where now you see only green on the tourist office's map. After Rome's fall these areas were never really rebuilt, and even substantial ruins such as Trajan's Baths remain unexcavated.

The **Second Rome**, that of the popes, had its centre in the Campus Martius, the plain to the west and north of the Capitoline Hill, later expanding to include the 'Leonine City' around St Peter's, and the Baroque district around Piazza del Popolo and the Spanish Steps.

The **Third Rome**, capital of United Italy, has expanded in all directions; the closest it has to a centre is Via del Corso.

self-inflicted satire and one of the world's apotheoses of kitsch. Its size and its solid marble walls are explained by the 1880s prime minister who commissioned it; he happened to have a marble quarry in his home district of Brescia. Recounting its sculptural allegories would take pages, but of the two big bronze imperial-style *quadrigae* on top, one represents Italian Liberty and the other Italian Unity. In the centre, the modest virtues of Vittorio Emanuele II have earned him a 38ft bronze equestrian statue. Beneath him, Italy's Unknown Soldier sleeps peacefully with a round-the-clock guard. It's worth the climb to the top terrace for staggering views across the city (without the blight of the Typewriter itself).

Il Vittoriano is home to a pair of **exhibition galleries** (*times depend on exhibition; adm*), another temporary exhibition space, and two military museums: the **Sacrario Militare della Bandiera** (a flag museum; *open Tues–Sun 9–1; free*) and the **Museo Centrale del Risorgimento** (*open Tues–Sun 10.30–6.30, last adm 5.30; free*). Left of the monument are the remains of the republican Roman tomb of C. Publius Bibulus.

Behind the Vittoriano, two stairways lead to the top of the **Capitoline Hill**. This is a fateful spot; in 121 BC reformer Tiberius Gracchus was murdered here by what today would be called a 'right-wing death squad'. Almost a millennium and a half later Cola di Rienzo was trying to escape Rome in disguise when a mob recognized him by the rings on his fingers and tore him to pieces. Rienzo built the left-hand staircase, and

Seven Hills

Originally these were much higher; centuries of building, rebuilding and river flooding have made the ground level in the valleys much higher, and emperors and popes shaved bits off their tops in building programmes. The **Monte Capitolino**, the smallest but most important, now has Rome's City Hall, the Campidoglio, roughly on the site of ancient Rome's greatest temple, that of Jupiter Greatest and Best. The **Palatino**, adjacent to it, was originally the most fashionable district, and got entirely covered by the palaces of the emperors.

The plebeian **Aventino** lies to the south of it, across the Circus Maximus. Between the Colosseum and the Stazione Termini, the **Esquilino**, the **Viminale** and the **Quirinale** stand in a row. The Quirinale was long the residence of the popes, and later of the Italian kings. Finally, there is the **Monte Celio** south of the Colosseum, now an oasis of parkland and ancient churches.

Rome has other hills not included in the canonical seven: **Monte Vaticano**, from which the Vatican takes its name, **Monte Pincio**, including the Villa Borghese, and the **Gianicolo**, the long ridge above Trastevere that the ancients called the Janiculum.

Fourteen Regions

Ancient Rome had neither street lights nor street signs; modern Rome has plenty of both. This being Rome, of course, the street signs are of marble. In the corner of each, you will notice a small number in Roman numerals; this refers to the *rione*, or ward. In the Middle Ages, there were 14 of these, descendants of the 14 *regii* of the ancient city; even after the fall of Rome they maintained their organization.

was the first to climb it. It leads to **Santa Maria in Aracoeli** (***t*** *06 679 8155; open 6.30–5.30*), begun in the 7th century over the temple of Juno Moneta – the ancient Roman Mint was next to it. The Aracoeli, in Rienzo's time a council hall for the Romans, is one of the most revered of churches; legend has it that one of the Sibyls of Tivoli prophesied the coming of Jesus and told Augustus to build a temple here to the 'first born of God'. Inside are frescoes by Pinturicchio (*San Bernardino of Siena*) and Gozzoli (*San Antonio of Padua*), and a tombstone by Donatello, near the entrance.

The second stairway takes you to the real heart of Rome, Michelangelo's **Piazza del Campidoglio**, passing a rather flattering statue of Rienzo on a bronze pedestal. Bordering the piazza, a formidable cast of statues includes the Dioscuri, who come from Pompey's Theatre, and Marforio (in the Musei Capitolini courtyard), a river god once employed as a 'talking statue', decorated with graffiti and placards commenting on current events. The great 2nd-century AD bronze equestrian statue of the benign and philosophical emperor **Marcus Aurelius**, which stood on the plinth in the middle of the piazza from the 16th century until 1981, has been fully restored and regilded and is now in the Musei Capitolini – fortunately enough, since it was an old Roman saying that the world would end when all the gold flaked off. The Christians of old only refrained from melting him down for cash because they believed he was not Marcus Aurelius, but Constantine. A faithful copy now stands in the piazza.

Passing the Time of Day in Ancient Rome

Recreating some of the atmosphere of the old days is not hard: a score of books have been written on the subject, of which one of the best is *Daily Life in Ancient Rome* by Jerome Carcopino. Roman poets such as Horace, Martial and especially Juvenal also have plenty to say about it.

Life in Rome at the height of Empire was an Imperial pain: ridiculously high rents, high taxes, street crime, noise around the clock, and neighbours from Baetica or Rhaetia with peculiar habits. Yet naturally everyone in the Empire dreamed of some day moving there. The most significant difference between the way they lived then and our times was the sharp contrast between the quality of life in public versus private places. The average Roman citizen, usually unemployed or underemployed, could loll about magnificent baths and forums all day; only with reluctance did he drag himself home to his nasty, cramped fourth-floor flat at night.

Public Rome

The Roman *forum*, developed from the Greek *agora*, took the form of an open space surrounded by temples, basilicas and colonnades. In the centre, the original Roman Forum and the Fora of Augustus and Trajan made up a single vast complex, the public stage of Roman life. A typical Roman citizen would be there in the morning, to transact business, meet friends, watch the cosmopolitan crowd go by, or indulge in the favourite pastime of watching court proceedings in the basilica. Often they would have their own actions running; the Romans were easily the most litigious nation in all history. Surrounding the *fora* would be the market-places, some of them imposing buildings such as the Market of Trajan (in its time not unlike today's covered market in Istanbul).

For all their skill at plumbing, the Romans never managed to bring running water into their flats. The baths, therefore, were a daily spot on any respectable Roman's agenda. He could have stayed all day, for these great establishments were a stage for public life, and cheap and accessible even to the poorest man. Every neighbourhood had some, and, counting the ones built by the emperors, they covered almost 10 per cent of Rome. The biggest ones, with bathing halls bigger than St Peter's, included parks, museums, libraries, lunch counters and *palaestrae* – athletic grounds for the Romans' favourite games. No civilization, perhaps, ever conceived a more useful way for its citizens to spend their leisure time. There were other places in which to pursue the classical *dolce vita* – the emperors' extensive gardens (usually open to the public),

The Musei Capitolini

***t** 06 6710 2071; open Tues–Sun 9–8, last adm 7; hols 9–1.45; adm, free last Sun of month, audioguides available for a small fee.*

Michelangelo's ideas may have been adapted and tinkered with by later architects, but his plan for the Campidoglio was one of the triumphs of Renaissance design. The centrepiece, the **Palazzo Senatorio**, Rome's city hall, with its distinctive stairway and bell tower, is built over the ruins of the Roman *tabularium*, the state archive. At the

the temples, which in an irreligious age were really glorified art museums, and the taverns – one on every block, usually with upstairs and gambling in the backroom. Romans were terrible gamblers; even the virtuous Augustus would regularly present his children, slaves and dinner guests with bags of *sestertii* to wager against him. Finally there were the races and games in the Colosseum or the Circus Maximus, all of them extraordinarily brutal and bloody, which occupied an average of around 90–100 days a year. These were free, though you needed a ticket just to remind you of the imperial largesse that made it all possible. You also needed a toga, unless you were in the plebeian cheap seats, for these were among this informal city's few dress-up occasions.

Private Rome

More than 90 per cent of Romans lived in flats, in pretty but generally poorly built *insulae* up to 10 storeys in height. From the outside they looked much the same as some of the older Roman apartment blocks today, only with more imaginative façades of brick, stucco and patterned timbers. Many had balconies, and every part of these balconies and windows that received any sun would be full of climbing vines and flowers. Unfortunately most of the streets were less than 12ft across.

Rich and poor Romans lived mixed together in every *regio*: the very rich in walled houses (like those at Pompeii), set perhaps next to a four-storey block with wine and oil shops, taverns and ironmongers on the ground floor, middle-class bureaucrats and clients of the rich on the first (with perhaps three or four slaves), and the very poor above them. These had the furthest to climb, and were doomed in case of fire or collapse. Both were constant worries. Crassus, who ruled Rome in the first Triumvirate with Caesar and Pompey, got his start as a weasling building contractor, following the fire squads.

People who lived in flats did not use them much for entertaining, or even for cooking. They had paid water-carriers, but no heating except braziers, no glass windows and little furniture. The shops that filled the ground floors of most buildings always spilled out into the narrow streets, joining the market barrows and the grammar-school classes, which rented space under shop awnings or in porticoes – learning to live with distractions was a part of any Roman's education. Traffic problems were probably Rome's biggest headache after the 2nd century BC; Julius Caesar decreed an end to chariots and carriages (the rich had to get by with slave-borne litters) and banished wagons during daylight hours.

base of the stair note the statue of Minerva, in her aspect as the allegorical goddess Roma. Flanking it, Michelangelo redesigned the façade of the Palazzo dei Conservatori on the right, and projected the matching building across the square, the Palazzo Nuovo, built in the early 18th century. Together they make up the **Capitoline Museums**. Founded by Pope Clement XII in 1734, the oldest true museum in the world reopened in 2000 after a massive restoration project that added an echoing subterranean corridor lined with sculpture, columns and sarcophagi, connecting the two palaces and giving access to the Tabularium, an arched gallery offering fantastic views of the Forum below. The Capitolini display both the heights and depths of ancient society and culture. For the former there are the reliefs from the triumphal arch of Marcus Aurelius in the **Palazzo dei Conservatori** – first-class work in scenes of the emperor's clemency and piety, and his triumphal receptions in Rome. Marcus always looks a little worried in these, perhaps considering his good-for-nothing son Commodus, and the empire he would inherit, sinking into corruption and excess. What was to come is well illustrated by the degenerate art of the 4th century, such as the colossal bronze head, hand and foot of Constantine, parts of a colossal statue in the Basilica of Maxentius, scattered around the courtyard or the immense frescoed halls of the 'Appartamento dei Conservatori' on the first floor. These halls also contain the *Capitoline She-Wolf*, the symbol of Rome (note that the suckling twins were added to the Etruscan bronze she-wolf in the Renaissance), and the gentle *Spinario*, a 1st-century BC bronze of a boy pulling out a thorn from his foot.

On the second floor is a small **Pinacoteca** with some dignified Velázquez gentlemen looking scornfully at the other paintings, and two major Caravaggios, the *Fortune Teller* and *John the Baptist*. There are also some lovely 18th-century porcelains – orchestras of monkeys in powdered wigs, and suchlike. As part of the millennial renovations, the Palazzo dei Conservatori was given new spaces for temporary exhibitions on the third floor, and there's an excellent café with a vast terrace and city views.

The **Palazzo Nuovo**, reached via the underground corridor, hasn't changed since the 18th century and holds statues of most of the emperors, busts of Homer, Sophocles and Pythagoras; the voluptuous *Capitoline Venus*; a big baby Hercules; and the *Muse Polyhymnia*, one of the most delightful statues of antiquity. Later works include lots of papal paraphernalia, a statue of Charles of Anjou by Arnolfo di Cambio, and the regilded statue of Marcus Aurelius.

Carcere Mamertino

The best overview of the Roman Forum is from behind Palazzo Senatorio. A stairway leads down from the left side to Via dei Fori Imperiali and the entrance to the Forum. On the way, on Via del Carcere Tulliano beneath the church of San Giuseppe Falegnami, is the **Carcere Mamertino** (*open daily 9–12 and 2.30–5; donation requested*), the small calaboose used by the ancient Romans for their most important prisoners – the Catiline conspirators, Vercingetorix (the Gaulish chief captured by Caesar), and St Peter. The southern end of the Capitol, one of the quietest corners of Rome, was the site of the temple of Jupiter Optimus Maximus, built originally by the Etruscan kings. At the time it was the largest in Italy, testimony to Rome's importance as far back as 450 BC. Along the southern edge of the hill, the cliffs are the reduced remains of the **Tarpeian Rock**, from which traitors and other malefactors were thrown in Rome's early days.

Along the Tiber

The early emperors did their best to import classical Greek drama to Rome, and for a while, with the poets of the Latin New Comedy, it seemed the Romans would carry on the tradition. Great theatres were built, such as the **Teatro di Marcello** (*open by prior* *arrangement only, f 06 689 2115*), begun by Caesar and completed by Augustus. By the second century AD, however, theatre had begun to degenerate into lewd music-hall performances complete with naked actresses and grisly murders (condemned prisoners were sometimes butchered on stage), and shows by celebrity actors. Marcellus' theatre survived into the Middle Ages, when the Orsini family converted it into their palace-fortress. You can still see the tall arches of the circumference surmounted by the rough medieval walls, forming a dramatic backdrop for occasional concerts.

The streets to the west contain a mix of some of Rome's oldest houses and new buildings; the latter have replaced the old walled **ghetto**. There has been a sizeable Jewish community in Rome since the 2nd century BC; after conquering the Jews at the end of the 1st century AD, Pompey and Titus brought them to Rome as slaves. They helped finance the career of Julius Caesar, who proved their greatest benefactor. For centuries they lived near this bend in the river and in Trastevere. Paul IV took time off from burning books and heretics to wall them into the tiny ghetto in 1555; he also forced them to wear orange hats and attend Mass on Sunday, and limited them to the rag and old iron trades. Tearing down the ghetto walls was one of the first acts of the Italian kingdom after entry into Rome in 1870. The eclectic main **synagogue** on Lungotevere dei Cenci was built in 1904; there are guided tours, and it contains a small **museum of the Jewish Community** (*t 06 6840 0661; open Mon–Thurs 9–7.30, Fri and Sun 9–1.30, closed Jewish hols; adm*), which includes a section on the Holocaust.

Opposite, the **Isola Tiberina** is joined to both sides of the river by ancient bridges. In imperial times the island was sacred to Aesculapius, god of healing; a legend records how serpents brought from the god's shrine in Greece escaped and swam to the spot, choosing the site by divine guidance. Now, as in ancient times, most of the lovely island is taken up by a hospital. In place of the Temple of Aesculapius is the church of **San Bartolomeo** (*t 06 687 7973; open daily 9–10.30 and 4–6.30*), rebuilt in the 1690s.

The **Velabrum**, in the earliest days of Rome, was a cattle market (interestingly, in the Middle Ages, the Roman Forum itself was used for the same purpose). In this area, east of the Isola Tiberina, is **San Giorgio in Velabro** (*open daily 9–1 and 3–6.30*), parts of which date back to the 7th century; there is a Cosmatesque altar, and early-Christian fragments on the left wall. The lovely portico has been restored after a Mafia bombing in 1993. Of the two ancient arches outside, the **Arco degli Argentari** was erected by the moneychangers in honour of Septimius Severus. The larger, the unfinished, four-sided **Janus Quadrifons**, dates from the time of Constantine.

Piazza Bocca della Verità

Tourists almost always overlook this beautiful corner along the Tiber, which is a shame because it is home to two well-preserved Roman temples. Both of them go under false names: the round **Temple of Vesta**, which was used as an Armenian church in the Middle Ages, and the **Temple of Fortuna Virilis** actually seem to have been dedicated to Hercules Victor and Portunus (the god of harbours) respectively. Some bits of an exotic Roman cornice are built into the brick building on Via Luigi Petroselli opposite, part of the **House of the Crescenzi**, a powerful family in the 9th century, descended from Theodora Senatrix. If you look over the side of the Tiber embankment here you can see the outlet of the **Cloaca Maxima** (*Lungotevere Pierleoni*), the sewer that was begun by King Tarquin. Big enough to drive two carriages through, it is still in use today.

Just upstream, past the Ponte Palatino, a single arch decorated with dragons is all that remains of the Pons Aemilius. Originally built in the 2nd century BC, it collapsed twice and was last restored in 1575 by Gregory XIII, only to fall down again 20 years later. Now it is known as the 'broken bridge', or **Ponte Rotto**.

Across from the temples, the handsome medieval church with the lofty campanile is **Santa Maria in Cosmedin** (***t*** *06 678 1419; open daily summer 10–6.30, winter 10–5*), built over an altar of Hercules in the 6th century and given to Byzantine Greeks escaping from the Iconoclast emperors in the 8th. The name means 'decorated' (like 'cosmetic'), but little of the original art has survived; most of what you see is from the 12th century, including some fine Cosmatesque work inside. In the portico, an ancient, ghostly image in stone built into the walls has come down in legend as the **Bocca della Verità** – the Mouth of Truth. Medieval Romans would swear oaths and close business deals here; if you tell a lie with your hand in the image's mouth he will most assuredly bite your fingers off. Try it.

The Heart of Ancient Rome

In the 1930s Mussolini built a grand boulevard between the Vittoriano and the Colosseum to ease traffic congestion and show off the ancient sites. He called it the Via del Impero, coinciding with his aspirations of returning Rome to greatness through a new empire in Africa. After Mussolini's demise the road was re-christened **Via dei Fori Imperiali**, after the Imperial Fora which it partly covers.

The **Imperial Fora** of Augustus, Nerva and Trajan were built to relieve congestion in the original Roman Forum. **Trajan's Forum** (*Foro Traiano*), which was built with the spoils of his conquest of Dacia (modern Romania), was perhaps the grandest architectural and planning conception ever built in Rome, a broad square surrounded by colonnades, with a huge basilica flanked by two libraries and a covered market outside (the world's first shopping mall). A large part of **Trajan's Markets** (*Mercati di Traiano*) still stands and has recently been expensively converted into a massive and very striking exhibition space (*entrance on Via IV Novembre;* ***t*** *06 679 0048; open Tues–Sun 9–5; adm*); the network of surrounding paths and viewing points that pick over the ruins are due to be expanded.

Behind it, you can see Rome's own leaning tower, the 12th-century **Torre delle Milizie**. All that remains of Trajan's great square is the paving and its centrepiece, **Trajan's Column** (*Colonna Traiana*). The spiralling bands of reliefs, illustrating the Dacian Wars, reach to the top, some 96ft high. They rank with the greatest works of Roman art. Behind the column on Piazza Madonna di Loreto, **Santa Maria di Loreto** (*open daily 7.30–12 and 4–6*) is a somewhat garish High Renaissance bauble, built by Bramante and Antonio da Sangallo the Younger. The Romans liked the church so much that in the 1730s they built another one just like it next door, the **Santissimo Nome di Maria**. Scanty remains of **Caesar's Forum** (*Foro di Cesare*) and **Augustus' Forum** (*Foro di Augusto*) can be seen along the boulevard to the south.

The Roman Forum

Entrances on Via dei Fori Imperiali at Via Cavour, and at the end of the ramp that approaches the Forum from the Colosseum side; **t** *06 699 0110; open daily 9–1hr before sunset. There's a visitor centre for the Fori Imperiali on the Via dei Fori Imperiali, with small exhibitions and an information desk.*

For a place that was the centre of the Mediterranean world, there is surprisingly little to see here; centuries of use as a quarry have seen to that. The word *forum* meant 'outside' (like the Italian *fuori*); this was a marketplace outside the original Rome that became the centre of both government and business as the city expanded.

The **Via Sacra**, ancient Rome's most important street, runs the length of the Forum. At the end of it beneath the Capitoline Hill you face the **Arch of Septimius Severus** (AD 203), with reliefs of some rather trivial victories over the Arabs and Parthians; conservative Romans of the time must have strongly resented this upstart African emperor planting his monument in such an important spot. The arch also commemorated Septimius' two sons, Geta and Caracalla; when the nasty Caracalla did his brother in, he had his name effaced from it. In front of it, the **Lapis Niger**, a mysterious stone with an underground chamber beneath it, is the legendary tomb of Romulus (*closed to the public*). The inscription down below – a threat against the profaning of this sacred spot – is one of the oldest ever found in the Latin language. The famous Golden Milestone also stood here, the 'umbilicus' of Rome and the point from which all distances in the Empire were measured.

To the right is the **Curia** (the Senate House), heavily restored after centuries' use as a church (the good Baroque church behind it is **SS. Luca e Martina** (*closed for restoration*), built by Pietro da Cortona in the 1660s). To the left of the arch the remains of a raised stone area were the **Rostra**, the speakers' platform under the Republic, decorated with ships' prows (*rostra*) taken in a sea battle in about 320 BC. Of the great temples on the Capitol slope only a few columns remain: from left to right, the **Temple of Saturn**, which served as Rome's treasury, the **Temple of Vespasian** (three standing columns) and the **Temple of Concord**, built by Tiberius to honour the peace – so to speak – that the emperors had enforced between patricians and plebeians.

In front of the Rostra, in the open area once decorated with statues and monuments, the simple standing **column** was placed in honour of Nikephoros Phocas, the Byzantine emperor in 608, and was the last monument ever erected in the Forum; the Romans had to steal the column from a ruined building. Just behind it a small pool once marked the spot of one of ancient Rome's favourite legends. In 362 BC, according to Livy, an abyss suddenly opened across the Forum, and the sibyls predicted that it would not close unless the 'things that Rome held most precious' were thrown in. A consul, Marcus Curtius, took this as meaning a Roman citizen and soldier. He leapt in fully armed, horse and all, and the crack closed over him.

This section of the Forum was bordered by two imposing buildings, the **Basilica Aemilia** to the north and the **Basilica Julia** to the south, the latter built by Caesar with the spoils of the Gallic Wars. The **Temple of Caesar** closes the east end, built by Augustus as a visual symbol of the new Imperial mythology.

Rome 300 AD

*before names of sights indicates significant remains

modern streets and squares are shaded in to help orientation

Campus Martius

1 Stadium of Domitian
2 Baths of Nero
3 *Temple of Hadrian
4 Domitian's Odeon
5 Stagnum Agrippae
6 *Pantheon
7 Baths of Agrippa
8 S{ae} pta Julia
9 Temple of Isis
10 Porticus Divorum
11 Portico of Vipsania
12 Pompey's Theatre
13 *Republican Temples (Largo Argentina)
14 Portico of Minucia
15 Theatre of Balbus
16 Porticus Philippi
17 *Portico of Octavia
18 Circus Flaminius
19 *Temple of Apollo
20 Temple of Bellona
21 *Temple of Marcellus
22 *Temple of Hope (S. Nicolo)
23 Forum Holitorium
24 Temple of Aesculapius
25 Warehouses

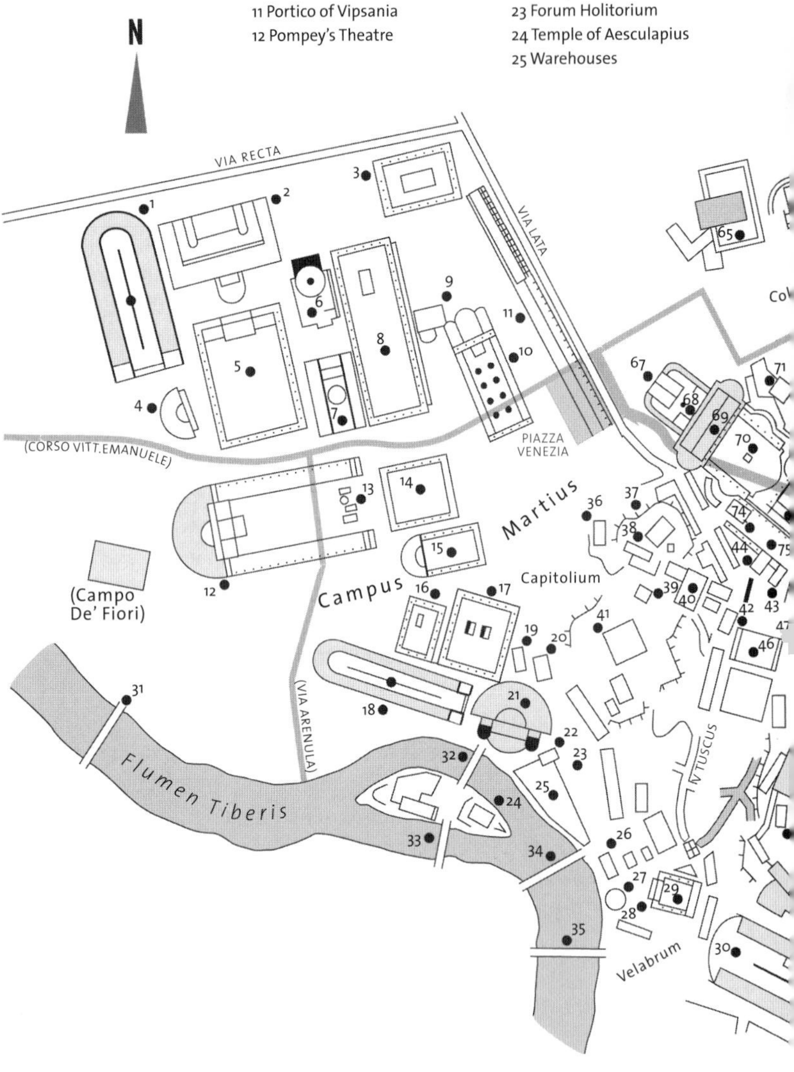

Velabrum and Tiber Island

26 *Temple of Portumnus
27 *Temple of Hercules Victor
28 Forum Boarium
29 Statio Annonae/ Altar of Hercules
30 Circus Maximus
31 Bridge of Valentinian
32 *Pons Cestius
33 *Pons Fabricius
34 * Pons Aemilius
35 Pons Probus

Capitol

36 *Insula (Apartment House)
37 Arx (Citadel)
38 Temple of Juno Moneta
39 Asylum - Temple of Veiovis
40 *Tabularium
41 Temple of Jupiter

Forum

42 *Temple of Saturn
43 *Arch of Septimius Severus
44 *Curia
45 Basilica Aemilia
46 Basilica Julia
47 *Temple of the Dioscuri
48 *House of the Vestal Virgins
49 *Basilica of Maxentius
50 *Arch of Titus
51 *Temple of Venus and Rome
52 Temple of Elagabalus
53 Nero's Colossus
54 *Arch of Constantine
55 *Colosseum

Palatine

56 *Palace of Tiberius
57 Temple of Cybele
58 *House of Augustus
59 *Staduim
60 Septizonium

Caelian and Quirinal

61 Temple of Claudius
62 *Ludus Magnus
63 Baths of Titus
64 Baths of Trajan
65 Temple of Serapis
66 Baths of Constantine

Imperial Fora

67 Temple of Trajan
68 *Trajan's Column
69 Basilica Ulpia
70 Forum of Trajan
71 *Trajan's Market
72 *Forum of Augustus
73 *Forum of Nerva – Temple of Minerva
74 Temple of Venus Genetrix
75 Forum of Caeser
76 Forum of Vespasian

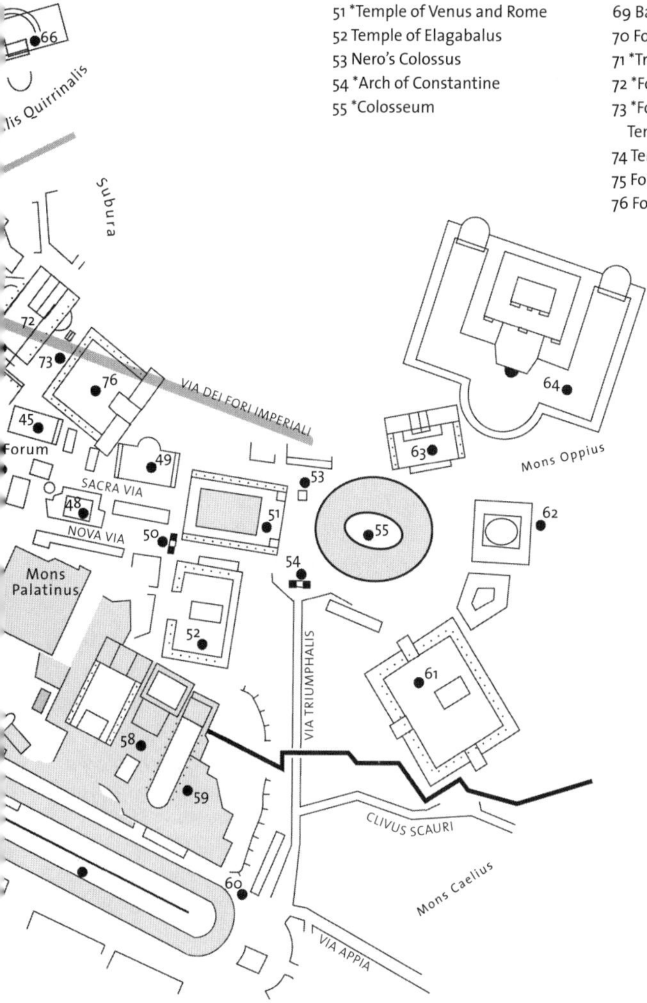

The adjacent **Temple of the Dioscuri** provides a good example of how temples were used in ancient times. This one was a meeting hall for men of the equestrian class (the knights, though they were really more likely to be businessmen); they had safe-deposit boxes in the basement, where the standard weights and measures of the Empire were kept. Between them, the round pedestal was the foundation of the small **Temple of Vesta**, where the sacred hearth fire was kept burning by the Vestal Virgins; ruins of their extensive apartments can be seen next door.

Two more Christian churches stand in this part of the Forum. **SS. Cosma e Damiano** (*open daily 9–1 and 3–6.30*) was built on to the **Temple of Antoninus Pius and Faustina** in the 6th century; most of the columns survive, with a fine sculptural frieze of griffons. **Santa Francesca Romana** (*open daily 9.30–12 and 4–7*) is built over a corner of Rome's largest temple, that of **Venus and Rome**. Built by Hadrian, this was a curious, double-ended shrine to the state cult, with one side devoted to the goddess Roma and the other to Venus – in Imperial mythology she was the ancestress of the Caesars.

The church entrance is outside the Forum, but the adjoining convent, inside the monumental area, houses the **Antiquarium Forense**, a tired collection of Iron-Age burial urns and other paraphernalia from the Forum excavations. Between the two churches the **Basilica of Maxentius**, finished by Constantine, remains the largest ruin of the Forum, its clumsy arches illustrating the ungainly but technically sophisticated 4th century. Near the exit, the **Arch of Titus** commemorates the victories of Titus and his father Vespasian over the rebellious Jews (AD 60–80). The reliefs show the booty being carted through Rome in the triumphal parade, including the seven-branched golden candlestick from the holy of holies in the Temple at Jerusalem.

South of the arch a path leads up to the **Monte Palatino** (***t*** *06 3996 7700; open daily 9–1hr before sunset; adm*). Here, overlooking the corner of the world that gave our language words such as *senate*, *plebiscite* and *magistrate*, you can leave democracy behind and visit the etymological birthplace of *palace*. The ruins of the imperial *Palatium* once covered the hill. As with the Forum, almost all the stone has been cannibalized, and there's little to see of what was once a complex half a mile long.

There are good views across the Circus Maximus from just above what was the portico from which the emperor watched the races. Take a stroll through the gardens planted by the Farnese family (*currently closed for renovation*) over what were the Imperial servants' quarters. The one modern building on the Palatino houses the **Museo Palatino** (*adm included in ticket for Palatine*), a good collection of relics found within a stone's throw of the building, plus a history of the hill.

The Colosseum

Piazza del Colosseo; open daily 9–1hr before sunset; adm; see Roma Archeologia Card p.770; audioguide in English for small fee. Daily guided tours in English at 3, plus 4.15 and 5.15 in summer.

Its real name was the Flavian Amphitheatre, after the family of emperors who built it, beginning with Vespasian in AD 72; Colosseum refers to the *Colossus*, a huge gilded statue of Nero (erected by himself, of course) that stood in the square in front. There doesn't seem to be much evidence that Christians were literally thrown to lions here – there were other places for that – but what did go on was perhaps the grossest and best-organized perversity in all history. Gladiatorial contests began under the republic, designed to make Romans better soldiers by rendering them indifferent to the sight of death. Later emperors introduced new displays to relieve the monotony – men versus animals, lions versus elephants, women versus dwarfs, sea-battles (the arena could be flooded at a moment's notice), public tortures of criminals, and even genuine athletics (a Greek import the Romans never much cared for). In the first 100 days of the Colosseum's opening, 5,000 animals were slaughtered. The native elephant and lion of North Africa and Arabia are extinct thanks to this.

However hideous its purpose, the Colosseum ranks with the greatest works of Roman architecture and engineering; all modern stadia have its basic plan. One surprising feature was a removable awning that covered the stands. Sailors from Cape Misenum were kept to operate it; they also manned the galleys during the mock sea-battles. Originally there were statues in every arch and a ring of bronze shields around the cornice. The concrete stands have eroded away, revealing the brick structure underneath. Renaissance and Baroque popes hauled away half the travertine exterior – enough to build the Palazzo Venezia, the Palazzo Barberini, a few other palaces and bridges and part of St Peter's. Almost all of the construction work carried out under Vespasian and Titus was performed by Jewish slaves after the suppression of their revolt.

Just outside the Colosseum, the **Arch of Constantine** marks the end of the ancient Triumphal Way (now Via di San Gregorio) where victorious emperors and their troops would parade their captives and booty. The arch, with a coy inscription mentioning Constantine's 'divine inspiration' (the Romans weren't sure whether it was yet respectable to mention Christianity), is covered with reliefs stolen from older arches and public buildings – a sad commentary on the state of art in Constantine's day.

Domus Aurea and the Monte Esquilino

When Nero decided he needed a new palace, money was no object. Taking advantage of the great fire of AD 64 (which he apparently did *not* start), he had a huge section of Rome (temporarily renamed Neropolis) cleared to make a rural estate. The **Golden House** (*Colle Oppio; **t** 06 3996 7700; open Weds–Mon 9–7.45; advance booking essential; adm; audioguide recommended*) was probably the most sumptuous palace ever built in Rome, decorated in an age when Roman art was at its height, but Nero never lived to see it finished – he committed suicide during an army coup by Spanish legions. When the dust settled, the new emperor Vespasian had this flagrant symbol of Imperial decadence demolished, and Titus and Trajan later erected great bath complexes on its foundations; Nero's gardens and vast lake became the site of the Colosseum. In the 1500s some beautifully decorated rooms of the Domus Aurea were discovered underground, saved for use as the basement of Titus' baths. Raphael and other artists studied them closely and incorporated some of the spirit of the fresco decoration into the grand manner of the High Renaissance (our word 'grotesque', originally referring to the leering faces and floral designs of this time, comes from the finds in this 'grotto').

The **Monte Esquilino** is better known today as the Colle Oppio. Much of it is covered with parks; besides the Domus Aurea there are very substantial ruins of the **Terme di Traiano**, still unexcavated. On the northern slope of the hill, **San Pietro in Vincoli** (**t** *06 488 2865; open daily 7–12.30 and 3.30–6*) takes its name from relics supposed to be the chains Peter was locked in before Nero had him crucified. They are kept over the main altar, though the real attraction of this church for non-Catholics is the famous, ill-fated **tomb of Julius II**, which tortured Michelangelo for many years. Of the original project, planned as a sort of tabernacle with 40 individual statues, the artist completed, as well as the statues of *Leah* and *Rachel*, the powerful figure of *Moses*, perhaps the closest anyone has ever come to capturing prophetic vision in stone. All the other statues on the tomb are the work of Michelangelo's students.

San Clemente

Via San Giovanni in Laterano; **t** *06 7045 1018; open Mon–Fri 9–12.30 and 3–6, Sat, Sun hols 10–12.30 and 3–6; adm to the excavations.*

This church, a little east of the Colosseum, is one of the more fascinating remnants of Rome's history. One of the first large building projects of the Christians in Rome, the original basilica of *c*. 375 burned with the rest of the quarter during a 1084 sacking by the Normans. It was rebuilt soon afterwards with a new Cosmatesque pavement, and the 6th-century choir screen from the original church. The 12th-century mosaic in the apse represents the Triumph of the Cross, and the chapel at the entrance contains a beautiful series of quattrocento frescoes by Masolino. From a vestibule, nuns sell tickets to the **Lower Church**, the lower half of the original San Clemente, with remarkable, though deteriorated, frescoes from the 900s and the 12th century. The plaque from Bulgaria, mentioned on p.765, commemorates SS. Cyril and Methodius, who went from this church to spread the Gospel among the Slavs; they translated the Bible into Old Slavonic, and invented the first Slavic alphabet (Cyrillic) to do it.

From here, steps lead down to the lowest stratum, with 1st- and 2nd-century AD buildings divided by an alley; this includes the **Mithraeum**, the best-preserved temple of its kind after Capua's. The neighbouring building was filled with rubble to serve as a foundation for the basilica, and the apse later added over the Mithraeum. Father Mulhooly of Boston started excavating in the 1860s, and later excavations revealed a Mithraic antechamber with a fine stuccoed ceiling, a Mithraic school, and the temple proper, a small cavern-like hall with benches for initiates to share ritual suppers.

Mithraism was a mystery religion, full of secrets closely held by the initiates (all male, and largely soldiers) and it is difficult to say what else went on down here. Two altars were found, each with the image of Persian-import god Mithras despatching a white bull. Underneath is a fourth building level, consisting of some foundations from the Republican era. At the end of the 1st-century building you can look down into an ancient sewer or underground stream, one of 1,000 entrances to the surreal sub-Roma of endless subterranean caves, buildings, rivers and lakes, mostly unexplored and unexplorable. A century ago a schoolboy fell in the water here; they found him, barely alive, in open country several kilometres from the city.

Corso Vittorio Emanuele

This street, chopped through the medieval centre in the 1880s, still hasn't quite been assimilated into its surroundings; nevertheless, this ragged, smoky traffic tunnel will come in handy when you find yourself lost in the tortuous, meandering streets of Rome's oldest quarter. Starting west from Piazza Venezia, the church of **Il Gesù** (1568–84; ***t** 06 697 001; open daily 7–12 and 3–7.30*) in Piazza del Gesù was a landmark for a new era and the new aesthetic of cinquecento Rome. The transitional, pre-Baroque fashion was often referred to as the 'Jesuit style', and here in the Jesuits' head church architects Vignola and Della Porta laid down Baroque's first law: an intimation of paradise through decorative excess. It hasn't aged well, though at the time it must have seemed to most Romans a perfect marriage of Renaissance art and a reformed, revitalized faith. St Ignatius is buried in the left transept right under the altar, Spanish-style; the globe in the sculpted Trinity is the biggest piece of lapis lazuli in the world.

Further west, the street opens into a ghastly square called Largo Argentina. Remains of several Republican-era temples, unearthed far below ground level, occupy the centre. The square teems with cats: tucked beneath the square at one end is the **Roman Cat Sanctuary** (**t** 06 687 2133). Take a short detour around the corner to find the newest addition to the Museo Nazionale d'Arte Romana halfway down Via delle Botteghe Oscure at No.31: the **Crypta Balbi** (*open Tues–Sun 9–7.45; adm*). This modern, glassy museum is built over the ruins of a theatre, which was almost as large as the huge theatres of Pompey and Marcellus. A medieval church grew up on the ruins, before becoming submerged by the modern street.

Back up on Via Corso Emanuele, just beyond the Largo Argentina, is another grand Baroque church, **Sant'Andrea della Valle** (***t** 06 686 1339; open daily 8–12 and 4.30–7*), boasting the city's second-tallest dome. Maderno, one of the architects of St Peter's, did the majority of the work. The curving façade across the street belongs to the **Palazzo Massimo alle Colonne** (*open 16 Mar only 7–1; adm*), the masterpiece of the Renaissance architect Baldassare Peruzzi; he transplanted something of the Florentine style of monumental palaces, adding some light-hearted proto-Baroque decoration. If you can, have a look inside the adjacent church of **San Pantaleo de Parione** (*open, rarely, for Mass*), with its outlandish sculptural frieze of shields, trays and popes' hats piled up like a rubbish heap. The sumptuous Palazzo Braschi next door at Piazza San Pantaleo 10 houses the **Museo di Roma** (***t** 06 8207 7384; open Tues–Sun 9–7; guided tours Sat and Sun, call for times; adm*), which reopened in 2002 after a decade of restoration but has a disappointing collection of artefacts that are virtually meaningless unless you hire the audioguide. There are good views over Piazza Navona however.

Right across the street is one of the earliest and best of the palaces on Corso Vittorio Emanuele, the delicate **Piccola Farnesina** by Antonio da Sangallo the Younger. It houses another little museum, the **Museo Barracco** (***t** 06 6880 6848; open Tues–Sun 9–7; adm*) with its collection of sculpture. Just around the corner from Sant'Andrea, the **Burcardo Library and Theatre Collection**, Via Sudario 44 (*open Sun–Fri 9–1.30, closed hols*) is a collection of fascinating relics from the Roman theatrical tradition.

The biggest palace on the street, attributed to Bramante, is **Palazzo della Cancelleria** (***t*** *06 6989 3405; open for visits by reservation at least 1 month in advance*), once the seat of the papal municipal government. St Philip Neri, the gifted, irascible holy man who is patron saint of Rome, built the **Chiesa Nuova** (*open daily 8–12 and 4.30–7*) near the eastern end of the Corso (1584). Philip was quite a character, with something of the Zen Buddhist in him. He forbade his followers from engaging in any sort of philosophical speculation, but made them sing and recite poetry; two of his pastimes were insulting popes and making initiates walk through Rome with a foxtail sewn to the back of their coat to learn humility. As was common in those times, sincere faith and humility were eventually translated into flagrant Baroque. The Chiesa Nuova is one of the larger and fancier of the species. Its altarpiece is a Madonna with Angels by Rubens. Even more flagrant, outside the church, is the curved arch-Baroque façade of the **Oratorio dei Filippini** by Borromini. The form of music called the *oratorio* takes its name from this chapel, a tribute to St Philip's role in promoting sacred music.

Campo de' Fiori

Few cities can put on such a variety of faces; depending on where you spend your time in Rome, you may come away with the impression of a city that is one great Baroque stage set, a city of grimy early 1900s *palazzi* and bad traffic, or a city full of nothing but ruins and parks. Around Campo de' Fiori, one of the spots dearest to the hearts of Romans themselves, you may think yourself in the middle of some scruffy south Italian village. Rome's market square, disorderly, cramped and chaotic, it is easily the liveliest corner of the city, full of barrows, buskers, teenage bohemians and the folkloresque types who have lived here all their lives. The best time to see it is during the morning market (*Mon–Sat dawn–1*) or at night along with the adjacent Piazza Farnese. During papal rule the old square was also used for executions – most notoriously the burning of Giordano Bruno in 1600. This well-travelled philosopher was the first to take Copernican astronomy to its logical extremes, positing an infinite universe with no centre, no room for Heaven, and nothing eternal but change. The Church had few enemies more dangerous. Italy never forgot him; the statue of Bruno in Campo de' Fiori went up only a few years after the end of papal rule.

Just east of the square, the heap of buildings around Piazzetta di Grottapinta is built over the cavea of **Teatro di Pompeo**, ancient Rome's biggest. This complex included a curia, where Julius Caesar was assassinated in 44 BC. Walk south from Campo de' Fiori into the heart of the High Renaissance with the **Palazzo Farnese**, a definitive work of that Olympian style. The younger Sangallo began it in 1514, and Michelangelo contributed to the façades and interiors. The building is now the French Embassy (*open for group visits by arrangement with the cultural section of the embassy*).

Most of the palaces that fill this neighbourhood have one thing in common – they were made possible by someone's accession to the papacy. Built on the pennies of the faithful, they provide the most outrageous illustration of Church corruption at the dawn of the Reformation. Alessandro Farnese, who as Pope Paul III was a clever and effective pope – though perhaps the greatest nepotist – managed to build this palace 20 years before his election, with the income from his 16 absentee bishoprics.

Palazzo Spada, just to the east on Via Capo di Ferro 13, was the home of a mere cardinal, but its florid stucco façade (1540) almost upstages the Farnese. Inside, the **Galleria Spada** (***t** 06 6880 9814; open Tues–Sat 9–7.30, Sun 9–6.30; adm*) is one of Rome's great collections of 16th- and 17th-century painting. Guido Reni, Guercino and the other favourites of the age are well represented. Don't miss the courtyard, which has decoration similar to the façade, and a glass window with a view through the library to one of Rome's little Baroque treasures: the recently restored *trompe l'œil* corridor, designed by Borromini to appear four times its actual length (the statue at the end of the path is actually less than three feet tall). To the south, close to the Tiber, **Via Giulia**, laid out by Pope Julius II, is a pretty thoroughfare lined with churches and *palazzi*. Many artists (successful ones) have lived here, including Raphael.

Piazza Navona

In 1477 the area now covered by one of Rome's most beautiful piazzas was a field full of huts and vineyards, tucked inside the imposing ruins of the Stadium of Domitian. A redevelopment of the area covered the long grandstands with new houses, but the decoration had to wait for the age of Baroque. In 1644, the Pamphili family won the papal sweepstakes with the election of Innocent X. Innocent, a great grafter and such a villainous pope that when he died no one – not even his newly wealthy relatives – would pay for a proper burial, built the ornate **Palazzo Pamphili** (now the Brazilian Embassy) and hired Borromini to complete the gaudy church of **Sant'Agnese in Agone** (*open Tues–Sun 10–7 and for Mass*), begun by Carlo and Girolamo Rainaldi.

Borromini's arch-rival, Bernini, got the commission for the piazza's famous fountains; the Romans still tell stories of how the two artists carried on. Borromini started a rumour that the tall obelisk atop the central **Fontana dei Fiumi** was about to topple; when the alarmed papal commissioners arrived to confront Bernini with the news, he tied a piece of twine around it, secured the other end to a lamppost, and laughed all the way home. The fountain is Bernini's masterpiece, Baroque at its flashiest and most lovable. Among the travertine grottoes and fantastical flora and fauna under the obelisk, the four colossal figures represent the Ganges, Danube, Rio de la Plata and Nile (with the veiled head because its source was unknown). Bernini also designed the smaller **Fontana del Moro**, at the southern end. The third fountain, that of *Neptune*, was an empty basin until the 19th century, when the statues by Giacomo della Porta were added to make the square seem more symmetrical. Off the southern end of the piazza, at the back of Palazzo Braschi, **Pasquino** is the original Roman 'talking statue', embellished with placards and graffiti ('*pasquinades*') since the 1500s – one of his favourite subjects in those days was the insatiable pigginess of families such as the Farnese; serious religious issues were usually too hot to touch.

Piazza Navona seems mildly schizoid these days, unable to become entirely part of high-fashion, tourist-itinerary Rome, yet no longer as comfortable and unpretentious as the rest of the neighbourhood. One symptom will be readily apparent should you step into any of the old cosy-looking cafés and restaurants around the piazza: they're as expensive as in any part of Rome. The best time to come to Piazza Navona is at night when the fountain is illuminated – or, if you can, for the noisy, traditional toy fair of the **Befana**, which is set up between just before Christmas and Epiphany. **Palazzo Altemps**, on Piazza Sant'Apollinare, now contains part of the excellent **Museo Nazionale Romano** (*t 06 683 3759; open Tues–Fri 9–7.45, Sun 9am–11pm; adm*). The beautiful palace makes a stunning setting for the collection of busts and statues: the *piano nobile* still contains fragments of 16th-century frescoes and there's a glorious painted loggia lined with busts of the Caesars, as well as a tiny, forlorn gilded theatre in the basement.

Some of the churches in the area are worth a look, such as **Santa Maria della Pace** at Vicolo del Arco della Pace 5 (***t** 06 686 1156; open Tues–Sat 10–12 and 4–6, Sun 9–11*), with Raphael's series of Sibyls and Prophets on the vaulting and a cloister by Bramante. **San Luigi dei Francesi** (***t** 06 688 271; open Mon–Weds and Fri–Sun 8.30–12.30 and 3.30–7; Thurs 8.30–12.30*), the French church in Rome, contains the great *Life of St Matthew* by Caravaggio in a chapel on the left aisle. Towards the Pantheon at Corso del Rinascimento 40, **Sant'Ivo alla Sapienza** (***t** 06 686 4987; open Sun am for Mass*) once served the English community in Rome. Borromini built them one of his most singular buildings (1660), with its dome and spiralling cupola.

The Pantheon

*Piazza della Rotonda; **t** 06 6830 0230; open Mon–Sat 8.30–7.30, Sun 9–6.*

When we consider the fate of so many other great buildings of ancient Rome, we can begin to understand what a slim chance it was that allowed this one to come down to us. The first Pantheon was built in 27 BC by Agrippa, Emperor Augustus' son-in-law and right-hand man, but was destroyed by fire and replaced by the present temple in AD 119–28 by the Emperor Hadrian, although curiously it retains Agrippa's original inscription on the pediment. Its history has been precarious ever since. In 609 the empty Pantheon was consecrated to Christianity as 'St Mary of the Martyrs'. Becoming a church is probably what saved it, though the Byzantines hauled away the gilded bronze roof tiles soon afterwards, and for a while in the Middle Ages the portico saw use as a fish market. The Pantheon's greatest enemy, however, was Gian Lorenzo Bernini. He not only took it upon himself to 'improve' it with a pair of Baroque belfries over the porch (demolished in 1887), he also had Pope Urban VIII take down the bronze covering on the inside of the dome to melt down for his *baldacchino* over the altar at St Peter's. Supposedly there was enough left over to make the pope 60 cannons.

You may notice that the building seems perilously unsound. There is no way a simple vertical wall can support such a heavy, shallow dome (steep domes push downwards, shallow ones outwards). Obviously the walls will tumble at any moment. That is a little joke the Roman architects are playing, showing off as shamelessly as in the Colosseum or the aqueduct with four storeys of arches that used to run *up* to the Monte Palatino. The wall that looks so fragile is really 23ft thick and the dome on top isn't a dome at all – the real hemispherical dome lies underneath, resting easily on the walls inside. The ridges you see on the upper dome are courses of cantilevered bricks, effectively almost weightless. The real surprise, however, lies behind the enormous original bronze doors: an interior of precious marbles and finely sculpted details, the grandest and best-preserved building to have survived from the ancient world. The movie directors who made all those Roman epics in the 1950s and '60s certainly took many of their settings from this High Imperial creation, just as architects from the early Middle Ages onwards have tried to equal it.

Brunelleschi learned enough from it to build his dome in Florence, and a visit here will show you at a glance what Michelangelo and his contemporaries were trying so hard to outdo. The coffered dome, the biggest cast concrete construction ever made before the 20th century, is the crowning audacity. At 141ft in diameter it is probably the largest in the world (a little-known fact – St Peter's dome is 6ft less, though much taller). Standing in the centre and looking at the clouds through the 28ft *oculus*, the hole at the top, provides an odd sensation you can experience nowhere else.

Inside, the niches around the perimeter held statues of the Pantheon's 12 gods, plus those of Augustus and Hadrian; in the centre, illuminated by a direct sunbeam at midsummer noon, stood Jove. Now the interior decoration is limited to an Annunciation, attributed to Melozzo da Forlì, and the tombs of eminent Italians such as Raphael and kings Vittorio Emanuele II and Umberto I. The Pantheon simply stands open, with no admission charges, probably fulfilling the same purpose as it did in Hadrian's day – no purpose at all, save that of an unequalled monument to art and the builder's skill.

Just behind the Pantheon, **Santa Maria sopra Minerva** (***t*** *06 679 1217; open daily 7am–7.30pm; cloister open Mon–Sat 8–1 and 4–7*) is one of the few medieval churches of Rome (*c.* 1280) to have escaped the Baroque treatment. Two Medici popes, Leo X and Clement VII, are buried here, as is Fra Angelico. Santa Maria's Florentine connection began with the Dominican monks who designed it; they also created Florence's Santa Maria Novella. A work of Michelangelo, *Christ with the Cross*, can be seen near the high altar; the Carafa Chapel off the right aisle, where you can pay your respects to Pope Paul IV, has a series of frescoes (1489) on the Life of St Thomas by Filippino Lippi, his best work outside Florence.

Via del Corso

The Campus Martius, the open plain between Rome's hills and the Tiber, was the training ground for soldiers in the early days of the Republic. Eventually the city swallowed it up and the old path towards the Via Flaminia became an important thoroughfare, *Via Lata* ('Broad Street'). Not entirely by coincidence, the popes of the 14th and 15th centuries laid out a new boulevard almost in the same place. **Via del Corso**, or simply the Corso, has been the main axis of Roman society ever since. Goethe left a fascinating account of the Carnival festivities of Rome's benignly decadent 18th century, climaxing in the horse-races that gave the street its name. Much of its length is taken up by the overdone palaces of the age, such as the Palazzo Doria (1780) at Piazza del Collegio Romano 2, where the **Galleria Doria Pamphili** (***t*** *06 679 7323; open Fri–Weds 10–5; adm, includes audioguide in English*), still owned by the Pamphili, has a fine painting collection – with Velázquez' *Portrait of Innocent X*, Caravaggio's *Flight into Egypt*, and works by Rubens, Titian, Brueghel and others. Guided tours of the apartments (available in English by request) help to convey an idea of the kind of lifestyle a family expected when one of its members hit the papal jackpot.

To the north, the palaces have come down in the world, now housing banks and offices. Look on the sidestreets for some hidden attractions: **Sant'Ignazio** on Piazza di Sant'Ignazio (*open daily 7.30–12.30 and 4–7.15*) is another Jesuit church with some spectacular *trompe l'œil* frescoes on the ceiling; a block north on Piazza di Pietra, columns of the ancient **Temple of Hadrian** are incorporated into the north side of the city's tiny stock exchange. **Piazza Colonna** takes its name from the column of Marcus Aurelius, whose military victories are remembered in a column (just like those of Trajan); on top is a statue of St Paul. The obelisk in adjacent Piazza di Montecitorio once marked the hours on a gigantic sundial in Emperor Augustus' garden; **Palazzo di Montecitorio**, begun by Bernini, now houses the Italian Chamber of Deputies.

A little way east of Piazza Colonna is the **Fontana di Trevi**, into which you throw coins to guarantee a return trip to Rome. The fountain was completed in 1762 to commemorate the restoration of Agrippa's aqueduct by Nicholas V in 1453. The source was called the 'Virgin Water' after Virgo, a young girl who had shown thirsty Roman soldiers the hidden spring. It makes a grand sight – enough to make you want to come back (not many fountains have an entire palace for a stage backdrop). The big fellow in the centre is Oceanus, drawn by horses and tritons through cascades of travertine and blue water. Across from the fountain, little **SS. Vincenzo and Anastasio** (***t** 06 678 3098; open daily 7–9am*) has the distinction of caring for the pickled hearts and entrails of dozens of popes, kept down in the crypt. A short walk from the fountain the **Museo delle Paste Alimentari** at Piazza Scanderbeg 117 (***t** 06 699 1119; open daily 9.30–5.30; adm*) has a small, modern display on the history of Italy's most famous food.

Further north, the Corso comes close to the Tiber and the dilapidated **Mausoleo di Augusto** (*closed to the public*), a cylinder of shabby brick once covered in marble and golden statues. All the Julian emperors except Nero were interred here, in the middle of what were Augustus' enormous gardens. After the centuries had despoiled the tomb of its riches, the Colonna family turned the hulk into a fortress. Further indignities were in store. Until 1823, when the pope forbade them, bullfights were popular in Rome, and a Spanish entrepreneur found the circular enclosure perfect for the *toreros*. After that the tomb was used as a circus, before Mussolini, wishing to afford the founders of Imperial Rome due respect (and perhaps intending to be buried there himself), declared it a national monument and had trees planted around it. Even so, no one quite seems to know what to do with it; it sits locked and empty.

Across the street, Augustus' **Ara Pacis**, Altar of Peace (*Via di Ripetta, **t** 06 6710 3819; currently closed for restoration*), has had a better fate. Bits and pieces of the beautiful sculpted reliefs, dug up in 1937, were joined with casts of others from museums around Europe to recreate the small building almost in its entirety, one of antiquity's noblest (and least pretentious) conceptions. Among the mythological reliefs, note the side facing the river, with the emperor and his family dedicating a sacrifice. At the time of writing it's shrouded in scaffolding while Richard Meier's glassy visitor centre takes shape around it.

Piazza di Spagna

This sophisticated piazza has been a favourite with foreigners since it was laid out in the early 16th century. The Spaniards came first, as their embassy to the popes was established here in 1646, giving the square and the steps their name. Later, the English Romantic poets made it their headquarters in Italy; typical mementos – locks of hair, fond remembrances, death masks – can be seen at the **Keats–Shelley Memorial House** at No.26 (***t*** *06 678 4235; open Mon–Fri 9–1 and 3–6, Sat 11–2 and 3–6; adm*). Almost every artist, writer or musician of the last century spent some time here, but today the piazza often finds itself bursting at the seams with refreshingly Philistine gawkers and wayward youth from all over the world, caught between the charms of McDonald's (the first in Rome) and the fancy shops around Via Condotti.

All these visitors need somewhere to sit, and the popes obliged them in 1725 with the construction of the **Spanish Steps** (*Scalinata di Trinità dei Monti*), an exceptionally beautiful and exceptionally Baroque ornament. At the top of the stairs the simple but equally effective church of **Trinità dei Monti** (***t*** *06 679 4179; open daily 9–8*) by Carlo Maderno (early 16th century) was paid for by the king of France.

At the southern end of Piazza di Spagna, a Borromini palace housed the papal office called the *Propaganda Fide*. The column in front (1857) celebrates the proclamation of the Dogma of the Immaculate Conception. Via del Babuino, a street named after a siren on a fountain so ugly that Romans called her the 'baboon', connects Piazza di Spagna with Piazza del Popolo. Besides its impressive antique shops, the street carries on the English connection, with All Saints' Church, a sleepy neo-pub and an English bookshop just off it.

Piazza del Popolo

If you have a choice of how you enter Rome, this is the way to do it, through the gate in the old Aurelian wall and into one of the most successful of all Roman piazzas. Valadier, the pope's architect after the Napoleonic occupation, gave the piazza the form it has today, but the big obelisk of Pharaoh Ramses II, punctuating the view down the boulevards, arrived in the 1580s. It is 3,200 years old but, like all obelisks, it looks mysteriously brand new. Augustus brought it to Rome from Heliopolis and planted it in the Circus Maximus; it was transferred here by Pope Sixtus V. The two domed churches designed by Rainaldi, set like bookends at the entrance to the three boulevards, are from the 1670s, and formed part of the original plan for the piazza to which Bernini and Fontana may have contributed. Nero's ashes were interred in a mausoleum here, at the foot of the Monte Pincio. The site was planted with walnut trees and soon everyone in Rome knew that Nero's ghost haunted the grove, sending out demons in the form of flocks of ravens to perform deeds of evil. In about 1100 Pope Paschal II destroyed the grove and scattered the ashes; to complete the exorcism he built a church on the site, **Santa Maria del Popolo** (***t*** *06 361 0636; open Mon–Fri 6–1 and 5–7.30, Sat–Sun 8–1 and 5–7.30*). Rebuilt in the 1470s, it contains some of the best painting in Rome: Caravaggio's stunning *Crucifixion of St Peter* and *Conversion of St Paul* (in the left transept), and frescoes by Pinturicchio near the altar. Raphael designed the Chigi Chapel, off the left aisle, including its mosaics.

Villa Borghese

From Piazza del Popolo, a winding ramp leads up to Rome's great complex of parks. The **Monte Pincio** once formed part of Augustus' imperial gardens; the adjacent **Villa Medici** at Viale della Trinità dei Monti 1 (***t** 06 676 1305, open for guided tours of the gardens 1 Mar–31 May and 6–25 Oct, Sun every half-hour 10–12.30*) occupies the site of the Villa of Lucullus, the 2nd-century BC philosopher and general who conquered northern Anatolia and brought cherries to Europe. Now the home of the French Academy, the Villa Medici was a posh jail of sorts for Galileo during his Inquisitorial trials. The Pincio, redesigned by Valadier as a lovely formal garden, offers rare views over Rome. It is separated from the **Villa Borghese** (*open daily dawn–sunset*) proper by the Aurelian wall and the modern sunken roadway that borders it; its name, Viale del Muro Torto (crooked wall), refers to a section that collapsed in the 6th century and was left as it was because it was believed to be protected by St Peter.

The vast spaces of the Villa Borghese contain charming vales, woods and a pond (with rowing boats for hire), an imitation Roman temple or two, rococo avenues where bewigged dandies and powdered tarts promenaded in the 1700s, bits of ancient aqueduct, a **Bioparco** or zoo at Piazzale del Giardino Zoologico (***t** 06 360 8211, open daily Mar–Oct 9.30–6, Nov–Feb 9.30–5; adm*), and the **Galleria Nazionale d'Arte Moderna** (***t** 06 322 981; open Tues–Sun 8.30–7.30; adm; guided tours in English Sun at 11am by reservation*), housed in one of Rome's most inexcusable buildings (1913) but containing some great works by Modigliani and the Futurists.

If you cannot make it to Tarquinia, the **Museo Etrusco Nazionale di Villa Giulia** on Piazzale di Villa Giulia (***t** 06 321 7224; open Tues–Sun 8.30–7.30; adm*) is the place to get to know the Etruscans. Some of their best art has been collected here, as well as some laboriously reconstructed terracotta façades giving an idea of how an Etruscan temple looked. The compelling attraction is the Etruscans' effortless talent for portraiture: expressive faces that bridge the gap between the centuries can be seen in terracotta ex-votos, sarcophagi and even architectural decoration. Serious art is often more stylized; fine examples are the charming couple on the *Sarcophago dei Sposi* from Cerveteri, and the roof statues from the Temple of Portonaccio at Veii. The museum building and its courts and gardens are attractions in themselves; Julius III had Vignola and Ammannati build this quirky Mannerist villa in 1553.

The ancient relics and late Renaissance and Baroque painting and sculpture – including masterpieces by Bernini and Caravaggio – at the **Museo e Galleria Borghese** (***t** 06 32810; open Tues–Sun 9–7; adm, booking recommended, essential in summer; guided visits Tues–Sun 9.10 and 11.10; guided tours of Secret Gardens Sat 10.30am, call to reserve, **t** 06 8107 7304*) is testimony to the greed and avarice of Cardinal Scipione Borghese, nephew of Pope Paul IV, who amassed one of the great private collections of the 17th century and built a magnificently decorated palace on the family's property to hold it. The display is all the more impressive in that a descendant of the Cardinal 'sold' many pieces to his brother-in-law, Napoleon Bonaparte, who put them in the Louvre.

The Museo Borghese (on the ground floor) offers an intriguing mix of great art and Roman preciosity. Often the two go hand-in-hand, as with the sensuously charged showpieces of Bernini: *Apollo and Daphne*, *The Rape of Proserpina* and especially his

David, which the artist modestly chiselled in his own image. Canova, the hot item among sculptors in Napoleon's day, contributes a titillatingly languorous statue of Pauline Borghese (Napoleon's sister) as the Conquering Venus. Also on the ground floor are several Caravaggios, including the *Madonna of the Palafrenier*.

No less impressive are the paintings in the gallery upstairs (entrance through the basement café), representing many of the finest 16th- and 17th-century painters: Titian, Bernini, Raphael, Correggio and Rubens.

Via Veneto and the Quirinale

This chain of gardens used to be much bigger, but at the end of the last century many of the old villas were lost to urban expansion. Perhaps the greatest loss was the Villa Ludovisi, praised by many as the most beautiful of all Rome's parks. Now the choice 'Ludovisi' quarter, it has given the city one of its most famous streets, Via Veneto, the long winding boulevard of grand hotels, cafés and boutiques. A promenade for the smart set in the 1950s, it now wears something of the forlorn air of a jilted beau. At southern end, the cellar of the **Convento dei Cappuccini** (*entrance halfway up the stairs of Santa Maria della Concezione; open daily 9–12 and 3–6; adm*) contains the bones and skulls of 4,000 monks carefully arranged by serious-minded Capuchins long ago to remind us of something we know only too well.

On the other side of Piazza Barberini, up a gloomy Baroque avenue called Via delle Quattro Fontane, is the Palazzo Barberini, decorated everywhere with the bees from the family arms. Maderno, Borromini and Bernini all worked on it, with financing made possible by the election of a Barberini as Pope Urban VIII in 1623. It now houses the **Galleria Nazionale d'Arte Antica** (***t*** *06 481 4591; open Tues–Sun 8.30–7.30; adm*) – a misleading title, as it is devoted to Italian works of the 12th–18th centuries. Often the original decoration steals the show from the pictures: Bernini's Great Hall, for example, has a ceiling fresco by Pietro da Cortona, the *Triumph of Divine Providence*. Works present include a Bernini self-portrait, Raphael's famous portrait of his beloved mistress *La Fornarina*, the 'baker's girl', and Lippi's *Madonna*.

San Carlino (***t*** *06 488 3261; open Mon–Fri 9–1 and 3–4, Sat 9–12.30, Sun 10.30–1*), situated on the corner of Via delle Quattro Fontane and Via Quirinale, is one of Borromini's best works – and his first one (1638). It's a flight of fancy built exactly the size of one of the four massive pillars that hold up the dome in St Peter's. Just down the street, his rival Bernini counters with **Sant'Andrea al Quirinale** (1658–70), a small, richly decorated elliptical church that constitutes one of the architectural *tours de force* of the Baroque.

Continue down **Via Quirinale** and you'll reach the summit of that hill, covered with villas and gardens in ancient times, and abandoned in the Middle Ages. During the reign of Sixtus V they were excavated to reveal monumental Roman statues of the **Dioscuri** (Castor and Pollux), probably copied from Phidias or Praxiteles. Together with a huge basin found in the Forum, they make a centrepiece for Piazza del Quirinale. Behind it is the dreary **Palazzo del Quirinale** (***t*** *06 46991; open late Sept–early July Sun 8.30–12.30; adm*), built in 1574 to symbolize the political domination of the popes, later occupied by the kings of Italy, and now the residence of the country's president.

Around Stazione Termini: Terme

Rome's great station takes its name from the nearby **Terme di Diocleziano** *(**t** 06 3996 7700; open Tues–Sun 9–7; adm)*, which is part of the **Museo Nazionale Romano**, the greatest Italian collection of antiquities after the museum in Naples. Until the popes dismantled the baths for building stone, this was by far Rome's biggest ruin; its outer wall followed the present-day lines of Via XX Settembre, Via Volturno and Piazza dei Cinquecento, and the big semi-circular **Piazza della Repubblica**, with its mouldering, grandiose 1890s *palazzi* and huge fountain, occupies the site of the baths' exercise ground, or *palaestra*. In all, the complex covered some 11 hectares. Michelangelo, not on one of his better days, converted a section of the lofty, vaulted central bathhouse into the church of **Santa Maria degli Angeli**, conserving some of the building's original form and adding a broad new cloister. The cloister and the adjoining building now house part of the Museo Nazionale Romano's vast collection.

Across the street are more of the Museo Nazionale's holdings at the unmissable **Palazzo Massimo alle Terme** (***t*** *06 3996 7700; open Tues–Sun 9–7; adm*). The basement, courtyard and first-floor rooms contain coins, jewellery, busts and statuary, but it's the delicate frescoes and mosaics from the Villa di Livia, the Villa della Farnesina and other aristocratic villas that which really stand out (*visits by guided tour only; time marked on admission tickets*). There's a shimmering sea-green forest of fruit trees and exotic birds that once covered the dining room of the Villa di Livia, and a lively fresco from the old fish market.

A block north of the baths, Piazza San Bernardo has two interesting churches: **San Bernardo**, built out of a circular library that once occupied a corner of the baths' walls, and **Santa Maria della Vittoria** (***t*** *06 482 6190; open daily 7–12 and 4.30–7*), home to one of the essential works of Baroque sculpture, the disconcertingly erotic *St Teresa in Ecstasy* by Bernini (in a chapel off the left aisle).

The Patriarchal Basilicas

Besides St Peter's there are three patriarchal basilicas – ancient and revered churches under the care of the pope that have always been a part of the Roman Pilgrimage. Santa Maria Maggiore, San Paolo Fuori le Mura (*see* p.816) and San Giovanni in Laterano are all on the edges of the city, away from the political and commercial centre; by the Middle Ages they stood in open countryside, and only recently has the city grown outwards to swallow them once more.

Santa Maria Maggiore

Santa Maria Maggiore, on Monte Esquilino, was probably begun about 352, when a rich Christian saw a vision of the Virgin directing him to build a church; Pope Liberius had received the same vision at the same time, and the two supposedly found the site marked out for them by a miraculous August snowfall. The church (***t*** *06 483 195; open 7–7; call for info on guided visits to the Loggia delle Benedizioni, which has some 13th-century mosaics depicting the legend of the church's foundation*) took its current form in the 1740s, with a perfectly elegant façade by Fernando Fuga and an equally impressive rear elevation by other architects; the obelisk behind it came from the

Santa Maria Maggiore

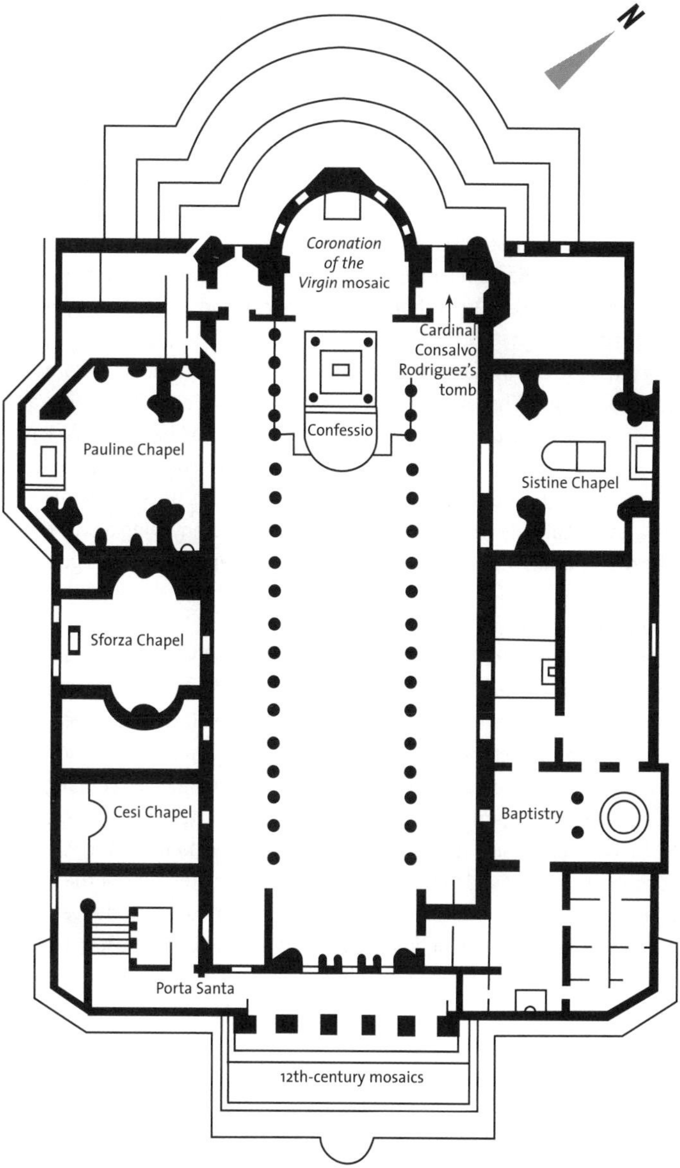

Mausoleum of Augustus. Above everything rises the tallest and fairest **campanile** in Rome, an incongruous survival from the 1380s. Inside, the most conspicuous feature is the coffered ceiling by Giuliano da Sangallo, gilded with the first gold brought back from the New World by Columbus, a gift from Ferdinand and Isabella of Spain. In the apse are splendid but faded mosaics from 1295 of the Coronation of the Virgin; others, from the 5th century, decorate the nave and the 'triumphal arch' in front of the apse. Santa Maria Maggiore has a prize relic – the genuine manger from Bethlehem, preserved in a sunken shrine in front of the altar. In front, kneeling in prayer, is a colossal, rather grotesque statue of Pope Pius IV added in the 1880s.

In 822, two decades after Charlemagne visited Rome, Pope Paschal I found the money and talent to build works he hoped would be compared to the magnificent ruins that lay on every side. The churches he had rebuilt near Santa Maria Maggiore commemorating two sisters, early Christian martyrs of the 1st century, were not large, but they were a start; to embellish them he imported Byzantine artists who originated a rebirth of mosaic work and painting in Rome. **Santa Pudenziana** at Via Urbana 160 (***t** 06 481 4622; open daily 7–7*) conserves a mosaic of Christ and the Apostles from the 4th century, a thoroughly classical work from the very beginnings of Christian art.

At **Santa Prassede** the mosaics reveal a different world: the shadowy Rome of the not-entirely Dark Ages. The jewel of Santa Prassede at Via Santa Prassede 9/a (***t** 06 488 2456; open daily 7–12 and 4–6.30*) is the small San Zeno Chapel, which Paschal intended as a mausoleum for his mother. The square vaulted chamber is entirely covered with gold-ground mosaics of Christ Pantocrator, saints and some very dignified, classical angels who look as if they never heard anything about the fall of Rome. The 9th-century mosaics around the altar are even better, if less golden.

San Giovanni in Laterano

Where is Rome's cathedral? It isn't St Peter's, and never has been. The true seat of the Bishop of Rome, and the end of a Roman Pilgrimage, is here in the shadow of the Aurelian wall, a church established by Constantine himself (***t** 06 6988 6433; open daily 7–6.45; Museo Sacro and cloister open 9–6*). The family of Plautius Lateranus, according to ancient records, had their property here confiscated after a failed coup against Nero in AD 66. It eventually became part of the imperial real estate, and Constantine and his wife Fausta once kept house in the Lateran Palace. Later he donated it to Pope Miltiades as a cult centre for the Christians of Rome. Almost nothing remains of the original basilica; the sacks of the Vandals and Normans, two earthquakes and several fires have resulted in a building made up of bits and pieces from each of the last 16 centuries.

Like Santa Maria Maggiore, this church has an 18th-century exterior that is almost miraculously good considering other Italian buildings from that age, with a west front by Alessandro Galilei (1736) that confidently and competently re-uses the High Renaissance architectural vernacular. The equally fine north façade is older, done by Domenico Fontana in 1586, and incorporates the twin medieval bell towers. Entering at the west front you pass an ancient statue of Constantine, found at the baths he built on the Quirinale; the bronze doors in the central portal once graced the Senate

House in the Forum. Inside, the nave is dominated by giant statues of the Apostles (*c.* 1720), glaring down like Roman emperors of old. There is some carefree Baroque work in the side chapels, as well as the remains of a fresco by Giotto, behind the first column on the right. Near the apse, decorated with 13th-century mosaics (of a reindeer worshipping the cross, an odd conceit probably adapted from older mosaics in Ravenna), the Papal Altar supposedly contains the heads of Peter and Paul. Below floor level is the tomb of Pope Martin V; pilgrims drop flowers and coins for luck.

Rome in the later Middle Ages had evolved an architectural style entirely its own, uninterested in Gothic or reviving classicism, or, for that matter, in anything else that was going on in the rest of Italy. Sadly, almost all of it disappeared in the Renaissance and Baroque rebuildings. The towers of Santa Maria in Cosmedin and Santa Maria Maggiore are good examples of it, as well as the expressive mosaics of Pietro Cavallini and his school and the intricate, geometrical Cosmatesque pavements in this church and so many others. Perhaps the most striking survival of this lost chapter in art is the Lateran **cloister** (*open daily 9–6, until 5 in winter; adm*), with its pairs of spiral columns and 13th-century Cosmatesque mosaics; it completely upstages everything else in the church. Around the cloister walls, fragments from the earlier incarnations of the basilica have been assembled – the hoard of broken pretty things includes a tomb of a 13th-century bishop, perhaps the work of Arnolfo di Cambio.

The Lateran's **baptistry** (*open daily 8–12.30 and 3.30–7*) is nothing less than the first one in Christendom, converted from an older temple by Constantine; its octagonal form has been copied in other baptistries all over Italy. Inside are unusual pairs of bronze doors on either side: one from 1196 with scenes of how the Lateran basilica appeared at that time, and the other from the Baths of Caracalla, 'singing' doors that make a low, harmonic sound when you open them slowly. Built around the baptistry are three venerable chapels with more mosaics from the early Middle Ages. The entrance to the baptistry is in Piazza San Giovanni in Laterano, behind the **Lateran Palace** (***t*** *06 6988 6452; open Mon–Sat 8–1; adm*), rebuilt in 1588 over the original building that had served as home for the popes from the 4th to the 14th centuries.

Across the piazza is the **Scala Santa** (***t*** *06 6988 6392; open daily 6.15–12 and 3.30–6.45, in winter 3–6*), supposedly the stairs of Pilate's palace in Jerusalem, ascended by Christ on his way to Judgement and brought to Rome by Constantine's mother, St Helena. Serious pilgrims ascend them on their knees. The Chapel of San Lorenzo at the top, part of the medieval Papal Palace, has two miraculous portraits of Jesus, painted by angels. The stretch of the Aurelian Wall behind the Lateran Palace probably looks much as it did originally, and the nearby **Porta Asinara** (next to Porta San Giovanni) is one of the best-preserved monumental ancient gateways.

Monte Celio

South of the Colosseum you can see nothing but trees, but on every inch of this vast tract of parkland, ancient neighbourhoods wait just a few feet beneath the surface. Modern Rome never expanded in this direction, and almost the whole of it has been preserved as open space. It's a fascinating place to walk around, if you can avoid the traffic thundering down the big boulevards towards the southern suburbs.

The Monte Celio is only a small part of it, but it is one of the least known and most delightful corners of Rome. Have a picnic in the **Villa Celimontana** on Piazza della Navicella (*open daily 7am–sunset*) and you may have only squirrels for company.

Some of Rome's most ancient churches repose in quiet settings here; all are worth a look inside if they are open. **Santo Stefano Rotondo** at Via di Santo Stefano Rotondo (***t** 06 7049 3717; open Mon 3.30–6; Tues–Sat 9–1 and 3.30–6*), the oldest circular church in Italy, was built around 470 over the ruins of a marketplace of Nero's time. Across the street more mosaics from the age of Paschal I (*c.* 820) can be seen in **Santa Maria in Dominica** (***t** 06 700 1519; open daily 9–12 and 3.30–7, in winter until 6*) in **Piazza della Navicella**, which has a fountain in the form of an ancient Roman ship.

Take the narrow road (just downhill from the church) that cuts down into the hill to **SS. Giovanni e Paolo** (*open daily 8.30–12 and 3–6.30*), built in the 4th century in the top floor of three Roman houses, which have just emerged from restoration and can be visited (*adm*). Down the western slope is **San Gregorio Magno** (***t** 06 5526 1617; open daily 8–12.30 and 4–6.30*), begun by Pope Gregory the Great in 590. St Augustine lived here before being sent by Gregory to convert the Angles and Saxons of Britain. Adjacent to the church are several chapels with frescoes.

Circus Maximus and Terme di Caracalla

Piazza Porta Capena, at the foot of the Monte Celio, was in Mussolini's time a showcase of imperial ambitions. In 1936, to commemorate the conquest of Ethiopia, it was decorated with an obelisk stolen from the holy city of Axum; after decades of negotiations, this was finally returned to Ethiopia in 2003. The piazza itself is a vortex of Mussolinian pretensions; the dictator built himself a new Triumphal Way (now Via San Gregorio) along the route of the original one, to celebrate his piddling triumphs in Roman imperial style. An enormous building that was to house the Ministry of Africa to administer Mussolini's colonies found a more agreeable use after the war – as home of the UN Food and Agricultural Organization (FAO).

To the west, a broad green lawn is all that remains of the **Circus Maximus**. Archaeologists have estimated that as many as 300,000 Romans could squeeze in here and place their bets on the chariot races. Founded by King Tarquin and completed by Trajan, the stadium proved simply too convenient a quarry; the banked, horseshoe-shaped depression, however, still follows the line of the grandstands.

The **Terme di Caracalla** (AD 206–20), in a large park south of Porta Capena, rank with those of Diocletian as the largest and most lavish (***t** 06 975 8626; open Mon 9–2, Tues–Sun 9–1hr before sunset; guided tours Sat and Sun 10.30; adm*). Roughly 1,000ft square, with libraries and exercise courts, the baths probably boasted more gold, marble and art than any building complex in Rome; here the Farnese family dug up such masterpieces as the *Hercules* and the *Farnese Bull*, now in the Naples museum. In the 1700s these baths were one of the obligatory sights of the Grand Tour; their lofty, broken arches and vaults appealed to the Romantic love of ruins like no other. Much of the central building survives, with its mosaic-decorated hot and cold rooms, great hall and swimming pool. A large tunnel connects the baths with the area around Palazzo Venezia, a kilometre and a half away; its purpose was to transport the vast amounts of wood that were needed to keep the baths hot. Mussolini initiated the custom (now provisionally discontinued owing to the frailty of the ruins) of holding summer operas here; he liked to drive his roadster through the tunnel and pop out dramatically on stage at the start of the festivities.

Behind the baths a stretch of the **Antonine Aqueduct** that supplied them can still be seen. On the other side, facing Via Terme di Caracalla, **SS. Nereo e Achilleo** (*open daily 10–12 and 4–6; ring bell for custodian*) has more mosaics from the time of Leo III (*c.* 800), a Cosmatesque floor and choir, and some gruesome 16th-century frescoes of the martydoms of the saints.

The Via Appia Antica: Rome's Catacombs

The hop-on, hop-off 'Archeobus' minibus departs hourly from Piazza Venezia and heads down the Via Appia to the Villa dei Quintili.

Rome's 'Queen of Roads', the path of trade and conquest to Campania, Brindisi and the east, was begun in 312 BC by Consul Appius Claudius. Like most of the consular roads outside Rome, over the centuries it became lined with cemeteries and the elaborate mausolea of the wealthy, since ancient Roman practice, inherited from the Etruscans, prohibited any burials within the *pomerium*, the sacred ground of the city itself. Later the early Christians built extensive catacombs here – the word itself comes from the location, *ad catacumbas*, referring to the dip in the Via Appia near the suburban Circus of Maxentius. The Via Appia Antica (as distinguished from the modern Via Appia Nuova) makes a pleasant excursion outside the city, especially on Sundays, when the road is closed to traffic all the way back to Piazza Venezia.

The road passes under the Aurelian wall at **Porta San Sebastiano**, which is one of the best-preserved of the old gates. It houses the **Museo delle Mura** (***t** 06 7047 5284; open Tues–Sun 9–7, in winter until 5.30; adm*), admission to which also gives you access to a well-preserved section of the 4th-century wall alongside it. Continuing along the road, past some ruined tombs, you'll come to the famous church of **Domine Quo Vadis** (***t** 06 512 0441; open daily 7.30–6.45*), on the spot where Peter, fleeing from the dangers of Rome, met Christ coming the other way. 'Where goest thou, Lord?' Peter asked. 'I am going to be crucified once more,' was the reply. As the vision departed the shamed Apostle turned back, to face his own crucifixion in Rome.

Another kilometre or so takes you to the **Catacombe di San Callisto**, off on a side road to the right (*open for guided tours summer Thurs–Tues 8.30–12 and 2.30–5, winter 8.30–12 and 2.30–5; closed Feb; adm*). Here the biggest attraction is the 'Crypt of the Popes', consisting of the burial places of 3rd- and 4th-century pontiffs with some well-executed frescoes and inscriptions. Popular romance and modern cinema notwithstanding, catacombs were never places of refuge from persecution, but simply burial grounds. The word 'catacombs' was only used after the 5th century; before that the Christians simply called them 'cemeteries'. The burrowing instinct is harder to explain. Few other places have ancient catacombs (Naples, Syracuse, Malta and the Greek island of Milos are among them). One of the requirements seems to be tufa, or some other stone that can be easily excavated. Even so, the work that was involved was tremendous, and not explainable by any reasons of necessity. Christians were still digging them after they had become a power in Rome, in Constantine's time. No one knows for certain what sort of funeral rites were celebrated in them, just as no one knows much about any of the prayers or rituals of the early Christians; we can only suspect that a Christian of the 4th century and one of the 16th would have had considerable difficulty recognizing each other as brothers in the faith.

Most catacombs began small, as private family cemeteries; over the course of generations some grew into enormous termitaries extending for several kilometres. Inside, the majority of the tombs that you see will be simple *loculi* – walled-up niches with only a symbol or short inscription. Others, especially the tombs of popes or the wealthy, may be embellished by paintings of scriptural scenes, though this is usually very poor work that reflects more on the dire state of the late Roman imagination than on the Christians.

From here you can make a detour another kilometre and a half to the west to see the **Catacombe di Santa Domitilla** at Via delle Sette Chiese 283 (***t*** *06 511 0342; open for guided tours Feb–Dec Weds–Mon 8.30–12 and 2.30–5.30; adm*). Domitilla was a member of a senatorial family, and, interestingly, the catacombs seem to incorporate parts of earlier pagan hypogea, including a cemetery of the Imperial Flavian family; the paintings include an unusual Last Supper scene, portraying a young and beardless Jesus and Apostles in Roman dress. There is an adjacent basilica, built about the tombs of SS. Nereus and Achilleus, on Via delle Sette Chiese.

Not far away on Via Ardeatina 174 is a monument to martyrs of a very different sort, the **Mausoleum of the Fosse Ardeatine** (***t*** *06 513 6742; open Mon–Fri 8.15–6.45, Sat and Sun 8.15–3.30*), dedicated to the 335 Romans who were massacred by the Nazis on this spot in 1944 in retaliation for a partisan attack. Back on the Via Appia Antica, near the corner of Via Appia Pignatelli, are several catacombs, including a Jewish one (*closed*); the largest are the **Catacombe di San Sebastiano** (***t*** *06 788 735; open for guided tours Fri–Weds 8.30–12 and 2.30–5.30, closed Nov; adm*). This complex, too, began as a pagan cemetery and has some intriguing paintings and incised symbols throughout. The place had some special significance for the early Christians, and it has been conjectured that Peter and Paul were originally buried here, before their removal to the basilicas in Constantine's time.

Further south, by now in fairly open country, are the ruins of the **Circus of Maxentius** (***t*** *06 780 1324; open Apr–Sept, Tues–Sat 9–7 and Sun 9–1; Oct–Mar Tues–Sat 9–5, Sun 9–1; adm*), built in the early 4th century. Then there's the imposing cylindrical **tomb of Cecilia Metella** (***t*** *06 780 2465; open Tues–Sun 9–7; adm*) dating from the time of Augustus. In the Middle Ages the Caetani family turned the tomb into a family fortress guarding the road to the south; at other times, before and since, it was a famous rendezvous for *banditti*.

The road continues, flanked by tombs and stately pines, with stretches of the original paving, for 16 kilometres beyond the walls of Rome. Further out still are the extensive, marble-strewn remains of the **Villa dei Quintili** (*open 9am–1hr before sunset; adm*), which was built in the 2nd century AD by the Quintilius brothers and was once the largest villa outside the city walls.

Monte Aventino

Every now and then, whenever a left-wing party walks out of negotiations, the Italian newspapers talk of an 'Aventine Secession', making reference to events that took place in Rome 2,500 years ago. Under the Republic, the Monte Aventino was the most solidly plebeian quarter of the city. On several occasions, when legislation proposed by the senate and consuls seriously threatened the rights or interests of the people, they retired en masse to the Aventino and stayed there until the plan was dropped. Rome's unionists are probably unaware that their ancestors had the honour of inventing the general strike.

The Aventino had another distinction in those times. In its uninhabited regions – the steep, cave-ridden slopes towards the south – Greek immigrants and returning soldiers introduced the midnight rituals of Dionysus/Bacchus. Though secret, such goings-on soon came to the attention of the senate, which rightly saw the orgies as a danger to the state and banned them in 146 BC. They must not have died out completely, however, as in the Middle Ages the Aventino had a reputation as a haunt of witches. The early Christian community also prospered here, and their churches are the oldest relics on the Aventino today.

Coming up from the Circus Maximus along Via Santa Sabina, you'll see **Santa Sabina** (*open daily 6.30–12 and 3.30–7*), a simple, rare example of a 5th-century basilica, with an atrium at its entrance like a Roman secular basilica, and an original door of cypress carved with scriptural scenes. This has been the head church of the Dominicans ever since a 13th-century pope gave it to St Dominic. Both Santa Sabina and the church of **Sant'Alessio** (*open daily 8.30–8*) further down the street have good Cosmatesque cloisters.

At the end of this street, one of the oddities that only Rome can offer stands on its quiet square, oblivious of the centuries: the **Priorato dei Cavalieri di Malta** (*open for guided tours by prior arrangement; call* ***t*** *06 577 9193*), a fancy rococo complex designed by Giambattista Piranesi. The Knights of Malta – or more properly, the Knights Hospitallers of St John – no longer wait here for the popes to unleash them against Saracen and Turk; mostly this social club for nobles bestirs itself to assist hospitals, its original job during the Crusades. The Order's ambassadors to Italy and the Vatican still live here. You can't go inside.

Elsewhere on the Aventino, **Santa Prisca** (***t*** *06 3996 7700; open by appointment only*) has beginnings typical of an early Roman church; its crypt, the original church, was allegedly converted from the house of the martyr Prisca, host to St Peter; the Apostle must have often presided over Mass here. **San Saba** on Via San Saba (*open daily 7–12 and 4–7*) was founded in the 7th century by monks fleeing the Arabs in Jordan and Syria and rebuilt in 1205. Highlights are some Cosmatesque details, a superb mosaic floor and a crypt with 7th–11th-century frescoes.

Monte Testaccio and Rome's Pyramid

Porta San Paolo, set in one of the best-preserved sections of the Aurelian wall, looks just as it did 1,700 years ago, when it was the *Porta Ostiense*; its change of name came about because Paul passed through it on the way to his execution. Near the gate is something unique – the 92ft **Pyramid of Caius Cestius** (AD 12), which may seem a strange self-tribute for a Roman, but at least Cestius, who had served in Egypt, paid for the tomb himself.

Behind it, inside the walls at Via Caio Cestio 6, the lovely **Cimitero Protestante** (***t*** *06 574 1900; open Tues–Sun 9–5.30, in winter until 4.30; ring the bell at the gate; donation requested*) is a popular point of Romantic pilgrimage. The graves of Shelley and Keats are there, joined by that of 400 British soldiers who died during the march on Rome in 1944. Just to the west is the youngest of Rome's hills, **Monte Testaccio**, made up almost entirely of pot-shards. In ancient times, wine, oil, olives and nearly everything else were shipped in big *amphorae*; here, in what was Rome's port warehouse district, all the broken, discarded ones accumulated in one place. The vast cellars the Romans left beneath it are now used as workshops, wine cellars and nightclubs that make Testaccio a swinging area after dark.

San Paolo Fuori le Mura (Outside the Walls)

t *06 541 0341; basilica open daily 7–6.30, cloister 9–1 and 3–6.*

Paul was beheaded near the Ostia road; according to an old legend, the head bounced three times, and at each place where it hit a fountain sprung up. The Abbazia delle Tre Fontane, near EUR, occupies the site today. Later, Constantine constructed a basilica alongside the road as a fitting resting place for the saint. Of the five patriarchal basilicas (*see* p.808), St Paul's was the grandest; 9th-century chroniclers speak of the separate walled city of 'Giovannipolis' that had grown up around it, connected to the Aurelian wall by a kilometre-and-a-half-long colonnade built by Pope John VIII in the 870s. The Norman sack of 1084, a few good earthquakes, and a catastrophic fire in 1823 wiped Giovannipolis off the map, and left us with a St Paul's that for the most part is barely more than a century old. Today it sits in the middle of factories, gasworks and concrete flats. Still, the façade of golden mosaics and sturdy Corinthian columns is pleasant to look at, and some features survive – the 11th-century door made in Constantinople; a Gothic *baldacchino* over Paul's tomb by Arnolfo di Cambio; a 13th-century Cosmatesque cloister; and 5th-century mosaics over the 'Triumphal Arch' in front of the apse, the restored remains of the original mosaics from the façade, contributed by Empress Galla Placidia. Art Deco is not what you would expect from those times, but Americans at least will have a hard time believing these mosaics were not done by President Roosevelt's WPA. The apse itself has some more conventional mosaics from the 13th-century Roman school, and the nave is lined with the portraits of all 263 popes. According to one Roman legend, when the remaining spaces are filled, the world will end.

On the same road as San Paolo (Via Ostiense) you'll find the **Centrale Montemartini** (*open Tues–Sun 9.30–7; adm; metro to Garbatella and cross flyover towards Via Ostiense, or bus to Via Ostiense*), which provides an unusual home for the overflow of the great hoard of ancient art from the Capitoline Museums. This converted power station makes a dramatic setting for a variety of busts, mosaics and statuary, which are arranged around two enormous power generators. There's a peaceful café on the top floor.

EUR

By the late 1930s Mussolini was proud enough of his accomplishments to plan a world fair. Its theme was to be the Progress of Civilization, measured no doubt from the invention of the wheel up to the invention of the Corporate State. A vast area south of Rome was cleared and transformed into a grid of wide boulevards broken up by parks and lagoons. Huge Mussolini-style pavilions were begun, and a design was accepted for an aluminium arch – the forerunner of the famous one in St Louis but many times bigger – that would overarch the entire fairground. War intervening, the arch never appeared, and the Esposizione Universale di Roma never came off.

After 1945 the Italians tried to make the best of it, turning EUR into a model satellite city and trade centre, on the lines of La Défense in Paris. The result will derange your senses as much as it does the average Roman's: it's a chilly nightmare of modernism complete with boulevards of Humanism, Electronics and Social Security. Still, for those who can appreciate the well-landscaped macabre, EUR can be fun. Some of the older corners reveal giant Fascist mosaics of heroic miners, soldiers, assembly-line workers and mothers, and at the end of the Boulevard of Civilization and Labour you can have a look at the modest masterpiece of Mussolini architecture – the small, elegantly proportioned **Palazzo della Civiltà del Lavoro**, nicknamed the Square Colosseum. Liberal, post-war Italy has rarely, if ever, been able to conceive anything with such a sure sense of design and a feeling for history.

EUR is also home to a few good museums. The **Museo della Civiltà Romana** at Piazza Giovanni Agnelli 10 (***t** 06 592 6041; open Tues–Sat 9–6.45, Sun 9–1.30; adm*), a collection of antiquities and exhibits that includes a huge scale-model of ancient Rome with every building present, is a great place to seed your imagination with visions of the old city's splendour. Others in the area include the **museum of prehistory and ethnography** at Piazza Marconi 14 (***t** 06 549 921; open Tues–Sun 9–8; adm*), covering civilizations before classical Rome, and the **museum of the early Middle Ages** at Viale Lincoln 3 (***t** 06 5422 8199; open Tues–Sat 9–8; adm*).

Trastevere

So often just being on the wrong side of the river encourages a city district to cultivate its differences and its eccentricities. Trastevere isn't really a Left Bank – it's more a pocket-sized Brooklyn, and as in Brooklyn those differences and eccentricities often turn out to be the old habits of the whole city, preserved in an out-of-the-way corner. The people of Trastevere are more Roman than the Romans. Indeed, they claim to be the real descendants of the Romans of old; one story traces their ancestry back to the sailors who worked the great awning at the Colosseum. Such places have a hard time surviving these days, especially when they are as trendy as Trastevere is. But even though such things as Trastevere's famous school of dialect poets may be mostly a memory, the quarter remains the liveliest in Rome.

Just over Ponte Garibaldi is Piazza Sonnino, with the **Torre degli Anguillara**, an uncommon survival of the defence towers that loomed over medieval Rome, and the 12th-century church of **San Crisogono** (***t** 06 581 8225; open Mon–Sat 7am– 7.30pm, Sun 8–1 and 4.15–7.30*), with mosaics by Pietro Cavallini, built over the remains of an earlier church. Near the bridge, the statue in the top hat is of Giuseppe Gioacchino Belli, one of Trastevere's 19th-century dialect poets. Turn left on to one of the narrow streets off Viale di Trastevere to get to the church of **Santa Cecilia in Trastevere** (*t 06 589 9289; open daily 9.30–1 and 4–7.15*), founded over the house of the 2nd-century martyr whom centuries of hagiography have turned into one of the most agreeable of saints, the inventor of the organ and patroness of music. Cecilia was disinterred in 1599 and her body found entirely uncorrupted. Clement VIII commissioned Maderno to sculpt an exact copy from sketches made before her body dissolved into thin air; this charming work can be seen near the altar.

Nearby is a Tabernacle by Arnolfo di Cambio similar to the one in St Paul's, and some 9th-century mosaics in the apse. The church has other treasures: Renaissance tombs, including one of a 14th-century cardinal from Hertford; frescoes by the school of Pinturicchio, in a chapel on the right; and a crypt built in the underlying Roman constructions, thought to be Cecilia's home (*adm*). Up in the singing gallery are the remains of the original church wall decoration – a wonderful fresco of the Last Judgement by Cavallini (*viewable Tues and Thurs 10–12, Sun 11.15–12; adm*).

Across Viale di Trastevere – an intrusive modern boulevard that slices the district in two – lies the heart of old Trastevere around **Piazza Santa Maria in Trastevere** and its church. Most of this building dates from the 1140s, though the original church, begun perhaps in 222, may be the first anywhere dedicated to the Virgin Mary. The medieval building is a treasure-house of Roman mosaics. The piazza, and the streets around it, has been for decades one of the most popular spots in Rome for restaurants; tables are spread out wherever there's room, and there is always a crowd in the evening.

Two Roads to St Peter's

One is broad and straight, the route of the many; the other tortuous and narrow, and after it but few enquire. **Via della Lungara**, the route of the slothful from Trastevere, takes you past **Villa Farnesina** (*open Mon–Sat 9–1; adm*), an early 1500s palace built for the Chigi family. Inside are some of the best frescoes in Rome: the *Galatea* by Raphael and the *Cupid and Psyche Gallery*, designed by Raphael; a prospect of the constellations and a room of false perspectives by Baldassare Peruzzi, who also designed the building; and works of Sodoma. Across the street, the **Palazzo Corsini** (*t 06 6880 2323; open Tues–Sat 8.30–6.30, Sun 9–1; adm*) contains an exceptional collection of 16th- and 17th-century art, including works by Caravaggio, Van Dyck, Guido Reni, Salvatore Rosa and many others. It's out of the way, but this may well be the best of all Rome's many small state picture galleries.

The other road may be more difficult to find, but repays the effort with lovely gardens and views over Rome from the Gianicolo, the ancient *Janiculum*. First find Via Garibaldi, in the backstreets behind Ponte Sisto, and continue up to the Renaissance church of **San Pietro in Montorio** (*t 06 581 3940; open daily 9–12 and 4–6; if closed, ring bell at door to right of church*), once believed to be the spot of St Peter's upside-down crucifixion. A popular church for weddings, it has several fine paintings in the shallow chapels, including a marvellous Flagellation by Sebastiano del Piombo. But the real draw here is Bramante's famed **Tempietto** in the adjacent courtyard. In so many

Renaissance paintings – Perugino's *Donation of the Keys* in the Sistine Chapel or Raphael's *Betrothal of the Virgin* in Milan – the characters in the foreground take second place in interest to an ethereal, round temple centred at the perspectival vanishing point. These constructions, seemingly built not of vulgar stone but of pure intelligence and light, could stand as a symbol for the aspirations of the Renaissance. Bramante was the first actually to try to build one; his perfect little Tempietto (1502), the first building to re-use the ancient Doric order in all of its proportions, probably inspired Raphael's painting two years later.

Via Garibaldi continues up the Janiculum to the gushing **Acqua Paola fountain**, where you should turn right along the Passeggiata del Gianicolo. The **Garibaldi monument** stands at the summit, overlooking the Botanical Gardens and the rest of Rome. At the other end of the hill, going towards the Vatican, the road curves downwards, passing the Renaissance church of **Sant'Onofrio** (*open daily 9–1*), with frescoes by Peruzzi in the apse. After descending the Passeggiata del Gianicolo, cross modern Piazza della Rovere into the Borgo district. On your right is the hospital of Santo Spirito and the church of **Santo Spirito in Sassia** (*open daily 7.30–12 and 3–7.30*). This name may ring a bell with antiquarians: 'Sassia' refers to the Saxons of England, who upon their conversion became among the most devoted servants of the Church. English princes founded this hospital in the 8th century. The Angles and Saxons who settled in Rome made up almost a small village unto themselves at this bend of the Tiber, and their 'burgh' gave its name to the neighbourhood called the Borgo today.

Castel Sant'Angelo

*Lungotevere Castello 50, **t** 06 3996 7600; open Tues–Sun 9–8; adm; English audioguide available. Guided visits (extra charge) in English available; reserve ahead.*

Though it was intended as a resting place for a most serene emperor, this building has seen more blood, treachery and turmoil than any other in Rome. Hadrian designed his mausoleum three years before his death in 138, on an eccentric plan consisting of a huge marble cylinder surmounted by a conical hill planted with cypresses. The marble, obelisks and gold and bronze decorations did not survive the 5th-century sacks, but *c.* 590, during a plague, Pope Gregory the Great saw a vision of St Michael over the mausoleum, ostensibly announcing the end of the plague, but perhaps also mentioning discreetly that here, if anyone cared to use it, was the most valuable fortress in Europe.

There would be no papacy, perhaps, without this castle – at least not in its present form. Hadrian's cylinder is high, steep and almost solid – impregnable even after the invention of artillery. With rebellions of some sort occurring on average every two years before 1400, the popes often had recourse to this place of safety. It last saw action in the sack of 1527, when the miserable Clement VII withstood a siege of several months while his city went up in flames. The popes also used Castel Sant'Angelo as a prison; famous inmates included Giordano Bruno, Benvenuto Cellini and Beatrice Cenci. Tosca tosses herself off the top at the end of Puccini's opera.

Inside, the recently restored spiral ramp leads up to the **Papal Apartments**, which were decorated as lavishly by 16th-century artists as anything in the Vatican. The **Sala Paolina** has frescoes by Perin del Vaga of events in the history of Rome, and the **Sala di Apollo** was frescoed with grotesques in an attempt to reproduce the wall decorations of Nero's Golden House. A mighty statue of Michael commemorates Gregory's vision.

Castel Sant'Angelo makes a great place to rest after the Vatican. The views from the roof are some of the best in Rome, and there's a café on the fourth floor. The three central arches of the **Ponte Sant'Angelo** were built by Hadrian, although the statues of angels added in 1688 steal the show; at once dubbed Bernini's Breezy Maniacs, they battle a never-ending Baroque hurricane to display the symbols of Christ's Passion.

Vatican City

The world's smallest country contains the world's largest museum, piazza and church. It is next to impossible to see the Vatican Museums, St Peter's and Castel Sant'Angelo in one day, let alone the **Vatican Gardens**, easily Rome's most beautiful park, with its remarkable Renaissance jewel of a villa – the Casino of Pius IV (1558–62) by Pietro Ligorio and Peruzzi (*open for morning guided tours May–Sept Mon, Tues and Thurs–Sat; Oct–Apr Sat; adm exp; reserve a few days in advance with the Vatican information office*). Nor will you fit in the afternoon tour of the ancient **necropolis** under the crypt of St Peter's, discovered by archaeologists in the 1940s perfectly preserved and boasting many beautiful paintings (*1½-hour guided visits in English by reservation; adm exp; call Ufficio degli Scavi on* **t** *06 6988 5318 for information; then fax them on* **f** *06 6988 5518, with your name, nationality, language you want a tour in, the dates you are in Rome, an email address and a contact number in Rome*).

Michelangelo designed the **wall** that since 1929 has marked the boundaries of the Vatican. Behind it lie things that most of us will never see: several small old churches, a printing press, the headquarters of *L'Osservatore Romano* and Vatican Radio (run, of course, by the Jesuits), a motor garage, a 'Palazzo di Giustizia' and even a big shop – in fact, everything that the world's smallest nation could ever need. Modern popes, in contrast to their predecessors, do not take up much space. The current Papal Apartments are situated in a corner of the Vatican Palace overlooking Piazza San Pietro; John Paul II usually appears to say a few electrically amplified words from his window at noon on Sundays.

St Peter's

Along Borgo Sant'Angelo, heading towards the Vatican, you will see the famous **covered passageway** used by the popes since 1277 to escape to the castle when things became dangerous. The customary route, however, leads up **Via della Conciliazione**, a broad boulevard drilled by Mussolini through the tangled web of medieval streets. Critics have said it spoils the surprise, but no arrangement of streets and buildings could really prepare you for Bernini's Brobdingnagian **Piazza San Pietro**. Someone has calculated that there's room for about 300,000 people in the piazza, with no crowding. Few people have ever noticed Bernini's little joke on antiquity; the open

Vatican Practicalities

The **museums** are *open Mar–Oct Mon–Fri 8.45–2.20, Sat 8.45–12.20, Nov–Feb Mon–Sat 8.45–12.20; adm; also open (and free) last Sun of each month 8.45–12.20*. These times are subject to change so confirm in advance. The entrance is on Viale Vaticano, to the north of Piazza San Pietro.

St Peter's is *open daily Apr–Oct 8–7, Nov–Mar 7–6*; the basilica is closed when there are official ceremonies in the piazza, although visitors are allowed in during Mass. The **dome** is *open daily summer 8.30–5.45, winter 8.30–4.45*, the **Treasury** *daily 9–6.15*. The dress code – no shorts, short skirts or sleeveless dresses – is strictly controlled by the papal gendarmes. There are free guided visits to St Peter's in English Mon, Weds–Sat 3, Sun 2.30.

The **Vatican Information Office, t** 06 6988 1662, in Piazza San Pietro (*open daily 8.30–7*) is very helpful. There are Vatican post offices on the opposite side of the square and inside the Vatican Museums for distinctive postcards home. The information office arranges 2hr morning tours of the **Vatican Gardens**; the rest of the Vatican is strictly off limits and patrolled by Swiss Guards (still recruited from the three Catholic Swiss cantons).

For tickets to the Weds morning **papal audience**, usually held at 10.30am in the piazza (*May–Sept*) or in the Nervi Auditorium (*Oct–Apr*), apply in advance at the Papal Prefecture through the bronze door in the right-hand colonnade of Piazza San Pietro (*open Mon–Sat 9–1.30*, **t** *06 6988 3114, collect tickets Mon–Sat 3–8 at the Portone del Bronzo on Piazza San Pietro*).

space almost exactly meets the size and dimensions of the Colosseum. Bernini's **Colonnade** (1656), with its 284 massive columns and statues of 140 saints, stretches around it like 'the arms of the Church embracing the world' – it's perhaps the biggest cliché in Christendom by now, but it's exactly what Bernini had in mind. Stand on either of the two dark stones at the foci of the elliptical piazza and you will see Bernini's forest of columns resolve into neat rows, in a subtly impressive optical effect like the one created by the hole in the top of the Pantheon.

Flanked by two lovely fountains, the work of Maderno and Fontana, the Vatican **obelisk** seems nothing special as obelisks go, but it is one of the most fantastical relics in all Rome. It comes from Heliopolis, founded as a capital and cult centre by Akhnaton, the half-legendary Pharaoh who, according to Sigmund Freud and others, founded the first monotheistic religion, influencing Moses and all that came after. Caligula brought it over to Rome in AD 37 to decorate the now-disappeared Circus Vaticanus (later referred to as the Circus of Nero), where it would have overlooked Peter's martyrdom. In the Middle Ages it was placed to the side of the basilica, but Sixtus V moved it to where it now stands in 1586.

It may be irreverent to say so, but the original St Peter's, begun over the Apostle's tomb by Constantine in 324, may well have been a more interesting building: it was a richly decorated basilica full of gold and mosaics, with a vast porch of marble and bronze in front and a lofty campanile topped by the famous golden cockerel that everyone believed would some day crow to announce the end of the world. This St Peter's, where Charlemagne and Frederick II received their imperial crowns, was falling to pieces by the 1400s, conveniently in time for the popes of the Renaissance to plan a replacement. In about 1450 Nicholas V conceived an almost Neronian building programme for the Vatican, 10 times as large as anything his ancestors could have contemplated. It was not until the time of Julius II, however, that Bramante was commissioned to demolish the old church and begin the new. His original plan called for a great dome over a centralized Greek cross. Michelangelo, who took over in 1546, basically agreed, and if he had had his way St Peter's might indeed have become the crowning achievement of Renaissance art that everyone hoped it would be.

Unfortunately, over the 120 years of construction, too many popes and too many artists got their hand in – Rossellino, Giuliano da Sangallo, Raphael, Antonio da Sangallo, Vignola, Ligorio, Della Porta, Fontana, Bernini and Maderno all contributed something to the hotchpotch we see today. The most substantial tinkering occurred in the early 17th century, when a committee of cardinals decided that a Latin cross was desired, resulting in the huge extension of the nave that blocks the view of Michelangelo's dome from the piazza. Baroque architects, mistaking size and virtuosity for art, found perfect patrons in the Baroque popes, interested in the power and majesty of the papacy. Passing through Maderno's gigantic façade seems like entering a Grand Central Station full of stone saints and angels. All along the nave, markers showing the length of other proud cathedrals prove how each fails to measure up to the Biggest Church in the World. This being Rome, not even the markers are honest – Milan's cathedral is actually 63ft longer.

The best feature is on the right: Michelangelo's *Pietà*, which is now restored and kept behind glass to protect it from future madmen. Sculpted when he was aged just 25, it helped make the artist's reputation. Its smooth and elegant figures, with the realities of death and grief sublimated on to some ethereal plane known only to saints and artists, were a turning point in religious art. From here the beautiful, unreal art of the religious Baroque was the logical next step. Michelangelo carved his name in small letters on the band around the Virgin's garment after overhearing a group of tourists from Milan who thought the *Pietà* the work of a fellow Milanese.

Not much else in St Peter's really stands out. In its vast spaces, scores of popes and saints are remembered in assembly-line Baroque; the paintings over most of the altars have been replaced by mosaic copies. The famous bronze statute of St Peter, its foot worn away by the touch of millions of pilgrims, is by the right front pier. Stealing the show, as he knew it would, is Bernini's great, garish **baldacchino** over the high altar, cast out of bronze looted from the Pantheon roof.

Many visitors head straight for Michelangelo's **dome** (*open daily 8.30–5.45, winter until 4.45*). There are 320 steps *after* the lift to get up to the cupola viewing terrace, but to be in the middle of such a spectacular construction is worth the climb itself. You can walk out on to the roof for a view over Rome; even more startling, however, is the chance to look down from the interior balcony over the vast church 250ft below.

In the **treasury** (*open daily 9–6.15; adm*), which was built in the 18th century, there are a number of treasures – those that the Saracens, the imperial soldiers of 1527, and Napoleon couldn't manage to steal. Do not pass up a descent to the **Sacred Grottoes** (*same hours as basilica*), the foundation of the earlier St Peter's converted into a crypt. Dozens of popes are buried here, along with distinguished friends of the Church such as Queen Christina of Sweden and James III, the Stuart pretender. Perhaps the greatest work of art here is the bronze tomb of Sixtus IV, a definitive Renaissance confection by Pollaiuolo, though the most visited is undoubtedly the monument to John XXIII.

The Vatican Museums

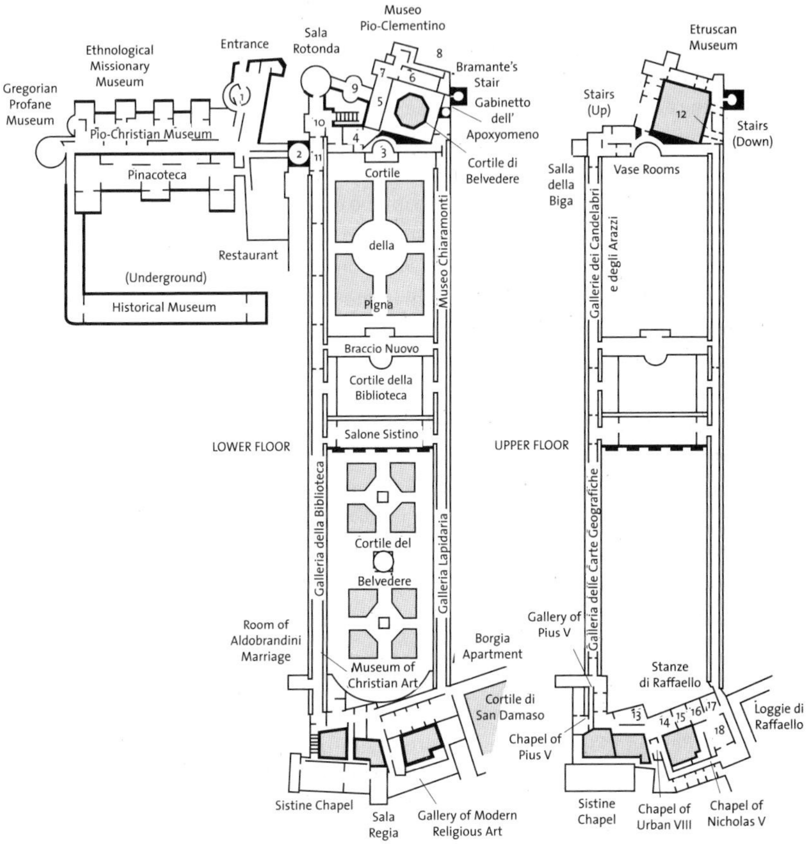

1 Spiral
2 Quattro Cancelli
3 La Pigna
4 Egyptian Museum
5 Room of the Animals
6 Gallery of Statues
7 Mask Room
8 Gallery of Busts
9 Hall of the Muses
10 Hall of the Greek Cross
11 Museum of Pagan Antiquities
12 Rooms of Greek Originals
13 Hall of the Immaculate Conception
14 Stanza dell'Incendio
15 Stanza della Segnatura
16 Stanza di Eliodoro
17 Sala di Costantino
18 Sala dei Chiaroscuri

The Musei Vaticani (Vatican Museums)

The admission price (*currently €10, audioguides €5*) may be the most expensive of any attraction in Italy, but for that you do get 10 museums in one, with the Sistine Chapel and the Raphael rooms thrown in free. Altogether, almost seven kilometres of exhibits fill the halls of the Vatican Palace, and unfortunately for you there isn't much dull museum clutter that can be passed over lightly. Seeing this infinite, exasperating hoard properly would be the work of a lifetime. On the bright side, however, the Pope sees to it that his museum is managed more intelligently and thoughtfully than anything run by the Italian state. A choice of two colour-coded itineraries, which you may follow according to the amount of time you have to spend, will get you through the labyrinth in two or four hours.

Near the entrance, the first big challenge is the large **Museo Egizio** – one of Europe's best Egyptian collections – and then some rooms of antiquities from the Holy Land and Syria, before the **Museo Chiaramonti**, which is full of Roman statuary (including famous busts of Caesar, Mark Antony and Augustus) and inscriptions. The **Museo Pio-Clementino** contains some of the best-known statues of antiquity: the dramatic *Laocoön*, dug up in Nero's Golden House, and the *Apollo Belvedere*. No other ancient works recovered during the Renaissance had a greater influence on sculptors than these two. A 'room of animals' captures the more fanciful side of antiquity, and the 2nd-century 'Baroque' tendency in Roman art comes out clearly in a group called 'The Nile', complete with sphinxes and crocodiles – it comes from a Roman temple of Isis. The bronze papal fig-leaves that protect the modesty of hundreds of nude statues are a good joke at first – it was the same spirit that put breeches on the saints in Michelangelo's *Last Judgement*, ordered by Pius IV once Michelangelo was safely dead.

The best things in the **Museo Etrusco** are a truly excellent collection of Greek vases imported by discriminating Etruscan nobles that includes the famous *Oedipus and the Sphinx*. Beyond that is a hall hung with beautiful high-medieval tapestries from Tournai (15th century), and the long, long **Galleria delle Carte Geografiche**, which is lined with carefully painted town views and maps of every corner of Italy; note the long scene of the 1566 Great Siege of Malta at the entrance.

Anywhere else, with no Michelangelos to offer competition, Raphael's celebrated frescoes in the **Stanza della Segnatura** would have been the prime destination on anyone's itinerary. The *School of Athens* is too well known to require any kind of introduction, but here is a brief guide to some of the figures: on Aristotle's side are Archimedes and Euclid surrounded by their disciples (Euclid, drawing plane figures on a slate, is a portrait of Bramante); off to the right, Ptolemy and Zoroaster hold the terrestrial and celestial globes. Raphael includes himself among the Aristotelians, between Zoroaster and the painter Sodoma. Behind Plato stand Socrates and Alcibiades, and to the left, Zeno and Epicurus. In the foreground, Pythagoras writes while Empedocles and the Arab Averroes look on. Diogenes sprawls philosophically on the steps, while isolated near the front is Heraclitus – who is really Michelangelo (Raphael put him in at the last minute, after seeing the work that was in progress in the Sistine Chapel).

Across from this apotheosis of philosophy, Raphael painted a Triumph of Theology to keep the clerics happy, the *Dispute of the Holy Sacrament*. The other frescoes include the *Parnassus*, a vision of the ancient Greek and Latin poets, the *Miracle of Bolsena*, the *Expulsion of Heliodorus*, an allegory of the triumphs of the Counter-Reformation papacy, the *Meeting of Leo I and Attila* and, best of all, the solemn, spectacularly lit *Liberation of St Peter*. Nearby, there is the **Loggia** of Bramante, also with decoration designed by Raphael, though executed by other artists (*only visitable with written permission*), and the chapel of **Nicholas V**, with frescoes by Fra Angelico. The **Appartamento Borgia**, a luxurious suite built for Pope Alexander VI, has walls decorated by Pinturicchio. These run into the **Opere d'Arte Religiosa Moderna**, a game attempt by the Vatican to prove that such a thing really exists.

The Sistine Chapel (Cappella Sistina)

To the sophisticated Sixtus IV, building this ungainly barn of a chapel may have seemed like a mistake in the first place. When the pushy, despotic Julius II sent Michelangelo up, against his will, to paint the vast ceiling, it might have turned out to be a project as hopeless as the tomb that Julius had already commissioned. Michelangelo spent four years of his life (1508–12) on the Sistine Ceiling. No one can say what drove him to turn his surly patron's whim into a masterpiece: the fear of wasting those years, perhaps; the challenge of an impossible task; or maybe just the desire to spite Julius – he exasperated the pope by making him wait, and refused all demands to hire assistants.

Everywhere on the Sistine Ceiling you will notice the austere blankness of the backgrounds. Michelangelo always eschewed stage props; one of the tenets of his art was that complex ideas could be expressed in the portrayal of the human body alone. With sculpture, that takes time. Perhaps the inspiration that kept Michelangelo on the ceiling so long was the chance of distilling out of the Book of Genesis and his own genius an entirely new vocabulary of images, Christian and intellectual. Like most Renaissance patrons, Julius had asked for nothing more than virtuoso interior decoration. What he got was the way the Old Testament looks in the deepest recesses of the imagination. The fascination of the Sistine Ceiling, and the equally compelling ***Last Judgement*** on the rear wall, done much later (1534–41), is that while we may recognize the individual figures we still have not captured their secret meanings. Hordes of tourists stare up at the heroic Adam, the mysterious *ignudi* in the corners, the Russian masseuse sibyls with their longshoremen's arms, the six-toed prophets, the strange vision of Noah's deluge. They wonder what they're looking at – it's a question that would take years of inspired wondering to answer. Mostly they direct their attention to the all-too-famous scene of the Creation, with perhaps the only representation of God the Father ever painted that escapes being merely ridiculous. One might suspect that the figure is really some ageing Florentine artist, and that Michelangelo only forgot to paint the brush in his hand.

The restoration of the ceiling and *Last Judgement*, paid for by a Japanese TV network, have accurately revealed Michelangelo's true colours – jarring, surprise hues that no interior decorator would ever choose, including plenty of sea-green, splashes of yellow and purple and dramatic shadows. No new paint was applied, only solvents to clear off the grime. Most visitors overlook the earlier frescoes on the lower walls, great works of art that would have made the Sistine Chapel famous by themselves: scenes from the *Exodus* by Botticelli, Perugino's *Donation of the Keys*, and Signorelli's *Moses Consigning his Staff to Joshua*.

More Miles in the Big Museum

There's still the **Vatican Library** to go, with its seemingly endless halls and precious manuscripts tucked neatly away in cabinets. The brightly painted rooms contain thousands of reliquaries and monstrances, medieval ivories, gold-glass medallions from the catacombs, and every sort of globe, orrery and astronomical instrument. If you survive this, the next hurdle is the new **Museo Gregoriano**, with its hoard of classical statuary, mosaics and inscriptions collected by Pope Gregory XVI. Then comes a museum of **carriages** (*closed for restoration*), the **Museo Pio-Cristiano** of early Christian art and, finally, one of the most interesting of all, the museum of **ethnology**, with wonderful art from every continent, brought home to Italy by missionaries.

By itself the Vatican **Pinacoteca** would be by far the finest picture gallery in Rome, a representative sampling of Renaissance art from its beginnings, with some fine works by Giotto (*Il Redentore* and the *Martyrdoms of Peter and Paul*) and contemporary Sienese painters, as well as Gentile da Fabriano, Sano di Pietro and Filippo Lippi. Don't overlook the tiny but electrically surreal masterpiece of Fra Angelico, the *Story of St Nicolas at Bari*, or the *Angelic Musicians* of Melozzo da Forlì, set next to Melozzo's famous painting of Platina being nominated by Sixtus IV to head the Vatican Library – a rare snapshot of Renaissance humanism. Venetian artists are not well represented, but there is a *Pietà* by Bellini and a *Madonna* by the fastidious Carlo Crivelli. Perhaps the best-known paintings are the *Transfiguration of Christ*, Raphael's last work, and the *St Jerome* of Da Vinci.

Peripheral Attractions

There are plenty of interesting things on Rome's outskirts; the following is a brief overview, running clockwise around Rome from the north.

By the Tiber, the **Foro Italico** was Mussolini's most blatant monument to himself: he left his mark everywhere, on a giant obelisk, in the paving stones and around the grandiose **Marble Stadium**, chiselled too deep ever to be eroded. The sports complex hosted the 1960 Olympics. Across the Tiber, on Via Salaria, **Villa Ada** was once the hunting reserve of Vittorio Emanuele III; it's now a huge city park. The **Catacombe di Priscilla**, Via Salaria 430, are well worth the nun-led tour of the 2nd-century frescoes and the tombs of many early popes and martyrs (***t** 06 8620 6272; open Mon, Tues, Thurs–Sun 8.30–12 and 2.30–5; Apr–Sept until 5.30; closed Feb; adm*).

Via XX Settembre, the big road out from Monte Quirinale, passes the Aurelian Wall at **Porta Pia**, redesigned by Michelangelo. Here it becomes Via Nomentana, a boulevard lined with villas not yet swallowed up by creeping urbanization.

A kilometre east, stop at the charming complex of **Sant'Agnese Fuori le Mura** (Outside the Walls; *open daily 7–12 and 4–8*), which includes a 4th-century church with an early mosaic of St Agnes in the apse, and 15 ancient marble columns. Along the stairway down to the church, early Christian reliefs and inscriptions are displayed; inside the church is the entrance to the small, aristocratic **catacombs** (3rd century), which absorbed parts of earlier pagan catacombs (***t** 06 861 0840; open Mon 9–12, Tues–Sat 9–12 and 4–6, Sun and hols 4–6; adm*).

Around the back, through gardens where neighbourhood children play, stands one of Rome's least known but most remarkable churches, **Santa Costanza**, built as a mausoleum for Constantia, Emperor Constantine's daughter. In this domed, circular building – one of the finest late Roman works – you can see the great religious turning point of the 4th century come alive; among the exquisite mosaics are scenes of a grape harvest, and motifs familiar to any ancient devotee of Dionysus or Bacchus. In the two side chapels are later mosaics of Christ and the Apostles.

At the end of Viale Regina Elena, behind the university, **San Lorenzo** is one of Rome's seven pilgrimage churches. The original building, begun under Constantine, was reconstructed in the early 13th century and contains fine Cosmati family work around the altar. From here you can re-enter the city through the impressive **Porta Maggiore**, built under Emperor Claudius; the walls here carry an aqueduct. You can also see the **Temple of Minerva** nearby, on Via Giolitti, a round brick ruin dating from the 3rd century AD, and **Santa Croce in Gerusalemme**, another of the seven churches, founded by Constantine but now thoroughly Baroqued.

Almost directly under the train tracks, the **Underground Basilica**, only unearthed in 1916, was built underground for a secret, possibly illegal religious sect in the 1st century AD. Scholars haven't guessed what the cult's beliefs were from its strange stucco reliefs but venture to call it 'neo-Pythagorian' (*contact the Sovrintendenza Archeologica di Roma on **t** 06 699 0110 to arrange a visit*).

Day-Trips from Rome

Ostia, the Port of Empire

According to archaeologists, Rome's port was founded in the 4th century BC, 400 years after Rome itself. But in the centuries of conquest Ostia grew into a major city in its own right, with a population of about 100,000 and nearly two kilometres of *horreae* (warehouses) near the mouth of the Tiber. In the 4th century, when the trade flow slowed and the grain supply from Africa was diverted to Constantinople, Ostia lost its raison d'être. Malaria thrived, and by AD 800 it was abandoned. Old Father Tiber obliged the future by burying it in sand and mud. Mussolini shovelled it out in the 1930s, recovering an ancient attraction (*open daily 9–4, until 6 in winter; adm*) that's often overlooked. It's easy to reach by train: get off at the Ostia Antica stop.

As in Pompeii, here can imagine life in a big ancient city; the temples, baths, frescoed houses, barracks and warehouses are amazingly intact. Ostia's **Forum**, with its columns of temples, is set around a little hill that's wistfully called the 'Capitol'.

Getting Around

There are frequent **trains** to Ostia and Ostia Lido from Roma–Lido station.

The best way to get to Tivoli and Villa Adriana is by COTRAL **bus** from Ponte Mammolo terminal. For the Castelli Romani, there are frequent COTRAL **buses** from Anagnina, at the end of Metro Line A (a 20min ride from the centre of town).

There are frequent COTRAL **buses** from Rome to Subiaco (from Stazione Ponte Mammolo on Metro Line B) and to Palestrina (from Stazione Anagnina at the end of Metro Line A) and the Castelli Romani (also from Anagnina).

Tourist Information

Tivoli: Largo Garibaldi, **t** 0774 334 249.
Subiaco: Via Cadorna 59, **t** 0774 822 013.
Frascati: Piazza Marconi, **t** 06 942 0331.

Where to Stay and Eat

Ostia Antica

Al Monumento, Piazza Umberto I 8, **t** 06 565 0021 (*cheap*). A decent restaurant near the castle, offering good grilled fish at lunchtime. *Closed Mon and last 2wks Aug.*

Tivoli ✉ 00019

*****Padovano**, Via Tiburtina 130, Tiburtina, **t** 0774 530 807 (*moderate*). A good place to stay, with bargain rates.

Sibilla, Via della Sibilla 50, **t** 0774 335 281 (*moderate*). A touristy restaurant that incorporates the Temple of the Sibyls in its building, with good food and fair prices. *Closed Mon.*

Frascati

San Martino Il Vicolo, Via San Martino 6, **t** 06 941 6102 (*moderate*). A romantic little restaurant with tables outside in summer and excellent local cuisine.

Zarazà, Via Regina Margherita 45, **t** 06 942 2053 (*moderate*). Lovely views, local cooking and good Frascati wine. *Closed Mon May–Sept, Sun and Mon Oct–Apr.*

Zapata Bar, Via Risorgimento 4 (*cheap*). Good trattoria-style food popular with trendy locals.

Nemi ✉ 00040

*****Culla del Lago**, Via Spiaggia del Lago 38, Castel Gandolfo, by Lago di Albano just outside town, **t** 06 936 8231 (*moderate*). A good place to stay if you have a car.

Da Baffone, Via dei Laghi km 15, **t** 06 963 3892 (*moderate*). Dishes with wild mushrooms, plus good roast meats and exceptional house wine. *Closed Mon.*

The small **theatre** has an interesting **Mithraeum**, like the one under San Clemente in Rome; there's a police station (*Caserma dei Vigili*) and the oldest **synagogue** in Italy. One vast square, the 'Piazzale delle Corporazion', has some mosaics symbolizing the trades. A floor mosaic in **Fortunatus's Tavern** boasts an early specimen of advertising: 'Fortunatus says: if you're thirsty, have a bowl of wine.'

Near the ruins is the sleepy hamlet of **Ostia Antica**, also called the 'Borgo'. Founded as a fortress town in 830 by Pope Gregory IV, it wasn't enough to keep the Saracens out when they sacked Rome 19 years later. It contains is a small Renaissance church dedicated to **Sant'Aurea** (a 3rd-century Ostian martyr), and the elegant **castello**, erected in 1483 by Julius II (still only a cardinal) to keep out the Turks.

Tivoli and the Villa Adriana

Ancient *Tibur*, set in a cliff with a beautiful view over the Roman Campagna, became a sort of garden suburb for the senatorial class in the early days of Empire. But a place with a view is also easily defensible, and by the early Middle Ages, despite all the dirty work of Goths and Huns, Tibur had changed its name to Tivoli and transformed itself from posh resort to feisty, independent hill town. Once, in its struggles with Rome, it even defeated its neighbour and captured a pope. Wealth returned in the Renaissance in the form of cardinals; one, Ippolito d'Este, son of Duke Ercole I of Ferrara, created perhaps the most fantastically worldly villa and gardens Italy has ever seen.

That is no small statement, but the **Villa d'Este** (*__t__ 0774 312 070; open Tues–Sun May–Sept 9–6.30, Oct–Mar 9–5; ticket office closes 1½ hours earlier; adm; check with Tivoli tourist office for days fountains are running*) still has the charm to attract hordes of day-trippers year round. The villa itself, designed by Pietro Ligorio and decorated with Mannerist frescoes, is upstaged by the gardens, set on a series of terraces on the slopes. Among palms and cypresses, flowers and lawns, every turn exposes a confectionery fountain – Bernini's 'Fountain of Glass', the 'Grotto of Diana', the 'Fountain of Dragons' – along with artificial waterfalls and pools. The cardinal's water organ and mechanical birds don't work, but you won't regret you came.

Tivoli has a gaudy 17th-century **cathedral** and a Romanesque church, **San Silvestro**, with early medieval frescoes, which you pass on the way to another Renaissance cardinal's fantasy, the **Villa Gregoriana** (*currently under restoration; normally open daily 9–1hr before sunset; adm*). Built in a natural chasm, the shady paths and gardens are irresistible to visitors, who trip gaily down then realize they face quite a climb back to ground level. It's worth the trip, if you're up to it, for the spectacular natural waterfall on the Aniene river, and a smaller, artificial one designed by Bernini.

On the edge of the abyss are two small, remarkably well-preserved Roman temples, one circular and the other rectangular, called the **Temples of the Sibyl** and **Vesta**. There was indeed a college of sibyls in Tibur, as at Cumae near Naples, and they may have kept one of these temples. Whatever, the presence of these oracular ladies, cousins to the oracle at Delphi, show the influence of Greek thought and religion in Latium from the earliest times.

Just outside town (CAT bus no.4 from Largo Garibaldi) are signs to **Hadrian's Villa**, the grandest palace complex ever built in Italy (*__t__ 0774 382 733; open daily Apr–Sept 9–6.30, Oct–Mar 9–5; last entry 1½ hours before closing; adm exp*). To get an idea of the scale on which a 2nd-century emperor could indulge his fantasies, stop at the model of the villa near the entrance. All marble and travertine, and the same size as the ancient centre of Rome, Hadrian's dream house shows the excess even an intelligent and useful emperor was capable of, and had features that would surprise even Californians – such as a heated beach with steam pipes under the sand.

Hadrian was an architect, whose design credits include the Pantheon; he travelled widely through the empire gathering inspiration for his villa, creating reproductions of the Canopic Temple of Alexandria, the Platonic Academy and Stoa Poikile of Athens, set among huge baths, libraries, a Praetorian barracks, temples, theatres and a little palace on an island in an artificial lagoon, which may have been his private retreat. Many of the best statues in the Vatican and other museums were found here.

Subiaco and Palestrina

To see any of the hill towns to the east and south, you'll need a car. Quite a few interesting little villages have managed so far to escape modern tourism, including lovely **Anticoli Corrado** on its steep cliff, and **Saracinesco**, founded on a nearly inaccessible crag by Saracen raiders in the 9th century (the present townspeople are their direct descendants). Few towns can claim as glorious a past as **Subiaco**, to which St Benedict retired in the late 5th century to write his *Rule* and set Christian monasticism on its way. All through the dark centuries, his monasteries (originally Subiaco had 12) provided a haven for learning and piety, and as late as the 1460s the first printed books in Italy were made here by two monks from Germany.

Today the oldest buildings are in the **convent of Santa Scolastica** (***t*** *0774 85525; open daily 9–12.30 and 3.30–7*), named after Benedict's twin sister, with cloisters from the 6th and 11th centuries, and a medieval church decorated by the Cosmati. Beyond this, in a dramatic setting above a river gorge (a two-and-a-half-kilometre walk from town), the **monastery of San Benedetto** (***t*** *0774 85039; open daily 9–12.30 and 3–6*) has a treasure of late medieval and Sienese quattrocento frescoes (including a rare life portrait of St Francis of Assisi) in a maze of chapels, passages and steps cut into the rock; at the bottom is the *Sacro Speco*, the cave where Benedict lived as a hermit for three years. Nearby, in the gorge of the Aniene, is a little lake with a waterfall, which may have been constructed by Nero, who had a villa at Subiaco.

South of Tivoli, **Zagarolo** has Baroque churches, a medieval citadel and a thoroughly strange Baroque gate, perhaps the work of Vignola. Nearby **Palestrina**, ancient *Praeneste*, occupies the site of the greatest Hellenistic temple in Italy, the sanctuary of Fortuna Primigenia. Originally home to an oracle of the Latin tribes, this complex, built on a series of mountainside terraces, was as large as the town built on top. Part of the highest terrace was used as a foundation for the 17th-century Colonna-Barberini Palace, now home to the **Museo Nazionale Archeologico Prenestino** (***t*** *06 953 8100; open daily 9–1hr before sunset; adm*); here the star attraction is a mosaic with scenes of Egypt, showing the flooding of the Nile. The ruins of the oracle chamber can be seen in the museum's grounds. On the way down to the town centre are some unusual relics: the ruins of a temple of Serapis, a treasury, and the cathedral, built over what was probably a temple of Jupiter.

The Castelli Romani

Before there was a Rome, these towns around the Alban Hills were the strongest members of the Latin Confederation. Since being pounded into submission some 2,200 years ago, their role has been reduced to that of providing the capital with wine, flowers and a place to spend summer weekends. The countryside is beautiful, though the Castelli are nearly surrounded by the Roman suburbs.

Frascati, the nearest and most popular of the Castelli, was a medieval replacement for the ancient Latin city of *Tusculum*, destroyed in 1191. Frascati took some hard knocks in the Second World War but is still lovely, with winding alleys and a great view of the countryside. The elegant park in the grounds of the 17th-century **Villa Aldobrandini** (*open Mon–Fri 9–1 and 3–6, winter until 5*) has famous views over Rome. Nearby **Grottaferrata** was built around the 11th-century abbey, founded by saints Nilus and Bartholomew and still in the care of Greek Catholic monks; its **Basilica di Santa Maria** combines Byzantine mosaics with Italian medieval frescoes; one chapel was painted by Domenichino, and outside is a fine columned campanile from the 1200s (***t*** *06 945*

9309; abbey open daily 7–6.30). **Marino**, like Frascati, is famed for its wine; the town fountains flow with it during the grape festival on the first Sunday of October. From here the Via dei Laghi passes **Lago di Albano** on the way to Velletri and the south. After the lake is a turn-off to **Rocca di Papa**, a dramatically sited town with a medieval citadel called the *Quartiere dei Bavaresi* after Emperor Ludwig's Bavarian troops stationed here in the 1320s. From the town you can drive up to the highest of the Alban Hills, **Monte Cavo** (3,228ft), passing a spot where Hannibal camped during the Punic Wars.

From Rome, the Via Appia Antica passes the other side of Lago Albano in a dead straight line as far as **Castel Gandolfo**, the Vatican enclave where popes take their summer holidays. After that comes **Albano Laziale**, named for the ancient Alba Longa, mother city of Rome. Septimus Severus built a huge army base for the second legion here, and its relics can be seen all over town, including a 3rd-century cistern – still in use – and the principal gate, which was rediscovered in 1944 when the houses that covered it were bombed. The town's two central churches were both originally part of a vast bath complex: **San Pietro**, with a fine Romanesque campanile, and **Santa Maria della Rotonda**, a remarkable miniature Pantheon that was a *nymphaeum* and still has some mosaics of sea-monsters and a relief of Mithras. Albano's museum, on Viale Risorgimento, stands near another strange relic, the so-called 'Tomb of the Horatii and Curiatii', built in an Etruscan style.

From Albano, the Appian Way (SS7) continues south to **Ariccia**. Anyone familiar with Sir James Frazier's *The Golden Bough*, the foundation work of modern anthropology, will remember the priest of Diana who ruled the Ariccian Grove, the 'King of the Wood', and how as late as Roman times any man who cared to could cut some mistletoe from one of the sacred oaks, kill the king and take his place. There are still oak groves around Ariccia, and 'Diana's Mirror', beautiful **Lake Nemi**, is still an enchanted spot, a deep blue oval surrounded by wooded hills and villas. The town of Nemi itself, a pretty place known for its violets and *fragoline* (tiny strawberries), is also worth a detour. Beyond Nemi, **Velletri** is the last of the Castelli, with a Baroque cathedral and an odd, 149ft striped tower of 1353 called the Torre del Trivio.

The Monti Lepini: Cori, Ninfa and Sermoneta

In the Middle Ages, the Monti Lepini was the closest people could live to the malaria-ridden coast; now the charming old hill towns are well off the beaten track. **Cori**, like Rome and so many other Latin towns, likes to trace its founding to Trojan refugees. It may well be 3,000 years old; that, at least, is the date archaeologists assign to its 'Cyclopean' walls, built of huge, neatly fitted polygonal stones, still visible in many places. There are also many Roman ruins, including an intact bridge and the Temple of Hercules (really of Jupiter), a small Doric building complete but for its roof.

Nearby **Ninfa** (***t** 0773 695 404; open by infrequent guided tour; a limited number of tickets are available at the site or at Rome's Palazzo Caetani porters' lodge at Via Botteghe Oscure 32,* ***t*** *06 6880 3231*) was once a powerful city, one that witnessed the election of two popes. Now it is called the 'medieval Pompeii'. Like many others, this city belonged to the Caetani, one of the most powerful of the great Roman families. After one family faction seized it from another and sacked it in 1382, it dwindled.

Malaria set in and the area was abandoned by the 17th century. In the 1920s, Caetani descendants began turning the site of the city into what has become a stunning botanical garden, where the ruins of the medieval monuments survive in a setting of small streams and lakes, overgrown with wildflowers and trees. It is now run by a foundation with the help of the WWF.

Norma, built on a steep, curving cliff, seems a city hanging in the air. Nearby are more Cyclopean walls around the ruins of **Norba**, once capital of Rome's enemies, the Volscians. It was destroyed by the legions in the Social Wars in 89 BC but has been reconstructed in a **Museo Virtuale** (*open Tues–Fri 9.30–12.30, Sat and Sun 4–7; adm*).

Many of the medieval refugees from Ninfa went just up the hill to **Sermoneta**, a lovely, dignified hill village where you can take a fascinating tour of the **Castello Caetani** and look upon one of the most transcendant Madonnas you'll ever see, by the cheerful Florentine Benozzo Gozzoli, in the 12th-century **Collegiata di Santa Maria**.

At the eastern end of the Monti Lepini, **Priverno** was another Volscian capital, and home to the warrior maiden Camilla who led them (at least in the *Aeneid*) against the Trojans. Now it has an excellent archaeology museum, a wealth of little churches with medieval frescoes (you'll have to ask around for keys), and the ruins of its ancestor, *Privernum*, down on the plain amid fields of the town's famous artichokes.

That Priverno has a Gothic cathedral is thanks to the French Cistercian architects from nearby **Fossanova** with its 12th-century abbey (***t** 0773 930 961; currently closed for restoration*). The Cistercians, masters at reclaiming swamplands, got these from the pope in 1130 and soon started work on the austere but graceful Gothic pile for their HQ. The Italians never were much interested in the style, of course, and Fossanova survives along with several other churches in southern Lazio, all built or inspired by the Cistercians, as rare examples on this side of the Alps. The church, of cathedral proportions, is a fine, sedate Burgundian Gothic work with a beautiful rose window. Not much is left inside, except the stately rows of piers and pointed arches. Fossanova was a great centre of learning in its day (St Thomas Aquinas spent time here), but after the 1400s wealth and talent deserted it. After centuries of decadence, it was expropriated in 1873, and its treasures were dispersed.

Up in the Monti Ausoni above Fossanova, **Sonnino** was bandit country even a century ago; the village commemorates its badmen in a Museo dei Briganti.

Southern Lazio

Down the Coast

The Pontine Marshes

...nowhere else has the creative power of Fascism left a deeper mark. The immense works can be summed up in the lapidary phrase of Il Duce:'You redeem the land, you found some cities.'

from a 1939 Italian guidebook

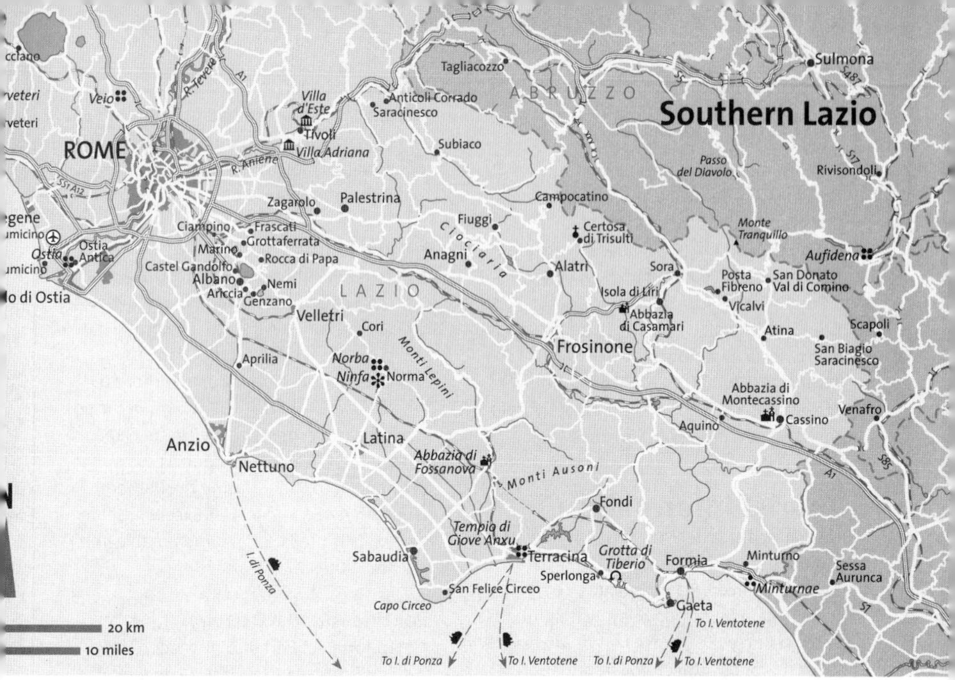

You wouldn't have been travelling this way 60 years ago, when the broad Pontine Marshes plain was the biggest no-man's-land in Italy, wracked by malaria and healthy only for the water buffalo. The Romans dug canals to reclaim the swamp, but they became blocked up in the Dark Ages. During the 13th century some of the marshes were drained again, but a few centuries of papal rule had the area back to its soggy emptiness when Mussolini decided to make it one of the showpieces of his regime.

Today, save the corner preserved as a park and wildlife refuge, the marshes no longer exist, and new towns such as Aprilia, Pomezia, Pontinia and Sabaudia sit amid miles of prosperous farms as monuments to the brighter side of Fascism. So does **Latina**, largest of the Pontine towns and Italy's youngest provincial capital, founded in 1932. It's a bright, busy place with plenty of trees and chunky Mussolini *palazzi*.

Down the Coast: Ánzio, Monte Circeo and Terracina

If you drive along the coast you'll pass plenty of beaches, including those of the small resort of **Ánzio**, ancient *Antium*, popular with the Romans. This Volscian town, from which Coriolanus made his rebellion against Rome, later became the home of one of Augustus' imperial palaces; ruins include that of a theatre. Later holiday-makers included a pope or two, and the Roman families that left a host of Liberty-style villas a century ago. Ánzio really became popular in January 1944, when British and US forces found its beaches an ideal spot for a landing; that bloody but successful end-run forced the Germans to abandon their Gustav Line and opened the way for the liberation of Rome. Large military cemeteries surround the town.

Between Ánzio and Cape Circeo the coast is a solid stretch of beaches and dunes. **Monte Circeo**, at the end, was an island in ancient times – one of many candidates for Homer's Isle of Circe from the *Odyssey*. Since 1934 much of this area has been in

Getting Around

The Rome–Naples **rail** line runs parallel to the coast. For Terracina and Sabaudia, get off at Priverno; for Sperlonga, at Fondi; for Gaeta, at Formia, and take local buses. There are also regular COTRAL **buses** from Roma EUR Fermi.

Formia is the year-round port for the **Pontine Islands**, with daily **ferries**. In summer you can also catch a **hydrofoil** and ferry from Ánzio or Terracina; in winter there's a ferry from Terracina (daily 8am) and a regular hydrofoil service from Ánzio (Sat, Sun and Mon).

Tourist Information

Latina: Via Duca del Mare 19, **t** 0773 695 404, *www.aptlatinaturismo.it*.

San Felice Circeo: Piazza Lanzuisi, **t** 0773 547 770.

Ponza: Molo Musco, on quay near lighthouse, **t** 0771 80031/809 866, *www.isolaponza.com*. Useful for ferry/hydrofoil information.

Where to Stay and Eat

Sperlonga ✉ 04029

*****La Playa**, Via C. Colombo, Loc. Fiorelle, **t** 0771 549 496 (*expensive*). A fine modern hotel with a pool and a bit of beach. *Closed Jan–Mar*.

*****Parkhotel Fiorelle**, Via C. Colombo, Loc. Fiorelle, **t** 0771 548 246 (*moderate*). A decent option close to the Playa.

La Bisaccia, Via Romita 25, **t** 0771 54576 (*moderate*). A charming little restaurant in town, serving fish and pasta dishes. *Closed Tues and Nov*.

Gaeta ✉ 04024

*****Summit**, on the coastal Via Flacca km 23, **t** 0771 741 741 (*very expensive–moderate*). A good modern resort hotel in a fine location. *Close Nov–Easter*.

Masaniello, Piazza Commestibili 6, t 0771 462 296 (*moderate*). A restaurant offering fish specialities prepared in a style more typical of Campania than Lazio.

Formia ✉ 04023

******Grande Albergo Miramare**, Via Appia 44, **t** 0771 320 047 (*moderate*). One of the best places on the coast, set in a beautiful old villa on the southern edge of the town, with extensive gardens on the shore, a beach, a swimming pool, and modernized but pleasant rooms, as well as an elegant restaurant in a little pavilion.

Zì Anna, Largo Paone, facing the harbour, **t** 0771 771 063 (*moderate*). Excellent seafood, classically prepared, and memorable *primi piatti*. *Closed Tues*.

Pontine Islands ✉ 04027

*****La Torre dei Borboni**, Via Madonna 1, **t** 0771 80135 (*very expensive–moderate*). The most picturesque place to stay on Ponza, with rooms and apartments in an 18th-century castle with great views, and its own beach. Prices double in high season. *Closed mid-Oct–Easter*.

*****Gennarino a Mare**, **t** 0771 80071 (*very expensive–moderate*). A good option close to Ponza's central beach. Prices double in summer. *Closed Thurs out of season*.

Da Luisa, Via Chiaia di Luna, **t** 0771 80128 (*moderate*). A reasonable hotel situated up a pedestrian street at the top of town.

Ristorante da Antonio, Via A Dante, **t** 0771 809 832 (*moderate*). A friendly and upmarket eatery set in a wooden hut on the beach of San Antonio close to the port. Diners can choose from a selection of seafood platters, or from a range of tasty, if rather overpriced, pasta dishes.

La Lanterna, Corso Carlo Pisacane (*cheap*). A family-run restaurant offering bargain home-style meals.

the **Parco Nazionale del Circeo**, an unspoilt watery landscape. Migratory birds stop here, and besides wildflowers and primeval forests you may see woodpeckers, peregrine falcons, herons and that overdressed seabird, the *Cavaliere d'Italia*.

This being Italy, the next compelling sight is never far; here, the Cooperativa La Mela Cotogna at Via Carlo Alberto 104 in Sabaudia organizes guided visits (***t*** *0773 511 206*) to the villa of **Emperor Domitian**, accessible by boat across the lake of Sabaudia, in the

National Park. **Sabaudia** itself is another of Mussolini's Art Deco new towns (1933), probably the most successful of them; as a publicity stunt, the Duce collared every loose labourer in Italy and got the town built in 253 days.

Further down the coast the Ausonian Mountains crowd the sea at **Terracina**, which was once the Volscian port of *Anxur* and later became a major node on the Appian Way and the biggest port between Rome and Naples. Now it's an attractive town scattered with ruins. The best are high up in the **Capitolium**: three Etruscan-style temples dating from the 1st century BC, including the gate at Albano Laziale, which was discovered when the buildings on top were destroyed in 1944. The hotchpotch **cathedral** began as a temple to Augustus and deified Rome; in places you can still see the ancient columns through the walls. There is an exotic 13th-century campanile, and mosaics and Cosmati work inside.

Down in the modern town, constructed around the harbour and an 18th-century ship canal that was built by the popes, are the ruins of a bath complex and an amphitheatre. **Terracina** is a resort with an enormous beach west of the centre along Lungomare Circeo. At the eastern entrance to town, Trajan cut a passage through the mountains, the 'Pisco Montano', to allow the Via Appia to continue along the coast. In Roman times, every sailor on the Tyrrhenian knew the landmark **temple of Giove Anxur**, high up on Monte Sant'Angelo above the city. Take the Strada Panoramica up to the top; the temple's mighty stone platform survives, affording views for miles along the coast.

From Terracina you can make a detour to **Fondi**, an old town on the plain that's surrounded by lakes, orchards and vegetable gardens. Fondi has stuck to its rectilinear Roman street plan; through the centuries it added a cathedral full of curiosities, and a bluff and businesslike 14th-century castle that contains a small museum.

Sperlonga and Gaeta

Towards Naples, **Sperlonga** is one of the most pleasant small resorts on the central Tyrrhenian coast, with a picturesque whitewashed medieval quarter on its steep promontory and miles of fine beaches to either side. About three kilometres beyond it lies the sea cave called the **Grotto of Tiberius** (*site and museum open daily 8.30–7.30; adm*), once fitted out as a pleasure dome for the hedonistic emperor (read the details in Suetonius' tell-all *Lives of the Caesars*). Outrageous sculpture has been found here, smashed to pieces and now reconstructed; the best bits are two vast compositions representing scenes from the *Odyssey*. Entry to the site is through the museum that has been built to house them.

At the end of this scenic stretch of coast, **Gaeta** stands behind its medieval walls on a narrow peninsula, forming the grandest sight between Monte Argentario and the Bay of Naples. In the early Middle Ages, this town was an important Mediterranean trading centre, a rival to Amalfi and Pisa. Its naturally defensible site made it a valued stronghold for centuries; it was briefly the last redoubt of the House of Bourbon in 1861, when the King of Naples and his palace guard withstood a siege from the army of the new Italy, hoping for help from France that never came. Now Gaeta gracefully juggles its two modern roles of romantic, evocative resort and US naval base.

The town has a quiet medieval atmosphere, with its 13th-century castle and crumbling old streets and alleys around the harbour. The much rebuilt **cathedral** boasts a spectacular 185ft **campanile** begun in the 11th century; its coloured tiles and interlaced arches betray the influence of the minarets of Spain and North Africa. The hill above Gaeta, **Monte Orlando**, is now a park closed to traffic, but you can take a shuttle bus up to the top for the views and the rich and well-preserved tomb of a Roman general named Munatius Planctus, founder of Lyon, France.

The resort strip spreads around the gulf to Gaeta's sister city **Formia**, the major port for ferries to the Pontine Islands, which enjoyed a blessed past as one of the gilded resorts of Imperial Rome, like Capri or Baiae. Mark Antony's men caught up with the virtuous but capitally tedious orator Cicero here, after the assassination of Caesar, and knifed him in the baths of his villa. Little of ancient Formia survived through the Dark Ages, and the little city that replaced it suffered grievously in 1944, but there are still some Roman ruins, including the so-called 'Tomb of Cicero'. Today Formia is a happy and growing place that seems to have a bright future.

Before Campania, the last town along the coast is **Minturno**, a medieval replacement for ancient *Minturnae*, the ruins of which, closer to the coast, include a restored theatre, bits of temples and an aqueduct.

Ponza and the Pontine Islands

An ancient volcano gave birth to the five small islands of the Pontine archipelago, and to it they owe much of their charm and eccentricities. Two are inhabited: **Ponza**, the larger and more popular, is stunningly beautiful and shaped like a crescent moon. The curve of its fishing harbour, with its oddly shaped sea rocks, arches and coves, shelters a charming pastel-tinted town and small tower. On the other side of the island, but within walking distance, is the island's famous 'moonlit' beach, the **Chiaia di Luna**, a curved strand beneath steep pale cliffs. Wandering (or, far better, sailing) along its long, jagged shores, you'll discover such wonders as a volcanically created swimming pool and the glaringly white Infernal Cove, both near **La Forna** (the only other real settlement on Ponza). Hire a boat at Ponza town or Santa Maria to visit the **Grotte di Pilato**, three grottoes connnected by tunnels dug in Republican times as part of a luxury villa, and used to store live fish for its kitchens.

The other inhabited island, tiny **Ventotene**, is a table of reddish tufa on the surface of the sea; Augustus' daughter Julia built a grand villa here to receive her many lovers far from the wagging tongues of Rome (though her behaviour eventually caught up with her and Ventotene became her rock of exile) and a few bits remain beyond the rocky beach of Cala Rossano. Later Julians found it a usefully isolated place to do their dirty work, too; Caligula's mother starved herself to death here, and Nero had his wife Octavia murdered in her bath; the meagre ruins of her villa stand evocative on windswept Punta Eolo. The town of **Porto Ventotene** is piled over the old Porto Romano, carved out of tufa. There is a small museum in the Municipio (*open Tues–Sun summer 9.30pm–midnight, winter 9–1 and 6–8.30*), with items found in Julia's villa. You can stroll round the island in less than an hour, past little fields of lentils. Here and there are little paths winding towards the sea, the cliffs and beaches.

Inland

The Ciociaria: Anagni and Ferentino

The quickest route from Naples from Rome is the Autostrada del Sole, following the route of the Roman Via Casilina behind the coastal mountains. After Velletri, in the Castelli Romani, however, there are still detours to delay you. This humble corner of Lazio is known as the **Ciociaria**, after the *ciocie*, or bark sandals, that were worn by the countrymen not so long ago, when this was one of the backwaters of Italy.

Anagni, small as it is, held centre stage in European politics several times in the Middle Ages. Four 14th-century popes were born here, and others made it their summer home. Greatest among them was Boniface VIII, a nasty intriguer from the Caetani family who loudly proclaimed the temporal supremacy of the popes long after anyone took the idea seriously. Parts of the **Palazzo di Bonifacio VIII** can still be seen (***t** 0775 727 053; open daily 9–1 and 3–7, winter until 6; adm*), along with the stout **cathedral**, one of the finest in central Italy. Outside, it is 11th-century Romanesque; a rebuilding in the 1300s left it tentatively Gothic within. There is a Cosmatesque pavement and a 13th-century stone baldaquin over the altar, but the real attraction is the 'Medieval Sistine Chapel', the **crypt of San Magno** (*open daily Apr–Oct 9–1 and 4–7, Nov–Mar 9–1 and 3–6; adm; you may have to wait for someone with the key*), entirely covered in blue and gold Byzantine-style frescoes from the 12th and 13th centuries. Underneath is one of the most richly detailed Cosmati pavements anywhere, signed by Master Cosma himself.

In the mountains above Anagni, **Fiuggi** has been a popular spa for centuries, and the 1900s left the town an ensemble of ornate hotels, tree-lined boulevards and a casino. East of Anagni, the attractive hill town of **Ferentino** sits inside a complete circuit of pre-Roman Cyclopean walls. Its landmark church is the refined French Gothic **Santa Maria Maggiore**, built by the Cistercians. Up on the old acropolis is a handsome **cathedral** with a complete set of Cosmatesque furnishings paid for by Innocent III.

Alatri and Arpino

Two and a half millennia ago, **Alatri** was one of the main cities of the Hernici, an Italic tribe that differed from its neighbours by being a firm ally of Rome, which spared it the destruction that befell many other ancient cities of Lazio. Consequently it remains the best example of a pre-Roman Italian town, with almost a complete circuit of Cyclopean walls from about the 6th century BC. Another set of walls at the top of Alatri's hill marks the boundaries of the acropolis, where the **cathedral** and the Bishop's Palace stand over the temples of the long-forgotten Hernici. In the lower town, Santa Maria Maggiore contains fine medieval polychromed woodcarvings and a Byzantine icon called the Madonna of Constantinople. Just outside town is an early Carthusian monastery, the **Certosa di Trisulti** (***t** 0775 47024; open Mon–Sat 9.30–12 and 3–5.30, Sun 3–5.30; longer afternoon hours in summer*), with some buildings dating back to 1210 and a preserved 18th-century pharmacy – this part of Lazio has been famed for medicinal herbs since ancient times, and you can learn more about them here, as well as in the **botanical garden** run by the WWF outside town.

Along the old Via Casalina, little **Frosinone** is the provincial capital of the Ciociaria. A side road (SS214) takes you to the delightful **Abbey of Casamari** (*open daily 9–12 and 3–6*), a 13th-century French Cistercian complex with a church much like the one at Fossanova, then to **Isola del Liri**, a town with a dramatic waterfall and a blues festival each July. Further down the Via Casalina, **Aquino**, the elegant home town of Cicero, has Roman-era ruins, including a small decorative arch, and two museums: one dedicated to lutes and mandolins, for which Arpino was once famous, and the other to the works of sculptor Umberto Mastroianni, uncle of the actor Marcello.

For something out of the way, venture up into the highest corner of Lazio, the valley of the Comino on the borders of the Abruzzo National Park. In this mountainous region there are beautiful **lakes** at Posta Fibreno and Biagio Saracinísco, and the ruins of a 12th-century castle at **Vicalvi**. **Atina** has been the most important town since the days of the Samnites; relics from its past are preserved in the municipal museum.

Montecassino

This may be the most famous monastery in Italy, but its dramatic location on a mountaintop over the Garigliano Valley has caused the honest monks nothing but trouble over the centuries. The latter were essential in keeping alive the traditions of letters and scholarship in the Dark Ages – a fact that is all the more remarkable when you consider that Montecassino has been utterly destroyed five times.

Benedict came in 529, but the Lombards wrecked the place only 60 years later. The Saracens and the Normans repeated the scene in the 9th and 11th centuries, and an earthquake finished off what must have been one of Italy's treasures of medieval architecture in 1348. Each time the place has been rebuilt, but the reason why Montecassino attracts so much strife was demonstrated again during the Italian Campaign of 1944 – the rock happens to be the most strategically important spot in central Italy, the key to either Rome or Naples, depending on which way your army is walking. In 1944 the Germans made it the western bastion of their Gustav Line and it held up the Allied advance for four months. Enough bombs were dropped to destroy the monastery and flatten the forests around it without seriously disconcerting the defenders. The polyglot Allied forces of New Zealanders, Indians, Moroccans, Canadians and Free French made unsuccessful attacks between January and May. It was the Poles who finally beat their way in, losing more than 1,000 men on the way up; their cemetery can be seen near the hill.

Rebuilding began almost immediately after the war. The Renaissance basilica and cloisters have been faithfully reconstructed, along with the 'Loggia del Paradiso' and its famous views, though the only surviving art is a set of remarkable mosaics in the crypt, made by German monks in 1913; a small museum holds shattered fragments of the rest (***t** 0776 311 529; open daily Apr–Oct 8.30–12 and 3.30–6, until 5 rest of year; ask at office about guided tours; no shorts or vests*).

On the way back down the mountain to Cassino town (also levelled in the fighting and completely rebuilt), you'll pass the site of Roman Cassino, with an archaeological museum and ruins that include a barbaric-looking amphitheatre in *opus reticulatum* (*open daily until 1hr before sunset; adm*).

Campania

19

Highlights

1 Pompeii and Herculaneum, ghost cities of the Roman Empire

2 Amalfi, and the famous Amalfi Drive

3 Procida, Ischia and Capri: jewels in the sea

4 Egyptian curiosities and Trajan's Arch in Benevento

5 The Greek temple at Paestum

The *Feste* of Campania

Any excuse will do for throwing a party in Campania, and the region plays host to some of Italy's most spectacular and colourful traditional festivals or *feste*. Most of the festivities are linked to religious events and feast days, and the Madonna features prominently, often decked out garishly with fairy lights and gaudy flowers and hauled through the streets on the top of tiny Fiats that have been hastily covered with red velvet (with peepholes for the driver), or on platforms borne by the village's fittest and strongest young men. But many of the celebrations also have a strong pagan flavour, especially those linked to the land and the harvest, and some of the feast-day paraphernalia is unmistakably phallic (spot the towers and obelisks).

Whatever the occasion, a village *festa* is a chance to see local traditions and ancient rites in full swing. This being Campania, where eating is in itself a second religion, a visit to a *festa* will invariably involve consuming vast quantities of food, often superbly cooked in makeshift kitchens organized by the local women and sold at knock-down prices. The following are some of the best *feste* to look out for, but keep a lookout for others by checking billboards in the piazzas of towns and villages.

La Sagra dei Gigli (lily festival), Nola, 27 June. The whole town commemorates the return of 5th-century bishop St Paulinus after his long imprisonment in Africa. The original Nolani welcomed him home with bunches of lilies. Today, the townspeople recall this by hauling 80ft wooden 'lilies' through the streets.

Festa di Sant'Anna, around Ischia, 26 July. A dazzling torchlit procession of hundreds of boats, transformed into floats, to honour the island's patron saint.

Festa dell'Obelisco di Paglia (feast of the straw obelisk), Fontanarosa, near Avellino, 14 August. A harvest thanksgiving ritual, with a giant 100ft spire of plaited straw, around which villagers dance and sing.

La Sagra del Grano (wheat festival), Foglianise, near Benevento, 16 August. A striking display of allegorical floats depicting famous churches and monuments, all made out of straw and cornstalks.

Festa dell'Assunta (feast of the Assumption), Positano, 15 August. An ancient celebration in honour of the Virgin, which also recreates the landing – and defeat – of the hated Saracens. Local townspeople dress in costumes and stage a parade of decorated boats, before the grand finale: a dramatic firework display over the sea. In neighbouring Montepertuso there is another attractive *festa* two weeks later, the **Sagra del Fagiolo** (feast of the bean).

Festa di San Gennaro, Naples, 19 September. A major event commemorating Naples' patron saint, with a service held in the cathedral to witness the miracle of the liquefaction of his blood (*see* p.861). Afterwards, citizens take to the streets to watch the silver statue of the saint being paraded through the streets. Needless to say, no one goes to work that day.

Festa dell'Immacolata (feast of the Immaculate Conception), Torre del Greco, December. A commemoration of the town's lucky escape from the 1861 eruption of Vesuvius, during which more than 100 local men carry a huge triumphal float, topped by the Madonna, through the streets.

The Italian south – the Mezzogiorno ('Noonday') – is one of the extremities of Europe, poised in a calm sea between the Balkans and the Sahara. The contrasts within the south are greater than in the other two-thirds of Italy; from the dreamy coastline of Amalfi and Positano it is only an afternoon's drive to the grimmest deforested wastelands of the Basilicata. Some sections of the south are prosperous and forward looking, and not too distant from their northern counterparts; others lag astonishingly behind, despite all the efforts of the government and the Cassa per il Mezzogiorno. Some areas are surprising, others surprisingly empty.

In Roman times, to distinguish the *Campania* around Naples from parts further north (the present Roman *Campagna*), the southern section acquired the name of *Campania Felix* – and a happy land it was, the richest and most civilized province in Italy, with a mix of Greek and Etruscan culture superimposed on the native Samnites and Ausones, not to mention the merry Oscans and their perfumed city of Capua. Campania's charm, then as now, starts with one of the most captivating stretches of coastline in Italy – the Amalfi Coast – followed by Capri and Ischia, Sorrento, Vesuvius, the Phlegraean Fields around Pozzuoli, and the beautiful but lesser-known Cilento Coast at the southern tip of the region. Roman emperors and senators spent as much time here as business would allow, and even today it is said that the dream of every Italian is to have a villa at Capri or Sorrento overlooking the sea.

In the middle of all this sprawls Italy's third-largest city, Naples, a place that may well be either your favourite or least favourite Italian city – or both at the same time. Campania shares fully in all the complexes and problems of the Italian south as a whole. It has large new industries, ambitious planning schemes to attract more, and substantial difficulties with pollution, poverty, soaring unemployment, corruption and crime. Though the potential certainly exists, there is a long way to go before the region can reclaim the position it had in the days of the Caesars.

Naples

The most loathsome nest of human caterpillars I was ever forced to stay in – a hell with all the devils imbecile in it.

John Ruskin

...it reveals itself only to the simpatici.

Peter Gunn

For many, Naples is the true homeland of a particular Italian fantasy, a bastion of singing waiters and red-checked tablecloths, operatic passion and colourful poverty, balanced precariously between Love's own coastline and the menace of Vesuvius. But mention Naples or the Neapolitans to any modern, respectable north Italian and, as they gesticulate and roll their eyes to heaven, you will get a first-hand lesson in the dynamics of Italy's 'Problem of the South'. Many Italians simply can't accept that such an outlandish place can be in the same country with them – a sentiment that probably contains as much envy as contempt. Naples, the city that has given the world Enrico Caruso, Sophia Loren, pizza and syphilis (the disease appeared here in 1495, and was immediately blamed on the French garrison), has also long been Italy's urban problem child.

Whatever it might have been that so spooked the delicate Ruskin, Naples used to conjure up a very different image among Italians – it was a city of grace and joy, laughter and song, and plenty of good food. 'You are the empire of harmony, O Naples', as the traditional song 'Santa Lucia' put it.

But the city of harmony got a rude jolt when it came to adjusting to the modern industrial world, and an even worse one with World War II and the poverty and depravity that accompanied the ensuing Allied occupation. In the decades that followed, visitors saw Naples at its worst: the Allies had allowed organized crime to reestablish itself, and it came to dominate the city and its institutions. In a world in which corruption ruled supreme, urban problems got out of hand – drugs and crime flourished (the contraband pack of Marlboros came to rival Vesuvius as the city's best-known symbol), and at one point smugglers formed a union to protect themselves against the police. Pollution and traffic problems became Italy's worst. Illegal building spoiled much of the Bay, while at the same time severe housing shortages left Neapolitans living in abandoned buses and stolen cargo containers.

In the 18th century, when the city and its incomparable setting were a highlight of the Grand Tour, the saying was 'See Naples and die...' By the 1970s and 1980s, when things were arguably at their worst, this had become a macabre joke. But signs that Naples is slowly, fitfully recovering its old graces are everywhere: long-neglected monuments are being restored, public services are run a little better, a new metro is under construction, and much of the centre has been closed to traffic. An enormous modern business centre, the Centro Direzionale, has materialized out of the old wastelands behind Piazza Garibaldi.

There's still no shortage of problems, though. Rubbish pick-up is a crying scandal, as you won't fail to notice, and the Camorra still makes the daily headlines with its grisly clan wars. As the man in the hotel put it: 'It's not quite Zürich yet', and we agreed that that was something to be thankful for –the thought of a tidy, orderly Switzerland on the Bay sends a chill through the soul. Naples's real attraction is the priceless insight it affords into humanity: its population of 2.2 million spirited anarchists may be among the few peoples of urban Europe who truly realize they are alive, and try to enjoy it as best they can.

Their history being what it is, this manifests itself in diverse ways. The Napoletani do not stand in lines, or fill out forms, or stop for traffic signals if they can get away with avoiding them; they will talk your ears off, run you over in their ancient Fiats, criticize the way you dress, whisper alarming propositions, give you sweets, try to pick your pockets with engaging artlessness, offer surprising kindnesses, and – with a reassuring smile – they will always, *always* give you the wrong directions. In an official capacity, they will either break the rules for you or invent new ones; in shops and restaurants they will either charge you too much or too little. A bus ticket officially costs 77 centesimi, but even the employees of the bus line round it down to 75; life is too short to worry about pennies.

Naples
VIA PIETRO CASTELLINO
VIA GIACINTO GIGANTE
VIA MATTEO RENATO IMBRIANI
VIA SALVATORE ROSA
V. M. D. VITO PISCICELLI
V. G. B. RUOPPOTO
PZA MEDAGLIE D'ORO
VIA SIMONE MARTINI
VIA G. SANTA GROCE
VIALE MICHELANGELO
CORSO VITTORIO EMANUELE
VIA ACITILLO
VIA LUCA GIORDANO
Montesanto Funicular
VIA TITO ANGELINI
PZA VANVITELLI
VIA A. SCARLATTI
Castel Sant'Elmo
Certosa di San Martino
VIA FRANCESCO CILEA
VIA DOMENICO CIMAROSA
VIA ANIELLO FALCONE
Funicolare Centrale
QUARTIER SPAGNUOL
Funicolare di Chiaia
Villa Floridiana
VIA ANIELLO FALCONE
VIA TORQUATO TASSO
VIA DI PARCO MARGERITA
PZA AMEDEO
CORSO VITTORIO EMANUELE
VIA DEI MILLE
VIA FRANCESCO CRISPI
VIA MICHELANGELO SCHIPA
Museo principe de Aragona Pignatelli
PZA DEI MARTIRI
RIVIERA DI CHIAIA
Villa Comunale
PZA VITTORIA
VIA FRANCESCO CARACCIOLO
PZA DELLA REPUBLICA
VIA PIEDIGROTTA
VIA GIORDANO BRUNO
VIALE ANTONIO GRAMSCI
VIA FRANCESCO CARACCIOLO
Tomba deVirgilo
PZA SANNAZZARO
Funicolare di Pesillipo
MERGELLINA

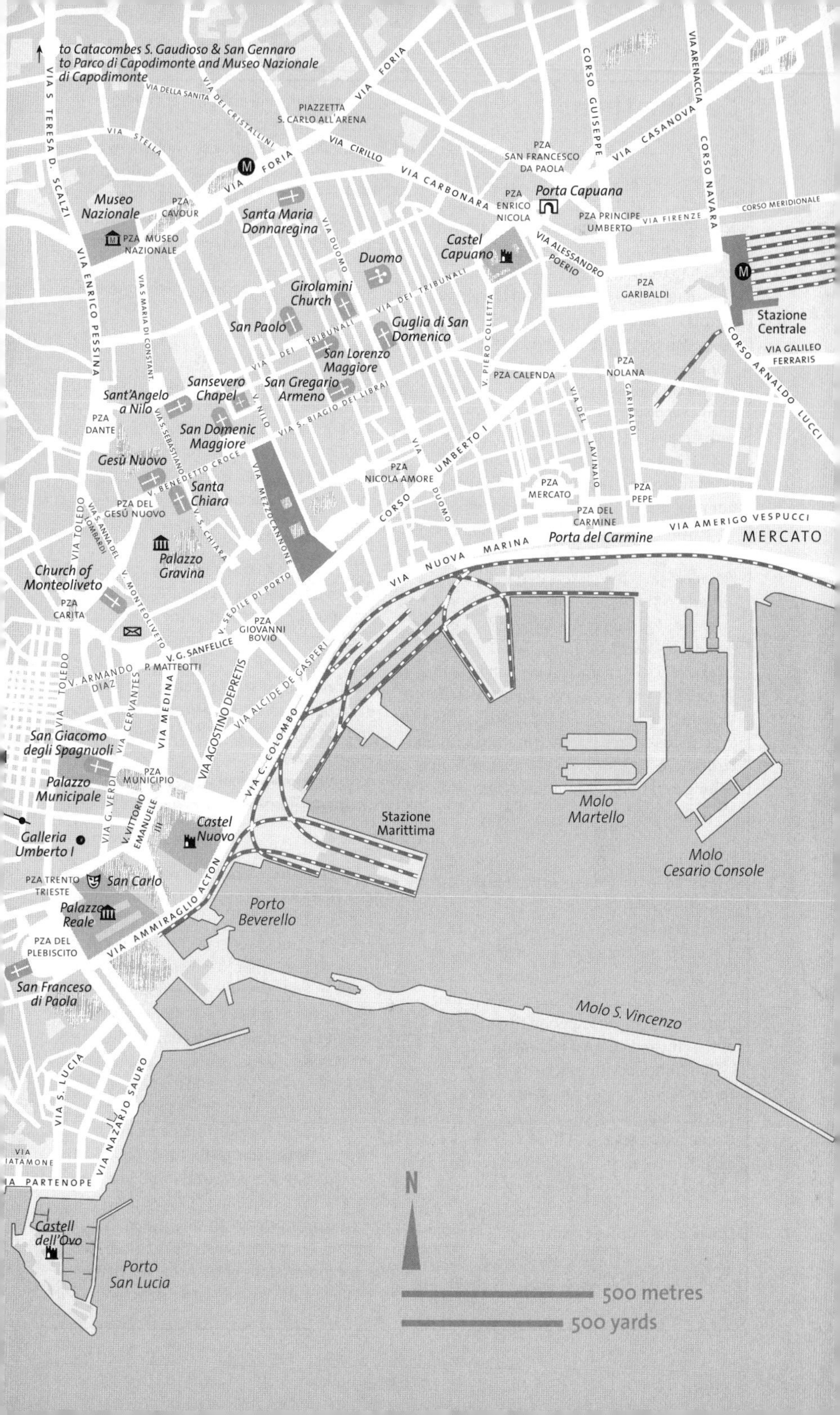
to Catacombes S. Gaudioso & San Gennaro
to Parco di Capodimonte and Museo Nazionale di Capodimonte
VIA S TERESA D. SCALZI
VIA DELLA SANITÀ
VIA DEI CRISTALLINI
VIA FORIA
PIAZZETTA S. CARLO ALL'ARENA
VIA STELLA
VIA CIRILLO
VIA CARBONARA
CORSO GUISEPPE
VIA ARENACCIA
VIA CASANOVA
CORSO NAVARA
PZA SAN FRANCESCO DA PAOLA
Porta Capuana
PZA ENRICO NICOLA
PZA PRINCIPE UMBERTO
VIA FIRENZE
CORSO MERIDIONALE
Museo Nazionale
PZA CAVOUR
PZA MUSEO NAZIONALE
Santa Maria Donnaregina
VIA DUOMO
Castel Capuano
VIA ALESSANDRO POERIO
Duomo
VIA DEI TRIBUNALI
PZA GARIBALDI
Stazione Centrale
VIA ENRICO PESSINA
VIA S MARIA DI CONSTANT.
Girolamini Church
San Paolo
Guglia di San Domenico
V. PIERO COLLETTA
CORSO ARNALDO LUCCI
VIA GALILEO FERRARIS
San Lorenzo Maggiore
PZA CALENDA
PZA NOLANA
Sansevero Chapel
San Gregario Armeno
VIA DEL LAVINAIO
GARIBALDI
Sant'Angelo a Nilo
V. NILO
VIA S. BIAGIO DEI LIBRAI
PZA DANTE
VIA S. SEBASTIANO
San Domenic Maggiore
CORSO UMBERTO I
Gesù Nuovo
V. BENEDETTO CROCE
VIA MEZZOCANNONE
PZA NICOLA AMORE
PZA MERCATO
PZA PEPE
Santa Chiara
PZA DEL GESÙ NUOVO
VIA TOLEDO
VIA S. ANNA DEI LOMBARDI
V. S. CHIARA
PZA DEL CARMINE
VIA AMERIGO VESPUCCI
Porta del Carmine
MERCATO
VIA NUOVA MARINA
Palazzo Gravina
Church of Monteoliveto
PZA CARITA
V. MONTEOLIVETO
V. SEDILE DI PORTO
PZA GIOVANNI BOVIO
V. G. SANFELICE
P. MATTEOTTI
V. ARMANDO DIAZ
VIA CERVANTES
VIA MEDINA
VIA AGOSTINO DEPRETIS
VIA ALCIDE DE GASPERI
VIA C. COLOMBO
San Giacomo degli Spagnuoli
PZA MUNICIPIO
Palazzo Municipale
VIA G. VERDI
V. VITTORIO EMANUELE III
Castel Nuovo
Molo Martello
Stazione Marittima
Galleria Umberto I
Molo Cesario Console
PZA TRENTO TRIESTE
San Carlo
VIA AMMIRAGLIO ACTON
Porto Beverello
Palazzo Reale
PZA DEL PLEBISCITO
San Franceso di Paola
Molo S. Vincenzo
VIA S. LUCIA
VIA NAZARJO SAURO
VIA CHIATAMONE
VIA PARTENOPE
Castell dell'Ovo
Porto San Lucia
N
500 metres
500 yards

Getting There

By Air

Naples' **Capodichino airport, t** 081 789 6259, on the north of the city, relatively close to the centre, has frequent direct links with all major Italian destinations and many foreign cities, including London (several flights daily).

The blue Alibus runs between the airport, Piazza Garibaldi (for the train station) and Piazza Municipio (for the ferry harbour) every 30mins 6.30am–11.30pm. Tickets (€2) can be bought on the bus.

The orange 3S bus also runs every 30mins but with frequent stops, including Piazza Garibaldi and Molo Beverello (for the ferry harbour). Tickets (€0.77) must be bought before travelling, from the *tabacchi* in the airport.

There are 3 daily Circumvesuviana buses, **t** 800 039 939, from the airport to Pompei (Pompei Scavi). Buy tickets (€4), on the bus. Curreri, **t** 081 801 5420, runs buses to Sorrento from the stop outside the Arrivals hall, on the right (every 1½hrs till 7pm, €6).

Taxis officially charge supplements for the airport trip and luggage on top of the meter fare; there may also be unexplained 'extras'. If in doubt, ask to see the price list, which should be displayed in the cab, or agree a fare before getting in. If traffic is not too heavy, the fare to the centre should not exceed €25.

By Rail

Most train travellers arrive at Stazione Centrale on Piazza Garibaldi, which is also a junction for the local Circumvesuviana railway and city buses. Trains for Rome or Reggio di Calabria pass through every 30mins or so. Many trains also stop at Napoli Mergellina and Napoli Campi Flegrei, on the western side of the city, and at other local stations.

Three other local lines serve the Bay of Naples: **Ferrovia Circumvesuviana** runs trains to Herculaneum, Pompeii and Sorrento; **Ferrovia Cumana** has services to the Campi Flegrei area, including Pozzuoli and Baia, from the station at Piazza Montesanto; and **Ferrovia Circumflegrea** runs to and from Piazza Montesanto west to Licola and Cuma. The last trains are: Circumflegrea 8.30pm, Cumana 9pm and Circumvesuviana 10.30pm. For more info on services around the Bay, call **t** 800 001 616.

Piazza Garibaldi station, from which the Circumvesuviana, metro and some mainline trains depart (Circumvesuviana trains also call at the nearby station in Corso Garibaldi), is in the basement of Stazione Centrale and poorly signposted (take stairs down from the main forecourt). Tickets can be purchased from machines (which rarely work), ticket desks or the pleasant travel agency on the ground floor behind the stairwell.

By Long-distance Bus

Most services to and from destinations in Campania operate from Piazza Garibaldi, in front of the Stazione Centrale. **SITA** (**t** 081 552 2176) runs a service to Amalfi and Salerno with stops on the Amalfi coast. Buses depart from the Varco Immacolatella by the port.

By Car

The A2 *autostrada* from Rome approaches Naples from the north, via Caserta. On the city's outskirts, just east of the airport, it meets a series of massive road junctions: the A16 turns east for Avellino and Bari, then 2 roads head west: the P1 for the coast, and Naples' inner ring road, the *tangenziale*, for Pozzuoli and the Campi Flegrei. The *tangenziale* lets you reach much of Naples while avoiding the centre. If you're heading further south, stay on the A2 until it meets the A3, avoiding the city.

By Sea

Naples' port has more sea connections than anywhere else in the Mediterranean, including the islands in the Bay of Naples, Sicily and the Aeolian Islands. Generally, ferries are cheaper than hydrofoils but take twice as long.

Ferries and hydrofoils leave from 3 points in Naples. Most long-distance ferries arrive and depart from **Stazione Marittima** in the centre of the port near the Castel Nuovo. Look in the daily newspaper *Il Mattino*, or in *Qui Napoli*, for timetables or consult the main companies: **Tirrenia** (**t** 199 123 199) for Palermo and Cagliari; **Siremar** (**t** 081 580 0340 or 199 123 199) for the Aeolian Islands and Milazzo in Sicily; **Lauro** (**t** 081 551 3352) for Tunisia; and **TTT Lines** (**t** 800 915 365) for Catania. **SNAV** (**t** 081 761 23 48) runs a daily hydrofoil from Mergellina quay to Palermo.

For more details of boat services to the Bay of Naples and its islands, *see* p.870 and p.896.

Getting Around

Naples' main **landmarks** are Castel Sant'Elmo and the huge monastery of San Martino, which are neighbours on the steep Vomero hill that slopes down to the sea near the port, dividing the city into old and new quarters. To the west is **modern Naples** – the busy but pleasant districts of Mergellina, Vomero and Fuorigrotta, to which middle-class Neapolitans retreat after work on their creaking old funiculars. East, towards Vesuvius, lies the **old centre**; the oldest districts are along and east of Via Toledo, where tall tenements jam into a grid of narrow streets, climaxing in the crowded markets around Piazza Garibaldi.

Walking is often the best and fastest way of getting around. Otherwise take public transport. The **Artecard** (*www.campaniaartecard.it*) gives 3 days' travel on the metro, buses, trains and funiculars, plus a return trip to Sorrento on the Circumvesuviana and travel on the Metro del Mare, for €13 (€8 under-25s). It also includes discounted car parking and free or half-price entry to major museums and sites throughout Campania, including Pompeii, Herculaneum and Paestum. You can buy it at the airport, museums or hotels. The 7-day version (€28) gives free entry to all sites in Naples and around the Bay but not transport. If you're staying longer, you can get a monthly pass (€23) covering buses, funiculars and the metro.

The Artecard also includes the Linea dei Musei hop-on-hop-off bus service every 45mins between main museums and sites Fri–Sun.

By Bus

Naples buses are slow, crowded and prime spots for pickpockets. That said, many stops now have electronic info boards telling you when buses are due to arrive, and if you buy the Artecard, the accompanying booklet has excellent maps and itineraries for key routes.

Most lines start at Piazza Garibaldi, Piazza Vittoria or Piazza del Plebiscito. Useful routes include: **R2** from Piazza Garibaldi to Corso Umberto and Piazza Municipio; **R3** from Piazza Municipio to Riviera di Chiaia and Mergellina; **137** or **160** from Piazza Garibaldi to Piazza Cavour and Capodimonte; **152** from Piazza Garibaldi to Pozzuoli; and **Tram 1** from Piazza Garibaldi to Piazza Vittoria past the ferry harbour.

The useful **Giranapoli** ('Around Naples') bus tickets come in two types, one lasting 90mins for €0.77 and a day ticket for €2.32.

By Metro and *Funicolare*

Much of the city is currently torn up as gigantic excavations make way for a major expansion of the formerly shabby single-line underground. For now, the metro is helpful for reaching the station (Piazza Garibaldi), the Museo Archeologico Nazionale, points in Vomero and Fuorigrotta, Solfatara and Pozzuoli. Note that the old line is no.2, while the new one being built will be no.1.

Ticket inspections are frequent and fines are issued if you fail to present a ticket. You must validate your ticket when you climb aboard. If the machine doesn't work, you must write the time and date on the reverse.

Middle-class Vomero is very well connected, with three *funicolari*. The Funicolare Centrale runs until 1am; the other *funiculari* and the metro stop at around 10pm. Tickets should be purchased from news vendors or *tabacchi*; machines inside stations rarely work.

By Taxi

In central Naples, the traffic is often so bad that relatively short journeys can take so long (and cost so much) that they're not worth it.

Naples taxi drivers are striving to improve their reputation for scamming tourists; most now display charges. There are plenty of ranks, or call **Radiotaxi Napoli, t** 081 556 4444. Don't get into a taxi that's trying to poach you from the queue (they'll rip you off), and check your change. Tipping is optional – €0.50 is plenty.

By Car

Leave your car elsewhere. Cars are broken into, or stolen, with alarming frequency. The traffic is abominable, and though drivers now occasionally stop for red lights, there's still plenty of the old anarchic spirit left.

If you do bring a car, try to find a hotel with secure parking (*parcheggio custodito*), or use a private car park (about €0.30/hr, €7.20/day). The Artecard (*see* above) gives 20% discounts for 2 car parks, one near the station at the Porto exit from the *tangenziale* (ANM Brin), one in Vomero (ANM Colli Aminei), **t** 800 639 525. Both have good bus links with the centre.

Tourist Information

The best place for information about Naples itself is the friendly booth run by the city's **Azienda Autonoma di Soggiorno** on Piazza del Gesù Nuovo, **t** 081 552 3328 or **t** 081 551 2701, in the old town (*open Mon–Sat 9–8, Sun and hols 9–3*). There are other tourist offices in the Royal Palace, **t** 081 252 5711, and opposite the Teatro San Carlo in Galleria Umberto I, **t** 081 402 394.

Details of excursions outside the city are available from the less helpful provincial tourist office **EPT**, Piazza dei Martiri 58, **t** 081 405 311. The EPT also has offices at the Stazione Centrale, **t** 081 268 779, which may help you find a hotel, at the airport, **t** 081 789 6259, and at Stazione Mergellina, **t** 081 761 2102. The EPT produce good free maps of the city and the Bay of Naples.

Crime

Naples' reputation for crime is exaggerated, but not entirely undeserved. Tips for a safe stay include leaving valuables in your hotel room or safe and avoiding looking too much like a tourist in poor areas. This means not waving your camera around or pulling out maps if you can avoid it. Keep your bag in front of you on buses and in crowds.

Areas where particular care is advised – especially after dark – are on buses and at train stations, around Piazza Garibaldi, the Forcella markets, the Quartieri Spagnuoli and near the botanical gardens.

Police: for an English-speaking operator, call **t** 112.

Shopping

No one thinks of Naples as one of Italy's prime shopping destinations, but there are as many things to be bought here as anywhere else, usually at lower prices. The backstreets around Spaccanapoli and other old sections are still full of artisan workshops. The Royal Factory at Capodimonte, founded by the Bourbons, still makes beautiful **porcelain and ceramic figures**, sold at the fancier shops in the city centre. Another old Naples tradition is the making of **cameos** from seashells; the shops outside the Certosa di San Martino have the best selection at relatively low prices.

Via San Biagio dei Librai – the middle stretch of the Spaccanapoli – contains some of the best antiquarian book-dealers in Italy, and the street is also full of odd surprises: the religious goods shops, for instance, have surprisingly good works in terracotta. The **Doll Hospital** at No.81, **t** 081 203 067, is one of the most charming shops in Naples.

Scriptura, at Vico San Domenico Maggiore 3, is a tiny shop that specializes in beautiful hand-made leather diaries, notebooks, photo albums and address books.

The backstreets near the archaeological museum contain many antiques and junk shops. The swankiest antiques shops tend to be along Via Morelli off Piazza dei Martiri in Chiaia. There's also a huge twice-monthly antiques market, the **Fiera dell'Antiquariato**, on alternate Sat and Sun mornings in the Villa Comunale gardens.

You can buy old prints at **Bowinkel**, Piazza dei Martiri 24, **t** 081 764 4344, while **Fonderia Chiurazzi**, Via Ponti Rossi 271, **t** 081 751 2685, makes artistic bronzes, including reproductions of works in the Museo Archeologico.

Intra Moenia, a publishing house and literary café in Piazza Bellini, has a good selection of cards, books and posters of old Naples.

For **clothes**, Via dei Mille, which runs from Piazza Amedeo down to Via Chiaia, has several local designer boutiques (such as Barbaro), while Via Calabritto off Piazza dei Martiri is the home of Prada and Versace. **Department stores** include COIN on Vomero's pedestrianized Via Scarlatti, or Il Rinascente on Via Toledo.

The **street markets** near Piazza Garibaldi are fascinating – especially the daily catch of fish, live squid and octopus at Via Ferrara, east of Corso Novara – although not very safe.

Where to Stay

Naples ✉ 80100

There's a shortage of good, affordable rooms in Naples, so book ahead if you can. The best area to stay is on the waterfront around Santa Lucia and Castel dell'Ovo, where you have easy access to shops, museums and good restaurants. It's less claustrophobic too. There are thousands of cheap rooms near Piazza Garibaldi, but most are in horrible dives.

The hotel booking service offered by the EPT at the station or airport (*see* above) can find you a room for a small fee.

Luxury

★★★★★**Excelsior**, Via Partenope 48, **t** 081 764 0111, *www.excelsior.it*. Naples' finest hotel, favoured by visiting sheikhs, kings and rock stars, with beautiful suites and a tradition of impeccable service since 1909. You pay for space here – in the elegant lounges, lovely rooftop solarium and restaurant, and rooms with large beds. It faces Vesuvius.

★★★★★**Parker's**, Corso Vittorio Emanuele 135, **t** 081 761 2474, *www.grandhotelparkers.com*. A delightful hotel – Naples' oldest – with airy rooms with polished wood, chandeliers and comfortable furniture. Sea-facing rooms have balconies and a vista of Vesuvius and Capri; the view is even more spectacular from the award-winning roof-terrace restaurant.

★★★★★**Santa Lucia**, Via Partenope 46, **t** 081 764 0666, *www.santalucia.it*. A beautifully restored 18th-century *palazzo*, aimed at the corporate crowd but with personal touches.

★★★★★**Vesuvio**, Via Partenope 45, **t** 081 764 0044, *www.vesuvio.it*. The grandiose hotel where Bill Clinton and the Italian football team stay, though it lacks the head-on view of Vesuvius implied by the name. There's a health spa and lovely roof-garden restaurant.

Very Expensive

★★★★★**Miramare**, Via Sauro 24, **t** 081 764 7589, *www.hotelmiramare.com*. A gem exuding the kind of old-world charm usually found outside cities. The 30 rooms have personal touches, and the atmosphere is cosy. Some rooms are small but the old lift and lavish breakfast laid out on the rooftop solarium more than make up for that. Rooms not facing the sea are quieter.

★★★★★**Paradiso**, Via Catullo 11, **t** 081 247 5111, *www.bestwestern.it/paradiso_na*. A good if slightly corporate bet with stunning views over the bay from its sea-facing rooms.

Expensive

★★★★★**Angioino**, Via Depretis 123, **t** 081 552 9500, *www.mercure.com*. A central option with 86 good-sized rooms and efficient service that makes it popular with the business crowd. The views are unspectacular, the furnishings functional, but all rooms are comfy and soundproofed, and it makes a good base.

★★★**Chiaia Hotel de Charme**, Via Chiaia 216, **t** 081 415 555, *www.hotelchiaia.it*. A quiet, clean, friendly and extremely comfortable hotel in an aristocratic *palazzo* 2mins' walk from San Carlo and the Piazza del Plebiscito. All 27 rooms are individually furnished with antiques; some have a Jacuzzi bathtub.

★★★**Palazzo Doria D'Angri**, Piazza 7 Settembre 28, **t** 081 210 907, *www.albergosansevero.it*. A hotel in a lovingly restored 18th-century palace designed by the Bourbons' favourite architect, Luigi Vanvitelli. There are 8 large bedrooms, a beautiful circular breakfast room, a bar and an oval ballroom with its original mirrors and friezes and frescoes by Fischetti.

Moderate

★★★**Cavour**, Piazza Garibaldi 32, **t** 081 283 122, *www.hotelcavournapoli.it*. A decent, well-run hotel in an otherwise desperate area. The top-floor suites, with their ample terraces and good views over Vesuvius, are a respite from the bustle below. Rooms are nicely decorated in the Liberty style, and bathrooms are good for an area where plumbing hasn't been overhauled since the Greeks. The restaurant has 2 Michelin *fourchettes*.

★★★**Rex**, Via Palepoli 12, **t** 081 764 9389, *www.hotel-rex.it*. Simple rooms with bare 1970s-style furnishings and no public areas (breakfast is brought to your room), in the Santa Lucia district near Piazza del Plebiscito.

★★**Albergo Sansevero**, Via S.M. di Costantinpoli 101, **t** 081 210 907, *www.albergosansevero.it*. A real find, tucked inside elegant *palazzo* near the archaeological museum. It is quiet and well furnished, with friendly staff. The family has 2 other hotels in the same price range in historic *palazzi* close: the **Soggiorno Sansevero**, Piazza San Domenico Maggiore 9, **t** 081 551 5742, and **Albergo Sansevero Degas**, Calata Trinità Maggiore 53, **t** 081 551 1276.

★★**Ausonia**, Via Caracciolo 11, **t** 081 682 278/664 536. A clean, comfortable *pensione* within a *palazzo*, with an interior courtyard and 20 rooms with a nautical theme. Rooms are well appointed, with TV and video recorder (tapes are also available in English). A quiet option in the Mergellina area.

★**Duomo**, Via Duomo 228, **t** 081 265 988. A *pensione* with a family feel and 12 clean and spacious rooms with bathrooms.

Cheap

Naples has a dearth of pleasant budget hotels; the cheap places around Stazione Centrale and Piazza Garibaldi are invariably substandard, and Via Mezzocannone, south of Spaccanapoli, is also a little grotty – and it borders the university, so rooms are often filled with students.

★★**Fontane al Mare**, Via N. Tommaseo 14, **t** 081 764 3811. Twenty-one rooms on the top 2 floors of an old *palazzo* next to the Chiaia gardens (you need 10c coins for the lift). The rooms without bathroom have a great sea view and are better value. It's popular with the local *carabinieri* college, so book ahead.

★**Margherita**, Via Cimerosa 29, **t** 081 556 7044/ 578 2852. Twenty basic but clean rooms on the 5th floor of a *palazzo* in a safe area high on Vomero hill (you need 5c coins for the lift), with 6 shared bathrooms. It is next door to the Funicolare Centrale, which takes you down to the Via Toledo in 10mins.

Hotel Ginevra, Via Genova 116, **t** 081 554 1757, or **t** (0039) 333 281 3802 (information in English), *www.hotelginevra.it*. A clean, friendly, modernized hotel in the least seedy corner of Piazza Garibaldi, with double en suite rooms with phone and TV.

Soggiorno Imperia, Piazza Miraglia 386, **t** 081 459 347. A friendly, wonderfully located option just around the corner from Piazza Bellini, with 9 rooms; No.8 is en suite with a TV; the others share 2 bathrooms (No.5 and No.6 have wonderful views). It's on the 5th floor without a lift.

Ostello Mergellina, Salita della Grotta 23, **t** 081 761 2346. Naples' youth hostel, near the Mergellina metro station.

Eating Out

Neapolitan cuisine is simple: a favourite dish is *spaghetti alle vongole*, and even in some of the swankier places you will see Neapolitan *cucina povera* sneaking onto the menu, in the form of *pasta e fagioli* and the like. There are few bad restaurants or tourist traps, and many excellent family-run *trattorie* or *pizzerie*.

Naples has some of the cheapest restaurants in Italy – they cheat on their taxes. Others can be alarmingly expensive, especially for fish. Restaurants in all price ranges are spread pretty evenly around town. For romantic meals, try **Borgo Marinara** beside the Castel dell'Ovo, where the whole marina is set aside for dining, or **Mergellina**. Nearer the old centre is where you'll find character; pokey streets with pokey restaurants with chefs who pop over to local street stalls for their veg.

Some of the cheapest and homeliest places are on or around **Via Speranzella**, a block west of Via Toledo in the Tavoliere, where few tourists go. Most restaurants around Piazza Garibaldi and the station are best avoided, but this area, and Piazza Mercato, is an open bazaar where you can snack from bars and stalls on slices of pizza, heavy *arancini* and the flaky pastries called *sfogliatelle*.

For authentic Naples **pizza**, look for the Neapolitan pizza oven – a built-in, bell-shaped affair made of stone with a broad, clean tile floor. The fire is at the back, nice and close to the pizza, not hidden underneath.

Watch out for house **wines**: in cheaper places this is likely to be Gragnano from nearby Monte Faito – rough and detestable. On the other hand, you can find some real surprises from Campania: a dry white called Greco di Tufo; Taurasi, a distinguished red; and Falerno, a descendant of the ancient Falernian that Latin poets never tired of praising.

Very Expensive

La Cantinella, Via Nazario Sauro 23, **t** 081 764 8684. *The* place to be seen, near the Castel dell'Ovo on the esplanade. *Linguine Santa Lucia*, made with home-made pasta, octopus, squid, prawns, clams and baby tomatoes, takes some beating, as does the risotto. The atmosphere is smart but relaxed, service welcoming and friendly. *Closed Sun*.

Da Cicciotto, Calata Ponticello a Marechiaro 32, Posillipo, **t** 081 575 1165. A romantically set fish place along from Mergellina, with the temple of Fortuna as a backdrop. There is no fixed menu – the waiter reels off what's on offer each day – but a typical meal may consist of *mozzarella di bufala* accompanying huge quantities of mixed grilled or fried seafood *antipasti*, followed by lobster. Book ahead.

Dora, Via Ferdinando Palasciano 30 (off Riviera di Chiaia), **t** 081 680 519. A cosy and convivial institution with a fish-only menu; the grilled prawns are to die for. Booking advised. *Closed Sun.*

Expensive

La Bersagliera, Borgo Marinara 10, **t** 081 764 6016. An elegant 1900s restaurant in an excellent location, with delicious fish and good wines. *Closed Tues.*

Ciro, Borgo Marinara, **t** 081 552 4072. A smart place beneath the Castel dell'Ovo, famous for its *pasta e fagioli* and other humble pasta dishes. *Closed Mon.*

Don Salvatore, Via Mergellina 5, **t** 081 681 817. A place with a reputation for its fine local fare, accompanied by some of the area's best wines. There are set menus for those who want an introduction to Naples' best cuisine, and pizza for those who want to keep the bill down. *Closed Weds.*

Jap-One, Via Santa Maria Cappella Vecchia 30, **t** 081 764 6667. A trendy sushi restaurant at the end of a narrow but safe road beside Feltrinelli at Piazza dei Martiri. Book ahead. *Closed lunchtimes, Mon and Aug.*

Mimì alla Ferrovia, Via Alfonso d'Aragona 19, **t** 081 553 8525. A popular place with the local media posse, serving honest dishes based on recipes handed down for generations, including *pasta e ceci*, a khaki soup of flat pasta and chick peas. *Closed Sun.*

La Sacrestia, Via Orazio 116, **t** 081 761 1051. A temple of local gastronomy overlooking the Bay from the heights at Mergellina, near San Gioacchino funicular station. Try *risotto con neonati di seppietta* (risotto with baby squid). *Closed Sun eve, Mon lunch and Aug.*

Moderate

La Cantina di Triunfo, Riviera di Chiaia 64, **t** 081 668 101. A small restaurant on the north of Piazza della Repubblica that raises *cucina povera* to an art form with its soups, *polpette di baccalà* (salt cod balls, fried or served in a tomato sauce) and mouthwatering pasta. Desserts are good, too – try *crostata d'arance e mandorle* (orange and almond tart). The wine list is exceptional, and there are 80 types of grappa, many home-made. Be sure to book. *Closed Sun.*

Taverna e Zi Carmela, Via Niccolò Tommaseo 11/12, **t** 081 764 3581. A seafood specialist on the Via Partenope esplanade. *Closed Sun.*

Cheap

Bellini, Via Santa Maria di Costantinopoli 80, **t** 081 459 774. A trattoria just beyond the Port'Alba, with good pizza and pasta dishes. Try *linguine al cartoccio (*oven-baked seafood pasta), or *pesce alla griglia*. *Closed Sun.*

Brandi, Salita Sant'Anna di Palazzo 1/2, **t** 081 416 928. A lively pizzeria off Via Chiaia that claims to have invented the *margherita*, Naples' most famous pizza (mozzarella, tomatoes and fresh basil) in honour of the 19th-century queen whose favourite dish it apparently was. The seafood option includes octopus cooked with their ink sacs intact.

Castel Nuovo, Piazza Francese 42, **t** 081 551 5524. A restaurant popular with staff from the nearby Navale university, and handy for the ferry to Capri (it's situated where Piazza Municipio meets Molo Beverello). The well-prepared pasta dishes include *spaghetti alle cozze*, and *rigatoni* with squash and prawns, and there are good pizzas.

Da Michele, Via Sersale 1, **t** 081 553 9204. A good place for a quick snack, one of the few where you'll see Neapolitans queuing. The superb giant pizzas come in 2 varieties: *margherita* and *marinara*.

Lombardi a Santa Chiara, Via Benedetto Croce 59, **t** 081 552 0780. A busy, noisy, friendly restaurant off Piazza del Gesù Nuovo, offering great pizza, *antipasti* of fried zucchini, baby mozzarella and artichokes, and great *bucatini al pomodoro*. Book ahead or be prepared to wait. *Closed Sun.*

Da Pietro, Via Luculliana 27. A little place with a handful of tables and no menu, but a prime position on the Borgo Marinara by the Castel dell'Ovo. The tasty fare is mainly seafood.

Pizzeria Port'Alba, Via Port'Alba 18, **t** 081 459 713. A little place in the historic centre, set up in 1830 and serving excellent pizzas and good full dinners, including a vast *linguine al cartoccio*. You can sit outside, under the Port'Alba, or inside (upstairs is cosier).

Trattoria Nennella, Vico Lungo Teatro Nuovo 103–105. An amazing bargain in the Quartieri Spagnuoli, offering true Naples food and spirit in a simple setting. *Closed Sun.*

Cafés and *Gelaterie*

Naples is hailed for its locally roasted coffee, such as Moreno, Passalacqua and Tico. The best (and cheapest) coffee is found in stand-up places, where you pay at the till, bang the receipt and a tip down on the bar and bark your order. If you like it without sugar, ask for a *caffè amaro*. Good stand-up bars include **Caffè del Professore** (Corso Novara opposite the station), **Bar Nilo** on Spaccanapoli (Via San Biagi dei Librai 129) and **Caffè Roma** (Via Toledo 325).

Of the crop of ornate but often faded 19th-century *gran caffè* by the Galleria and Piazza del Plebiscito, the best is **Gambrinus**, Piazza Trieste e Trento, **t** 081 417 582. For people-watching, try **La Caffetteria** (Piazza Vanvitelli 10, Vomero, and Piazza dei Martiri 30, Chiaia) and **Cafè San Domenico** (Piazza San Domenico di Maggiore).

Scimmia, Piazza della Carità 4, just off Via Toledo near Spaccanapoli, has long been regarded as one of the city's best *gelaterie*; also try **La Tortiera** (Via Filangieri 75 in Chiaia) and **Soave** (Via Scarlatti in Vomero).

For *sfogliatelle*, **Scaturchio** (Piazza San Domenico Maggiore) is acclaimed as the best *pasticceria* in Naples.

Entertainment and Nightlife

For concerts, shows and other events, see *Il Mattino* newspaper, the excellent monthly *Qui Napoli*, free from tourist offices and some hotels,and daily freesheets *Metro* and *Leggo*.

Opera, Classical Music and Theatre

Tickets for operas at **San Carlo** (**t** 081 797 2331/2412) are hard to come by and pricey; hotels may be able to get them most easily. You may have more luck catching a concert at the **Auditorium RAI-TV**, Via Guglielmo Marconi (Fuorigrotta), **t** 081 725 1111; **Conservatorio San Pietro a Maiella**, Via San Pietro a Maiella, **t** 081 564 4411; or **Associazione Alessandro Scarlatti**, Piazza dei Martiri 58, **t** 081 409 494. City churches also put on concerts, often free. Look for street billboards with details of events.

Tickets for many events are sold at the **Box Office**, Galleria Umberto I 15–16, **t** 081 551 9188, and **Concerteria**, Via Schipa 23, **t** 081 761 1221.

The best theatres are the **Politeama**, Via Monte di Dio, **t** 081 764 5016; **Cilea**, Via S. Domenico, **t** 081 714 3110; **Bracco**, Via Tarsia 40, **t** 081 564 5323; and **Sannazzaro**, Via Chiaia 157, **t** 081 411 723.

Clubs, Bars and Discos

Some areas are best avoided after midnight, notably the Forcella–Piazza Garibaldi area near the station and the Quartieri Spagnuoli, the narrow sidestreets off Via Toledo.

Neapolitans are nightowls; many don't even think about going out to dinner until 10pm. For late-night **bars**, Piazza Bellini, a block north of Santa Chiara in the old town, is where the young and trendy come to see and be seen; try to get a table at **Intra Moenia**, the literary café-cum-publishing house, **t** 081 200 720. Bars at Mergellina and on the Borgo Marinara stay open until 2am and are lively in summer, and Via Martucci, just off Piazza Amedeo in Chiaia, is good for a bar crawl.

A list of **nightclubs** can be found in *Qui Napoli*. It's worth checking with locals where the current most popular haunts are, but Borgo Marinara is generally a good spot. Very few places open during the week. You will rarely pay more €15 to get in, including a free drink; women often get in for less or for free. Things never kick off until after midnight.

Ferdinandstrasse, Piazza Porta Nova 8, **t** 081 207 390. A gay disco-bar, very crowded on Sun.

Madison Street, Via Sgambati 47, **t** 081 546 6566. Naples' biggest club, attracting an affluent young crowd with its theme nights and Sat gay nights.

La Mela, Via dei Mille 41, **t** 081 413 881. A spot beloved by the young and beautiful.

My Way, Via Cappella Vecchia 30/c, **t** 081 764 4735. A popular long-standing nightspot.

Otto Jazz Club, Piazzetta Cariati 32, **t** 081 552 4373. A place hosting a brand of jazz that looks for inspiration as much to Neapolitan folk songs as to New Orleans. It also serves pasta and light meals, and has a well-stocked bar offering 200 cocktails. It's in a hard area, so get a taxi home. *Closed Mon–Weds.*

Velvet, Via Cisterna dell'Olio, old town. An alternative club with a rougher edge.

Virgilio Sporting Club, Via Tito Lucrezio Caro 6, **t** 081 769 5261. A sophisticated club in its own park on Posillipo hill, with tables outside in fine weather. *Closed Mon–Thurs.*

If the accounts of long-ago travellers are to be believed, Naples has always been like this. Too much sunshine, and living under such a large and ill-mannered volcano, must contribute much to the effect. It would be somewhat harder to explain some of Naples' ancient distinctions. First and foremost, this is Italy's city of philosophers – its greatest, Giambattista Vico, was a Neapolitan, and others, such as St Thomas Aquinas and Benedetto Croce, spent much of their time here. Naples can also claim to be first in music: among native composers are Gesualdo, Domenico Scarlatti and Leoncavallo, and Neapolitans claim that their conservatory is the oldest in Europe. Even today, members of the opera company at San Carlo look down on their colleagues at Milan's La Scala as a band of promising upstarts who could stand to take their jobs a little more seriously. Neapolitan popular song, expressive and intense, is an unchained Italian stereotype; the Napoletani maintain its traditions as jealously as they do their impenetrable dialect – flavoured with Arabic and Spanish galore, and one of the most widely spoken and robust in modern Italy.

Along with these, the aural ambience takes in plenty of fireworks, slamming doors, impromptu arias, screams, ambulance sirens and howling cats. The only thing subtle about Naples is its charm, and the city may win your heart at the same time as it is deranging your senses.

History

Naples' rise to become the metropolis of Campania was largely the result of the lucky elimination of her rivals over centuries. Capua, *Cumae* and Benevento rose and fell, and *Pompeii* and *Herculaneum* disappeared under volcanic ash, but fortune has always seemed to protect Naples from the really big disasters. As a Greek colony founded by Cumae in 750 BC, the city began with the name *Neapolis* ('New City'), and prospered moderately throughout the periods of Greek, Samnite and Roman rule. Belisarius, Justinian's famous general, seized the region for Byzantium in 536 after invasions by the Goths and Vandals, but a duke of Naples declared the city independent in 763, acknowledging only the authority of the pope.

The chronicles are understandably slim for this period; early medieval Naples offers us more in the way of fairy tales than facts. Many of its early legends deal with none other than the poet Virgil. Somehow, folklore during the Dark Ages had transformed the greatest Latin poet into Master Virgil, a mighty magician who was given credit for many of the inexplicable engineering feats of the ancient Romans. Naples claimed him for its founder, and its legends told of how he built the Castel dell'Ovo, balancing it on an egg at the bottom of the harbour. Master Virgil also built a talking statue that warned the city of enemies, earthquakes or plagues, and medieval chroniclers mention the bronze horses and bronze fly that he built over two of the city's gates, still to be seen then, and said to be magical charms on which the city's fortunes depended.

Naples lost its independence to the Normans in 1139, later passing under the rule of the Hohenstaufen emperors along with the rest of southern Italy. Charles of Anjou took over in 1266, and lopped off the head of the last Hohenstaufen, Conradin, in what is now Naples' Piazza del Mercato.

Under the Angevins, Naples assumed the status of a capital for the first time. The Angevin kings of Naples, however, did little to develop their new realm, expending most of their energy in futile attempts to recapture Sicily, lost to them after the Sicilian Vespers revolution of 1282. After their line expired in 1435 with the death of Giovanni II, the kingdom fell to Alfonso V of Aragon – a fateful event that provided Spain's first foothold on the Italian mainland.

Habsburgs and Bourbons

Aragonese rule seemed promising at first, under the enlightened Alfonso. Later it became clear that the Spaniards were mainly interested in milking Italy for taxes with which to finance further conquests. The city itself, as the seat of the viceregal court, prospered greatly; by 1600 its population of 280,000 made it the largest city on the Med. The long period of Spanish control did much to give Naples its distinct character, especially in the 17th and 18th centuries, when the city participated almost joyfully in the decadence and decay of the Spanish Empire. This period saw the construction of the scores of frilly, gloomy Baroque churches, now half-abandoned, that add so much to the Neapolitan scene. In manners especially, the imperial Spanish influence was felt. 'Nothing', in the words of one observer, 'is cheaper here than human life.'

In 1707, during the War of the Spanish Succession, Naples passed under the rule of Archduke Charles of Austria. Prince Charles of Bourbon snatched it away from him in 1734, and for the next century and a half mouldering, picturesque Naples made the perfect backdrop for the rococo shenanigans of the new Bourbon kingdom. The new rulers were little improvement over the Spaniards, but immigrants from all over the south poured in, chasing the thousands of ducats dropped by a free-spending court. Naples became the most densely populated city in Europe (a distinction it still holds today); crime and epidemics became widespread.

Nevertheless, this was the Naples that attracted 18th- and 19th-century aesthetes doing the Grand Tour. Goethe flirted with contessas here, while English poets flirted with dread diseases and Lord Nelson made eyes at Lady Hamilton. The Neapolitans are frank about it: Naples at the time was the easiest place in Europe to find sex, and everyone knew it, saving Goethe and the rest the trouble of mentioning the subject in their travel accounts and letters home.

The Bourbon restoration after Napoleon's occupation meant a return of political decadence and reaction. Neapolitans rebelled in 1821 and forced Ferdinand I to grant a charter, though he soon took it back. Still, the city was generally happy under the light Bourbon rule. And neither Naples nor its rulers were as backward as their reputation had it: under the last Bourbons Naples built Italy's first railroad and first steamship.

Garibaldi's army entered Naples in February 1861. As the new Italy's biggest basket case, the city has since received considerable assistance with its planning and social problems, but not nearly enough to make up for the centuries of neglect. The Second World War didn't help: for four days in late September 1944 the city staged a heroic and successful revolt against the Germans, the 'Quattro Giornate'; more damage was done by Allied bombing; and the retreating Nazis rounded off the destruction by destroying the city's port and utilities as they left.

While the post-war period saw considerable rebuilding, it also brought fresh calamity. Illegal and speculative building projects grabbed most of the crowded city's free space (you'll notice the almost total absence of parks), and turned the fringe areas and much of the once-beautiful Bay of Naples shore into a nightmare of human detritus.

In the post-war era organized crime ran the city directly, under the shadowy mayor Achille Lauro (1950–8) or in partnership with the major parties. In the political turmoil of the 1990s, with the collapse of the old parties, Naples saw a big rise in support for both the Communists and the neo-Fascist MSI. Crime interests countered attempts at reform with political obstruction and, occasionally, violence. Nevertheless, much has been accomplished: in 1993 the state dissolved Naples' crooked government; and in mayoral elections the next year Communist reformer Antonio Bassolino narrowly beat Alessandra Mussolini, Benito's granddaughter (and Sophia Loren's niece). Bassolino was overwhelmingly re-elected for a second term in 1998, and his two terms saw the worst of the ghettos around the port demolished, while tourist trails across Spaccanapoli were encouraged, and long-closed churches and sites were reopened. The grand Piazza del Plebiscito, long choked by traffic and seemingly fated to remain the city's car park, was emptied and cleaned up.

Most spectacularly, Naples planned and built the Centro Direzionale, a modernistic skyscraper development on the lines of Paris's La Défense. In spite of a few hiccups, most notably when the new palace of justice was mysteriously burnt to the ground (no prizes for guessing by whom), the project is a striking new centre for the regional economy. Though the excitement has fizzled out – Camorra families are still collecting extortion money and bombing each other in the middle of town, and Bassolino, accused of addressing only the outer layer of Naples' problems rather than tackling major issues, lost his halo – the left is holding on. Bassolino's successor, Rosa Iervolina Russo, still occupies the Municipio and has become a politician of national stature, while Bassolino is President of the Campania regional council.

But while things are looking up, you may still find discussions of the city's problems in the press conducted in apocalyptic tones – leave room for exaggeration, because the Napoletani probably couldn't enjoy life without a permanent state of crisis.

The City

Piazza del Plebiscito and the Palazzo Reale

The immense **Piazza del Plebiscito**, the centre of modern Naples, has been rescued and restored to the city – children now come here to kick a football under the eyes of adoring parents, and shows staged here by the city for the benefit of national TV have forced some northern Italians to admit that Naples may not be all bad after all. The huge domed church embracing the piazza in its curving colonnades is **San Francesco di Paola**. King Ferdinand IV, after the British restored him to power in 1815, vowed to construct it; the classical portico and great dome were modelled after Rome's Pantheon. There's little to see inside; anyone with an understanding of Naples won't be surprised to find the colonnades given over to light manufacturing and warehouse space.

Across the square rises the equally imposing bulk of the **Palazzo Reale** or Royal Palace (***t*** *081 580 8111; open Thurs–Tues 9–8; adm*). Begun by the Spanish viceroys in 1600, this was expanded by the Bourbons and finished by the kings of Italy. Umberto I added the eight giant figures on the façade, representing the eight houses that have ruled at Naples. It seems the 19th-century sculptors had trouble taking some of them seriously; note the preposterous figures of Charles of Anjou, whom the Neapolitans never liked, and Vittorio Emanuele II, the latter probably an accurate portrayal. There are Ruritanian stone sentry boxes and stone peacocks in the courtyard to recall the Bourbons.

A number of rooms inside have been restored and can be visited, including a grand staircase, a theatre and several chambers in the 18th-century style. The theatre saw the premières of many works of Alessandro Scarlatti. In the Palatine chapel there is a lovely 1674 altar of semi-precious stone and an outstanding 18th-century crib or *presepio* – a handful of its 210 figures are by master sculptor Sammartino.

The restored roof garden offers wonderful views over the Bay, while the rear of the palace, now home to Naples' important **Biblioteca Nazionale**, faces a pretty, little-visited garden, across from the Castel Nuovo, where you can eat a pizza in tranquillity.

Teatro San Carlo and Galleria Umberto I

The Bourbons were opera buffs and built Italy's largest opera house, the **Teatro San Carlo**, next to their palace. Begun in 1737 (making it older than La Scala in Milan), this was sumptuously restored after a fire in 1816, at a time when Naples was the capital of opera. So important was the theatre to the people of Naples that King Ferdinand made sure the workmen got the job done in record time – 300 days. Today San Carlo is still among the world's most prestigious opera houses (the Neapolitans, of course, place it first). Each season at least one lesser-known Neapolitan opera is performed. Tickets are as expensive as opera anywhere – they can cost more than €100 on an opening night. Brief weekend tours (***t*** *081 797 2331*) cost considerably less.

Opposite the San Carlo is the grandest interior in southern Italy, that of the **Galleria Umberto I**. This great glass-roofed arcade, perhaps the largest in the world, was begun in 1887, nine years after the Galleria Vittorio Emanuele in Milan. The arcade is cross shaped, with a pretty mosaic of the zodiac on the floor at the centre, and its arching dome is 184ft tall. The complex covers an entire block; tucked in the corner facing Piazza Trieste e Trento is the old Bourbon court church, **San Ferdinando**, with a wild Baroque interior in the manner of Cosimo Fanzago.

Castel Nuovo

t *081 795 2003; open Sat 9–1.30, Sun–Fri 9–7; adm.*

The port of Naples has been protected by this odd, beautiful castle, looming over the harbour behind the Palazzo Reale and San Carlo, for some 700 years now. Charles of Anjou built it in 1279; many Neapolitans still call it by the curious name of Maschio Angioino ('the Angevin Boy'). Most of what you see today, however, including the eccentric, ponderous round towers, is the work of Guillermo Sagrera, the great Catalan architect who built the famous Exchange in Palma de Mallorca.

The conquering Aragonese hired the finest sculptors from all over Italy to build Alfonso's Triumphal Arch, a masterpiece of Renaissance sculpture and design inspired by the triumphal arches of the ancient Romans, between two of these towers at the entrance. The symbolism, as in the Roman arches, may be a little confusing: the figure at the top is Saint Michael; below him are a matched pair of sea gods, and, further down, allegorical virtues and relief panels portray Alfonso's victories and wise governance.

The castle currently houses parts of the city administration and various cultural societies. If you come during office hours, someone will probably show you the **Sala dei Baroni**, where the city council meets, which has a cupola with an unusual Moorish vaulting – an eight-pointed star made of interlocking arches. King Ferrante used this as his dining hall: it takes its name from the evening he invited a score of the kingdom's leading barons to a ball, then arrested the lot. There are also **two museums**: one, in the Gothic **Cappella Palatina** next to the council hall, contains some lovely 14th- and 15th-century frescoes; the other, in the **south wing**, has paintings and a collection of silver and bronzes from the 15th century to the present.

Castel dell'Ovo

The hill called **Pizzofalcone** rises directly behind Piazza del Plebiscito. This was the site of *Parthenope*, the Greek town that antedated Neapolis and was eventually swallowed up by it (though Neapolitans still like to refer to themselves as 'Parthenopeans'). Parthenope had a little harbour, formed by an island that is mainly covered by the strangely shaped fortress of the Castel dell'Ovo (***t** 081 246 4334*) – the one Master Virgil is said to have built balanced on an egg (hence the name). Most of it was really built by Frederick II, and expanded by the Angevins. It holds regular art exhibitions and conferences. If you ask, you should be able to go in and have a look round: the views across the Bay are wonderful.

The island contained the villa of Roman general and philosopher Lucullus, victor over Mithridates in the Pontic Wars; Lucullus curried favour with the people by throwing his sumptuous gardens, and famous library, open to the public. In the 5th century AD the villa became a home in exile for Romulus Augustulus, last of the Western Roman emperors. The Goths spared him only because of his youth and simple-mindedness, and pensioned him off here.

Squeezed onto the rest of the island below the castle, **Borgo Marinara** is a small harbour flanked by cafés and restaurants. In the evenings, it's a safe and pleasant area, full of romancing couples, fortune-tellers and buskers.

Via Toledo

From the landward side of Piazza del Plebiscito and the palace, Naples' most imposing street, Via Toledo, runs northwards past the Galleria Umberto I through Piazza Carità (*marked on some maps as Piazza San d'Aquisto*). The name of the street commemorates its builder, Don Pedro de Toledo, Spanish viceroy at the beginning of the 16th century, and a great benefactor of Naples. Stendhal, in 1817, called this 'the most populous and gayest street in the world'; now pedestrianized, it is still the city's main business and shopping street, eventually leading up to Capodimonte and the northern suburbs. Don Pedro's elegant Renaissance tomb, among others, can be seen in little **San Giacomo degli Spagnuoli**, now swallowed up by the 19th-century **Palazzo Municipale** (*marked on some maps as Palazzo San Giacomo*) complex, originally home to the Bourbon royal bureaucracy.

Right of Via Toledo, Naples' half-crumbling, half-modern business centre contains a few buildings worth a look. The **Palazzo Gravina** on Via Monteoliveto is a fine palace in the northern Renaissance style, built in 1513–49. It now houses Naples university's faculty of architecture. Almost directly across the street, the church of **Sant'Anna dei Lombardi** (*marked on some maps as Chiesa di Monteoliveto; open Tues–Thurs and Sat 8.30–12.30*) is a little treasure house of late Renaissance sculpture and painting, with tombs and altars in the chapels by southern artists such Giovanni da Nola and Antonio Rossellino, as well as some frescoes by Vasari.

After passing Spaccanapoli, Via Toledo continues northwards to **Piazza Dante**, one of the most delightful and animated corners of the city.

The Spacca

The district east of Via Toledo is called after the familiar name of its main street: *Spaccanapoli* means 'Split-Naples', and that is what this long, narrow thoroughfare has done for the last 2,600 years. On the map it changes its name with alarming frequency – Via Benedetto Croce and Via San Biagio dei Librai are two of the most prominent sections – but in Roman times you would have found it by asking for the Decumanus Inferior, the second east–west street in planned Roman cities.

No large city has maintained its Roman street plan as completely as Naples (the Greeks laid out these streets, but the Romans learned their planning from them), and it is easier to imagine the atmosphere of a big ancient city here than in Rome, or even in Pompeii. The narrow, straight streets and tall *insulae* can't have changed much; only the forum and temples are missing.

This is the heart of old Naples – and what a street it is, lined with grocery barrows, scholarly bookshops, and shops selling old violins, plaster saints, pizza or used clothes pegs. Not so long ago, the Spacca was a Felliniesque stage for arch-Neapolitan characters, manic motorists; and long alleys of impossibly tall tenements with clothes lines swelling bravely in the breeze. This is the Naples that was the most densely packed city in Europe, courtesy of a 1555 Spanish decree that forbade building outside the walls. Increasing prosperity is thinning it out now; you won't see nearly as many clothes lines. What's more, the city has banished the cars, and made fair headway in fixing up the scores of historic churches and palaces. The Spacca that had decayed to a picturesque slum is now, slowly, regaining its place as Naples' proud *centro storico*.

Piazza del Gesù Nuovo

Your introduction to the Spacca, off Via Toledo, is the most characteristic of Naples' squares, decorated by the gaudiest and most random of the city's monuments, the **Guglia dell'Immacolata** – a *guglia* (pinnacle) is a kind of rococo obelisk, dripping with frills, saints and putti.

The unsightly and unfinished façade behind the Guglia, covered with pyramidal extrusions in dark basalt, belongs to the church of **Gesù Nuovo**. As strange as it is, this façade, which was originally part of a late 15th-century palace, has become one of the landmarks of Naples. The interior is typically lavish Neapolitan Baroque, gloriously overdone in acres of coloured marbles and frescoes, some by Solimena. One of his best works is here, above the main door inside. Dating from 1725, it depicts three angels driving the Syrian magician Eliodorus out of the Temple of Jerusalem. In the second chapel on the right you is a bronze statue of Naples' newest saint, Saint Giuseppe Moscati, a doctor who lectured at Naples university and otherwise devoted himself to caring for the poor. He died in 1927.

Chiesa di Santa Chiara

This church, just across the piazza, dates from the early 14th century. It once had a Baroque interior as good as the Gesù's, but Allied bombers remodelled it to suit modern tastes in 1943, and only a few of the original Angevin tombs have survived. To get some idea of what the interior must have been like, stop in and see the restored **Majolica cloister**, which is nothing less than the loveliest and most peaceful spot in Naples – especially in contrast to the neighbourhood outside. It can be visited as part of the **Complesso di Santa Chiara** (***t*** *081 797 1256; open Mon–Sat 9.30–1 and 2.30–5.30, Sun and hols 9.30–1; adm*), which includes a museum housing the church treasures, marbles and an area of archaeological excavations from the Roman period. So much in Naples shows the Spanish influence (such as the use of the title 'Don', now largely limited to Camorra bosses), and here someone in the 1740s transplanted the Andalucían love of pictures done in painted *azulejo* tiles, turning a simple monkish cloister into a little fairyland of gaily coloured arbours, benches and columns, shaded by orange and lemon trees (the only trees in the whole district).

During the restoration of a vestibule off the cloister (reached via the back of the church), it was discovered that the indifferent 17th-century frescoes hid some earlier, highly original paintings of the Last Judgement. Now uncovered and restored, they reveal an inspired 16th-century vision of the event in a style utterly unlike the slick virtuosity of the time, with plenty of novel tortures for the damned, and angels welcoming cute naked nuns among the elect.

Piazza San Domenico and Around

A few streets further down Via Benedetto Croce, Piazza San Domenico has monuments from Naples' three most creative periods. **San Domenico Maggiore**, built in 1283–1324, was the Dominican church in Naples; St Thomas Aquinas lived in the adjacent monastery. Later this became the favourite church of the Spanish, and it contains some interesting Renaissance funerary monuments. A better one, however, lies across the square in the church of **Sant'Angelo a Nilo** – the tomb of Cardinal Brancaccio, designed by Michelozzo, with a relief of the Assumption of the Virgin by Donatello (the two artists had collaborated before, on the baptistry in Siena). The second of the area's three Baroque pinnacles decorates the piazza, the **Guglia di San Domenico**, built after a plague in 1650.

Near San Domenico, a block south of the Spacca, is Naples' **university**, one of Europe's oldest and most distinguished. The Emperor Frederick II founded it in 1224, as a 'Ghibelline' university to counter the pope's 'Guelph' (*see* **Historical Terms**, p.974) university at Bologna, as well as to provide scholars, and train officials, for the new state he was trying to build. It still occupies its ancient, overcrowded quarters around Via Mezzocannone. Four little **museums** (of mineralogy, zoology, anthropology and palaeontology) are hidden behind the university walls at Via Mezzacannone 8 (***t** 081 253 5205; open Mon 9–1.30 and 3–5, Tues–Sun 9–1, closed Aug*).

Sansevero Chapel

***t** 081 551 8470; open Mon–Fri 10–7, until 5 in winter; Sat and Sun 10–1.30; adm.*

Just around the corner from Piazza San Domenico, on Via Francesco de Sanctis, inspect Neapolitan Rococo at its queerest in the Sansevero Chapel. Prince Raimondo di Sangro (*b.* 1701) was responsible for the final form of this, his family's private chapel. He was a strange bird, a sort of aristocratic dilettante mystic, and there is supposedly a grand allegorical scheme behind the arrangement of the sculptures and frescoes he commissioned, but a work like this, though only 200 years old, seems as foreign to our modern understanding as a Mayan temple. The sculptures, by little-known Naples artists such as Giuseppe Sammartino and Antonio Corradini, are inscrutable allegories in themselves, often executed with a breathtakingly showy virtuosity. Francesco Queirolo's *Il Disinganno* ('Disillusion') is an extreme case – a fishing net, and the pages of a book, carved out of marble. There are a dozen or so of these large sculptural groups under the crazy heavenly vortex of the ceiling fresco by Francesco Mario Russo.

Down in the crypt are two complete human cardiovascular systems, removed and preserved by Prince Raimondo in the course of his alchemical experiments.

Sansevero to the Duomo

Continue east on the Spaccanapoli (now Via San Biagio dei Librai); just around the corner on Via San Gregorio is **San Gregorio Armeno** church, with another gaudy Baroque interior. If the gilding and the painting by Luca Giordano of the Arrival of Saint Basilio are not your cup of tea, try the cloister (*open daily 9.30–noon*), an oasis of tranquillity and a step back to the 16th century. Since the 1500s it has served the convent of Benedictine nuns. At its centre is a fountain sculpted in 1733 and depicting Christ meeting the Samaritan woman. On your way out, note the revolving drums used for communicating with the outside world before 1922, when the monastic order was closed off from the profane. A caustic note by the nuns on one of them dismisses the popular misconception that they were for abandoned newborn babies.

This street and others around it have become Naples' famous **Christmas Market**, where everyone comes to buy figurines of the Holy Family, the Three Kings and all the other accessories required for their Christmas *presepi*, or manger scenes – one of the most devotedly followed of local traditions. For several weeks leading up to Christmas, hundreds of stands fill up the neighbourhood's narrow streets; the rest of the year, it's the place to find Neapolitan souvenirs.

A little further north up Via San Gregorio is late 13th-century **San Lorenzo Maggiore** (*open Mon–Sat 9–5, Sun and hols 9.30–1.30*), one of Naples' finest medieval churches; Petrarch lived for a while in the adjacent monastery. Excavations have uncovered extensive Greek and Roman remains on the site; entering through the cloister, where the base of a Roman *macellum* (market place) is being excavated, head down the stairs at the back to see this fascinating piece of subterranean Naples.

San Paolo, across the street, isn't much to see now; before an earthquake wrecked it in the 17th century, its façade was the portico of an ancient Roman temple to Castor and Pollux. Andrea Palladio studied it closely and it provided some of the inspiration for his classical villas and churches in the Veneto.

After Spaccanapoli, **Via dei Tribunali** has been the busiest street in old Naples since it was the Roman Decumanus Major. The arcades that line it in places, a sort of continuous covered market, are 1,000 years old or more. Here, the **Girolamini** church (*open daily 9.30–1*) has frescoes by Luca Giordano, paintings by Ribera and Guido Reni, among others, and the modest tomb of philosopher Giambattista Vico. Northwest of the Girolamini, around **Via Anticaglia**, are a few crooked streets – the only ones in old Naples that do not stick to the rectilinear Roman plan. These follow the outline of the **Roman theatre**, much of which still survives, hidden among the tenements; a few arches are all that is visible from the street.

Duomo

Wide Via Duomo is a breath of fresh air in this crowded district – which is exactly what the city intended when they ploughed it through Old Naples after the cholera epidemic of 1884. The Duomo itself is another fine medieval building, though hidden behind an awful pseudo-Gothic façade pasted on in 1905. The best things are inside: the Renaissance **Cappella Minùtolo**, the tomb of Charles of Anjou and the **Cappella San Gennaro** (of Il Tesoro), glittering with the gold and silver of the cathedral treasure, and with frescoes by Domenichino and Lanfranco.

The **Basilica Santa Restituta**, a sizeable church, is tacked on to the side of the Duomo. Its columns are thought to be from the temple of Apollo that once occupied the site. Begun in 324, though often rebuilt, this is the oldest building in Naples. The ceiling frescoes are by Luca Giordano. Just off the basilica, the 5th-century **baptistry** contains a good Byzantine-style mosaic by 14th-century artist Lello di Roma; the baptismal font probably comes from an ancient temple of Dionysus. From Santa Restituta's chapel you can access a collection of archaeological remains dating from the Greeks to the Middle Ages (*open Mon–Sat 9–12 and 4.30–7, Sun and hols 9–12; adm*).

The last and most elaborate of the area's *guglie*, the **Guglia San Gennaro**, designed by Cosimo Fanzago, is just outside the south transept. You can also visit the **crypt of San Gennaro**, patron of Naples, with elaborate Renaissance marble decoration and the tomb of Pope Innocent IV. On a small piazza just north of the Duomo, 17th-century **Santa Maria Donnaregina** offers more overdone Baroque. To the side of it is the smaller original church, built in 1307 by Queen Mary of Hungary (wife of Charles of Anjou), whose elaborate tomb is inside, along with some good frescoes from the first half of the 12th century.

The Market Districts

In Naples, market stands or *bancarelle* are as much a part of everyday life as they must have been in the Middle Ages, and the city probably has as many of them as the rest of Italy put together. The greatest concentration can be found in the **Forcella market district**, in the narrow streets to the east of the Via Duomo, where you can buy everything from stereos to light bulbs. According to government economists, at least one-third of Naples' economy is underground – outright illegal, or at the least not paying taxes or subject to any regulation. In the post-war decades, specialities included bootleg cassette tapes, untaxed American cigarettes and plenty of designer labels (if they're real, don't ask where they came from). There's been a strong crackdown lately, and the Forcella is smaller, calmer and much more respectable, but eventually this will pass and things will get back to normal.

Piazza Mercato, one of the nodes of the Neapolitan bazaar, has probably been a market square since medieval times. Today it's well out of the mainstream, home to sellers of ladders, cement mixers and garden furniture. In the old days this was also the site of major executions, most notably that of 16-year-old Conradin, the rightful heir to the throne, by Charles of Anjou in 1268 – an act that shocked the whole of Europe. Charles ordered him buried underneath the piazza – he couldn't be laid in consecrated ground since he had just been excommunicated for political reasons by Charles' ally the pope.

In 1647 Masaniello's Revolt started here; Masaniello (Tommaso Aniello), a young fisherman from Amalfi, had been chosen by his fellow conspirators to step up in the middle of a festival and proclaim to the people and the viceroy that the new tax that the viceroy had introduced 'no longer existed'. As the plotters had hoped, a spontaneous rising followed, and for a week Masaniello ruled Naples while the frightened viceroy hid in Castel Sant'Elmo.

In Naples, unfortunately, such risings can burn out as quickly as a match. The viceroy's spies first secretly drugged Masaniello, so that he appeared drunk or mad to the people, and then, in an unguarded moment, they murdered him and sent his head to the viceroy. Masaniello met his end in the convent of **Santa Maria del Carmine**, on adjacent Piazza del Carmine; where the church has the most spectacular Baroque campanile (1631) in Naples.

The narrow streets between the port and Corso Umberto I are on the main route for smuggled contraband, be it drugs, guns or fake Prada. Keep a low profile when walking around the Piazza Mercato area, and don't go near it after dark.

Porta Capuana

To the northwest of the Piazza Garibaldi, some of Naples' shabbiest streets lead towards the **Piazza Enrico de Nicola**, once the city's main gate. The **Porta Capuana**, built in 1484, seems like a smaller version of the Castel Nuovo's triumphal arch, crowded in by the same squat round towers. Here it is traditional to eat *zuppa alle cozze* (mussel soup) – in summer about a dozen pavement restaurants appear in the square, heaving with assertive locals. Get a ticket and stand in line for a truly Neapolitan experience.

The **Castel Capuano** began life as a residence for the Hohenstaufen kings. Since its construction in the 13th century it has been reshaped so many times it doesn't look like a castle any more; for four centuries it has served as Naples' law courts.

Facing the Porta Capuana is **Santa Caterina a Formello**, a church by the obscure architect Romolo Balsimelli that is one of the masterpieces of 16th-century Italian architecture. Completed in 1593, the church's bulky, squarish form was an important stepping stone towards the Baroque. Despite long neglect (during which its dome seemed to tilt at an ever-more precarious angle), it has reopened to the public and further projects are underway for the conservation of its interior.

Museo Archeologico Nazionale

Open Weds–Mon 9–8; adm.

Naples has the most important collection of Roman art and antiquities in the world, thanks to Vesuvius (for burying Pompeii and Herculaneum) and to the sharp eyes and deep pockets of the Farnese family. Many of the best works here come from the collection they built up over 300 years.

On the ground floor, room after room is filled with **ancient sculpture**, most of it in need of a good dusting. Many of the pieces on view are the best existing Roman-era copies of lost Greek statues, including some by Phidias and Praxiteles. Some are masterpieces in their own right, such as the huge, dramatic ensemble called the Farnese Bull, the Tyrannicides (with other statues' heads stuck on them) and the truly heroic Farnese Hercules that once decorated the Baths of Caracalla. A number of provocative Aphrodites compete for your attention, along with several formidable Athenas, the famous Doryphoros (spear-bearer) and enough Greek and Roman busts to populate a Colosseum.

The museum's famous collection of Roman pornography, the **Gabinetto Segreto** (Secret Room), contains a veritable cornucopia of embarrassing expressions and inflated manhoods, providing a fascinating insight into the love life of ancient Rome. The room has been regularly closed by outraged royals and curators since 1819 (it was shut from 1971 until 2000, supposedly for 'restoration') but now welcomes sniggering visitors over the age of 11. Book your visit at the ticket desk when you arrive.

Upstairs, most rooms are given over to finds from **Pompeii**. The collection of Roman mosaics, mostly from Pompeii and Herculaneum, is one of the best anywhere; the insight it provides into the life and thought of the ancients is priceless. One feature that it betrays clearly is a certain silliness – there are plenty of chickens, ducks and grinning cats, the famous *Cave canem* ('beware of the dog') mosaic from the front of a house, comic scenes from the theatre, and a wonderful panel of crocodiles and hippopotami along the Nile. Some of the mosaics are very consciously 'art', including one showing a detailed scene of the Battle of Issus, where Alexander the Great defeated the Persian king, and another with a view of the Academy of Athens that includes a portrait of Plato.

A recent addition is a section devoted to the Temple of Isis at Pompeii, discovered in 1765, with five rooms displaying sculpture, frescoes and paintings from it.

The museum also has a superb collection of **Roman murals**. Much of it is fascinatingly modern in theme and execution; many walls of Pompeiian villas were decorated with architectural fantasias that seem strangely like those of the Renaissance. Other works show an almost Baroque lack of respect for the gods, such as *The Wedding of Zeus and Hera*. Scholars do indeed denote a period of 'Roman Baroque' beginning around the 2nd century; from it come paintings graced by genuine winged putti, called *amoretti* in Roman days. Among the most famous pictures are *The Astragal Players* – young girls shooting craps – and the beautiful *Portrait of an Unknown Woman*, a thoughtful lady holding her pen to her lips.

Other attractions of the museum include large collections of jewellery, coins, gladiators' fancy armour, Greek vases, decorative bronzes and a highly detailed, room-sized scale model of all excavations up to the 1840s at Pompeii (lovingly restored since the memorable assault on it by the authors' baby boy back in 1980).

The Egyptian collection is not a large one, but it is fun, with a dog-headed Anubis in a Roman toga, some ancient feet under glass and a mummified crocodile.

Museo Nazionale di Capodimonte

Open Weds–Mon 8.30–7.30; adm.

At the top of the hill north of the archaeological museum, the **Parco di Capodimonte** is a well-kept, exotic park created as a hunting preserve by the Bourbons in the 18th century. Charles III built a royal palace here in 1738; it's now Naples' art gallery, the Museo Nazionale di Capodimonte.

On the first floor, the **Royal Apartments** are much the way the Bourbons left them. Persevere through the overdecorated chambers to the **Salotto di porcellana** of Queen Maria Amalia. Built for the royal palace at Portici in 1757 and dismantled and moved to Capodimonte in 1866, it contains more than 3,000 pieces of Capodimonte porcelain.

The collection of **paintings** on the second floor is the best in the south of Italy, and is especially rich in works of the late Renaissance. Some of the pieces that you shouldn't miss are: an Annunciation by Filippino Lippi; a Botticelli Madonna; the mystical portrait of the mathematician Fra Luca Pacioli by an unknown quattrocento artist; Giovanni Bellini's *Transfiguration*; two wry homilies by the elder Brueghel, *The Misanthrope* and *The Blind*; Masaccio's *Crucifixion*; Caravaggio's *Flagellation of Christ;* Titian's *Danae*; and a hilarious picture by Lotto of St Peter Martyr nonchalantly conversing with the Virgin Mary with a hatchet sticking out of his head. Look out, too, for paintings by Neapolitan artists Luca Giordano and Artemesia Gentileschi. The fiery Gentileschi, one of the few female artists of her day, was the victim of a well-publicized rape; she exorcized her demons with violent paintings of avenging women, such as *Judith and Holofernes*. The top floor showcases contemporary art; it's worth a look just for Andy Warhol's *Vesuvius*, erupting Pop Art style.

The museum also contains a fine **armoury** collection, and there's an entire wing filled with delightfully frivolous 18th-century **porcelain** figurines. The Bourbons maintained a royal factory for making such things at Capodimonte, which now houses an institute for the porcelain and ceramics industry.

Certosa and Museo Nazionale di San Martino

Open Tues–Fri and Sun 8.30–7.30, Sat 9–11; adm.

When you start to feel that Naples is closing you in, ride the Montesanto Funicular up to the top of the city; a short walk (bear right) from there will take you to the 17th-century **Castel Sant'Elmo**, the impressive Baroque fortification built by Don Pedro de Toledo to watch over the Neapolitans; the city now uses it for art exhibitions.

Next to it, hogging the best view in Naples, the Carthusians built their original, modest **Certosa di San Martino** some time during the early 14th century. Two centuries later, like most Carthusian branch offices, they were rolling embarrassingly in lucre, and building the poshest monastery in all Italy was the only thing to do. The rebuilt *certosa* (charterhouse) is only marginally smaller than Castel Sant'Elmo. Built on the slope of the mountain, it is supported by a gargantuan platform that is visible for miles out to sea and contains enough stone to construct a small pyramid. Inside, the **Museo Nazionale di San Martino** is a museum of Naples, its history, art and traditions. Most of the museum's collections are in the halls surrounding the cloister (*see* below); here you'll find costumes, paintings, ships' models and curiosities of many different kinds.

The monastery itself was built in bits and pieces from the 1500s through the 1700s, with many of Naples' finest architects and artists contributing; inside the entrance, the first attraction is the **church**, one of the glories of Neapolitan Baroque, with an excess of lovely coloured inlaid marble to complement the overabundance of painting. The work over the altar, the *Descent from the Cross*, is one of the finest by José Ribera. This tormented artist, often called *Lo Spagnuolo* in Italy, has paintings all over Naples. His popularity does not owe everything to his artistic talent; apparently he formed a cartel with two local artists and cornered the market by hiring a gang of thugs to harry other painters out of town.

The **Chiostro Grande** – the grand cloister – is a stately work by a Florentine Renaissance architect named Dosio. Thanks to a sculptural scheme carried out by Cosimo Fanzago, it is also the creepiest cloister east of Seville. Fanzago (who was also one of the architects of San Martino) gives us eight figures of saints that seem more like vampires in priestly robes and mitres. They form a perfect background for his little enclosed cemetery garden, its wall topped with rows of gleaming marble skulls.

At the corners of the cloister are belvederes from which you can look down over Naples (outside the complex is a series of lovely terraced gardens offering a similar view). The *presepi* (cribs) occupy what was once the Certosa's lavish kitchens.

Chiaia

To the west of Castel dell'Ovo, Chiaia district occupies a handsome sweep of waterfront. This is one of the most pleasant parts of the new city. Here, the long, pretty **Villa Comunale**, central Naples' only park, follows the shore. Inside the park, the **aquarium** (***t*** *081 583 3263; open Tues–Fri 9–6, until 5 in winter; Sun 9–2; adm*), which was built by the German naturalist Dr Anton Dohrn in the 1870s, may be the oldest in the world. All the fish, octopi and other marine delicacies here are from the

Bay of Naples; depending on the hour, you'll find them either fascinating or appetizing. When the Allies marched into town in 1943, the Neapolitans put on a party for the officers; there being practically nothing left to eat anywhere in Naples, they cleaned out the aquarium and managed to put on an all-seafood feast. General Mark Clark, the commander, is reputed to have got the aquarium's prize specimen, a baby manatee, but how they prepared it is not recorded.

If you ask, you will be taken upstairs to see murals of Dohrn (who was, incidentally, a friend and colleague of Charles Darwin) and other buddies depicted by German artist Hans von Marees. The wall opposite has local boys frolicking naked under the orange groves. Restored after the 1980 earthquake, the murals are an insight into the secret life of aquariums.

Behind the park, on the Riviera di Chiaia, the **Museo Principe di Aragona Pignatelli Cortes** (***t** 081 761 2356; open Tues–Sun 9–2; adm*) has the same kind of decorative porcelain as at Capodimonte, as well as a number of 18th- and 19th-century carriages, furniture and art.

Mergellina and Posillipo

Beginning a few streets beyond the western end of the Villa Comunale, **Mergellina** is one of the brightest and most popular quarters of Naples, and makes a good place for dinner or a *passeggiata* around busy **Piazza Sannazzaro**. Its centre is the **marina**, where besides small craft there are hydrofoils to Sorrento and the islands in summer, and excursion boats for tours of the shore between Castel dell'Ovo and Posillipo.

From the harbour, Mergellina rises steeply into the surrounding hills; there is a funicular to the top (every 15 minutes), although it is somewhat run down and not entirely safe. On the hillside, between the railway bridge and the tunnel that leads under the hill to Fuorigrotta, is a small park containing a Roman funerary monument that tradition has always held to be the **Tomb of Virgil** (*open Tues–Sun 9–1*). The poet died in Brindisi in 19 BC on his way back from a trip to Greece. Naples was a city dear to him – he wrote most of the *Aeneid* here – and Virgil was brought here for burial, though ancient authors attest that the tomb was closer to the aquarium.

Just below the monument is the entrance to one of the little-known wonders of the ancient world, the **Crypta Neapolitana** (*open daily 9–1*), a 1,988ft road tunnel built during the reign of Augustus to connect Neapolis with Pozzuoli and Baia – it was the longest such work the Romans ever attempted.

To the west of Mergellina lies the upmarket suburb of **Posillipo**, on a hill overlooking the Bay. The area was popular during Roman times and is dotted with 17th-century aristocratic villas; however, as with Vomero, unregulated post-war development has lessened the natural beauty of the area. On the clifftop at the western end of Posillipo, reached by bus no.140 from Santa Lucia or the C27 from Piazza Amedeo, is the beautifully restored **Parco Virgiliano** with amazing views over the Bay of Naples. You can also peer down on the devastated beauty around Italsida, the huge, defunct steel plant at Bagnoli. Afterwards, meander down the narrow lanes to **Marechiaro**, where you can eat like a king and bathe safely – it's one of the few places in Naples where the water is clean enough.

Around the Bay of Naples

Against any other part of the monotonous Italian coastline, the Campanian shore seems almost indecently blessed, possessing the kind of distracting beauty that seduces history off the path of duty and virtue. Today, for all the troubles that come seeping out of Naples, this coast is still one of the capitals of Mediterranean languor.

In Roman days, this was the California of the ancient world: fantastically prosperous, lined with glittering resorts and as favoured by artists and poets as by rich patricians. Like California, though, its perfume was mixed with a little whiff of insecurity. Vesuvius would be enough, but even outside the regularly scheduled eruptions and earthquakes, the region is Vulcan's own curiosity shop. West of Naples, especially, there are eternally rising and sinking landscapes, sulphurous pools, thermal springs and even a baby volcano – altogether, it's a most unstable corner of the earth's crust.

West of Naples

The pretty coastal road leaving the city has views of Vesuvius all through the district of Posillipo. Naples' suburbs continue through **Agnano**, a town of spas and hot springs set around a kilometre-and-half-wide extinct crater, and stretch as far as Pozzuoli.

Pozzuoli

Sophia Loren's birthplace is a modest little city with only its ruins to remind it of the time when Roman *Puteoli*, not Naples, was the metropolis of the Bay. In the time of Caesar and Augustus it was the main port of Italy; at one point the Senate considered the bizarre idea of digging a canal all the way to Rome to make shipping safer. The city's decline began in the 2nd century with Emperor Trajan's expansion of the port of Ostia, closer to Rome. During the 5th-century barbarian invasions, most of Puteoli's citizens took refuge in better-defended Naples.

The **amphitheatre** (***t*** *081 526 6007; open Weds–Mon 9–1hr before sunset; adm*) on Via Domiziana near the train station was the third largest in the Roman world (after Rome and Capua), with 60 gates for letting in the beasts. It is remarkable for the preservation of its subterranean structure, where the scenery, changing rooms and cells for storing wild animals prior to shows were. The long central cavity was for hoisting up scenery. Unlike the chambers beneath, which were buried in mud and landslides, the exposed stands were stripped of their masonry through the ages. The amphitheatre was started by Nero and finished by Vespasianus, who renamed the city *Colonia Flavia Augusta Puteoli*, in thanks to Puteoli for its aid in the civil war that made him emperor. It was the second amphitheatre in Pozzuoli – a few broken arches of the older one, probably used for gladiatorial combats, survive 100 metres to the north.

Pozzuoli's other important ruin is a bit of an embarrassment. For centuries people here showed off the ancient Serapeum – temple to the popular Egyptian god Serapis – until some killjoy archaeologist proved it to be a lavish *macellum*, or market. Only the foundations remain, now forming the centrepiece of Piazza Serapide.

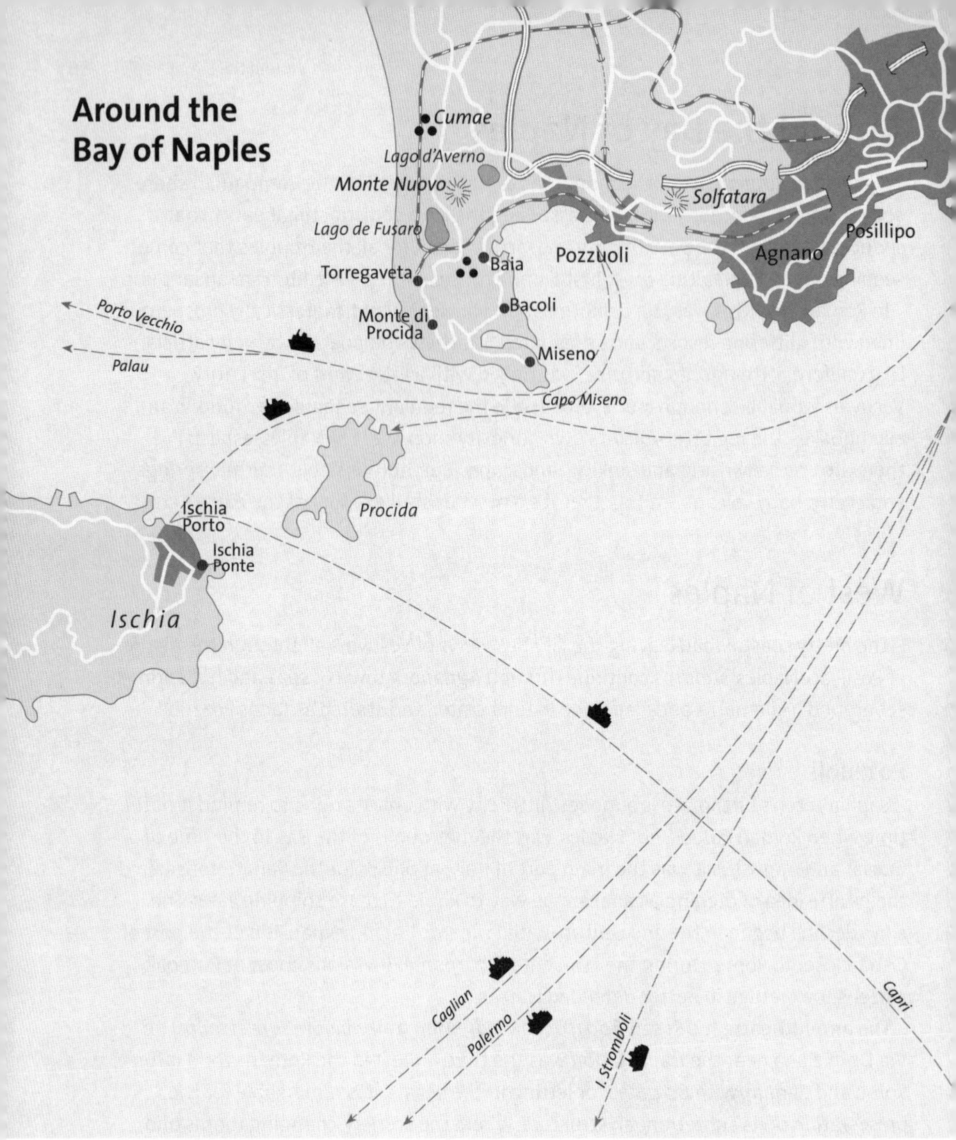

For all ancient Puteoli's size and wealth, little else remains. The reason is *bradyseism*, a rare seismic phenomenon that manifests itself in the form of 'slow' earthquakes. The level of the land fell nearly 20ft in the 1,000 years after the fall of Rome, only to begin rising again in the 15th century. It's currently falling again, and the bits of ancient Puteoli that have not been gently shaken to pieces over the centuries are now underwater. Roman *moles* and docks can sometimes be made out under the surface.

Works for the development and restoration of the historical area of **Rione Terra** (***t*** *848 800 288; open Sat and Sun 9–2 and 4–9*) started in 2002. The site has disclosed the remains of a Roman settlement dating from 194 BC, and it should become a larger archaeological site within a few years.

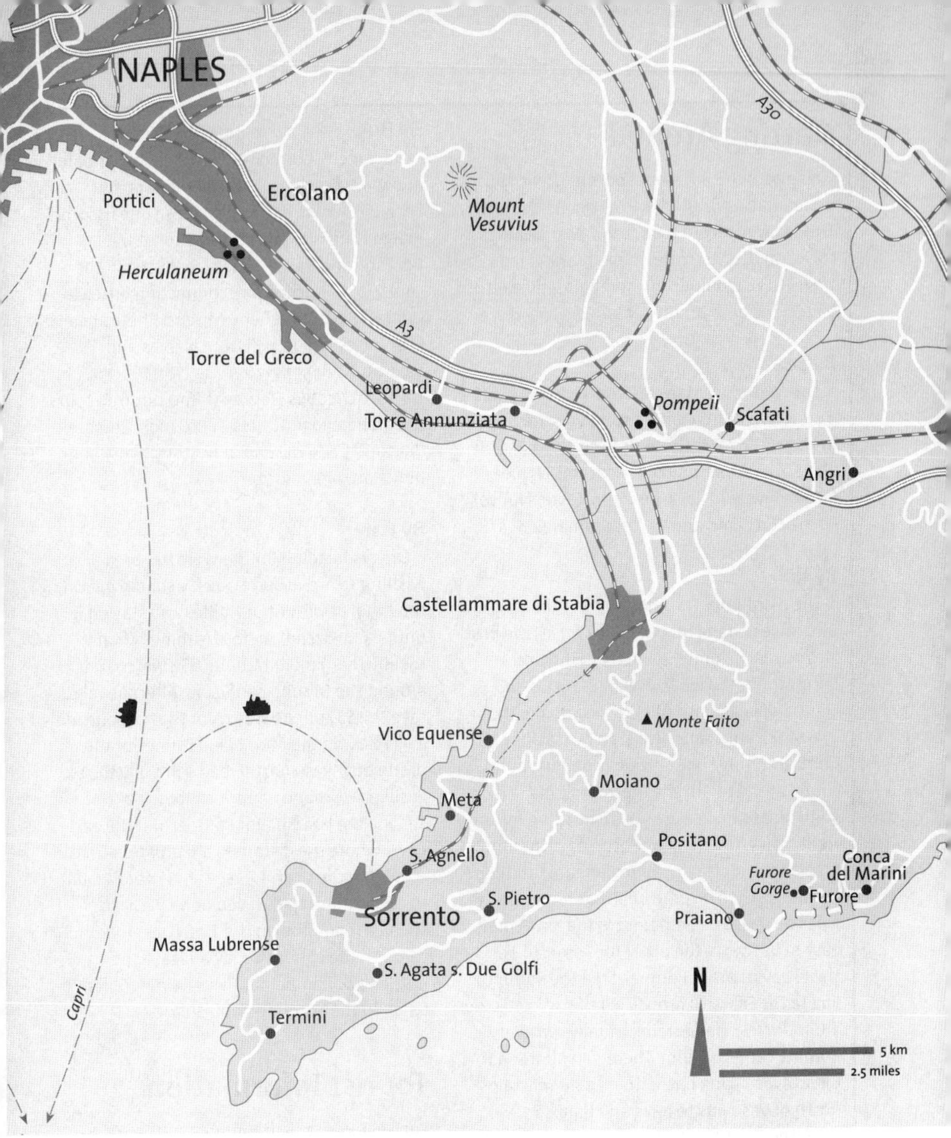

Solfatara

t 081 526 2341; open daily 8.30–7; adm.

What's troubling Pozzuoli can be seen clearly just outside the town at Solfatara, the storm centre of what the Greeks called the **Phlegraean (fiery) Fields** (*Campi Flegrei* in Italian). To the Romans, this was the *Forum Vulcani*, a major attraction of the Campanian coast. It hasn't changed much since. Solfatara is the crater of a collapsed volcano, but one that just can't be still; sulphur gas vents, bubbling mud pits and whistling superheated steam fumaroles decorate the eerie landscape. Dangerous spots are fenced off, and guides are sometimes available to lead you round.

Getting Around

Naples is the Bay's transport hub, with buses, ferries and local rail lines to all points (*see* p.846). The 3-day **Artecard** pass (*see* p.847) includes travel on the Metrò del Mare, bus and rail travel to Pozzuoli, Cuma and Baia, and a return trip to Sorrento on the Circumvesuviana.

By Sea

The **Metrò del Mare** ferry service (**t** 199 446 644, *www.metrodelmare.com*) was introduced in 2002. The MM1 route runs between Bacoli and Sorrento, stopping at Pozzuoli, Naples (Molo Beverello dock, near the Castel Nuovo), Portici/Ercolano and Castellammare.

By Rail

The most important local line is the efficient **Circumvesuviana** (*www.vesuviana.it*), the best way to reach Pompei, Herculaneum and Sorrento. Its station is in Naples on Corso Garibaldi just south of Piazza Garibaldi (**t** 081 772 2444), but trains also stop at Stazione Centrale (where the station is underground, sharing space with the Metropolitana – ask someone to make sure you're heading for the right train). The main lines run east through Ercolano (the stop for Herculaneum) and Torre del Greco, then diverge near Torre Annunziata. One line heads for Sarno, out in the farm country east of Vesuvius, the other for Sorrento. For the excavations at Pompei, take the Sorrento line to the Scavi di Pompei/Villa dei Misteri stop.

Circumvesuviana trains usually run every 30mins 5am–10.45pm. There's an additional Circumvesuviana line with infrequent trains north of Vesuvius to Nola and Baia.

For the west bay, Naples' own **Metropolitana FS** (**t** 800 568 866; trains every 15 mins) goes as far as Pozzuoli-Solfatara. The 2 other regional lines have trains about every 30mins from Piazza Montesanto station, near Piazza Dante. The **Ferrovia Cumana** (**t** 800 001 616) runs along the shore through Fuorigrotta, Bagnoli, Pozzuoli and Baia to Torregáveta (trains every 10mins). The **Circumflegrea** (**t** 800 001 616; trains every 20mins) also finishes at Torregáveta, but usually goes only as far as Licola. Six trains a day stop at the archaeological site of Cumae.

By Bus

Naples city bus no.152 from Piazza Garibaldi and Via Mergellina goes to Solfatara and Pozzuoli. A blue bus run by **Sepsa** departs from Piazza Garibaldi and stops at Solfatara, Pozzuoli and Baia. From the bus stop in the centre of Baia, there are connecting buses to Cumae, Bacoli and Cape Miseno. There are also SITA buses to Pompeii from Naples and Salerno. **t** 081 552 2176.

The **Archeobus Flegreo** (**t** 800 001 616) tours the archaeological sites of Pozzuoli, Cumae, Baia and Capo Miseno in 16 stops, every hour between 9am and 7pm.

By Car

Drivers heading for the west bay area and wishing to arrive quite quickly should get on the *tangenziale* out of Naples and stay on it until past Pozzuoli, before turning off on to the (by then) more tranquil SS7, which runs around the Miseno peninsula. Alternatively, take the SS7 all the way from the harbourside in Naples via the Mergellina tunnel, or the pretty but slow coastal road – initially the Via Posillipo – around Cape Posillipo.

If you are heading for Pompei and the east bay – where the distances are greater, so a car is much more useful – use the A3 *autostrada* to get out of Naples if you don't want to spend a long time on the SS18 coast road through the suburbs. You can leave the A3 at Ercolano or Pompeii, or Castellammare for SS145 to the Sorrento peninsula.

Tourist Information

Pozzuoli: Piazza Matteoti 1/A, **t** 081 526 6639, (*open daily 9–2; also 4–8 June–Sept*).

Pompei: Via Sacra 1, 80045, **t** 081 850 7255, *www.pompeiisites.org* (*open Mon–Sat 8.30–7*). There's a branch near the Porta Marina entrance to the Pompeii site. Guidebooks are sold outside the ruins.

Where to Stay

With the picturesque Sorrentine peninsula and its excellent hotels only 40mins away in one direction, and with Naples about the same distance away in the other, there's little point staying overnight in this built-up and semi-industrial area.

Eating Out

If you're travelling west to visit the classical sites, you may just want to grab a sandwich; the mini-market in **Solfatara** is a good place to pick up a *panino* for a picnic on the acropolis at Cuma (modern Cumae). At **Baia** there is a mini-market opposite the station.

As well as the following, the harbour at **Castellammare di Stabia** is favoured by locals, who come to dine alfresco on summer evenings.

Pozzuoli

Il Capitano, Via Cristoforo Colombo 10, **t** 081 526 2283 (*expensive*). A good spot for fish-lovers, with five rooms if you decide to stay overnight. *Closed Thurs lunch.*

La Granzeola, Via Cupa delle Fescine 33, on the way out of town along the coastal road, **t** 081 524 3430 (*expensive*). Tasty dishes made from fish bought directly off the boats. Try *rigatoni con ragù di cozze* – short pasta with a delicious mussel sauce. *Closed Sun eve and Mon.*

Baia to Cuma

L'Altro Cucchiaro, Via Lucullo 13, **t** 081 868 7196 (*very expensive*). Divine seafood and pasta in a restaurant between Baia's railway station and harbour, perfectly placed if you're visiting the archaeological park. *Closed Mon and Aug.*

La Ninfea, Via Italia 1, Lake Lucrino, between Baia and Pozzuoli, **t** 081 866 1326 (*expensive*). A restaurant with a lakeside terrace where you can dine on fresh fish and simple grilled meats. Try the linguine with prawns.

Villa Chiara, Via Torre di Cappella 10, **t** 081 868 7139 (*expensive*). One of several decent seafood places between Cuma and Fusaro. *Closed Weds low season.*

Giardino degli Aranci, Via Cuma 75, **t** 081 854 3120 (*moderate*). A decent fish restaurant that's handily situated for those visiting the archaeological site at Cuma. *Closed Tues low season.*

Anfiteatro Cumano, Via Cuma 576, **t** 081 854 3119 (*cheap*). Another good fish restaurant near the archaeological site. *Closed Tues.*

Torregáveta

Villa Aragonese, Via Spiaggia Torregáveta, **t** 081 868 9180 (*expensive*). A good place for full meals, in a slightly shabby town. *Closed Tues, and 2wks Aug and Dec.*

Ercolano

There are no restaurants or cafés inside the **Herculaneum** ruins.

Bar degli Amorini, opposite entrance to ruins (*cheap*). A deceptively small frontage behind which lurks a reasonable dining area that's good for a snack or pizza.

Cagnano, Via Roma 17 (*cheap*). A simple trattoria a short walk up the hill from the ruins, serving huge bowlfuls of pasta, including a memorable *spaghetti alle vongole*.

Pompei

There is a restaurant in the ruins, just beyond the forum area through the Arch of Tiberius. The self-service food is nothing special; to escape the crowds opt for waiter service and sit out under the colonnade adjoining the ancient baths.

Restaurants in modern Pompei tend to cater for the captive tourist market. Among the better ones are:

Al Gamberone, Via Piave 36, **t** 081 850 6814 (*moderate*). An option close to Pompei's main church, where you can feast on prawns doused in cognac and other tasty fish dishes (there's also good cannelloni and the likes if you're not in the mood for fish). In summer there are tables outside under the lemon and orange trees. *Closed Tues.*

Anfiteatro, Via Plinio 9, **t** 081 850 6042 (*moderate*). One of the few places in Pompei where you'll see *baccalà* (salt cod) on the menu, along with truly good *spaghetti alle vongole*. It is just outside the excavations exit next to the amphitheatre.

Zi Caterina, Via Roma 20, **t** 081 850 7447 (*moderate*). Good seafood dishes, including lobsters plucked live from the tank. It's also a good place to try Lacrima Christi wine from the slopes of Vesuvius. *Closed Tues eve.*

Their favourite trick is to hold a smoking torch to one of the fumaroles, making a dozen others nearby go off at the same time. (The effect is produced by the steam condensing around smoke particles.) Solfatara is perfectly safe, though the ground underneath feels hot and sounds strangely hollow. (It is; scientists keep a close watch on the huge plug of cooled lava that underlies the area around Pozzuoli, and they say the pressure from below is only about a third as much as it was under Vesuvius in AD 79).

The easiest way to reach Solfatara is on bus no.152 from Naples. Otherwise it is a 25-minute trudge uphill from Pozzuoli train station.

Baia

Baia, the next town along the coast, was the greatest pleasure dome of classical antiquity. Anybody who was anybody in the Roman world had a villa here, with a view of the sea, beach access and a few hundred slaves to dust the statues and clean up after the orgies. You'll find little hint of that today: Goths, malaria and earthquakes have done a thorough job of wrecking the place. Most of ancient Baia is underwater, a victim of the same *bradyseism* that afflicts Pozzuoli. In summer, a **glass-bottomed boat** departs from Baia harbour to see this Roman Atlantis (***t** 081 526 5780; Sat 12 and 4, Sun 10.30, 12 and 4*) and there are also scuba-diving trips to the ruins.

Modern Baia is a pleasant little town, though its lovely bay is used as a graveyard for dead freighters. Nevertheless, the extensive but humble remains of the imperial villa can be visited at the **Parco Archeologico** (***t** 081 868 7592; open Tues–Sun 9–1hr before sunset; adm*), including part of the famous baths – a thermal spa for wealthy Romans that was probably the largest and poshest such establishment in the ancient world.

The wonderful **Baia castle** (***t** 081 523 3310; open daily 9–1hr before sunset*) dominates the Golfo di Pozzuoli, with views as far as Capri. Begun by the Aragonese in 1495 to protect the bay from a feared French invasion, it was rebuilt by Pedro di Toledo after the earthquake of 1538 and contains the **archaeological museum of the Phlegraean Fields**, with some impressive Roman frescoes and statues.

Bacoli to Cumae via Capo Miseno

The coast curves south towards **Bacoli**, a pleasant village with a covered Roman reservoir called the **Piscina Mirabile**, a vaulted chamber like the one in Istanbul; and the **Cento Camerelle**, the 'hundred little rooms', a vast ruin of a villa that might have belonged to Julius Caesar (***t** 081 523 3690; open daily 9–1hr before sunset*).

South of Bacoli lies **Capo Miseno** (Cape Misenum), a beautiful spot that for centuries was the greatest naval base of the Roman Empire. As at Baia, foundations and bits of columns and cornices are everywhere, though nothing of real interest has survived intact. Nearby **Lake Miseno**, also called the 'Dead Sea', was once part of the base, joined to the sea by a canal dug by Augustus' right-hand man Cornelius Agrippa in 37 BC.

More lakes, created by volcanic action, lie north of Cape Miseno. **Lago di Fusaro** is a large, shallow oyster farm, cut off from the sea by a sand bar near the woebegone fishing village of **Torregáveta**, the terminus of the Circumflegrea and Cumana railways. The decaying rococo palace on an island in the centre is the **Casina** (*open Thurs, Sat and Sun 9–1*), built in 1782 by the Bourbon kings' favourite architect, Luigi Vanvitelli.

Nearby is the baby volcano of **Monte Nuovo** (460ft tall); it's an an easy climb up to the crater, inside which you can have a picnic. **Lago d'Averno** (Lake Avernus) may ring a bell from your schooldays – it's the mouth of Hell, according to the ancient Greeks, who believed any passing bird would be suffocated by the infernal fumes rising from it. Cornelius Agrippa didn't have much respect for mythology; he turned the lake into a part of the naval base by cutting another canal.

Cumae

Open daily 9–1hr before sunset; adm.

North of Monte Nuovo and the lakes, near the modern town of Cuma, is the main archaeological site west of Naples. As one of the first Greek settlements in Italy, Cumae was the mother colony for Naples and many other cities of Magna Graecia. In 421 BC it lost its independence to the Samnites and declined steadily. Arab raiders wiped it off the map in the 9th century AD, and there's little to see at the site – only the foundations of a few temples on the high acropolis, worth the climb for the views around Capo Miseno, and the famous **Cave of the Cumaean Sibyl**, discovered by accident in 1932. This was the setting of Aeneas' famous encounter with the Sibyl who leads him into the underworld, described in Book 6 of Virgil's *Aeneid*. It is a place of mystery, a long series of strange, trapezoidal galleries cut out of solid rock – impressive enough, even stripped of the sumptuous decoration they must once have had (all ancient oracles were marvellously profitable). Nobody has a clear idea how old it is, but by classical times it took the form of an oracle quite like the one at Delphi. At its far end, a plain alcove with two benches marks the spot where the Sibyls would inhale fumes over the sacred tripod, chew laurel leaves and go into their trance.

East of Naples: Vesuvius and Pompeii

Naples' eastern suburbs and satellite towns spread along the shore of the Bay in the shadow of Mount Vesuvius as far as Torre Annunziata. The coastal road passes through unattractive industrial zones and modern housing blocks, many thrown up to rehouse the homeless after the 1980 earthquake. Tempting though it is to bypass all this and head straight for Pompeii on the A3 *autostrada*, the area does have two great attractions: the splendid Roman ruins at Herculaneum, and Vesuvius itself, which is accessed from Ercolano, the modern town built on top of those ruins. There are also traces of the splendid villas of the Bourbon aristocracy along the once-glorious Golden Mile, and another fine Roman villa at Oplontis.

Vesuvius

Open daily 9–5; adm.

Despite its fearsome reputation and formidable appearance looming over Naples, Mount Vesuvius is a midget as volcanoes go – only 4,202ft. No one even suspected it was a volcano until 24 August 79, when a titanic eruption buried Herculaneum under mud and Pompeii and Stabiae under cinders and ash, while coating most of Italy with a thin layer of dust. More than 100 eruptions have since destroyed various towns and villages, some more than once, but, as at Mount Etna in Sicily, people just can't stay away from Vesuvius' slopes. Volcanic soil grows grapes and olives in abundance, though the novelty of it often makes the Italians exaggerate their quality.

Vesuvius was last heard from in 1944, when an eruption left the lava flows that are visible on the upper slopes. It also sealed the main fissure, putting an end to the permanent plume of smoke that was once a landmark. You can bet the scientists are watching Vesuvius, but there is no reason to expect another eruption soon. If it were to explode now, however, it would cause a catastrophe, as the area around the volcano has become one of the most densely populated in all Italy; today, the Campania region is paying big money to people in the 'red zone' to move out.

To visit the main crater (between the two peaks), take the Vesuvius bus from the Circumvesuviana stop in Ercolano. You then have a stiff half-hour climb up the ash path. Dismiss all hopes of an easy ascent to the top singing 'Funiculi, funicula' from the legendary Thomas Cook cable railway, long since defunct. The white scar on the side of the crater is the result of work on a second funicular, which was meant to have replaced the old chairlift. Work halted after an argument over its control between the communes of Torre del Greco and Ercolano – while they were arguing, the money mysteriously 'disappeared'.

Herculaneum

Open daily Apr–Oct 8.30–7.30, Nov–Mar 8.30–5; last tickets 90mins before closing; adm.

The drab suburb of Ercolano is built on the mass of rock that imprisons ancient Herculaneum, a smaller and less famous victim of the great AD 79 Vesuvius eruption than Pompeii, but one that's equally worth visiting.

Where Pompeii was buried under layers of ash, Herculaneum, much closer to the volcano, drowned in a sea of mud. Over time this hardened to a soft stone, preserving the city and nearly everything in it as a sort of fossil – furniture, clothing and even some goods in the shops have survived. Like Pompeii, Herculaneum was discovered by accident. In the early 1700s, an Austrian officer, Prince Elbeuf, had a well dug here, and not far down, the workmen struck a stone pavement – the stage of the city's theatre. The Bourbon government began some old-fashioned destructive excavation; serious archaeological work began only under Mussolini, though only about eight blocks of shops and villas have been excavated. The rest is covered not only by tens of yards of rock, but by a dense modern neighbourhood. New digs are still going on, and at any given time, most buildings will be locked, though the guards wandering about have the keys and will show you almost any upon request (they often seem to expect tips).

Unlike Pompeii (which was an important commercial centre), Herculaneum seems to have been a wealthy resort, and is only about a third of Pompeii's size. Many of the most interesting houses can be found along **Cardo IV**, in the centre of the excavated area. On the corner of the Decumanus Inferior, the **House of the Wooden Partition** may be the best example we have of the façade of a Roman house: inside there is an amazingly preserved wooden screen used for separating the *tablinum* – the master's study – from the atrium. Next door, **Trellis House** was a much more modest dwelling, with a built-in workshop; the **House of the Mosaic Atrium**, down the street, is another luxurious villa built with a mind to the sea view from the bedrooms upstairs. On the other side of the Decumanus, Cardo IV passes the **Samnite House** (so named because of its early-style atrium), and further up, a column with police notices painted on it stands near the **House of Neptune**, with a lovely mythological mosaic in the atrium.

The **suburban baths**, near the entrance to the site, were built not long before Vesuvius erupted, and are probably the best-preserved baths of antiquity. Inside are stucco reliefs of warriors, remarkably well-preserved wooden doors and window frames, an intact central furnace, and marble floors and seats. Other buildings worth a visit include the **House of the Deer**, with its infamous statue of a drunken Hercules relieving himself, the well-preserved **forum baths**, and the **Palaestra** (gym), with its unusual serpent fountain and rather elegant, cross-shaped swimming pool.

Villa Poppaea at Oplontis

Open daily Apr–Oct 8.30–7.30, Nov–Mar 8.30–5; last tickets 90mins before closing.

Torre Annunziata is another sorry place with a serious drug problem and a penchant for pasta production, but the Roman villa excavated on Via Sepolcri, known as the Villa Poppaea at Oplontis, is well worth a detour. If you are arriving on the Circumvesuviana, when you leave the station walk downhill over the crossroads and head for the open area on the left opposite the military zone.

Two-thirds of the villa has been fully excavated, revealing an extremely opulent pad with a private bath complex, servants' quarters, monumental reception rooms and an ornamental pool. There are beautiful wall paintings (*see* box, p.876) depicting scenes of monumental halls hung with military arms, a magnificent tripod set between a receding colonnade, bowls of figs and fresh fruit, and vignettes of pastoral idylls, including one showing Hercules under a tree with the apples of the Hesperides that he persuaded Atlas to retrieve for him during his penultimate labour.

The part of the villa near the road is dominated by the great atrium hall and the family quarters. The wing further from the road seems to have been the servants' quarters. Here you can still see amphorae stacked up in a store room. Outside the latrines, partitioned for each sex, it may have been one of the slaves who left his name, scrawled in Greek, 'Remember Beryllos'.

An amphora marked with the name Poppaea has given rise to the suggestion that the villa may have belonged to the *gens* Poppaea, the wealthy Roman family who also owned the House of Menander at Pompeii. The most infamous member of this family was Sabina Poppaea, a woman with everything but virtue. She used her charms to captivate the emperor Nero, leaving her second husband Otho – another future emperor – who was rapidly dispatched to Lusitania. Spurred on by her, Nero killed off his mother Agrippina and his first wife. Nero eventually killed Sabina by mistake in a fit of rage in AD 65, viciously kicking her in the abdomen while she was pregnant.

Roman Frescoes

Pompeii and Herculaneum have been of prime importance in the study of Roman painting. It's impossible to know how much of this art was borrowed from the Greeks or Etruscans, although by the time of Augustus it appears that Rome and Campania were in the vanguard. New fashions set in the palaces of the Palatine Hill were quickly copied in the villas of Roman Campania – or perhaps it was the other way round.

Wealthy Romans tended to regard their homes as domestic shrines rather than a place to relax after a hard day at the forum (the public baths served that role – the ancient Italians behaved much like the modern ones, who do everything in groups of 10). At home they used as many mosaics and wall paintings as they could afford to lend the place the necessary dignity. In Pompeii and Herculaneum, four styles of painting have been defined by art historians, although they often overlap.

Style I (2nd century BC) was heavily influenced by Hellenistic models, especially from Alexandria. Walls are divided into three sections, often by bands of stucco, with a cornice and frieze along the top and square panels (*dados*) on the bottom. The middle sections are skilfully painted to resemble rich marble slabs. A predilection for deep colours, combined with a lack of windows, often makes these small rooms seem somewhat claustrophobic (*see* the Samnite House, Herculaneum, p.875).

Later Romans must have felt the same lack of air and space for, in about 90 BC, they moved on to the 'architectonic' **Style II**. Columns and architraves were painted round the edges of the wall, and an architectural screen added to give an illusion of depth and space on the large central panels. At first the centres consisted of more fake

Pompeii

Open daily Apr–Oct 8.30–7.30, Nov–Mar 8.30–5; last tickets 90mins before closing.

Herculaneum may have been better preserved, but to see an entire ancient city come to life, the only place on earth you can go is this magic time capsule, left to us by the good graces of Mount Vesuvius. Pompeii is no mere ruin. Walking down the old Roman high street, you can peek into the shops, read the graffiti on the walls, then wander off down the backstreets to explore the homes of the inhabitants and appraise their taste in painting – they won't mind a bit if you do. Almost everything that we know for sure concerning the daily life of the ancients was learned here, and the huge mass of artefacts and art dug up over the course of 200 years is still helping scholars re-evaluate the Roman world.

Though a fair-sized city by Roman standards, with a population of some 20,000, Pompeii was probably only the third or fourth city of Campania, and a trading and manufacturing centre of no special distinction. Founded perhaps in the 7th century BC, the city came under the Roman sphere of influence around 200 BC. In the fateful year of AD 79 it was still a cosmopolitan place, culturally more Greek than Roman. Vesuvius' rumblings and the tall, sinister-looking cloud that began to form above it gave those Pompeiians with any presence of mind a chance to leave, and only about a tenth of the population perished.

marble, but landscapes and mythological scenes soon became more popular. The Villa of the Mysteries (*see* p.879) near Pompeii is a prime example.

Vitruvius, the architecture writer, sternly disapproved of Style III, which abandoned pretence and architectural dissimulation in favour of more playful compositions in perspective, still always done with a strict regard for symmetry. A favourite motif was patterns of foliage, fountains and candelabras decorated with delicate, imaginative figures. These would be called 'grotesques' in the Renaissance, when Raphael and his friends rediscovered some in part of Nero's Golden House. The middle panels are often done in solid colours, with small scenes at the centre to resemble framed paintings. In Pompeii, examples include the Houses of Lucretius Fronto and the Priest Amandus, the latter done by a remarkable artist who comes close to scientific perspective.

The last fashion to hit Pompeii before Vesuvius did, Style IV, combines the architectural elements of Style II and the framed picture effects of Style III, but with a much greater degree of elaboration and decoration. Additional small scenes are on the sides – among subjects covered are landscapes, still lifes, genre scenes from everyday life and architectural *trompe l'œil* windows done with a much more refined use of perspective (*see* the House of the Vettii, p.878). Sometimes an entire stage would be painted, with the curtain pulled aside to show a scene from a play. Borders are decorated with garlands of flowers, leering satyrs, grotesques and frolicking cupids (*amoretti*). Humorous vignettes of the gods and incidents from Virgil's *Aeneid* were popular, along with images of Pompeii's divine patroness, Venus. She also inspired the subject matter of the frescoes you have to bribe the guards to see.

After the city was buried under stones and ash, the upper floors stuck out. These were looted and gradually cleared by farmers, and eventually the city was forgotten. Engineers found it while digging an aqueduct in 1600, and excavations began in 1748 – they were a four-star attraction on the Grand Tour. Early digs were far from scientific; archaeologists today complain they did more damage than Vesuvius. Resurrected Pompeii has had other problems: theft of artworks, a fair dose of bombs in the Second World War, and the earthquake of 1980, the damage from which is still being repaired today, though almost all the buildings are once more open to visitors.

You can spend two or three hours on the main sights, or devote a day to scrutinizing details for a total immersion in this ancient world that you won't find anywhere else. Your ticket also entitles you to entrance to the Villa of the Mysteries, five minutes' walk up the Viale Villa dei Misteri (to the left when you exit the Circumvesuviana).

As long as daylight lasted, Pompeii would have been crowded with improvized *bancarelle*; any wagon-driver who wished to pass would need all manner of creative cursing. At least the streets were well paved – better than those in Rome itself in fact. Campania's cities, the richest in western Europe, could well afford such luxuries. All the pavements were much smoother and more even than you see now. The purpose of the flat stones laid across the streets should not be hard to guess – they were places to cross when it rained (streets here were also drains), and the slots in them allowed wagon wheels to pass through.

The shops, open to the street in the day, would be sealed up behind shutters at night, just as they are in old parts of Mediterranean cities today. Houses, on the other hand, turned a blank wall to the street: they got their light and air from skylights in the *atrium*, the roofed court around which rooms were arranged. Later, fancier villas have a second, open court directly behind the first, designed after the Greek *peristyle*.

As in Rome, there was no 'fashionable district'. Elegant villas are everywhere, often between two simple workmen's flats. And don't take the street names too seriously – often they were bestowed by the archaeologists, as with the Via di Mercurio (Mercury Street), after mythological subjects depicted on the street fountains.

Around the Forum

Past the throng of hawkers and refreshment stands, the main site entrance takes you through the walls at the **Porta Marina**. Just inside the gate, the **Antiquarium** displays some of the artworks that haven't been spirited off to the museum in Naples, as well as some gruesome casts of fossilized victims of the eruption.

Two blocks beyond the Antiquarium and you're in the **Forum**, orientated towards a view of Vesuvius. Unfortunately this is the worst-preserved part of town. Here you can see the tribune from which orators addressed public meetings and the pedestals that held statues of heroes and civic benefactors, as well as the once-imposing **Basilica** (law courts), **temples to Apollo and Jupiter**, a public latrine and a **Macellum** (market) decorated with frescoes.

Around Mercury Street

The real attractions in this part of town are a few lavish villas in the sidestreets, including the enormous **House of Pansa**, the **House of the Faun**, which boasts the world's oldest-known welcome mat (set in the pavement, really), and the wonderful **House of the Vettii**, owned by a pair of rich brothers who were oil and wine merchants. It contains several rooms of excellent, well-preserved paintings of mythological scenes, as well as the famous picture of Priapus. This over-endowed character, in legend the son of Venus and Adonis, has made Pompeii something more than a respectable tourist trap, along with a couple of wall paintings along the lines of the *Kama Sutra*. There are a few paintings of Priapus showing it off in the houses of Pompeii, besides the phallic images that adorn bakers' ovens, wine shops and almost every other establishment in town.

The Pompeiians would be terribly embarrassed, however, if they knew what you are thinking. They were a libidinous lot, like anyone else fortunate enough to live on the Campanian coast during recorded history, but the omnipresent phalluses were never meant as decoration. Almost always they are found close to the entrances, where their job was to ward off the evil eye. This use of phallic symbols against evil probably dates from the earliest times in southern Italy; the horn-shaped amulets that millions of people wear around their necks today are their direct descendants. Even so, not so very long ago, women visiting Pompeii were not allowed to set eyes on the various erotic images around the site, and were obliged by the guides to wait chastely outside while their spouses or male companions went in for a peek.

Nearby Via di Nola, one of Pompeii's main streets, leads northwest past the **Temple of Fortuna Augusta**, the **central baths** – uncompleted when Vesuvius went off – and the **House of Marcus Fronto**, with more good paintings and a reconstructed roof.

The Triangular Forum

Beginning in 1911, the archaeologists cleared a vast area of Pompeii around what was probably the most important thoroughfare of the city, now called the Via dell'Abbondanza. Three blocks west of the Forum, this street leads to the **Via dei Teatri** and the Triangular Forum, bordering the southern walls.

Two **theatres** here are worth a visit: a large, open one that seated 5,000 and a smaller, covered one for concerts. The big quadrangle, originally a lobby for the theatres, seems to have been converted into a gladiators' barracks. This is only one of the disconcerting things about Pompeii. The ruined temple in the Triangular Forum was already long ruined in AD 79, and scholars who study the art of the city find the last (fourth) period betrays a growing lack of skill and coarseness of spirit. It seems that 1st-century Pompeii had its share of urban problems and cultural malaise.

Next to the theatres, a small **Temple of Isis** testifies to the religious diversity of Pompeii; elsewhere around town is graffiti satirizing that new and troublesome cult, the Christians.

The Via dell'Abbondanza and Via delle Tombe

The Via dell'Abbondanza is one of Pompeii's most fascinating streets. Among its shops are a smith, a grocer, a weaver and a typical Roman tavern with its modest walk-up brothel. The most common are those with built-in tubs facing the street – shops that sold wine, or oil for cooking and lamps. Notices painted on walls announce coming games at the amphitheatre or recommend candidates for public office.

Some of the best-decorated villas in this neighbourhood are on the sidestreets: the **House of Loreius**, the **House of Amandus** and an odd underground chamber called the **Cryptoporticus**. Pompeii's two most impressive structures occupy a corner just within the walls: the **Palaestra**, a big colonnaded exercise yard, and the **amphitheatre**, the best preserved in Italy, with seating for about 20,000. Tacitus records that a fight broke out here between the Pompeiians and rival supporters from Nocera during games staged in AD 59; Nero exiled those responsible for the games and forbade further spectacles for 10 years.

The Romans buried their dead outside their cities. The manner of burial depended on wealth and status, but around the **Via delle Tombe** (or 'Necropoli'), which lies outside the town walls through the **Porta di Nocera** (near the Palaestra), you can see some impressive funerary monuments to local dignitaries and their families.

The Villa dei Misteri

The famous **Villa dei Misteri** is a country villa northwest of the city through the Porta di Ercolano. It is thought to have been a place of initiation in the forbidden Bacchic (or Dionysiac) Mysteries, one of the cults most feared by Rome's Senate, and later by the emperors. On the walls are scenes from the myth of Dionysus and of the ritual itself.

Pompei to Sorrento

Modern Pompei

Pompei (the modern town has one 'i') is an important pilgrimage centre worth a visit for its wonderfully overdone church, dedicated to the **Madonna di Pompei** (*open daily 6–2 and 3–6.30*). For a good view over the town and the excavations take the lift up the tower (*open daily 9–1 and 3–5; adm*). The Madonna of the church holds a special place in the affections of Neapolitan women, who you'll probably see busily saying their rosaries, asking for the Madonna's intercession to help sort out their problems. If they have bare feet, this is not poverty but devotion (usually the fulfilment of a pledge to the Madonna in thanks for a favour received): Neapolitans who ask for the Madonna's help often promise to walk here barefoot from Naples (26 kilometres) if their prayers are met.

It is only just that Pompei is host to the **Vesuvian museum** on Via Colle San Bartolomeo (*open Mon–Sat 8–2*), which has plenty to satisfy most basic volcano questions.

Along the Coast to Sorrento

Beyond Pompei the coastline begins to curve out towards Sorrento. At the foot of the peninsula lies **Castellammare di Stabia**, which little suggests the beauty further on. Roman Stabiae was the port of Pompeii and the third big town to be destroyed by Vesuvius. Most famously it was where Pliny the Elder, in command of the fleet at Misenum during the AD 79 eruption, met his end as he tried to bring help to those fleeing the catastrophe. Today, beneath a 12th-century **Hohenstaufen castle**, you'll find the modern shipyards of the Italian navy.

From Castellammare it's a short cable-car ride (*open Apr–Oct*) up to **Monte Faito**, a broad, heavily forested mountain that may be the last really tranquil spot on the Bay. – though a few hotels have already appeared. It is a good starting point for some pleasant walks in the hills of the Sorrento peninsula.

Back down on the coast, the first clue that you're entering one of the most beautiful corners of Italy comes when the busy road from Castellammare begins to climb into a corniche at **Vico Equense**, a pretty village that is fast becoming a small resort.

Sorrento

Sorrento began its career as a resort in the early 19th century, when Naples began to grow too piquant for English tastes. The English, especially, have never forsaken it. The town's secret is a certain cosiness, a sense of comfort like that you get from old shoes or a favourite cardigan, a reassuring sense that nothing distressing is going to happen. It helps that this is a lovely, civilized old town. Not many resorts can trace their ancestry back to the Etruscans or claim a native son such as poet Torquato Tasso, though today Sorrento is more proud of songwriter De Curtio, whose *Come Back to Sorrento,* according to a local brochure, ranks with *O Sole Mio* as one of the 'two most familiar songs in the world'. There's a bust of him in front of the Circumvesuviana station.

Getting There and Around

One line of the Circumvesuviana (*see* p.870) goes to Sorrento; the terminal is in Piazza Lauro, two streets east of Piazza Tasso. Trains usually run every 30mins 5am–10.45pm. On a *direttissima* (several daily), Naples–Sorrento takes 1hr 10mins; locals are much slower.

Though the Circumvesuviana makes buses unnecessary for most of the east bay, there's a bus from the **airport** to Sorrento 3 times a day.

Ferry services around the Bay are:

Alimar, 3 round trips a day from Naples' Molo Beverello dock to Sorrento.

Linee Marittime Partenopee, t 081 806 3024, 8 daily return trips from Naples to Sorrento, 9–9, plus ferries from Sorrento to Capri (40mins return, 5 daily), Positano (6 daily), Ischia (1 daily, 9.30am) and Amalfi (3 daily), and a hydrofoil from Sorrento to Capri (20mins return, 16 daily). Winter services only run between Sorrento, Capri and Naples.

Alilauro, t 081 551 3236 or **t** 081 507 1345, a fast hydrofoil service from Naples' Molo Beverello and Mergellina docks (30mins, 7 daily, 9–7.30) to Sorrento.

Caremar, t 081 807 3077, ferries between Sorrento and Capri (20mins return, 4 daily).

Tourist Information

Vico Equense: Via San Ciro 16, **t** 081 801 5752, *www.vicoturismo.it*.

Sorrento: Via L. de Maio 35, **t** 081 807 4033, *www.sorrentotourism.it*.

Massa Lubrense: Viale Filangieri 11, **t** 081 808 9856.

Where to Stay

Vico Equense ✉ 80069

★★★★**Capo La Gala**, Loc. Scrajo, **t** 081 801 5758, *www.capolagala.com* (*very expensive*). A beautiful modern resort hotel near some sulphur springs. Bedrooms have terraces overlooking the beach and there's a pool. *Closed Oct–Apr.*

Sorrento ✉ 80067

Sorrento, a good base for exploring Campania, isn't the status resort it was. Rates are still high, but many upmarket places – almost indecently elegant converted villas by the sea – are good value.

Luxury

★★★★★**Excelsior Vittoria**, Piazza Tasso 34, **t** 081 807 1044, *www.exvitt.it*. The place to stay if you want a taste of the Grand Tour – Byron, Wagner, Nietzsche, Wilde, Monroe and Loren all stopped by. It's set in its own park, with olive and orange groves, overlooking the sea.

★★★★**Ambasciatori**, Via Califano 18, **t** 081 878 2025, *www.manniellohotels.it*. A palatial hotel with pool, lush gardens and a sea-bathing platform that compensate for the location away from the centre. *Closed Jan–Mar.*

★★★★**Imperial Tramontano**, Via V. Veneto, **t** 081 878 2588, *www.tramontano.com*. A place long favoured by British travellers, from Byron and Shelley, with incredible tropical gardens, a private beach and a pool. *Closed Jan–Mar.*

★★★★**President**, Via Nastro Verde, Colle Parise (take coast road past Marina Grande, turning left up SS145), **t** 081 878 2262, *www.acampora.it*. A good option if you have a car, in its own park with lovely views and good-sized pool.

★★★★**Royal**, Via Correale 42, **t** 081 807 3434, *www.manniellohotels.it*. A beautiful hotel on the cliffs above the Riviera Massa, with a pool and beach access. *Closed Nov–Apr.*

Very Expensive

★★★★**Bellevue-Syrene**, Piazza della Vittoria 5, **t** 081 878 1024, *www.bellevuesyrene.it*. A villa-hotel with lush gardens, beautifully restored rooms and a lift to the beach. The

Sorrento doesn't flagrantly chase after your money, unlike many other places in Italy, and it lacks the high-density garishness of, say, Rimini. Its one big drawback is its lack of a decent beach, though at some of the fancier hotels you can take a lift down to the sea. There are also several piers (*stabilimenti*) that are kitted out with loungers and beach umbrellas for hire.

cliff-top colonnade is a lovely spot for a drink even if you're not staying, though staff can be pompous.

★★★**Minerva**, Via Capo 30, east out of town, **t** 081 878 1011, *www.acampora.it*. Fifty good rooms, some with stunning sea views. *Closed Nov–Mar.*

Expensive

★★**La Tonnarella**, Via Capo 31, **t** 081 878 1153, *www.latonnarella.com*. An attractive villa with great views, a private beach and a good restaurant. Book early. *Closed Jan and Feb.*

Moderate

★★**Loreley et Londres**, Via Califano 2, **t** 081 807 3187. A place with dreary décor but friendly staff, a sea-bathing platform and a terrace with the most romantic sunsets in town. Half board is compulsory in summer if you want a room with a sea view, away from the noisy road. *Closed mid-Nov–mid-Mar.*

★**City**, Corso d'Italia 221, **t** 081 877 2210. A simple hotel in the centre. *Closed mid-Nov–mid-Dec.*

★**Nice**, Corso Italia 257, **t** 081 807 2530. A good find on the main road just in front of the Circumvesuviana station, with clean, pleasant rooms. *Closed Nov–Feb.*

Cheap

Ostello delle Sirene, Via degli Aranci 160, **t** 081 807 2925, *www.hostel.it*. A budget hostel near the train station; follow the signs.

Massa Lubrense

Il Giardino di Vigliano, Via Vigliano 3, Loc. Villazzano, **t** 081 533 9823, *www.massalubrense.it/vigliano.htm*. An *azienda agrituristica* in a 17th-century building with a Saracen tower, up on the hill and good for those with cars (there's a sign on the wall marking the turn-off from the main road). The view of Capri from the roof terrace is breathtaking..Half board and apartments are available.

Eating Out

Sorrento ✉ 80067

Very Expensive

Don Alfonso, Piazza Sant'Agata, Sant'Agata sui Due Golfi, 9km outside town, **t** 081 878 0026. A fantastic Michelin 3-starred restaurant that is reckoned by many food critics to be the best in southern Italy. There are also 3 beautiful apartments that you can stay in. *Closed Mon, Thurs except high season, and Jan and Feb.*

Expensive

Caruso, Piazza Tasso, **t** 081 807 3156. A vast, inventive menu, attentive service and an extensive wine list. Booking essential. *Closed Mon except high season.*

Maria Grazia, Via Marina del Cantone 65, Nerano, **t** 081 808 1011. A restaurant with a reputation for serving up melt-in-the-mouth *spaghetti con le zucchine. Closed Dec and Jan.*

O'Parrucchiano, Corso Italia 71, **t** 081 878 1321. A restaurant that claims to have invented cannelloni, back in 1870. *Closed Weds except high season.*

Moderate

Da Pappone, Via Marina del Cantone 23, Nerano, **t** 081 808 1209 (*moderate*). An elegant placing specializing in fish and elaborate (but pricey) *antipasto*.

Trattoria da Emilia, Via Marina Grande 62, **t** 081 807 2720. A bustling trattoria with a terrace overlooking the sea and good local fare such as pasta and beans with mussels. *Closed Tues except high season.*

Cheap

Panetteria-Pizzeria Franco, Corso Italia 265, **t** 081 877 2066. A convivial place where you sit at long wooden tables beneath hanging hams and watch your pizza being prepared in front of you.

Sorrento sits on a long cliff overlooking the bay and is chopped in half by a narrow ravine. On one side is a suburban area of quiet, mostly expensive hotels, around Via Correale; on the other is the old town, still preserving its grid of narrow Roman streets. Sorrento was never a large town, though for a while in the Middle Ages it was an important trading post. The Sorrentini recall with pride that their fleet once defeated Amalfi's fleet, even though it was in 897. Today the population is only 15,000, but this figure is inflated in summer by the scores of coaches and cruise ships disgorging British and American passengers.

Tiny **Via San Cesareo** is the heart of the old town, dubbed by the sizeable community of British ex-pats 'The Drain' and the focus of the town's *passeggiata*, which goes on until late at night. Half of the shop windows here seem to be displaying *intarsia* – fine pictures in inlaid woods, which have been a local craft for centuries. The **Museo-Bottega della Tarsialignea** on Via San Nicola (***t*** *081 877 1942; open Tues–Sun 9.30–1 and 4–8*) is an interesting woodcarving museum-workshop.

Also look out for the laboratories, open to the street, producing perfume and *limoncello*, the distinctive lemon liqueur made from the lemons grown throughout the peninsula. The church of **San Francesco** stands in the piazza of the same name, next to a small 14th-century arched cloister with arabesques. In summer there are art exhibitions (*free*) and impromptu concerts here. The nearby public gardens offers the classic Sorrentine view along the cliff tops, with the sea and Vesuvius in the distance. You can get down to the *stabilimenti* by taking the lift from here.

Around Sorrento

As far as the mountains allow, the area surrounding Sorrento is one of the great garden spots of Campania – a lush little plain full of vines and lemon groves tucked beneath a backdrop of soaring hills. From the town, you can follow the winding path to the west to the **Bagni Regina Giovanna**, a natural triangular seapool where you can see the scanty ruins of the Roman **Villa di Pollio**. You can also take the short trip west to **Massa Lubrense**, an uncrowded fishing village with fine views stretching as far as the tip of the peninsula and the rugged outline of Capri beyond. There are some lovely walks from Massa and the nearby village of **Termini**, exploring the rugged tip of the peninsula with stupendous views of Capri, the Bay of Naples and the Amalfi Coast: ask at Massa Lubrense tourist office for a walking map.

The Amalfi Coast

...the only delectable part of Italy,
which the inhabitants there dwelling do call the coast of Malfie,
full of towns, gardens, springs and wealthy men.

Boccaccio

Along this coast, where one mountain after another plunges sheer into the sea, there is a string of towns that not long ago were accessible only by boat. Today the Amalfi Drive, a spectacular corniche road of 'a thousand bends', covers the route; necessity makes it so narrow that every encounter with an oncoming vehicle is an adventure, but everyone except the driver will have a treat. Nature here has created an amazing vertical landscape, a mix of sharp crags and deep green forests. In doing so she inspired the Italians to add three of their most beautiful towns.

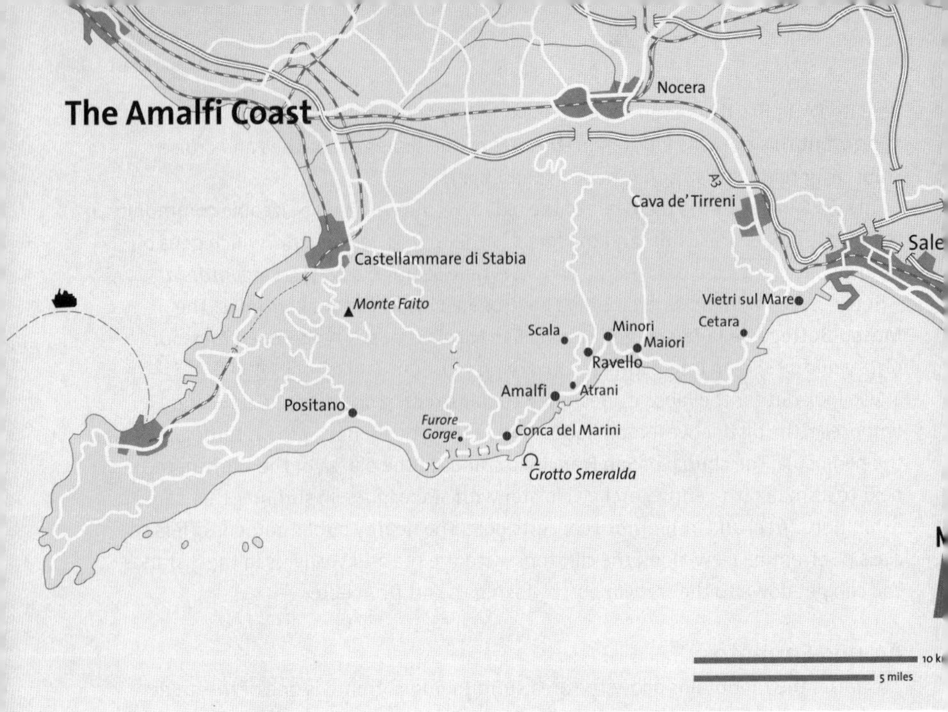

This coast, generally acclaimed to be the most beautiful stretch of scenery in the entire Mediterranean, has always attracted foreigners, but only relatively recently have places such as Positano become haunts for the rich, with swarms of day-trippers likely to descend at any moment. Prices are high, the traffic is terrible and there are plenty of tacky souvenir shops. But tourism is unlikely to ever really spoil this area – its natural beauty outshines anything humans could inflict on it. All the engineers in Italy couldn't widen the Amalfi road, and the steepness of the terrain leaves no room at all for new development.

Positano

Complementing the vertical landscape is Italy's most nearly vertical town, spilling down from the corniche in a waterfall of pink, cream and yellow villas. The day-trippers may well walk down to the sea, but only the alpinists among them make it back up (fortunately, there is a regular bus service along the one main street).

After the Second World War, Positano became a well-known hideaway among artists and writers – many of them American, following John Steinbeck's lead – and fashion was not slow to follow. These days, even though it's infested with coach parties in summer, the town reverts to the Positanesi in the off-season and quietens down considerably.

Parking here, as on most of the Amalfi coast, is extremely limited and you may be forced to hand over a fat wad of euros if you bring your car. Off the main thoroughfare, the road spirals down to the town centre – avoid bringing your car this far if you can. There are usually more spaces further from the centre, and even when it looks to be a fair hike into town steps often provide a short cut down the hillside.

Getting Around

The SS145 coast **road** is tortuous, narrow and slow, with endless hairpins, cliff-edge sections and too much traffic. Overtaking is dangerous. The views, though, are truly stunning.

SITA runs buses from Salerno for the Amalfi coast, with regular departures for Sorrento (in front of the Circumvesuviana station), stopping at Amalfi, Ravello and other towns en route. They are usually so frequent that it is easy to see all the main coast towns on a day-trip, hopping from one to the next. Buses are the best way to do it; driving can be a hair-raising experience.

You can also get to Positano, Amalfi and Salerno by **sea** on the Metrò del Mare's MM2 service (**t** 199 446 644, 2 return trips daily). **Linee Marittime Partenopee, t** 081 807 1812, runs ferries from Sorrento to Positano (6 daily) and Amalfi (3 daily).

A ferry called the *Faraglione* leaves Salerno's Molo Manfredi (at the western end of town) at 7.30am daily, calling at Amalfi and Positano on the way to Capri.

You can explore much of the area on **foot**; see *www.villagesoftradition.it/cost-itin.htm*.

Tourist Information

Positano: Via Saracino 4, **t** 089 875 067 (*open daily June–Sept 8–2 and 3.30–8, Oct–May 8–2*).
Amalfi: Corso Roma 19, **t** 089 871 107, *www.azienturismoamalfi.com* (*open daily 8.30–1.30 and 3–5.15*).
Ravello: Piazza Duomo, **t** 089 857 096, *www.ravello.it/aziendaturismo* (*open Mon–Sat 9–7, 9–8 in summer*).
Maiori: Corso Regina 73, **t** 089 877 452.
Salerno: Piazza V. Veneto, near station, **t** 089 231 432, *www.azienturismosalerno.com*.

See *www.giracostiera.com* for further useful information on the Amalfi coast.

Where to Stay

Positano ✉ 84017

With Positano's high-fashion status come some of the highest hotel prices in Italy. A few cheap *pensioni* can be found on Via Fornillo and other streets leading down to the beach.

*******Covo dei Saraceni**, Via Regina Giovanna 5, **t** 089 875 400, *www.starnet.it* (*luxury*). A comfortable hotel in a great location at the bottom of the hill right on the harbour. Rooms are simple and spacious, with antique furniture. *Closed Nov–Mar.*

*******San Pietro**, Via Laurito 2, 1½km outside town, **t** 089 875 455, *www.ilsanpietro.it* (*luxury*). An intimate paradise believed by many to be the finest resort hotel in Italy, with 58 immaculate rooms, superb facilities, including a private beach, and spectacular views. The entrance is hidden behind an old chapel. *Closed Nov–Mar.*

*******Le Sirenuse**, Via Cristoforo Colombo 30, **t** 089 875 066, *www.sirenuse.it* (*luxury*). The stylish former home of a noble Naples family, to whom it still belongs, with a pool with mosaic tiles, a Jacuzzi anda fitness area.

******Palazzo Murat**, Via dei Mulini 23, **t** 089 875 177, *www.palazzomurat.it* (*luxury*). An 18th-century *palazzo* that once belonged to Napoleon's brother-in-law Joachim Murat, in the heart of town. There's plenty of old-world charm, antiques in many rooms and a courtyard shaded by palms. *Closed Nov–Mar.*

*****Casa Albertina**, Via Tavolozza 3, **t** 089 875 143, *www.casalbertina.it* (*very expensive*). A family-run place with lovely, understated décor, great views and a rooftop restaurant. Half board is compulsory in high season.

*****California**, Via Cristoforo Colombo 141, **t** 089 875 382 (*expensive*). A well-located and charmingly run option with 15 good rooms and a terrace restaurant. *Closed Nov–Mar.*

***Maria Luisa**, Via Fornillo 42, **t** 089 875 023 (*moderate*). A small, friendly, family-run hotel. *Closed Nov.*

***Ostello Brikette**, Via G. Marconi 358, **t** 089 875 857 (*cheap*). A lovely hostel facing the sea, with some private rooms.

Amalfi ✉ 84011

Amalfi has been a resort for much longer than Positano, and its older establishments are some of the most distinctive in the Med, though prices are generally higher than average.

*******Santa Caterina**, SS Amalfitana 9, **t** 089 871 012, *www.hotelsantacaterina.it* (*luxury*). A cliff-top villa just outside town, with lovely gardens. and fabulous sea views from most rooms. *Closed Jan and Feb.*

★★★★**Luna**, Via P. Comite 33, **t** 089 871 002, *www.lunahotel.it* (*luxury*). A former monastery above the main road on Amalfi's eastern edge. Wagner stayed here, and they can show you the room where Ibsen wrote *A Doll's House*. Deftly modernized, it has comfortable rooms and attentive service.

★★★★**Cappuccini Convento**, Via Annunziatella 46, **t** 089 871 877, *www.hotelcappuccini.it* (*very expensive*). A former monastery on a hillside overlooking town, built by Emperor Frederick II in the 12th century. The bedrooms were monks' cells and the chapel and cloister remain. The food is wonderful.

★★★★**Miramalfi**, Via Quasimodo 3, between Positano and Amalfi, **t** 089 871 588, *www.miramalfi.it* (*very expensive*). An efficient 1960s-style hotel with parking, a beach and a swimming pool.

★★★**Amalfi**, Via dei Pastai 3, **t** 089 872 440, *www.starnet.it/hamalfi* (*expensive*). A central hotel, popular with package tours and good for those without transport.

★★**Lidomare**, Largo Duchi Piccolomini 9, **t** 089 871 332, *www.lidomare.it* (*expensive*). A pleasant hotel not far from the cathedral but away from the crowds, with bright rooms and obliging staff.

★★**Fontana**, Piazza Duomo 7, **t** 089 871 530 (*moderate*). Sixteen clean and spacious rooms near the cathedral. The piazza hums until the early hours. *Closed Oct–Easter.*

★★**Sant'Andrea**, Via Santolo Camera 1, **t** 089 871 145 (*moderate*). A tiny, elaborately furnished hotel with views of the cathedral and a warm welcome. *Closed Nov–May.*

★★**Sole,** Largo della Zecca 2, **t** 089 871 147, *www.starnet.it/hsole* (*moderate*). A small, clean, airy option in a quiet piazza behind the beach, with parking. Book in advance.

Ravello ✉ 84010

Hotels in Ravello have no beaches, but many have unforgettable gardens and some of the most spectacular views in the Mediterranean.

★★★★★**Palazzo Sasso**, Via S. Giovanni del Toro 28, **t** 089 818 181, *www.palazzosasso.com* (*luxury*). A top hotel in a 12th-century villa, with plush décor, a renowned restaurant, astonishing views and friendly staff. It was here that Wagner fixed on paper the vision he caught in Villa Rùfolo. *Closed Nov–Feb.*

★★★★★**Palumbo**, Via S. Giovanni del Toro 16, **t** 089 857 244, *www.hotelpalumbo.it* (*luxury*). A fine hotel with a guestbook full of famous names. The 11 rooms are set around an Arab courtyard, and there's a simpler *dipendenza* with 6 cheaper rooms. The famous restaurant (booking advisable) serves wine made on the premises. There's a pool and parking.

★★★★**Villa Cimbrone**, Via Santa Chiara 26, **t** 089 857 459, *www.villacimbrone.it* (*luxury*). An elegant old villa on the cliffs, with the lushest gardens on the coast. The 10 rooms (5 with sea views) are beautifully decorated, and the view from the breakfast terrace is stunning. Drawbacks are the 10min walk from the car park and the lack of restaurant (though there is a pool). *Closed Nov–Apr.*

★★★**Hotel Giordano**, Via Trinità 14, **t** 089 857 255, *www.giordanohotel.it* (*very expensive*). A comfortable modern hotel with a heated outdoor pool and solarium, and parking. *Closed Nov–Easter.*

★★★★**Villa Maria**, Via Santa Chiara 2, **t** 089 857 255, *www.villamaria.it* (*very expensive*). A gracious villa, a favourite among many celebrities, with a restaurant that has won a *gambero rosso* award. Guests can use the facilities at Hotel Giordano a few mins' walk away.

★★**Villa Amore**, Via dei Fusco 5, **t** 089 857 135 (*moderate*). A delightful little hotel with 5-star views, 12 clean, simple rooms, a lovely terrace and a homely atmosphere.

Scala ✉ 84010

★★★**Villa Giuseppina**, Via Torricella 39, **t** 089 857 106 (*moderate*). A charming, tranquil place with good food and great views from the pool.

Minori ✉ 84010

The pleasant beach lidos of Minori and Maiori are a little dull compared to Amalfi and Positano but they can be useful bases.

★★★★**Villa Romana**, Corso Vittorio Emanuele 90, **t** 081 877 237 (*expensive*). A stylish, comfortable modern hotel in the heart of town (but not on the sea). with a rooftop pool away from the crowds and fumes, and clean, pleasant rooms. Parking is difficult.

★★★**Santa Lucia**, Via Nazionale 144, **t** 089 877 142, *www.hotelsantalucia.it* (*moderate*). A hotel by the beach and archaeological park, with 1960s décor. *Closed Nov–Mar.*

Eating Out

Positano

Cheap places to eat are hard to find here, though there are some decent pizzerias around Via Fornillo, and some of the restaurants below, such as Chez Black, also offer pizzas.

La Cambusa, Piazza Vespucci 4, **t** 089 875 432 (*very expensive*). A restaurant looking out onto the beach, with excellent seafood. *Closed Jan.*

Chez Black, Via Brigantino 19, **t** 089 875 036 (*expensive*). A slick joint by the beach, with good Neapolitan favourites such as *spaghetti alle vongole*, and pizzas. *Closed Jan.*

Lo Guarracino, Via Positanesi d'America 12, **t** 089 875 794 (*expensive*). A friendly, informal pizzeria/trattoria perched over the sea on the cliff path leading to Fornillo beach. *Closed Tues, Nov–Mar.*

Da Adolfo, Via Laurito, Laurito, **t** 089 875 022 (*moderate*). A delightful trattoria on a small beach, serving old-fashioned recipes such as *totani con patate* (squid with potatoes in oil and garlic), washed down with white wine spiked with fresh peaches. There's a free ferry service from Positano's jetty (look for boats marked 'Da Laurito'). *Closed Oct–May.*

O'Caporale, Via Regina Giovanna 12, **t** 089 811 188 (*moderate*). Simple and well-cooked seafood just off the beach. *Closed Oct–Mar.*

Amalfi

Some of Amalfi's best restaurants are in its hotels; *see* above.

La Caravella, Via Matteo Camera 12, **t** 089 871 029 (*very expensive*). A busy restaurant near the tunnel by the beach, serving generous helpings of home-made pasta, including ravioli with seafood, and good homemade desserts, including *tiramisù*. The cellar has more than 1,000 wines. *Closed Tues except high season, and Nov.*

Da Gemma, Via Fra Gerardo Sasso 9, **t** 089 871 345 (*very expensive*). One of Amalfi's oldest restaurants, with an attractive terrace and an excellent fish-based menu. The *zuppa di pesce* is superb; try also *melanzane al cioccolato* (grilled aubergines in chocolate sauce), a heavenly combination. *Closed Weds.*

Lo Smeraldino, Piazzale dei Protontini 1, **t** 089 871 070 (*expensive*). A popular eatery on the water's edge towards the far end of the port. Try the local speciality, *scialatielli ai frutti di mare* (fresh pasta with mixed seafood). The good *secondi* include an excellent *fritto misto. Closed Weds, and Jan and Feb.*

La Taverna del Duca, Largo Spirito Santo 26, **t** 089 872 755 (*expensive*). A relaxing lunch offering pizza, pasta and traditional Amalfi cooking, with tables scattered around a small piazza. *Closed Thurs.*

Tarì, Via P. Capuano, **t** 089 871 832 (*moderate*). A cool, welcoming trattoria north of the cathedral. *Closed Tues.*

Da Barracca, Piazza dei Dogi, **t** 089 871 285 (*moderate*). Everything an Italian trattoria should be, with tables spilling out on to a tranquil, shaded piazza just west of the cathedral, and friendly waiters proffering tasty snacks and plates of steaming pasta. *Closed Weds, and Jan and Feb.*

Da Maria, Via Lorenzo di Amalfi 14, **t** 089 871 880 (*moderate*). A trattoria and pizzeria near the cathedral, with a multilingual menu to entice travellers. The waiters are cheerful and helpful, and the food is better than at some of the other reasonably priced places. *Closed Mon.*

San Giuseppe, Via Ruggiero II 4, **t** 089 872 640 (*moderate*). A family-run hostelry serving up sublime pizza (the owner is a baker) and homely bowls of pasta amid the noise of television and shrieking children. *Closed Thurs.*

Ravello

Most of the best dining in Ravello is in the hotels, notably Palazzo Sasso and Villa Maria, which welcome non-residents.

Cumpà Cosimo, Via Roma 44–6, **t** 089 857 156 (*expensive*). A traditional restaurant with a homely atmosphere, and walls lined with framed recommendations from national and international newspapers, enthusing over the recipes handed down by the owner–cook's grandmother. The menu is based on fresh produce grown on the family farm in Scala.

Vittoria, Via dei Rufolo 3, **t** 089 857 947 (*expensive*). A large trattoria off the main piazza, serving delicious food in generous portions; try the rich, gooey *risotto ai funghi porcini*. There's a shady patio at the back. *Closed Tues except high season.*

A highlight of Positano's year is the spectacular **Feast of the Assumption** on 15 August – the main holiday of the summer throughout Italy – when locals recreate the Amalfi coast's centuries-long battles with the Saracens (*see* p.841).

Amalfi

Can this minuscule village really once have had a population of 80,000? There's no room among these jagged rocks for even a fraction of that, but then in Campania anything is possible, and in fact most of the old town simply slid into the sea during a storm and earthquake in 1343. Until that moment, Amalfi was a glorious place, the first Italian city to regain its balance after the Dark Ages, the first to recreate its civic pride and its mercantile daring, showing the way to Venice, Pisa and Genoa, though she kept few of the prizes for herself.

It is only natural that the Amalfitani would try to embroider their history a little to match such an exquisite setting. Legends tell of a nymph named Amalphi who haunted this shore and became the lover of Hercules. As for their city's founding, locals will tell you about a party of Roman noblemen, fleeing the barbarians after the fall of the Empire, who found the site a safe haven to carry on the old Roman culture.

Amalfi first appears in the 6th century; by the 9th it had achieved independence from the dukes of Naples and was probably the most important trading port of southern Italy, with a large colony of merchants at Constantinople and connections with all the Muslim lands. In 849 the chroniclers record Amalfi's fleet chasing off an Arab raid on Rome.

To begin with, the Amalfitani Republic was ruled by officers called *giudici*, or judges. The year 958 brought a change in constitutions, and Amalfi elected its first doge, in imitation of Venice. At about the same time, the city's merchants developed the famous *Tavola Amalfitana*, a book of maritime laws that was widely adopted around the Mediterranean. All of this came at a time for which historical records are scarce, but Amalfi's merchant adventurers must have had as romantically exciting a time as those of Venice. Their luck was to turn sour in the 11th century, however. The first disaster was a sacking by Robert Guiscard in 1073. Amalfi regained its freedom with a revolt in 1096, but the Normans of the new Kingdom of Sicily came back to stay in 1131. Unfortunately they proved unable to protect the town from two further terrible sackings at the hands of its arch-enemy Pisa in 1135 and 1137. Today, Amalfi only gets to relive its glory days once every four years, when it hosts the Pisans, Genoese and Venetians in the antique boat race of the Four Maritime republics: the next race is in 2005.

The earthquake of 1343 completed Amalfi's decline, but what is left of the place today – with its 5,000 or so people – is beautiful almost to excess. Above the little square around the harbour, a conspicuous inscription brags: 'Judgement Day, for the Amalfitani who go to heaven, will be a day like any other day.' The square is called **Piazza Flavio Gioia**, after Amalfi's most famous merchant adventurer (his statue looks as if he's offering you a cup of tea). He's probably another fictitious character – more Amalfitani embroidery – but they claim that he invented the compass in the 12th century.

From here, an arch under the buildings leads to the centre of the town, **Piazza del Duomo**, with a long flight of steps up to what may be the loveliest cathedral in south Italy (9th–12th centuries). Not even in Sicily was the Arab–Norman style carried to such a flight of fancy as in this delicate façade, with its four levels of interlaced arches in stripes of different-coloured stone. Much restored a century ago, the open, lace-like arches on the porch are unique in Italy, although common enough in Muslim Spain, one of the countries with which Amalfi had regular trade relations.

The cathedral's greatest treasure is its bronze doors, cast with portraits of Christ, Mary, St Peter and Amalfi's patron St Andrew. The first of such doors in Italy, they were made in Constantinople in 1066 by an artist named Simon of Syria (he signed them) and commissioned by the leader of the Amalfitan colony there. The interior, sadly, was restored in the 18th-century Baroque style, with plenty of frills in inlaid coloured marble. The red porphyry baptismal font in the first chapel on the left is believed to have come from the ruins of Paestum. In the crypt is more coloured marble work and frescoes, a gift of Philip II of Spain, as well as the head of St Andrew; this relic was part of Amalfi's share of the loot in the sack of Constantinople in 1204.

One of the oldest parts to survive is the **Chiostro del Paradiso** (*open daily 9–7, until 5 in winter; adm*), a whitewashed quadrangle of interlaced arches with an African air. To the side is the **Basilica del Crocifisso**, the original cathedral. Here, among the surviving frescoes, are many of the bits and pieces of old Amalfi that have endured its calamities: classical sarcophagi, medieval sculptures and coats of arms. Best of all are the fragments of Cosmatesque work – brightly coloured geometric mosaics that once were parts of pulpits and pillars, a speciality of this part of Campania. Don't miss the lovely 16th-century Madonna col Bambino by the stairs down to the crypt.

From the centre of Amalfi, it's a few minutes walk to the northern edge of the city and the narrow **Valley of the Mills**, along a stream bed between steep cliffs. Some of the mills that made medieval Amalfi famous for paper-making are still in operation, and there is a small **paper museum** (*open daily 10–6; adm*) in the town. You can also see paper being made and buy products at Amatruda, Via Fiume, near the museum.

One of the best ways to spend time in this area is by walking the lovely paths that navigate the steep hills into the interior of the peninsula, passing through groves of chestnut and ash. These were the main roads in this area in the days of the Republic. A particularly good one is the **Sentiero degli Dei** ('Footpath of the Gods') from Agerola to Positano in the green heart of the coast, a lovely 9-kilometre walk. Another is the **Amalfi–Pontone path**, passing the ruins of the old monastery of Sant'Eustacchio. There are many other paths around Ravello and Scala; ask at the tourist offices.

Villages Inland: Ravello and Scala

As important as it was in its day, the Amalfitan Republic was never large. At its greatest extent it could only claim a small part of the coast, plus Ravello and Scala in the hills. Like Amalfi, both were once much larger and richer than they are today. **Ravello** enjoys a beautiful location, perched on a balcony overlooking the Amalfi Coast. The sinuous climb can be made by bus or car, but be warned that parking here is a nightmare – expect to pay through the nose if you bring your car.

The village seems to have been a resort even in Roman times, for numerous remains of villas have been found. Later, as second city of the Amalfitan Republic, medieval Ravello's population reached 30,000. Today it is an example of a typically Italian phenomenon – a village of 2,000 with a first-rate cathedral. Its chief glories are its wonderful gardens, treasure houses of tropical botany. The **Villa Cimbrone** (*open daily 9–1hr before sunset; adm*) was laid out by Lord Grimthorpe, the Englishman who designed Big Ben. Its priceless view over the Amalfi Coast is now owned by the Swiss Vuillemier family, who also own the Palumbo hotel (*see* p.886). The villa is without doubt one of the most beautiful properties in all Italy.

Fans of Wagner will be interested to know the **Villa Rùfolo** (*open daily 9–8, until 6 in winter; adm*) is none other than Klingsor's magic garden. Wagner says so himself, in a note scribbled in the villa's guestbook. He came here looking for the proper setting in which to imagine the worldly, Faustian enchanter of Parsifal, and his imagination was fired. The villa is a remarkable 11th-century pleasure palace, the temporary abode of Charles of Anjou, various Norman kings and Adrian IV, the only English pope (1154–9), who came here when fleeing a rebellion in Rome. Even in its present, half-ruined state it is worth a visit. It houses a small collection of architectural fragments, including a Moorish cloister and two crumbling towers, one of which can still be climbed. The garden, with more fine views, is a semi-tropical paradise: in summer it reverberates with 'sounds and sweet airs' as the setting for open-air concerts.

The **cathedral** is named after Ravello's patron, San Pantaleone, an obscure early martyr. There is a phial of his blood in one of the side chapels; it 'boils' like the blood of San Gennaro in Naples when the saint is in the mood. Lately he hasn't been, which worries the Ravellans. The cathedral has two treasures: a pair of bronze doors by Barisano of Trani (1179),inspired by the Greek ones at Amalfi, and a pair of marble *ambones* (pulpits) that rank among the outstanding examples of 12th- and 13th-century sculptural and mosaic work. The more elaborate one, with columns resting on six curious lions, dates from 1272. The sacristy contains two paintings by the southern Renaissance artist Andrea da Salerno.

Downstairs is a small **museum** (*open daily Apr–Oct 9–1 and 3–7; adm*) with more bits of the original Cosmatesque interior and an intriguing bust of Sigilgaida Rufolo by Bartolomeo di Nicola, the sculptor of the lions' *ambone*. In this cathedral in 1149 the English pope, Adrian IV, crowned William the Bad King of Sicily. You can see decorative work similar to the cathedral's at the churches of **Santa Maria a Gradillo** and **San Giovanni del Toro**.

From Ravello, it's a lovely half-hour's walk to **Scala**, smallest and oldest of the three Amalfitan towns and a genteel option for the traveller seeking peace and parsimony in the refreshing mountain air. Perched on the hillside across from Ravello, it's unfettered by the glitz of other resorts. It has another interesting old cathedral, **San Lorenzo**, housing a 13th-century wooden crucifix. The town is also the birthplace of Gerardo da Sasso, who started out running a small hostel for pilgrims in Jerusalem and ended up founding the Knights Hospitallers, or Knights of St John (1118); his family's **ruined palace** is near the village. Above Scala, the chapel of San Pietro in **Campoleone** has medieval carvings of St Michael and St Catherine, if you can find someone with the key.

Salerno

Anywhere else in the south, a city like Salerno would be an attraction in itself; here it gets lost among the wonders of the Campanian coast and few people pay more than a brief visit. But this is a clean and orderly place, which should endear it to those who hate Naples, and it's also a town where you can rub shoulders with real Italians in shops, restaurants and bars – a nice change from the Amalfi Coast. Its setting against a backdrop of mountains is memorable, too. The Italian highway engineers, showing off as usual, have brought the highway to Salerno across a chain of viaducts, one lofty span after another, creating an unusual and pleasing ornament for the city; at night the road lights hang on the slopes like strings of fairylights on a Christmas tree.

Getting There

There's an express bus from Naples to Salerno, usually every 30mins; it leaves from the **SITA** office on Via Pisanelli, just off Piazza Municipio, **t** 081 552 2176, and arrives in Salerno at Corso Garibaldi 117, **t** 089 226 604.

Where to Stay

Salerno ✉ 84100

Salerno's hotels, although generally modest and utilitarian, are a cheaper alternative to the Amalfi Coast and are also more accessible by car, with secure parking facilities. You could easily base yourself here and explore the towns of the Amalfi Coast by bus on day-trips.

Expensive

★★★★Jolly Hotel delle Palme, Lungomare Trieste 1, **t** 089 225 222, *www.jollyhotels.it*. A pleasant, reliable choice on the seafront.

Moderate

★★★Plaza, Piazza Vittorio Veneto 42, **t** 089 224 477, *www.plazasalerno.it*. Modern and comfortable rooms opposite the station.

★★★Fiorenza, Via Trento 145, **t** 089 338 800, *www.hotelfiorenza.it*. A clean and well-run 30-room hotel convenient for the beach.

Cheap

★★Salerno, Via G. Vicinanza 42, **t** 089 224 211. A simple but comfortable budget option.

Ostello per la Gioventù' Irno, Via Luigi Guercio 112, **t** 089 790 251, Salerno's youth hostel, with a 1am curfew. *Closed daily 10.30–5.*

Eating Out

Expensive

Alla Brace, Lungomare Trieste 11–13, **t** 089 225 159. Fish dishes, plus delicious local specialities such as stuffed peppers, ravioli with ricotta and a remarkable potato soufflé. *Closed Tues.*

Al Cenacolo, Piazza Alfano I 4/6, **t** 089 238 818. A place beside the cathedral, recommended by locals for its fine seafood. Book ahead. *Closed Sun and Mon eves.*

Nicola dei Principati, Corso Garibaldi 201, **t** 089 225 435. An eatery in the old centre, serving mainly fish, including an excellent *linguine con astice* (linguini with lobster).

Il Timone, Via Generale Clark 29, Mercatello, a few km east of town, **t** 089 335 111. A restaurant offering a delicious speciality of *tubetti alla pescatrice* (short pasta with fish sauce). *Closed Mon and Sun eves, last 2wks Aug.*

Cheap

Vicolo della Neve, Vicolo della Neve 24, **t** 089 225 705. A lively restaurant in the *centro storico*, with local art on the walls. Try regional favourites such as *melanzane alla parmigiana* (aubergines with tomato, mozzarella, parmesan and basil). classic *pasta e fagioli* or excellent pizza. *Open lunchtimes and Weds.*

Da Sasa, Via degli Orti 9, **t** 089 220 330. A good trattoria with traditional home cooking. *Closed Fri and Sat lunch, Mon, and Aug.*

Pantaleone, Via dei Mercanti 75, **t** 089 227 7825. The oldest pastry shop in town.

Pinocchio, Lungomare Trieste 56–8, **t** 089 229 964. Great-value pizza and seafood, popular with locals. *Closed Fri.*

Salerno's ancient distinction was its medical school, the oldest and finest in medieval Europe, and of the greatest importance in the transmission of Greek and Muslim science to Europe. Most people, however, recognize the town better as the site of the Allied invasion in September 1943, one of the biggest such operations of the war. Seven months later, Salerno became capital of Italy, until liberation was completed.

Salerno's port is on the outskirts of town, and the shore all through the city centre is graced with a pretty park, the **Lungomare Trieste**. Parallel to it two streets back, Corso Vittorio Emanuele leads into the old town, where it changes its name to Via dei Mercanti, most colourful of Salerno's old streets. The **cathedral**, a block north on Via del Duomo, is set behind a courtyard with a central fountain and a detached campanile, as if it were not a church at all, but a mosque. The Corinthian columns around the church come from the ancient Greek city of Paestum, a short way down the coast (*see* p.906). Its treasures include bronze doors from Constantinople and a pair of Cosmatesque pulpits, though the biggest surprise is the overwhelming mosaic floor, a vast expanse of marble and polychrome tiles of Byzantine inspiration. Many of the best original details have been preserved in the adjacent **Museo del Duomo** (*open daily 9–6.30*).

The Islands of the Bay of Naples

The islands in the Bay of Naples – Capri, Ischia and, to a far lesser extent, Procida – are the holiday queens of the Italian islands. Every schoolchild has heard of Capri, the playground of Emperor Tiberius and Norman Douglas' 'gentlemanly freaks'. Ischia, 50 years ago, was the favourite island of jet-setters jaded by Capri. Renowned in ancient times for its mud baths, it has become a home-from-home for the German bourgeoisie. If anyone tries to tell you it's still 'unspoiled', remind them that it's Italy's biggest buyer of spaghetti-flavoured ice cream. Procida, on the other hand, has hardly been developed at all, though not through lack of charm. For many Italians the name of the island, for years home to a high-security prison, conjures up the associations that Alcatraz does for Americans – which has kept developers away until very recently.

Ischia and Procida are part of the enormous submerged volcano of Campano, which stretches from Ventotene in the Pontine Islands down to Strómboli and the Aeolian Islands. In not too ancient times, the islands were connected to each other and, if Greek geographer Strabo is to be believed, to the Phlegraean Fields on the mainland. He records how, during an eruption of now-dormant Epomeo on Ischia, an earthquake split Ischia–Procida from the mainland, then, in another upheaval, jolted the island in twain. In this same geological cataclysm, Capri broke off from the Sorrentine peninsula, a blow that shattered its coasts to form the island's famous cliffs.

Capri

Capri can lay fair claim to being the most beautiful island in the Mediterranean, a delicious garden of Eden with more than 800 species of flowers and plants cascading over a sheer chunk of limestone. Yet it's an Eden where the angels have definitely let down their guard. Unlike Ischia and other, more recent, tourist haunts, it has the relaxed air of having seen it all. No room remains for property speculators; everything has been built and planted. The tourists come and go every day, almost invisible to the Capriots and other residents, who have learned to turn a blind eye to them.

Between June and September you understand why the word 'trash' is inscribed on the bins in 30 languages. If you don't mind the trendy shops being closed, try coming in November or February instead, when you may enjoy a few brilliant days between the rains, and feel like Adam or Eve (well, almost). It's worth the risk of a soaking or two.

Capri's most famous tourist sight, the **Grotta Azzurra** ('Blue Grotto'), is well named if nothing else – its shimmering, iridescent blueness is caused by the reflection of light on the water in the morning. Similar caverns are fairly common in the Mediterranean, but Capri's is the yardstick by which they are measured. In summer (*1 June–30 Sept*), boats for the grotto leave Marina Grande at 9am, provided the sea is calm. The entrance to the cave is quite low and if there's any swell on the sea at all someone is sure to get a nasty knock on the head.

The architecture of the charming white town of Capri complements the island's natural beauty – much of what is typical and 'home-made' in Mediterranean building can be seen here in the older quarters: the moulded arches and domes; the narrow streets and stairways crossed by buttresses supporting the buildings; the ubiquitous whitewash; the play of light and shadow, and sudden little squares, just large enough for a few children to improvize a game of football. Most of the island's hotels, generally very tasteful and surrounded by gardens. are scattered throughout the town.

If you go up to Capri by *funicolare*, you'll surface next to the much-photographed **cathedral**, with its joyful campanile and clock. Built in the 17th century in the local Baroque style, it has a charming buttressed roof. The little square in its shadow is Piazza Umberto, commonly known as **La Piazzetta**; its outdoor cafés have been frequented by such a variety of eccentrics, dilettantes and celebrities that each chair should have a historical plaque on it (beware – drinks are extraordinarily expensive). On the other side of the piazza is a sheer drop down to Marina Grande.

From Capri Town, the narrow Via Krupp (built by the German arms manufacturer of that name, who spent his leisure hours studying lamprey larvae off the Salto di Tiberio) takes you down the cliffs in 100 hairpin turns to the **Marina Piccola**, the charming little port containing most of Capri's bathing establishments: Da Maria, La Canzione del Mare, Le Sirene and Internazionale (all but the last connected to restaurants). On one side are the ruins of a **Saracen tower**, on the other is the **Scoglio delle Sirene** (Sirens' Rock); if you read the books of Norman Douglas and Edwin Cerio, son of archaeologist Ignazio Cerio, they will convince you that this really was the home of the Sirens. There is a bus, luckily, that makes the steep climb back up the cliffs to Capri Town.

East of Marina Piccola, back past the Certosa, the **Faraglioni** are three enormous limestone pinnacles that tower straight up in the blue-green sea. These rocks are home to the rare blue lizard (*Lacerta coerulea Faraglionensis*) and an unusual species of seagull that supposedly guffaws. From Via Tragara a stairway descends to the point and the **Porto di Tragara** where, for a price, you can take a swim from the platforms beneath the vertical rocks.

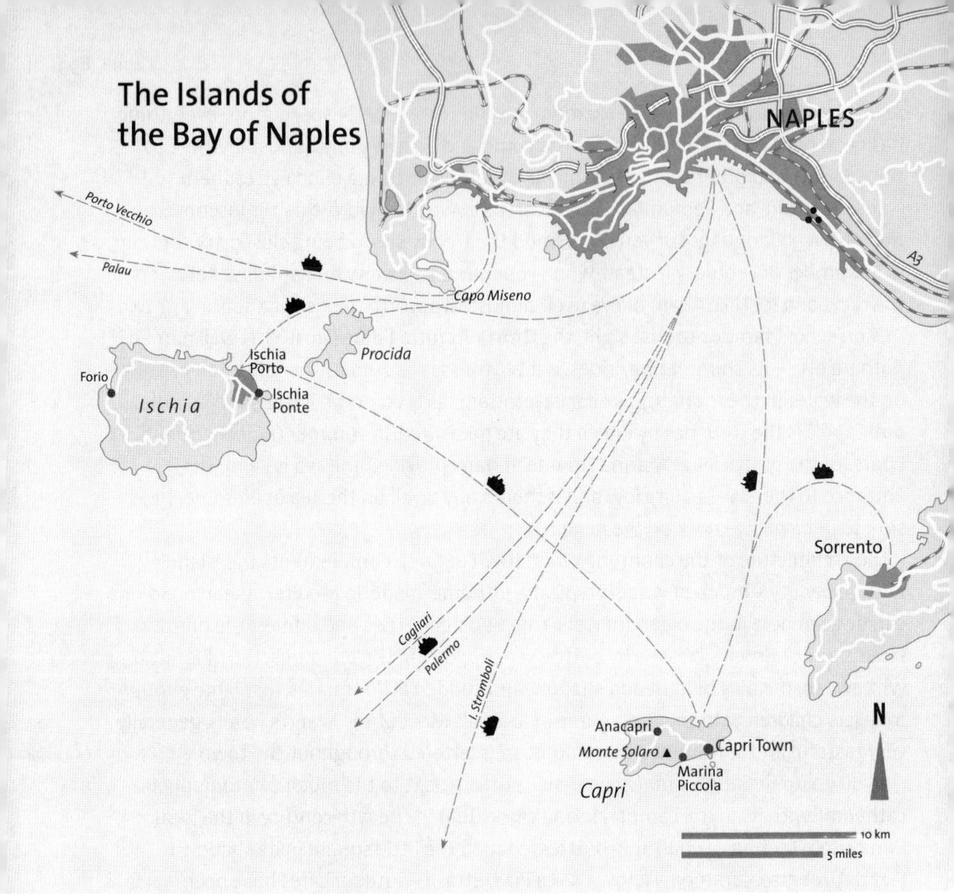

Nearby is the Tragara Terrace, from which there are magnificent views, and the tall skinny rock known as the Pizzolungo. Follow the main track along the coast and up the stairway to the **Grotta di Matromania**, which was the centre of the cult of the goddess Cybele (Mater Magna), whose worship was banned in Rome itself. Part of Capri's reputation as an island of orgies may derive from this ancient eastern cult's noisy hypnotic rituals, which would culminate with the self-castration of the priest. Only vestiges remain of the cave's elaborate décor.

From the Grotta di Matromania, a stepped path leads down to yet another famous eroded rock, the **Arco Naturale**, where dark pines – found everywhere on Capri – cling to every tiny ledge. On the way back to town you'll pass some of the island's vineyards, which produce the rare and famous *Lacrimae Tiberii*.

The **Villa Jovis** (*open daily 9–1hr before sunset; adm*) on Punta del Capo (1,017ft) was the most important of the 12 imperial villas constructed on Capri: from here Tiberius governed the Roman Empire for his last 10 years. Although much has been sacked over the course of the centuries, the extent of the remaining foundations and walls gives you a fair idea of the scale on which the imperial pervert lived. The centre of the villa was occupied by vast cisterns for supplying the private baths, scene of so many naughty capers.

On top of the green plateau above the escarpment spreads the town of **Anacapri**, once a fierce rival to Capri. The construction of the roads in 1874 slowly taught them to reconcile their differences. Although it has its share of hotels, Anacapri retains a rustic air, with its many olive trees and surrounding vineyards and its simple style of architecture – rather Moorish in style with cubic, flat-roofed houses. From Piazza Vittoria, a chairlift travels to the summit of **Monte Solaro**, the highest point on the island at 1,919ft, from which there are stunning views.

Ischia

Ischia is a remarkably lovely island, able to hold its own with Capri in the glitterati sweepstakes. The sea of vineyards encircling its highest peak, volcanic Monte Epomeo (2,601ft), produces excellent wine named after the mountain, and the villages high on its slopes, such as Fontana and Buonopane, remain untouched by the international onslaught at the resorts of Casamicciola, Forio, Lacco Ameno and Ischia Porto.

Unlike Capri, Ischia has many long, first-class beaches. On one – Maronti – the island's volcanic origins are more than evident. The hot mineral springs that gush all year round have attracted cure-seekers since Roman times, and are still recommended for sufferers of rheumatism, arthritis, neuralgia and obesity. Because many of the springs are radioactive, a doctor's permission is often required before you soak (there are physicians on the island who specialize in prescribing such treatments, and they charge a pretty penny). The hottest spring on the island is Terme Rita at Casamicciola, which belches from the earth at around 180°F. Try the renovated Terme Comunali at the port or the unique baths at Cavascura above Sant'Angelo.

The first hint of Ischia's volcanic origins comes at the almost perfectly round harbour of Ischia Porto, formed by a sister crater of Monte Epomeo. It was only linked to the sea in 1855, when Ferdinand II's engineers carved a narrow outlet. Full of yachts and lined with restaurants, it is everything a Mediterranean port should be. Ships dock to the left (as you look out to sea), hydrofoils dock to the right, near the **Terme Comunali**. Via Roma, the main shopping street, with cafés and boutiques, passes the **Chiesa dell'Assunta**, built in 1300 and given a Baroque makeover.

Further on, when Via Roma becomes the more fashionable Corso Vittoria Colonna, turn down Via V. F. d'Avalos for the numerous seaside *pensioni*, or down Via V.E. Cortese for the **Pineta** (pine wood) – the lovely shady divider between Ischia Porto and Ischia Ponte. From the summit of the extinct volcano behind the town, **Montagnone** (836ft), views stretch to the Phlegraean Fields on the mainland. **Ischia Ponte** – once a separate fishing village – is slowly being gobbled up by the tourist sprawl of Ischia Porte. 'Ponte' refers to the causeway built by Alfonso (Il Magnifico) of Aragon in 1441 to the Castello d'Ischia on its offshore rock. Popular **beaches** line many of the town's shores.

In Ischia Porte there are private beaches, Ciro, Medusa, Lauro and Starace, for which you have to pay. Others, such as Spiaggia degli Inglesi (named after the English occupation at the beginning of the 18th century) and Dei Pini, are free. On the tiny islet across the causeway from Ischia Ponte, the fortress of the **Castello d'Ischia** (or Castello Aragonese; ***t*** *081 991 956; open 9.30–7.30; adm*) is on a rugged outcrop.

Getting to the Islands

In summer, there are frequent ferries and hydrofoils from Naples, plus services from Sorrento to Capri and Pozzuoli to Procida and Ischia. In Naples, ferries and hydrofoils leave from Molo Beverello or Mergellina dock in Chiaia.

From Molo Beverello, Naples

Alilauro, **t** 081 761 1004, *www.alilauro.it*, hydrofoil to Ischia Forio and Ischia Porto (daily, every hour).

Caremar, **t** 081 551 3882, *www.caremar.it*, 4 hydrofoils and 6 ferries daily to Capri; 6 hydrofoils and 8 ferries to Ischia via Procida.

Linea Jet, **t** 081 550 763, *www.navlib.it*, ferries to Capri (daily, about every 90mins).

Linee Lauro, **t** 081 552 2838, *www.lineelauro.it*, ferries to Ischia (7 daily, every 90mins).

From Mergellina, Naples

Alilauro, *see* Molo Beverello.

SNAV, **t** 081 761 2348, *www.snavali.com*, hydrofoil to Capri (5 daily), Ischia (6 daily) and Procida (4 daily).

From Sorrento

Linee Marittime Partenopee, **t** 081 807 1812, ferries (20mins, 5 daily) and hydrofoils (10mins, 16 daily) to Capri.

Caremar, **t** 081 807 3077, *www.caremar.it*, fast ferry service to Capri (10mins, 4 daily).

From Salerno, Amalfi, Positano

A ferry service called the *Faraglione* leaves Salerno's Molo Manfredi (towards the western end of town) at 7.30am daily, calling at Amalfi and Positano on the way to Capri.

Getting Around

Capri

From Marina Grande, you can go up to Capri or Anacapri on one of the frequent **buses**, or take the **funicular** up to Capri Town (*daily 6.30am–12.30am, Oct–Apr until 9pm; every 15mins*), although it's crowded in summer.

Regular **buses** run from Capri Town to Anacapri, Marina Piccola and Damecuta, and from Anacapri to Faro, the Grotto Azzurra, Marina Grande and Marina Piccola.

There's a **chairlift** from Anacapri to Monte Solaro (*12mins; Mon and Weds–Sun summer 9.30–sunset; Nov–Feb 10.30–3*).

Finally, you can **walk** to most places. The trails across the island are major attractions, but pack a mac out of season, just in case.

Ischia

Ischia is considerably larger than Capri. **Buses** and **taxis** around the island depart from the square next to Santa Maria di Portosalvo in Ischia Porto. **SEPSA** runs buses along the SS270 (which circles the island) in both directions: CD buses run clockwise, CS anti-clockwise.

Cars can be hired relatively cheaply. In Ischia Porto, try **Autonoleggio Balestrieri**, Via Jasolino 27, **t** 081 985 691 (inside a harbourfront bar); in Forio, try **Davidauto**, Via G. Mazzella 104, **t** 081 998 043. Or rent a *motorino* (moped) – traffic here is less threatening than on the mainland.

Procida

There are **buses** every 20mins or so between the harbour and Chiaiolella at the other end of Procida, stopping more or less everywhere, or there are diesel buggies that serve as **taxis**.

Tourist Information

Capri Town: Piazza Umberto 1, **t** 081 837 0686 (*open daily 9–8.30*).

Marina Grande: Banchina del Porto, **t** 081 837 0634 (*open Mon–Sat 8.30–8.30, Sun 8.30–2*).

Anacapri: Via G. Orlandi 59/a,**t** 089 837 1524 (*open Mon–Sat 9.15–1 and 1.30–5*).

Ischia Porto, Via Jasolino, **t** 081 507 4211. Or try the friendlier **Centro Servizi Turistici**, Via Jasolino 72, **t** 081 98 061. A good website for information on Ischia is *www.ischiaonline.it*.

Marina Grande: Via Roma 92 (by ticket office near ferry departure point), **t** 081 810 1968 (*open daily summer 9–1 and 3.30–7.30, winter 9–1*).

Where to Stay

Capri ✉ 80073

Hotel prices on Capri are well above average, and rooms for the summer often get booked up months in advance.

Luxury

*****Grand Hotel Quisisana, Via Camerelle 2, Capri Town, t 081 837 0788, *www.quisi.com*. The place to stay if money's no object, set in its own grounds and equipped with a pool, a gym, tennis courts and more. *Closed Nov–Mar.*

*****La Scalinatella, Via Tragara 8, Capri Town, t 081 837 0633, *www.scalinatella.com*. A jewel of a hotel with stunning views, 31 beautifully decorated rooms, a pool and a good restaurant.

****Hotel Punta Tragara, Via Tragara 57, Punta Tragara, t 081 837 0844, *www.hoteltragara.com*. A de luxe resort hotel in a building designed by Le Corbusier, with a pool, gym, a lovely veranda restaurant, a nightclub in the rocks and spectacular views. *Closed Nov–Mar.*

****La Palma, Via V. Emanuele 39, Capri Town, t 081 837 0133, *www.lapalma-capri.com*. A hotel in its own gardens, with majolica-tiled floors in the rooms and an airy feel. Staff are charming. *Closed Nov–Easter.*

****Villa Brunella, Via Tragara 24a, on way up to Punta Tragara, t 081 837 0122, *www.villabrunella.com*. A pretty hotel with private villa-style accommodation on terraces that overlook Monte Solaro. There is a good restaurant and a pool. *Closed Nov–Mar.*

Very Expensive

***Floridiana, Via Campo di Teste 16, Capri Town, t 081 837 0166, *www.lafloridiana-capri.com*. A hotel boasting fine sea panoramas. Lone travellers pay half the cost of a double room. *Closed Nov–Mar.*

Expensive

**Villa Krupp, Viale Matteotti 12, Capri Town, t 081 837 0362. A lovely historic hotel with enviable views, antique furniture and a relaxed and welcoming ambience. Trotsky stayed and left a samovar. Book well ahead. *Closed Nov–Feb.*

*Stella Maris, Via Roma 27, Capri Town, t 081 837 0452. A cosy, clean, well-run family-run affair close to the bus station. Most rooms look down to the Marina Grande below and across to distant Ischia.

*La Tosca, Via D. Birago, Capri Town, t 081 837 0989, *www.latoscahotel.com*. A recently refurbished hotel with clean tiled rooms and high ceilings. Ask for a room with a view. *Closed Nov–Mar.*

Ischia Porto ✉ 80077

*****Excelsior Belvedere, Via E. Gianturco 1, t 081 991 522, *www.excelsiorischia.it* (*expensive*). A fine, stylish hotel in a sidestreet, with a fine pool and garden. *Closed Nov–Mar.*

****Mare Blu, Via Pontano 44, t 081 982 555, *www.hotelmareblu.it* (*expensive*). A sleek hotel in a charming position on the waterfront, a short walk from the centre. There's a private beach over the road, two pools and a great view of the castle. *Closed Nov–May.*

****Villa Rosa, Via G. Gigante 5, t 081 991 316, *www.lavillarosa.it* (*expensive*). An elegant hotel screened from the outside world by a leafy forecourt. Tastefully furnished, it has a small pool and a garden, and offers thermal treatments. *Closed Nov–Mar.*

***Parco Verde, Via Mazzella 43, t081 992 282, *www.parcoverde.com* (*expensive*). A hotel in an attractive park amidst shady pines, with full thermal facilities and trained staff. There's a pool in the grounds and it's a short walk from the beach.

**Macrì, Via Jasolino 78a, t 081 992 603 (*moderate*). A well-run, relaxed hotel a couple of steps from the harbour front, popular with young, independent travellers. Rooms on the first floor are best.

Ischia Ponte ✉ 80077

***Monastero, Castello Aragonese 39, t 081 992 435, *www.castelloaragonese.it* (*expensive*). A hotel within the Castello Aragonese itself, with 14 clean and simple en suite rooms in the cells where monks once slept. It's a bit of a climb, but the view is unforgettable. *Closed Nov–Mar.*

Ischia, Lacco Ameno ✉ 80076

*****Regina Isabella, Piazza Santa Restituta, t 081 994 322, *www.reginaisabella.it* (*luxury*). A swanky hotel on the waterfront, with a beach, superb gym and some well-known spas. Service is impeccable, if lacking true warmth. *Closed Nov–Mar.*

*****San Montano, Via Monte Vico, t 081 994 033, *www.sanmontano.com* (*luxury*). A resort hotel with a pool, tennis courts and other comforts, plus thermal baths. *Closed Nov–Mar.*

**Bristol, Via Fundera 88, t 081 994 566 (*cheap*). The best budget bet, with a small garden, a pool and friendly staff. *Closed Nov–Mar.*

Procida ✉ 80079

Though there are few places to stay on Procida, it's a tranquil spot away from the crowds.

***Crescenzo**, Via Marina Chiaiolella 33, short walk from Chiaiolella beach, **t** 081 896 7255, *www.hotelcrescenzo.it* (*moderate*). A landmark harbourfront hotel with simple but pleasant rooms, most with showers, and a good restaurant. The sunroof offers a great view.

***Riviera**, Via Giovanni da Procida 36, a 10min walk from Chiaiolella, **t** 081 896 7197, *www.hotelrivieraprocida.it* (*moderate*). A pretty hotel on the bus route through the centre of the island, with 23 rooms in a relaxed sunny environment, and extremely friendly owners. Half or full board is required in high season. *Closed Nov–Mar.*

Eating Out

Capri Town

Very Expensive

I Faraglioni, Via Camerelle 75, **t** 081 837 0320. A place with good house specialities such as *crêpes al formaggio* (thin pancakes filled with cheese) and *risotto ai frutti di mare*.

Expensive

La Capannina, Via delle Botteghe 12–14, **t** 081 837 0732. Capri's best restaurant, set in a secluded garden and offering wonderful pasta, fish and desserts. *Closed Weds and Nov–Mar.*

Da Paolino, Via Palazzo a Mare 11, between Capri Town and Marina Grande, **t** 081 837 6102. A restaurant where you can eat in an arbour of lemon trees; most dishes were inspired by the fruit. *Closed lunchtimes and Feb–Easter.*

Moderate

Da Gemma, Via Madre Serafina 6, **t** 081 837 0461. A welcoming trattoria offering superb local dishes and good pizza. *Closed Mon except Aug, and Jan and Feb.*

Anacapri

Da Gelsomina alla Migliara, Via La Migliara 72, **t** 081 837 1499 (*expensive*). A trattoria about a half-hour walk from the Piazzetta, with home-made wine to go with its home-cooked island specialities. *Closed Tues except high season and Jan.*

Ischia Porto

Island rabbit is prominent on local menus.

Zi Nannina a Mare, Lungomare Cristoforo Colombo 1, **t** 081 991 350 (*very expensive*). A delightful family-run restaurant offering local specialities. *Closed Nov–Mar.*

Gennaro, Via Porto 66, **t** 081 992 917 (*expensive*). A convivial place that has attracted the likes of Tom Cruise and Andrew Lloyd Webber, with delicious Ischian specialities. *Closed Nov–Mar.*

Il Damiano, Via delle Vigne, on SS270 towards Casamicciola, **t** 081 983 093 (*expensive*). Superb sea views and beautifully cooked seafood. *Closed lunchtimes and Oct–Easter.*

Da Cocò, Piazzale Aragonese, **t** 081 981 823 (*moderate*). A relaxed, noisy eatery on the seafront, run by a retired fisherman. *Closed Weds except high season, and Jan and Feb.*

Ischia Ponte ✉ 80077

Giardini Eden, Via Nuova Cartaromana 68, **t** 081 985 015 (*expensive*). Fantastic views and excellent seafood. There's a free taxi-boat (*eves only*) from Via Pontana. *Closed Oct–Apr.*

Pirozzi, Via Seminario 51, **t** 081 991 121 (*moderate*). A bustling pizzeria. *Closed Mon except high season, and Dec.*

Ciro e Caterina, Via Luigi Mazzella 80, **t** 081 993 122 (*cheap*). A decent restaurant not far from the castle, with tables spilling out beneath a palm tree. *Closed Thurs except high season.*

Ischia, Lacco Ameno

Al Delfino, Corso A. Rizzoli 116, **t** 081 900 252 (*expensive*). A glass-fronted harbourfront restaurant with delicious food. *Closed Weds except high season, and Nov–Mar.*

Procida

La Medusa, Via Roma 116, Marina Grande, **t** 081 896 7481 (*very expensive*). A good restaurant along the port. Try the speciality, *spaghetti ai ricci di mare* (with sea urchins). *Closed Tues except high season, and Jan and Feb.*

Il Cantinone, Via Roma 55, Marina Grande, **t** 081 896 8811 (*moderate*). A low-key eatery serving pizza, homely dishes and great *fritto misto di pesce*. *Closed Tues except high season.*

With the large dome of its **abandoned church** in the centre, the fortress where Vittoria Colonna spent so many years looks like an illustration from a book of fairy tales. There are atmospheric narrow streets and 500-year-old houses, and the views from the walls are superb. Don't miss the **crypt** with its lovely frescoes by Giotto's disciples. Come on 26 July for the festival of Sant'Anna to see the island's traditional *'ndrezzata*, a dagger dance dating from the time of Vittoria Colonna, accompanied by clarinets and tambours.

Procida

Lovely, uncomplicated and tiny, Procida is in many ways the archetypal 'Italian island' of many holiday-makers' dreams. Scented by groves that produce the finest lemons in Italy (the *granita* served in almost every local bar is a treat) and embellished with colourful houses as original as they are beautiful, it has been the setting for two famous love stories and, more recently, the Oscar-winning *Il Postino*. Most people here still earn a living from the sea, as sailors or fishermen, or from carving lovely models of historic ships. Its very proximity to the glamour and chaos of Naples, Capri and Ischia has saved it from the worst ravages of touristic excess, and the pace of life is delightfully slow: when there was talk of converting the prison into a hotel, locals shuddered, preferring the cons to any Capri-like transformation of their idyllic life.

The main settlement of Procida is at the north of the island and includes the port, the high walled district of Terra Murata and the old fishing village of Corricella. Connected to Procida by a modern bridge is the minute islet of Vivara, officially a natural park of Naples, which teems with wild rabbits, an important ingredient in Procida's cuisine, along with the more obvious fruits of the sea.

Ships and hydrofoils call at the port of **Marina Grande**. Walk up Via Roma to Piazza Sancio Cattolico (also called Sent'Co). The church here, **Santa Maria della Pietà** (1616), gives you a taste of Procida's delightful architecture – wide arches in random rhythms and exterior rampant stairs crisscrossing the façades, all in softly moulded lines. North of Marina Grande is Via Annunziata, named after the **Chiesa dell'Annunziata**. The church was reconstructed in 1600 and contains a miraculous Madonna, to whom are given the many votive offerings that adorn the interior. It has pretty views to the lighthouse and Punta Pioppeto, where people often swim. Nearby is the remaining watchtower of three constructed in the 16th century. From **Punta Cottimo** you can see the island of Ventotene, halfway to Rome and part of the same volcano as Procida.

Back towards the port is **Piazza dei Martiri**, where twelve Procidanese were executed in 1799 by the Bourbons for plotting a revolt. Near the piazza is the domed 17th-century **Madonna delle Grazie**, with a revered statue of the Virgin.

South of the piazza, through the Porta Mezz'Olmo, is the walled **Terra Murata** quarter. This section of town, which occupies the highest ground on the island, was fortified as a protection against Saracen pirates, and the island's inhabitants would retreat here in times of danger. The walls that you can see today date from different periods – the latest portions are from 1521; the oldest parts, around the Porta, were built in medieval times.

At the highest point of the Terra Murata, past the romantic if roofless ruins of **Santa Margherita Nuova** (*currently under restoration*), built in 1586 at the edge of the Punta dei Monaci, the **abbey of San Michele Arcangelo** perches on a cliff edge and has magnificent views. Despite its exotic, almost Saracen appearance from a distance, it wears a simple unadorned façade. The domes are untiled – Procida receives so little rain that tiles aren't strictly necessary, or at least not worth the cost. Of the original pre-16th-century structure, only part of the ceiling in the Sala del Capitolo remains. Many works of art in the three-naved church attest to the former splendour of the Benedictines; the painted wooden ceiling dates from the 17th century, as do the apse paintings by Nicola Rosso, the most interesting of which shows God's aide-de-camp, Michael, and his putti swooping down to save Procida from the Turks. Pride of place goes to a splashy canvas by Neapolitan Luca Giordano.

Near the abbey, in Piazza d'Armi, is the Cardinal of Aragon's 1563 **Castello d'Avalos**. Bought by the Bourbons in 1744 as a royal hunting residence, it was converted into a prison in 1818 and abandoned in 1988. Around here, too, you can see sections of the Terra Murata walls, inside which are tortuous alleyways and steep narrow houses.

In the protected cove beneath the citadel is the fishing village of **Corricella**, the oldest settlement on the island. It can only be reachd on foot via steep stone stairways that cascade down among the arches and pastel-painted houses. Some of the homes here have been extensively remodelled over the centuries, providing proof of an old island saying, that 'a house isn't only a house. A house is a story.'

Some old palaces may be seen along the escarpment overlooking Chiaia beach – including the **Palazzo Minichini** on Via Marcello Scotti, next to the fine old church of **San Tommaso d'Aquino**, and the **Casa di Graziella**.

Campania Inland

There's more to the region than the Bay of Naples, yet the coast and its endless attractions draw off most of the tourists, and it's a rare soul who makes it up to old Capua, or the excellent little city of Benevento.

Capua

This is a double city, consisting of the modern town, founded in the 9th century, and the ancient one, once the second city of Italy but deserted in the Dark Ages and now modestly reborn as **Santa Maria Capua Vetere.** Capua was founded by the Oscans, blithe folk of ancient Italy who introduced farce to the theatre, and gave us the word *obscene*. The Oscan farces, banned by all decent Roman emperors, carried the seed of *commedia dell'arte* stock characters – which should give you an idea of the spirit of old Capua, a city as renowned for loose morals in its day as Sybaris. All but the jealous Roman historians gave Capua credit for defeating Hannibal. The Capuans had always hated the dreary dour Romans and eagerly took the Carthaginians' part. Hannibal's men enjoyed Capuan hospitality in the winter of 216 BC; they came so dreamy-eyed and dissipated they never beat the Romans again.

Of course there was hell to pay when the Romans came back, but Capua survived, and even flourished for several more centuries as the greatest city of the region. Finally, though, some even worse enemies than the Romans arrived – the Arabs, who utterly destroyed the city in about AD 830. The survivors refounded Capua on a new site, a few kilometres to the north.

At Santa Maria Capua Vetere, you can see the remains of the second-largest **amphitheatre** in Italy (***t*** *848 800 288; open 9–1hr before sunset; adm*) – it was the largest of all before Rome built its Colosseum. A short walk away is something much more interesting – perhaps the best example of a ***mithraeum*** discovered in the Mediterranean (*open Tues–Sun 9–1hr before sunset*). The cult of the god Mithras, imported from Persia by the legionaries, was for a while the most widespread of the cults that tried to fill the religious vacuum of the imperial centuries. Some scholars see in it much in common with Christianity, but the resemblance isn't obvious; Mithraism was an archaic, visceral cult, with mystery initiations and bull's blood. Though it took hold in the army, and always remained a men-only affair, as late as the 3rd century AD it still claimed more adherents than Christianity. The upper classes were never too impressed with it, which is why it lost out to the Christians, and why such well-executed frescoes as these are rare. The *mithraeum* is an underground hall used in the initiations and dominated by a large scene of Mithras, a typical Mediterranean solar hero, slaying a white bull with a serpent under its feet; the fresco representing the moon on the opposite wall is less well preserved.

The **archaeological museum of Ancient Capua** on Via Roberto D'Angio (*open Tues–Sun 9–7*) provides a convenient introduction to the site, complementing the more important Museo Campano at new Capua. Also around Santa Maria, you'll find a crumbling triumphal arch, and some elaborate Roman tombs, situated off the road to Caserta.

The new Capua has all the most interesting finds from the old one at the **Museo Provinciale Campano** at Via Principi Longobardi 1/3 (*open Tues–Sat 9–2, Sun 9–1; adm*) though most people will probably make do with the museum at Santa Maria Capua Vetere. Just to the north of the town, on the slopes of Mount Tifata, a site that was once occupied by a temple of Diana now contains the 11th-century basilica of **Sant'Angelo in Formis**. The 12th-century frescoes here are some of the best in the south – they are oddly archaic figures that would seem much more at home in Constantinople than in Italy. And, more than mere artistry, there is an intense spiritual vision about these paintings – note especially the unearthly, unforgettable face of the enthroned St Michael above the portal.

North of Capua, near the border with Lazio, the last town in Campania along the Via Appia is **Sessa Aurunca**, with a Roman bridge and some other scanty ruins, as well as a 12th-century cathedral, interesting for its surviving ancient and medieval sections.

Caserta

In one shot, you can see the biggest palace in Italy, and also the most wearisome; both distinctions belong uncontestably to the **Reggia**, or Royal Palace, built here by the Bourbon King of Naples, Charles III (*royal apartments open Tues–Sun 8.30–7.30;*

Getting Around

The 3 main towns of Campania's interior are all provincial capitals, but none is on the main **rail** lines; you have to scrutinize schedules in Naples carefully to find your way round. For **Capua** take the Piedimonte Matese train from Naples to Santa Maria Capua Vetere. Trains to **Caserta** are more frequent and convenient for the Reggia. Remote **Benevento** is not well linked with any of Italy's main transport systems; it is on the Naples–Foggia rail line, but some Naples–Benevento trains are run by a faster private railway, and you need to buy the right ticket (ask at the info booth in the station).

Buses for Caserta, Capua, Avellino and Benevento leave Naples from Piazza Garibaldi, in front of the Stazione Centrale. The Consorzio Trasporti Pubblici, **t** 081 700 1111, runs regular buses to **Caserta** station (1hr). From here there are buses to Santa Maria Capua Vetere. Benevento is best reached by bus. Consorzio Trasporti Irpini, **t** 081 553 4677, has regular buses to **Avellino** (50min) and **Benevento** (1½hrs) from Naples' Piazza Garibaldi. In Benevento, buses to Naples and a variety of other places (including one daily to Rome) leave from Piazza Pacca. There are several companies; check at the EPT for schedules.

Tourist Information

Caserta: in the Reggia, **t** 0823 277 320, *www.reggiadicaserta.org* (*open daily 8.30–6.30*).

Benevento: Via Nicola Sala 31, **t** 0824 319 911 (*open Mon–Fri 8–2 and 3–6*), information office in Palazzo Bosco, Piazza Roma 11, **t** 0824 319 938 (*open Sat 9–4*).

Avellino: Piazza Libertà 83100, **t** 0825 74732 (*open daily 8.15–1.30*).

Where to Stay and Eat

Capua and Caserta are not tempting places for an overnight stay, but there are some good restaurants around Caserta. Benevento is little visited by tourists but is all the more attractive for that, making an ideal base for forays into inland Campania, as well as Caserta and Capua. Its several good restaurants are better value than those on the coast and in Naples; menus are strong on rabbit, duck, lamb and veal. Samnium makes some good but little-known wines; try Solopaca red.

Around Caserta

Rocca di Sant'Andrea, Via Torre 8, Casertavecchia, **t** 0827 971 232 (*expensive*). Delicious pasta dishes, meat grilled on the open fire, and good home-made desserts. *Closed Mon.*

La Castellana, Via Torre 4, near Rocca di Sant' Andrea, **t** 0823 371 230 (*moderate*). A trattoria offering wild boar and venison in season, plus innovative soup and pasta *primi*. *Closed Thurs.*

Ritrovo dei Patriarchi, Via Conte Landolfo 14, Loc. Sommana, outside Casertavecchia, **t** 0823 371 510 (*moderate*). A good place for game in season, plus good hearty soups and vegetable dishes. *Closed Thurs.*

Benevento ✉ 82100

******Gran Hotel Italiano**, Viale Principe di Napoli 137, **t** 0824 24111 (*moderate*). The best hotel in town, with 1970s architecture and décor, and 2 original prints by Piranesi. Staff are helpful and prices provincial, but the 20-min walk to the historic centre is a drawback.

****Della Corte**, Piazza Piano di Corte, **t** 0824 54819 (*cheap*). A charming, characterful *pensione* in the heart of the historic quarter. The 7 rooms are clean and quiet.

Ristorante Teatro Gastronomico, Via Traiano-Palazzo L. Andreotti, **t** 0824 54605 (*moderate*). A fun restaurant in the piazza in front of Trajan's Arch, with a gastronomic menu of local specialities. *Closed Mon.*

Pizzeria Rodolfo, Via Meo Martini, **t** 0824 51761, (*cheap*). A place considered by many to be the best pizzeria in town.

Pizzeria Romana, Viale Spinelli 27 (*cheap*). A stand-up *tavola calda* on the corner of Corso Dante and Corso Vittorio Emanuele, a block west of the cathedral, with an excellent selection of affordable delicacies for picnics in the gardens of the Reggia at Caserta and other sites.

Trattoria Nunzia, Via Annunziata 152, **t** 0824 29431 (*cheap*). A third-generation trattoria situated in the pretty medieval area, offering a range of surprising specialities such as delicious *cavatielli fagioli e cozze* (home-made pasta with beans and mussels). *Closed Sun.*

adm). His architect, Luigi Vanvitelli, spared no expense; like the Spanish Bourbons, those of Naples were envious of Versailles, and wanted to show the Louies back home that they, too, deserved a little respect.

The Reggia, begun in 1752, has some 1,200 rooms – this is not many compared with the 2,800 of the Bourbon palace in Madrid, but it is larger than its Spanish cousin just the same (it's also bigger than Versailles); the façade is 804ft across. Inside, as in Madrid, everything is tasteful, ornate and soberingly expensive; the only good touches from Vanvitelli's heavy hand are the elegant grand staircases.

The **park** (*open Tues–Sun 8.30–1hr before sunset; adm*) is what makes the trip worthwhile – an amazingly long axis of pools and cascades climbs up to the famous **Diana fountain**, with a lifelike sculptural group of the goddess and her attendants catching Actaeon in the act. There is also an **English garden**, the sort fashionable in the 18th century and a good place for a picnic.

The village of **San Leucio**, three kilometres north of Caserta, was founded by the Bourbon kings as a paternalistic utopian experiment, and for the manufacture of silk. Ferdinand IV, for most of his life, saw to every detail of its operation, even christening the children of the workers. The successor of his Real Fabbrica is still a silk centre.

Some nine kilometres to the east there is the half-deserted town of **Casertavecchia**. The building of the Reggia drew most of the population down to modern Caserta, but the old town still has the 12th-century **cathedral** (*open daily 9–1 and 5.30–6*) with an octagonal *ciborium* (a cylindrical or prismatic dome) that is one of the glories of Arab-Norman architecture.

The Duchy of Benevento

Ever since the Middle Ages, the land around Caserta and Capua has been called the Terra del Lavoro – cultivated land, a broad garden plain that is one of the most fertile corners of Italy. Today its lush landscapes have suffered creeping industrialization, though it's to the south, between Caserta and Naples, that the worst depredations can be seen. The Napoletani call the towns around Afragola, Acerra and Secondigliano the 'Triangle of Death' – a wasteland of shanties and power lines, ruled by the Camorra, that has Italy's worst unemployment, and its worst social problems.

Go east instead, up into the foothills of the Apennines towards Benevento, yet another small city that has often played a big role in Italian history. On an old tower in the centre of town, the city fathers have put up maps of southern Italy, showing the boundaries of the two important states of which Benevento was capital. At first, as *Malies* or *Maloenton*, it was the main town of the Samnites, warlike mountain people who resisted Roman imperialism for so long. The Romans later made a big city of it, an important stop along the Appian Way. They Latinized the name to *Maleventum* – ill wind – but after a lucky defeat of Pyrrhus of Epirus here in 275 BC they thought it might just be a *Beneventum* after all. In AD 571, the city was captured by the bloodthirsty Lombards, becoming their southern capital. After the Lombards of the north fell to Charlemagne, the Duchy of Benevento carried on as an independent state; at its greatest extent, under relatively enlightened princes such as Arechi II (*c.* 800), it ruled almost all southern Italy. The Normans put an end to it in the 1060s.

If you come to Benevento in winter, you're bound to think the Romans were crazy to change the name. When the Salernitani are ready to hit the beaches, the Beneventani are still shivering on street corners in fur caps, victims of the worst weather in southern Italy. It is claimed that this makes them more serious and introspective than people on the coast – certainly it seems a thousand miles away. Benevento has often been shaken by earthquakes, and the city took plenty of hard shots during the battles of 1943, but there are still attractions to make a stop worthwhile.

Benevento's **cathedral** is in the lower town, the part that suffered most bombings. The cathedral itself was a near total loss; only its odd 13th-century façade remains, built of bits of Roman buildings – reliefs, friezes and pillars – arranged every which way. In the old streets behind it is a dismally kept **Roman theatre** (*t 0824 29970; open daily 9–1hr before sunset; adm*) – not an amphitheatre but a place for classical drama, something rare this far north. By the time the Romans conquered them, the culture of the Samnites was almost completely Hellenized. This theatre, built under Hadrian, originally seated 20,000; it is still used. All through this quarter, the **Triggio**, you will see bits of Roman brick and medieval masonry in the walls of houses. There is half a Roman bridge (the Ponte Leproso – leper's bridge) over the river Sabato, ruins of baths, remains of a triumphal arch, and gates and fortification walls built by the Lombards. On Via Posillipo, a Baroque monument houses the *Bue Apis*, a sacred Egyptian bull sculpture found in Benevento's Temple of Isis.

Trajan's Arch

Some people claim Benevento's triumphal arch to be better than Rome's; built in AD 117, it is a serious piece of work with more than 50ft of expensive Parian marble from Greece, and it is better preserved than the ones in the capital. It marks the spot where the Appian Way entered *Beneventum* (now Via Traiana on the edge of the old town); the carved reliefs on both faces record major events in the emperor's career.

Trajan (AD 98–117), conqueror of Dacia (modern-day Romania) and Mesopotamia, ranks among the greatest of the emperors, and a little commemoration would not seem out of hand; nevertheless cynics will enjoy the transparent and sometimes heavy-handed political propaganda of ornaments such as this. In one of the panels, Trajan (the handsome fellow with the curly beard) is shown distributing gifts to children; in another he presides over the *institutio alimentaria* – the dole. Most of the scenes are about victories: Trajan announcing military reforms, Trajan celebrating a triumph, Jove handing Trajan one of his thunderbolts, and finally the Apotheosis, where the late emperor is received among the gods while the goddess Roma escorts Hadrian to coronation as his divinely ordained successor.

The Museo Sannio

Corso Garibaldi is Benevento's main street, just south of Trajan's Arch. Near its eastern end is the city's oldest church, **Santa Sofia**, built in the late 8th century. It is unusual for its plan – an irregular six-pointed star – and was built for the Lombard Prince Arechi II by an architect grounded in the mystic geometry of the early Middle Ages. The vaulting is supported by recycled Roman columns; other columns have been

Some Samnite Curiosities

Two rooms in the Museo Sannio are filled with objects from the Temple of Isis. Anyone who has read Apuleius' *The Golden Ass* will remember just how important the cult of the transcendent goddess Isis was throughout the Roman world. This Egyptian import certainly seems to have found a home in Beneventum; nowhere in Europe has so much fine Egyptian statuary been retrieved. The temple had imperial backing. One of the statues is of the founder, Emperor Domitian himself, in Egyptian dress. Other works portray priestesses, sacred boats and sphinxes, another Apis bull, and a porphyry '*cista mistica*', carved with a snake. The image of Isis is also there, formidably impressive, even without a head.

Somehow this leads naturally to Benevento's more famous piece of exotica – the witches. In the days of the Lombards, women by the hundreds would dance around a sacred walnut tree on the banks of the Sabato ('sabbath') river. Even after the official conversion to Christianity in 663, the older religion persisted, and Benevento is full of every sort of 'witch' story as a result. The best piece of modern sculpture in the Museo Sannio is a representation of the witches' dance. Of course the city has found ways to put the legend to use. In any bar in Italy, you can pick up a bottle of 'liquore Strega' (*strega* means witch) and read on the label the proud device: 'Made next to the train station in Benevento, Italy.'

hollowed out for use as holy water fonts. The church cloister contains one of the south's more interesting provincial museums, the randomly open **Museo Sannio** (***t*** *0824 21812; open in theory Tues–Sun 9–1*). Sannio refers to Samnium, as Benevento's province is still officially called. The 12th-century cloister has a variety of strange twisted columns under pulvins carved with even stranger scenes: monster-hunting, dancing, fantastical animals, bunnies and a camel or two. The best things are in the archaeological section: classic Campanian copies of Greek vases – ceramics production was the engine that drove Campania Felix's economy in its glory days.

Over the road is the little-known **Hortus Conclusus**, a small enclosed garden. The dedicatory **obelisk** from the Isis temple stands in front of the town hall. The Corso takes you to the **Rocca de' Rettori**, a fortress built by the popes in the 14th century; for centuries Benevento was a papal enclave surrounded by the Kingdom of Naples. The fortress is now a part of the museum. Behind it is a lovely park, the **Villa Comunale**.

Samnium

Samnium is one of Italy's smallest provinces, but there are a few towns and villages of interest; the countryside, full of oak and walnut forests, is often reminiscent of a corner of Umbria. **Morcone**, to the north, has a memorable setting, draped on the curving slope of a hill like a Roman theatre. **Telese**, to the west on the road towards Lazio, is near a small but pretty lake with a popular spa. The ruins of the Samnite–Roman town of *Telesia* are remarkable for their perfectly octagonal walls, with gates at the cardinal points. Further north you'll find **San Lorenzello**, famous for its ceramics and for being transformed into an antiques market the last weekend of every month.

Best of all is the town of **Sant'Agata dei Goti**, north of the Via Appia between Benevento and Caserta, with its long line of buildings like a man-made cliff overhanging a little ravine. Sant'Agata takes its name from the Goths who founded it in the 6th century; it was badly damaged in the 1980 earthquake, and its *castello* and the 12th-century church of Santo Menna are still undergoing restoration, though of the former you can see the Salone di Diana and Atteone, and the latter can be viewed by appointment (***t*** *082 717159 or* ***t*** *338 923 8541*).

Southern Campania

Continuing this broad arc around Naples, there are few attractions to the south and east of Benevento, and some attractive mountain scenery in the region of **Irpinia** – most of the province of Avellino. In places, the mountains bear fine forests of chestnuts and oaks, and plantations of hazelnut trees; other parts are grim and bare, testimony to the 19th-century deforestation that ruined so much of southern Italy. Irpinia was also the region that was worst affected by the 1980 earthquake. The provincial capital of **Avellino**, important in Norman times, has been wrecked so many times by earthquakes and invaders that little remains. In the centre, though, the 17th-century Palazzo della Dogana retains its façade of ancient statues and its original clock tower.

The main highway south from Caserta, around the back of Vesuvius, isn't much more promising. Nola, the main town here, began as another Oscan foundation. It had a famous early bishop, St Paulinus, a friend of St Augustine also said to be the inventor of the bell (bells are *campane* in Italian, from their Campanian origin). To celebrate the anniversary of St Paulinus' return from imprisonment by the Vandals, every 27 June the people of **Nola** put on one of the south's more spectacular festivals, the 'lily festival' (*see* p.841).

Further south, in the hills above **Nocera Inferiore**, the ancient hamlet of **Nocera Superiore** has kept intact its 4th-century church, an unusual round building with a cupola that may have been converted from a pagan sanctuary.

Paestum and the Cilento

Paestum: A Lost City

t *0828 811 023; site open daily 9–1hr before sunset; closed 1st and 3rd Mon of month for restoration work; museum open Tues–Sun 9–2; adm.*

The coastal route begins in a fertile plain that meets the Cilento near the ruins of Paestum, site of the only well-preserved Greek temples north of Sicily, and of another key Mediterranean player, the anopheles mosquito. In fact the mosquito gets the credit for preserving Paestum's ruins so well. By the 9th century, this once-great city was breathing its last, a victim of economic decline and Arab raiders. As its people abandoned it for safer settlements in the hills, it was swallowed up by thick subtropical forests; when the people left, malarial mosquitoes took over. By the Middle Ages, the site was uninhabitable and the city's very existence was forgotten. After being hidden away, like the Mayan temples, for almost 1,000 years, the city was rediscovered in the 18th century; a crew of Charles III's road builders stumbled on the huge temples in the midst of the forest.

Originally *Poseidonia*, the city was founded in the 7th century BC by the Sybarites, as a station on the important trade route up Italy's west coast. The Romans took over in 273 BC, and the name became Latinized to Paestum. Famous for its roses, it prospered until the end of the Roman era. Today the forests have been cleared, and the ruins of the city stand in the open. Not only the celebrated temples have survived; much of the five-kilometre circuit of walls still stands, along with some of the towers and gates.

Most of Paestum's important buildings were grouped along an axis between the **Porta Aurea** and the **Porta Giustizia**, with the forum at its centre. The two grand temples are at the southernmost end, two Doric edifices in the finest classical style, known as the **Basilica** and the **Temple of Neptune** – the names are guesses by early archaeologists.

The Neptune temple, the best preserved, was built about 450 BC. It is 200ft long, and the whole structure survives except for the roof and the internal walls. It may have been dedicated to Apollo, like a similar temple at Tarentum, but Hera and Zeus are also possible contenders. The Basilica was divided to house two cults, connected with Hera, the tutelary goddess of the city. It is a century older, and a little smaller. Missing its Doric frieze and pediment, it was not recognized as a temple by the first archaeologists – hence the name Basilica.

The aesthetic may not be quite what you would expect – the dimensions are squat and strong rather than tall and graceful. Still, this is the classic austerity of Greek architecture at its best, and there is more to it than meets the eye. If you look closely along the rows of columns, or the lines of the base, you may notice that nothing in either of them is perfectly straight; the edges bulge outwards, as they do in the Parthenon and every other Greek building – this is an architectural trick called *entasis*, which creates an optical illusion, making the lines seem straight at a distance.

Based on a simple system of perfect proportion, temples like this are the most sober and serious buildings in western architecture. With some imagination you can picture them in their original beauty, covered in a sort of enamel made of gleaming ground marble, setting off the brilliant colours of the polychromed sculptural reliefs on the pediments and frieze.

To the north, around the broad **Forum** – really a simple rectangular space in the manner of a Greek *agora* – are the remains of an ampitheatre, a round *bouleterion*, or council house, and other buildings. Still further north is the third and smallest of the surviving temples, the **Temple of Ceres**.

Paestum's **museum** holds most of the sculptural fragments and finds from the town. Some of the best reliefs are not from Paestum at all, but from the **Sanctuary of Hera**, discovered at the mouth of the Sele river. This temple, which was mentioned by many ancient writers, is said to have been founded by Jason and the Argonauts.

Getting There and Around

Paestum has a **station** on the main **rail** line between Naples and Reggio di Calabria, but only local trains stop. More convenient are the frequent **buses** from Piazza Concordia in Salerno (on the shore, by the Porto Turistico), run by several companies; some follow the coast route, others go through Battipaglia, and some of these continue on to various resort towns on the Cilento coast.

All **Cilento towns** are linked by **bus** to Salerno's Piazza Concordia; there is a bewildering list of companies, towns and schedules; the EPT in Salerno publishes a full list at the front of their annual hotel book. The **railway** line only touches the Cilento coast at two points – Ascea and Pisciotta – and, as at Paestum, not too many trains stop.

There are 2 main **road** routes: the SS18 coast road and the A3 *autostrada* further inland (with the SS19 running alongside it through the Tanagro valley). At Agropoli, the SS267 leaves the SS18 and runs around the Cilento coast. North of Paestum is another turn off the SS18, the SS166 to the east – a long and winding road across the Cilento interior that eventually links up with the A3 *autostrada*.

Tourist Information

Paestum: Piazza V. Veneto, near main station, **t** 089 231432.
AAST: in central Piazza Amendola, 84100, **t** 089 224 744; information office, Via Magna Grecia 155 (near archaeological zone), **t** 0828 811 016, *www.fromitaly.it/Paestum*.
Palinuro: Piazza Virgilio, **t** 0974 938 144.

Where to Stay and Eat

Most people think of Paestum as a day-trip, but there are enough hotels around the site, and by nearby beaches, to make an overnight stay possible and convenient. Some of the best accommodation is at Laura beach, about 5km north of Paestum.

Hotels on the Cilento are mainly modern and unremarkable. Most restaurants are in the hotels, and in summer most hotels insist on full or half board (often an excellent deal).

If you're travelling through Battipaglia make sure you stop at one of the shops selling the unbelievable local *mozzarella di bufala*.

Paestum ✉ 84063

★★★★**Ariston**, Via Laura 13, **t** 0828 851 333 (*expensive*). A modern, businesslike hotel on the main road into Paestum from Salerno, with comfy rooms and all amenities.

★★★★**Le Palme**, Via Sterpina 33, **t** 0828 851 025 (*moderate*). A popular hotel with a private beach a short walk away.

★★★**Laura**, Via Marittima 10, **t** 0828 851 068 (*moderate*). A pretty and relaxed family hotel just north of Le Palme, with its own beach.

Nettuno, Via Nettuno 2, **t** 0828 811 028 (*moderate*). An excellent family-run seafood restaurant in the archaeological zone, under the city walls near Porta Giustizia.

Bar Anna, **t** 0828 811 196 (*moderate*). A friendly bar offering good cold *antipasti* and local buffalo mozzarella in a tomato salad (*insalata alla caprese*). *Closed Mon in winter.*

Palinuro ✉ 84064

★★★★**King's Residence**, Via Piano Faracchio, **t** 0974 931 324, *www.hotelkings.it* (*moderate*). A hotel in a stunning setting just outside town, perched high on the cliffs overlooking the Buondormire ('sleep well') bay. Every room has a terrace or balcony, and there's a pathway leading down to a pretty little private beach, where there's a small bar serving drinks and light meals. *Closed Nov–Feb.*

Da Carmelo, just outside town, 1km along road towards Camerota, **t** 0974 931 138 (*moderate*). A lively trattoria offering good dishes prepared according to traditional old recipes. The seafood comes highly recommended by locals, who throng the place. Don't miss the excellent *antipasti*. Above the restaurant are some self-catering apartments you can rent. *Closed Weds out of season and 15 Oct–30 Nov.*

Taverna del Porto, Via Porto 50, **t** 0974 931 278 (*cheap*). A two-tiered bar and restaurant down by the harbour in Palinuro, with tables a stone's throw from the water's edge, making it ideal for a post-swim light lunch. Dinner is served on the more formal upper level.

From tombs excavated just outside the city come examples of Greek fresco painting – the only ones in existence. Look out for the most famous fresco, *The Diver*, which you will have seen reproduced innumerable times elsewhere. The Greeks took painting as seriously as they did sculpture, but surviving examples are rare. While you are exploring Paestum, keep an eye out for the famous roses (*bifera rosaria Paestum*). More than one 19th-century traveller claimed to have found them growing wild.

The Cilento Coast

For many people, part of Paestum's attraction will be the fine, long beaches that line this part of the coast. Further south, the shore becomes jagged and mountainous, passing groves of pines alternating with cliffs and pocket-sized beaches. Most of the villages along it have become quiet, cosy resorts that cater mostly to Italians. **Agropoli** comes first, then **Santa Maria di Castellabate**, **San Marco** and **Punta Licosa**, situated on the western point of the Cilento and named after the siren Leucosia – legend has it that she threw herself into the sea after failing to entice Ulysses on to the rocks. From here, you can take a boat out to see the unidentified ancient ruins on the uninhabited islet of Licosa. Further down the coast, **Acciaroli** and **Pioppi** are among the more pleasant resorts.

Further south still, inland from Ascea Marina, you can visit the ruins of another Greek city, *Velia*. Don't expect anything spectacular of the order of Paestum – Velia disappeared gradually, and most of its remains were carried off for building stone long ago. *Elea*, as it was known then, was a colony of the Ionian city of Phocaea, and a sister city of another important Phocaean foundation – Marseille, in France. Elea's name lives on in philosophy; the Elean school produced some of the most brilliant minds of the ancient world: logical grinds such as Parmenides, who proposed the first theory of atoms, and wiseacres such as Zeno, with his pesky paradoxes. Fortifications survive, including one well-preserved gate, the Porta Rosa, and just enough of the *agora*, baths and streets to enable us to guess at how the city may have looked.

Both **Ascea Marina** and its neighbouring *località* of **Casalvelino** have some pretty beaches, but the best ones, perhaps, are to be found in the rocky terrain around **Palinuro**. This town, which has a small **museum** of archaeological finds, takes its name from Aeneas' pilot Palinurus, who is supposedly buried here – Virgil in fact made the whole story up for the *Aeneid*, but that hasn't stopped it from sticking fast in local legend. Beyond Palinuro, the sandy coast curves back north into the Gulf of Policastro; here two more pleasant beach villages, **Scario** and **Sapri**, mark the southern boundary of Campania.

The Inland Route: Around the Cilento

South from Salerno, the *autostrada* skirts the back of the Cilento down to Calabria. Christ may have stopped at **Eboli**, but there's no reason you should – and that goes for **Battipaglia** and **Polla** too. The delights of this region are subterranean: two first-rate caves on opposite slopes of the Monti Alburni. **Pertosa** (***t*** *0975 397 037; open daily Apr–Sept 8–7, Oct–Mar 9–4; adm*), near the highway, is the better choice, with guided tours by boat and on foot; potholers (spelunkers) suspect it is connected to the other one, at **Castelcivita**, near the village of **Controne**, which is part of the **National Park of Cilento**, a conservation project established locally to attract tourists. The national park has an attractive mountain landscape that makes good trekking terrain (*call* **t** *0974 952 135 for more information*).

At **Teggiano** there is a 13th-century castle and cathedral, as well as a little museum. **Padula**, just off the highway, is the unlikely location of the **Certosa di San Lorenzo**, after San Martino in Naples probably the biggest and richest monastery in the south. The Certosa has been closed for more than a century, but in its heyday it would have held hundreds of Carthusians, in a complex laid out in the form of a gridiron (recalling the martyrdom of St Lawrence; the same plan was used in El Escorial in Spain, which is also dedicated to the saint). Though it was expanded and rebuilt over the course of 400 years, its best parts are Baroque: an enormous, elegant cloister, some wonderfully garish frescoes and lavish stucco figures in and around the chapel, and various eccentric but well-executed decorative details throughout. There is a small **archaeological museum**.

Calabria and the Basilicata

20

Calabria and the Basilicata

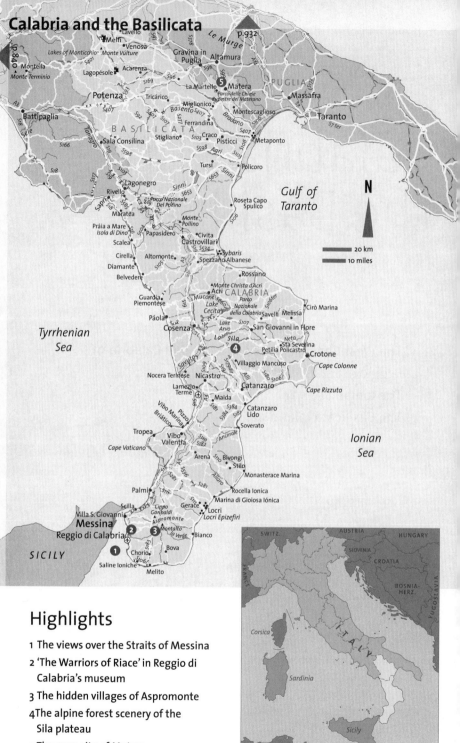

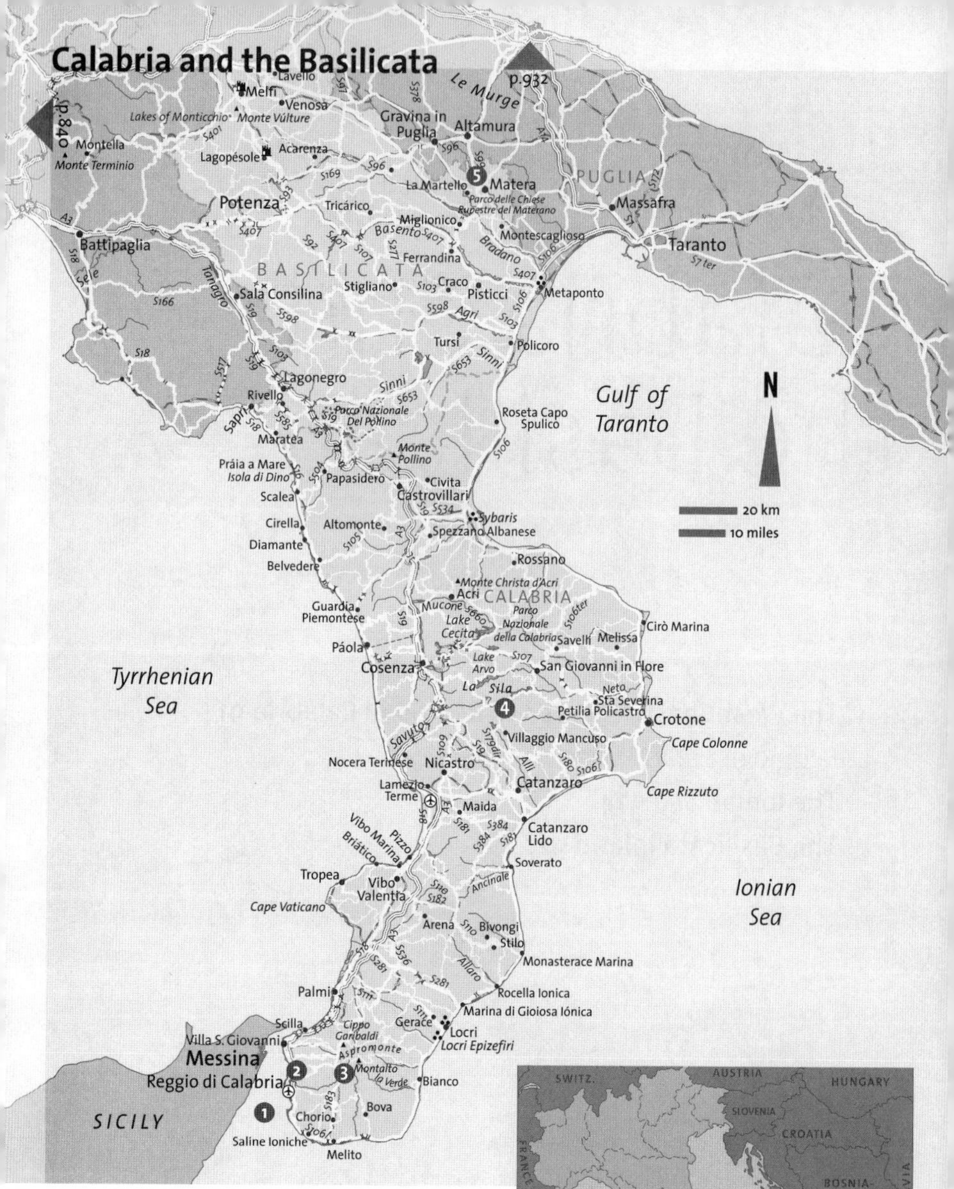

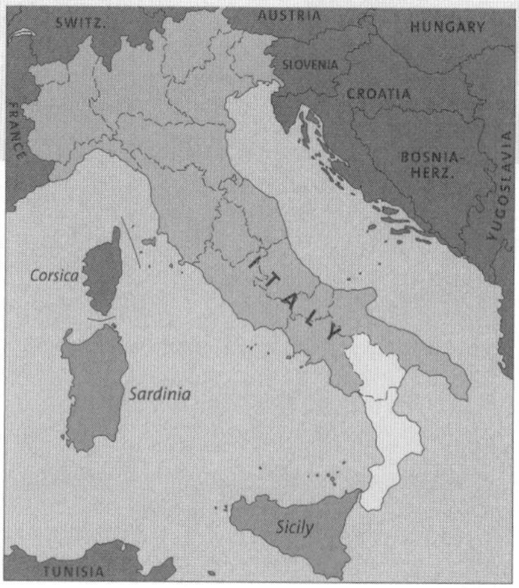

Highlights

1 The views over the Straits of Messina

2 'The Warriors of Riace' in Reggio di Calabria's museum

3 The hidden villages of Aspromonte

4 The alpine forest scenery of the Sila plateau

5 The cave-city of Matera

Italy may be a country unusually blessed, but her favours are by no means evenly distributed. To balance regions such as the Veneto or Campania with their manifold delights, nature has given Italy its own empty quarter, the adjacent regions of Calabria and the Basilicata.

Calabria is the toe of the Italian boot, a gnarled, knobbly toe amply endowed with corns and bunions and pointed accusingly at neighbouring Sicily. Almost all of it is mountainous, leaving just enough room at the edges for the longest, broadest, emptiest beaches in Italy. It can claim three natural attractions: a scenic western coast, the forested highland regions of Aspromonte at the toe, and the Sila, in the centre. Most man-made attractions have been shaken to bits by Calabria's eternal plague of earthquakes, and there are plenty of ruins and ghost towns.

The Basilicata, still better known to many people under its old name of *Lucania*, takes on all comers for the title of Italy's most obscure region. It offers plenty of lonely, Wild West landscapes and two increasingly popular destinations, the resort of Maratea and the strange city of Matera, where people used to live in caves.

Magna Graecia

It was not always this way. Starting in about 750 BC, the Greeks extensively colonized southern Italy. *Rhegium*, today's Reggio di Calabria, came first, followed in short order by *Sybaris, Croton* and *Locris*, among others. These towns, happily situated along the major trade route of the Mediterranean, rapidly became as cultured as those of Greece itself – and far wealthier. It was a brilliant hour, and a brief one. After a time, blessed with a lack of external enemies, the cities of 'greater Greece' took to fighting among themselves in a series of ghastly, cruel wars over the most trivial of causes, often resulting in the total destruction of a city and the massacre of its inhabitants. Weakened by their own barbarous behaviour, the Greek cities then became pawns between Rome and Carthage in the Punic Wars; the victorious Romans wreaked a terrible vengeance on those such as *Taras* (Taranto, in modern Puglia) that supported the wrong side. Roman rule meant a slow decline for the survivors, and by the 6th century the beautiful cities of Magna Graecia had been abandoned to the malarial mosquitoes.

Don't, however, come to Calabria looking for classical ruins. The great museum at Reggio gives a hint of what these cities were, but at the sites themselves almost nothing remains. Golden Sybaris has only just been found by the archaeologists, and only at *Metapontum* will you see so much as a few standing columns. Some may call the emptiness a monument to Greek hubris, or perhaps somehow these cities were doomed from the start. Considering Magna Graecia can be profoundly disconcerting: even in the ancient Mediterranean it is strange and rare for so many big cities to disappear so completely.

Nor has this corner of Italy been any more hospitable to civilization in the centuries since. Calabria in particular has suffered more at the hands of history than any region deserves. Since the Romans and the malaria mosquito put an end to the brilliant, short-lived civilization of Magna Graecia, Calabria has endured one terrible earthquake after another, not to mention Arab raiders and Norman bully boys,

Spaniards and Bourbons, the most vicious of feudal landlords and the most backward and ignorant of monks and priests. By the 18th century, these elements had combined to effect one of the most complete social breakdowns ever seen in modern Europe. Calabria staggered into anarchy, its mountains given over to bands of cut-throats while the country people endured almost subhuman poverty and oppression. Not surprisingly, everyone who was able to chose to emigrate; today there are several times as many Calabresi living in the Americas as in Calabria itself.

A New Land

While famine, disease and misgovernment were putting an end to old Calabria, natural disasters such as the terrible earthquake of 1783, and the even worse one in 1908 that destroyed the city of Reggio, were erasing the last traces of it. Calabria's stage was cleared for a modest rebirth, and the opportunity for it came after the Second World War, when Mr Rockefeller's DDT made the coasts habitable for the first time in more than a millennium. Within a few years, government land reform had improved the lives of thousands of people in both regions, and the Cassa per il Mezzogiorno's roads and industrial projects had set out to pull their economies into the 20th century.

Today, despite the many problems that remain, it's possible to see the beginnings of an entirely new Calabria. A thousand years or more ago, the Calabrians deserted their once-great port cities for wretched though defensible villages in the mountains. Now they are finally moving back, and everywhere around Calabria's long and fertile coasts you will see new towns and cities; some, like Locri or Metaponto, are built over the ruins of the Greek cities that are their direct ancestors.

Most of this new Calabria isn't much to look at yet; the bigger towns, in fact, can be determinedly ugly (as is the case with Crotone). Calabria these days, for all its history, has an unmistakable frontier air about it. The people are simple, suspicious and a little rough. Unlike other Italians, they seem to have lots of children; they work hard, fix their own cars and tractors, and lay their concrete everywhere. So far, the changes have amounted to such a humble revolution that few people have even noticed, and the emigration rate remains enormous. But both these regions are, if anything, lands of survivors, and by now they may be taking their first steps on the road to reclaiming their ancient prosperity and distinction.

The West Coast: Maratea to Reggio di Calabria

Just south of Campania's Cilento peninsula, a little corner of the Basilicata stretches out to touch the Tyrrhenian Sea. The scenery here differs little from the steep cliffs and green slopes of the Cilento; after Sapri, the SS18 becomes a spectacular and rugged corniche road, passing over cliffs covered with scrubby *macchia*, and soft grey beaches on coves that are not so hidden as they once were, as a few hotels have been springing up on them, as at Acquafredda, just over the border.

Getting There and Around

The main regional **airport** is at Lamezia-Terme on the plain of Sant'Eufemia near the SS280 Catanzaro turn-off from the SS18; it has scheduled flights to most of major Italian cities. Reggio di Calabria airport just south of the city has regular links with Rome and Milan.

Two major **rail** lines pass through these regions: the Rome–Naples–Villa San Giovanni/Reggio di Calabria route along the west coast (15 trains a day), and the branch from Battipaglia in Campania to Táranto, via Potenza and Metaponto (6 trains a day). A third line follows the long Ionian shore from Reggio to Táranto. Reggio di Calabria has 2 rail stations: Stazione Marittima, with crossings to Messina in Sicily, and Stazione Centrale; if you're making a quick stop for the museum, the Marittima is closer.

Rail connections to anywhere in the **interior** are chancy at best: a few trains go through to Cosenza, but you'll usually have to change at Paola or Sibari. There are also regular **buses** from Paola to Cosenza. At Catanzaro it's the same; most trains stop only at Catanzaro Lido, 9km away (though there is a regular local bus to the centre). In Cosenza buses leave from Piazza L. Fera, at the north end of Corso Mazzini, for Catanzaro (several daily) and points round the province, including towns in the Sila.

A pleasant way to see the **Sila** is on the old private FCL narrow-gauge railway between Cosenza and San Giovanni in Fiore (3 trains a day). The FCL station in Cosenza is behind the now disused FS station in the town. Near the tip of Calabria is another attractive local rail line, around the Tropea peninsula between Pizzo and Rosarno.

Matera is served by another FCL private line that runs 12 trains a day from Bari in Puglia – a day trip from Bari, 46km away, may be a convenient way to see Matera. The station there is on Via Nazionale on the western edge of town. There is also a very slow FCL line between Potenza and Bari, via Altamura. FCL and other companies operate daily bus services from Matera's Piazza Matteotti to Ferrandina, Potenza, Naples and Metaponto.

Car and passenger **ferries** to Sicily leave from Villa San Giovanni – the quickest route, with the most frequent services – and Reggio di Calabria. There are two companies: Caronte, **t** 0965 793 131, and Tourist Ferry, **t** 0965 751 413. Service are frequent and when you arrive you'll be directed to whichever ferry is leaving next.

Tourist Information

See *www.regione.basilicata.it* and *www.aptbasilicata.it*.

Maratea: (AAST), Piazza del Gesù 32, **t** 0973 877 455/876 908.

Cosenza: Corso Mazzini 92, **t** 0984 27485, *www.costadei.net*

Vibo Valentia: Galleria Vecchio, **t** 0963 42008.

Reggio di Calabria: Via Roma 3, **t** 0965 892 512, (*open Mon and Weds 8.30–1 and 2–7, Tues, Thurs and Fri 7.30–4*); there are branches at the Stazione Centrale and the airport.

Gambarie: Piazzale Mangiaruca, **t** 0965 743 295.

Where to Stay and Eat

Seldom will you see a hotel older than the 1960s here, but there are acceptable hotels almost everywhere; if you are just passing through, there are plenty of options along the SS18. If you have a car, the best deals are often in the family-run *aziende agrituristiche*, where you can taste the famed southern Italian hospitality and some of the region's best food.

Maratea ✉ 85046

*****__Santavenere__, Via Santavenere, Fiumicello–Santa Venere, 1½km north of Porto di Maratea, **t** 0973 876 910, *www.santavenerehotel.com* (*luxury*). A modern building furnished with unusual elegance, in a fine setting on cliffs above the sea, with a private beach and a pool. It also has an excellent restaurant.

****__Villa del Mare__, Acquafredda, just up the coast from town via the SS18, **t** 0973 878 007, *www.bestwestern.it* (*luxury*). A clifftop choice with a lift down to its own beach.

***__Villa degli Aranci__, Via Profiti 12, Maratea-Fiumicello, **t** 0973 876 344 (*moderate*). A good cheaper hotel near the Santavenere.

Za Mariuccia, Via Grotte 2, Maratea Porto, **t** 0973 876 163 (*expensive*). A good seafood trattoria with tables overlooking the sea. The extensive menu includes excellent risotto and pasta dishes featuring scampi, lobster and the very best of whatever Maratea's fishermen have come up with that day. *Closed Fri.*

Rovita, Via Rovita 13, **t** 0973 876 588 (*expensive*). Excellent fish matched with equally good pasta and meat dishes, all making the most of local Basilicata produce – rocket, aubergines and so on. *Closed Tues and Dec–Feb.*

La Torre, Largo Immacolata, **t** 0973 876 227 (*cheap*). The most popular trattoria in the historic centre, on the main piazza. Arrive early to bag an outside table.

Caffè e Dolcezze, Piazza Raglia 19 (*cheap*). A great place to stop for a coffee in the old town. There's only one table inside, amidst glass-fronted drawers packed with colourful sweets, liquorice and candied fruits.

Práia a Mare ✉ 87028

This is good place to look for a cheap room, with at least 10 other places like the Calabria.

****Calabria**, Via Roma 58, **t** 0985 72350 (*cheap*) A simple place near the sea, with its own stretch of beach.

Pian delle Vigne, in the hamlet of the same name, **t** 0985 74190 (*cheap*). A wide choice of fresh grilled fish and seafood served with *porcini* mushrooms or rocket. *Closed Tues.*

Cosenza ✉ 87100

There are no hotels in the old citadel.

******Royal**, Via Molinella 24/e, **t** 0984 412 165, *www.hotelroyalsas.it* (*moderate*). A comfy, reasonably priced hotel, the smartest option in town.

L'Arco Vecchio, Piazza Archi di Ciaccio 21, **t** 0984 72564 (*moderate*). A sophisticated eatery in the heart of the old quarter. *Closed Sun.*

Bella Calabria, Piazza Duomo, **t** 0984 793 531 (*cheap*). A restaurant that's lent a smart feel by its waiters in tuxedos, where you eat alfresco at the foot of the cathedral. Afterwards stroll over to the **Artcafé**, **t** 0984 3268, for a drink and some jazz.

***Bruno**, Corso Mazzini 27, **t** 0984 73889 (*cheap*). The best budget option, very basic but only a short walk from the centre.

Da Giocondo, Via Piave 53, **t** 0984 22199 (*cheap*). A restaurant serving good meals in an informal and busy atmosphere in the new town.

The Sila ✉ 87100

There is very modest accommodation to be had at Bocchigliero and Longobucco, to the north near the Sila Greca. Around the Albanian villages, accommodation is mostly in Spezzano Albanese.

Alternatively, a good base for exploring the Sila is Tiriolo, at its southern end, not far from Catanzaro.

*****Grande Albergo Parco della Fate**, Villaggio Mancuso, **t** 0961 922 057 (*moderate*). A stylish hotel set in alpine forests.

*****Dino's**, Viale della Repubblica 166, Pirainella, just outside San Giovanni in Fiore, **t** 0984 992 090 (*cheap*). A comfortable enough hotel for a short stopover, with a great-value restaurant (the best in the area), specializing in roast kid, trout and other delights of the upland.

*****Due Torri**, on the SS19 near Spezzano Albanese, **t** 0984 953 613 (*cheap*). A cheerful budget option.

Vibo Valentia ✉ 89900

****Terrazzino**, Largo Marinella 6, Fraz. Bivona, **t** 0963 571 091 (*cheap*). A very basic *pensione* on the coast near the castle.

L'Approdo, Via Roma 22, Vibo Marina, **t** 0963 572 640 (*very expensive*). A locally celebrated seafood establishment and the area's best restaurant. The elaborate *frutti di mare, antipasti*, grilled fish and swordfish *involtini* make it a worthwhile splurge.

Pizzo ✉ 88026

*****Murat**, Piazza della Repubblica 41, **t** 0963 534 201 (*moderate*). A rare old-fashioned establishment in the heart of the old village and a very pleasant place to stay.

Casa Janca, Riviera Prangi, Loc. Marinella, **t** 0963 534 890 (*moderate*). A quirkily decorated *agriturismo*. Full board is obligatory in summer but you'll be grateful – people flock here from Catanzaro for the glorious Calabrian cooking (*cheap*).

Tropea/Cape Vaticano ✉ 88038

The best places to stay are around Tropea and nearby Parghelia – there are scores of new resort hotels in all price ranges around Tropea itself, as well as at Parghelia and Zambrone to the east, where the beaches are.

★★★★★**Baia Paraelios**, **t** 0963 600 300, *www.baiaparaelios.com* (*expensive*). A group of well-furnished cottages set on a terraced hill overlooking a beautiful beach on one of the prettiest parts of the coast. Like many places along this coast, you need to reserve some time ahead. Full board is obligatory. *Closed Oct–Apr.*

Da Isabella, Zambrone, off the coastal road towards Tropea, **t** 0963 392 891/0333 524 5467 (*cheap*). A pretty villa set in its own lush garden on a hillside, with an English-speaking proprietress and an intimate atmosphere. The rooms are cosy and you can start your day with an English breakfast – a rarity amidst the region's *cucina povera.*

Al Centro Storico, Via Pietro Vanea, Tropea (*moderate*). A seafood restaurant with outside tables on a little square.

Terra di Dentro, Via Roma. Calabrian specialities to take home, from fine wines to hot peppers and *'nduja*, the spicy hard salami that is an essential component of Calabrian soul food.

Scilla ✉ 89058

★★★**Del Pino**, Loc. Melia, Via Boccata 11, **t** 0965 755 126 (*moderate*). A fancy option for the area, with a pool, set up in the hills above the village. *Closed Jan and Feb.*

★★**Sirene**, Via Nazionale 57, **t** 0965 754 019 (*cheap*). The only hotel in Scilla itself, with simple rooms and a great position just off the beach. Book in advance.

Il Castello di Alta Fiumana, Villa S. Giovanni, Loc. S. Trada, **t** 0965 759 804 (*very expensive*). A good eating option on a hill with great views over the straits.

Alla Pescatora, Marina di Scilla, **t** 0965 754 147 (*moderate*). A place right on the beach, offering alfresco dining and a great octopus *antipasto* among other seafood specialities. *Closed Weds, Dec and Jan.*

Pizzeria S. Francesco, Via Cristoforo Colombo 29 (*cheap*). Generous pizzas on the seafront, and very friendly service.

Reggio di Calabria ✉ 89100

★★★**Lido**, Via III Settembre 6, **t** 0965 25001, (*moderate*). A modest, well-positioned hotel, a short walk from the beach.

★★**Eremo**, Via Eremo Botte 12, **t** 0965 22433 (*cheap*). A pleasant, plant-filled hotel up the hill, one of the very few in the vicinity with wheelchair access.

★★**Diana**, Via Vitrioli 12, **t** 0965 891 522 (*cheap*). A funky, friendly hotel in a mouldering *palazzo* just off Corso Garibaldi.

Bracieria, Via Tripepi 81–3, **t** 0965 29361 (*expensive*). A warm, cosily furnished restaurant on a street parallel to Corso Garibaldi in the centre, serving a variety of local dishes. Highly recommended by locals.

Il Ducale, Corso Vittorio Emanuele III 13, **t** 0965 891 520 (*moderate*). An attractive restaurant in the centre, beside the Museo Nazionale, though many dishes may be unavailable on any given day, and the food doesn't quite live up to the elegant décor.

Il Mio Ristorante, Via Provinciale 41, Gallina, **t** 0965 682 654 (*moderate*). A smart option just outside town, affording beautiful views of the straits and offering first-class swordfish, *aragoste* and good desserts. *Closed Mon.*

Villeggiante, Via Condera Vallone Mariannazzo 31, **t** 0965 25021 (*cheap*). A large, popular restaurant up the hill towards Chiesa Eremo, with views over the straits, serving traditional Calabrian cuisine. *Closed Sun eve.*

Aspromonte ✉ 89050

★★★**Centrale**, Piaza Mangeruca 22, Gambarie, **t** 0965 743 133 (*cheap*). A large and adequate choice, if a bit characterless.

Ristorante Nunziatina, Sant'Alessio di Aspromonte, on the road up to Gambarie, **t** 0965 741 006 (*cheap*). A few tables under the trees, and good simple cooking for next to nothing. It's a local favourite and a stronghold of mountain cooking, with home-made Calabrian pastries for dessert. *Open summer only.*

Villa Rosa, on the road to Gambarie, just beyond Santo Stefano, **t** 0965 740 500 (*moderate*). A wonderful place with outdoor dining on a panoramic terrace covered with flowers, and delicious dishes served by cheery staff; try the pasta with *porcini* mushrooms, or something from the sizzling barbecue. Book in advance.

Sapori di Calabria, on Gambarie's main square, **t** 0965 743 168. A very friendly delicatessen where you can buy gift-wrapped *porcini* mushrooms, or order delicious chunky sandwiches for a picnic.

Maratea and the Coast

The centre of the Basilicata's coast is **Maratea**, a pretty hill village of tiny alleys and steps, with more modern additions tucked between the cliffs by the sea far below it. In the last few years it's become quite sophisticated and expensive, though it's still pretty laid-back. Besides some of the best coastal scenery in the deep south, you can enjoy relatively uncrowded beaches and modest hotels at Acquafredda, Maratea Marina (where trains on the main Rome–Reggio line stop), and several other points along the coast. The town lies under the queerest hilltop Jesus in Italy; all marble, and 66ft tall. Designed by Bruno Innocenti in 1963 at the start of Maratea's push to become a resort, it looks more like a perfume bottle with wings from a distance.

Some of the twistiest roads in the Basilicata take you up to the A3 *autostrada*, or to the sleepy village of **Lagonegro**, with its Baroque churches, and **Rivello**, a charming, isolated hilltop village that's well worth exploring, though in its steep alleys you'll be doing a good deal more climbing than walking.

Some 10 kilometres further down the coast you're in Calabria, on the outskirts of another resort on a less dramatic stretch of coast: **Práia a Mare**, with its 14th-century castle. From the beach you can rent a boat to visit the 'Blue Grotto' on the **Isola di Dino**, an uninhabited islet just offshore. Further south along the road is the now overdeveloped **Scalea**. Further into the mountains, beyond **Papasidero**, is the **Grotta del Romito** (*guided tours daily 9–1 and 4–8 in summer; 9–5 in winter; adm*), which was inhabited into the early palaeolithic period. A rock at the entrance is decorated with an unusually clear image of a bull, the extinct Bos Primigenius, with the head of a smaller bull visible beneath. Several feet away, two tombs have been uncovered, each revealing the remains of a couple locked in an embrace. One of the pairs, thought to be 11,000–12,000 years old, appears to have been deformed by rickets. The position of the tomb suggests they were given an elevated position in society as a result of their disabilities, which may have been attributed to supernatural intervention.

South of Scalea is **Cirella**; from here you can take a boat trip to another uninhabited islet, the **Isola di Cirella**, or climb up to visit the overgrown remains of **Cirella Vecchia**, a village founded by the Greeks that survived until a French bombardment in the Napoleonic Wars; bits of a Greek mausoleum remain, with streets of half-ruined homes and churches. Next comes **Diamante**, a picturesque village of narrow streets, stacked on a rock above the sea. **Páola**, where the road from Cosenza meets the coast, is a larger, somewhat dishevelled resort, a fitting introduction to the 'Calabrian Riviera' to the south. Above it stands the 15th-century **Santuario di San Francesco di Pola**, dedicated to the town's most famous son, Calabria's patron saint (not the same Francis as the saint of Assisi) and the object of pilgrimages from all over southern Italy.

Cosenza

This may not be a stellar attraction, but as cities go it's the best Calabria can do. One of its chief towns through most of recorded history, it began as the capital of the Bruttians, the aboriginal nation from whom today's Calabrians are descended. Medieval Cosenza was busy: the Arabs took it twice, Norman freebooters fought over it, and at least one king of France passed through on his way to the Crusades.

The **Busento** divides Cosenza between the flat modern town and the old citadel on the hill. The river is famous, if only because beneath it is Alaric the Goth. Alaric – no drooling barbarian, just another scheming Roman general with a Teutonic accent – came here in 410, fresh from his sack of Rome and on his way to conquer Africa. He died of a fever here, and his men diverted the Busento and buried him under it, probably with a fair share of the Roman loot. Archaeologists are still looking for it.

For all its history, Cosenza has little to show; even in Calabria, no place is more prone to earthquakes – there have been four big ones in the last 200 years – and then there was added destruction by Allied bombers in 1943. The **cathedral**, a simple Gothic structure, has survived the latest earthquakes, although it didn't back in 1184 – what we see now was rebuilt under Frederick II on the ruins of the 7th-century basilica. Inside lie buried one of Frederick's sons and Isabella of Aragon. Its best bits have been moved to the cloister of the church of **San Francesco d'Assisi**, down the hill on Via San Francesco. This contains two real treasures: a Byzantine-style crucifix in gold and enamel, made in Sicily in the 12th century and given by Frederick himself on the occasion of the cathedral's consecration in 1222; and the shiny 13th-century Byzantine icon of the Madonna del Pilerio, believed to have saved the city from the bubonic plague of 1576 and thus made patron of Cosenza.

A few blocks south of the cathedral, on Piazza XV Marzo, is a small **Museo Civico** (***t*** *0984 813 324; open Mon and Thurs 9–1.30 and 3.30–6.30; Tues, Wed and Fri 9–1.30; adm*), with paintings and archaeological finds. From there you can climb up to the **castle** overlooking the city (*open daily July and Aug 8–midnight, Sept–June 8–8*). Built by the Normans, it was modified by Frederick II, the Aragonese and the Angevins. The medieval 'reception room' has capitals with floral motifs carved in pink sandstone.

West of Cosenza, the large village of **Rende** has a Museo Civico (*open Tues and Thurs 8.30–5.30; adm*) with a very good collection on all aspects of Calabrian life and folklore.

The Sila

Cosenza makes the best base from which to explore this region – a lovely, peaceful plateau between mountains that offers an unusual experience of alpine scenery close to the southern tip of Italy. Much of the Sila is still covered with trees – beeches, oaks and pines. In summer you can find wild strawberries, and in winter – if you're lucky, or perhaps unlucky – wolves. Some of Italy's last specimens make their stand in the Sila's wilder corners. Artificial lakes, built since the war as part of Calabria's hydroelectric schemes, add to the scenery, notably **Lake Arvo** and **Lake Cecita**, between Cosenza and the town of **San Giovanni in Fiore**, which owes its founding to another celebrated Calabrian mystic, the 12th-century monk and devotional writer Joachim of Fiore. Emperor Henry IV granted the privileges of Joachim's new abbey in 1195, and throughout the Middle Ages it was one of the most important communities of the south. The austere abbey complex has been restored and now contains the oddly titled **Demographic Museum of the Silan Economy, Labour and Social History** (***t*** *0984 970 059; open June–Sept Mon–Sat 8.30–6.30, Sun 9.30–12.30 and 3.30–6.30; adm*). Much of the economy, labour and history in this town has to do with hand-made carpets and fabrics, an old speciality.

The Sila is the best place in Calabria for motoring or hiking; maps and information are available from Cosenza tourist office. Most likely you will see only the largest and prettiest section, the **Sila Grande** in the middle, though more adventurous souls can press on to the barely accessible **Sila Greca**, to the north, or south to the **Sila Piccola**, around the little mountain resort of **Villaggio Mancuso**.

On the southern edge of the Sila, on the road to Catanzaro, **Taverna** was the birthplace of Mattia Preti, the only notable artist from Calabria. The best work of this 17th-century follower of Caravaggio can be seen in Naples and Malta, but he left a number of paintings here; these have been restored and removed from the village's churches to the Museo Civico, in the cloister next to San Domenico (*open Tues–Fri Apr–Oct 9.30–12 and 4–7.30, Nov–Mar mornings only; adm*).

On the eastern flank of the Sila Piccola, not far from **Crotone**, is the interesting little town of **Santa Severina**, with a Norman castle and a cathedral with a Byzantine baptistry. Despite the name, the Sila Greca is inhabited by Albanians of the Greek Orthodox faith, who came to Calabria and Sicily as refugees from the Turks in the 15th century and today constitute one of Italy's largest ethnic minorities. Albanians can be found all over Calabria, especially here and in the north around Castrovillari; you'll know you've stumbled on one of their villages if you see a Byzantine-domed church or a statue of Skanderbeg, the Albanian national hero.

Castrovíllari has an Aragonese castle, a small archaeological museum and the church of Santa Maria del Castello – interesting for its odd bits of art from various centuries (there's a small museum in the sacristy) and for the views it offers over the mountains. **Civita**, just to the east, has a small museum dedicated to the life and history of the Albanians in Calabria, the **Museo Etnografico Arbërësh** (*open daily June–Sept 2–8; rest of the year by request, call* **t** *0981 73043*).

South of Castrovíllari, tortuous mountain roads connect a string of Albanian villages. One, **Spezzano Albanese**, is a small spa with some accommodation. West of the *autostrada*, **Altomonte** is an unpromising village, remote even by Calabrian standards before the building of the motorway, that contains one of the most unusual churches in the south – **Santa Maria della Consolazione**, a genuine 14th-century Gothic structure with a big rose window. Most likely it was the work of architects from Siena. Its works of art include a painting by Tuscan master Simone Martini, and the fine tomb of Duke Filippo Sangineto by a follower of Tino di Camaino. Sangineto was a local boy who made good fighting for Charles of Anjou. As well as a duke here, Sangineto was Seneschal of Provence – his descendants financed this church.

South of Cosenza

Back towards the coast south of Cosenza, just a few kilometres from the main road up in the hills, is **Nocera Terinese**, a town famous for its Easter festival in which processions of flagellants go around town beating themselves into a bloody mess with thorn bushes. It's one of the local events most regularly deployed to demonstrate Calabria's distance from the modern world. Further south again, the road descends to the plain of Sant'Eufemia, one of the new agricultural areas reclaimed from the mosquito. The town of **Maida**, site of one of the first French defeats in the Napoleonic

Wars, gave its name to London's Maida Vale. **Pizzo** also has its Napoleonic association: the great cavalry commander, Marshal Murat, whom Bonaparte had made King of Naples, tried after Waterloo to regain his throne by beginning a new revolution in Calabria. When his boat landed here in 1815, the crowd almost tore him to pieces. The Bourbons executed him a few days later in the castle, built in the 1480s by Ferdinand of Aragon. By the port is a small **Museo del Mare** (*open summer daily 8pm–midnight*).

The best of Calabria's coast begins near Capo Vaticano. **Vibo Valentia**, a new provincial capital, has views over the coast, a 12th-century castle, remains of the fortifications of the ancient Greek city of *Hipponion*, and some overwrought Baroque churches. Finds from the excavations of Hipponion are on view in the museum in the castle (*open daily 9–7; adm*). South of Vibo the main road cuts inland. **Mileto** stands next to the ruins of Mileto Vecchia, destroyed in the earthquake of 1783. The extensive ruins include the cathredral and the Abbazia della Trinità, also built by the Normans.

The railway and some backroads head around Cape Vaticano, a district of fashionable, pretty beach resorts and difficult mountains. **Tropea** is a lovely town along the coast; next to it, on a rocky peninsula that was once an island, is the romantically ruined Benedictine monastery of Santa Maria dell'Isola. The town offers some spectacular views, taking in on a clear day the island volcano of Strómboli and Sicily's north coast.

Further south, the towns along the coast are more accessible; some have grown into fair-sized holiday spots. Outside Palmi is a museum and cultural complex, the **Casa di Cultura Leonida Repaci**, that, among other collections, houses the best folk museum in Calabria, and a modern art gallery with works by De Chirico and other 20th-century Italians (***t*** *0966 262 248; open Mon and Thurs 8–2 and 3–6, Tues, Weds and Fri 8–2*).

Scilla, at the entrance to the Straits of Messina, marks the spot where the mythological Scylla, daughter of Hecates, changed into a dog-like sea monster and seized some of Odysseus' crewmen near the end of the *Odyssey*. In classical times Scylla meant the dangerous rocks of the Calabrian side of the straits, a counterpart to the whirlpool Charybdis towards the Sicilian shore. So many earthquakes have rearranged the topography since then that nothing remains of either. Still, the narrow straits are one of the most dramatic sights in Italy, with Messina and the Monte Peloritani visible over in Sicily, neatly balancing Reggio and the jumbled peaks of Aspromonte in Calabria. The view as you approach Scilla from the west is dominated by the town's late-medieval **castle** (*open Tues–Sun 9.30–12.30 and 5.30–8.30*), perched high on a rock that plunges into turbulent waters at the mouth of the straits.

Reggio di Calabria

The last big earthquake came in 1908, when more than 100,000 people died here and in Messina across the straits. Both these cities have a remarkable will to survive, considering the havoc quakes have played on them in the last 2,000 years. Perhaps the setting is irresistible. Fortune has favoured them unequally in the rebuilding; though both are about the same size, Messina has made of itself a slick, almost beautiful town, while Reggio has chosen to remain swaddled in Calabrian humility.

The Warriors of Riace

Reggio's museum, directly north of the city centre on Corso Garibaldi, is a classic of Mussolini architecture built in chunky travertine. Containing a hoard as precious as anything in Greece itself, the museum would make a trip to Reggio worthwhile just for the Warriors of Riace – two bronze masterpieces that rank among the greatest productions of antiquity to have come down to us. If you haven't heard of them, it is because they were only found in 1972, by divers exploring an ancient shipwreck off Riace on Calabria's Ionic coast. They are normally kept in the basement in a room of their own, next to a big exhibition detailing the tremendously complex original restoration job done in the 1970s. These fellows, both about six-foot-seven and quite indecently virile, may have come from a temple at Delphi; no one really knows why they were being shipped to Magna Graecia. One of them has been attributed to the great sculptor Phidias.

The Warriors share the basement with a few other rare works of Greek sculpture, notably the unidentified, 5th-century BC 'Philosopher', as well as anchors and ship fittings, and *amphorae* that once held wine or oil – all recovered from the shipwreck, from mud well over a metre deep. The divers are convinced that the dangerous waters around Calabria may hold dozens of such treasures, so more artefacts may have found their way to the museum by the time you arrive.

Its plain grid of dusty streets and low buildings was laid out only after the earthquake of 1783, when the destruction was even greater than in 1908 and the city had to be rebuilt from scratch.

The Allies also did a pretty thorough job of bombing Reggio in the Second World War; after all that, it's not surprising that there is little left to see of the city that began its life as Greek *Rhegium* in the 8th century BC. Some bits of Greek wall and Roman baths, and some once-grand 19th-century buildings along the waterfront promenade, are almost the only things in the city older than 1908.

Part of Reggio's shabbiness is without question due to the corrosive social effect of the local Calabrese mafia, known in dialect as the *'ndrangheta*, who continue to have a hold here stronger even than those that its wealthier partners in crime, the Sicilian Mafia and the Neapolitan Camorra, exert over their own respective backyards. In recent years, however, thought and effort have gone into the development of the city centre, most noticeably on the seafront. The city's main attraction is its **Museo Nazionale della Magna Graecia** (***t*** *0965 812255; open Mon–Sat 9–7, Sun 9am–10pm; closed 1st and 3rd Mon of month; adm*), which houses the finest collection of Greek art between Naples and Sicily. Besides the Warriors of Riace (*see* above), some of the best things in the collection are the terracotta **ex-voto plaques**, recovered from the temples of Magna Graecia. Most of these offerings show goddesses in the magical archaic Greek style – usually Persephone, who had influence over death – being abducted by Hades, receiving propitiatory gifts, or accepting souls into the underworld. Chickens are a recurring motif, not too surprisingly – to the ancient Greeks a soul rises out of its burial urn the same way a chicken hatches from an egg.

Other works help complete the picture of life and art in Magna Graecia: Greek painted ceramics from Locris and Attica, fragments of architectural decoration from temples, records of city finances on bronze tablets, coins, treasure recovered from tombs, and a rare early Hellenistic mosaic of a dragon, made in Calabria. The museum also has a collection of paintings, including two works by Antonello da Messina.

Aspromonte

All around the toe of Italy, from Palmi as far as Locri, the interior of the peninsula seems impenetrable, a wall of rough peaks looming over the narrow coastal plain. In fact all of the toe is really one great round massif, Aspromonte. The tortuous roads allow few easy opportunities for climbing inland, but from the north end of Reggio the 30-kilometre SS184 takes you up to **Gambarie**, with pine forests and views over the straits and Sicily. In winter this is Calabria's unlikely ski resort, with just enough snow to get by in an average year; in summer it's a good starting point for walkers. There's a chairlift to the top (*daily 9–12 and 3.30–6.30; adm*).

Aspromonte, with its 22 summits and its Greek-speaking villages, was the haunt of the chivalrous 19th-century bandit Musolino, a sort of Calabrian Robin Hood. His well-tended grave is in the cemetery in his birthplace, **Santo Stefano**, just below Gambarie. Scholars who have studied the Greeks here speculate that they may be descendants of the original Greek population of Magna Graecia, retaining their cultural identity thanks only to the barely accessible locations of their mountain villages.

One popular summer excursion follows a passable road to just under the tallest summit of Aspromonte, **Montalto** (6,412ft); look for a small sign ('Montalto Redentore'). The easy 15-minute walk is rewarded, on a clear day, with incredible views of two seas and three volcanoes (the Aeolian islands of Strómboli and nearby Vulcano, along with Mount Etna). Seven kilometres from Montalto, the **Santuario di Polsi** is a popular pilgrimage site for the 'Madonna della Montagna'.

Aspromonte's coastal plain is one of Italy's gardens, a panorama of lemon and orange groves. Two more exotic crops have also given fame to the region: jasmine, which grows so well nowhere else in Italy; and bergamot, a small, hard, green orange, discovered some 200 years ago and now an indispensable ingredient in the making of the finest perfumes (it's also used to flavour Earl Grey tea). On a clear day the straits around Reggio offer some of the grandest views in the south; much of the Sicilian coast is visible, and perhaps even Mount Etna will peek out from behind its clouds.

If you are especially lucky, you may be treated to an appearance of the famous **Fata Morgana** – the mirages of islands or many-towered cities that often appear over the straits. The name comes from the enchantress Morgan le Fay. Arthurian romance came to southern Italy with the Normans, and rooted itself deeply in these parts; old Sicilian legends have a lot to say about King Arthur. In one of the tales, Arthur sleeps and awaits his return not up in chilly England, but deep in the smoky bowels of Etna. Roger de Hauteville, a close relation of William the Conqueror, is said to have seen the Fata Morgana, and his learned men interpreted the vision as a divine invitation to invade Sicily. Roger demurred, thinking it would be better to wait and take Sicily on his own than do it with the aid of sorcery.

Tourist Information

Locri: Pro Loco, Via Raffaele Macri, **t** 0964 330 742.

Catanzaro: Galleria Mancuso, **t** 0961 741 764.

Metaponto Lido: Viale delle Sirene, **t** 0835 741 933. This is one of the coastal resorts that open local information desks in summer.

Where to Stay and Eat

Marina di Gioiosa Iónica ✉ 89046

*****San Giorgio**, Via I Maggio 3, **t** 0964 415 064 (*cheap*). One of the more pleasant spots on Calabria's Ionian shore, just north of Locri. with a nice garden, a private stretch of beach and a pool. *Closed Oct–May.*

Gerace ✉ 89048

******La Casa di Gianna**, Via Paolo Frascà 4, **t** 0964 355 024, *www.lacasadigianna.it* (*very expensive*). A 16th-century villa converted into a luxurious 10-roomed hotel, hidden down a narrow medieval street and centred around an atrium that bathes the upper floors in light. Bedrooms are tasteful; the restaurant is cool and elegant.

A Squella, Viale della Resistenza, on the Locri road into town, **t** 0964 356 086 (*cheap*). A little trattoria that serves good pizza as well as a full menu featuring favourites such as bean and chicory casserole, and pasta with chick peas and hot peppers.

Stilo ✉ 89900

*****San Giorgio**, Via Citarelli 8, **t** 0964 775 047 (*moderate*). The only hotel in town, but one with an unusual degree of character, occupying a former cardinal's palace. Furnished partly in period style, it has a pool and a terrace with panoramic views. Full board is obligatory in Aug. *Closed Nov–Mar.*

La Vecchia Miniera, just outside Bivongi, near the Cascate del Marmárico, **t** 0964 731 869 (*cheap*). A place where you can sample local fare such as mountain trout or pasta with stewed kid sauce. The owner organizes tours of the falls and other sites. *Closed Mon.*

Catanzaro ✉ 88100

*****Grand Hotel**, Piazza Matteotti, **t** 0961 701 256 (*moderate*). An attractive modern place in the centre of town.

****Belvedere**, Via Italia 33, **t** 0961 720 591 (*cheap*). A comfortable budget option.

The Ionian Sea

Italy's Longest Beach

From Reggio as far as Taranto, the coasts of Calabria and later the Basilicata are one long beach – about 500 kilometres of it, broken in only a few places by mountains or patches of industry. All along this route, the pattern is the same: sleepy new concrete settlements on the shore, within sight of their mother towns just a few kilometres further up in the mountains. In summer, you will see great rivers, such as the Amendola, filled not with water but with pebbles; the terrible deforestation of Calabria in the 19th century (committed mostly by northern Europeans with the assistance of corrupt Italian governments) denuded much of the interior, and made its rivers raging torrents in the spring. Recent governments have worked sincerely to reforest vast tracts, especially on Aspromonte, but wherever you see bare rock on the mountains, there is land that can never be redeemed.

Many of the new villages and towns on the bottom of the toe have become little resorts, with two *pensioni* and a pizzeria, on average. None is worth special mention, but you'll never have trouble finding clean water and a kilometre or so of empty (usually rubbish-strewn) beach. About three kilometres south of **Locri** there are the fragmentary ruins of the Greek city *Epizefiri* (**t** *0964 390 023; open 9–1hr before sunset;*

*Coniglio d'Oro, Loc. Vaccariti, Tiriolo (on the main street north of the centre), **t** 0961 991 056 (*cheap*). A small, welcoming place in a pretty village at the south end of the Sila, a good base for exploring the interior. It has a good and very reasonable *pizzeria-ristorante*.

La Corteccia, Via Indipendenza 30, **t** 0961 746 130 (*moderate*). As good a place as any to fill up on traditional cuisine at reasonable prices.

Due Romani, Via Murano, Catanzaro Lido, off the coastal SS106, **t** 0961 32097 (*cheap*). A seafood place offering a wonderful, copious *griglia mista. Closed Sun.*

Wine shop, Vicolo San Rocchello (*cheap*). A rough-and-ready place in which to sample powerful local specialities.

Crotone ✉ 88900

Restaurants along this stretch of coast take the form of seafood shacks open in summer, and small, lively pizzerias with sunny terraces.

Da Annibale, Via Duomo 35, Le Castella, Capo Rizzuto, south of town, **t** 0962 795 004 (*expensive*). One of the few places on the Ionian coast serving elaborate meals.

Il Girrarosto, Via Vittorio Veneto 30, **t** 0962 22043 (*moderate*). A very good restaurant in the centre of town. The cook specializes in roast lamb and kid but knows what to do with swordfish and other seafood too. There's a very pleasant terrace.

Da Peppino, Piazza Umberto (*cheap*). A simple, bustling trattoria serving pizza and seafood at tables on a leafy piazza near the cathedral.

Policoro and Metaponto ✉ 75025

Policoro is the most convenient place to stop over along the Basilicata's short stretch of Ionian coast.

****Degli Argonauti**, Marina di Pisticci, **t** 0835 470 242, *www.argonauti.com* (*expensive*). A plush hotel centred around an enormous, lagoon-like swimming pool. In summer a week's stay and full board are minimum requirements; this may be lifted at the very beginning and end of the season. *Closed Oct–Apr.*

***Callà**, Corso Pandosia 1, Policoro, **t** 0835 972 129 (*cheap*). A decent middle-range hotel.

***Kennedy**, Viale Jonio 1, Metaponto Lido, **t** 0835 741 960 (*cheap*). A bargain right on the beach.

Ragno Verde, Via Colombo 13, Policoro, **t** 0835 971 736 (*cheap*). A good family trattoria. *Closed Sun.*

closed 1st and 3rd Mon of month), consisting of a few bits of wall and temple bases. Most of the art excavated here has been taken to the Reggio museum and further afield (it may include the famous Ludovisi throne in Rome, but some have called that a fake). Enough was left behind to make the Antiquarium near the sea worth a visit (*open daily 9–8; adm*).

When pirates and malaria forced the Locrians to abandon their city in the 8th century, they fled to the nearby mountains and founded **Gerace**. Though the population of its melancholy medieval centre today is only about 300, Gerace was an important centre in the Middle Ages; it has Calabria's biggest cathedral, an 11th-century Norman Romanesque work supported by columns from the ruins of Locri. The church has an interesting display on the restoration and a *tesoro* with a 12th-century cross from Constantinople. Other churches worth a look here are San Francesco, a big Franciscan barn, and the small Oratorio dell'Addolorata with its ornate rococo interior. Older churches such as Santa Cuore show a strong Byzantine–Norman influence.

Roccella Iónica is an up-and-coming little town, its hilltop setting and half-ruined castle providing a rare break from the monotony of beach along the coast road. Up in the hills above Monasterace Marina, the Greek village of **Stilo** is famous for its 10th-century Byzantine church, La Cattólica, with five small domes and the remains of medieval frescoes. Another good church nearby is San Giovanni Theresti (*open

July–mid-Sept 5pm–sunset; mid-Sept–June Sat 10–12 and 3–5), just outside the village of **Bivongi**. Nearby there's a beautiful waterfall on the Torrente Stilo, the **Cascate del Marmàrico** (though not much water falls in summer).

Further inland, **Serra San Bruno**, a pretty and refined village surrounded by forests, grew up around the huge 11th-century Carthusian monastery, or **Certosa**, two kilometres outside it. The founder of the Carthusians, Bruno of Cologne, lived and died here. Much of the monastery was destroyed by an earthquake in 1783, but it still has the remains of a lavish Baroque complex, a **museum** (*open summer daily 9–1 and 3–8; winter Tues–Sun 9.30–1 and 3–6; adm*) and a church façade, now freestanding like a stage prop. In the village, the rococo San Biagio, or Chiesa Matrice, has reliefs with scenes from Bruno's life and an unusual altarpiece.

Further north, there is little to detain you along the shore of the Gulf of Squillace as far as **Catanzaro**, the Calabrian capital. Really an overgrown mountaintop village that has straggled gradually down to the sea since the war, it is the kind of place where the young men call you *capo* or *cavaliere* and ask for a light while they give you the once-over. Its park, the Villa Trieste, has nice views, and there is a museum of carriages (*open Mon–Fri 8.30–12 and 4–6; adm*) at Località Siano, in the north of the town.

Crotone: The City of Pythagoras

As you head into the gulf of Taranto, the ghost cities of Magna Graecia are the only distractions along a lonely coast. **Crotone**, the Greek Croton, is a dismal mid-sized industrial city. The old Croton was often the most powerful of the Greek cities in Calabria, though it was more famous in the ancient world as the adopted home of the philosophere Pythagoras. With his scientific discoveries, mathematical mysticism and belief in the transmigration of souls, Pythagoras cast a spell over the Greek world, and particularly over Magna Graecia. He was hardly a disinterested scholar in an ivory tower; around the middle of the 6th century BC he seems to have led, or merely inspired, a mystic-aristocratic government in Croton based on his teachings. When a democratic revolution threw him out, he took refuge in Metapontum.

Croton also had a reputation for its medical school, for the success of its athletes at the Olympic games, and, especially, for its aggressive and unyielding attitude towards its neighbours. From all this, nothing is left but the **Museo Archeologico** at Via Risorgimento 20 (***t*** *0962 23082; open daily 9–8; closed 1st and 3rd Mon of month*), which includes a large collection of terracotta ex-votos like those at Reggio. On a promontory south of Crotone, a single standing column from a temple of Hera makes a romantic ruin on **Capo Colonne**. The **Museo Civico** (*open Tues–Sat 9–1 and 3–7, Sun 9–12.45*), within the ramparts of the 16th-century castle, houses a small collection of maps and local relics.

Some 80 kilometres north, you can dip easily into the mountains at **Rossano**, one of the better-kept hill towns. The town's particular treasure, originally in the cathedral, is a beautiful 6th-century manuscript called the *Purple Codex*, believed to be the oldest illuminated gospel anywhere, made in Syria and almost certainly brought here by eastern monks fleeing their Muslim invaders. It can be seen in the **Museo Diocesano**, next to the cathedral (***t*** *0983 520 282; open Tues–Sat 10–12 and 4.30–6, Sun 9.30–12*).

Past Rossano, the mountains recede into the **plain of Sybaris**, named after the Greek city so renowned for decadence that even today it is echoed in the word 'sybarite'. The misfortune of Sybaris was to have jealous Croton for a neighbour, which besieged Sybaris and took it in 510 BC. After razing it to the ground, they diverted the Crati river over the ruins so it could never be rebuilt. They did such a good job that until a few years ago modern archaeologists could not even find the site; some scholars became convinced Sybaris was a myth. Excavations are now feverishly underway, and it's hoped that the richest city of Magna Graecia may yield the archaeologists something worth the trouble it has caused them. Above Sybaris proper, levels of excavation reveal ruins of *Thurii*, an Athenian colony and base in the Peloponnesian Wars, and a Roman town above that, *Copia*. You can wander round the excavation site with a guide (*open daily 9–1hr before sunset*), or visit the **museum** (***t*** *0981 7991; open daily 9–8; adm*) a kilometre further north, which houses ceramics, gold and silverware from the Sybaris site and findings from two Bronze Age settlements in the Siberi plain.

Sybaris stands at the mouth of the Crati, which is now a wildlife preserve for a small colony of the increasingly rare Mediterranean seal.

Policoro and *Metapontum*

Nearing the northern boundaries of Calabria, castles frown down over the sea at Roseto and Rocca Imperiale (*open summer only*), the latter built by Frederick II. The Basilicata's share of the Ionian coast offers little change from Calabria. Two areas have been excavated, showing a long, tidy grid of streets with the foundations of houses but, so far, no important temples. The new town of Policoro stands near the ancient city of *Eraclea*; its **Museo Nazionale della Siritide** (*open Weds–Mon 9–7, Tues 2–7, until 6 in Oct–Mar; adm*) has a good collection of Greek vases and terracottas. North of Policoro, Metapontum was a city grown prosperous from cultivating and shipping wheat; today its famous silver coins, decorated with an ear of wheat, are prized by collectors. It has more ruins to show than any of the other Calabrian sites, but do not expect anything like Paestum or Pompeii. On the banks of the Bradano, facing the coastal SS106, stands the Temple of Hera, which used to be called the *Tavole Palatine* by locals – the Round Table of King Arthur. Fifteen columns remain.

The Basilicata Inland

Matera and its Province

The interior of the Basilicata has never been one of the more welcoming regions of Italy. Divided roughly equally between mountains and rolling hills, it is an isolated land that has usually remained cut off from the major events of Italian history. The territory may be familiar if you have read Carlo Levi's *Christ Stopped at Eboli*, a novel written when the Basilicata was a national scandal, the poorest and most backward corner of Italy – the writer had been sent into internal exile there by the Fascists. None of the famous 18th- and 19th-century travellers ever penetrated deeply into the region, and even today it is a part of the country few foreigners ever visit.

Tourist Information

Matera: Via Viti de Marco 9, **t** 0835 331 983 (*open Mon and Thurs 8.30–1 and 4–6m Tues, Weds, Fri and Sat 8.30–1*), *www.hsh.it.*

Potenza: Via Cavour 2, **t** 0971 274 485, and Via Alianelli 4, **t** 0971 21812.

Venosa: Via F. Frusci 7, off Piazza Municipo, **t** 0972 36542.

Where to Stay and Eat

Matera and Potenza are the only places equipped for visitors; with the exception of Venosa, expect simple lodgings elsewhere.

Matera ✉ 75100

***__Hotel Sassi__, Via San Giovanni Vecchio 89, **t** 0835 331 009, *www.hotelsassi.it* (*moderate*). *The* place to stay in Matera, in the heart of the Sasso Barisano. A restructured 18th-century complex, it has 15 rooms differently shaped to respect the original layout, all with balconies overlooking the Sassi. The decor is simple but tasteful and the service friendly and efficient.

***__Italia__, Via Ridola 5, **t** 0835 333 561 (*moderate*). A pleasant hotel; some rooms have good views over the Sassi.

*__Roma__, Via Roma 62, **t** 0835 333 912 (*cheap*). A clean, spartan *pensione*, with shared baths.

Basilico, Via San Francesco 33, **t** 0835 336 540 (*moderate*). A restaurant that looks a bit out of place here, with its modern pastel décor and *cuisine soignée*; most people come for the really good pizza. *Closed Fri.*

Lucana, Via Lucana 48, **t** 0835 336 117 (*moderate*). A popular trattoria serving local favourites. The *antipasti della casa* is a meal in itself.

Il Castello, Via Castello 1, **t** 0835 333 752 (*cheap–moderate*). One of several good restaurants in town, with an interesting *orecchiette* with mushrooms and sausage. *Closed Weds.*

Il Terrazzino, Vico S. Giuseppe 7, just off Piazza Vittorio Veneto, **t** 0835 332 503 (*cheap–moderate*). A wide choice of simple but tasty Basilicatan dishes, and a terrace overlooking the Sassi. *Closed Tues.*

Del Corso, Via Luigi La Vista 12, **t** 0835 332 892 (*cheap*). A budget place in which to gorge yourself in the company of discerning locals. *Closed Fri eve.*

Potenza ✉ 85100

This is the kind of place where you will share a quiet hotel with a small group of government inspectors and travelling *salami* salesmen – all on expense accounts, so there are no bargains.

Not that they've been overlooking anything. The only Basilicata town worth stopping at is Matera, a lively provincial capital of 55,000 people that has become a kind of freak show attraction. Until recently, it also had a certain notoriety as the most desperately poor provincial capital in Italy, and the scene of Carlo Levi's book.

Matera has been inhabited since before recorded history in these parts began, and for centuries, probably millennia, its people built cave-homes and cave-churches in the tufa. Times are better now, but Matera has chosen to preserve its terrible past by turning its poorest sections, the **Sassi**, into a sort of open-air museum – one that has made UNESCO's list of World Heritage Sites. Sassi are the cave neighbourhoods that line the two ravines between which Matera is built. Visitors as recently as 40 years ago reported people living in their cave-homes in almost inconceivable poverty, sharing space with pigs and chickens, their children imploring outsiders for quinine.

You may think it macabre, visiting the scenes of past misery, but the Sassi are fascinating in their own way. There are two parts, the wealthier **Sasso Barisano** north of the town centre, and the poorer **Sasso Caveoso** to the east. If you visit, before long a child or old man will come up and approach you with the offer of guide service – this is worth the trouble and slight expense if you have the time. The guides know where the old churches with the Byzantine frescoes are (some as old as the 9th

★★★**Degli Ulivi**, outside Ferrandina on the SS407, 25km south of Matera, **t** 0835 757 020 (*moderate*). A comfortable stopover if you're passing through on the way to Táranto.

★★**Margariello**, Corso Umberto 55, Stigliano, **t** 0835 561 225 (*cheap*). A modest hotel with shared bathrooms.

★★**Miramonti**, Via Caserma Lucana 30, **t** 0971 22987 (*cheap*). A straightforward hotel in Potenza itself.

Taverna Oraziana, Via O. Flacco 2, **t** 0971 21851 (*expensive*). An exceptional restaurant, with fine fresh pasta and local produce, used to recreate traditional old local recipes. *Closed Fri and Aug.*

Fuori le Mura, Via 4 Novembre 34, **t** 0971 25409 (*moderate*). A singular, employee-owned restaurant renowned locally for its huge choice of *antipasto* treats and good roast pork and lamb. *Closed Mon.*

Falcon Castel Lagopesole, **t** 0971 86239 (*cheap*). A trattoria just below the castle serving hearty local specialities.

Melfi ✉ 85025

★★★**Due Pini**, outside town by the station, **t** 0972 21031 (*moderate*). A travelling salesmen's haunt that's an adequate option for an overnight stay.

Il Tratturo Regio, Contrada del Casonetto, **t** 0972 239 295 (*cheap*). A reasonably well-signposted *azienda agrituristica* run by an enthusiastic young English-speaking family who will feed you their fresh ricotta and mamma's best home-cooking. You may be tempted to stay longer than planned.

Il Pescatore, Monticchio Laghi, **t** 0972 731 036 (*moderate*). A restaurant that's worth tracking down if you're visiting the lakes of Monticchio to the south of Melfi (it's on the road round the smaller of the two lakes).

Vaddone, Corso da Sant'Abruzzese, **t** 0972 24323 (*moderate*). A family-run restaurant offering good regional cuisine accompanied by local Aglianico and Vúlture wines. *Closed Sun eve and Mon.*

Venosa ✉ 85029

★★★**Orazio**, Corso Vittorio Emanuele II 142, **t** 0972 31135 (*cheap*). A beautifully restored *palazzo* and a real bargain – rooms are fully equipped, there's a communal terrace with lovely views over the valley, and a lounge area where you can watch TV or read the verses of local poet Horace.

Il Grifo, Via delle Fornci, **t** 0972 35188 (*cheap*). A busy restaurant beside the castle. Try the *lagane*, a delicious local pasta.

century), and, if you can pick out enough of their southern dialect, they have plenty of stories to tell. They are also a better option than the maps and itineraries from the tourist office. Alternatively, the very good Tour Service Matera on the main Piazza Vittorio Veneto 42 (***t*** *0835 334 633*) offers a wide range of tailor-made guided tours.

Not all of Matera's sights are in the Sassi; there's also a 13th-century **cathedral**, a fine Romanesque building with some richly decorated side chapels; the churches of **San Francesco** and **San Giovanni Battista**, both with good façades; a 15th-century castle, the gloomy **Castello Tramontano** above the city; an eccentric 18th-century church, the **Purgatorio**, with a leering skull over the main portal; and a first-class local archaeological museum, the **Museo Ridola** (*open Mon 2–7, Tues–Sun 9–7; adm*) in the Baroque former convent of Santa Chiara.

The austere countryside around Matera is full of tufa quarries, caves and churches. Across the Gravina ravine from the Sasso Caveoso (the one south of the cathedral), the cliffs called the **Murgia Timone** hold some more interesting cave-churches, some with elaborate fronts, even domes, cut out of the tufa, and medieval frescoes. You'll need a map and some help from the provincial tourist office, or else a guide, to find them. Among the most interesting are those of **Santa Maria della Palomba**, **La Vaglia**, the **Madonna delle Tre Porte** and **Santa Barbara**.

In the remote south of Matera province, the village of **Tursi** boasts the sanctuary of **Santa Maria d'Anglona,** out in the country on the road to Policoro, and **Stigliano** has the 17th-century **church of San Antonio** with an odd waffle-iron rococo façade that's even better than the one on the Gesù Nuovo in Naples. South of Stigliano, the wild countryside around **Aliano** has some of the more outlandish scenery in southern Italy. Deforestation and consequent erosion have turned parts of it into a lunar landscape, exposing weirdly twisted rock formations called *calanchi*. Aliano is the village where Carlo Levi stayed during the time described in *Christ Stopped at Eboli*; the house where he lived at the bottom of the village is a **museum** (***t*** *0835 314 139; call in advance*) dedicated to the writer and to local folklore, customs and traditional life.

Monte Vúlture and the Castles of Emperor Frederick

The western Basilicata is a province to itself, with a capital at **Potenza**, a plain modern hilltop city regularly rattled by earthquakes. The northern end of the province, astride the important routes between Naples and Puglia, was very busy in the Middle Ages, full of castles and fought over by Normans, Angevins and Holy Roman Emperors. Frederick II, in particular, haunted these bleak hills; he spent three months here, just before moving on to Puglia, where he died of dysentery. His son Manfred and Elena of Epirus spent their honeymoon at the well-preserved castle of **Lagopésole**, halfway between Potenza and Melfi. Earlier in his reign, the great Hohenstaufen had spent some time at the castle at **Melfi**, a fortress that two centuries before had been the De Hautevilles' first Italian headquarters, where Robert Guiscard was crowned Duke of Puglia and Calabria. There's none of Frederick's geomantical mysticism here; unlike Castel del Monte, this was built for defence. Little remains of the original furnishings, but there is a small **archaeological museum** (***t*** *0972 238 726; open Tues–Sat 9–2, Sun 9–1; adm*). Melfi itself is a sleepy town, with little but the castle and its 11th-century cathedral to remind it of times when it occupied the centre stage of European politics.

Looking out from Melfi's castle, the horizon to the south is dominated by the faintly menacing outline of **Monte Vúlture**, a long-extinct volcano with a forest where once it had a smoking crater. Around the back of the mountain is one of the Basilicata's few beauty spots, the little **lakes of Monticchio**, with lovely woods and a funicular to the top of the mountain. Out east from Melfi is another old castle at **Venosa**, an important town in Roman times and the birthplace of the poet Horace, with a museum (***t*** *0972 36095; open daily 9–8, except Tues am; adm*).

Just outside town, on the road to Puglia, are the remnants of one of the most ambitious church building projects ever undertaken in the south. The Benedictine **Abbazia della Trinità** (*open daily Apr–Sept 9–7, rest of year 9–1hr before sunset*), begun in the 1050s, was never completed, but it became the resting place of four of the five famous Norman brothers: William, Drogo, Robert (Guiscard) and Humphrey de Hauteville. Their tombs are in the older, completed church, along with some very fine surviving frescoes and carved capitals. Among the heaps of stones tumbled about you may notice some Hebrew inscriptions; ancient and medieval Venosa both had important Jewish communities, and some Jewish catacombs have been discovered along with Christian ones on the hill east of the abbey.

Puglia

21

Puglia

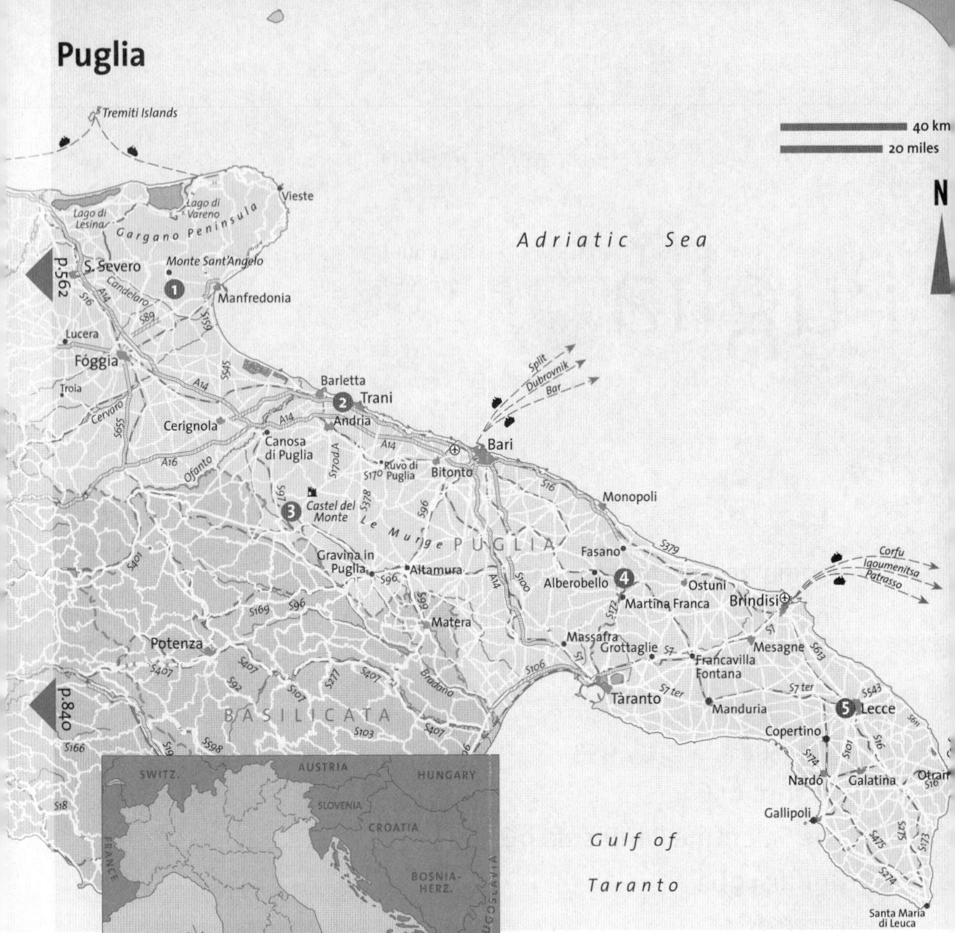

Highlights

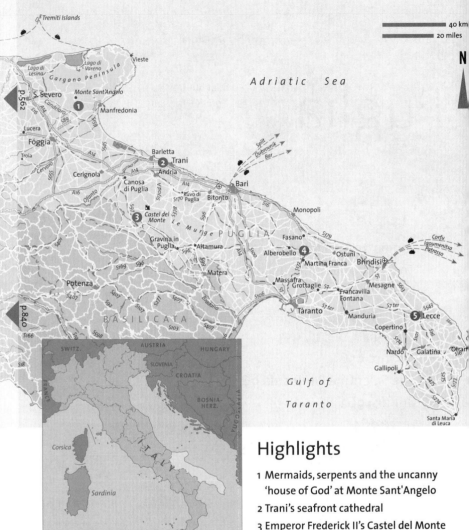

1 Mermaids, serpents and the uncanny 'house of God' at Monte Sant'Angelo
2 Trani's seafront cathedral
3 Emperor Frederick II's Castel del Monte
4 The land of the *trulli* around Alberobello
5 Lecce, the Baroque pearl of the south

In many ways this region is the biggest surprise of Italy's south. From the forests and shining limestone cliffs of the beautiful Gargano Peninsula in the north, through the long plain of the *Tavoliere* to the southernmost tip of Italy's heel, Puglia offers the most variety of any of the southern regions, not only in nature, but in its towns and in its art: you can see Byzantine art around Taranto, a score or so of Europe's finest Romanesque cathedrals, Santa Claus' tomb, the end of the Appian Way, the loveliest Baroque city in the Mediterranean, and a town of buildings with roofs shaped like oilcans.

Ancient Puglia was home to a number of quiet, modestly cultured and prosperous nations, notably the Daunii around Foggia and the Messapians in the south. Under Roman rule it was a quiet and predominantly agricultural province, Rome's gateway to the east, and one of the parts of Italy most heavily influenced by the proximity of Greek culture. During the Middle Ages, it was the home of a unique culture influenced by Normans, Arabs and Greeks. In a brief but intense period of prosperity, helped along greatly by the Crusades, its cities were fully equal in wealth and artistic talent to those of the north.

Puglia's greatest artistic productions are the medieval cathedrals and churches of Trani, Bari, Ruvo, Altamura, Molfetta, Bisceglie, Bitonto and Barletta, all of which are situated close together in Bari province. The fascinating Castel del Monte, to the west of Bari, and the great castle at Lucera, are only two of the important sites that are associated with the reign of the *Stupor Mundi* – 'wonder of the world' Emperor Frederick II.

To get to know Puglia better, keep an eye open for some of its less important sights – pre-classical ruins, dolmens, relics of Greek Italy, religious centres, and especially the unique rural civilization of the *trulli* country. Puglia is not often spectacular, but the depth and meaning of its culture will come as a surprise; it is one of the regions most worth knowing.

Food and Wine in Puglia

La cucina pugliese makes use of all the natural resources at its disposal. Bari is particularly famous for its fish, while Táranto has excellent mussels, mostly from the Mare Grande, called *mitili* (instead of *cozze* as they are in the rest of Italy); they feature prominently on the menus of virtually all Taranto's restaurants. In the hill towns of the interior, fish is replaced by meat, especially pork, rabbit and lamb. The 'national' dish of Puglia is *fave e cicoria*, a delicious purée of dry broad beans served with sautéed wild chicory.

Puglia produces vast amounts of good olive oil – to the point that the big boys in Tuscany buy a lot of their oil from here and label it as their own. Puglian oil varies considerably, from fruity and strong (south Puglia and the area around San Severo) to mild and pure enough for babies (the Gargano). Many agronomists reckon that some of the finest oil in Italy is from near Castel del Monte near Bari.

As in most of southern Italy, sheep make up a great part of the livestock here, and the region's sheep's cheeses include the local styles of *pecorino* and ricotta – look out for the strongly flavoured *ricotta forte*, which goes particularly well in sauces with the local pasta, *orecchiette* ('little ears'), formed by shaping the uncooked pasta with the thumb. Another cheese speciality is *burrata*, a tear-shaped mozzarella shell filled with a heart of shredded mozzarella and cream. Puglia also grows some of the best almonds in the world, used in the preparation of delicious cookies and desserts.

Pugliese wine, strong and full-bodied like the cuisine, has had a good reputation since Roman times. Today about 24 wines are produced, including the sweet Muscat. Two worth looking out for are the powerful red, *Cacc'e mmitte*, from Foggia province, and the comparatively light, delicate dry white from Locorotondo.

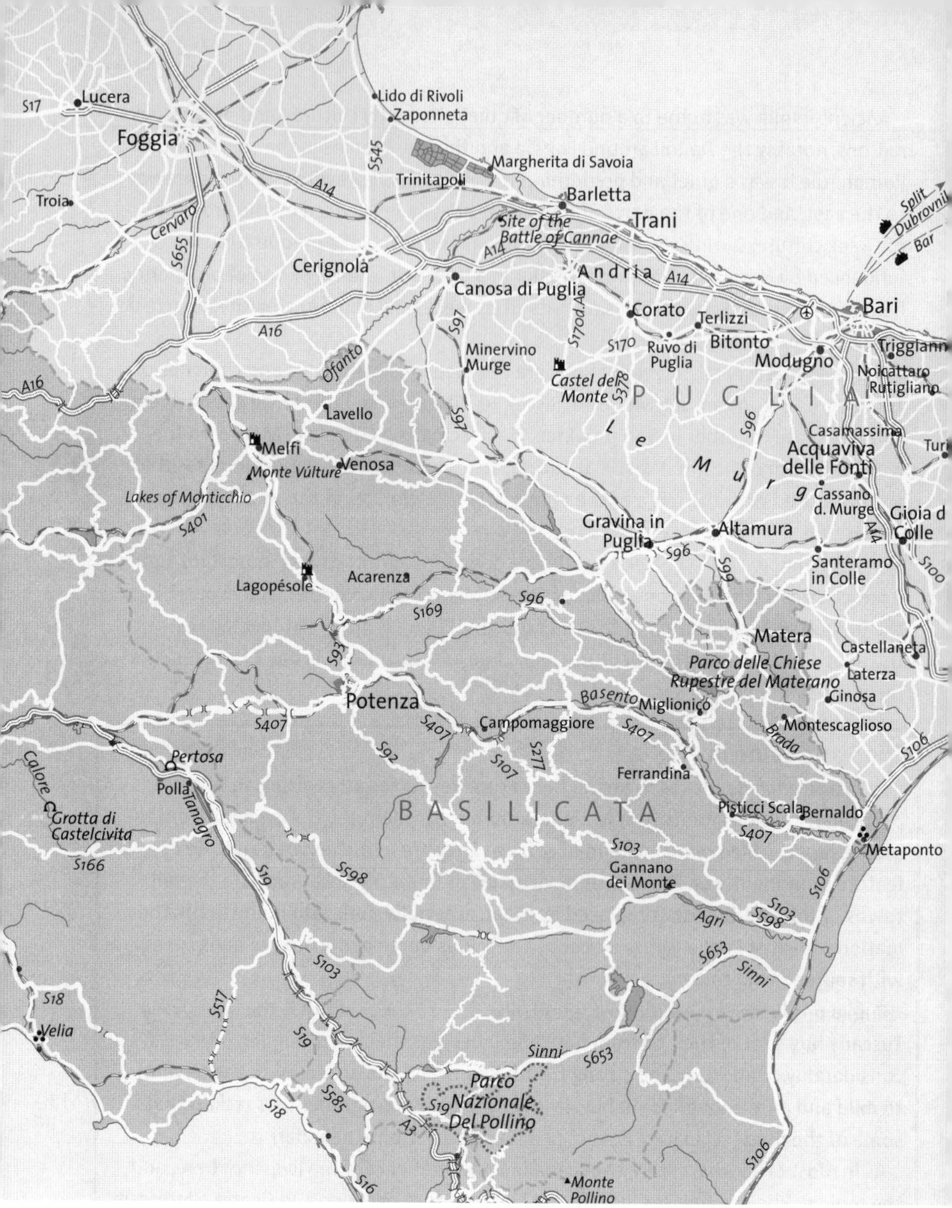

Foggia and its *Tavoliere*

Foggia

Foggia, the third city of Puglia, was once Frederick's capital, where he enjoyed quiet moments with his English wife, his harem, his falcons and his Muslim sorcerers. It must have been quite a place, but old Foggia has been obliterated by two southern plagues: earthquakes have levelled it on several occasions, and the French sacked it in 1528. Allied bombers finished off the remains, and the city suffered some of the

Central Puglia and the Salentine Peninsula

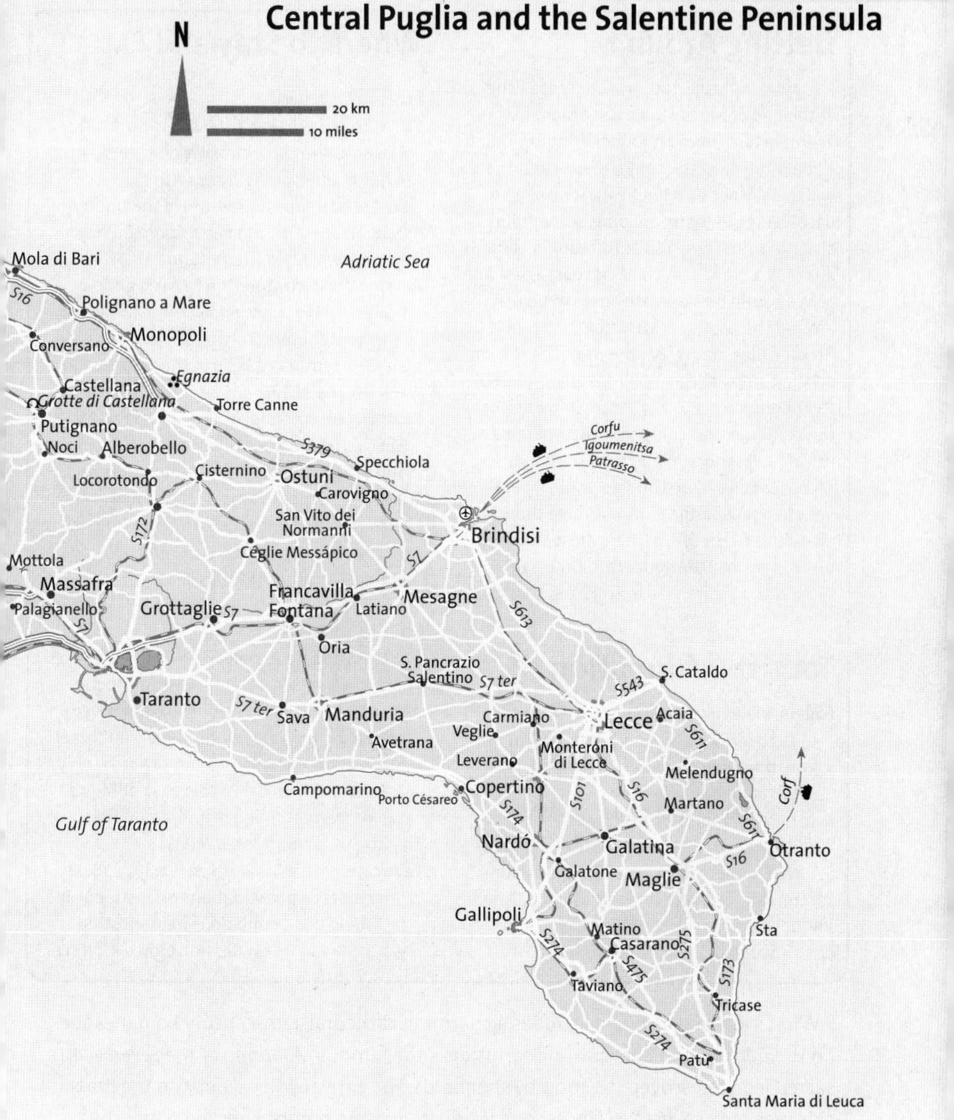

highest civilian losses anywhere in World War II – in two separate bombardments half the population was killed. The Foggia you see today is a newborn – homely and awkward yet endearing. Its citizens haven't forgotten Frederick but seem more proud of a composer of operas named **Umberto Giordano**, born here in 1867. The municipal theatre is named after him, and there is a big statue of him in Piazza Giordano in the centre, among an eccentric set of more statues of characters from his works. Giordano's big hit was *Andrea Chénier*; you'll be able to see it or other of his works during Foggia's autumn opera season.

Getting Around

Foggia's **railway** station is on Piazza Veneto, at the end of central Viale XXIV Maggio. It is an important junction for north–south trains – you often have to change there – and there will usually not be a long wait for trains to Bari, Naples, Bologna or Rome. Some trains also run from Foggia to Manfredonia, though it is only a branch off the main east-coast line.

Two companies operate **buses** to points around the province: **SITA**, **t** 0881 773 117 (ticket office at Kiwi Bar opposite the station, on the corner of Viale XXIV Maggio), and **FG**, freephone **t** 167 296 247 (ticket office left of the station entrance), which also operates a private rail service in northern Gargano. All buses leave from the side of the Piazza Veneto opposite the station, where there is also a bus ticket office. There are also several buses a day to Manfredonia, Monte Sant' Angelo and Vieste, and to Troia and Lucera.

Tourist Information

Foggia: Via Emilio Perrone 17 (*open Mon–Fri 9–12.30 but inconveniently situated far from anything of interest*), **t** 0881 723 141, *www. pugliaturismo.com.*

Lucera: Via Zuppetta 7, **t** 0881 522 762 (*open daily May–Sept 9–2 and 3–8, Oct–Apr 9–2*)

Tutto Gargano is an excellent publication for tourists in Italian and English, published annually before the summer season and stocked at good newspaper vendors.

Where to Stay and Eat

Foggia ✉ 71100

******Cicolella**, Viale XXIV Maggio 60, **t** 0881 688 890, *www.hotelcicolella.it* (*very expensive*). A rather uninspiring hotel with one of the best restaurants (*expensive*) in town, offering Puglian specialities such as *orecchiette. Restaurant closed Sat and Sun.*

Albergo del Cacciatore, Via P Mascagni 12, **t** 0881 771 839, *www.paginegialle.it/ albergocacciatore* (*cheap*). En suite rooms in an 18th-century *palazzo* in the heart of old Foggia. The restaurant offers good local fare.

Pompeo (ex Giordano), Vicolo al Piano 14, **t** 0881 724 640 (*moderate*). A fine restaurant for local and seasonal specialities. *Closed 2wks Aug.*

Trillusa, Via Tenente Iorio 50, **t** 0881 709 253 (*cheap*). A popular pizzeria with excellent pizzas (available by the slice) and delicious *antipasti, frittini* and *dolci. Closed Weds.*

Lucera ✉ 71036

*****La Balconata 2**, Viale Ferrovia 15, **t** 0881 546 725 (*moderate*). A decent choice for stopovers.

*****Milano**, Via Teano Appulo 10, San Severo, **t** 0882 375 643 (*moderate*). A pleasant hotel north of Lucera.

Al Passetto, Piazza del Popolo 24, **t** 0881 542 213 (*moderate*). A fine restaurant in the centre of Lucera. *Closed Mon.*

Le Arcate, Piazza Cavalotti 29, **t** 0882 226 025 (*moderate*). Light variations on rustic cuisine, including good lamb done in interesting ways. Save room for dessert. *Closed Mon eves.*

What's left of old Foggia includes a charming **cathedral**, 12th-century Romanesque on the bottom and Baroque on top. Inside is the famous *Madonna of the Seven Veils*, a sacred icon rediscovered *c.* 1000 by shepherds. The early medieval door on the north side was rediscovered in the Second World War, when bombs knocked down the adjacent building that was hiding it. A few twisting streets to the north, on Piazza Nigri, the **Museo Civico** (*open daily 9–1, also Tues, Thurs and Fri 5–7*) is devoted to archaeological finds. The scientific section has been relocated to the **Museo di Storia Naturale**, Via Bellavia (*open Mon–Sat 9–1, Mon and Fri also 4.30–7; adm*). The single portal with an inscription incorporated into one side of the building is the last surviving remnant of Frederick's palace. Near the museum, on Piazza Sant'Egidio, the **Chiesa della Croce** (1693–1742) is one of Puglia's more unusual churches: an elegant Baroque gate leads to a long avenue, which passes under five domed chapels that represent stages in the passion of Christ before arriving at the church itself.

Lucera and Troia

Why does Lucera have a cathedral from the 14th century when almost all other Puglian towns built theirs in the 12th century or earlier? Well, there's a story. In the 1230s Frederick II was hard pressed. Excommunicated by his devious rival, Pope Gregory IX, and at war with all the Guelph towns of Italy, Frederick needed allies he could trust. At the same time he had a problem with brigandage in some of the mainly Muslim mountain areas of Sicily. His solution: induce 20,000 Sicilian Arabs to move to Puglia, with land grants and promises of imperial employment and favours.

The almost abandoned town of *Luceria*, once an important Roman colony, was the spot chosen, and before anybody knew it Frederick had conjured up an entirely Muslim metropolis 290 kilometres from Rome. The Emperor felt right at home in Lucera and the new city became one of his favourite residences; later it would be the last stronghold of his son, Manfred, in the dark days that followed Frederick's death. Charles of Anjou took the city in 1267; attempts at forced Christianization, and the introduction of settlers from Provence, caused revolts among the people, which the Angevins finally settled in 1300 by butchering the lot.

Little remains of Muslim Lucera, or even of the Lucera of the French; most of the Provençals could not take the summer heat, though some of their descendants still live in the hills to the south. Charles II began the simple, Gothic **cathedral** of 1300 directly after the massacre of the Saracens. Other monuments include the church of **San Francesco**, a typical barn-like Franciscan church built from recycled Roman ruins, as well as parts of a gate and an amphitheatre from Roman Luceria on the edge of town. Smaller fragments reside at the **Museo Civico** (*closed for repairs after the 2002 earthquake; scheduled to reopen at the end of 2004; call* **t** *800 767 606 for updates*), just behind the cathedral.

Frederick's **castle** (*open Tues–Sun May–Sept 9–2 and 3–8; Oct–Apr 9–2*), two kilometres north of the centre (it's signposted), one of the largest ever built in Italy, was begun in 1233, the same year as the importation of the Saracens. It is still a highly impressive sight, with its score of towers and walls nearly a kilometre in circumference, set on a hill looking out over Lucera and the Foggia plain. Only ruins are left of Frederick's palace inside.

South and west of Foggia, in the foothills of the Apennines bordering the Molise and the Basilicata, lies Troia. Its famous **cathedral** is one of the oldest and most spectacular of its kind in Puglia, and an excellent introduction to the glories of the Puglian Romanesque. Troia, once the Roman town of *Aecae*, was refounded in 1017, and prospered from the start. Popes held two small church councils here in the 11th and 12th centuries; and the cathedral was begun in 1093, though not finished until the time of Frederick. Much of the inspiration for the Puglian style came from Pisa, and the Pisan trademark – blind arcades decorated with circle and diamond shapes – is in evidence here. There's also the most beautiful rose window in Italy – a unique, Arab-inspired fantasy from Frederick's time, with a circle divided into 11 sections, each with carved stone lattice-work in a different geometric design. Inside, the cathedral is strangely and intentionally asymmetrical, with everything on the right side just slightly out of alignment.

Bovino is a resolutely medieval-looking village with a 13th-century cathedral and some Roman remains, and **Ascoli Satriano** has a very well-preserved triple-arched Roman bridge over the Carapelle (*call* **t** *0885 652 811 to arrange a visit or ask tourist office in Via San Donato*). Nearby, close to **Ordona**, there are substantial remains of the abandoned Roman town of *Herdonia*.

The Gargano Peninsula

The 'spur' of the Italian boot is a lost chip of the former Yugoslavia, left behind when two geological plates separated to form the Adriatic several million years ago. For a long time, before silt washed down by the rivers gradually joined it to the mainland, the Gargano was an island. It might as well have remained so – it's as different from the adjacent lands in attitude as it is in its landscape, and constitutes the only stretch of scenic coast between Venice and the tip of Calabria.

Manfredonia

If you're coming from the north, you'll enter the Gargano via Lesina and the region's two lakes, the **Lago di Lesina** and the **Lago di Varano**, two large lagoons cut off from the sea by broad sand spits. From Foggia, the logical base for attacking the Gargano would be Manfredonia, a dusty port town with a beach and a pretty centre at the southern end of the peninsula. Founded by Frederick's son Manfred, it prospered well enough until Dragut's Turkish pirates sacked and razed it in 1620 (a local girl ended up the favoured wife of the sultan). Of old Manfredonia, all that is left is Manfred's castle, rebuilt by Charles of Anjou; it houses a small **archaeological museum** (*open Tues–Sun 8.15–7.30, until 7 in winter; adm*) with some valuable ancient stones with carvings by the Daun people of the 6th–7th century BC. There's also a brash 17th-century **cathedral**.

Along the Foggia road, about two kilometres south of the centre of Manfredonia, are the ruins of *Sipontum*, a Roman town that was finally abandoned to the malaria mosquitoes when Manfred moved the population to his healthier new city. The more recent town of **Siponto**, next to it, is a popular beach resort.

Evidence of how important Sipontum was in the early Middle Ages is provided by the 11th-century church of **Santa Maria di Siponto**, in the same style of decoration as the cathedral at Troia but built on a square, Byzantine–Greek plan. It is constructed over an underground Christian building from around the 5th century. A similar but even better 11th-century church is **San Leonardo** nine kilometres up the road, with finely sculpted portals and a small dome. At certain times in summer, a ray of sunshine enters the hole in the centre of its rose window, splitting into 17 rays on the floor.

Monte Sant'Angelo

Those who come for the beaches probably never notice, but this peninsula is holy ground, and has been perhaps since the time of the ancient Daunians. Sanctuaries, ancient and modern, are scattered all over it; there are many stories of the apparitions of saints and angels.

The Gargano Peninsula

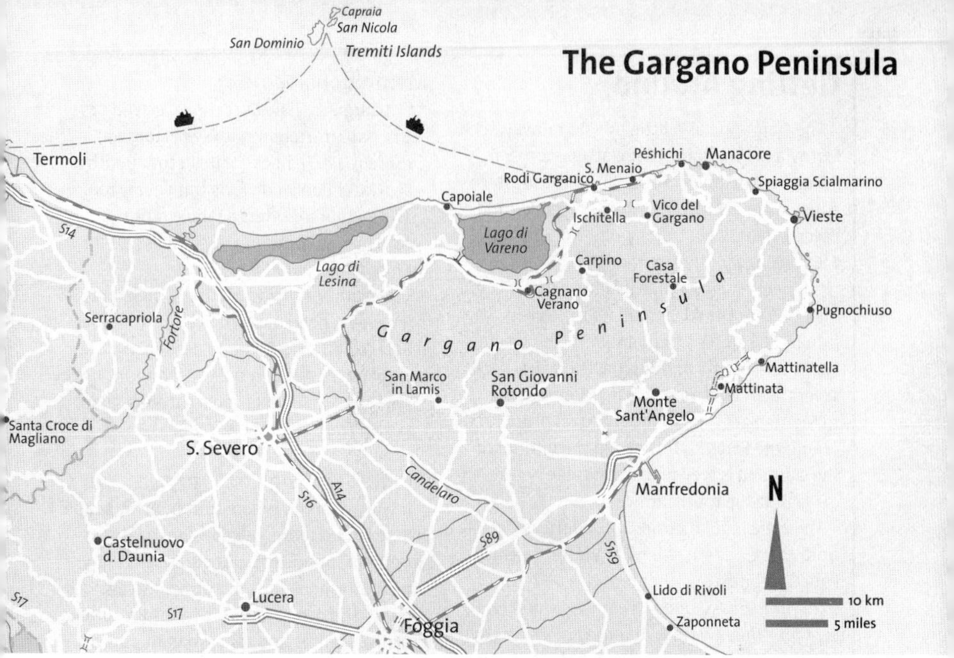

The centre of all this, for the last 1,000 years at least, has been **Monte Sant'Angelo**, one of the most important pilgrimage towns in Italy. Before Christianity, the cavern dedicated to Saint Michael was the site of a dream oracle; a 5th-century bishop of Sipontum had a vision of the archangel, who left his red cloak as a token and ordered that the sanctuary be converted to Christian worship. Early on, the new Monte Sant'Angelo was attracting pilgrims from all over Europe, continuing a tradition that had begun long before the site was Christianized. Among the pilgrims were the first Normans, in the 9th century. They returned home with tales of a rich and civilized Puglia, a place they suspected just might be a pushover for mounted, heavily armoured knights. The first Norman adventurers were not slow in taking up the challenge. All the other sites dedicated to St Michael around the coasts of Europe – including Mont St-Michel in Normandy – are the spiritual descendants of this one, founded as the cult of St Michael spread across Christendom in the early Middle Ages.

That Monte Sant'Angelo is a special place becomes evident even before you arrive. The trip up from Manfredonia passes through an uncanny landscape of chalky cliffs dotted with caves, ancient agricultural terraces, and a strange clarity in the light and air. After much twisting and grinding of gears, you arrive at a quiet, whitewashed city, a maze of steps and tunnels. Its medieval centre, the **Junno**, is one of the loveliest old quarters in southern Italy, a nonchalant harmony of colour and form. Here you'll find the **Santuario di San Michele** (*open daily Easter–Oct 7–7; Nov–Mar 7–1 and 3–5*), behind an eight-sided tower built by Charles of Anjou that reproduces the proportions (on one level) and much of the decoration of Frederick's Castel del Monte. The exterior has a Gothic porch and portals (mostly built in the 19th century; try to guess which of the identical portals is the 12th-century original). Above the doors is a Latin inscription: 'Terrible is this place; this is the house of God and the Gate of Heaven.'

Getting Around

The Gargano has a little **private railway**, the Ferrovia del Gargano, that clatters from San Severo, 30km north of Foggia, up the western edge of the peninsula to Rodi Garganico and Péschici (about six trains a day; freephone **t** 167 296 247 for information).

Connecting **buses** take you from Péschici to Vieste along the coast road (SP52). Buses (run by FG) are less frequent between Vieste and Manfredonia and Foggia. There are several **SITA** buses a day from Manfredonia to Monte Sant'Angelo (**t** 0881 773 117), but seeing the Foresta Umbra and the interior of the Gargano is well nigh impossible without a car (ask at the tourist office).

There are regular **ferries** around the peninsula from Manfredonia, calling at Vieste, Péschici, Rodi Garganico and the Tremiti Islands (*mid-June–mid-Sept daily; early June and late Sept four times weekly; Apr–May twice weekly*); the rest of the year, the islands are reachable only from Termoli and Manfredonia.

Tourist Information

Manfredonia: Piazza del Popolo 10, **t** 0884 581 998 (*open Mon–Sat 8.30–1.30*).

Vieste: Corso Fazzini 8, **t** 0884 708 806 (*open Mon–Fri 8–2, Tues and Thurs also 4–7*), and Piazza Kennedy, **t** 0884 708 805 (*often open longer hours and at weekends*).

Vieste hosts a film festival in the last 2wks of July, and in Sept there are 3 days of international windsurfing and kitesurfing competitions and parties at Spiaggialunga.

Where to Stay and Eat

The Gargano has a great many *aziende agrituristiche* – some simple country B&Bs, others offering delicious home-cooked meals at very reasonable prices. If you are travelling by car, they are an inexpensive alternative to hotels. Lists are available at tourist offices.

Manfredonia ✉ 71043

****__Gargano__, Viale Beccarini 2, **t** 0884 587 621, *www.tuttogargano.com/hgargano* (*expensive*). The best hotel in town, with a seawater pool and views from every room. The restaurant offers a whole range of fish dishes, from soup to *fritto misto*. *Closed Tues and most of Nov.*

*__Sipontum__, Via di Vittorio 229, **t** 0884 542 916 (*cheap*). A good basic choice.

Il Baracchio, Corso Roma 38, **t** 0884 583 874 (*expensive*). A cool modern restaurant by the port, with an unbelievable octopus salad. *Closed Thurs and 1st 2wks July.*

Monte Sant'Angelo ✉ 71037

If you ask about where to stay, most people will send you to the religious hostel (the Forestiera) beside the cathedral/sanctuary, which you should do your utmost to avoid: it's gloomy and overpriced, with an 11pm curfew, crucifixes galore and sanctimonious staff.

***__Hotel Michael__, Via R. Basilica 86, **t** 0884 565 519, *www.hotelmichael.com* (*cheap–moderate*). A wonderful new hotel with cosy, smartly furnished rooms opposite the cathedral, with balconies facing the square. Breakfast is served on a panoramic terrace overlooking the old town down to the sea. Everything in the restaurant is locally produced; try the pasta with *funghi* and *porcini* from the Foresta Umbria.

Al Grottino, Corso Vittorio Emanuele 179, **t** 0884 561 132 (*cheap*). A restaurant where you can get dinner for half what it's really worth. The goodies on offer include roast lamb and kid, and truly elegant *antipasti*. *Closed Mon.*

Vieste ✉ 71019

Nearby Péschici and Rodi Garganico have increasing numbers of hotels similar to those in Vieste itself.

Rodi is famous for its very sweet oranges and lemons (*agrumi*); if you're offered a *limoncello* don't think it's a tourist gimmick borrowed from Naples.

Inside is a long series of steps leading down to the cavern, passing a beautiful pair of bronze doors made in Constantinople in 1076. In the darkness most scenes are hard to make out, but Jacob's ladder and the expulsion from Eden stand out clearly. In the

★★★★**Pizzomunno**, Lungomare Enrico Mattei, **t** 0884 708 741, *www.ventaglio.it* (*expensive–luxury*). A gorgeous place just south of the centre, with sailing and sports activities, a pool, a beautiful beach, a disco and a highly rated restaurant (*expensive*). *Closed Nov–Mar.*

★★★**Falcone**, Lungomare Enrico Mattei 5, **t** 0884 708 251, *www.gtfalcone.it* (*cheap–moderate*). Vieste's second choice, with a private beach and most resort amenities.

★**Al Centro Storico**, Via Mafrolla 32, **t** 0884 707 030, *www.viesteonline.it/cstorico* (*cheap–moderate*). A gem of a *pensione* right in the centre of old Vieste, with friendly, efficient staff, clean rooms and sea views. Breakfast is served on a beautiful sunny terrace.

★★★**Gabbiano Beach**, **t** 0884 706 376, 7km north of town on the road to Péschici, *www.gabbianobeach.it* (*moderate*). A beautifully sited hotel, convenient only if you have a car, with its own beach, a nice swimming pool and sailing facilities. Some rooms are *cheap*, others *expensive*. *Closed end Oct–Mar.*

★★★**Albano**, Via Scalo Marittimo 33, Rodi Garganico, **t** 0884 965 138 (*moderate*). A reasonable option south of the historic centre of Rodi, with air-conditioned rooms and a good if unexciting restaurant.

★★**Hotel Maremonti**, Via della Resistenza, just outside Vico del Gargano, **t** 0884 991 418 (*cheap–moderate*) A small hotel high on a clifftop just outside the Foresta Umbra, with a pool and the ultimate sea view.

★★**Péschici**, Via San Maritino 31, Péschici, **t** 0884 964 195, *www.residencem3.com* (*cheap*). Good views, and more facilities and services than most two-stars. Full board is mandatory in August. *Closed mid-Oct–Easter.*

★**Roccamare**, Via Varano, Rodi Garganico, **t** 0884 965 461 (*cheap*). A special budget hotel on a cliff-face below the centre of Rodi. The four smaller rooms share a terrace with sea views.

Dragone, Via Duomo 8, **t** 0884 701 212 (*expensive*). One of Vieste's best restaurants, in a natural cave in the centre of the old town. Book ahead. *Closed Tues in low season, and Nov–Mar.*

La Scogliera, Largo S. Pietro 3, **t** 0884 708 107 (*expensive*). A bar, pizzeria and restaurant serving excellent seafood inside a Norman tower, with an outside terrace.

San Michele, Viale XXXIV Maggio 72, **t** 0884 708 143 (*moderate*). The finest restaurant in Vieste, according to many locals. Come here for fish grilled or in soups. *Closed Mon in low season; winter usually Nov–Feb.*

Box 19, Via Santa Maria di Merino 19, **t** 0884 705 229 (*moderate*). Reasonably priced seafood and grilled meats. *Closed Mon in low season, and Nov.*

Al Castello, Piazza Castello 29, Péschici, **t** 0884 964 038 (*moderate*). A hotel restaurant serving good seafood and meat dishes, with tables outdoors in Péschici's old quarter.

Regina, Corso Madonna della Libera 46, Rodi Garganico, **t** 0884 965 463 (*cheap*). A restaurant and *birreria* offering a bargain set menu, with plenty to choose from, including 'Regina' penne with mushrooms, tomatoes, mozzarella and *pancetta*, and fragrant mounds of *cozze* (mussels).

Il Trabucco, Loc. Monte Pucci, outside Péschici, **t** 0884 911 008 (*cheap*). A very basic fish restaurant overlooking a picturesque bay, set inside a *trabucco* (a wooden fishing hoist on a clifftop, peculiar to the Gargano) and serving its own freshly caught fish.

Tremiti Islands ✉ 71100

The grocer beside the chemist near the main square wraps up slices of delicious steaming potato pizza – just right for beach picnics.

★★★**Gabbiano**, near main square on San Domino, **t** 0882 463 401 (*moderate–expensive*). A good choice. Booking is essential.

★★**Al Faro**, near the main square on San Domino, **t** 0882 463 424 (*cheap–moderate*). A *pensione* with 8 rather cramped rooms but an excellent-value restaurant serving good home-cooking influenced by the food traditions of the San Nicola monastery, accompanied by some quality wines. Half board is obligatory. Book in advance. *Closed Oct–Easter.*

old days pilgrims would come down here on their knees, shuffling through the puddles to kiss the image of the archangel. The grotto is laid out like a small chapel. Of the medieval sculptural work around, the best is a 12th-century bishop's chair.

The town records give us an almost endless list of celebrity pilgrims: a dozen popes, King Ferdinand of Spain, four Holy Roman emperors, saints Bernard, Thomas Aquinas and Catherine of Siena, and even St Francis (attendants can show you the mark he made on the cavern wall). Behind the altar is the little well that made this a holy site in the first place. Long before there was a St Michael, indigenous religions of Europe had a great interest in springs and underground streams. Many scholars believe the idea of dragons began with a primeval fascination with buried streams and lines of telluric forces beneath the earth's surface; the sleepless 'eye' of the dragon is the fountain, where these forces come to the surface. In the icons of Monte Sant'Angelo, as well as in the endless souvenir figurines hawked outside the sanctuary, Michael is shown dispatching Lucifer in the form of a dragon.

Downhill from the sanctuary, next to the half-ruined church of San Pietro, is the 12th-century **tomb of Rotari** (*open daily 9–1 and 4–7; adm*). The idea that this was the tomb of 'Rotarus', a Lombard chief, stems from a misreading of one of the inscriptions. It is now believed it was intended as a baptistry – a very large and unusual baptistry, if so. Some of the sculpted detail is extremely odd; note the figures of a woman suckling a serpent – or a dragon.

Also in the Junno district is a small museum of Gargano folk arts and culture, the **Museo Tancredi** (*open Tues–Sun 9.30–1 and 5–7.30; adm*). At the top town is a ruined Norman castle, rebuilt by the Aragonese kings, then left quite alone.

San Giovanni Rotondo and Padre Pio

From the back of Monte Sant'Angelo, a narrow road leads into the heart of the Gargano, eventually branching off to the 'Forest of Shadows' (*see* p.943) or **San Giovanni Rotondo**, a little town on the slopes of Monte Calvo. Here, besides the strange round temple that gives the town its name (believed, like the tomb of Rotari, to have been intended as a baptistry), is a 16th-century monastery that for more than 50 years was home to Padre Pio da Pietralcina, a simple priest who not only received the stigmata on his hands, feet and side, but also had the ability to appear before cardinals in Rome while his body was sleeping back in the Gargano. The Church always has its suspicions about phenomena like these, but over the last 30 years veneration of Padre Pio has spread all over the world, and San Giovanni is a major pilgrimage site. After careful 'research', Vatican experts have decreed that the devil had nothing to do with Padre Pio's healing powers and he was beatified in May 1999.

West of San Giovanni and also an old stop on the pilgrimage route to Monte Sant'Angelo is the town of **San Marco in Lamis**, which has similarly always been a monastic centre. The present, huge Franciscan house dates from the 16th century.

Vieste

Past Monte Sacro, on the coast north of Monte Sant'Angelo, you're in the holiday Gargano, on an exceptionally lovely coastline of limestone cliffs, clean blue sea and good beaches decorated with old watchtowers, or stumps and columns of rock and other curious formations. Vieste, at the tip of the peninsula, is a lively and beautiful white town on white cliffs, surrounded by beaches. Though retaining its old charm, it has become the major resort of the southern Adriatic, and boutiques and restaurants crowd the centre. On Via Duomo, near the middle of the old town, is the **Chianca Amara** or 'bitter stone', where, it is believed, 5,000 townspeople were beheaded by the Turks when they sacked Vieste in 1554. Nearby is the 11th-century **cathedral**, with 18th-century additions, and, beyond that, another **castle** built by Frederick II, and the **Grotta Sfondata** ('bottomless lagoon'), one of a few marine grottos and lagoons accessible by boat tour from Vieste. There is also an odd early Christian *hypogeum* (cave for burials) on the coast, at the site of the long-disappeared town of *Merinum*.

On the Gargano's northern coast, **Péschici** and **Rodi Garganico** are pretty fishing villages that are now fast-developing resorts, particularly crowded in August. Boats call at both for the Tremiti Islands, and from either village, or from Vieste, it is an easy excursion by bus or car up the mountains to the **Foresta Umbra** ('forest of shadows'), a thick, primeval forest of beeches, oaks and pines, similar to those that covered most of Puglia in the Middle Ages. Across the forest is **Vico del Gargano**, untouched by tacky tourism, with tiny alleys, streets and squares that are well worth exploring.

The Tremiti Islands

In winter this minuscule archipelago 40 kilometres from the coast has a population of about 50; August finds it crawling with most of the 100,000 holiday-makers who annually spill over from the resorts of the Gargano. The islands have the same scoured limestone coasts as the peninsula, though there is only one beach, on the larger island of **San Domino**.

The islands entered the history books as a place of exile – Augustus' daughter and Charlemagne's troublesome Italian father-in-law were confined here – and a monkish retreat. From the 18th century they were used as a penal colony. The only sight on the smaller island of **San Nicola**, where ferries from the mainland disembark, is a huge half-ruined fortress-monastery begun by Benedictines in the 11th century. Local ferries run from there to San Domino, which has the only hotels. It's a beauty, forested and surrounded with wonderful coves and lagoons set in a translucent blue-green sea. If you can avoid coming in July or August, when day-trippers and ravenous mosquitoes sail in, the Tremitis can be a perfect spot to let your watch wind down.

Down the Coast to Bari

If you take the main route, a little bit inland you pass through more of the *Tavoliere*, the long, dull plain that stretches the length of Puglia. *Tavoliere* means chessboard; 2,000 years ago, when the Romans first sent in surveyors to apportion the land among their Punic War veterans, this flat plain – the only one south of the Po – gave the methodical rectangularity of the Roman mind a chance to express itself. They turned the plain into a grid of neatly squared roads and farms; many of their arrow-straight roads survive, and the succeeding centuries have managed to throw only a few kinks into the rest. If it weren't for the olive groves and vineyards, you might think you were in Iowa.

Barletta's Colossus

The coastal road, though just as flat, has more to see than the inland route, passing as it does through a string of attractive medieval port towns, each of which bears its contribution to the Puglian Romanesque in the shape of a grand old cathedral. You'll also see ancient salt marshes that are still being farmed, and marble salesrooms galore by the roadside.

Barletta, the first of the port towns as you come from the north and the best introduction, contains a unique and astounding sight. On Corso Vittorio Emanuele, beside the church of San Sepolcro, stands the largest surviving ancient bronze statue, locally known as the **Colosso**. To come upon this 20-foot figure in the middle of a busy city street, wearing an imperial scowl and a pose of conquest, with a cross and a sphere in his hands, is like lapsing into a dream. Scholars have debated for centuries who it might be. It's obviously a late Roman emperor, and the guesses have included Valentinian, Heraclius and Marcian; the last is most probable, and especially intriguing, since the triumphal column of Marcian (a useless emperor with no real successes to commemorate) still stands in Istanbul, and the statue of the emperor that once stood on top of it was probably carried away by the Venetians after the sack of Constantinople in 1204. A ship full of booty from that sack foundered off Barletta's coast, and the Colosso washed up on a nearby beach; the superstitious citizens let it stay there for decades before they got up enough nerve to bring it into the city. The figure is surpassingly strange, a monument to the onset of the Dark Ages; the costume the emperor wears is only a pale memory of the dress of Marcus Aurelius or Hadrian, with a pair of barbaric-looking leather boots instead of imperial buskins.

San Sepolcro, finished in the 13th century, is interesting in its own right. Above the plain French-Gothic vaulting is an octagonal dome recalling the Holy Sepulchre in Jerusalem. Corso Garibaldi leads from here into the heart of old Barletta and the 12th-century **cathedral**. Look on the left-hand wall, between the façade and the campanile, and you will see a cornice supported by 13 strange figures. If you are clever and have a good eye, you may make out the letters on them that make an acrostic of *Richardus Rex I* – Richard the Lionheart, who contributed to the embellishment of the cathedral on his way to the Crusades.

Nearby is the 13th-century church of **Sant'Andrea**, with another fine façade, the main portal of which, dating from 1240, was the work of Dalmatian sculptor Simon di Ragusa. The Third Crusade was launched from Barletta's often-rebuilt **Castello** (*open Tues–Sun 9–1 and 4–7; adm*), in a great council of Frederick and his knights. Apart from a collection of antiques, coins and armour, the castle also houses the **Pinacoteca Giuseppe de Nittis**, which has in its collection the only surviving statue of Frederick II – a little the worse for wear, poor fellow – as well as a large collection of works by the local, Impressionist-influenced painter Giuseppe de Nittis (1846–84). The admission ticket to the castle will also get you into the **Cantina della Disfida**, in Via Cialdini, where in 1503, after much drinking and brawling, 13 'Italian' knights challenged 13 French knights to a duel for control of the besieged town. The Italians won, and Barletta's siege was lifted. The historical event gets re-enacted in one of Puglia's largest pageants on the second weekend in September.

Getting There and Around

Two FS **railways** serve this area and you're more likely to find a train than a bus to many places. All coastal towns from Barletta to Monópoli are on the main FS east-coast route. From Barletta, there is an FS branch line to the south with infrequent services to Spinazzola and Altamura. One of the three private lines that operate from Bari, the Ferrovia Bari-Nord, **t** 080 578 9511, runs a frequent service through inland towns such as Andria, Ruvo and Bitonto.

There are also reasonably regular **buses** along the coast road, and inland from Barletta or Bari. Unfortunately, Castel del Monte is just about the hardest place to reach in Puglia: call the castle or the tourist office in Andria for timetables for the infrequent bus service.

Tourist Information

Barletta: Corso Garibaldi 208, **t** 0883 331 331 (*open Mon–Fri 9–1, Tues and Thurs also 5–7*).

Trani: Piazza Trieste 10, **t** 0883 588 830 (*open Mon–Sat 8.30–1.30, Tues also 3–6*).

Ruvo di Puglia: Via Vittorio Veneto 48, **t** 080 361 549 (*open Mon–Fri 9.30–12 and 5.30–7.30, Sat and Sun 9.30–12*).

Andria, Piazza Caturna, **t** 0883 290 293.

Where to Stay and Eat

The area north of Bari is famous for its sea urchins, eaten raw. Barletta is also known for its watermelons, sold by the roadside. Corato, on the road to Castel del Monte, is one of Italy's finest olive oil producing zones. Its oil cooperative at Via Castel del Monte 184, **t** 080 872 1024, sells wine and oil out of vast pumps.

Barletta ✉ 70051

******Artù**, Piazza Castello 67, **t** 0883 332 121 (*moderate*). An adequate central option.

Antica Cucina, Via Milano, **t** 0883 521 718 (*expensive*). Light, tasty fish dishes and good desserts. *Closed Sun eve, Mon and July.*

Trani ✉ 70059

******Régia**, Piazza Mons. Addazi 2, **t** 0883 584 444 (*expensive*). A *palazzo* by the cathedral, with a good-value restaurant. *Closed Mon.*

******Royal**, Via De Robertis 29, **t** 0883 588 777, *www.hotelroyaldam.com* (*expensive*). A rather corporate choice, with quiet rooms.

***Lucy**, Piazza Plebliscito 11, **t** 0883 481 022 (*cheap*). An excellent *pensione*, with high-ceilinged rooms and balconies overlooking a nice square, round the block from the harbour.

Padri Bernabiti, Piazza Tiepolo, **t** 0883 481 180 (*cheap*). Basic, clean rooms with views. The fathers will only let married couples share a room. Reserve. *Closed 1–5pm; curfew 1am.*

Torrente Antico, Via Fusco 3, **t** 0883 487 911 (*very expensive*). Local fish and fowl prepared in interesting ways, and the best local wines. *Closed Sun eve, Mon and 2wks Aug.*

La Nicchia, Via S. Gervasio 69, **t** 0883 482 020 (*cheap*). Good-value shellfish. *Closed Thurs.*

Il Pozzo dei Desideri, Via Zanardelli 36, **t** 0883 481 902 (*cheap*). An attractive restaurant on a cobbled street just off the harbour, with free home-baked *focaccia. Closed Mon.*

Molfetta ✉ 70056

*****Molfetta Garden**, Via Provinciale per Terlizzi, **t** 080 334 1722, *www.gardenhotel.org* (*moderate*). A good-value, modern hotel.

Bufi, Via Vittorio Emanuele 15, **t** 080 397 1597 (*expensive*). Old recipes presented in innovative ways, plus a great wine cellar. *Closed Mon, Sun eve and 2wks Jan and Aug.*

Bistrot, Corso Dante 33, **t** 080 397 5812 (*moderate*). An adventurous place offering specialities such as chef's *gamberi. Closed Weds and middle 2wks Aug.*

Andria

Archo Marchese, Via Arco Marchese 1, **t** 0883 557 826 (*expensive*). A family-run fish restaurant in old Andria, with charming service and inventive cuisine. Try cuttlefish with aubergine, or beef with almond cream sauce. *Closed Sun eve, Tues and Aug.*

Gravina in Puglia

Madonna della Stella, Via Madonna della Stella, **t** 080 325 6383 (*moderate*). A panoramic restaurant offering strictly local fare. *Closed Tues and Feb.*

Osteria Cucco, Piazza Pellicciari 4, **t** 080 326 1872 (*moderate*). Eclectic Pugliese/Emilian specialities such as pumpkin or walnut ravioli. *Closed Mon and last 2wks Aug.*

Trani

The next town along the coast, Trani is a sun- and sea-washed old port with a large and prosperous fishing fleet. It was an important merchant town in the early Middle Ages – it fought a war with Venice, and its merchant captains created what may have been the first code of laws of the sea since ancient times. Its famous **cathedral** (*open Mon–Sat 8–12.30 and 3.30–6.30, Sun and hols 9–12.45 and 2–7*) in an open piazza on the edge of the sea is an excellent work of the Puglian Romanesque, and a monument to the age of the Crusades. At the centre of the façade is a pair of 12th-century bronze doors like the ones in many other cities of the south. But these ones are special – the artist who did them and several others in the town was a native, Barisano of Trani.

Inside, the most remarkable things are underground. This cathedral is in fact three buildings stacked on the same site; the lower church, **Santa Maria della Scala**, is the earlier, Byzantine cathedral; below it is the **crypt of San Leucio**, an unusual early Christian church or catacomb with solid marble columns and bits of medieval frescoes. Other notable buildings include the **Castello Svevo** (*open daily 8.30–7.30; adm*), another of Frederick II's symmetrical fortresses, on the seafront; the **Ognissanti** (*if it's closed, ask the Knights if they will let you have a look inside*), a typical church of the 12th-century Knights Templar; the **Palazzo Caccett1**, a rare (for southern Italy) example of late Gothic architecture from the 1450s; and two small churches that were once synagogues, **Santa Maria di Scuola Nova** and **Sant'Anna**, converted after the Spaniards expelled Trani's long-established Jewish community in the 16th century.

From Trani, **Bisceglie** is the next town, with another good Romanesque cathedral. Then comes **Molfetta**, a city with a reputation for drugs and gangsters. Molfetta has a cathedral like Trani's on the harbour's edge, the **Duomo Vecchio**. This may be the most peculiar of them all: its plan, subtly asymmetrical like that of Troia, has a wide nave covered by three domes, the central one being elliptical. The west front is almost blank, while the back side has elaborate carved decoration, and a door that leads into the apse. Molfetta also has another cathedral, the Baroque **Duomo Nuovo**, from 1785.

Castel del Monte

Open daily Mar–Sept 10–7.30; Oct–Feb 9–7; adm; tours in Italian and English (donations appreciated), call **t** *0883 569 848 summer, Andria tourist office winter.*

In Enna, the 'navel of Sicily', Emperor Frederick built a mysterious octagonal tower at the highest point of the town. In Puglia, this most esoteric of emperors erected an equally puzzling palace. It, too, is a perfect octagon; if you've been travelling through the region, you'll have noticed that nearly every town has at least one eight-sided tower, bastion or campanile, and that often enough Frederick was behind them. Castel di Santa Maria del Monte, to give it its original title, was begun by Frederick in the 1240s on a high hill overlooking the Puglian *Tavoliere*, south of the town of Andria.

At each of the eight corners of Castel del Monte is a slender octagonal tower. The 80ft-tall building has only two storeys; each with eight rooms, all interconnected, and each facing the octagonal courtyard. Historians have tried to pass off the castle as one of Frederick's hunting lodges. This is implausible: the rooms each have only one small window, and in spite of the wealth of sculpted stone it would have seemed more like a prison than a forest retreat – in fact the emperor's grandsons, the heirs of his son Manfred, were imprisoned here for 30 years. Neither is it a fortification: there are no ramparts, no arrow slits, and not even a defensible gate. Some writers suggest that Frederick had an artistic monument in mind. The entrance to the castle, the so-called 'triumphal arch', is a work unique for the 13th century: an elegant classical portal that prefigures the Renaissance. Inside, every room was decorated with friezes, columns and reliefs in Greek marble, porphyry and precious stones. Almost all have gone, vandalized by the noblemen who owned the castle over the last five centuries. Only the delicately carved Gothic double windows survive, one to each room.

At Castel del Monte, however, it is the things you can't see that are most interesting. This is nothing less than the Great Pyramid of Italy, and the secrets Frederick built into it have for centuries attracted the attention of cranks and serious scholars. The guides are full of opinions; one suggests that the castle was built for meetings of a secret society, and considering the atmosphere of eclectic mysticism that surrounded the emperor and his court, this is entirely plausible. Whole books have been written about the measurements and proportions of the castle, finding endless repetitions of the Golden Section, its square and cubic roots, relations to the movements of the planets and the stars, the angles and proportions of the Pythagorean five-pointed star, and so on. A link between the castle and the ancient surveying of the Puglian plain is a fascinating possibility. Frederick's tower in Enna has been found to be the centre of an enormous rectilinear network of alignments uniting scores of ancient temples, towers and cities in straight lines that crisscross Sicily. That tower may have been built on the site of a forgotten holy place; the alignments and vast geometrical temple they form probably predate the Greeks. No one has suggested that Castel del Monte replaced any ancient site, but the particular care of Puglia's ancient surveyors – and the arrangement of the region's holy places, sanctuaries and Frederick's castles – suggest that something similarly strange may be hidden here.

Around the *Tavoliere*

The nearest town to Castel del Monte is Andria, a thriving market centre. Another city associated with Frederick, it has an inscription from the emperor on its St Andrea's Gate, honouring it for its loyalty. Two of Frederick's wives, Yolande of Jerusalem and Isabella of England, daughter of King John, are buried in the cathedral crypt.

Back towards the northwest, on the banks of the Ofanto between Barletta and Canosa di Puglia (SS93), is the site of the **Battle of Cannae**; here, in 216 BC, Hannibal annihilated four Roman legions. Military strategists still study the Carthaginians' brilliant ambush – the last serious defeat Rome suffered for centuries. Hannibal and his elephants had been in Italy for two years. Cannae was the opportunity he was waiting for, and historians are puzzled as to why he didn't follow it up with a march on Rome – probably it was due to a lack of siege equipment. The chance was missed; Hannibal spent eight years campaigning successfully but fruitlessly in Italy, while the Romans locked themselves up in their towns and sent their armies off to conquer Spain and North Africa.

In Roman times, **Canosa di Puglia** was one of the region's most important towns; reminders of its former status include three large tombs on the outskirts, excavated in 1843, and some archaeological relics in the **Museo Civico** (*open summer Tues–Sat 9–1 and 4–6, Sun 8–2; winter 9–1 and 2–5, Sun 8–2*). Its otherwise undistinguished five-domed cathedral has in its courtyard the **tomb of Bohemund**, a striking marble chapel with a small cupola (octagonal, of course) that holds the remains of the doughty Crusader. Bohemund was the son of Robert Guiscard; renowned for valour and chivalry, he seized the main chance when the First Crusade was being preached, and ended up Prince of Antioch. The most remarkable feature of his tomb is the pair of bronze doors, signed by an artist named Roger of Melfi. The one on the left, inscribed with geometrical arabesques, is a single slab of bronze. Inside the cathedral, notice the early medieval bishop's chair, resting on two weary-looking elephants.

Four Towns, Four More Cathedrals

In this corner of Bari province there are eight noteworthy cathedrals on a narrow strip of land just 64 kilometres long. They're the only real monuments – nothing has been built ambitiously and well around here since the 14th century – and they are the best evidence of Puglia's greatest period of culture and prosperity. One of the best is at **Ruvo di Puglia**, an ancient settlement famous in classical times for pottery – reproducing Greek urns at a lower price, above all between the 5th and the 3rd centuries BC when the trade was at its height. Locally made urns, and some Greek imports, can be seen at the **Museo Jatta** in Piazza Bovio (*open Mon–Thurs 8.30–1.30*). The **cathedral** is a tall, almost Gothic work, with a richly decorated façade containing a fine rose window. The little arches along the sides are decorated with intricate figures of pagan gods, copied from surviving pieces of ancient Ruvo's pottery.

Bitonto, the centre of olive oil production in Puglia, has a **cathedral** considered by many the classic of Puglian Romanesque; the best features of the exterior are the side galleries and the carvings of fantastical animals and scriptural scenes over the three front portals. Inside is a famous pulpit of 1226 displaying a fierce eagle; on one side a primitive relief shows Emperor Frederick, Isabella of England, and their family.

Puglia's southern borders make up a jumble of plain and rolling hills, **Le Murge**. The biggest town, **Altamura**, producing bread that's shipped all over Italy, was founded by Frederick on the site of an ancient city. For centuries it was a town of some distinction, with its own university. Its advanced outlook led Altamura to support the French and the short-lived Parthenopean Republic in the Napoleonic Wars. As a result, the Army of the Holy Faith, a mob led by a cardinal and egged on by monks, sacked and burned the city in 1799. The university never recovered, but there's still a beautiful **cathedral**, begun by Frederick in 1232; damage in a 1316 quake accounts for departures from the Puglian norm. It retains its exceptional rose window and portal, but the twin towers were added in the Renaissance, when the cathedral was turned backwards – the old portal and rose window were taken apart and placed where the apse used to be.

The **Museo Archeologico** at Via Santeramo 88 (***t*** *080 314 6409; open Mon–Sat 8.30–1.30 and 2.30–7.30, Sun 8.30–1.30 only*) houses first-rate finds related to the people of the Murge from prehistoric times to the Middle Ages.

Gravina in Puglia, on the road towards Potenza, has the fourth cathedral, but it is only a dull 15th-century replacement for the Norman original. Gravina does have other charms, though. The town is set above a steep ravine, lined with caves where the inhabitants took refuge from pirates and barbarians during the Dark Ages. One of its churches, **San Michele dei Grotti**, is a cave too (*contact Cooperative Benedetto XIII*, **t** *338 567 8017, inside the cathedral, for free tours in English of San Michele and other cave-churches such as Madonna della Stella; donations appreciated*), with a heap of human bones believed to be those of victims of Arab pirates during the 8th century. Other churches show somewhat eccentric versions of Renaissance styles, notably the **Madonna delle Grazie**, near the railway station. On Piazza Santomasi there's a **museum** (*open Tues–Sat 9–1 and 4–7, Sun 9–1*), with a full-size reconstruction of another ancient cave-church, with fragments of Byzantine frescoes.

Bari

The second city of the peninsular Mezzogiorno is a bustling town full of sailors and fishermen, and also boasts a university and a long heritage of cultural distinction, but it will disappoint if you come expecting Mediterranean charm and medieval romance. If, on the other hand, you'd like to see a southern city that has come close to catching up with the rest of Italy economically, Bari is just the place. Its newer districts, jammed with noisy traffic, exhibit a thoroughly northern glitter, and the good burghers who stroll down the Corso Cavour for their evening *passeggiata* are among the most overdressed in Italy. Be warned, though – and you probably will be – that the city has one of the highest street-crime rates in the country.

The Town that Stole Santa Claus

Bari traces its history back to before the Romans but began to make a name for itself only in the 10th century. As an important trading city, and seat of a nominally independent Byzantine governor, it was sometimes a rival to Venice but more often its ally. Robert Guiscard and his Normans, who took the city in 1071, favoured Bari and helped it become the leading town of Puglia.

Sixteen years later, in 1087, a fleet of Barese merchantmen in Antioch got word that some of their Venetian counterparts were planning a little raid on Myra, on what is now the southern coast of Turkey. Their intention was to pinch the mortal remains of St Nicholas, Myra's 4th-century bishop, canonized for his generosity and good deeds. Relic-stealing was a cultural imperative for medieval Italians, and the Baresi sneaked in by night and beat the Venetians to their prey – something that didn't happen often in those days. The Greek Christians of Myra were disgusted by the whole affair, but the Baresi had them outmatched, and so St Nicholas went west (his sarcophagus was too heavy to move, and you can still see it today in the museum at Antalya, Turkey). Every year on 8 May the Baresi celebrate their cleverness with a procession of boats in the harbour, and an ancient icon of the saint is held up to receive the homage of the crowds on shore, recreating the scene of Nicholas' arrival 900 years ago.

Getting There and Around

Bari's **airport** (**t** 080 021 9172), about 9km west of the city at Palese, has regular links to Rome, Milan, Turin, Pisa and other destinations. There is a special bus to the airport from the central train station.

Bari is an important junction on the main FS east-coast **railway** line, with many long-distance services; there is also a busy branch line from Bari to Táranto, and three private regional railways that run from the city. The Ferrovie Sud-Est (FSE), **t** 080 546 2111, runs a line from Via Amendola 106 near Bari's central FS station (on Piazza Aldo Moro) to Lecce and Táranto (competing with the FS) and towns in the *trulli* country. Nearby, the Ferrovia Bari-Nord station, **t** 080 521 3427, runs frequent trains to Andria and towns en route; while Ferrovie Appulo-Lucane (FCL), **t** 080 572 5228, on Corso Italia, goes to Altamura and to Matera in the Basilicata. The Ferrovia del Gargano, **t** 080 520 7311, is at Via Zuppetta 7.

There are long-distance **buses** to Rome, Naples and other major Italian cities, most of which also leave from Piazza Aldo Moro, though services to coastal towns north of Bari operate from Piazza Eroi del Mare (on the east side of the port). SITA buses (Via Capruzzi, behind the FS train station, reached via the subway) connect Bari with inland and southern towns, while the private rail lines' bus services (FCL and FSE) leave respectively from stations on Corso Italia and Largo Ciaia.

Regular **ferries** to Corfu, mainland Greece (Igoumenitsa and Patras), Albania, Croatia and Turkey leave from the Stazione Marittima on the Mole San Vito, at the opposite end of the city from the main FS rail station (connected by bus no.20). **Car ferries** to Greece are run by the **Ventouris line**, c/o Pan Travel, Via 24 Maggio 40, **t** 080 521 7699 (June–Sept daily; rest of the year 3 times a week) and **Superfast**, **t** 080 528 2828. **Adriatica**, Via Liside 4, **t** 080 553 1555, and **Stazione Marittima**, **t** 080 553 0360, run ferries to Dubrovnik (Fri and Sun) and Montenegro (Tues, Fri and Sat). **CTS**, Via Postiglione 27, **t** 080 555 9916, is a helpful travel agent.

Bari is compact and it doesn't take long to see the sights on foot. Orange **city buses** run 5.30am–11pm; their main terminus is Piazza Aldo Moro. The traffic and parking are horrible.

Tourist Information

Piazza Aldo Moro 33, **t** 080 542 361, next to FS station (*open Mon–Sat 8.30–1*).

Stop Over, Via Nicola 47, **t** 080 523 2716 (*open Mon–Fri 9.30–1 and 4.30–8*). A more useful resource.

Where to Stay

Bari ✉ 70100

Bari is a convenient base but also a business centre, full of bad hotels at absurd prices.

****__Villa Mercure Romanazzi Carducci__, Via Capruzzi 326, **t** 080 542 7400, *www.villaromanazzi.com* (*expensive*). The one upmarket hotel here that is not a rip-off, with ample, comfortable rooms.

***__Grand Hotel Moderno__, Via Crisanzio 60, **t** 080 521 3313 (*moderate*). A pleasant hotel.

***__Costa__, Via Crisanzio 12, **t** 080 521 9015 (*moderate*). A decent if unremarkable option.

__Albergo Giulia__, **t 080 521 6630, *www.hotelpensionegiulia.it* (*moderate*). A good inexpensive option.

Eating Out

Bari is famous for its fish; it still sends its own fishing fleet out each morning.

Murat de l'Hotel Palace, Via Lombardi 13, **t** 080 521 6551 (*expensive*). A highly rated restaurant with daring and innovative Italian cuisine and panoramic views of old Bari. *Closed Sun and Aug.*

Al Pescatore, Via Federico II di Svevia 6, **t** 080 523 7039 (*moderate*). Excellent grilled fish served in informal surroundings. *Closed Mon.*

Taverna Verde, Largo Adua 19, **t** 080 554 0870 (*moderate*). A popular place for fish and beer – good if you've overdosed on wine. *Closed Sun, last 2wks Aug, and 24 Dec–6 Jan.*

Terranima, Via Putignani 213, **t** 080 521 9725 (*moderate*). Arguably the best trattoria in town, with a limited daily menu of solid dishes. *Closed Sun eve and Aug.*

Da Tommaso, Palese Marina, **t** 080 530 0038 (*moderate*). A good seafood place outside town. *Closed Mon.*

Enzo e Ciro, Via Imbriani 79, **t** 080 554 1535 (*cheap*). Good pizzas.

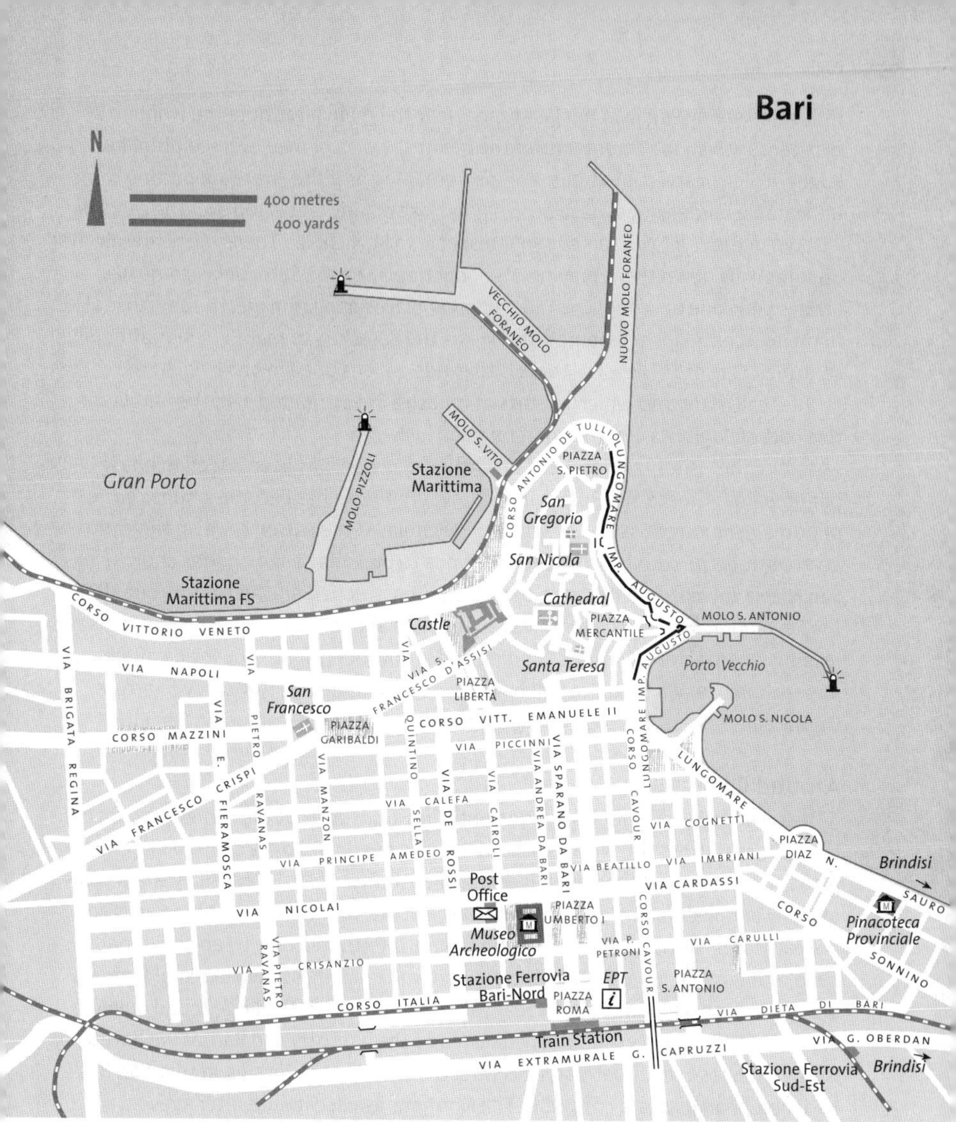

To provide a fitting home for such an important saint, Bari began almost immediately to construct the **Basilica di San Nicola** (*open Tues–Fri 10–12 and for Mass daily*) at the centre of the old town. Unfortunately, the original ambition overreached the ability of succeeding generations to finish the job. The two big towers remain unfinished. and much of the decorative scheme was abandoned, giving the church a dowdy appearance. Still, this is the first of the great Puglian churches, the place where the style was first translated from Norman French to southern Italian. Inside, the only surprise is the tomb of Bona Sforza, Queen of Poland and Duchess of Bari. The daughter of a 16th-century Duke of Milan, she inherited Bari on her mother's side and as a teenager was packed off to marry Sigismund, one of Poland's greatest kings. She survived him, and had a brief but eventful career as a dowager queen before retiring to sunny Puglia in her last years. Near the main altar, note the wonderful 11th-century bishop's throne, one of the greatest works of medieval sculpture in Puglia; its legs, carved into figures of men groaning as if they were supporting some unbearable burden, must have been a good joke on any fat bishop over the centuries.

Down in the crypt you can pay your respects to St Nicholas. There will nearly always be somebody down there, praying or conducting a service; St Nicholas' tomb has always been one of the south's most popular places of pilgrimage. The church is also home to a centre for ecumenical studies, as the Baresi try to make amends after nine centuries. One of St Nicholas' tricks is to exude gallons of a brownish liquid the faithful call manna, to which all sorts of miracles are attributed; half the families in this part of Puglia have a phial of it for good luck.

Most of the visitors are local, but an Orthodox chapel has been added to house pilgrims from Greece and Russia. Indeed, over time Bari has become a huge centre of pilgrimage among Russians, of whom St Nicholas is the patron saint. In the early 20th century the country provided the funds to build its own orthodox church, **San Nicola Taymaturgo**, on Corso Benedetto. Construction finished in 1913 but after the Revolution four years later it was abandoned and fell rapidly into disrepair. It has recently been restored with EU funding and is now open again. The inside of the upper church on Via Bottalica will be frescoed by contemporary Moscovite artists. On the same street, at No.34, you'll find an elegant Russian restaurant, Rasputin.

Around Old Bari

The **cathedral** (*closed for restoration until Christmas 2004 at the earliest*) is difficult to distinguish from San Nicola, although it was begun almost a century later. The plan is the same, as is the general feeling of austerity, which is broken by small areas of richly detailed carving around some of the doors and windows. Unlike San Nicola, the cathedral still has its original beam ceiling, interrupted only by an octagonal cupola, and much more suited to its Romanesque plainness. Two unusual features are the stone baldaquin over the main altar, and the *trullo*, the large round building adjacent to the north wall that once served as the baptistry. Old Bari, as we have said, is a bit drab for a medieval historic centre. There is a reason for this, in that Bari has had more than its share of trouble. The Normans levelled it once after a revolt; a plague in the 1650s wiped out nearly the entire population; and the port area was heavily bombed in the Second World War.

As a result, old Bari in some parts has the air of a new town. The buildings in the old centre may have all been rebuilt or restored, but at least the labyrinthine old street plan survives – it's famous, in fact, for being one of the easiest places in all Italy in which to get lost. There will be no trouble, however, finding the **castle** (*open Mon–Sat 9–1 and 3.30–7, Sun and hols 9–1; adm*), just across Piazza Odegitria from the cathedral. The Normans began it, Frederick II completed it, and in later centuries the polygonal bastions were added to deflect cannonballs. Inside, some sculpted reliefs and windows survive from Frederick's time, along with bits of sculpture and architectural fragments from all over Puglia. Excavations have revealed parts of Roman Bari, which lies directly underneath.

Modern Bari

On your way to the railway station, you'll cross the Corso Vittorio Emanuele, site of the city hall and Bari's famous fish market, and the boundary between the old city and the new. When Bari's fortunes began to revive, at the beginning of the 19th century, Murat's Napoleonic government laid out this broad rectilinear extension to the city. It has the plan of an old Greek or Roman town, only with wider streets, and it fits Bari well; many of the streets have an open view to the sea. Via Sparano di Bari and Corso Cavour are the choicest shopping streets.

Bari's museums are in the new town. The **Pinacoteca Provinciale** (*open Tues–Sat 9–1 and 4–7, Sun 9–1; adm*), in the Palazzo della Provincia on Lungomare Nazario Saura, has a good selection of southern Italian art. The **Museo Archeologico** (*closed for restoration; call* **t** *080 521 1559 for an update*) occupies a corner of the university's sprawling, crowded palace on Piazza Umberto I, near the station. The star exhibits are classical ceramics: painted vases from Attica, including a very beautiful figure of the Birth of Helen from Leda's egg, and Puglian copies, as good as the best of the Greeks. Much of the rest of the collection is devoted to the pre-Greek Neolithic cultures of Puglia.

The *Trulli* Country

Southeast of Bari is an attractive region of small towns set amid an extraordinary man-made landscape, given its character by one of the oldest forms of building in Italy still in regular use – the whitewashed dome-roofed houses known as *trulli*.

Alberobello, Locorotondo and Ostuni

The **Valle d'Itria**, between the towns of Putignano and Martina Franca, is the best place for *trullo*-hunting. Alberobello, the *trullo* capital, has more than 1,000 (and nearly as many craft shops) in two adjacent neighbourhoods, the Rione Monti and Ala Piccola. Even the modern church of Sant'Antonio has been built in *trullo*-fashion. There are plenty more out in the countryside, particularly around **Locorotondo**, a gleaming white hill town with views around the Itria valley, topped with tidy rows of distinctive gables. The street plan, from which the town takes its name, is neatly circular, built around an ancient well dedicated to St George.

Towns and villages in this district are among the most beautiful in southern Italy. In each, white arches and steps climb the hillsides, sometimes punctuated by *trulli* and topped with surprisingly grand Baroque churches. **Ostuni** is one of the loveliest, with an ornate 16th-century cathedral and a handful of other Renaissance and Baroque confections in its white streets, including even a Neapolitan-style *guglia* (spire). The **Chiesa delle Monacelle** (*open daily 9–1, Tues, Thurs and Sun also 4–7; longer hours in summer; adm*) is home to Delia, the archaeological highlight of Ostuni, a well-preserved skeleton of a pregnant young woman found in a crouched position, her skull decorated with coloured beads and stones before burial during what must have been a mystic, religious ceremony. The church also hosts a permanent display on prehistoric agriculture in southern Italy.

Getting Around

One of the best ways to see the area is on the Ferrovie Sud-Est **rail** line between Bari and Táranto or Lecce, which stops at most of the *trulli* country towns, including Putignano, Alberobello, Locorotondo and Martina Franca, where the Lecce and Táranto lines divide.

The FSE also operates **bus** services to the area from Táranto and Bari.

Tourist Information

Ostuni: Corso Giuseppe Mazzini 6, **t** 0831 301 268 (*open Mon–Fri summer 8.30–1.30 and 5.30–8.30, winter 8.30–1.30 and 3.30–6.30*).

Martina Franca: Piazza Roma 37, **t** 080 480 5702 (*open Mon–Sat 9–1 and 6–7.30*).

Fasano: Piazza Ciaia 10, **t** 080 441 3086 (*open Mon–Fri 8–1.30 and 3.30–7, Sat 8–1.30 and 3.30–9*).

Where to Stay and Eat

Across this area there are dozens of private *trulli* that are rented out as part of the local *agriturismo* programme and are perfect for those with kids. You can get more information from local tourist offices. In Alberobello, try **Trullidea**, Via Monte Nero 15, **t** 0804 323860, *www.trullidea.it*, for moderately priced, basic apartments in *trulli*.

Alberobello ✉ 70011

***** **Hotel dei Trulli**, Via Cadore 32, **t** 080 432 3555, *www.hoteldeitrulli.it* (*very expensive*). A group of *trulli* set in a garden with a pool. Each beautifully furnished cottage has its own patio.

* **Hotel Lanzillotta**, Via Ferdinando IV 31, **t** 080 432 1511 (*cheap*). A budget hotel situated right in the town square, with a family-run restaurant, the **Cucina dei Trulli**, that has been in business for more than a century and offers excellent home-cooking. *Restaurant closed Tues in winter.*

Il Poeta Contadino, Via Indipendenza 21, **t** 080 432 1917 (*very expensive*). One of Puglia's finest 'creative' restaurants, with a soothing atmosphere and top-notch food and wine. *Closed Mon in winter, and Jan.*

Trullo d'Oro, Via Cavallotti 27, **t** 080 432 3909 (*moderate*). An old *trullo* where you can enjoy fancy cuisine such as *spiedini* Puglian-style. *Closed Mon and 3wks Jan.*

Locorotondo ✉ 70010

This village is at the centre of Puglia's most famous wine region, and a bottle of

Martina Franca, the highest town in Puglia, has a garland of Baroque monuments, including the old Palazzo Ducale and a cathedral at the top. During July and August, the town becomes an important point on the cultural map when it hosts the Valle d'Itria Festival – an international music festival that attracts major opera, classical and jazz performers from around the world (*call* **t** *080 480 5100 for details of performances, or contact tourist office for information about tickets*).

Caves, *Laure* and a Dolmen

The attractions of this area are not limited to *trulli* and white towns. The people around the **Castellana Grotte** never tire of bragging that their famous grottoes are the most beautiful in Italy. They may be right: the deepest section of the grotto tour, called the **Caverna Bianca**, is a glistening wonderland hung with thousands of bright glassy stalactites (*open daily Apr–Sept 8.30–12.30 and 2.30–6.30, Oct–Mar until 4.30; tours hourly, lasting about 1hr 45mins; Aug also tours at 9pm; adm exp*). Like much of Puglia, this region is what geologists call karst topography: made of easily dissolving limestone, the territory is laced with caves, accompanied by streams and rivers that disappear into the ground, only to pop back up to the surface a few miles away.

Locorotondo – a pale, dry white, much more delicate than most Puglian wines – is mandatory with dinner.

Casa Mia, Via Cisternino, a few km along road towards Ostuni, **t** 080 431 1218 (*moderate*). A fine establishment serving the likes of stuffed peppers and *coniglio al forno*. *Closed Tues.*

Centro Storico, Via Eroi di Dogali 6, **t** 080 431 5473 (*moderate*). An intimate trattoria with careful cooking and presentation. *Closed Weds in winter.*

Ostuni ✉ 72017

****Hotel Rosa Marina, along shoreline at Rosa Marina, on SS379 north of town, **t** 0831 350 411, *www.grandhotelrosamarina.com* (*very expensive*). A sharply designed modern hotel that stands out from the crowd, with a pool, beach and all amenities. Some rooms are *luxury*, some *expensive*.

Tre Torri, Corso Vittorio Emanuele 298, **t 0831 331 114 (*cheap*). A pleasant enough hotel for a short stay.

*Orchidea Nera, Corso Mazzini 118, **t** 0831 301 366. The only real option for those without a car; you couldn't be better placed to walk around town. The hotel is old-fashioned and clean if a little spartan, with an eccentric owner in her 90s who speeds around in a sports car and does her shopping on horseback. Some of the rooms are en suite.

Martina Franca ✉ 74015

***Dell'Erba, Via dei Cedri 1, **t** 080 430 1055 (*moderate–expensive*). A reasonable option with a child-minding service, a garden, a pool and an excellent restaurant.

Castellana Grotte ✉ 70013

Fontanina, Via Alcantarini 14, on Alberobello road outside town, **t** 080 496 8010 (*moderate*). A welcoming restaurant in a lovely spot, offering generous portions of traditional food. *Closed Mon.*

Taverna degli Artisti, Via Matarrese 23, **t** 080 496 8234 (*moderate*). A friendly place with particularly good cannelloni and lamb *torcini*. *Closed Thurs eve and Jan–mid-Mar.*

Savelletri di Fasano ✉ 72010

*****Masseria San Domenico, on Strada Litoranea not far from Egnazia, **t** 080 482 7990 (*luxury*). One of the most relaxing and luxurious hotels in Puglia, in the renovated buildings of an old country house set amid the olive groves. The beautiful swimming pool in the shape of a natural lake is filled with filtered sea water. Prices reach eyewatering levels.

In the Middle Ages the more inviting of the caves filled up with Greek Basilian monks. Here, following their burrowing instinct just as they did in Asia Minor and elsewhere, the Greek hermits turned literally dozens of caves into hidden sanctuaries and chapels. The best are around Taranto, but there are a couple, the **Grotto di San Biagio** and **Grotto di San Giovanni**, outside the town of San Vito dei Normanni, and some more along the ravines near the town of Fasano, where they are called *laure*.

Also near Fasano, just off the Ostuni road at the village of Montalbano, is what may be the most impressive **dolmen** in the south. Puglia's earliest cultures were not often great builders, but they could be counted among the most sophisticated of all the Mediterranean Neolithic peoples. Much of their geometric pottery, which you can see scattered among Puglia's museums, is distinctively beautiful. This dolmen, a chamber formed by one huge slab of rock propped horizontally over two others, has acquired an odd local nickname: the **Tavole Palatine**, or Table of the Knights – the Round Table of King Arthur.

Along the coast near Fasano is the small resort of **Torre Canne**, and to the north of that, in an isolated setting by the sea, straddling the coastal road, the ruins of the Messapian-Roman town of **Egnazia**. The site is worth a brief visit, if only to admire

The Love of *Trulli*

Turning a corner of the road or passing the crest of one of the low hills of the Murge, all at once you meet a kind of landscape you have never seen before, with smooth whitewashed structures in a bewildering variety of shapes and forms, each crowned with one or more tall conical stone roofs. These are *trulli*, and when there are enough of them in one place, they make a picture that might be at home in Africa, or in a fairytale, but certainly nowhere else in Italy.

The *trulli* are still built; the dome is easier to raise than it looks, and the form is adaptable to everything from tool sheds to petrol stations. It is anybody's guess as to their origins; some scholars have mentioned the Saracens, others, less probably, the Mycenaean Greeks. None of the *trulli* you see today are more than a century or two old. They are exotically beautiful; if the form has any other advantage, it is that the domes give warmer air a chance to rise, making the houses cooler in the broiling Puglian summers.

Trulli are built of limestone, with thick, whitewashed walls and only a few tiny windows. The domes are limestone too, a single row of narrow slates wound in a gradually decreasing spiral up to the top. The 'pinnacles' on the roof are symbolic, indating family name, religion and the like, and have proven helpful when a census has been taken. *Trulli* seem only to come in one size; when a *trullo*-dweller needs more room, they simply have another unit added on. In this way, some of the fancier trullo palaces come to resemble small castles – Loire châteaux built for hobbits. Grandest of all is the one on Piazza Sacramento in Alberobello, the only specimen with a second floor; they call it the Sovrano, or Supreme *Trullo*.

Alberobello has a tourist office approved cultural association offering guided tours of the *trulli* in various languages. It's at Via Montenero 1, t 080 432 371 9525.

the stupendous polychromatic mosaics with geometrical patterns and wild beasts, currently housed in the small museum, which also contains a number of Messapian artefacts, pottery and architectural fragments (***t*** *080 482 9056; open daily 8.30–7, until 3.30 in winter; Oct–June closed Sun pm; adm; to book an English-speaking guide call* ***t*** *080 482 7895*).

Taranto

According to legend, Taranto was founded by Taras, a son of Poseidon who came riding into the harbour on the back of a dolphin. According to the historians, however, it was only a band of Spartans, shipped here in 708 BC to found a colony. They chose a good spot: it's probably the best harbour in Italy, and the only good one at all on the Ionian Sea. Not surprisingly, their new town of Taras did well. Until the Romans cut it down to size, it was the metropolis of Magna Graecia, a town feared in war but more renowned in philosophy. Taras, now called Taranto, is still an interesting place with an exotic old quarter, a good museum and excellent seafood. Nevertheless, the best part of the story is all in the past.

History: Rotten Shellfish, Sheep with Overcoats

With its harbour, and with the help of a little Spartan know-how on the battlefield, Taras had little trouble acquiring wealth and political power. By the 4th century BC, the population had reached 300,000. In its balmiest days, Taras' prosperity depended on an unusual variety of luxury goods. Its oysters were a highly prized delicacy as far away as Rome, while another shellfish, the murex, provided the purple dye – really a deep scarlet – used for the robes of Roman emperors and every other style-conscious ruler across the Mediterranean. This imperial purple, the most expensive stuff of the ancient world, was obtained by allowing masses of murex to rot in the sun; a huge heap of the shells, with perhaps the mollusc who coloured Caesar's cloak somewhere near the bottom, was mentioned by travellers only a century ago. For a similarly high price the Tarantines would have been happy to provide you with the cloth, too. Their sheep were known for the softest and best wool available, and Tarantine shepherds actually put coats on their flocks to keep it nice.

If contemporary historians are to be believed, Taras avoided most of the terrible inter-city conflicts of Magna Graecia simply by being much larger and more powerful than its neighbours. And it was spared civil troubles by a sound constitution, with a mix of aristocratic and democratic elements. Pythagoras spent part of his life in Taras, an exile from his native Croton, and helped set a philosophical tone for the city's affairs. The height of Taras' glory was perhaps the long period of rule under a Pythagorean mathematician and philosopher named Archytas (*c.* 400 BC), a paragon of wisdom and virtue in the ancient world. Plato himself came to visit Archytas.

When Taras and Rome went to war in 282 BC, they did so as equals. Taras called in Pyrrhus of Epirus as an ally, but after 10 years of inconclusive Pyrrhic victories, the Romans gained the upper hand and ended Taras' independence. Rome graciously refrained from razing the city after Taras helped Hannibal in the Second Punic War; just the same, the Tarantines felt the iron grip of the victors, and their city quickly dwindled in wealth and importance. Of all the Greek cities of the south, Taras, along with Reggio, proved the best survivor. Throughout the Dark Ages the city never quite disappeared, and by the time of the Crusades it was an important port once more.

First impressions of modern Taranto inevitably call to mind the old expression 'how the mighty are fallen' – despite its noble history, the first thing any visitor sees is the heavily industrial and intimidating Italsider steel site. The bridge brings you to the old heart of Taranto, once home to splendid Greek temples, now housing Piazza Fontana and the crumbling and seedy fishing port, although if you arrive on a hot sunny day, the smell of the sea and the sight of the fishermen going about their daily business is captivating. And the unique position of the city, which straddles two 'seas', combined with its impressive history, gives the place another dimension. After a visit to the Palazzo Pantaleo and one of the fish restaurants at the port you'll be enamoured.

This is the city that gave its name to the country quick-dance called the *tarantella*, and also to the *tarantula*, but there are no large hairy poisonous spiders in Puglia – just a few innocent little brown ones. Their bite isn't much, but a little notoriety still clings to them, thanks to the religious pathology of the south Italians. Throughout antiquity and the Middle Ages various cults of dancing were current around the

Getting There and Around

The two **rail** lines use the central station on Piazzale Duca d'Aosta at the far westof town, between the old town and the steel mills. There are regular FS trains for Lecce, Bríndisi, Bari and further north, as well as for Reggio di Calabria (an endless trip around the Ionian Sea). On one or another of the FS lines you can get to Massafra, Castellaneta, Grottaglie and Manduria. FSE (Ferrovie Sud-Est) local trains go from one side of the station to Locorotondo, Martina Franca and Alberobello.

The FSE also operates a large proportion of the province's **bus** services (**t** 099 471 5901): there are several a day for Alberobello, Bari and Lecce from Piazza Castello. FSE buses for Ostuni and Manduria leave from Via di Palma. SITA buses to Matera also leave from Piazza Castello, and there are daily buses to Naples run by Miccolis from the bus station. Buses to Metaponto leave from Piazza Castello.

Between the train station and around Piazza Fontana, the gateway to old and modern Táranto, is where local heroin addicts and criminals congregate. If you arrive after dark, take a bus or taxi if you are heading for the modern city over the swinging bridge – don't walk through the old town.

Moving about old Táranto can also be a little intimidating – the extremely narrow streets, (many less than a metre wide) are easy to get lost in, and you could end up meeting someone not so nice and being literally in a tight corner. It may be best to explore it in the morning, when there are lots of children playing in the street and housewives shopping and chatting on every corner.

Tourist Information

Corso Umberto I 113, **t** 099 453 2392 (*open Mon–Fri 9–1 and 4.30–6.30, Sat 9–12*).

Where to Stay and Eat

Taranto ✉ 74100

★★★**Plaza**, Via d'Aquino 46, opposite Piazza Archita, **t** 099 459 0775 (*moderate*). A well-run if dated spot in the centre. Most rooms have a balcony overlooking the square.

★★**Sorrentino**, Piazza Fontana 7, **t** 099 470 7456 (*cheap*). A wonderful *pensione* by the fish market, run by a delightful old couple, with high walls founded in the sea and rooms with glorious views of the water and the mussel nets. Get an early night though, because Piazza Fontana can get seedy.

Le Vecchie Cantine, Via Girasoli 23, Loc. Larna, **t** 099 777 2589 (*expensive*). A sophisticated place a fair way from town (get a taxi), with a daily-changing menu focused on fish. *Closed lunchtimes, Weds in winter, and Jan.*

L'Approdo, Via Matteotti 4, **t** 0994 533 524 (*moderate*). A smart option opposite the castle, with creative cuisine such as fresh *tubettini* with tomato and mussels, and baked *seppie* (cuttlefish). *Closed Mon.*

Trattoria del Pescatore, Piazza Fontana, **t** 0994 707 121 (*cheap–moderate*). A dark, cool spot next door to its owner – one of Taranto's finest fishmongers. Choose from pasta dishes, lobster, prawns and the day's catch.

Da Mimmo, Via Giovinazzi 18, **t** 099 459 3733 (*cheap*). A good seafood restaurant with lots of local mussels. *Closed Weds and 2wks Aug.*

Santa Caterina al Borgo, Via Acclavio 35, **t** 0994 525528 (cheap). Creative and classic *pizze* and *pucce* (Tárantese calzone). *Closed Mon.*

Trattoria D. Bari, Largo San Nicola 5 (*cheap*). A long, whitewashed cantina tucked in a corner of Piazza Fontana, full of locals feasting on the cheapest seafood in town.

Ceglie Messapica ✉ 72013

★★★★**La Fontanina**, on Ostuni–Francavilla road (km 9), **t** 0831 380 932, *www.lafontanina.it* (*expensive*). A hotel and fish restaurant, the latter popular with locals.

★★**Tre Trulli**, Contrada Montevicoli 115, **t** 0831 381 312 (*cheap*). A simple hotel, fine for a stopover.

Al Fornello da Ricci, Contrada Montevicoli, **t** 0831 377 104 (*expensive*). One of the finest restaurants in Puglia. *Closed Mon eve, Tues, and last 2wks in Feb and Sept.*

Messapica, Piazza del Plebescito 27 (*cheap*). A trattoria serving typical home-made dishes.

Castellaneta Marina ✉ 74011

★★★★**Golf Hotel**, Loc. Riva dei Tessali, **t** 099 843 9251, *www.rivadeitessali.it* (*expensive–very expensive*). A resort complex of cottages in a grove near the links.

Mediterranean. Everything from the worship of Dionysus to the medieval Dance of Death touched this region and, when the Catholic church began to frown on such carryings on, the urge took strange forms. People bitten by spiders became convinced that they would die and that their only salvation was to dance the venom out of their system – dance until they dropped, in fact. Sometimes they would dance for four days or more, while musicians played for them and their friends sought to discover the magic colour – the 'colour' of that particular spider – that would calm the dancer. *Tarantism*, as 19th-century psychologists called it, is rarely seen anywhere in the south these days; nor for that matter is the *tarantella*, a popular style of music first in vogue around the beginning of the 1800s that took its name from this bit of folklore.

The Città Vecchia

Taranto's harbour consists of two large lagoons, the **Mare Grande** and the **Mare Piccolo**; the city is on a narrow strip of land between them, broken into three pieces by a pair of narrow channels. Directly below the railway station in the westernmost section, along the Via Duca d'Aosta, a bridge takes you over to the old town – a nearly rectangular island that is only four blocks wide but does its best to make you lose your way. The ancient Tarantines, lacking any sort of hill, made the island their acropolis, though in those days it was attached to the mainland. Most of the temples were here, along with a famous gold-plated bronze statue of Zeus that was the second-largest piece of sculpture in the world, surpassed only by the Colossus of Rhodes.

Today all that remains of ancient Taras are some columns from a **temple of Poseidon**, which have been re-erected in the main square next to Taranto's **Castello**, built in the 1480s by King Ferdinand of Spain and now the navy headquarters. From the square, a **swinging bridge**, something rare in Italy, connects the old town with the new. The Mare Piccolo, besides being an enormous oyster and mussel farm for the fishermen of Taranto, is also the home of one of Italy's two main naval bases. Very early in the morning, when the bridge is open, you may see big warships waiting their turn with little fishing boats to squeeze their way through the narrow channel.

Follow the fishermen home, and you'll end up in the **fish market** on Via Cariati, near the docks at the opposite end of the Città Vecchia. In sometimes slick and up-to-date Italy, this is one place where you can most truly believe you are in the Mediterranean: it's a wet and mildly grubby quay awash with the sounds and smells of the sea, where tired fishermen appear each morning at dawn to have coffee, sort out the catch, and bang the life out of octopuses on the stones. Of course there are plenty of cats around; true 'aristocats' they are, the descendants of the first cats of Europe. Ancient historians record how the ancient Tarantines imported them from Egypt.

From the fish market, pick your way a short distance across the Città Vecchia to the **cathedral**, built and rebuilt in a hotchpotch of styles, beginning in the 11th century. Most of the last, florid Baroque remodelling has been cleared away, saving only a curious coffered ceiling, with two golden statues suspended from it. Roman columns and capitals support the arches, and there's a good medieval baptismal font under a baldaquin. Some bits of mosaic survive on the floor; mosaics in the Byzantine manner were important in all Puglia's medieval churches.

The cathedral is dedicated to San Cataldo, an Irish priest who was passing through Taranto on his way to the Crusades but was so appalled at the drunken, lecherous behaviour of the locals that he decided to stay put. There's a beautiful intarsio marble and onyx chapel to the saint, whose holy day, 8 May, is a good time to be in Taranto – the silver statue of the saint is carried on a flower-strewn cart to the port, then taken on a boat from one 'sea' to the other, accompanied by a fireworks display at the castle, then brought back to the cathedral. A medieval necropolis that was discovered in the cathedral's crypt, where his tomb lies, is scheduled to open to the public in mid to late 2004; the major excavation work means that some parts of the building may be inaccessible.

The rest of the Città Vecchia holds few surprises. The area is extremely down at heel and was half-forgotten for a long time, although with Taranto's newfound prosperity a good deal of money is being poured into housing rehabilitation and into restoring old palaces and other monuments – a process that is already making quite a difference. As in Bari, when you cross from the sleepy old town into the hyperactive new centre, the contrast is startling. Taranto has no need to envy Bari these days; its new town is bright and busy, with as many grey-suited businessmen as blue-clad sailors.

Palazzo Pantaleo (including Museo Nazionale collection)

Lungomare Vittorio Emanuele; open daily 8.30–7.30. The Museo Nazionale at Piazza Archita (entrance at Corso Umberto 41) will remain closed for major restoration work for a further 2 or 3 years, although some rooms have recently re-opened and are used for free temporary touring exhibitions.

This elegantly restored and finely frescoed *palazzo* a five-minute walk from Piazza Fontana is the current home of a small part of the Museo Nazionale's priceless collection, which is probably the finest anywhere on Magna Graecia (and with building activity going full blast around Taranto, new discoveries are being made all the time). You can currently see a fine array of Greek vases finely decorated with snarling panthers, inscrutable sphinxes, Dionysian orgies, carriage races, battles and religious processions; exquisite and incredibly intact blown-glass perfume bottles and wine glasses; gold earrings with tiny dolphins and ducks; and large plates and amphorae with long-necked geese, noble eagles or cavorting dolphins, recalling Taranto's vibrant and noble past.

The ground floor has ancient Neolithic ceramics with etched or painted patterns, as well as copper and bronze tools and utensils from the Bronze Age (3,500 BC). A selection of the museum's huge collection of Greek terracotta figures, believed to be the largest in the world, can be seen on the mezzanine. The playful and beautifully executed items on show include a gladiator, a boxer and dozens of little cherubs.

The nearby church of **San Domenico** (*open same hours as* palazzo) boasts a wonderfully dramatic façade hiding a peaceful cloister, which in turn reveals the recently uncovered remains of a Greek temple dating from the 6th century BC. On 25 November (St Katherine's Day) and Maunday Thursday, major processions set out from San Domenico.

Towns Around Taranto

Grottaglie, just 15 minutes by train to the east of the city, is the ceramics capital of southeast Italy. The town's potters continue to produce plates, vases and pots in enormous quantities, and attract throngs of visitors on summer weekends, eager to buy their traditional, and sometimes more modern, styles.

Further along the road and rail line towards Bríndisi, **Francavilla Fontana** takes its title of 'free town' from a favour granted by King Ferdinand IV. The town has several 14th–18th-century palaces, including a small one belonging to the 18th-century Bourbon kings, as a reminder of its days as a feudal stronghold. Nearby **Oria** has a similar history; Frederick II built a strong **castle** here in 1227–33 (***t*** *0831 840 009; open summer Mon–Fri 4.30–7.30, Sat 9.30–12; winter Mon–Fri 3.30–6.30, Sat 9.30–12; hours may vary so check in advance; adm; free guided visits in English*), with three tall round towers, which holds a collection of antiquities and bric-à-brac. In the Middle Ages, Oria had an important Jewish community; the ghetto and its buildings are still intact.

Oria is believed to have been the capital of the ancient Messapians, a civilized people who suffered many indignities at the hands of the Greek colonists, and finally succumbed to the allure of classical culture. **Ceglie Messapica**, south of Ostuni, was another of their cities, and it is here you can see the *specchie* , the Messapians' most noteworthy surviving monuments. These conical stepped towers, which get their name from the Latin *speculum* (mirror), were supposedly used for measuring distances (as in 'Taranto is six *specchie* from here'). Inside were mirrors that glittered in the sun – travellers would count these off as they approached their destination. One *specchia* is in Ceglie, the other two are out in the country. The most impressive, the 36ft **Specchia Miano**, is seven kilometres down the road to Francavilla – turn right up the road to Masseria Bottari farm and walk through the field on the right.

Manduria was another Messapian city, mentioned in the histories as fighting continuous wars with the Greeks of Taras. Ruins of its fortifications can still be seen – three concentric circuits of which the outermost is five kilometres around – along with caves, necropolises and a well mentioned in Pliny's *Natural History* (turn right in front of the church of the Cappuccini, on Via Sant'Antonio). The new city has a cathedral with a beautifully carved Renaissance rose window and portals.

Massafra

West of Taranto, a short distance back toward Le Murge and Matera, is one of the most unusual cities of Puglia. Massafra, even more than Matera, was a city of troglodytes and monks. A steep ravine, the **Gravina di San Marco**, cuts it in two; the ravine and surrounding valleys are lined with caves, many of which were expanded into cave-chapels, or *laure*, by Greek monks in the early Middle Ages. Between the caves and the old church crypts, it has been estimated that there are more than 100 medieval frescoes in, around and under Massafra – some of considerable artistic merit. One of the best is a beautiful Byzantine Virgin called *La Vergine della Scala*, in the Santuario della Scala reached from Via del Santuario in the old town by a long naïf-Baroque set of stairs. The Madonna is shown receiving the homage of two kneeling deer, the subject of an old legend. Adjacent to the sanctuary are some

13th-century paintings in the Cripta della Bona Nova. At the bottom of the ravine is the Farmacia del Mago Greguro, a rather neglected complex of caves that it is believed were used by the monks to store and prepare medicinal herbs.

Other cave-churches and frescoes can be seen at **Mottola**, **Palagianello** and **Ginosa**, built like Massafra over a ravine full of caves. **Laterza**, perched on a 650ft-deep gorge near the border with the Basilicata, has about 180 caves and *laure*, of which some 30 can be visited. **Castellaneta** also has a ravine, the steepest and wildest of them all, and some cave-churches, but this town cares more to be known as the birthplace, in 1895, of Rudolph Valentino. There's a monument to him in the main square, with a life-size ceramic statue of the old matinée idol dressed as the Sheikh of Arabia.

The Salentine Peninsula

This has lovely Lecce and cheerful Bríndisi, some flat but unusual countryside, the sun-bleached and sea-washed old towns of Gallipoli and Otranto, and lots of caves and Neolithic remains. Its coastline, while not as ruggedly beautiful as that of the Gargano, does have its charms, not least of which is that it is relatively uncrowded. Not many foreign tourists make their way to this distant Land's End, although it teems with Italians in August. If you are beachcombing or backpacking, and can resist the temptation presented by the ferries to Greece, this might be a perfect place to spend a lazy week or so.

Bríndisi

The word *brindisi* in Italian means to toast. It's just a coincidence; the name comes from the original Greek colony of *Brentesion*. In Roman times this was the gang-plank to the boat for Greece; today it's a clean, pedestrianized port with well-restored buildings and lots of flowers. On Viale Regina Margherita, to the right of the harbour, a small piazza at the top of a formal stairway holds a magnificent **Roman column**, once topped by the statue of an emperor, that marked the end of the Appian Way.

For six centuries, all Rome's trade with the East, all its legions heading toward new conquests, and all its trains of triumphant or beaten emperors and generals passed through *Brundisium*. From the 11th century on, the city reassumed its old role when it became one of the most important Crusader ports. A memory of this survives too; if you enter the city from the north or west, you will pass the **Tancredi Fountain**, an Arab-inspired work built by the Norman chief, Tancred. Here the Christian knights watered their horses before setting out for the Holy Land.

As a city where people have always been more concerned with coming and going than settling down, Bríndisi has not saved up a great store of monuments and art. Travel agents and shipping offices are more in evidence than anything else. But if you're staying, there are a few things to look at. Alongside the 12th-century **cathedral**, rebuilt in warmed-over Baroque, there's a small, exotic-looking portico with striped pointed arches; this is all that remains of the **Temple**, headquarters church of the

Getting There and Around

Bríndisi's Casale **airport** is 4km north of the city and has regular flights to Rome, Milan and Verona. There are frequent buses between the airport and the main FS rail station in the centre.

Sleeper **trains** travelling across Italy to Rome and Milan pass through Bríndisi, which also has very frequent trains to Bari and Taranto.

Buses to all provincial towns and nearby cities leave from Viale Porta Pia. Marozzi, **t** 0831 521 684, and Miccolis, **t** 0831 560 678, run bus services to Rome and Naples respectively, with several daily departures from Lungomare Regina Margherita, near the tourist office.

Bríndisi is the most important Italian port for **ferries** to Greece, with daily connections almost year round to Corfu, Patras and Igoumenitsa (several a day in summer). All ferries leave from the Stazione Marittima, in the centre of the port. The EPT office has up-to-date information on schedules and prices, but this may not be much help in summer – as frequently as boats run, it is a good idea in July and Aug to book a passage before you get to Bríndisi.

If you buy a ticket here, avoid the ticket touts round the train station and the Stazione Marittima; even the huge number of agencies in Bríndisi offering ferry tickets are notoriously unreliable. Buy tickets from the boat companies or an approved agent. The most established ferry companies are **Adriatica**, Via Provinciale per Lecce, **t** 0831 548 340; **Blue Star**, Molo Costa Morena, **t** 0831 548 115; and **Hellenic Mediterranean**, Molo Costa Morena, **t** 0831 524 921. The most reliable agents are **UTAC Viaggi**, Via Santa Lucia 11, **t** 0831 560 780, and **Grecian Travel**, Corso Garibaldi 79, near the harbour, **t** 0831 597 884.

Between June and Sept ferries also operate between the little port of Otranto and Corfu and Igoumenitsa. They are faster than many Bríndisi boats but more expensive.

The Via Appia (roughly following today's SS7) reaches its end in Bríndisi, as it has done for more than 2,000 years. Traffic leaving the port can be very slow in summer; it's better to get away from the city on the SS16.

Tourist Information

Bríndisi: Piazza Dionisio, off Lungomare Regina Margherita, **t** 0831 523 072 (*open Mon–Sat 7.30–2 and 3–7*).

Where to Stay and Eat

Bríndisi ✉ 72100

If all you want is some cheap, filling and quick food while you're waiting to jump on a train or a ferry, there are any number of *pizzerie* and *trattorie* along Corso Umberto and Corso Garibaldi.

******Internazionale**, Lungomare Regina Margherita 26, **t** 0831 523 473, *www.albergointernazionale.com* (*expensive*). A well-kept older hotel with rather grandmotherly furnishings, convenient for the ferry docks. Some rooms have marble fireplaces, and there's a very good restaurant, **La Valigia delle Indie**. *Restaurant closed July and Aug.*

*****Barsotti**, Via Cavour 1, **t** 0831 560 877 (*moderate*). A plain but acceptable place near the train station.

Carpe Diem, Via Nicola Brandi 2, **t** 0831 418 418, *www.hostelcarpediem.it* (*cheap*). A newly opened and excellent hostel with both rooms and dorms, a restaurant and a bar, and a free pick-up service from the airport, train station and port. There's also a handy day-hostel option whereby you can have a bed and make use of the showers and other facilities while you're waiting for a night ferry.

La Lanterna, Via G. Tarantina 14, **t** 0831 564 026 (*expensive*). The city's most elegant restaurant, combining traditional and new ways of cooking and presenting meat, seafood and pasta. *Closed Sun and 3wks Aug.*

Trattoria Pantagruele, Via Salita di Ripalta 1–3, **t** 0831 560 605 (*expensive*). A trattoria offering simple but good fare, including delicious home-made desserts. *Closed Sat lunch, Sun and 2wks Aug.*

Già Sotto l'Arco, Corso Vittorio Emanuele 71, Carovigno, about 25km north of town, **t** 0831 996 286 (*very expensive*). An interesting traditional restaurant. Book the table on the balcony if you can. *Closed Mon and Jan.*

Knights Templar, and closely related to the Temple in London. Nearby, a small collection of ancient Puglian relics has been assembled at the **Museo Archeologico** (*open Tues–Sat 8.30–1*). Down Via San Giovanni, a few blocks south, another curious souvenir of the Templars has survived – the round church of **San Giovanni al Sepolcro**, built in the late 11th century, with fanciful carvings of dancers and lions on the portal. Back on the waterfront, on Viale Regina Margherita, a small local ferry runs across the harbour to the 150ft **monument to Italian sailors**, erected by Mussolini in 1933. A lift goes up to the top, from where there are good views of the comings and goings of the port.

Santa Maria del Casale

The greatest of Bríndisi's attractions lies just north of the city, near the sports complex on the way to the airport. Santa Maria del Casale (*ring bell at gate*) is a church unlike any other in Italy; built in the 1320s, in an austere, almost modern economy of vertical lines and arches, it has a façade done in two shades of sandstone, not striped as in so many other Italian churches, but shaped into a variety of simple, exquisite patterns. The interior, a simple, barn-like space, is painted with equally noteworthy frescoes in the Byzantine manner. The wall over the entrance is covered with a remarkable visionary Last Judgement by an artist named Rinaldo of Taranto, full of brightly coloured angels and apostles, saints and sinners; a river of fire washes the damned into the inferno while, above, the fish of the sea disgorge their human prey to be judged. Many of the other frescoes, in the nave and transepts, are badly faded, though they are still of interest.

Also north of Bríndisi, halfway to Carovigno, is the recently created **marine park and nature reserve of Torre Guaceto** (***t*** *0831 989 885*), where you can walk, cycle and dive.

Lecce

You will have to come a long way – to the furthest corner of Puglia – to find the most beautiful town in southern Italy. Lecce is worth the trip, though; its history, and its tastes, have given it a fate different from that of any other Italian town.

FIrst and foremost, this is the capital of southern Baroque – not the chilly, pompous Baroque of Rome, but a sunny, frivolous style Lecce created on its own. It started life as a Messapian town, and flourished as the Roman *Lupiae*, but only really came into its own during the Middle Ages, as the centre of a semi-independent county comprising most of the Salentine Peninsula. It went on to enjoy royal favour under the Spaniards in the 16th century. Located near the front lines of the continual wars between Habsburg and Turk, the town often found itself the centre of attention even though it was not a port. During the Spanish centuries, while every other southern city except the royal seat of Naples was in serious decline, 'the Athens of Puglia' was enjoying a golden age, attaining distinction in literature and the arts. Lecce also found the wealth to rebuild itself, and took the form we see today with the construction of dozens of palaces, churches and public buildings in the city's own distinctive style.

Getting There and Around

Despite its location, Lecce is well served by **rail**; the city is a terminus for long sleeper runs across Italy to Rome and Milan. There is also the **FSE** (**t** 0832 668 233), which has services from Lecce to Otranto, Gallipoli and Nardò, and some to Bari and Taranto via Manduria.

Most **buses** to towns in the Salentine, run by **STP**, **t** 0832 302 873, leave from Via Adua near the old western walls. The **FSE**, Via Torre del Parco, near Porta Napoli, **t** 0832 347 634, connects Lecce with Taranto, from where you can reach other destinations in the region. Salento in Bus, **t** 0832 217 077, has regular services between the main towns south of Lecce and lays on guided tours of the peninsula. Tickets are sold at newsagents, bars and tobacconists (look for 'SalentoInBus' signs); buses leave from 9 stops around town.

Tourist Information

Lecce: Via Vittorio Emanuele II 23, **t** 0832 332 463 (*open Mon–Fri 9–1 and 5–7*).

Where to Stay and Eat

Lecce ✉ 73100

Lecce is overrun by B&Bs, most with just 1 or 2 rooms. There's a room-finding service at Via dei Mocenigo 12, **t** 0832 279 195.

*****Patria Palace Hotel**, Piazzetta Riccardi 13, **t** 0832 245 111, *www.patriapalacelecce.com* (*very expensive*). A comfortable place with the full range of facilities. Many rooms have a view of Santa Croce.

****Grand Hotel Tiziano**, Viale Porta D'Europa, **t** 0832 272 111, *www.grandhoteltiziano.it* (*expensive*). A smart modern hotel on the fringes of the old centre, with a lovely rooftop swimming pool and bar and an elegant restaurant in the cellar.

B&B Prestige, Via S. Maria del Paradiso 4, **t** 0832 243 353, *www.bbprestige-lecce.it* (*moderate*). A centrally located B&B with three lovely rooms (all of them en suite), a beautiful little terrace overlooking the church of Sand Giovanni, and a charming host. Book ahead.

Cappello, Via Montegrappa 4, **t** 0832 308 881, *www.hotelcappello.it* (*cheap*). A cheerful budget option between the station and the *centro storico*.

B&B Centro Storico, Via Andrea Vignes 2b, **t** 0883 242 828. *www.bedandbreakfast.lecce.it* (*cheap*). The first B&B in Lecce, and one of the nicest. Very central and clean, it has 7 rooms and a tiny panoramic roof terrace. Book ahead.

Gino e Gianni, Via Adriatica, **t** 0832 399 210 (*moderate*). A popular place a short way from the centre, with a wide choice of local seafood dishes. *Closed Weds and 2wks Aug.*

Villa Giovanni Camillo Della Monica, Via SS. Giacomo e Filippo 40, **t** 0832 458 432 (*moderate*). A fine restaurant in the marbled courtyard of a 16th-century *palazzo*, with beautifully presented food. Try the luscious entrecôte with asparagus and Chardonnay sauce, or bream wrapped in aubergine.

Casareccia, Via Colonnello Archimede Costadura 19, **t** 0832 245 178 (*cheap*). A friendly, reliable trattoria with excellent home-cooking. *Closed Sun eve and Mon.*

Even though Lecce was doing very well for itself under the Spaniards and Bourbons, it hardly enjoyed the privilege of being ruled by them. On the contrary, the town's resistance to the new order manifested itself in four serious revolts. First, in 1648, came a popular revolution that coincided with Masaniello's revolt in Naples and that, like it, was bloodily repressed by Spanish troops. A second rebellion, which occurred in 1734, almost succeeded; the rebels were tricked into submitting by the Bourbons, who offered them reforms that were later withdrawn. In the wake of the French Revolution, another revolt took place, and the last one came in 1848; the Leccesi worked hard for the unification of Italy, and contributed both men and ideas to the fight.

Leccese Baroque

Lecce, like southern Sicily, some parts of Spain, and Malta – places where southern Baroque styles were well developed – was fortunate to have an inexhaustible supply of a perfect stone. Pietra di Lecce, a kind of sandstone of a warm golden hue, has the additional virtues of being extremely easy to carve and becoming hard as granite after a few years in the weather. Almost all the town is built of it, giving it the appearance of one great, delicately crafted architectural ensemble.

The artists and architects who made Lecce's buildings were almost all local talent, most notably Antonio and Giuseppe Zimbalo, who designed many of its finest buildings in the mid 17th century, and carried the style to its wildest extremes. Leccese Baroque does not involve any new forms or structural innovations; the ground plans of the Zimbalos' buildings are more typical of late Renaissance Italy. The difference is in the decoration; there's an emphasis on vertical lines and planes of rusticated stonework, broken by patches of the most intricate and fanciful stone-carving Baroque ever knew.

These churches and palaces, along with the hundreds of complementary details that adorn almost every street – fountains, gates, balconies and monuments – combine to form an elegant and refined cityscape that paradoxically seems all gravity and restraint. Leccese Baroque owes more than a little to Spanish influences, and the town itself still has an air of Spanish reserve. As a king of Spain described a similar Baroque city – Valletta, in Malta – Lecce is a 'town built for gentlemen'.

Piazza Sant'Oronzo

A Baroque city was conceived as a sort of theatre set, its squares as stages on which its decorous gentlemen could promenade. An odd chance has given Lecce's main piazza something even better – in 1901 workmen digging the basement for a bank building discovered a **Roman amphitheatre**, with seats for some 15,000, directly under the city centre. In the 1930s, the half under the piazza was excavated; occasionally the city uses it for concerts and shows. Only the lower half of the grandstands survived; the stones of the top levels were probably carted away for other buildings long ago.

In Bríndisi, by the column that marked the end of the Appian Way, you may notice the pedestal of a vanished second column. Lightning toppled that one in 1528, and the Bríndisians let it lie until 1661, when Lecce bought it and moved it here, attaching a copper statue of their patron, Sant'Oronzo (Orontius), the first bishop of Lecce, and supposedly a martyr during the persecutions of Nero. What appears to be a small pavilion in the middle of the square, overlooking the amphitheatre, is the **Sedile**, an elegant early masterpiece of the Leccese style (1596) that once served as the town hall.

Santa Croce and San Matteo

North of Piazza Sant'Oronzio, the most outrageous Baroque of all awaits along Via Umberto I. **Santa Croce** was begun in 1549, but not completed until 1680, giving Lecce's Baroque berserkers a chance at the façade. The lower half of it is original, done mainly in a sober Renaissance style. The portal, however, and every thing above it, is a fond fancy of Zimbalo and his colleague Cesare Penna. Among the florid cake-icing decoration the rose window stands out, made of concentric choirs of tiny angels. Look carefully at the figures on the corbels supporting the second level: among the various cartoon monsters can be made out Romulus' and Remus' she-wolf, a few dragons, a Turk, an African, and an equally exotic German. Santa Croce's interior is one of Lecce's best, with beautiful altars in the transept chapels by Penna and Antonio Zimbalo. Giuseppe Zimbalo also designed the **Palazzo del Governo**, originally a monastery.

Behind Santa Croce, the pretty **Giardino Pubblico** and the nearby **castello**, built by Emperor Charles V, mark old Lecce's eastern edge. The castle (*open daily 9–1, until 9pm July and Aug*) is used to host conferences and exhibitions, and also has a tourist information desk. For an interesting walk, start from Piazza Sant'Oronzio and follow Via Augusto Imperatore (Augustus was in Lecce when he got news of Julius Caesar's assassination). This street passes another Baroque church, **Santa Chiara** (*open daily 9.30–12 and 4.30–7*), and a Salesian convent with a skull and crossbones over the portal – the ultimate Spanish touch. In a small garden opposite the church is the most preposterous statue of **Vittorio Emanuele** in all Italy, surpassing even the bronze colossus on the Altar of the Nation in Rome (*see* p.786). This Vittorio is smaller, but the contrast between his ponderous moustaches and jaunty stance leaves him looking half like a pirate, half like the leader of a firemen's band.

The next Baroque church is **San Matteo** (1700), one of the last, and architecturally the most adventurous of the lot, with an elliptical nave and a complex façade that is convex on the lower level and concave above. Continue straight down Via Perroni and you will come to one of Lecce's fine Baroque town gates, the **Porta San Biagio**. To prove that this city's curiosities are not all Baroque, we can offer the neoclassical **war memorial**, across Piazza Roma near the gate, and off to its right a block of mansions, built around the turn of the 19th century, in a style that imitates the Alhambra in Spain, complete with pointed arches, minarets and Koranic inscriptions.

Piazza del Duomo

Leaving Piazza Sant'Oronzo by Via Vittorio Emanuele, you pass **Santa Irene**, a relatively modest Baroque church from the 1720s, with a splendid statue of the saint above the main portal. Be careful not to miss the little alley off to the left that leads to the **Piazza del Duomo**, one of the finest Baroque architectural groups anywhere. It was the intention of the designers to keep this square cut off from the life of the city, making it a sort of tranquil stone park; the alley off Via Vittorio Emanuele is the only entrance.

The **cathedral** (1659–70) is one of the finest works of Giuseppe Zimbalo. To make the building stand out in the L-shaped medieval piazza, the architect gave it two façades: one on the west front and a more gloriously ornate one facing the open end of the piazza. The angular, unusually tall campanile (240ft), with its simple lines and baby obelisks, echoes the Herreran style of imperial Spain. If you can get in, the long climb is worth the trouble, culminating in an exceptional view over most of the Salentine Peninsula. Adjoining the cathedral are the complementary façades of the **Palazzo Vescovile** and the **Seminario**, the latter the work of Giuseppe Cino, a pupil of Zimbalo.

Behind the cathedral, in the backstreets off Via Paladini, is the small, well-preserved **Teatro Romano** with an adjacent **museum** (*closed for restoration*). In the opposite direction, Via Libertini passes several good churches, including **Rosario** (1691–1728), also known as **San Giovanni Battista**, the last and most unusual work of Giuseppe Zimbalo. Just beyond it, the street leaves the city through the **Porta Rudiae**, the most elaborate of its gates, bearing another statue of Sant'Oronzo. Leading away to the right from here, Via Adua follows the northwestern face of this diamond-shaped city, passing the remains of the walls Charles V rebuilt to keep out Turkish corsairs; further up, at the **Porta di Napoli**, is another relic of Charles' in the **triumphal arch**, erected in 1548. Charles erected monuments like this all around the Med, usually after failed revolts, to remind the people who was boss. This one, featuring crowned screaming eagles and a huge Spanish coat of arms, is a grim reminder of the militaristic, almost totalitarian government with which the Habsburgs tried to conquer Europe.

In a little park in front of the Porta di Napoli is the **Obelisk**, an attractive monument to the less grisly, though thoroughly useless, King Ferdinand I. From here, a road off to the right leads to the city cemetery, home to a tribe of contented cats who pass in and out through an elegant 19th-century neoclassical gate; next to it stands the church of **SS. Nicolò e Cataldo** (*currently closed for restoration; may open for Mass Sat pm and Sun am*), founded in 1180 by Count Tancred. The façade is typical Baroque, but if you look carefully you'll notice that the portal and rose window are much older. Behind the 18th-century front is one of the best Puglian Romanesque churches, and one of the only medieval monuments to survive in Lecce. The nave and the dome are unusually lofty; the carvings on the side portal and elsewhere are especially good, with a discipline and tidiness unusual for medieval sculpture (to see these, you'll have to enter the cemetery, around the left side of the church).

Museo Sigismundo Castromediano

Viale Gallipoli, at the southern end of the old town, not far from railway station; museum currently closed for restoration; Pinacoteca open Mon–Sat 9–1 and 2.30–7.30, Sun 9–1.30.

The founder of this collection, now Lecce's city museum, was a duke, and also a famous local patriot who fought against the Bourbons and earned long spells in the Neapolitan dungeons. His prison memoirs shocked Europe in the 1850s and moved William Gladstone to a few rousing anti-Bourbon speeches. Duke Sigismundo would be happy if he could see his little collection, now one of the best-arranged and most modern museums in Italy – a corkscrew-shaped ramp through its middle makes it accessible to wheelchair-users, and virtually all the exhibits are clearly labelled. The most prized works are several excellent Puglian and Greek vases, found all over the Salentine Peninsula, though there is also a good collection of medieval art and architectural fragments, and a small picture gallery.

An interesting sight betweem the museum and the train station is an extremely rare UNESCO/WWF-protected 700-year-old Valonia oak, a survivor from the botanic gardens that were destroyed in 1929 (there are also some in the Foresta Umbra).

The Tip of the Salentine

Italy's furthest southeastern corner is one of the quieter parts of the country, with a low, rocky coastline like that of the Gargano but without the mountains, some towns in the Leccese Baroque style, and a lonely beach or two. One of its most noticeable features – and this is true for all of the Salentine Peninsula – is the eccentricity of the rural architecture. There are a few of the predecessors to *trulli*, low-domed houses of unknown age, some little houses with flat roofs curled up at the corners, some recent experiments in cinder-block, and many tiny pink Baroque palaces in a prairie landscape of olive trees, tobacco and wild flowers.

Towns here show an almost African austerity, excepting perhaps **Nardò**, with its lovely Piazza Salandra, home to a *guglia* (spire) as frilly as those in Naples. Its much-rebuilt 11th-century cathedral retains some medieval frescoes. Near the town walls, on Via Giuseppe Galliano, is an unexplained circular temple, the Osanna, built in 1603.

Among other interesting towns and villages around Lecce are **Acaia**, with a ruined Renaissance castle, **Galatina** with wonderful Renaissance frescoes in the 1392 church of Santa Caterina, and **Calimera**, one of the centres of Puglia's tiny Greek community (its name means 'good morning' in Greek). Very few people in Puglia still speak Greek, though their dialect has led many writers to think so; any Greeks left are more likely to be descendants of 16th-century refugees from Albania than survivors of Magna Graecia.

In the early 17th century, nearby **Copertino** was the home of St Joseph, a carpenter's son born in a stable who was canonized for his talent for levitating. Thousands saw him do it, including the Pope's emissaries, a king of Poland, and a Protestant German duke, who immediately converted. Joseph's heart is buried under the altar of the little church named after him. Copertino also has a large Angevin castle.

Gallipoli

It's hard to imagine sleepy, sunny Gallipoli as a bustling port nowadays, although as soon as you arrive at the station you can sense the sea. A short walk down from the station, if you follow the road to the right, is the fish market, where the road bends round into the heart of old Gallipoli, shimmering across the bridge. This tiny island, centred around the main street of Via della Pace, contains all the sites of interest and is very easy to find your way around. The curious fountain in the little square, built in a hotchpotch of styles from Renaissance to Baroque, features three stories on forbidden love from Ovid's *Metamorphoses*, in which three miscreant nymphs, Dirce, Salamacis and Biblide, were transformed into fountains by kindly gods to end the misery their excessive passion had engendered. Some believe that the lowest figures may be ancient Greek, which would make them amongst the oldest surviving sculptures in Italy.

Gallipoli gets its name from the Greek *kalli polis*, or 'beautiful city', and justifiably so. An independent city-state under the Normans, it fought off marauding pirates and enemies for years, its castle protecting the island-city from threats from both terra firma and the sea: it was only in 1484 that Gallipoli finally fell to the ferocious Venetians, who punished it dearly for its heroic resistance.

Tourist Information

Gallipoli: Piazza Imbriani, **t** 0823 265 259 (*open daily 8–2, and also 4–10 in summer*).

Otranto: Piazza Castello, **t** 0836 801 436 (*open June–Sept daily 8–2 and 4–8; shorter hours rest of year*).

Where to Stay and Eat

Gallipoli ✉ 73014

*******Hotel Palazzo del Corso**, Corso Roma 145, Gallipoli, **t** 0833 264 040, *www.hotelpalazzodelcorso.it* (*very expensive*). A delightfully intimate hotel in a restored 19th-century *palazzo* in the centre, with a lovely roof terrace and very elegant rooms.

******Costa Brada**, **t** 0833 202 551, Baia Verde, on Via Litoranea to S. Maria di Leuca, *www.grandhotelcostabrada.it* (*very expensive–luxury*). A fine modern resort hotel.

*****Le Sirenuse**, Litoranea S. Maria di Leuca, **t** 0833 202 536, *www.attiliocaroli.it* (*expensive*). A typical white Mediterranean palace with a good restaurant.

*****Al Pescatore**, Riviera Colombo 39, **t** 0833 263 656, *www.al-pescatore.it* (*moderate*). The best place to stay in the old town, with 16 rooms around a courtyard and a seafront restaurant that draws in crowds every night. Half board is obligatory in Aug and Sept.

***Nardo**, Via A. de' Gasperi 35, Nardo, t 0833 571 994 (*cheap*). A friendly hotel above a café, with comfy modern rooms and big balconies. It makes a good base for lazing on the coast or exploring further inland if you have a car.

Il Capriccio, Viale Bovio 14, **t** 0833 261 545 (*moderate*). A restaurant serving a great variety of seafood dishes. Try the local speciality, *orecchiette alla Gallipolina*. *Closed Mon and 10–30 Jan.*

Rossini, Via Lamarmora 25, along coastal road towards Porto Cesáreo, **t** 0833 573 009 (*moderate*). A fish restaurant with a terrace. Specialities include *gnocchi con crema di gamberetti e rucola* (with creamed shrimp and rocket).

Scoglio delle Sirene, Riv. N. Sauro 83, **t** 0833 261 091 (*moderate*). A cheerful seafood trattoria overlooking the beach in the old town, and a quiet alternative to the restaurants behind the castle, where you often have to queue.

Zia Fernanda, Via XXV Aprile I, **t** 0836 801 884 (*cheap*). A friendly trattoria with excellent local seafood and meat dishes cooked in terracotta dishes on an old hearth, including marinated sardines, delicious *ciceri e tria* (half-cooked pasta fried in olive oil), and tripe or horsemeat *involtini*. Finish with *spumone*, a dessert made from egg whites and cream. *Closed Mon in winter, Nov and Feb.*

Otranto ✉ 73028

*****Albania**, Via S. Francesco di Paola 10, **t** 0836 801 183, *www.hotelalbania.com* (*moderate–expensive*). A pleasant 10-roomed place.

****Miramare**, Viale Lungomare 55, **t** 0836 801 023, (*moderate–expensive*). A newish hotel near the beaches.

Da Sergio, Corso Garibaldi 9, **t** 0836 801 408 (*expensive*). A good fish restaurant, though Sergio can be patronizing to foreigners. *Closed Weds, Jan and Feb.*

But Gallipoli is renowned not so much for its military history as for its olive oil, which from the 16th century brought the small city fortune for more than 300 years. The oil produced here and around southern Puglia was deemed the best for burning in lamps, and was used to light the capital cities of Europe for more two centuries. At its peak, Gallípoli had hundreds of vice-consulates and shipping agents, and in 1741 the port was given the title of second city of the Kingdom of Naples. This heyday came to an end in the mid 1800s, when gas lighting was introduced.

During the prosperous times, however, Gallípoli's nobility had summoned the finest artists and architects of the kingdom to build and adorn their *palazzi* and create one of southern Italy's most beautiful cathedrals. Indeed, one of the city's finest churches was built by one of the confraternities that sprang up after the Counter-Reformation of Trent. A far cry from J.R. Ewing and his cronies at the oil barons' ball, these built oratories (distinguishable from churches by the fact they have two entrances) to the glory of God. These whitewashed buildings verge on the austere externally, but some have colourful majolica-tiled panels and frivolous roofs. Inside are sumptuous paintings, majolica-tiled floors, painted wooden seats and altars adorned with silver and gold.

The most famous oratory is **Della Purità** (*open summer daily 9–12.30 and 4–9.30; winter Mon–Fri 5pm–9.30, Sat and Sun 9–12*), set up by a confraternity of dockers opposite the beautiful beach of the same name. Built around 1650, it is filled to the brim with oil paintings by the Neapolitan School – the painting of the Madonna della Purità above the altar is believed to be by Neapolitan golden boy Luca Giordano. The original majolica-tiled paving remains, as do sculptures by Leccese papier-mâché master Achille de Lucrezi. The **Oratorio dei Nobili** (*open daily 9–1 and 4–7*), which belonged to the Confraternità dell'Immacolata and San Vicenzo, patrician noblemen, was built in 1613 on top of an existing church and covered inside with delicate stucchi in 1732. Its dramatic staircase-entrance came later, in 1790. It now holds the public library and historical archives of the city. Seven chalk panels decorated in silver and gold, which used to be inside, can be seen in the Seminario (*closed for restoration*).

Tiny, beautiful **Santa Teresa** (*only open for morning Masses*) was built by Spanish bishop Perez De La Lastra, for which he delayed the completion of the city's cathedral, to the horror of locals. It contains a rare surviving Baroque altar in the Lecce style in pale Lecce tufo. Gallípoli buildings are constructed from *carparo*, a darker tufo, which originated under the sea and contains a high level of salt. This meant the masterful frescoes in local churches were consumed by salt over time. Paintings were therefore often carried out on wood, hung a short distance from the wall to avoid erosion (in Della Purità, the paintings were done three times – on the walls, on wood and on canvas).

Gallípoli's cathedral, the **Basilica of Sant'Agata** (*open daily 7–12 and 4–8*), contains works of art by great painters of the Gallipolese school, including G. Andrea Coppola, G. Malinconico and G. Domenico Catalano, who all studied under masters of the Neapolitan school. Begun in 1629 and finished almost 70 years later, it was designed by local architects Scipione Lachibari and Francesco Bischettini with decoration by Bernardino Genuino. The façade has two very different styles; the lowest part is austere, while the top, believed to be by Lo Zimbalo of Lecce, is more expressive. Inside, the layout is late Renaissance. The corners near the altar are white with brick stucco akin to a *trullo*; the 18th-century altar is made from precious stones and marble decorated with lapis lazuli and mother of pearl; and the choir is made from rich walnut. No single inch of wall or ceiling is unpainted.

Gallípoli retains its original sloping Byzantine cobbles, and wherever you look you can see enchanting architectural detail: it is a remarkably preserved city, precisely because it was so rarely rampaged. As testimony to its noble oil heritage stand two recently restored **presses** or *frantoi*, one at Via de la Pace (***t** 0833 264 242; open daily May, June and Sept 10–12.30 and 4–7.30; July and Aug 10–1 and 4.30–11; adm*) and one at Via Angeli south of Palazzo Briganti (*open daily July–mid-Sept 10–1 and 4.30–11, mid-Sept–Oct 10–12.30 and 4–8, Dec 8–12 and 4–8; tours by request at the Frantoi della Pace; shared adm*). Both display 15th–18th-century oil presses and implements used in the extraction of the oil, located in cool caves dug out from the local rock.

Otranto

This is an ancient and beguiling town of whitewashed houses cascading around squat, turreted walls protecting a noble cathedral and castle and facing a sea as iridescent as a peacock's feather. Horace Walpole chose its name at random for his Gothic novel *Castle of Otranto*, but in 1480 the city had witnessed a real-life (albeit delicately embroidered) horror story, when, during Naples' wars with the Turks and their Venetian allies, Turkish pirates sacked the city, killing some 12,000 or so, and massacring the 800 survivors when they refused, to a man, to forsake Christianity.

It's now a popular resort, and the biggest threat around are the legions of high-season holiday-makers wielding ice-cream cones. The best reason for visiting is the **cathedral** (*open daily 8–12 and 3–7*), begun in the 11th century by the Normans, and the only one in the south to have conserved an entire medieval mosaic pavement, the work of a priest named Pantaleone in about 1165. Once described as 'the Bayeux Tapestry in stone', the lovely mosaic depicts three giant Trees of Life, their roots supported by two elephants, bearing extraordinary fruits. Among the fantastical animals are figures from mythology and history, as well as scenes of the local Labours of the Months. Far less playfully, set behind glass in the altar, is the massive stone where the beheadings took place during the Turkish attack; the small chapel to the right contains the mortal remains of the 800 martyrs in large glass cases.

The **castle** (*open daily 8–1; also mid-June–mid-Sept 5–11*), built by the Aragonese in the 1490s, was probably already in ruins in Walpole's times. Now restored, it is used as a meeting point for cultural events. Giant Turkish cannonballs remain in the moat, and a panoramic terrace high above the ramparts has beautiful views over the coast.

The oldest church in Otranto, and Puglia's finest remaining example of Byzantine art, the **Chiesetta di San Pietro** on Via Leondari (*ask at tourist office for opening times or request key from custodian at Piazza del Popolo*) was built *c.* 1000 and belonged to a community of Greek monks, who lived side by side with their Latin-speaking brothers in Otranto for centuries. Facing Jerusalem, it has a Greek cross, three small naves, a simple cupola and walls covered in 10th–13th-century frescoes, many with Greek inscriptions. According to legend, St Peter landed at Otranto before heading to Rome.

The End of the Earth

The Salentine's southern tip is called Land's End – *Finibus Terrae*. The spot is marked by the church of **Santa Maria di Leuca**, built over the ruins of a temple of Minerva that must have been a familiar landmark to ancient mariners. The church's altar stone fulfilled the same purpose in the original temple. As in the Land's Ends of Celtic Europe, this corner of the Salentine has quite a few standing stones and dolmens, left from the days of the Messapians or earlier. The most important Neolithic monument is the *Centopietre* – 'hundred stones' – near the village of **Patù**; it is a small temple of two aisles divided by columns, with flat stone slabs for a roof.

Coming back up the Adriatic side towards Otranto, the coast is lined with caves, many showing evidence of Stone Age habitation or later religious uses. The **Grotta Zinzulusa**, hung with stalactites, is one worth visiting. Just to the north is a thermal spa, **Santa Cesarea Terme**, built on an old neo-Moorish bath-house.

Historical Terms

Acroterion: decorative protrusion on the rooftop of an Etruscan, Greek or Roman temple. Known as *antefixes* at the corners of the roof.

Ambones: twin pulpits in some southern churches (singular: *ambo*), often elaborately decorated.

Atrium: the entrance court of a Roman house or early church.

Badia: *abbazia*, an abbey or abbey church.

Baldacchino: baldaquin, a columned stone or fabric canopy above the altar of a church.

Basilica: a rectangular building usually divided into three aisles by rows of columns. In Rome this was the common form for law courts and other public buildings, and Roman Christians adapted it for their early churches.

Borgo: a suburb (from the Saxon *burh* of Santo Spirito in Rome).

Bucchero ware: black, delicately thin Etruscan ceramics, usually incised or painted.

Calvary chapels: a series of outdoor chapels, usually on a hillside, that commemorate the stages of the Passion of Christ.

Campanile: a bell-tower.

Campanilismo: local patriotism; the Italians' own word for their historic tendency to be more faithful to their home towns than to the abstract idea of 'Italy'.

Camposanto: a cemetery.

Cardo: a transverse street of a Roman *castrum*-shaped city, at right angles to the Decumanus Major.

Carroccio: a wagon carrying the banners of a medieval city and an altar; it served as the rallying point in battles.

Cartoon: the preliminary sketch for a fresco or tapestry.

Caryatid: a supporting pillar or column carved into a standing female form; male versions are called *telamones*.

Castrum: a Roman military camp, always neatly rectangular, with straight streets and gates at the cardinal points. Later, the Romans founded or refounded cities in this form, hundreds of which survive today. (Lucca, Aosta, Florence, Pavia, Como, Brescia, Ascoli Piceno and Ancona are examples.)

Cavea: the semicircle of seats found in a classical theatre.

Cenacolo: a fresco of the Last Supper, often on the wall of a monastery refectory.

Ciborium: a tabernacle; the word is often used for large freestanding tabernacles, or in the sense of a *baldacchino* (q.v.).

Comune: commune, or commonwealth, referring to the governments of the free cities of the Middle Ages. Today it denotes any local government, from the Comune di Roma down to the smallest village.

Condottiere: the leader of a band of mercenaries during the late Middle Ages and the Renaissance.

Confraternity: a religious lay brotherhood, often serving as a neighbourhood mutual-aid and burial society, or following some specific charitable work (Michelangelo, for example, belonged to one that cared for condemned prisoners in Rome).

Cosmati work: a distinctive style of inlaid marble or enamel chips used in architectural decoration (pavements, pulpits, paschal candlesticks, etc.) in medieval southern Italy. The Cosmati family of Rome were its greatest practitioners – hence the name. 'Cosmatesque' describes work in this style.

Cupola: a dome.

Cyclopean walls: fortifications built of enormous, irregularly-shaped polygonal blocks, as in the pre-Roman cities of Latium.

Decumanus: the street of a Roman *castrum*-shaped city parallel to the longer axis, the central, main avenue called the Decumanus Major.

Duomo: cathedral.

Forum: the central square of a Roman town, with its most important temples and public buildings. The word means 'outside', because the original Roman Forum was outside the first city walls.

Fresco: wall painting, the most important Italian artistic medium since Etruscan times. The artist draws the *sinopia* (q.v.) on the wall, which is then covered with plaster, a little at a time (the paint must be on the plaster before it dries). Leonardo da Vinci's endless attempts to find clever shortcuts ensured that little of his work survived.

Ghibellines: (see *Guelphs*). One of the two great medieval parties; supporters of the Holy Roman emperors.

Gonfalon: the banner of a medieval free city; the *gonfaloniere*, or flag bearer, was often the most important public official.

Grotesques: carved or painted faces used in Etruscan and later Roman decoration; Raphael and other artists rediscovered and copied them from the 'grotto' of Nero's Golden House in Rome.

Guelphs: (see *Ghibellines*). The other great political faction of medieval Italy; supporters of the pope.

Hypogeum: an underground burial cavern, usually of pre-Christian religions.

Intarsia: work in inlaid wood or marble.

Laura: a Greek cave-chapel or monastic cell of southern Puglia, often with frescoes.

Lozenge: the diamond shape, a trademark of Pisan architecture.

Narthex: the enclosed porch of a church.

Naumachia: mock naval battles, such as those staged in the Colosseum.

Opus reticulatum: Roman masonry consisting of diamond-shaped blocks.

Palazzo: any large, important building (the word comes from the Imperial *palatium* on Rome's Palatine Hill).

Palio: a banner, and the horse race in which city neighbourhoods contend for it in their annual festivals. The most famous is at Siena, but they have been revived elsewhere.

Pantocrator: Christ 'ruler of all', a common subject for apse paintings and mosaics in areas influenced by Byzantine art.

Pietra dura: rich inlay work using semi-precious stones, perfected in post-Renaissance Florence.

Pieve: a parish church, especially in the north.

Predella: smaller paintings on panels below the main subject of a painted altarpiece.

Presepio: a Christmas crib.

Pulvin: a stone, often trapezoidal, that supports or replaces the capital of a column; decoratively carved examples can be seen in many medieval southern cloisters.

Putti: flocks of plaster cherubs with rosy cheeks and bums that infested much of Italy in the Baroque era.

Quadriga: a chariot pulled by four horses.

Quattrocento: the 1400s (the Italian refer to centuries as quattrocento, cinquecento, etc.).

Sinopia: the layout of a fresco (q.v.), etched by the artist on the wall before the plaster is applied. Often these are works of art in their own right.

Stigmata: a miraculous simulation of the bleeding wounds of Christ that appeared in holy men such St Francis in the 12th century, and Padre Pio of Puglia in recent times.

Telamon: see Caryatid.

Thermae: Roman baths.

Tondo: a round relief, painting or terracotta.

Transenna: a marble screen separating the altar area from the rest of an early Christian church.

Travertine: hard, light-coloured stone, sometimes flecked or pitted with black, sometimes perfect, and the most widely used material in ancient and modern Rome.

Triclinium: the main hall of a Roman house, used for dining and entertaining.

Triptych: a painting, especially an altarpiece, in three sections.

Trompe l'oeil: art that uses perspective effects to deceive the eye – for example, to create the illusion of depth on a flat surface, or to make columns and arches painted on a wall seem real.

Tympanum: the semicircular space, often bearing a painting or relief, above the portal of a church.

Language

The fathers of modern Italian were Dante, Manzoni and TV. Each helped create a national language from myriad regional and local dialects; Florentine Dante, the first 'immortal' to write in the vernacular, did much to put the Tuscan dialect in the foreground of Italian literature with his *Divina Commedia* ('Divine Comedy'). Manzoni's revolutionary novel, *I Promessi Sposi* ('The Betrothed'), heightened national consciousness by using an everyday language everyone understood in the 19th century. Television in the last few decades has performed an even more spectacular linguistic unification; though most Italians speak a dialect at home, school and at work, their screen idols insist on proper Italian.

Perhaps because they are so busy learning their own beautiful but grammatically complex language, Italians are not especially apt at learning others. English lessons, however, have been the rage for years, and at most hotels and restaurants there will be someone who speaks some English. In small towns and out of the way places, finding an Anglophone may prove more difficult. The words and phrases below should help you out in most situations, but the ideal way to come to Italy is with some Italian under your belt; your visit will be richer, and you're much more likely to make some Italian friends.

For a list of foods, *see* **Food and Drink**, pp.62.

Pronunciation

Italian words are pronounced phonetically. Every vowel and consonant (except 'h') is sounded. Consonants are the same as in English, except 'c', which, when followed by an 'e' or 'i', is pronounced like the English 'ch' (*cinque* thus becomes 'cheenquay'). Italian 'g' is also soft before 'i' or 'e' as in *gira*, pronounced 'jee-ra'. The letter 'h' is never sounded, and 'z' is pronounced like 'ts'.

The consonants 'sc' before the vowels 'i' and 'e' become like the English 'sh' as in 'sci', pronounced 'shee'; 'ch' is pronouced like a 'k' as in Chianti, kee-an-tee; 'gn' as 'ny' in English (*bagno*, pronounced 'ban-yo'); while 'gli' is pronounced like the middle of the word 'million' (Castiglione, for example, is pronounced 'Ca-steely-oh-nay').

Vowel pronunciation is: 'a' as in English father; 'e' when unstressed like 'a' in 'fate' as in *mele*, when stressed can be the same or like the 'e' in 'pet' (*bello*); 'i' is like the 'i' in 'machine'; 'o', like 'e', has two sounds, 'o' as in 'hope' when unstressed (*tacchino*), and usually 'o' as in 'rock' when stressed (*morte*); 'u' is pronounced like the 'u' in 'June'.

The stress usually (but not always!) falls on the penultimate syllable. Accents indicate if it falls elsewhere (as in *città*). Also note that, in the big northern cities, the informal way of addressing someone as you, *tu*, is widely used; the more formal *lei* or *voi* is commonly used in provincial districts, *voi* more in the south.

Useful Words and Phrases

yes/no/maybe *si/no/forse*
I don't know *Non lo so*
I don't understand (Italian) *Non capisco (italiano)*
Does someone here speak English? *C'è qualcuno qui che parla inglese?*
Speak slowly *Parla lentamente*
Could you assist me? *Potrebbe aiutarmi?*
Help! *Aiuto!*
Please/Thank you (very much) *Per favore/(Molte) grazie*
You're welcome *Prego*
It doesn't matter *Non importa*
All right *Va bene*
Excuse me/I'm sorry *Permesso/Mi scusi; Mi dispiace*
Be careful! *Attenzione!*

Nothing *Niente*
It is urgent! *È urgente!*
How are you? *Come sta?*
Well, and you? *Bene, e Lei?*
What is your name? *Come si chiama?*
Hello *Salve or ciao* (both informal)
Good morning *Buongiorno* (formal hello)
Good afternoon, evening
Buonasera (also formal hello)
Good night *Buona notte*
Goodbye *ArrivederLa* (formal), *arrivederci, ciao* (informal)
What do you call this in Italian?
Come si chiama questo in italiano?
What?/Who?/Where? *Che?/Chi?/Dove?*
When?/Why? *Quando?/Perché?*
How? *Come?*
How much? *Quanto?*
I am lost *Mi sono smarrito*
I am hungry/thirsty/sleepy
Ho fame/sete/ sonno
I am sorry *Mi dispiace*
I am tired *Sono stanco*
I am ill *Mi sento male*
Leave me alone *Lasciami in pace*
good/bad *buono; bravo/male; cattivo*
hot/cold *caldo/freddo*
slow/fast *lento/rapido*
up/down *su/giù*
big/small *grande/piccolo*
here/there *qui/lì*

Travel Directions

One (two) ticket(s) to Naples, please
Un biglietto (due biglietti) per Napoli, per favore
one way *semplice; andata*
return *andata e ritorno*
first/second class *Prima/seconda classe*
I want to go to... *Desidero andare a...*
How can I get to...? *Come posso andare a...?*
Do you stop at...? *Si ferma a...?*
Where is...? *Dov'è...?*
How far is it to...? *Quanto siamo lontani da...?*
What is the name of this station?
Come si chiama questa stazione?
When does the next ... leave?
Quando parte il prossimo...?
From where does it leave? *Da dove parte?*
How much is the fare? *Quant'è il biglietto?*
Have a good trip! *Buon viaggio!*

Shopping, Services, Sightseeing

I would like... *Vorrei...*
Where is/are... *Dov'è/Dove sono...*
How much is it? *Quanto costa questo?*
open/closed *aperto/chiuso*
cheap/expensive *a buon prezzo/caro*
bank *banca*
beach *spiaggia*
bed *letto*
church *chiesa*
entrance/exit *entrata/uscita*
hospital *ospedale*
money *soldi*
newspaper (foreign) *giornale (straniero)*
pharmacy *farmacia*
police station *commissariato*
policeman *poliziotto*
post office *ufficio postale*
sea *mare*
shop *negozio*
room *camera*
tobacco shop *tabaccaio*
WC *toilette; bagno*
men *Signori; Uomini*
women *Signore; Donne*

Days

Monday *lunedì*
Tuesday *martedì*
Wednesday *mercoledì*
Thursday *giovedì*
Friday *venerdì*
Saturday *sabato*
Sunday *domenica*
Holidays *festivi*

Transport

airport *aeroporto*
bus stop *fermata*
bus/coach *autobus/pullman*
railway station *stazione ferroviaria*
train *treno*
platform *binario*
taxi *tassì*
ticket *biglietto*
customs *dogana*
seat (reserved) *posto (prenotato)*

Numbers

one/two/three/four *uno (una)/due/tre/quattro*
five/six/seven/eight *cinque/sei/sette/otto*
nine/ten/eleven *nove/dieci/undici*
twelve/thirteen *dodici/tredici*
fourteen/fifteen *quattordici/quindici*
sixteen/seventeen *sedici/diciassette*
eighteen/nineteen *diciotto/diciannove*
twenty *venti*
twenty-one/twenty-two *ventuno/ventidue*
thirty *trenta*
forty *quaranta*
fifty *cinquanta*
sixty *sessanta*
seventy *settanta*
eighty *ottanta*
ninety *novanta*
hundred *cento*
one hundred and one *centouno*
two hundred *duecento*
one thousand *mille*
two thousand *duemila*
million *milione*

Time

What time is it? *Che ore sono?*
day/week *giorno/settimana*
month *mese*
morning/afternoon *mattina/pomeriggio*
evening *sera*
yesterday *ieri*
today *oggi*
tomorrow *domani*
soon *fra poco*
later *dopo; più tardi*
It is too early/late *È troppo presto/tardi*

Driving

near/far *vicino/lontano*
left/right *sinistra/destra*
straight ahead *sempre diritto*
forwards/backwards *avanti/indietro*
north/south *nord/sud*
east *est; oriente*
west *ovest; occidente*
crossroads *incrocio*
street/road *strada/via*
square *piazza*
car hire *noleggio macchina*
motorbike/scooter *motocicletta/Vespa*
bicycle *bicicletta*
petrol/diesel *benzina/gasolio*
garage (parking and repairs) *garage*
This doesn't work *Questo non funziona*
mechanic *meccanico; autorimessa*
map/town plan *carta/pianta*
Where is the road to...? *Dov'è la strada per...?*
breakdown *guasto*
driving licence *patente di guida*
driver *guidatore; autista*
speed *velocità*
danger *pericolo*
parking *parcheggio*
no parking *sosta vietata*
narrow *stretto*
bridge *ponte*
toll *pedaggio*
to slow down *rallentare*

Useful Hotel Vocabulary

I'd like a double room please *Vorrei una camera doppia (matrimoniale), per favore*
I'd like a single room please
Vorrei una camera singola, per favore
with bath, without bath
con bagno, senza bagno
for two nights *per due notti*
We are leaving tomorrow morning
Partiamo domani mattina
May I see the room, please?
Vorrei vedere la camera, per cortesia?
Is there a room with a balcony?
C'è una camera con balcone?
There isn't (aren't) any hot water, soap,
Manca/Mancano acqua calda, sapone,
...light, toilet paper, towels
...luce, carta igienica, asciugamani
May I pay by credit card?
Vorrei pagare con carta di credito?
May I see another room please?
Per favore, vorrei vedere un'altra camera?
Fine, I'll take it *Bene, la prendo*
Is breakfast included?
È' compresa la prima colazione?
What time do you serve breakfast?
A che ora è la colazione?
How do I get to the town centre?
Come raggiungo il centro città?

Further Reading

General and Travel

Barzini, Luigi, *The Italians* (Hamish Hamilton, 1964). A clever (perhaps too clever) account of the Italians by an Italian journalist then living in London.

Douglas, Norman, *Old Calabria* (Century, 1983). The reprint of a rascally travel classic.

Goethe, J.W., *Italian Journey* (Penguin Classics, 1982). An excellent demonstration of a genius turned to mush by Italy; brilliant insights and big, big mistakes.

Haycraft, John, *Italian Labyrinth* (Penguin, 1987). An attempt to unravel the Italian mess.

Hutton, Edward, *Florence; Assisi and Umbria Revisited; Venice and Venetia; Siena and Southern Tuscany; Naples and Campania Revisited* and *Rome* (Hollis & Carter).

Keates, Jonathan, *Italian Journeys* (Picador, 1991). The neglected charms of northern Italy.

McCarthy, Mary, *The Stones of Florence* and *Venice Observed* (Penguin, 1986). Brilliant evocations of Italy's two great art cities that make many other works on the subject seem sluggish and pedantic.

Morris, James, *Venice* (Faber & Faber, 1960). A classic account of 'the world's most beautiful city'.

Morton, H.V., *A Traveller in Rome* and *A Traveller in Southern Italy* (Methuen, 1957, 1969). Some of the most readable and delightful accounts of the regions in print, by a scholar and gentleman.

Newby, Eric, *Love and War in the Apennines* (Picador, 1983). Memories of wartime, when Apennine villagers hid Newby from Nazis.

History

Acton, Harold *The Bourbons of Naples* (Methuen, 1956).

Baranski, Zygmunt G. and West, Rebecca J. (eds), *The Cambridge Companion to Modern Italian Culture* (Cambridge Companions to Culture; 2001). Essays on various aspects of contemporary Italy culture.

Burckhardt, Jacob, *The Civilization of the Renaissance in Italy* (Harper & Row, 1975). The classic work on the subject (first published in 1860), and the mark against which scholars still level their poison arrows of revisionism.

Carcopino, Jérome, *Daily Life in Ancient Rome* (Penguin, 1981). A thorough, lively account of Rome at the height of Empire, guaranteed to evoke empathy from modern urbanites.

Hale, J.R. (ed.), *A Concise Encyclopaedia of the Italian Renaissance* (Thames & Hudson, 1981). An excellent reference guide, with many concise, well-written essays.

Hibbert, Christopher, *Benito Mussolini; Rise and Fall of the House of Medici and Rome* (Penguin, 1965, 1979, 1985).

Holland, Tom, *Rubicon, The Triumph and Tragedy of the Roman Republic* (Little, Brown, 2003). A fascinating new account of the disintegration of the Roman Republic.

Joll, James, *Gramsci* (Fontana, 1977). A look at the father of modern Italian communism.

Jones, Tobias, *The Dark Heart of Italy: Travels . Through Space and Time Across Italy* (Faber & Faber, 2003). A brand-new look at a complex, contradictory nation and its troubling undercurrents

Masson, Georgina, *Frederick II of Hohenstaufen* (London, 1957).

Morris, Jan, *The Venetian Empire* (Faber & Faber, 1980). A fascinating account of the Serenissima's glory days.

Norwich, John Julius, *The Normans in the South* (Thames & Hudson, 1967).

Origo, Iris, *The Merchant of Prato* (Penguin, 1963). An evocation of life in medieval Tuscany with the father of modern accounting, Francesco di Marco Datini.

Parks, Tim, *An Italian Education* (Vintage, 2001). A expat's view of the modern Italian family at school, home, work and play.

Rand, Edward Kennard, *Founders of the Middle Ages* (Dover reprint, New York). A little-known but brilliant work that explains Jerome, Augustine, Boethius and other intellectual currents of the decaying classical world.

Sciascia, Leonardo, *The Moro Affair* (Granta, 2002). A dissection of the events of March 1978, when Aldo Moro, former Italian PM, was ambushed by the Red Brigades.

Art and Literature

Boccaccio, Giovanni, *The Decameron* (Penguin). A classic by a father of Italian literature, with an irreverent worldliness that still provides a salutary antidote to whatever dubious ideas persist in visitors' mental baggage.

Calvino, Italo, *Invisible Cities* and *If Upon a Winter's Night a Traveller* (Picador). Provocative fantasies that could only have been written by an Italian.

Cellini, *Autobiography of Benvenuto Cellini* (Penguin, trans. by George Bull). Fun reading from the pen of a swashbuckling braggart.

Clark, Kenneth, *Leonardo da Vinci* (Penguin).

Dante Alighieri, *The Divine Comedy* (there are plenty of equally good translations). A poem with a rare mythical significance for a nation. Anyone serious about understanding Italy and the Italian world view needs more than a passing acquaintance with Dante.

Forster, E.M., *A Room with a View* (Penguin). A classic social comedy about middle-class English tourists and expats in Florence.

Gadda, Carlo Emilio, *That Awful Mess on Via Merulana* (Quartet). Italy in the Fascist era.

Gilbert and Linscott, *Complete Poems and Selected Letters of Michelangelo* (Princeton Press, 1984).

Henig, Martin (ed.), *A Handbook of Roman Art* (Phaidon, 1983). Essays on all aspects of ancient Roman art.

Lawrence, D.H., *Etruscan Places* (Olive Press).

Levi, Carlo, *Christ Stopped at Eboli* (Penguin). Disturbing post-war realism.

Levy, Michael, *Early Renaissance* (Penguin, 1967) and *High Renaissance* (Penguin, 1975). Old-fashioned accounts of the period, with a breathless reverence for the 1500s, yet full of intriguing interpretations.

Murray, Linda, *The High Renaissance* and *The Late Renaissance and Mannerism* (Thames & Hudson, 1977). Excellent introductions to the periods; see also Peter and Linda Murray, *The Art of the Renaissance* (Thames & Hudson, 1963).

Pavese, Cesare, *The Moon and the Bonfire* (Quartet). A post-war classic.

Petrarch, Francesco, *Canzoniere and Other Works* (Oxford). The most famous poems by the 'First Modern Man'.

Vasari, Giorgio, *Lives of the Artists* (Penguin). Readable, anecdotal accounts of the Renaissance greats by the father of art history (and first professional Philistine).

Wittkower, Rudolf, *Art and Architecture in Italy 1600–1750* (Pelican, 1986). The Bible on Baroque, erudite and full of wit.

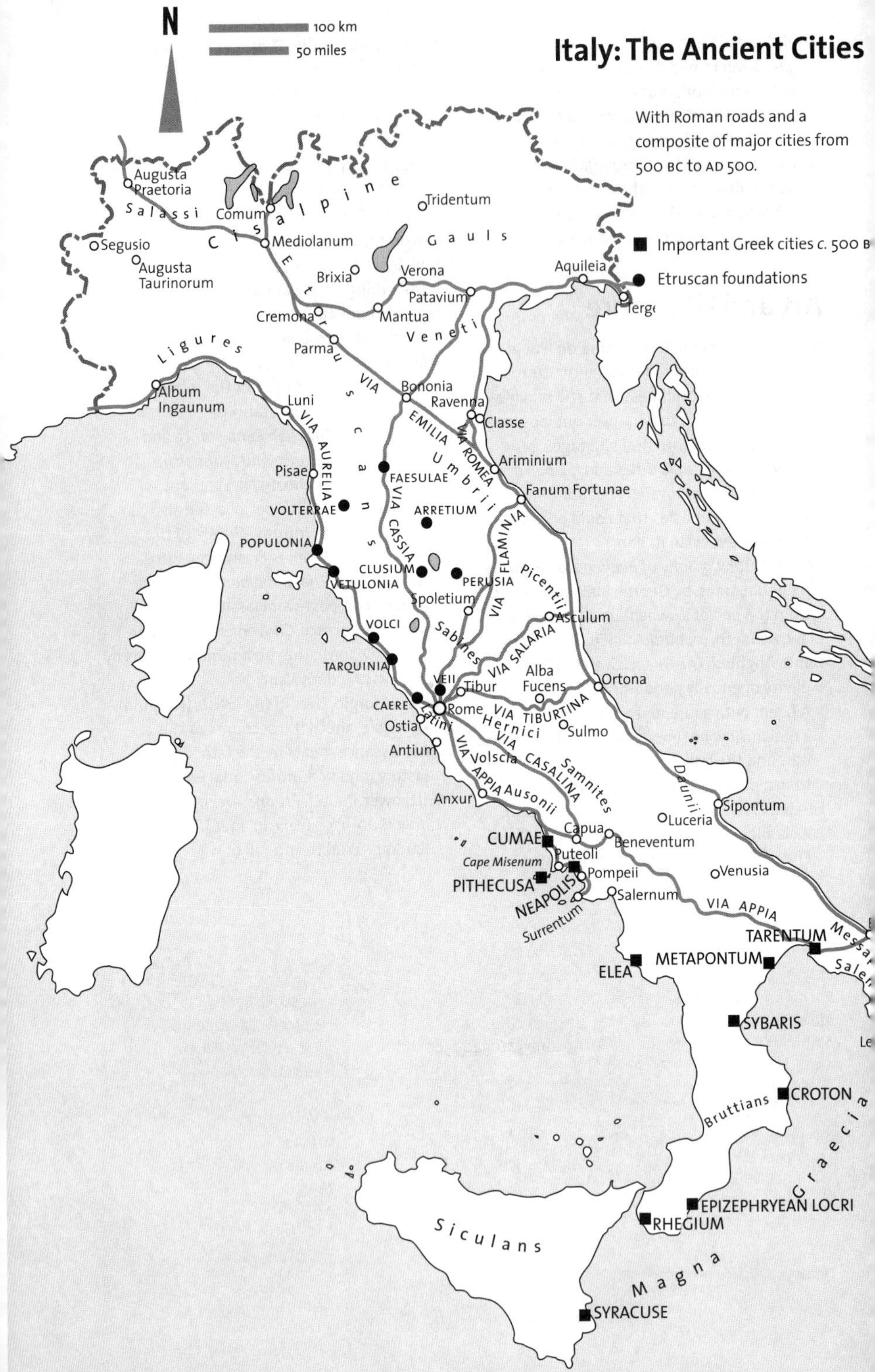
Italy: The Ancient Cities
With Roman roads and a composite of major cities from 500 BC to AD 500.
Important Greek cities c. 500 B
Etruscan foundations
N
100 km
50 miles
Augusta Praetoria
Salassi
Comum
Cisalpine Gauls
Tridentum
Segusio
Augusta Taurinorum
Mediolanum
Brixia
Verona
Aquileia
Patavium
Terge
Cremona
Mantua
Veneti
Parma
Ligures
Etruscans
VIA EMILIA
Bononia
Ravenna
Classe
Album Ingaunum
Luni
VIA AURELIA
VIA ROMEA
Umbrii
Ariminium
Pisae
FAESULAE
Fanum Fortunae
VOLTERRAE
VIA CASSIA
ARRETIUM
VIA FLAMINIA
POPULONIA
CLUSIUM
PERUSIA
Picentii
VETULONIA
Spoletium
VOLCI
Asculum
Sabines
VIA SALARIA
TARQUINIA
VEII
Tibur
Alba Fucens
Ortona
CAERE
Rome
VIA TIBURTINA
Ostia
Latini
Hernici
Sulmo
Antium
VIA APPIA
Volscia
VIA CASALINA
Samnites
Ausonii
Anxur
Daunii
Sipontum
Luceria
CUMAE
Capua
Beneventum
Cape Misenum
Puteoli
PITHECUSA
Pompeii
Venusia
NEAPOLIS
Salernum
VIA APPIA
Surrentum
TARENTUM
Messa
Sale
ELEA
METAPONTUM
SYBARIS
Le
CROTON
Bruttians
Magna Graecia
EPIZEPHRYEAN LOCRI
RHEGIUM
Siculans
SYRACUSE

Index

Main page references are in **bold**. Page references to maps are in *italics*.

Italy touring atlas

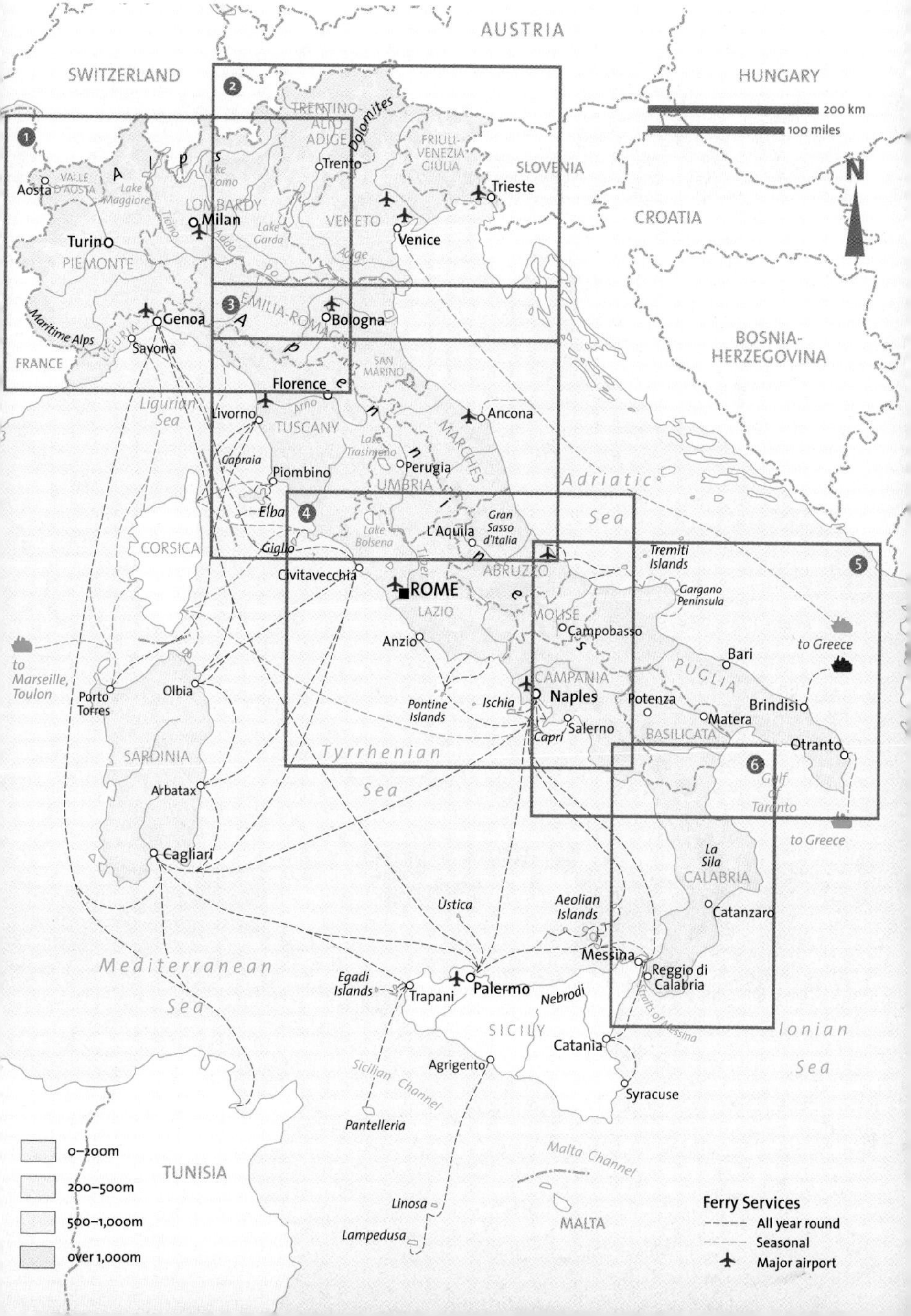

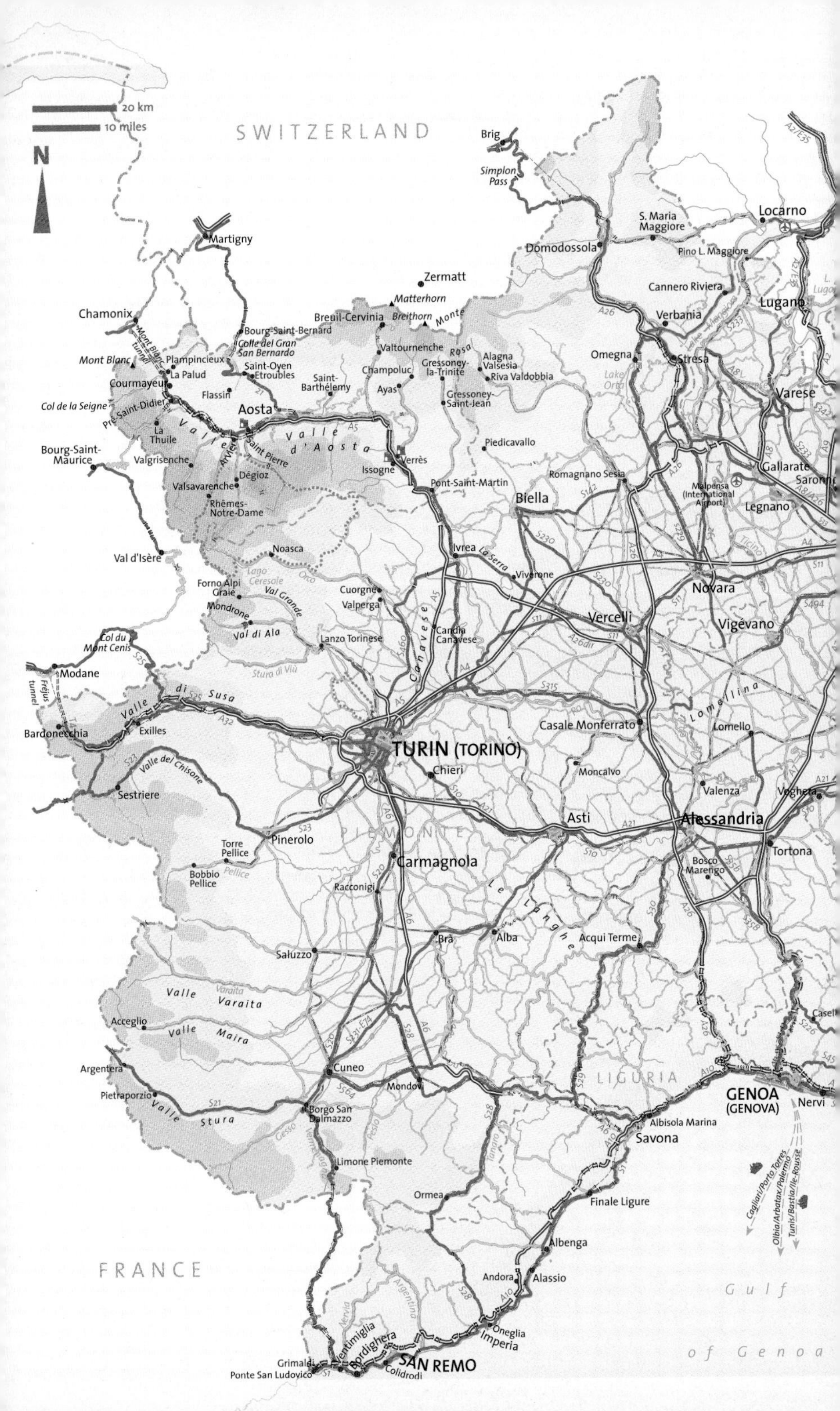

20 km
10 miles
N
SWITZERLAND
FRANCE
Brig
Simplon Pass
Locarno
S. Maria Maggiore
Domodossola
Pino L. Maggiore
Martigny
Zermatt
Matterhorn
Cannero Riviera
Lugano
Chamonix
Breuil-Cervinia
Breithorn
Monte Rosa
Verbania
Mont Blanc tunnel
Bourg-Saint-Bernard
Colle del Gran San Bernardo
Valtournenche
Mont Blanc
Plampincieux
Saint-Oyen
Etroubles
Gressoney-la-Trinité
Alagna Valsesia
Riva Valdobbia
Omegna
Stresa
Lake Maggiore
Lake Orta
La Palud
Champoluc
Courmayeur
Saint-Barthélemy
Ayas
Flassin
Gressoney-Saint-Jean
Varese
Col de la Seigne
Pré-Saint-Didier
Aosta
La Thuile
Valle d'Aosta
Arvier
Saint Pierre
Piedicavallo
Bourg-Saint-Maurice
Valgrisenche
Issogne
Verrès
Romagnano Sesia
Gallarate
Dégioz
Malpensa (International Airport)
Saronno
Valsavarenche
Pont-Saint-Martin
Biella
Legnano
Rhêmes-Notre-Dame
Noasca
Ivrea
La Serra
Val d'Isère
Ticino
Lago Ceresole
Orco
Viverone
Novara
Forno Alpi Graie
Val Grande
Cuorgnè
Valperga
Mondrone
Val di Ala
Vercelli
Vigévano
Candia Canavese
Canavese
Col du Mont Cenis
Lanzo Torinese
Stura di Viù
Modane
Fréjus tunnel
Valle di Susa
Lomellina
Bardonecchia
Exilles
Casale Monferrato
Lomello
TURIN (TORINO)
Valle del Chisone
Chieri
Moncalvo
Sestriere
Valenza
Voghera
Asti
Alessandria
Pinerolo
PIEMONTE
Torre Pellice
Tortona
Carmagnola
Bobbio Pellice
Pellice
Bosco Marengo
Racconigi
Le Langhe
Brà
Alba
Acqui Terme
Saluzzo
Valle Varaita
Acceglio
Valle Maira
Argentera
Cuneo
LIGURIA
Mondovì
Pietraporzio
Valle Stura
Borgo San Dalmazzo
GENOA (GENOVA)
Nervi
Gesso
Vermenagna
Pesio
Tanaro
Albisola Marina
Savona
Limone Piemonte
Cagliari/Porto Torres
Olbia/Arbatax/Palermo
Tunis/Bastia/Ile-Rousse
Ormea
Finale Ligure
Albenga
Andora
Alassio
Gulf of Genoa
Nervia
Argentina
Oneglia
Imperia
Ventimiglia
Bordighera
Grimaldi
Ponte San Ludovico
SAN REMO
Colidrodi

SWITZERLAND
TRENTINO-ALTO ADIGE
Parco Nazionale della Stelvio
Bolzano
Nove Levante
Sanzeno
Val di Sole
Val di Non
Predazzo
Cavalese
Val di Fiemme
Chiavenna
L. Mezzola
Tirano
Sondrio
Edolo
Alpi Orobie
Malonno
Adamello Mts
Madonna di Campiglio
Lago di Molveno
Val di Cembra
Bellano
L. Como
Trento
Vetriolo Terme
Lago di Caldonazzo
Dezzo
Valle Seriana
Valle Camonica
Valli Giudicarie
Riva del Garda
Arco
Rovereto
Asiago
Lecco
S. Pellegrino Terme
Boario Terme
Lago di Ledro
Limone sul Garda
Tremosine
Lake Iseo
Bergamo
Gardone Val Trompia
Gargnano
Schio
Thiene
Clusane
Toscolano-Maderno
Giazza
Valdagno
Monza
Salò
Lago di Garda
Garda
Vicenza
LOMBARDY
Brescia
Bardolino
MILAN
Desenzano del Garda
Sirmione
Montecchio Maggiore
Rivolta d'Adda
Verona
VENETO
Crema
Lodi
Asola
Pavia
Montagnana
Cremona
Mantua
Legnano
Piacenza
Po
Busseto
VIA AEMILIA
Fidenza
Salsomaggiore
Bobbio
Parma
Reggio nell'Emilia
Carpi
Montecchio Emilia
Cento
EMILIA-ROMAGNA
Bardi
Modena
Canossa
Sassuolo
Bologna
Vignola
Rapallo
Varese Ligure
Pontremoli
Pavullo nel Frignano
Chiavari
Sestri Levante
Moneglia
Deiva Marina
Pieve di Monti
Fivizzano
Sestola
Fiumalbo
Abetone
Piazza al Serchio
Cinque Terre
Sarzana
La Spezia
Castelnuovo di Garfagnana
Riviera di Levante
Portovenere
I. Palmaria
Carrara
Massa
Alpi Apuane
Gulf of Spezia
Marina di Massa
Forte dei Marmi
Olbia/Bastia
Borgo a Mozzano
TUSCANY
Pistoia
Borgo S. Lorenzo
Montecatini Terme
Viareggio
Lucca
Prato
Torre del Lago Puccini

AUSTRIA
SWITZERLAND
Brenner Pass/
Passo del Brennero
Vipiteno
Campo Tures
Brun
Lago di
Resia
Malles Venosta
Merano
Bressanone
Chiusa
Ponte
Gardena
Ortisei
La
Villa
Corvara
Bolzano
Renon
Isarco
S244
S242
S38
S41
S38
Parco Nazionale
della Stelvio
TRENTINO-ALTO
ADIGE
Val di Sole
Val di Non
Sanzeno
Nove
Levante
Val di Fassa
Pozza di Fassa
Vigo di Fassa
Pieve di
Livinallongo
S241
S48
S346
Predazzo
Cavalese
Val di Fiemme
Val di Cembra
S42
A22
Sondrio
Tirano
Edolo
S38
S39
Alpi Orobie
Malonno
Madonna di
Campiglio
Adamello Mts
Lago di
Molveno
Adige
Avisio
S239
Trento
Vetriolo
Terme
Feltre
S47
Lago di
Caldonazzo
Valle Seriana
Dezzo
Valle Camonica
Valli Giudicarie
Riva del
Garda
Arco
Rovereto
Asiago
S350
Brenta
S.Pellegrino
Terme
Boario
Terme
Lago
di Ledro
Limone sul Garda
Tremosine
S46
Bassano
del Grappa
S248
Valle
Bergamo
Lake
Iseo
Lago
d'Idro
Gargnano
Thiene
Schio
S53
S42
Gardone Val
Trompia
Toscolano-
Maderno
A22
Valdagno
S46
A31
A246
S47
1
Clusane
LOMBARDY
Salò
Lago
di
Garda
Garda
Vicenza
A4
Brescia
Bardolino
Montecchio
Maggiore
VENETO
S11
Desenzano
del Garda
Sirmione
Verona
A4
Padua
A4
S307
Crema
Abano Terme
A21
S236
A22
Asola
Mincio
Monselice
Montagnana
Legnano
Cremona
Mantua
A13
S434
Adige
Piacenza
A21
Po
Po
Rovigo
A21D
A1
Busseto
S9 VIA AEMILIA
A22
A13
Po
Fidenza
Ferrara
Salsomaggiore
S63
A1
Parma
Carpi
EMILIA ROMAGNA
Reggio
nell'Emilia
Montecchio
Emilia
Cento
A13
Bardi
Modena
Argenta
S513
S63
R. Reno
A15
S62
Canossa
Sassuolo
S12
Bologna
Vignola
R. Secchia
S253
A1
3

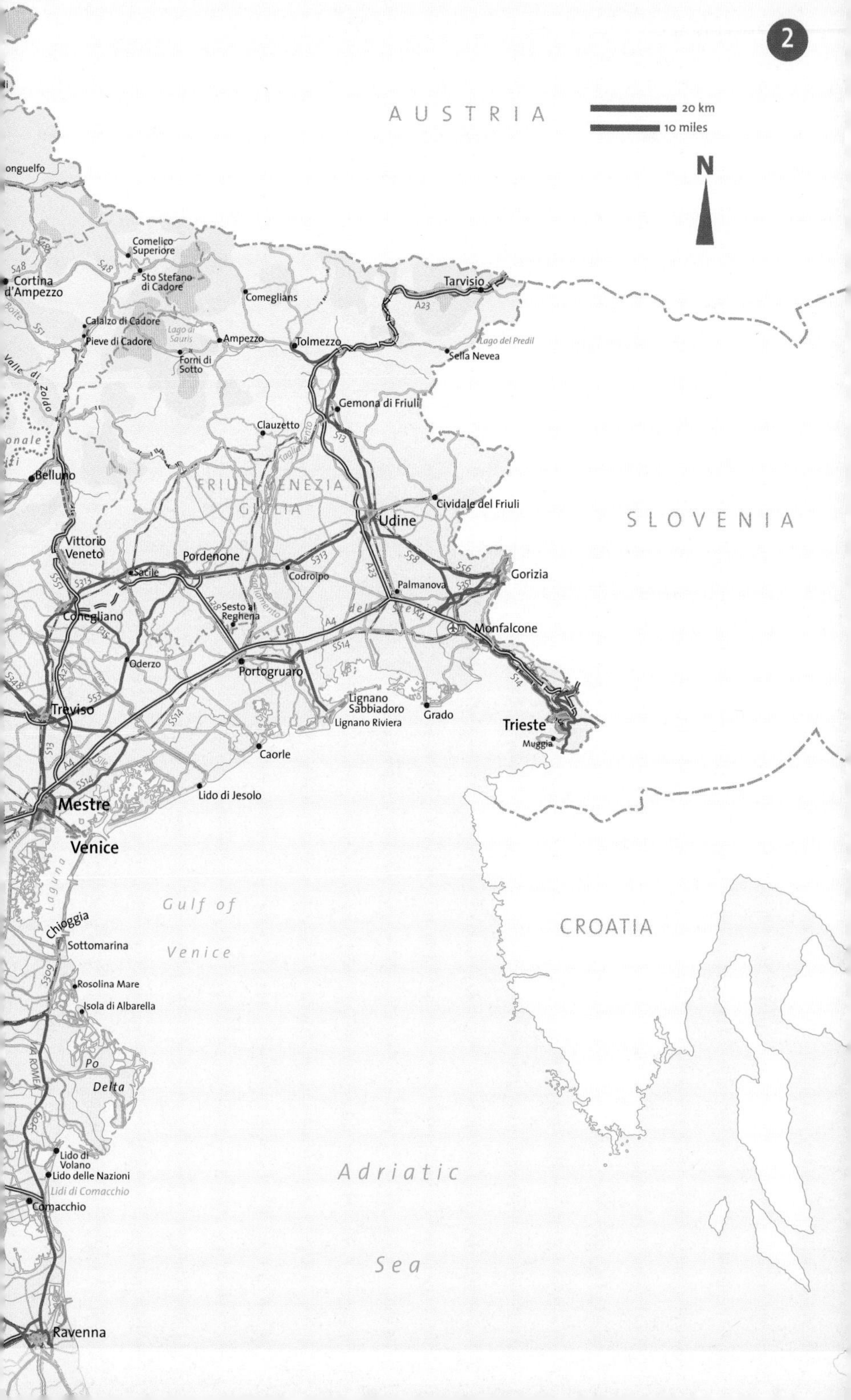

AUSTRIA
20 km
10 miles
N
SLOVENIA
CROATIA
FRIULI-VENEZIA GIULIA
Tarvisio
Sella Nevea
Lago del Predil
Tolmezzo
Comeglians
Ampezzo
Forni di Sotto
Lago di Sauris
Comelico Superiore
Sto Stefano di Cadore
Cortina d'Ampezzo
Calalzo di Cadore
Pieve di Cadore
Gemona di Friuli
Clauzetto
Belluno
Udine
Cividale del Friuli
Gorizia
Palmanova
Monfalcone
Trieste
Muggia
Vittorio Veneto
Pordenone
Sacile
Codroipo
Conegliano
Sesto al Reghena
Oderzo
Portogruaro
Lignano Sabbiadoro
Lignano Riviera
Grado
Treviso
Caorle
Lido di Jesolo
Mestre
Venice
Gulf of Venice
Chioggia
Sottomarina
Rosolina Mare
Isola di Albarella
Po Delta
Lido di Volano
Lido delle Nazioni
Lidi di Comacchio
Comacchio
Ravenna
Adriatic Sea
A23
A4
A28
A27
S13
S14
S48
S51
S52
S56
S58
S313
S309

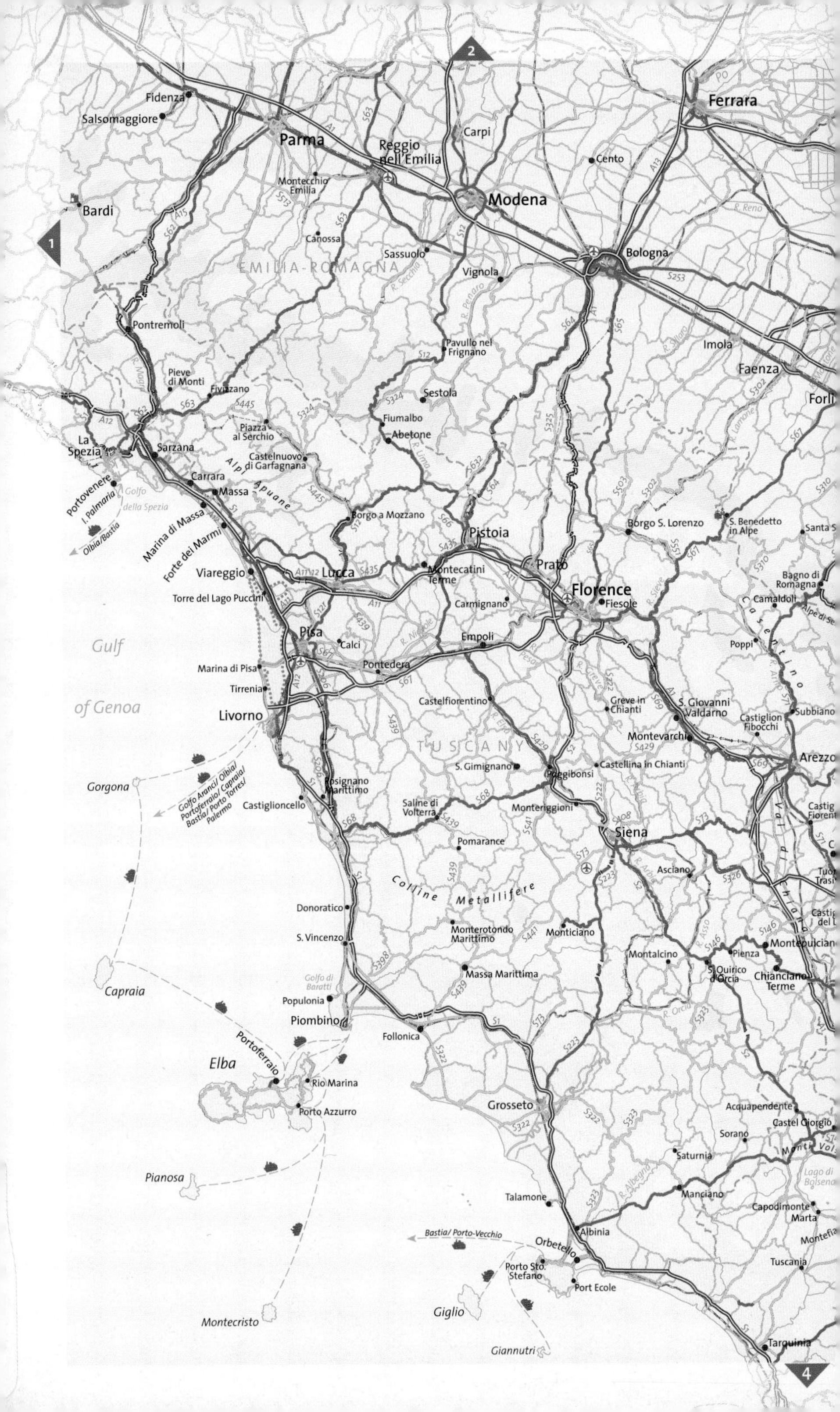

2
1
4
Fidenza
Salsomaggiore
Parma
Reggio nell'Emilia
Carpi
Ferrara
Po
Cento
Montecchio Emilia
Modena
Bardi
Canossa
Sassuolo
Bologna
R. Reno
EMILIA-ROMAGNA
Vignola
R. Secchia
R. Panaro
S253
Pontremoli
Pavullo nel Frignano
Imola
Faenza
Forlì
Pieve di Monti
Fivizzano
Sestola
Fiumalbo
Abetone
R. Lima
La Spezia
Sarzana
Piazza al Serchio
Castelnuovo di Garfagnana
Alpi Apuane
Carrara
Massa
Portovenere
I. Palmaria
Golfo della Spezia
Olbia/Bastia
Marina di Massa
Forte dei Marmi
Borgo a Mozzano
Pistoia
Borgo S. Lorenzo
S. Benedetto in Alpe
Santa S
Viareggio
Lucca
Montecatini Terme
Prato
Florence
Fiesole
Bagno di Romagna
Camaldoli
Torre del Lago Puccini
Carmignano
Casentino
Alpe di Se
Gulf of Genoa
Pisa
Calci
Empoli
Poppi
Marina di Pisa
Pontedera
Tirrenia
Castelfiorentino
Greve in Chianti
S. Giovanni Valdarno
Castiglion Fibocchi
Subbiano
Livorno
TUSCANY
Montevarchi
Arezzo
S. Gimignano
Poggibonsi
Castellina in Chianti
Gorgona
Golfo Aranci/ Olbia/ Portoferraio/ Capraia/ Bastia/ Porto Torres/ Palermo
Rosignano Marittimo
Castiglioncello
Saline di Volterra
Monteriggioni
Siena
Val di Chiana
Pomarance
Colline Metallifere
Asciano
Donoratico
S. Vincenzo
Monterotondo Marittimo
Monticiano
Montalcino
Pienza
Montepulciano
S. Quirico d'Orcia
Chianciano Terme
Capraia
Golfo di Baratti
Populonia
Massa Marittima
Piombino
Follonica
R. Orcia
Portoferraio
Elba
Rio Marina
Porto Azzurro
Grosseto
Acquapendente
Castel Giorgio
Sorano
Saturnia
Pianosa
Monti Volsini
Lago di Bolsena
Talamone
Manciano
R. Albegna
Capodimonte
Marta
Albinia
Bastia/ Porto-Vecchio
Orbetello
Porto Sto. Stefano
Port Ecole
Tuscania
Giglio
Montecristo
Giannutri
Tarquinia
A1
A11
A12
A13
A15
S1
S2
S12
S62
S63
S64
S65
S66
S67
S68
S69
S71
S73
S146
S222
S223
S322
S323
S324
S325
S326
S398
S429
S435
S439
S441
S445
S503
S541
S551
S632

3
20 km
10 miles
N
Adriatic
Sea
Lido di Volano
Lido delle Nazioni
Lidi di Comacchio
Comacchio
Ravenna
Milano Marittima
Cesenatico
Cesena
Savignano sul Rubicone
Rimini
Riccione
Cattolica
S. Marino
Pesaro
Fano
Perticara
S. Agata Feltria
Macerata Feltria
Urbino
Fermignano
Fossombrone
Senigallia
To Greece
Falconara Marittima
Ancona
Corinaldo
Chiaravalle
Mercatello s. Metauro
Acqualagna
Sansepolcro
Pergola
Jesi
Numana
Osimo
Castelfidardo
Porto Recanati
Loreto
Recanati
Citta di Castello
Sassoferrato
Filottrano
Cingoli
Poggio S. Romualdo
Montecassiano
THE MARCHES
Gubbio
Fabriano
Macerata
Civitanova Marche
Umbertide
Fossato di Vico
Porto S. Elpidio
Gualdo Tadino
S. Severino Marche
Porto S. Giorgio
Passignano s. Trasimeno
Massa Fermana
Fermo
Perugia
Camerino
S. Ginesio
Assisi
Nocera Umbra
Lago Trasimeno
Sarnano
Cupra Marittima
Parco Nazionale dei Monti Sibillini
Montalto di Marche
S. Benedetto del Tronto
Foligno
Montefortino
Porto d'Ascoli
UMBRIA
Montemonaco
Ascoli Piceno
Trevi
Alba Adriatica
Castelluccio
Norcia
Civitella del Tronto
Giulianova
Prodo
Todi
Spoleto
Arquata del Tronto
Campli
Orvieto
Acquasparta
Cascia
Morro d'Oro
Roseto degli Abruzzi
Teramo
Canzano
Ferentillo
Pineto
Montefranco
Montorio al Vomano
Silvi Alta
Amelia
Fano Adriano
Castel Castagna
To Split
Lugnano in Teverina
Leonessa
Tossicia
Isola del Gran Sasso d'Italia
Pescara
Terni
Prato Selva
Castelli
Narni
Lago di Campotosto
Penne
Moscufo
Francavilla al Mare
Orte
Fonte Cerreto
Loreto Aprutino
Antrodoco
Assergi
Rieti
Castel del Monte
Ortona
Viterbo
Soriano nel Cimino
L'Aquila
Chieti
Monti Sabini
Bazzano
Caprarola
LAZIO
Rocca di Cambio
Capestrano
San Giovanni in Venere
Bominaco
Lanciano
Lago di Salto
Capranica
4

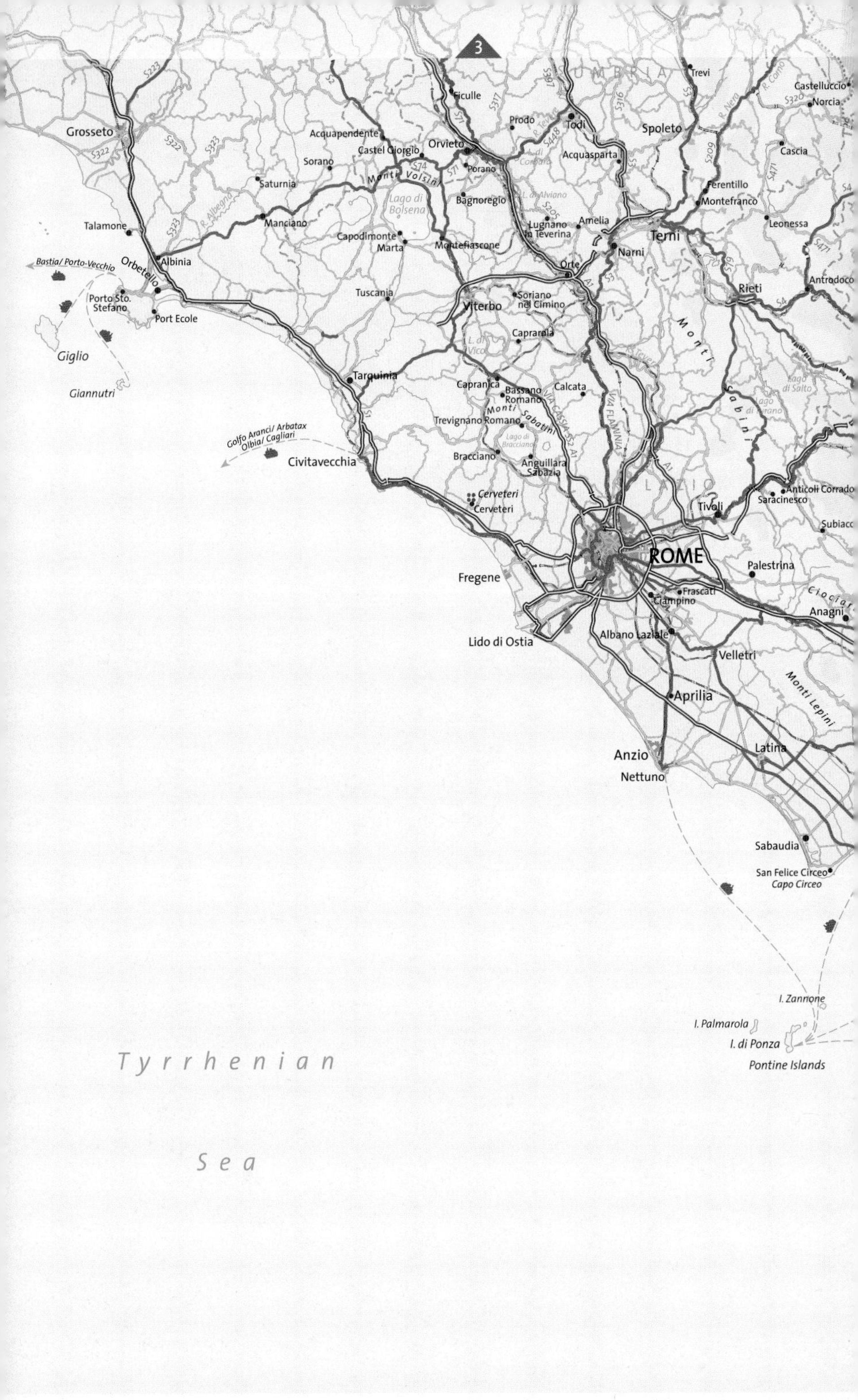
3
UMBRIA
Trevi
Castelluccio
Norcia
Ficulle
Prodo
Todi
Spoleto
Grosseto
Acquapendente
Castel Giorgio
Orvieto
Acquasparta
Cascia
Sorano
Porano
Saturnia
Monti Volsini
Lago di Bolsena
Bagnoregio
Ferentillo
Montefranco
Talamone
Manciano
Capodimonte
Marta
Montefiascone
Lugnano in Teverina
Amelia
Terni
Leonessa
Narni
Bastia/ Porto-Vecchio
Orbetello
Albinia
Orte
Antrodoco
Rieti
Porto Sto. Stefano
Port Ecole
Tuscania
Viterbo
Soriano nel Cimino
Giglio
Caprarola
Monti
Giannutri
Tarquinia
Capranica
Bassano Romano
Calcata
Sabini
Trevignano Romano
Monti Sabatini
Golfo Aranci/ Arbatax
Olbia/ Cagliari
Civitavecchia
Bracciano
Anguillara Sabazia
LAZIO
Anticoli Corrado
Saracinesco
Cerveteri
Cerveteri
Tivoli
Subiaco
ROME
Palestrina
Fregene
Frascati
Ciampino
Anagni
Lido di Ostia
Albano Laziale
Velletri
Monti Lepini
Aprilia
Anzio
Nettuno
Latina
Sabaudia
San Felice Circeo
Capo Circeo
I. Zannone
I. Palmarola
I. di Ponza
Pontine Islands
Tyrrhenian
Sea

3
4
20 km
10 miles
N
Adriatic
Sea
To Split
Ascoli Piceno
Alba Adriatica
Civitella del Tronto
Giulianova
Campli
Teramo
Morro d'Oro
Roseto degli Abruzzi
Canzano
Pineto
Montorio al Vomano
Silvi Alta
Fano Adriano
Castel Castagna
Tossicia
Prato Selva
Isola del Gran Sasso d'Italia
Castelli
Pescara
Penne
Moscufo
Francavilla al Mare
Fonte Cerreto
Loreto Aprutino
Assergi
Castel del Monte
Ortona
Aquila
Bazzano
Chieti
Capestrano
San Giovanni in Venere
Fossacesia Marina
Torino di Sangro Marina
Rocca di Cambio
Caporciano
Bominaco
Navelli
Torre de' Passeri
Lanciano
Caramanico Terme
Tremiti Islands
Isole Tremiti
Capraia
San Nicola
San Dominio
Vasto
Parco
Nazionale
Montagna della
della Maiella
Ovindoli
Celano
Forca Caruso
Sulmona
Termoli
Avezzano
Anversa d'Abruzzi
Campo di Giove
Taranta Peligna
Lido di Campomarino
Lago di Lesina
Frattura
Portocannone
Acquaviva Collecroce
Scanno
Pescocostanzo
Rivisondoli
Roccaraso
Ururi
Campocatino
Capracotta
Larino
Pescasseroli
Opi
Lago di Barrea
Castel di Sangro
Agnone
Pietrabbondante
Alfedena
Montenero Val Cocchiara
Alatri
Posta Fibreno
San Donato Val di Comino
Pescolanciano
S. Severo
MOLISE
Castel San Vincenzo
Isernia
Frosinone
San Biagio Saracinesco
Campobasso
Ferrazzano
Lucera
Foggia
Cassino
Venafro
Monti del Matese
Monti del Sannio
Lago del Matese
Passo del Prete Morto
Piedimonte Matese
Monti Ausoni
Minturno
Sessa Aurunca
Terracina
Sperlonga
Formia
Gaeta
Benevento
5
Casertavecchia
Capua
Caserta
CAMPANIA
Nola
Avellino
NAPLES
Pozzuoli
Agnano
Ercolano
Porto Vecchio
Palau
I. Ventotene
Torre Annunziata
Castellammare di Stabia
Nocera Inferiore
Ischia
Ischia Porto
Sorrento
Ravello
Amalfi
Salerno
Positano
Eboli
Battipaglia
Pertosa
Cagliari
Palermo
I. Stromboli
Capri
Capri Town
Castelcivita
Polla
Paestum
Agropoli
Santa Maria di Castellabate
San Marco
Punta Licosa
Acciaroli
Pioppi
Casalvelino
Ascea Marina

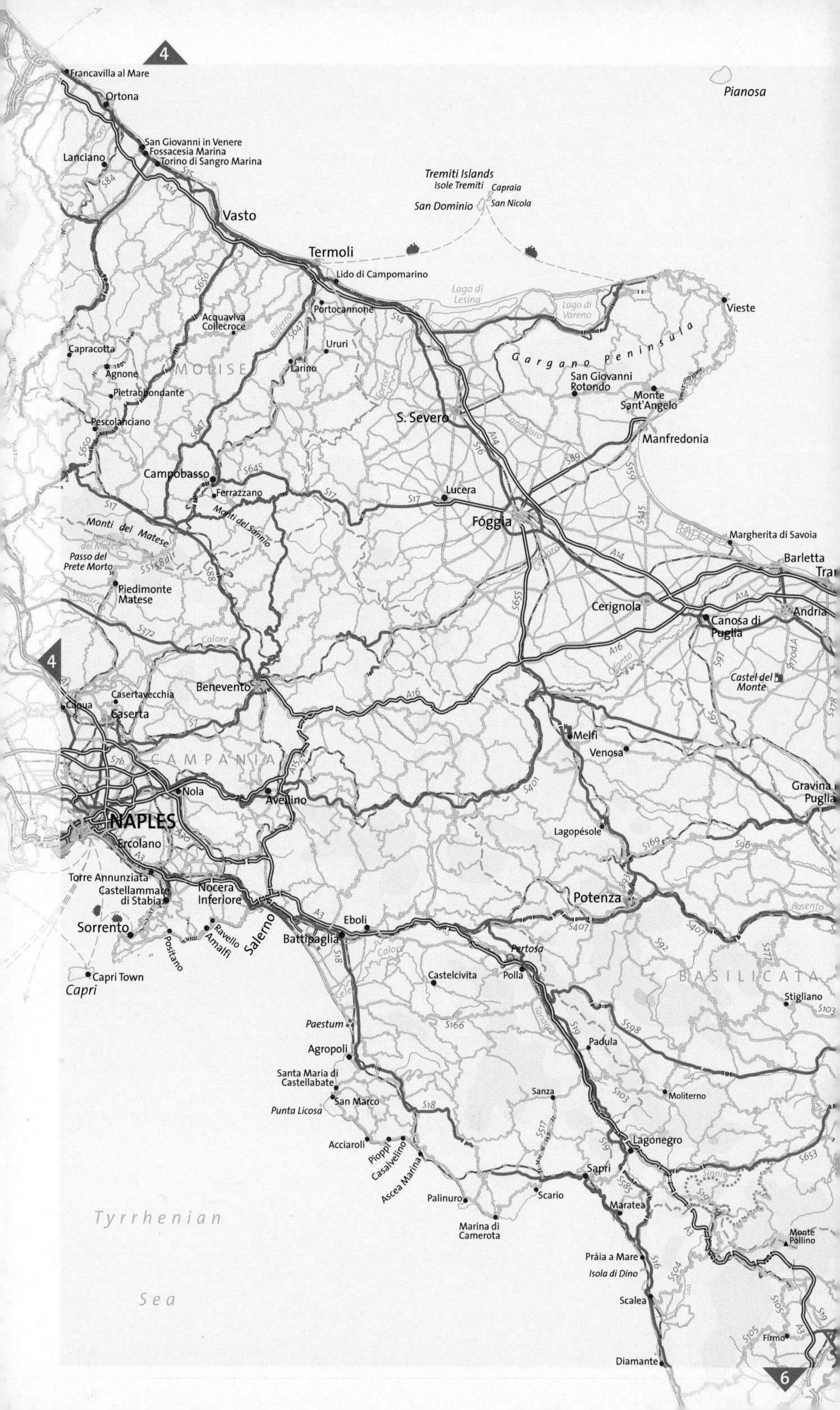
4
Francavilla al Mare
Ortona
Pianosa
San Giovanni in Venere
Fossacesia Marina
Torino di Sangro Marina
Lanciano
S84
A14
Tremiti Islands
Isole Tremiti
Capraia
San Dominio
San Nicola
Vasto
Termoli
Lido di Campomarino
Lago di Lesina
Lago di Vareno
Vieste
Portocannone
Acquaviva Collecroce
S650
Biferno
S647
S14
Ururi
Capracotta
Agnone
MOLISE
Larino
Gargano Peninsula
San Giovanni Rotondo
Monte Sant'Angelo
Pietrabbondante
Pescolanciano
S. Severo
Manfredonia
Candelaro
S16
S89
S159
Campobasso
S645
Ferrazzano
Lucera
S17
Monti del Sannio
Monti del Matese
Lago del Matese
Fóggia
S545
Margherita di Savoia
Passo del Prete Morto
S158dir
S88
Barletta
Piedimonte Matese
S655
Cerignola
Canosa di Puglia
Andria
S372
Calore
A16
Ofanto
S97
S170dA
4
Benevento
Castel del Monte
Casertavecchia
Capua
Caserta
S7
Melfi
Venosa
CAMPANIA
S7b
A15
Nola
Avellino
S401
Gravina in Puglia
NAPLES
Ercolano
A30
A3
Lagopésole
S169
S96
Torre Annunziata
Castellammare di Stabia
Nocera Inferiore
Potenza
Basento
Sorrento
Ravello
Amalfi
Salerno
Eboli
S407
Positano
Battipaglia
S18
Pertosa
Capri Town
Capri
Calore
Castelcivita
Polla
S92
BASILICATA
Stigliano
Paestum
S166
S598
Agropoli
S19
Padula
Santa Maria di Castellabate
San Marco
Punta Licosa
Sanza
S103
Moliterno
S517
Acciaroli
Pioppi
Casalvelino
Ascea Marina
Lagonegro
S653
Sapri
S585
Palinuro
Scario
Maratea
Tyrrhenian Sea
Marina di Camerota
Monte Pollino
Práia a Mare
Isola di Dino
S504
Scalea
S105
Firmo
Diamante
6

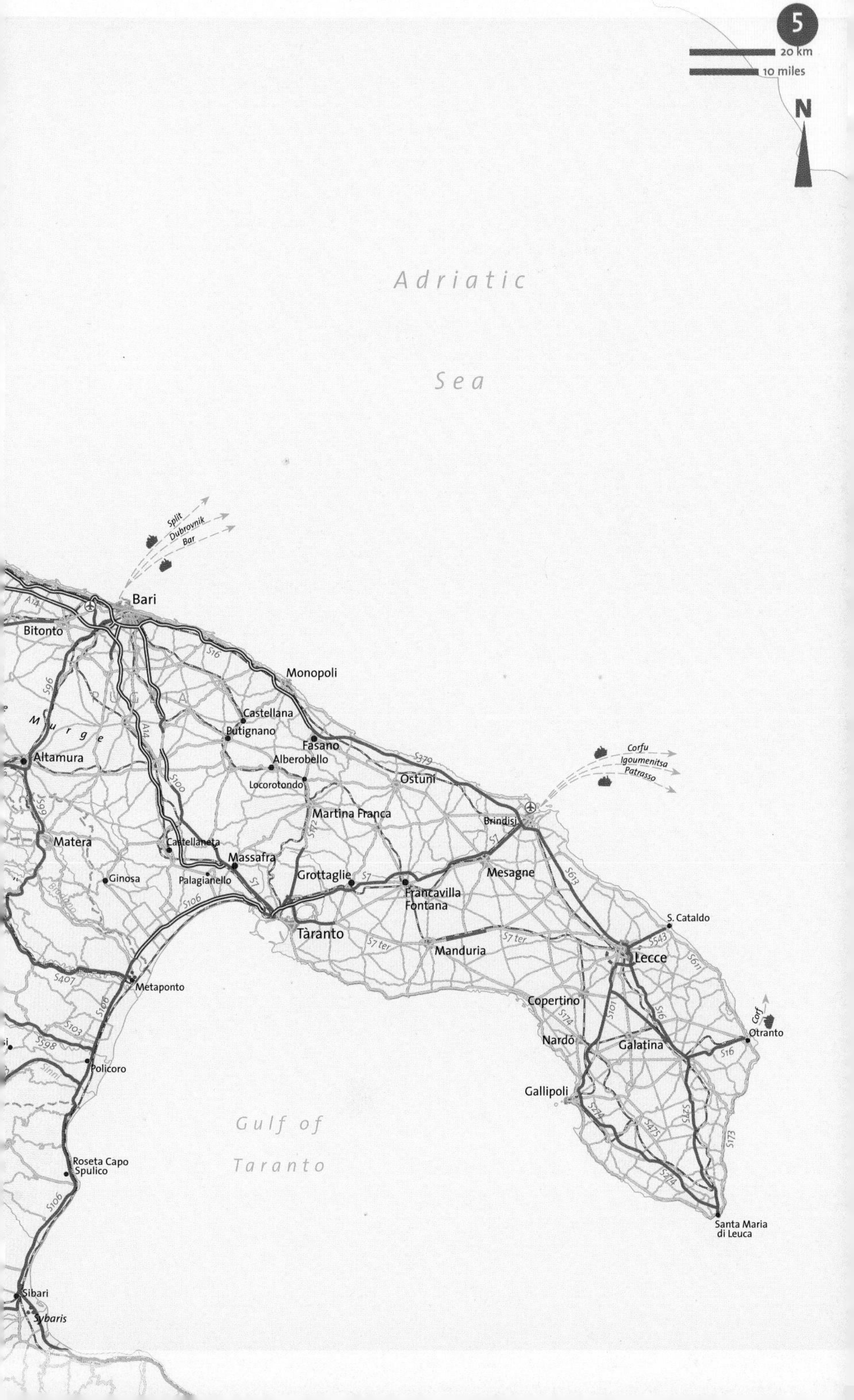
5
20 km
10 miles
N
Adriatic
Sea
Split
Dubrovnik
Bar
Bari
Bitonto
A14
S16
Monopoli
S96
PUGLIA
Murge
Castellana
Putignano
Fasano
Altamura
Alberobello
S379
Locorotondo
Ostuni
S100
Martina Franca
Corfu
Igoumenitsa
Patrasso
Brindisi
S172
Matera
Castellaneta
Massafra
S7
Mesagne
Ginosa
Palagianello
Grottaglie
Francavilla Fontana
S613
S106
Tàranto
S. Cataldo
S7 ter
Manduria
S543
Lecce
S611
S407
Metaponto
Copertino
S174
S101
S16
Corf
Otranto
S103
S598
Nardò
Galatina
Policoro
Sinni
Gallipoli
S274
S475
S275
S173
Gulf of
Taranto
Roseta Capo Spulico
Santa Maria di Leuca
Sibari
Sybaris

6
5
20 km
10 miles
N
Gulf of Taranto
Tyrrhenian Sea
Ionian Sea
BASILICATA
CALABRIA
La Sila
Aspromonte
Monti Peloritani
Padula
Sanza
Moliterno
Tursi
Policoro
Lagonegro
Sapri
Palinuro
Scario
Marina di Camerota
Maratea
Monte Pollino
Roseta Capo Spulico
Práia a Mare
Isola di Dino
Scalea
Sibari
Sybaris
Firmo
Diamante
Rossano
Crucoli Torretta
Acri
Longobucco
Parco Nazionale della Calabria
Lake Cecita
Marina di Fuscaldo
Páola
Cosenza
Melissa
Marina di Strongoli
San Giovanni in Flore
Lake Arvo
Sta Severina
Crotone
Cape Colonne
Petilia Policastro
Villaggio Racise
Villaggio Mancuso
Amantea
Nocera Terinese
Catanzaro
Cape Rizzuto
Maida
Catanzaro Lido
Soverato
Pizzo
Vibo Marina
Vibo Valentia
Tropea
Cape Vaticano
Serra San Bruno
I. Stromboli
Naples
Vibo Valentina
Reggio di Calabria
Palmi
Roccella Iónica
Gerace
Locri
Locri Epizefiri
Capo Peloro
Capo di Milazzo
Milazzo
Scilla
Straits of Messina
Gambarie
MESSINA
Barcellona
Reggio di Calabria
Ali Terme
Sta. Teresa di Riva
Mélito di Porto Salvo
Capo Taormina
Taormina
Capo Schisò
Fiumefreddo di Sicilia
Catania
S19
S598
S103
S106
S653
S517
S585
S504
S105
S534
S660
S177
S107
S106ter
S108bis
S179dir
S109
S180
S280/E848
S384
S181
S18
A3
S110
S182
S536
S281
S111
S670
S184
S183
S106/E90
S114
A18
A20
Agri
Sinni
Lao
Coscile
Mucone
Lese
Neto
Savuto
Alli
Ancinale
Allaro
Marro
Mesima
La Verde
S Agata

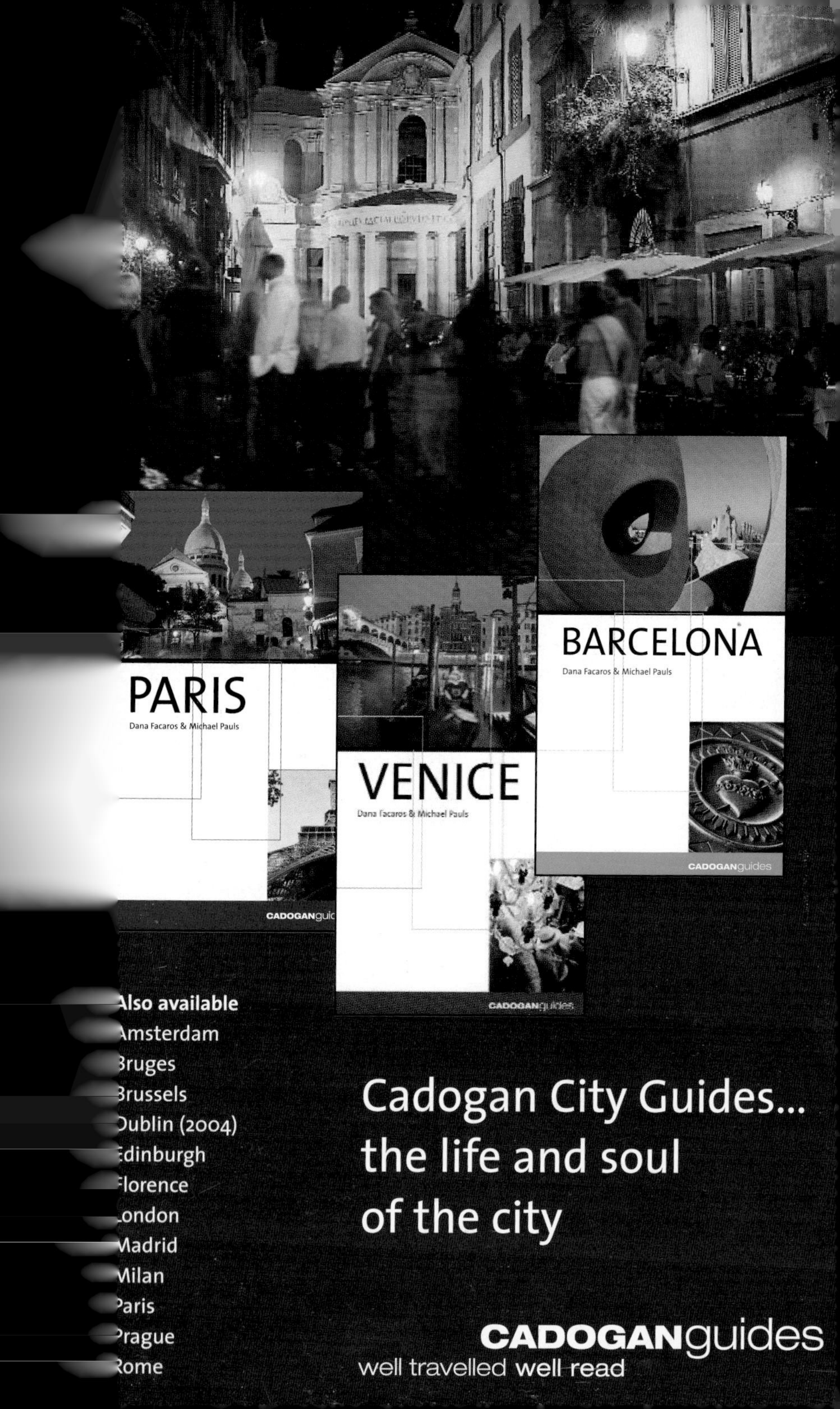
PARIS
Dana Facaros & Michael Pauls
CADOGANguides
VENICE
Dana Facaros & Michael Pauls
CADOGANguides
BARCELONA
Dana Facaros & Michael Pauls
CADOGANguides
Also available
Amsterdam
Bruges
Brussels
Dublin (2004)
Edinburgh
Florence
London
Madrid
Milan
Paris
Prague
Rome
Cadogan City Guides...
the life and soul
of the city
CADOGANguides
well travelled well read